5.5   Entrepreneurs and Their Risk-Return Preferences: 49ers and e-49ers

5.6   Risk Aversion While Standing In Line

6.1   The Benefits of Exchange and the Growth of C2C and B2B E-Commerce

6.2   Water Allocation in California

6.3   The Benefits and Costs of Rationing by Waiting

7.1   Marginal and Average Products in Major League Baseball

7.2   The Law of Diminishing Marginal Returns and Home Horticulture

7.3   Adam Smith and Pin Production

7.4   Decreasing Returns to Scale and the Demise of People Express

7.5   Why Oil Shippers Are Compartmentalizing Their Firms and Fliers Are Building Their Own Planes

8.1   American Airlines and Cost Minimization

8.2   The Cost of Public Versus Private Provision

8.3   The Economics of Raising and Razing Buildings

8.4   Why the Necks Are Thicker in New Haven

8.5   Economies of Scale and the "Network Society"

8.6   Minimum Efficient Scales in Suds, Suits, and Soft Drinks

8.7   The Cost of Dealing With Global Warming

8.8   Economies of Scope and the Marriage of AOL and Time Warner

9.1   Are American Executives Underpaid?

9.2   Continental Airlines, MR, and MC

9.3   Continental Airlines, AR, ATC, and AVC

9.4   The Competitive Firm's Supply Curve in the Very Short Run

9.5   Why Electric Bulls in California Increased After Deregulation

9.6   Increasing Input Costs in the Information Technology Industry

9.7   The Bidding War for MIS and Finance Professors

10.1   The Allocation of Producer Surplus in Trucking

10.2   Why Cigarette Company Profits Did Not Get Smoked by a Recent Punitive-Damages Award

10.3   The Long and the Short (Run) of the Deadweight Loss of Rent Control

10.4   The Contestability of Airline Markets

10.5   Gypsy Vans and Super Shuttles

10.6   Should Imports of Sunlight Be Banned?

10.7   Evading Quantity Restrictions: Virgin Atlantic's Interest in the Airbus A380

(Continued on inside back cover)

Microeconomics: Theory & Applications

● **Edgar K. Browning**
Texas A&M University

● **Mark A. Zupan**
University of Arizona

John Wiley & Sons, Inc.
New York • Chichester • Weinheim • Brisbane • Singapore • Toronto

WILEY

ACQUISITIONS EDITOR	Leslie Kraham
MARKETING MANAGER	Charity Robey
SENIOR PRODUCTION EDITOR	Petrina Kulek
ART DIRECTION	Dawn L. Stanley
TEXT DESIGNER	Michael Jung
COVER DESIGNER	Norm Christiansen
ILLUSTRATION COORDINATOR	Anna Melhorn
PHOTO EDITORS	Hilary Newman & Sara Wight

This book was set in Goudy by UG / GGS Information Services, Inc. and printed and bound by Von Hoffman Press. The cover was printed by Von Hoffman Press.

Opener Photo Credits

Chapter 1: ©Marjory Dressler. **Chapter 2**: Gene Peach/Stone. **Chapter 3**: John Riley/Stone. **Chapter 4**: J.L. Bulcao/Liaison Agency, Inc. **Chapter 5**: George Diebold/The Stock Market. **Chapter 6**: ©AP/Wide World Photos. **Chapter 7**: Mathew McVay/Stone. **Chapter 8**: Charlie Westerman/Liaison Agency, Inc. **Chapter 9**: Z & B Baran/Stone. **Chapter 10**: A & L Sinibaldi/Stone. **Chapter 11**: ©AP/Wide World Photos. **Chapter 12**: Andy Caulfield/The Image Bank. **Chapter 13**: Bruce Byers/FPG International. **Chapter 14**: Courtesy U.S. Army. **Chapter 15**: ©AP/Wide World Photos. **Chapter 16**: Bruce Ayers/Stone. **Chapter 17**: Bob Kusel/Stone. **Chapter 18**: Jeff Baker/FPG International. **Chapter 19**: Charles Gupton/Stone. **Chapter 20**: Peter Lamberti/Stone.

This book is printed on acid free paper. ∞

Library of Congress Cataloging in Publication Data:
Browning, Edgar K.
    Microeconomic theory & applications / Edgar K. Browning, Mark A. Zupan.—7th ed.
        p. cm.
    Includes bibliographical references and index.
    ISBN 0-471-38916-1 (cloth : alk. paper)
        1. Microeconomics. 2. Microeconomics—Examinations. questions, etc.   I. Title:
    Microeconomic theory and applications.   II. Zupan, Mark A.   III. Title.

HB172.B864 2001
338.5—dc21

2001017650

Printed in the United States of America

10 9 8 7 6 5 4 3 2 1

PREFACE

In early 2000, horror writer Stephen King opted to bypass the assistance of a traditional publisher and to sell his latest novel, "The Plant," in serial form directly to readers through the Internet. King distributed the novel a chapter at a time through an honor-system payment plan. Namely, readers were asked to voluntarily pay $1 for each chapter downloaded. In turn, King promised to keep publishing additional chapters so long as at least 75 percent of all readers complied with the payment plan. Much to the writer's chagrin (and, need we say, horror), only 46 percent of the chapter downloads ended up being paid for. As a consequence, publication of "The Plant" was discontinued in late 2000.

A thorough knowledge of microeconomics would have served to forewarn Stephen King about the possible pitfalls associated with his Internet publishing experiment (as we show in Chapter 20). This is because the "free-rider" problem that resulted in less than 50 percent of the readers paying for the chapters they downloaded, is a principle of microeconomics that has been both theoretically demonstrated and empirically documented. The "free-rider" problem can plague Internet-based initiatives such as Stephen King's much as it historically has hindered the effective provision of, among other things, roads, dams, defense, vaccinations, and technological innovations.

More broadly, we show throughout this text how microeconomics can help students understand how markets operate. Our intention with this edition of the text is to give students the fundamental tools of analysis and to show how the tools can be used to analyze "Old Economy" as well as "New Economy" markets. To this end, we present basic microeconomic principles in a clear, thorough way, using numerous applications to illustrate the use of theory and to reinforce students' understanding of it.

We believe that microeconomics is the most important course in the undergraduate economics curriculum. We also believe that understanding microeconomics provides an essential foundation to any bachelor's or master's degree business student. As a result, our text is written so that both economics and business students will learn microeconomic theory and how to use it correctly.

ORGANIZATION AND CONTENT

The seventh edition of *Microeconomics: Theory and Applications* continues to reflect our belief that it is better for students to be exposed to thorough coverage of fundamental microeconomic concepts and techniques than to skim through a superficial treatment of a great number of topics, many of which they will never encounter again. The enthusiastic reception given the first six editions suggests that a large number of instructors also share this view. Apart from the emphasis on the core principles of microeconomics and how to use them, the text is by and large conventional in structure and organization except for one feature: Four chapters are devoted exclusively to applications. These are Chapter 5, "Using Consumer Choice Theory"; Chapter 10, "Using the Competitive Model"; Chapter 15, "Using Noncompetitive Market Models"; and Chapter 18, "Using Input Market Analysis."

A distinguishing feature of the text is the attention we give to input market analysis. Traditionally, this has been a weak area in most microeconomics texts, with seldom more than two, and frequently only one, chapter(s) on the subject. Yet in a fundamental quantitative sense, input markets and product markets are of equal importance, because the sum of incomes generated in input markets (national income) equals total outlays on goods and services (national product). Moreover, public policy issues relating to input markets have become increasingly important, as suggested by recent attention given to managerial compensation, income distribution, welfare programs, discrimination, comparable worth, interest rates and investment, and minimum wage legislation. Consequently, we devote three chapters to the subject of input market analysis (Chapters 16 through 18).

Because all microeconomics courses are not taught the same way, the text is designed to give instructors great flexibility in adapting the book to their requirements. For example, in a short course emphasizing the theoretical underpinnings of partial equilibrium analysis, the instructor might cover only Chapters 1 through 4, 7 through 11, 16, and 17. A longer, more theoretically oriented course could include all chapters except that most instructors will steer a middle course and select three or four applications from each of these chapters (the way we normally use the material). In addition, instructors can either assign the applications as they appear in the text—following the development of the theory—or integrate them into their presentations of the theory chapters.

APPLICATIONS

We believe that a large dose of applications is an essential ingredient in any microeconomics course. Although economists know that microeconomics is important and often exciting, students often need to be convinced that this is so. Applications serve this purpose. In addition, they enliven the subject for students and help them better appreciate the theory. Time permitting, the more applications covered, the better prepared students will be to use the theory on their own.

Each of the four applications chapters (Chapters 5, 10, 15, and 18) contains four to seven longer applications that use and reinforce the graphical and logical techniques developed in the theory chapters. In Chapter 10, for example, the competitive model is employed to analyze taxicab licensing, airline regulation, and international trade. In Chapter 18, "Using Input Market Analysis," the theory is applied to discrimination, the incidence of the Social Security payroll tax, and the effects of the National Collegiate Athletic Association on college football players.

Applications are not relegated exclusively to the four applications chapters; all other chapters contain several shorter applications. We feel, however, that it is appropriate to use more applications in some areas than in others. For example, it seems a misallocation of limited textbook space to include as many applications for general equilibrium theory as for the competitive and monopoly models. Not only are the applications in the latter two areas likely to be more interesting to students, they are also likely to provide more useful background for students' later work.

CHANGES IN THE SEVENTH EDITION

Based on comments from users and reviewers of the sixth edition, as well as our own desire to improve the text we have revised it to provide the most cutting-edge illustrations of microeconomic theory at work. There is a wealth of new and enhanced applications, a focus on the New Economy, and organizational changes users have asked for.

Only the Best Applications (and More of Them)

When asked to identify strengths of this text, reviewers and users overwhelming cite the applications—the four chapters devoted to longer applications as well as the 100-plus shorter applications sprinkled through other chapters. To build on this hallmark of our text, we implemented a rating system whereby we asked reviewers to evaluate each of the applications in the sixth edition. Based on their responses, we have added more than thirty new applications. The topical issues they address include electricity bills in California since deregulation; the effect of Napster on economic efficiency; the wealth of New Economy entrepreneurs compared with the wealth of Old Economy tycoons in real terms; the benefits of exchange and the growth of B2B and C2C markets; network effects and how they lead to the dominance of particular products such as Windows in software markets; an economic analysis of the Microsoft antitrust case; the effect on cigarette company profits following an unfavorable $246 billion jury verdict; adverse selection and the American Red Cross; and the Bay Area real estate frenzy brought about by the growth of the New Economy.

We also retained (and enhanced, whenever possible) the top 75 percent of the applications in the previous edition. These cover topics such as: the Rolex cartel; yield management by airlines; the consumer surplus associated with free television; and demand elasticity and cable television pricing. Other issues include the profitability of demolishing a "profitable" Hong Kong hotel; the long and the short (run) deadweight loss of rent control; water allocation in California; cures for traffic externalities; monopsony in Major League baseball; the returns to investing in a BA and an MBA; the costs of engaging in price discrimination at Disneyland; moral hazard in the savings and loan industry; and the disemployment effect associated with minimum wage hikes.

By culling the cream of the applications in the preceding edition and adding numerous interesting demonstrations of the way microeconomic theory can be employed to analyze real-world phenomena, we've made the book's outstanding feature—its applications— stronger than ever in this revision.

A Focus on the New Economy

What is the *New Economy*? We believe that it is not limited to information technology and that it more broadly reflects the growing importance of human capital as the engine of economic progress. Studies indicate that human capital now accounts for more than 75 percent of the U.S. net worth. This percentage is expected to continue increasing over the coming decades, while more traditional sources of a nation's net worth, such as natural resources, diminish in importance. Indeed, the word *capital* comes from the Latin word *capitalis*, "of the head," reflecting that it is the ideas that emanate from individuals' heads that are the wellsprings of economic development, rather than the more common conceptions of capital such as bricks and mortar, machinery, and financial instruments.

In our judgment, the growth of the New Economy doesn't invalidate existing microeconomic theory. If anything, it provides further confirmation of time-tested theory while highlighting particular aspects such as network effects, economies of scale, static versus dynamic views of efficiency, public goods, and property rights. Accordingly, in this edition of the text we stress how knowledge of microeconomics is critical to understanding the New Economy. And, through the new applications, end-of-chapter questions, and revisions of the main text, we show that microeconomics applies now more than ever.

Enhanced User Friendliness

We have made the seventh edition as user friendly as possible. For example, because reviewers indicated that in covering consumer choice theory they typically addressed preferences before introducing budget constraints, we revised the text to correspond with this sequence. As another example, numerous users requested that we not wait until the end of the text to cover the benefits of exchange and introduce the concept of efficiency. In response to this request, we have added a chapter (Chapter 6) early in the text to address these topics— along the lines of some earlier editions of this book.

PEDAGOGICAL AIDS

Several other in-text pedagogical aids help students to structure and retain information.

Chapter Outlines and Learning Objectives
Each chapter begins with an outline as well as a list of key learning objectives. These offer a preview of the chapter content and help structure study and review.

Glossary
A running glossary has been added in the margins of the text as a way to cement students' understanding of key concepts and terms.

Graphs
We have paid careful attention to the graphs used in the text. Unusually thorough explanations of graphs are given. Furthermore, the explanatory captions and liberal use of color will help students follow the text discussion and understand graphical analysis.

End-of-Chapter Aids
A summary at the end of each chapter highlights the important points of the chapter to help students review their knowledge of the basic material. More than 400 review questions and problems test students on chapter material and require them to solve analytical exercises. Answers to questions and problems with asterisks are provided at the end of the book.

ANCILLARIES

A *Study Guide*, prepared by John Lunn, Hope College, is available to give students further review and practice in the use of microeconomic theory. The Study Guide features chapter-by-chapter analysis of key concepts, applications of the theory, review questions, multiple-choice questions, and discussion questions, problems and answers.

An *Instructor's Manual*, written by the text authors and Andrew Foshee, McNeese State University, also accompanies the text. Each chapter in the manual features a chapter outline, general comments on the chapter, specific section-by-section comments, and suggestions that may help in developing lectures and class discussion topics. The Appendix in the Instructor's Manual contains the answers to those questions and problems in the text that are not already answered at the end of the text.

A set of Powerpoint presentations, which consists of enlarged versions of all the figures contained in the text, is also available. This set can be used to create overhead transparencies for viewing in the classroom or they can be copied and used as handouts for students.

The *Test Bank* prepared by Mark Foley, Davidson College, contains 1,500 multiple-choice questions with answers. This Test Bank is also available electronically, which shows instructors how to customize their exams.

A dedicated *Web site* with extensive resources for both students and professors (http//www.wiley.com/college/browning) is also available.

ACKNOWLEDGMENTS

We have been fortunate to have had the assistance of many able economists in the preparation of this book. Those who have worked at various stages in the development of the first six editions include:

Gary Anderson, *California State University, Northridge*
Peter Aranson, *Emory University*
Jeff Baldani, *Colgate University*
David Black, *University of Delaware*
David Blau, *University of North Carolina*
Larry Blume, *University of Michigan*
Wayne Boyet, *University of Mississippi*
Charles Breeden, *Marquette University*
Charles A. Capone, *Baylor University*
Richard Caves, *Harvard University*
David Chaplin, *State of Wyoming*
Alvin Cohen, *Lehigh University*
Patrice Karr Cohen, *University of Mississippi*
Darius Conger, *Central Michigan University*
David Conn, *University of Kansas*
Robert Connolly, *University of North Carolina at Greensboro*
Keith J. Crocker, *University of Michigan*
Carl Davidson, *Michigan State University*
Cliff Dobitz, *North Dakota State University*
Rich Eastin, *University of Southern California*
Robert Ekelund, *Auburn University*
David Emmons, *Wayne State University*
Maxim Engers, *University of Virginia*
Ian Gale, *University of Wisconsin*
David Gay, *University of Arkansas*
Charles Geiss, *University of Missouri*
Soumen Ghosh, *New Mexico State University*
James Giordano, *Villanova University*
John Goddeeris, *Michigan State University*
Robert Goldfarb, *George Washington University*
Warren Gramm, *Washington State University*

Lawrence H. Goulder, *Stanford University*
James M. Griffin, *Texas A&M University*
Timothy Gronberg, *Texas A&M University*
Robert G. Hansen, *Amos Tuck School, Dartmouth College*
John Harford, *Cleveland State University*
Mehdi Haririan, *Bloomsburg University*
Glenn Heuckel, *Purdue University*
Barry Hirsch, *University of North Carolina at Greensboro*
W. L. Holmes, *Temple University*
Joseph Hunt, *Shippensburg University*
Joseph Jadlow, *Oklahoma State University*
Joseph P. Kalt, *Harvard University*
Art Kartman, *San Diego State University*
Philip King, *San Francisco State University*
Edward Kittrell, *Northern Illinois University*
Leonard Lardaro, *University of Rhode Island*
Daniel Y. Lee, *Shippensburg University*
Tom Lee, *California State University, Northridge*
Al Link, *Auburn University*
Christine Loucks, *Boise State University*
R. Ashley Lyman, *University of Idaho*
William McEachern, *University of Connecticut*
Mark Machina, *University of California, San Diego*
Robert Main, *Butler University*
Robert Maness, *Louisiana State University*
D. E. Mills, *University of Virginia*
Robby Moore, *Occidental College*
Roger Morefield, *University of Saint Thomas*
William Novshek, *Stanford University*
Richard E. Olsen, *Washburn University*

William O'Neil, *Colby College*
Patrick B. O'Neill, *University of North Dakota*
Lydia Ortega, *San Jose State University*
H. Craig Petersen, *Utah State University*
Jeffrey Pliskin, *Hamilton College*
Michael Reclam, *Virginia Military Institute*
John Riley, *University of California, Los Angeles*
Radwan Shaban, *Georgia Institute of Technology*
Stephen Shmanske, *California State University at Hayward*
David Sisk, *San Francisco State University*
Gene Smiley, *Marquette University*
Scott Smith, *George Mason University*
William Doyle Smith, *University of Texas at El Paso*
Hubert O. Sprayberry, *Howard Payne University*
Stanley Stephenson, *Pennsylvania State University*
Douglas Steward, *San Diego State University*
Shirley Svorny, *California State University, Northridge*
Wayne Talley, *Old Dominion University*
Bryan Taylor, *California State University, Los Angeles*
Roger Trenary, *Kansas State University*
Roy Van Til, *Bentley College*
Nicholas Vonortas, *George Washington University*
Don Waldman, *Colgate University*
Doug Walker, *Louisiana State University*
Donald Wells, *University of Arizona*

In addition, the following economists assisted with the development of the seventh edition manuscript:

Hamid Bastin, *Shippensburg University*
Richard Butler, *Trinity University*
Bruce Caldwell, *University of North Carolina, Greensboro*
Eddie Dekel, *Northwestern University*
Cliff Dobitz, *North Dakota State University*
David E. R. Gay, *University of Arkansas*

Sumit Joshi, *George Washington University*
Larry Kenny, *University of Florida*
Greg Lemon, *DePauw University*
Armando Levy, *North Carolina State University*
Charles Mason, *University of Wyoming*
James McClure, *Ball State University*

Robert Michaels, *California State University, Fullerton*
Michael Ransom, *Brigham Young University*
Stephen Shmanske, *California State University, Hayward*
Eric Stout, *Brandeis University*

These reviewers were generous with their time, and their comments have greatly enhanced the quality of the book. To them we extend our gratitude and our hope that the final product meets with their approval.

Special mention should be made of the late Jacquelene M. Browning, who was the co-author of the first four editions. Her pedagogical skills, together with her insistence that the text be one from which students could learn effectively, continue to have a profound influence in the present edition.

Edie Trimble provided outstanding research and editorial assistance. We would also like to thank the people at John Wiley who made important contributions to this edition, in particular, Publisher Susan Elbe, Acquisitions Editor Leslie Kraham, Associate Director of Development Johnna Barto, Associate Editor Cindy Rhoads, Senior Production Editor Petrina Kulek, and Senior Marketing Manager Charity Robey.

This book is dedicated to our families without whose unflagging encouragement and support our vision for the book would have never become a reality.

Edgar K. Browning
Mark A. Zupan

TABLE OF CONTENTS

PREFACE iii

ACKNOWLEDGMENTS vi

CHAPTER 1: AN INTRODUCTION TO MICROECONOMICS   1

1.1   The Scope of Microeconomic Theory 2
1.2   The Nature and Role of Theory 2
1.3   Positive Versus Normative Analysis 3
1.4   Market Analysis and Real Versus
     Nominal Prices 4
     Application 1.1 The Old Rich Versus the
     New Rich: A Real Comparison 5
1.5   Basic Assumptions About Market
     Participants 5
1.6   Opportunity Cost .6
     Application 1.2 The Rise of Mail-Order
     and Online Shopping 7
     Application 1.3 Never on Sunday 7
     Economic Versus Accounting Costs 8
     Application 1.4 Why It Was Profitable to
     Demolish a Profitable Hong Kong Hotel 8
     Sunk Costs 8
     Application 1.5 Measuring Economic
     Costs and Benefits 9
1.7   Production Possibility Frontier 9

CHAPTER 2: SUPPLY AND DEMAND   15

2.1   Demand and Supply Curves 16
     The Demand Curve 16   Shifts in the Demand
     Curve 17
     Application 2.1 The Effect of Traffic
     Schools on Speeding 20
     The Supply Curve 20   Shifts in the Supply
     Curve 21
2.2   Determination of Equilibrium Price
     and Quantity 22
     Application 2.2 Is There a Parking
     Shortage in Major American Cities? 23

2.3   Adjustment to Changes in Demand
     or Supply 24
     Application 2.3 Supply, Demand,
     and Babysitting .25
     Using the Supply–Demand Model to Explain
     Market Outcomes 26
2.4   Government Intervention in Markets:
     Price Controls 27
     Rent Control 27   Who Loses, Who Benefits? 29
     Application 2.4 Why Web Surfing Can
     Turn into Web Crawling 31
     Application 2.5 Why the Doctor
     Is Not In 31
2.5   Elasticities 32
     Price Elasticity of Demand 32   Calculating
     Price Elasticity of Demand 34
     Application 2.6 Demand Elasticity
     and Cable Television Pricing 36
     Demand Elasticities Vary Among Goods 36
     The Estimation of Demand Elasticities 37
     Application 2.7 D.C. Learns about
     Demand Elasticity 38
     Three Other Elasticities 39
     Application 2.8 It Takes Time 40

CHAPTER 3: THE THEORY OF CONSUMER CHOICE   45

3.1   Consumer Preferences 46
     Consumer Preferences Graphed as Indifference
     Curves 47   Curvature of Indifference Curves 49
     Individuals Have Different Preferences 52
     Graphing Economic Bad and Economic Neuters
     52   Perfect Substitutes and Complements 54
3.2   The Budget Constraint 55
     Geometry of the Budget Line 56   Shifts in
     Budget Lines 57
3.3   The Consumer's Choice 59
     A Corner Solution 61   The Composite-Good
     Convention 61
     Application 3.1 Consumers' Valuation
     of Air Bags 63
     Application 3.2 Convex (Indifference)
     Curves and Cellular Charges 64

3.4 Changes in Income and Consumption
Choices 64
Normal Goods 64   Inferior Goods 66
*Application 3.3 Running Towards the Border
in a Recession* 68
The Food Stamp Program 68
*Application 3.4 Keeping Bugs Bunny
and the Back Street Boys at Bay
in Canada* 70
*Application 3.5 The Allocation of
Commencement Tickets* 71
3.5 Are People Selfish? 72
Application 3.6 The New Philanthropy ...74
3.6 The Utility Approach to
Consumer Choice 74
The Consumer's Optimal Choice 75
Relationship to Indifference Curves 76

**CHAPTER 4: INDIVIDUAL
AND MARKET DEMAND   81**

4.1 Price Changes and Consumption
Choices 82
The Consumer's Demand Curve 83   Some
Remarks About the Demand Curve 84
*Application 4.1 Using Price to Deter
Youth Alcohol Abuse* 84
*Application 4.2 Young Techies Say
No to College* 85
Do Demand Curves Always Slope
Downward? 86
4.2 Income and Substitution Effects of a
Price Change 86
Income and Substitution Effects Illustrated:
The Normal-Good Case 87   The Income
and Substitution Effects Associated with a
Gasoline-Tax-Plus-Rebate Program 89
4.3 Income and Substitution Effects:
Inferior Goods 92
The Giffen Good Case: How Likely? 94
*Application 4.3 Do Rats Have
Downward-Sloping Demand Curves?* 95
4.4 From Individual to Market Demand 95
*Application 4.4 Aggregating Demand
Curves for a UCLA MBA* 97
4.5 Consumer Surplus 98
*Application 4.5 The Consumer Surplus
Associated with Free TV* 101
Consumer Surplus and Indifference Curves 102

4.6 Price Elasticity and the
Price-Consumption Curve 103
*Application 4.6 The P-C Curve for
a Non-P-C Good* 104
4.7 Network Effects 105
The Bandwagon Effect 105   The Snob
Effect 106
*Application 4.7 Getting on the Bank
ATM Bandwagon* 108
*Application 4.8 Network Effects, the
New Economy, and the Microsoft
Antitrust Case* 108
4.8 The Basics of Demand Estimation 109
Experimentation 109   Surveys 109
Regression Analysis 110
*Application 4.9 Demand Estimation:
McDonald's Versus Burger King* 113

**CHAPTER 5: USING CONSUMER
CHOICE THEORY   117**

5.1 Excise Subsidies, Health Care, and
Consumer Welfare 118
*Application 5.1 Why are Company
Health Benefits Tax Exempt?* 120
Using the Consumer Surplus Approach 121
*Application 5.2 Burning Up Resources
in Moscow* 122
5.2 Public Schools and the
Voucher Proposal 122
5.3 Paying for Garbage 125
Does Everyone Benefit? 127
*Application 5.3 Trash Pricing
and Recycling* 128
5.4 The Consumer's Choice to Save
or Borrow 128
A Change in Endowment 130
*Application 5.4 The New Economy
and a Negative U.S. Saving Rate* 132
Changes in the Interest Rate 132
5.5 Investor Choice 134
*Application 5.5 Entrepreneurs
and Their Risk-Return Preferences:
49ers and e-49ers* 136
Investor Preferences Toward Risk 137
*Application 5.6 Risk Aversion While
Standing In Line* 140
Minimizing Exposure to Risk 140

CHAPTER 6: EXCHANGE, EFFICIENCY, AND PRICES   145

6.1 Two-Person Exchange 146
Application 6.1 The Benefits of Exchange and the Growth of C2C and B2B E-Commerce 147
The Edgeworth Exchange Box Diagram 148
The Edgeworth Exchange Box Diagram with Indifference Curves 149
6.2 Efficiency in the Distribution of Goods . .151
Efficiency and Equity 154
6.3 Competitive Equilibrium and Efficient Distribution 155
Application 6.2 Water Allocation in California .158
6.4 Price and Nonprice Rationing and Efficiency 159
Application 6.3 The Benefits and Costs of Rationing by Waiting 161

CHAPTER 7: PRODUCTION   165

7.1 Relating Output to Inputs 166
7.2 Production When Only One Input is Variable 167
Total, Average, and Marginal Product Curves 168   The Relationship Between Average and Marginal Product Curves 169
Application 7.1 Marginal and Average Products in Major League Baseball 170
The Geometry of Product Curves 170   The Law of Diminishing Marginal Returns 172
Application 7.2 The Law of Diminishing Marginal Returns and Home Horticulture 172
7.3 Production When All Inputs are Variable 173
Production Isoquants 173   *MRTS* and the Marginal Products of Inputs 176   Using *MRTS*: Speed Limits and Gasoline Consumption 176
7.4 Returns to Scale 178
Application 7.3 Adam Smith and Pin Production 178
Application 7.4 Decreasing Returns to Scale and the Demise of People Express 180

Application 7.5 Why Oil Shippers Are Compartmentalizing Their Firms and Fliers Are Building Their Own Planes 181
7.5 Empirical Estimation of Production Functions 182

CHAPTER 8: THE COST OF PRODUCTION   189

8.1 The Nature of Cost 190
8.2 Short-Run Cost of Production 191
Measures of Short-Run Cost 191   Behind Cost Relationships 192
8.3 Short-Run Cost Curves 194
Marginal Cost 195   Average Cost 196
Marginal-Average Relationships 196   The Geometry of Cost Curves 197
8.4 Long-Run Cost of Production 197
Isocost Lines 197   Least Costly Input Combinations 199   Interpreting the Tangency Points 200
Application 8.1 American Airlines and Cost Minimization 201
The Expansion Path 202   Is Production Cost Minimized? 202
Application 8.2 The Cost of Public Versus Private Provision .203
8.5 Input Price Changes and Cost Curves . . .204
Application 8.3 The Economics of Raising and Razing Buildings 205
Application 8.4 Why the Necks Are Thicker in New Haven 206
8.6 Long-Run Cost Curves 207
Application 8.5 Economies of Scale and the "Network Society" 208
The Long Run and Short Run Revisited 209
8.7 Importance of Cost Curves to Market Structure 210
Application 8.6 Minimum Efficient Scales in Suds, Suits, and Soft Drinks 212
8.8 Using Cost Curves: Controlling Pollution 213
Application 8.7 The Cost of Dealing With Global Warming 215
8.9 Economies of Scope 216
Application 8.8 Economies of Scope and the Marriage of AOL and Time Warner . .217
8.10 Estimating Cost 217

CHAPTER 9: PROFIT MAXIMIZATION IN PERFECTLY COMPETITIVE MARKETS 223

9.1 The Assumptions of Perfect Competition . .224
9.2 Profit Maximization 225
  Application 9.1 Are American Executives Underpaid? 227
9.3 The Demand Curve Facing the Competitive Firm 227
9.4 Short-Run Profit Maximization 229
  Short-Run Profit Maximization Using Per-Unit Curves 231
  Application 9.2 Continental Airlines, MR, and MC 232
  Operating at a Loss in the Short Run 232
  Application 9.3 Continental Airlines, AR, ATC, and AVC 234
9.5 The Perfectly Competitive Firm's Short-Run Supply Curve 234
  Application 9.4 The Competitive Firm's Supply Curve in the Very Short Run 236
  Output Response to a Change in Input Prices 236
9.6 The Short-Run Industry Supply Curve . .237
  Price and Output Determination in the Short Run 238
  Application 9.5 Why Electric Bills in California Increased After Deregulation . .239
9.7 Long-Run Competitive Equilibrium 241
  Zero Profit When Firms' Cost Curves Differ? 244
9.8. The Long-Run Industry Supply Curve . .245
  Constant-Cost Industry 245 Increasing-Cost Industry 247
  Application 9.6 Increasing Input Costs in the Information Technology Industry . .249
  Decreasing-Cost Industry 249
  Application 9.7 The Bidding War for MIS and Finance Professors 251
  Comments on the Long-Run Supply Curve 251
9.9 When Does the Competitive Model Apply? 253

CHAPTER 10: USING THE COMPETITIVE MODEL 259

10.1 The Evaluation of Gains and Losses 260
  Producer Surplus 260
  Application 10.1 The Allocation of Producer Surplus in Trucking 262

Consumer Surplus, Producer Surplus, and Efficient Output 262 The Deadweight Loss of a Price Ceiling 264
10.2 Excise Taxation 266
  Who Bears the Burden of the Tax? 269
  Application 10.2 Why Cigarette Company Profits Did Not Get Smoked by a Recent Punitive-Damages Award 271
  The Deadweight Loss of Excise Taxation 271
  Application 10.3 The Long and the Short (Run) of the Deadweight Loss of Rent Control 273
10.3 Airline Regulation and Deregulation 274
  What Happened to the Profits? 275 After Deregulation 276
  Application 10.4 The Contestability of Airline Markets .277
  The Push for Reregulation 278
10.4 City Taxicab Markets 279
  The Illegal Market 281
  Application 10.5 Gypsy Vans and Super Shuttles 282
10.5 Consumer and Producer Surplus, and the Net Gains from Trade 283
  The Gains from International Trade 285
  Application 10.6 Should Imports of Sunlight Be Banned? 286
  The Link Between Imports and Exports 287
10.6 Government Intervention in Markets: Quantity Controls 288
  Sugar Policy: A Sweet Deal 288
  Application 10.7 Evading Quantity Restrictions: Virgin Atlantic's Interest in the Airbus A380 291

CHAPTER 11: MONOPOLY 295

11.1 The Monopolist's Demand and Marginal Revenue Curves 296
11.2 Profit-Maximizing Output of a Monopoly . .298
  Graphical Analysis 299 The Monopoly Price and Its Relationship to Elasticity of Demand 301
  Application 11.1 Demand Elasticity and Home Video Prices 304
11.3 Further Implications of Monopoly Analysis 304
  Application 11.2 Life Is Not Always a Box of Chocolates 307

11.4 The Measurement and Sources of
Monopoly Power 308
Measuring Monopoly Power 309   The Sources
of Monopoly Power 309   Barriers to Entry 310
*Application 11.3 Regulatory Barriers
in the Philippines* 311
Strategic Behavior by Firms: Incumbents
and Potential Entrants 312

11.5 The Efficiency Effects of Monopoly 313
A Dynamic View of Monopoly and Its
Efficiency Implications 315
*Application 11.4 The Dynamics of
Developing an AIDS Vaccine* 317

11.6 Public Policy Toward Monopoly 317
*Application 11.5 What Not to Say
to a Rival on the Telephone* 318
*Application 11.6 Static Versus Dynamic
Views of Monopoly and the Microsoft
Antitrust Case* 319
Regulation of Price 320

CHAPTER 12: PRODUCT PRICING WITH MONOPOLY POWER   325

12.1 Price Discrimination 326
Other Degrees of Price Discrimination 328
*Application 12.1 Giving Frequent Shoppers
the Second Degree* 329
*Application 12.2 The Third Degree by
Car Dealers* 330

12.2 Three Necessary Conditions for
Price Discrimination 330
*Application 12.3 Arbitrage in the
International Phone Calling Market* 331

12.3 Price and Output Determination with
Price Discrimination 331
*Application 12.4 Why Hotel and Apartment
Building Owners Get Cable Television
Service for a Lower Price* 334
*Application 12.5 The Cost of Being Earnest
When It Comes to Applying to Colleges* ..335

12.4 Two-Part Tariffs 335
Many Consumers, Different Demands 337
*Application 12.6 The Costs of Engaging
in Price Discrimination* 340

12.5 Intertemporal Price Discrimination
and Peak-Load Pricing 340
*Application 12.7 Yield Management
by Airlines* 342

*Application 12.8 Priceline.com, Project
Purple Demon, and Online Intertemporal
Price Discrimination* 343
Peak-Load Pricing 343
*Application 12.9 Peak-Load Pricing
Goes to College* 346

CHAPTER 13: MONOPOLISTIC COMPETITION AND OLIGOPOLY   351

13.1 Price and Output Under Monopolistic
Competition 352
Determination of Market Equilibrium 352
Monopolistic Competition and Efficiency 355
*Application 13.1 Ready-to-Regulate
Ready-to-Eat* 357
*Application 13.2 Monopolistic Competition
Is in the Eye of the Beholder* 357

13.2 Oligopoly and the Cournot Model 358
The Cournot Model 359   Evaluation of the
Cournot Model 362
*Application 13.3 Strategic Interaction
on Duopoly Air Routes* 362

13.3 Other Oligopoly Models 363
The Stackelberg Model 363   The Dominant
Firm Model 365   The Elasticity of the
Dominant Firm's Demand Curve 367
*Application 13.4 The Dynamics of the
Dominant Firm Model in Pharmaceutical
Markets* 368

13.4 Cartels and Collusion 368
Cartelization of a Competitive Industry 369
*Application 13.5 Will the Internet Promote
Competition or Cartelization?* 370
Why Cartels Fail 371
*Application 13.6 The Difficulty of
Controlling Cheating* 373
Application 13.7 The Rolex "Cartel" 373
Oligopolies and Collusion 374
*Application 13.8 Firm Count, Market
Concentration, and Successful Collusion* ..375
The Case of OPEC 375

CHAPTER 14: GAME THEORY AND THE ECONOMICS OF INFORMATION   383

14.1 Game Theory 384
Determination of Equilibrium 384

Application 14.1 Dominant Strategies in Baseball 386

14.2 The Prisoner's Dilemma Game 388

Application 14.2 The Congressional Prisoner's Dilemma 389

The Prisoner's Dilemma and Cheating by Cartel Members 390   A Prisoner's Dilemma Game You May Play 392

14.3 Repeated Games 393

Application 14.3 Cooperation in the Trenches of World War I 395

Do Oligopolistic Firms Always Collude? 395   Game Theory and Oligopoly: A Summary 396

14.4 Asymmetric Information 397

The "Lemons" Model 397   Market Responses to Asymmetric Information 398

Application 14.4 Is There a Lemons Problem in Used Car Markets? 399

14.5 Adverse Selection and Moral Hazard 400

Adverse Selection 400

Application 14.5 Adverse Selection and the American Red Cross 402

Moral Hazard 402

Application 14.6 Moral Hazard in the S&L Industry 403

Application 14.7 Moral Hazard on the Road and at the Plate 404

14.6 Limited Price Information 404

14.7 Advertising 405

Advertising as Information 406

Application 14.8 A Newspaper Strike's Effect on Food Prices 408

CHAPTER 15: USING NONCOMPETITIVE MARKET MODELS   **411**

15.1 The Size of the Deadweight Loss of Monopoly 412

Other Possible Deadweight Losses of Monopoly 414

Application 15.1 Software and Soft-Money Political Contributions 415

15.2 Do Monopolies Suppress Inventions? 416

Application 15.2 Hollywood and Home Videos 418

15.3 Natural Monopoly 419

Regulation of Natural Monopoly 420 Regulation of Natural Monopoly in Practice 421

Application 15.3 Regulating Natural Monopoly Through Public Ownership: The Case of USPS 422

15.4 Government-Established Cartels: The Case of the British Columbia Egg Marketing Board 423

Estimating the Deadweight Loss: The First Round 424   Estimating the Deadweight Loss: The Second Round 425

Application 15.4 The International Air Cartel 427

15.5 More on Game Theory: Iterated Dominance and Commitment 428

Iterated Dominance 428   Commitment 430

Application 15.5 Why It May Be Wise to Burn the Bridges Behind You 432

CHAPTER 16: EMPLOYMENT AND PRICING OF INPUTS   **435**

16.1 The Input Demand Curve of a Competitive Firm 436

The Firm's Demand Curve: One Variable Input 436   The Firm's Demand Curve: All Inputs Variable 438   The Firm's Demand Curve: An Alternative Approach 439

16.2 Industry and Market Demand Curves for an Input 441

A Competitive Industry's Demand Curve For an Input 441   The Elasticity of an Industry's Demand Curve for an Input 443

Application 16.1 Explaining Sky-High Pilot Salaries Under Airline Regulation 444

The Market Demand Curve for an Input 444

16.3 The Supply of Inputs 444

16.4 Industry Determination of Price and Employment of Inputs 446

Process of Input Price Equalization Across Industries 447

Application 16.2 The Net Benefits of High-Tech Immigrants 449

16.5 Input Price Determination in a Multi-Industry Market 450

16.6 Input Demand and Employment by an Output Market Monopoly 452

16.7 Monopsony in Input Markets 454

Application 16.3 Major League Monopsony 455

CHAPTER 17: WAGES, RENT, INTEREST, AND PROFIT   459

17.1 The Income-Leisure Choice
of the Worker 460
Is This Model Plausible? 461
17.2 The Supply of Hours of Work 462
Is a Backward-Bending Labor Supply Curve
Possible? 463   The Market Supply Curve 465
17.3 The General Level of Wage Rates 465
*Application 17.1 The Malaise
of the 1970s* 467
17.4 Why Wages Differ 468
Compensating Wage Differentials 469
*Application 17.2 Twelve Hours' Pay
for Ten Minutes' Work* 470
Differences in Human Capital Investment 470
*Application 17.3 The Returns to Investing
in a BA and an MBA* 471
Differences in Ability 471
*Application 17.4 What's on the Outside
Also Counts* 472
17.5 Economic Rent 472
*Application 17.5 The Bay Area Real Estate
Frenzy: Economic Rents at Ground Zero* . .474
17.6 Monopoly Power in Input Markets:
The Case of Unions 474
*Application 17.6 The Decline
and Rise of Unions* 477
17.7 Borrowing, Lending, and the
Interest Rate 478
17.8 Investment and the Marginal Productivity
of Capital 479
The Investment Demand Curve 480
17.9 Saving, Investment, and the
Interest Rate 481
Equalization of Rates of Return 483
17.10 Why Interest Rates Differ 484
17.11 Valuing Investment Projects 485
*Application 17.7 Why Lottery Winners
May Not Be "Millionaires"* 487

CHAPTER 18: USING INPUT MARKET ANALYSIS   491

18.1 The Minimum Wage Law 492
Further Considerations 493   How Large Are
The Effects of the Minimum Wage? 494
*Application 18.1 The Disemployment Effect
of the 1990–1991 Minimum Wage Hike* . .495

The Minimum Wage: An Example of an
Efficient Wage? 496
18.2 Who Really Pays for Social Security? 497
But Do Workers Bear All the Burden? 498
*Application 18.2 Mandated Retirement
Benefits and Corporate America's
Increasing Reliance on "Permatemps"* . . .500
18.3 The NCAA Cartel 500
An Input Buyers' Cartel 500   The NCAA as a
Cartel of Buyers 502   Eliminate the Cartel
Restrictions on Pay? 503
*Application 18.3 The "Collusion Era"
in Major League Baseball* 505
18.4 Discrimination in Employment 505
What Causes Average Wage Rates to
Differ? 508
*Application 18.4 Male Versus Female
Earnings Among Self-Employed
Workers* 509

CHAPTER 19: GENERAL EQUILIBRIUM ANALYSIS AND ECONOMIC EFFICIENCY   513

19.1 Partial and General Equilibrium
Analysis Compared 514
The Mutual Interdependence of Markets
Illustrated 514   When Should General
Equilibrium Analysis Be Used? 516
19.2 Economic Efficiency 517
Efficiency as a Goal for Economic
Performance 518
19.3 Conditions for Economic Efficiency 519
19.4 Efficiency in Production 520
The Edgeworth Production Box 520   The
Production Contract Curve and Efficiency in
Production 522   General Equilibrium in
Competitive Input Markets 522
19.5 The Production Possibility Frontier
and Efficiency in Output 523
Efficiency in Output 525   An Economy's PPF
and the Gains from International Trade 526
*Application 19.1 The Effects of Trade
Restrictions on an Economy's Consumption
and Production Possibilities* 528
19.6 Competitive Markets and
Economic Efficiency 529
The Role of Information 530
*Application 19.2 Can Centralized
Planning Promote Efficiency?* 531

19.7 The Causes of Economic Inefficiency 532
Market Power 532   Imperfect Information 533
*Application 19.3 Deterring Cigarette
Smoking* 533
Externalities/Public Goods 534

**CHAPTER 20: PUBLIC GOODS
AND EXTERNALITIES**   **537**

20.1 What Are Public Goods? 538
The Free-Rider Problem 539
Application 20.1 Paying for NATO 540
Application 20.2 An Online Horror Tale . .540
20.2 Efficiency in the Provision
of a Public Good 541
*Application 20.3 Promoting Truthful
Revelation in China* 542
Efficiency in Production and Distribution 543
Patents 543
*Application 20.4 Napster: Nipping
or Nudging Economic Efficiency?* 544

20.3 Externalities 545
External Costs 546
*Application 20.5 Cures for Traffic
Externalities* 547
External Benefits 548
20.4 Externalities and Property Rights 550
*Application 20.6 Radio Waves
and Property Rights* 551
The Coasean Theorem 551
*Application 20.7 Coasean Bargaining
in Movie Making* 552
20.5 Controlling Pollution, Revisited 553
The Market for Los Angeles Smog 555

MATHEMATICAL APPENDIX 561

**ANSWERS TO SELECTED
PROBLEMS** 571

INDEX 581

CHAPTER 1

An Introduction to Microeconomics

Microeconomic theory helps us to understand
the New Economy as well as the Old.

Chapter Outline

1.1 The Scope of Microeconomic Theory
1.2 The Nature and Role of Theory
1.3 Positive Versus Normative Analysis
1.4 Market Analysis and Real Versus Nominal Prices
    Application 1.1 The Old Rich Versus the New Rich: A Real Comparison
1.5 Basic Assumptions About Market Participants
1.6 Opportunity Cost
    Application 1.2 The Rise of Mail-Order and Online Shopping
    Application 1.3 Never on Sunday
    Economic Versus Accounting Costs
    Application 1.4 Why It Was Profitable to Demolish a Profitable Hong Kong Hotel
    Sunk Costs
    Application 1.5 Measuring Economic Costs and Benefits
1.7 Production Possibility Frontier

Learning Objectives

- Convey the scope of microeconomic theory and why theory, in general, is essential to the understanding and prediction of real-world outcomes.
- Distinguish between positive and normative analysis.
- Differentiate between real and nominal prices.
- Introduce the concept of opportunity cost and explain how economic costs differ from accounting costs.
- Explain how a production possibility frontier graphically depicts the basic assumptions economists make about market actors as well as the concept of opportunity cost.

If employers are required by the government to provide health care for their employees, who will bear the cost of the mandate? When quotas are placed on imports of Japanese cars, is the United States better off? Why is the World Wide Web often dubbed the World Wide Wait? Will issuing firms tradeable permits to pollute be an effective way to control smog in the Los Angeles Basin? Will per-bag billing charges in trash collection encourage greater recycling? Does rate regulation lead to lower rates for cable television service? Why do dry cleaners charge more to launder women's blouses than men's shirts? And, should apparent monopolies such as Microsoft be praised for their efficiency and profitability or subject to antitrust prosecution and broken up?

As these questions suggest, there are many interesting issues that microeconomic theory can help us understand—in the *New Economy* as well as the *Old*. This text presents the analytical techniques of microeconomics and shows how to apply them to explain or predict real-world phenomena.

This chapter introduces the subject of microeconomic theory by first discussing its nature and the role of theory in general. The remainder of the chapter covers the basic assumptions economists make about market participants and introduces a central microeconomic concept: opportunity cost.

1.1   THE SCOPE OF MICROECONOMIC THEORY

MACROECONOMICS
the study of aggregate
economic factors

MICROECONOMICS
the study of the behavior of
small economic units such
as consumers and firms

PRICE THEORY
another term for
microeconomics

The prefix *micro-* in microeconomics comes from the Greek word *mikros*, meaning small. It contrasts with macroeconomics, the other branch of economic theory. **Macroeconomics** deals primarily with aggregates, such as the total amount of goods and services produced by society and the absolute level of prices, while **microeconomics** analyzes the behavior of "small" units: consumers, workers, savers, business managers, firms, individual industries and markets, and so on. Microeconomics, however, is not limited to "small" issues. Instead, it reflects the fact that many "big" issues can best be understood by recognizing that they are composed of numerous smaller parts. Just as much of our knowledge of chemistry and physics is built on the study of molecules, atoms, and subatomic particles, much of our knowledge of economics is based on the study of individual behavior.

Individuals are the fundamental decision makers in any society. Their decisions, in the aggregate, define the economic environment of that society. Consumers decide how much of various goods to purchase, workers decide what jobs to take, and business people decide how many workers to hire and how much output to produce. Microeconomics encompasses the factors that influence these choices and the way these innumerable small decisions merge to determine the workings of the entire economy. Because prices have important effects on these individual decisions, microeconomics is frequently called **price theory**.

1.2   THE NATURE AND ROLE OF THEORY

In disciplines from physics to political science, using a theory to make sense of a complex reality is essential. Facts do not always "speak for themselves." In economics, facts may describe a historical episode, but facts can never explain why the episode occurred or how things would have been different had, for example, the government pursued another policy. Moreover, facts can never demonstrate how, for instance, a change in agricultural price supports will affect agricultural production next year. For purposes of explanation or prediction, we must employ a theory that shows how facts are related to one another.

Theory in economics, as in other sciences, is based on certain assumptions. For example, economists assume that firms strive to maximize profit. Based on this assumption, the economic theory of the firm explains what mix of steel and plastic firms such as Toyota and General Motors (GM) employ in production as well as what amount of cars and trucks they produce. The theory also explains how Toyota's and GM's desired input mixes and final output levels are affected by changes in, say, the price of steel or the price received per car sold.

Economic theory can be used to predict as well as to explain real-world outcomes. For instance, the basic supply–demand model (discussed in Chapter 2) can be used to explain the effects observed in cities that have enacted rent control laws. It can also be used to predict the effects should the federal government impose similar price ceilings on health care services.

How do we know if a theory, whether it be in economics, physics, or political science, is a "good" theory? Basically, *a theory is considered to be valid and useful if it successfully explains and predicts the phenomena that it is intended to explain and predict*. In keeping with this litmus test, theories are continually stacked up against real-world data. Depending on how well a theory matches the data, the theory is maintained, refined, or sometimes even discarded (perhaps in favor of a competing explanation). The continual process of testing theories against real-world data is critical to the advancement of any science, not just economics.

In testing a theory, it is important to note that imperfection tends to be the norm. That is, "good" theories typically do not explain the observed data perfectly nor are the assumptions upon which they are based entirely realistic. For example, consider the *calorie theory*, one accepted by millions of people. The calorie theory holds that a person's weight depends on the number of calories consumed per day: the more calories ingested, the heavier the person will be.

The calorie theory predicts that to lose weight, a person should cut his or her calorie intake. Is this a valid and useful theory? Consider two criticisms: First, the calorie theory is based on assumptions that are not completely realistic. That is, no one has ever seen a calorie, much less observed the human body convert it into weight. Second, the theory is not perfect. Reducing your calorie intake will not necessarily make you thin. Other factors, besides calories, influence a person's weight: heredity, exercise, metabolism, ratio of fat to protein consumption, and so on.

Does this mean that people who count calories are wrong? Not at all. In fact, the calorie theory is quite useful for millions of weight watchers around the world. For them, the general relationship between calories and weight tends to hold and becomes even stronger once the calorie theory is refined to account for other factors such as heredity, exercise, metabolism, and so forth.

Such is the case with economics. While firms may not appear to maximize profit (think about Amazon.com or Biogen), and refinements accounting for special features of particular markets may be necessary (long-run versus short-run profitability in industries where firms must make substantial up-front research and development investments), the economic theory of the firm based on the assumption of profit maximization successfully explains and predicts a wide range of real-world phenomena. Thus the theory is useful to both business managers and public policymakers.

1.3 POSITIVE VERSUS NORMATIVE ANALYSIS

Economic theory is a tool for understanding relationships in the economy. While it can explain the behavior of market actors, it cannot determine which public policies are desirable and which are not. Economics can help us evaluate the results of public policies, but it never, by itself, demonstrates whether the results are good or bad.

Consider the federal minimum wage—first set in 1938 at $0.25 per hour and periodically increased over the years (to $5.15 per hour by 1997). Evaluating the desirability of this policy requires three steps. First, one must determine the qualitative effects of the policy. For example, how does it affect the employment of workers by firms? Does it increase or decrease employment? Second, one must determine the magnitude of the effects. If the minimum wage leads to less employment, how much less? How many workers lose their jobs and how many retain their jobs at the higher wage rate? Finally, a judgment needs to be made as to whether the policy's effects are desirable. Does the benefit to workers who remain employed outweigh the costs to those workers whose jobs are cut by employers on account of the minimum wage law?

The first step involves identifying the qualitative nature of the consequences of the policy. This step is in the realm of **positive analysis**, assessing the expected, objective outcomes. The distinguishing feature of positive analysis is that it deals with propositions that can be tested with respect to both their underlying logic and the empirical evidence. It deals with what is, or what might be, without deciding whether something is right or wrong, good or bad. Positive analysis is scientific because it draws on accepted rules of logic and evidence, of both a qualitative and quantitative nature, that can be used to determine the truth or falsity of statements. Microeconomic theory is a form of positive analysis; it can be used, for example, to make the qualitative prediction that a minimum wage law will reduce employment.

If we want to resolve the question of desirability, however, identifying the qualitative nature of the effects is not sufficient. We also need some idea of the size of the effects. It may

POSITIVE ANALYSIS
assessment of expected objective outcomes

matter a great deal whether the minimum wage causes 1 percent or 25 percent of unskilled workers to lose their jobs. Note that this step still involves positive analysis, but in quantitative terms rather than qualitative terms.

Knowing the consequences of an action, both qualitatively and quantitatively, is still not sufficient to determine whether a policy is desirable. A final step is necessary: we must decide whether the consequences themselves are, on balance, desirable. To make this evaluation, each person must make a **normative analysis**, or value judgment. By nature, such a judgment is nonscientific. It cannot be proved to be right or wrong by facts, evidence, or logic. It stems from the value system of the person who makes the judgment. For example, a belief that it is desirable to raise the wages of the lowest-paid workers, even at the expense of others, falls into this category. People may agree that a particular policy has this effect, but some may hold that the outcome is desirable and others that it is not. Their value judgments differ.

NORMATIVE ANALYSIS
a nonscientific value judgment

Microeconomic theory cannot demonstrate that a particular set of economic institutions or policies is desirable—and neither, for that matter, can any other scientific branch of knowledge. A belief that something is desirable requires a nonscientific judgment of what constitutes *desirability*, and that value judgment is the domain of normative analysis. Nonetheless, microeconomic theory can assist each of us in reaching such normative judgments by helping us determine the likely outcomes. In other words, microeconomics helps us take the first two of the three steps necessary to make an evaluation of real-world phenomena.

1.4   MARKET ANALYSIS AND REAL VERSUS NOMINAL PRICES

Most of microeconomics involves the study of how individual markets function. **Markets** involve the interplay of all potential buyers and sellers of a particular commodity or service. Most economic issues concern the way particular markets function. For example, an economist's wages are likely to be higher than those of a gas station attendant but lower than those of a doctor. This situation reflects the workings of the three labor markets.

MARKETS
the interplay of all potential buyers and sellers of a particular commodity or service

To analyze markets, we concentrate on factors having the greatest influence on the decisions of buyers and sellers. Prices receive special attention. Prices result from market transactions, but they also strongly influence the behavior of buyers and sellers in every market.

In microeconomics the term *price* always refers to the relative or real price of the item. The **nominal price**, or *absolute price*, by itself does not tell us how costly an item really is. Is a 10-cent cup of coffee expensive? In 1900 it would have been outrageously expensive; today it would be a bargain. The problem with nominal prices is that the dollar is an elastic yardstick. *The **real price** of a good reflects its nominal price adjusted for the changing value of money.* Table 1.1 clarifies the distinction between real and nominal prices. Between 1983 and 2000, the price level, or average price of goods and services, rose by 71 percent according to the Consumer Price Index (CPI). [The CPI for all items in 2000 was 171; it was 100 in the base year, 1983, so it rose by $(171 - 100)/100$, or 71 percent.] The CPI measures the change in nominal prices. Table 1.1 indicates that the nominal prices of some goods, such as college tuition, rose by much more than the average 71 percent, and the prices of others, like gasoline, rose less.

NOMINAL PRICE
the absolute price, not adjusted for the changing value of money

REAL PRICE
the nominal price adjusted for the changing value of money

The last column in Table 1.1 lists the change in each item's price compared with the change in the average of all prices. Although the *nominal price* of cereal rose by 98 percent, the overall price level rose by 71 percent over the same period, so the *real price* of cereal rose by only 16 percent $[(198 - 171)/171]$. No matter how the nominal price changed between 1983 and 2000, an economist would say that the prices of the first five individual items rose while the prices of the last three fell. The term *price* always refers to a real price. The prices

TABLE 1.1

NOMINAL AND REAL PRICE CHANGES, 1983 TO 2000

	Index of Nominal Prices in 2000 (1983 = 100)	Change in Real Prices, 1983 to 2000
All items	171	—
College tuition	326	+91%
Medical care	259	+51%
Cereal	198	+16%
Residential rent	182	+6%
Beer and ale	182	+6%
Gasoline	128	−25%
Women's shoes	122	−29%
Interstate telephone calls	70	−59%

Source: U.S. Department of Labor, *CPI Detailed Report*, April 2000.

we use in discussion and in various diagrams refer to real prices, unless otherwise noted. But these prices are generally measured in dollar units. This practice is legitimate as long as we are using dollars of *constant purchasing power*—which is the same as measuring each price in comparison with the general price level.

APPLICATION 1.1 THE OLD RICH VERSUS THE NEW RICH: A REAL COMPARISON

John D. Rockefeller, the early-twentieth-century oil tycoon, was worth $1.1 billion in nominal dollars in 1910. By contrast, in mid-2000, fifty-one Americans were multibillionaires according to a *Forbes* survey. Does this mean that Rockefeller was a financial lightweight relative to today's business executives? Hardly. Rockefeller's nominal wealth of 1910 is the equivalent of $21 billion in today's dollars, an amount surpassed by only four of the "New Rich": Microsoft co-founders Bill Gates and Paul Allen (worth $100 billion and $28 billion as of mid-2000, respectively), Oracle's founder Larry Ellison ($47 billion), and Warren Buffett, chairman of Berkshire Hathaway ($28 billion).

1.5 BASIC ASSUMPTIONS ABOUT MARKET PARTICIPANTS

GOAL-ORIENTED BEHAVIOR
the behavior of market participants interested in fulfilling their own, personal goals

Economists make three basic assumptions about buyers and sellers in markets. First, market participants are presumed to be **goal-oriented**—that is, interested in fulfilling their own, personal goals. For example, the Emir of Kuwait may desire an opulent personal jet and advanced medical care for the people of his country. Former basketball star Michael Jordan might long for greater privacy and the opportunity to play more golf. The late film star Marilyn Monroe hoped for ever greater success on the screen and stage, an Academy Award, and children of her own.

The assumption of goal-oriented behavior often is taken to indicate that individuals are self-interested. This assumption, however, does not imply that market participants care solely about their own pocketbooks. As economists use this term, the behavior of Mother Teresa could accurately be described as goal-oriented. Although Mother Teresa's actions clearly indicated that she had little interest in worldly possessions, they did reflect her own personal desire to help the poor of Calcutta. The assumption of goal-oriented behavior does not rule out altruistic goals.

The second assumption economists make about market participants is that they engage in **rational behavior**. For example, we presume that Toyota's decision to build a car production plant in the United States is the outcome of a careful, deliberative process that weighs the expected benefits and costs. We presume an individual buys a new home based on knowledge of its market value and an honest appraisal of what he or she can afford.

The third, and most important, assumption made by economists about market participants is that they confront **scarce resources**. For example, there is simply not enough time, money, or other resources for the typical consumer to satisfy all of his or her desires. Most economists argue that human beings have relatively limitless desires, and that no matter how wealthy individuals become, resources will never be plentiful enough to ensure that all their desires can be fulfilled.

If individuals rationally pursue their goals but have limited resources with which to pursue them, choices must be made. Specifically, one must decide which goal to pursue and how far to pursue it. Microeconomics explores this process of making choices subject to resource constraints.

RATIONAL BEHAVIOR
the behavior of market participants based on a careful, deliberative process that weighs expected benefits and costs

SCARCE RESOURCES
insufficient time, money, or other resources for individuals to satisfy all their desires

1.6 OPPORTUNITY COST

Whenever you pursue one goal, you limit the extent to which your other goals can be satisfied with your scarce resources. For example, suppose that after getting your bachelor's degree and working for a few years, you enroll in a full-time, two-year MBA program. What would the cost of this choice be? You would incur some **explicit costs**, such as tuition, books, and parking. The dollars spent on such items could have been devoted to the pursuit of other goals. You would also face **implicit costs** associated with your own use of time. For example, instead of going to business school, you could have continued working and making $40,000 per year. The $40,000 in annual forgone wages would be an implicit cost associated with pursuing an MBA. In other words, the time and effort devoted to pursuing the MBA could have instead been used to generate $40,000 in each of the two years that you attend graduate business school.

To understand why implicit costs matter, assume that, relative to the option of remaining at work, the MBA entails explicit costs (such as tuition) of $50,000 and will increase your postgraduation lifetime earnings by $60,000. In this case you will probably not leave your job to pursue the MBA. The $60,000 increase in postgraduate net earnings would be outweighed by the combined $50,000 in explicit costs and $80,000 in the implicit cost of two years' lost wages.

The concepts of explicit and implicit costs also apply to the production side of a market. For firms making production decisions, explicit costs are those that are usually counted as costs in conventional accounting statements. They include payroll, raw materials, insurance, electricity, interest on debt, and so on. Implicit costs reflect the fact that a firm's resources can be allocated to other uses—AOL-Time-Warner, for example, can reallocate its resources from magazine publishing to the production and distribution of interactive video products.

The sum of the explicit and implicit costs associated with using some resource in a particular way is defined to be the resource's **economic cost** or **opportunity cost**. The concept of opportunity cost forces us to recognize that costs are not just money payments but also sacrificed alternatives. Where more than two uses for a resource exist and the resource can be devoted to only one use at a time, the opportunity cost of using the resource in a particular way is the

EXPLICIT COSTS
money used in the pursuit of a goal that could otherwise have been spent on an alternative objective

IMPLICIT COSTS
costs associated with the individual's use of his or her own time

ECONOMIC COST OR OPPORTUNITY COST
the sum of explicit and implicit costs

value of the resource in its best alternative use. So, if your options are business school, continuing to work in your current job for $40,000 per year, and switching to a similarly demanding job that only pays $30,000 per year, you would take into account only the implicit cost of giving up your current job in determining the opportunity cost of pursuing the MBA.

APPLICATION 1.2 THE RISE OF MAIL-ORDER AND ONLINE SHOPPING

By any absolute or relative measure mail-order shopping has increased dramatically over the past few decades. An important reason for this development involves a change in the implicit cost of shoppers' time. With the rapid growth over the past few decades of two-wage-earner families and the greater work commitments faced by such families, the implicit cost of shoppers' time has increased significantly. By comparison, earlier in the twentieth century, one-wage-earner families were more common and the "nonworking" spouse typically specialized in taking care of the family's household needs, including shopping. As the implicit cost of time spent on shopping has increased, families have economized on the amount of time devoted to shopping through devices such as mail-order catalogs and the Internet. The increase in the implicit cost of shoppers' time also helps explain the growth of fast-food restaurants, convenience stores being bundled together with gasoline stations, and one-stop shopping hypermarkets such as Sam's Club. More recently, the increase in the implicit cost of consumers' time has fueled the growth of distance learning (typically accessed asynchronously through the Internet at a student's preferred location and time) and online shopping.

Of course, as households have shifted to buying everything from clothing and furniture to food and books through mail-order and Web sites, the mailboxes of those households have had to adjust. For example, one of the authors' mailboxes has collapsed twice from the sheer weight and wear and tear associated with the increased volume of mail-order catalogs over the years. It had to be replaced by an ultra-durable, supersized version. Moreover, households are soon expected to have "home delivery portals" the size of hotel guest-room refrigerators, costing about $300 apiece to produce, and much more agreeable to customers who cannot be there or want things delivered while they are asleep. These state-of-the-art computerized mailboxes will be able to remember who delivered and when and connected to security systems to deter thieves (perhaps even hidden underground to pop up only on a delivery driver's signal). They will have several components: some refrigerated to protect perishables; others heated to keep croissants and cappucino at serving temperatures.

APPLICATION 1.3 NEVER ON SUNDAY

In determining the opportunity cost of pursuing any objective, both monetary and nonmonetary costs need to be taken into account. For example, in 1995, former Brigham Young University football star Eli Herring turned down a three-year, $500,000-per-year offer to play professional football with the Oakland Raiders. Herring instead chose to pursue a career as a high school math teacher, earning $22,000 per year. Why did he make this choice? Playing professional football would have come at a high nonmonetary cost. Herring is a devout Mormon who believes that the Sabbath should be strictly observed. Because most professional football games are played on Sunday, accepting the Raiders' offer would have violated what Herring believes is the Bible's prohibition of working on a day that should be devoted to going to church and spending time with family.

Economic Versus Accounting Costs

Because opportunity costs are not always readily apparent (especially their implicit components), they often are not accurately reflected in companies' net income statements. For example, consider a family-run grocery store in downtown Tokyo whose owners acquired the property several generations ago for almost nothing. From an accounting perspective, the grocery store may appear to be generating positive net income: revenue exceeds the sum of **accounting costs** comprising payroll, electricity, insurance, wholesale grocery costs, and so on. Still, the grocery store may be losing money from an economic perspective once the opportunity cost of the land on which it sits is taken into account. That is, the land could be sold or rented to someone else. This choice would generate payments to the family that are sacrificed when the family uses the land itself. These forgone earnings represent an opportunity cost—and this cost can be significant. For example, the value of just the Imperial Palace grounds situated in the heart of Tokyo has been estimated to exceed the total value of real estate in the state of California.

ACCOUNTING COSTS
costs reported in companies' net income statements generated by accountants

---

APPLICATION 1.4   **WHY IT WAS PROFITABLE TO DEMOLISH A PROFITABLE HONG KONG HOTEL**

In June 1995, the 26-story Hong Kong Hilton, the first five-star hotel in the central business district of Hong Kong, was smashed to rubble. The hotel was demolished despite the facts that accounting statements showed the hotel earning $25 million in profit on $58 million in revenue in 1994; $16 million had recently been spent to rebuild the hotel's lobby—more than the hotel cost to build in 1963; and the owner of the hotel, real estate tycoon Li Ka-Shing, had to pay $125 million to Hilton's parent company to break the last 20 years of the hotel's management contract. Why did the demolition make sense? With the astronomically high rental prices for office space in Hong Kong, property consultants estimated that Mr. Li Ka-Shing could earn an extra $70 million in rental income per year by constructing an office tower on the site historically occupied by the 750-room hotel.

Sunk Costs

Although opportunity costs may not be readily apparent, they should always be taken into account when making economic decisions. The opposite is the case for **sunk costs**—costs that have already been incurred and are beyond recovery. Even though sunk costs are usually quite apparent, they need to be ignored when making economic decisions.

Consider the case of the Los Angeles Lakers, who negotiated a seven-year, $120 million contract with center Shaquille O'Neal in 1996. The contract involved a signing bonus of $22 million, plus annual payments averaging $14 million, should the Lakers exercise their option of playing O'Neal. But, suppose that after the contract is signed, a center comparable in talent to O'Neal offers his services to the Lakers for $105 million for the next seven years—annual payments of $15 million. What should the Lakers management do? The answer is, stick with O'Neal. Once the $22 million signing bonus has been paid to O'Neal, it is a sunk cost. The opportunity cost of exercising the O'Neal option is thus $98 million (the remaining amount that must be paid to O'Neal) versus the $105 million it would cost to hire the rival center.

SUNK COSTS
costs that have already been incurred and are beyond recovery

APPLICATION 1.5 — MEASURING ECONOMIC COSTS AND BENEFITS

Although important, measuring the economic costs and benefits associated with using resources in a particular way is not always easy. Take the case of intangibles that have no established market price, such as clean air, virgin wilderness, and endangered species. For example, how can we put a dollar value on the amount of damage (crude-oil-covered beaches, dead sea life, and so on) caused by Exxon's *Valdez* oil spill? Measuring intangibles is easiest when environmental problems cause direct harm to users: the value of lost recreational opportunities (such as less fishing, swimming, and hiking) can be estimated. It is more difficult when consumers have no contact with a natural resource but still place a positive value on its existence. For example, you may get a real "existence" value from knowing that sea otters or bald eagles exist, even though you may never have actually seen one. Of course, the benefit is likely to vary, depending on how strong an environmentalist you are.

When resources have no established market price, economists rely on a variety of methods to account for the economic costs and benefits associated with using the resources in a particular way. For example, techniques drawn from psychology and market research are employed to determine how much people who don't come into contact with a resource (such as a bald eagle) would be willing to pay to keep the resource in existence. The statistical tool of regression analysis (covered in Chapter 4) is utilized in other cases, such as determining the cost, in terms of noise pollution, of being located in an airport's flight path. Specifically, economists examine housing prices while holding constant all other factors (such as square footage, quality of area schools, and proximity to shopping centers). Any remaining difference between the price of homes that sit in airport flight paths and those that don't is assumed to reflect the cost of airport noise pollution.

But remember that the cost of sitting in the same location along an airport's flight path may vary across individuals. A case in point involves a bottler of wines whose shop is located in the flight path of Los Angeles International Airport. The bottler produces two types of wine: Runway Red and Runway White. He claims that the location of his business is ideal because the sound of planes overhead taking off and landing shakes the bottles in a way that speeds the sedimentation process. Thus, what may be a cost to one individual can be a benefit to another.

1.7 PRODUCTION POSSIBILITY FRONTIER

PRODUCTION POSSIBILITY FRONTIER (PPF)
a depiction of all the different combinations of goods that a rational actor with certain personal goals can attain with a fixed amount of resources

We can display in graphical form the basic assumptions we have made about market actors as well as the concept of opportunity cost. Specifically, a **production possibility frontier (PPF)** depicts all the different combinations of goods that a rational actor with certain personal goals can attain with a fixed amount of resources. For example, suppose you are president of a university. By effectively employing the resources on your campus, such as the faculty and staff, classrooms, libraries, laboratories, dorms, cyclotron, and so on, you can produce two possible services: research and teaching.

Based on the resources at your disposal, assume that the different combinations of research and teaching services that your university can produce each year are represented by the *PPF* depicted in Figure 1.1. At one extreme, if your university were devoted solely to research, you could produce 1,000 units of research and 0 units of teaching (point A) with your limited resources. At the other extreme, if classroom instruction were the overriding objective, your university could produce a maximum of 500 units of teaching and 0 units of research (point Z). Of course, you need not be at either of the two extremes on your *PPF*.

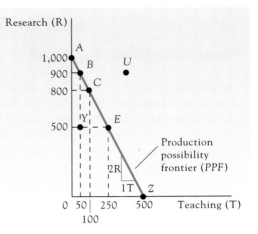

FIGURE 1.1

A Production Possibility Frontier (PPF)
A *PPF* depicts the three basic assumptions made by economists about market participants (goal-oriented behavior, scarce resources, and rationality) as well as the concept of opportunity cost. With a nonsatiable desire for both research (R) and teaching (T), a university president would prefer to be as far to the northeast as possible on the graph. Scarce resources limit the president to any combination on or below the *PPF* boundary *AZ*. Rational behavior implies that the president will choose to be on the boundary as opposed to below it. Opportunity cost is reflected by the slope of the *PPF*.

You also have the option of producing a mix of 500 units of research and 250 teaching units (point *E*) or, for that matter, any point lying on or inside (such as *Y*) the straight-line segment that we have drawn connecting endpoints *A* and *Z* of the *PPF* shown in Figure 1.1.

How does a *PPF* such as the one shown in Figure 1.1 reflect the three basic assumptions that we have made about market actors? Your desire as university president to encourage both research and teaching, if unlimited, would imply that you would like to be as far to the northeast as possible in the graph—generating an infinite amount of both research and teaching. But scarce resources, represented by the boundary, segment *AZ*, of your *PPF*, keep you inside the *PPF*. Points such as *U*, beyond your *PPF*'s boundary, thus are unattainable. Finally, rational behavior presumes that you will choose a point on the boundary of your *PPF* rather than inside the boundary. Why choose a mix of output involving 500 research and 50 teaching units (point *Y*), when the same resources at your disposal can get you more of both research and teaching (such as at point *C*)? Rational behavior implies that you will select a point on the boundary (segment *AZ*) of your *PPF*.

The three basic assumptions that we have made about market actors imply that you will be on the boundary of your *PPF*, but you must still choose a specific combination of research and teaching on the boundary. The three basic assumptions (positive analysis) can place you only on the *PPF* boundary. Once on the boundary, a value judgment (normative analysis) is necessary to determine the "best" point for you along the boundary. For example, if you believe that a good university should focus solely on research, you will probably opt for point *A* on the *PPF* boundary. If, instead, you believe that a university is distinguished exclusively by the quality of its classroom instruction, point *Z* is likely to be your selection.

Figure 1.1 also depicts the concept of opportunity cost. Consider the movement between points *A* and *B* on the boundary of the *PPF*. If you, as the university president, start off at point *A* with 0 teaching units and move to point *B* with 50 teaching units, 100 research units will have to be given up (from 1,000 research units at *A* to 900 at *B*). Thus, if the three basic assumptions that we have outlined about market participants hold and you are forced to move along the boundary of your *PPF*, you confront a tradeoff of 100 research units lost per 50 teaching units gained, moving between points *A* and *B*. This tradeoff is the opportunity cost of using your resources to increase the number of teaching units from 0 to 50. By expanding output of teaching from 0 to 50, you are implicitly giving up 100 units of research. The opportunity cost of each additional teaching unit gained between 0 and 50 teaching units is 2 research units. And, since the boundary of the *PPF* as we have drawn it is

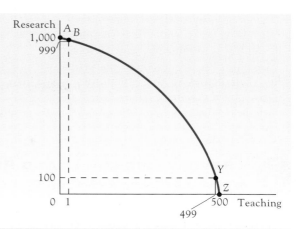

FIGURE 1.2

The Typical-Case *PPF*: Concave to the Origin
With a concave *PPF*, the per-unit opportunity cost of an additional unit of teaching increases with the more teaching one produces. A one-teaching-unit increase between points *A* and *B* along the boundary of the *PPF* is associated with an opportunity cost equal to 1 research unit. A one-teaching-unit increase between points *Y* and *Z* carries with it an opportunity cost of 100 research units.

a straight line, this per-teaching-unit opportunity cost is constant over the entire AZ boundary of the depicted *PPF*.

Constant per-unit opportunity costs occur only where the boundary of the *PPF* is a straight line. But the more typical *PPF* is a concave-shaped boundary bowed out from the origin, as in Figure 1.2. With a concave-shaped *PPF*, the slope of the boundary AZ becomes steeper (that is, more negative) as one moves from point A, where the university is producing just research and no teaching, to point Z, where the reverse is true. The per-unit opportunity cost of producing additional teaching, in terms of the research that must be given up to produce those added teaching units, grows with the total output of teaching. For example, if you are producing 0 teaching units and want to expand output to 1 teaching unit, moving from point A to B in Figure 1.2, you would have to drop 1 research unit. The first teaching unit produced would have an opportunity cost of 1 research unit. When you are producing 499 teaching units, however, and want to expand teaching output by the same additional unit, the opportunity cost in terms of research that must be given up is much higher—100 research units must be given up to move from point Y to Z.

Why does the per-unit opportunity cost associated with expanding the output of any particular commodity typically increase in this way? The reason stems from differences in relative productivity across resources as related to various commodities. For example, some faculty are relatively better researchers, others do better in the classroom. When a university is at point A, the per-unit opportunity cost of increasing teaching output is fairly low. There are bound to be some faculty who are not prolific researchers, but who are adept at teaching. Reallocating such faculty to increasing teaching output will not involve much of a per-unit loss in terms of research (one research unit between points A and B). By contrast, when one is already producing 499 units of teaching and contemplating increasing production to 500 (that is, moving from point Y to point Z), one has to move the most talented researchers full-time into the classroom, a far more costly undertaking in terms of forgone research.

SUMMARY

• Microeconomic theory is the branch of economics that begins with the study of the behavior of individual economic units, primarily consumers and business firms.

• Microeconomics considers how the decisions of individuals and firms are coordinated through interactions in markets.

• Economists make three assumptions about the behavior of market participants: It is goal-oriented, it is rational, and it is constrained by scarce resources.

• Because of scarce resources, market participants can't fulfill their desires to the extent they would like, and choices must therefore be made.

• Whenever one alternative is chosen, an opportunity cost is involved.

• A production possibility frontier (*PPF*) allows us to graphically depict the basic assumptions made by economists about market participants, as well as the concept of opportunity cost.

REVIEW QUESTIONS AND PROBLEMS

Questions and problems marked with an asterisk have solutions given in Answers to Selected Problems at the back of the book (page 571).

1.1. In 1997, the citizens of Tucson, Arizona, voted on whether the minimum wage within the city should be raised to $7 per hour. Explain how one would use positive and normative analysis to evaluate the desirability of this proposed policy.

1.2. What economic forces might explain why the relative price of interstate telephone calls fell while the relative price of medical care increased between 1983 and 2000?

1.3. Explain why it is important to look at a good's real price as opposed to its nominal, or absolute, price.

1.4. Suppose that Jack Welch, the successful CEO of General Electric, who is paid an annual salary of $10 million, were to leave General Electric and start his own management consulting company. If, in the new venture, Welch chose not to pay himself a salary, the net income statement for his venture would not report an accounting cost associated with such a decision. Would there be an economic cost—an opportunity cost—associated with Welch's new position in the management consulting firm?

*1.5. The RAND (short for "research and development") Corporation is a think tank located on 15 prime acres of seaside property in the center of Santa Monica, California. RAND purchased the land for its offices from the city in 1952 for $250,000. "Given that the money RAND paid for its land in 1952 can be treated as a sunk cost, the cost of the land to RAND is zero and RAND would thus be foolish to consider purchasing a new site in Las Vegas and relocating there." Is this statement true, false, or uncertain? Explain your answer.

1.6. Tokyo's streets are characterized by a plethora of vending machines—dispensing everything from soft drinks, candy bars, and cigarettes to magazines, personal toiletries, and beer. Unlike other major cities such as New York and London, virtually every downtown street corner seems to have at least one vending machine. Relying on the concept of opportunity cost, explain why vending machines are so prevalent in Tokyo versus more traditional purveying mechanisms such as newsstands, grocery stores, and liquor stores.

1.7. Reconsider the example in the text of whether you should pursue an MBA. Suppose that prior to making a decision you are robbed of $5,000. Should this theft affect your decision? How will the theft affect the accounting and economic costs associated with pursuing the MBA?

1.8. Instead of being robbed of $5,000, suppose that you win $50 in the state lottery prior to making your decision about whether to pursue an MBA. Should this windfall affect your decision?

1.9. Some people have argued that the United States cannot afford a volunteer army in which wages are high enough to attract competent enlistees. Instead, they suggest paying lower wages and drafting the required number of recruits. Would such a policy change lower the accounting and economic costs to the United States government from maintaining an army? Explain your answer.

1.10. Say that the city of Los Angeles grants, for a price of $0, a sizable tract of land to Hughes Aircraft Company. The grant does not restrict Hughes to using the land only to produce military aircraft. Explain what the economic cost is to Hughes of using the granted land to produce military aircraft.

1.11. A university produces two commodities: research and teaching. The resources the university uses include faculty and staff, libraries, classrooms, and so on. The following schedule indicates some points on the university's *PPF*:

	A	B	C	D	E	F	G
Research	900	750	600	450	300	150	0
Teaching	0	20	45	75	110	150	200

a. Does research production by the university exhibit increasing, constant, or decreasing per-unit opportunity costs?

b. Graph the university's *PPF* (assuming that straight-line segments connect the points specified above). Indicate which areas of the graph correspond to unattainable production points, production points that make the most effective use of the university's resources, and points where there are unemployed resources.

c. Suppose that the university is at point B but would like to alter production to point C. What would be the per-teaching-unit opportunity cost of producing the extra teaching units?

d. Suppose that the university is at point C but would like to alter production to point B. What would be the per-research-unit opportunity cost of producing the extra research?

e. What will happen to the university's *PPF* if the main laboratory burns down (assume that the laboratory is not used to produce teaching but is used solely to produce research)? Graph the new *PPF*.

f. What will happen to the *PPF* if all of the campus resources are cut in half? Graph the new *PPF*.

g. Suppose the university is at point F. The university president proposes to move the school to point B; she claims that B is a more desirable choice since the total output is 750 + 20 = 770 total units of output at B versus 150 + 150 = 300 output units at C. Is the president correct?

1.12. Preparation time for the typical family meal has dwindled from two and a half hours in the early 1960s to 15 minutes today. Over the same time period, brown-bag lunches for school kids have yielded to prefabricated "meal kits." For example, Oscar Mayer launched its packaged Lunchables in 1988 and by 2000 was making nearly $600 million in meal-kit profits. Using the concept of opportunity cost, explain these phenomena.

1.13. "Motorola and other backers sank more than $5 billion in the 1990s into the development of Iridium, a globe-covering satellite communications system to connect wireless telephone users anywhere on earth. Although the number of subscribers signing up for the service has fallen significantly below projections and operating costs vastly exceed revenues, this is no reason for Motorola and its partners to back out of the venture. Indeed, it would be foolish to quit now, given the large amount of money that has already been invested in Iridium." True, false, or uncertain? Explain why.

1.14. Abraham Lincoln was paid $25,000 as president. Today, the president earns $400,000 a year. Does this mean that President Lincoln was relatively underpaid for his service? (*Hint:* The CPI in 1863 was 9.)

1.15. A study by Professor Gerald Scully of the University of Texas finds that government-sponsored killing of its own people—an act that claimed the lives of 170 million people in the twentieth century (7.3 percent of the total population and four times as many individuals as claimed by international and civil wars combined)—is less likely to occur the more productive is a country's populace (as measured by real gross domestic product per capita). Explain why this is consistent with the concept of opportunity cost.

CHAPTER 2

Supply and Demand

The supply–demand model shows how the competitive interaction of sellers and buyers determines a good's market price and quantity.

● Chapter Outline

2.1 Demand and Supply Curves
The Demand Curve   Shifts in the Demand Curve
***Application 2.1** The Effect of Traffic Schools on Speeding*
The Supply Curve   Shifts in the Supply Curve
2.2 Determination of Equilibrium Price and Quantity
***Application 2.2** Is There a Parking Shortage in Major American Cities?*
2.3 Adjustment to Changes in Demand or Supply
***Application 2.3** Supply, Demand, and Babysitting*
Using the Supply–Demand Model to Explain Market Outcomes
2.4 Government Intervention in Markets: Price Controls
Rent Control   Who Loses, Who Benefits?
***Application 2.4** Why Web Surfing Can Turn into Web Crawling*
***Application 2.5** Why the Doctor Is Not In*
2.5 Elasticities
Price Elasticity of Demand   Calculating Price Elasticity of Demand
***Application 2.6** Demand Elasticity and Cable Television Pricing*
Demand Elasticities Vary Among Goods   The Estimation of Demand Elasticities
***Application 2.7** D.C. Learns about Demand Elasticity*
Three Other Elasticities
***Application 2.8** It Takes Time*

● Learning Objectives

- Understand how the behavior of buyers and sellers can be characterized through demand and supply curves.
- Explain how equilibrium price and quantity are determined in a market for a good or service.
- Analyze how a market equilibrium is affected by changes in demand or supply.
- Explore the effects of government intervention in markets and how a price ceiling impacts the prevailing price, quantity supplied, quantity demanded, and the welfare of buyers and sellers.
- Show how elasticities provide a quantitative measure of the responsiveness of quantity demanded or supplied to a change in some other variable such as price or income.

● As personal computers and word processing programs proliferate, what will happen to the demand for paper? Why have home prices in the San Francisco Bay Area risen so much more than elsewhere in the United States with the growth of the New Economy? Why have fixed retail prices become less common with the advent of the Internet and online shopping? If a cable company raises its rates, will total revenues and profit also increase? Will a hike in the government sales tax on cigarettes have an appreciable effect on teen smoking?

A solid grounding in the basics of supply and demand can help us address these and many other real-world questions. The supply–demand model reviewed in this chapter indicates how the competitive interaction of sellers and buyers determines a good's market price and quantity. In addition, the model indicates how the market price and quantity of a good respond to changes in other economic variables such as the cost of inputs, technology, consumer preferences, and the prices of other goods. Furthermore, the basic supply–demand model can be used to analyze the effects of various forms of government intervention in markets. Price controls are the form of government intervention that we will analyze in this chapter. Finally, we will examine how markets operate from a *quantitative* as well as a *qualitative* perspective. In the business world especially, we often need a quantitative answer to the question of how a change in one economic variable such as consumer income, price, price of another good, or price of an input affects the quantity demanded or supplied of a particular good.

2.1 DEMAND AND SUPPLY CURVES

Markets are composed of buyers and sellers. Our analysis of the behavior of buyers relies on demand curves; supply curves depict the behavior of sellers. Let's begin with the buyer, or demand, side of the market.

The Demand Curve

The amount of a good that a consumer or a group of consumers wishes to purchase depends on many factors: income, age, occupation, education, experience, buyer preferences, taxes, subsidies, expectations, and so on. It also depends on the price of the good. According to the **law of demand**, *the lower price of a good, the larger the quantity consumers wish to purchase.* To this law we must add an important condition. The relationship will hold only if the other factors affecting consumption, such as income and preferences, do not change at the same time that the price of the good changes. The assumption that all other factors remain constant is an important one to keep in mind when examining many relationships in economics.

Figure 2.1 shows a hypothetical market demand curve for digital video (or versatile) disc players (DVD players). At each possible price the curve identifies the total quantity desired by consumers. So, at a per-unit price of $250, the *quantity demanded* will be 400,000, while at a per-unit price of $200 the *quantity demanded* will be 550,000. Note that we do not say that *demand* is higher at the lower price, only that the *quantity demanded* is. When economists use the term *demand* by itself (as in demand and supply), we are referring to the entire relationship, the demand curve. *Quantity demanded*, however, refers to one particular quantity on the demand curve.

The negative slope of the demand curve—higher prices associated with lower quantities—is the graphical representation of the law of demand. Economists believe that the demand curves for all, or virtually all, goods and inputs slope downward. As a consequence, the proposition that demand curves have negative slopes has been elevated in economic jargon to the position of a "law." It is probably the most universally valid and strongly supported proposition in economics.

A demand curve for a product pertains to a particular period of time. For example, the demand curve in Figure 2.1 may refer to consumer buying behavior for July of this year. Another demand curve may be relevant for a different period of time. In addition, the information conveyed by the demand curve refers to alternative possibilities for the same time

LAW OF DEMAND
the economic principle that says, the lower the price of a good, the larger the quantity consumers wish to purchase

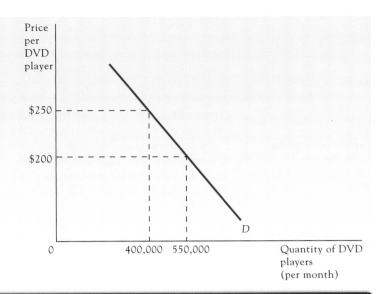

FIGURE 2.1

A Demand Curve
The demand curve *D* shows the quantity of DVD players that consumers will purchase at alternative prices. Its negative slope reflects the law of demand: more DVD players are purchased at a lower price.

period. If the per-unit price is $250 in July of this year, consumers will purchase 400,000 DVD players; if, instead, it is $200 for the same time period, consumers will purchase 550,000 DVD players.

Although economists usually interpret the curve as showing *the quantities purchased at various prices*, they sometimes use an equivalent interpretation. The demand curve also identifies *the price that consumers will pay for various quantities*. If the demand curve in Figure 2.1 is correct and 400,000 DVD players are placed on the market, consumers will be willing to pay $250 per unit up to the marginal, 400,000th player (400,001 DVD players will not be purchased, according to Figure 2.1, if the per-unit price is $250). If the larger quantity, 550,000, is offered on the market, consumers will purchase the quantity only at the lower per-unit price of $200. That a larger quantity can be sold only at a lower price is another, and equivalent, way of stating the law of demand.

A final point about demand curves: their negative slope is not due only to the presence of more consumers at lower prices. For some goods, like water, the number of consumers will be the same regardless of price, though the amount they use may vary. Increased water consumption when the price is lower reflects greater consumption per person, not more people consuming water. At the other extreme are goods for which more consumption at lower prices results mainly from new consumers entering the market. Personal computers might be such a good. Most goods fall between these extremes—more consumers entering the market, and more consumption per consumer occurring at lower prices. The downward-sloping demand for DVD players is probably due mostly to additional families buying DVD players at lower prices, but some families may purchase more than one because they either have more than one television set or are giving them away as gifts.

Shifts in the Demand Curve

As mentioned earlier, many factors influence consumer purchases. A demand curve focuses just on the effect of changes in a product's own per-unit price, with other factors held constant. For example, consumers' incomes are taken to be invariant at all points on a particular demand curve. Now let's consider the other factors, besides the good's price, that might

NORMAL GOODS
those goods for which an
increase in income leads
to greater consumption

INFERIOR GOODS
those goods whose
consumption falls when
income rises

COMPLEMENTS
two goods that tend to be
consumed together, so
consumption of both
tends to rise or fall
simultaneously

SUBSTITUTES
goods that can replace one
another in consumption

**TASTES OR
PREFERENCES**
the feelings of consumers
about the desirability of
different goods

affect the consumption of it. First are the *incomes* of consumers. The level of income is al-most certain to affect the amount of goods consumers will purchase; usually, they wish to purchase more when income rises. The term **normal goods** refers to those for which an in-crease in income leads to greater consumption. Most studies indicate that DVD players fall in this category. There are, however, certain goods, called **inferior goods**, whose consump-tion falls when income rises. Examples of this latter, more rare, category might include ham-burger, cheap wine (e.g., André's), and public transportation. If you won $10 million in the state lottery, would you continue to take the bus?

In addition to incomes, the *prices of related goods* also affect the quantity of DVD players consumers will purchase. Related goods fall into two distinct groups: *complements* and *substi-tutes*. Two goods are **complements** if they tend to be consumed together, so consumption of both goods tends to rise or fall simultaneously. Examples of complements to DVD players in-clude television sets, DVDs, and popcorn. After all, trying to use a DVD without a televi-sion set or discs is difficult. And popcorn, for many consumers, increases the pleasure of using a DVD player. *If two goods are complements, an increase in the price of one leads to a de-crease in the demand for the other, and vice versa.* If the price of television sets rises, DVD player consumption will decrease (the demand curve for DVD players shifts in).

Substitutes, on the other hand, are goods that can replace one another in consumption. Their consumption is frequently an "either-or" choice since they serve similar purposes, and one or the other may be chosen. For instance, live theater and the VCRs are, in the eyes of many consumers, substitutes for DVD players. If two goods are substitutes, an increase in the price of one leads to an increased demand for the other. If the price of movie passes rises sharply, DVD player consumption will increase (the demand curve shifts out); DVD players are substituted for going out to the movies when going out to the movies becomes more ex-pensive.

It is not always readily apparent whether two goods are complements or substitutes for one another. For example, one might think that personal computers and word processing programs would be substitutes for paper since virtual text can be used in lieu of hard copy. If anything, however, personal computers and word processing programs have proved to be complements to paper in practice. That is, paper usage has increased sharply with the ad-vent of virtual text. This is so because as technology has made it easier to create and revise text, individuals can obtain hard copies of more files (through the printers, of course, that typically accompany personal computers).

Consumers' tastes or preferences also affect consumption. By **tastes** or **preferences** we mean the subjective feelings of consumers about the desirability of different goods. Should consumers decide that outdoor exercise is more appealing than watching DVDs—a change in tastes—the purchases of players would drop off. A real-world example occurred in Min-nesota, where analysts have found that television entertainment is less popular among con-sumers than it is, on average, in the other 49 states. The phenomenon appears to reflect the fact that Minnesota was settled disproportionately by Scandinavians, who do not regard television entertainment as highly as do the other ethnic groups constituting the U.S. popu-lation.

Because tastes are a harder-to-quantify factor than price or income, it may be tempting to omit them from an analysis of demand for a product. To do so, however, can lead to incom-plete explanations and inappropriate conclusions. For example, the law of demand applies to the market for beef in India: namely, if the price of beef rises in India, the quantity de-manded of beef will fall. Price, by itself, however, cannot explain why per capita beef con-sumption is so low in India relative to the United States. To understand this requires some knowledge of factors such as religious beliefs and cultural taboos that influence consumer preferences regarding beef in India.

The preceding factors (incomes, prices of related goods, and tastes) are not the only influences on demand beyond the price of the good in question. They are, however, almost certain to be significant for virtually all goods. Thus, we will concentrate on them in the remainder of our analysis.

In drawing a demand curve, we assume that incomes, the prices of related goods, and preferences are the same at all points on the curve. The purpose of holding them constant is not to deny that they change but to identify the independent influence of the good's own price on consumer purchases. If incomes, prices of related goods, or preferences do change, the entire demand curve shifts. Figure 2.2 illustrates such a shift. (Note that we begin to use shorthand terms on the axes, *price* and *quantity*. It should be understood that we mean *price per unit* and *quantity per time period*.) Demand curve *D*, for example, reflects conditions when consumers' annual incomes average $35,000 and the other factors are held constant. If consumers' annual incomes rise to an average of $45,000 and DVD players are a normal good, consumers will wish to purchase more players at every price than they did before. The change in income produces a *shift in the demand curve* from *D* to *D'*. An increase in income *increases demand* for the good (in the normal good case), meaning that the entire demand curve shifts outward or rightward. A *decrease in demand* refers to an inward, or leftward, shift in the demand curve toward the origin. If consumers' preferences shift from being a couch potato and watching DVDs to exercising outdoors, the demand for DVD players will decrease.

To use demand curves correctly, we must distinguish clearly between situations that involve a **movement along a given demand curve** and those that involve a **shift in demand**. A movement along a given demand curve occurs when the quantity demanded changes in response to a change in price of a particular good while the other factors affecting consumption are held constant. This is not a change in the demand curve. An example would be the movement from point A to point B along demand curve *D* in Figure 2.2. A shift in demand, a movement of the curve itself, occurs when there is a change in income, the price of a related good, or tastes, affecting the quantity demanded at each possible price. An example is the movement of the entire demand curve from *D* to *D'* in Figure 2.2.

MOVEMENT ALONG A GIVEN DEMAND CURVE
a change in quantity demanded that occurs in response to a change in price, other factors holding constant

SHIFT OF A DEMAND CURVE
a change in the demand curve itself that occurs with a change in income, in the price of a related good, or in tastes and affecting the quantity demanded at each possible price

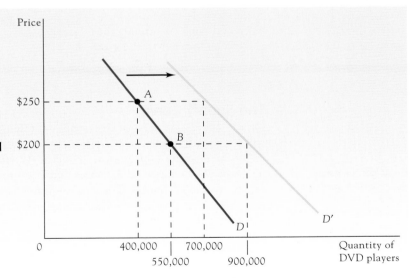

FIGURE 2.2

An Increase in Demand
For a demand curve, other influences besides the price of the good being examined (consumers' incomes, consumers' preferences, prices of related goods, and so on) are held constant at all points along the curve. Changes in these underlying factors normally cause the demand curve to shift. Here, an increase in consumers' incomes causes the demand curve to shift from *D* to *D'* because DVD players are assumed to be a normal good.

APPLICATION 2.1　　THE EFFECT OF TRAFFIC SCHOOLS ON SPEEDING

Traffic schools, which exist in most states of the United States, provide a useful way to remember the distinction between a movement along a given demand curve and shifts of the demand curve. Traffic schools reflect both a movement along a given demand curve for traffic infractions (such as speeding) and an attempt to shift the entire demand curve for traffic infractions leftward. In the case of speeding, a driver's demand to exceed the speed limit can be taken to depend on factors such as the price of exceeding the limit, the driver's preferences and income, and so on. The price of speeding itself depends on the likelihood of being caught, the cost of a traffic ticket, and the effect of a ticket on a motorist's insurance premium.

In California, individuals who have been issued a moving violation are eligible to attend traffic school once every 18 months. To participate, a traffic violator must pay the moving violation, remit tuition to the traffic school, and spend eight hours in "class". The benefit from attending can be substantial, especially in a state such as California, where auto insurance rates are high. Attending allows the "student" to erase one moving violation from his or her driving record and keeps the violation from resulting in a higher insurance premium.

The effect of traffic schools on the cost of speeding violations is surprising: traffic schools lower the cost. Even though it costs money and time to attend, the price of traffic school appears to be lower than the cost

of higher insurance rates. To the degree that they lower the price of speeding, traffic schools produce a downward movement along a given demand curve for speeding, thus increasing the quantity of speeding demanded.

In addition to lowering the price of speeding, however, traffic schools also attempt to decrease drivers' tastes for committing moving violations. They do so in a variety of ways. Some employ comedians as instructors in an attempt to promote better driving behavior through humor. Others rely on gore (movies of past accident scenes) or embarrassment (berating individual violators in front of their classmates for their driving mistakes).

Are traffic schools effective at shifting leftward the demand curve for speeding? Studies by the California Department of Motor Vehicles suggest not.[1] Comparing subsequent records of first-time speeders who attend traffic school versus those who do not, and holding constant other factors such as age and gender, the studies find no improvement in driving behavior. Moreover, since traffic schools reduce the price of speeding and move drivers down a given demand curve for speeding, the net effect of traffic schools is to increase the quantity demanded of speeding.

[1]"The Effectiveness of Accredited Traffic Violator Schools in Reducing Accidents and Violations," Department of Motor Vehicles, State of California, September 1979, and *Business Week*, April 28, 1997, p. 120.

The Supply Curve

LAW OF SUPPLY
the economic principle that says the higher the price of a good, the larger the quantity firms want to produce

On the selling side of a market, we are interested in the amount of a good that business firms will produce and sell. According to the **law of supply**, the higher the price of a good, the larger the quantity firms want to produce. As with the law of demand, this relationship will necessarily hold only if other factors that affect the firms' decisions remain constant when the price of the good changes. The amount firms offer for sale depends on many factors, including the technological know-how concerning production of the good, the cost and productivity of inputs required for production, expectations, employee-management relations, the goals of firms' owners, the presence of any government taxes or subsidies, and so on. The price of the good is also important because it is the reward producers receive for their efforts. The supply curve summarizes the effect of price on the quantity that firms produce and offer for sale.

Figure 2.3 shows a hypothetical market supply curve for DVD players. For each possible price the supply curve identifies the *sum of the quantities offered for sale by the separate firms*. Because all the firms that produce a particular product constitute the industry, this curve is

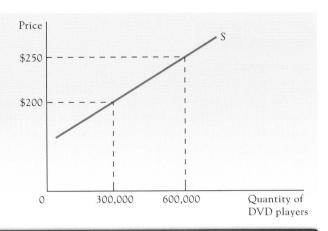

FIGURE 2.3

A Supply Curve
The supply curve S shows the quantity of DVD players producers will be willing to sell at alternative prices. It generally slopes upward, indicating that a higher price will result in increased output.

generally called the industry, or market, supply curve. It shows, for example, that at a price of $200 per DVD player the *quantity supplied* will be 300,000, whereas at a price of $250 the *quantity supplied* will be 600,000. Note that we do not say that *supply* is greater at the higher price, only that the *quantity supplied* is. The term *supply* by itself refers to the entire supply curve, while *quantity supplied* refers to one particular quantity on the curve. This parallels the terminology used for the demand curve.

Supply curves for most goods slope upward. Basically, this upward slope reflects the fact that per-unit opportunity costs rise when more units are produced, so a higher price is necessary to elicit a greater output.[2]

Like the demand curve, the supply curve pertains to a particular period of time. In addition, different points on the supply curve refer to alternative possibilities for the same period of time. Finally, the number of firms producing the good may vary along the supply curve. At low prices some firms may halt production and leave the industry; at high prices new firms may enter the industry.

Shifts in the Supply Curve
The supply curve shows the influence of price on quantity supplied when other factors that also influence output are held constant. When any of the other factors change, the entire supply curve shifts.

Beyond a good's own price, two determinants of quantity supplied deserve special emphasis. First is the *state of technological knowledge* concerning the various ways a good can be manufactured. Second are the *conditions of supply of inputs*, like labor and energy, that are used to produce the good. Supply conditions for inputs relate to the prices that must be paid for their use. Other factors may be important in particular cases—for example, government in the case of health care, weather in the case of agriculture, and an organization's goals in the case of nonprofit institutions like the Red Cross—but technology and input supply conditions influence all output markets.

In drawing a supply curve, we assume that factors such as technological knowledge and input supply conditions do not vary along the curve. The supply curve shows how variation in price alone affects output. If technology or input supply conditions do change, the supply curve shifts. For instance, if a new technology allows manufacturers to produce DVD players

[2]In Chapter 9, though, we will see that supply curves for some products may be horizontal. Upward-sloping supply curves, however, are thought to be the most common shape, and we draw them this way here.

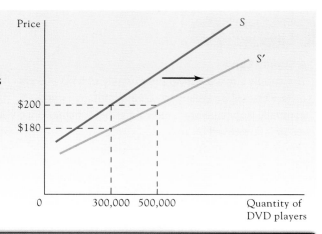

FIGURE 2.4

An Increase in Supply

For a supply curve, technology and input supply conditions are held constant at all points along the curve. Changes in these underlying factors normally cause the supply curve to shift. Here, a technological change causes the supply curve to shift from S to S'.

MOVEMENT ALONG A GIVEN SUPPLY CURVE

a change in quantity supplied that occurs in response to a change in the good's selling price, other factors holding constant

SHIFT OF A SUPPLY CURVE

a change in the supply curve itself that occurs when the other factors, besides price, that affect output change

at a lower cost, the supply curve shifts to the right, as illustrated in Figure 2.4. Because producers' costs are now lower due to the technological advance, individual producers will want to produce more at any price. After the technological advance, the quantity supplied is greater at each possible price, as shown by the shift in the supply curve from S to S'. The rightward shift in the supply curve reflects an *increase in supply*. If there is an increase in supply, each quantity will be available at a lower price than before. For example, before the technological advance, 300,000 DVD players would have been produced only if the price were at least $200; afterward, 300,000 would be produced at a price of $180.

Just as with demand curves, we must distinguish a **movement along a given supply curve** from a **shift in supply**. A movement along a supply curve occurs when the quantity supplied varies in response to a change in the good's selling price while the other factors that affect output hold constant. A shift in the supply curve occurs when the other factors that affect output change.

2.2 DETERMINATION OF EQUILIBRIUM PRICE AND QUANTITY

The demand curve shows what consumers wish to purchase at various prices, and the supply curve shows what producers wish to sell. When the two are put together, we see that there is only one price at which the quantity consumers wish to purchase exactly equals the quantity firms wish to sell. In Figure 2.5, that price is $220, where consumers wish to purchase 475,000 DVD players and firms wish to sell the same quantity. It is identified by the point of intersection between the supply and demand curves.

The intersection identifies the **equilibrium** price and quantity in the market. Upon reaching equilibrium, price and quantity will remain there. Of course, if the supply or the demand curve shifts, the equilibrium point will change, too. A basic assumption of microeconomic theory is that the independent actions of buyers and sellers tend to move the market toward equilibrium. We can see how this happens if we first imagine that the price is not at its equilibrium level. Suppose, for example, that the price is $180 in Figure 2.5. At $180 the demand curve indicates that consumers want 600,000 DVD players, but the supply curve shows that firms will produce only 200,000 DVD players. This situation is a **disequilibrium**; the quantity demanded exceeds the quantity supplied, so the plans of buyers and sellers are inconsistent. The excess of the amount consumers want over what firms will sell—in this case 400,000 DVD players—is called the *excess demand* (*XD*), or **shortage**, at the price of $180.

How will the people involved—both consumers and business managers—react in this situation? Consumers will be frustrated by not getting as much as they wish and will be willing

EQUILIBRIUM

a situation in which quantity demanded equals quantity supplied at the prevailing price

DISEQUILIBRIUM

a situation in which the quantity demanded and the quantity supplied are not in balance

SHORTAGE

excess demand for a good

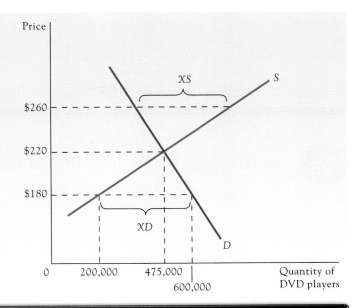

FIGURE 2.5

Determination of the Equilibrium Price and Quantity
The intersection of the supply and demand curves identifies the equilibrium price and quantity. Here, at the price of $220, the quantity demanded by consumers exactly equals the quantity supplied by firms. Market forces tend to produce this outcome.

SURPLUS
excess supply of a good

to pay a higher price to obtain more DVD players. Business managers will see that quantity demanded is greater than quantity supplied and will be prompted to hike their selling price. Consequently, whenever there is a shortage at some price, market forces—defined as the behavior of buyers and sellers in the market—tend to produce a higher price. In this example the price rises to $220. As the price rises, quantity demanded falls below 600,000 (a movement along the demand curve), and quantity supplied increases beyond 200,000 (a movement along the supply curve). The process continues until quantity demanded equals quantity supplied at a price of $220.

Alternatively, if for some reason the price is above $220, the quantity firms wish to sell will be greater than the quantity consumers are willing to buy. An *excess supply* (XS), or **surplus**, will exist at a higher-than-equilibrium price. Unsold goods pile up. In this case market forces exert a downward pressure on price, because firms cut prices rather than accumulate unwanted inventories and consumers realize that they do not have to pay as high a price for the commodity.

Therefore, at any price other than the equilibrium price, market forces will tend to cause price and quantity to change in the direction of their equilibrium values. The equilibrium position itself will change whenever demand or supply curves shift, so actual markets may, in effect, be pursuing a moving target as they continually adjust toward equilibrium.

APPLICATION 2.2

IS THERE A PARKING SHORTAGE IN MAJOR AMERICAN CITIES?

There are more than 190 million passenger cars and trucks in operation in the United States at any given time, but only slightly more than 100 million controlled (nonprivate) parking spaces. The average car is parked more than 95 percent of the time.

Most urban planning experts disagree with the popular impression that severe parking shortages exist in major cities such as New York, San Francisco, and Boston, saying that no parking shortage is evident. The experts argue that there is plenty of parking, provided that you are willing to pay the prevailing price for a space or walk—two options that many U.S. motorists dislike. As the editor of the *Parking Professional*, a trade magazine for private and municipal parking operators, puts it: "It's not that there is a shortage of spaces, just a shortage of free spaces where people want them to be." Namely, while parking spaces are available at the prices charged by major cities for them, few spaces are available at the lower price of zero that drivers would prefer to see charged.

2.3 ADJUSTMENT TO CHANGES IN DEMAND OR SUPPLY

The most common application of the supply and demand model is to explain or predict how a change in market conditions affects equilibrium price and output. In Figure 2.6a, we see an increase in demand but no change in supply. Demand might increase, for instance, following a report from the Surgeon General's office that watching at least two hours of DVDs per day reduces the risk of heart attack. This report would shift the demand curve for DVD players to the right but leave the supply curve unaffected.

Before demand increases, the equilibrium price and quantity are $220 and 475,000 DVD players, respectively. When the demand curve shifts to D', a shortage will temporarily exist at the original price of $220—quantity demanded (650,000) will exceed quantity supplied (475,000). As a consequence, there will be upward pressure on price. Price will rise, quantity supplied will increase, and quantity demanded will decline until a new equilibrium price and quantity of $250 and 600,000 DVD players, respectively, are determined, as indicated by the intersection of D' and S. Note that the higher output is not described as an increase in supply; only the quantity supplied has increased.

Figure 2.6b shows the effects of an increase in supply when there is no change in demand. Suppose that an advance in technology reduces production costs in the DVD player industry. This event will cause the supply curve of DVD players to shift rightward. At the initial

---

FIGURE 2.6

Market Adjustments to Changes in Demand and Supply
(a) An increase in demand from D to D', with supply unchanged, leads to a higher equilibrium price and output. (b) An increase in supply from S to S', with demand unchanged, leads to a lower equilibrium price and a higher equilibrium output.

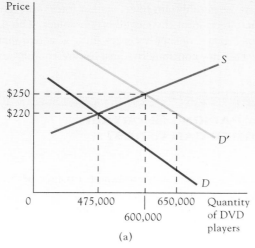

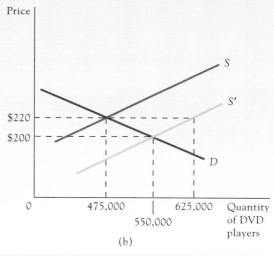

price of $220 firms would now wish to sell more players than consumers would be willing to buy, and a temporary surplus would result. Price would fall, and a new equilibrium with a price of $200 and an output of 550,000 would be established. Note that the greater purchases by consumers at the new equilibrium are not described as an increase in demand. Demand has not increased; quantity demanded has increased because of a lower price.

Do real-world markets respond to the forces of supply and demand in the way suggested by the theory? Over time, economists have accumulated and evaluated a great deal of evidence indicating that they do.

Some recent confirmations of the theory come from such disparate applications as variable-price parking meters and soft-drink vending machines; online shopping; and the San Francisco Bay Area housing market. For example, the next generation of parking meters and vending machines are being armed, through computer chips, to adjust the price charged in response to changes in demand—a higher price when traffic is more congested or when the weather is hotter and, consequently, consumer thirsts are greater. The Web has also increased the speed at which market equilibrium adjusts to changes in supply and demand across section after section of the economy. In contrast to traditional retail models, where fixed prices for relatively long periods of time are the norm, the Internet allows for quicker updating of prices and customer feedback. By bringing information about supply and demand together at the moment of sale, online shopping increases the alacrity with which equilibrium prices and quantities adjust, in predictable ways, to a change in demand or supply.

The San Francisco Bay Area housing market further testifies to how market equilibrium responds to underlying changes in supply and demand. For the last few years the price of an average home has risen by at least twice as much in and around San Francisco as elsewhere in the country—indeed, by a whopping 25 percent in 1999 relative to 5 percent for the United States as a whole. The reason for this disparity appears to lie with the growth of the New Economy. Silicon Valley, which is an economic engine for the San Francisco Bay Area, has been vastly outpacing the rest of the United States in terms of job growth, minting more millionaires per year over the last decade than any other place on the planet. As people pour into the area, demand for houses outstrips supply. Houses are a normal good; prices predictably rise as the market seeks equilibrium.

APPLICATION 2.3   SUPPLY, DEMAND, AND BABYSITTING

According to the *Wall Street Journal*: "Finding spot babysitters—teens who can pick up where day care or full-time nannies leave off—has gotten so hard that many parents wouldn't think twice about picking a sitter up at softball practice or scheduling their own social events around student government meetings. To hold on to sitters, parents sometimes behave pretty childishly, outbidding rivals, refusing to give the sitter's number to friends, and loading up their refrigerators with bribes."[3] In New York City, the base rate for sitters is

$10 per hour, with bonuses if a sitter works beyond the normal week's hours.

Why are parents going to greater lengths to keep good sitters and why is the going rate for babysitting services increasing? The answer boils down to supply and demand. There are more than 7 million girls who are 12 to 15 years old—the prime sitter pool—and roughly 35 million U.S. families with kids 11 years old and younger who need sitters. This imbalance—more families with an interest in babysitting services and fewer potential babysitters—did not exist a few decades ago when the Baby Boom generation (children born after the end of World War II) had yet to enter their prime child-rearing years.

[3]"Why Teenage Sitters Have So Much Power," *Wall Street Journal,* September 26, 1996, pp. B1 and B9.

Using the Supply–Demand Model to Explain Market Outcomes

We have focused so far on how the supply–demand model can be employed to *predict* market outcomes. An increase in the price of gasoline, for example, can be forecast to shift the demand curve for cars leftward (since gasoline and cars are complements) and thus to reduce the equilibrium price and quantity in the market for cars. However, the supply–demand model can also *explain* market outcomes. For example, why has the equilibrium price for, and per capita consumption of, medical care increased so dramatically over the last fifty years? Why is the price of gasoline so high and per capita consumption so much lower in Western Europe than the United States?

We can use the supply–demand model "in reverse" to explain such puzzling market outcomes in a fairly straightforward way. The first step involves determining how the equilibrium in a market has changed. Suppose, for example, that, as shown in Figure 2.7, we start off with an initial equilibrium price and quantity (P^* and Q^*) determined by the intersection of supply and demand curves (S and D). The initial equilibrium can be altered in four ways, represented by four quadrants.

Once we have determined what quadrant the new equilibrium is in, we can see whether demand or supply has produced the new market outcome. For example, if the new equilibrium is to the northeast of the initial equilibrium, we know that the demand curve has altered the equilibrium: The demand curve shifts to the right to produce a new equilibrium located northeast of the initial one. After we know which curve has produced the new equilibrium, we can attempt to isolate the factor that produced the observed change in market outcome.

Take the case of gasoline in Western Europe. As anybody who has traveled there knows, the per-unit price of gasoline is usually two to three times as high there as it is in the United States. Moreover, per capita consumption of gasoline is significantly lower in Western Europe than in the United States. Why is this the case? In Figure 2.7, the Western European per capita equilibrium for gasoline is located to the northwest of the equilibrium in the United States. Its location to the northwest means that the supply curve must be explaining the Western European market outcome. Specifically, the supply curve has to shift to the left to induce a movement in the gasoline market equilibrium to the northwest in the case of Western Europe. Now that we have isolated the supply curve as playing the dominant explanatory role, we can focus on what determinant of supply might be producing such a left-

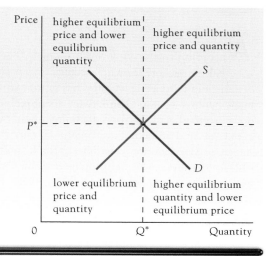

FIGURE 2.7

Using the Supply–Demand Model to Explain Market Outcomes
The supply–demand model can be used "in reverse" to explain market outcomes. By determining where the new equilibrium is relative to the initial equilibrium, it is possible to determine whether the demand or supply curve has produced the new market outcome.

ward shift in the supply curve. The culprit turns out to be the taxes levied by Western European governments on the sale of gasoline—taxes that significantly raise the cost of supplying gasoline to the market.

The supply–demand model also can be applied, in reverse, to explain the market for medical care. By most measures, per capita consumption and the per-unit price (adjusted for inflation) of medical care have increased over the past half-century in the United States. What is behind this phenomenon? We are clearly to the northeast, in terms of Figure 2.7, of the equilibrium that prevailed at the end of World War II. The demand curve, by shifting to the right, must be playing the explanatory role. One likely reason the demand curve has shifted is growth in consumers' incomes and the fact that medical care is a normal good. As people get richer, they appear to be spending more money on medical care for themselves and their families. (As we shall see in later chapters, however, the full explanation is a bit more complicated.)

GOVERNMENT INTERVENTION IN MARKETS: PRICE CONTROLS

Markets can be thought of as self-adjusting mechanisms; they automatically adjust to any change affecting the behavior of buyers and sellers in the market. But for this mechanism to operate, the price must be free to move in response to the interplay of supply and demand. When the government steps in to regulate prices, the market does not function in the same way. We can use the supply–demand framework to analyze this form of government intervention.

Policy makers may believe that market-determined prices are either too high or too low. In the former case, they may impose a legislated maximum price, or **price ceiling**. Under a legislated price ceiling it is illegal to charge a price higher than the ceiling. In the latter case, a minimum price, or **price floor**, may be legislated. In this section, we'll analyze price ceilings and show how their economic effects may be directly contrary to the stated objectives of the policymakers who impose them.

Price ceilings are not uncommon. In the twentieth century, broad-ranging price controls were established at the federal level during several major crises, including World War II, the Korean War, and the Vietnam War. Other examples of price ceilings on specific items include rent control, caps on automobile insurance rates in some states, and federal constraints on the prices that may be charged for human body organs for transplant. We will examine rent control in detail, but keep in mind that the effects of government intervention can be generalized to other markets where price ceilings prevent competitive market forces from determining the equilibrium.

PRICE CEILING
a legislated maximum price for a good

PRICE FLOOR
a legislated minimum price for a good

Rent Control

During World War II, many local governments in the United States applied price ceilings to rental housing units, a policy generally referred to as **rent control**. New York City was the only major city to continue rent control after World War II, and it still uses it today. Apart from New York, relatively few cities experimented with rent control until the 1970s, when an increasing number of cities adopted the practice. By 1990, more than two hundred cities were using some form of rent control, including Los Angeles, Washington, Boston, and Newark (although in the last few years the state legislatures in both Massachusetts and California have voted to end local rent control).

RENT CONTROL
price ceilings applied to rental housing units

We can examine the effects of rent control with the aid of Figure 2.8, which shows the supply and demand curves for rental housing units in a particular city. As shown in Figure 2.8, in the absence of rent control, the equilibrium monthly price is P, or $800, and Q is the equilibrium quantity. Rent control imposes a maximum price on a rental unit below the

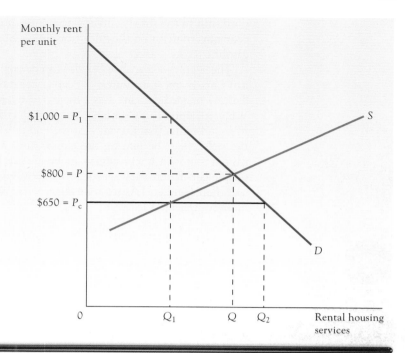

FIGURE 2.8

Rent Control
With a legal maximum rent of $650 set below the market equilibrium level of $800, quantity supplied falls from Q to Q_1, and quantity demanded rises to Q_2. The difference, Q_2 minus Q_1, is the excess demand, or shortage, created by the rent control policy.

equilibrium level. Suppose that the price is not allowed to rise above P_c, or $650. The first question to answer is whether the law can be effectively enforced. Because tenants are willing to pay a higher price, landlords have an incentive to extract side payments from tenants. Such side payments might include a nonrefundable key deposit; purchase of a parking space or furniture as a condition for renting; or paying for one's own repairs. All these practices have been observed to occur under rent control. In this way, a landlord might charge the regulation $650 in explicit rent, but receive enough extra in side payments to get the effective price closer to the market price.

Let's assume that these methods of circumventing the law are not allowed. (They are, in fact, illegal under most rent control laws.) The price that consumers must pay is lower, and at a lower price the quantity demanded is greater, namely, Q_2. At the lower price, however, the quantity supplied falls to Q_1, because investment in this market becomes less profitable. Fewer new rental units are constructed. New York City, for example, has the lowest rental vacancy rate in the country. And, the number of new rental housing units (per capita) added to the city's total supply of such units is the lowest in the nation. Moreover, owners allow existing units to deteriorate more rapidly by spending less on maintenance for those units. One study found repair expenditures in New York City on rent-controlled apartments to be only half as large as the repair expenditures made on comparable apartments not subject to rent control.[4]

The result of rent control, like that of any other price ceiling applied in a competitive market, is a shortage. The quantity that potential tenants would like to rent, Q_2, is greater than the quantity available, Q_1, and the excess of quantity demanded over quantity supplied, Q_1Q_2, measures the shortage. Because only Q_1 units are actually available, the marginal value of housing units to consumers must be at least $1,000 (the height of the demand

[4]G. Sternlieb, *The Urban Housing Dilemma* (New York: New York Housing and Development Administration, 1972), p. 202.

curve at Q_1). Price, however, cannot legally rise above $650 per month, so producers have no incentive to increase quantity beyond Q_1.

Rent control has effects on other markets, too. Not all people who wish to rent are able to do so, so they must make other living arrangements. Apart from living in a different community, the major alternative is some form of owner-occupied housing. Therefore, the demand for such housing will increase as frustrated apartment hunters turn to home ownership. At the same time the owners of rent-controlled apartments have an incentive to convert their rental units into owner-occupied units, or condominiums, and sell them to tenants. Typically, communities with rent controls resort to limitations on condominium conversion to prevent the supply of rental units from drying up completely. Because landlords also have an incentive to convert rental units to commercial units (such as stores and business offices) that are not subject to rent control, most communities with rent control also outlaw this practice.

Who Loses, Who Benefits?

Those obviously harmed by rent control are the owners of rental units at the time the policy is implemented. They have invested in the construction or purchase of units in the expectation of being able to charge $800 per month (in our example), but they find their return reduced by law. Although landlords are often depicted as wealthy and easily able to bear the losses imposed by rent control, this is often not the case. While the evidence is sketchy, landlords often have incomes that are no greater than those of their tenants. For example, a 1988 survey of New York landlords found that 30 percent had incomes below $20,000, and half had incomes below $40,000.[5]

Now consider who benefits from rent control. The intended beneficiaries are clear. In virtually all cases proponents of rent control expressly seek to benefit tenants. Economists, however, are skeptical about the degree to which this benefit actually occurs. Indeed, some economists believe that tenants, on average, are worse off under rent control. While lower rents by themselves are good for tenants lucky enough to get a rent-controlled apartment, other changes in the market are not so advantageous.

First, the lower rental price is necessarily accompanied by a lower quantity (quantity falls from Q to Q_1 in Figure 2.8). A lower price is good for tenants, but fewer rental units are not, and the net effect of the two is uncertain. It is conceivable that all tenants are made worse off. To see this, suppose that the quantity of available rental units falls to zero under rent control. A lower price does tenants little good if they cannot find housing. Moreover, all tenants likely will not be affected in the same way. Some tenants may find what they want at the lower rents, while others may not. For example, while former New York Mayor Ed Koch had a rent-controlled apartment in Greenwich Village in 1989 for $352, a recent college graduate was paying $300 to live in a pantry in another person's apartment.[6] (Pantries are apparently not subject to rent control.) The biggest losers among the tenants are, of course, the "potential tenants" who are unable to find rental apartments and must either purchase housing or live elsewhere.

Another disadvantage to tenants of rent control involves its impact on quality. Just as a quantity reduction acts to the detriment of tenants, so does the decrease in quality. Landlords have an incentive to lower costs by reducing maintenance. Normally, they would not do this because they would lose tenants, but because of the rent-control–created shortage they can reduce the value of rental units without driving tenants away. Consequently, tenants get a lower-quality product for the lower price.

[5]Irving Welfeld, *Where We Live* (New York: Simon and Schuster, 1988), p. 146.
[6]William Tucker, "It's a Rotten Life," *Reason* (February 1989), p. 23.

Quality is also likely to suffer when rent control laws have provisions permitting landlords to raise the rent on a unit that becomes vacant. Because such provisions give landlords an incentive to evict tenants, the law typically also has strong anti-eviction provisions. In turn, anti-eviction provisions give landlords the incentive to make tenants as unhappy as possible so they will choose to leave, and one way to do that is to let the rental unit deteriorate. The normal incentive of landlords—to provide a quality unit so tenants will stay a long time—is turned upside down by rent control.

Under rent control, nonprice rationing becomes more prevalent. Since price is not allowed to ration the available quantity among competing consumers, quantity supplied does not equal quantity demanded, and some other way of determining who gets the good and who doesn't must arise. Nonprice rationing can take many forms and works to the disadvantage of some tenants. Because there are many more potential tenants than apartments, landlords can be highly selective. For example, they are likely to favor tenants without children or pets (children and pets increase maintenance and repair costs) and tenants with histories of steady employment at good wage rates (who can be counted on to pay on time).[7] Minorities may not fare well under rent control if landlords have prejudices against them and choose to indulge such prejudices in selecting tenants.

Another form of nonprice rationing that becomes more important is rationing on a first-come, first-served basis. Because of the lack of available units, potential tenants incur the cost of waiting in line (or in a pantry) and searching for that rare commodity, a vacant rent-controlled unit. This factor, of course, adds to the true cost of rental housing since not only the rent but also the cost of time spent waiting and searching must be paid by prospective tenants.

A more obvious form of nonprice rationing is the payment of bribes to secure a rent-controlled apartment. Because a rent-controlled apartment is often worth more to tenants than the rent they must pay, they are willing to pay a "finder's fee" to anyone who secures a rental unit for them.

BLACK MARKET
an illegal market for a good

Under rent controls, **black markets** may emerge, with units renting for more than $650 per month. This occurs because prospective tenants are willing to pay more than the legal price for an apartment. In Figure 2.8, when the quantity Q_1 is legally available, tenants are willing to pay as much as P_1—the height of the demand curve at that quantity—for an apartment. Landlords benefit by renting a unit at more than $650 per month, so there is room for transactions that benefit both consumers and producers—which is why black market exchanges are likely to occur. The extent of black market activities will depend on the penalties the government applies to this behavior and how rigorously the penalties are enforced.

While most local governments vigorously police against black market exchanges between landlords and initial tenants, they often look the other way when it comes to the practice of subletting. *Subletting* occurs when the initial tenant rents the apartment to a secondary tenant (generally without the landlord's knowledge). New York City does not actively police against this practice, and as a result most subletting rental rates are at least double the official rent control rates for the same apartments. Since subletting is essentially a black market in rental units, to the extent that cities condone the practice, the rental rates paid by tenants (at least secondary tenants) can end up higher than they would be were there no rent control—P_1 versus P in Figure 2.8.

Rent controls also involve administrative costs. For example, in Santa Monica, California, the Rent Control Board's annual budget has exceeded $5 million in certain years. To pay for this budget, each tenant is levied an annual fee of $132. Furthermore, since property

---

[7]Landlords in rent-controlled cities often screen for and attempt to avoid renting to law students. It seems that such students are prone to practice their future trade on existing landlords.

taxes are the most important source of revenue for most cities, and rent control lowers the market values of rental properties, a city's tax base is eroded. This loss can be substantial. It has been estimated, for example, that property tax revenues fell by 10 to 20 percent in Cambridge, Massachusetts, as a result of rent controls.[8] This means that residents, including tenants, either receive fewer services provided by the city or have to pay higher income taxes.

For all these reasons the benefits to tenants from the lower rents under rent control are likely to be a good deal smaller than it appears on the surface. Generalizing the outcomes for tenants as a group is difficult because particular tenants are likely to be affected in different ways. Probably some tenants benefit, especially those occupying rental units at the time rent control takes effect, but the deterioration of the quality of the units diminishes even their benefits. Other tenants are almost certainly worse off because of the side effects that accompany the lower rents.

APPLICATION 2.4 WHY WEB SURFING CAN TURN INTO WEB CRAWLING

When typing in the address for a site on the World Wide Web, many of us experience what has been dubbed the "World Wide Wait" before the requested information is displayed on the computer screen. Why are delays prevalent when one is attempting to surf the Internet? The primary reason stems from the role played by the government in starting the Internet (through the Defense Department and the National Science Foundation) and the government's resistance to levying charges based on usage of the Internet. With a price ceiling basically set at zero (apart from some typically minor hookup charge) for Internet usage, the supply–demand framework developed in this chapter predicts the outcome: a shortage of Internet capacity and delays confronting those who wish to use it.

APPLICATION 2.5 WHY THE DOCTOR IS NOT IN

Delays are the norm in the United States when trying to see a doctor for medical conditions that are covered by a patient's third-party underwriter—either government-funded programs such as Medicare/Medicaid or insurers and health maintenance organizations (HMOs), whose growth over the past half century has been fueled through a tax break provided by the government to companies who offer their employees health benefits. As you might have guessed, the delays are the result of caps placed by the third parties on doctor reimbursement. The caps lead to a shortage of doctor services relative to the amount that is desired by patients.

And, for reasons that we will cover in this book's concluding chapter, the shortage is exacerbated by the fact that patients typically pay only a small portion of the reimbursed amount directly to the doctor (a $5 or $10 copayment per visit), with the remainder of the reimbursement coming indirectly through the third-party underwriter.

The delays have grown to such an extent that more and more patients are turning to urgent-care facilities and hospital emergency rooms for prompter medical attention. Notwithstanding the higher fees patients must pay directly out of their own pockets for such alternative

[8]Peter Navarro, "Rent Control in Cambridge, Massachusetts," *The Public Interest*, 78 (Winter 1985), pp. 83–100.

ways to see a doctor (the copayments typically range from $50 to $150), the timelier service may be worth it. Of course, as growing numbers of patients turn to urgent care and emergency rooms, the delays for services provided by these sites (which face analogous caps by third-party underwriters) have also increased.

The delays faced by patients in the United States, however, have yet to rival those in Canada, where universal "free" health care is provided by the government to its citizens and user fees have been outlawed since 1984.[9] "Hallway medicine" has become so routine in hospitals across Canada, with patients either waiting for attention or recuperating from operations on hallway stretchers, that the stretcher locations have permanent

numbers. An official at a Vancouver hospital estimates that 20 percent of heart attack patients who should be treated within 15 minutes now wait at least an hour. In Toronto, at the nation's most prestigious cancer hospital, hospital lawyers have drawn up a protective waiver for patients to sign indicating that they fully understand the danger of delaying radiation treatment.

There is no comparable crisis in dental and veterinary care in Canada because these sectors still operate without government intervention. As Michael Bliss, a medical historian, notes: "So we have the absurdity in Canada that you can get faster care for your gum disease than your cancer, and probably more attentive care for your dog than your grandmother." Indeed, in the Canadian province of Ontario one man on a lengthy wait list for magnetic resonance imaging (MRI) tests recently reserved a session for himself at a private animal hospital with a machine. He registered under the name Fido.

[9]The remainder of this application is based on "Full Hospitals Make Canadians Wait and Look South," *New York Times*, January 16, 2000, p. 3.

2.5 ELASTICITIES[10]

We have so far focused on specifying qualitative relationships between determinants of supply and demand and the actual quantity demanded and quantity supplied of a good. Although qualitative relationships provide meaningful information, they cannot measure the impact produced by a change in a particular determinant on the quantity demanded or supplied of a commodity. In the business world especially, we need to know the quantitative impact of a change in one determinant such as price, income, or the price of inputs on the quantity demanded or quantity supplied of a commodity. Quantitative impacts are also often important in the public policy arena. For instance, when considering an increase in the sales tax on cigarettes, government decisionmakers may be concerned about the magnitude of the effect of the tax on the quantity of cigarettes demanded by smokers (perhaps, in particular, by teenage smokers). **Elasticities** measure the magnitude of the responsiveness of any variable (such as quantity demanded and quantity supplied) to a change in particular determinants.

ELASTICITIES

measures of the magnitude of the responsiveness of any variable (such as quantity demanded or supplied) to a change in particular determinants

Price Elasticity of Demand

Even though we assume that all market demand curves have negative slopes (implying that at a lower price a greater quantity will be purchased), the degree of responsiveness varies widely from one commodity to another. A reduction in the price of cigarettes may lead to an infinitesimal increase in purchases while a reduction in airplane fares may produce a veritable explosion in air travel. The law of demand tells us to expect *some* increase in quantity demanded, but not how much.

PRICE ELASTICITY OF DEMAND

a measure of how sensitive quantity demanded is to a change in a product's price

The **price elasticity of demand** is a measure of how sensitive quantity demanded is to a change in a product's price. It can be defined as *the percentage change in quantity demanded divided by the percentage change in price*. The ratio will always be negative for any downward-

[10]A mathematical treatment of some of the material in this section is given in the appendix at the back of the book (pages 561–562).

sloping demand curve. For example, if a 10 percent price increase brings about a 20 percent reduction in quantity demanded, the price elasticity of demand is −20 percent/+10 percent, or −2.0. Economists usually drop the minus sign on the understanding that price and quantity demanded always move in different directions and simply refer to the elasticity as being, in this case, 2.0.

Price elasticity of demand provides a quantitative measure of the price responsiveness of quantity demanded along a demand curve. The higher the numerical value of the elasticity, the larger the effect of a price change on quantity. If the elasticity is only 0.2, then a 10 percent price increase will reduce quantity demanded by just 2 percent (2 percent/10 percent = 0.2). Alternatively, if the elasticity is 4.0, a 10 percent price rise will reduce quantity demanded by 40 percent (40 percent/10 percent = 4.0).

If the price elasticity of demand exceeds 1.0, then demand is said to be **elastic**. Elasticity is greater than 1.0 whenever the percentage change in quantity demanded is greater than the percentage change in price, implying that the quantity demanded is relatively responsive to a price change. If the price elasticity of demand is less than 1.0, then demand is said to be **inelastic**. Elasticity is less than 1.0 whenever the percentage change in quantity demanded is less than the percentage change in price, implying that quantity demanded is relatively unresponsive to a price change. When the price elasticity of demand is equal to 1.0, then demand is said to be **unit elastic**, or of unitary elasticity. Unitary elasticity occurs whenever the percentage changes in price and quantity demanded are equal.

Whether demand is elastic, unit elastic, or inelastic determines how a price change will affect total expenditure on the product. Total expenditure equals price times quantity, or $P \times Q$. A change in price affects these terms in offsetting ways. A higher price increases the P term but reduces the Q term (quantity demanded is lower at a higher price). The net effect on total expenditure, therefore, depends on the relative size of the two changes. Put differently, the net effect on total expenditure depends on how responsive quantity is to the price change; it depends on the price elasticity of demand. If a 10 percent increase in price reduces quantity by 10 percent (the unit elastic case), then total expenditure, $P \times Q$, remains unchanged. If a 10 percent increase in price reduces quantity by more than 10 percent (the elastic demand case), then total expenditure will fall because of the sharper reduction in quantity purchased. Finally, if a 10 percent increase in price reduces quantity by less than 10 percent (the inelastic demand case), then total expenditure will rise.

Figure 2.9a depicts a case where a small change in the per-gallon price of gasoline has a large effect on quantity purchased. Demand is elastic in this case since the percentage change in quantity demanded exceeds the percentage change in price. If, for example, price falls from $1.00 to $0.90 per gallon, quantity increases sharply from 100 to 200 gallons. The price reduction increases total expenditure on gasoline from $100 ($1.00 per gallon multiplied by 100 gallons) to $180 ($0.90 multiplied by 200 gallons). Conversely, if the price rises from $0.90 to $1.00, total expenditure falls from $180 to $100. Thus, we see graphically how a price change affects total expenditure when demand is elastic.

Figure 2.9b examines the relationship between price and total expenditure if the demand for gasoline is very inelastic: a change in price has little effect on quantity. When the price falls from $1.00 to $0.50 per gallon, total expenditure falls from $100 to $60. When price rises from $0.50 to $1.00, total expenditure rises. Figure 2.9c shows the intermediate case of unit elasticity.[11] In this case total expenditure remains unchanged when price varies. Consumers purchase 100 gallons at a price of $1.00 per gallon (total expenditure of $100) and 200 gallons at a price of $0.50 per gallon (total expenditure still $100).

---

[11]Because the product of price and quantity is unchanged at all points along a demand curve with unit elasticity, such a curve must satisfy the equation $P \times Q = K$ (a constant). This equation describes a rectangular hyperbola.

ELASTIC
the situation in which price elasticity of demand exceeds 1.0 or unity

INELASTIC
the situation in which price elasticity of demand is less than 1.0 or unity

UNIT ELASTIC
the situation in which price elasticity of demand equals 1.0 or unity

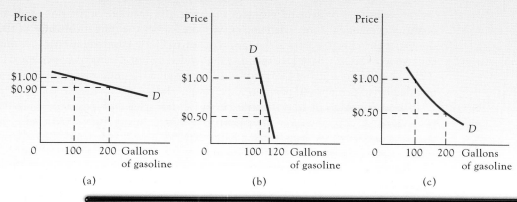

FIGURE 2.9

Price Elasticity of Demand and Total Expenditure
(a) If demand is elastic, a lower price increases total expenditure. (b) If demand is inelastic, a lower price decreases total expenditure. (c) If demand is unit elastic, a lower price leaves total expenditure unchanged.

In short, when demand is elastic (elasticity greater than 1.0), price and total expenditure move in opposite directions. When demand is inelastic (elasticity less than 1.0), price and total expenditure move in the same direction. And when demand is unit elastic, total expenditure remains constant when the price varies.

Calculating Price Elasticity of Demand

Calculating price elasticity of demand from a pair of price–quantity points is frequently necessary. Suppose that we are given the following price–quantity values for gasoline (where quantity demanded is measured in gallons):

$$P_1 = \$1.00 \qquad P_2 = \$0.99$$
$$Q_{d1} = 1,000 \quad Q_{d2} = 1,005.$$

Our definition of price elasticity of demand is the percentage change in quantity demanded divided by the percentage change in price. This relationship is expressed as a formula, letting η (the Greek letter eta) stand for price elasticity of demand:

$$\eta = \frac{(\Delta Q_d/Q_d)}{(\Delta P/P)}.$$

Here, $\Delta Q_d/Q_d$ is the percentage change in quantity demanded, and $\Delta P/P$ is the percentage change in price.[12] In applying this formula—called the **point elasticity formula**—we encounter an ambiguity. While ΔQ_d and ΔP are unambiguously determined (a 5 gallon change in quantity and a $0.01 change in the per-gallon price), what values should be used for Q_d and P? If we enter the values for P_1 and Q_{d1} into the formula, we obtain:

$$\frac{(\Delta Q_d/Q_{d1})}{(\Delta P/P_1)} = \frac{(5/1,000)}{(\$0.01/\$1.00)} = 0.50.$$

Alternatively, if we use P_2 and Q_{d2}, we obtain:

$$\frac{(\Delta Q_d/Q_{d2})}{(\Delta P/P_2)} = \frac{(5/1,005)}{(\$0.01/\$0.99)} = 0.49.$$

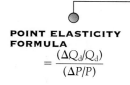

POINT ELASTICITY FORMULA
$$= \frac{(\Delta Q_d/Q_d)}{(\Delta P/P)}$$

[12]The Greek letter Δ as in ΔQ_d simply means "change in."

Because we are dealing with small changes in this case, which values we choose makes little quantitative difference. There is, however, a slight difference, and it reflects the fact that the percentage change between two prices depends on the direction of the change. If price falls from $1.00 to $0.50 per gallon, this is referred to as a 50 percent decrease (a $0.50 change in price divided by the *initial* price, $1.00). Alternatively, if the price rises from $0.50 to $1.00 per gallon, this is a 100 percent increase (a $0.50 change in price divided by the *initial* price, $0.50). Don't be sidetracked by this arithmetical obscurity. The important point is that some base Q_d and P must be employed in the formula, but for small changes in Q_d and P, which base is chosen makes no significant difference to the results.

There is a substantial difference, however, when a large change in price and quantity is involved. Suppose, for example, that we have the following values:

$$P_1 = \$1.00 \qquad P_2 = \$0.50$$

$$Q_{d1} = 1{,}000 \qquad Q_{d2} = 2{,}000.$$

By inspection we see that total expenditure is $1,000 (quantity demanded is once again being measured in gallons) at both prices, so we know that demand is unit elastic. Surprisingly, though, it now makes a great deal of difference what base values of P and Q_d we use if we try to apply the point elasticity formula:

$$(\Delta Q_d/Q_{d1})/(\Delta P/P_1) = (1{,}000/1{,}000)/(\$0.50/\$1.00) = 2.0 \text{ and}$$

$$(\Delta Q_d/Q_{d2})/(\Delta P/P_2) = (1{,}000/2{,}000)/(\$0.50/\$0.50) = 0.5.$$

According to one calculation, price elasticity of demand is 2.0; according to the other it is 0.5. Both are wrong, and the true value, unity, lies between these estimates. The basic problem in this case is that the elasticity of demand tends to vary from one point (one P, Q_d combination) to another on the demand curve, and for a large change in price and quantity we need an average value over the entire range. Consequently, when we deal with large changes in price and quantity, we should use the following **arc elasticity formula**:

ARC ELASTICITY FORMULA

$$= \frac{\left[\dfrac{\Delta Q_d}{(\frac{1}{2})(Q_{d1} + Q_{d2})}\right]}{\left[\dfrac{\Delta P}{(\frac{1}{2})(P_1 + P_2)}\right]}$$

$$\eta = \frac{\left[\dfrac{\Delta Q_d}{(\frac{1}{2})(Q_{d1} + Q_{d2})}\right]}{\left[\dfrac{\Delta P}{(\frac{1}{2})(P_1 + P_2)}\right]}.$$

Note that this formula differs from the point elasticity formula only in using the average of the two quantities, $(1/2)(Q_{d1} + Q_{d2})$, and the average of the two prices, $(1/2)(P_1 + P_2)$. Applying this formula to the preceding figures yields the true value of the elasticity over the entire range of prices considered:

$$\frac{\left[\dfrac{\Delta Q_d}{(\frac{1}{2})(Q_{d1} + Q_{d2})}\right]}{\left[\dfrac{\Delta P}{(\frac{1}{2})(P_1 + P_2)}\right]} = \frac{\left[\dfrac{1{,}000}{(\frac{1}{2})(1{,}000 + 2{,}000)}\right]}{\left[\dfrac{\$0.50}{(\frac{1}{2})(\$0.50 + \$1.00)}\right]} = 1.0.$$

Thus, we have two formulas. The first works well when small changes in P and Q_d are involved because, in that case, which P and Q_d are used makes little difference. The second formula avoids the problem of having to pick one specific point by using the average values of price and quantity demanded and should be used with large changes in price and quantity demanded.

APPLICATION 2.6 — DEMAND ELASTICITY AND CABLE TELEVISION PRICING

C able systems historically have offered two tiers of service: a "basic" tier numbering 10 or more channels, including programming such as CNN, ESPN, and MTV; and "pay" tiers featuring movie channels such as HBO and Showtime. Subscribers purchase the basic tier as a package. Pay tiers are available separately for an additional specified fee per channel.

While pay tiers have never been subject to government rate control, basic tiers were regulated prior to 1987 and reregulated between 1992 and 1999. From 1987 to 1991 as well as after 1999, however, basic rates were deregulated and cable operators had to determine what price they should charge. Elasticity of demand considerations helped them decide.

As we saw earlier in this section, whether demand is inelastic, unit elastic, or elastic determines how a price change will affect the total expenditure on a product. Calculating basic tier demand elasticity was thus vital to operators interested in finding out whether the rates they were charging under regulation were too low in terms of maximizing profit.

Studies conducted by cable operators found that basic tier demand elasticity at the time of rate deregulation in 1987 was less than unity—between 0.1 and 0.5. The estimated elasticity indicated that profits would increase if basic rates were raised. Two factors are at work here. First, if a firm is operating along an inelastic portion of its demand curve, the total revenue earned from basic subscribers will increase if the basic rate is raised. The effect on revenue of a decrease in the number of subscribers will be more than compensated for by the higher rate earned per remaining subscriber when demand is inelastic. Second, at the higher rate, fewer subscribers will be served and the total cost of providing service will be lower. Between the increase in total revenue and the decrease in total cost, the profit earned on basic service will increase (profit is the difference between total revenue and total cost). In sum, operators stood to lose some subscribers but to more than make up for that from the ones they kept.

Had operators estimated demand elasticity to equal unity, profits on basic service could also be increased by raising rates. With unit elastic demand, basic tier revenue remains unchanged with a rate increase since the effect of a decrease in the number of subscribers exactly offsets the higher rate earned per remaining subscriber. Total cost, however, decreases due to a smaller number of subscribers at the higher rate. Consequently, an operator's profit on basic service is enlarged by an increase in the basic rate with unit elastic demand.

Finally, had operators estimated demand for basic service to be price elastic, it would have been unclear whether rates should be raised or lowered following deregulation. A demand elasticity exceeding unity implies that total revenue will fall in the wake of a rate increase—the effect on basic tier revenue of a smaller number of subscribers more than offsets the higher rate earned per remaining subscriber. By itself, this would suggest that rates should not be raised and, in fact, need to be lowered. However, the total cost of providing basic service also declines with a higher price and fewer subscribers. What happens to a firm's profit in a case where demand is elastic thus depends (as we will see in a later chapter) on the magnitude of the total cost decrease versus the total revenue decrease associated with a higher price.

Relying on estimates that demand elasticity was less than unity, operators began to raise rates following deregulation. Average basic rates increased roughly 75 percent during the five-year period (1987 to 1991) they were first free of government control—an amount significantly greater than the inflation rate, even after adjustments made for improvements in programming quality. Cable operators' profits on basic service increased along with the rates. Analogous changes in basic rates and profits occurred under the more recent period of deregulation (post 1999) as operators once again estimated demand elasticity to be less than unity.

Demand Elasticities Vary Among Goods

We can never know why people respond exactly as they do. Nonetheless, two general factors seem to have a pronounced effect on the elasticity of demand for a particular product.

The first, and most important, factor is the availability and closeness of substitutes. *The more substitutes there are for some product, and the better the substitutes, the more elastic the demand for the product will be.* When there are good substitutes, a change in the price of the product will lead to considerable substitution among products by consumers. The demand for margarine, for example, would probably be quite elastic, because when its price rises, many people would switch to butter. Remember that when we evaluate the elasticity of demand for margarine, we assume the price of butter to be unchanged. Thus, a higher price of margarine (with an unchanged price of butter) leads people to shift from margarine to butter, because they are close substitutes.

The degree to which a good has close substitutes depends in part on how specifically it is defined. A narrowly defined good will frequently have close substitutes, and elasticity will tend to be higher. For example, the elasticity of demand for Zest soap (a very narrowly defined good with many substitutes) will be greater than the elasticity of demand for soap. Along these lines, the demand for any particular brand of some product (such as Budweiser beer) will be more elastic than the demand for all brands taken together (beer).

In addition to the number and the quality of substitutes, a second factor that can be important in determining elasticity of demand is the time period over which consumers adjust to a price change. *The longer the time period involved, the fuller is the adjustment consumers can make.* In part, this reflects the fact that it takes time for consumers to learn about a price change, but there are other reasons, too. Consider an increase in the price of electricity. In the month following the price increase, people can cut back their use somewhat by switching lights off more conscientiously, turning thermostats down (if electric heating is used), or turning air conditioners off. The number of ways people can economize on electricity, however, is greater when we consider what they can do over a longer period. Over a year, for example, they can substitute lower-wattage light bulbs for existing light bulbs, convert electric furnaces to oil or gas furnaces, insulate their houses, use portable kerosene heaters, buy appliances that require less electricity, and so on. In short, demand will be more elastic the longer the time period over which consumers can adjust and, in essence, find substitutes.

For many goods, consumers will not require much time to make a full adjustment to a change in price. In these cases the long-run and short-run responses will not differ substantially. Changes in the prices of electricity and gasoline will necessitate major alterations in the consumption of very durable goods (houses, appliances, and cars) before consumers have fully adjusted, and those alterations take time. But for most goods (such as beer, shoes, wristwatches, meat, televisions, compact discs, and so on) we would not expect the short- and long-run elasticities of demand to be much different.

The Estimation of Demand Elasticities

In practice, estimating elasticities of demand is problematic because elasticity of demand refers to a *given demand curve*, but the demand curve itself is likely to shift over time. Economists and statisticians have developed some sophisticated techniques (briefly overviewed in Chapter 4) to deal with this problem and to permit estimation of demand elasticities. Table 2.1 lists some selected estimates of elasticities of demand for a variety of products.

As Table 2.1 indicates, the estimates of demand elasticities differ widely among goods. Not surprisingly, cigarettes are in inelastic demand (an elasticity of 0.35). Although people commonly think of medical care consumption as almost totally unresponsive to price, the elasticity of demand for physicians' services is 0.6. While this demand is inelastic, it does imply that a 50 percent increase in price would reduce consumption by fully 30 percent. Some products, such as air travel and automobiles, are apparently in highly elastic demand (in the long run).

One implication of these estimates (and many others that could be cited) should not be missed: they all support the law of demand. Consumers purchase more at a lower price, other things being equal.

TABLE 2.1

SELECTED ESTIMATES OF DEMAND ELASTICITIES

	Short-Run	Long-Run
Cigarettes	—	0.35
Water	—	0.4
Beer	—	0.8
Physicians' services	0.6	—
Gasoline	0.2	0.5–1.5
Automobiles	—	1.5
Chevrolets	—	4.0
Electricity (household utility)	0.1	1.9
Air travel	0.1	2.4

Sources: Hendrik S. Houthakker and Lester D. Taylor, *Consumer Demand in the United States, 1929–1970* (Cambridge, Massachusetts: Harvard University Press, 1966 and 1970 editions); Kenneth G. Elzinga, "The Beer Industry," in *The Structure of American Industry*, edited by Walter Adams (New York: Macmillan, 1977); and James L. Sweeney, "The Response of Energy Demand to Higher Prices: What Have We Learned?" *American Economic Review*, 74, No. 2 (May 1984), pp. 31–37.

APPLICATION 2.7   D.C. LEARNS ABOUT DEMAND ELASTICITY

Two decades ago, Washington, D.C., city officials, hard-pressed for tax revenues, levied a 6 percent tax on the sale of gasoline. As a first approximation (and a reasonable one, it turns out), this tax could be expected to increase the price of gasoline by 6 percent. The elasticity of demand is a key factor in the consequences of this action, because the more sharply the sales of gasoline fall, the less tax revenue the city will raise. Presumably, city officials hoped that gasoline sales would be largely unaffected by the higher price.

Within a few months, however, the amount of gasoline sold had fallen by 33 percent.[13] A 6 percent price increase producing a 33 percent quantity reduction means the price elasticity was about 5.5. And this reaction was only the immediate, or short-run, response. The sharp sales drop meant that added tax revenue was not raised. Further indications were that when consumers had fully adjusted to the tax, tax revenues would actually fall lower. (There had been a 10 cent per gallon tax before the 6 percent tax was added, so although the 6 percent levy was raising revenue, the gain was largely offset by the loss in revenue from the initial 10-cent tax following the reduction in sales.)

In interpreting this episode, we must recognize that demand elasticities of the type reported in Table 2.1 for gasoline are irrelevant in this case. This was not a general increase in gasoline prices but a rise only within the Washington city limits. Gasoline sold in the District of Columbia is a narrowly defined product that has good substitutes—gasoline sold in nearby Virginia and Maryland. Higher gasoline prices in the District of Columbia, when the prices charged in Virginia and Maryland are unchanged, will obviously be highly elastic. No economist would be surprised at the results of this tax, but apparently city officials were. Observed one city councilman: "We think of ourselves here in the District as an island to ourselves. But we've got to realize that we're not. We've got to realize that Maryland and Virginia are right out there, and there's nothing to stop people from crossing over the line."

The 6 percent gasoline tax was repealed five months after it was levied. At that time, the mayor of Washington cited "overwhelming evidence" that the tax had not worked and that it had caused "undue hardships both to the consumers of gas . . . and those who operate retail gas businesses."

[13]"Barry Asks Gasoline Tax Repeal," *Washington Post*, November 2, 1980, p. A1.

Three Other Elasticities

Price elasticity of demand is the most important elasticity concept in economics, but we can define elasticity in general as a measure of the response of any variable to the change in some other variable. Two other common elasticity measures that relate to consumer behavior are the income elasticity of demand and the cross-price elasticity of demand. On the supply side, the most important elasticity is price elasticity of supply. The price elasticity of supply measures the responsiveness of quantity supplied to price.

Income Elasticity

The **income elasticity of demand** measures how responsive consumption of some item is to a change in income (I), assuming that the price of the good itself remains unchanged. We define *income elasticity* as the percentage change in consumption of a good Q_d divided by the percentage change in income or (in point elasticity form):

$$\text{income elasticity of demand for a good} = \frac{(\Delta Q_d/Q_d)}{(\Delta I/I)}.$$

For example, if income rises by 10 percent, and a consumer increases purchases of gasoline by 5 percent, then the income elasticity of gasoline is 0.5. Note that the algebraic sign of this elasticity distinguishes between normal and inferior goods. Whenever income elasticity is positive, consumption of the good rises with income, so the good must be normal. Whenever income elasticity is negative, consumption of the good falls when income rises, and the good must be inferior. A unitary income elasticity means the consumer continues to spend the same percentage of income on the good when income rises.

Cross-Price Elasticity of Demand

The **cross-price elasticity of demand** measures how responsive consumption of one good is to a change in the price of a related good. We define *cross-price elasticity* as the percentage change in consumption of one good, X, divided by the percentage change in the price of a different good, Y, or (in point elasticity form):

$$\text{cross-price elasticity of demand for X with respect to the price of Y} = \frac{(\Delta Q_{dX}/Q_{dX})}{(\Delta P_Y/P_Y)}.$$

For example, if the price of BMW automobiles rises by 10 percent, and the quantity of Mercedes cars purchased increases by 5 percent, then the cross-price elasticity of demand for Mercedes cars with respect to the price of BMWs is 0.5. Note that cross-price elasticity will be positive when the goods are substitutes (as are BMW and Mercedes cars) and negative when the goods are complements (for example, gasoline and cars). Indeed, the major use of this elasticity is to measure the strength of the complementary or substitute relationship between goods. The concept of cross-price elasticity is widely used in antitrust cases. How a market is defined and how competitive it is depends on the availability of substitutes. One way to ascertain substitutability is with a measure of the cross-price elasticity of demand.

Elasticity of Supply

The **price elasticity of supply**, or *elasticity of supply*, is a measure of the responsiveness of the quantity supplied of a commodity to a change in the commodity's own price. It is defined as the percentage change in quantity supplied, Q_s, divided by the percentage change in price. Using the Greek letter ϵ (epsilon) to represent price elasticity of supply, we can express it as (in point elasticity form):

$$\epsilon = \frac{(\Delta Q_s/Q_s)}{(\Delta P/P)}.$$

INCOME ELASTICITY OF DEMAND

a measure of how responsive consumption of some items is to a change in income, assuming the price of the good itself remains unchanged

CROSS-PRICE ELASTICITY OF DEMAND

a measure of how responsive consumption of one good is to a change in the price of a related good

PRICE ELASTICITY OF SUPPLY

a measure of the responsiveness of the quantity supplied of a commodity to a change in the commodity's own price

Any upward-sloping supply curve—the increasing per-unit cost case—has a positive elasticity of supply because price and quantity supplied move in the same direction. If per-unit production costs are constant, the supply curve is horizontal, and the price elasticity of supply is infinity. For example, the supply of dimes in terms of nickels is a horizontal curve with a height of 2 at most banks (banks are willing to provide you an additional dime so long as you give them 2 nickels per dime). As the price of dimes rises from 1.99 nickels per dime (a rate at which banks would be unwilling to sell you any dimes in exchange for nickels) to 2 nickels per dime (a rate at which banks would become willing to supply you quite a few dimes in exchange for nickels), the percentage change in quantity supplied (from zero to a lot of dimes) is infinite relative to the percentage change in price (from 1.99 to 2 nickels per dime).

At the opposite extreme, if supply is entirely unresponsive to price, the supply curve is vertical and the elasticity of supply is equal to zero. For example, no matter how high the price gets, it is impossible to produce more original Picasso paintings (although several imposters have attempted to copy the dead artist's style and pass off the result as a Picasso original). The responsiveness of the quantity of Picasso paintings supplied to increases (or decreases) in the price of Picasso paintings is thus zero.

Finally, as in the case of elasticity of demand, when the ratio of the percentage change in quantity supplied to the percentage change in price is greater than unity, we say that supply is *elastic*. When supply is elastic, an increase in price produces a more than proportionate increase in quantity supplied. When the elasticity of supply is less than unity, supply is *inelastic* and a higher price produces a less than proportionate increase in quantity supplied. When the ratio equals unity, supply is *unit elastic* and a higher price produces a proportionate increase in quantity supplied.

APPLICATION 2.8   IT TAKES TIME

Just as with demand, supply tends to become more elastic the longer the time period over which producers can adjust to a price change. For example, Hurricane Andrew struck southern Florida in 1992, destroying or damaging more than 75,000 homes. In the first week after the hurricane hit, the price of lumber doubled in southern Florida. We would expect this kind of effect when demand increases dramatically for a product that, at least in the short run, is in relatively fixed supply. Recall that a given supply (or demand) curve is drawn for a specific time period. The supply curve for lumber was close to vertical in the days immediately after the hurricane, as producers were unable to supply appreciably more lumber despite the doubling in lumber's price. With more time to adjust and ship lumber from elsewhere in the country, however, Hurricane Andrew led to a significant increase in the quantity of lumber supplied to the southern Florida market. Supply elasticity, in other words, became greater as producers had more time to adjust to the hurricane-induced change in the price of lumber.

Note that while many people regarded the doubling in the price of lumber immediately following Hurricane Andrew as *price gouging*, the so-called "gouging" gave lumber suppliers an incentive to ship additional lumber to southern Florida. A legal proscription against an increase in the price of lumber following the hurricane would have wiped out the incentive to ship additional lumber to southern Florida and created a shortage of a commodity critical to the rebuilding process. The so-called price gouging also had a beneficial effect on the demand side: it gave consumers a greater incentive to conserve in their use of lumber and thereby helped bring quantity demanded into equality with quantity supplied in the local lumber market following the hurricane.

SUMMARY

• Most economic issues involve the workings of individual markets.

• In the supply–demand model we analyze the behavior of buyers by using the demand curve.

• The demand curve shows how much people will purchase at different prices when other factors that affect purchases are held constant. The demand curve slopes downward, reflecting the law of demand.

• Analysis of the sellers' side of the market relies on the supply curve, which shows the amount that firms will offer for sale at different prices, other factors being constant. The supply curve typically slopes upward.

• The intersection of the demand and supply curves, reflecting the behavior of buyers and sellers, identifies the equilibrium price and quantity.

• A shift in the supply or demand curve produces a change in the equilibrium price and quantity.

• For the market mechanism to operate, price must be free to adjust to any change affecting the behavior of buyers and sellers in the market. Thus when the government steps in to regulate prices, the market does not function in the same way.

• A government-imposed price ceiling results in a shortage and may lead to diminution in product quality, nonprice rationing, an incentive for black markets to emerge, administrative costs, and increased demand for and supply of substitute goods. Sellers are clearly harmed by the imposition of a price ceiling, and the effect on buyers as a group may not be beneficial.

• Elasticities provide a quantitative measure of the magnitude of the responsiveness of quantity demanded or supplied to a change in some other variable.

• The most important elasticity in economics is price elasticity of demand, which measures how responsive the quantity demanded of a commodity is to a change in the commodity's own price. It is measured by the percentage change in quantity demanded divided by the percentage change in price.

• When price elasticity exceeds unity, demand is elastic and a lower price expands purchases so sharply that total expenditure rises.

• When price elasticity is less than unity, demand is inelastic, and a lower price leads to a reduction in total expenditure.

• When price elasticity equals unity, demand is unit elastic, and total expenditure is unchanged at a lower price.

• Three other important elasticities are the income elasticity of demand, cross-price elasticity of demand, and price elasticity of supply. They are constructed in a manner analogous to that employed to construct price elasticity of demand and measure, respectively, the responsiveness of quantity demanded to income, the responsiveness of quantity demanded of one good to the price of a related good, and the responsiveness of the quantity supplied of a commodity to the commodity's own price.

REVIEW QUESTIONS AND PROBLEMS

Questions and problems marked with an asterisk have solutions given in Answers to Selected Problems at the back of the book (page 571).

*2.1. A newspaper article points out that the price of economics textbooks is up 10 percent this year over last year, and yet the number of textbooks sold is higher this year. The article claims that these figures show that the law of demand does not apply to textbooks. Is there a flaw in this argument?

2.2. A demand curve is drawn holding "other things constant." What does the "other things constant" provision mean, and why is it important to a correct interpretation of the law of demand?

2.3. "Because demand curves and supply curves are always shifting, markets can never attain an equilibrium." Does this imply that the concept of equilibrium is not useful?

2.4. If we know that the (real) price of tennis rackets is higher now than last year, can we conclude that the demand curve shifted out over the year? Explain.

*2.5. The supply and demand schedules for apples are as follows:

Demand		Supply	
Price per Pound	Quantity Demanded per Year	Price per Pound	Quantity Supplied per Year
$0.90	100,000	$0.60	100,000
0.80	110,000	0.70	120,000
0.70	120,000	0.80	140,000
0.60	135,000	0.90	150,000

Use graphs to answer the following questions.

a. What is the market equilibrium price and quantity?

b. The government agrees to purchase as many pounds of apples as growers will sell at a price of $0.80 per pound. How much will the government purchase, how much will consumers purchase, and how much will be produced?

c. Suppose the government policy in part b remains in effect, but consumer demand increases by 10 percent (consumers will purchase 10 percent more at each price than they did before). What will be the effect on total apple output, purchases by consumers, purchases by the government, and the price of apples?

2.6. In economics, what do we mean by the term *shortage*? In unregulated competitive markets, are there ever shortages? Have you ever heard noneconomists use the term *shortage* with a different meaning?

2.7. "A decrease in supply will lead to an increase in the price, which decreases demand, thus lowering price. Thus, a decrease in supply has no effect on the price of a good." Evaluate this statement.

*2.8. Consider the market for taxi service in a city. Explain, by using supply and demand curves, how each of the following actions will affect the market. (Consider each case separately.)

a. Bus drivers go on strike.

b. Bus fares increase after a strike by bus drivers.

c. Taxi drivers must pass a competency test, and one-third fail.

d. Gasoline prices increase.

e. Half the downtown parking lots are converted to office buildings.

f. The population of the city increases.

2.9. As a regional manager for American Airlines you have recently undertaken a survey of economy-class load factors (the percentage of economy-class seats that are filled with paying customers) on the Chicago–Columbus, Ohio, route that you service. The survey was conducted over five successive months. For each month, data collected include the one-way fare you charge per economy seat, the price charged by rival United Airlines, the average (monthly) per capita income in the combined Chicago–Columbus market, and the average economy-class load factor for both American and United Airlines. Assume that all other factors (the price charged by Southwest Airlines, the number of flights, the size of planes flown, and so on) have remained constant.

Month	AA Price	UA Price	Income	AA Load Factor	UA Load Factor
1	$110	$112	$2,000	65	60
2	109	110	1,900	62	63
3	110	112	2,100	70	66
4	109	111	1,900	70	61
5	108	110	1,900	68	59

a. On the Chicago–Columbus route, identify the arc price elasticity of demand for American economy seats, the arc income elasticity of demand for American economy seats, and the arc cross-price elasticity of demand for American economy seats with respect to United prices.

b. Based on the data that you have collected, is United a substitute or complement for American in the Chicago–Columbus market? Explain your answer.

c. Are American's economy seats a normal or inferior good in the Chicago–Columbus market? Explain your answer.

d. Would the estimated demand elasticity for your product be larger or smaller if consumers had been given more time to respond to any price change (for example, one year versus one month)?

e. Compared with the price elasticity of demand for United and American economy seats, is the demand elasticity for economy seats in general in the Chicago–Columbus market (regardless of which airline provides them) larger or smaller?

*2.10. Suppose that the demand elasticity for cigarettes is equal to 2.0. If the demand elasticity for Camel cigarettes is equal to 6.0, must there be at least some cigarette brands with a demand elasticity less than 2.0?

2.11. Suppose that the typical economics student is interested in consuming (and spends all her money on) only two commodities: economics study guides and horror movie passes. An unlimited supply of horror movie passes is available at a price of $5 per pass while an equally unlimited supply of study guides covering endlessly different (and interesting) nuances in economics can be purchased for $30 each. The student currently purchases 20 horror movie passes and 10 study guides per semester. If the typical student's price and income elasticities of demand for horror movie passes are both unity, what is the student's cross-price elasticity of demand for study guides with respect to changes in the price of horror movie passes?

2.12. Suppose that the demand curve for corn is downward sloping but that the supply curve is perfectly price inelastic at a quantity of Q^* once the corn is harvested. Furthermore, assume that the equilibrium price is $5 per bushel.

a. If the U.S. government decides to enter the market for corn and purchase enough so that the price doubles to $10 per bushel (assume that the corn is given away to Russia), indicate on a supply–demand diagram the amount spent on corn by private American consumers and the amount spent on corn by the U.S. government. If the demand for corn by private American consumers is price inelastic (suppose that demand elasticity is equal to 0.5), which amount is larger—that spent by the government or that spent by private consumers? Explain your answer.

b. An alternative method for helping corn farmers is to have the government pay them a subsidy of $5 per bushel of corn. Show graphically the amount spent on corn by private consumers under this proposal as well as the amount spent by the

U.S. government. Again assuming that the demand elasticity for corn is 0.5, is the cost to the government of the subsidy program greater or less than the cost of the program described in part a? Explain your answer.

2.13. Heidi spends all her income on going to the movies regardless of her income level or the price of movie passes. What is her income elasticity of demand for movie passes? What is her price elasticity of demand for movie passes?

*2.14. Assume that the demand for crack cocaine is inelastic and that users get the funds to pay for crack cocaine by stealing. Suppose that the government increases penalties on suppliers of crack cocaine and thereby reduces supply. What will happen to the amount of crime committed by crack cocaine users?

2.15. If the price of gasoline is $2.00 and the price elasticity of demand is 0.4, how much will a 10 percent reduction in the quantity placed on the market increase the price? Will total spending on gasoline rise? If so, by what percentage?

2.16. Given two parallel, downward-sloping, linear demand curves, is the demand elasticity the same at any given price? Given two downward-sloping, linear demand curves, with one showing consumption to be 50 percent greater than the other demand curve at each price, is the demand elasticity the same at any given price?

2.17. In 1999, the bidding for a human kidney offered on the Internet auction site eBay hit $5.7 million before the company put a stop to it citing a federal law that makes it illegal to sell one's own organs. Using a supply and demand graph, explain this bidding phenomenon given that the federal law mandates a price of zero for the sale of body organs.

2.18. Some opponents of the death penalty are opposed to executing individuals who have been convicted of murder because they believe that murder is an irrational act and that raising the price of murder through capital punishment thus will not have a deterrent effect on prospective murderers. If these opponents are correct in their view of murder being an irrational act, depict what the demand curve for murder looks like. What is the price elasticity of demand for murder according to this view?

2.19. In the antitrust case brought by the Justice Department against Microsoft, explain why the cross-price elasticity of demand between rival operating systems such as Linux and Microsoft's own MS-DOS system might have been of interest in determining Microsoft's ability to control the prevailing price in the operating system market.

CHAPTER 3

The Theory of Consumer Choice

How do prices, incomes, and preferences affect consumers' choices to purchase some goods and not others?

Chapter Outline

3.1 Consumer Preferences
Consumer Preferences Graphed as Indifference Curves   Curvature of Indifference Curves   Individuals Have Different Preferences   Graphing Economic Bads and Economic Neuters   Perfect Substitutes and Complements

3.2 The Budget Constraint
Geometry of the Budget Line   Shifts in Budget Lines

3.3 The Consumer's Choice
A Corner Solution   The Composite-Good Convention
***Application 3.1** Consumers' Valuation of Air Bags*
***Application 3.2** Convex (Indifference) Curves and Cellular Charges*

3.4 Changes in Income and Consumption Choices
Normal Goods   Inferior Goods
***Application 3.3** Running Toward the Border in a Recession*
The Food Stamp Program
***Application 3.4** Keeping Bugs Bunny and the Back Street Boys at Bay in Canada*
***Application 3.5** The Allocation of Commencement Tickets*

3.5 Are People Selfish?
***Application 3.6** The New Philanthropy*

3.6 The Utility Approach to Consumer Choice
The Consumer's Optimal Choice   Relationship to Indifference Curves

Learning Objectives

- Develop an approach for analyzing consumer preferences.
- Explain how a consumer's income and the prices that must be paid for various goods limit consumption choices.
- Understand how the market basket chosen by a consumer reflects both the consumer's preferences and the budget constraints imposed on the consumer by income and the prices that must be paid for various goods.
- Determine how changes in income affect consumption choices.
- Show how altruism can be explained by the theory of consumer choice.
- Relate the utility approach to the indifference curve method of analyzing consumer choice.

Consumers spend more than $4 trillion annually in the United States. These outlays reflect countless decisions by consumers to buy or not to buy various goods. Why do consumers purchase some things and not others? How do incomes, prices, and tastes affect consumption decisions? In this chapter we develop the fundamentals of the theory economists use to explain how these factors interact to determine consumption choices.

One use of consumer choice theory is to explain why demand curves slope downward. But if the theory of consumer behavior provided nothing more than a justification for drawing demand curves with negative slopes, it would hardly be worth discussing. The basic principles of the theory, however, have far broader applications. For example, in business, the theory yields information for: car companies worried about the extent to which consumers value safety versus fuel mileage; railroad and bus firms facing rising consumer incomes; financial managers concerned about how best to structure their clients' portfolios; cable operators seeking to determine whether rates charged for the basic service package should increase proportionately with the number of channels of programming added to the package; and suppliers wondering how minutes of phone service sold and profits will be affected by billing customers a constant amount per minute versus offering a flat monthly service fee irrespective of usage. In the public policy arena, consumer choice theory can assist in the design of programs to promote health care and encourage recycling. Furthermore, it can shed light on the school choice debate and whether vouchers that can be used to help underwrite the education of a child at a school of a family's choosing enhance household well-being relative to the historical model of public provision of a particular school in each family's district.

Economists also have extended consumer choice theory to individuals' decisions concerning labor supply, saving and investment, charitable contributions, voting, and even marriage. Indeed, some believe it provides the basis for a general theory of all human choices, not just consumer choices among goods in the marketplace. Several applications will be examined later in Chapter 5, but first we develop the theory fully as it pertains to the simple choices, among goods, made by a consumer.

The basic model focuses on two important factors that influence a consumer's behavior. First are the consumer's preferences, or tastes, over various combinations of goods. Second is the consumer's ability to acquire goods, which is determined by income and the prices of the goods.

3.1 CONSUMER PREFERENCES[1]

Everyday observation tells us that consumers differ widely in their preferences: some like liver, others despise it; some smoke cigarettes, others avoid cigarette smoke like the plague; some want a different pair of shoes for every occasion, others wear running shoes everywhere. Given such diversity in preferences about goods, how should we incorporate the obviously important influence they have on consumer choices? To deal with this problem, economists base their analysis on some general propositions about consumer behavior that are widely believed to be true. These propositions do not explain why people have the exact tastes they do; they only identify some characteristics shared by the preferences of virtually everyone.

Economists make three assumptions about the preferences of the typical consumer. First, we assume that preferences are *complete* in the sense that a consumer can rank (in order of preference) all market baskets. In other words, between a McDonald's Big Mac and a Burger King Whopper hamburger, the consumer prefers the Big Mac to the Whopper, prefers the Whopper to the Big Mac, or is *indifferent* between the two. We say a consumer is indifferent between two options when both are equally satisfactory. Importantly, this preference ranking reflects the relative desirability of the options themselves and ignores their cost. For example, it is not inconsistent for a consumer to prefer a Mercedes to a Saturn automobile but

---

[1]A mathematical treatment of some of the material in this section is given in the appendix at the back of the book (page 562).

to buy the Saturn. A purchase decision reflects both the preference ranking and the consumer's ability to acquire goods, which is determined by income and the prices of the goods; the consumer purchases the Saturn because its lower purchase price makes it more attractive when both cost and the intrinsic merits of the vehicles are considered. Preferences and budgets both influence consumer choice, but for the moment we will be concerned only with preferences.

Second, we assume that preferences are *transitive*. Transitivity means that if a consumer prefers market basket A to B, and B to C, then the consumer prefers A to C. For example, if Cindy Crawford likes Pepsi better than Coke, and Coke better than 7-Up, then logically she likes Pepsi better than 7-Up. In a sense this condition simply requires that people have rational or consistent preferences.

Third, a consumer is presumed to prefer more of any good to less. For example, given a choice between one vacation in Tahiti and two vacations in Tahiti, a consumer will prefer the latter provided that the choices are otherwise identical. This characteristic is termed *nonsatiation* and is expressed as "more is preferred to less."

Are the preceding three assumptions about preferences valid? In general, yes, although there are exceptions. For example, the assumption of transitivity is violated in the case of individuals with a schizophrenic disorder and has been found to be less likely to hold the younger the consumer. Researchers attribute the latter phenomenon either to a willingness to experiment in one's formative years or to the fact that being able to rank order preferences in a consistent manner is an acquired skill.

The assumption that more is better is also not universally true. Hot dogs might be appealing to most individuals, but more may not always be preferred to less if they have to be consumed all at once. That is, two hot dogs may be preferred to one hot dog, but fifty hot dogs are less appealing than two hot dogs—even to the heartiest eaters—if the hot dogs have to be eaten in one fell swoop.

Moreover, there are other goods such as pollution and liver (for some people), where less is preferred to more over all possible ranges of consumption. We call such commodities **economic "bads"** to distinguish them from the more frequently encountered economic "goods." An **economic "good"** is one for which more is better than less; in effect it is a desirable commodity in the consumer's view.

Notwithstanding the exceptions, completeness, transitivity, and nonsatiation appear to be reasonable and robust characteristics of consumer preferences. We start with these assumptions as a basis and show that a theory that is quite versatile can be developed without having to resort to more and stronger assumptions. Along the way, we point out how exceptions to the basic assumptions, such as economic "bads," can be accommodated by the theory.

Consumer Preferences Graphed as Indifference Curves

We can show a consumer's preferences across various **market baskets** or combinations of goods in a diagram with indifference curves. An **indifference curve** plots all the market baskets that the consumer views as being equally satisfactory. In other words, it identifies the various combinations of goods among which the consumer is indifferent. Figure 3.1 shows an indifference curve, U_1, for a student-consumer interested in two goods: movie passes (M) and compact discs (C). The student is equally satisfied with 10M plus 4C (basket A) or 5M plus 12C (basket B)—or any other combination of movie passes and compact discs along U_1.

From our basic assumptions we can deduce several characteristics that indifference curves must have. First, an indifference curve must slope downward if the consumer views the goods as desirable. To see this, start with point A on U_1 in Figure 3.1. If we change the composition of the market basket so that it contains more compact discs but the same amount of

ECONOMIC "BADS"
commodities of which less is preferred to more over all possible ranges of consumption

ECONOMIC "GOODS"
commodities of which more is better than less

MARKET BASKETS
combinations of goods

INDIFFERENCE CURVE
a diagram that plots all the markets baskets the consumer views as being equally satisfactory

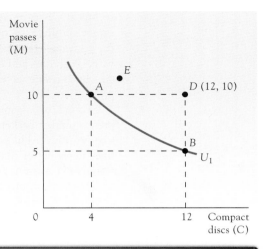

FIGURE 3.1

An Indifference Curve
The indifference curve, U_1, shows all the combinations of movie passes and compact discs that the consumer considers equally satisfactory. The consumer prefers any market basket lying above U_1 (like point E) to all market baskets on U_1, and any market basket on U_1 is preferred to any market basket lying below U_1.

movie passes (so the new basket is at a point such as D), the student will be better off—more compact discs are preferred to less. Note, though, that the consumer will no longer be on U_1, the original indifference curve. If we are required to keep the consumer indifferent between alternative combinations of movie passes and compact discs, we must find a market basket that contains *more* compact discs but *fewer* movie passes. Market baskets that are equally satisfactory must contain more of one good and less of the other; in other words, the curve must have a negative slope.

A second characteristic of indifference curves is that a consumer prefers a market basket lying above (to the northeast of) a given indifference curve to every basket on the indifference curve. (Similarly, the consumer regards a basket below the indifference curve as less desirable than any on the indifference curve.) In Figure 3.1, pick any point above U_1—for instance, E. There must be a point on U_1 that has less of both goods than E—point A, for example. Basket E will clearly be preferred to A because it contains more of both goods, and more is preferred to less. Because A is equally preferred to all points on U_1, point E must also be preferred to all points on U_1, from the transitivity assumption. Similar reasoning implies that every basket on U_1 is preferred to any basket lying below the curve.

So far we have examined only one indifference curve. To show a consumer's entire preference ranking, we need a set of indifference curves, or an **indifference map**. Figure 3.2 shows three of the consumer's indifference curves. Because more is preferred to less, the consumer prefers higher indifference curves. Every market basket on U_3, for example, is preferred to every basket on U_2. Likewise, every basket on U_2 is preferred to every basket on U_1.

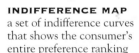

INDIFFERENCE MAP
a set of indifference curves that shows the consumer's entire preference ranking

A set of indifference curves represents an ordinal ranking. An *ordinal ranking* arrays market baskets in a certain order, such as most preferred, second-most preferred, and third-most preferred. It shows order of preference but does not indicate by how much one basket is preferred to another. There is simply no way to measure how much better off the consumer is on U_2 compared with U_1. Fortunately, we do not need this information to explain consumer choices when using indifference curves: knowing how consumers rank market baskets is sufficient. The numbers used to label the indifference curves measure nothing; they are simply a means of distinguishing more-preferred from less-preferred market baskets.

Now that we have described how preferences can be represented by a set of indifference curves, a third characteristic of these curves can be stated: two indifference curves cannot intersect. We can see this by incorrectly assuming that two curves intersect and then noting

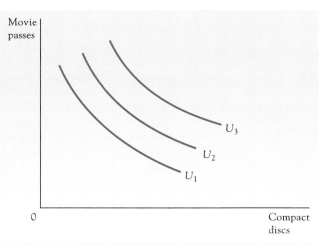

FIGURE 3.2

An Indifference Map
A set of indifference curves, or an indifference map, indicates how a consumer ranks all possible market baskets. Market baskets lying on indifference curves farther from the origin are preferred to those on curves closer to the origin.

that this proposition violates our basic assumptions. In Figure 3.3, two indifference curves have been drawn to intersect. Consider three points: the intersection point E and two other points such that one (B) has more of both goods than the other (A). Now, because B and E lie on U_2, they are equally preferred. Also, because E and A lie on U_1, they are equally preferred. Thus, B is equal to E, and E is equal to A, so by transitivity B should equal A. However, because B has more of both goods than A, B must be preferred to A (more is preferred to less). We arrive at a contradiction: B cannot be equal to A and preferred to A simultaneously. Intersecting indifference curves violate our transitivity and nonsatiation assumptions. In short, they don't make sense.

Curvature of Indifference Curves

We have discussed three features of indifference curves: they slope downward, higher curves are preferred to lower ones, and they cannot intersect. These features are implied by the assumptions about consumer preferences made earlier. Convexity is a fourth feature of indif-

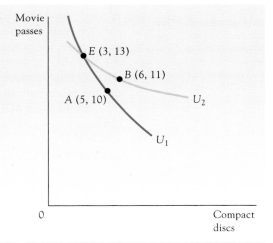

FIGURE 3.3

Why Intersecting Indifference Curves Are Inconsistent
Intersecting indifference curves are inconsistent with rational choice; they violate the assumptions of nonsatiation and transitive preferences.

ference curves, but because we cannot logically deduce it from the basic assumptions about preferences, further explanation is required.

So far we have seen indifference curves that are convex to the origin; that is, they bow inward toward the origin, so the slope of the curve becomes flatter as you move down the curve. To explain why indifference curves have this shape we introduce the concept of **marginal rate of substitution**, or **MRS**. A student's marginal rate of substitution between, for example, compact discs and movie passes (MRS_{CM}) is *the maximum amount of movie passes the consumer is willing to give up to obtain an additional compact disc*. Because it is a measure of the *willingness* to trade one good for another, the MRS depends on the initial quantities held: holding the number of movie passes constant, the student's willingness to exchange movie passes for compact discs will likely differ if the student has ten compact discs rather than five. Thus, a consumer's MRS is not a fixed number but will vary with the amount of each good the consumer has.

The marginal rate of substitution is related to the slope of the consumer's indifference curves. In fact, the slope of the indifference curve (multiplied by −1) is equal to the MRS. For example, say a market basket contains fifteen movie passes and five compact discs. Let's assume that a student is willing to trade a maximum of four movie passes for one more compact disc. In other words, the MRS at this point is 4M per 1C. What happens to the student's well-being if 4M are lost and 1C is gained, so that the market basket contains 11M and 6C? The student will be no better off and no worse off than before. This is so because we have taken away the maximum amount of movie passes (4) that the student was willing to give up for another compact disc. In other words, if the student's MRS is four movie passes per compact disc, and we take away four movie passes and add one compact disc, the new market basket will be preferred equally to the original one. Both market baskets lie on the same indifference curve.

This relationship is illustrated in Figure 3.4. Market baskets A (15M and 5C) and B (11M and 6C) are both on indifference curve U_1. Note that the curve's slope between points A and B is −4M/1C. The slope—or, more precisely, −1 times this slope—measures the consumer's MRS. Purely for ease of communication, we define the MRS as a positive number so that the slope of the indifference curve, which is negative, must be multiplied by −1. Don't let this definitional complication confuse you: the MRS and the indifference curve slope are identical concepts, both measuring the willingness of a consumer to substitute one good for another. The indifference curve slope shows how many movie passes can be exchanged for a compact disc without changing the consumer's well-being—which is precisely what the MRS measures.[2] Because an indifference curve's slope and the MRS measure the same thing, drawing an indifference curve as convex (i.e., with a flatter slope as we move down the curve) means that the MRS declines as we move down the curve. In Figure 3.4, the MRS declines from 4M per 1C at basket A to 3M per 1C at B, and so on. To justify drawing indifference curves as convex, we need to explain why the MRS can be expected to decline as we move down the curve.

A **diminishing MRS** means that as more and more of one good is consumed along an indifference curve, the consumer is willing to give up less and less of some other good to obtain still more of the first good. Look at point F in Figure 3.4. Here the student has a large number of compact discs and very few movie passes; in comparison with points such as A

MARGINAL RATE OF SUBSTITUTION (MRS)
a measure of the consumer's willingness to trade one good for another

DIMINISHING MRS
a consumer's willingness to give up less and less of some other good to obtain still more of the first good

---

[2]The slope of the indifference curve at point A is not exactly −4M/1C. A curved line has a different slope at each point on it; its slope is measured by the slope of a straight line drawn tangent to the curve. As shown in the figure here, the slope at point A is $\Delta M/\Delta C$. Identifying the slope as we do in Figure 3.4 is an approximation to the correct measure, but for small movements along the curve the two measures are approximately equal.

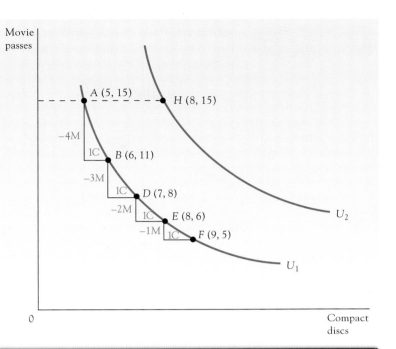

FIGURE 3.4

Diminishing *MRS* Along an Indifference Curve

Indifference curves are convex toward the origin, implying that the slope of each curve becomes flatter as we move down the curve. The (absolute value of the) slope of U_1 at A is $4M/1C$; at E it is $1M/1C$. The indifference curve's slope measures the consumer's marginal rate of substitution between goods. The convexity of indifference curves thus embodies the assumption of diminishing *MRS* along an indifference curve.

farther up the curve, compact discs are relatively plentiful and movie passes are relatively scarce. Under these circumstances the student will probably be unwilling to exchange many movie passes (already scarce) for more compact discs (already plentiful). Thus, it seems reasonable to suppose that the MRS is lower at F than at A. At A, movie passes are more plentiful and compact discs more scarce, so we might anticipate that the student will place a higher value on compact discs—that is, be willing to sacrifice a larger amount of movie passes to obtain an additional compact disc. In other words, *the assumption of a declining* MRS *embodies the belief that the relative amounts of goods are related systematically to the consumer's views about their relative importance.* In particular, the more scarce one good is *relative* to another, the greater its *relative* value in terms of the other good.

This discussion is merely an appeal to the intuitive plausibility of convex indifference curves; it is not proof. Thinking along these lines, however, has convinced many people that indifference curves generally reflect a declining MRS. We therefore assume that indifference curves are convex to the origin, which implies that the consumer's MRS declines as we move down any one of these curves.

Two final points related to the convexity of indifference curves should also be mentioned. First, we have assumed implicitly that both goods in the student's market basket are economic "goods" (that is, more is preferred to less), which is the general case. In other cases, as with economic "bads," indifference curves need not be convex. Second, a declining MRS pertains only to a movement along a given indifference curve, not to a movement from one curve to another. For example, we might be tempted to argue that if the student has more compact discs and the same number of movie passes, the MRS_{CM} will be lower. For Figure 3.4, this argument implies that curve U_2 is flatter at point H than U_1 is at point A. This is not what we are assuming; we are only assuming that the slope of each curve becomes flatter as we move down that curve.

Indifference Map of Two Consumers

People have different preferences, and these differences show up in the shapes of their indifference maps. Oprah Winfrey's preferences are graphed in part (a) and George W. Bush's in part (b). The indifference maps show that Bush has a stronger preference for tacos than Winfrey does.

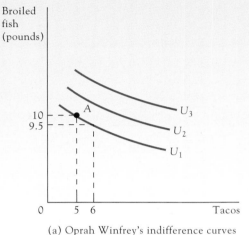

(a) Oprah Winfrey's indifference curves

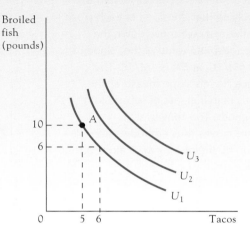

(b) George W. Bush's indifference curves

Individuals Have Different Preferences

People have different preferences, and those differences are indicated by the shapes of their indifference curves. Consider the preferences of two consumers, Oprah Winfrey and George W. Bush, for tacos and broiled fish. Figure 3.5a shows Winfrey's preferences with several of her indifference curves relating broiled fish and taco consumption. Figure 3.5b shows Bush's indifference curves. Bush's curves being steeper than Winfrey's indicates that Bush has a stronger preference for tacos than Winfrey does. To understand this idea, suppose they were both consuming the same market basket shown by point A in each graph. Because Bush's indifference curve through this point is steeper than Winfrey's, Bush's MRS of fish for tacos is greater than Winfrey's. Bush (who said on Oprah that tacos are his favorite fast food) would be willing to trade four pounds of broiled fish for one more taco, but Winfrey (with her preference for fish over tacos) would give up only half a pound of broiled fish for another taco.

Indifference curves indicate the *relative* desirability of different combinations of goods, so to say that Bush values tacos in terms of broiled fish more than Winfrey does is the same as saying that Winfrey values broiled fish in terms of tacos more than Bush does. They say nothing about how much either of them values roast turkey, for example.

Graphing Economic Bads and Economic Neuters

Although our discussion of indifference curves has been restricted to the most generally encountered case of choices among desirable goods, where more is preferred to less, we may depict *any* type of preferences with a set of indifference curves. Indeed, a good test of your understanding of indifference curves is to analyze some other situations.

For example, how would you show a person's preferences relating weekly income and pollution with indifference curves? For a typical person, income is a desirable good, but smog is an economic "bad." Figure 3.6a shows income and smog on the axes. To determine the

FIGURE 3.6

Indifference Maps for a "Bad" and a "Neuter"
(a) Indifference curves have the shapes shown here when a "good" is on the vertical axis and a "bad" on the horizontal axis. (b) They have the shapes shown here with a "good" on the vertical axis and a "neuter" on the horizontal axis.

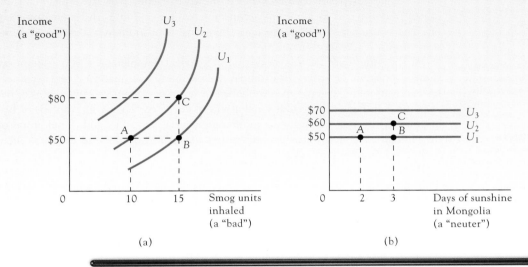

(a)   (b)

shapes of the indifference curves, we start by picking an arbitrary market basket, point A, for example, composed of 10 units of smog and $50 in income. If we hold income constant at $50 but increase units of smog—a move from A to B—the person will be worse off (that is, on a lower indifference curve) because smog is a "bad." If a person inhales more smog and is to remain on the same indifference curve, more of the "good," income, is necessary to compensate for the additional smog, as at point C. Thus, the indifference curve must slope upward. In addition, greater levels of well-being are shown by indifference curves above and to the northwest: U_2 is preferred to U_1 if the "good" is on the vertical axis. This result can be seen by focusing on horizontal movements (more smog with the same income makes the consumer worse off) and vertical movements (more income with the same smog level makes the consumer better off).

Most things are either "goods" or "bads," but an intermediate case is possible where the consumer doesn't care one way or another about something. For example, we suspect most people don't care how many days a week the sun shines in Mongolia (unless they live in Mongolia). Yet we can still draw indifference curves for Mongolian days of sunshine (an **economic "neuter"**) and a second good such as income. Figure 3.6b shows these indifference curves as horizontal straight lines. Starting at A, we see that a horizontal move to B— more sunshine but the same income—leaves the consumer on the same indifference curve. Thus, the indifference curves are horizontal, implying that the MRS is zero: the consumer is unwilling to give up any income for more days of Mongolian sunshine. Any vertical movement—more income and the same amount of sunshine—will put the consumer on a higher indifference curve.

By thinking of horizontal and vertical movements, you may deduce the shape of indifference curves that relate various goods under different conditions. The most important thing, however, is to understand the general case where desirable goods are on both axes, since this case is the one most frequently encountered.

ECONOMIC "NEUTER"
a case in which the consumer doesn't care one way or another about a particular good

Perfect Substitutes and Complements

The shapes of indifference curves in general indicate the willingness of consumers to substitute one good for another and remain equally well off. At one extreme, certain goods are **perfect substitutes** in consumption. For example, for most consumers, any dime offers the same satisfaction as any two nickels. As shown in Figure 3.7a, the typical consumer is willing to trade nickels for dimes at a constant two-for-one rate while remaining equally well off. The consumer's indifference map thus consists of indifference curves all having a constant slope of -2 nickels per dime.

At the other extreme are goods that are **perfect complements** in consumption. To consume a molecule of water, for example, we need an exact match of two atoms of hydrogen for every atom of oxygen. Once we have one atom of oxygen and two atoms of hydrogen, as at point A in Figure 3.7b, additional atoms of either oxygen (as at point B) or hydrogen (as at point C) keep us on the same indifference curve, U_1. Only additional atoms of both hydrogen *and* oxygen, at a two-to-one rate, are sufficient to move us to points such as D and higher indifference curves such as U_2.

Perfect complements are associated with sharply kinked, L-shaped indifference curves. The indifference curves undergo abrupt changes in slope (from infinity to zero) at their kinks. In our water molecule example, the kink indicates that consumers would be infinitely willing to substitute surplus oxygen for additional hydrogen atoms when they are above point A on indifference curve U_1. Conversely, consumers would be entirely unwilling to substitute oxygen for hydrogen atoms if they are located to the right of A on indifference curve U_1 and have surplus hydrogen atoms. The reason for the sharp slope change at the kink reflects the desire to get a precise combination of the goods in question in the act of consumption.

The typical goods on which we focus in this book fall somewhere between being perfect substitutes and perfect complements. Namely, the typical indifference curve has a slope that

FIGURE 3.7

Perfect Substitutes and Perfect Complements
(a) Indifference curves are straight lines when goods are perfect substitutes in consumption. (b) With perfect complements, indifference curves are L-shaped.

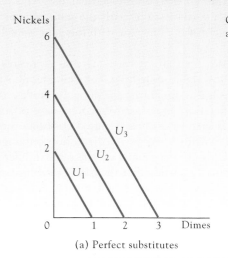

(a) Perfect substitutes

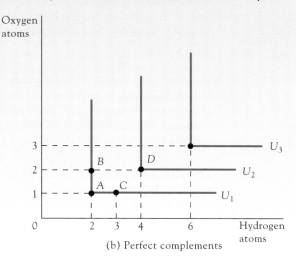

(b) Perfect complements

PERFECT SUBSTITUTE
the case where a consumer is willing to substitute one good for another at some constant rate and remain equally well off

PERFECT COMPLEMENTS
goods that must be consumed in a precise combination in order to provide a consumer a given level of satisfaction

becomes gently flatter as one moves down the curve. The curve is not characterized by a constant slope (as with perfect substitutes). Neither does the typical indifference curve's slope change in an abrupt manner (as with perfect complements).

3.2 THE BUDGET CONSTRAINT[3]

BUDGET CONSTRAINT
the way in which a consumer's income and the prices that must be paid for various goods limit choices

The preceding section examined consumer's preferences, or tastes, for various goods. Now, we turn to understanding **budget constraints** or how a consumer's income and the prices that must be paid for various goods limit choices. Let's begin with a simple example. Consider a student who has a weekly discretionary income of $60 that she uses to purchase only two goods, compact discs and movie passes.[4] The price of each compact disc (P_C) is $12, and the price of each movie pass (P_M) is $6. What combinations of compact discs and movie passes may be purchased given the student's income and the prices of the two goods? Table 3.1 provides one way of identifying the various market baskets that the consumer can purchase under these conditions.

Market basket A in Table 3.1 shows what can be purchased if all the student's income goes to purchase movie passes. A weekly income of $60 permits the student to buy 10 movie passes at a price of $6 each, with nothing left over for compact discs. Basket Z shows the other extreme, when the student spends the entire $60 on compact discs. Because compact discs cost $12 each, a maximum of 5 can be purchased per week, with nothing left over for movie passes. All the intermediate baskets, B through Y, indicate the other mixes of compact discs and movie passes that cost a total of $60. In short, Table 3.1 lists all the alternative combinations of the two goods that the student can purchase with $60.

BUDGET LINE
a line that shows the combinations of goods that can be purchased at the specified prices and assuming that all of the consumer's income is expended

Figure 3.8 shows a more convenient way of presenting the same information. In this diagram the amount of movie passes consumed per week is measured on the vertical axis, and the number of compact discs is measured on the horizontal axis. Both axes, therefore, measure *quantities* (in contrast to a supply–demand diagram that has price on one axis). The line AZ plots the various market baskets the student may purchase from the data in Table 3.1. This line is called the **budget line**, and it shows all the combinations of movie passes and compact discs the student can buy at the specified prices and assuming that the student spends all of her income.

TABLE 3.1   ALTERNATIVE MARKET BASKETS THE CONSUMER MAY PURCHASE

Market Basket	Composition of Market Baskets	
	Movie Passes per Week	Compact Discs per Week
A	10	0
B	8	1
W	6	2
X	4	3
Y	2	4
Z	0	5

Note: Income = $60; P_M = $6/movie pass; P_C = $12/compact disc.

---

[3]A mathematical treatment of some of the material in this section is given in the appendix at the back of the book (page 562).

[4]Note that we are defining income (and, later, consumption) as a "flow" variable—the amount of income the student receives per week—as opposed to a "stock" variable—the wealth at the disposal of the student.

FIGURE 3.8

The Budget Line
A consumer's budget line shows the combinations of goods that can be purchased with a given income and prices of goods held constant. Line *AZ* shows the budget line when income is $60, P_M = $6/movie pass, and P_C = $12/compact disc. The line's slope is $-P_C/P_M$.

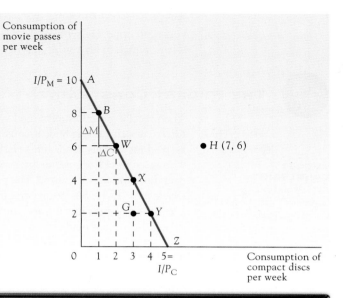

The budget line is drawn as a continuous line, not a collection of discrete points such as A and B, reflecting an assumption of continuous divisibility; that is, fractional units may be purchased. Although the assumption of continuous divisibility may be questioned—we can buy zero or one haircut in a week, for example, but can we buy half a haircut?—a little reflection shows that we can buy half a haircut per week by buying one every other week. Viewing consumption as the average consumption per week, rather than the precise level of consumption in any specific week, makes the assumption of a continuous budget line acceptable in most cases.

The consumer's budget line identifies the options from which the consumer can choose. In our example, the student can purchase any basket on or inside line AZ. Any basket inside the line, such as G, involves a total outlay that is smaller than the student's weekly income. Any point outside the line, such as H (7 compact discs and 6 movie passes), requires an outlay larger than the student's weekly income and is therefore beyond reach. Consequently, the budget line reinforces the concept of scarcity developed in Chapter 1: the student cannot have unlimited amounts of everything, so choices among possible options, which are shown by the budget line, must be made.

Geometry of the Budget Line

A thorough understanding of the geometry of a budget line will prove helpful later on. Note that the intercepts with the axes show the maximum amount of one good that can be purchased if none of the other is bought. Point A indicates that 10 movie passes can be bought if income is devoted to movie passes alone. The vertical intercept equals the student's weekly income (*I*) divided by the price of movie passes (I/P_M, or [$60/($6/movie pass)]) = 10 movie passes), since $60 permits the purchase of 10 movie passes costing $6 each. Similarly, point Z equals weekly income divided by the price of compact discs (I/P_C, or [$60/($12/compact disc)] = 5 compact discs).

The budget line's slope indicates how many movie passes the student must give up to buy one more compact disc. For example, the slope at point B in Figure 3.8 is $\Delta M/\Delta C$, or -2 movie passes/1 compact disc, indicating that a move from B to W involves sacrificing 2 movie passes to gain an additional compact disc. (Because AZ is a straight line, the slope is constant at −2 movie passes per 1 compact disc at all points along the line.) Note that the slope indicates the relative cost of each good. To get 1 more compact disc, the student must give up 2 movie passes. A budget line's slope is determined by the prices of the two goods. In fact, the slope is equal to (minus) the ratio of prices:

$$\Delta M/\Delta C = -P_C/P_M.$$

In this example we have:

$$\Delta M/\Delta C = (-2 \text{ movie passes})/(1 \text{ compact disc});$$

because:

$$-P_C/P_M = -[(\$12/\text{compact disc})/(\$6/\text{movie pass})];$$
$$= (-2 \text{ movie passes})/(1 \text{ compact disc}).$$

To understand this important relationship, note that because movie passes cost $6 each, the student has to purchase two fewer movie passes (ΔM) to have the $12 required to buy one more compact disc (ΔC). Thus, the slope of the budget line, which equals two movie passes per compact disc, reflects the fact that compact discs are twice as expensive as movie passes. The slope is equal to the price ratio: $12 per compact disc divided by $6 per movie pass equals two movie passes per compact disc. Put somewhat differently, the slope of the budget line is a measure of relative price—the price of one unit of a good in terms of units of the other.[5]

Shifts in Budget Lines

We have seen how income together with the prices of goods determines a consumer's budget line. Any change in income or prices will cause a shift in the budget line. Let us explore how the budget line shifts in response to a change in these two underlying factors.

Income Changes

We'll begin with the budget line described before, where the student's weekly income is $60, the price of each compact disc is $12, and the price of each movie pass is $6. We again draw the budget line as AZ in Figure 3.9. (Note that from now on, we will use the shorthand term *compact discs* instead of *weekly consumption of compact discs*. We also will use *income* instead of *weekly income* and *price* instead of *per-unit price*.) Now suppose the student's income rises to $120, but the prices of compact discs and movie passes do not change. The new budget line is A'Z'. Point A' shows the new maximum number of movie passes that can be bought if all income is allocated to movie passes. Because income is now $120 ($2I$) and P_M is still $6, the student can buy 20 movie passes. (Recall that the vertical intercept, A', equals income, now $2I = \$120$, divided by P_M.) Similarly, the student can buy a maximum of 10 compact discs if all income is spent on compact discs.

Note that a change in income with constant prices produces a parallel shift in the budget line. The slope of the budget line has not changed, because prices have remained fixed. Even with a higher income, the student must still give up 2 movie passes, at $6 per pass, to consume 1 more compact disc at $12 each (as shown by the move from *J* to *K* on the new budget line). The slope of any budget line—regardless of the income level—equals the price

---

[5] We summarize this idea with a bit of algebra. The budget line shows market baskets where the sum of expenditures on compact discs and movie passes equals income. Thus, $I = P_C C + P_M M$, where $P_C C$ is the per-unit price times the quantity of compact discs consumed. That is, $P_C C$ is the expenditure on compact discs. Similarly, $P_M M$ is the expenditure on movie passes. Because I, P_C, and P_M are constants, this equation defines a straight line. If we solve for M we have $M = I/P_M - (P_C/P_M)C$. The slope of this line is the coefficient of C, or $-P_C/P_M$.

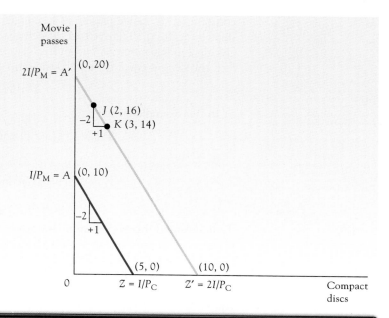

FIGURE 3.9

Effect of an Income Change on the Budget Line
A change in income when product prices remain unchanged results in a parallel shift in the budget line. When income increases from $60 to $120, the budget line shifts outward from *AZ* to *A'Z'*, but its slope does not change.

ratio; because prices are unchanged, so is the slope. With a higher income the student can purchase more of both goods than before, but the cost of one good in terms of the other remains the same.

Price Changes
Now consider a change in the price of one good, with income and the price of the other good held constant. Starting again with the same initial budget line *AZ*, reflecting a budget of $60, Figure 3.10 shows the effect of a reduction in the price of compact discs from $12 to $6 (from P_C to P'_C). *The price reduction causes the budget line to rotate about point A and become flatter, producing the new budget line AZ'*. The maximum number of movie passes that can be

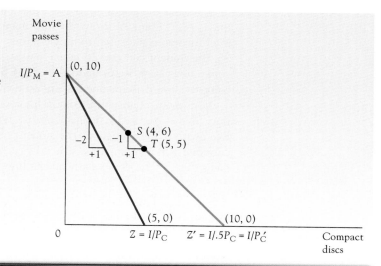

FIGURE 3.10

Effect of a Price Change on the Budget Line
A change in the price of one good, with income and the other good's price remaining unchanged, causes the budget line to rotate about one of the intercepts. When the price of compact discs declines from $12 to $6, the budget line rotates from *AZ* to *AZ'*.

bought is unaffected, because income is still $60 and P_M is still $6. However, the maximum number of compact discs that can be bought increases when the price of compact discs falls. At the new price of $6 ($P_C' = .5P_C$), the student can buy a maximum of 10 compact discs (point Z') if the entire $60 is spent on compact discs. A price change causes the budget line to rotate, so the slope of the line changes. When the price of compact discs falls, the new budget line becomes flatter because its slope, $-P_C'/P_M$, is now equal to -1 movie pass per 1 compact disc. With the price of both movie passes and compact discs at $6, the purchase of an additional compact disc now involves a sacrifice of only one movie pass: this tradeoff is illustrated by the move from S to T on the new budget line. *A flatter budget line means that the real or relative price of the good on the horizontal axis is lower*.

Now is an appropriate time to emphasize why the slope measures the *real* price. A slope of $-2/1$, like the slope for line AZ, means the compact disc price is double the movie pass price. Note, however, that the slope does not tell us what the nominal (absolute) prices are. If both prices change by the same proportion—both double or are cut in half, for instance— the price ratio does not change, so the cost of one good in terms of another is unaffected. For example, see how pure inflation (in which all prices, including wage rates, rise proportionately) affects the budget line. Suppose all prices and income double: the student's income rises to $120 (or $2I$), and prices increase so that $P_M' = \$12$ (or $2P_M$) and $P_C' = \$24$ (or $2P_C$). Despite the nominal increases in income and prices, the budget line does not change. The budget line intercepts are now $2I/2P_M$ and $2I/2P_C$, and the slope is $-2P_C/2P_M$, which all reduce to the original values. The position and the slope of budget lines always reflect real, not nominal, prices.

We have confined our attention to simple budget lines in which the consumer can buy as much of each good as desired without affecting its price. Since individual consumers usually buy only a tiny portion of the total quantity of any good, their purchases generally have no perceptible effect on price. Thus, the consumer can treat price as constant, and with prices constant the budget line is a simple straight line. As we will see later, there are cases where budget lines are not straight lines, but they are easily dealt with after the standard case has been thoroughly examined.

3.3   THE CONSUMER'S CHOICE[6]

Indifference curves represent the consumer's preferences toward various market baskets; the budget line shows what market baskets the consumer can afford. Putting these two pieces together, we can determine what market basket the consumer will actually choose.

Figure 3.11 shows the student-consumer's budget line AZ along with several indifference curves. Remember from the foregoing section that the budget line AZ is based on income (I) of $60 and prices ($P_C$ and P_M, respectively) of $12 per compact disc and $6 per movie. We assume that the student will purchase the market basket, choosing from among those that can be afforded, that will place him or her on the highest possible (most preferred) indifference curve. In other words, the consumer will select the market basket that best satisfies preferences, given a limited income and prevailing prices. Visual inspection of this diagram shows that the student will choose market basket W (2 compact discs and 6 movie passes) on indifference curve U_2. Indifference curve U_2 is the highest level of satisfaction the student can attain, given the limitations implied by the budget line. Although the student would be better off with any market basket on U_3, none of those baskets is affordable because U_3 lies entirely above the budget line. Any basket other than W on the budget line is

---

[6]A mathematical treatment of some of the material in this section is given in the appendix at the back of the book (pages 562–563).

FIGURE 3.11

The Consumer's Optimal Consumption Choice
The market basket the consumer will choose is shown by point *W*, where the budget line is tangent to (has the same slope as) indifference curve U_2. Among market baskets that can be afforded—shown by budget line *AZ*—basket *W* yields the greatest satisfaction because it is on the highest attainable indifference curve. At point *W*, $MRS_{CM} = P_C/P_M$.

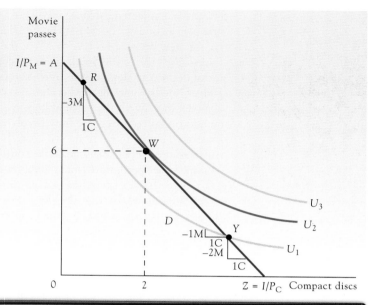

affordable but yields less satisfaction because it lies on an indifference curve below U_2. For example, basket *R* can be purchased, but then the student is on U_1, so basket *R* is clearly inferior to basket *W*.

Note that the highest indifference curve attainable is the one that just touches, or is tangent to, the budget line: U_2 is tangent to *AZ* at *W*. The consumer's optimal point is *W*. Since U_2 and *AZ* are tangent at this point, the slopes of the curves are equal. Because the slopes equal the consumer's *MRS* and price ratio, respectively, the consumer's optimal choice is characterized by the following equality:

$$MRS_{CM} = P_C/P_M.$$

This equality indicates that the student equates the rate that he or she is willing to substitute compact discs for movie passes (MRS_{CM}) to the rate at which the market allows the student to make the substitution (P_C/P_M). To see why this equality characterizes the student's optimal choice, suppose that the student buys some market basket other than point *W* on the budget line—for example, the basket at point *R*. The indifference curve through any point above *W* on the budget line will intersect the budget line from above, as U_1 does at point *R*.[7] Thus, at *R* the student's MRS_{CM} (three movie passes per compact disc) is greater than the price ratio (two movie passes per compact disc). At point *R* the student's preferences indicate a willingness to exchange as many as three movie passes for another compact disc, but at the given market prices the student needs to give up only two movie passes per compact disc—a bargain.

In effect, the *MRS* measures the **marginal benefit** or value the student derives from consuming one more unit of a good. At point *R*, for example, the marginal benefit of another compact disc is three movie passes, or the number of movie passes the student would give up for another compact disc. On the other hand, the price ratio measures marginal cost: the **marginal cost** of another compact disc is two movie passes. At *R*, therefore, the marginal

MARGINAL BENEFIT
the value the consumer derives from consuming one more unit of a good

MARGINAL COST
the cost of consuming one more unit of a good

[7]If we tried to draw an indifference curve through *R* intersecting from below, we would find that it would intersect U_2, and intersecting indifference curves are impossible.

benefit of another compact disc in terms of movie passes is greater than the marginal cost, and the student will be better off consuming more compact discs (and fewer movie passes). Thus, by moving along the budget line in the direction of point W, the student will reach a higher indifference curve. In these terms, the optimal point indicates that the student has chosen a market basket so that the marginal benefit of compact discs in terms of movie passes (MRS_{CM}) equals the marginal cost of compact discs in terms of movie passes (P_C/P_M).

At points below W on the budget line, similar reasoning shows that the student would be better off consuming fewer compact discs and more movie passes, so none of these points is optimal. At point Y, the student's MRS is less than the price ratio. The last compact disc consumed is worth 1 movie pass to the student, yet its marginal cost is 2 movie passes, so the student is better off by moving back up toward point W.

A Corner Solution

When a consumer's preferences are such that some of both goods will be consumed, the optimal consumption choice is characterized by an equality between the MRS and the price ratio, as described earlier. In reality, however, there are some goods individual consumers do not consume at all. You may wish you had a Maserati, tickets to the Super Bowl, or a posh condominium in Palm Beach, but in all likelihood your consumption of these, and many other, goods is zero. The reason is that the first unit of consumption of these goods, however desirable, fails to justify the cost involved.

Figure 3.12 shows a situation in which a consumer purchases only one of the two goods available. The optimal consumption point is A, where all the consumer's income goes to purchase clothing. Because the slope of the indifference curve at A is less than the slope of the budget line, the first unit of Dom Perignon champagne (arguably the world's finest) is not worth its cost to the consumer (roughly $100 per bottle). In this situation, known as a **corner solution**, the consumer's optimal choice is not characterized by an equality between the MRS and the price ratio, because the slopes of the indifference curve and the budget line differ at point A. The equality condition holds only between pairs of goods consumed in positive amounts.

The Composite-Good Convention

We developed our analysis for a two-good world, but the general principles apply to a world of many goods. Unfortunately, many goods cannot be shown on a two-dimensional graph. Still, it is possible to deal with a multitude of goods in two dimensions by treating a number

CORNER SOLUTION
a situation in which a particular good is not consumed at all by an individual consumer because the value of the first unit of the good is less than the cost

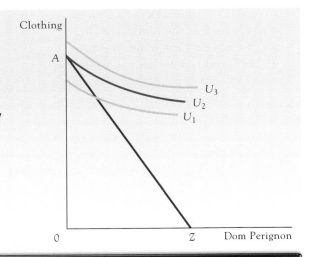

FIGURE 3.12

A Corner Solution
Possibly, the consumer will not buy any of one good. In this case, the optimal choice lies at one of the intercepts of the budget line, with the consumer's entire income spent on only one good. Here the choice is point *A*, with only clothing purchased.

of goods as a group. Suppose there are many goods: compact discs, movie passes, cellular telephone minutes, Big Macs, and so on. We can continue to measure compact disc consumption, or whatever specific good we wish to analyze, on one axis, but then treat all other goods as if they were one good—that is, as a **composite good**. Consumption of the composite good is gauged by total outlays on it—in other words, total outlays on all goods *other than compact discs*.

COMPOSITE GOOD
a number of goods treated as a group

Figure 3.13 illustrates this approach. The consumer has $120 in weekly income and the price of each compact disc is $12. The budget line's vertical intercept occurs at $120, because total outlays on other goods will be $120 if compact disc consumption is zero. The consumer's income is equal to A. As noted earlier, the budget line's slope equals the ratio of prices, but because a $1 outlay on other goods has a price of one, the ratio reduces to the price of compact discs ($P_C/1 = P_C$). Thus, at any point on the budget line, such as Y, consuming one more compact disc (which costs $12) means that outlays on other goods must be reduced by $12.

Convex indifference curves can also be drawn to relate outlays on other goods and compact discs, because both are presumed to be desirable goods to the consumer. We must now state an important assumption associated with this approach: We assume that the prices of all the other goods are constant. This assumption allows us to treat them as a single good. We want outlays on other goods to serve as an index of the quantities of other goods consumed, and if prices were allowed to vary, it would become a rubbery index. (A larger outlay would not necessarily mean more goods were consumed unless prices were fixed.) When other prices are held constant, the consumer's preferences can be shown as indifference curves that identify a unique level of well-being for each combination of compact discs and outlays on other goods.

FIGURE 3.13

The Composite-Good Convention
To deal graphically with the consumption of many goods, we group together all goods but one and measure total outlays on this composite good on the vertical axis. The slope of the budget line is then the dollar price of the good on the horizontal axis. The consumer's optimal point, *W*, is once more a tangency between an indifference curve and the budget line.

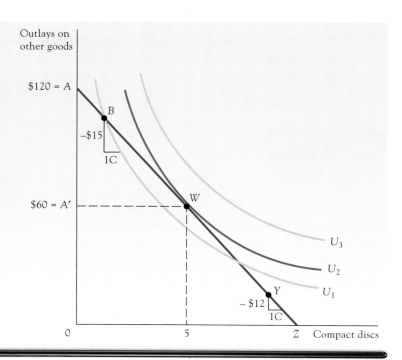

The slope of an indifference curve, the MRS, now shows how much the consumer is willing to reduce outlays on other goods to obtain one more compact disc. With market basket B, for example, the consumer is willing to give up $15 worth of other goods in exchange for an additional disc. Note that this MRS is still a measure of the consumer's willingness to substitute among real goods, but now dollar outlays measure the quantity of other goods the consumer is willing to sacrifice in return for compact discs.

Figure 3.13 shows the optimal point for the consumer is W, where the budget line is tangent to an indifference curve. At W, the consumer is just willing to give up $12 worth of other goods for another compact disc, indicating that his or her MRS is $12 per compact disc. This figure equals the market price that must be paid for another compact disc (that is, the slope of the budget line, $P_C/1$, equals $12 per compact disc).

The optimal market basket W consists of five compact discs and $60 ($A'$) devoted to the purchase of other goods. The total outlay on compact discs can also be shown as the distance AA'. Because the consumer has an income of A ($120) and, after buying compact discs, has A' ($60) left to spend on other goods, the difference ($A - A' = AA'$), or $60, is the total cost of the five compact discs. The difference between the consumer's total income and the amount spent on everything else except compact discs reflects the amount of the consumer's income spent on compact discs.

Thus, we see that using the composite-good convention does not change the substance of our analysis. The consumer's optimal point still involves a balancing of the relative desirability of goods with their relative costs.

APPLICATION 3.1 CONSUMERS' VALUATION OF AIR BAGS

In 1988, only 2 percent of the new cars sold in the United States were equipped with air bags. By 1996, more than 90 percent of all new cars sold came with this safety feature. Why the dramatic increase?

Surprisingly, perhaps, the increase does not reflect a government mandate—a federal requirement that automakers install air bags in their vehicles did not take effect until 1998. Rather, an analysis of a sample of households that purchased a new car during 1990–1993 reveals that consumers were willing to trade increasingly more of their total outlays on other goods in exchange for an air bag over this time period. Moreover, the increase in the amount of the composite good consumers were willing to exchange for an air bag appears to reflect information about actual experiences with air bags, which was spread through the media and by friends. According to the analysis, the average willingness to pay for a driver-side air bag increased from $331 in 1990 to $512 in 1993. The amount a particular consumer in the sample was willing to pay for a driver-side air bag was posi-

tively related to the consumer's reported number of hours of television viewing per day and the number of friends owning cars equipped with air bags. According to the study's authors: "Friends provide opportunities for demonstration effects, while television viewing provides opportunities to obtain hard evidence of air bag effectiveness through automakers' advertisements and occasional news stories that feature people who actually survived serious automobile crashes because of air bags."[8]

Although some more recent news has questioned the extent to which air bags promote the safety of vehicular occupants and has negatively affected the extent to which drivers are willing to pay for air bags, it remains clear that consumers' valuation of air bags is a key reason why such a safety feature became commonplace in motor vehicles in the United States.

[8]Fred Mannering and Clifford Winston, "Automobile Air Bags in the 1990s: Market Failure or Market Efficiency?" *Journal of Law and Economics*, 38 No. 2 (October 1995), pp. 265–280.

APPLICATION 3.2 CONVEX (INDIFFERENCE) CURVES AND CELLULAR CHARGES

S ome evidence in support of the assumption of diminishing marginal rate of substitution and the resulting convex shape of indifference curves is provided by the fee structure offered by most cellular phone service providers. For example, in 2000 AT&T offered One Rate calling plans that consisted of charges of $59.99 per month for 500 minutes (an average price of 12 cents per minute across the 500 minutes); $89.99 for 800 minutes (11.25 cents per minute); $119.99 for 1,200 minutes (10 cents per minute); and $149.99 for 1,600 minutes (9.4 cents per minute). To sign up for packages that feature greater usage, cellular phone customers appear to have to be enticed by lower (average) fees per minute of service. As more cellular phone service minutes are consumed, consumers are willing to give up less and less in terms of dollar outlays on other goods to obtain still more cellular phone service minutes. How budget lines can be depicted when suppliers charge varying prices depending on consumption, and the reason suppliers may find it profitable to offer consumers such fee schedules, will be addressed later in this book.

3.4 CHANGES IN INCOME AND CONSUMPTION CHOICES

A change in income affects consumption choices by altering the set of market baskets a consumer can afford—that is, by shifting the budget line. To examine the impact of a change in income, we assume that the consumer's underlying preferences do not change and the prices of goods remain fixed; only income varies.

In Figure 3.14a, the student's original optimal choice is at point W, where indifference curve U_1 is tangent to budget line AZ. Consumption of compact discs is C_1 and consumption of all other goods is A_1. Now suppose that income increases such that the budget line parallel shifts out from AZ to $A'Z'$. The budget line's slope (the price ratio) is unchanged since only income is assumed to vary.

The outward shift in the budget line means that the consumer is able to buy market baskets that were previously unaffordable, but which market basket will be chosen? The answer depends on the nature of the consumer's preferences. For the set of indifference curves in Figure 3.14a, the most preferred market basket along the $A'Z'$ budget line is at point W', where U_2 is tangent to the budget line. The consumer is better off (that is, attains a higher indifference curve) and consumes C_2 compact discs and A_2 of other goods. For the specific indifference curves shown, an increase in income with no change in prices leads to an increase in compact disc consumption, from C_1 to C_2.

If income increases further such that the budget line shifts to $A''Z''$, the new optimal consumption choice becomes point W''. Proceeding in the same way, we find that each possible income level has a unique optimal market basket associated with it. Only three optimal consumption points are shown in the diagram, but others can be derived by considering still different levels of income for the student. The line that joins all the optimal consumption points generated by varying income is the **income-consumption curve**. It passes through points W, W', and W'' in the diagram.

INCOME-CONSUMP-TION CURVE
the line that joins all the optimal consumption points generated by varying income

Normal Goods

The relationship in Figure 3.14a is fairly typical of what happens to the consumption of a good (compact discs, in this case) when income increases. As noted in Chapter 2, when more of a good is purchased by an individual as income rises (prices and preferences being

Income Changes and Optimal Consumption Choice

An increase in income parallel-shifts the budget line outward and leads the consumer to select a different market basket. Connecting the optimal consumption points (W, W', W'') associated with different incomes yields the income-consumption curve in part (a). Part (b) shows how the consumer's demand curve shifts when income changes.

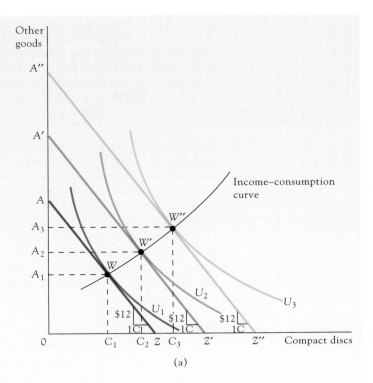

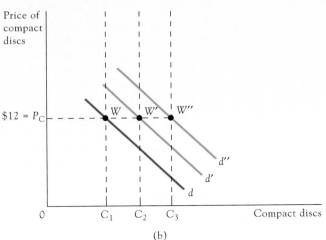

unchanged) and less is purchased as income falls, the good is defined to be a normal good. Calling such a good *normal* reflects the judgment that most goods are like this.

Figure 3.14a indicates that compact disc consumption increases with income even though the price of compact discs (P_C) is unchanged. We can illustrate the same thing by using a different graph that shows the consumer's demand curve, d, for compact discs (we use a lowercase d to indicate that it is the demand curve for an individual consumer). We have not derived an entire demand curve yet, but we can identify one point on the demand curve corresponding to each income level. For example, at the original income level, when the budget constraint is AZ and the price of a compact disc is P_C, the student consumes C_1 compact discs. Therefore, one point on the demand curve d in Figure 3.14b can be identified: point W indicates that compact disc consumption is C_1 when the compact disc price is P_C. (The other points on the curve will be taken for granted at the present.)

When an increase in income combined with no change in prices leads to greater consumption, it is represented by a shift in the demand curve. Thus, when income rises such that the budget line shifts from AZ to $A'Z'$, the entire demand curve shifts to d', which shows an increased consumption of compact discs, C_2, at an unchanged compact disc price. Recall that a demand curve shows how price affects consumption when other factors are held constant. One of the more important factors held fixed is the consumer's income, so a change in income can be expected to shift the entire demand curve. Put another way, d is a demand curve that holds income constant (at the level associated with budget line AZ in Figure 3.14a) at all points along it, while d' holds the income constant at a different level (the level associated with budget line $A'Z'$).

While our major emphasis here is on the way budget lines and indifference curves can be used to examine consumer choices, we should not lose sight of the fact that there are alternative ways to approach the same problem. Both parts of Figure 3.14 show the same thing but from different perspectives. Which approach is better depends on the problem being examined.

Inferior Goods

Does an increase in income always lead to increased consumption? As discussed in Chapter 2, not necessarily. The consumption of certain goods, termed inferior goods, is inversely related to income. For example, consumption of Saturn cars may fall (and consumption of Mercedes cars rise) for an individual whose income increases sharply. Rail and bus transportation have declined over the past several decades due to rising income levels and consumers traveling by air instead.

For the student whose preferences are shown in Figure 3.15a, hamburger is an inferior good. At the original income level, when the budget line is AZ, the student's optimal consumption point is W. Hamburger consumption is H_1. When income rises such that the budget line parallel shifts out to $A'Z'$, the optimal point, W', on the new budget line, shows that hamburger consumption drops to H_2. When a good is an inferior good, the income-consumption curve connecting the optimal points, W, W', and so on, is negatively sloped, implying lower consumption at higher income levels. In Figure 3.15b, note that the demand curve shifts inward for an inferior good when income increases: lower consumption at an unchanged price of hamburger (P_H) implies a reduction in demand.

Several other subtle points concerning normal and inferior goods should also be kept in mind. First, a good may be inferior for some people and normal for others. Your hamburger consumption may go up if your income rises, but someone else's may go down if their income rises. Goods themselves are not intrinsically normal or inferior: the definitions refer to individuals' responses to income changes, and the responses depend ultimately on the shapes of the individuals' indifference curves.

Second, a good may be a normal good for an individual at some income levels but an inferior good at other income levels. In Figure 3.15a, at a low level of income, the good is normal (as shown by the positively sloped income-consumption curve when income is low), but it becomes inferior at higher income levels. For example, you might consume more hamburger if your weekly income increases by $10, but you might consume less if your weekly income increases by $1,000.

Third, an inferior good should not be confused with an economic "bad." An inferior good is not a "bad" (where less is preferred to more), as shown by the normally shaped indifference curves in Figure 3.15a.

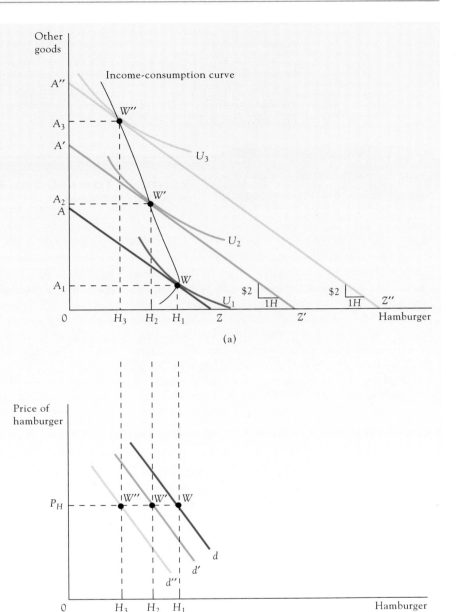

FIGURE 3.15

Income Changes and Purchases of an Inferior Good

(a) An inferior good is one that the consumer will purchase less of at a higher income and unchanged price, and is characterized by a negatively sloped income-consumption curve. (b) At a higher income, the demand for an inferior good shifts inward.

Fourth, inferior goods tend to have certain common characteristics, and understanding these characteristics is helpful in evaluating their significance. For example, most inferior goods are narrowly defined goods in a general category that includes several other higher-quality (and higher-priced) goods. Take hamburger: hamburger is a narrowly defined good belonging to the general category, meat. In the meat category there are other higher-quality and higher-priced options, such as filet mignon, prime rib, and veal. Understandably, some people would consume less hamburger when their incomes go up, because they could afford the better-quality alternatives that serve the same basic purposes but satisfy them better.

In contrast, intuition and evidence both suggest that broadly defined goods are usually normal. Meat is more likely to be a normal good than hamburger is, and food is more likely to be a normal good than meat. Many applications of economic theory necessarily involve broadly defined goods, which means that the normal-good case is likely to be the most relevant one. For example, the food stamp program subsidizes consumption of all kinds of food, not just hamburger; and food, considered as a composite commodity composed of many specific items, is surely a normal good.

APPLICATION 3.3   RUNNING TOWARD THE BORDER IN A RECESSION

During the economic downturn of the late 1980s and early 1990s, Taco Bell increased sales per outlet and gained overall market share in the fast-food market. By contrast, competitors such as McDonald's and Burger King saw their sales and market share decline over the same period. Assume that the relative prices of the items sold by the various fast-food chains as well as all other factors remain unchanged. Taco Bell's increase in per-outlet sales and gain in overall market share thus would appear to reflect the fact that the products sold by Taco Bell are inferior goods for the average fast-food consumer: their consumption in-creased as the economy went into recession and consumer income decreased. By contrast, the products sold by McDonald's and Burger King appear to be normal goods for the average fast-food consumer. As the average fast-food consumer's income decreased during the recession, the average fast-food consumer appears to have spent more on the relatively lower-priced items sold by Taco Bell and spent less on the relatively more expensive items sold by McDonald's and Burger King. The reverse was the case as the average fast-food consumer's income increased in the boom years of the mid-to late-1990s.

The Food Stamp Program

Under the federal food stamp program, eligible low-income families receive free food stamps, which can be used only to buy food, F. To show how consumer theory can be used to examine this program, we'll use a specific example in which a consumer receives $50 worth of food stamps each week. We assume that the consumer has a weekly income of $100 and that the per-unit price of food (P_F) is $5.

Consider Figure 3.16a. The presubsidy budget line is AZ and the consumer purchases 8 units of food prior to receiving food stamps. The food stamp subsidy shifts the budget line to $AA'Z'$. Over the AA' range the budget line is horizontal since the $50 in free food stamps permits the recipient to purchase up to 10 units of food while leaving the consumer his or her entire income of $100 to be spent on other goods. If, however, food purchases exceed 10 units, the consumer must buy any additional units at the full market price of $5. Thus, the $A'Z'$ portion of the budget line has a slope of $5 per unit of food, indicating the price of food over this range.

In this case, the budget line is not a straight line throughout but is kinked at point A', since the subsidy terminates at the point where the $50 in food stamps is used up. Another way of visualizing this budget line is by contrasting it with the budget line associated with an increase in income of $50, which would result if the government gave the consumer $50 to spend on any good desired. With a $50 cash grant the budget line would be $A''Z'$. The only way the food stamp subsidy differs from an outright cash grant is that options indicated on the upper part of the line, $A''A'$, are not available to the recipient, since food stamps cannot be used to purchase nonfood items.

FIGURE 3.16

Effects of the Food Stamp Program on Consumption

If a consumer is given AA' in food stamps, the budget line shifts to $AA'Z'$. The result is identical to giving the consumer cash if preferences are like those in part (a), but the consumer would be better off if given cash for preferences like those in part (b).

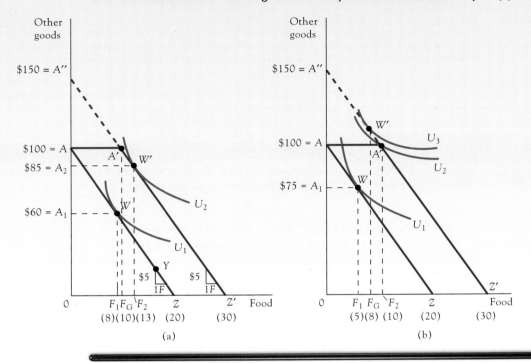

(a)

(b)

The food stamp subsidy will affect the recipient in one of two ways. Figure 3.16a shows one possibility. In this case, the consumer chooses market basket W' when the budget line is $AA'Z'$ under the food stamp program. If the consumer receives instead a cash grant of $50, the budget line is $A''Z'$, and the same market basket W' would be chosen. Food consumption increases, but only because food is a normal good, and more of a normal good is consumed at a higher income. Note, however, that food consumption rises by less than the amount of the subsidy. For the preferences shown in Figure 3.16a, food consumption increases by 5 units, or $25 worth. The consumer uses the remainder of the subsidy to increase purchases of other goods, from $60 to $85 worth. (Because other goods, taken as a group, are certainly normal goods, too, the purchase of these goods will also increase.)

Figure 3.16b, where the indifference curves differ from those in Figure 3.16a, shows another possible outcome of the food stamp subsidy. In this case, with a direct cash grant of $50, the consumer prefers to consume at point W', where U_3 is tangent to the budget line $A''A'Z'$. The food stamp subsidy prohibits such an outcome, however; the consumer must choose among the options shown by the $AA'Z'$ budget line. Faced with these alternatives, the best the consumer can do is choose point A', because the highest indifference curve attainable is U_2, which passes through the market basket at point A'.

When the situation shown in Figure 3.16b occurs, the subsidy increases the consumer's purchases of both food and nonfood items. Indeed, regardless of whether Figure 3.16a or Figure 3.16b is the relevant case, the food stamp subsidy cannot in reality avoid being used in part to finance increased consumption of nonfood items. This result is particularly interesting because many proponents of subsidies of this sort emphasize that the subsidy should not be used to finance consumption of "unnecessary" goods (such as vodka or junk food). In practice, it is difficult to design a subsidy that will increase consumption of only the subsidized good and not affect consumption of other goods at the same time.

Note also that the consumer in Figure 3.16b will be better off if given $50 to spend as he or she wishes instead of $50 in food stamps. The budget line will then be $A''A'Z'$, and the consumer will choose the market basket at point W', on indifference curve U_3. This observation illustrates the general proposition that recipients of a subsidy will be better off if the subsidy is given as cash. The situation in Figure 3.16a illustrates why there is a qualification to this proposition: in some cases the consumer is equally well off under either subsidy. There is no case, however, where the consumer is better off with a subsidy to a particular good than with an equivalent cash subsidy.

APPLICATION 3.4 — KEEPING BUGS BUNNY AND THE BACK STREET BOYS AT BAY IN CANADA

The food stamp program focuses on providing a minimum amount of a particular good, food, to consumers through a subsidy. Government decisionmakers, of course, have other policy instruments at their disposal with which to affect consumption. Among these instruments are taxes, price controls, and quantity controls. An example of a quantity control intended to ensure that consumption exceeds a minimum threshold is the Canadian approach toward limiting the influence of U.S. pop culture. Namely, television stations must offer at least 60 percent Canadian content in their programming. Radio stations must ensure that at least 35 per-

cent of the popular songs that they play have a Canadian connection (for example, the music is performed by a Canadian, the lyrics are written by a Canadian, and so on).

Although intended by policymakers to bolster a distinct national culture, the mandates to promote consumption of domestically produced programming have predictable effects on individual consumer welfare. As shown in Figure 3.17, suppose that, based on other demands on his time, a consumer has only 100 minutes to devote to television viewing and that the only cost associated with viewing either Canadian or non-Canadian

FIGURE 3.17

A Minimum Purchase Mandate and Consumer Welfare

A Canadian television viewer is worse off if he would have chosen a point such as *B* on the *AF* portion of the budget line *AZ* prior to the government mandating that at least 60 percent of the programming consumed must have Canadian content.

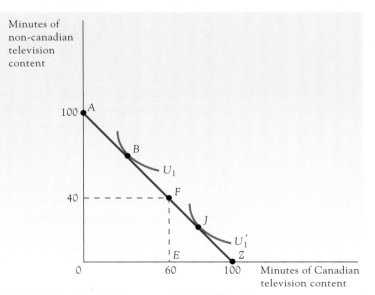

programming is the time that must be given up to do so. In the simplified case where the government successfully mandates that at least 60 percent of the consumer's viewing be devoted to Canadian programming, the consumer's budget line is constricted from AZ to EFZ. Restricted from accessing the AF portion of the original budget line, the viewer is worse off than if he had cho-

sen less than 60 percent Canadian programming absent government interference (as with an indifference curve such as U_1 and an optimal point of B). And the consumer is no better off with the mandate if he would have chosen more than 60 percent Canadian programming on his own (such as with indifference curve U_1' and optimal consumption point J).

APPLICATION 3.5 THE ALLOCATION OF COMMENCEMENT TICKETS

At most colleges, commencement tickets are rationed to seniors at a zero cash price. For example, each senior may be given four tickets for family and friends. We can depict the effects of such an allocation scheme in Figure 3.18a. The typical senior's budget line is ABCE: from zero to four tickets the slope of the budget line is $0 per ticket since the first four tickets are free; the budget line

becomes perfectly vertical to the right of four tickets since no more than four tickets can be obtained; and, assuming that the college is the only source of tickets (we rule out, for now, students exchanging tickets between themselves), the price of a ticket becomes infinite beyond four tickets.

Relative to the case where the college sets a positive price for tickets such that the average senior would buy

FIGURE 3.18

The Allocation of Commencement Tickets
(a) If given 4 free tickets rather than being charged $10 per ticket, the average senior is better off. (b) However, some students may prefer the $10-per-ticket pricing scheme to receiving 4 free tickets.

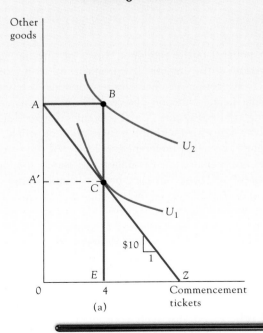

(a)

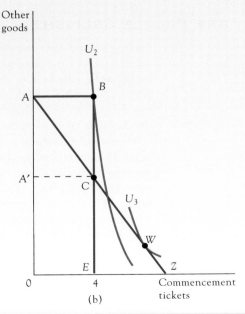

(b)

exactly four tickets, the average senior is definitely better off if four tickets are given away instead. Suppose, for example, that, as shown in Figure 3.18a, a price of $10 per ticket would result in the average senior choosing market basket C along the budget line AZ; the senior would purchase four commencement tickets at $10 each and spend A' on other goods. Under the $10-per-ticket pricing scheme, the average senior is able to attain only indifference curve U_1. In contrast, when the college provides four free tickets the senior is able to attain indifference curve U_2 and thus is better off.

While the average senior depicted in Figure 3.18a may be better off, is every senior better off? The answer is no, and Figure 3.18b shows why. There are some students who may have steeply sloped indifference curves at point B—four free tickets and an income level of A. Because they come from large families and/or have many friends they may dearly want more than the allocated four tickets. These students will be willing to exchange a considerable amount, in terms of dollars that could be spent on other goods, for some additional tickets (the MRS at point B of the student depicted in Figure 3.18b is much greater than for the student shown in Figure 3.18a). Under a $10-per-ticket pricing scheme, they would select market basket W on indifference curve U_3 and be better off than under the existing system where they get four free tickets and can attain only indifference curve U_2.

We have so far ruled out seniors exchanging tickets among themselves. At most colleges, however, just such a resale market emerges every spring. The reason is fairly easy to see. Under the allocation scheme employed by most colleges, seniors will tend to select a point such as B on the northeast corner of their budget line (the northeast corner is the market basket of choice so long as their indifference curves are not either perfectly horizontal or perfectly vertical). Having opted to be on the same northeast corner (a point such as B) of their budget line, however, does not imply that the slopes of the indifference curves of all seniors are identical at their chosen market baskets. As can be seen by comparing Figures 3.18a and 3.18b, some students have flatter indifference curves than others at their optimal consumption points (U_2 is flatter at point B in Figure 3.18a than in Figure 3.18b). Variations in indifference curve slopes imply differences across consumers in their willingness to exchange dollars spent on other goods for commencement tickets (that is, differences in their marginal rates of substitution). Such differences create an opportunity for mutually beneficial exchange between the various consumers in a market. In a later chapter we will show something you may be surprised to learn: that although a resale market results in what seems like high prices for otherwise "free" tickets, both individuals buying and selling the tickets gain from the development of such a market.

3.5 ARE PEOPLE SELFISH?

Having set out the basic components of the economic theory of consumer choice, we may now reconsider the general nature of the analysis. In particular, we wish to evaluate a commonly made objection to the way economists characterize individual behavior in economic theory. You may already have heard someone observe: "Economics assumes people are greedy and care only about material possessions;" or "Economics disregards the fact that individuals are benevolent and are concerned with the welfare of other people."

A review of our basic assumptions about preferences reveals that these criticisms are not valid. Economic analysis does not prejudge what commodities, services, or activities people consider to be economic "goods" or "bads." In fact, because many things are "goods" for some people and "bads" for others (e.g., liver, liquor, big-time wrestling, ballet, chewing tobacco, video games, cigarettes, reading economic theory), any attempt to specify in advance what all people consider desirable would frequently lead to mistakes.

If we are unable to specify which goods people find desirable, though, how can we apply the theory to concrete situations? The answer is simple: People reveal that some commodities are desirable by the way they allocate their spending. When we observe some consumers giving up money in return for Internet service, the evidence is fairly conclusive that Internet service is a desirable good for them. We would then draw convex indifference curves between Internet service and other goods for such consumers and investigate how their incomes, the price of Internet service, and so on, affect consumption decisions.

People give up time and resources to pursue charitable endeavors, sacrifice material wealth for a quiet life, or campaign for politicians. To show how economic theory can be applied to examine the factors that influence such decisions, consider a hypothetical situation.

Samantha (Sam) and Oscar are friends. Sam earns $90,000 a year; Oscar earns only $10,000 a year. Let's assume that Sam cares about the material well-being of Oscar—or, more precisely, that Oscar's income (which determines the material comforts he can enjoy) is an economic good for Sam. Does this concern imply that Sam will give some of her income to Oscar?

Figure 3.19 illustrates how we can apply indifference curve analysis to this situation. Figure 3.19a shows Sam's budget line AZ, relating her income and Oscar's. Sam's budget line does not intersect the vertical axis because we suppose she can't take income from Oscar. Point A shows their initial incomes. Obviously, Sam can increase Oscar's income by giving Oscar some of her income, but every dollar she gives to Oscar reduces her own income by a dollar, so the slope of the budget line is -1. Figure 3.19a shows two of Sam's indifference curves, and because both her income and Oscar's are economic goods, they have the usual shapes. Given the preferences indicated by Sam's indifference curves, at point A she would be willing to pay more than $1 to raise Oscar's income by $1. Thus, it is in her interest to give some of her income to Oscar, and the best-sized gift from her point of view is $5,000.

The fact that Sam cares about Oscar's income is not sufficient to imply that she will always donate money to Oscar's cause. Figure 3.19b shows an alternative set of indifference curves that Sam might have. Because these curves slope downward, they imply that Sam still views Oscar's income as an economic good. At point A, however, the slope of U_1 is less than the slope of the budget line. Thus, Sam might be willing to give up, for example, $0.25 in return for Oscar having $1 more in income; unfortunately, however, it would cost her $1 to increase Oscar's income by $1 (the slope of the budget line), so she decides not to contribute anything to the Oscar fund. A corner equilibrium results.

Both parts of Figure 3.19 show preferences implying that Sam views Oscar's income as an economic good, but the intensity of preferences differs. The differing intensity is shown by

FIGURE 3.19

Transferring Income to Another Person
Altruistic preferences can also be accommodated in the analysis. In part (a) Sam chooses to give $5,000 of her income to Oscar. When Sam's preferences are different, as in part (b)—still altruistic but less so than in part (a)—she will not give any of her income to Oscar.

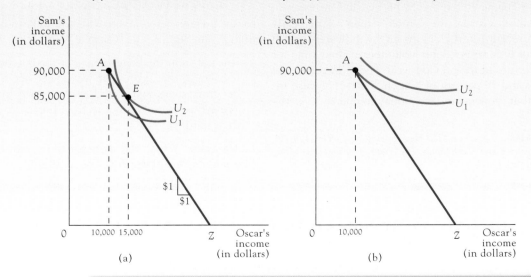

the different slopes of the indifference curves (the MRSs) at point A in the two diagrams. Thus, the fact that Sam cares about Oscar's income does not allow us to conclude that she will necessarily transfer any of her income to Oscar: the intensity of her preferences and the cost of giving play critical roles.

APPLICATION 3.6   THE NEW PHILANTHROPY

The increase in wealth created by the technology boom has affected charitable giving in the United States.[9] Charitable gifts by U.S. citizens totaled $190 billion in 1999—2 percent of national income and equal to one third of the domestic federal budget. That giving rate represented the highest level in nearly three decades and was led by some notable gifts from New Economy magnates. For example, as of 1999, Microsoft co-founder Bill Gates and his wife Melinda had given $22 billion to their foundation. In real terms Bill and Melinda Gates have given money away faster and in greater amounts than anyone else in history. By comparison, the charitable contributions of Old Economy oil tycoon and noted benefactor John D. Rockefeller total $5.8 billion in 1999 dollars. Steel magnate and philanthropist Andrew Carnegie's giving amounts to $4.8 billion in 1999 dollars.

Although significant, modern-day altruism is similar in three important ways to the philanthropy of previous generations. First, U.S. citizens have consistently distinguished themselves, at least from their European counterparts, by their willingness to give of their time and money. This was a cultural trait that Frenchman Alexis de Tocqueville noted in his classic *Democracy in America* after visiting the United States in the early 1800s. A recent Johns Hopkins survey indicates that 49 percent of U.S. respondents volunteered their time for civic activities in the previous year, versus 13 percent of Germans and 19 percent of French. The survey also indicated that 73 percent gave money to charity over the last year versus 44 percent of Germans and 43 percent of French.

Second, much like the federal food stamp program described in a preceding section, philanthropic gifts typically come with strings attached and restrictions about who the intended beneficiaries will be, and in what particular dimensions those beneficiaries are meant, by the donor, to be better off. For example, one of Gates's first big commitments was made in 1997 and involved paying billions to help children specifically through wiring every library in the country to the Internet. Many of the libraries wired through the Gates Foundation gift had been started earlier in the century through the munificence of Andrew Carnegie, who similarly wanted to provide opportunity to U.S. youth through a subsidy of a particular good (namely, libraries) rather than an equivalent cash subsidy.

Finally, the intensity of preferences for giving to others differs, as it always has, across individuals. Unlike Gates, for instance, Larry Ellison, the founder of Oracle, is skeptical about the extent to which philanthropy can solve the world's problems. Worth about $50 billion as of 2000, Ellison does not give as much—about $100 million per year—because he believes that the profit motive is the best tool for solving the world's problems. His apparent preferences comport with the well-known quote from Adam Smith's *The Wealth of Nations*:

> It is not from the benevolence of the butcher, the brewer, or the baker that we expect our dinner, but from their own regard to their own interest. We address ourselves not to their humanity but to their self-love.

Ellison asks, "Which did more for the world? The Ford Motor Company or the Ford Foundation?"

[9]This application is based on "The New Philanthropy," *Time* (July 24, 2000), pp. 49–59, and Adam Smith, *The Wealth of Nations* (New York: Modern Library, 1937), p. 14.

3.6   THE UTILITY APPROACH TO CONSUMER CHOICE

An alternative way to understand consumer choice theory is through the concepts of total and marginal utility. In this section we explain this alternative approach and relate it to the indifference curve approach emphasized earlier.

Let's assume we can measure the amount of satisfaction a consumer gets from any market basket by its utility. Units in which utility is measured are arbitrary, but they are commonly referred to as *utils*: a util is one unit of utility.

In consumers' minds, consumption of goods provides them with utility. But we must distinguish between the concepts of total utility and marginal utility. Table 3.2 illustrates the difference. Suppose Marilyn, the consumer, purchases only champagne (C), so for the moment consider only the first three columns. **Total utility** from champagne consumption (TU_C) is the total utils Marilyn gets from a given number of glasses of champagne. If two glasses are consumed, total utility is 38 utils. Total utility is obviously greater at higher levels of consumption, because champagne is an economic good. The **marginal utility** of champagne (MU_C) refers to the amount total utility rises when consumption increases by one unit. When champagne consumption increases from three to four glasses, total utility rises from 53 to 65 utils, or by 12 utils. The marginal utility of the fourth glass is thus 12 utils.[10]

Table 3.2 also illustrates the assumption of **diminishing marginal utility**. This assumption holds that as more of a given good is consumed, the marginal utility associated with the consumption of additional units tends to decline, other things being equal. (In particular, the other-things-being-equal condition means that consumption of other goods is held fixed as consumption of the good in question is varied.) In Table 3.2, the marginal utility of the first glass of champagne is 20 utils, but it is 18 utils for the second glass (the increase in TU_C from 20 to 38 utils) and so on. Note that the MU_C of each successive glass is smaller.

Table 3.2 also shows the total and marginal utility associated with different levels of consumption of a second good, perfume (F). The total utility of a market basket containing champagne and perfume is then the sum of TU_C and TU_F. (This statement assumes that the utility derived from perfume consumption is independent of champagne consumption, and vice versa. While this assumption will not always be true, its use simplifies the explanation of the theory without materially affecting the results.) With consumption of five glasses of champagne and three ounces of perfume, total utility is 185 utils. Obviously, the consumer will choose the market basket yielding the greatest total utility, subject to the limitation implied by her income and the prices of the two goods.

The Consumer's Optimal Choice

If the consumer's income and the prices of champagne and perfume are specified (P_C and P_F), we could consult Table 3.2 and by trial and error eventually find the market basket of champagne and perfume that produces the greatest total utility. With an income of $65 and

TOTAL UTILITY
assuming that it is measurable, the total satisfaction a consumer receives from a given level of consumption

MARGINAL UTILITY
the amount by which total utility rises when consumption increases by one unit

DIMINISHING MARGINAL UTILITY
the assumption that as more of a given good is consumed, the marginal utility associated with the consumption of additional units tends to decline, other things equal

TABLE 3.2

TOTAL AND MARGINAL UTILITY

Champagne (glasses)	TU_C	MU_C	Perfume (ounces)	TU_F	MU_F
1	20	20	1	50	50
2	38	18	2	85	35
3	53	15	3	110	25
4	65	12	4	130	20
5	75	10	5	145	15
6	83	8	6	155	10

[10]In Table 3.2, the marginal utility when consumption is 6 glasses is in the same row as 6 glasses of champagne. Because marginal utility refers to the change in going from 5 to 6 glasses, however, some writers prefer to place marginal utility halfway between the fifth and sixth rows. Either procedure is acceptable as long as the correct meaning is communicated.

the prices of champagne and perfume at $5 and $10, we would eventually find that the market basket composed of five glasses of champagne and four ounces of perfume produces more total utility (205 utils) than any other market basket costing $65.

There is a simpler way to proceed. As it turns out, the utility-maximizing market basket is one for which the consumer allocates income so that the marginal utility divided by the good's price is equal for every good purchased:

$$MU_C/P_C = MU_F/P_F.$$

A market basket of 5C and 4F satisfies this equality: MU_C/P_C is equal to ten utils per glass/$5 per glass, or two utils per dollar, and MU_F/P_F is equal to twenty utils per ounce/$10 per ounce, or two utils per dollar. These ratios measure how much additional utility is generated by spending $1 extra on each good. With MU_C/P_C equal to two utils per dollar, $1 more spent on champagne (purchasing one-fifth of a glass) will generate two utils in additional utility (one-fifth of the MU associated with the fifth champagne glass). Put slightly differently, MU/P is the marginal rate of return, in terms of utility, earned by the consumer if she invests $1 extra in a good. The rule for maximizing utility thus can equivalently be stated as allocating income among goods so that the marginal rates of return, measured in terms of utils per dollar "invested," are equalized across all the goods in which the consumer invests.

If this equality is not satisfied, total utility can be increased by a rearrangement in the consumer's purchases. Suppose that Marilyn buys 3C and 5F. This market basket also costs $65, but total utility is now 198 utils, according to Table 3.2. With this market basket we have $MU_C/P_C > MU_F/P_F$ or 15 utils/$5 > 15 utils/$10. This inequality shows that the marginal dollar devoted to champagne yields 3 utils, while the marginal dollar devoted to perfume yields only 1.5 utils. Since $1 spent on champagne generates a higher return in terms of utility, shifting $1 from perfume to champagne consumption will increase total utility. Spending $1 less on perfume reduces utility by 1.5 utils, but spending $1 more on champagne increases it by 3 utils, a net gain of 1.5 utils. As long as an inequality persists, the consumer should reallocate purchases from the good with a lower marginal utility per dollar of expenditure to the good with a higher marginal utility per dollar of expenditure. Shifting dollar outlays from perfume to champagne will eventually reestablish the equality condition. As champagne consumption increases, its MU falls (reducing MU_C/P_C) because of the assumption of diminishing marginal utility; as perfume consumption falls, its MU rises (increasing MU_F/P_F). When the equality condition is reestablished, at 5C and 4F in this example, the consumer is maximizing utility with the given income and prices.

An analogy from the world of finance may help cement your understanding of the foregoing rule for maximizing consumer utility. Suppose that you have a total portfolio of $1 million invested partly at Bank A and partly at Bank B. Your investment at Bank A earns a 3 percent annual rate of return while dollars saved at Bank B earn 1.5 percent per year. What would be wrong with such a financial strategy provided that investing at either bank is riskless? The answer is probably clear. You would be better off by shifting money out of Bank B and into Bank A so long as the rate of return at A is higher. The same principle applies if you are trying to maximize utility by purchasing various goods (investing in various "banks") with your limited budget.

Relationship to Indifference Curves

As noted earlier in this chapter, an indifference curve is simply a curve showing alternative market baskets that yield the same total utility to the consumer. Figure 3.20 shows two indifference curves. The consumer's MRS_{FC} between points R and T along indifference curve U_2 is $\Delta C/\Delta F$. This slope, however, can also be explained in terms of the marginal utilities of the two goods.

Along an indifference curve, the slope $\Delta C/\Delta F$ *equals the ratio of the marginal utilities of the two goods.* Suppose $\Delta C/\Delta F = 2C/1F$. That is, one ounce of perfume will replace two glasses of

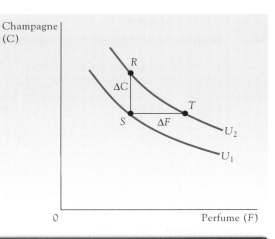

FIGURE 3.20

MRS and Marginal Utilities
The slope of an indifference curve is related to the marginal utilities of the two goods. At point _R_ the slope is Δ_C_/Δ_F_, and this ratio equals _MU__F/_MU__C.

champagne without affecting total utility. If $1F$ will replace $2C$, then the marginal utility of one ounce of perfume must be twice as great as the marginal utility of one glass of champagne. Thus, the slope $\Delta C/\Delta F$ equals MU_F/MU_C. The indifference curve slope measures the relative importance of the two goods to the consumer, which in turn is equal to their relative marginal utilities.

We can demonstrate this conclusion more formally. In Figure 3.20, the movement from R to S, ΔC, reduces total utility by an amount equal to $\Delta C \times MU_C$. (If ΔC is two glasses and the MU per glass of C is 5 utils, then total utility falls by 10 utils.) Similarly, the movement from S to T, ΔF, increases total utility by an amount equal to $\Delta F \times MU_F$. Because R and T lie on the same indifference curve, the loss in utility associated with a move from R to S must be exactly offset by the gain in utility in going from S to T. Therefore, we have:

$$\Delta C \times MU_C = \Delta F \times MU_F.$$

Rearranging these terms, we find:

$$\Delta C/\Delta F = MU_F/MU_C.$$

Because $\Delta C/\Delta F$ equals MRS_{FC}, we can substitute terms and obtain:

$$MRS_{FC} = MU_F/MU_C.$$

Earlier in this chapter, we noted that, so long as there is not a corner solution, the consumer's optimal choice is where her indifference curve slope equals the slope of her budget constraint:

$$MRS_{FC} = P_F/P_C.$$

Since MRS_{FC} equals MU_F/MU_C, we can substitute terms and rewrite the optimality condition as:

$$MU_F/MU_C = P_F/P_C.$$

Then, by rearranging terms, we obtain:

$$MU_F/P_F = MU_C/P_C;$$

which is the condition for the optimal consumption choice when using the utility theory approach.

An equality between the marginal utility per dollar's worth of both goods is the same as an equality between the MRS and the price ratio. The utility theory and the indifference curve approach are thus simply different ways of viewing the same thing.

SUMMARY

• The theory of consumer choice is designed to explain why consumers purchase the goods they do. The theory emphasizes two factors: the consumer's preferences over various market baskets and the consumer's budget line, which shows the market baskets that can be bought.

• An indifference curve graphically depicts all the combinations of goods considered equally desirable by a consumer.

• For economic "goods," indifference curves are assumed to be downward-sloping, convex, and nonintersecting.

• The slope of an indifference curve measures the marginal rate of substitution (MRS), which is the willingness of the consumer to trade one good for another.

• A budget line shows the combinations of goods a consumer can purchase with given prices for the good and assuming all the consumer's income is spent on the good.

• The consumer's income and the market prices of the goods determine the position and slope of the budget line. The slope of the budget line is equal to the ratio of the prices of the goods and measures the relative price of one good compared with another.

• From among the market baskets the consumer can purchase, we assume the consumer will select the one that results in the greatest possible level of satisfaction or well-being. Graphically, this optimal choice is shown by the tangency between the budget line and the indifference curve, where the consumer's MRS equals the price ratio.

• A change in the consumer's budget line leads to a change in the market basket selected.

• An increase in income when the prices of goods are held constant parallel shifts out the budget line. This can lead to either an increase or a decrease in the consumption of a good.

• When the consumption of a good rises with an increase in income, the good is a normal good.

• An inferior good is one for which consumption falls as income increases.

• The utility approach to consumer choice does not differ in any significant way from the indifference curve approach.

REVIEW QUESTIONS AND PROBLEMS

Questions and problems marked with an asterisk have solutions given in Answers to Selected Problems at the back of the book (pages 571–572).

3.1. Imelda spends her entire income on shoes and hats. Draw the budget line for each of the following situations, identifying the intercepts and the slope in each case.
a. Monthly income is $1,000, the price of a pair of shoes is $8, and the price of a hat is $10.
b. Same conditions as in part a, except that income is $500.
c. Same conditions as in part a, except that income is $2,000 and the price of a pair of shoes is $16.
d. Same conditions as in part a, except that hats cost $5 each.

*3.2. In most cases, a consumer can purchase any number of units of a good at an unchanged price. Suppose, however, that a consumer must pay $10 per visit to an amusement park for the first five visits but only $5 per visit in excess of five visits. What does the budget line relating amusement park visits and other goods look like?

*3.3. Bill's budget line relating hamburgers and french fries has intercepts of 20 hamburgers and 30 orders of french fries. If the price of a hamburger is $3, what is Bill's income? What is the per-order price of french fries? What is the slope of the budget line?

3.4. Under what conditions, if any, would a consumer's budget line be convex toward the origin? If a consumer has a convex budget line, is it possible for an indifference curve to be tangent to it at two different points? Which point would the consumer select?

3.5. Elton says, "To me, Coke and Pepsi are both the same." Draw several of Elton's indifference curves relating Coke and Pepsi.

3.6. People's rankings of activities are sometimes described in terms of their "priorities." For example, some students claim that getting good grades takes priority over watching television or dating. Does this ranking mean they never engage in the latter activities and spend all their time studying? If people do consume both high-priority and low-priority goods, what do we mean when we say that some goods have higher priorities than others?

3.7. Draw a set of indifference curves relating two "bads" such as smog and garbage. What characteristics do these curves have?

3.8. With the per-unit prices of broccoli (B) and pork rinds (R) equal to $2 and $1, a consumer, George, with an income of $1,000 purchases $400R$ and $300B$. At that point, the consumer's $MRS_{BR} = 2R/1B$. Does this mean that George would be just as well off consuming $200R$ and $400B$? Support your answer with a diagram.

*3.9. Marilyn spends her entire monthly income of $600 on champagne ($C$) and perfume ($F$). The price of a bottle of champagne is $30 and the price of an ounce of perfume is $10. If she consumes 12 bottles of champagne and 24 ounces of perfume, her MRS is $1C/1F$. Is her choice optimal? Explain your answer with a diagram.

*3.10. Seat belts in cars were available as options before they were required by law. Most motorists, however, did not buy them. Assuming that motorists were aware that seat belts reduced injuries from accidents, were motorists irrational in not purchasing them?

3.11. Is it inconsistent to claim that (a) people's preferences differ and (b) at their current consumption levels, their marginal rates of substitution are equal?

3.12. In a recent study of charitable giving in the United States it was found that households with annual income under $10,000 gave 5.2 percent of their income to charity. Households with income between $10,000 and $49,999 gave an average of 2.5 percent and households with at least $50,000 in income gave 2.1 percent. Does this evidence indicate that charitable giving is an inferior good?

*3.13. Is it possible for all goods a consumer buys to be normal? Is it possible for all goods a consumer buys to be inferior?

*3.14. Consider two market baskets, A ($100 worth of other goods, O, and 10 video rentals, V) and B ($150 worth of other goods and 10 video rentals). If video rentals are a normal good, will the consumer's MRS_{VO} be greater when basket A or basket B is consumed? What if video rentals are an inferior good? Depict in a diagram.

3.15. Explain why the food stamp program can have the same effect on the consumption pattern and well-being of recipients as an outright cash transfer of the same cost. Why do you think it is not converted into an explicit cash transfer program, thereby saving the cost of printing and redeeming food stamps?

3.16. Prior to 1979, the food stamp program required families to pay a certain amount for food stamps. Suppose a family can receive $150 in food stamps for a payment of $50; no other options are offered. How would this policy affect the budget line? Compared with an outright gift of $100 in food stamps, which is the way the program now works, would this policy lead to more, less, or the same food consumption?

3.17. Suppose that Thurston, a color-blind consumer, has $80 to spend on either pink or lime-green sweaters. Thurston does not care what color sweater he wears but deems it very important to buy as many sweaters as possible with the $80. Pink sweaters cost $40 each and lime-green ones cost $20 each.
a. Draw Thurston's budget line and indifference map. What is Thurston's optimal consumption choice?
b. A sale on pink sweaters begins: if a consumer buys two pink sweaters at the regular price, he or she can get two additional pink sweaters for free. Two pink sweaters must be purchased to get the deal. Otherwise prices are unchanged. With the sale, depict Thurston's new budget line and preferred consumption point.

3.18. Explain why the fact that most parents would prefer having one boy and one girl rather than two boys or two girls is consistent with diminishing MRS.

3.19. An Engel curve is a relationship between the consumer's income and the quantity of some good consumed (the price of the good fixed). Income is measured on the vertical axis, and the quantity of the good consumed is measured on the horizontal axis. Draw the Engel curves for compact discs and hamburger from Figures 3.14 and 3.15. How does the slope of an Engel curve identify whether the good is normal or inferior?

3.20. Measure the income of Samantha on the vertical axis and the income of Oscar on the horizontal axis, as we did in Figure 3.19. Draw several of Sam's indifference curves under the following circumstances.
a. Sam doesn't care about Oscar's income, but the higher her own income is, the better off she is.

b. Sam considers both her own income and Oscar's income to be economic "goods," but only as long as her income exceeds Oscar's. When Oscar's income exceeds hers, Sam considers Oscar's income to be an economic "bad."

3.21. If Sam's preferences relating her own income and Oscar's income conform to the Golden Rule ("Love thy neighbor as thyself"), what would her indifference curves in a diagram like Figure 3.19 look like?

3.22. Sam is subject to a 40 percent tax on income, and her after-tax income is $90,000, as in Figure 3.19. Now suppose the government permits her to deduct her contributions (to Oscar) from her income before the 40 percent tax rate is applied. How will this deduction affect her budget line?

3.23. When we use the composite-good convention, what do we mean by a *composite good* and how do we measure it? What is the slope of the budget line? What is the slope of an indifference curve? Does the consumer equilibrium involve an equality between MRS and a price ratio?

3.24. The text argues that the preferences of an individual can be represented with indifference curves. Can the preferences of a group of people, such as a family or an entire society, be represented by a set of indifference curves? Why or why not?

3.25. Suppose that you have only 9 hours left to cram for final exams and you want to get as high an average numerical grade as possible in three courses: marketing, accounting, and microeconomics. Your grade in each course depends on the time devoted to studying the subjects in the following manner:

Marketing		Accounting		Microeconomics	
Hours of Study	Grade	Hours of Study	Grade	Hours of Study	Grade
0	90	0	80	0	0
1	97	1	90	1	40
2	98	2	97	2	60
3	99	3	98	3	70
4	100	4	99	4	79
5	100	5	100	5	87
6	100	6	100	6	94
7	100	7	100	7	100

How many hours should you devote to studying each subject?

3.26. Depict the relevant budget line associated with AT&T's fee schedule in Application 3.2, assuming that the prices are charged on a per-minute basis and are 12 cents per minute for the first 500 minutes, 11.25 cents per minute for the next 300 minutes, 10 cents per minute for the next 400 minutes, and 9.4 cents per minute for minutes 1,201 to 1,600.

3.27. The actual pricing plan offered by AT&T and described in Application 3.2 involves *block pricing*: $59.99 for the first block of 500 minutes; $30 more for the next 300-minute-block; and so on. Depict the relevant budget line associated with this block-pricing schedule.

3.28. Relying on the concept of diminishing marginal utility, explain why coin-operated newspaper racks differ from vending machines for candy bars and sodas (the latter dispense one item at a time while the former consist of a stack of newspapers inside with no limit on how many a consumer can take once the first paper has been paid for).

CHAPTER 4

Individual and Market Demand

How do individuals' consumption choices respond to price changes and how is the market demand curve derived from individual consumers' demand curves?

Chapter Outline

4.1 Price Changes and Consumption Choices
  The Consumer's Demand Curve   Some Remarks About the Demand Curve
  ***Application 4.1** Using Price to Deter Youth Alcohol Abuse*
  ***Application 4.2** Young Techies Say No to College*
  Do Demand Curves Always Slope Downward?
4.2 Income and Substitution Effects of a Price Change
  Income and Substitution Effects Illustrated: The Normal-Good Case   The Income and Substitution Effects Associated with a Gasoline-Tax-Plus-Rebate Program
4.3 Income and Substitution Effects: Inferior Goods
  The Giffen Good Case: How Likely?
  ***Application 4.3** Do Rats Have Downward-Sloping Demand Curves?*
4.4 From Individual to Market Demand
  ***Application 4.4** Aggregating Demand Curves for a UCLA MBA*
4.5 Consumer Surplus
  ***Application 4.5** The Consumer Surplus Associated with Free TV*
  Consumer Surplus and Indifference Curves
4.6 Price Elasticity and the Price-Consumption Curve
  ***Application 4.6** The P-C Curve for a non–P-C Good*
4.7 Network Effects
  The Bandwagon Effect   The Snob Effect
  ***Application 4.7** Getting on the Bank ATM Bandwagon*
  ***Application 4.8** Network Effects, the New Economy, and the Microsoft Antitrust Case*
4.8 The Basics of Demand Estimation
  Experimentation   Surveys   Regression Analysis
  ***Application 4.9** Demand Estimation: McDonald's Versus Burger King*

Learning Objectives

- Understand how price changes affect consumption choices.
- Differentiate between the income and substitution effects associated with a price change on the consumption of a particular good.
- Explain the relation between income and substitution effects in the case of inferior goods.
- Show how individual demand curves are aggregated to obtain the market demand curve.
- Demonstrate how consumer surplus represents the net benefit, or gain, served by an individual from consuming one market basket instead of another.
- Investigate the relationship between own-price elasticity of demand and the price-consumption curve.
- Examine network effects: the extent to which an individual consumer's demand for a good is influenced by other individuals' purchases.
- Overview the basics of demand estimation.

n Chapter 3, we developed a model using indifference curves and budget lines to explain consumer behavior and used it to examine how changes in income affect consumer choices. In this chapter we use the consumer choice model to analyze the effects of price changes and show how a consumer's demand curve can be derived using the model. We also discuss how individual demand curves are aggregated to obtain the market demand curve. In addition, we explain the concept of consumer surplus, which relates to how areas under the demand curve can be used to measure the net benefits or costs to consumers from changes in consumption. And finally, we cover demand estimation to show how individuals' or market demand curves can be estimated from real-world data.

This chapter completes our discussion of the basic elements of the *theory* of consumer choice. Chapter 5, however, will illustrate the wide range of *applications* of this theory to such diverse problems as pricing garbage collection, deciding how much to save and borrow, and determining how much to invest in various financial assets.

4.1 PRICE CHANGES AND CONSUMPTION CHOICES[1]

Let's examine the way a change in the price of a good affects the market basket the consumer will choose. Because we wish to isolate the effect of a price change on consumption, we hold constant other factors such as income, preferences, and the prices of other goods.

Figure 4.1a depicts a consumer deciding how to allocate a given amount of annual income between college education (C) and all other goods. The per-credit-hour price of college education, $250, is indicated by the slope of the budget line since the per-dollar price of outlays on all other goods can be taken to be unity. With an initial budget line of AZ, the consumer's optimal consumption point is W. The consumption of college education is C_1, and outlays on other goods are A_1.

If the price of college education falls from $250 to $200, the budget line rotates around point A and becomes flatter. With a price of $200, the budget line becomes AZ', where Z' equals the consumer's constant income divided by the lower price of college education. Confronted with this new budget line, the consumer selects the most preferred market basket from among those available on AZ'. For the particular preferences shown, the preferred basket is point W', where the slope of U_2 (the marginal rate of substitution) equals the slope of the flatter budget line AZ'. Consumption of college education has increased to C_2 in response to the reduction in its price. If the price of college education falls still further to $150, then the budget line becomes AZ'', and the consumer will choose point W'', with the amount of credit hours of college education consumed equal to C_3.

Proceeding in this way, we can vary the price of college education and observe the market basket chosen by the consumer. For every possible price, a different budget line results and the consumer selects the market basket that permits attainment of the highest possible indifference curve. Points W, W', and W''' represent three market baskets associated with prices of $250, $200, and $150, respectively. If we connect these optimal consumption points, and those associated with other prices (not drawn in explicitly), we obtain the **price-consumption curve**, shown as the P-C curve in the diagram. The price-consumption curve identifies the optimal market basket associated with each possible price of college education, holding constant all other determinants of demand.

**PRICE-CONSUMP-
TION CURVE**
a curve that identifies the optimal market basket associated with each possible price of a good, holding constant all other determinants of demand

---

[1]A mathematical treatment of some of the material in this section is given in the appendix at the back of the book (page 563).

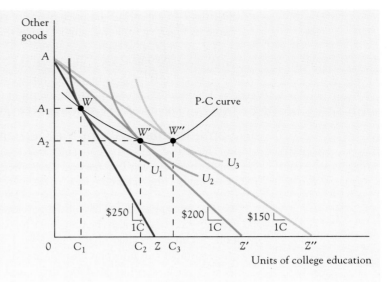

FIGURE 4.1

Derivation of the Consumer's Demand Curve

A reduction in the price of college education, with income, preferences, and the prices of other goods remaining fixed, leads the consumer to purchase more units of college education. (a) The optimal market baskets associated with alternative prices for college education are connected to form the price–consumption curve. (b) The same information is plotted as the consumer's demand curve for college education.

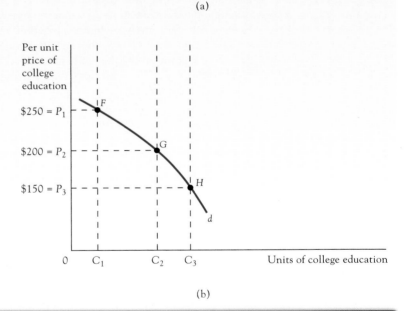

The Consumer's Demand Curve

Using the procedure just described, we can determine the consumer's demand curve for college education. The demand curve relates consumption of college education to its price, holding constant such factors as income, the prices of related goods, and preferences. The price-consumption curve does the same thing although it is not itself the demand curve. To convert the price-consumption curve to a demand curve, we simply plot the price-quantity relationship identified by the price-consumption curve in the appropriate graph.

Figure 4.1b shows the consumer's demand curve d (as before, we use lowercase letters to indicate the individual consumer's demand curve); it indicates the quantity of college education the consumer will buy at alternative prices, other factors held constant. The demand curve is determined by plotting the price-quantity combinations identified by the price-consumption curve in Figure 4.1a. For example, when the price of college education is $250 (the slope of AZ), consumption of college education is C_1 at point W in Figure 4.1a. Figure 4.1b shows the price of college education explicitly on the vertical axis. When the price is $250, consumption is C_1, so point F locates one point on the demand curve. When the price is $200 (the slope of AZ'), consumption is C_2, which identifies a second point, G, on the demand curve. Other points are obtained in the same manner to plot the entire demand curve d.

Some Remarks About the Demand Curve

We have just derived a consumer's demand curve from the individual's underlying preferences (with a given income and fixed prices of other goods). This approach clarifies several points about the demand curve:

1. The consumer's level of well-being varies along the demand curve. This point is clear from Figure 4.1a, where the consumer reaches a higher indifference curve when the price of college education falls. The diagram specifies why the consumer benefits from a lower price: the consumer can now purchase market baskets that were previously unattainable.

2. The prices of other goods are held constant along a demand curve, but the quantities purchased of these other goods can vary. For example, in Figure 4.1a, consumption of all other goods falls from A_1 to A_2 when the price of college education falls from $250 to $200. Because all other goods are lumped together and treated as a composite good, the way in which consumption of any other specific good may change is not shown explicitly.

3. At each point on the demand curve, the consumer's optimality condition $MRS_{CO} = P_C/P_O$ is satisfied. (The subscript O refers to *other goods*, the composite good measured on the vertical axis.) As the price of college education falls, the value of P_C/P_O becomes smaller, and the consumer chooses a market basket for which MRS_{CO}, the slope of the indifference curve, is also smaller.

4. The demand curve identifies the marginal benefit associated with various levels of consumption. The height of the demand curve from the horizontal axis, at each level of consumption, indicates the marginal benefit of the good. For example, when consumption is C_2 at point G on the demand curve (Figure 4.1b), the distance GC_2 (or $200) is a measure of how much the marginal unit of college education consumed is worth to the consumer. Why? Refer to Figure 4.1a; for a market basket selected by a consumer to be optimal, such as W' when the price of college education is $200, MRS_{CO} equals P_C/P_O. Since P_O can be taken to equal unity, this implies that $MRS_{CO} = P_C$. Thus, at point W' in Figure 4.1a, MRS_{CO} is equal to $200 per unit of college education. Because the MRS is a measure of what the consumer is willing to give up for an additional credit hour of college education, it is a measure of the marginal benefit. *Note that at every point on the demand curve the height of the demand curve equals the* MRS, *thereby indicating the marginal benefit of the good to the consumer.* For this reason economists refer to the price at which people purchase a given good as revealing the relative importance of the good to them.

APPLICATION 4.1   USING PRICE TO DETER YOUTH ALCOHOL ABUSE

Although economists ascribe an important role to price in determining the quantity demanded of a product, policymakers often do not. A case in point is the campaign that policymakers have been waging since the mid-1970s to discourage alcohol abuse and thereby decrease the number of traffic-related deaths. One of the main objectives of the campaign has been to raise the legal age for purchase and consumption of alcohol to 21 years. The reason behind this is that while people under the age of 25 represent 20 percent of all licensed drivers, they account for more than 35 percent of all drivers involved in fatal accidents. Alcohol is involved in more than half the driving fatalities accounted for by young drivers.

By raising the legal age for the purchase and consumption of alcohol to 21, policymakers hope to shift the demand curve for alcohol to the left (diminishing the portion of the population with legal access to alcohol) and thereby reduce both alcohol abuse and driving fatalities.

Shifting the demand curve for alcohol to the left is one way to reduce alcohol abuse and traffic fatalities. However, economic research suggests that a more effective method, even among teenagers, would be to raise the price of alcohol through higher taxes, thereby producing a movement along the demand curve for alcohol.

The federal tax on alcohol was constant in nominal dollar terms between 1951 and 1991 ($9 per barrel of beer, $10.50 per proof gallon of distilled spirits such as vodka, and so on) and has only been increased modestly since then. In real terms, consequently, the federal tax on alcohol has decreased since 1951. For examples, the real federal tax on beer has declined by 70 percent since 1951 while the real tax on distilled spirits has decreased by 81 percent. The decline, in real terms, of the federal

tax on alcohol is a major factor behind the substantial decrease in the real price of alcohol since 1951—40 percent in the case of beer and 70 percent for hard liquor.

A national survey of teenagers finds that, holding constant other factors such as a state's minimum drinking age, religious affiliation, and proximity to bordering states with lower minimum drinking ages, the amount of alcohol consumed by the average teenager in a state is significantly influenced by the price of alcohol there.[2]

The survey findings suggest that raising taxes on alcohol offers a potent mechanism for deterring alcohol abuse and traffic fatalities among teenagers. Specifically, based on the survey's results, had federal taxes on alcohol remained constant since 1951 in real purchasing power terms rather than in dollar terms, teenage drinking would have fallen more than if the minimum drinking age had been raised to 21 in all states. Raising the price of drinking and moving along the demand curve for alcohol thus promises to be more effective at reducing teenage drinking than the policy pursued by most policymakers—shifting the demand curve for alcohol to the left by imposing age restrictions.

[2]According to Douglas Coate and Michael Grossman, "Effects of Alcoholic Beverage Prices and Legal Drinking Ages on Youth Alcohol Use," *Journal of Law and Economics*, 31 No. 1 (April 1988), pp. 145–172, the estimated price elasticity of demand for teenage drinking ranges from 0.5 to 1.2.

APPLICATION 4.2   YOUNG TECHIES SAY NO TO COLLEGE

According to Census figures, the percentage of high school graduates attending college fell to 63 percent in 1999 from 67 percent in 1997.[3] One of the reasons for this decline appears to be the strength of the economy and its information technology engine during the latter half of the 1990s. In the last decade, the annual employment growth for computer systems analysts (a broad category that includes Web designers, network administrators, computer scientists, and computer security professionals) has averaged 17 per-

cent. By comparison, overall employment growth averaged 1.5 percent per year over the same time period.

Salaries in the information technology arena have risen in conjunction with the growth in demand for workers. According to Census data, the median income for computer systems analysts was $1,008 per week. This amount is nearly double the $550 median weekly wage for all workers in the United States.

As opportunities and salaries in information technology have increased so has the price of going to college for young "techies" given that the opportunity cost of forgoing job opportunities for the sake of attending college has risen. Predictably, therefore, a higher price

[3]This application is based on "Young Techies Say No to College," *New York Times on the Web*, September 7, 2000.

has led to fewer high school graduates opting to pursue a college degree.

Corey Ganett, 20, is an example of the phenomenon. Corey graduated from high school in 1998 with less than a 2.0 grade point average because he spent more of his time hanging out on the Internet and learning about network security. By 2000, Corey was working as a junior network administrator at Juniper Networks in Silicon Valley making $50,000 annually and with stock options in his company worth around $350,000. According to Corey, "in this field, if you go to college, you're outdated."

Do Demand Curves Always Slope Downward?

For the specific indifference curves shown in Figure 4.1, we derived a downward-sloping demand curve. But does the demand curve always slope downward? Is it possible for a consumer to have indifference curves so that the law of demand does not hold for some goods?

Figure 4.2 suggests such a possibility. When the budget line is AZ, consumption of good X is X_1 units. If the price of X falls so that the budget line becomes AZ', consumption of X falls to X_2, an apparent violation of the law of demand. Note that the indifference curves that produce this result are downward-sloping, nonintersecting, and convex; that is, they do not contradict any of our basic assumptions about preferences.

Just because we can draw a diagram that shows reduced consumption at a lower price does not mean such an outcome will ever be observed in reality. It does suggest, however, the importance of carefully considering exactly why consumption of a good varies in response to a change in its price. We illustrate this idea in the following sections.

4.2   INCOME AND SUBSTITUTION EFFECTS OF A PRICE CHANGE

When the price of a good changes, the change affects consumption in two different ways. Normally, we cannot observe these two effects separately. Instead, when the consumer alters consumption in response to a price change, all we see is the combined effect of both factors.

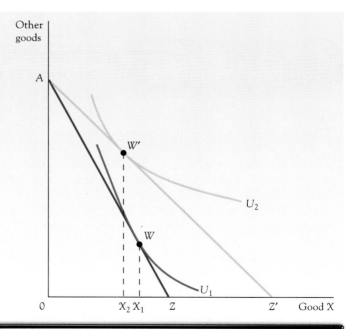

FIGURE 4.2

A Lower Price Leading to Less Consumption
A consumer purchases less of good *X* when its price falls, an apparent violation of the law of demand. In this case the demand curve will be upward-sloping.

Nevertheless, it is useful to analytically break down the effects of a price change into these two components.

The first way a price change affects consumption is the **income effect**. When the price of a good falls, a consumer's real purchasing power increases, which affects consumption of the good. A price reduction increases *real* income—that is, makes it possible for the consumer to attain a higher indifference curve.

The second way a price reduction affects consumption is the **substitution effect**. When the price of one good falls, the consumer has an incentive to increase consumption of that good at the expense of other, now *relatively* more expensive, goods. The individual's consumption pattern will change in favor of the now less costly good and away from other goods—in short, the consumer will substitute the less expensive good for other goods—hence the name *substitution effect.*

To see intuitively that two different factors are at work when a price changes, compare Figure 3.14 from Chapter 3 and Figure 4.1. In Figure 4.1, a price reduction results in the consumer reaching a higher indifference curve. In Figure 3.14, an increase in income, with no change in prices, also results in consumers reaching a higher indifference curve. Apparently, a common factor is at work: Both a reduction in price and an increase in income raise the consumer's real income, in the sense of permitting attainment of greater well-being. In both cases the budget line moves outward, allowing consumption of market baskets that were not previously attainable. This points to one of the two ways a price reduction affects consumption: It augments real income (by increasing the purchasing power of a given nominal income), which obviously affects consumption. This is the income effect.

Although a price reduction and an income increase both have an income effect on consumption, there is a significant difference between them. With a price reduction the consumer moves to a point on a higher indifference curve where the slope is lower than it was at the original optimal consumption point (see Figure 4.1). In effect, the consumer has moved down the indifference curve to consume more of the lower-priced good. This result illustrates the substitution in favor of the less costly good. When income increases, however, the consumer moves to a point on a higher indifference curve where the slope (the MRS) is the same as it was prior to the income increase. This is so because if only income changes, the slope of the consumer's budget line does not change. The precise distinction between these two effects and the way they help us understand why the demand curve has the shape it does are clarified next with a graphical treatment.

Income and Substitution Effects Illustrated: The Normal-Good Case

In Figure 4.3, the consumer's original budget line AZ relates annual credit hours of college education and outlays on all other goods. At a per-credit-hour price of $250, the optimal market basket is W, with C_1 credit hours bought by the consumer. If the price of college education falls to $200, the budget line becomes AZ', and the consumer buys C_2 units. The increase in consumption of college education (from C_1 to C_2) in response to the lower price is the *total effect* of the price reduction on purchases of college education. The demand curve shows the total effect. Now we wish to show how this total effect can be decomposed conceptually into its two component parts—the income effect and the substitution effect.

The substitution effect illustrates how the change in relative prices *alone* affects consumption, independent of any change in real income or well-being. To isolate the substitution effect, we must keep the consumer on the original indifference curve, U_1, while at the same time confronting the individual with a lower price of college education. We do so by drawing a new budget line with a smaller slope, which reflects the lower price, and then imagining that the consumer's income is reduced just enough (while holding the price of college education at $200) so that the student can attain indifference curve U_1. In other words, we move the AZ' budget line toward the origin parallel to itself until it is tangent to

INCOME EFFECT
a change in a consumer's real purchasing power brought about by a change in the price of a good

SUBSTITUTION EFFECT
an incentive to increase consumption of a good whose price falls, at the expense of other, now relatively more expensive, goods

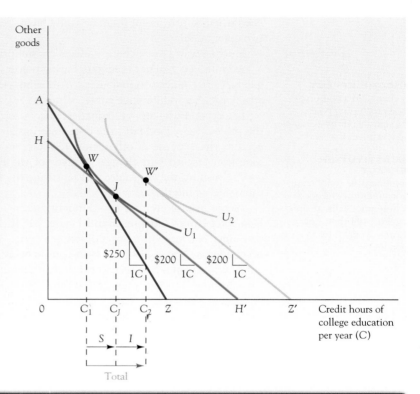

FIGURE 4.3

Income and Substitution Effects of a Price Reduction

The total effect (from C_1 to C_2) of a reduction in the price of college education can be separated into two components, the income effect and the substitution effect. A hypothetical budget line HH' is drawn parallel to the new (after-price-change) budget line but tangent to the initial indifference curve U_1 at point J. The substitution effect is then C_1 to C_J, and the income effect is C_J to C_2, which together give the total effect of the price decrease on the consumption of college education by the consumer.

U_1. The result is the *hypothetical* budget line HH', which is parallel to AZ' (both reflect the $200 price) and tangent to U_1 at point J. This new budget line shows that if, after the price decrease, the consumer's income is reduced by AH, the preferred market basket will be at point J on U_1, the indifference curve attained by the consumer prior to the price decrease. (Remember from the last chapter that the height of the budget line's intercept on the vertical axis represents the consumer's income when dollar outlays on all other goods are measured on the vertical axis.)

This manipulation permits us to separate the income and substitution effects so that each can be identified independently. *The substitution effect is shown by the difference between the market baskets at points W and J.* The lower price of college education, looked at by itself, induces the consumer to increase consumption of college education from C_1 to C_J and reduce consumption of other goods. In effect, the substitution effect involves sliding down the original indifference curve from point W, where its slope is $250 per credit hour, to point J, where its slope is $200 per credit hour. Consequently, the substitution effect of the lower price increases consumption from C_1 to C_J.

The income effect is shown by the change in consumption when the consumer moves from point J on U_1 to point W' on U_2. This change involves a parallel movement in HH' out to the AZ' budget line. Recall that a parallel shift in the budget line indicates a change in income but no change in the price of college education. Thus, the income effect of the lower price causes consumption of college education to rise from C_J to C_2.

The sum of the substitution effect (C_1 to C_J) and the income effect (C_J to C_2) measures the total effect (C_1 to C_2) of the lower price on the consumption of college education. Any change in price can be separated into income and substitution effects in this manner.

Although this analysis may seem esoteric, it is highly significant. Ultimately, we are seeking a firm basis for believing that people will consume more at lower prices—that is, that the law of demand is valid. Separating the income and substitution effects allows us to look at the issue more deeply.

Note that the substitution effect of any price change will always mean more consumption of a good at a lower price or less consumption at a higher price. This relationship follows directly from the convexity of indifference curves: With convex indifference curves, a lower price always implies a substitution effect that involves sliding down the initial indifference curve to a point where consumption of the good is greater. Thus, the substitution effect conforms to the law of demand.

The income effect of a price change, however, implies greater consumption at a lower price only if the good is a normal good. In Figure 4.3, when the budget line shifts from *HH'* to *AZ'* (a parallel shift), consumption of college education will rise if college education is a normal good.

The demand curve for a normal good must therefore be downward-sloping. Both the substitution effect and the income effect of a price change involve greater consumption of the good when its price is lower.[4] Because the total effect is the sum of the income and substitution effects, people will consume more of a normal good when its price is lower. This conclusion is a powerful one, because we know that most goods are normal goods. Some goods are inferior goods, however. In Section 4.3 we will explore whether the law of demand applies universally to them. ✒

The Income and Substitution Effects Associated with a Gasoline-Tax-Plus-Rebate Program

Ever since the Arab oil embargo in 1973 and the quadrupling of oil prices that resulted from it, there have been numerous proposals designed to encourage or force U.S. consumers to cut back on their use of gasoline. One such proposal involves the use of a large excise tax on gasoline (roughly 50 cents per gallon) to raise its price and thereby reduce consumption. An **excise tax** is a tax on a specific good such as gasoline that allows the consumer to purchase as many units of the good at the taxed price as desired.

EXCISE TAX
a tax on a specific good

Realizing that a large excise tax on gasoline would place a heavy burden on many families, most proponents of the proposal recommend that the revenues raised by the tax be returned to the consumers in the form of unrestricted cash transfers, or tax rebates. Alternatively, the excise tax revenues could be used to reduce the federal government's outstanding debt.

Although a sizable increase in gasoline taxes has not yet been enacted into law, it poses an interesting problem. One objection commonly raised to this plan questions whether it would really cause gasoline consumption to fall. If the revenues from the tax are simply distributed to the general public, why would gas consumption be curtailed? We can use consumer choice theory to show that gasoline consumption will, in fact, be reduced by a combination of an excise tax and a tax rebate.

The key to analyzing this policy package is realizing that the tax rebate would be a cash transfer to each family that is completely unrelated to its gasoline consumption. In other words, the proposal would not give a rebate of 50 cents for every gallon of gasoline purchased by a family, because that policy would leave the effective price of gasoline un-

---

[4]Figure 4.3 shows the substitution and income effects for a price reduction. An increase is handled in a slightly different way. If we were considering an increase in the price of college education from \$200 to \$250 in the diagram, we would accomplish the separation into substitution and income effects by drawing a hypothetical budget line with a slope of \$250 (the new price) tangent to the indifference curve, U_2, the consumer is on before the price increase.

changed and completely negate the effect of the tax. Instead, a family would receive a check for $500 a year, for example, regardless of how much gasoline it purchased. On average for all families, the rebate would equal the total tax paid, but some families would be overcompensated for the tax while others would be undercompensated.

Now let's examine the gasoline tax and rebate plan for a representative consumer. Figure 4.4a focuses on the effects of such a plan on the representative consumer's budget line AZ. The excise tax by itself will increase the price from $1.00 to $1.50 per gallon and therefore rotate the budget line inward to AZ'. This is not the end of the analysis, however, because the budget line to which the consumer will adjust must reflect both the tax and the rebate. The rebate is shown as the outward parallel shift in AZ' to $A'Z''$, similar to an increase in income, while the price of gasoline remains constant at $1.50 per gallon.

Figure 4.4b depicts what happens to the consumer's optimal consumption point under the tax and rebate plan. Initially, the consumer selects point E, along the original budget line AZ, with G_1 gallons being purchased. With the gasoline tax and rebate the consumer selects point E', where U_1 is tangent to the new budget line $A'Z''$. Gasoline consumption has fallen from G_1 to G_2, while consumption of other goods has increased.

How far out will the tax rebate shift the after-tax budget line, AZ'? If everyone receives a rebate of the same size, and it is determined by dividing total tax revenue by the number of consumers, then the average consumer will receive a rebate equal to the tax he or she pays. Thus, it seems reasonable to focus the analysis on a consumer who receives a rebate equal to the tax paid, the situation shown in Figure 4.4b.

To see that the tax and rebate are equal when the consumer's optimal choice is point E', note that G_2 units of gasoline will be purchased at that point. Because the AZ' budget line shows the effect of the tax by itself, the total tax revenue is the vertical distance, $E'T$, between the original budget line, AZ, and the budget line, AZ', incorporating the tax. We can see that $E'T$ is the total tax bill by noting that if G_2 gallons were purchased when the market price was $1.00, outlays on other goods would have been vertical distance, $E'G_2$. Once the tax is levied, only TG_2 in income is left (before the rebate). The vertical difference, $E'T$, is thus the total tax. Because the rebate equals the tax, the budget line must shift up by an amount equal to $E'T$, and so it passes through point E'. Finally, we have already seen that point E' represents the consumer's optimal choice under the tax and rebate plan because the indifference curve is tangent to the final budget line at that point. By experimentation, you can determine that if the rebate were any larger, it would be greater than the amount of tax paid and, conversely, less than the tax paid if it were smaller.

The geometry of this case is slightly complicated, but the final outcome fits with common sense. The excise tax by itself (without a rebate) has an income effect and a substitution effect. Both effects reduce gas consumption—provided, of course, that gas is a normal good in the case of the income effect. The rebate thus offsets most of the income effect of the tax (but not quite all of it, because the consumer does not return all the way to the original indifference curve). Thus, the substitution effect determines the final result. Because a higher price leads the consumer to substitute away from gasoline, the final outcome is reduced gasoline consumption (G_2 versus G_1).

Finally, note that this combination of tax and rebate necessarily harms the consumer. This result is true, at least, for any consumer who receives a rebate exactly equal to the tax, because the final outcome will be a market basket on the original budget line that is inferior to the one selected in the absence of the tax and rebate. Why does anyone propose a policy that will make the average family worse off? A good question. Perhaps some consequences are not fully reflected in this analysis. For example, decreased gasoline purchases mean decreased oil imports from the Middle East, and possibly decreased dependence on imported oil is beneficial in and of itself. In addition, reduced gasoline consumption means lower au-

FIGURE 4.4

Tax-Plus-Rebate Program
An excise tax will reduce gasoline consumption even if the revenue is returned to taxpayers as lump-sum transfers. (a) The tax pivots the budget line to *AZ′* and the tax rebate shifts it to *A′Z″*. (b) The combined effect reduces gasoline consumption from G_1 to G_2.

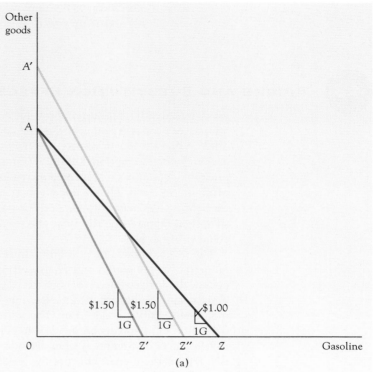

(a)

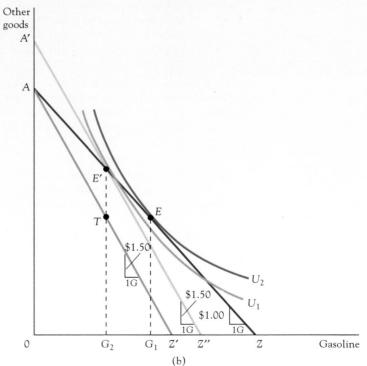

(b)

tomobile emissions and possibly improved air quality. These benefits are not incorporated into this analysis, and if they were it is possible that consumers would be better off on balance.

4.3   INCOME AND SUBSTITUTION EFFECTS: INFERIOR GOODS

Mechanically, the separation of income and substitution effects for a change in the price of an inferior good is accomplished in the same way as for a normal good. The results, however, differ in one significant respect. With a price reduction, the substitution effect still encourages greater consumption, but the income effect works in the opposite direction. At a lower price the consumer's real income increases, and this fact, by itself, implies less consumption of an inferior good. Thus, a price reduction for an inferior good involves a substitution effect that encourages *more* consumption but an opposing income effect that encourages *less* consumption. Apparently, the total effect—the sum of the income and substitution effects—could go either way.

Figure 4.5a shows one possibility. Initially, the budget line is AZ, with the price of hamburger at \$2 per pound and H_1 pounds being purchased. When the price falls to \$1 per pound, the budget line pivots out to AZ', and hamburger consumption rises to H_2 pounds. Once again, the hypothetical budget line HH' that keeps the consumer on U_1, the original indifference curve, is drawn in. The substitution effect is the movement from point W to point J on U_1, implying an increase in consumption from H_1 to H_J. Now see what happens to hamburger consumption when we move out from budget line HH' to AZ', a movement that reflects the income effect of the lower price of hamburger. Because hamburger is an inferior good for this consumer, the income effect reduces hamburger consumption, from H_J to H_2. Overall, however, the total effect of the price reduction is increased consumption, because the substitution effect (greater consumption) is larger than the income effect (lower consumption). In this situation the consumer's demand curve for hamburger will slope downward.

For an inferior good there is another possibility, illustrated in Figure 4.5b. Good X is also an inferior good for some consumers, and a reduction in its price pivots the budget line from AZ to AZ'. Here, however, the total effect of the price decrease is a reduction in the consumption of X, from X_1 to X_2. When the income and substitution effects are shown separately, we see how this outcome occurs. The substitution effect (point W to point J, or increased consumption of X) still shows greater consumption at a lower price. However, the income effect for this inferior good not only works in the opposing direction (less consumption, from X_J to X_2), but also overwhelms the substitution effect. Because the income effect more than offsets the substitution effect, consumption falls. This consumer's demand curve for good X, at least for the prices shown in the diagram, will slope upward.

GIFFEN GOOD
the result of an income effect being larger than the substitution effect for an inferior good, so that the demand curve will have a positive slope.

Thus, for inferior goods, there are two possibilities. If the substitution effect is larger than the income effect when the price of the good changes, then the demand curve will have its usual negative slope. If the income effect is larger than the substitution effect for an inferior good, then the demand curve will have a positive slope. This second case represents a theoretically possible (but rarely observed) exception to the law of demand. It can happen only with an inferior good and, moreover, only for a subset of inferior goods in which income effects are larger than substitution effects. We refer to a good in this class as a **Giffen good**, after the nineteenth-century English economist Robert Giffen, who believed that, during the years of famine, potatoes in Ireland had an upward-sloping demand curve. Giffen observed that as the blight diminished the supply of potatoes in Ireland and drove up their price, the quantity demanded of potatoes appeared to increase. (The evidence in support of Giffen's observation is a matter of debate among economists.)

FIGURE 4.5

Income and Substitution Effects for an Inferior Good

(a) Hamburger is an inferior good with a normally shaped, downward-sloping demand curve, because the substitution effect is larger than the income effect. (b) Good X is an inferior good with an upward-sloping demand curve, because the income effect is larger than the substitution effect. Good X is called a Giffen good.

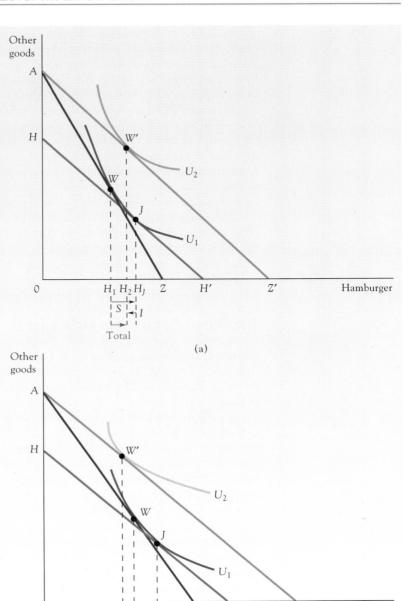

(a)

(b)

Finding an intuitively plausible example in which the demand curve slopes upward is difficult, but consider the following hypothetical situation.[5] The Shuherk family lives in Alaska and traditionally spends the month of January in Hawaii. One year the price of home heating oil increases sharply. The Shuherks cut back on their use of heating oil during the other winter months, but, nonetheless, their total heating costs rise to a point where they can no longer afford a tropical vacation. Because they stay at home in January, their use of heating oil for that month increases dramatically over the amount they would have used had they been in Hawaii. On balance, annual heating oil purchases will rise if the increased use in January is greater than the reduction achieved during the remaining winter months. Consequently, an increase in the price of heating oil can conceivably lead to greater use of heating oil by the Shuherks. (Conversely, a decrease in the price of heating oil can result in lower consumption of heating oil by the Shuherks.)

This contrived scenario illustrates the type of situation shown in Figure 4.5b. Heating oil is an inferior good for the Shuherks; a reduction in income will lead them to spend more time at home, which causes an increase in the use of heating oil. A price increase has an income effect that induces them to forgo their January vacation. If the expected consumption in January exceeds the reduced consumption of heating oil during the other winter months, a net increase in consumption of heating oil at a higher price results.

The Giffen Good Case: How Likely?

We might conceive of cases where the income effect for an inferior good exceeds the substitution effect, producing an upward-sloping demand curve. However, economists believe that most, if not all, real-world inferior goods have downward-sloping demand curves, as shown in Figure 4.5a. This belief stems from both theoretical considerations and empirical evidence.

At a theoretical level the question is whether the income effect or the substitution effect of a price change for an inferior good will be larger. If the substitution effect is larger, then the demand curve will slope downward, even for an inferior good. There are good reasons for believing that the substitution effect is larger. Consider first the income effect. Its size relates closely to the fraction of the consumer's budget devoted to the good. If the price of some good falls by 10 percent, the price reduction will benefit a consumer much more (have a larger income effect) if 25 percent of the consumer's income is spent on the good than if only 1 percent is spent on it. For example, a 10 percent reduction in the price of housing will probably influence housing consumption greatly by its income effect, but a 10 percent reduction in the price of computer diskettes will have a much smaller, almost imperceptible income effect. Income effects from a change in price are quite small for most goods because they seldom account for as much as 10 percent of a consumer's budget. This observation is especially true of inferior goods, which are likely to be narrowly defined goods.

In contrast, there is reason to believe that substitution effects for inferior goods will be relatively large. Inferior goods usually belong to a general category that contains similar goods of differing qualities. Take hamburger: we would expect a reduction in its price to result in a rearrangement of the consumer's purchases away from chicken, pork, pot roast, and so on, in favor of hamburger, thus resulting in a large substitution effect. Consequently, we expect price changes for inferior goods to involve relatively large substitution effects but small income effects. Therefore, the demand curve will slope downward, and the case shown in Figure 4.5a will be typical. The Giffen good remains an intriguing but remote theoretical possibility.

[5]This example is adapted from E. G. Dolan, *Basic Economics*, 4th ed. (Hinsdale, Ill.: Dryden Press, 1986).

APPLICATION 4.3   DO RATS HAVE DOWNWARD-SLOPING DEMAND CURVES?

L ogical reasoning and empirical evidence support the proposition that humans have downward-sloping demand curves. The inquiring reader may wonder whether the law of demand also applies to the behavior of animals. Experimental evidence suggests that it does. Consider the results of a study on rats done by researchers at Texas A&M University.[6] The rats were found to have downward-sloping demand curves for root beer and Tom Collins mix.

Researchers confronted each rat with a budget line relating root beer and Collins mix. They charged a "price" by requiring the rats to press a lever to receive 0.05 milliliter of each beverage. The "incomes" of the rats were determined by allocating each rat a certain number of lever presses per day. With an income of 300 lever presses and equal prices for root beer and Collins mix, rats expressed a decided preference for root beer and spent most of their incomes on it. Then, the price of Collins mix was cut in half (half as many lever presses required per unit of Collins mix) and the price of root beer doubled, with income set so that each rat could still consume its previously chosen market basket if it wished. Economic theory predicts that consumption of Collins mix will rise and root beer fall given the new

"prices." The theory proved correct: The rats chose to consume more than four times as much Collins mix as before and less root beer.

In a more recent study, researchers attempted to create a situation in which the rats would consume less at a lower price (and, conversely, more at a higher price)—the Giffen good case.[7] Economic theory suggests that this can occur only when the good is strongly inferior and occupies a large portion of the budget (so the income effect is large). When consumption of fluids was restricted to root beer and quinine water, the researchers found that quinine water was an inferior good for the rats. They then lowered the rats' "incomes" to the point where most of their budget was devoted to quinine water; a change in the price of quinine water would then have a large income effect. Next came the crucial experiment: The price of quinine water was reduced. The rats consumed less quinine at the lower price and used their increased real income to increase their root beer consumption. A Giffen good case finally had been found. What is particularly interesting about the experimental results is that the Giffen good case was demonstrated in exactly the circumstances that theory emphasizes are necessary—a strongly inferior good, with most of the budget devoted to purchases of that good.

[6]John Kagel et al., "Experimental Studies of Consumer Demand Behavior Using Laboratory Animals," *Economic Inquiry*, 13 No. 1 (March 1975), pp. 22–38.

[7]Raymond C. Battalio, John H. Kagel, and Carl Kogut, "Experimental Confirmation of the Existence of a Giffen Good," *American Economic Review*, 81 No. 3 (September 1991), pp. 961–970.

4.4 FROM INDIVIDUAL TO MARKET DEMAND

We have seen how to derive an individual consumer's demand curve and why the concepts of income and substitution effects imply that it will typically slope downward. But most practical applications of economic theory require the use of the market demand curve. We begin with a discussion of individual demand because the individual demand curves of all the consumers in the market added together constitute the market demand curve. We will show that, if the typical consumer's demand curve has a negative slope, then the market demand curve must also have a negative slope.

Figure 4.6 illustrates how individual demand curves are aggregated to obtain the market demand curve. Assume that there are only three consumers who purchase an MBA educa-

FIGURE 4.6

Summing Individual Demands to Obtain Market Demand
The market demand curve *D* is derived from the individual consumers' demand curves by horizontally summing the individual demand curves. At each price we sum the quantities each consumer will buy to obtain the total quantity demanded at that price.

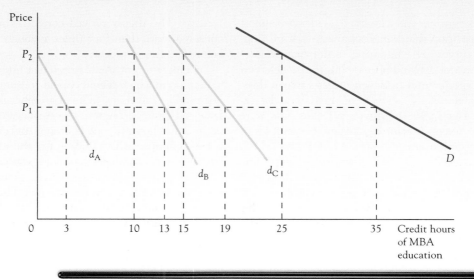

tion, although the process will obviously apply to the more important case where there are a great many consumers. The individual demand curves are d_A, d_B, and d_C. To derive the market demand curve, we sum the quantities each consumer will buy at alternative prices. For example, at P_2 consumer B will buy 10 credit hours of MBA education, consumer C will buy 15, and consumer A will buy none. (Note that when the price is P_2, consumer A will be at a corner optimum.) The combined purchases of all consumers total 25 credit hours when the price is P_2, and this combination identifies one point on the market de-mand curve D.

Other points on the market demand curve are derived in the same way. If the price is P_1, A will buy 3 credit hours, B will buy 13, and C will buy 19, so total quantity demanded at a price of P_1 is 35 credit hours of MBA education. The process of adding up the individual de-mand curves to obtain the market demand curve is called *horizontal summation*, because the quantities (measured on the horizontal axis) bought at each price are added. Note that when the individual demand curves slope downward, the market demand curve also slopes downward. If all consumers buy more at a lower price, then total purchases will rise when the price falls.

A market demand curve, however, can slope downward, even if some consumers have upward-sloping individual demand curves. In a market with thousands of consumers, if a few dozen happened to have upward-sloping demand curves, then their contribution to the market demand curve would be more than offset by the normal behavior of the other consumers. So we have yet another reason not to be particularly concerned about the Giffen good case. It is possible to imagine that the Shuherk family in Alaska will buy more heating oil at a higher price, but it is difficult to believe that their behavior is typical.

APPLICATION 4.4 AGGREGATING DEMAND CURVES FOR A UCLA MBA

Many business schools offer both a full-time and an evening MBA program. The degrees are the same but the length of time it takes to obtain the degree often differs: a full-time program lasts two years, while earning an MBA at night (and retaining one's job during the day) requires an average of three years of study. Suppose, as shown in Figure 4.7, that at UCLA's Graduate School of Management, the demand for the full-time MBA program is represented by the equation $Q_F = 20,000 - 40P$ where Q_F is the annual number of credit hours demanded by students qualified for admission and P is the per-credit-hour price. Demand for UCLA's evening MBA program is given by the equation $Q_E = 20,000 - 20P$ where Q_E is the annual number of credit hours demanded by students qualified for admission and P is the per-credit-hour price.

If UCLA charges the same per-credit-hour price for the MBA offered by its full-time and evening MBA programs, we can obtain the aggregate quantity demanded of credit hours for UCLA's MBA (Q_M) across the two programs. We can do this by horizontally adding up the quantity of credit hours demanded for each program at alternative prices. Therefore, $Q_M = Q_F + Q_E = (20,000 - 40P) + (20,000 - 20P) = 40,000 - 60P$.

In horizontally adding up the full-time and evening MBA demand curves at any price, of course, we must take into account the fact that at all prices above $500,

the quantity demanded of full-time MBA program credit hours is zero. Thus, as shown in Figure 4.7, the aggregate demand curve for the UCLA MBA is the same as the evening MBA demand curve above the price of $500 ($Q_M = Q_E = 20,000 - 20P$ along segment EG). Below $500, there is full-time MBA program demand, and the aggregate demand curve is obtained by horizontally summing the evening and full-time MBA demand curves (the segment GH of the aggregate demand curve below the price of $500 is given by the equation calculated in the preceding paragraph, $Q_M = Q_F + Q_E = 40,000 - 60P$). As Figure 4.7 shows, the aggregate demand for a UCLA MBA across the two programs is equal to EGH and is kinked at point G—at the price above which there is no full-time MBA program demand.

In horizontally summing the individual demand curves to obtain the aggregate demand curve, we have assumed that UCLA charges the same price for its MBA in both programs. As we will see in a later chapter, however, this need not be the case. Producers interested in maximizing profit may find it advantageous to focus on individual demand curves rather than the aggregate demand curve. By "segmenting" the aggregate market, producers can charge different prices to the individual demand curve segments that are inversely related to how sensitive those segments are to the price charged.

FIGURE 4.7

The Aggregate Demand for a UCLA MBA
The demand for UCLA's evening MBA program is represented by *EE'* while the demand for UCLA's full-time MBA program is represented by *FF'*. The aggregate demand curve for a UCLA MBA across these two programs is *EGH*.

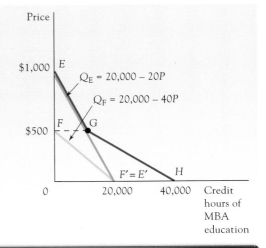

4.5 CONSUMER SURPLUS

CONSUMER SURPLUS
the net benefit or gain
from consuming one
market basket instead
of another

TOTAL BENEFIT
the total value a consumer
derives from a particular
amount of a good and thus
the maximum amount the
consumer would be
willing to pay for that
amount of the good.

MARGINAL BENEFIT
the incremental value a
consumer derives from
consuming an additional
unit of a good and thus
the maximum amount the
consumer would pay for
that additional unit

Consumers purchase goods and services because they are better off (that is, on a higher indifference curve) after the purchase than they were before; otherwise, the purchase would not take place. The term **consumer surplus** refers to the net benefit, or gain, secured by an individual from consuming one market basket instead of another. For example, suppose that around exam time you purchase six cups of espresso coffee per day at $3 per cup from the campus coffeeshop. You have chosen to spend $18 per day on espresso, allocating the rest of your budget to other items. Alternatively, you could choose to not buy espresso, cut your pulse rate in half, and spend the $18 on something else; this is another possible allocation of your budget. Because you clearly feel you are better off by consuming espresso, we say that you secure a consumer surplus from being able to purchase six espressos per day at $3 per cup. We now wish to see how this surplus, or net benefit, can be measured in dollar terms.

To obtain a measure of consumer surplus associated with espresso purchases, first ask yourself this question: What is the maximum amount you would be willing to pay for six cups per day from the campus coffeeshop during exam time? Your answer will be the **total benefit** (or total value) of the six cups per day. Your total cost is the $18 per day that you pay to the campus coffeeshop for the espressos. The difference between these two sums is the net benefit, or consumer surplus, you receive.

The demand curve provides another, and more direct, way to measure consumer surplus. To see how the demand curve relates to consumer surplus, consider how, in our hypothetical example, your demand curve for espresso from the campus coffeeshop is actually generated. To simplify the analysis, let's initially assume that espressos are sold only in uniform unit-cups, and start with a price so high that you wouldn't buy any. We gradually lower the price until you purchase one cup per day—say, when the price reaches $8. Thus, the incremental value, the **marginal benefit**, to you of the first cup is $8; this price is the maximum amount you would pay for the first cup. Because you are willing to pay $8 for the first cup, the $8 reflects the value you place on the first cup; that is, it is a measurement, in dollar terms, of the benefit you derive from the espresso. Lowering the price further, suppose that we find that at a price of $7 you will purchase a second cup; that is, the marginal benefit of the second cup is $7. Consequently, the price at which a given unit will be purchased measures the marginal benefit of that unit to you.

Continuing this process, we can generate your entire daily demand curve for espresso at the campus coffeeshop. In our hypothetical example (where fractions of a cup cannot be purchased), your demand curve is the step-like curve *d* shown in Figure 4.8. The *area* of each of the tall rectangles measures the marginal benefit to you, the consumer, of a specific cup. For instance, the tallest rectangle has an area of $8 ($8 per cup multiplied by one cup, or $8). The marginal benefit of the first cup is $8; of the second, $7; of the third, $6; and so on. The *total benefit* of consuming a given quantity is the sum of the marginal benefits. If two cups are consumed, the total benefit is $15, because you would have been willing to pay as much as $8 for the first cup and $7 for the second. By determining the maximum amount you will pay, we can calculate the total benefit of the espresso to you, which is equal to the area under the demand curve up to the quantity purchased.

Now suppose, more realistically, that you can purchase each espresso cup at a price of $3. As a rational consumer, you purchase cups up to the point where the marginal benefit of a cup is just equal to the price. Now compare the total benefit from purchasing six cups at $3 per cup with the total cost:

$$\text{Total benefit} = \text{sum of marginal benefits}$$
$$= \$8 + \$7 + \$6 + \$5 + \$4 + \$3 = \$33.$$

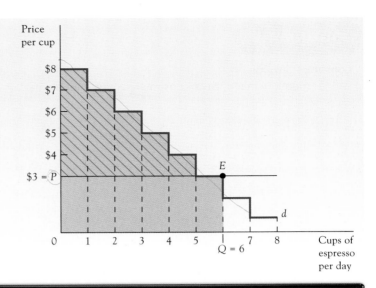

FIGURE 4.8

Consumer Surplus
The total benefit from purchasing six units at a price of $3 per unit is the sum of the six shaded rectangles, or $33. Since the six units involve a total cost of $18, the consumer surplus is $15 and is shown by the striped area.

$$\text{Total cost} = \text{sum of cost of each unit}$$
$$= \$3 \times 6 = \$18.$$

$$\text{Net benefit (consumer surplus)} = \text{total benefit} - \text{total cost}$$
$$= \$15.$$

The total daily benefit of six cups is $33 but you have paid only $18 for the espresso, so a consumer surplus, or a net gain of $15, accrues. Put simply, the consumer surplus is the difference between what you would have been willing to pay for the espresso and what you actually did.

Geometrically, we add the areas of the six rectangles reflecting the marginal benefits; then we subtract the total cost (price times quantity) represented by the area of the large rectangle, $PEQ0$, or $3 times six cups. The area that remains—the striped area in Figure 4.8 between the price line and the demand curve—is the geometric representation of consumer surplus. An alternative way to see that this area measures consumer surplus is to imagine purchasing the units of the good sequentially. The first cup is worth $8, but it costs only $3, so there is a net gain of $5 on that unit; this gain is the first striped rectangle above the price line. The second cup is also purchased for $3, but because you would have been willing to pay as much as $7 for the second cup, there is a net gain of $4 on that cup. (This gain is the second striped rectangle above the price line.) Adding up the excess of benefit over cost on each unit purchased, we have $5 + $4 + $3 + $2 + $1 + $0 = $15, which is shown by the area between the price line and the demand curve. Note that there is no net gain on the last unit purchased. Purchases are expanded up to the point where the marginal benefit of the last unit is exactly equal to the price. Previous units purchased are worth more than their price—which, of course, is why you receive a net gain.

Figure 4.9 shows the same situation, but now we assume that espresso is divisible into small units so that a smooth demand curve D can be drawn. We also allow for more than just a single consumer of espresso (thus the uppercase D is used to express demand). Indeed, at a price of P, we assume that, across all consumers, the total amount of espresso purchased equals Q. Consumer surplus is the striped triangular area TEP between the demand curve and the price line. It is analogous to the areas of the rectangles above the price line in Figure

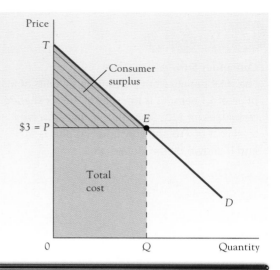

FIGURE 4.9

Consumer Surplus
With a smooth demand curve, consumer surplus equals area *TEP*.

4.8, but by letting the width of the rectangles become smaller and smaller (fractional units may be purchased), we now have a smooth line rather than discrete steps. In Figure 4.9, the total benefit from consuming Q units is *TEQ0*, the sum of the heights of the demand curve from 0 to Q. (Instead of a *rectangular area*, the maximum amount that consumers are willing to pay for a particular unit is represented by the *height of the demand curve at that unit* when the units employed to measure purchases become very small.) The total cost is *PEQ0*, and the difference, *TEP*, is the consumer surplus garnered by all consumers, as a group, of the espresso sold by the campus coffeeshop.

As you might imagine, consumer surplus has many uses. To managers of business firms, consumer surplus indicates the benefits obtained by buyers over and above the prices the buyers are charged. As we will see in a later chapter, many product pricing strategies reflect an effort by firms to capture more of the consumer surplus generated by their products and to convert such surplus into profit.

The concept of consumer surplus can also be used to identify the net benefit of a change in the price of a commodity or in its level of consumption. For example, Figure 4.10 shows the U.S. demand curve for sugar. Suppose that at a price of 25 cents per pound, U.S. buyers purchase Q pounds per year. The consumer surplus is given by area *TAP*. Now, due to trade

FIGURE 4.10

The Increase in Consumer Surplus with a Lower Price
At a price of 25 cents per pound, consumer surplus is *TAP*. At a price of 15 cents per pound, consumer surplus is *TEP′*. The increase in consumer surplus from the price reduction is thus the shaded area *PAEP′*: this area is a measure of the benefit to consumers of a reduction in the price from 25 to 15 cents.

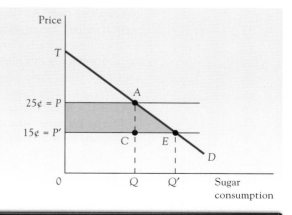

liberalization and the possibility of imports from overseas, suppose that the price falls to 15 cents per pound. How much better off are U.S. buyers because of the decrease in the price of sugar? There are two equivalent ways to arrive at the answer. One is to note that the consumer surplus will be *TEP'* at the lower price, which is greater than the initial consumer surplus, *TAP*, by the area *PAEP'*. Thus, the area *PAEP'* is the increase in consumer surplus, and it identifies the net benefit to U.S. buyers from the lower price.

A second way to reach the same answer is to imagine U.S. buyers adjusting to the lower price in two steps. First, total consumption is tentatively held fixed at *Q*. When the price falls, the same *Q* units can be purchased for 10 cents less per pound than before; this amount is equal to area *PACP'*, and it is part of the net benefit from the lower price. Second, the lower price also makes it advantageous for buyers to expand their purchases from *Q* to *Q'*. A second net benefit is associated with this expansion because the marginal benefit of each of these pounds is greater than the per-pound price. For instance, the first pound of sugar beyond *Q* pounds has a marginal benefit of just slightly under 25 cents, but it can be purchased for 15 cents thanks to trade liberalization—a net benefit of about 10 cents for that unit. The net benefit to buyers from expanding their sugar consumption from *Q* to *Q'* pounds is the area *AEC*. Combining the two areas of net benefit once again yields *PAEP'* as the net benefit from the lower price.

In later chapters we will see other examples of how the concept of consumer surplus can help us to evaluate the benefits and costs of various economic phenomena.

APPLICATION 4.5   THE CONSUMER SURPLUS ASSOCIATED WITH FREE TV

Until the advent of cable, television was not sold directly to viewers. The price of viewing broadcast programming was zero (apart from the opportunity cost of the viewer's time and the electricity necessary to power the set) for a household with a television and clear reception of the signal. Most of the costs of operating over-the-air networks and stations were, and still are, covered by sales of broadcast time to advertisers.

In the heyday of free television, viewing options were limited but the consumer surplus accruing to viewers was not. In 1968, for example, the average U.S. household had access to three network stations and one independent station. The estimated annual consumer surplus garnered by viewers was $32 billion ($158 billion in 2000 dollars) due to a price of zero for broadcast television.[8] The estimated consumer surplus vastly exceeded the $3.5 billion in advertising revenues earned by all television stations in 1968.

A prominent economic study published in 1973 indicated that an expansion in viewing options, in terms of the consumer surplus generated through such an expansion, would be highly valued. According to the study, a fourth network would add $4.2 billion in consumer surplus as of 1968 ($21 billion in 2000 dollars). Expansion, however, was precluded by regulations as well as by the fact that it was not technologically feasible to charge viewers for the additional programming.

The study's results suggest why cable television has grown so rapidly over the past 30 years. Namely, by figuring out a way to exclude nonpayers and charge subscribers for their service, cable operators have been able to capture some of the television consumer surplus from either existing or newly developed programming and convert it into cable company profits. Television owners have found subscribing to cable attractive because it allows them to expand their viewing options (experiments involving cable systems with up to 500 channels of programming have recently been undertaken), enhanced options that generate consumer surplus. Currently, 67 percent of U.S. households subscribe to cable, and the average subscribing household spends approximately $45 per month on cable. In comparison, the amount of advertising revenues earned by broadcast stations averages roughly $33 per month per household.

[8]This application is based on Roger G. Noll, Merton J. Peck, and John J. McGowan, *Economic Aspects of Television Regulation* (Washington, D.C.: Brookings Institution, 1973).

Consumer Surplus and Indifference Curves

Consumer surplus can also be represented in our indifference curve and budget line diagrams. Let's return to our original example in which a consumer purchases six cups of espresso at a price of $3 per cup. Figure 4.11 shows the optimal consumption at point W, the familiar tangency between an indifference curve and the budget line. Note that the consumer is on a higher indifference curve, U_2, when purchasing six cups of espresso than when buying no espresso at all. If no espresso is bought, the optimal point would be A on U_1. The net benefit, or consumer surplus, from purchasing six units is clearly shown by the consumer reaching a higher indifference curve at point W than at point A.

Thus, the consumer receives a net benefit from purchasing six units instead of none. Now let's try to measure the net benefit in dollar terms. Starting at point A, where no espresso is purchased, let's ask this question: What is the maximum amount of money the consumer would give up for six cups of espresso? Paying the *maximum* amount means the consumer will remain on U_1, the original indifference curve, and move down to point R, where six units are consumed. The distance AA_2 identifies the maximum amount the consumer would be willing to pay. Note that this amount is equal to the sum of the amounts that would be paid for each successive unit; that is, in moving from point A to point S, the consumer would pay $8 for the first unit, $7 for the second unit ($S$ to T), and so on. The sum of these amounts equals AA_2, or $33. The distance AA_2 measures the *total benefit* from consuming six units, and it corresponds to the area under the demand curve in a demand curve diagram.

Total benefit is AA_2. However, the consumer actually purchases six units at a cost of only AA_1, or $18. The total benefit, AA_2, exceeds total cost, AA_1, by the distance A_1A_2 (also equal to the distance WR). The difference between total benefit and total cost—in this case $15—is the consumer surplus from purchasing six cups of espresso at a price of $3 per cup. The consumer surplus can be shown either by the area between the demand curve and the price line or as a vertical distance between indifference curves. Both this diagram and Figure 4.8 therefore show the same thing but from different perspectives.

Note one qualification: Under certain conditions consumer surplus, as measured by the area under a demand curve, is exactly equal to the measure obtained in Figure 4.11. The certain conditions, however, require a special assumption: The income effect of price changes on consumption of the good in question must be zero. This assumption is reflected by the indifference curves being vertically parallel, having the same slope as you move up a vertical line. In Figure 4.11, for example, the slope of U_1 at point R is the same as the slope of U_2 at

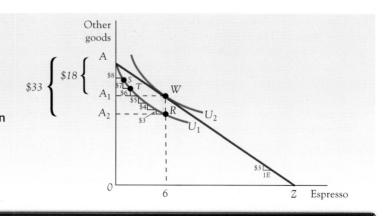

FIGURE 4.11

Consumer Surplus and Indifference Curves
The consumer surplus associated with being able to purchase espresso at $3 per cup is shown by the consumer being on U_2 rather than U_1. In dollars, this net gain, or surplus, is the distance *WR*.

point W. When this assumption does not hold, the area under the demand curve is only an approximation of the true measure of consumer surplus. The approximation is still generally close enough for most applications.[9]

4.6   PRICE ELASTICITY AND THE PRICE-CONSUMPTION CURVE

Price elasticity can be computed for any demand curve, whether it is the market demand curve or an individual consumer's curve. Admittedly, the price elasticity of market demand is generally of greatest interest, but that elasticity depends on the underlying elasticities of the demand curves of various consumers. In terms of our treatment of individual demand, we can now show that the slope of the individual's price-consumption curve provides important information about the elasticity of demand.

Figure 4.12 shows four hypothetical price-consumption curves. In Figure 4.12a, the curve slopes downward. This means that the price elasticity exceeds unity; that is, the consumer's demand curve will be elastic if plotted in a price–quantity diagram. A downward-sloping price-consumption curve shows that the consumer's total expenditure on college education rises when the price of such education falls, which, by definition, is an elastic demand. (When demand is elastic, the percentage change in quantity associated with a price change is larger, in absolute value terms, than the percentage change in price. Total expenditure, or price times quantity, thus moves in the same direction as quantity and in the opposite direction from price anytime the price is altered.) Recall that the distance AA_1 shows total expenditure on college education when the price of college education is given by the slope of the budget line AZ. (This is because $A0$ represents the consumer's income and A_10 indicates outlays on all other goods. Thus, AA_1 must represent the amount that is left to spend on college education.) When price falls, the budget line rotates to AZ', and at the new optimal point total expenditure on college education is now AA_2—an increase from the original level.

Figures 4.12b and 4.12c show the cases of unit elastic and inelastic demand, respectively. In Figure 4.12b, the price-consumption curve is a horizontal line, showing that total expenditure on college education remains unchanged at AA_1 when the price of college education is varied. This situation is, by definition, one of unit elastic demand. Figure 4.12c has an upward-sloping price-consumption curve. In this case a reduction in price reduces total expenditure on college education, by definition an inelastic demand. Expenditure is initially AA_1 but falls to AA_2 when the price is reduced. Therefore, if the price-consumption curve slopes downward, then the consumer's demand is elastic. If it is horizontal, demand is unit elastic. If it slopes upward, it is inelastic.

Finally, Figure 4.12d shows a U-shaped price-consumption curve. The elasticity of demand varies along this curve. It is elastic along the negatively-sloped AJ portion of the curve; becomes unit elastic at point J, where the slope of the curve is zero; and is inelastic along the upward-sloping portion of the curve to the right of point J. This type of price-consumption curve is probably typical. It begins at point A because at a high enough price no college education would be purchased. Thus, it must be negatively-sloped at relatively high prices (implying an elastic demand). On the other hand, there will generally be a finite quantity the consumer would consume even at a zero price, so the price-consumption curve must slope upward at relatively low prices (implying an inelastic demand). Therefore, a consumer's demand curve tends to be elastic at high prices and inelastic at low prices. This knowledge does not help us determine elasticity at a specific price because we don't know whether that specific price is "high" or "low" in this sense.

---

[9]Robert D. Willig, "Consumer Surplus Without Apology," *American Economic Review*, 65 (1976), pp. 589–597.

FIGURE 4.12

Price-Consumption Curves and the Elasticity of Demand

The slope of a consumer's price-consumption curve tells us whether demand is elastic, inelastic, or unit elastic. (a) When the price-consumption curve is negatively-sloped, demand is elastic. (b) When it is zero-sloped, demand is unit elastic. (c) When it is positively-sloped, demand is inelastic. (d) When it is U-shaped, demand is elastic at high prices and inelastic at low prices.

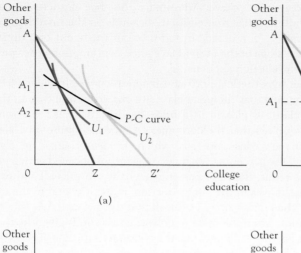

(a)

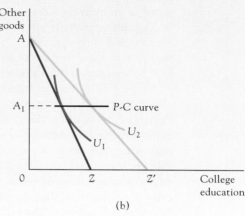

(b)

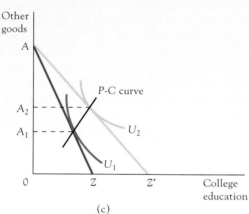

(c)

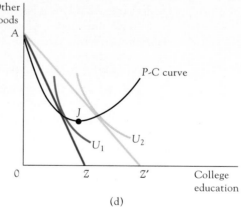

(d)

APPLICATION 4.6   THE P-C CURVE FOR A NON-PC GOOD

Cigarettes are near the top of the list when it comes to things that are not politically correct (PC). This makes the tobacco industry fair game in the minds of many legislators and attorneys. Indeed, juries have slapped tobacco companies with several multibillion punitive damages verdicts in recent years. How- ever, the effect on company profits has been less signif- icant than commonly assumed.[10] The adverse effect on profits has been mitigated in part because payment of

[10]"Yes, $145 Billion Deals Tobacco a Huge Blow, But Not a Killing One," *Wall Street Journal* (July 17, 2000), pp. A1 and A8.

the damages will be made over a long period of time. For instance, in 1997–1998 cigarette makers settled suits brought by the attorneys general of all 50 states by agreeing to pay the huge-sounding sum of $246 billion. For reasons that we will explain in a later chapter, however, the real cost of these damages is much smaller because the bill is due in installments over 25 years.

More importantly, the effect of the verdicts on profits has been lessened by the ability of companies to raise the extra revenue they need to pay the damages by raising prices. Because the demand for cigarettes is estimated to be inelastic (between 0.3 and 0.5), the relevant *P-C* curve is downward-sloping as in Figure 4.12a, and total expenditures made by consumers on cigarettes increase as the price of cigarettes is raised.

4.7 NETWORK EFFECTS

NETWORK EFFECTS
the extent to which an individual consumer's demand for a good is influenced by other individuals' purchases

BANDWAGON EFFECT
a positive network effect

SNOB EFFECT
a negative network effect

Until now we have assumed that a particular consumer's demand for a good is unrelated to the demand for the good by other consumers. However, this need not be the case. To the extent that an individual consumer's demand for a good is influenced by other individuals' purchases, there is a **network effect**. Network effects can be positive or negative. The positive case, or **bandwagon effect**, exists whenever the quantity of a good demanded by a particular consumer is greater the larger the number of other consumers purchasing the same good. The negative case, or **snob effect**, occurs when the quantity of a good demanded by a particular consumer is smaller the larger the number of other consumers purchasing the same good.

The Bandwagon Effect

Capitalizing on bandwagon effects is critical to the marketing of some goods. For example, clothing, toy, and food manufacturers realize that their ability to sell certain products to a particular consumer will be enhanced the greater the number of other consumers purchasing the same products. Tommy Hilfiger jeans, Barbie dolls, Pokémon cards, Nike running shoes, and Evian water are all products characterized by such positive network effects. In some cases, the positive network effects stem from consumers' desires to be in fashion and the utility that is derived from owning products that are popular with other consumers. In other cases, a bandwagon effect derives from the fact that the inherent value of a good to a consumer is enhanced by widespread usage of the good among other consumers. Take the case of America Online (AOL). The value of AOL to an individual consumer is increased when other consumers also use AOL if a larger customer base leads to more services, more chat rooms, and more e-mail contacts. The extent of a business school's alumni network similarly can increase the inherent value of attending the school to a particular applicant. This is so because, all other things being equal, a greater number of alums translates into more possible connections when the applicant searches for a job after graduating.

Figure 4.13 depicts the case of a bandwagon effect. If consumers believe that only 1,000 people own a good, the demand curve is $d_{1,000}$. If consumers believe that more people own the good and, consequently, the good is more desirable—either because it is in greater fashion or because its inherent value is increased—the demand curve is located farther to the right at any price: $d_{2,000}$ if 2,000 people are believed to own the good; $d_{3,000}$ if 3,000 people are believed to own the good; and so on.

With a bandwagon effect, the market demand curve, *D*, is more price elastic. To see why, suppose that consumers initially are willing to purchase 1,000 units if the price is $50. Now

FIGURE 4.13

Bandwagon Effect
A bandwagon effect leads to greater consumer purchases of a good the more other consumers are believed to desire the same good. The market demand curve, *D*, is more elastic because the bandwagon effect increases the response in quantity demanded to any change in price.

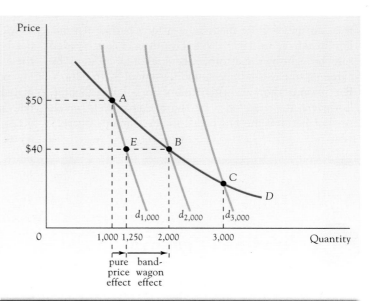

consider a decrease in price from $50 to $40. Without any bandwagon effect, the quantity demanded would increase to 1,250 along curve $d_{1,000}$. The bandwagon effect, however, results from more people purchasing the good at the lower price, and this, in turn, increases consumers' willingness to purchase the good for its greater fashion or inherent value.

In the case of Figure 4.13, 2,000 units are purchased at a price of $40, and the bandwagon effect accounts for the increase in quantity demanded from 1,250 to 2,000 in response to the decrease in price from $50 to $40. The market demand curve is derived by connecting the points on the curves $d_{1,000}$, $d_{2,000}$, and $d_{3,000}$ corresponding to the quantities 1,000, 2,000, and 3,000. A, B, and C are the only points consistent with the expected quantities associated with each of the curves. By contrast, point E, representing a quantity of 1,250 on the curve $d_{1,000}$, is inconsistent with consumers' beliefs that overall purchases total 1,000 units and thus cannot lie on the market demand curve.

The market demand curve is more elastic that the individual curves $d_{1,000}$, $d_{2,000}$, and $d_{3,000}$ because the bandwagon effect increases the response in quantity demanded to any change in price. In other words, the total response in quantity demanded to a change in price is the sum of the pure price effect and the bandwagon effect. Thus, it exceeds the pure price effect in magnitude.

The Snob Effect

The snob effect is the opposite of the bandwagon effect. It occurs when a consumer is less willing to purchase a good the more widespread its usage. A vintage Jaguar car, an original copy of the Declaration of Independence, a custom-made Versace evening gown, a Picasso painting, and a hand-crafted Piaget watch are all possible examples of goods associated with snob effects. A consumer's valuation of such goods may be greater the more exclusive are the goods, on account of the prestige and admiration derived by the consumer from the goods being selectively owned.

Figure 4.14 depicts a snob effect in the case of vintage Jaguar cars. The relevant demand curves are d_{10}, d_{20}, and d_{30} if consumers believe that only 10, 20, and 30 people, respectively, own a particular model. Note that the demand curve is farther to the right at any given price the more exclusive the ownership of the vintage Jaguar model is believed to be—d_{20} is to the right of d_{30} and d_{10} is to the right of d_{20}. This reflects a snob effect: The quantity of a good demanded by a particular individual falls the more widely owned the good is considered to be by other consumers.

The market demand curve is more inelastic in the case of goods characterized by a snob effect. To see why, note that the market demand curve connects the points on curves d_{10}, d_{20}, and d_{30} associated with the quantities 10, 20, and 30. F, G, and H are the only points consistent with the expected purchases associated with curves d_{10}, d_{20}, and d_{30}. Point I cannot lie on the market demand curve because a quantity of 5 is inconsistent with the expectation of 30 purchases associated with d_{30}.

An alternative, and perhaps clearer, manner of understanding why the market demand curve is more inelastic in the case of goods characterized by a snob effect is to examine the effect of a price increase, such as from $50,000 to $150,000 in Figure 4.14. The pure price effect of this increase would be to decrease consumption from 30 to 5 Jaguar vintage cars along curve d_{30}. However, the snob effect associated with the enhanced exclusivity resulting from the price increase would work to counteract the pure price effect and increase consumption from 5 to 20 units. On net, therefore, the increase in price of a particular model of Jaguar cars would lead to a decrease in the quantity demand from 30 to only 20 units and would be less than the decrease associated with the pure price effect. Because the snob effect runs counter to the pure price effect, the market demand curve is less price elastic—the cumulative impact of the pure price and snob effects on quantity demanded is less than the pure price effect.

FIGURE 4.14

Snob Effect
A snob effect leads to smaller consumer purchases of a good the more other consumers are believed to desire the same good. The market demand curve, D, is less elastic because the snob effect decreases the response to quantity demanded for any change in price.

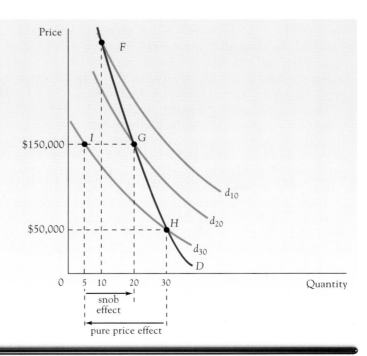

The diffusion of automated teller machines (ATMs) in the retail banking industry was significantly influenced by a bandwagon effect. The value of an ATM system to depositors depends on the number of locations included in a bank's network, so a bank with more branches stands to earn more from installing ATMs. A study by Garth Saloner and Andrea Shepard of Stanford supports this assertion.[11] During the 1970s, 55 percent of banks with more than 15 branches installed ATMs, as opposed to 16 percent of banks with only 2 branches.

[11]Garth Saloner and Andrea Shepard, "Adoption of Technologies With Network Effects," *Rand Journal of Economics*, 26 No. 3 (Autumn 1995), pp. 479–501.

Network effects are not all that new. For example, early in the last century, the diffusion of the telephone and automobile was aided by a bandwagon effect. In other words, the inherent value of a telephone or automobile to a particular consumer increased the more other consumers there were who had the same goods. More people could be called on the phone, and the spread of car ownership spurred the development of paved roads and gas stations. Positive network effects similarly spurred the development of railroads, the telegraph, airlines, radio, television, and postal systems.

There is no question, however, that network effects appear to be more prevalent in the New Economy.[12] The value of information goods at the core of the New Economy depends significantly on the extent of the networks for such goods. Consider the case of one of the most popular information goods over the past decade, Microsoft's Windows operating system. Because the value of using Windows increases the more other consumers there are who already use the same operating system, a positive network effect has been an important reason behind the success of Windows.

Of course, the same positive network effects that led to Windows' success also were an important factor in

[12]Carl Shapiro and Hal R. Varian, *Information Rules* (Boston: Harvard Business School Press, 1999).

the Department of Justice's antitrust case against Microsoft. The Justice Department alleged that a positive network effect allowed Microsoft to capture a dominant share of the personal computer operating system market. Its built-in customer base gave Microsoft a significant edge in the browser market for its Internet Explorer product over rival Netscape Navigator, said the court, because, at no extra charge to consumers, Microsoft packaged Internet Explorer with its Windows operating system.

We will explore the Microsoft antitrust case more fully in Chapter 11, but one point that deserves mention here is that positive network effects can be a two-edged sword for suppliers. Although a bandwagon effect enhances the possibility that a supplier will capture a dominant market share, it simultaneously limits the supplier's ability to exploit that position through a price increase. As we saw in Figure 4.13, the market demand curve is more price elastic when there are positive network effects present. In the case of Windows, this implies that Microsoft's ability to exploit, through a price increase, the dominant customer base that a bandwagon effect helped to build is limited by the same bandwagon effect. Should Microsoft attempt to raise Windows' price, customers would run toward alternative operating systems more quickly than they would without the bandwagon effect being present.

4.8   ## THE BASICS OF DEMAND ESTIMATION

Although indifference curves and budget lines together provide an appealing theoretical model of consumer choice, our ability to test the validity of the model and apply it to the real world rests critically on the extent to which we are able to empirically estimate individual consumers' or market demand curves. There are three methods generally relied upon to estimate demand. These are experimentation, surveys, and regression analysis. We briefly outline each of these methods as well as their accompanying pitfalls.

Experimentation

McDonald's will often run a controlled experiment to test how the demand for one of its fast-food items responds to a change in its price or to a change in the price of a complement. For example, McDonald's executives will select a number of franchises at which the price of french fries is lowered to determine the effect of such a change on Big Mac sandwich sales. Based on the results, the managers can estimate the sensitivity of Big Mac demand to the price of the complement, french fries, and thereby derive a relevant cross-price elasticity of demand.

While a valid mechanism for estimating demand, experimentation carries with it some limitations. Among these is that to run a true, controlled experiment, only one determinant, such as the price of french fries, should be changed at a time to determine its impact on Big Mac sales. Suppose that the price charged by Burger King for its products rises or the local income level falls at the same time that the McDonald's french fries price is altered. If this is the case, McDonald's managers will get a contaminated and unreliable measure of the impact of the price of their french fries on Big Mac sales.

Another limitation is one of generalizability. It may be incorrect to assume that the experimental results obtained in one sample of McDonald's franchises apply to all. The effect on Big Mac sales of a change in the price of french fries may be much different in Ohio than in Osaka, Japan. Experimental results from a sample of Ohio franchises thus may not generalize to those in Osaka.

Surveys

To anticipate the market reaction to a price increase, the Ford Motor Company regularly conducts consumer surveys—either by mail, telephone, or focus groups. A Californian will be contacted by telephone, for instance, and asked about the extent to which her likelihood of purchasing a Taurus automobile over the next 12 months will be diminished if the price is raised by $400.

As with experimentation, customer surveys can generate valuable information. They are not, however, foolproof. As with experimentation, one must be careful to choose a representative sample. A good example of what can happen if this rule is not heeded involves one of the first U.S. presidential polls—a survey taken prior to the 1936 election that predicted Republican Alf Landon would crush Democrat Franklin Delano Roosevelt. The exact opposite occurred. The poll surveyed citizens whose names had been taken from telephone directories and automobile registration rolls. Since the rich were more likely to have telephones and cars in 1936 and were also more likely to be Republican, the poll was based on a nonrepresentative sample of the voting population.

Furthermore, a survey's reliability is dependent on respondents telling the truth. For example, there is considerable evidence that polls will not accurately predict election results where political candidates and voters are of different ethnic backgrounds. While those surveyed say they will vote for a candidate whose ethnicity is different from their own, once in the privacy of the voting booth they are much more likely to actually pull the lever for a candidate similar to themselves.

Perhaps the classic case of misreporting by respondents involves the story of a researcher who surveyed Americans regarding their sex lives. According to the research, there was a significant difference between the number of sexual partners that males and females in the sample reported having over their lifetimes. Men reported an average of fourteen female sex partners. Women responded that they had four male sex partners. The samples, moreover, appeared to be representative.

While the difference in the averages across the genders may at first blush appear provocative, some further thought should convince you that, from a statistical perspective, there cannot be such a difference. The averages for both genders should be identical. After all, every time heterosexual intercourse occurs with a new partner it should raise both genders' averages equally—regardless of how the averages are distributed within each gender.

Which gender is not telling the truth? Probably both of them. In response to this particular question, men likely have a tendency to overstate whereas women may undercount. If this is the case, the true, common average falls in between.

Regression Analysis

Private and public decisionmakers regularly rely on existing data to statistically estimate demand. To see how this is done, suppose that you operate cable systems in 10 equal-sized communities (10,000 homes in each community). The systems are characterized by the data in Table 4.1. The quantity demanded of your basic tier service (Q) is represented by the number of basic tier subscribers in each community—where the basic tier features retransmitted local broadcast signals and other networks such as ESPN, MTV, and CNN. The other columns in Table 4.1 reflect the monthly basic tier price charged in each community (P), the monthly per capita income level of a community's residents (I), and the monthly price charged per additional pay tier ($PPAY$) such as HBO and Cinemax.

To determine whether it would be profitable to raise or lower basic tier prices, you would want to know how sensitive basic service demand is to its price, holding constant other determinants such as per capita income and the pay tier price. **Regression analysis**, also called **econometrics**, is a statistical method that allows you to estimate this sensitivity based on existing data. It begins by assuming that we can specify an equation for the underlying data and that the data do not "fit" the equation perfectly.

REGRESSION ANALYSIS (ECONOMETRICS)
a statistical method that allows one to estimate, among other things, the sensitivity of the quantity demanded of a good to determinants such as price and income

TABLE 4.1	CABLE DEMAND DATA			
System Number	Basic Tier Subscribers (Q)	Basic Tier Price (P)	Per Capita Income (I)	Pay Tier Price (PPAY)
1	3,300	$18	$3,900	$22
2	6,600	10	5,560	10
3	3,900	18	8,900	18
4	5,000	14	8,200	16
5	5,100	15	7,950	10
6	6,900	9	6,500	7
7	6,400	12	5,900	8
8	5,900	13	7,500	15
9	5,800	12	7,864	12
10	4,800	18	4,500	12
Average	5,370	$13.90	$6,677.40	$13

Take the case of the information in Table 4.1. Let us start by supposing that only P influences Q and that the demand for basic cable in a community is best described by the following linear relationship:

$$Q_i = a + bP_i + e_i; \qquad (1)$$

where the subscript i refers to the number of the system or the "observation" being considered. The variable Q that the equation is seeking to explain is called the dependent variable. Any variable such as P employed to explain the dependent variable is called an explanatory variable. The error term, e, is included in the equation to account for either mistakes in data collection; determinants of demand other than P that are inadvertently or, due to a lack of data, intentionally omitted from the relationship; or the possibility that the demand for basic cable is, to a certain extent, random and thus not predictable by economic models. The term a is the intercept of the linear equation—the number of subscribers a system will have if the basic price and the error term equal zero. And b, the coefficient on the basic tier price, indicates by how much the number of subscribers will change per dollar change in the basic tier price ($b = \Delta Q/\Delta P$).

Regression analysis usually employs the **ordinary least-squares** or **OLS** technique to estimate equations such as the one we have specified for the demand for basic cable. OLS estimates the "best fitting" intercept and coefficient for the specified relationship and the employed data. *Best fitting* means that the estimated equation will be "as close as possible" to the observed data points. The technical criterion for "as close as possible" involves the distances between the various data points and the estimated equation.

The specific manner in which OLS determines the equation that best fits the data is beyond the scope of this book.[13] Suffice it to say that the intercept and coefficient estimated by OLS (where estimated is signified with a "∧" as in $\hat{a}$ and $\hat{b}$) serves to minimize the distances between the data points and the estimated equation. The distances between the data points and the estimated equation represent the errors made by the estimated equation across the various data points.

Figure 4.15 graphically depicts how OLS regression works. In the simple demand relationship assumed by equation (1), the intercept and coefficient for the estimated equation that best fits the data across the ten systems turn out to be $\hat{a} = 9{,}970.1$ and $\hat{b} = -330.9$, respectively. The intercept estimate $\hat{a}$ implies that for the sample examined and the demand relationship assumed, if price were set equal to 0, the forecast number of basic subscribers, $\hat{Q}$, would be 9,970.1. The coefficient estimate $\hat{b}$ means that for every \$1 increase in the monthly basic tier price, the number of basic subscribers decreases by 330.9 ($\hat{b} = \Delta Q/\Delta P$). The slope of the estimated regression line is $\Delta P/\Delta Q$ and thus equals $1/\hat{b} = -0.003$.

The dots in Figure 4.15 represent the actual prices and quantities of the 10 systems in our sample. For the tenth system, for example, the price, P_{10}, is \$18 and the number of basic subscribers, Q_{10}, is 4,800. The OLS-estimated number of basic subscribers for the tenth system, $\hat{Q}_{10}$, is equal to the value obtained for Q when one plugs in the tenth system's price into the estimated regression line. Thus, $\hat{Q}_{10} = 9{,}970.1 - 330.9(18) = 4{,}013.9$. The error made by OLS in estimating demand for the tenth system, $\hat{e}_{10}$, is the difference between the actual and forecast number of basic subscribers and equals 786.1 ($Q_{10} - \hat{Q}_{10} = \hat{e}_{10} = 786.1$). The OLS regression has calculated $\hat{a}$ and $\hat{b}$ so as to minimize the sum of the squares of such errors across the ten systems in the sample. From the perspective of Figure 4.15, OLS positions the regression line, $\hat{a} + \hat{b}P_i$, so as to best fit the scatterplot of data points—where the "fit" reflects the horizontal distances of the observed data points from the estimated equation.

ORDINARY LEAST-SQUARES (OLS)
a technique for estimating the equation that "best fits" the data

---

[13]Most beginning econometrics texts explore the derivation of the intercept and coefficients through OLS in considerable detail. So long as you understand the intuition behind their calculation, that will suffice for the material in our book.

FIGURE 4.15

Ordinary Least-Squares Regression
Ordinary least-squares positions the regression line, $\hat{Q}_i = \hat{a} + \hat{b}P_i$, so as to "best fit" the sample data points.

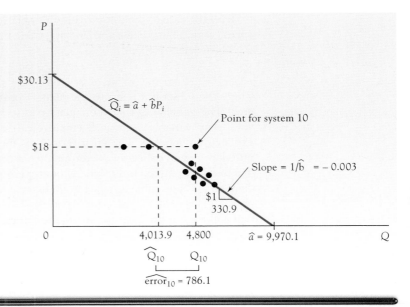

The estimated OLS equation provides valuable demand-side information. For instance, if we wanted to calculate the elasticity of demand for basic cable service at the average basic tier price and number of basic subscribers in our sample we would use the now-familiar formula:

$$\eta = (\Delta Q/\Delta P)(\overline{P}/\overline{Q});$$

where $\overline{P}$ and $\overline{Q}$ are the average basic tier price and number of subscribers, respectively, for the sample. The first part of the right-hand side of the elasticity formula, $\Delta Q/\Delta P$, is the rate at which the number of a system's subscribers changes per dollar change in the basic price. This is none other than the $\hat{b}$ or -330.9 estimated by OLS. Employing the average values for P and Q reported in Table 4.1, one obtains an elasticity of demand of 0.9. Since this is less than unity, demand for basic cable is inelastic when evaluated at the price and number of subscribers for the average system in the sample. This indicates that profit could be increased by raising the average basic price.

Suppose that we estimated a more extensive basic cable demand relationship, such as:

$$Q_i = a + bP_i + cI_i + dPPAY_i + e_i. \tag{2}$$

This more extensive model tries to control explicitly for more of the factors that might affect demand for basic cable. OLS regression proceeds in a fashion analogous to the one employed in estimating the simpler equation (1). OLS calculates the intercept $\hat{a}$ and coefficients $\hat{b}$, $\hat{c}$, and $\hat{d}$ so as to best fit the observed data—now incorporating information on income, I, and the price of pay tier service, $PPAY$, in the estimation process. In this more extensive model, the estimated coefficient $\hat{c}$, for example, measures the independent effect of a $1 increase in per capita income on the number of basic subscribers in a community. Its value indicates whether basic cable is a normal or an inferior good across the systems in the sample. The estimated coefficient $\hat{c}$ associated with the pay tier price variable, $PPAY$, likewise reflects the impact of a $1 increase in the pay tier price on the demand for basic cable, holding constant the basic tier price and the per capita income level. It tells us whether pay service is a complement or substitute for basic cable in our sample of systems.

Controlling explicitly for more variables can affect the estimate of the effect of basic price on the demand for basic service. When equation (2) is estimated, $\hat{a} = 9,931.0$, $\hat{b} = -230.0$, $\hat{c} = -0.01$, and $\hat{d} = -99.5$. By comparison, the estimated basic price coefficient, $\hat{b}$, was larger in magnitude when equation (1) was used. Use of equation (2) rather than equation (1) causes the estimated demand elasticity to fall as well. This is probably a truer estimate of the elasticity because it controls for additional causal factors.

We close this chapter by noting that while regression analysis is a powerful tool allowing one to employ existing data and estimate the effects of individual determinants on demand while holding constant other determinants' effects, it also has its difficulties. For one, the intercepts and coefficients estimated by OLS regression are only as good as the data and the models to which the analysis is applied. "Garbage in, garbage out," as the saying goes. If the sample data are nonrepresentative of the larger population or if the assumed demand relationship is incorrect (for example, linear when it should be nonlinear), unreliable estimates will result.

APPLICATION 4.9   DEMAND ESTIMATION: MCDONALD'S VERSUS BURGER KING

cDonald's makes extensive use of regression analysis in determining where to locate franchises. Sales are estimated for any possible location as a function of factors such as the prices that will be charged; demographics (including the surrounding community's income level, average family unit size, and ethnic composition); the availability of substitutes; traffic flows; and the side of the street on which the franchise will be located (sales are higher if a franchise is on the side of the street with the heaviest home-bound traffic at day's end).

By contrast, McDonald's rival Burger King has a smaller demand forecasting staff and often relies on a different, much simpler mechanism for determining franchise locations. Burger King waits for McDonald's to make the first move. After McDonald's statistically determines that a location will be profitable and begins operations on that site, Burger King opens up its own franchise nearby.

SUMMARY

- By rotating the budget line confronting a consumer, we can determine the market basket the consumer will select at different prices, while factors such as income, preferences, and the prices of other goods are held constant. The various price–quantity combinations identified in this way can be plotted as the consumer's demand curve.
- To determine whether a demand curve must have a negative slope, we separate the effect of a change in price on quantity demanded into two components, an income effect and a substitution effect.
- For a normal good, both income and substitution effects imply greater consumption at a lower price. Thus the demand curve for a normal good must slope downward.
- For an inferior good, the income and substitution effects of a price change operate in opposing directions. If

the income effect is larger, the demand curve will slope upward. However, both theoretical reasoning and empirical evidence suggest this case is quite rare.
- Consumer surplus is a measure of the net benefit a consumer receives from consuming a good. It is shown graphically by the area between the consumer's demand curve and the price line.
- Consumer surplus can also show the benefit or cost a consumer receives as a result of a change in the price of the good.
- Individual consumers' demand curves can be aggregated to obtain the market demand.
- An individual's price-consumption curve provides important information about the person's elasticity of demand.

• An individual consumer's purchases of a good may be influenced by other individuals' purchases through network effects.

• Three methods allow us to estimate individuals' or market demand curves: experimentation, surveys, and regression analysis or econometrics.

 ## REVIEW QUESTIONS AND PROBLEMS

Questions and problems marked with an asterisk have solutions given in Answers to Selected Problems at the back of the book (pages 572–573).

4.1. Explain how the indifference curve and budget line apparatus are used to derive a consumer's demand curve. For a demand curve, certain things are held constant. What are they, and how does this approach hold them constant?

4.2. If the per-unit price of college education rises and the prices of all other items fall, is it possible for the consumer to end up on the same indifference curve as before the price changes? If so, will the consumer be purchasing the same market basket? Support your answer with a diagram.

4.3. "A Giffen good must be an inferior good, but an inferior good need not be a Giffen good." Explain this statement fully, using the concepts of income and substitution effects.

*4.4. Assume that Joe would like to purchase 50 gallons of gasoline per month at the price of $1.50 per gallon. However, the $1.50 price is the result of a government price ceiling, so there is a shortage, and Joe can only get 25 gallons. Show what this situation looks like by using indifference curves and the budget line. Then, show that Joe will be willing to pay a price higher than $1.50 to get additional units of gasoline. (This result is the demand-side reason for the emergence of a black market.)

4.5. Delores has a different price-consumption curve associated with each possible income level. If two of these curves intersect, are Delores' preferences rational?

*4.6. If Edie's income rises by 50 percent and, simultaneously, the price of automobile maintenance increases by 50 percent, can we predict how Edie's consumption of automobile maintenance will be affected? Can we predict how, on average, Edie's consumption of other goods will be affected? Use the concepts of income and substitution effects to answer this question.

4.7. Assume that Dan's income-consumption curve for potatoes is a vertical line when potatoes are on the horizontal axis. Show that Dan's demand curve for potatoes must be downward-sloping.

4.8. Given the OLS estimates for the coefficient and intercept in the basic tier cable demand equation (1), calculate the point demand elasticity for system number 7.

4.9. Given the OLS estimates for the coefficients and intercept in the basic tier cable demand equation (2), calculate the following:

a. Income elasticity of demand for basic service evaluated at the average values for monthly per capita income and the number of basic subscribers across the sample of ten systems. Based on your calculation, is basic cable a normal or an inferior good?

b. Cross-price elasticity of demand for basic service with respect to the pay tier price evaluated at the average values for the pay tier price and the number of basic subscribers across the 10 systems in the sample. Based on your calculation, is pay tier service a substitute or a complement for basic service?

c. The income elasticity of demand for basic service evaluated at the income-quantity data for system number 3.

4.10. Suppose that Lorena consumes only three different goods: steak knives, butter knives, and butcher knives. If, according to Lorena's preferences, butter and butcher knives are inferior goods, must steak knives be a normal good? Explain your answer.

4.11. Suppose that there are only five consumers of a software game program. The demand curve for each of the individual consumers is identical. Will the market demand curve that is obtained by horizontally summing across the five individual consumers' demand curves be less or more price elastic at any price than the demand curve for any of the individual consumers?

4.12. Suppose that the Downtown Athletic Club increases its monthly membership charge from $150 to $200. Among the businesspeople belonging to the Club, would you expect that lower-level business managers would be more sensitive to the price increase than senior managers? Explain your answer using indifference curves.

4.13. Suppose that George is interested in only two goods, cigars and scotch. Employ the indifference curve/budget line apparatus to show a case where a decrease in the price of cigars leads to an increase in George's scotch consumption. Does this imply that cigars and scotch are complements to George? Explain your answer.

4.14. Repeat the preceding question but assume that a decrease in the price of cigars leads to a decrease in George's scotch consumption. Does this imply that scotch is an inferior good in George's case?

4.15. In the tax-plus-rebate example discussed in the text, suppose that the government adjusts the size of the rebate so that the consumer stays on her initial indifference curve (U_2 in Figure 4.4). Show the results in a diagram. Can the government achieve this result for all consumers? Why or why not?

*4.16. When the price of gasoline in Italy is $5 per gallon, Fabio consumes 1,000 gallons per year. The price rises to $5.50 and, to offset the harm to Fabio, the Italian government gives him a cash transfer of $500 a year. Will Fabio be better or worse off after the price rise plus transfer? What will happen to his gasoline consumption?

4.17. Left and right shoes are perfect complements for most people. If only the price of right shoes increased, what would be the substitution effect of such a price change on the typical consumer's consumption of right shoes (assume that the only two goods that the consumer cares about are right and left shoes)? What about the income effect?

4.18. If Clint's elasticity of demand for cigars is equal to zero, are cigars a normal or an inferior good for Clint? Explain.

4.19. Define consumer surplus, and explain how you would show it in a diagram containing a demand curve for some product. What would consumer surplus equal in Figure 4.8 if the demand was perfectly elastic at the market price of $3 per espresso cup?

4.20. Diamonds clearly satisfy less important needs than water, which is essential to life. Yet according to market prices, the essential commodity, water, is worth less than the less essential commodity, diamonds. Why would a vital commodity such as water sell for so much less than diamonds? Does this imply that there is something wrong with a market system that values diamonds more than water? Explain using demand and supply curves for water and diamonds. In your explanation, distinguish between the marginal and total benefit of the two commodities.

4.21. Noneconomists sometimes refer to medical care as "invaluable" or "priceless." Do you think these terms may be simply imprecise ways of saying that the consumer surplus associated with medical care is very large? Suppose that the consumer surplus is immense. Explain why this is irrelevant in deciding whether to provide more medical care. What is relevant?

4.22. "The price of water is a measure of water's marginal benefit to consumers." Is this statement true for all consumers of water? If a government price ceiling is set below the equilibrium price, will the price equal the marginal benefit of water?

4.23. Could the snob effect ever overpower the combined substitution and income effects associated with an increase in the price of a good? Explain why or why not.

4.24. Explain how a bandwagon effect might speed up the rate at which DVD players are adopted by consumers. Do likewise for the case of cable television subscriptions.

4.25. Suppose that the P-C curve associated with a pharmaceutical drug is downward-sloping. If the government underwrites a certain percentage of consumers' drug purchases, will the government outlays associated with such a program be greater the larger the percentage of the purchases underwritten? Explain why or why not. What if the P-C curve is upward-sloping?

CHAPTER 5

Using Consumer Choice Theory

Consumer choice theory can be used to analyze many interesting and important questions. For example the theory shows the impact of per-bag charges versus a fixed annual fee on the amount of trash generated by a community and recycling.

Chapter Outline

5.1 Excise Subsidies, Health Care, and Consumer Welfare
Application 5.1 Why Are Company Health Benefits Tax Exempt?
Using the Consumer Surplus Approach
Application 5.2 Burning Up Resources in Moscow
5.2 Public Schools and the Voucher Proposal
5.3 Paying for Garbage
Does Everyone Benefit?
Application 5.3 Trash Pricing and Recycling
5.4 The Consumer's Choice to Save or Borrow
A Change in Endowment
Application 5.4 The New Economy and a Negative U.S. Saving Rate
Changes in the Interest Rate
5.5 Investor Choice
Application 5.5 Entrepreneurs and their Risk-Return Preferences: 49ers and e-49ers
Investor Preferences Toward Risk
Application 5.6 Risk Aversion While Standing in Line
Minimizing Exposure to Risk

Learning Objectives

- Determine how an excise subsidy affects consumer welfare and why it results in a deadweight loss.
- Examine how the public provision of a certain quantity of a good such as education may lead to less consumption of the good.
- Analyze how a voucher program would affect the quantity of educational services chosen by parents for their children.
- Explore the impact of per-bag charges versus a fixed annual fee on the amount of trash generated by a community, recycling, and household welfare.
- Develop an intertemporal model that illuminates the consumer's choice to save or borrow and shows how changes in endowment and the interest rate affect that choice.
- Understand how the theory of consumer choice can explain what types of financial assets an individual intent on saving for the future should purchase, or invest in.

In the development of economic theory the most important use of consumer choice analysis is to justify the negative slope of demand curves. Once consumer choice theory provides us with a firm basis for believing the law of demand, many problems can be analyzed by using the demand curve, without having to look more deeply into consumer behavior. Some issues, though, are better analyzed through using the budget lines and indifference curves developed by consumer choice theory.

In this chapter we will see how we can apply consumer choice theory to several interesting and important questions. For example, we will see how providing "free" public schools may lead to less consumption of education, why higher interest rates can lead people to save less, and why lump-sum "medisave" accounts could make workers better off than the current excise subsidy policy toward health care. Although some of the applications in this chapter are important in themselves, they are included primarily to illustrate how the theory of consumer choice can be applied to analyze a wide variety of problems.

5.1   EXCISE SUBSIDIES, HEALTH CARE, AND CONSUMER WELFARE

EXCISE SUBSIDY
a form of subsidy in which the government pays part of the per-unit price of a good and allows consumers to purchase as many units as desired at the subsidized price

An **excise subsidy** is a form of subsidy in which the government pays part of the per-unit price of a good and allows the consumer to purchase as many units as desired at the subsidized price. For example, the government might pay half a consumer's housing costs, which effectively lowers the per-unit price of housing services by 50 percent. The most common examples of excise subsidies are found in the income tax code. A tax credit for child care expenses, for instance, reduces the taxpayer's tax liability when these items are purchased, and this lowers the price to the taxpayer in the same way as an outright excise subsidy. Health care provides another example. Business has been the largest underwriter of health care costs in the United States over the past several decades largely because the costs of providing health care to employees have been tax exempt—in effect, subsidized by the government. If company health benefits were not tax exempt, state and federal tax revenues would be at least $60 billion higher per year.

Let's look at an excise subsidy applied to the health care purchases of a particular consumer. Suppose that the consumer has a weekly income of $100, the market price of health care is $5 per unit, and the consumer will purchase 9 units of health care without any subsidy. The pre-subsidy optimal consumption point is shown in Figure 5.1 by the tangency between indifference curve U_1 and the budget line AZ. The consumer's optimal choice is

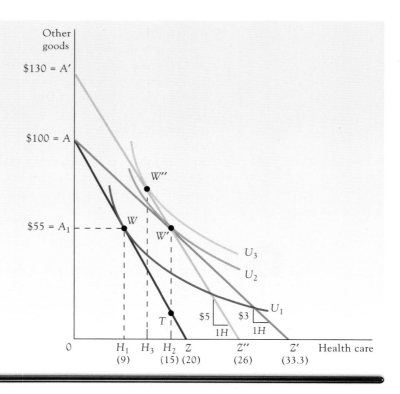

FIGURE 5.1

Excise Versus Lump-Sum Subsidy
A $2 per-unit excise subsidy to health care pivots out the budget line to AZ'; the optimal consumption point is W', with a total cost of $W'T$. An equal-cost, lump-sum subsidy produces the budget line $A'Z''$, and the consumer is better off at point W'' at no additional cost to the government.

point W, consuming 9 units of health care and $55 worth of other goods. Note that total outlays on other goods, which is normally measured by A_1, is also equal to the vertical distance WH_1; this will be helpful to keep in mind later.

To subsidize the individual's health care consumption, suppose that the government pays $2 of the $5 per-unit cost of health care. The subsidy effectively lowers the price of health care to the recipient from $5 to $3 and, as with any price reduction, causes the budget line to rotate. The new budget line is AZ'. Because health care is now less costly to the consumer, more will be consumed. Given the preferences shown in the diagram, the new optimal point is W', where U_2 is tangent to AZ', and health care consumption is 15 units. What is the total cost to the government of supplying this subsidy? Because the subsidy is $2 per unit, and the consumer purchases 15 units per week, the total cost is $30 per week. Figure 5.1 shows total government outlays on the subsidy as the vertical distance $W'T$, the distance between the subsidized and unsubsidized budget lines at the level of consumption chosen by the recipient. To see this, note that if the consumer had to pay the unsubsidized market price for health care (still shown by budget line AZ) and purchased 15 units, there would only be TH_2 dollars remaining to spend on other goods. With the subsidy, however, there are $W'H_2$ dollars left to spend on other goods, or $W'T$ dollars more than if the consumer had to pay the entire cost of 15 units of health care. Thus, the total cost to the subsidy recipient of consuming 15 units has fallen by $W'T$, or $30, because the government is absorbing that amount.

So far in our analysis of an excise subsidy, we haven't done anything that couldn't be accomplished just as easily by using the consumer's demand curve instead of indifference curves. We have shown that when a subsidy lowers the price of a good to the consumer, consumption of the good will increase. Now, however, consider some related issues that are better analyzed by using consumer choice theory. Suppose that instead of using an excise subsidy, the government gives the consumer the same amount of assistance, $30 per week, in the form of a cash grant to be spent any way the recipient wants. (Economists refer to a transfer of a fixed amount as a **lump-sum transfer**.[1]) How will this change in the nature of the subsidy affect the individual's consumption pattern, and will the consumer be better or worse off with the lump-sum grant? These questions are important policy questions, and we can answer them by using consumer choice theory.

LUMP-SUM TRANSFER

a form of subsidy in which the government gives the consumer a cash grant to be spent in any way the recipient wants

Substituting an unrestricted cash grant of $30 for the excise subsidy will shift the consumer's budget line in a different way. Since the lump-sum cash grant is the same as an increase in the recipient's income, it produces a parallel outward shift in the budget line, from AZ to $A'Z''$. *Note that $A'Z''$ passes through point W', the optimal market basket under the excise subsidy.* The reason is that both subsidies involve the same total cost to the government. As we saw, the total cost of the excise subsidy is $W'T$, or $30; with a cash grant of $30 the new budget line, $A'Z''$, lies exactly $30 (vertically) above AZ at all points, including point T. For example, $A'A$ equals $W'T$; both measure the size of the cash grant. Put differently, when the government uses a lump-sum cash grant instead of an excise subsidy, the consumer still has the option to purchase the same market basket chosen under the excise subsidy of the same total cost.

With the new budget line $A'Z''$ the consumer's preferred market basket is at point W''. The effects of substituting the cash transfer for the excise subsidy can easily be determined. *The consumer purchases less health care and more of other goods under the cash transfer and is better off* (that is, reaches a higher indifference curve). These results must be true: because U_2 is tangent to AZ' at W', it must intersect the $A'Z''$ budget line at point W', indicating that preferred positions lie to the northwest of W' on the $A'Z''$ line.

[1]An excise subsidy is not a lump-sum transfer because it is linked to consumption of a specific good and the amount of the subsidy varies with the amount of that good consumed.

These conclusions can be explained in a different way. Although both subsidies have an income effect that tends to expand health care consumption, only the excise subsidy has a substitution effect (because of the relatively lower price of health care) that further stimulates health care consumption. Confronted with a price of only $3 per unit with the excise subsidy, the recipient purchases health care up to the point where its marginal benefit (the MRS between health care and other goods) is only $3, at point W'. Thus, the fifteenth unit of health care purchased is worth only $3 to the recipient, but its true market cost is $5; it was purchased only because the government absorbed $2 of its cost. The recipient would rather have $5 worth of other goods instead of the fifteenth unit of health care. With a cash transfer, this option is available.

This analysis generally implies that a consumer will be better off if given a cash grant instead of an excise subsidy linked to the consumption of a particular good. This result explains why many economists favor converting welfare programs such as Medicaid, food stamps, and housing subsidies into outright cash grants. If given cash, the recipients could still afford to buy the same quantities of health care, food, and housing. And if they choose to purchase something else, the presumption is that they prefer the alternative to the subsidized good they were consuming.

Our analysis does not demonstrate that cash transfers are better; it only shows that the recipients will be better off, *according to their own preferences*, if they receive cash. Of course, a person can take a paternalistic view, assume "subsidy recipients don't know what's good for them," and favor overriding their preferences when providing them with a subsidy. Some people, for example, believe the poor wouldn't spend enough of the cash welfare payments on "necessities." Existing data, however, indicate that low-income families actually devote a larger proportion of their incomes to food, housing, and medical care than do upper-income families.

APPLICATION 5.1   WHY ARE COMPANY HEALTH BENEFITS TAX EXEMPT?

The origins of deductible corporate health care lie in World War II, when the government imposed wage and price controls while simultaneously printing more money to pay for the expenditures associated with fighting a two-front war. Shortages for various goods, including labor, developed. Limited by what they could offer in terms of wages, companies sought to attract workers by offering fringe benefits such as health care.

At first, employers did not report the value of the added fringe benefits to the Internal Revenue Service (IRS). It took some time for the IRS to catch on. By the time the agency issued regulations requiring firms to include the value of any medical benefits in reported employees' income, workers had become so accustomed to the tax-free status of company-sponsored medical care that they raised a hue and cry with their elected representatives. The outcry prompted Congress to pass legislation ensuring that employer-sponsored medical care would remain tax exempt, even when wage and price controls were lifted.

By not requiring taxpayers to report the health care benefits provided by their employers, the government in effect subsidizes health care. Individual taxpayers, that is, have an incentive to be paid by their employers through corporate-sponsored health care benefits (that are tax-free) versus wages (that are subject to personal income taxes).

Economists have proposed retaining the tax-exempt status of health care while lifting the requirement that employees spend all of the tax-free fringe benefits solely on health care. According to this proposal, workers and their employers could agree on a specified amount above actual wages to be allocated to employees' "medisave" accounts. This lump-sum amount would be at the complete discretion of employees. It could be accumulated over time and under specified conditions be withdrawn for other, nonmedical purposes. As shown by the analysis in Figure 5.1, lump-sum medisave accounts that could be allocated to purposes other than health care would make workers better off than the current excise subsidy policy.

Using the Consumer Surplus Approach

The same analysis can be conducted from a different perspective using the concept of consumer surplus. Figure 5.2 illustrates this. The individual consumer's demand curve is shown as d, and he or she is initially purchasing H_1 units of health care at the market price of \$5. When the government introduces the excise subsidy the price becomes \$3, and the consumer now purchases H_2 units at the lower price. As we explained in Chapter 4, the benefit to the consumer from the lower price can be shown in the graph as area $PEBP'$. Now consider the cost to the government of providing this benefit. It is shown as area $PCBP'$, or the \$2 subsidy per unit (PP') times the quantity purchased with the subsidy in place (H_2, or 15 units). It is clear that the cost to the government exceeds the benefit to the consumer by triangular area ECB. This area is the **deadweight loss** of the excise subsidy. It is a measure of the loss in well-being that results from the use of the excise subsidy.

DEADWEIGHT LOSS
a measure of the loss in well-being resulting in this case from the use of an excise subsidy

Referring to area ECB as a deadweight loss does not mean that the consumer is worse off under the excise subsidy than with no subsidy at all. Obviously, the consumer benefits from the lower price; the benefit, in fact, is shown by area $PEBP'$. Instead, it means that the consumer could be better off by area ECB under an alternative subsidy of the same cost to the government. That is what we showed in Figure 5.1, with the consumer attaining a higher indifference curve when an equal-cost, lump-sum cash transfer is used instead of the excise subsidy. Indeed, the area ECB in Figure 5.2 is a measure of the monetary value to the consumer of being on U_3 rather than U_2 in Figure 5.1.

We can understand that area ECB constitutes a net loss in potential well-being in another way. The effect of the excise subsidy is to increase consumption from H_1 to H_2. How much are those additional units of health care worth to the consumer? That is shown in Figure 5.2 by the area EBH_2H_1. (Recall that the height of the demand curve is a measure of marginal benefit, so adding the marginal benefit of each additional unit from H_1 to H_2 yields area EBH_2H_1 as the combined value of the entire increase in consumption of health care stimulated by the excise subsidy.) In contrast, the cost of these additional units is equal to the market price of health care times the additional units consumed, or area ECH_2H_1. (This cost is not borne fully by the consumer under the excise subsidy, but that part not paid for by the consumer has to be paid for by someone—in this case, taxpayers in general.) We can now see that the additional units consumed as a result of the excise subsidy have a cost

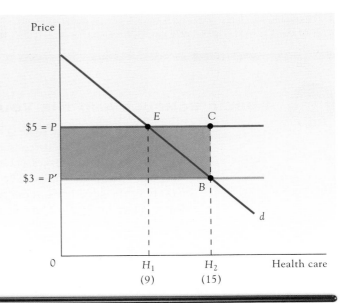

FIGURE 5.2

Excise Subsidy Using Consumer Surplus
The excise subsidy reduces the price from *P* to *P'*. The benefit to the consumer (the increase in consumer surplus) equals area *PEBP'*, but the cost to the government is area *PCBP'*. The excess of cost over benefit is the deadweight loss, area *ECB*.

(ECH_2H_1) that exceeds their benefit to the consumer (EBH_2H_1) by area ECB. By offering the consumer an artificially low price, the excise subsidy prompts him or her to purchase units that are worth less than their true cost.

A final connection between Figures 5.2 and 5.1 deserves mention. In Figure 5.2, the increase in consumer surplus produced by a $2 per-unit excise subsidy could be replicated with a lump-sum subsidy equal to $PEBP'$. The excise subsidy thus costs the government more, by an amount equal to area ECB, to produce the identical enhancement in consumer welfare. This offers another way to see why improving the consumer's lot from U_1 to U_2 in Figure 5.1 (as measured by $PEBP'$ in Figure 5.2), through a lump-sum subsidy, requires less government expenditure than an excise subsidy. Whereas the excise subsidy approach requires $30 in government expenditure (distance $A'A$ on the vertical axis of Figure 5.1) to move the consumer from U_1 to U_2, a lump-sum subsidy would require parallel shifting out the original budget line AZ by less than $30 on the vertical axis to move the consumer from U_1 to U_2. Do you see why?

APPLICATION 5.2   BURNING UP RESOURCES IN MOSCOW

Central heating in Moscow means something different than in the United States.[2] The city's 10 million residents are warmed by a few giant government-operated heating plants that pump steam into virtually every school, workplace, and apartment building. The heat is turned on at the end of October and remains on through early May. A few central administrators determine the overall heating level. The price of heating is significantly subsidized—as a result, the average Moscow apartment owner pays only $7 per month for heat.

[2]This application draws on "Central Heat Saps Moscow Economy," *Los Angeles Times* (March 23, 1997), pp. A1, A8, and A9.

As one might expect, Muscovites have little incentive to conserve energy under the existing system. Moscow's central heating system annually consumes more natural gas than does all of France (which has a population of roughly 60 million). If it becomes too hot, most residents of Moscow find it less expensive to open their windows and let the heat escape, even in the dead of winter, than to install thermostats.

A Russian deputy prime minister recently noted, "All of our salaries and pensions are burning up in the stoves of municipal heating stations." In the context of our consumer choice analysis, Moscow's residents would be better off if they were granted a cash grant equivalent to the existing excise subsidy for heating.

5.2   PUBLIC SCHOOLS AND THE VOUCHER PROPOSAL

Paying part of the price of some good, thereby reducing the price the consumer must pay, is not the only way to subsidize consumption. In fact, a more common form of subsidy is one in which the government makes a certain quantity of a good available at no cost, or perhaps at a cost below the market price. The essential characteristic of this type of subsidy is that the quantity of the good being subsidized is beyond the control of the recipient. Probably the most significant example is the public school system. Public schools make a certain quantity of educational services available to families at no direct cost;[3] if a larger quantity or a differ-

[3]Public schools are usually financed by property taxes, but the taxes paid typically bear no relationship to the amount of schooling consumed. Senior citizens with no children may pay the same taxes as a family with four school-age children.

ent type of schooling is desired, the only alternative is for families to use private schools and pay the market price (tuition), because the government subsidizes only public schools.

In some cases, this type of subsidy may actually reduce consumption of the subsidized good; that is, the provision of education through the public school system may decrease the amount of education consumed. This paradoxical outcome can occur when it is impossible, or very difficult, for the consumer to supplement the subsidized quantity of the good provided by the government—as is true with public schooling. To make this point clear, let's assume that we can measure the quantity of educational services by the expenditure per pupil and that the public school provides services at a cost of $3,000 per pupil. Now suppose that a family prefers to spend $3,500 per child on schooling (perhaps involving smaller class sizes or more computer training for students) and is willing to pay the $500 difference in cost for the greater quantity. This option, however, is not available at the public school; the government provides only a fixed quantity of services at the public school. Moreover, the family cannot utilize the services of the public school and, by paying $500 extra, obtain a $3,500 education for its child. The family must either accept the public school subsidy as is or forgo it altogether and seek out a private school that will deliver the $3,500 in educational services it desires. In such a "take it or leave it" situation, it would cost the family $3,500 to get $500 more in educational services. In this setting the family may decide to send the child to the public school; in the absence of the public school subsidy, however, it would have chosen to purchase a $3,500 education.

The way public schools can lead to reduced consumption of schooling is clarified further in Figure 5.3. The pre-subsidy budget line relating educational services and all other goods is

FIGURE 5.3

Fixed-Quantity Subsidy: Education
(a) With no subsidy, the family confronts budget line *AZ* and consumes S_1 units of schooling and A_1 units of all other goods. (b) If the family cannot augment the quantity of the subsidized good, the result is a budget line like *AA'RZ*. This situation can actually lead to lower consumption of the subsidized good than would occur with no subsidy at all. The optimal consumption point with the subsidy is *A'* with S_2 units of schooling, less than the S_1 units that would be purchased without the subsidy.

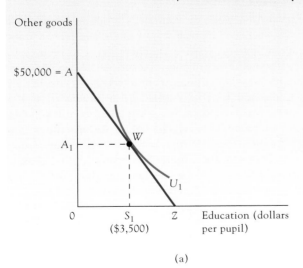

(a)

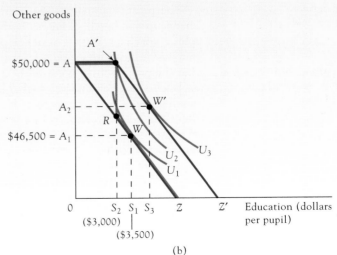

(b)

AZ. In drawing this budget line, we assume that alternative quantities of educational services are available at private schools. In the absence of any public school subsidy the family will choose to consume S_1 of educational services (the amount referred to earlier as \$3,500), and the total outlay on other goods is A_1 (\$46,500).

By providing a public school that children can attend at no cost, the government offers the lower-quantity educational services of S_2 (the amount referred to earlier as \$3,000). As shown in Figure 5.3b, the budget line confronting the family becomes *AA'RZ*. The initial S_2 units of educational services (\$3,000, or the length of segment *AA'*) are available to the family at no cost. To consume more schooling than the subsidized quantity S_2, the family must forgo the public school subsidy and bear the entire cost of schooling along the *RZ* portion of the original budget line. If the family sends its child to the public school, it can consume S_2 of schooling, leaving vertical distance *A* (the family's entire disposable income of \$50,000) available to spend on other goods. However, to consume more than S_2 units of schooling—for example, S_2S_1 extra units (or \$500)—the family will have to give up AA_1 (\$3,500) in other goods. This is because to consume \$3,500 of educational services, the family must forgo the public school subsidy altogether and enroll its child at a private school at a cost of \$3,500. Thus, there is a very high marginal cost associated with consumption beyond S_2. In other words, S_2 units of educational services can be consumed with no sacrifice in income, but to consume a larger quantity, the family must pay the *total* (not the marginal) cost of the desired education. Thus, the budget line is drawn as *AA'RZ*.

Confronted with the *AA'RZ* budget line in Figure 5.3b, the family will choose to send its child to the public school and consume at point *A'*; this choice places the family on a higher indifference curve, U_2, which is preferable to consuming at point *W* on indifference curve U_1. Although the family is consuming S_1S_2 (\$500) less of educational services, there is a gain of AA_1 (\$3,500) in other goods, and the indifference curves show the net effect to be an improvement. This analysis illustrates how the provision of public schools can lead to a reduction in the amount of education received by some children. Keep in mind that this analysis has been conducted for a family with a high demand for educational services, as shown by its preference for a larger quantity of schooling than that provided by the public schools. Other families will be affected differently. For instance, a family that may have chosen a point along the *AR* portion of the *AZ* budget line in the absence of the public school will actually consume more education when the public school subsidy is available. Which type of outcome is more common is not known.

The preceding analysis also provides a framework to examine a proposal for a major change in public school financing that has attracted a great deal of interest in recent years, school vouchers. With a **voucher program**, parents receive vouchers that can be used to purchase education at any school they choose. The program operates as follows: Assume that the public school is currently spending \$3,000 per pupil. Parents receive a voucher for each school-age child; the voucher is redeemable for \$3,000 when spent on education. If a family decides to continue to send its child to the public school, it turns in the voucher there and nothing changes. In a voucher program, however, the family also has the option of taking the public school subsidy to a different school (either public or private) and using the voucher to pay for all or part of the cost of education there. For instance, to purchase a \$3,500 education at a private school, the family turns in the voucher there (and the private school receives \$3,000 from the government) and pays \$500 of its own money.

Figure 5.3b can also be used to illustrate some of the effects of a school voucher. With the voucher the budget line becomes *AA'Z'*. The family can continue to use the public school system, staying at point *A'*; note, however, that consuming less education is not possible because the voucher can be used only to purchase educational services. Alternatively, the family can use the voucher to help purchase a greater quantity of educational services along the *A'Z'* portion of the budget line. The exact outcome depends on the preferences of families

VOUCHER PROGRAM
a form of subsidy in which parents receive vouchers that can be used to purchase education at any school they choose

and will vary from one family to another. The preferences shown in the diagram depict a family who will move its child to a private school offering S_3 units of educational services and pay for it with the voucher plus AA_2 of its own income.

Thus, we expect the voucher program to lead some families to purchase a larger quantity of educational services for their children—or at any rate a type of education they view as superior to that offered in the public schools. These families will be better off, because they are on a higher indifference curve at point W'. Other families would choose to continue receiving the same educational services at the public school.

This is a good place to emphasize that an analysis using budget lines and indifference curves is incomplete in some cases, because it assumes that the supply side of the market adjusts passively to consumer demands, which is not always true. Here, at least two types of changes on the supply side of the market have been predicted to occur: one favorable to the voucher proposal, the other not. First, with the voucher program in place, public schools would be in direct competition among themselves, and with private schools, for students. Under the current system public schools do not have a strong incentive to improve educational services, because they are giving away what their competitors must sell. Increased competition could lead to a better quality of education at both public and private schools. On the other hand, the voucher program may lead to an education system that is more segregated by income, race, or religion. Parents with higher incomes, for example, might use their vouchers (as well as their financial resources) to purchase very expensive private educations for their children, reducing the resources of public schools and thereby lowering the quality of education for children who continue to attend public schools. Of course, lower-income families may also use the vouchers to purchase a better-quality education for their children than their neighborhood public schools can provide, because they have the option of using the voucher at any public school as well as at a private school. We will not try to evaluate these consequences here because our main purpose is to show how consumer choice theory can be used to analyze effects of various options on consumer behavior.

5.3   PAYING FOR GARBAGE

The Borough of Perkasie, a small Pennsylvania town, had a problem: throughout the 1980s its trash collection costs rose rapidly.[4] The local government devised an innovative solution to the problem by changing the way residents paid to have their trash picked up. Historically, Perkasie residents paid a fixed annual fee of $120 per residence for garbage collection, a system of payment typical of many U.S. communities. Under the new plan introduced in 1988, there is no annual fee but garbage is picked up only when it is placed in specially marked, black plastic bags. The bags are sold by the town at a price greater than their cost; for example, each large bag costs $1.50. The net revenue from sale of the bags (revenue less the cost of the bags to the town) is used to finance the town's trash collection services.

This change in the system of paying for garbage collection produced some dramatic effects in Perkasie. The amount of trash collected per person dropped nearly 50 percent, the average household spent about 30 percent less on garbage collection, and the town saved 40 percent on its garbage collection costs. Why did these changes occur? The answer lies in considering the incentives faced by households under the two payment systems. With a fixed annual fee, households faced an effective price of zero for the trash collection service: if a household doubled the amount of its trash, it bore no additional cost. In effect, the fixed fee gave no incentive to cut down on the amount of trash generated. By contrast,

---

[4]Timothy Tregarthen, "Garbage by the Bag: Perkasie Acts on Solid Waste," *The Margin* (September/October 1989), p. 17.

under the bag system, when more trash is generated, more bags have to be purchased and households bear a cost directly associated with generating more trash. Basically, switching to the bag system increased the price per unit households had to pay for trash collection services, and that increase gave them an incentive to cut down on the amount of trash they generated.

We can gain a better understanding of how Perkasie's new trash collection payment system affected households by applying the theory of consumer choice. In Figure 5.4, the amount of trash disposal "consumed" by a typical household is measured (in pounds) on the horizontal axis and its consumption of all other goods is measured vertically. The household's income is indicated by A'—the vertical height of the budget line when no trash disposal is consumed. Now consider the budget line under the original $120 annual fee system. Payment of the fee reduces the disposable income of the household to A ($A'A =$ $120). After paying that fee, the household could dispose of any amount of trash it wanted at no additional cost. Thus, the budget line becomes the horizontal line AZ, implying a zero price per unit (that is, the line has a zero slope) for trash disposal. Confronted with that budget line, the consumer's optimal point is W, where the indifference curve U_1 is tangent to AZ.

Before going further, we should explain the shape of U_1. Note that we have drawn it with the usual shape to the left of point W, but its slope at point W is zero and then the indifference curve becomes positively-sloped to the right of point W. Normally, only the downward-sloping portion of indifference curves is relevant. When consumption of a good (measured horizontally) becomes large enough, however, it can become so abundant that it is a nuisance—that is, an economic "bad." Then the indifference curve takes on a positive slope. When positive prices are paid for all goods we have to be concerned with only the downward-sloping portions of indifference curves, but in this case the household is confronted with a zero price. Thus, the household will expand consumption up to the point where the marginal benefit (MRS) of another unit of trash disposal is zero, equal to the marginal cost, as shown at point W.

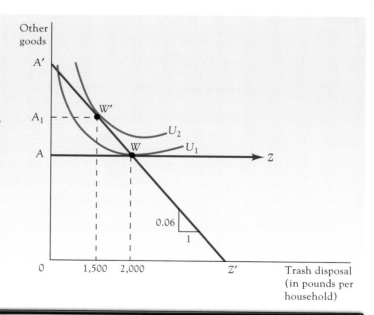

FIGURE 5.4

Consumer Choice: Garbage Disposal
Under the fixed annual fee, the consumer's optimal consumption point is W, where indifference curve U_1 is tangent to budget line AZ. When trash disposal is sold at a price per unit, the budget line becomes $A'Z'$, and the optimal consumption point becomes W'; thus, less trash is generated.

Now let's consider how the situation changes when the town introduces the bag system. In effect, having to purchase bags is analogous to having to pay a price per unit of trash disposal. Suppose that the price of trash disposal implicit in the price of the bags is $0.06 per pound, and that this is equal to the cost of the city's trash disposal service. Then the household will be confronted with the budget line $A'Z'$, which has a slope of $0.06. We have drawn this budget line through point W to reflect the assumption that the total cost to the household of the bag system will be the same as the annual fee if the household continues to generate the same amount of trash. (At $0.06 per pound, 2,000 pounds of trash will cost $120, or $A'A$.) Basically, we want to assume that this is an average household, so that the annual fee ($120) just covers the cost of trash disposal ($120) under the fee system. Under the bag system, of course, the payments made will also cover the city's cost of trash collection.

Thus, with the introduction of the bag system, the household's budget line shifts from AZ to $A'Z'$, reflecting an increase in the price per unit of trash disposal from zero to $0.06 per pound. Even though the household could continue disposing of 2,000 pounds of trash for $120, just as it was doing under the annual fee system, the graph makes it clear that the household will cut back on the amount of trash. The new optimal consumption point under the bag system is W', where the amount of trash disposal has been reduced to 1,500 pounds, and the total annual cost to the household has fallen to $A'A_1$ ($90). This analysis explains the dramatic effects observed in Perkasie in response to the bag system: when residents have to pay for each unit of trash generated, they have an incentive to cut down on the amount of trash they generate. But the graph also makes another point clear: the average household is likely to benefit from this change in the pricing arrangement. Note that the household attains a higher indifference curve under the bag system. This will necessarily be the case for the average household that was previously generating an amount of trash that cost the town $120 (the amount of the annual fee) to eliminate.

Does Everyone Benefit?

Why would anyone object to a system that leads to less garbage and also benefits people? The problem is that not everyone benefits when switching from a fixed annual fee to a per-bag pricing system. The average household—one that generates the average amount of trash—can be expected to benefit, but not all households are average.

To see how the effects differ when households differ, consider two households with the same income but with different amounts of trash. Suppose that under the initial fixed annual fee system household M generates 2,500 pounds of trash and household N generates 1,500 pounds of trash. Both households confront the AZ budget line in Figure 5.5, but M's optimal consumption point is W'_M and N's is W'_N. (Note that the two sets of indifference curves are for two different households. We assume they have the same income so both confront the same budget line.)

When the price-per-bag system is introduced, the budget line becomes $A'Z'$ for both households but affects them in different ways. Household N benefits from the change, moving to a new optimal consumption point W''_N on a higher indifference curve (U_2^N). In contrast, household M becomes worse off because of the change, moving to point W''_M on a lower indifference curve (U_1^M). In general, households that generate the average amount of trash (2,000 pounds) or less will benefit from changing to a price-per-bag arrangement, while households that generate more than the average amount are likely to be harmed. Under the annual fee system, households that generate little trash tend to pay more than the cost of disposing of their trash, and that excess implicitly subsidizes heavy users of the trash disposal service. The price-per-bag system makes each household pay the cost of its own trash disposal, thereby removing the implicit subsidy arrangement of the annual fee and harming those who were on balance being subsidized.

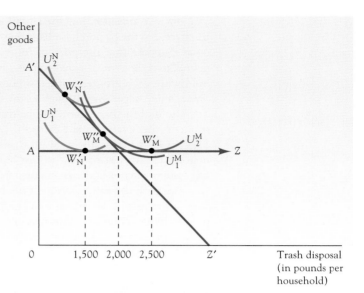

FIGURE 5.5

Trash Disposal: The Bag System
With the same income, both households confront the same initial budget line. Household M has trash disposal of 2,500 pounds and household N, 1,500 pounds. With the bag system, the common budget line becomes $A'Z'$, and this change benefits household N but harms household M.

APPLICATION 5.3   TRASH PRICING AND RECYCLING

There have been numerous news stories in recent years concerning the problem of garbage disposal in the United States. Despite the many admonitions to moderate their trashy habits, Americans generate nearly 4 pounds of garbage per day, up from 2.6 pounds per day in 1960. In part, this behavior results from the fact that most communities use systems like the fixed annual fee to finance trash collections, so residents don't have to pay more when they discard more trash. The Perkasie experience shows that some pricing policies can give people an incentive to generate less trash. Starting from close to the national average in terms of the trash produced on a per-citizen basis, Perkasie was able to cut its trash collections in half by switching to a per-bag pricing scheme.

Charging by the bag not only can reduce a municipality's garbage collection costs and more fairly allocate expenses across households based on the amount of garbage generated, but it also encourages recycling, a substitute for trash generation. For example, the largest and oldest per-container billing system in the United States is in Seattle. Since the billing program's inception in 1981, the percentage of trash recycled in Seattle has risen from 5 to 42 percent.

The principal complaint regarding per-bag billing is that it provides an incentive for illegal dumping. Some Seattle homeowners, for example, routinely leave their garbage in apartment house dumpsters. In response, the owners of such dumpsters have begun padlocking them.

5.4   THE CONSUMER'S CHOICE TO SAVE OR BORROW

Saving involves consuming less than one's current income, which makes it possible to consume more at a later date. Borrowing makes it possible to consume more than current income, but consumption in the future must fall below future income to repay the loan. A decision to save (or borrow) is therefore a decision to rearrange consumption between various time periods. By suitably adapting the theory of consumer choice, we can examine the factors that influence decisions to save or borrow.

Let's confront this topic in the simplest possible way. Imagine a short-lived individual, Ms. Cher Noble, whose lifetime spans two time periods, year 1 (this year) and year 2 (next year). Ms. Noble's earnings in year 1 (I_1) are $10,000, but they will fall to $2,200 in year 2 ($I_2$). The interest rate, r, at which she can borrow or lend is 10 percent per year. We assume there is no inflation in the general price level so that a dollar will purchase the same quantity of goods both years. (If there is inflation, the earnings in each year can simply be expressed in dollars of constant purchasing power, and the real rate of interest can be used instead of the nominal rate.)

This information allows us to plot Ms. Noble's budget line. In Figure 5.6, consumption in year 1 is measured on the vertical axis and consumption in year 2 (next year's consumption) on the horizontal axis. Any point in the diagram therefore represents a certain level of consumption in each year. The budget line indicates what combinations are available to the consumer. Point N, for example, identifies the consumption mix where the individual's entire earnings are spent in each year: a market basket containing $10,000 in consumption in year 1 (equal to year 1 earnings of $10,000) and $2,200 in consumption in year 2 (equal to year 2 earnings). Point N is sometimes called the **endowment point**, showing the consumption mix available to the individual if no saving or borrowing takes place. Alternatively, by saving or borrowing, the consumer can choose a different market basket.

ENDOWMENT POINT
the consumption mix available to the individual if no saving or borrowing takes place

To identify another point on the budget line, suppose that Ms. Noble's entire year 1 income of $10,000 is saved. In this case consumption in year 1 is zero, but in year 2 she could consume $13,200, equal to the sum saved the year before ($10,000), plus interest on that sum at a 10 percent rate ($1,000 in interest), plus earnings in year 2 ($2,200). Thus, point Z shows the horizontal intercept of the budget line; if consumption in year 1 is zero, Ms. Noble can consume $13,200 in year 2. The vertical intercept, A, shows the maximum possi-

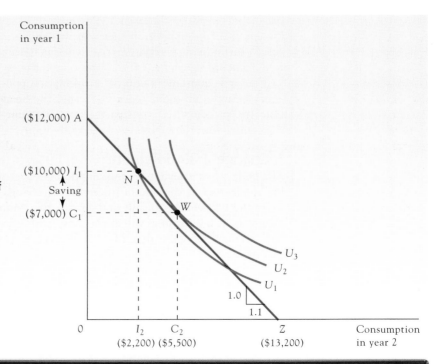

FIGURE 5.6

Consumer Choice Over Two Time Periods
With an interest rate, r, of 10 percent and with earnings of $10,000 in year 1 and $2,200 in year 2, the budget line relating consumption in the two years is AZ with a slope of $1/(1 + r)$. The optimal point is W, with saving of I_1C_1 in year 1. In year 2, consumption exceeds that year's income by I_2C_2, which is equal to the amount saved ($3,000) plus interest on this sum ($300).

ble consumption in year 1. This maximum is achieved by borrowing as much as possible, limited by how much can be repaid in year 2. That is, if $2,000 is borrowed, year 1 consumption can be $12,000 ($2,000 plus year 1 earnings). Ms. Noble can borrow $2,000 at a maximum because $2,000 plus 10 percent interest, or $2,200, must be repaid the next year. This amount equals total year 2 earnings with nothing left over for consumption. So the budget line's vertical intercept is $12,000.

Points A, N, and Z represent three points on the consumer's budget line. Connecting these points yields AZ as the entire budget line. If the consumer, Ms. Noble, chooses a point along the NZ portion of the line, she will be consuming less than earnings in year 1, or saving, and consuming more than earnings in year 2 (consuming the previous year's saving plus interest). Along the AN portion of the budget line, Ms. Noble is borrowing in year 1 and repaying the loan in year 2.

Notice how the slope of this budget line relates to the interest rate. In fact, the slope is equal to $1/(1 + r)$, where r is the interest rate. Thus, if Ms. Noble reduces consumption by $1.00 in year 1 (saves $1.00), she can increase consumption in year 2 by $1.00 plus the interest of $0.10, or by $1.10. With an interest rate of 10 percent the slope is equal to $1/(1 + 0.10)$, or 0.91 (rounded). This result tells us that the present cost of $1.00 consumed in year 2 is $0.91 in year 1, since $0.91 saved today grows to $1.00 a year later at a 10 percent interest rate—or, conversely, to have $1.00 to spend in year 2, the consumer must save $0.91 in year 1.

Now let's bring Ms. Noble's preferences into the picture. Because consumption in both years is desirable (more is preferred to less), the indifference curves have the usual shape. The slope of an indifference curve at any point is the marginal rate of substitution between consumption in year 1 and consumption in year 2, and it shows the willingness of Ms. Noble to reduce consumption in year 1 to have greater consumption in year 2.

For the indifference curves shown in Figure 5.6, the consumer's optimal choice is point W. Consumption in year 1 is $7,000, and consumption in year 2 is $5,500. Note that Ms. Noble is saving some of her year 1 earnings, as indicated by the choice to consume less than her income of $10,000 in year 1. The amount of saving in year 1 is the difference between income and consumption in that year, which is shown by the distance I_1C_1, or $3,000. In year 2, the individual's consumption is $3,300 greater than year 2 earnings; this sum is equal to the amount saved, $3,000, plus interest on the saving.

Thus, the consumer's optimal consumption point is once again characterized by a tangency between an indifference curve and the budget line. The only novel feature here is that the "commodities" consumed refer to consumption in different time periods, but that does not change the substance of the analysis.

A Change in Endowment

The budget line relevant for consumption choices over time depends on current and future income as well as the rate of interest. Any change in one or more of these variables will cause the budget line to shift and change the market basket chosen. Let's examine how a change in year 2 earnings will affect consumption and saving. Continuing with the example just discussed, suppose that Ms. Noble expects year 2's earnings to be zero rather than $2,200.

A change in earnings in either year moves the endowment point in the graph. In Figure 5.7, budget line AZ is reproduced from Figure 5.6; it shows the opportunities available when earnings are $10,000 in year 1 and $2,200 in year 2. When year 2 earnings fall to zero, the endowment point moves from N to I_1 on the vertical axis: if Ms. Noble's consumption equals earnings in each year, consumption will be $10,000 in year 1 and nothing in year 2. The new budget line is I_1Z', and it is parallel to AZ because the interest rate remains unchanged [both lines have a slope of $1/(1 + r)$].

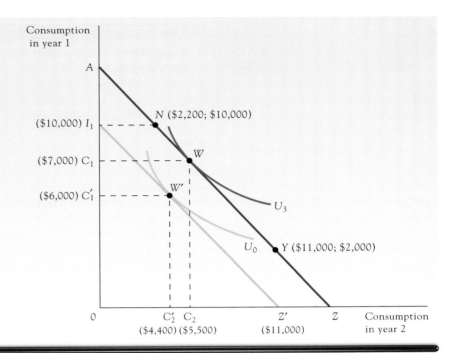

FIGURE 5.7

An Income Change and Intertemporal Choice

If year 2 income is zero instead of $2,200, the budget line shifts from *AZ* to I_1Z', a parallel shift. The result is an increase in saving in year 1, from I_1C_1 to I_1C_1'. Consumption in both years falls, assuming that consumption in each year is a normal good.

A reduction in future income will not alter the relative cost of future and present consumption, but it will influence behavior through its income effect. If consumption in each year is a normal good—which is almost certain to be true because consumption is a very broadly defined good—then the shift in the budget line will lead to reduced consumption in both years. Ms. Noble spreads the loss over both years, cutting back on consumption in year 1 and year 2. The new optimal consumption point, W', illustrates this situation, with consumption reduced from $7,000 to $6,000 in year 1 and from $5,500 to $4,400 in year 2.

This analysis implies that a reduction in expected future earnings causes saving in year 1 to increase. Recall that saving is the difference between consumption and income. Before the income loss, saving was I_1C_1, or $3,000; after the loss, saving increases to I_1C_1', or $4,000. Current saving, therefore, doesn't depend exclusively on current income (which is unchanged in this example); it is also affected by the expected level of future income.

So far we have been looking at a person who saves in year 1. Yet some people borrow in the present and repay the loan later. Under different circumstances the individual shown to be a saver in Figure 5.7 could become a borrower. For instance, suppose that instead of an income in year 1 of $10,000 and an income in year 2 of $2,200 (point *N*), earnings are $2,000 in year 1 and $11,000 in year 2 (point *Y*). *The budget line doesn't change*: only the endowment point changes, from *N* to *Y* on *AZ*. The optimal consumption point remains at *W*, but to reach that position, the individual borrows $5,000 in year 1 and repays the loan plus interest in year 2.

This analysis shows how the pattern of earnings over time is likely to affect saving and borrowing decisions. A relatively high present income but sharply reduced future income (such as endowment point *N*) is typical of middle-aged persons approaching retirement, and we expect to see them save part of their current income. A low present income but a higher expected future income (such as endowment point *Y*) is typical of students and young workers, and it is not uncommon to see such persons acquiring debt and consuming above their present income.

APPLICATION 5.4   **THE NEW ECONOMY AND A NEGATIVE U.S. SAVING RATE**

In 1999, the U.S. saving rate became negative for the first time since 1933. That is, U.S. consumers were spending more in 1999 than they were earning. The negative saving rate appears to reflect how the average U.S. household's endowment point was altered by the rising stock market of the 1990s. The greater wealth associated with a rising stock market resulted in an outward shift of the typical household's intertemporal budget line, such as AZ in Figure 5.7. However, households devoted only a small portion of the wealth increase (on the order of 3 percent) to current spending.[5] The re-

maining portion of the wealth increase brought about by the New Economy appears to have been treated, in the context of a simplified two-period intertemporal model, as future income. The relevant endowment point, consequently, moved further down to the southeast along the shifted out budget line—closer to a point such as Y and further from point N in Figure 5.7. And a comparatively higher expected future income resulted in the optimal consumption point's involving borrowing (negative saving) relative to the new endowment point.

[5]James M. Poterba, "Stock Market Wealth and Consumption," *Journal of Economic Perspectives* 14, No. 2 (Spring 2000): pp. 99–118.

Changes in the Interest Rate

Will people save more at a higher interest rate? The answer to this question may not be the yes response commonly expected. Let's see why.

A higher interest rate changes the relative cost of present versus future consumption, which is reflected in a change in the slope of the budget line. If the interest rate rises from 10 to 20 percent, the slope of the budget line, $1/(1 + r)$, changes from $1/(1 + 0.1)$ to $1/(1 + 0.2)$, so the new budget line will have a slope of $1/1.2$, or 0.83. Reducing consumption by $1.00 in year 1 (saving $1.00) permits consumption of $1.20 more in year 2. Put somewhat differently, the present cost of consuming $1.00 in year 2 is $0.83 in year 1, because $0.83 will grow to $1.00 in one year at a 20 percent interest rate. Or, conversely, to have $1.00 to spend in year 2, the consumer need save only $0.83 now at the higher interest rate. Thus, a higher interest rate reduces the cost of future consumption in terms of the present sacrifice required.

Figure 5.8a shows the way the budget line changes. The initial budget line AZ once again reflects the 10 percent interest rate, and the endowment point is N. *When the interest rate rises to 20 percent, the budget line rotates about point* N *and becomes* A′Z′. Point N is also on the new budget line because the individual can still consume I_1 in year 1 and I_2 in year 2 if no borrowing or saving takes place. The slope of the budget line becomes flatter through point N because an increase in the interest rate from 10 to 20 percent increases the cost of present versus future consumption. At the higher interest rate, that is, increasing present consumption by $1.00 (through borrowing) now requires $1.20 to be paid back in year 2. And increasing future consumption by $1.00 (through saving) now requires only $0.83 to be banked in year 1.

Incorporating the indifference curves of the individual, we can determine the preferred market basket associated with the new budget line. For the indifference curves shown in Figure 5.8a, the initial optimal levels of consumption are C_1 and C_2, with I_1C_1 saving in year 1. When the interest rate rises to 20 percent, the new optimal point W′ involves consumption of $C_2′$ in year 2 and $C_1′$ in year 1. A lower consumption in year 1 means an increase in saving

FIGURE 5.8

A Change in Interest Rates and Intertemporal Choice

A change in the interest rate rotates the budget line at endowment point N. When the interest rate rises from 10 to 20 percent, the budget line rotates from AZ to A'Z'. Whether saving rises or falls depends on the magnitude of the income effect (encourages less saving provided that year 1 consumption is a normal good) relative to the substitution effect (encourages more saving). (a) If the substitution effect outweighs the income effect, saving rises with the interest rate increase. (b) If the income effect outweighs the substitution effect, saving falls with the interest rate increase.

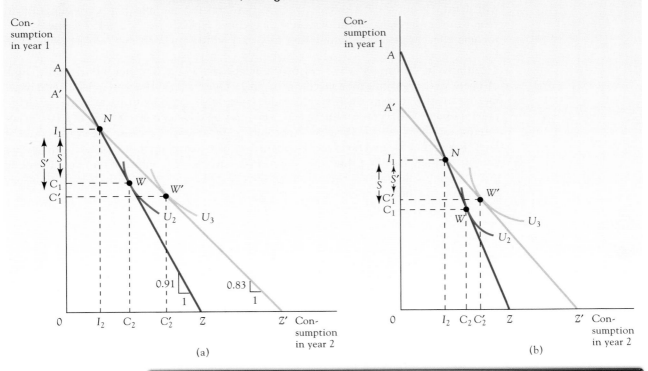

(a)

(b)

from I_1C_1 to I_1C_1'. Consequently, this individual will save more when the interest rate rises from 10 to 20 percent.

The case depicted in Figure 5.8a, however, is not the only possible outcome. For example, if the individual's indifference curves are as depicted in Figure 5.8b, an increase in the interest rate from 10 to 20 percent actually leads to less saving. With the new budget line A'Z', the optimal point is W', involving more consumption in both years than at W. (Note that a higher interest rate allows a saver to increase consumption in the present and still consume more in the future.) Because consumption increases in year 1, saving falls when the interest rate rises from 10 to 20 percent for an individual with indifference curves as shown in Figure 5.8b.

What factors determine whether saving rises or falls when the interest rate increases from 10 to 20 percent? Once again, they are the familiar income and substitution effects. (To avoid complicating the diagram, we do not show these effects explicitly in Figure 5.8 but, instead, give a verbal explanation.) The substitution effect associated with a higher interest rate results from the change in the relative cost of present versus future consumption. A higher interest rate reduces the cost of future consumption, which implies a substitution effect that favors future consumption at the expense of present consumption. So the substitution effect encourages future consumption instead of present consumption. In contrast, the income effect associated with a higher interest rate enriches the saver, who is able to attain a higher indifference curve. A higher real income enables the individual to consume more in both periods, so the income effect favors increased consumption in both periods if consumption in each period is a normal good.

Because both the substitution and income effects favor more consumption in year 2, it will definitely increase. However, substitution and income effects for consumption in year 1 are in opposing directions, so the outcome depends on their relative sizes. If the income effect is greater, consumption in year 1 will rise, which implies that saving will fall.

Intuitively, we can see why some people might save less at a higher interest rate. Think of a person who is saving for a specific good, like a cruise around the world. A higher interest rate means the consumer can purchase the cruise without committing as many dollars to present saving. If the cruise costs $6,000, a person would have to save $5,454 at a 10 percent interest rate but only $5,000 at a 20 percent interest rate to purchase the cruise one year later. For such a focused saver the income effect of a higher interest rate (favoring greater current consumption and thus less saving) may outweigh the substitution effect (favoring greater future consumption through more saving). Saving for such an individual thus may decrease as the interest rate rises.

5.5 INVESTOR CHOICE

The theory of consumer choice not only helps to illuminate the decision to save or borrow but also can be applied to explain what types of financial assets an individual intent on saving for the future should purchase, or invest in. That is, should such an individual invest in stocks, U.S. Treasury bills, gold, cattle futures, or the local bank? At first glance, investing in stocks would appear to be quite desirable given the returns generated historically by such financial assets. For example, a portfolio composed of stocks of the 500 largest publicly traded companies in the United States averaged an annual real rate of return of 9.8 percent between 1926 and 1998.[6] (The real rate of return is the nominal rate of return less the inflation rate.) The annual real rate of return on a portfolio composed of the smallest 20 percent of the companies listed on the New York Stock Exchange averaged 14.5 percent over the same time period. By contrast, three-month U.S. Treasury bills provided an average annual real rate of return of only 0.6 percent.

The historical data on annual rates of return also indicate that a dollar invested in a portfolio of small company stocks in 1926 would have grown, in real terms, to a whopping $613 by 1998.[7] A dollar invested in U.S. Treasury bills ("T-bills" for short) in 1926 would have grown to only $1.58 by 1998 after adjusting for inflation.

Given the historical data on the rates of return of various financial assets, a natural question arises. Namely, why would a rational investor ever choose to purchase T-bills as op-

[6]Stephen A. Ross, Randolph W. Westerfield, and Jeffrey Jaffe, *Fundamentals of Corporate Finance*, 5th ed. (Boston: Irwin McGraw-Hill, 1999).

[7]This growth is based on the actual annual real rates of return between 1926 and 1997 and assumes that all dividends are reinvested. The estimated growth would differ if the return on a portfolio of small company stocks had been a constant 14.5 percent per year as opposed to a nonconstant amount averaging out to 14.5 percent per year.

posed to small company stocks? It would seem logical to place all one's financial eggs in the asset basket offering the highest return.

The reason investors do not typically allocate all of their portfolios to the asset with the highest rate of return involves the risk associated with such an action. If higher rates of return are associated with greater risk and investors are averse to risk (that is, risk is a "bad"), a tradeoff exists between return and risk. While it may be true that *in retrospect* small company stocks display higher returns than T-bills, a person contemplating purchasing small company stocks does not know *beforehand* what next year's return will be.

Small company stocks may average a 14.5 percent annual real rate of return. The average, however, may be arrived at by a return of -14.5 percent in one year and 43.5 percent in another, with the dramatic and unpredictable gyrations averaging out to 14.5 percent over a two-year period. By contrast, T-bills have a lower average return but may be a very sure thing from period to period. There is very little chance, that is, that the U.S. government will default on its borrowing obligations by not paying the promised amount to purchasers of T-bills that mature (must be paid off) in three months. An average annual real rate of return on T-bills of 0.6 percent thus may be arrived at by a constant and more predictable return of 0.6 percent in year one and 0.6 percent in year two. Indeed, between 1926 and 1998, the volatility of returns has been significantly lower for T-bills than for small company stocks.

Figure 5.9 displays what an investor's indifference map looks like if higher expected returns are associated with greater volatility or risk, and risk is a bad in the eyes of the investor. As discussed in Chapter 3, the indifference curves are upward-sloping if the expected return on an asset is a good while the risk associated with the asset's return is a bad. Holding constant the expected return on an asset at $return_1$, a rise in the risk associated with the return on the asset, such as a move from point A to point B, places the risk-averse investor on a lower indifference curve (U_1 versus U_2). Furthermore, as the risk of an asset's return rises from $risk_1$ to $risk_2$, the expected return on the asset must rise from $return_1$ to $return_2$, as at point C, to compensate for the added risk and leave the investor's utility level unchanged at U_2. Greater levels of well-being are shown by indifference curves above and to the northwest: U_2 is preferred to U_1.

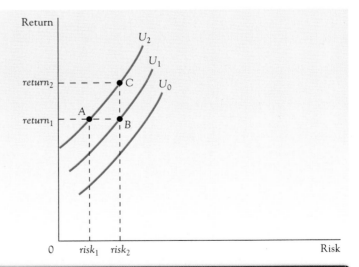

FIGURE 5.9

The Return-Risk Tradeoff
Since volatility or risk is a bad and expected return is a good, the investor's indifference curves are upward-sloping.

ENTREPRENEURS AND THEIR RISK-RETURN PREFERENCES: 49ERS AND E-49ERS

Studies indicate that small, entrepreneurial ventures were responsible for more than 90 percent of the net new jobs created in the United States in the last few decades.[8] Concurrently, interest in entrepreneurship has grown. Over 1,000 colleges and universities now offer courses in entrepreneurship, and a recent Gallup poll indicates that 7 out of 10 high school students in the United States want to start and own their own businesses in their adult years.

Entrepreneurs are characterized by their willingness to take risks and their ability to pursue and seize opportunity to create value, notwithstanding apparent re-

source constraints, through a new or existing company. Figure 5.10 depicts the observed differences in risk-return preferences for a representative entrepreneur and nonentrepreneur. The indifference curves are flatter in the case of the entrepreneur because the entrepreneur is willing to take on more risk for a given increase in the expected return (for example, from $return_1$ to $return_2$). That is, the difference between $risk_1^E$ and $risk_2^E$ (as the entrepreneur moves between points B and C along indifference curve U_1^E in Figure 5.10a) is greater than the difference between $risk_1^{NE}$ and $risk_2^{NE}$ (as the nonentrepreneur moves between points Y and Z along indifference curve U_1^{NE} in Figure 5.10b).

The willingness of entrepreneurs to forsake a secure established position for a relatively riskier new venture is nothing new. After all, this is what led so many individuals, called 49ers, to California to pursue the opportunities opened up by the discovery of gold at Sutter's Mills near Sacramento in 1848. Nearly 75 percent of the adults living in San Francisco left their established jobs

[8]This application is based on: Mickie P. Slaughter, "Entrepreneurship: Economic Impact and Public Policy Implications," Kauffman Center for Entrepreneurial Leadership, March 1996; Alberta Charney and Gary D. Libecap, "The Impact of Entrepreneurship Education: An Evaluation of the Berger Entrepreneurship Program at the University of Arizona, 1985–1999," Kauffman Center for Entrepreneurial Leadership (July 2000); and "San Francisco's E-49ers: Those Yearning to IPO," *Time* (September 27, 1999), p. 82.

FIGURE 5.10

Differences in Individuals' Risk-Return Preferences
An entrepreneur (a) has flatter indifference curves than a nonentrepreneur (b) because the entrepreneur is less risk averse.

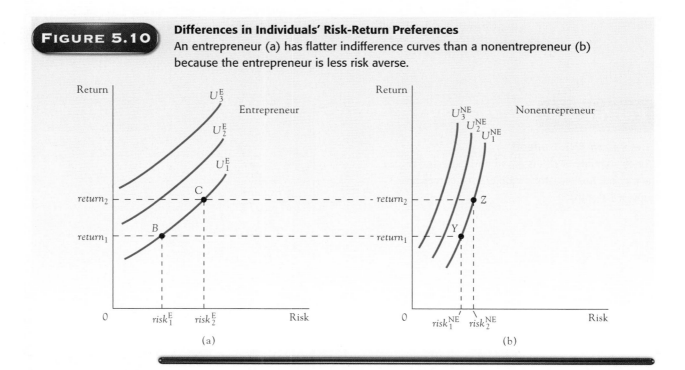

in 1849 to head for the gold fields near Sacramento. San Francisco's local paper, the *California Star*, was forced to shut down because the staff ran off to try to strike it rich.

A similar phenomenon is at work more recently with the opportunities opened up for "e-49ers" by the Internet. For example, as profiled recently by *Time*, four 1998 graduates of the Harvard Business School left their six-figure-salary starting jobs with prestigious, established organizations such as McKinsey, Porsche, and Bain in 1999 to launch their own firm, Simplexis.com, in the San Francisco Bay area. The venture's goal is to save $10 billion by 2005 for U.S. K–12 school districts, which annually spend nearly $100 billion on supplies. The partners intend to accomplish this by aggregating individual school district purchases, through the Internet, and thereby bringing some buying power to bear for the benefit of the districts (most school districts have historically bought their supplies on their own). The co-founders of Simplexis.com realize the risks associated with forsaking their Old Economy jobs. The expected return on the new venture, however, appears to more than justify the decision to go for the "new gold." And, at least as of the writing of this text, the venture's realized returns have matched the expected returns.

Investor Preferences Toward Risk

We have so far mentioned that, other things being equal, risk-averse investors prefer a sure thing—an asset promising the same return at lower volatility. As the volatility of an asset's return increases, risk-averse investors must be compensated with a greater expected return to remain equally well off (that is, to remain on the same indifference curve, as shown in Figure 5.9). In addition to looking at an indifference map, we can also examine what is meant by "risk aversion" by graphing the total utility curve of an investor as a function of the expected return per dollar invested in the stock of a company such as IBM.

As depicted in Figure 5.11a, the total utility curve has a positive but diminishing slope for risk-averse investors. To see why this is the case, let's investigate the properties of such a total utility curve. The height of the curve at each possible return indicates the utility of that return to the investor. For example, as drawn, the utility of a return of 2 percent equals 100 while the utility of a return of 8 percent equals 300.

Suppose that, per dollar invested, IBM stock will provide either a return of 2 or 8 percent and that the probability of either outcome is 0.5. The **expected return** on IBM stock can be designated as $E(r_i)$ where E is shorthand for "expected," r represents return, and the subscript i reflects the fact that the return can take on different possible values. $E(r_i)$ is the average return that the investor can anticipate receiving from IBM stock; it is equal to the summed value of each possible rate of return weighted by its probability $E(r_i) = 2(0.5) + 8(0.5) = 5$.

The **expected utility** from holding IBM stock, $E[U(r_i)]$, is the average utility the investor can anticipate receiving from among the different possible returns on IBM stock; it is equal to the summed value of each possible utility weighted by its probability. The expected utility from holding IBM stock in our example is consequently 200, $E[U(r_i)] = 100(0.5) + 300(0.5) = 200$.

Graphically, the expected utility from investing in IBM stock with an equally likely return of 2 and 8 percent can be determined by constructing a dashed chord, AZ, that connects the heights of the total utility curve at returns of 2 and 8 percent. The height of chord AZ at the expected return of IBM stock (5 percent in our example) indicates the average or expected utility from investing in IBM stock, $E[U(r_i)]$. In Figure 5.11a total utility rises from 100 to 300 between returns of 2 and 8 percent. Thus, to achieve a 200-unit increase in total utility ($300 - 100 = 200$) as the return increases by 6 percent ($8 - 2 = 6$), the average utility when we are at a return of 5 percent—halfway between a return of 2 and 8 percent—must be half the distance between 100 and 300 units of total utility. As a result, the expected utility of holding IBM stock is given by the height of chord AZ at the expected return of 5 percent: $E[U(r_i)] = 200$ in the case of Figure 5.11a.

Now compare the height of the risk-averse investor's total utility curve with the height of chord AZ at a return of 5 percent. The height of the total utility curve at 5 percent in Figure

EXPECTED RETURN the summed value of each possible rate of return weighted by its probability

EXPECTED UTILITY the summed value of each possible utility weighted by its probability

FIGURE 5.11

Investor Preferences Toward Risk

(a) A risk-averse investor's total utility curve has an upward, but diminishing slope. For every return between the equally likely returns of 2 and 8 percent, the height of the total utility curve exceeds the height of the expected utility chord, AZ. (b) A risk-neutral investor has a total utility curve that is an upward-sloping straight line. The total utility curve and the expected utility chord have the same height at every return between 2 and 8 percent. (c) A risk-loving investor's total utility curve has an upward and increasing slope. The height of the expected utility chord exceeds the height of the total utility curve over the relevant range of returns.

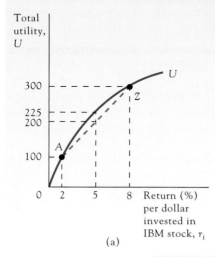

(a)

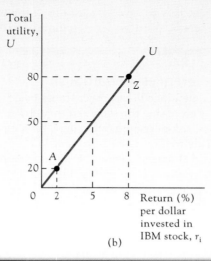

(b)

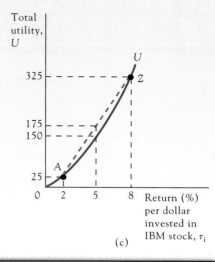

(c)

5.11a (225) indicates the utility the investor would derive were IBM stock to provide a sure return (with no variance or risk) of 5 percent per dollar invested. Because the height of the total utility curve (225) exceeds the height of the straight-line segment AZ (200) at a return of 5 percent, this shows that the risk-averse investor gets more utility from a sure return of 5 percent (and no variance) than from investing in IBM stock that generates the same average return of 5 percent but through varying between returns of 2 and 8 percent. In general, an individual is deemed to be **risk averse** if he or she prefers a certain return to an uncertain prospect generating the same expected return.

We can define risk aversion more formally by using some symbols for the heights of the total utility curve and the expected utility chord AZ. While the return on IBM's stock varies in our example, the average or expected return, $E(r_i)$, is 5 percent and is a fixed number. The height of the total utility curve at 5 percent thus can be written as $U[E(r_i)]$—the utility that would be generated by a sure return of 5 percent. Since a risk-averse investor prefers a sure return to an uncertain prospect generating the same expected return, this implies that the height of the total utility curve exceeds the height of the expected utility chord AZ at the expected return of the risky investment:

$$U[E(r_i)] > E[U(r_i)].$$

The preceding inequality will be true whenever an investor's total utility curve has a positive, but diminishing slope. Since the slope of the total utility curve is the marginal utility associated with various returns (see Chapter 3), risk aversion is present whenever the mar-

RISK AVERSE
a state of preferring a certain return to an uncertain prospect that generates the same expected return

ginal utility of payoffs to an individual declines as a function of the size of those payoffs. With diminishing marginal utility, an investor will prefer a sure payoff of 5 percent per dollar invested to the prospect of earning 8 percent (3 percent above the average) half of the time and earning 2 percent (3 percent below the average) the other half. The marginal utility associated with each unit increase in the return between 5 and 8 percent will not be as great as the marginal utility associated with each unit decrease in the return between 5 and 2 percent if diminishing marginal utility applies to an asset's payoffs.

Among investors making choices involving uncertain payoffs, aversion appears to be the most common attitude toward risk, especially when the size of the payoffs involved is significant. For example, consider the risk of losing one's home to a fire. Most families would rather pay a $1,000 annual premium for an insurance policy covering loss due to fire than to face the prospect that in any given year the probability of losing their home valued at $100,000 to fire is 0.01 while the probability of there being no fire is 0.99. Most families, that is, would prefer a sure loss of $1,000 to an insurance company in the form of a premium than to take the gamble of not having fire insurance, even though the latter gamble involves the same expected return, $E(r_i)$, of $-$1,000 per year, $E(r_i) = (-100,000)(0.01) + 0(0.99) = -1,000$.

Although risk aversion may be the most common attitude toward risk, it is not the only possible attitude. Indeed, there are two other views people can take toward risk. They can be neutral toward it or they can seek it out. These two alternatives are depicted by Figures 5.11b and 5.11c, respectively.

In the case of a risk-neutral investor (Figure 5.11b), the total utility curve is an upward-sloping straight line. For the same example involving IBM stock whose return is equally likely to be 2 or 8 percent, a risk-neutral investor will be indifferent between a sure return of 5 percent and investing in the risky IBM stock generating an expected return of 5 percent. Graphically, the height of the investor's total utility curve (50) equals the height of the expected utility chord, $A\overline{Z}$, at the expected return of 5 percent. In general, an individual who is **risk neutral** gets the same utility from a certain return, $U[E(r_i)]$, as from an uncertain prospect generating the same expected return, $E[U(r_i)]$. Formally, that is, the following equation holds for a risk-neutral investor:

$$U[E(r_i)] = E[U(r_i)].$$

For a risk-loving investor (Figure 5.11c), the total utility curve has an upward, but ever-increasing slope. In our IBM example, a risk-lover will prefer investing in the risky IBM stock generating an expected return of 5 percent over a sure return of 5 percent. Graphically, the height of the investor's total utility curve (150) is less than the height (175) of the expected utility chord, $A\overline{Z}$, at the expected return of 5 percent. In general, an individual who is **risk loving** gets less utility from a certain return, $U[E(r_i)]$, than from an uncertain prospect generating the same expected return, $E[U(r_i)]$. Formally, the following equation holds for a risk lover:

$$U[E(r_i)] < E[U(r_i)].$$

An example of risk-loving behavior involves the purchase of state lottery tickets even when one knows that the return on each dollar invested in such tickets is -50 percent. That is, the typical dollar invested in a state lottery has an expected payback of 50 cents. The return of -50 percent is much lower than the sure return of 0 percent one could obtain by keeping the money spent on lottery tickets in one's pockets instead.[9] While such risk-

RISK NEUTRAL
a state of deriving the same utility from a certain return as from an uncertain prospect generating the same expected return

RISK LOVING
a state of deriving less utility from a certain return than from an uncertain prospect generating the same expected return

[9]State lotteries make most of their money, and impose such a highly negative return on investors, by stretching out payments to lottery winners. For example, you may win $10 million in a state lottery drawing but that winning will be paid to you in equal installments over a period of 20 years. As we saw in Section 5.4, any dollars earned in the future are equal to less than their face value in terms of today's dollars. By contrast, the major casinos at Las Vegas pay gamblers an average return of -2 percent per dollar invested. That is, the typical dollar bet in a Las Vegas casino has an expected payoff of 98 cents. The less negative return in Las Vegas is due to the fact that casinos pay immediately when an "investor" gets lucky at a slot machine or blackjack table.

loving behavior certainly does occur, it tends to diminish as the gambling stakes increase. For example, more individuals at the casinos in Las Vegas play the $0.25 slot machines than the $100 blackjack tables.

APPLICATION 5.6   RISK AVERSION WHILE STANDING IN LINE

Many airline ticket counters, department of motor vehicles offices, federal customs checkpoints, banks, postal branches, college financial aid departments, and fast-food restaurants have a single line feeding to multiple clerks as opposed to separate lines for each clerk. This is the case even though a single-line system is unlikely to alter the average time a customer must spend waiting to see a clerk. After all, the line is not likely to affect either the total number of clerks or the number of customers waiting to see them.

A single line, however, does reduce the variance of a customer's waiting time since a customer is less likely to get into a "slow" or "fast" line. Holding constant the expected waiting time, the reduction in the variance of the waiting time will be appealing to customers if they are risk averse to spending time in lines. If a sure wait of 5 minutes is preferred to the prospect of a 0.5 probability

each of a 2-minute and an 8-minute wait, customers will be happier under the single-line system. According to operations researchers, at least part of the reason customers prefer less variance when waiting in line is their sense of social justice. Specifically, relative to an expected wait of 5 minutes, experiencing only a 2-minute wait because one is fortunate enough to get into a "fast" line appears to add less to total utility than experiencing an 8-minute wait in a "slow" line subtracts from total utility, since the longer wait brings with it the added aggravation of seeing more recent arrivals who get into a fast line receive service first.[10]

[10]Richard C. Larson, "Perspectives on Queues: Social Justice and the Psychology of Queuing," *Operations Research*, 35 No. 6 (November–December 1987), pp. 895–905.

Minimizing Exposure to Risk

Living in a world where risk abounds, how can risk-averse individuals minimize their exposure to it? One method already mentioned is **insurance**. By paying a premium in return for the promise that the insurer will provide compensation for losses due to an accident, illness, fire, and so on, one effectively exchanges a gamble for a sure return. And risk-averse individuals would prefer a sure loss of $1,000 per year in the form of a premium paid to an insurance company over being uninsured and confronting the gamble of a 0.01 probability they will suffer a $100,000 loss versus the 0.99 probability they will not.

INSURANCE
an arrangement by which the consumer pays a premium in return for the promise that the insurer will provide compensation for losses due to an accident, illness, fire, and so on

What is the maximum price that a risk-averse individual would be willing to pay for an insurance premium against a 0.01 probability of suffering a $100,000 loss? We can show that it is larger than $1,000, the expected value of the loss—$100,000(0.01) + $0(0.99) = $1,000. Figure 5.12 displays the total utility curve for an individual who owns a $100,000 home and faces the chance that the home will burn down with probability 0.01 in any given year. The expected utility from such a prospect is given by the height (U^*) of the expected utility chord, AZ, at an income of $99,000 (the expected payoff or income is $99,000 since with probability 0.99 there will be no fire and the individual's $100,000 home will be undamaged while with probability 0.01 the home will be reduced to ash and a value of $0). Note that the same utility of U^* would also be provided by a certain income of $98,300 since the height of the total utility curve equals U^* at an income of $98,300. Thus, the individual whose total utility curve is depicted in Figure 5.12 would be willing to pay up to $1,700 per year to insure against a fire loss. The homeowner is indifferent between (a) paying $1,700 ($PP''$) per year in exchange for a certain income of $98,300 (the insurance company will fully compensate the individual for the $100,000 loss in case of a fire), and (b) the prospect of remaining uninsured and facing an expected, but not certain, loss of $1,000 (P'P'') and an income of $99,000.

Will an insurance company be willing to supply coverage against fire loss to the homeowner for less than the maximum the homeowner is willing to pay for such coverage? The answer is in all likelihood yes. This is because insurance companies typically insure a large pool of individuals with respect to the same risk. While the probability that any one home will burn down in a given year may be subject to significant variability and therefore be difficult to predict, it is possible to predict much more precisely the total number of similarly situated homes in a large pool that will burn down in a given year. If the probability of any one house burning down is 0.01, for example, then an insurance company can be reasonably confident that, out of a pool of 10 million homes it insures, 100,000 will burn down in any given year. An apt analogy involves flipping coins. The deviation in the actual number of heads from the theoretically predicted probability will be much greater if a coin is flipped only once versus if the coin is flipped a large number of times.

By pooling a large enough number of similar fire risks, an insurance company will be able to predict reasonably well (that is, with very low variance) the total expected payments it will have to make on the fire insurance policies that it writes—$1,000 per home insured in our example. At the bare minimum, therefore, the insurance company should be willing to supply an insurance policy for $1,000 (plus any cost associated with administering the policy)—distance P'P'' in Figure 5.12. And since the maximum the risk-averse homeowner is willing to pay for such insurance (PP'') exceeds the minimum the insurance company needs to be paid (P'P''), an opportunity exists for mutually beneficial exchange.

In addition to insurance, another method of minimizing one's exposure to risk is through diversifying one's asset holdings. **Diversification** involves investing a given amount of resources in numerous independent projects instead of one single project. What may be an unacceptably large risk can thus be translated into more palatable small ones. The larger the number of independent projects, the more predictable the expected return on investment (as in our earlier coin-flipping example) and the lower the overall risk.

Organizational structures that promote the risk-spreading advantages attendant to diversification include partnerships and corporations whose stock is publicly traded. Suppose, for

DIVERSIFICATION
investing a given amount of resources in numerous independent projects instead of a single project in order to minimize exposure to risk.

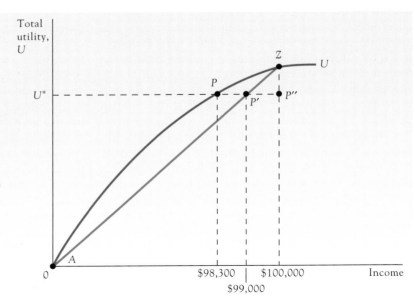

FIGURE 5.12

Pricing Insurance
In our example, a risk-averse homeowner is willing to pay up to $1,700 (PP'') per year to insure against a 0.01 probability of losing a $100,000 home to fire. By pooling a large enough number of equal risks, the minimum the insurance company will be willing to write an insurance policy for is $1,000 (P'P'') plus any costs associated with administering the policy.

example, that a promising start-up company requires $100,000 in funds to get off the ground but there is some probability that the venture will not succeed and that any invested funds will be lost. If you are risk-averse, you are likely to find investing in the venture more palatable if you can do it jointly with 10 other equal partners each chipping in $10,000 than if you have to underwrite the entire venture by yourself.

As with business partnerships, public trading of corporate stocks allows investors to diversify their asset portfolio by buying up a small number of shares of stock in a large number of companies. By not putting their financial eggs in a single asset basket, investors are able to mitigate their exposure to risk. This is because certain risks uniquely affect a single stock or a small group of stocks. And the investor's overall vulnerability to such unique risks will be lower the more diffuse a portfolio's holdings.

For example, take the case of the unexpected death in 1983 of Henry "Scoop" Jackson, a senator from the state of Washington with considerable clout on defense-spending issues. Jackson's death had no impact on most stocks but produced a decline in the price of Boeing Aircraft Company stock—Senator Jackson had been known as the "Senator from Boeing" for his lobbying efforts on behalf of the Washington-state-based firm.[11] Jackson's death also led to a rise in Lockheed Corporation's stock price since Lockheed was the largest defense manufacturer in Georgia, home to the senator expected to replace Jackson as ranking member of the Senate Armed Services Committee, Sam Nunn. An investor holding only Boeing *or* Lockheed stock at the time of Jackson's death would have confronted much greater risk (more volatility in asset returns) than would an investor with a more diversified portfolio. A well-diversified portfolio would include (a) many stocks that were not affected at all by Jackson's death, and (b) other stocks whose movement in the wake of Jackson's passing away would work to cancel each other out (such as Boeing and Lockheed), thereby lowering the volatility of the overall portfolio.

SUMMARY

- Consumer choice theory can be applied to a wide range of interesting and important policy questions.
- An excise subsidy is a form of subsidy in which the government pays part of the per-unit price of a good and allows the consumer to purchase as many units as desired at the subsidized price. Subsidies can also be made in the form of cash, as a lump-sum transfer. Consumer choice theory helps us discover that according to their own preferences, consumers will be better off if they receive cash.
- Public schools offer another common form of subsidy in which the government makes a certain quantity of a good available at no cost, or below the market price. Voucher programs allow parents to purchase education (with vouchers) at any school they choose. A variety of possible consequences of a school voucher program can be identified with the tools of consumer choice theory.

- When consumers directly bear the cost of such services as trash collection instead of paying a fixed annual fee, they have an incentive to cut down on the amount of the service they use, eliminating what was in effect a subsidy for heavy users of the service. Light users may pay more, however.
- A decision to save (or to borrow) is a decision to rearrange consumption between various time periods. Adaptations of consumer choice theory allow us to examine this decision and to see how it is affected by changes in earnings and in the interest rate.
- Consumer choice theory can also be applied to explain what types of financial assets an individual who is saving for the future should purchase—stocks, Treasury bills, gold, futures, or a savings account. Indifference curves demonstrate the tradeoffs between expected risk and return. Utility chords shed light on the way in which insurance operates to reduce individuals' risk.

[11]Brian E. Roberts, "A Dead Senator Tells No Lies: Seniority and the Distribution of Federal Benefits," *American Journal of Political Science*, 34 No. 1 (February 1990), pp. 31–58.

REVIEW QUESTIONS AND PROBLEMS

Questions and problems marked with an asterisk have solutions given in Answers to Selected Problems at the back of the book (page 573).

5.1. Tony currently goes to the dentist twice a year at $50 per visit. His employer, the University of Arizona, subsidizes Tony's purchases by paying half the cost of each dental visit *in excess of one visit per year.* (No subsidy is granted on the first visit.) Show how this affects Tony's budget line and his purchases of dental services. Identify in a diagram how much Tony spends on dental work and how much the University of Arizona spends in subsidizing his consumption.

*5.2. The government has $100 per month with which to subsidize waif-like supermodel Kate Moss's food consumption. It is considering two alternatives: giving Kate $100 worth of food stamps per month, or paying part of the price of food, thereby lowering the price to Kate. In the case of the excise subsidy, the price is lowered to the point where the total cost of the subsidy is $100 per month. Which type of subsidy will benefit Kate more? Under which type of subsidy will she consume more food?

5.3. With an excise tax of $0.20 per six-pack, Kristine purchases three six-packs of Diet Coke per day. If the government eliminates the excise tax and, instead, requires Kristine to pay $0.60 per day as a lump-sum tax (the daily tax liability is $0.60 regardless of how much Diet Coke Kristine consumes), how will Kristine's consumption pattern and welfare be affected?

5.4. How can the government reduce a consumer's consumption of schooling by providing schooling at no cost? Explain in words and show in a diagram.

5.5. We assumed in the text that families receive the public school subsidy at no direct cost. Yet families pay property (and other) taxes that are used to finance schools. Does this fact invalidate the analysis in the text?

5.6. At the "All You Can Eat" brunch buffet offered by Chez Paul's Cajun Restaurant, consumers pay a price of $15 and then can consume all they want. Show a consumer's optimal consumption point with a budget line and indifference curve. Explain the shape of both curves.

5.7. Based on the assumptions of Figure 5.5, is it possible for a person to benefit from shifting from the fixed annual fee to the price-per-unit system if that person is initially (under the annual fee arrangement) consuming more than 2,000 units of trash disposal? Justify your answer with a diagram.

5.8. In terms of a graph similar to Figure 5.2, explain why holiday gift-giving may generate a deadweight loss. Specifically, suppose that the recipients of gifts estimate that they would have been willing to pay only 75 percent of the estimated amount of money spent by the givers of the holiday gifts.

5.9. Draw the budget line for Beth, a consumer who must pay a higher interest rate to borrow than the interest rate she receives on her saving.

5.10. In a two-year period, Anna has earnings of $6 million this year (year 1) and earnings of $10 million next year (year 2). She can borrow or lend at an interest rate of 25 percent. Suppose that Anna decides to borrow $1 million in year 1. Show Anna's optimal consumption point in a diagram. Identify the amount borrowed in year 1, the amount repaid in year 2, consumption in year 1, and consumption in year 2.

*5.11. From the position described in the preceding question, Anna's earnings in year 1 fall to $4 million due to an unfavorable tax court ruling. How will this change in income affect the amount she borrows, her consumption in year 1, and her consumption in year 2? If her earnings fall by $2 million in year 1, will her year 1 consumption fall by the same amount? Explain your answer.

5.12. "A higher interest rate lowers the present cost of future consumption." "A higher interest rate raises the future cost of present consumption." Use an example to show that both statements are correct.

5.13. "For a person who saves in year 1, a higher interest rate will increase consumption in year 2 but may either increase or reduce the amount saved in year 1." Explain this statement, using the concepts of income and substitution effects. Use a diagram like Figure 5.8, and separate the income and substitution effects geometrically.

5.14. Why are the indifference curves depicted in Figure 5.10 flatter for the less risk-averse individual, the entrepreneur?

5.15. What would an indifference map (with expected *return* on the vertical axis and *risk* on the horizontal axis) look like for a risk-neutral investor? For a risk-loving investor?

5.16. How does the marginal utility of payoffs vary with the size of those payoffs for a risk-neutral investor?

5.17. Even though they enter graduate school at roughly the same age, law students typically own nicer cars than do Ph.D. students. Assuming that there is no difference across the two groups in terms of preferences and current incomes, explain this phenomenon. Rely on the intertemporal choice model developed in Section 5.4 for your explanation.

5.18. What is the maximum price that a risk-neutral individual would be willing to pay for an insurance premium against a 0.01 probability of suffering a $100,000 loss?

5.19. Based on historical data presented in this chapter on the annual real rates of return for a portfolio of stocks versus U.S. Treasury bills, would a risk-averse investor ever want to invest in stocks? Explain why or why not. Would a risk-neutral investor ever want to invest in Treasury bills? Explain.

5.20. Explain why the delays associated with surfing the Web are greater because users are charged a flat monthly fee to access the Web instead of per-unit use charges. Suppose that the per-unit use charge was set at a level such that the average Internet user ends up paying the same total amount if her consumption remains unchanged subsequent to the per-unit charge system being implemented. What will be the effect on total units of Internet usage if the per-unit charge system is adopted? Will the average user be better off? Explain. Will all users be better off? Explain.

5.21. Rocker Bruce Springsteen insured his vocal cords for $6 million. Dancer Fred Astaire insured his legs for $75,000 each. And, in 1999, singer and actress Jennifer Lopez reportedly took out a $1 billion insurance policy on her entire body. Why might stars such as these find it advantageous to take out these insurance policies? Why might insurance companies be willing to offer the policies?

CHAPTER 6

Exchange, Efficiency, and Prices

Voluntary exchange, or trade, is mutually beneficial to the parties
involved in the transaction.

Chapter Outline

6.1 Two-Person Exchange
Application 6.1 The Benefits of Exchange and the Growth of C2C and B2B E-Commerce
The Edgeworth Exchange Box Diagram   *The Edgeworth Exchange Box Diagram with Indifference Curves*
6.2 Efficiency in the Distribution of Goods
Efficiency and Equity
6.3 Competitive Equilibrium and Efficient Distribution
Application 6.2 Water Allocation in California
6.4 Price and Nonprice Rationing and Efficiency
Application 6.3 The Benefits and Costs of Rationing by Waiting

Learning Objectives

- Understand why voluntary exchange is mutually beneficial.
- Define what economists mean by efficiency in exchange and delineate the benefits associated with the promotion of such efficiency.
- Show how competitive markets promote efficient distributions of goods between consumers.
- Explore the extent to which price and nonprice mechanisms for rationing goods across consumers serve to promote efficiency.

In Chapters 3 through 5 we concentrated on the way a typical consumer reacts to changes in his or her budget line. Higher or lower prices or incomes, subsidies, and taxes produce generally predictable responses. The consequences of a consumer's choices for participants on the selling side of markets have so far been ignored. Of course, the budget line itself, indicating relative prices, reflects the willingness of others to trade with the consumer on specified terms, but now we will emphasize more explicitly that a consumer's market choices involve exchanges between the consumer and other people.

To investigate the essential two-sidedness of market transactions, we examine pure exchange. At the outset our analysis will focus on two consumers who start with specified quantities of two goods and engage in barter. This model may seem remote from real-world behavior, and to some extent, it is. But the intention here is to focus on the nature and consequences of voluntary exchanges between people, and the pure exchange model provides the simplest means possible.

Most economic activity occurs through a series of voluntary exchanges. U.S. consumers buy Sony products with some of their dollars. The dollars spent on Walkmans are eventually used by the various Sony stakeholders (workers, management, stockholders, and so on) in the pursuit of consumer goods of interest to them. Indirectly, therefore, Sony stakeholders exchange consumer goods for consumer goods. General Electric workers exchange their labor for money and then exchange money for various consumer goods, so indirectly they exchange labor for consumer goods. A model that permits us to see why voluntary exchanges occur and what their consequences are thus turns out to be quite useful.

ECONOMIC EFFICIENCY
with regard to exchange, economic efficiency represents a distribution of goods across consumers in which no one consumer can be made better off without hurting another consumer

The model presented in this chapter is useful for two fundamental reasons. First, it allows us to demonstrate one of the most important principles of economics: namely, that voluntary exchange, or trade, is mutually beneficial to the parties involved in the transaction. Although the principle that such exchange represents a "win–win" for the parties involved is often questioned, especially in the public policymaking arena, it is one of the most critical lessons to be learned from the study of economics.

Second, the model developed in this chapter allows us to introduce the concept of **economic efficiency**. A central tenet of economics, efficiency in exchange means that goods are distributed across consumers such that no one consumer can be made better off without hurting another consumer. We will show why pursuing such distributions of goods is a desirable objective, and how competitive markets promote efficiency in exchange.

6.1 TWO-PERSON EXCHANGE

People engage in exchanges, or trades, because they expect to benefit. When an exchange is voluntary, with parties in agreement on the terms of the trade, the strong presumption is that both benefit. Such a presumption follows from the fact that each party had the option of refusing to trade but instead chose to engage in the exchange. If Jean-Claude van Damme rents a tearjerker movie from a Blockbuster video store, his action must mean he prefers the movie rental to the money he exchanges for it. Also, the sale must mean Blockbuster prefers the money to keeping the movie in the store. Both parties benefit from the exchange.

The fundamental point can be stated simply: *Voluntary exchange is mutually beneficial.* The truth of this basic economic proposition may seem obvious, but it is widely doubted. For example, many people assume that the prosperity of successful businesspeople must have come at the expense of their customers or workers. Economic activity, however, is not like a sports contest in which, if there are winners, there must be losers. The voluntary exchanges through which economic activity is organized can generate win–win outcomes.

There are, of course, some qualifications to the basic proposition that voluntary exchange is mutually beneficial. First, it presupposes that fraud or trickery has not taken place. If van Damme pays for his video rental with a bad check, Blockbuster will be worse off. Second, the benefit achieved refers to the expectations of the parties at the time of the transaction. Van Damme may rent a tear-jerker but after watching it decide he would have been better off keeping the money. Nonetheless, at the time he rented the movie, he must have believed the opportunity to view it was worth more than the money.

Setting aside these qualifications, let's look at the nature of voluntary exchange in more detail. Suppose that there are only two consumers, Mr. Edge and Ms. Worth, and only two goods, ballet and football tickets. Assume that Edge and Worth begin each year with specific quantities of each good. Edge's initial market basket (endowment) is 35 ballet and 5 football tickets; Worth's initial market basket is 5 ballet and 45 football tickets. In the end Mr. Edge and Ms. Worth may choose not to consume their initial market baskets. Instead, they may decide to trade with one another and end up with different combinations of football and ballet tickets.

Under what conditions will Edge and Worth find it advantageous to trade? In this setting, whether trade occurs depends crucially on the relative importance of the two goods to each consumer. Let's suppose that Mr. Edge, given his initial basket, would be willing to give up five ballet tickets to obtain one more football ticket: his marginal rate of substitution is 5B/1F. Ms. Worth, on the other hand, would be willing to give up only one ballet ticket for one more football ticket: her marginal rate of substitution is 1B/1F. In this case the relative importance of the goods differs between Edge and Worth, as indicated by their different MRSs; thus, a mutually beneficial exchange can take place. Let's see how. (The numerical data of this example are summarized in Table 6.1 for convenience.)

TABLE 6.1	GAINS FROM EXCHANGE			
Consumer	Initial Market Basket	MRS$_{FB}$	Trade	New Market Basket After Trade
Mr. Edge	35B + 5F	5B/1F	−3B + 1F	32B + 6F
Ms. Worth	5B + 45F	1B/1F	+3B − 1F	8B + 44F

Given their initial holdings, Edge values football more highly than Worth does relative to ballet. He is willing to give up as many as five ballet tickets to obtain another football ticket. Worth, in contrast, is willing to give up one football ticket if she receives at least one ballet ticket in return. (Note that if Worth's MRS is 1B/1F, she will give up 1B for 1F, or, alternatively, 1F in return for 1B. For a small movement in either direction along the indifference curve, 1F trades for 1B without affecting her well-being.) Put differently, Edge would pay 5B to get 1F, while Worth would be willing to sell him 1F for 1B. There is room for a mutually beneficial trade. Suppose that Edge offers Worth three ballet tickets for one football ticket, and she accepts. Edge will be better off after the exchange because he would have been willing to pay as much as 5B for the football ticket, but he got it for 3B. Worth will also be better off because she would have sold the football ticket for as little as 1B but instead received 3B. Therefore, this exchange will leave both parties better off: they prefer their new market baskets to their initial holdings. (See Table 6.1.)

APPLICATION 6.1   THE BENEFITS OF EXCHANGE AND THE GROWTH OF C2C AND B2B E-COMMERCE

Testament to the proposition that voluntary exchange represents a win–win for participating parties is provided by the growth of consumer-to-consumer (C2C) and business-to-business (B2B) e-commerce.[1] The largest initial supplier of C2C services, eBay, was founded in 1995 by Pierre Omidyar, a 31-year-old software developer who wanted to help his fiancée trade Pez dispensers online. Through the Web-based community pioneered by eBay, buyers and sellers can socialize, discuss topics of common interest, and ultimately conduct business in an online trading environment. By 2000, eBay had more than 2 million registered users, had earned more than $400 million in total revenues, and featured more than 1,000 categories of goods including collectibles, antiques, sports memorabilia, Beanie Babies, jewelry, and books.

While eBay offers the marketplace, the consumers who connect through the marketplace do all the work.

When the auction is over, the high bidder and the seller contact each other, usually by e-mail, to finalize the purchase. eBay's earnings come from fees paid by sellers to post items and a commission that is tied to the sale price.

B2B promises to be at least as great an opportunity as C2C for online commerce. For example, while U.S. consumers spend $180 billion each year on collectibles at auctions, it is estimated that B2B transactions of all types will grow from $145 billion in 1999 to $7.3 trillion by 2004. A cut of, say, 0.25 percent in transaction fees would yield nearly $20 billion in annual revenue.

Of course, there are some challenges associated with ensuring that Internet-based exchange is mutually beneficial. In the C2C case, for example, a seller may misrepresent the quality of an item put up for auction. In an attempt to address such potential problems, eBay allows sellers and buyers to rate each other at the end of each transaction. eBay also offers transaction insurance and escrow arrangements and allows users, through a partnership with Equifax, to validate their identities and post their credit histories.

[1]This application is based on: "Why eBay is Flying," *Fortune*, December 7, 1998, pp. 255–256; "Riding the Internet's Latest Wave," *Money*, May 2000, pp. 42 and 44; and "The Powers Behind the Auctions," *New York Times*, August 20, 2000, Section 3, pp. 1 and 11.

The stock market has rewarded firms that promise to establish the deepest, most competitive Internet markets. For instance, CommerceOne, one of the early leaders in the B2B market, generated only $34 million in revenue in 1999 but had a market valuation of roughly $15 billion as of early 2000. Later in this chapter we will see why competitive markets promote the gains from exchange and economic efficiency. We will thereby see why firms that promise to develop the most competitive online markets have reaped the greatest rewards in terms of their own market valuations.

EDGEWORTH EXCHANGE BOX

a diagram for examining the allocation of fixed total quantities of two goods between two consumers

The Edgeworth Exchange Box Diagram

The way two parties may both gain from exchange illustrates a simple idea: "You have what I want, and I have what you want, so let's trade!" While this statement conveys intuitively what is involved, a deeper understanding of the nature and consequences of voluntary exchange is important. A new graphical device, the Edgeworth exchange box, can give us that understanding.

The **Edgeworth exchange box** diagram can be used to examine the allocation of fixed total quantities of two goods between two consumers.[2] Figure 6.1 shows the box diagram appropriate for the numerical example just discussed. The horizontal and vertical dimensions of the box indicate the total quantities of the two goods. The length of the box diagram indicates the total amount of football tickets held by the two consumers, 50, and the height of the diagram indicates the total amount of ballet tickets, 40.

FIGURE 6.1

The Edgeworth Exchange Box

The horizontal dimension of the box measures the total number of football tickets, and the vertical dimension measures the total number of ballet tickets. When the origins of the consumers are O_E and O_W, each point in the box represents a specific division of the goods between the consumers.

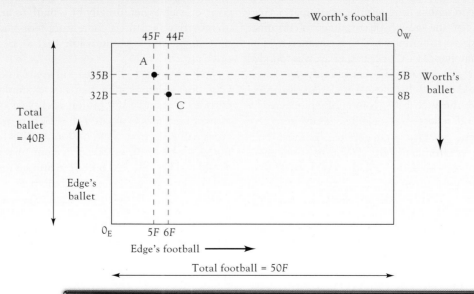

---

[2]The Edgeworth box is named for F. Y. Edgeworth, who hinted at such a construction in 1881 in his *Mathematical Psychics: An Essay on the Application of Mathematics to the Moral Sciences* (New York: August Kelly, 1953).

By interpreting the box diagram in a certain way, we can show all the possible ways 50 football tickets and 40 ballet tickets can be divided between Mr. Edge and Ms. Worth. Let's measure Edge's holdings of football tickets horizontally from point 0_E and his holdings of ballet tickets vertically from the same point. In effect, 0_E is the origin of the diagram for purposes of measuring the number of football and ballet tickets possessed by Edge. Point A shows the market basket for Edge that contains 35B and 5F; it is, in fact, his initial market basket from our numerical illustration.

One ingenious aspect of the box diagram is that point A also indicates Worth's market basket. Because the number of football tickets held by both parties is fixed at 50, placing Edge at point A with 5 football tickets means Worth holds the remaining 45 tickets. This amount is shown in the diagram by measuring Worth's football holdings to the left from point 0_W. Worth has 45 football tickets: point A in effect divides the horizontal dimension of the box, 50F, between Edge (5F) and Worth (45F). Point A also indicates Worth's ballet holdings by measuring them down from point 0_W. Since combined ballet holdings equal 40, Edge has 35, and the remaining 5 tickets belong to Worth.

Now consider point C, which identifies a different market basket for both Edge and Worth. Edge's market basket at C contains 32B and 6F, while Worth's contains 8B and 44F. (The totals still add to 50F and 40B.) In fact, the movement from point A to point C illustrates the exchange between Edge and Worth in our numerical example. In moving from A to C, Edge has given up 3B and gained 1F, while Worth has gained 3B and given up 1F. The movement from A to C shows graphically what happens when Edge buys one football ticket from Worth and pays for it with three ballet tickets.

The Edgeworth Exchange Box Diagram with Indifference Curves

Because the points in the Edgeworth box identify alternative market baskets that each party may consume, we can use indifference curves to represent each person's preferences regarding the alternatives, as in Figure 6.2a. Edge's indifference curves, U_{E3} and U_{E4} require little explanation. Because Edge's market baskets are measured in the normal way, from his origin at the southwest corner, these curves have their familiar shapes.

Worth's indifference curves, U_{W3}, U_{W4}, and so on, may appear odd at first glance. Recall that the origin, for purposes of measuring Worth's consumption, is the northeast corner, 0_W, and her indifference curves are relative to this origin. Compared with the usual graphic representation, all we have done is rotated Worth's indifference map 180 degrees and placed the origin in the northeast corner. The small insert in Figure 6.2a should make this manipulation clear: it shows how the normal indifference map has been inverted to place the origin at 0_W in the box diagram. Worth's indifference curves also have normal shapes; we are just looking at them upside down.

Now let's use this construction for our original example once again. Point A in Figure 6.2a identifies Edge's and Worth's initial market baskets. The indifference curves corresponding to the initial market baskets (passing through point A) are U_{E3} and U_{W3}. Note that these curves intersect at point A, because we assume that the marginal rates of substitution differ for the two consumers. The slope of U_{E3} at point A is 5B/1F, while the slope of U_{W3} is 1B/1F. The area that lies between these two curves—the shaded area in the graph—is highly significant. *Every point inside the shaded area represents a market basket for each consumer that is preferred to basket A.* In other words, within this area both consumers would be on higher indifference curves compared with their initial curves at point A.

The shaded lens-shaped area in Figure 6.2a illustrates the potential benefit from exchange, and it is possible to arrange exchanges between Worth and Edge so that they move into this area and both benefit. For example, if Edge purchases one football ticket from Worth and pays for it with three ballet tickets (as we discussed earlier), then they move from A to C. Note that both Edge and Worth are better off (that is, on higher indifference curves) at point C than they were at point A.

FIGURE 6.2

Gains from Trade

(a) Point *A* shows the initial division of goods. Edge's and Worth's indifference curves through point *A* intersect, transcribing the shaded lens-shaped area. Both parties would be better off with any division of goods lying inside the lens-shaped area. It is thus in the interest of both parties to work out an exchange that will move them into this area. (b) Once the two parties reach a point such as *E*, where their indifference curves are tangent, no further trade is possible that will benefit both parties. Any movement from point *E* would harm at least one of the two parties.

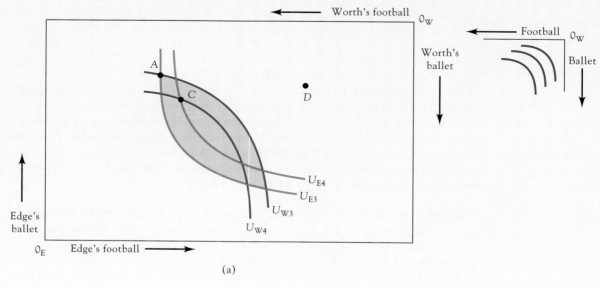

(a)

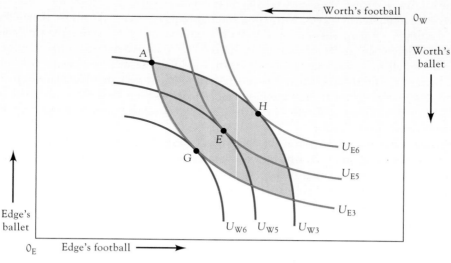

(b)

Starting at point A, any voluntary exchanges that occur will necessarily involve movements into the lens-shaped area of mutual gain. If they moved outside the shaded area, one or both parties would be worse off (on lower indifference curves), so such a trade would never be mutually agreed to. For example, a move from point A to point D (lying outside the shaded area) would never be agreed to by Worth. It would put her on a lower indifference curve than the one that she is on, U_{W3}, at point A. The basic economic proposition illustrated here is that exchanges will tend to take place as long as both parties continue to benefit. After moving from point A to point C, both parties may still benefit from further exchanges: U_{E4} and U_{W4} intersect at point C, carving out a smaller lens-shaped area of mutually beneficial potential exchanges. For example, Edge might trade his ballet tickets for Worth's football tickets again in such a way as to move into this smaller lens-shaped area and make both parties better off than they are at point C.

We have seen that, starting at point A, voluntary exchange can benefit both parties by moving them into the lens-shaped area defined by indifference curves U_{E3} and U_{W3}. However, once they reach a point such as E in Figure 6.2b, where their indifference curves are tangent, no further trade is possible that will benefit both. Any movement from point E would harm at least one of the two (as an inspection will show), so the injured party would never agree to such an exchange. A tangency of indifference curves implies that the two consumers' marginal rates of substitution are equal. The process of trading from point A, where the MRSs differ, tends to bring the MRSs into equality. As Edge acquires more football tickets and gives up ballet tickets, his MRS becomes lower: his indifference curve is flatter at point E than it is at A. As Worth gets more ballet tickets and gives up football tickets, her MRS becomes greater: her indifference curve is steeper at point E than at A.

Where the marginal rates of substitution differ, mutually beneficial trade between the parties is possible. Differing MRSs imply intersecting indifference curves and a corresponding lens-shaped area of potential mutual gain in the Edgeworth box diagram. Predictably, then, voluntary exchanges will occur to realize the potential gain.

We should mention one final point. Our theory does not permit us to predict exactly where in the lens-shaped area the consumers will end up. Although there should be a tendency for trade to continue until it is no longer mutually beneficial—until a tangency is reached—this condition does not identify a *unique* outcome. For example, if Edge is a very astute trader, he might persuade Worth to agree to an exchange from point A to a point near H in Figure 6.2b where Worth is scarcely any better off (she would be no better off at H); then the lion's share of the potential mutual benefit goes to Edge. Conversely, if Worth is a sharp bargainer, they might end up at a point near G.

The reason for the indeterminacy is that we are assuming only two potential traders, one buyer and one seller, so this setting is not a competitive one (many buyers and sellers). When only two parties participate in the exchange process, elements of haggling and strategy appear, because each tries to conceal from the other how much he or she wants the trade so as to get the best terms. Thus, we are unable to predict the exact terms of the exchange, except to note a tendency for any exchanges that occur to benefit both parties to some degree.

6.2   EFFICIENCY IN THE DISTRIBUTION OF GOODS[3]

PARETO OPTIMALITY
another term for economic efficiency

Economic efficiency—or, as it is sometimes called, **Pareto optimality**[4]—is a characteristic, highly regarded by economists, of some resource allocations. Noneconomists do not generally hold it in such high esteem; they frequently disparage it because they believe it relates

---

[3]A mathematical treatment of some of the material in this section is given in the appendix at the back of the book (pages 563–564).

[4]Named after the Italian economist Vilfredo Pareto (1848–1923), who first systematically formulated the concept in *Cours d'Economie Politique* (Lausanne: F. Rouge, 1897).

only to materialistic values or monetary costs and ignores human needs. This criticism misconstrues the meaning of *economic efficiency* as economists use the term. Quite the opposite of a materialistic focus, efficiency is defined in terms of the well-being of people. Roughly speaking, an efficient outcome is one that makes people as well off as possible. A full treatment of the concept of efficiency is important in appreciating its use in economic analysis.

In this chapter we consider economic efficiency as it relates to the way fixed total quantities of goods are distributed among consumers. Two consumers and two goods are analyzed, just as before, but the results generalize easily to larger numbers. Moreover, the concept of economic efficiency can be applied in other settings, such as deciding what level of output of a particular good is most efficient. Clearly, overall efficiency in resource allocation involves more than just an efficient distribution of goods, but an efficient distribution is an important part of the overall concept. We discuss other aspects of economic efficiency in later chapters.

Suppose that we have 50 football tickets and 40 ballet tickets to divide between our friends, Mr. Edge and Ms. Worth. There are innumerable ways to distribute 50F and 40B between two consumers. The Edgeworth box diagram not only identifies all the possibilities but also shows how alternative distributions affect the well-being of both parties. Previously, we used the Edgeworth box to show how Edge and Worth, starting with certain market baskets, could exchange products to reach a preferred position. Now, however, the box diagram is used in a different way; we wish to consider all the points in the diagram, not just those that Edge and Worth can reach by voluntary trade starting from some initial endowment. In other words, let's imagine that a philanthropist is going to give 50F and 40B to Edge and Worth and is devising ways that this might be done. Some ways are efficient, and some are inefficient, as we will see.

Figure 6.3 is an Edgeworth box diagram that shows different ways of dividing the given quantities of football and ballet tickets between Edge and Worth. Several indifference curves for both people have been drawn so that we can see their preferences among the various possibilities. We begin by defining efficiency relative to this setting. *An efficient distribution of fixed total quantities of goods is one in which it is not possible, through any change in the distribution, to benefit one person without making some other person worse off.*

In the diagram, the points where Edge's and Worth's indifference curves are tangent show efficient distributions. Point E, for example, satisfies the definition of efficiency. If we change the distribution from point E by moving to any other point, either Edge or Worth will be worse off (that is, on a lower indifference curve). For example, a move to point L makes Ms. Worth worse off, a move to point M makes Mr. Edge worse off, and so forth. Thus, point E is an efficient distribution of football and ballet tickets. Note, though, that it is not unique; indeed, any point of tangency between indifference curves defines an efficient distribution. At point J, for example, U_{W7} is tangent to U_{E2}. Any move from point J will harm at least one of the two consumers, so point J is an efficient distribution. Point K also represents an efficient distribution, as do other points of tangency not drawn in. A line drawn through all the efficient distributions is called the **contract curve**. It is shown as CC in Figure 6.3, and it identifies all the efficient ways of dividing the two goods between the consumers.

An alternative but equivalent way of defining *efficiency* may be helpful. An efficient distribution is one that makes one party as well off as possible for a given level of well-being for the second party. For example, suppose that we consider the given level of well-being indicated by U_{W2} for Worth. She is equally well off at points L and K, or any other point on U_{W2}. Among all the possible combinations of football and ballet tickets that keep Worth on U_{W2}, Edge is best off at point K. Point K places him on the highest indifference curve possible, assuming Worth stays on U_{W2}. Because point K makes Edge as well off as possible for a given level of well-being (U_{W2}) for Worth, it is an efficient distribution. Similarly, if we hold Worth on U_{W5}, point E is best for Edge. Consequently, the same set of tangency points is defined when we look at efficiency in this way.

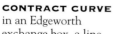

CONTRACT CURVE
in an Edgeworth exchange box, a line drawn through all the efficient distributions

FIGURE 6.3 **Efficient Distributions and the Contract Curve**
A distribution of goods for which the consumers' indifference curves are tangent is efficient. We cannot change the distribution without making at least one of them worse off. There are many efficient distributions, as shown by the contract curve *CC*, which connects the points of tangency.

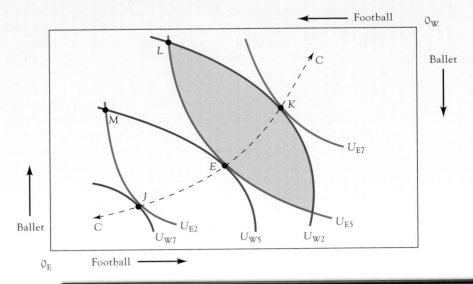

The contract curve defines the set of all efficient ways to divide football and ballet tickets between Edge and Worth. In contrast, all points off the contract curve are inefficient allocations. **Inefficiency** may be defined as follows: an inefficient distribution of goods is one in which it is possible, through a change in the distribution, to benefit one party without harming the other.

INEFFICIENCY
a distribution of goods in which it is possible, through a change in the distribution, to benefit one party without harming the other

In Figure 6.3, all points off the contract curve satisfy this definition of inefficiency. Consider point *L*. If we change the distribution from point *L* to point *K*, Edge will be better off without harming Worth—she remains on the same indifference curve, U_{W2}. Alternatively, we can move from point *L* to point *E*, which benefits Worth while leaving Edge's well-being unchanged. Note, in fact, that an inefficient allocation, such as point *L*, permits a change that benefits both parties. That is, a move from point *L* to any point on the contract curve between points *E* and *K* will leave both Edge and Worth on higher indifference curves than the ones that they are on at point *L*.

If we select any point off the contract curve and draw Edge's and Worth's indifference curves through this point, the curves will intersect. The intersecting indifference curves will circumscribe a lens-shaped area within which both parties will be on higher indifference curves. Because this is true of every point off the contract curve, all these points represent inefficient distributions of the goods.

By this means, all the ways that the goods can be divided between Edge and Worth can be characterized as either efficient or inefficient. Inefficient distributions are shown as points where the indifference curves of the two parties intersect, that is, where $MRS_{FB}^{E} \neq MRS_{FB}^{W}$. This inequality implies, just as with our initial numerical example (Table 6.1), that the consumers place different values on the two goods, so both will prefer a different distribution. Efficient distributions are shown by the contract curve, which connects the points of tangency between indifference curves. Thus, efficient distributions are characterized by an equality between marginal rates of substitution, or $MRS_{FB}^E = MRS_{FB}^W$. At those points the consumers' relative valuations of the two goods are equal, and no further change that will benefit both parties is possible.

Efficiency and Equity

For any inefficient point there are many efficient points on the contract curve that *both* parties prefer. This can be seen by looking at any point such as L located off the contract curve in Figure 6.3. In this case points between E and K on the contract curve are better from both Edge's and Worth's viewpoints than point L. Most people would probably agree that the efficient points between E and K are preferred to the inefficient point L.

Now suppose that two efficient points are compared, points E and K, for instance. Which of these is "better?" Because both points are efficient, the concept of efficiency provides no help in choosing between the two, yet there is a marked difference between E and K. Edge is better off at point K than at point E, while Worth is better off at point E than at point K. Moving from K to E benefits Worth at Edge's expense; moving from E to K benefits Edge at Worth's expense. To judge one efficient point superior to another requires deciding whose well-being is more important, and there is no objective basis for such a decision. In the economist's jargon, *interpersonal comparisons of utility* cannot be made scientifically, so there is no objective way to demonstrate that one efficient point is preferred to another.

If a philanthropist has to choose how to divide the football and ballet tickets between Edge and Worth, on what basis could the choice between points E and K be made? The decision would have to be based on something other than efficiency because both points are efficient. **Equity**, or fairness, might provide the basis for the decision. However, although we all have views of what is equitable or fair, our views differ: there is no agreed-upon definition of what constitutes equity. For that reason economics does not provide a formula that allows us to state that one efficient point is better than any other.

EQUITY
the concept of fairness

Note also the critical role that the initial endowment plays in determining which of all of the efficient points on the contract curve in Figure 6.3 are attainable through voluntary exchange. For example, starting from endowment point L, all points between E and K on the contract curve are attainable through voluntary exchange. Any other points on the contract curve, however, are not attainable. Edge would never agree voluntarily to move to point J if the initial endowment is L. Point J lies on a lower indifference curve for Edge than does point L. Nevertheless, Edge may end up at point J if we start from an initial endowment that is less favorable to Edge than L, an endowment such as M (point M lies on a lower indifference curve for Edge than does point L).

While voluntary exchange serves to promote efficiency starting from any initial endowment of goods, we can see that the "fairness" of any efficient distributive outcome hinges critically on the initial endowment. The economist's objective criteria of Pareto optimality does not provide us a means of judging the relative desirability of different initial endowments. Much as there are no objective criteria for deciding on the relative worth of all the different efficient outcomes lying on a contract curve, there are no objective criteria for evaluating the desirability of different endowments such as points L and M. Once again, this judgment must be based on normative, or equity, considerations. And people disagree on what equity implies for initial endowments, as they do over the desirability of various possible distributive outcomes that can emerge from voluntary exchange.

In sum, economics offers an objective means to see why for any initial inefficient point there always exist efficient points preferred by all parties. A choice among initial endowment points or between different efficient distributive outcomes, however, requires that normative considerations be brought into play: some subjective judgment about which of the parties is more deserving relative to others. The objective dictates of Pareto optimality cannot help us make these normative judgments.

6.3   COMPETITIVE EQUILIBRIUM AND EFFICIENT DISTRIBUTION

In the two-person model of exchange, the exact outcome of bargaining cannot be predicted. We can expect the parties to haggle over the terms of exchange (the price), with the result depending on which one is the superior negotiator. In the real world, however, buyers and sellers might not haggle over prices, especially when there are many buyers and sellers in any given market. In such cases, each party is not limited to dealing with another specific party—there are alternatives. It would do you little good, for example, to try to bargain over the price of a video rental; if you offer a price below the going rate, the video rental store manager will simply wait for another customer. Similarly, if the manager tries to extract a higher price from you, you will probably rent your movies from another store. The existence of alternative buyers and sellers greatly limits the influence any one of them can have on the price. People simply find alternative sources if the deal offered by one person is not as good as what can be obtained elsewhere.

PRICE TAKER
an individual who cannot affect the prevailing market price

With many buyers and sellers, each individual will behave like a **price taker**. Consumers acting individually cannot affect the price perceptibly by haggling. They take the price as given and buy or sell whatever quantities they wish at that price. What determines the given price in this many-person setting? It is, of course, the interaction of supply and demand, because we are now dealing with a competitive market. Namely, the overall demand for and supply of a good across all individual market participants with their respective initial holdings and preferences determine the market price for the good. Once this market price is determined, individual participants must decide how much of the good they wish to buy or sell.

Let's rejoin Edge and Worth and extend our two-person model to show the outcome when the competitive equilibrium is attained and market participants are price takers. We can illustrate the nature of this equilibrium for Edge and Worth by using the Edgeworth box diagram. In Figure 6.4, Edge and Worth begin with the initial holdings shown at point A. Suppose that the market-determined price of one football ticket is three ballet tickets. Then, both Edge and Worth confront the budget line ZZ', which has a slope of 3B/1F. At that price, Edge prefers to move to point E, purchasing 4 football tickets in exchange for 12 ballet tickets. Confronted with ZZ', Worth also prefers point E, selling 4 football tickets for 12 ballet tickets. If both Edge and Worth take the price (3B/1F) as given and are the only two market participants, the quantity of football tickets demanded by Edge (4) is exactly equal to the quantity Worth wants to sell at that price. The price of 3 ballet tickets per football ticket is therefore an equilibrium price.

Remember that the preceding example investigates price-taking behavior, while assuming that there are still only two market participants. In general, price-taking behavior results from the presence of many market participants. And the equilibrium price will be one where the total amount of football tickets demanded by buyers such as Edge in our preceding example exactly equals the quantity sellers such as Worth are willing to supply. If the price were lower, there would be a shortage in the football ticket market, and the price would rise. If the price were higher, there would be a surplus of tickets, and the price would fall. The tangency of indifference curves at point E in Figure 6.4 simply illustrates the balance between quantities demanded and supplied at the competitive equilibrium price in a two-person setting.

Another implication of the competitive equilibrium should not be missed: *the final equilibrium point is an efficient allocation.* This can be seen in Figure 6.4 by noting that point E is a point of tangency between indifference curves and therefore lies on the contract curve. In a pure exchange model, this conclusion illustrates Adam Smith's famous "invisible hand" theorem: each trader, concerned only with furthering his or her own interest, is led to exchange to a socially efficient result. All the potential gains from voluntary exchange are realized in a competitive market.

FIGURE 6.4

Competitive Exchange
In a competitive equilibrium, market actors are price takers—they all confront a uniform price for football tickets equal to 3 ballet tickets per football ticket. Each party faces the budget line ZZ', and the equilibrium is at point E—an efficient outcome.

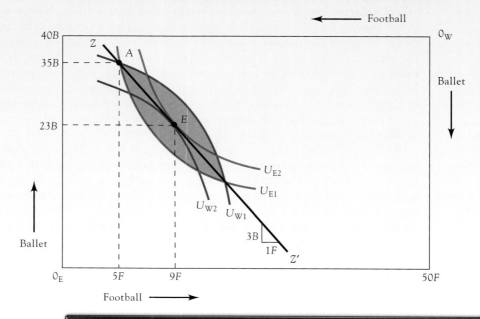

There is an alternative way of showing that a competitive equilibrium produces an efficient allocation. Specifically, recall from earlier in this chapter that an efficient distribution in our two-person (Edge and Worth), two-good (football and ballet tickets) case requires that:

$$MRS_{FB}^E = MRS_{FB}^W. \qquad (1)$$

Because Edge and Worth make their consumption decisions independently of one another in a competitive market setting, it might seem unlikely that this condition will be satisfied. Consider, however, the equilibrium conditions that result when each person allocates his or her income in the appropriate way:

$$MRS_{FB}^E = P_F/P_B; \ and \qquad (2)$$

$$MRS_{FB}^W = P_F/P_B. \qquad (3)$$

Chapter 3 demonstrated that each consumer purchases a market basket such that his or her marginal rate of substitution equals the price ratio. Because the prices are the same for both consumers, each consumer's MRS is equal to the same price ratio, and so the MRSs are equal to one another. Thus, condition (1) is satisfied.

Let's look at this matter graphically. Panels a and b in Figure 6.5 show Mr. Edge and Ms. Worth in competitive equilibrium. In panel a, on his budget line ZZ', Edge is at point E consuming 23 ballet tickets and 9 football tickets. Worth is consuming 17 ballet and 41 football tickets at point E in panel b. Note, however, that the slopes of their budget lines are equal. Because they face the same market prices for football and ballet, P_F/P_B (equal to

FIGURE 6.5

A Market-Determined Distribution Is Efficient
(a) Edge's optimal consumption point is *E*. (b) Worth's optimal point is also *E*. Even though each consumer acts independently, they both seek to equate their *MRS* to the same market-determined price of ballet passes per football ticket, *ZZ'*. An efficient distribution results.

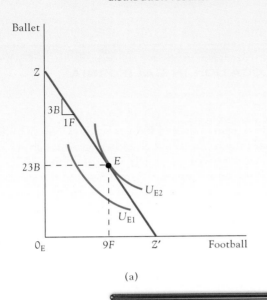

(a)

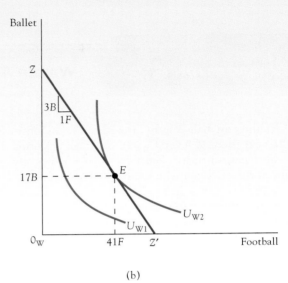

(b)

3B/1F in the diagram) is the same for both of them. Thus, the slope of Edge's indifference curve at his optimal consumption point, 3B/1F, equals the slope of Worth's indifference curve at her optimal point.

Panels a and b of Figure 6.5, of course, are nothing more than the components of Figure 6.4, the Edgeworth box diagram for the total quantities of football and ballet, 50F and 40B, consumed by Edge and Worth. To see this, start with Edge's budget line, *ZZ'*, from panel a of Figure 6.5. Then, rotate Worth's indifference map from panel b 180 degrees, superimposing her optimal consumption point, *E*, on Edge's optimal point and ensuring that her rotated indifference curve U_{W2} is tangent to Worth's budget line *ZZ'* at *E* in panel a. Because they are tangent to the same budget line *ZZ'*, Edge's and Worth's indifference curves U_{E2} and U_{W2} are also tangent to each other at point *E*. Thus, the distribution of goods described by points *E* in the two graphs is an efficient one: there is no other way to divide 50F and 40B that would not make at least one of the two consumers worse off.

Over any period of time the market distributes, or rations, goods among consumers. Although each consumer acts independently in choosing a market basket, the result is an efficient distribution of the goods. This outcome depends on two conditions. First, the prices of goods must be the same for all consumers; this condition ensures that every consumer's budget line will have the same slope. Second, consumers must be able to purchase whatever quantity they want at those prices; this condition ensures that every consumer can select a market basket for which the marginal rate of substitution equals the ratio of the prices of the goods.

Reaching an efficient distribution, albeit not the only possible efficient distribution, is no small feat. No philanthropist or government agency knows the preferences of millions of consumers. To attain any efficient outcome in this setting is a considerable achievement. When consumers must pay for the products they consume, self-interest leads them to utilize their knowledge of their own preferences, and these preferences are reflected in the market basket they select. Because their decisions are guided by the same relative prices confronting other consumers, the result is a coordination among purchase plans that would be difficult to achieve any other way.

APPLICATION 6.2   WATER ALLOCATION IN CALIFORNIA

Over the past half-century, the state of California has experienced several water "shortages." During these shortages, quantity demanded exceeds quantity supplied at the prices for which water is sold by the federal and state government to California's various water districts and ultimately to consumers. Rather than relying on price and exchange mechanisms to deal with the shortages, policymakers have discouraged water use (through either voluntary or mandatory conservation programs) and spent tax dollars on the procurement of additional water supplies, such as through desalination of seawater. There has even been talk of building a massive pipeline to transport glacial water from Alaska to California.

Water is sold in units called acre-feet. An acre-foot is the amount of water it takes to flood an acre of land to a depth of one foot. The prices for which water is sold vary substantially by district. Agricultural districts are allocated 85 percent of the state's water at prices ranging from $20 to $80 per acre-foot. Urban districts account for 85 percent of the state's population but are allocated only 15 percent of the water at prices that typically exceed $100 per acre-foot (the resource cost of producing water generally ranges from $100 to $200 per acre-foot). Trade in allocated water rights by consumers in the state's various districts is prohibited.

As one can imagine, the manner in which water is priced and allocated in California produces some tremendous inefficiencies. The low prices and relatively plentiful allocations to agricultural districts make it profitable to grow hay in Death Valley; allow California to be one of the major rice-producing states in the country—despite the fact that the cultivation of rice requires a monsoon climate while California is generally classi-

fied as semi-arid; lead farmers in the Central Valley to water their crops through either open-trough irrigation systems or aerial spraying (processes through which over half the water evaporates); and result in the state's cows consuming more water (either directly or indirectly through crops such as alfalfa and hay) than does the state's human population.

In California's cities, the relatively scarce allocations of water and the policy of either encouraging or mandating conservation result in water "police" being hired to crack down on leaking faucets and lush lawns; lead newspapers to publish the names of the 100 largest water "hogs" in town; and necessitate the establishment of special judiciary panels to hear cases of residents appealing their allotted water quotas (for reasons such as additional children or a booming business). More than 175,000 appeals were filed the last time the Metropolitan Water District of Los Angeles instituted mandatory, nonprice rationing. Perhaps the funniest one involved a man who wanted to start a worm farm: Policymakers had to check with researchers at several area universities to determine the right amount of water to allot the appellant.

Given the existing pricing and allocation policies, Californians would be better off if urban residents could purchase some of the water allocated to farmers. Under existing endowments and preferences for water versus other goods, in other words, the residents in urban water districts would be willing to pay more for additional acre-feet than the value those acre-feet generate for farmers through the production of agricultural products. The prohibition on trading of allocated water supplies, however, prevents California's water consumers from being on their contract curve and thereby achieving Pareto optimality.

6.4 PRICE AND NONPRICE RATIONING AND EFFICIENCY

In open markets, prices serve a rationing function in determining how much of available quantities each consumer will get. The rationing function and whether it is accomplished efficiently or inefficiently are what this chapter is all about. We conclude our analysis with an example that illustrates the relationship between the demand curve treatment of rationing problems and the Edgeworth box approach emphasized in previous sections.

Figure 6.6b shows the market demand and supply curves for gasoline. Because our emphasis is on the rationing of fixed supplies, the supply curve is drawn as vertical (perhaps reflecting a very short-run situation). With the S supply curve, the per-gallon price is $1.00 and quantity is 150 gallons. Now suppose that there is a sharp reduction in supply to 100 gallons so that the supply curve shifts from S to S' (because of a foreign oil embargo, perhaps). The market response is an increase in price to $2.00 per gallon. Consumers are induced by the higher price to restrict their use of gasoline to the available quantity.

By looking at Figure 6.6a, we see what this price increase means for the individual consumers in the market. Once again, we consider only two consumers, Edge and Worth, whose demand curves are d_E and d_W. When the price reaches $2.00, each consumer moves up his or her demand curve, cutting back on any gasoline use that is valued at less than $2.00 per gallon. The final optimal consumption points are A and B, with Worth purchasing 70 gallons and Edge purchasing 30 gallons. The sum of their purchases, 100 gallons, is, of course, the total quantity purchased, shown in Figure 6.6b.

Their adjustment to the higher price represents an efficient rationing of the reduced quantity available. Consider how this result would appear if the final equilibrium were shown in an Edgeworth box diagram. Edge, in purchasing 30 gallons, consumes at a point where his marginal rate of substitution between outlays on all other goods and gasoline is $2.00 per gallon. Similarly, Worth, in purchasing 70 gallons, consumes at a point where her

---

FIGURE 6.6

Gasoline Rationing
Nonprice rationing will generally lead to an inefficient distribution. We can illustrate an inefficient distribution by differences in the demand prices of consumers. When each consumer receives 50 gallons of gasoline, Worth's demand price is $3.00 and Edge's is $1.20, implying that both would be better off with a different distribution.

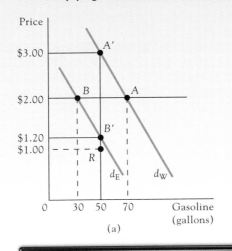

(a)

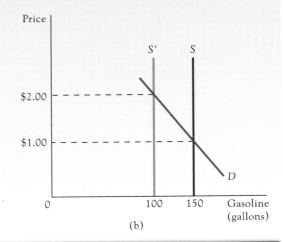

(b)

marginal rate of substitution between outlays on all other goods and gasoline is $2.00 per gallon. Their marginal rates of substitution are equal, and if this situation were depicted in an Edgeworth box, it would look qualitatively like point E in Figure 6.4.[5] Edge's and Worth's indifference curves would have the same slope at their optimal consumption points and so would be tangent in the box diagram. Consequently, allowing the market price to ration the available quantities between the consumers leads to an efficient distribution of goods.

We can better appreciate the significance of the rationing problem by speculating on how it might be resolved if price were not allowed to perform this function. For example, suppose that when the supply of gasoline falls, the government does not allow the price to rise but instead imposes a price ceiling at $1.00 per gallon. In that event the total quantity demanded exceeds the total quantity available, but somehow the combined use of Edge and Worth must be restricted to 100 gallons. Suppose that the government implements a rationing scheme by using ration coupons, as it did in World War II. (In fact, during the Arab oil embargo of 1973–1974, the government again proposed the use of ration coupons and printed 3.8 billion, but the coupons were never used.) One hundred ration coupons will be printed and distributed to Edge and Worth. To purchase a gallon of gasoline, the consumer must pay $1.00 and turn in one ration coupon; because only 100 coupons are available, gasoline purchases will not exceed the available supply. Resale of the coupons is not permitted.

The problem, then, is how to divide the ration coupons between Edge and Worth. Suppose that each receives 50 coupons: then neither could purchase more than 50 gallons. In Figure 6.6a, this solution puts both Edge and Worth at point R, each paying $1.00 per gallon and receiving 50 gallons. Both, however, place a value greater than $1.00 on gasoline at that level of consumption. When Worth consumes 50 gallons, her marginal value of gasoline is $3.00 per gallon. This marginal value is indicated by A', the height of her demand curve at 50 gallons. (Remember from Chapter 2 that the height of a demand curve reflects the maximum a consumer is willing to pay for an incremental unit of a good.) A marginal value of $3.00 per gallon also implies that Worth's marginal rate of substitution between outlays on all other goods and gasoline is $3.00 per gallon when only 50 gallons are available. In other words, it is the maximum dollar of outlay on all other goods that she is willing to give up to get an additional gallon of gasoline at 50 gallons. Edge's marginal value of gasoline is $1.20 at 50 gallons as reflected by the height of his demand curve at B'. Because Worth places a higher marginal value on gasoline than Edge does, this method of rationing gasoline is inefficient.

We could also depict this coupon-rationing equilibrium in an Edgeworth box diagram; it would be shown by a point where Edge's and Worth's indifference curves intersect. (Qualitatively, it would look like point A in Figure 6.4.) Because Worth would be willing to pay just under $3.00 for another gallon of gas, and Edge would be willing to give up a gallon for just over $1.20, both would be better off if Worth could purchase gasoline (or coupons) from Edge. The government will not allow her to do so in our example, however, so mutually advantageous trades cannot occur. In this situation a black market in gasoline (or coupons) would probably arise.

Thinking about how to distribute gasoline ration coupons suggests how difficult it is to reach an efficient outcome if voluntary exchange and market-determined prices are not allowed to perform their rationing function. The essence of efficient rationing is to distribute a good so that its marginal value is the same among consumers, but without knowing the

---

[5]In this case, however, the vertical dimension of the Edgeworth box would measure the total amount of gasoline across the two consumers while the horizontal dimension measured the total dollar outlay on all other goods.

preferences of all consumers, it is a virtually impossible task. For this reason any type of non-price rationing system is almost certain to involve some inefficiency in the way goods are distributed among consumers.

Pointing out the inefficiency associated with nonprice rationing programs is not to claim that these forms of rationing are undesirable. The purpose of price ceilings is generally to benefit consumers at the expense of producers. Clearly, producers are harmed, but the significance of this inefficiency is that it also diminishes the benefit to consumers. In our example, both consumers would be better off—without harming producers any further—if they could exchange gasoline until their marginal values are brought into equality.

Of course, the longer-run effect of the price ceiling on the quantity supplied has been neglected in order to emphasize the rationing problem. Our purpose in this section has been to illustrate inefficiency in the distribution of a given supply by using the consumers' demand curves, because this approach provides an alternative to the use of Edgeworth box diagrams.

APPLICATION 6.3   THE BENEFITS AND COSTS OF RATIONING BY WAITING

An equal allocation of ration coupons or a lottery are not the only nonprice ways of rationing a good that is in short supply at the existing price. Sometimes, as in the example of rent control discussed in Chapter 2, a price-controlled good is allocated to buyers on a first-come, first-served basis. This rationing-by-waiting approach has the advantage that, if there are no costs to waiting, consumers placing the highest marginal value on a good have the greatest incentive to get in line to purchase the good. To the extent that consumers placing the highest marginal value on a good are at the head of the line, efficiency in the distribution of the good among consumers is promoted.

Rationing by waiting, however, has its costs if consumers have something else that they could be doing with their time besides waiting in line. For example, a study examined the effects of a price ceiling applied to a Chevron station in Ventura, California, in 1980 versus two competing stations not subject to the same price ceiling.[6] (Stations owned and operated by integrated oil companies were subject to the price ceiling while those operated by independent or franchised dealers were

not.) The study found that the price at the Chevron station was $0.19 per gallon lower than at the competing stations. Because of the lower price, long lines formed at the Chevron station—the average time a consumer spent waiting in line was 15 minutes. By contrast, there was no waiting at the competing stations.

The study surveyed customers at the various stations and estimated the customers' opportunity cost of time based on their employment and income characteristics. The study found that a significant percentage of the increase in consumer surplus generated by the price ceiling was dissipated through the costs of having to wait in line to buy the low-priced Chevron gasoline. Specifically, once the costs of waiting were accounted for, consumers received only 49 percent of the increase in consumer surplus generated by the price ceiling at the Chevron station. Moreover, the study pointed out that there is no guarantee that if costs are associated with waiting, the consumers placing the highest marginal value on a good will also be the ones with the lowest opportunity cost of time. To the extent that high-marginal-value customers also have a high opportunity cost of time, they will be discouraged from waiting in line and a rationing-by-waiting scheme will not allocate the good across consumers in an efficient manner.

[6]Robert T. Deacon and Jon Sonstelie, "Rationing by Waiting and the Value of Time: Results From a Natural Experiment," *Journal of Political Economy*, 93 No. 4 (October 1985), pp. 627–647.

SUMMARY

- Voluntary exchange is mutually beneficial.
- The Edgeworth exchange box diagram shows that differing marginal rates of substitution (MRS) imply the possibility of mutually beneficial exchange. The prospect of mutual gain gives rise to voluntary exchange.
- A distribution of goods between consumers is efficient if any change in the distribution will harm at least one of them. The many distributions that satisfy this definition are shown as points on the contract curve in the Edgeworth exchange box diagram, along which consumers' MRSs are equal.

- Equity is another criterion for evaluating economic arrangements, especially when determining whether one efficient distribution is to be preferred to another.
- The distribution of goods implied by a competitive market equilibrium is efficient. Because each consumer strives to equate his or her MRS to the same price ratio that confronts other consumers, consumers' MRSs end up being equal to one another.
- Some economic arrangements can lead to an inefficient distribution of goods. The allocation of water in California across various users coupled with a prohibition of trade in allocated water supplies is an example.

REVIEW QUESTIONS AND PROBLEMS

Questions and problems marked with an asterisk have solutions given in Answers to Selected Problems at the back of the book (page 573–574).

6.1. What do the dimensions of the Edgeworth exchange box diagram signify? How does a point in the box identify the distribution of goods between two consumers? What does a point on one of the sides of the box indicate? What does it mean if we are located at one of the corners of the box? (Examine each corner separately.)

6.2. What does a vertical movement inside the Edgeworth exchange box diagram signify? Would a voluntary trade ever be shown by a vertical movement? What does a horizontal movement signify? Would a voluntary trade ever be shown by a horizontal movement?

*6.3. John has 40 gallons of gasoline (G) and 20 bags of sugar (S); for that market basket, John's MRS_{SG} is 3G/1S. Maria has 40 gallons of gasoline and 50 bags of sugar; for that market basket, Maria's MRS_{SG} is 1G/1S. Use a numerical example to explain how a trade can benefit both of them. Illustrate the trade by using an Edgeworth exchange box diagram, showing that both consumers reach higher indifference curves.

6.4. Define *efficiency* and *inefficiency* in the context of the distribution of goods between two consumers. If the distribution lies inside the Edgeworth box diagram, how does knowledge of the consumers' marginal rates of substitution permit us to tell whether the distribution is efficient?

*6.5. John has 40 gallons of gasoline and no bags of sugar; for that market basket his MRS_{SG} is 1G/1S. Maria has 20 gallons of gasoline and 20 bags of sugar; Maria's MRS_{SG} is 3G/1S. Is this arrangement an efficient distribution of goods? Show, using the Edgeworth box diagram.

6.6. When John has 40 gallons of gasoline and 20 bags of sugar, his MRS_{SG} is 5G/1S. When Maria has 40 gallons of gasoline and 50 bags of sugar, her MRS_{SG} is 1G/1S. If John exchanges nine of his gallons of gasoline for three of Maria's bags of sugar, both their MRS after the exchange are 3G/1S. Are they both better off? Show, using the Edgeworth box diagram.

*6.7. Given his initial endowment of gasoline and sugar, John's MRS_{SG} is 4G/1S; given Maria's initial endowment, her MRS_{SG} is 2G/1S. If the government collects a tax of 3G for each unit of S traded, can John and Maria engage in mutually beneficial exchange? Compared to the absence of the tax, who is harmed by it? Who benefits?

6.8. Bill and Hillary confront the same market prices for health care and hamburgers. Bill's optimal consumption point is a corner equilibrium where he consumes only hamburgers; Hillary's optimal point involves consumption of both health care and hamburgers. Are their MRSs equal? Does the distribution lie on the contract curve? Support your answer by constructing the relevant Edgeworth box diagram.

*6.9. How is an equal distribution of goods shown in the Edgeworth box diagram? Is an equal distribution efficient?

6.10. Scrooge is the only moneylender in town—a monopolist—and he charges exorbitant interest rates. If you borrow money from Scrooge, does this practice illustrate the principle that voluntary trade is mutually beneficial?

*6.11. An owner of an apartment building converts the units into condominiums, evicting the current tenants. Is this situation an example of voluntary trade? Is it an example of mutually beneficial trade?

6.12. "Private markets ration goods among consumers in an efficient way." Explain what this statement means and why it is so.

Does it imply that there is no basis for thinking that some other distribution would be better?

6.13. Tickets to the National Football League's (NFL's) championship game, the Super Bowl, are sold by the League at a below-market-clearing price. This policy produces a shortage. To allocate the relatively scarce tickets, the NFL typically employs a nonprice rationing scheme. For example, during a recent season, the League allowed all interested buyers to submit an application for up to two Super Bowl tickets. The NFL then conducted a lottery to determine which of the submitted applications would be honored. Explain why the nonprice rationing scheme employed by the NFL results in an inefficient distribution of goods. Can the NFL's insistence that the state in which the Super Bowl is played prohibit ticket scalping be justified on efficiency or equity grounds? Explain. (*Hint:* Ticket scalping involves the operation of a secondary market and the resale of tickets by original recipients to other interested consumers.)

6.14. Use the analytical framework of this chapter to explain why ticket scalping frequently occurs at college athletic events. (Why does it occur at some events and not at others?) Who benefits and who is harmed by this practice? Should steps be taken to suppress ticket scalping?

*6.15. Denny gives each of his two daughters a glass of milk and six cookies for lunch. The two daughters want to trade so that one will drink the two glasses of milk and the other will eat the dozen cookies. Does economic analysis imply that Denny should allow his children to engage in this trade?

6.16. Why is water allocated the way it is in California? Why don't policymakers allow trading of rights to water allocations across the state's various water districts? Why might farmers not support the allowance of such trading?

6.17. Landing fees at many airports are based on aircraft weight. However, these fees do not accurately measure the cost associated with a landing or takeoff. This is because the opportunity cost of a plane using a runway primarily reflects the amount of time that other aircraft no longer have access to the runway and this amount of time is largely independent of the weight of a plane. If landing fees at heavily-used airports are set below market-clearing levels and are based on aircraft weight, explain why there may be some significant costs associated with such an approach.

6.18. The U.S. government designates particular amounts of the electromagnetic spectrum for certain telecommunications uses: broadcast television; wireless; radio; and so on. In the interest of economic efficiency, should trade be allowed between holders of government-sanctioned rights to the various portions of the spectrum? That is, should the owner of a certain amount of spectrum targeted for radio be allowed to sell the asset to another individual who believes that the value of the spectrum would be greater if it was devoted to cellular phone service?

CHAPTER 7

Production

How does a firm minimize the total cost of producing a given output
level of a good such as airplanes?

Chapter Outline

7.1 Relating Output to Inputs

7.2 Production When Only One Input Is Variable

Total, Average, and Marginal Product Curves   *The Relationship Between Average and Marginal Product Curves*

Application 7.1 *Marginal and Average Products in Major League Baseball*

The Geometry of Product Curves   *The Law of Diminishing Marginal Returns*

Application 7.2 *The Law of Diminishing Marginal Returns and Home Horticulture*

7.3 Production When All Inputs Are Variable

Production Isoquants   MRTS *and the Marginal Products of Inputs*   *Using* MRTS:

Speed Limits and Gasoline Consumption

7.4 Returns to Scale

Application 7.3 *Adam Smith and Pin Production*

Application 7.4 *Decreasing Returns to Scale and the Demise of People Express*

Application 7.5 *Why Oil Shippers Are Compartmentalizing Their Firms and Fliers Are Building Their Own Planes*

7.5 Empirical Estimation of Production Functions

Learning Objectives

- Establish the relationship between inputs and output.
- Distinguish between variable and fixed inputs.
- Define total, average, and marginal product.
- Understand the Law of Diminishing Marginal Returns.
- Investigate the ability of a firm to vary its output in the long run when all inputs are variable.
- Explore returns to scale: how a firm's output response is affected by a proportionate change in all inputs.
- Overview how production relationships can be estimated through surveys, experimentation, or regression analysis.

In Chapters 3 through 6 we concentrated on consumer behavior, with the supply of goods taken for granted. Now we begin to analyze the factors that determine the quantities of goods firms will produce and offer for sale.

We begin our examination of the supply side of the market by assuming that firms maximize profit. If a firm is interested in maximizing profit, two important steps must be taken. First, for any potential output level, total cost needs to be minimized. In other words, no more resources than necessary should be employed to produce any given level of output. Second, having minimized the cost of producing a given output, the firm must select the price and corresponding output level that maximizes profit. As we will see, the optimal price-output choice will depend on the market structure in which the firm operates.

This chapter and Chapter 8 focus on the first step that a firm must take to maximize profit. Namely, we examine the firm's technology and the input prices the firm confronts to develop an intuitive rule for minimizing the total cost of producing a given output level. Chapters 9 through 15 address the second step toward profit maximization—choosing the right price–output combination once the total cost of producing a given output level has been minimized.

To arrive at an intuitive rule for cost minimization, the logical starting place is to identify the underlying technological relationships between inputs employed and output produced. This chapter explains how economists represent the technological possibilities available to the firm. The productivity of inputs is an important determinant of output: it specifies how much can be produced. As we will see in later chapters, the productivity of inputs underlies both the cost curves of the firm and the firm's demand curves for inputs.

7.1   RELATING OUTPUT TO INPUTS

**FACTORS OF
PRODUCTION**
inputs or ingredients
mixed together by a firm
through its technology to
produce output

Inputs—sometimes called **factors of production**—are the ingredients mixed together by a firm through its technology to produce output. For example, a motion picture studio uses inputs such as producers, directors, actors, costume and sound designers, technicians, and the capital invested in its lots, sound stages, and equipment to produce movies.

Inputs may be defined broadly or narrowly. A broad definition might categorize all inputs as either labor, land, raw materials, or capital. When considering some questions, however, it may be helpful to use more narrow subdivisions within the broader categories. For example, the labor inputs employed by a firm might include engineers, accountants, programmers, secretaries, and managers. Raw materials may involve electricity, fuel, and water. Capital inputs may include buildings, trucks, robots, and automated assembly lines.

For any good, the existing state of technology ultimately determines the maximum amount of output a firm can produce with specified quantities of inputs. By *state of technology*, we mean the technical or organizational "recipes" regarding the various ways a product can be produced. The **production function** summarizes the characteristics of existing technology. The production function is a relationship between inputs and output: it identifies the maximum output that can be produced per time period by each specific combination of inputs.

**PRODUCTION
FUNCTION**
a relationship between
inputs and outputs that
identifies the maximum
output that can be
produced per time period
by each specific
combination of inputs

Consider the case of a firm that employs two inputs, labor (L) and capital (K), to produce output (Q). Input usage and output are measured as *flows*: for example, the units of capital and labor employed *per day* and the firm's *daily* output. For simplicity, however, we generally will omit the time period and refer to units of inputs or output rather than units of inputs or output per relevant time period.

Mathematically, the firm's production function can be written as

$$Q = f(L,K).$$

**TECHNOLOGICALLY
EFFICIENT**
a condition in which the
firm produces the
maximum output from any
given combination of labor
and capital inputs

This function indicates what is **technologically efficient**—the maximum output the firm can produce from any given combination of labor and capital inputs. The production function identifies the physical constraints with which the firm must deal. We assume that the firm knows the production function for the good it produces and always uses this knowledge to achieve maximum output from whatever combination of inputs it employs. This assumption of technological efficiency may not always be valid, but there is reason for believing it to be generally correct. Any firm operating in a technologically inefficient way is not making as much money as possible. The firm's cost of using a given level of inputs is the same whether or not it uses the inputs wisely, but the revenue from the sale of the product (and hence the profit) will be greatest when the firm produces the maximum output given these inputs. Consequently, any profit-oriented firm has an incentive to seek out and use the best available production technique.

7.2 PRODUCTION WHEN ONLY ONE INPUT IS VARIABLE[1]

Naturally, the example of a firm using the two inputs of labor and capital to produce output is exceedingly simple and glosses over many of the subtleties of real-world production technologies. Still, this simple example allows us to illustrate several key features of the relationship between inputs and output that does characterize real-world production. One of these features is what happens to output when a firm can vary the use of only one of its inputs over a given time period.

Resources that a firm cannot feasibly vary over the time period involved are referred to as **fixed inputs**. These inputs need not be fixed in the sense that varying their use is literally impossible; rather, they are any inputs that are prohibitively costly to alter in a short time period. For example, a commercial real estate developer in New York City may be largely unable to supply additional office space over the coming month in response to an increase in market demand. This is because acquiring land and/or building permits in New York over such a short time frame is virtually impossible. DaimlerChrysler's physical plant provides another example. In response to strong consumer demand, DaimlerChrysler might be able to expand capacity for production of its PT Cruiser car in a month. Doing so, however, would require around-the-clock employment of large numbers of engineers and contractors at exorbitant cost. In that case, practically speaking, the physical manufacturing plant associated with the PT Cruiser car is a fixed input that Chrysler will not vary in the event that quick output adjustments are required.

Suppose that in our simple scenario, the firm is stuck with a certain amount of capital for the time being and can vary only the number of workers—the amount of labor—that it employs. For the sake of simplicity, we assume that capital is held constant at 3 units and examine how output or **total product** varies as the firm employs different quantities of labor.

Table 7.1 shows a hypothetical relationship between output and various labor quantities. The first column is included merely to emphasize that the amount of capital input is held

FIXED INPUTS
resources a firm cannot feasibly vary over the time period involved

TOTAL PRODUCT
the total output of the firm

TABLE 7.1

PRODUCTION WITH ONE VARIABLE INPUT

Amount of Capital	Amount of Labor	Total Product	Average Product of Labor	Marginal Product of Labor
3	0	0	—	—
3	1	5	5	5
3	2	18	9	13
3	3	30	10	12
3	4	40	10	10
3	5	45	9	5
3	6	48	8	3
3	7	49	7	1
3	8	49	6.1	0
3	9	45	5	−4

[1]A mathematical treatment of some of the material in this section is given in the appendix at the back of the book (pages 564–565).

constant at 3 units regardless of the labor used. The second and third columns contain the important data, showing how much total product can be produced with alternative quantities of labor. With zero workers, total product is zero. As the amount of labor increases, total product rises. One worker combined with 3 units of capital results in a total product of 5, using 2 workers raises output to 18, 3 workers further increases output to 30, and so on. There is, however, a limit to the total product that the firm can produce by increasing labor input if capital input is held constant at 3 units. In our example the limit is reached when 8 workers are employed and total product is 49. The eighth worker adds nothing to output, and using 9 workers actually causes output to fall.

Although these figures are hypothetical, the general relationship they illustrate is quite common. To examine the relationship further, we introduce the concepts of average product and marginal product of an input. The **average product** of an input is defined as the total output (or total product) divided by the amount of the input used to produce that output. For example, 3 workers produce 30 units of total product, so the average product of labor is 10 units of output at that employment level. The average product for each quantity of labor is therefore derived by dividing the total product in column 3 by the corresponding amount of labor in column 2. Note that total product, and thus the average product of labor, depends on the amount of other inputs—in this case, capital—being used and that the amount of nonlabor inputs is held constant throughout Table 7.1.

The **marginal product** of an input can be defined as the change in total output that results from a one-unit change in the amount of the input, holding the quantities of other inputs constant. To illustrate, when labor is increased from 4 to 5 units, total output rises from 40 to 45, or by 5 units. So the marginal product of labor, when the fifth worker is employed, is 5 units of output. What the marginal product of an input measures should be thoroughly understood. In many applications it is the crucial economic variable, because most production decisions relate to whether a little more or a little less of an input should be employed. The way total output responds to this variation is what the marginal product measures.[2]

AVERAGE PRODUCT
the total output (or total product) divided by the amount of the input used to produce that output

MARGINAL PRODUCT
the change in total output that results from a one-unit change in the amount of an input, holding the quantities of other inputs constant

Total, Average, and Marginal Product Curves

The information from Table 7.1 can be conveniently graphed. Figure 7.1 shows the result. (We have assumed that labor and output are divisible into smaller units in drawing the graphs, so the relationships are smooth curves rather than 10 discrete points.) The total product (*TP*) curve in Figure 7.1a shows how the output varies with the quantity of labor employed. Just as indicated in Table 7.1, output increases as more labor is used and reaches a maximum at 49 units, when 8 workers are employed; beyond 8 workers, output declines.

Figure 7.1b shows the average product (AP_L) and marginal product (MP_L) curves for labor. Note that these curves measure the output per unit of input on the vertical axis rather than total product, which is what the vertical axis measures in Figure 7.1a. As employment of labor increases, MP_L increases at first, reaches a maximum at 2 workers, and then declines. The average product of labor also increases at low levels of employment, reaches a maximum height of 10 units per worker, and then declines.

The two panels of Figure 7.1 highlight the relationship between total and marginal product. As long as marginal product is positive, total product rises. That is, as long as an extra unit of labor produces some extra output (however small), the total amount produced increases (up through 7 units of labor in Figure 7.1). When marginal product is negative, total product falls (beyond 8 units of labor), and when marginal product is zero, total product is at its maximum (at 8 units of labor).

---

[2]Note that the marginal product figures in Table 7.1 pertain to the interval between the indicated amount of labor and 1 unit less. Thus, the marginal product at 4 units of labor is 10, because total output rises from 30 to 40 when labor increases from 3 to 4 units.

FIGURE 7.1

Total, Average, and Marginal Product Curves
(a) The total product curve shows the output produced with various amounts of labor, assuming that other inputs are held constant. (b) Average and marginal product curves are derived from the total product curve.

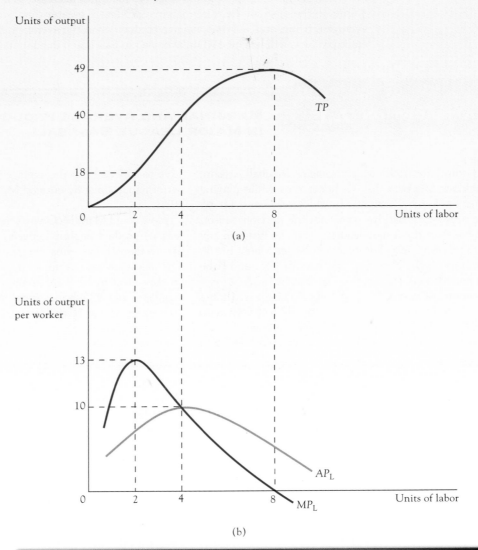

(a)

(b)

A rational producer, of course, will never operate where marginal product is negative (beyond 8 workers in Figure 7.1). This is so because employing a variable input at a level where its marginal product is negative is technologically inefficient. The firm can increase its total product and lower its production cost (provided that the price of the variable input is positive) by using less of the variable input.

The Relationship Between Average and Marginal Product Curves

A definite relationship exists between the average and marginal product curves. When marginal product is greater than average product, average product must be increasing, as is shown between 1 and 4 units of labor in Figure 7.1b. This relationship follows directly from the meaning of the terms. If the addition to total product (marginal product) is greater than the average, the average must rise. Think of the average height of people in a room. If another person enters who is taller than the average (the marginal height of the extra person is greater than the average), the average height will increase. Similarly, when marginal product is less than average product, average product must decrease, as is shown for labor beyond 4 units in the diagram. Because marginal product is greater than average product when the average is rising, and less than average product when the average is falling, marginal and average products will be equal when average product is at a maximum.

APPLICATION 7.1 MARGINAL AND AVERAGE PRODUCTS IN MAJOR LEAGUE BASEBALL

During the 1998 Major League Baseball season, Mark McGwire hit 70 home runs while playing for the St. Louis Cardinals. In 1999, McGwire hit 65 home runs—less than his own total the previous season but more than the league-leading total of a hitter in any other preceding year. For example, Roger Marris hit 61 home runs for the New York Yankees in 1961 and Babe Ruth recorded 60, also for the Yankees, in 1927.

In terms of home runs, McGwire's marginal (home run per season) product declined from 70 to 65 between the 1998 and 1999 seasons. However, McGwire's average (home runs per season) product increased from 35 in 1998 to 37 in 1999—the average is based on McGwire's performance since he entered Major League Baseball in 1986.

How could Mark McGwire's marginal (home runs per season) product decline between 1998 and 1999 while his average (home runs per season) product increase? The reason is straightforward. Since McGwire's marginal product in 1999 (65 home runs) exceeded the average product (35 home runs) through his preceding seasons in Major League Baseball, McGwire's average product ended up being pulled from 35 to 37 by the 65-home-run season.

The Geometry of Product Curves

As we saw in discussing Table 7.1, knowing how total output varies with the quantity of the variable input allows us to derive the average and marginal product relationships. Similarly, we can use geometrical relationships to derive the average and marginal product curves from the total product curve.

Figure 7.2 illustrates how average product is derived geometrically from the total product curve, TP. The average product of labor is total output divided by the total quantity of labor. At point B on the total product curve, average product is equal to Q_2/L_2, or 9 units of output per worker. Note, however, that Q_2/L_2 equals the slope of the straight-line segment $0B$ drawn from the origin to point B on the total product curve. Thus, the average product at a particular point is shown geometrically by the slope of a straight line from the origin to that point on the total product curve.

Now consider points B, C, and D on the total product curve. As output expands from B to C to D, the straight-line segments $0B$, $0C$, and $0D$ become successively steeper, so that the slopes of these segments become successively greater. This shows that the average product of labor rises over this region. At point D, in fact, average product reaches a maximum, because the straight-line segment $0D$ is the steepest such segment from the origin that still touches the total product curve ($0D$ is tangent to the total product curve at point D). Beyond point D, the slope of the straight-line segment connecting the origin to the total product curve begins to decline as the employment of labor is increased. For example, at point H,

FIGURE 7.2

Deriving Average and Marginal Product

The average product of labor equals the slope of a straight-line segment from the origin to any point on the total product curve. Thus, at point *B*, the average product is shown by the slope of straight-line segment 0*B*, or 9 units of output per unit of labor. The marginal product of labor is equal to the slope of the total product curve at each point. Thus, at point *A*, the marginal product is equal to 5 units of output per unit of labor.

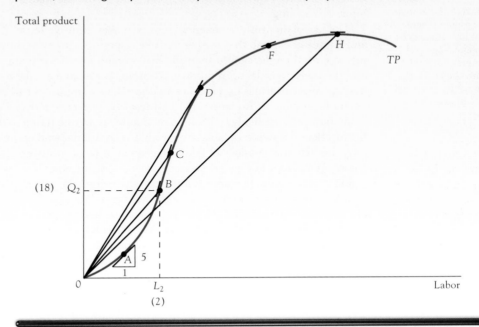

the slope of straight-line segment 0*H* is less than the slope of segment 0*D*. This indicates that the average product of labor is smaller at point *H* than at point *D*.

Marginal product measures how much total output changes with a small change in the use of an input, holding the use of other inputs constant. Figure 7.2 also shows how marginal product is derived geometrically from the total product curve. *The marginal product of labor at any point on the total product curve is shown by the slope of the total product curve at that point.* The slope of the total product curve is, in turn, equal to the slope of a line tangent to the curve. At point *A*, for example, we have drawn a line tangent to the total product curve, with a slope of 5/1. Thus, the marginal product of labor at point *A* is 5 units of output.

The steeper the total product curve, the faster output rises when more input is used, which implies a larger marginal product. In the diagram, marginal product rises as we move up the curve from the origin to point *B*, but it declines (the slope becomes smaller) as we go beyond point *B*. At point *B* the total product curve is steepest, and marginal product is at a maximum. Beyond point *B* output rises less and less when more and more input is used. Note that at point *D* marginal and average product are equal since the slope of the total product curve (marginal product) equals the slope of a straight-line segment from the origin (average product). This is the graphic representation of the proposition, noted earlier, that when average product is at a maximum, marginal and average product are equal. When marginal product falls to zero at point *H*, as implied by the zero slope of the total product curve there, total output is at a maximum.

The Law of Diminishing Marginal Returns

The shapes of the product curves in Figures 7.1 and 7.2 reflect the **law of diminishing marginal returns**, an empirical generalization about the way output responds to increases in the employment of a variable input. The law of diminishing marginal returns holds that as the amount of some input is increased in equal increments, while technology and other inputs are held constant, the resulting increments in output will eventually begin to decrease. Put more briefly, the law holds that beyond some point the marginal product of the variable input will decline.

The law of diminishing marginal returns makes intuitive sense. If we begin with 1 worker and 3 units of capital, that worker must be responsible for everything. A second worker may increase total product more than the first worker does if there are advantages to teamwork and the division of labor in producing output. For example, take the case of a firm that delivers pianos to various buyers in a city using the two inputs of trucks (assumed to be fixed at one unit) and labor. A piano is hard for just one worker to move. Two workers working as a team, however, are likely to be more productive than one trying to do the work alone. More teamwork and division of labor are possible as additional workers are employed, but, eventually, the marginal product of additional units of labor falls, because the workers' tasks become redundant and they get in each other's way. Imagine 20 workers crowded around and trying to move a single piano! Ultimately, the marginal product of an extra unit of labor becomes negative when there are so many workers relative to the other, fixed inputs that their efforts actually lower total output. If 20 workers had to squeeze into the firm's one moving truck (the fixed input) there would be little room left for pianos.

In Figure 7.1b, diminishing marginal returns set in when the amount of labor increases beyond two workers. Each additional worker beyond the second adds less to total product than the previous one; the marginal product curve slopes downward. Note that the law of diminishing marginal returns does not depend on workers being different in their productive abilities. We are assuming that all workers are alike.

It is entirely possible that diminishing marginal returns will occur from the very beginning, with the second unit of labor adding less to total output than the first. More commonly, marginal returns increase at very low levels of output and then decline, as in Figure 7.1b. Note also that the law of diminishing returns applies to labor so long as the marginal product of labor curve is downward sloping (as it is beyond two workers). The height of the curve does not have to be negative (as it is beyond eight workers) for the law of diminishing returns to hold.

In applying the law of diminishing marginal returns, two conditions must be kept in mind. First, some other input (or inputs) must stay fixed as the amount of the input in question is varied. The law does not apply, for example, to a situation where labor and capital are the only inputs and the usage of both is increased. It does apply if the amount of capital is held constant while workers and raw materials, for example, are varied. The key point is that some important input is not varied. Second, technology must remain unchanged. A change in technical know-how would cause the entire total product curve to shift.

APPLICATION 7.2   THE LAW OF DIMINISHING MARGINAL RETURNS AND HOME HORTICULTURE

Although the Romans were the first to use special indoor growing areas to speed up plant growth, houseplants did not become widely popular until the seventeenth century. Among the key inputs to a houseplant's success are light, temperature, humidity, soil quality, nutrients, pest control, and water. An increase in any of the inputs, however, is generally subject to the law of diminishing marginal returns. For example, improper watering, especially overwatering, is the biggest cause of problems with houseplants. Although the absence of water is fatal and initial increases in water supply may be associated with increasing marginal products in terms of a houseplant's success, further increases in watering are associated with diminishing, and perhaps even negative, marginal products. If its roots are constantly embedded in waterlogged soil, a houseplant is subject to root rot and becomes more susceptible to disease. Moreover, if the soil becomes saturated from overwatering, the roots will suffocate and the plant will die.

7.3 PRODUCTION WHEN ALL INPUTS ARE VARIABLE[3]

SHORT RUN
a period of time in which changing the employment levels of some inputs is impractical

LONG RUN
a period of time in which the firm can vary all its inputs

VARIABLE INPUTS
all inputs in the long run

By investigating the case where one input (capital) is fixed, the previous section was in fact focusing on the short-run output response by a firm. The **short run** is defined as a period of time in which *changing the employment levels of some inputs is impractical*. By contrast, the **long run** is a period of time in which *the firm can vary all its inputs*. A commercial real estate developer in New York City can acquire the additional land and building permits necessary to supply more office space. DaimlerChrysler has sufficient time to expand its capacity to produce PT Cruisers. There are no fixed inputs in the long run; all inputs are **variable inputs**.

Of course, the distinction between the short run and the long run is necessarily somewhat arbitrary. Six months may be ample time for the clothing industry to make a long-run adjustment to a change in prevailing fashions but insufficient time for the automobile industry to switch from production of large to small cars. Even for a given industry no specific time period can be identified as *the* short run since some inputs may be variable in three months, others in six months, and still others only after a year. Despite this unavoidable imprecision, the concepts of short run and long run do emphasize that quick output changes are likely to be accomplished differently from output changes that can take place over time.

Production Isoquants

ISOQUANT
a curve that shows all the combinations of inputs that, when used in a technologically efficient way, will produce a certain level of output

In the long run all inputs may be varied, so it is necessary to consider all the possibilities identified by the firm's production function. When we consider a product produced by using two inputs, the production options when both inputs can be varied may be shown with isoquants. An **isoquant** is a curve that shows all the combinations of inputs that, when used in a technologically efficient way, will produce a certain level of output. Figure 7.3 shows several isoquants for the case of a firm interested in maximizing output by using the two inputs of capital and labor. Isoquant IQ_{18}, for example, shows the combinations of inputs that will produce 18 units of output. (Note that the axes measure the quantities of the two inputs used per time period.) Combining 5 units of capital with 1 unit of labor will result in 18 units of output (point B); so will 2 units of capital and 3 units of labor (point C) or, indeed, any other combination on the IQ_{18} isoquant. Isoquants farther from the origin indicate higher output levels.

The isoquants in Figure 7.3 portray an important economic assumption: a firm can produce a specified level of output in a variety of different ways—that is, by using different combinations of inputs, as indicated by points A, B, C, and D on IQ_{18}. The firm can produce 18 units of output with a small amount of capital combined with a relatively large amount of labor (point A) or with more capital coupled with less labor (point B). For example, an au-

---

[3]A mathematical treatment of some of the material in this section is given in the appendix at the back of the book (page 565).

FIGURE 7.3

Production Isoquants

Production isoquants show how much output a firm can produce with various combinations of inputs. A set of isoquants graphs the production function of the firm. Isoquants have geometric properties that are similar to those of indifference curves: they are downward-sloping, nonintersecting, and convex. The slope of an isoquant measures the marginal rate of technical substitution between the inputs. Between points *B* and *D* the $MRTS_{LK}$ equals $2K/1L$, implying that 1 unit of labor can replace 2 units of capital without reducing the firm's output.

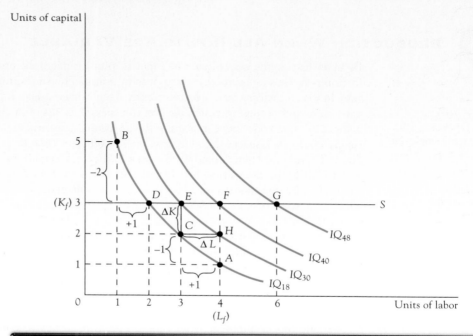

tomobile can be custom-built in a local garage with very little equipment and a great deal of labor, or it can be produced in a factory with a large quantity of specialized equipment and far less labor.

It should be emphasized that *every* combination of inputs shown on the isoquants in Figure 7.3 is technologically efficient: each combination shows the maximum output possible from given inputs. Since a given product can be produced in many different technologically efficient ways, knowing the technological input–output relationships does not by itself allow us to identify the best, or least costly, input combination to use. To determine the lowest-cost way to produce a given level of output, we also need to know input costs, as we will see in the next chapter.

Isoquants are very similar to indifference curves in their characteristics. While indifference curves order levels of a consumer's satisfaction from low to high, isoquants order levels of a producer's output. In contrast to indifference curves, however, each isoquant reflects a measurable output level. As we discussed in Chapter 3, there is no meaningful way to measure the level of satisfaction associated with each indifference curve. The numerical labels associated with each indifference curve are useful only to the extent that they show that higher indifference curves reflect higher levels of consumer satisfaction.

Four characteristics of the isoquants depicted in Figure 7.3 are worth noting. First, the isoquants must slope downward as long as both inputs are productive—that is, they both have positive marginal products. If we increase the amount of labor employed (which, presumably, would by itself raise output) and wish to keep output unchanged, we need to reduce the amount of capital. This relationship implies a negative slope.

Second, isoquants lying farther to the northeast identify greater levels of output. Assuming, again, that inputs are productive, using more of both inputs means a higher output.

Third, two isoquants can never intersect. Intersecting isoquants would imply, at the point of intersection, that the same combination of inputs is capable of producing two different *maximum* levels of output—a logical impossibility.

Fourth, isoquants will generally be convex to the origin. In other words, the slope of an isoquant (in absolute value) becomes smaller as we move down the curve from left to right. To see why this is likely to be true, note that the slope of an isoquant measures the ability of one input to replace another in production. At point B in Figure 7.3, for example, 5 units of capital and 1 unit of labor result in 18 units of output. The input combination at point D, though, can also produce the same output. The slope of the isoquant between B and D is $(-2$ units of capital$)/(+1$ unit of labor$)$, meaning that at point B, 1 unit of labor can replace, or substitute for, 2 units of capital without affecting output.

Without the minus sign the slope of an isoquant measures the marginal rate of technical substitution between the inputs. The **marginal rate of technical substitution** of labor for capital ($MRTS_{LK}$) is defined as *the amount by which capital can be reduced without changing output when there is a small (unit) increase in the amount of labor.* Between points B and D the $MRTS_{LK}$ is 2 units of capital per 1 unit of labor, which equals the slope when we drop the minus sign.

MARGINAL RATE OF TECHNICAL SUBSTITUTION
the amount by which one input can be reduced without changing output when there is a small (unit) increase in the amount of another input

Convexity of isoquants means that the marginal rate of technical substitution diminishes as we move down each isoquant. Between points C and A on IQ_{18} in Figure 7.3, for example, the $MRTS_{LK}$ is only 1 unit of capital per unit of labor, less than it is between points B and D. The assumption of convexity of isoquants, just as with convexity of indifference curves, is an empirical generalization that cannot be proven correct or incorrect on logical grounds. It does, however, agree with intuition. At point B, capital is relatively abundant, and labor is relatively scarce, compared with point C. Between points B and D, 1 unit of the scarce input (labor) can replace 2 units of the abundant input (capital). Moving down the isoquant, labor becomes more abundant and capital more scarce. It makes sense that it becomes increasingly difficult for labor to replace capital in these circumstances, and this is what is implied by the convexity of the curve.

We have been focusing on the long-run scenario in which a firm can vary the use of all of its inputs, but the isoquants depicted in Figure 7.3 also show that there are diminishing returns to both labor and capital. For example, if we hold capital constant at 3 units (as we did in Section 7.2), and increase the use of labor along line K_fS (K_f signifies that capital is fixed), each additional unit of labor beyond 2 units can be seen to add less and less to output. Increasing labor from 2 to 3 units results in output increasing from 18 to 30 units (from point D on IQ_{18} to point E on IQ_{30} along line K_fS), thus implying that the third worker's marginal product is 12 units of output. Adding a fourth worker raises output from 30 to 40 units (from point E on IQ_{30} to point F on IQ_{40} along line K_fS), indicating that the fourth worker's marginal product is 10 units of output. Since the fourth worker contributes less to output than does the third worker, there are diminishing returns to labor over this range of employment.

The firm also faces diminishing returns to capital. For example, holding labor employment constant at 4 units (L_f where the subscript "f" indicates that labor is being held fixed) and increasing the use of capital from 1 to 2 units raises output from 18 to 30 units (from point A on IQ_{18} to point H on IQ_{30} along segment L_fF). This indicates that the marginal product of the second unit of capital is 12 units of output. Further raising capital from 2 to 3 units, assuming that labor employment is still held constant at L_f, increases output from 30 to 40 units (from point H on IQ_{30} to point F on IQ_{40} along segment L_fF). Since the third unit of capital has a lower marginal product (10 units of output) than does the second unit of capital (12 units of output), the law of diminishing marginal returns applies to capital over this range of capital use.

MRTS and the Marginal Products of Inputs

The degree to which inputs can be substituted for one another, as measured by the marginal rate of technical substitution, is directly linked to the marginal productivities of the inputs. Consider again the MRTS, or slope, between points B and D in Figure 7.3. Between these two points one unit of labor can replace two units of capital, so labor's marginal product must be two times as large as capital's marginal product when the slope of the isoquant ($MRTS_{LK}$) is two units of capital to one unit of labor. To check this reasoning, note that between points C and A in Figure 7.3 the slope of the isoquant is unity. Here the marginal products must be equal because the gain in output from an additional unit of labor (that is, labor's marginal product) must exactly offset the loss in output associated with a 1-unit reduction in capital (that is, capital's marginal product).

Consequently, the marginal rate of technical substitution, which is equal to (minus) the slope of an isoquant, is also equal to the relative marginal productivities (MPs) of the inputs. Thus:

$$MRTS_{LK} = (-)\, \Delta K/\Delta L = MP_L/MP_K.$$

Note that the isoquant's slope does not tell us the absolute size of either marginal product but only their ratio.

We can also derive this relationship more formally. In Figure 7.3, consider the slope of isoquant IQ_{30} between points E and H, $\Delta K/\Delta L$. With a move from point E to C, the reduction in capital, ΔK, by itself reduces output from 30 to 18 units. This reduction in output must equal ΔK times the marginal product of capital. For example, if $\Delta K = -1$ unit, and the marginal product of the incremental unit of capital is 12 units of output, reducing the amount of capital by 1 unit reduces output by 12 units. Expressing the change in output as ΔQ, we have

$$\Delta Q = \Delta K \times MP_K.$$

Similarly, when labor increases from point C to H, or by ΔL, output increases by ΔL times labor's marginal product:

$$\Delta Q = \Delta L \times MP_L.$$

For a movement along an isoquant, the output decrease from reducing capital must equal the output increase from employing more labor, so the ΔQ terms are equal. The right-hand terms in the two expressions are therefore equal, and, by substitution, we obtain:

$$\Delta K \times MP_K = \Delta L \times MP_L.$$

Then rearranging terms yields the suggested relationship:

$$\Delta K/\Delta L = MP_L/MP_K.$$

Using MRTS: Speed Limits and Gasoline Consumption

Using isoquants can clarify a wide range of issues. Let's say a person drives 6,000 miles per year to and from work. The speed at which the car is driven affects both the amount of gasoline used (driving faster reduces gas mileage) and the amount of time spent commuting. We can think of gasoline and time as inputs in the production of transportation. Driving slower means using less gasoline but taking more time to get to work. This relationship is shown by the isoquant in Figure 7.4. Suppose that the car gets 25 miles per gallon if driven 60 miles per hour. In that case, commuting at 60 miles per hour uses 240 gallons of gasoline and 100 hours, as shown by point A. If the car gets 26 miles per gallon when driven 55 miles per hour, commuting at 55 miles per hour uses 231 gallons and 109 hours, as shown at point B. Driving at the slower speed saves 9 gallons but takes 9 additional hours of commuting time: the MRTS is 9 gallons/9 hours, or 1 gallon per hour.

In debates over whether gas savings justify lower speed limits, this isoquant forces us to recognize that there is a tradeoff between gasoline saved by a lower speed limit and additional time spent in transit. The tradeoff is measured by the MRTS: here 1 gallon of gasoline per hour spent commuting (between A and B). Because reducing the speed limit from 60 to 55 miles per hour means using less of one scarce resource (gasoline) but more of another (driver's time), we cannot determine from the MRTS alone which speed limit is preferable. Put differently, both A and B represent technologically efficient points.

Nonetheless, the MRTS is one critical piece of information in comparing different speed limits. What else do we need to know? Basically, we need to know the relative importance of the scarce resources, gasoline and time. If gasoline costs $1.00 per gallon, the 55-mile-per-hour speed limit saves our commuter $9.00. But if the commuter values time at anything more than $1.00 an hour (less than one-fifth the minimum wage), the lower speed limit costs the commuter more in lost time than is saved through reduced gasoline use. Another tradeoff is also relevant here: lower speed limits mean greater safety. Once again, the size of the tradeoff between greater safety and time, the MRTS, is important. That tradeoff, though, is much harder to measure.

FIGURE 7.4

Isoquant Relating Gasoline and Commuting Time
When driving faster reduces gas mileage, there is a conventionally shaped isoquant relating gas consumption and time. The slope, or *MRTS*, shows the tradeoff between gas and time implied by a change in speed.

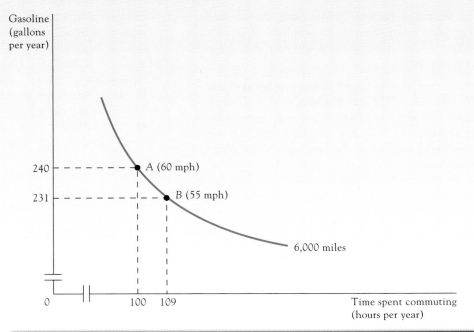

7.4 RETURNS TO SCALE[4]

CONSTANT RETURNS TO SCALE
a situation in which a proportional increase in all inputs increases output in the same proportion

INCREASING RETURNS TO SCALE
a situation in which output increases in greater proportion than input use

DECREASING RETURNS TO SCALE
a situation in which output increases less than proportionally to input use

What relationship exists between output and inputs in the long run? Because all inputs can be varied in the long run, economists approach this problem by focusing on the overall scale of operation. Specifically, we will look at how output is affected by a proportionate change in all inputs—for example, when the quantities of both labor and capital are doubled.

In this case three possibilities arise. First, a proportionate increase in all inputs may increase output in the same proportion; for example, a doubling of all inputs exactly doubles output. Here production is said to be subject to **constant returns to scale**. Second, output may increase in greater proportion than input use: output more than doubles when inputs double. Production is then subject to **increasing returns to scale**. Finally, output may increase less than in proportion to input use. We then have **decreasing returns to scale**.

These are the possibilities, but the actual relationship is not as easy to pin down. Some factors lead to increasing returns and others lead to decreasing returns; which ones predominate in a particular case is an empirical question.

To begin with, what factors may give rise to increasing returns? First, in a large-scale operation workers can specialize in specific tasks and carry them out more proficiently than they could if they were responsible for a multitude of jobs. This factor, the specialization and division of labor within the firm, was emphasized by the Scottish political economist Adam Smith.

APPLICATION 7.3   **ADAM SMITH AND PIN PRODUCTION**

In *Wealth of Nations*, Adam Smith noted the increasing returns that division of labor is capable of providing in a business as seemingly simple as the production of pins:[5]

> A workman not educated to this business (which the division of labour has rendered a distinct trade), nor acquainted with the use of the machinery employed in it (to the invention of which the same division of labour has probably given occasion), could scarce, perhaps, with his utmost industry, make one pin in a day, and certainly could not make twenty. But in the way in which the business is now carried on, not only the whole work is a peculiar trade, but it is divided into a number of branches, of which the greater part are likewise peculiar trades. One man draws out the wire, another straights it, a third cuts it, a fourth points it, a fifth grinds it at the top for receiving the head; to make the head requires two or three distinct operations; to put it on, is a peculiar business, to whiten the pins is another; it is even a trade by itself to put them into the paper; and the important business of making a pin is, in this manner, divided into about eighteen distinct operations, which, in some manufactures, are all performed by distinct hands, though in others the same man will sometimes perform two or three of them. I have seen a small manufactory of this kind

[5]Adam Smith, *The Wealth of Nations* (New York: Modern Library, 1937), pp. 4–5.

---

[4]A mathematical treatment of some of the material in this section is given in the appendix at the back of the book (pages 565–566).

where ten men only were employed, and where some of them consequently performed two or three distinct operations. But though they were very poor, they could, when they exerted themselves, make among them about twelve pounds of pins in a day. There are in a pound upwards of four thousand pins. . . . Those ten persons, therefore, could make among them upwards of forty-eight thousand pins in a day. Each person, therefore, making a tenth part of the forty-eight thousand pins, might be considered as making four thousand eight hundred pins in a day. But if they had all wrought separately and independently, and with-

out any of them having been educated to this peculiar business, they certainly could not each of them had made twenty, perhaps not one pin in a day; that is, certainly, not the two hundred and fortieth, perhaps not the four thousand eight hundredth part of what they are at present capable of performing in consequence of a proper division and combination of their distinct operations.

As evident in this famous passage, increases in the scale of production in the pin industry allowed firms to realize output increases that were significantly more than in proportion to the increases in input use.

Second, certain arithmetical relationships underlie increasing returns to scale. For example, a 100-foot square building (with 10,000 square feet of floor space) requires 400 feet of walls, but a 100 × 200-foot building, with *twice* the floor space, requires 600 feet of walls, or only 50 percent more material. For another example, a natural gas pipeline's circumference (and hence the amount of material that must be employed to create a unit of pipeline) equals the constant "pi" (approximately 3.14) times twice the radius of the pipeline. In contrast, the volume of goods such as crude oil that a pipeline is able to carry depends on the unit area of the pipeline, which equals pi times the pipeline's squared radius. If a pipeline's radius is expanded from 1 to 10 feet, therefore, its circumference (and approximate construction cost) will go up by a factor of 10 while the pipeline's carrying capacity increases by a factor of 100.

Third, the use of some techniques may not be possible in a small-scale operation. Airline hubs, magnetic resonance imaging (MRI) machines, an Internet backbone, assembly lines, direct broadcast satellite television systems, and other similarly complex and expensive techniques or equipment may be feasible only when output is sufficiently high.

The foregoing three factors (division and specialization of labor, arithmetical relationships, and large-scale technologies) are generally what is meant by a phrase such as the "advantages of large-scale or mass production." These factors, however, are inherently limited: after a certain scale of operation is reached, further expansion makes more economies impossible. Even the arithmetical factors may be limited: as a building becomes larger, the ceiling and walls may have to be built with stronger materials; and as a pipeline is enlarged, stronger materials may have to be employed as well as proportionately greater amounts spent on pumping crude oil through the pipeline.

Set against the factors that tend to produce increasing returns to scale is one factor that tends to produce decreasing returns to scale: the inefficiency of managing large operations. With large operations, coordination and control become increasingly difficult. Information may be lost or distorted as it is transmitted from workers to supervisors to middle management and on to senior executives, and the reverse may be equally likely. Channels of communication become more complex and more difficult to monitor. Decisions require more time to make and implement. Problems of this sort occur in all large organizations, and they suggest that the managerial function can be a source of decreasing returns to scale.

APPLICATION 7.4   **DECREASING RETURNS TO SCALE AND THE DEMISE OF PEOPLE EXPRESS**

People Express, once the darling of both economists for its success in the wake of airline deregulation, and organizational behaviorists, for its innovative management techniques, was sold in September 1986 to Texas Air Corporation after running hopelessly into debt.[6] Started in 1981, People Express quickly grew from 3 to almost 80 planes, reached both U.S. coasts and Europe, earned positive profits in its initial years of operation, drew widespread accolades for its human resource practices (minimal hierarchy, profit

sharing, extensive training, and pay for performance), and spent $305 million in 1985 to purchase Denver-based Frontier Airlines. The rapid growth, however, proved to be the undoing of People Express as decreasing returns to scale set in. People's top management team found it more difficult to effectively apply their management practices when the company was composed of over 5,000 employees in 1985 versus a few hundred in 1981. In the early days, the top management team was personally involved in the training and selection of employees and this participation was key to instilling spirit and dedication among the staff. Such active involvement became more difficult to coordinate and implement as the company (including the top management team) expanded. More hierarchy, with its accompanying problems, had to be imposed. People Express's output began to increase less than in proportion to its input use.

[6]This example is based on Debra Whitestone and Leonard A. Schlesinger, "People Express (A)," (Boston: HBS Case Services, 1983); Daniel R. Denison, "The Rise and Fall of People Express Airlines: A Case Study in Organizational Behavior and Effectiveness," Working Paper, Graduate School of Business Administration, University of Michigan, November 1988; and "Rise and Fall of a Discounter," *Washington Times* (June 7, 1992), p. A7.

The relative importance of the factors leading to increasing and decreasing returns to scale is likely to vary across industries. As a general rule, increasing returns to scale are likely to apply when the scale of operation is small, perhaps followed by an intermediate range when constant returns prevail, with decreasing returns to scale becoming important for large-scale operations. In other words, a production function can embody increasing, constant, and decreasing returns to scale at different output levels. In fact, this condition is probably the general case.

Figure 7.5 shows isoquants reflecting such a production function. Because we are talking about returns to scale, we are interested in how output varies as we move along a ray from the origin, like OR in the diagram. Along this ray the proportion of capital to labor is constant: the ratio of capital to labor is one-to-one at all points. At low rates of output, increasing returns to scale are prevalent: when capital and labor are both doubled, in a move from point A to point D, output more than doubles (that is, it quadruples since we move from IQ_{10} to IQ_{40}). Between points D and F, a range of constant returns to scale occurs: increasing both capital and labor by a half, in a move from D to F, increases output by exactly a half (that is, from IQ_{40} to IQ_{60}). Finally, beyond point F, decreasing returns to scale result: a doubling of inputs increases output by only one-third (that is, from IQ_{60} to IQ_{80}) in a move from F to H.

Figure 7.5 shows that as inputs are increased proportionately, the spacing of isoquants provides a graphical method of ascertaining returns to scale. With increasing returns to scale, that is, isoquants become closer and closer to one another as inputs are scaled up proportionately (that is, moving from A to D). The spacing between isoquants is equidistant with constant returns to scale (moving from D to F). And the spacing between isoquants grows farther apart with decreasing returns to scale (moving from F to H).

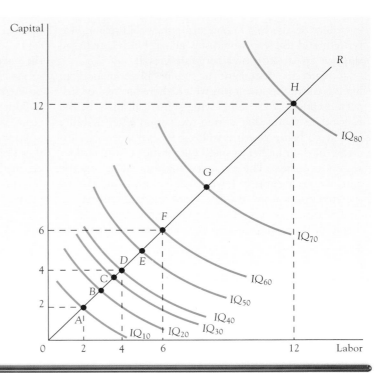

FIGURE 7.5

Returns to Scale
The spacing of isoquants indicates whether returns to scale are increasing, constant, or decreasing. From *A* to *D*, there are increasing returns to scale; from *D* to *F*, constant returns to scale; and beyond *F*, decreasing returns to scale.

Of course, saying that returns to scale generally will be increasing at first, then constant, and then decreasing is not saying a great deal. The exact output range over which these relations hold is very important; as we will see in the next chapter, it helps determine the number of firms that can survive in an industry.

APPLICATION 7.5

WHY OIL SHIPPERS ARE COMPARTMENTALIZING THEIR FIRMS AND FLIERS ARE BUILDING THEIR OWN PLANES

Recent oil-spill legislation allows unlimited liability in the case of an accident.[7] Namely, it allows state governments to take companies to court for the entire worth of their assets if a spill occurs. Due to the legislation it does not pay to be big if one is in the oil shipping business; the cost of insurance/warranty (an important input in the business) increases dramatically with the size of the oil shipping firm. Prior to the imposition of unlimited liability rules, shippers could petition courts to limit liability to the value of the cargo and vessel only. The request was typically approved provided there was not evidence of gross negligence or willful misconduct.

Confronted by legally imposed decreasing returns to scale, oil shippers have been seeking to minimize their insurance/warranty costs. Many of the world's largest tanker fleets, often owned by families whose entire fortunes are invested in them, have restructured into a group of smaller firms, each with a tanker as its sole asset. The liability risk (and associated insurance/warranty cost) is thereby localized should an oil spill occur. The strategy is much like that of the builders of the *Titanic*, who divided their ship into many compartments in an attempt to ensure that if one compartment was

---

[7]"Oil Firms, Shippers Seek to Circumvent Laws Setting No Liability Limit for Spills," *Wall Street Journal*, July 26, 1990, pp. B1 and B4.

ever flooded, the other compartments would remain watertight and the ship would stay afloat. Undoubtedly oil shippers are banking on a better end result.

Researchers document a similar phenomenon in manufacturing industries in which there are real or suspected cancer risks.[8] Employing statistical analysis, the researchers found that during the period when liability laws were being rewritten (1967 to 1980), a large increase in the number of small corporations in hazardous sectors occurred. The evidence suggests efforts on the part of corporations to lower legal exposure and the associated insurance/warranty costs through divestiture.

The production of small airplanes provides a final example of decreasing returns to scale due to liability issues. The once dominant firm in the industry, Cessna, ceased production of single-engine craft between 1986 and 1995. Another significant supplier, Piper Aircraft,

entered bankruptcy in 1991. Both firms cited liability issues and high insurance/warranty costs as the reason for their actions.[9]

As large producers have been exiting the small plane business, entry has taken place in the form of individuals building their own planes at home from kits. In recent years, sales of such airplane kits have been roughly twice as large as sales of already-built small planes. According to a 1949 rule, it is legal to fly a plane that has not been certified as airworthy by the Federal Aviation Administration provided that you have built at least half the plane.

We know of at least one former student who has constructed a small plane at home from a kit. He keeps inviting us to drop by for a ride in his self-made craft. So far we have managed to come up with some other plans on the days that he has asked us to visit.

[8]Al H. Ringleb and Steven N. Wiggins, "Liability and Large-Scale, Long-Term Hazards," *Journal of Political Economy*, 98 No. 3 (June 1990), pp. 574–595.

[9]"Liability Costs Drive Small-Plane Business Back Into Pilots' Barns," *Wall Street Journal* (December 11, 1991), pp. A1 and A8. Cessna reentered the market in 1995 when Congress passed a law restricting liability for manufacturers of small aircraft.

7.5   EMPIRICAL ESTIMATION OF PRODUCTION FUNCTIONS[10]

As with demand, production relationships can be estimated through surveys, experimentation, or regression analysis. For example, a former student of ours was employed as a consultant by McKinsey & Company a few summers ago and assigned to a client interested in entering the pig chow (food for pigs) business in certain Midwestern states. One of his tasks was to determine the extent of increasing returns to scale in the production of pig chow. That is, over what range would output continue to go up more than in proportion to the increase in overall input use? The easiest way for the student to determine this range was through telephone surveys of existing producers. Even though most existing producers were reluctant to talk to him regarding the size of their operations for fear of releasing trade secrets, a surprising number provided the relevant data.

Regression analysis offers another method for estimating production functions. Of course, as noted in Chapter 4, such a method is not without its difficulties. Differences in technology across firms must be taken into account. Measures of the amount of each input employed by a firm may not be easy to calculate. In the case of "labor," for instance, most firms employ a wide variety of different types of labor (engineers, clerical assistants, accountants, and so on) at different wage rates. The measurement of output may also involve some difficulties. For example, organizations may not produce a single output, as in the case of universities, which supply both research and teaching services (we discuss multiproduct firms in

[10]A mathematical treatment of some of the material in this section is given in the appendix at the back of the book (pages 565–566).

the next chapter). Moreover, firms may have access to the same technology but face different regulatory environments. The ability to transform a given amount of inputs into output may be more limited in a restrictive regulatory environment.

In employing regression analysis, care also must be exercised in selecting a functional form for the relationship between inputs and output. Take the case of the following linear relationship between output (Q) and the two inputs of labor (L) and capital (K):

$$Q = a + bL + cK.$$

Such a linear production function is straightforward to interpret and easy to estimate, but presumes that the law of diminishing returns does not apply to either input. To see why, suppose that the estimated intercept and coefficients are $\hat{a} = 0$, $\hat{b} = 4$, and $\hat{c} = 3$ (as noted in Chapter 4, the "$\wedge$" signifies an estimated value). If we start off employing 1 unit of both inputs, the estimated output ($\hat{Q}$) would be 7:

$$\hat{Q} = \hat{a} + \hat{b}(1) + \hat{c}(1) = 0 + 4(1) + 3(1) = 7.$$

Fixing the level of capital at 1 unit, and varying the level of labor to 2 units would increase output by 4 units to 11:

$$\hat{Q} = \hat{a} + \hat{b}(2) + \hat{c}(1) = 0 + 4(2) + 3(1) = 11.$$

Upon reaching this output level, varying labor further to 3 would increase output an additional 4 units to 15:

$$\hat{Q} = \hat{a} + \hat{b}(3) + \hat{c}(1) = 0 + 4(3) + 3(1) = 15.$$

And so on. The law of diminishing returns thus can be seen not to apply to labor because each additional unit of labor does not add a diminishing amount but the same amount—4 units—to output. An analogous result applies to capital. Holding fixed the level of labor, say at 1 unit, each additional unit of capital increases output by a constant ($\hat{c} = 3$), rather than a diminishing, amount.

Of course, there are more elaborate mathematical forms of production functions that do not imply constant marginal products for inputs. Among the most common is the **Cobb–Douglas production function**.[11] In the case of our two-input example, the Cobb–Douglas production function takes this form:

COBB–DOUGLAS PRODUCTION FUNCTION
a production function that does not imply constant marginal products for inputs

$$Q = aL^bK^c.$$

Such a multiplicative form allows the law of diminishing returns to either apply or not apply to individual inputs. To see why, suppose that the estimated constant a and powers associated with the inputs labor and capital (b and c, respectively) are $\hat{a} = 2$, $\hat{b} = 0.5$, and $\hat{c} = 1$. If we start off employing 1 unit of both inputs, the estimated output ($\hat{Q}$) would be 2:

$$\hat{Q} = \hat{a}L^{\hat{b}}K^{\hat{c}} = 2(1^{0.5})(1^1) = 2.$$

Fixing the level of capital at 1 unit, and varying the level of labor to 2 units would increase output by 0.83 units to 2.83:

$$\hat{Q} = \hat{a}L^{\hat{b}}K^{\hat{c}} = 2(2^{0.5})(1^1) \approx 2(1.414)(1) \approx 2.83.$$

[11]This type of production function is named after Charles W. Cobb, a mathematician, and Paul H. Douglas, an economist and U.S. senator. Cobb and Douglas did pioneering work in estimating production functions in the early part of the twentieth century.

Upon reaching this output level, varying labor further to 3 units would increase output by 0.63 units from 2.83 to 3.46:

$$\hat{Q} = \hat{a}L^{\hat{b}}K^{\hat{c}} = 2(3^{0.5})(1^1) \approx 2(1.732)(1) \approx 3.46.$$

The law of diminishing returns can thus be seen to apply to labor for the input levels we have considered because, holding constant employment of capital, the third unit of labor adds less to total output (0.63 units) than does the second unit (0.83 units).

In the case of capital, however, the law of diminishing returns does not apply for the assumed Cobb–Douglas production function and estimated constant a and powers b and c. Suppose that we start off once again by employing 1 unit of both inputs. As we have seen before, the estimated output ($\hat{Q}$) is 2:

$$\hat{Q} = \hat{a}L^{\hat{b}}K^{\hat{c}} = 2(1^{0.5})(1^1) = 2.$$

Now instead of holding capital constant, let's fix labor at 1 unit and vary the level of capital to 2 units. Total output would increase by 2 units to 4:

$$\hat{Q} = \hat{a}L^{\hat{b}}K^{\hat{c}} = 2(1^{0.5})(2^1) = 2(1)(2) = 4.$$

Upon reaching this output level, varying capital further to 3 units would increase output by 2 units to 6:

$$\hat{Q} = \hat{a}L^{\hat{b}}K^{\hat{c}} = 2(1^{0.5})(3^1) = 2(1)(3) = 6.$$

The law of diminishing returns thus can be seen not to apply to capital because, holding constant employment of labor, the third unit of capital raises output by the same amount (2 units) as does the second unit of capital.

In general, if the power associated with an input in a Cobb–Douglas production function is less than unity, the law of diminishing returns applies to that input over all possible levels of input usage (do you see why?). If the power associated with an input is equal to or greater than unity, the law of diminishing returns does not apply to that input.

Furthermore, the sum of the powers associated with the inputs in a Cobb–Douglas production function has economic significance. If the sum of the powers exceeds unity (that is, $b + c > 1$), the production function is characterized by increasing returns to scale. If the sum of the powers equals unity ($b + c = 1$), constant returns to scale apply. Decreasing returns to scale apply when the sum of the powers is less than unity ($b + c < 1$).

To see why the sum of the powers associated with the inputs in a Cobb–Douglas production function is related to returns to scale, consider what would happen to output if we scaled up employment of all inputs by some factor, s. The scaling factor s is some number greater than unity because we are contemplating "scaling up" use of all inputs. For example, if we considered doubling all inputs, $s = 2$. To check on returns to scale, we want to compare the output we get when we scale up all inputs by s:

$$a(Ls)^b(Ks)^c,$$

with the original output, Q, scaled up by the same factor s:

$$sQ = saL^bK^c.$$

Written side by side, we are comparing whether the output we get when we scale up all inputs is more than the scaled-up initial output:

$$a(Ls)^b(Ks)^c \text{ versus } saL^bK^c.$$

With some simple rearrangement, we can thus see that the comparison boils down to the following:

$$s^{b+c}aL^bK^c \text{ versus } saL^bK^c.$$

If the sum of the powers associated with the inputs of labor and capital exceeds unity (that is, $b + c > 1$), the foregoing comparison indicates that scaling up all inputs (the left-hand side) will get us more than the scaled-up initial output (the right-hand side). This is the case when increasing returns apply. For example, if the sum of the powers associated with the inputs exceeds unity and $s = 2$, doubling all inputs will get us more than double the initial output.

If the sum of the powers associated with the inputs labor and capital equals unity ($b + c = 1$), scaling up all inputs (the left-hand side of the comparison) will get us the same amount as the scaled-up initial output (the right-hand side). This holds in the case of constant returns to scale. If $s = 2$ in such a case, doubling all inputs will produce an output that is exactly double the initial output.

Finally, if the sum of the powers associated with the inputs labor and capital is less than unity ($b + c < 1$), scaling up all inputs (the left-hand side of the comparison) will get us less than the scaled-up initial output (the right-hand side) and decreasing returns to scale apply. Were we to double the use of all inputs in such a case (that is, $s = 2$), output would less than double.

SUMMARY

- There are two relationships between the quantities of inputs used and the amount of output produced. In the first, the quantities of some inputs are not changed (fixed inputs), while the quantities of other inputs (variable inputs) are. This is normally a short-run output response, when varying the quantities of some inputs is not practical.

- In the second relationship, the quantities of all inputs can be varied, which is normally the case when long-run output responses are considered.

- With some inputs held fixed, the total product curve shows the relationship between the quantity of the variable input and output.

- The law of diminishing marginal returns holds that beyond some level, the marginal product of the variable input will decline as more of the input is used. This law implies that the total, average, and marginal product curves will have the general shapes shown in Figure 7.1.

- Isoquants depict all combinations of two inputs that will produce a given level of output. They show the relationship between inputs and output when both inputs can be varied.

- A set of isoquants is effectively a graphical representation of the firm's production function.

- Isoquants and indifferences curves have the same geometric characteristics.

- The marginal rate of technical substitution shows the technological feasibility of trading one input for another and is equal to the slope of an isoquant.

- Returns to scale refer to the relationship between a proportionate change in all inputs and the associated change in output. If output increases in greater proportion than input use, production is said to be subject to increasing returns to scale.

- Constant and decreasing returns to scale are defined analogously. In general, increasing returns to scale are common at low levels of output for a firm, possibly followed by constant returns over a certain range.

- At high levels of output, decreasing returns to scale will exist.

- Although it is not without its difficulties, regression analysis offers one means for estimating the relationship between inputs employed and output.

REVIEW QUESTIONS AND PROBLEMS

Questions and problems marked with an asterisk have solutions given in Answers to Selected Problems at the back of the book (page 574).

7.1. Fill in the spaces in the accompanying table associated with the firm William Perry, Inc., that delivers refrigerators in the Chicago area, using the two inputs of labor and trucks.

Number of Trucks	Amount of Labor	Total Output	Average Product of Labor	Marginal Product of Labor
2	0	0	—	—
2	1	75		
2	2		100	
2	3			100
2	4	380		
2	5			50
2	6		75	

7.2. State the law of diminishing marginal returns. How is it illustrated by the data in the table of the preceding question? There is a proviso to this law that certain things be held constant: What are these things? Give examples of situations where the law of diminishing marginal returns is not applicable because these "other things" are likely to vary.

*7.3. If the total product curve is a straight line through the origin, what do the average product and marginal product curves look like? What principle would lead you to expect that the total product curve would never have this shape?

*7.4. Is it possible that diminishing marginal returns will set in after the very first unit of labor is employed? What do the total, average, and marginal product curves look like in this case?

*7.5. Deloitte & Touche is thinking of hiring an additional employee. Should the firm be more concerned with the average or the marginal product of the new hire?

7.6. Consider your time spent studying as an input in the production of total points on an economics test. Assume that other inputs (what could they be?) are not varied. Draw the total, average, and marginal product curves. Will they have the general shapes shown in Figure 7.1? Why or why not?

7.7. Define *isoquant*. What is measured on the axes of a diagram with isoquants? What is the relationship between the isoquant map and the production function?

7.8. Assume that the marginal product of each input employed by Microsoft depends only on the quantity of that input employed (and not on the quantities of other inputs), and that diminishing marginal returns hold for each input. Explain why Microsoft's isoquants must be convex if these assumptions hold.

*7.9. When United Airlines uses equal amounts of pilots and mechanics, must the isoquant drawn through this point have a slope of −1? Could the isoquant have a slope of −1? If so, what would this characteristic tell us?

7.10. Isoquants are downward-sloping, nonintersecting, convex curves. Explain the basis for each of these characteristics.

*7.11. For a particular combination of capital and labor we know that the marginal product of capital is 6 units of output and that the marginal rate of technical substitution is 3 units of capital per unit of labor. What is the marginal product of labor?

7.12. Show how a total product curve for an input can be derived from an isoquant map. Why does the question specify "a" total product curve rather than "the" total product curve?

7.13. If the firm's isoquants in Figure 7.3 were straight lines, what would this imply about the two inputs?

7.14. In the commuting example in the text, we assumed that the car in question got 25 miles per gallon if driven at 60 mph and 26 miles per gallon if driven at 55 mph. If the car gets 1 more mile per gallon for each 5-mile-per-hour reduction in speed, will the isoquant be convex? Support your answer by identifying several more points on the isoquant in Figure 7.4.

7.15. Does the concept of technological efficiency permit us to determine at which point on an isoquant a firm should operate?

7.16. Suppose that the number of points on an economics midterm (P) can be characterized by the following production function:

$$P = 15 + 2HB,$$

where H is the number of hours spent studying for the exam and B is the number of beers consumed the week before the exam. Does the law of diminishing returns apply to H? To B? What does the typical isoquant look like for such a production function? Is the production function characterized by increasing, decreasing, or constant returns to scale? Explain your answers.

7.17. Answer all of the questions in the preceding problem if the production function is characterized as follows:

$$P = 5H - 4B.$$

7.18. American Airlines produces round-trip transportation between Dallas and San Jose using three inputs: capital (planes), labor (pilots, flight attendants, and so on), and fuel. Suppose that American's production function has the following Cobb–Douglas form:

$$T = aK^bL^cF^d = 0.02K^{0.25}L^{0.2}F^{0.55},$$

where T is the number of seat-miles produced annually, K is capital, L is labor, and F is fuel.

a. If American currently employs $K = 100$, $L = 500$, and $F = 20{,}000$, calculate the marginal products associated with K, L, and F.

b. What is American's marginal rate of technical substitution (*MRTS*) between *K* and *L*? How about the *MRTS* between *K* and *F*? Should American try to ensure that all its *MRTS*s are equal? Explain.

c. Does the law of diminishing returns apply for *K* in the production of seat-miles between Dallas and San Jose by American? For *L* or *F*? Explain. Would the law of diminishing returns apply to *L* if $c = -0.2$ instead of 0.2? If $c = 1.2$?

d. Given that the exponent associated with *F* is larger than the exponent associated with *L*, would it be wise for American to spend all its money on either fuel or capital and none on labor? Explain.

e. Does American's production function exhibit constant, increasing, or decreasing returns to scale? Explain. How would your answer change if $c = -0.2$ instead of 0.2? If $c = 1.2$?

f. Does the law of diminishing returns imply decreasing returns to scale? Explain. Would decreasing returns to scale imply the law of diminishing returns?

g. In the real world, do you think that the production of seat-miles between Dallas and San Jose is characterized by a multiplicative, Cobb–Douglas technology? If not, explain the nature of the production function that might characterize a typical firm producing seat-miles in this city-pair market.

7.19. Economists classify production functions as possessing constant, decreasing, or increasing returns to scale. Yet, from a cause-and-effect point of view, it is not readily apparent why decreasing returns to scale should ever exist. That is, if we duplicate an activity we ought to get duplicate results. Hence, if we truly duplicate all of the inputs, we ought to get double the output. Can you reconcile the apparent contradiction between this logic and the expectation of the economist that beyond certain output ranges firms will confront decreasing returns to scale?

7.20. Suppose that you estimated a production function for various professional tennis players. The measure of output is the percentage of matches played by a player that are won by the player. Inputs include the average number of hours per week spent practicing tennis. Suppose that your results indicate that

for the 2000 season, the marginal product associated with practice time is 0.07 for Anna Kournikova, 0.09 for Venus Williams, and 0.16 for Monica Seles. If the law of diminishing marginal returns holds, which of the three players would you say spent the most time practicing during the 2000 season?

7.21. The Los Angeles Lakers were the champions of the National Basketball Association during the 1999–2000 season. Two of the Lakers' leading players, Shaquille O'Neal and Kobe Bryant, made 57 and 44 percent, respectively, of the field goal shots they took on the way to capturing the championship. Given these different marginal products, wouldn't the Lakers have done even better in terms of overall scoring had O'Neal taken more shots and Bryant fewer?

7.22. A fellow student states that it is best to stop studying once you reach the point of diminishing returns with regard to the number of hours spent studying. Assess the validity of her statement.

7.23. Nineteenth-century British economist Thomas Malthus reasoned that because the amount of land is fixed, as population grows and more labor is applied to land, the productivity of labor in food production would decline, leading to widespread famine. This prediction is what led economics to be called the "dismal science". Malthus's prediction failed to come to pass as advances in technology, such as the Green Revolution, greatly increased labor productivity in food production. Do such technological advances contradict the law of diminishing marginal returns?

7.24. In 1965, Gordon Moore, the co-founder of Intel, predicted that the number of transistors per square inch on integrated circuits, and thus the computing speed of a given size microprocessing chip, would continue to double every year for the foreseeable future. In subsequent years the pace has slowed down a bit, but data density has doubled approximately every 18 months. This is the current definition of *Moore's Law*. Does Moore's Law contradict the law of diminishing marginal returns?

CHAPTER 8

The Cost of Production

How can a firm minimize its cost of production?

Chapter Outline

8.1 The Nature of Cost

8.2 Short-Run Cost of Production

Measures of Short-Run Cost   *Behind Cost Relationships*

8.3 Short-Run Cost Curves

Marginal Cost   *Average Cost*   *Marginal–Average Relationships*   *The Geometry of Cost Curves*

8.4 Long-Run Cost of Production

Isocost Lines   *Least Costly Input Combinations*   *Interpreting the Tangency Points*

Application 8.1 American Airlines and Cost Minimization

The Expansion Path   *Is Production Cost Minimized?*

Application 8.2 The Cost of Public Versus Private Provision

8.5 Input Price Changes and Cost Curves

Application 8.3 The Economics of Raising and Razing Buildings

Application 8.4 Why the Necks Are Thicker in New Haven

8.6 Long-Run Cost Curves

Application 8.5 Economies of Scale and the "Network Society"

The Long Run and the Short Run Revisited

8.7 Importance of Cost Curves to Market Structure

Application 8.6 Minimum Efficient Scales in Suds, Suits, and Soft Drinks

8.8 Using Cost Curves: Controlling Pollution

Application 8.7 The Cost of Dealing with Global Warming

8.9 Economies of Scope

Application 8.8 Economies of Scope and the Marriage of AOL and Time Warner

8.10 Estimating Cost

Learning Objectives

- Delineate the nature of a firm's cost—explicit as well as implicit.
- Outline how cost is likely to vary with output in the short run and various measures of short-run cost.
- Detail the typical shapes of a firm's short-run cost curves.
- See how a firm will choose to combine inputs in its production process in the long run when all inputs are variable.
- Show how input price changes affect a firm's cost curves.
- Differentiate between a firm's long-run and short-run cost curves.
- Understand how the minimum efficient scale of production is related to market structure.
- Spell out economies of scope—whether it is cheaper for one firm to produce products jointly than it is for separate firms to produce the same products independently.
- Overview how cost functions can be empirically estimated through surveys and regression analysis.

I n determining how to transform inputs into output, a firm must not only determine what inputs are necessary to produce various levels of output, as we saw in Chapter 7, but it must also consider the cost of acquiring the inputs used to produce the product. Because production cost is important in determining a firm's output, we should understand several aspects about a firm's cost: how cost is defined (what it includes), how cost varies with the output produced, and how cost can be empirically estimated. After examining cost, we develop an intuitive rule for minimizing the cost of producing any given output. Then, in Chapter 9, we will discuss how revenue from a product's sale can be incorporated into the analysis and how production cost and sales revenue jointly determine the profit-maximizing output for the competitive firm.

8.1 THE NATURE OF COST

Although a firm's cost of production is commonly thought of as its monetary outlay, this view of cost is too narrow for our purposes. Because, as economists, we wish to study the way cost affects output choices, employment decisions, and the like, cost should include several factors in addition to outright monetary expenses. As discussed in Chapter 1, the relevant cost to a firm of using its resources in a particular way is the opportunity cost of those resources—the value the resources would generate in their best alternative use. *Opportunity cost reflects both explicit and implicit costs.* Recall that *explicit costs* arise from transactions in which the firm purchases inputs or the services of inputs from other parties; they are usually recorded as costs in conventional accounting statements and include payroll, raw materials, insurance, electricity, interest on debt, and so on. *Implicit costs* are those associated with the use of the firm's own resources and reflect the fact that these resources could be employed elsewhere. Although implicit costs are difficult to measure, we must take them into account in analyzing the actions taken by a firm. Consider farmers, who not only personally supply manual labor to their operations but also frequently own the hundreds of thousands of dollars in land and machinery they use. Implicit costs are associated with the use of the land for farming even if no explicit payment is being made for it. Land, for instance, can be sold or leased; the revenue that a farmer would realize through sale or lease is sacrificed when the farmer uses the land for farming and so reflects an implicit cost associated with its use.

For the modern large corporation the most important implicit cost is associated with the use of the firm's productive assets, its capital. These resources are ultimately owned by the stockholders, who have provided funds to the corporation and expect to receive a return on their investment. Let's suppose that the stockholders could have invested their funds elsewhere and earned an annual return of 10 percent. If the corporation does not pay at least 10 percent of the invested capital (in dividends or higher market valuation of the stock), the stockholders have an incentive to withdraw their investments (by selling their stock) and place the funds elsewhere where they are guaranteed a 10 percent return. Although there is no contractual agreement, an implicit cost is associated with the firm's use of its own (or, more precisely, its stockholders') capital; the same resources could have earned 10 percent if invested elsewhere. Viewing the rate of return that could be obtained from investing elsewhere as an implicit cost means that an average market return on investment is treated as part of the firm's normal production cost.

That a firm's production cost will equal the opportunity cost of the firm's resources emphasizes that those resources can be used to produce many things: steel can be used to make cars, refrigerators, homes, or many other goods; mechanical engineers can be used in the production of roads, airplanes, and toys, among other things. When a resource is used to produce one good, it can't be used to produce something else. For example, when we use steel to make a car, we sacrifice other products that could have been produced with that steel. For another example, consider the firm's employment of workers. The firm must pay workers enough that they don't leave and go elsewhere. If the firm's wage is less than a worker's opportunity cost—that is, what the worker could earn in the best alternative job—the worker will quit and take the better-paying alternative. Thus, to hire a worker who could work elsewhere for $35,000, the firm must pay at least $35,000, and this wage is the opportunity cost of the worker's services.

8.2 SHORT-RUN COST OF PRODUCTION

A firm's production cost will vary with its rate of output. Exactly how cost is likely to vary with output in the short run is discussed in this and the following section. First, though, we will work through a numerical example that shows how short-run cost varies with output for a hypothetical firm. For the moment, understanding why cost varies with output exactly as it does in the example is not essential; our purpose is to introduce the terminology and explain the relationships among the various measures of cost.

TOTAL FIXED COST (TFC)

the cost incurred by the firm that does not depend on how much output it produces

TOTAL VARIABLE COST (TVC)

the cost incurred by the firm that depends on how much output it produces

Measures of Short-Run Cost

Recall that the short run is a period of time over which the firm is unable to vary all its inputs. Thus, some inputs are effectively fixed in the short run, whereas others are variable. There are, however, costs associated with the use of both fixed and variable inputs. Let's examine Table 8.1, which shows how production cost varies at different rates of output for the firm.

Total fixed cost (*TFC*) is the cost incurred by the firm that does not depend on how much output it produces. Fixed cost includes expenditures on inputs the firm cannot vary in the short run—normally, its plant and equipment. The fixed cost will be the same regardless of how much output the firm produces; in particular, if the firm shuts down and produces nothing, it still incurs its total fixed cost. In Table 8.1, the firm faces a total fixed cost of $60 per day.

Total variable cost (*TVC*) is the cost incurred by the firm that depends on how much output it produces. This cost is associated with the variable inputs; more output requires the

TABLE 8.1

SHORT-RUN COSTS ($) FOR A HYPOTHETICAL FIRM

Output	Total Fixed Cost	Total Variable Cost	Total Cost	Marginal Cost	Average Fixed Cost	Average Variable Cost	Average Total Cost
	(1)	(2)	(3)	(4)	(5)	(6)	(7)
0	60.00	0	60.00	—	—	—	—
1	60.00	30.00	90.00	30.00	60.00	30.00	90.00
2	60.00	49.00	109.00	19.00	30.00	24.50	54.50
3	60.00	65.00	125.00	16.00	20.00	21.67	41.67
4	60.00	80.00	140.00	15.00	15.00	20.00	35.00
5	60.00	100.00	160.00	20.00	12.00	20.00	32.00
6	60.00	124.00	184.00	24.00	10.00	20.67	30.67
7	60.00	150.00	210.00	26.00	8.57	21.43	30.00
8	60.00	180.00	240.00	30.00	7.50	22.50	30.00
9	60.00	215.00	275.00	35.00	6.67	23.89	30.56
10	60.00	255.00	315.00	40.00	6.00	25.50	31.50

use of more variable inputs, so total variable cost rises with output. To produce more in the short run, the firm must hire more workers, use more electricity, purchase more raw materials, and so on—all of which add to total variable cost as output rises. Total variable cost is shown in column (2) of the table.

Five other measures of cost are identified in the table. Before looking at them, we should emphasize that they are all derived from the total fixed and total variable cost relationships. No new types of costs are involved: everything that we are assuming about the firm's costs is shown in columns (1) and (2). The remaining columns are just different ways of presenting the same basic cost information in a more convenient and workable form.

Total cost (TC) is the sum of total fixed and total variable cost at each output level. For example, at 5 units of output, total fixed cost is $60, and total variable cost is $100, so total cost is $160. Total cost identifies the cost of all the inputs, fixed and variable, used to produce a certain output. Since total variable cost rises with output, so does total cost.

Marginal cost (MC) is the change in total cost that results from a one-unit change in output. When output increases from 7 to 8 units, for example, total cost rises from $210 to $240: the $30 increase in total cost is the marginal cost of producing the eighth unit. Marginal cost can also be defined as the change in total variable cost that results from a one-unit change in output, because the only part of total cost that rises with output is variable cost. Basically, then, the marginal cost relationship shows how much additional cost a firm will incur if it increases output by one unit, or how much cost saving it will realize if it reduces output by one unit. As we shall see, marginal cost is the most important cost concept for many purposes.

Finally, there are three measures of average cost per unit of output.

Average fixed cost (AFC) is total fixed cost divided by the amount of output. Because fixed cost is constant, the greater the output, the lower the average fixed cost. For example, the average fixed cost associated with the first unit of output is $60 at an output of one, but it falls to $6.67 for the ninth unit.

Average variable cost (AVC) is total variable cost divided by the amount of output. If 8 units are produced, total variable cost is $180, so average variable cost is $180/8, or $22.50 per unit.

Average total cost (ATC) is total cost divided by the output. We can also define it as the sum of average fixed cost and average variable cost. At 8 units of output, for instance, total cost is $240, so the average total cost is $30. Alternatively, average total cost is also the sum of average fixed cost, $7.50, and average variable cost, $22.50.

So far we have defined the various measures of cost and explained the arithmetical relationships among them. Having covered these matters, we can now turn to the important question of what factors determine the exact way cost varies with output for the various cost measures.

Behind Cost Relationships

A firm's costs are determined by its production function, which identifies the input combinations that can produce a given output, and the prices that must be paid for these inputs. In the short run the production function relates output to the quantity of variable inputs; fixed inputs do not vary. Recall that in a short-run setting the law of diminishing marginal returns is relevant. It specifies that increasing the variable input (or inputs) will, beyond some point, result in smaller and smaller increases in total output. This assumption is the only one we need to make about production relationships in the short run. As we will see, it largely determines how total variable cost varies with output.

The production function indicates how much of the variable input (or inputs) the firm needs to produce alternative levels of output. Because the total variable cost is the total amount of money the firm must spend to acquire the necessary quantity of the variable

TOTAL COST (TC)
the sum of total fixed and total variable cost at each output level.

MARGINAL COST (MC)
the change in total cost that results from a one-unit change in output

AVERAGE FIXED COST (AFC)
total fixed cost divided by the amount of output

AVERAGE VARIABLE COST (AVC)
total variable cost divided by the amount of output

AVERAGE TOTAL COST (ATC)
total cost divided by the output

FIGURE 8.1

From Total Product to Total Variable Cost

The quantity of the variable input is related to output through the total product curve. The total product (*TP*) curve can be transformed into the total variable cost (*TVC*) curve by multiplying each quantity of the variable input by its per-unit price.

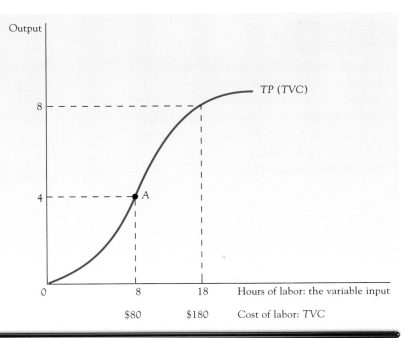

input, the price per unit of the variable input is crucial in determining the firm's short-run cost. We assume here that the firm can employ any quantity of the variable input at a given price per unit.

Figure 8.1 illustrates how these two factors—the law of diminishing marginal returns and a fixed price per unit of the variable input—combine to determine the way total variable cost varies with output. Suppose that the variable input is hours of labor and the total product (*TP*) curve relates the quantity of hours worked to total output. Note that the shape of the *TP* curve reflects diminishing marginal returns beyond point *A* (where the slope of the curve reaches a maximum).

The total product curve shows the amount of labor used to produce each level of output. If labor is the only variable input, the cost to the firm of hiring labor is the total variable cost of production. Total variable cost can also be measured on the horizontal axis by multiplying each quantity of labor by its unit cost, here assumed to be $10 per hour. For example, from the *TP* curve we know that producing 8 units of output requires 18 hours of labor, and at $10 per hour the total variable cost associated with 8 units of output is $180.

Thus, when inputs are measured in terms of their cost, the same curve relates input to output and cost to output. *The shape of the* TVC *curve is determined by the shape of the* TP *curve, which in turn reflects diminishing marginal returns*. This relationship explains why understanding the law of diminishing marginal returns is important; it ultimately determines how total variable cost is related to output. In addition, the law also determines the behavior of marginal cost and average variable cost since they are derived from the *TVC* relationship. We will discuss these relationships in more detail in Section 8.3.

By convention, we draw the total variable cost curve with *TVC* on the vertical axis and output on the horizontal axis, the reverse of the situation in Figure 8.1, which is why the *TVC* curve may not look right at first glance. To see its more conventional appearance, refer to Figure 8.2a, which represents Figure 8.1 after its axes have been interchanged.

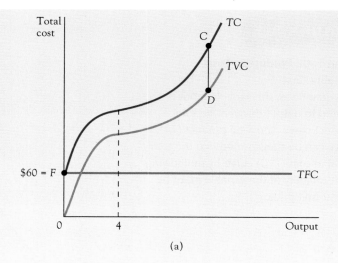

FIGURE 8.2

Short-Run Total and Per-Unit Cost Curves
(a) Adding total fixed cost (*TFC*) of *F0* to the *TVC* curve yields the short-run total cost curve.
(b) Four per-unit cost curves—average total cost (*ATC*), average variable cost (*AVC*), average fixed cost (*AFC*), and marginal cost (*MC*)—are derived from the total cost curve.

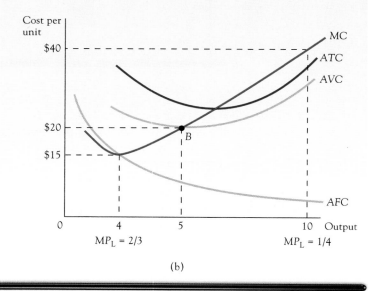

8.3 SHORT-RUN COST CURVES[1]

Now let's take a more careful look at the relationship between cost and output by using the firm's cost curves. Figure 8.2a shows the firm's total cost curves and Figure 8.2b shows the per-unit cost curves. The curves have the shapes implied by the data in Table 8.1, but now we wish to see why all short-run cost curves are expected to have these same general shapes.

Little more need be said about the total variable cost curve. In the previous section we explained the way the total variable cost curve is derived from the production function. Total fixed cost, *TFC*, is a horizontal line at $60, indicating a $60 fixed cost regardless of

[1]A mathematical treatment of some of the material in this section is given in the appendix at the back of the book (page 566).

output. The *TC* curve shows total cost, the sum of fixed and variable costs. Note that the *TC* curve is $60 higher than the *TVC* curve at each rate of output. The vertical distance between *TVC* and *TC* is total fixed cost: both *F0* and *CD* equal $60.

Marginal Cost

Economic analysis relies more heavily on the per-unit cost curves shown in Figure 8.2b, so we devote more attention to them here. Examine the marginal cost curve first. It is U-shaped, with the cost of additional units of output first falling, reaching a minimum, and then rising. Marginal cost falls at first because the fixed plant and equipment are not designed to produce very low rates of output, and production is very expensive when output is low. Consider a striking example: the marginal cost of printing a second newspaper may be trivial compared with the marginal cost of the first (which includes composing the pages and setting the press). Declining marginal cost comes to an end at some point (4 units of output in Figure 8.2b), and thereafter marginal cost rises with output. Eventually, marginal cost must rise because the plant will ultimately be overutilized as output expands beyond the level for which it was designed. At that point and possibly before, marginal cost begins to rise, and each additional unit of output costs more than the previous one.

The shape of the marginal cost curve is attributable to the law of diminishing marginal returns. To see exactly why, recall that marginal cost (MC) can be defined as the change in total variable cost (ΔTVC) that is associated with a small change in output (Δq):

$$MC = \Delta TVC/\Delta q.$$

A one-unit increase in output, for example, requires some additional amount of the variable input (labor), ΔL, to be employed. Using more labor increases the total variable cost by ΔL times the wage rate w. Thus, we have:

$$MC = \Delta TVC/\Delta q = w(\Delta L)/\Delta q = w/MP_L;$$

because the marginal product of labor (MP_L) equals $\Delta q/\Delta L$, so the reciprocal, $\Delta L/\Delta q$, equals $1/MP_L$.

This relationship states that short-run marginal cost equals the price of the variable input (in this case, the wage rate) divided by its marginal product. Let's check to see why this relationship makes sense. Suppose that at the output level of 4 units, $w = \$10$, and $MP_L = 2/3$ units of output. If an additional unit of labor increases output by 2/3 units (MP_L), then one additional unit of output requires 3/2 units of labor, at a cost of $10 per unit of labor. So the marginal cost at an output level of 4 units is $15, or $w/MP_L = \$10/(2/3)$.

Because of the law of diminishing marginal returns, the marginal product of labor varies with the amount of output and, therefore, so must marginal cost. At low levels of output MP_L is rising, so, correspondingly, marginal cost (w/MP_L) must be falling. When MP_L reaches a maximum, then MC must be at a minimum. This minimum occurs at 4 units of output in the diagram, the rate of output at which marginal returns begin to fall. At output levels where MP_L is declining, MC must be rising. For example, at an output of 10 units in the diagram, MP_L has declined to 1/4 units of output. Producing another unit of output, therefore, requires 4 more units of labor at a cost of $10, so the marginal cost is $40.

If the marginal product of the variable input rises (at low rates of output) and then falls, the marginal cost curve will first fall and then rise. Thus, the law of diminishing marginal returns lies behind the MC curve. Indeed, we can restate the meaning of diminishing marginal returns in a way that makes this relationship obvious. In the region of diminishing marginal returns, each additional unit of the variable input adds less to total output. That is, each additional unit of output requires more of the variable input than the previous unit. More of the variable input per unit of output means higher cost, so marginal cost will rise in the region where marginal product is falling.

Average Cost

There are three average cost curves. To begin, let's look at average variable cost in Figure 8.2b; average variable cost is equal to total variable cost divided by output. For the very first unit of output, total variable cost, average variable cost, and marginal cost are all equal (see Table 8.1). Then, marginal cost falls, causing the average cost to fall as well. In fact, average cost will decline as long as marginal cost lies below it and pulls it down. Put differently, per-unit production cost tends to fall at low rates of output (remember the second newspaper), but beyond some point (B in Figure 8.2 or 5 units of output in Table 8.1), average variable cost will rise.

The physical production relationships implied by the law of diminishing marginal returns are also responsible for the shape of the average variable cost curve. Average variable cost is total variable cost divided by output:

$$AVC = TVC/q.$$

Total variable cost is simply the total amount of the variable input (L) times its unit cost (w). Thus, we have

$$AVC = TVC/q = wL/q = w/AP_L;$$

because the average product of labor (AP_L) equals q/L (total output divided by total labor), and so the reciprocal, L/q, is equal to $1/AP_L$.

In the previous chapter we saw that the law of diminishing marginal returns leads to an average product curve shaped like the inverted letter "U"; that is, average product rises, reaches a maximum, and then falls. As a result, the AVC curve must be U-shaped. Over the region where AP_L is rising, w/AP_L (AVC) is falling. Similarly, when AP_L is falling, AVC must be rising. Point B, where AVC is at a minimum, therefore corresponds to the point at which AP_L is at a maximum. The law of diminishing marginal returns dictates the shape of both the MC and AVC curves—not a surprising conclusion since we saw that it determines TVC, and MC and AVC are derived from TVC. The shapes of the per-unit cost curves reflect the underlying physical requirements of production. As fewer units of the variable input are required per unit of output (on average for the AVC curve and for marginal changes on the MC curve), per-unit costs fall. Conversely, they rise when input requirements per unit of output increase.

There are two other average cost curves, average fixed cost (AFC) and average total cost (ATC). Average fixed cost declines over the entire range of output as the amount of total fixed cost is spread over ever-larger rates of output. The AFC curve has an intriguing property: if its height at any output is multiplied by that output, the area of the resulting rectangle (height times width) is the same regardless of the output level selected. Do you understand why?

The ATC curve shows average total cost. It is the sum of AFC and AVC and measures the average unit cost of all inputs, both fixed and variable. The ATC curve must also be U-shaped, although its minimum point is located at a higher output than the minimum point of AVC. This difference occurs because $ATC = AVC + AFC$, and at the output where AVC is at a minimum, AFC is still falling, so the sum of AVC and AFC will continue to fall. At some point, however, the rising AVC offsets the falling AFC, and thereafter ATC rises. Finally, because $AVC + AFC = ATC$, the average fixed cost is the vertical distance between ATC and AVC. Note that this vertical distance becomes smaller as more output is produced, since AFC declines as output rises.

Marginal–Average Relationships

All marginal curves are related to their average (total and variable) curves in the same way. Because we encounter average and marginal cost curves frequently in later chapters, the relationships bear repeating here.

When marginal cost is below average (total or variable) cost, average cost will decline. Equivalently, when average cost is declining, marginal cost must be below average cost. If average cost is currently $20, and producing one more unit costs $15, then the average cost of all units will fall.

When marginal cost is above average cost, average cost rises. Equivalently, when average cost is rising, marginal cost must be above average cost. If average cost is currently $20, and producing another unit costs $30, then the average cost of all units will be pulled up.

When average cost is at a minimum, marginal cost is equal to average cost. This is implicit in the other relationships, but we can explain it in a different way. At the point where average cost is at a minimum, the curve is essentially flat over a small range of output. When the curve is neither falling nor rising, a small change in output does not change average cost. If an additional unit of output leaves the average cost unchanged, the marginal cost must equal average cost. For example, if average cost is $20, and it is still $20 after output increases by a unit, then the marginal cost of that unit must also be $20. If it were not $20, then it would have changed average cost.

The Geometry of Cost Curves

The graphical derivation of the average and marginal cost curves from a total cost curve closely parallels the derivation of average and marginal product curves from a total product curve explained in Chapter 7. Note that although we use the short-run total variable cost (*TVC*) curve here, the same procedure applies to the derivation of the related average and marginal cost curves from any total cost curve, either short-run or long-run.

Figure 8.3a shows a total variable cost curve; Figure 8.3b shows the average variable cost and marginal cost curves derived from it. To derive *AVC* from the *TVC* curve, we draw a ray from the origin to each point on the *TVC* curve; the slope of the ray measures *AVC* at that output. At output q_1, for example, ray 0A has a slope equal to $Aq_1/0q_1$ or $21.67 per unit ($65/3). The slope of the ray in Figure 8.3a is shown by the height of the *AVC* curve in Figure 8.3b. The flatter the ray from the origin, the lower the *AVC*. For example, *AVC* is at a minimum ($20) when output is q_2, since the ray 0C is the flattest ray that touches the *TVC* curve. Thus, *AVC* falls as output increases from zero to q_2 and then rises at greater rates of output.

Marginal cost is shown by the slope of the total variable cost curve at each rate of output. At q_3, for instance, producing another unit of output adds $24 to cost, as indicated by the slope of *TVC* at point *D* in Figure 8.3a. The height of the marginal cost curve is thus $24 in Figure 8.3b. Starting from the origin, the *TVC* curve becomes flatter as we move up to point *B*, implying that MC is falling; beyond point *B* it becomes steeper, indicating that MC is rising. At point *C*, where average variable cost is at a minimum, MC equals AVC.

8.4   LONG-RUN COST OF PRODUCTION[2]

In the long run a firm has sufficient time to adjust its use of all inputs to produce output in the least costly way. Because a firm can augment office space and equipment by leasing or purchasing additional facilities, all inputs are variable. Our first task is to see how a firm will choose to combine inputs in its production process when all factors are variable.

ISOCOST LINE
a line that identifies all the combinations of capital and labor that can be purchased at a given total cost

Isocost Lines

Consider a firm that uses just two inputs, capital (its office space and equipment) and labor, to produce its product. The firm's costs of production can be represented by isocost lines. An **isocost line** (equal-cost line) identifies all the combinations of capital and labor that can be

---

[2]A mathematical treatment of some of the material in this section is given in the appendix at the back of the book (pages 566–567).

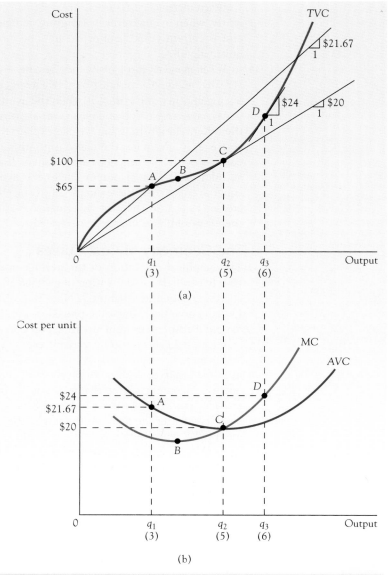

FIGURE 8.3

Graphical Derivation of Average and Marginal Cost Curves
(a) Average variable cost equals the slope of a ray from the origin to a point on the total variable cost curve. For example, at point *A*, *AVC* equals the slope of the ray *0A*, or $21.67 per unit. Marginal cost is the slope of the *TVC* curve at each point. For example, at point *D* marginal cost is $24 per unit. (b) The entire average variable cost and marginal cost curves are shown.

purchased at a given total cost. Figure 8.4a shows three isocost lines corresponding to three different levels of total cost.

Because the isocost line is a new relationship, let's carefully examine one. Look at the middle isocost line in Figure 8.4a. Suppose that a firm has total funds of TC_2 to pay its inputs. The prices the firm must pay for inputs are w for labor (the wage rate) and r for capital (the per-unit rental rate for office space and equipment, which may be an implicit cost if the firm owns the assets). If the firm devotes all the funds to capital, it can employ TC_2/r units of capital, leaving no money to hire workers. Thus, TC_2/r is the vertical intercept of the isocost line. Alternatively, if the firm devotes all the funds to hiring labor, it can hire TC_2/w units of labor, leaving no money for capital, so TC_2/w is the horizontal intercept. All the intermediate positions on the line show the combinations of labor and capital the firm can hire at a cost of exactly TC_2.

FIGURE 8.4

Isocost Lines and the Long-Run Expansion Path
(a) Three different isocost lines are shown corresponding to three different levels of total cost. (b) The point of tangency between an isoquant and an isocost line indicates the least costly combination of inputs that can produce a specified output. For example, employing L_2 units of labor and K_2 units of capital is the cheapest way to produce 6 units of output. The expansion path, which shows the least costly way of producing each output level when all inputs can be varied, is formed by connecting all points of tangency.

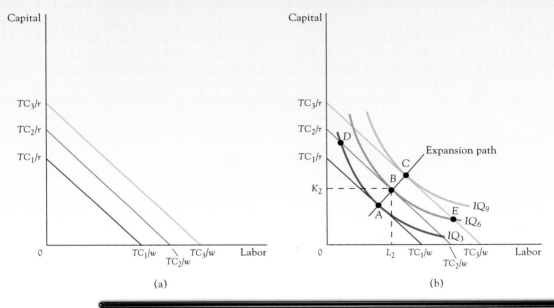

(a)   (b)

The slope of an isocost line is (minus) the ratio of input prices, w/r, indicating the relative prices of inputs. For example, if the wage rate is twice the rental rate of capital ($w/r = 2$), then hiring 1 more unit of labor, without incurring any additional cost, means the firm must employ 2 units less of capital. Thus a close analogy exists between the consumer's budget line and a firm's isocost line. In one respect, however, the analogy breaks down. Consumers are usually restricted to operating within a given budget, but firms are not. Firms can expand their use of all inputs and finance the expansion by selling the increased output. The total cost of operation of a firm is not a constant but varies with output, which explains why there are three isocost lines in Figure 8.4a (among the many that could be drawn) and not just one.

Least Costly Input Combinations

Analyzing isocost lines and isoquants together allows us to determine what combinations of inputs the firm will actually use to produce various rates of output. We have seen how a firm's production function can be represented by isoquants, and three (IQ_3, IQ_6, and IQ_9) are shown in Figure 8.4b. Suppose that the firm plans to spend exactly TC_2 to hire inputs. From among the input combinations it can employ (shown by the middle isocost line), the firm will clearly want to choose the combination of labor and capital that yields the greatest output. The firm could employ the input combination at point D, but only 3 units of output would be produced (since point D is on isoquant IQ_3). By using less capital and more labor at point B, the firm can produce 6 units of output at the same total cost. Indeed, 6 units of output is the maximum output possible at a total cost of TC_2, as shown by the fact that higher isoquants like IQ_9 lie entirely above the middle isocost line. To produce the maximum output possible at a given total cost, a firm should operate at a point where an isocost line is tangent to the highest isoquant attainable: IQ_6 is tangent to the middle isocost line at point B.

In the same manner we see that 9 units is the maximum output possible at the higher total cost of TC_3, where the firm would operate at point C. Similarly, 3 units is the maximum output possible at a total cost of TC_1. We can interpret these points in a different way: *they also show the least costly way of producing each specified level of output.* Suppose, for instance, that the firm wishes to produce 6 units of output: it must employ an input combination that lies on IQ_6. It could operate at point E and produce 6 units of output, but that combination of labor and capital costs TC_3, because it lies on a higher isocost line and requires a larger outlay than TC_2. In fact, every other way of producing 6 units of output involves a higher total cost than point B. Point B thus identifies the least costly combination of inputs that the firm can use to produce 6 units of output. *Points of tangency show the maximum output attainable at a given cost as well as the minimum cost necessary to produce that output.*

Interpreting the Tangency Points

Let's look at the tangency points more closely. At the tangencies, the isoquants and isocost lines have the same slopes. Recall that the slope of an isoquant is the marginal rate of technical substitution, $MRTS$, and the slope of the isocost line is the ratio of the input prices. Therefore, when the firm produces an output in the least costly way, it will satisfy the following condition:

$$MRTS_{LK} = w/r.$$

This condition indicates that the firm will adjust its employment of inputs so that the rate at which one input can be traded for another in production ($MRTS_{LK}$) will equal the rate at which one input can be substituted for the other in input markets (w/r).

Let's explore why this equality holds. Recall that the marginal rate of technical substitution equals the ratio of the marginal products of the inputs. Thus we can write the previous expression as:

$$MP_L/MP_K = w/r.$$

Rearranging terms, we obtain:

$$MP_L/w = MP_K/r.$$

GOLDEN RULE OF COST MINIMIZATION
a rule that says that to minimize cost, the firm should employ inputs in such a way that the marginal product per dollar spent is equal across all inputs

The last equality is sometimes termed the **golden rule of cost minimization**. It is equivalent to the tangency condition and indicates that to minimize cost, the firm should employ inputs in such a way that the marginal product per dollar spent is equal across all inputs. To illustrate, suppose that the firm is employing inputs at a point where $MP_L = 50$ (units of output) and $MP_K = 60$. Furthermore, suppose that the wage rate of labor is $10, and the rental cost of capital is $60. In this case, $MP_L/w = 50/\$10 = 5/\$1$, implying that an additional dollar spent on labor will produce 5 more units of output. For capital, $MP_K/r = 60/\$60 = 1/\$1$, indicating that an additional dollar spent on capital will produce only 1 more unit of output. For this allocation of inputs, $MP_L/w > MP_K/r$; that is, a dollar's worth of labor adds more to output than does a dollar's worth of capital. The firm is not producing as much output as it could given its cost (or, equivalently, it is not producing the current output at the lowest possible cost). If the firm spends $1 less on capital, it loses 1 unit of output ($MP_K/r = 1$), but spending this dollar on labor increases output by 5 units ($MP_L/w = 5$). So, on balance, output will rise under such a reallocation by 4 units with no change in cost.

Whenever MP_L/w is greater than MP_K/r, a firm can increase output without increasing production cost by shifting outlays from capital, where output per dollar spent is lower, to labor, where output per dollar spent is higher. This shifting should continue until the terms become equal. The law of diminishing returns serves to bring the terms into equality as the input mix is adjusted. That is, if the law of diminishing returns holds, hiring more labor tends to reduce MP_L, and hiring less capital tends to increase MP_K. Note that the initial situation described could be shown in Figure 8.4b by a point like D, because at that point $MRTS_{LK} > w/r$.

Perhaps the most intuitive way to think about the golden rule of cost minimization is to remember what the ratio of an input's marginal product to its price means. Take the case of labor. The ratio MP_L/w signifies the increase in output per dollar spent on labor. Although it's true that each unit of labor costs $10, *each* of those 10 dollars increases output by 5 units in our example. In an important sense then, MP_L/w represents the rate of return per dollar invested in labor. And the golden rule of cost minimization states that for a producer interested in maximizing profit, the rates of return across all the possible inputs should be identical at any selected level of output.

As an analogy, suppose that Larry Ellison, CEO of Oracle, has $10 billion split equally between two banks, Bank K and Bank L. Suppose also that Bank K offers a 1 percent annual interest rate on any money invested in it while Bank L offers a 5 percent annual interest rate. If there are no risk-diversification reasons for Larry to split his $10 billion total investment equally between the two banks, the financial advice that we would give him would be clear: namely, to maximize the total return on the investment, Larry needs to reallocate dollars from Bank K to Bank L as long as Bank L offers the higher interest rate.

The same principle applies to allocating dollars between inputs. Investing in different inputs is like investing in different banks. If, at Oracle's current level of output, the rate of return offered by an MBA exceeds the rate of return provided by a software engineer, the firm would be wise to reallocate dollars from the engineer "bank" to the MBA "bank" so as to maximize total output per dollars spent on inputs.

APPLICATION 8.1   AMERICAN AIRLINES AND COST MINIMIZATION

After the deregulation of the domestic airline industry in the late 1970s, American Airlines became one of the largest and most profitable airlines in the United States.[3] To a great extent, American Airlines' success reflected the strategic changes implemented by CEO Robert Crandall and his management team in the wake of deregulation. The key changes included developing the best information system (SABRE) in the industry, effective marketing strategies (such as the AAdvantage frequent-flyer program), high-quality customer service, and a passion for cost minimization.

In terms of cost minimization, American has been among the industry leaders, switching to modern, shorter-range, and more fuel-efficient aircraft; developing hub-and-spoke route structures that diminish overhead costs and are compatible with shorter-range and more fuel-efficient aircraft; increasing seating densities per plane; reducing labor costs through renegotiated labor contracts and a two-tier wage structure offering new workers employment at lower wages than existing staff; and thinking about every possible way to cut fuel and other nonlabor variable costs.

Most of the planes flown by American Airlines, for example, are not painted beyond their red, white, and

[3]This example is based on: "Airlines Resort to Penny-Pinching Ploys to Bring Their Fuel Bills Back to Earth," *Wall Street Journal* (September 28, 1990), pp. B1 and B3; "The Man Who Fired a Dog to Save a Buck," *Time* (October 28, 1990); and "Hold the Olives, Bring on the Lobster," *Time* (May 13, 1991), p. 57.

blue logo stripes. This tactic lowers cost in terms of both paint and fuel. An unpainted DC-10 is approximately 400 pounds lighter and as a result costs roughly $12,000 less to fly per year.

In the mid-1980s, American reduced the internal weight of each plane by at least 1,500 pounds. The reduction was achieved by installing lighter seats, replacing metal food carts with reinforced plastic ones, relying on smaller pillows and less bulky blankets, using lighter utensils in first class, and redesigning the service galleys. The reduction has saved American at least $22,000 per year per plane in fuel costs.

Not even the smallest stone remained unturned by Crandall and his management crew in their pursuit of cost minimization. While on board an American flight, Crandall dumped his leftover lettuce into a plastic bag and sent it off to the director of his firm's catering division with the message "Shrink the dinner salads!" Still not satisfied, the cost-conscious CEO then ordered the removal of one black olive from each passenger's salad (Crandall believed customers wouldn't notice if the olive was missing) and in the process saved the company $70,000 per year in reduced food and fuel costs. Crandall once even fired a watchdog to save a buck. As recounted by the CEO in an interview:

It's true. We had a cargo warehouse in the Caribbean, and we had a guy there guarding it all night long. I was reviewing the budget and wanted to reduce costs. My people said we needed him to prevent thefts. So I said, Put him on part time and rotate his nights so nobody knows when he will be there. And the next year I wanted to reduce costs, and I told them, Why don't we substitute a dog? Turn a dog loose in the warehouse. So we did, and it worked. Now the following year, I needed to get the costs down some more, and my guy said, Well, we're down to a dog! So I said, Why don't you just record the dog snarling? And we did. And it worked! Nobody was really sure whether there was a dog in there or not.

The Expansion Path

The points of tangency in Figure 8.4b show the least costly way of producing each indicated output. Producing 6 units of output as cheaply as possible, for instance, involves hiring L_2 units of labor and K_2 units of capital. The line formed by connecting these tangency points is the firm's **expansion path**. It identifies the least costly input combination for each output and will generally slope upward, implying that the firm will expand the use of both inputs (in the long-run setting) as it increases output. Note that input prices are assumed to remain constant as the firm varies its output along the expansion path.

EXPANSION PATH
a line formed by connecting the points of tangency between isocost lines and the highest respective attainable isoquants

Is Production Cost Minimized?

It is generally assumed that business firms produce output at the lowest possible cost. In terms of Figure 8.4b, the assumption is that firms will operate somewhere on the expansion path (exactly where depends on what output they choose to produce, as explained in the next chapter). Because there are many ways a given output can be produced, and because only one of these ways results in the minimum cost, what is the basis for assuming that the firm will choose the least costly method?

The assumption that firms minimize cost is based on the belief that firms are attempting to maximize profit. To maximize profit, a firm must produce its output at minimum cost. If a firm could produce the same output at a lower cost, it would reduce total cost without changing total revenue (because output is unchanged), and therefore realize a greater profit. Of course, firms may not always be successful in minimizing cost; this is a difficult task when input prices and technology both change over time. Nonetheless, firms do have a substantial profit incentive to hold cost down, so the assumption that they minimize cost seems warranted. The basis for assuming profit maximization itself will be discussed in the next chapter. It should be noted that cost minimization, while a necessary condition for profit maximization, is not the same as profit maximization. Cost minimization occurs at all points on the expansion path, but profit maximization also involves selecting the most profitable output from among those on the expansion path.

That the profit motive is important in spurring organizations to minimize cost is suggested by comparisons of costs of production by private firms and government agencies that produce the same, or similar, products. More than 50 studies have made such a comparison. For example, one study concluded that the construction cost for public housing was 20 percent higher than comparable privately produced housing. Another concluded that municipal fire departments had a 39 to 88 percent higher cost per capita than did communities contracting with a private firm to provide the services. More than 40 studies have found government provision to be more costly than private provision; only 2 have found government provision to be less costly.[4] The most likely explanation for this cost disparity seems to be that the profit incentive is absent in government organizations; public policymakers do not profit from reducing production cost.

APPLICATION 8.2 THE COST OF PUBLIC VERSUS PRIVATE PROVISION

A big reason behind the push for greater competition in primary and secondary education markets is the high cost associated with public schools.[5] For example, after holding other factors constant, the per-pupil cost of private school education in Chicago is estimated to be 45–77 percent lower than the cost of public education. The higher cost in public schools stems partly from greater administrative overhead. In Los Angeles, for instance, one-third of the public school system's budget of well over $1 billion per year is spent on central administrators who are not based on school campuses. There is one central administrator for every 153 students in the public schools of Los Angeles. By contrast, there is one central administrator for every 4,000 students in the privately managed Los Angeles Catholic School system.

Furthermore, the quality of education offered at higher-cost public schools appears to be inferior to that provided by private schools. Researchers find that private schools do better at emphasizing academic instruction and achievement, getting teachers and students to work hard, and getting parents involved—even after accounting for the socioeconomic status of a student's family.

Similar cost and quality differences between private and public firms are present in the postal market. About 10 percent of the $50 billion United States Postal Service (USPS) annual budget is already contracted out to private firms. For example, 10 percent of rural routes are franchised out to private carriers. According to USPS's own studies, contracting out leaves customers more satisfied and achieves an average cost saving of 50 percent.

That the private sector does a better job of delivering the mail was demonstrated to one of the authors during a cross-country move to Los Angeles when he shipped most of his books, research materials, and personal papers by the U.S. Postal Service. Of the 45 cartons shipped, 38 were delivered. The remaining 7 never arrived, save for a few items that would occasionally surface, much like the remnants of a ship that had been dashed to pieces against a reef. Among the flotsam was a copy of the author's 1983 tax return, which turned up badly mutilated in an envelope with a note from the Postal Service: "The enclosed item was found in the bottom of one of our mail trucks at our Mojave Station. We hope that this delay hasn't caused you any great inconvenience." It goes without saying that the author has relied on private firms to do his shipping ever since.

[5]This application draws on: John E. Chubb and Terry M. Moe, *Politics, Markets, and American Schools* (Washington, D.C.: Brookings Institution, 1990); and Mark A. Zupan, "Let the Market Deliver the Mail," *New York Times* (August 7, 1993), p. 11.

[4]These studies are discussed in T. E. Borcherding, W. W. Pommerehne, and F. Schneider, "Comparing the Efficiency of Private and Public Production: The Evidence from Five Countries," *Zeitschrift fur Nationalökonomie*, 89 (1982), pp. 127–156.

8.5 INPUT PRICE CHANGES AND COST CURVES

Remember that input prices are assumed to be constant when we construct a firm's cost curves. Per-unit costs vary with output along a cost curve because the productivity of the inputs varies with the rate of output, not because the costs of inputs vary. Economists generally assume that one firm's output will not by itself influence input prices. Rarely does a single firm use a large portion of the total quantity of any input. Consequently, if a firm increases its employment of land, MBAs, or gasoline, this expansion will not cause a perceptible increase in the market demand for these inputs, and their prices will not be affected.

Although input prices generally do not change because of any single firm's output decision, they do occasionally change on account of underlying market forces. For example, let's take a look at a commercial real estate developer, Coldwell Banker (CB). Coldwell Banker produces as part of its product line parking spaces using two inputs, concrete (C) and land (L). Importantly, these two inputs can be substituted for one another to a certain extent. Land can be conserved, for example, by using more concrete and building multistory parking garages. Because the two inputs are substitutes, CB's isoquants will have the typical shape—that associated with a production function in which different input combinations can produce the same total output.

Figure 8.5a illustrates the firm's input choices. Initially, Coldwell Banker is producing an output of 1,000 by employing land and concrete at point E on isoquant $IQ_{1,000}$ and isocost line MN. The firm's original expansion path passes through point E, and from it we can derive the per-unit cost curves MC and AC, shown in Figure 8.5b. Along these curves, as along the expansion path, the prices of inputs are unchanged.

Now suppose that the price of land increases. First, let's see how this change affects the way inputs are combined in the least costly manner to produce the same output, 1,000, in

FIGURE 8.5

A Higher Input Price Shifts Cost Curves Upward

(a) With a higher price of land the cost of producing each level of output increases. Input combination E' becomes the least costly way to produce $IQ_{1,000}$ after the increase in the land price. (b) The change in the land price shifts the AC and MC curves upward to AC' and MC', respectively.

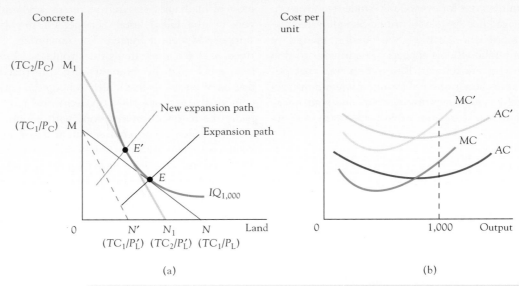

(a)   (b)

Figure 8.5a. A higher price of land means the slopes of isocost lines become steeper, because the slope is P_L/P_C. If CB were to continue to incur the same total cost in hiring land and concrete, the relevant isocost line would be MN'. If, however, CB operates on MN', it would produce less output, and we want to consider production of the original level of output, 1,000. To produce 1,000 units in the least costly way at the new price of land, CB should operate at point E', where $IQ_{1,000}$ is tangent to the isocost line M_1N_1. Note that M_1N_1 is parallel to MN', reflecting the higher price of land. Consequently, the higher land price increases the total cost to Coldwell Banker of producing the same output as before; MN' shows an unchanged total cost, so M_1N_1, which is further from the origin, represents a higher total cost. Note also that CB will use less of the more expensive input, land, and more of the now relatively less costly input, concrete, in its production. What the movement from E to E' really shows is the **input substitution effect** that results from a change in the relative cost of inputs. Because of the higher land price, a new expansion path is defined.[6]

INPUT SUBSTITUTION EFFECT

the effect of a change in the price of an input on a firm's relative use of the input to produce a given level of output

A higher price of land increases the total cost of producing a given number of parking spaces. In turn, an increased total cost also implies that Coldwell Banker's AC and MC curves shift upward to AC' and MC', as illustrated in Figure 8.5b. For example, a higher land price increases average cost since average cost equals total cost divided by output. The AC' and MC' curves are, of course, based on the new expansion path in Figure 8.5a, which shows the least costly method of producing each number of parking spaces at the higher land price. This result is not particularly surprising, but it highlights an important distinction. Per-unit costs can vary as a result of changing output when input prices are constant (a movement along given cost curves), or they can vary as a result of a change in input prices (a shift in the cost curves). Just as in the case of distinguishing between a movement along and a shift in a demand curve, keeping this distinction in mind for cost curves is important, too.

APPLICATION 8.3   THE ECONOMICS OF RAISING AND RAZING BUILDINGS

To minimize the cost of producing any given level of output, the golden rule of cost minimization implies that, at the margin, firms should equate rates of return across inputs. To see this rule in action and to show how the input substitution effect works, take the case of a commercial real estate developer producing the parking spaces associated with shopping malls. Assume that the developer uses two inputs, concrete (C) and land (L), and successfully equates the marginal rates of return across the inputs, $MP_C/P_C = MP_L/P_L$, in the production of parking spaces in suburban locations. If the developer moves production from a suburban to an urban setting, then the price of land will likely be higher while the other factors in the equation will not change appreciably. As the price of land rises to P_L', the marginal rate of return on land becomes lower than the marginal rate of return on concrete, $MP_C/P_C > MP_L/P_L'$. The inequality in rates of return gives the developer an incentive to shift away from land and toward concrete—hence, the phenomenon of high-rise parking structures taking up relatively little space in central business districts versus suburban parking lots that occupy a lot of land and use a minimal amount of concrete. In Tokyo, where the price of land is very high, so are some of the parking structures: 40-story buildings which hold four cars per floor and rely on elevators to transport cars to upper levels.

---

[6]In passing, we should warn against a common error. It is tempting to say that we can derive the firm's demand curve for land by identifying the point at which an isoquant is tangent to MN', by analogy to the way we derive a consumer's demand curve. This approach is incorrect, because the firm need not continue to operate at an unchanged level of total cost; it can choose any point on the new expansion path. The point that is most profitable, which will depend on demand conditions, would occur at the same total cost only by coincidence. In a later chapter we will see how the demand curve for an input such as land is derived.

While concrete-intensive, they are parsimonious in their use of expensive, horizontal real estate.

Building demolition provides another example of the golden rule of cost minimization and the input substitution effect at work. Most large, old buildings in the United States are razed through implosion or the strategic employment of dynamite. Not too long ago in Hong Kong, however, a very different method was employed. A firm charged with demolishing a building hired numerous workers who started on the building's top story, broke down the story into small pieces with pick-axes, and then carried the pieces away in sacks on their backs.

The process was repeated for each successive story from the top down to the bottom until the entire building had been manually broken apart and carted away.

Why the difference in techniques? As you probably guessed, the price of labor, P_L, was lower in Hong Kong. Firms in the razing business were trying to equate marginal rates of return on dynamite (D) and labor (L), $MP_D/P_D = MP_L/P_L$ and, due to the lower price of labor, P'_L, the marginal rate of return on dynamite was lower than that marginal rate of return on labor, $MP_D/P_D < MP_L/P'_L$. As a result, Hong Kong firms substituted toward labor and away from dynamite.

APPLICATION 8.4   WHY THE NECKS ARE THICKER IN NEW HAVEN

Sometimes it's not the price of an input but the input's marginal product that changes as one moves from location to location. Take the case of college hockey. Two of the perennially top-ranked teams in the country are Harvard and Yale. While tending to be alike in their national standing, they differ greatly in their playing style. Harvard consistently opts for fast but small players while Yale fields slower but brawnier skaters. This difference in playing styles has persisted over the past several decades despite coaching changes and turnover in player personnel.

What accounts for the difference? The answer may not be obvious but is certainly interesting: not all hockey rinks are the same size. Harvard's rink is large and this serves to increase the marginal product of speedy versus brawny players—there is more room to play a fast-paced version of hockey. By contrast, Yale's rink is smaller and thereby favors brawn over speed. Since there is less room to run, it becomes easier for larger players to hunt down smaller opposition and beat it to a pulp.

The Harvard and Yale teams both try to amplify their advantages during home games. Inside the Harvard arena, the temperature is always kept near freezing and spectators have to wear winter coats. The colder the temperature, the faster the ice, and therefore the more advantageous for the speed-oriented Harvard team. In comparison, at Yale's arena, the temperature hovers at a much higher level. A warmer temperature makes the ice choppier and lessens the pace at which a game can be

played, thereby giving a further edge to the slower-skating but brawnier Yale team.

Very often the outcome of the national college hockey championship tournament will hinge on the site at which the tournament is held. A large tournament rink plays into the hands of faster teams while a smaller rink helps brawnier outfits.

The same phenomenon of marginal products differing by location occurs in baseball. For example, the Florida Marlins typically employ players who are good singles hitters and speedy on the basepaths while the Boston Red Sox opt for slower players who are better at hitting home runs. The difference reflects the facts that there is no regulation-size baseball field and Florida has the larger field.[7] Both teams are attempting to equate the marginal rates of return on speed (S) and brawn (B), $MP_S/P_S = MP_B/P_B$. As one moves from Boston to Florida and a larger field size, the marginal product of brawn declines to MP'_B while the marginal product of speed increases to MP'_S. These alterations make the marginal rate of return on speed higher than the marginal rate of return on brawn, $MP'_S/P_S > MP'_B/P_B$. As a consequence, the Marlins feature more speed and less brawn than the Red Sox.

---

[7]At the Marlins' Pro Player Stadium, the distances between home plate and the left field, center field, and right field walls are 330, 434, and 345 feet, respectively. By contrast, the analogous distances are 310, 420, and 302 feet at Boston's Fenway Park.

8.6 LONG-RUN COST CURVES

In many respects the firm's long-run cost curves are easier to handle than short-run cost curves. In the short run we must distinguish among three total cost curves: total fixed cost, total variable cost, and total (combined) cost. Because all inputs are variable in the long run, there is only one long-run total cost curve. There is also only one long-run average cost curve, in contrast to three in the short run.

Figure 8.6a shows a long-run total cost curve (*LTC*); Figure 8.6b shows the associated long-run marginal cost (*LMC*) and average cost curves (*LAC*). (To distinguish between long-run and short-run cost curves, the long-run curves are prefixed with an *L* and the short-run curves with an *S*.) Since the graphical derivation of the average and marginal cost curves from the total cost curve is the same for the long run as for the short run (see Figure 8.2), we will not repeat it here.

Our primary concern now is to explain why the curves have the shapes they do. We have drawn the *LTC* curve to imply a U-shaped long-run average cost curve, but why would it have this shape? With the short-run average variable cost curve, the law of diminishing marginal returns was responsible for its U shape. In the long run there are generally no fixed inputs, so the law is not directly applicable.

Nonetheless, just as the relationship between inputs and output underlies the short-run curves, it also underlies the long-run curves. In the long run, however, returns to scale are

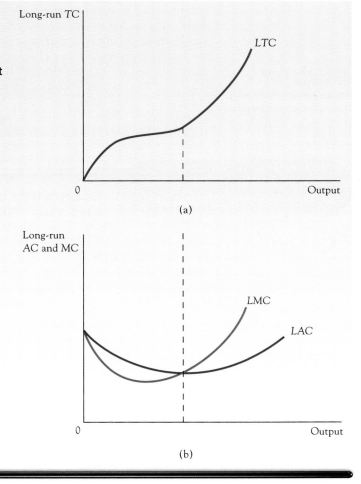

FIGURE 8.6

Long-Run Cost Curves
(a) The long-run total cost shows the minimum cost at which each rate of output may be produced, just as the expansion path does. (b) The long-run marginal and average cost curves are derived from the total cost curve in the same way the short-run per-unit curves are derived from the short-run total cost curve.

the factors that determine how output varies when all inputs are varied in proportion. As we explained in the previous chapter, increasing returns to scale are likely to be common at low output levels, while decreasing returns to scale are likely to prevail at high output levels. Under such plausible conditions, the long-run average cost curve will have a U shape.

Let's see why increasing returns to scale imply a declining average cost per unit of output. Suppose that 1 unit of capital (1K) and 6 units of labor (6L) produce an output of 3. With increasing returns to scale, a proportionate increase in inputs increases output more than in proportion. So suppose that doubling inputs more than doubles output. That is, suppose that employing 2K and 12L results in an output of 8. Note what this implies. When output is 3, the average amount of capital per unit of output is 0.33K, and the average amount of labor is 2L. At 8 units of output average input requirements have fallen to 0.25K and 0.67L. Increasing returns to scale mean that at higher output levels each unit of output requires (on average) a smaller quantity of all inputs. Because inputs are available at fixed prices, however, smaller average input requirements imply smaller average unit costs. *Therefore, increasing returns to scale imply that average unit cost is falling.*

By the same reasoning, *constant returns to scale imply a constant average cost, and decreasing returns to scale imply a rising average cost.* Insofar as returns to scale are first increasing and thereafter decreasing, the long-run average cost curve will be U-shaped. Once again, the cost curves reflect the firm's underlying production technology.

It is important to note that as a firm alters its level of output in the long run, it may also want to alter its input proportions. If input proportions are changed, then the concept of returns to scale does not apply—since not all inputs will be "scaled" up or down proportionately. Instead, economists use the term **economies of scale** to refer to the case where a firm can increase its output more than in proportion to its total input cost. **Diseconomies of scale** are said to apply when a firm's output increases less than in proportion to its total input cost. Increasing returns to scale thus imply economies of scale, but the reverse need not be true. That is, if firms find it advantageous to alter their input proportions with their output, then they may confront economies of scale but not increasing returns to scale. In the more general case, therefore, a firm's long-run average cost curve will be U-shaped if economies of scale are present at low rates of output and diseconomies of scale prevail at high output levels.[8]

ECONOMIES OF SCALE
a situation in which a firm can increase its output more than proportionally to its total input cost

DISECONOMIES OF SCALE
a situation in which a firm's output increases less than proportionally to its total input cost

---

APPLICATION 8.5   **ECONOMIES OF SCALE AND THE "NETWORK SOCIETY"**

S|ome business gurus have asserted that the theoretical principles upon which the New Economy operates are novel.[9] One of the main claims is that we live in a *network society*—one in which companies can benefit as never before from increasing output and lower per-unit production costs. The fax machine is a frequently cited example. One fax machine is useless, but when there are two or more, there is a network. If there are 100,000 fax machines, there are 10 billion possible relationships. A producer of fax machines, so the reasoning goes, thus stands to benefit more from any initial invest-

[9]This application is based on Carl Shapiro and Hal R. Varian, *Information Rules* (Boston: Harvard Business School Press, 1999); and Jeff Madrick, "The New Economy's 'Network Society' Plays by Old-Economy Rules," *New York Times* (July 6, 2000), p. C2.

---

[8]While a U shape is typical, the long-run average cost curve could have a somewhat different shape. Several studies have suggested that for some firms, economies of scale occur at low rates of output, but once output reaches a certain threshold level, neither economies nor diseconomies of scale hold over an extended region before diseconomies of scale set in. When this result is true, the firm's long-run average cost curve would have this shape: ⊔. When average cost reaches a minimum, it stays at that level over a wide range of output before it begins to rise. Do you see what the corresponding LMC curve will be shaped like in this case?

ment the greater is the network. And the ultimate network, according to these gurus, is the World Wide Web. The Web permits manufacturers of hardware or software products whose distribution can be tied to the Web to experience unrivaled profit opportunities.

Upon some reflection, however, it is unclear whether there are any new economic principles underlying the New Economy. Network effects were present in earlier times with products such as television and telephones much as they are today with fax machines and the World Wide Web. Moreover, the production cost advantages associated with today's network society appear to be nothing more than the economies of scale that have characterized prior industrial revolutions. For example, consider steel. In 1888, steel rails cost $68 per ton to produce. Primarily because of economies of scale, the real price of steel rails fell to $18 per ton by 1900. While the fixed cost associated with constructing a steel mill was high, the cost of producing extra rails was small. Thus, the more rails sold, the lower the average cost.

If anything, it is unclear whether production-side, economies of scale considerations play a more important role in today's markets than they have historically. Carl Shapiro and Hal Varian of Berkeley's Haas School of Business argue that, if anything, demand-side, bandwagon effects (covered in Chapter 4) may be more important in explaining the market dominance of a firm such as Microsoft than any production-side economies of scale. After all, any economies of scale associated with designing software are rather quickly exhausted. In contrast, bandwagon effects on the demand side appear to be much more important determinants of why an individual consumer will buy a product such as Microsoft's Windows operating system.

The Long Run and Short Run Revisited

It is convenient to think of the long run as a planning or investment horizon. In making long-run decisions, the firm decides what scale of plant to build or purchase, how much and what type of specialized equipment to install, whether to train existing workers for the new equipment or hire new workers, and so on. The firm is planning ahead in making such decisions. In effect, the firm is selecting what type of short-run situation it will be in later. Once the plant is built, the firm must operate with that fixed input for a certain time period (the short run) until enough time passes for a subsequent long-run adjustment to be made.

To clarify the relationship between the short run and the long run, let's suppose that there are only five scales of plant the firm can build, and associated with each plant size is a short-run average total cost curve. Figure 8.7 shows the five short-run average cost curves as SAC_1, SAC_2, and so on. The firm can choose only one plant size: Which will it be? The plant size depends on what output the firm expects will be appropriate—which, of course, depends on demand conditions not yet considered. Suppose, however, that the firm believes q_1 to be the appropriate output. The firm could build the smallest-sized plant (SAC_1) and produce q_1 at a unit cost of $50,000, or it could build the next larger plant (SAC_2) and produce at a unit cost of $55,000. Of course, the firm will build the plant size that permits it to produce q_1 at the lowest average (and hence total) cost—in this instance, the smallest-sized plant.

The long-run average cost curve is defined as the lowest average cost attainable when all inputs are variable—that is, when any plant size can be constructed. In this case, with only five options, point A on SAC_1 is one point on the long-run average cost curve, because it shows the lowest unit cost for q_1. Similarly, point C on SAC_2 is a second point on the *LAC* curve. With only five options the entire *LAC* curve is shown as the heavy scalloped sections of the *SAC* curves, because each of the segments indicates the lowest unit cost possible for the corresponding level of output.

Once the firm builds the plant, its options in the immediate future will be dictated by the *SAC* curve selected when the long-run decision was implemented. If the firm builds the smallest-sized plant, it is temporarily stuck with that decision even if q_1 turns out to be an inappropriate level of output after all. In that event the firm must determine whether to make another long-run decision to change its scale of operations.

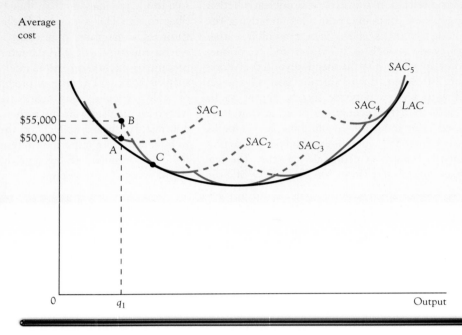

Short- and Long-Run Average Cost Curves
When the firm has five scales of plant from which to choose, the long-run average cost curve is the heavy scalloped portion of the five *SAC* curves. As the number of possible scales of plant increases, the long-run average cost curve becomes the smooth U-shaped *LAC* curve.

In general, the firm will have many more than five scales of plant to choose from. When a large number of options exist—for example, when there are a dozen scales of plant between SAC_1 and SAC_2—the long-run average cost curve effectively becomes a smooth curve, such as *LAC* in Figure 8.7. Each point on this curve is associated with a different short-run scale of operation that the firm could choose.

8.7 IMPORTANCE OF COST CURVES TO MARKET STRUCTURE

Although most firms have U-shaped long-run average cost curves, the level of output at which cost per unit reaches a minimum varies from firm to firm and from industry to industry. The scale of operations at which average cost per unit reaches a minimum, called the **minimum efficient scale,** may be immense for automobile producers but relatively small for apparel makers. These differences occur because the increasing returns to scale that are responsible for the declining portion of the long-run average cost curve primarily reflect technological factors, and the technology governing production differs significantly from one good to another.

The minimum efficient scale for a typical firm in an industry has a major impact on the structure of the industry—the number of firms in the industry and thus the proportion of overall industry output accounted for by each member firm. More precisely, what matters is the level of output where average cost reaches a minimum in comparison with the total in-

MINIMUM EFFICIENT SCALE
the scale of operations at which average cost per unit reaches a minimum

dustry demand for the product. Figure 8.8 illustrates this point. When the demand curve for legal services, for example, is D, suppose that the typical firm has a long-run average cost curve shown by LAC_1. Average cost reaches a minimum at $30,000 per unit of output, and at a price of $30,000 the total quantity demanded by consumers is L_1. The representative law firm can produce a total $0.05L_1$ at a unit cost of $30,000, or one-twentieth of the total quantity demanded by consumers. Insofar as LAC_1 is typical for firms producing legal services, the industry can accommodate 20 firms, each producing approximately 5 percent of the total output. With such a large number of firms, the industry is likely to be highly competitive.

In contrast, suppose that production technology dictates a cost curve like LAC_2. The minimum efficient scale is then half the total quantity demanded at a price of $30,000. With such cost curves, the industry would tend to become dominated by a few (probably two in this case) large law firms. Suppose that a small firm tried to compete in this market. Operating on a small scale, the firm would have a unit cost of more than $30,000; it might, for example, be operating at point A, where average cost is $50,000 per unit. Such a firm would tend to be driven out of business because it could easily be undersold by a larger operation producing at a unit cost of $30,000. For this reason the industry inevitably gravitates toward a small number of large firms. Thus, technology of production, which largely determines at what output unit cost is at a minimum for a firm, is an important factor in determining whether an industry is composed of a large or small number of firms, although other factors may prove influential as well.

FIGURE 8.8

Cost Curves and the Structure of Industry
The level of output at which long-run average cost is at a minimum relative to market demand has important implications for the structure of the industry. If all firms have *LAC* curves like *LAC*$_1$, 20 firms can coexist in the industry; if the *LAC*$_2$ curve is typical, only 2 firms are likely to survive.

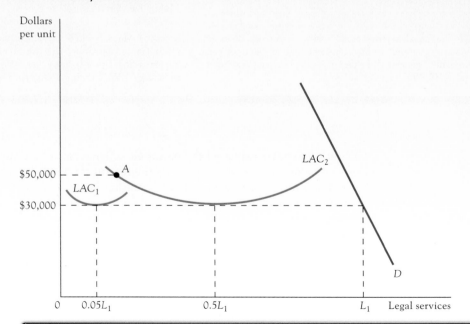

APPLICATION 8.6   MINIMUM EFFICIENT SCALES IN SUDS, SUITS, AND SOFT DRINKS

The minimum efficient scale of production varies across industries as well as over time within them. Take the case of the domestic beer industry. In 1914, there were almost 1,400 breweries in the United States versus fewer than 40 by 1980.[10] While demand-side changes affected the number of beer producers over this time period, several important technological changes also served to increase the minimum efficient scale of production. Pasteurization and the advent of at-home consumption from cans and bottles (versus a tavern's nonpasteurized draft) favored large brewers. Moreover, the number of bottles or cans that a brewery's filling and sealing line could produce per minute increased dramatically. In addition to the increased economies to operating single plants, greater economies also developed in multiplant operation—economies in the form of lower advertising and regulatory compliance costs. For example, with the advent of television, it is cheaper for Anheuser-Busch to buy a 30-second commercial for nationwide broadcast on a major network than it is for 50 smaller breweries, each producing one-fiftieth the output of Anheuser-Busch, to purchase the same length advertisements to air on their local television stations.

The minimum efficient scale of production has also been rising over time in the legal services and soft-drink industries. Smaller-size law firms have been dying out due to their inability to provide the diverse array of human and technological resources large corporations demand in today's litigious society.[11] Soft-drink producers such as Coca-Cola and Pepsi have moved from relying on independent bottlers to a system of "captive" bottlers.[12] Because the coordination of pricing and promotion strategies is more readily accomplished if bottlers are owned by Coke and Pepsi, the size of soft-drink firms has been growing. It is much easier for a single, large, soft-drink manufacturer to roll out a national promotion such as the "Pepsi Challenge" or to negotiate a single, nationwide contract with major retailers such as McDonald's and Wal-Mart than it is for a set of smaller bottlers to develop a coordinated promotion plan or negotiate individually with retailers.

---

[10]Kenneth G. Elzinga, "The Beer Industry," in *The Structure of American Industry*, 4th ed., edited by Walter Adams (New York: Macmillan, 1971). Recently, the number of breweries has risen with the advent of microbreweries and self-breweries. Self-breweries at least partly reflect an attempt by consumers to avoid taxes on beer. In Canada, where alcohol taxes are higher than in the United States, self-brewing is quite prevalent. In the Canadian province of Ontario, for instance, there are 250 self-breweries churning out an estimated 6 million gallons of beer per year—roughly 3 percent of the province's total output (*Wall Street Journal* (August 19, 1993), pp. A1 and A6).

[11]"Midsize Law Firms Struggle to Survive," *Wall Street Journal* (October 19, 1988), p. B1.

[12]Timothy J. Muris, David T. Scheffman, and Pablo T. Spiller, "Strategy and Transaction Costs: The Organization of Distribution in the Carbonated Soft Drink Industry," *Journal of Economics and Management Strategy*, 1 No. 1 (Spring 1992), pp. 83–128.

Economists have estimated the minimum efficient scale in different industries using a variety of techniques. Table 8.2 reports the results of one such study. The second column shows the minimum efficient scale of operation for several major manufacturing industries. The last column gives these outputs as a percentage of U.S. quantity demanded. Although there are substantial variations, in all cases except the refrigerator industry the minimum efficient scale tends to be small relative to the size of the market. Other studies have also reached the conclusion that most industries can accommodate a relatively large number of firms each operating at the minimum efficient scale. There are exceptions, of course. For example, the production of civilian airplanes has been estimated to require plant sizes that are large relative to the market to realize minimum unit production costs.

TABLE 8.2	MINIMUM EFFICIENT PLANT SCALES		
Industry	Minimum Efficient Scale (Per Year)	Percentage of U.S. Quantity Demanded
Beer brewing	4.5 million barrels	3.4
Cigarettes	36 billion cigarettes	6.6
Petroleum refining	73 million barrels	1.9
Glass bottles	133,000 tons	1.5
Cement	7 million barrels	1.7
Steel	4 million tons	2.6
Refrigerators	800,000 units	14.1
Car batteries	1 million units	1.9

Source: Frederic M. Scherer, Alan Beckenstein, Erich Kaufer, and R. D. Murphy, *The Economics of Multi-Plant Operation: An International Comparison Study* (Cambridge, Mass.: Harvard University Press, 1975), pp. 80–94.

8.8 USING COST CURVES: CONTROLLING POLLUTION[13]

Many problems can be clarified if we pose them in terms of marginal cost. Let's take an example of some practical importance. Two oil refineries located in the Los Angeles basin release some pollutants into the air in the process of distilling products such as gasoline from petroleum. Because the pollutants harm people living in the Los Angeles basin (for example, they increase the likelihood of respiratory illness), the government steps in and requires each refinery to curtail its pollution to 100 units (measured in some appropriate way). This restriction limits the total pollutants discharged into the air to 200 units.

An important question here is whether the government's program to reduce pollution to 200 units accomplishes the intended result at the lowest possible cost. To answer it, we must think in terms of the marginal cost each refinery bears in reducing pollution. Figure 8.9 illustrates the situation. In this diagram the amount of pollution generated by each refinery is measured from *right to left*. For example, before the government restricts its activities, refinery A discharges OP_1 (300 units), and refinery B discharges OP_2 (250 units). Measuring pollution from right to left is the same as measuring pollution abatement—the number of units by which pollution is reduced from its initial level—from left to right. For example, if refinery B cuts back its pollution from 250 to 100 units, it has produced 150 units of pollution abatement, the distance P_2X.

The reason for adopting these units of measurement along the horizontal axis is that each refinery incurs costs from reducing air pollution. The more pollution abatement, the greater the total cost to a refinery. In fact, we can think of each refinery as having a marginal cost curve, starting from its initial position, that measures the marginal cost of pollution abatement (cutting pollution by one unit) at each level of "output." Exactly what form this cost takes is immaterial; it may involve switching to a higher grade of petroleum, installing scrubbers on the refinery's smokestacks, or building a more modern plant. Each refinery would, of course, choose the least costly way of cutting back. The information we require to find the cost of complying with the government's regulation is each firm's marginal cost curve of pollution abatement. We expect these curves to rise if the law of diminishing returns applies to

[13]A mathematical treatment of some of the material in this section is given in the appendix at the back of the book (page 567).

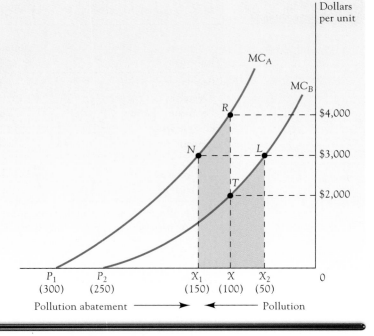

FIGURE 8.9

Cost of Pollution Abatement
To produce a given output at the lowest possible cost, separate firms must be producing at a point where their marginal costs are equal. This condition is also true for pollution abatement. To reduce pollution to 200 units in the least costly way, refinery A should discharge 150 units and refinery B, 50 units.

pollution abatement; as more pollution is abated, eliminating additional units becomes more expensive. In Figure 8.9 refinery A's marginal cost curve is MC_A, and refinery B's is MC_B. (Because air pollution is a by-product of the production of other goods such as gasoline, these curves are likely to start at zero and rise throughout. Do you see why?)

When the government limits each refinery to 100 units of pollution, refinery A will operate at point R on MC_A, and refinery B will be at point T on MC_B. (We assume that this restriction is not so costly that either refinery is put out of business.) Now only 200 units of pollution are released into the air, a reduction from 550. Is this the least costly way to limit pollution to 200 units? To see that it is not, we must consider the refineries' marginal costs. At 100 units of pollution, the marginal cost of reducing pollution to refinery A is $4,000, but refinery B's cost is only $2,000. If refinery B were to cut back pollution by 1 more unit, it would add only $2,000 to its cost. If refinery A increased pollution by 1 unit (produced 1 unit less of abatement), its cost would fall by $4,000. Having refinery B pollute 1 unit less and refinery A 1 unit more leaves the total amount of pollution unchanged, but it reduces the refineries' combined cost by $2,000 (plus $2,000 for refinery B and minus $4,000 for refinery A).

As long as the marginal costs differ, the total cost of pollution abatement can be reduced by increasing abatement where its marginal cost is less and reducing it where its marginal cost is greater. So shifting the production of abatement from refinery A to refinery B should continue until B's rising marginal cost just equals A's falling marginal cost. In the diagram this equality occurs where refinery B cuts back pollution to 50 units at point L on MC_B and refinery A increases pollution by 50 units to point N on MC_A. At these points the marginal cost to both refineries equals $3,000. Each step of this reallocation reduces A's cost by more than it increases B's cost, so the two refineries still generate the same amount of total pollution (200 units) but at a lower total cost. Any further shifting of pollution abatement from

A to B would increase total cost. To limit pollution to 200 units in the least costly way, the refineries should produce at a level where their marginal costs are equal.

When refinery B increases its pollution abatement from P_2X to P_2X_2, its total cost rises by the shaded area TLX_2X. This area in effect sums the marginal cost of each successive unit of abatement from P_2X to P_2X_2. For instance, the first unit (reduction in pollution from 100 units) beyond P_2X adds \$2,000 to total cost; the next, perhaps \$2,050; the third, \$2,100; and so on. So the addition to total cost from the first 3 units in this case is \$6,150. (In general, the area under a marginal cost curve between two levels of output measures how much total cost rises when moving from the lower to the higher output.) Refinery A's total cost falls by $NRXX_1$ when it reduces its abatement from P_1X to P_1X_1. The cost saving to refinery A, $NRXX_1$, is clearly larger than the additional cost to refinery B, TLX_2X (recall that $XX_2 = XX_1$).

If the government simply mandates that each refinery restrict its pollution to the same level, this policy will normally result in a higher cost for pollution control than necessary. The only exception would be if the marginal costs of the refineries are equal when they are polluting the same amount, and this is unlikely to happen. Our analysis, therefore, leads to an important conclusion: to minimize the cost of pollution control, firms should operate where their marginal costs are equal. The same rule also applies to emissions by other stationary sources as well as mobile sources of air pollutants. For example, emission standards for automobiles should take into account the fact that the marginal cost of limiting emissions varies from one make of automobile to another and between older and newer automobiles. Applying the same standards to all automobiles (as is done now) imposes a higher total cost than is necessary.

Realistically, can the government apply this rule? In terms of Figure 8.9, to allocate pollution abatement responsibility in the least costly way, the government needs to know both refineries' marginal cost curves, and such information would be virtually impossible to obtain with any degree of accuracy. Without knowledge of the MC curves, the government cannot place a limit on each refinery's pollution so that all refineries' marginal costs are equal. Does this conclusion mean that our economic analysis is of little practical value? Not at all. As we will see in Chapter 20, there is a way for the government to limit pollution efficiently without knowing the MC curves.

APPLICATION 8.7 THE COST OF DEALING WITH GLOBAL WARMING

E vidence that the law of diminishing returns applies to pollution abatement comes from some recent studies of the cost associated with mitigating global warming.[14] The central strategy for mitigating global warming focuses on limiting greenhouse-gas concentra-

tions in the atmosphere. Limiting greenhouse-gas concentrations requires curtailing activities that release carbon dioxide, methane, and other greenhouse gases into the atmosphere—gases that trap heat in the atmosphere and thereby promote global warming. The burning of fossil fuels (e.g., through automobile and airplane travel and home heating) is a human activity that has greatly increased the amount of greenhouse gases released into the atmosphere.

Several analyses have shown that the economic cost of limiting greenhouse-gas emissions increases appreciably as the target reduction in emissions is raised. Specifi-

[14]This application is based on Robert W. Hahn, *The Economics and Politics of Climate Change* (Washington, D.C.: The AEI Press, 1998); and Ian Parry, Roberton Williams, and Lawrence Goulder, "When Can Carbon Abatement Policies Increase Welfare?: The Fundamental Rate of Distorted Factor Markets," unpublished paper, Resources for the Future, 1996.

cally, the marginal cost of controlling emissions rises from \$10 to \$80 per ton as reductions increase from 5 to 25 percent. The law of diminishing returns thus appears to be a factor that will impede efforts to mitigate global warming—the more so as the intended reductions in greenhouse gas emissions are raised.

8.9   ECONOMIES OF SCOPE

So far we have been focusing on the cost to firms of producing single products. Most real-world firms, however, produce more than one product. For example, airlines typically provide different classes of service on a given city-pair route as well as serving numerous city pairs. Most business schools produce research and teaching. And telecommunications firms are capable of providing voice and video services through the same fiber-optic cable.

Economies of scope are present if it is cheaper for one firm to produce products jointly than it is for separate firms to produce the same products independently. Take the case of business schools. Economies of scope are likely to be present because certain inputs such as the library, administration, office space, and faculty are capable of contributing to both the teaching and research output of an institution. Were separate firms to produce the two independently, they would have to build their own individual facilities and employ separate faculty and administrators. Such duplication would in all likelihood make the overall cost of production across the separate research and teaching schools higher than the cost of joint production of research and teaching by a single school.

Suppose that the total cost to a business school of producing research (R) and teaching (T) can be represented by $TC(R,T)$. If only research is produced by the school, total cost equals $TC(R,0)$. Conversely, if teaching is the only output, total cost equals $TC(0,T)$. Economies of scope can be said to be present if the following inequality holds:

$$TC(R,T) < [TC(R,0) + TC(0,T)].$$

In other words, when it is more expensive to produce research and teaching independently than jointly, production is characterized by economies of scope. **Diseconomies of scope** would characterize production if the above inequality were reversed: if it was cheaper for research and teaching to be produced independently by separate entities than jointly under the same institutional roof.

Economies of scope are important since they provide an efficiency reason for the existence of multiproduct conglomerates. For example, if there are inputs such as fiber-optic cable and management that contribute to the provision of both voice and video services, it will be advantageous for telecommunications firms to span both markets. If hubs lower the total cost of providing air service between a set of different city-pair markets, it will be cheaper to have one airline serve all city pairs through a single hub-and-spoke system than to have separate airlines provide independent service to each particular city-pair route.

There is, of course, no relationship between economies of scope and economies of scale. That is, the Wharton School of Business may face economies of scope in producing teaching and research jointly yet face diseconomies of scale in the production of research (holding constant the amount of teaching performed, doubling research output may require more than a doubling of total input cost). Conversely, if Wharton faces economies of scale in the production of both teaching and research, it does not imply that the joint production of the two products is less expensive than if they are produced separately.

ECONOMIES OF SCOPE
a case where it is cheaper for one firm to produce products jointly than it is for separate firms to produce the same products independently

DISECONOMIES OF SCOPE
a case where it is cheaper for separate products to be produced independently than for one firm to produce the same products jointly

APPLICATION 8.8   **ECONOMIES OF SCOPE AND THE MARRIAGE OF AOL AND TIME WARNER**

In 2000, America Online (AOL) and Time Warner agreed to the biggest deal in history, creating a company worth $350 billion through their merger. At the time of the merger, AOL was the most profitable Internet company, providing interactive services, Internet technologies, and e-commerce services. Time Warner was a 75-year-old blue-chip entertainment company known for its programming content such as CNN and the television series *Friends*, *Time* magazine, and a record label with stars such as Alanis Morissette.

The prospect of economies of scope appear to have been the primary reason behind the merger. The CEOs of the merging companies, Steve Case (AOL) and Gerald Levin (Time Warner), believed that the combined company would be better able to take advantage of the growth of broadband delivery of television and Internet at home than would the two companies on their own. Time Warner's content and AOL's Internet distribution network were perceived by the CEOs to be more productive if operating in unison, as part of one company, than if operating individually as two separate companies.

8.10 ESTIMATING COST

As with demand and production functions, cost functions can be empirically estimated in a variety of ways. Surveys are a commonly used method to determine the minimum efficient scale of production in an industry. The case described in the preceding chapter of the McKinsey & Company summer intern charged with investigating the pig chow industry provides an example. The student used a telephone survey to determine plant sizes that the current firms in the industry were using. This method is sometimes known as the **new entrant** or **survivor technique**.[15]

Econometric estimation is another vehicle for estimating cost functions. For example, a *cubic total cost function* will generate conventional U-shaped MC and AC curves such as those shown earlier in this chapter. A cubic total cost function takes the following form:

$$TC = a + bq + cq^2 + dq^3;$$

NEW ENTRANT/SURVIVOR TECHNIQUE
method for determining the minimum efficient scale of production in an industry based on investigating the plant sizes either being built or used by firms in the industry

where q represents output; and a, b, c, and d are numerical values to be estimated. The term *cubic* derives from the fact that, in the assumed equation, total cost is taken to be a function of output, q, up to the third power. Based on the estimated constant and coefficients for the above cubic cost function it is possible to determine a number of things about a firm's production cost. For example, if the assumed cubic total cost function is valid, the intercept, a, indicates the firm's total fixed cost—it does not vary as a function of output, q; the firm's average total cost and marginal cost curves are $ATC = (a/q) + b + cq + dq^2$ and $MC = b + 2cq + 3dq^2$, respectively; and the firm's minimum efficient scale (and the extent of any economies of scale confronted by the firm) can be determined by finding the output level at which ATC is minimized.[16]

Suppose that for the above cubic total cost function $a = 0$, $b = 400$, $c = -50$, and $d = 5$. The average total cost and marginal cost curves would look as depicted in Figure 8.10a. The

---

[15]The survivor technique was first proposed by economist George Stigler in his article "Economies of Scale," *Journal of Law and Economics*, 1 No. 2 (October 1958), pp. 54–71. The idea helped win him the 1990 Nobel Prize in economics.

[16]The marginal cost curve is derived by using calculus.

FIGURE 8.10

Different Possible Cost Functions

(a) A cubic total cost function such as $TC = a + bq + cq^2 + dq^3$, where q is output, is associated with U-shaped average total cost and marginal cost curves. In the case depicted, the intercept and coefficients are assumed to be $a = 0$, $b = 400$, $c = -50$, and $d = 5$. (b) A quadratic total cost function such as $TC = a + bq + cq^2$ is associated with a U-shaped ATC curve, but generates an upward-sloping, straight-line MC curve.

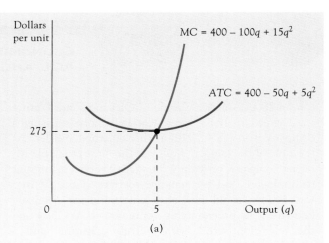

Dollars per unit

$MC = 400 - 100q + 15q^2$

$ATC = 400 - 50q + 5q^2$

275

0   5   Output (q)

(a)

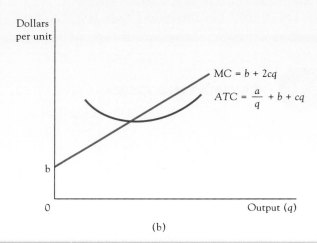

Dollars per unit

$MC = b + 2cq$

$ATC = \dfrac{a}{q} + b + cq$

b

0   Output (q)

(b)

minimum efficient scale of the firm would be where ATC is minimized—the output where $ATC = MC$. Setting ATC equal to MC and solving for q gives us an estimated minimum efficient scale of 5 (the corresponding height of the ATC and MC curves at this output is $275).

If a *quadratic total cost function* was more appropriate than a cubic total cost function, we would estimate an equation of the following form:

$$TC = a + bq + cq^2;$$

where the term *quadratic* derives from the fact that total cost is a function of output, q, up to the second power. A quadratic total cost function is also associated with a U-shaped ATC curve, but not a U-shaped MC curve. As depicted in Figure 8.10b, the MC curve generated by a quadratic total cost function is an upward-sloping straight line and is equal to, in our case, $MC = b + 2cq$.[17]

---

[17]As before, this MC curve is derived by using calculus.

SUMMARY

•   Cost is ultimately associated with the use of inputs that have alternative uses.

•   To economists, cost means opportunity cost—sacrificed alternatives when inputs are used to produce one product rather than some other product.

•   In the short run, firms cannot change the quantities of some inputs, so output can be altered only by varying the use of variable inputs.

•   The law of diminishing marginal returns applies here and dictates short-run cost curves' shapes.

•   The short-run marginal cost curve rises beyond the point at which diminishing marginal returns set in, and it intersects the U-shaped average variable and average total cost curves at their minimum points.

•   In the long run, firms can vary all inputs.

•   The expansion path in an isocost-isoquant diagram shows the least costly combinations of inputs required to produce various levels of output. It identifies the lowest total cost at which each output can be produced when all inputs can be varied. The same information is also conveyed by firms' long-run cost curves.

•   If input proportions are held constant, returns to scale determine the shape of a firm's long-run cost curves. With increasing returns to scale at low output and decreasing returns to scale at high outputs, the long-run average cost curve will be U-shaped. It shows the lowest per-unit cost at which each output can be produced.

•   The level of output at which the long-run average cost curve reaches a minimum depends on technological conditions and varies across products and firms.

•   In the more general case, when firms can alter input proportions with output, the shape of their long-run cost curves will depend on whether output changes are more than proportionate to any change in total input cost.

•   Economies of scale are present when a firm's output increases more than proportionally with a change in total input cost.

•   All cost curves for individual firms are drawn on the assumption that input prices are given. A change in one or more input prices causes the cost curves to shift.

•   Although economies of scale determine a long-run average cost curve's shape as a function of a particular product's output, firms often produce an array of products.

•   If it is cheaper for a single firm to produce an array of products than it is for an array of separate firms to independently produce distinct products, economies of scope apply. There is no necessary relationship between economies of scale and economies of scope.

•   A variety of techniques may be relied upon for empirical estimation of cost functions, including surveys, experimentation, and regression analysis.

REVIEW QUESTIONS AND PROBLEMS

Questions and problems marked with an asterisk have solutions given in Answers to Selected Problems at the back of the book (pages 574–575).

8.1. No Pain No Gain (NPNG), Inc., is a dental practice advocating a "natural" approach to dentistry. Namely, NPNG specializes in providing root canal operations without the administration of pain-killing drugs such as Novocain. If output (q) is measured as the number of root canals performed on a daily basis, define the following measures of NPNG's short-run cost: TFC, TVC, TC, MC, AFC, AVC, and ATC. Then fill in the spaces in the accompanying table.

q	TFC	TVC	TC	MC	AFC	AVC	ATC
1	$100	$50					
2				$30			
3						$40	
4		$270					
5							$70

*8.2. How is the law of diminishing marginal returns related to the shape of the short-run marginal cost curve? If the marginal product of the variable input declines from the very start, what will the short-run marginal cost and average cost curves look like? If the marginal product first rises and then falls, what will the cost curves look like?

8.3. Using the data from Question 7.1, construct the following relationships: (a) the average amount of labor used per unit of output at each level of output, and (b) the additional amount of labor required for each additional unit of output. Show these relationships as curves, with labor per unit of output on the vertical axis and output on the horizontal axis. How can these curves be converted into AVC and MC curves?

*8.4. Why do we assume that a firm will try to produce its output by using the lowest-cost combination of inputs possible? Does this reason also hold for production carried out by the U.S. Postal Service and the American Red Cross?

8.5. If the long-run marginal cost curve is U-shaped, must the long-run average cost curve also be U-shaped?

8.6. What is the significance of a tangency between an isoquant and an isocost line?

8.7. When a firm produces an output in the least costly way, using labor and capital, $MRTS_{LK} = w/r$. Does this relationship mean that the firm sets input prices so that the ratio equals $MRTS_{LK}$?

8.8. At point E in Figure 8.4, is MP_K/r greater or less than MP_L/w? How do you know? Use this inequality to explain how the firm can increase output without increasing its total cost by using a different combination of inputs.

*8.9. Coldwell Banker is employing 10 acres of land and 50 tons of cement to produce 1,000 parking spaces. Land costs $4,000 per acre and cement costs $12 per ton. For the input quantities employed, $MP_L = 50$ and $MP_C = 4$. Show this situation in an isoquant-isocost diagram. Explain, and show in the diagram, how Coldwell Banker can produce the same output at a lower total cost.

8.10. Why do we assume that the prices of inputs are constant when we draw a firm's cost curves? How does a change in the price of an input affect the AC and MC curves?

8.11. Suppose that the long-run average cost curve declines at first, then reaches a minimum at which level it is horizontal over an extended region, and then rises. Draw such a curve and the associated LMC curve.

8.12. In Figure 8.4, assume that the firm is currently producing 6 units of output at point B on isoquant IQ_6. Suppose now that the firm plans to expand output to 9 units by hiring more workers while continuing to use K_2 units of capital (capital is assumed to be a fixed input in the short run). Identify the combination of workers and capital that will be used. Is the total cost of producing 9 units of output in this way greater than, less than, or the same as the cost at point C? Support your answer by showing what has happened using LAC and SAC curves.

8.13. "Every point on Ford's long-run cost curve corresponds to a point on some short-run cost curve, but not every point on one of Ford's short-run cost curves corresponds to a point on the long-run cost curve." Explain.

8.14. "In the United States more than 50 firms produce textiles, but only 2 produce automobiles. This statistic shows that government antimonopoly policy has been applied more harshly to the textile industry than to the automobile industry." Can you give an alternative explanation for the difference in the number of firms in the two industries?

8.15. Suppose that Marriott's production function is characterized by constant returns to scale at all output levels. What will the firm's long-run total, average, and marginal cost curves look like?

8.16. If the Michigan Business School faces economies of scope in producing research and teaching, what does its production possibility frontier (PPF) look like? If the University of Phoenix faces diseconomies of scope in the provision of research and teaching, what does its PPF look like?

8.17. If the cubic total cost function described in the text applies to the production of output by a firm, and $a = 0$, $b = 400$, $c = -50$, and $d = 5$, what are the equations for the firm's TFC, TVC, MC, AFC, AVC, and ATC?

8.18. Suppose that for the cubic total cost function discussed in the text, $a = 0$, $b = 4$, $c = -5/2$, and $d = 5/3$. At what output level is average total cost minimized? At what output level is average variable cost minimized? Marginal cost? Average fixed cost?

8.19. Suppose that a firm's total cost is best described by the following quadratic cost function:

$$TC = a + bq + cq^2.$$

What are the equations for the firm's TFC, TVC, MC, AFC, AVC, and ATC?

8.20. Suppose that for the quadratic total cost function in the preceding problem, $a = 100$, $b = 6$, and $c = 1$. At what output level is average total cost minimized? At what output level is average variable cost minimized? Marginal cost? Average fixed cost? Provide a graph of the firm's TFC, TVC, MC, AFC, AVC, and ATC curves.

8.21. In comparing farming in Virginia with that in Europe, President Thomas Jefferson observed: "In Europe, the object is to make the most of their land, labor being abundant: here (in Virginia) it is to make the most of our labor, land being abundant." Explain how Jefferson's observation is consistent with the golden rule of cost minimization.

8.22. Recently technology has been a key factor in promoting cost minimization by airlines. For example, Internet ticket sales accounted for nearly 25 percent of Southwest Airlines' revenue in 2000. Historically, such sales had typically been made by travel agents who charged airlines a commission for their services. For another example, Continental Airlines has been testing software that will shift around aircraft as often as several times a day to match seats to backings. In the case of Internet ticket sales, explain how such a technological improvement allows an airline to minimize costs using an isoquant-isocost diagram.

8.23. Among the types of advertising that an advertising agency might provide are network television; radio; general magazines; business periodicals; and billboards. Provide an intuitive explanation as to why there may be economies of scope in the provision of services by one advertising agency across these various categories. Also explain why there may be an advantage for companies supplying the various categories of media services to merge (e.g., why might advertising economics of scope explain the 1997 purchase by Clear Channel Communications, a company with one of the largest holdings of radio stations in the United States, of Eller Media Company, one of the largest operators of outdoor advertising?).

CHAPTER 9

Profit Maximization in Perfectly Competitive Markets

How does a firm's optimal output choice in a perfectly competitive
market structure respond to changes in price and cost?

Chapter Outline

9.1 The Assumptions of Perfect Competition

9.2 Profit Maximization

Application 9.1 *Are American Executives Underpaid?*

9.3 The Demand Curve Facing the Competitive Firm

9.4 Short-Run Profit Maximization

Short-Run Profit Maximization Using Per-Unit Curves

Application 9.2 *Continental Airlines, MR, and MC*

Operating at a Loss in the Short Run

Application 9.3 *Continental Airlines, AR, ATC, and AVC*

9.5 The Perfectly Competitive Firm's Short-Run Supply Curve

Application 9.4 *The Competitive Firm's Supply Curve in the Very Short Run*

Output Response to a Change in Input Prices

9.6 The Short-Run Industry Supply Curve

Price and Output Determination in the Short Run

Application 9.5 *Why Electric Bills in California Increased After Deregulation*

9.7 Long-Run Competitive Equilibrium

Zero Profit When Firms' Cost Curves Differ?

9.8 The Long-Run Industry Supply Curve

Constant-Cost Industry   *Increasing-Cost Industry*

Application 9.6 *Increasing Input Costs in the Information Technology Industry*

Decreasing-Cost Industry

Application 9.7 *The Bidding War for MIS and Finance Professors*

Comments on the Long-Run Supply Curve

9.9 When Does the Competitive Model Apply?

Summary

Learning Objectives

- Outline the conditions that characterize perfect competition.
- Explain why it is appropriate to assume profit maximization on the part of firms.
- Show why the fact that a competitive firm is a price taker implies that the demand curve facing the firm is perfectly horizontal.
- Explore a competitive firm's optimal output choice in the short run and how the firm's short-run supply curve may be derived through this output selection.
- Delineate how the short-run industry supply curve is determined from individual firms' short-run supply curves.
- Define the conditions characterizing long-run competitive equilibrium.
- Understand how the long-run industry supply curve describes the relationship between price and industry output over the long run, taking into account how input prices may be affected by an industry's expansion/contraction.
- Analyze the extent to which the competitive market model applies.

As we have seen, the basic determinants of cost are the prices and the productivities of inputs. But a knowledge of cost conditions alone does not explain the level of a firm's output. Cost curves identify only the minimum cost at which the firm can produce various outputs.

For a firm interested in maximizing profit, cost and demand conditions jointly determine the optimal output level. So, to complete the model of output determination, we need to specify the demand curve confronting the firm. The demand curve determines the sales revenue at different volumes of output. In this chapter we concentrate on perfect competition and the demand curve facing a firm operating in such a market structure. Later chapters focus on the demand curve confronting a firm and the firm's optimal output choice when competition is imperfect.

We will explore how a firm's optimal output choice within a perfectly competitive market structure responds to changes in price and cost. This information can be employed to derive the firm's supply curve and, in turn, the industry supply curve. We also address the long-run outcome in perfect competition and contrast it with short-run responses.

9.1 THE ASSUMPTIONS OF PERFECT COMPETITION

In common usage, *competition* refers to intense rivalry among businesses. Microsoft and Sun Microsystems, Nike and Reebok, Pepsi and Coke are all competitors in this sense. Each firm makes a business decision—whether to introduce a new product, advertise existing products more forcefully, or enhance product quality—only after considering the effect on competitors and their likely response.

PERFECT COMPETITION
an economic model characterized by the assumption of (1) a large number of buyers and sellers, (2) free entry and exit, (3) product homogeneity, and (4) perfect information

FREE ENTRY AND EXIT
a situation in which there are no differential impediments across firms in the mobility of resources into and out of an industry

HOMOGENEOUS PRODUCTS
standardized products that, in the eyes of consumers, are perfect substitutes for one another

The economist's model of perfect competition, especially in its formal description, bears little resemblance to this picture. **Perfect competition** is distinguished largely by its impersonal nature. More specifically, four conditions characterize a perfectly competitive industry.

1. *Large numbers of buyers and sellers.* The presence of a great many independent participants on each side of the market, none of whom is large in relation to total industry sales or purchases, normally guarantees that individual participants' actions will not significantly affect the market price and overall industry output. In a market with many firms, each firm recognizes that its impact on the overall market is negligible, and consequently does not view other firms as personal rivals.

2. *Free entry and exit.* Industry adjustments to changing market conditions are always accompanied by resources entering or leaving the industry. As an industry expands, it uses more labor, capital, and so on; resources enter the industry. Similarly, resources leave a contracting industry. A perfectly competitive market requires that there be no differential impediments across firms in the mobility of resources into, around, and out of an industry. This condition is sometimes called **free entry and exit**. Examples of barriers to entry and exit include an incumbent firm with an exclusive government patent or operating license and economies of scale that impede the entry of new firms.

3. *Product homogeneity.* All the firms in the industry must be producing a standardized or **homogeneous product**. In the eyes of consumers, the goods produced by the industry's various firms are perfect substitutes for one another. This assumption allows us to add the outputs of the separate firms and talk meaningfully about the industry and its total output. It also contributes to the establishment of a uniform price for the product. One farmer will be unable to sell corn for a higher price than another if the products are viewed as interchangeable, because consumers will always purchase from the lower-priced source.

4. *Perfect information.* Firms, consumers, and resource owners must have all the information necessary to make the correct economic decisions. For firms, for example, the relevant information is knowledge of the production technology, input prices, and the price at which the product can be sold. For consumers, the relevant information is a knowledge of their own preferences and the prices of the various goods of interest to them. Moreover, the consumers, in their role as suppliers of inputs, must know the remuneration they can receive for supplying productive services.

Probably no industry completely satisfies all four conditions. Agricultural markets come close, although government involvement in such markets keeps them from fully satisfying the four conditions. Most industries satisfy some conditions well but not others. Even though the number of market participants in the gasoline retailing business is large and entry into the business is fairly easy, for example, not all gasoline brands are the same. Some brands have higher octane and more detergents, and are better for the environment. Certain stations are closer to particular consumers and thereby more convenient, or offer better complements such as full service, food-marts, and pumps that allow customers to pay for their purchases by inserting a credit card. Moreover, consumers are rarely perfectly informed about the prices all retailers are charging.

The fact that only a few industries may fully satisfy the four conditions does not mean that the study of perfect competition is unwarranted. Many industries come close enough to satisfying the four conditions to make the perfectly competitive model quite useful. Take the case of gasoline retailing. Although product homogeneity and perfect information may not fully apply, the extent to which an individual gas station has some choice over what price to charge per gallon is probably limited to a very narrow band of just a few cents. Such a narrow pricing power band is pretty close to having no significant impact over price, as predicted by the competitive model.

9.2   PROFIT MAXIMIZATION

**PROFIT
MAXIMIZATION**
the assumption that firms
select an output level so
as to maximize profit

In perfectly (as well as imperfectly) competitive markets, is it appropriate to assume **profit maximization** on the part of firms? At the outset we should recognize that any profit realized by a business belongs to the owner(s) of that business. For the millions of small businesses with only one owner-manager, decisions concerning what products to carry, whom to employ, what price to charge, and so on, will be heavily influenced by the way the owner's profit is affected. Owners of such businesses may well have goals such as early retirement or expensive educations for their children. These goals, however, are not inconsistent with the assumption of profit maximization. Since money is a means to many ends, early retirement or college educations can more easily be afforded when the owner makes more money.

A possible problem with assuming profit maximization is that the owner-manager cannot possibly have detailed knowledge of the cost and revenue associated with each conceivable action that could be taken to maximize profit. Economic theory, however, does not require that firms actually know or think in terms of marginal cost and revenue, only that they behave as if they did. Firms may come close enough to maximizing profit by trial and error, emulation of successful firms, following rules of thumb, or blind luck for the assumption to be a fruitful one.

When we move from the small, owner-managed firm to the large, modern corporation, another potential criticism of the assumption of profit maximization arises. A characteristic of most large corporations is that the stockholder-owners themselves do not make the day-to-day decisions about price, employment, advertising, and so on. Instead, salaried personnel of the corporation—managers—make these decisions. And so there is a separation of ownership and control in the corporation; managers control the firm, but stockholders own it. It is safe to assume that stockholders wish to make as much money on their investment as possible, but it is virtually impossible for them to constantly monitor their managers' actions. Therefore, managers will have some discretion, and some of their decisions may conflict with the profit-maximizing goals of the stockholder-owners.

While managers may have some discretion to deviate from the profit-maximizing goals of firms' shareholder-owners, several factors limit the exercise of such discretion. For example, stockholder-owners often relate compensation of business managers to profits, sometimes paying them in part with shares of stock or stock options, in order to give managers an incentive to pursue profits more actively. In addition, the profitability managers achieve in a given enterprise will affect their job prospects with others. And, finally, if managers do not make as large a profit as possible, stock prices, which tend to reflect profitability (especially projected profitability), will be lower than need be. Undervalued stock creates an incentive for outsiders, or "raiders," to buy up a controlling interest in the firm and replace the inefficient management team. A firm that neglects profit opportunities too often leaves itself open to such a takeover bid, a fairly common occurrence in the corporate world.

Operating in a competitive market provides yet another reason it is safe to assume that a firm will pursue profit maximization as a goal. Consider firms in the hospitality industry, such as Hilton, Marriott, and Sheraton. Suppose some of them virtually ignore profit, either through ignorance, negligence, bad luck, or intention. Their cost of labor is too high, they fail to minimize waste in their food service, they neglect training for the staff who serve customers, and so forth. Other firms, whether through superior management, close attention to costs, or the good luck of being closest to a newly enlarged convention center, produce the right type of hotel lodging in the appropriate quantity and in the least costly way. What will happen when these firms compete for customers? Clearly, the firms that come closer to maximizing profit will make money and prosper; the others will suffer losses. In general, in competitive markets, firms that do not approximate profit-maximizing behavior fail; the survivors will be the firms that, intentionally or not, make the appropriate, profit-maximizing decisions. This observation is sometimes called the **survivor principle** and it provides a practical defense for the assumption of profit maximization.

While it goes without saying that firms must pay close attention to profit, some deviation from single-minded profit maximization may still occur. Most economists, however, believe that the assumption of profit maximization provides a close enough approximation to be useful in analyzing many problems, and it has become the standard assumption regarding the behavior of the firm. While the assumption may not adequately explain why Billy, the company president, hires his ne'er-do-well brother-in-law, Roger, or why RJR Nabisco appears to have an excessively large fleet of corporate jets, it does not pretend to try. Instead, it is designed to explain how a firm's output will respond to a higher or a lower price, a tax or a government regulation, a cost change, and so on. Recall that the ultimate test of a theory is whether it explains and predicts well, and theories based on the assumption of profit maximization have passed that test.

SURVIVOR PRINCIPLE
the observation that in competitive markets, firms that do not approximate profit-maximizing behavior fail, and that survivors are those firms that, intentionally or not, make the appropriate profit-maximizing decisions

APPLICATION 9.1   ARE AMERICAN EXECUTIVES UNDERPAID?

In recent years, the pay received by senior business executives in the United States has grown much more rapidly (in percentage terms) than the average worker's pay, corporate earnings, and the gross national product.[1] Moreover, counting bonuses and stock options, the pay received by some executives has been truly spectacular. For example, Oracle's CEO Larry Ellison and Microsoft's Bill Gates earned billions of dollars from their stock options in the 1990s.

Although the high level and rate of increase in senior executive compensation have received much criticism in the media and the political arena, leading academic studies suggest that the monetary incentives offered by firms to their managers may still be inadequate. A study by Michael Jensen and Kevin Murphy of the Harvard Business School, for instance, finds that CEO wealth rises by just $3.25 for each $1,000 increase in shareholder wealth. Jensen and Murphy argue that their estimated sensitivity figures are too small to entirely solve the **principal–agent problem** confronting a firm's stockholders: namely, stockholders' agents (the managers or principals of the firm) do not have sufficient incentive to maximize the firm's profit if they receive only $3.25 per $1,000 of stockholder wealth that is generated. Based on the Jensen-Murphy results, a CEO would find it worthwhile to use $1 million of the shareholders' potential wealth on a private jet or rare artwork if such an item generated $3,250 in purely personal pleasure for the CEO. Jensen and Murphy propose that CEOs' pay should be tied more closely to stockholders' wealth to improve corporate performance, but they acknowledge that opposition in the media and the political arena may limit such a change.

Support for Jensen and Murphy's proposal is provided by a study by John Abowd of Cornell. Abowd examined 16,000 executives in 250 large U.S. corporations over the 1981–1986 time period. He found that increases in the sensitivity of executive pay to corporate performance improved corporate performance in terms of the rate of return earned by a firm's stockholders. In conjunction with the Jensen-Murphy results, Abowd's findings thus suggest that linking managerial compensation more closely to corporate performance can increase shareholder wealth. The existing link between managerial compensation and corporate performance, that is, is not yet sufficiently strong to completely eliminate the principal-agent problem confronted by the stockholders of U.S. firms.

PRINCIPAL–AGENT PROBLEM
a situation in which a principal's agent (such as the manager of a firm representing the firm's stockholders) may have an incentive that is not entirely consonant with the interests of the principal

[1]This application is based on Paul Milgrom and John Roberts, *Economics, Organization and Management* (Englewood Cliffs, NJ: Prentice Hall, 1992); Michael C. Jensen and Kevin J. Murphy, "Performance Pay and Top-Management Incentives," *Journal of Political Economy*, 98 No. 2 (April 1990), pp. 225–264; and John M. Abowd, "Does Performance-Based Managerial Compensation Affect Corporate Performance?" *Industrial and Labor Relations Review*, 43 No. 1 (February 1990), pp. 52S–73S.

9.3   THE DEMAND CURVE FACING THE COMPETITIVE FIRM

Assuming that firms are interested in maximizing profit, let's examine the implications of this assumption in a competitive market setting. Since a competitive market is characterized by a large number of firms selling the same product, each firm supplies only a small fraction of the entire industry output. For example, one farmer may account for only one-millionth of the entire corn industry's output or one building contractor may supply 1 percent of the total construction services in a particular city.

The nature of the demand curve confronting a single competitive firm follows directly from the relatively insignificant contribution its output makes toward total supply. The product's price is determined by the interaction of the market supply of and demand for the product. Because each firm produces such a small portion of the total supply, its output decisions have a correspondingly small effect on the market price. For simplicity the "small" effect is taken to be a "zero" effect, and the demand curve facing a competitive firm is drawn to be perfectly horizontal. A horizontal demand curve means the firm can sell as much output as it wants without affecting the product's price. Stated differently, a competitive firm is a **price taker**: the firm takes the price as given and does not expect its output decisions to affect price.

PRICE TAKER
a firm that takes prices as given and does not expect its output decisions to affect price

Figure 9.1 helps clarify why the firm's demand curve is drawn horizontally. In Figure 9.1b, the total output of corn, the good in question, is measured horizontally, and the per-unit price is measured vertically. The market demand curve is shown as D. The premise is that the total quantity offered for sale by all farms together interacts with this demand curve to determine price. If the combined output of all corn farms is 15 billion bushels, the market price per bushel is $3.

Assume that the Costner farm is one of 1 million identical farms supplying corn, and it is currently selling 15,000 bushels for $3 each, as shown in Figure 9.1a. The farm's demand curve is drawn horizontally as d in Figure 9.1a because its output variations will not have an appreciable effect on the market output and price. That is, if the Costner farm produced 15,000 fewer (an output of zero bushels) or more bushels (an output of 30,000 bushels), it would have an insignificant influence on the total industry output of 15 billion bushels. Consequently, the market price will not be altered by the output actions of this single farm. It is stuck with having to charge the market price of $3 no matter what output level it selects.

A horizontal demand curve has an elasticity of infinity. Since there are many homogeneous substitutes for any one farm's output and customers are perfectly informed in a perfectly competitive market, the quantity of corn demanded from the Costner farm will equal zero if the farm attempts to charge even so much as a penny over the prevailing market price.

FIGURE 9.1

The Competitive Farm's Demand Curve
(a) Because an individual farm supplies only a small portion of the market output, its demand curve, d, is perfectly elastic. (b) The interaction of market supply, S, and demand, D, determine the prevailing market price ($3) and output (15 billion bushels).

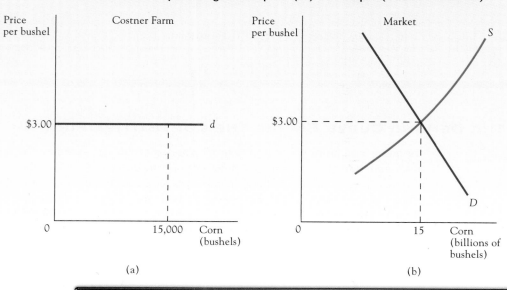

AVERAGE REVENUE (AR)
total revenue divided by output

MARGINAL REVENUE (MR)
the change in total revenue when there is a one-unit change in output

A firm's **average revenue** (AR), or total revenue divided by output, is the same as the prevailing market price. As Figure 9.1 shows, if the market price is $3, then the Costner farm will on average make $3 per bushel.

When a firm faces a horizontal demand curve, the market price also equals the firm's marginal revenue. **Marginal revenue** (MR) is defined as the change in total revenue when there is a one-unit change in output. A firm in a competitive market can sell one more unit of output without reducing the price it receives for its previous units, so total revenue will rise by an amount equal to the price. For example, if a farm is selling 15,000 bushels of corn at a price of $3 per bushel, total revenue is $45,000. If the farm sells 15,001 bushels at a price of $3 per bushel, as it can with a horizontal demand curve, total revenue rises from $45,000 to $45,003, or by $3. Once again the familiar average-marginal relationship can be seen to apply. Where the average revenue (AR) is flat or constant, the marginal revenue equals the average revenue (MR = AR).

Note that the assumption of a horizontal demand curve confronting a competitive firm does not mean that the price never changes. It just means that the firm, acting by itself, cannot affect the going price. The market price may vary from time to time due to changes in consumers' incomes, technology, consumers' preferences, and so on, but not because of changes in the amount sold by a particular firm.

9.4 SHORT-RUN PROFIT MAXIMIZATION[2]

TOTAL REVENUE (TR)
price times the quantity sold

In the short run, a competitive firm operating with a fixed plant can vary its output by altering its employment of variable inputs. To see how a profit-maximizing firm decides on what level of output to produce, let's begin with a numerical illustration. The information in Table 9.1 allows us to identify the output (q) that maximizes profit for a hypothetical competitive firm; it includes the short-run cost of production and revenue from the sale of output. We know the firm is selling in a competitive market because the price (P) is constant at $12 regardless of the output level. Note that **total revenue** (TR) is equal to price times the

TABLE 9.1

SHORT-RUN COST AND REVENUE OF A COMPETITIVE FIRM (IN DOLLARS)

q	P	TR	TC	TVC	ATC	AVC	π	π/q	MC	MR	
0	12	0	15	0	—	—	215	—	—	—	
1	12	12	25	10	25	10	−13	−13	10	12	
2	12	24	33	18	16.50	9	−9	−4.50	8	12	
3	12	36	40	25	13.30	8.30	−4	−1.30	7	12	
4	12	48	46	31	11.50	7.80	2	0.50	6	12	MC < MR
5	12	60	54	39	10.80	7.80	6	1.20	8	12	
6	12	72	63	48	10.50	6	9	1.50	9	12	
7	12	84	73	58	10.40	8.30	11	1.57	10	12	
8	12	96	84.90	69.90	10.61	8.70	11.10	1.39	11.90	12	MC ≈ MR
9	12	108	98	83	10.90	9.20	10	1.25	13.10	12	
10	12	120	113	98	11.30	9.80	7	0.70	15	12	MC > MR
11	12	132	132	117	12	10.60	0	0	19	12	

[2]A mathematical treatment of some of the material in this section is given in the appendix at the back of the book (pages 567–568).

quantity sold, and it rises in proportion to output since the price is constant. Total cost (TC) rises with output in the familiar fashion, slowly at first and then more rapidly as the plant becomes more fully utilized and marginal cost rises. Total cost, when output is zero, is $15, reflecting the total fixed cost.

Total profit (π) is the difference between total revenue and total cost. At low and high rates of output, profit is negative; that is, the firm would suffer losses. In particular, note that the firm loses $15 if it produces no output at all because it still must pay its fixed cost when it shuts down. At an intermediate rate of output in this example, profit is positive. The firm, however, wishes to make as large a profit as possible, and maximum profit occurs at an output of eight units where profit equals $11.10.

Note that maximizing total profit is generally not the same thing as maximizing **average profit per unit** (π/q) sold. The firm's goal is to maximize its total profit, and that is achieved at an output of 8 units. Profit per unit at that output is $1.39, but it could have an even higher average profit, $1.57, by producing just 7 units. Total profit is profit per unit times the number of units sold, so a lower average profit can correspond to a higher total profit if enough additional units are sold, as is true in the example of Table 9.1.

Figure 9.2 shows how we identify the most profitable level of output by using the total revenue and total cost curves. The total revenue curve is a new relationship, but it is a relatively simple one when we are dealing with a competitive firm. With the price per unit constant, total revenue rises in proportion to output and is, therefore, drawn as a straight line emanating from the origin. Its slope, showing how much total revenue rises when output changes by one unit, is marginal revenue.

In terms of Figure 9.2, the firm wishes to select the output level where total revenue exceeds total cost by the largest possible amount—that is, where profit is greatest. This situation occurs at output q_1, where total revenue, Aq_1, exceeds total cost, Bq_1, by AB. The vertical distance AB is total profit at q_1. At lower and higher output levels, total profit is

TOTAL PROFIT (π)
the difference between total revenue and total cost

AVERAGE PROFIT PER UNIT (π/q)
total profit divided by number of units sold

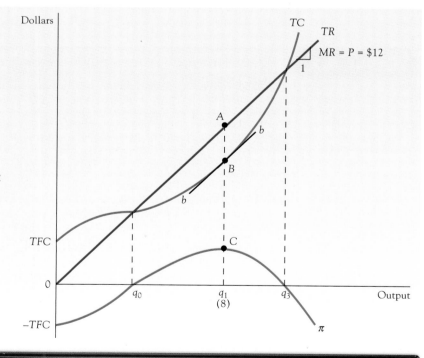

FIGURE 9.2

Short-Run Profit Maximization: Total Curves
Profit is maximized at the output where total revenue (TR) exceeds total cost (TC) by the largest possible amount. This occurs at output q_1, where profit is equal to AB. The total profit curve (π), which plots total profit explicitly at each rate of output, also shows the point of profit maximization.

lower than AB. Note that at a lower output level, q_0, for example, the TR and TC curves are diverging (becoming farther apart) as output rises, indicating that profit is greater at a higher output. This reflects the fact that marginal revenue (the slope of TR) is greater than marginal cost (the slope of TC) over this range. At q_1, when the curves are farthest apart (with revenue above cost), the slopes of TR and TC (the slope of TC at B is equal to the slope of bb) are equal, reflecting an equality between marginal revenue and marginal cost.

In Figure 9.2, the level of total profit at each rate of output is also shown explicitly by the total profit curve (π), which reaches a maximum at q_1. The total profit curve is derived graphically by plotting the difference between TR and TC at each output level. For example, AB is equal to Cq_1; alternatively, when output is zero, profit is negative and equal to minus total fixed cost (TFC).

Short-Run Profit Maximization Using Per-Unit Curves

Figure 9.3 presents the same information shown in Figure 9.2, but now we use the familiar per-unit cost and revenue relationships. With the vertical axis measuring dollars per unit of output, the firm's demand curve is shown as a horizontal line, because the firm may sell any number of units at the $12 price. The figure also shows the average total cost (ATC), average variable cost (AVC), and marginal cost (MC) curves. The most profitable output level occurs where marginal cost and marginal revenue are equal, at q_1 in the figure (eight units in Table 9.1). The shaded rectangle $BCDA$ shows total profit for that output. The height of

FIGURE 9.3

Short-Run Profit Maximization: Per-Unit Curves
In terms of the per-unit curves, the output that maximizes profit in the short run is where $MC = MR$, or q_1. At lower levels of output such as q_0, $MC < MR$, and the firm can increase profit by expanding output. At higher outputs like q_2, $MC > MR$, and the firm can increase profit by reducing output.

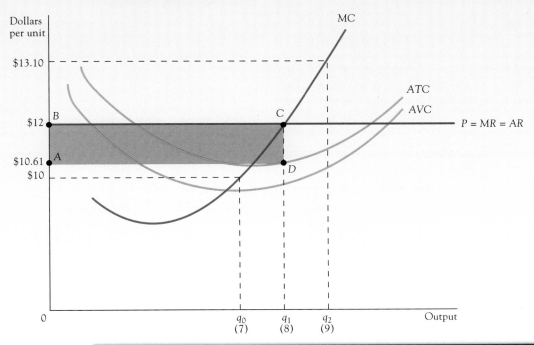

the rectangle, CD, is average revenue ($12) minus average total cost ($10.61 ≈ $84.9/8), or the average profit per unit of output ($1.39 = $12 − $10.61). Multiplying the average profit per unit by the number of units sold (the length of the rectangle) yields total profit ($11.10).

Understanding why the firm's profit is at a maximum where marginal cost and marginal revenue are equal is very important. Consider what it would mean if the firm were operating at a lower output where $MC \leq MR$, such as q_0 (7 units) in Figure 9.3. At q_0, marginal revenue is still $12, but marginal cost is lower ($10). Consequently, the seventh unit of output adds $12 to revenue but increases total cost by only $10; with revenue increasing more than cost, profit (the difference) will rise from $9 (at 6 units) to $11 when the seventh unit is sold. At any rate of output where marginal revenue is greater than marginal cost, the firm can increase its profit by increasing output. As output expands, marginal cost rises, so the addition to profit from each successive unit becomes smaller (but is still positive) until q_1 is reached, where $MC = MR$.

At output levels beyond q_1 the firm would be producing too much output. At q_2 (9 units in Table 9.1), for example, marginal cost is $13.10 and is greater than marginal revenue ($12). Thus, total profit could be increased by reducing output. If the firm produces 1 unit less, it loses $12 in revenue. But cost falls by $13.10, so the net effect is a $1.10 increase in profit. Thus, the firm's profit will increase by decreasing output if $MC > MR$.

In summary, the rule for profit maximization is to produce where $MC = MR$. Because marginal revenue equals price for a competitive firm, we can also express this condition as $MC = P$. This rule does *not* mean that the firm intentionally sets price equal to marginal cost since, for a competitive firm, price is given and beyond its control. Instead, the firm will adjust its production until the marginal cost is brought into equality with price.[3]

APPLICATION 9.2   CONTINENTAL AIRLINES, MR, AND MC

In 1962, Continental Airlines filled only 50 percent of the seats on its Boeing 707 flights—a number 15 percent below the industry average. As it turned out, however, this level was actually profit-maximizing. Each of the marginal flights that Continental considered dropping—which would have raised its percentage of seats filled—had a marginal cost of only $2,000, while the mar- ginal revenue equaled $3,100. By keeping these flights, Continental raised total profit by $1,100 per flight.[4]

[4]"Airline Takes the Marginal Route," *BusinessWeek* (April 20, 1963), pp. 111–114. Assuming that all other factors such as the price charged passengers are held constant, increasing the number of flights should lead to a reduction in the percentage of seats filled by an airline.

Operating at a Loss in the Short Run

A firm in a perfectly competitive market may find itself in the unenviable situation of suffer- ing a loss no matter what level of output it produces. In that event the firm has two alterna- tives: It can continue to operate at a loss, or it can shut down. (Recall that we are dealing with a short-run setting; halting production may be only a temporary move until market conditions improve and is not necessarily the same as going out of business.) Yet shutting

[3]Because the MC curve is U-shaped, MC may equal P at two different output levels. In this case the lower level is not the profit-maximizing output; in fact, it is the minimum-profit (or maximum-loss) output. If it is necessary to distinguish these two outputs, the profit-maximizing output is where $MC = P$ *and* MC cuts P from below (that is, MC is rising).

down will not avoid a loss since the firm is still liable for its fixed cost whether or not it operates. The relevant question is whether the firm will lose *less* by continuing to operate or by shutting down.

Figure 9.4 illustrates the case where the firm's best option is to operate at a loss rather than shut down. With the price at $8 per unit and the cost curves as shown, the firm's "most profitable" output (which can also mean its "least unprofitable" output, as it does here) is the point where price equals marginal cost at q_1. Because the average total cost curve lies above the price line everywhere, the firm incurs losses at all output levels. But at q_1 the loss is the smallest, as indicated by the rectangle BCFE. The height of this rectangle, CF, is the difference between average cost and average revenue, or the "negative profit margin" per unit, and the length of the rectangle, EF, is the number of units sold at a loss.

How do we know that the firm loses less by producing at q_1 than by shutting down? Consider the larger rectangle BCDA. The height of the rectangle, CD, is the difference between ATC and AVC at q_1. Thus, CD measures average fixed cost. Recall that AVC + AFC = ATC; therefore, ATC − AVC = AFC, and average fixed cost multiplied by the number of units produced (the length of the rectangle) equals total fixed cost (or the area of rectangle BCDA). Even if the firm shuts down, it will still incur a loss, namely, total fixed cost. But because that loss (BCDA) is larger than the loss (BCFE) incurred if the firm continues to operate, the firm loses less by producing q_1 than by shutting down. It is better to operate and lose $100 per week than to shut down and lose $200 per week.

FIGURE 9.4

Operating at a Loss in the Short Run
In the short run, a firm may continue to produce even though its best output yields a loss. As long as average revenue covers average variable cost, it is in the firm's interest to continue operating. Output will be q_1 even though the firm's loss is *BCFE*, because the loss would be even greater—*BCDA*—if it shut down.

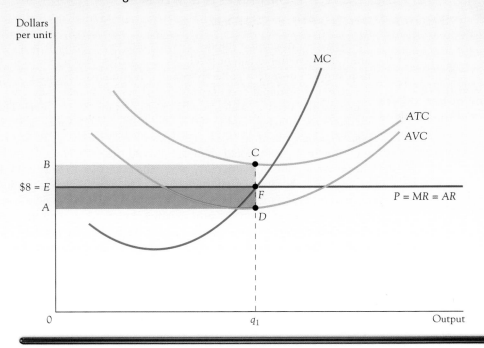

If the price falls sufficiently, however, the firm may lose less by shutting down, as we will see in the following section. Moreover, even when it is in the firm's interest to produce at a loss, as in Figure 9.4, this equilibrium can be only temporary (short run). If the price remains at $8, the firm will ultimately go out of business. The point here is that a firm will not immediately liquidate its assets the moment it begins to suffer losses.

APPLICATION 9.3   CONTINENTAL AIRLINES, AR, ATC, AND AVC

The previous application noted how Continental Airlines increased the number of Boeing 707 flights in 1962 up to the point where the marginal revenue contributed by a flight equaled its marginal cost. Despite applying an incremental profit analysis to its 707 fleet, Continental Airlines found itself still operating in the red. Specifically, because of significant fixed costs, Continental's average total cost per 707 flight exceeded average revenue.

Instead of filing for bankruptcy, Continental's managers opted to remain in business. This was the correct profit-maximizing choice, because although the average total cost of a 707 flight exceeded the average revenue, the average revenue per flight was greater than the average variable cost. By keeping its 707 fleet in operation, Continental thus earned more than it cost to keep the fleet going. And Continental's 1962 loss ended up being less than it would have been (that is, the size of total fixed cost) had the company shut down.

9.5   THE PERFECTLY COMPETITIVE FIRM'S SHORT-RUN SUPPLY CURVE

SHORT-RUN FIRM SUPPLY CURVE
a graph of the systematic relationship between a product's price and a firm's most profitable output level

The previous discussion implies a systematic relationship between a product's price and a firm's most profitable output level. We can analyze this relationship to derive the **short-run firm supply curve** in a perfectly competitive industry. Figure 9.5 depicts the firm's average variable and marginal cost curves. Note that the average total cost curve is not shown because it is not needed to identify the most profitable output level. The ATC curve is primarily useful for showing total profit or loss. If the per-unit price is $8, the firm will produce at point B, where marginal cost equals $8, so output will be q_1. If the price rises from $8 to $12, then the firm's profit would change, as would the most profitable output level. Suppose that the firm maintains an output of q_1 when the price rises to $12. Its profit will increase because revenue rises, but its cost will not change. The firm, however, can increase profit by increasing output. At q_1, marginal revenue ($12) now exceeds marginal cost ($8), signaling that an output increase will add more to revenue than to cost. The new profit-maximizing output occurs where output has expanded until marginal cost equals the $12 price, at point C on the MC curve. Thus, a higher price gives the firm an incentive to expand output from q_1 to q_2.

The MC = P (= MR) rule for maximizing profit in a competitive market structure therefore implies that a firm will produce more at a higher price because increased production becomes profitable at a higher price. In fact, we can think of the MC curve as the firm's supply curve in the short run, since it identifies the most profitable output for each possible price.

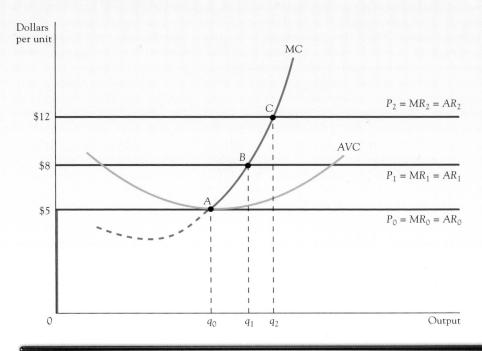

FIGURE 9.5

The Competitive Firm's Short-Run Supply Curve
The part of the *MC* curve lying above the minimum point on the *AVC* curve identifies the firm's most profitable output at prices above $5. Below a price of $5, the firm will be better off shutting down. Above a price of $5, the firm maximizes profit by producing where price equals marginal cost. Because the *MC* curve slopes upward, the firm increases output at a higher price. The solid, dark red curve represents the competitive firm's short-run supply curve.

For example, at a price of $8 output is q_1 at point B on MC, at a price of $12 output is q_2 at point C on MC, and so on.

One important qualification to this proposition should be mentioned. If price is too low, the firm will shut down. At a price of $5 the firm can just cover its variable cost by producing at point A, where average variable cost equals the price. At this point the firm would be operating at a short-run loss; in fact, the loss would be exactly equal to its total fixed cost, because revenue just covers variable cost, leaving nothing to set against fixed cost. At a price below $5 the firm is unable to cover its variable cost and would find it most advantageous to shut down. Consequently, point A, the minimum level of average variable cost, is effectively the **shutdown point**: if price falls below that level, the firm will cease operations.

As a consequence of this qualification, only the segment of the marginal cost curve that lies above the point of minimum average variable cost is relevant. Stated differently, the marginal cost curve above point A identifies the firm's output at prices above $5; at any lower price output will be zero.

SHUTDOWN POINT
the minimum level of average variable cost below which the firm will cease operations

APPLICATION 9.4   **THE COMPETITIVE FIRM'S SUPPLY CURVE IN THE VERY SHORT RUN**

We have been examining cases in which a competitive firm can vary its output in the short run by altering its employment of variable inputs. What if, in the very short run, it is not possible for the firm to alter its use of any inputs? What does the competitive firm's supply curve look like under such a scenario? For example, consider a producer of shovels immediately following the discovery of gold in 1848 at Sutter's Mill near then sparsely populated Sacramento, California. The discovery sparked a tremendous rush to mine the precious metal and dramatically increased the demand for and price of such mining implements as shovels. A shovel, whose nominal price had been only $1 in the Sacramento area prior to the gold discovery, sold for as much as $50 immediately following the discovery.

In the days just after the gold discovery, a supplier of shovels to the Sacramento area could not appreciably alter its output even though the demand for and price of shovels sharply increased. In 1848, it took more than a few days for the manufacturer to hear news of the gold discovery, manufacture additional shovels, and then ship the additional shovels to the Sacramento area (the relevant communication, manufacturing, and transportation times were much greater 150 years ago).

In a very-short-run scenario when no inputs can be altered, the firm's marginal cost curve is effectively vertical above the shutdown point (not upward-sloping, as it is in Figure 9.5 above point A). With a vertical marginal cost curve, no matter how high the price rises for the product, the firm cannot alter its output. Consequently, the competitive firm's supply curve is also vertical or perfectly price inelastic in a very-short-run setting where the firm cannot alter the use of its inputs.

Output Response to a Change in Input Prices

Many factors can affect the competitive firm's output decision, but perhaps the two most common are variations in the product price and variations in the prices of inputs used in production. In reality, product and input prices frequently change at the same time, but at the outset, examining each factor in isolation is best. In the preceding paragraphs we examined the way a product price change affects output when input prices are constant (reflected in the fact that the cost curves did not shift). Now let's study the impact of an input price change while holding constant the product price.

Figure 9.6 illustrates a competitive firm initially producing the output q_1 where marginal cost, shown by MC, equals the $12 product price. Note that only the marginal cost curve above the shutdown point, point A, is drawn in. Now suppose that the price of one (or more) of the variable inputs falls. As we saw in Chapter 8, lower input prices cause the cost curves to shift downward, indicating a lower cost associated with each rate of output than before. This change is depicted in the diagram by a shift in the marginal cost curve from MC to MC'. The rule for profit maximization in competitive markets, MC = P, determines the new output level q_2. To proceed to this conclusion somewhat more slowly, note that at the initial output level, a lower input price decreases the marginal cost from $12 to $6. After the reduction in cost, the price ($12) is higher than marginal cost ($6), indicating that an expansion in output will now (at the lower input price) add more to revenue than to cost and thereby increase profit. Consequently, the firm will expand output along the new MC' curve until marginal cost once again equals marginal revenue at q_2.

In this section we have reviewed the competitive firm's reactions to changes in its economic environment—changes that are communicated to the firm through variations in input or product prices. A competitive firm by itself does not influence these prices; it is a price taker. Nonetheless, the combined actions of all the competing firms affect product and

FIGURE 9.6

How the Firm Responds to Input Price Changes
An input price change, with an unchanged product price, alters the profit-maximizing output. If an input price falls, *MC* shifts to *MC'*, and output increases to q_2, where *MC'* equals the unchanged price.

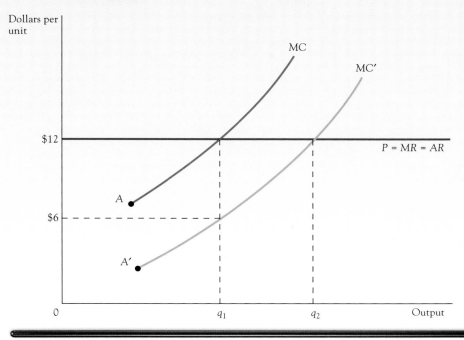

THE SHORT-RUN INDUSTRY SUPPLY CURVE

input prices, as we will see in the following sections. Each firm's response to price changes is an integral part of the adjustment process by which the overall market strives to reach equilibrium.

9.6 THE SHORT-RUN INDUSTRY SUPPLY CURVE

Moving from the determination of the most profitable output of the competitive firm to the short-run industry supply curve is a short step. In the short run a competitive firm will produce at a point where its marginal cost equals the price, as long as the price is above the minimum point of the average variable cost curve. In other words, each firm's marginal cost curve indicates how much the firm will produce at alternative prices. *As a first approximation, the* **short-run industry supply curve** *is derived by simply adding the quantities produced by each firm—that is, by summing the individual firms' marginal cost curves horizontally.* We assume for now that variable input prices remain constant at all levels of industry output.

Figure 9.7 illustrates how a short-run industry supply curve is derived for the three firms (A, B, and C) composing the cement industry. Although three firms may not be enough to constitute a competitive industry, the derivation is the same regardless of the number of firms involved. The figure shows the portion of each firm's marginal cost (MC) curve lying above its minimum average variable cost (AVC). Because the supply curve identifies the total quantity offered for sale at each price, we will add the outputs each firm chooses to produce individually.

SHORT-RUN INDUSTRY SUPPLY CURVE
the horizontal sum of the individual firms' marginal cost curves

FIGURE 9.7

The Short-Run Competitive Industry Supply Curve
Each firm will produce an output where marginal cost equals price to maximize profit. To derive the short-run industry supply curve, *SS*, we must horizontally sum the amounts produced by the industry's various firms, as shown by their respective marginal cost curves.

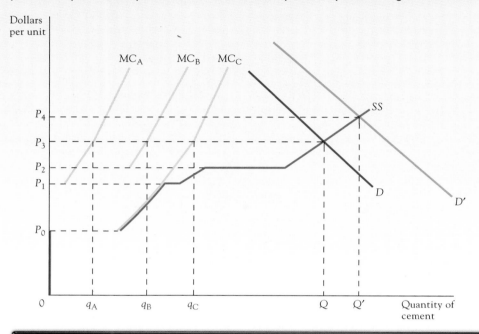

At any price below P_0, the minimum point on firm C's AVC curve, industry output is zero because all three firms shut down. At P_0, firm C begins to produce. Note that its output is the only output on the market until price reaches P_1, because the other companies will not operate at such low prices. Thus, the lower portion of firm C's MC curve reflects the total industry supply curve at low prices. When price reaches P_1, however, firm A begins to produce, and its output must be added to C's—hence, the kink in the industry supply curve at P_1. When price reaches P_2, firm B begins production, and its output is included in the supply curve at prices above P_2. We refer to this derivation of the short-run industry supply curve as a horizontal summation of the individual firms' short-run marginal cost curves because we are horizontally summing quantities across firms. For example, at a price of P_3, total industry supply is Q, the sum of the amounts each company produces at that price ($q_A + q_B + q_C$).

Note that the short-run industry supply curve, SS, slopes upward. Remember that each firm's MC curve slopes upward because it reflects the law of diminishing marginal returns to variable inputs. Thus, the law of diminishing marginal returns is the basic determinant of the shape of the industry's short-run supply curve.

Price and Output Determination in the Short Run
Incorporating the market demand for the product completes the short-run competitive model. Because the market demand relates total purchases (from all firms) to the price of cement, it interacts with the supply curve to determine price and quantity. In Figure 9.7, the intersection of the demand curve D with the supply curve identifies the price where total quantity demanded equals total quantity supplied. Thus, price P_3 is the short-run equilib-

rium price, and total industry output is Q. Each firm, taking price as given, produces an output where marginal cost equals P_3. Firm A thus produces q_A; firm B, q_B; firm C, q_C; the combined output, $q_A + q_B + q_C$, equals Q.

Given the Figure 9.7 supply and demand relationships, if price were at a level other than P_3 for some reason, familiar market pressures would work to push price toward its equilibrium level. For example, at a price lower than P_3, total quantity demanded by consumers would exceed the total amount supplied, a temporary shortage would exist, and price would be bid up. As price rises toward P_3, quantity demanded becomes smaller while quantity supplied becomes larger, until the two eventually come into balance at price P_3. Conversely, if price were higher than P_3, quantity supplied would exceed quantity demanded, a temporary surplus would exist, and competition among firms would drive the price down.

In the short run an increase in market demand leads to a higher price and a higher output. Suppose that we begin with the equilibrium just described, and then demand increases to D'. A shortage will exist at the initial price of P_3, and price will rise. The higher price will elicit a greater output response from the individual firms as they move up along their MC curves. The new short-run equilibrium will be price P_4 and quantity Q'.

Note that in Figure 9.7 we do not explicitly identify the profits, if any, realized by the firms. If we drew in each firm's average total cost curve, we could show them, but we do not need to use the average cost curves to explain the determination of price and quantity in the short run. All the necessary information is contained in the industry supply and demand curves.

APPLICATION 9.5 WHY ELECTRIC BILLS IN CALIFORNIA INCREASED AFTER DEREGULATION

Traditionally, electricity generation was assumed to be subject to economies of scale.[5] To allow consumers to realize the cost-side benefits of increased output by an individual supplier, electric utilities typically were granted exclusive rights to generate electricity for particular service territories. The utilities were placed under price regulation or state ownership to ensure that these lower average costs associated with a single company's generating electricity were passed on to consumers in the form of lower electric bills.

The extent to which there are economies of scale in the generation of electricity, however, has come under serious scrutiny over the last two decades. Indeed, most economists now believe that such economies are insufficient to justify granting utilities exclusive rights to generate power for particular service territories. Indeed,

although there may be important cost-side advantages to having a single, existing utility *distribute* power in a given locality, there also appear to be significant advantages associated with promoting competition between different companies to *generate* the power that will be distributed within the locality. A fitting analogy is the supply of gasoline for your car. It is desirable to have only one fuel system in your car, but competition between gas stations serves to keep your gasoline bills down.

To promote the benefits of competition, most states either already had deregulated electricity or were considering taking such a step by 2000. California initiated its deregulation in 1999, starting with San Diego. Instead of going down, however, electric bills went up. During the summer of 2000, for example, the typical San Diegan's electric bill was two to three times greater than it had been the previous summer.

Consider Figure 9.8a to understand why bills for electricity, measured in kilowatt hours (kWh), increased. Everything else being equal, suppose that deregulation allows for sources of power other than the public utility that

[5]This application is based on: Paul L. Joskow and Richard Schmalensee, *Markets for Power* (Cambridge, MA: MIT Press, 1983); James Flanigan, "Deregulation Is the Answer, Not the Problem," *latimes.com* (August 27, 2000); and Betsy Streisand, "Power to the People," *U.S. News Online* (August 21, 2000).

FIGURE 9.8

The Short-Run Electricity Supply Curve in California and Why the Price of Electricity Increased in 2000
(a) The short-run electricity supply curve is derived by horizontally summing the supply curves from traditional public utility sources (MC_{PU}) and new outside providers (MC_O). In and of itself, allowing in outside suppliers puts downward pressure on the price of electricity from P_2 to P_1.
(b) Instead of decreasing subsequent to deregulation, the price of electricity ends up increasing due to a simultaneous shift in demand (from D to D') and a leftward shift in the short-run supply curve (from SS to SS').

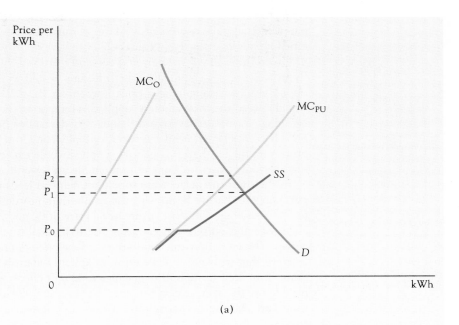

(a)

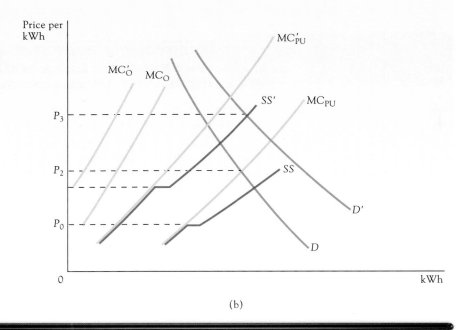

(b)

has traditionally served San Diego. The short-run supply curve to San Diego subsequent to deregulation, SS, thus is derived by horizontally summing the traditional public utility's marginal cost curve (MC_{PU}) with the marginal cost curve associated with other power companies from outside the traditional service territory (MC_O). As you can see in Figure 9.8a, deregulation puts downward pressure on price. Assuming that prior to deregulation regulators set the price at P_2 (where the demand curve, D, intersects the traditional utility's marginal cost curve, MC_{PU}), competition for electricity generation lowers the price to P_1 (where demand intersects the supply curve, SS).

In reality, however, deregulation failed to introduce sizable downward pressure on price because California didn't encourage entry by new suppliers as actively as did some other states. For example, Pennsylvania, with an electricity market less than 12 percent the size of California's, aggressively promoted competition and attracted more than 100 new suppliers. By contrast, California drew only a handful. The added potential output from the new suppliers (represented by MC_O) thus is small relative to the existing supply curve from traditional sources (represented by MC_{PU}). Consequently, the potential decrease in price brought about by deregulation, from P_2 to P_1 in Figure 9.8a, is smaller than it would have been had competition been more aggressively promoted.

More importantly, two changes in the market put appreciable upward pressure on electric bills. First, the price of fossil fuels such as oil, natural gas, and coal increased significantly due to cutbacks in the supply of crude oil by the members of the Organization of Petroleum Exporting Countries (OPEC). Since utilities rely extensively on fossil fuels to generate electricity, the increase in the price of these inputs shifts the relevant marginal cost curves upward from MC_{PU} to MC'_{PU} and MC_O to MC'_O in Figure 9.8b. As a result of the increase in the cost of generating electricity in both traditional and outside suppliers, the short-run supply curve shifts leftward from SS to SS'.

Second, demand for electricity in California has been growing nearly 5 percent a year, but no new power plants have been built in the state for more than 10 years (due to environmental concerns and a cumbersome regulatory process). In fact, California has grown disproportionately on account of the New Economy because it is home to Silicon Valley, prominent suppliers of media content in Los Angeles, and leading biotechnology firms in San Diego. The economic boom has shifted the demand for electricity rightward—from D to D' in Figure 9.8b.

Between the rightward shift in demand and the leftward shift in short-run supply, the price of electricity ends up rising to P_3 in Figure 9.8b (where SS' and D' intersect). And, as we can now see, the increase in the price of electricity reflects the workings of the familiar forces of supply and demand rather than a consequence of deregulation.

Of course, knowing that the forces of supply and demand are at work is little solace to a consumer whose electricity bill has suddenly doubled. As has happened in other cases where the price of a good has increased appreciably, pressure quickly mounted in California political circles to force utilities to roll back rates and/or to lower electricity prices through taxpayer subsidies. Moreover, in keeping with the law of demand, consumers quickly began to look for ways to lower the amount of electricity they demanded in the wake of the price increase. Even Sea World's star attraction, Shamu, began to feel the heat. The chillers that keep the killer whale's 7-million-gallon tank at a comfortable 55 degrees began to be shut down periodically to save on the park's $2.5 million annual electric bill.

9.7 LONG-RUN COMPETITIVE EQUILIBRIUM[6]

At any time, the short-run scale of plant a firm has built reflects a previous long-run decision. As a result, we must consider how the goal of profit maximization guides firms' long-run decisions and what that implies, in turn, about long-run competitive equilibrium. The same principles we used for the short-run setting apply to long-run profit maximization, but now we employ long-run cost curves, which allow a sufficient period of time to vary all inputs.

Figure 9.9 shows the long-run cost curves LAC and LMC for a representative firm in a perfectly competitive industry. If the firm believes the price will remain at $12, it will want to select an output level of q_3, where long-run marginal cost equals price. Producing q_3 involves building a scale of plant having a related short-run average cost curve (not depicted) tangent to LAC at point A. After building the plant, the firm realizes a total profit shown by area $EFAC$. No other size plant yields as much profit, since the long-run cost curves reflect all possible scales of plants the firm can select.

---

[6]A mathematical treatment of some of the material in this section is given in the appendix at the back of the book (pages 567–568).

FIGURE 9.9

Long-Run Profit Maximization
The competitive firm maximizes its profit by producing where $LMC = P$. With a price of $12, output will be q_3. By building a larger-scale plant and adjusting its output from q_1 to q_3, the firm increases its profit from $EGHI$ to $EFAC$.

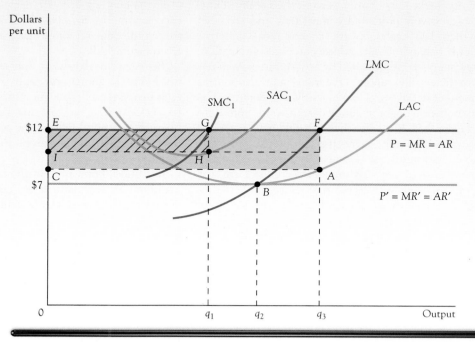

Figure 9.9 also illustrates why a short-run profit-maximizing outcome may be only a temporary equilibrium. Suppose that the price is $12 but the representative firm currently has a scale of plant with the short-run cost curves SAC_1 and SMC_1. With that size plant the firm's short-run profit-maximizing equilibrium is q_1, with the firm earning profit equal to the striped rectangular area $EGHI$. If the firm expects the price of $12 to persist, however, it would immediately begin making plans to enlarge its scale of plant, because it could earn significantly higher profit, area $EFAC$, by building the appropriate long-run scale of plant identified by point A. By its very nature, a short-run equilibrium is only temporary unless the firm's scale of plant is consistent with the price that is expected to persist in the market.

Suppose now that the expected price over the long run is $7 instead of $12. The horizontal demand curve at this price is just tangent to LAC at point B. For this demand curve the most profitable long-run output is q_2, where price equals long-run marginal cost. Total profit, however, is zero since price just equals the average cost of production.

The firm's long-run equilibrium at q_2, with price just covering average cost, has great significance. For one thing, the q_2 equilibrium indicates **zero economic profit**. Since the long-run cost curves take into account the opportunity costs of inputs, this implies that the return from employing inputs in the firm is as high as from the best alternative use of those inputs. In the case of capital, for instance, a firm's owners must be earning as great a return as the one they could make if their capital was employed elsewhere. Although the firm's books may show a positive accounting profit, the q_2 equilibrium involves a "normal" economic return being earned by inputs such as capital and thus zero economic profit.

Should a firm stay in business if it is earning zero economic profit at an output such as q_2 in Figure 9.9? The answer to this question is an emphatic *yes*. Zero economic profit means

ZERO ECONOMIC PROFIT
the point at which total profit is zero since price equals the average cost of production

that the various inputs, including capital provided by the owners, can earn just as much somewhere else. Although this is true, the relevant consideration is that they can't earn any *more* elsewhere, which is why the firm has an incentive to continue production.

The q_2 equilibrium is also significant because it is precisely the type of equilibrium competitive markets tend toward in the long run. To see why, remember that free entry and exit of resources is one of the characteristics of a perfectly competitive market. Figure 9.9 indicates how a price of $12 creates an incentive for the firm to expand output from q_2 to q_3 and provides the firm with a positive economic profit. Positive economic profit implies that resources invested in the industry generate a return higher than what could be earned elsewhere. Without barriers to entry, the abnormally high return results in new firms entering the industry; investors can make more money by shifting their resources into an industry affording positive economic profits. As shown in Figure 9.10, however, new entry also results in the industry short-run supply curve shifting to the right and a decrease in price. This process continues until the market demand curve and the new industry supply curve (SS′) intersect at the same price (P′) where long-run marginal cost equals the minimum point on the representative firm's long-run average total cost curve. Entry continues, in other words, until any positive economic profit signal and hence incentive for entry are eliminated. There is no incentive to enter the industry (that is, economic profit equals zero) when long-run average cost equals average revenue where long-run marginal cost equals price.

The long-run equilibrium shown in Figure 9.10 has three characteristics. First, the representative firm is maximizing profit and producing where *LMC* equals price. This condition must hold for a simple reason. If firms are not producing the appropriate amounts, they have an incentive to alter their output levels to increase profit. A change in firms' outputs, however, affects the total quantity offered for sale by the industry, which in turn changes the price at which the output is sold. Thus, the initial price cannot be an equilibrium price if firms are not producing where *LMC* equals price.

FIGURE 9.10

Long-Run Competitive Equilibrium
(b) An industry in long-run competitive equilibrium where *SS′* and *D* intersect.
(a) The equilibrium from the perspective of a representative firm. The firm is producing the most profitable output (*LMC* = *P′*) and is making zero economic profit (*LAC* = *AR′*).

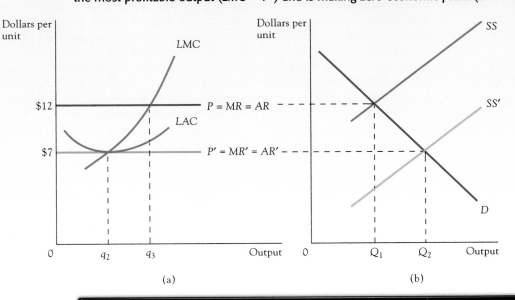

Second, there must be no incentive for firms to enter or leave the industry. This condition occurs when firms are making zero economic profits. If profits were higher, other firms seeking higher returns would enter the industry; if profits were lower, firms would leave the industry because they could do better elsewhere. This entry or exit would affect the level of industry output and change the price. If, however, profits in this industry are comparable to profits in other industries, there is no reason for entry or exit to occur, and price and output will remain stable.

Third, the combined quantity of output of all the firms at the prevailing price equals the total quantity consumers wish to purchase at that price. If this condition were violated, there would be either excess demand or excess supply at the prevailing price, so the price would not be an equilibrium one.

Zero Profit When Firms' Cost Curves Differ?

When all firms in a competitive industry have identical cost curves, every firm must be making zero economic profit in long-run equilibrium. Cost curves, however, may differ among firms. Some businesses may have access to superior technology, patents, or more skilled workers vis-à-vis other firms. These differences will be reflected as differences in production costs. While firms' LAC curves may be shaped and positioned differently, their minimum points will still end up at the same cost per unit through the process described below.

If firms' cost curves differ, we must reconsider the proposition that *every* firm makes zero economic profit in a long-run equilibrium. As it turns out, this proposition is still correct, but the reason it is deserves attention. To see why, consider the case of two firms that are both in the business of raising corporate executives' IQs, Densa Inc. and Mensa Inc. Let's suppose that Mensa has some especially productive input that Densa does not have. For example, suppose that Mensa and Densa both purchase office space to begin their operations. Through foresight or chance, Mensa's selected office site proves to be more favorable. Suppose that government policymakers unexpectedly encourage businesses to set up shop in Mensa's vicinity while locating a nuclear waste dump adjacent to Densa, thereby scaring off potential corporate neighbors. Because of the government actions, Mensa's location is more productive, even though both firms originally may have paid the same price for the office space. The better location accounts for Mensa's lower production cost.

Due to the unexpectedly productive location, Mensa's income statement will indicate a positive accounting profit. The original price Mensa paid for the space understates its real economic value; that is, the cost of using the space is greater than its purchase price. Remember, however, that cost reflects forgone opportunities, and once it is known that Mensa's location is highly productive, its market value—what other firms would pay for the space—will rise. Provided that input markets are perfectly competitive, the opportunity cost to Mensa of its office space will be bid up to reflect its full economic value. Once Mensa's office space is valued at its true opportunity cost, Mensa's economic profit falls to zero.

In this analysis it makes no difference whether Mensa rents or owns the office space. If Mensa rents the space, and it becomes apparent that the space is unusually productive, the rental cost will go up because other firms will be willing to pay more for highly productive office space. If Mensa owns the office space, the same principle applies; the original purchase price is irrelevant. What counts is how much the office space is worth to other potential users—that is, its opportunity cost. In this case the cost of using the office space is an implicit cost, and, as explained in an earlier chapter, we include implicit costs in the cost curves.

The process by which unusually productive inputs receive higher compensation is not restricted to office space. Suppose that you go to work for a business as a manager and are promised a salary of $40,000. When the firm hires you, it doesn't know whether you'll be any good at your job. Fortunately, you turn out to be brilliant, and even after paying your salary, the firm's net revenue rises by $25,000 due to your extraordinary managerial skills. The firm's owner is delighted, and the firm's books show a $25,000 profit increase. Once your managerial skills are recognized, however, you are in a position to command and receive a $25,000 raise, which will effectively eliminate the firm's accounting profit. You will be in such a position so long as your managerial skills are transferable across firms and there is a competitive market for your managerial talents. Provided these conditions hold, if you don't get a raise, you can resign and accept a position with another firm that will pay you a salary closer to what you're worth—your best alternative—and your former employer's profit will decline to its original level.

Needless to say, this process doesn't work instantaneously or with exact precision. There is a tendency, however, for inputs to receive compensation equal to their opportunity costs, that is, what they are worth to alternative users. This process leads to the zero-profit equilibrium. One implication of this analysis is that the accounting measure of profit may vary widely among firms in an industry even though economic profit is zero for each firm. This variation arises because a firm's assets are frequently valued on the books at their original purchase prices instead of their opportunity costs. In our earlier example, Mensa's accounting profit would be higher than Densa's if they both counted only the purchase price of the office space as a cost.

9.8 THE LONG-RUN INDUSTRY SUPPLY CURVE

LONG-RUN INDUSTRY SUPPLY CURVE
the long-run relationship between price and industry output, which depends on whether input prices are constant, increasing, or decreasing as the industry expands or contracts

CONSTANT-COST INDUSTRY
an industry in which expansion of output does not bid up input prices, long-run average production cost per unit remains unchanged, and the long-run industry supply curve is horizontal

INCREASING-COST INDUSTRY
an industry in which expansion of output leads to higher long-run average production costs and the long-run supply curve slopes upward

DECREASING-COST INDUSTRY
a highly unusual situation in which the long-run supply curve is downward sloping

To derive the competitive industry's short-run supply curve we horizontally sum individual firms' supply curves. We cannot similarly derive a competitive industry's long-run supply curve, however, because in the long run firms enter or exit the industry in response to the economic profits being earned. So we do not know which firms' supply curves to sum horizontally. Moreover, as an industry expands or contracts due to firm entry or exit, the prices that firms pay for their inputs may change. For example, as the movie business expands due to firm entry, the prices of actors and directors may be bid up. As the oil producing industry shrinks due to firm exit, the prices of petroleum engineers and drilling rigs may decline.

As we will see, the derivation of a **long-run industry supply curve** in a competitive market depends centrally on what happens to input prices as the industry expands or contracts. Based on the three possible effects of industry size on input prices, competitive industries are classified as **constant-cost**, **increasing-cost**, or **decreasing-cost**. We address each of these cases in turn, starting with the simplest of the three: when input prices remain constant regardless of an industry's overall size.

Constant-Cost Industry

To derive the long-run supply curve for a constant-cost industry, we start from a position of equilibrium and trace the effects of a demand change until the industry once again returns to a long-run equilibrium. As our example, let's assume that the market for MBA education is perfectly competitive, with business schools being the representative firms. We begin by examining the industry when it is in long-run equilibrium (say in 1970).

Figure 9.11b shows the industry's initial long-run equilibrium: when demand is D, output is Q_1, and price is P. Assuming that we start in long-run equilibrium, point A is then one point on the long-run supply curve, LS. Figure 9.11a shows the representative firm's position—say that of New York University (NYU). It is producing its most profitable output, q_1, and making zero economic profit at price P.

To identify other points on the long-run supply curve, let's imagine that there is an unexpected increase in demand to D' and work through the consequences for the industry. Demand for MBA education has grown over the past three decades for a number of reasons, including more women joining the work force and seeking a business education, worldwide

FIGURE 9.11 **Long-Run Supply in a Constant-Cost Industry**
The long-run industry supply curve LS of a constant-cost competitive industry is horizontal. Expansion of industry output does not bid up input prices. Thus, when industry output expands from Q_1 to Q_3, firms' cost curves do not shift and the long-run average production cost per unit remains unchanged.

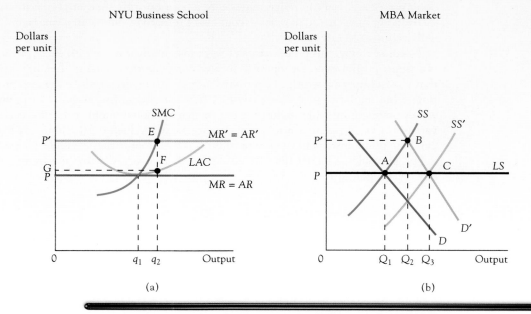

(a) (b)

economic growth and entrepreneurship (while domestic applications to U.S. MBA programs have increased slightly in recent years, international applications have boomed), and the ever-advancing state of business management knowledge.

Reflecting the increased demand, existing business schools have an immediate short-run response—they increase output by expanding operations in their existing plants and increasing employment of variable inputs such as faculty and staff. The response appears as a movement along the short-run industry supply curve, SS, from point A to point B. (Note that the initial long-run equilibrium is also a short-run equilibrium. Every school is operating its existing plant at the appropriate level—where SMC equals P—so point A is also a point on the short-run supply curve.) In the short run, price rises to P', and output increases to Q_2 as the industry expands along SS.

In Figure 9.11a, we can see what this adjustment means for NYU, a representative firm in the industry. The higher price induces NYU to increase output along its short-run marginal cost curve SMC and produce q_2 where SMC = P'. (Recall that the summation of all the schools' SMC curves yields the SS curve.) At this point every business school is making an economic profit (equal to area $P'EFG$).

The industry, however, has not fully adjusted to the increase in demand; this position is only a short-run equilibrium. *The key to the long-run adjustment is profit-seeking by firms.* In the short-run equilibrium, existing schools are making economic profits. The return on investment in the MBA education market is now greater than in other industries. Whenever economic profits exist in an industry, investors will realize that they can make more money by moving resources into the industry. If entry is costless, as it is assumed to be in the case of perfect competition, resources will be shifted into the MBA education market, thereby increasing its productive capacity.

Suppose that new schools enter the industry in an attempt to share in the market's profitability. The entry increases the industry's total output, which, in Figure 9.11b, is shown as a rightward shift in the short-run supply curve. Recall that a short-run supply curve represents a fixed number of schools with given plants. When the number of firms increases, the total output at each price is greater (there are more "member" firms with their corresponding MC curves in the industry "club")—implying a shift in the short-run supply curve. As output expands in response to entry, price falls from its short-run level along D' since the higher output can be sold only at a lower price. This process of firms entering, total output increasing, and price falling continues so long as the industry is generating a positive economic profit signal. In other words, a new long-run equilibrium emerges when schools are once again making only a "normal profit"—that is, zero economic profit.

For a constant-cost industry the increased employment of inputs associated with expanding output occurs without an increase in the price of individual inputs. This means business school cost curves do not shift. Thus, price must fall back to its original level before profits return to a normal level: if price is higher than P economic profits will persist, and entry of new schools will continue. Figure 9.11b shows the process of entry as a rightward shift in SS; it continues until SS' intersects the demand curve D' at point C and price has returned to its original level P.

Point C is a second point on the long-run supply curve LS. With demand curve D', industry output expands until it reaches Q_3 and price is P. Each school once again makes zero economic profit. In Figure 9.11a, NYU is again confronted with price P and can do no better than cover its average cost by producing q_1. The increase in industry output from Q_1 to Q_3 is the result of entry by new schools.

A constant-cost competitive industry is characterized by a horizontal long-run supply curve. Given time to adjust, the industry can expand with no increase in price along LS. The crucial assumption producing this result is that input prices are not affected by an industry's size, so new schools can enter the market and produce at the same average cost as existing schools. The term *constant cost* refers to the fact that schools' cost curves do not shift as the industry expands or contracts; it does *not* mean that each school in the industry has a horizontal LAC curve.

Increasing-Cost Industry

We can derive the long-run supply curve for an increasing-cost industry in the same way we derived it for a constant-cost industry. We assume an initial long-run equilibrium; then the demand curve shifts, and we follow the adjustment process through to its conclusion. Figure 9.12 illustrates this case. The initial industry long-run equilibrium price and quantity are P and Q_1, respectively. The typical firm, NYU, is producing q_1 and just covering its costs, shown by LAC, at the market price.

Once again, we assume an unexpected demand increase to D'. The short-run equilibrium is determined by the intersection of the short-run supply curve SS and D'. Price rises to P', and output increases to Q_2. The representative school expands output along its SMC curve to q_2 and realizes economic profit. In the long run, the profit attracts resources to the industry.

Up to this point the analysis is identical to the constant-cost case. Moreover, the attainment of a new long-run equilibrium involves further expansion of industry output until economic profits return to zero, just as in a constant-cost industry. However, in an increasing-cost industry the expansion of output leads to an increase in some input prices. To produce

FIGURE 9.12

Long-Run Supply in an Increasing-Cost Industry

For an increasing-cost competitive industry, the long-run supply curve *LS* slopes upward. Expansion of industry output bids up some input prices. Thus, when industry output expands from Q_1 to Q_3, firms' cost curves shift upward from *LAC* to *LAC'*, and the output expansion leads to a higher long-run average production cost.

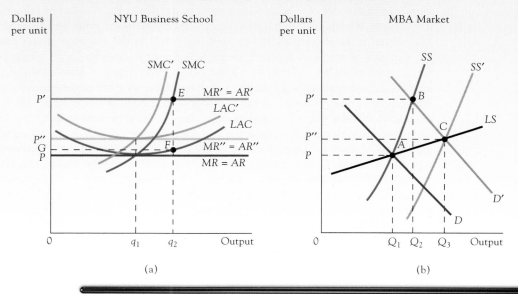

(a)   (b)

more output, schools must increase their demand for inputs, and some inputs such as finance professors are assumed to be available in larger quantities only at higher prices. This situation contrasts sharply with that of the constant-cost case, where schools can hire larger quantities of all inputs without affecting their prices.

Let's see how this difference affects the long-run adjustment process. At the short-run equilibrium, positive economic profits lead to entry by new schools and an expansion in industry output—a rightward shift in the short-run supply curve. Increased industry output now tends to reduce profits in two ways. First, as we saw earlier, the higher output causes price to fall, which reduces profits. Second, the increased demand for inputs that accompanies the expansion in industry output leads to higher input prices. Higher input prices mean higher production costs, which also reduce profits. Profits are thus caught in a two-way squeeze as the industry expands. The two-way squeeze continues until economic profits equal zero and a new long-run equilibrium is attained.

Figure 9.12 shows the two-way squeeze on economic profits. Starting with the short-run equilibrium at point *B* (panel b), as new schools enter the market, *SS* shifts to the right and price falls. Each school's horizontal demand curve shifts downward as price declines from *P'* to *P''*, and this decline reduces profits. At the same time, however, higher input prices shift the firms' cost curves upward, from *LAC* to *LAC'*. In Figure 9.12a, NYU's profit (area *P'EFG*) is squeezed from above by the decline in the product price and from below by the rising unit cost of production. A rising cost and falling price eventually eliminate NYU's economic profit. This occurs at price *P''*, when NYU can just cover its average cost by producing at the minimum point on *LAC'*. Once profit is eliminated, there is no longer an incentive for industry output to increase further, and a new long-run equilibrium is reached. In Figure 9.12b, SS has shifted rightward to SS', producing a price of P″ and an output of Q_3. No further shift in the short-run supply curve will occur, because economic profits have fallen to zero. Thus, point C is another point on the long-run industry supply curve.

An *increasing-cost competitive industry is characterized by an upward-sloping long-run supply curve*. This industry can produce an increased output only if it receives a higher price, because the cost of production rises (cost curves shift upward) as the industry expands. The term *increasing cost* indicates that the cost curves of all schools shift upward as the industry expands and input prices are bid up.

APPLICATION 9.6 — INCREASING INPUT COSTS IN THE INFORMATION TECHNOLOGY INDUSTRY

The information technology industry is based, to a significant extent, in California's Silicon Valley. As the industry has expanded dramatically in recent years, firms in the industry have bid up the price of computer software engineers and managers with expertise in running information technology companies. The expansion of the industry has also bid up the price of land in Silicon Valley, a relatively scarce input, which has increased the cost of housing sought by the software engineers and managers employed by the industry. In 2000, for example, the average fixer-upper in Palo Alto (in the heart of Silicon Valley) sold for more than $700,000. The cost of housing has been driven up so much by the expansion of the information technology industry that some employees find it convenient to commute daily by air from Phoenix, Arizona, or Las Vegas, Nevada. For an appreciable number of employees, then, the daily cost of commuting by air from cities more than 500 miles away is less than the cost of either buying a house or staying in a hotel in Silicon Valley. The scarcity of land in Silicon Valley thus has worked to make the information technology industry an increasing-cost industry. Of course, improvements in technology, discussed in the following subsection, have worked to counteract the effect that an expansion in the information technology industry has had on the cost of production.

Decreasing-Cost Industry

A *decreasing-cost* competitive industry is one that has a downward-sloping long-run supply curve. You might think that such a situation is impossible, and, in fact, some economists believe that it is. Others claim that a decreasing-cost industry is theoretically conceivable but admit that it is a remote possibility. Because all agree that it is, at best, highly unusual, we will deal with it only briefly here.

A decreasing-cost industry adjusts to an increase in demand by expanding output, just as industries in the other two cases. In this instance, though, the expansion of output by the industry in some way lowers the cost curves of the individual schools, leading to a new long-run equilibrium with a higher output but a lower price. The tricky part is to try to explain why the cost curves shift downward. A downward shift in cost curves usually reflects a decrease in input prices, but for that to happen we have to explain how an increase in demand for some input leads to an increased quantity supplied at a lower price—not an easy task.

Although economists are in agreement about how rare decreasing-cost industries must be, many noneconomists find the concept appealing. The reason for its appeal stems from the observation that prices have declined sharply as output has expanded in some industries. For example, color televisions, VCRs, and pocket calculators have all fallen in price in real terms by 80 to 90 percent since they were first introduced. More recently, there have been dramatic reductions in personal computer prices.

Before concluding that such evidence reflects decreasing-cost industries, we should explore some other possibilities. One common feature in these examples is that the price was high when the product was first marketed but later fell dramatically. This suggests two possible explanations. First, the firm initially marketing the product is a monopoly and thus has some pricing power. The price that the monopoly firm sets may be fairly high. As other firms enter the market and begin to compete, price falls and output increases. This process suggests that what we may be seeing is the rise of competition from an initial monopoly position and not a movement along an industry's long-run supply curve.

Second, the passage of time after a product's introduction makes technological improvements in production possible. Particularly in the case of new and complex products, technological know-how is frequently rudimentary when firms first market a product. With experience in production over time, technological improvements may occur quickly. We emphasize that technological know-how is assumed to be unchanged along a supply curve. An improvement in technology shifts the entire supply curve to the right.

Consider Figure 9.13. In conjunction with demand, the long-run supply curve for pocket calculators in 1970, LS_{70}, determined a price of $300. This price was, in fact, the approximate price of a calculator that performed only the basic functions—when expressed in constant 1990 dollars. After 10 years firms developed improved methods that lowered production cost, and the 1980 long-run supply curve was LS_{80}. We assume that demand is unchanged, although it was probably increasing over the period. This shift in supply led to a price of $100 in 1980. Further improvements in technology shifted the supply curve once again, and price fell to $10 in 1990. The combination of lower prices and higher outputs over time resulted here from shifts in an upward-sloping long-run supply curve, not from a slide down the negatively-sloped supply curve of a decreasing-cost industry. This explana-

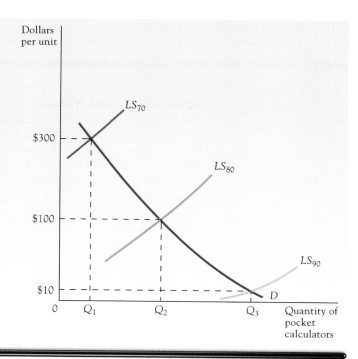

FIGURE 9.13

Technological Advances Shift the Long-Run Supply Curve
A price reduction and output increase over time need not imply that the long-run supply curve has a negative slope. Technological advances can occur over time, which shift the entire long-run supply curve downward, producing lower prices and higher outputs.

tion of the phenomenon is especially appealing because new high-technology items are known to show rapid improvements in technical knowledge in the first years of their production.

These remarks do not rule out the possibility of decreasing-cost industries, but if they exist, like the Giffen good case in demand theory, they are extremely rare. For all practical purposes the increasing- and constant-cost cases are the relevant possibilities.

APPLICATION 9.7 THE BIDDING WAR FOR MIS AND FINANCE PROFESSORS

Each year, the country's 700-plus business schools produce a total of 80,000 MBAs.[7] The number of business schools has more than doubled and the number of MBA graduates per year has increased fifteen-fold since 1970. As the industry has expanded, certain inputs have been bid up in price. Among the inputs that have been bid up most in price are faculty in disciplines such as management information systems (MIS) and finance, in which student enrollments have witnessed the largest increases. For example, top new finance assistant professors garnered starting salaries of more than $130,000 in 2000—36 percent higher than in 1997. Leading rookie MIS faculty members were earning $116,000 in 2000—37 percent more than in 1997. Annual salaries for the most respected senior faculty members in both fields rose from roughly $120,000 in the mid-1980s to well over $300,000 by 2000.

Of course, as the business school market has expanded, not all inputs have risen in price. Some have remained constant or perhaps even decreased. For example, schools' applicant screening costs have been reduced due to widespread reliance on the Graduate Management Admissions Test (GMAT) as a candidate-screening mechanism.

On average, however, real input prices have increased since the 1960s. This suggests that the long-run supply curve in the MBA education market is upward-sloping and provides at least a partial explanation for the rise in annual tuition at private business schools.[8] For example, annual MBA tuition at USC, a representative private business school, rose from $1,950 in 1970 to $30,000 in 1998. The 2000 annual USC MBA tuition equals roughly $6,756 in constant 1970 dollars. Although other factors (such as increased reliance by universities on their business schools to generate an operating surplus) have certainly affected MBA tuition, the growth of the MBA industry and the attendant increases in demand for industry inputs and the (real) prices of those inputs surely also played a role.

[7]This application is based on *AACSB Newsline*, Vol. 30 No. 3 (2000), pp. 1–5.

[8]Tuition at public business schools is generally controlled and subsidized by the state.

Comments on the Long-Run Supply Curve

An industry's long-run supply curve summarizes the results of a complex and subtle process of adjustment. Once the underlying determinants of the supply curve are understood, it becomes a powerful tool of analysis. To use the supply curve correctly, however, we must have a firm understanding of its underpinnings. To that end, we discuss several frequently misunderstood points.

1. We do not derive the long-run supply curve by summing the long-run marginal cost curves of an industry's firms. Admittedly, every firm is producing where $LMC = P$ at each point on LS, but as the industry adjusts along LS, firms are entering or leaving the market. Therefore, we cannot sum firms' LMC curves as we did in the short run. In addition, for an increasing-cost industry the LMC curves themselves shift because of changes in input prices.

2. Just as we did with a demand curve, we assume certain things remain unchanged at all points on the long-run supply curve. For one we assume technology is constant. An industry expanding along its *LS* curve is using the same technical know-how but employing more inputs to increase output. A change in technology causes the entire supply curve to shift, as we saw in the example about pocket calculators discussed earlier. We also assume that at all points on the long-run supply curve the supply curves of inputs to the industry remain unchanged. Note that we are not assuming that the prices of inputs are unchanged but rather that the conditions of supply remain constant. In a constant-cost industry, input prices remain constant not because we assume them to be fixed but because the input supply curves facing the industry are horizontal. In contrast, in an increasing-cost industry input prices change because the input supply curves facing the industry are upward-sloping, a condition that gives rise to an upward-sloping, long-run industry supply curve. When relevant, other factors like government regulations or the weather must also be assumed constant along the supply curve.

3. In reality, an industry is not likely to fully attain a position of long-run equilibrium. Real-world industries are continually buffeted by changes. For instance, input supplies, demand, technology, and government regulations frequently change. A long-run adjustment takes time, and if underlying conditions change often, an industry will find itself moving toward a long-run equilibrium that is continually shifting. Recognizing the reality of frequent change, however, does not undermine the usefulness of the long-run equilibrium concept. Although the industry may never attain a long-run equilibrium, the tendency for the industry to move in the indicated direction is what is important, and the outcome is correctly predicted by the theory.

4. Economic profit is zero all along a competitive industry's long-run supply curve. This point is often misunderstood. For example, someone may say that when industry output expands due to an increase in demand, the industry's firms benefit. We have seen, however, that after an increase in demand, all firms will make zero economic profits in the long run. There may be temporary economic profits in the short run, but the benefit is not permanent.

Who does benefit as we move along the long-run supply curve? Owners of inputs whose prices are bid up by the industry-wide expansion. With a constant-cost industry no input prices rise, and no input owners receive a permanent gain. If firms own some of the inputs and thus gain as input prices increase, the gain accrues to them on account of their input ownership and not because they are firms in an increasing-cost industry. It is also possible that firms own none of the inputs whose prices rise. It may be, for example, that finance professors whose wages go up as the MBA industry expands are the sole beneficiaries on this market's supply side.

The tendency toward zero economic profit means that the rate of return on invested resources will tend to equalize across industries. If invested resources yield an annual return of 10 percent in the restaurant industry, which is comparable to earnings elsewhere, then the restaurant industry is earning zero economic profit. Accountants, of course, generally call the 10 percent return a "profit," but economists regard the 10 percent return as a cost necessary to attract resources to the restaurant industry.

5. In deriving the long-run supply curve, we assumed that a short-run equilibrium was first established and then long-run forces came into play. Price first went up to a short-run high and then came down to a long-run equilibrium level. The actual process of adjustment to demand changes may not follow this pattern exactly. Identifying a short-run equilibrium and then tracing out long-run effects is merely an expedient way of explaining the determination of the final equilibrium. In fact, following a demand increase, price may never reach its short-run level and may never go above the ultimate long-run level. This can happen if, for example, firms anticipate the demand increase and make adjustments before demand actually rises.

These remarks also suggest that some care must be taken in using the short-run supply curve. We can use the short-run supply curve to identify the initial effects of a change in demand under only two conditions: when the demand change is unexpected, and when it is expected to be temporary. If firms anticipate the demand change, they can adjust their scales of plants or ready themselves to move into or out of a market before the demand change actually occurs. An unexpected demand change catches firms unaware, and they must operate temporarily with whatever scales of plants they have at that time. If firms expect a demand change to be temporary, they will not expand capacity or enter a market on the basis of conditions they know will not persist. Thus, any output change will result from the firms utilizing existing plants more or less intensively, and a short-run analysis is appropriate.

Even when appropriate, a short-run analysis identifies only an industry's temporary resting place, and subsequent long-run adjustments will continue moving the industry toward long-run equilibrium. So in most supply-demand applications we generally use the long-run supply curve.

9.9 WHEN DOES THE COMPETITIVE MODEL APPLY?[9]

The assumptions of perfect competition are stringent and are likely to be satisfied fully in very few real-world markets. Still, many markets come close enough to satisfying the assumptions of perfect competition to make the model quite useful. As we mentioned earlier, product homogeneity and perfect information may not apply in the case of gasoline retailing, yet the industry may be very close to being perfectly competitive since representative firms have only limited pricing power.

How close is "close enough" in terms of the assumptions of perfect competition being satisfied to make the model applicable? This question has no easy answer. For example, consider the assumption that there must be "many" small firms, an assumption that can be readily verified: firms can be counted. The relationship between the number of firms and an industry's competitiveness is not obvious. As we will see in Chapter 13, a relatively large number of firms producing a homogeneous product may collude to fix prices above the competitive level.

Conversely, even if there are only a few firms in an industry, each firm may face a highly elastic demand curve if the market demand curve is very elastic or if the elasticity of supply by rival firms is high. For example, suppose that United is one of four suppliers of air travel between Los Angeles and San Francisco, and that each of the four suppliers accounts for one-fourth of the total air passenger travel between the two cities. Although it is by no means a small player in this market, United may still face a highly elastic demand curve if when it raises its price, the rivals are quick to increase their output in response to United's price increase. A high elasticity of supply by rival airlines can thus severely limit United's pricing power. In Chapter 13 we will explore in greater depth how the output responses of rivals to a firm's price changes affect the elasticity of the firm's demand curve.

---

[9]A mathematical treatment of some of the material in this section is given in the appendix at the back of the book (page 568).

With regard to other assumptions of perfect competition, such as free entry and exit of resources, the competitive model frequently can be adapted to take the violations of these assumptions into account. This adaptability is another reason why the model is important: it can be extended to analyze the implications of specified departures from perfect competition. For example, suppose that an industry is in long-run equilibrium and demand increases, but new firms are blocked from entering the market. It is easy to show that output will increase by less in this case, price will be higher, and economic profit will persist after the industry's firms have made the appropriate long-run adjustment.

Consider as well the assumption that firms produce a homogeneous product. This assumption serves two purposes in the competitive model: it implies that a uniform price will prevail, and it affects the elasticity of demand facing a particular firm. What if the product homogeneity assumption is not fully satisfied? A good example of this is provided by comparison-shopping surveys that find food prices higher in the inner city than in the suburbs. For those who expect the competitive model to be an accurate description of reality, this result violates the uniform-price implication and suggests monopoly pricing in the inner cities. Further investigation, however, reveals profits to be no higher for inner-city food stores than for suburban markets, a result consistent with competition but not with monopoly.

What is going on? Basically, food sold in the inner city and food sold in the suburbs are not homogeneous products. To city residents, food sold in the inner city is worth more than food sold farther away. People are willing to pay something for the convenience of shopping nearby, and when convenience costs the retailer something, the price of the "same" product will differ. In comparison with costs in the suburbs, the cost of operating a food store in the inner city is higher because rent, fire and theft insurance, and the salaries of personnel all tend to be higher there. As a result, inner-city residents pay a higher price for shopping near their homes.

Dropping the homogeneous product assumption means that differentials in price can exist, but that is not often a serious problem and the competitive model can still be used. Suppose, for example, that a city government passed a law that food prices in the inner city cannot exceed prices in the suburbs. The competitive model applied to this setting would predict that output (food sales) would fall in the inner city, shortages would exist, some food stores would go out of business, and many inner-city residents would be worse off because no food was locally available at the mandated lower price—the familiar effects of a price ceiling. These predictions would, we suspect, be borne out in practice.

Finally, the assumption that firms and consumers have all the relevant information is also necessary if markets are to behave exactly as the competitive model predicts. For example, if consumers are ignorant of price, even homogeneous products can sell for different prices.

Dropping the assumption of full information does not mean, however, that we have to replace it with one of complete ignorance. One of the results of real-world markets is that firms and consumers have incentives to acquire the information that is important for their economic decisions. Although they may not become fully informed, because there are costs associated with acquiring information, we can easily suppose that they will become well enough informed that the assumption of complete information is not too great a distortion.

Economists have only recently begun to systematically analyze the acquisition of information and the way "information costs" influence the workings of markets. It is too early to make any sweeping generalizations in this area, but we do not want to suggest that the degree of information is irrelevant to the functioning of a market. Lack of information on the part of consumers may result in market outcomes that deviate significantly from the competitive norm. We will discuss issues related to information in more detail in Chapter 14.

SUMMARY

•   A perfectly competitive industry is characterized by a large number of buyers and sellers, free entry and exit of resources, a homogeneous product, and perfect information. Although few industries fully satisfy all these conditions, the model of perfect competition remains quite useful in analyzing many markets.

•   Since a competitive firm sells a product similar to that sold by many other firms, the firm's output decision has a negligible effect on the product's prices. Thus, the competitive firm's demand curve can be approximated by a horizontal line at the level of the prevailing price.

•   For any firm, the most profitable output occurs where the marginal cost of producing another unit of output just equals the marginal revenue from selling it.

•   For a competitive firm with its horizontal demand curve, price equals marginal revenue, so it maximizes profit by producing where marginal cost equals price. Price, however, must be at least as high as average variable cost or the firm suffers losses.

•   If price does not cover AVC in the short run, the firm will shut down; if price does not cover LAC in the long run, the firm will go out of business.

•   The competitive firm's short-run supply curve is its marginal cost curve, so long as marginal cost exceeds average variable cost.

•   The assumption of profit maximization allows us to predict how a competitive firm will respond to changes in the product price or in input prices. An increase in the product price (with unchanged cost curves) will lead the firm to expand output as it moves up its marginal cost curve.

•   A reduction in one or more input prices will shift the cost curves downward and so will lead the firm (with an unchanged product price) to expand output.

•   The competitive industry's short-run supply curve is the horizontal summation of the short-run marginal cost curves (above AVC) of an industry's firms.

•   Because the law of diminishing marginal returns implies that each firm's marginal cost curve slopes upward, the short-run industry supply curve also slopes upward.

•   In the long run, firms have sufficient time to alter plant capacity and to enter or leave the industry. The long-run supply curve takes these adjustments into account, with firms always guided by the search for profit.

•   Two shapes of the long-run industry supply curve are most likely. First, an increasing-cost industry has an upward-sloping long-run supply curve, reflecting the increase in the prices of one or more inputs as the industry expands.

•   Second, a constant-cost industry has a horizontal long-run supply curve, reflecting a situation where the industry can expand its use of inputs without affecting their prices.

•   At all points along a long-run supply curve, economic profit is zero, because only when profit is zero is there no incentive for firms to enter or leave the industry.

•   Input supply curves and technology are assumed as givens in deriving a long-run supply curve; changes in these underlying factors shift the long-run supply curve.

REVIEW QUESTIONS AND PROBLEMS

Questions and problems marked with an asterisk have solutions given in Answers to Selected Problems at the back of the book (page 575).

9.1. What are the four assumptions of the perfectly competitive model? Critics are fond of pointing out that few, if any, real-world markets satisfy all four conditions, implying that the competitive model has little relevance for real-world markets. How would you respond to these critics?

9.2. How can consumers of apartments in Atlanta have a downward-sloping demand curve for apartments, and yet each Atlanta rental property owner face a horizontal demand curve?

*9.3. Assume that a competitive firm has the short-run costs given in Table 8.1. What is the firm's most profitable output, and how large is profit if the price per unit of output is (a) $15? and (b) $26?

9.4. "IBM should never sell its product for less than it costs to produce." If "costs to produce" is interpreted to mean IBM's average total cost, is this correct? If it is interpreted to mean average variable cost, is the statement correct? If it is interpreted to mean marginal cost, is the statement correct?

9.5. In Table 9.1, suppose that variable input prices increase by 50 percent. Will the firm's profit-maximizing output level change? Illustrate your answer with a graph.

9.6. "If Conagra is a competitive firm, it will never operate at an output where its average total cost curve is downward-sloping." True or false? Explain.

*9.7. "The difference between price and marginal cost is the amount of profit per unit of output, which the firm wishes to be as large as possible." True, false, or uncertain? Explain.

9.8. Suppose that through laziness and/or sheer stupidity, Densa Inc. always falls 10 percent short of producing the profit-maximizing output. Would a higher product price lead to greater output? Would an increase in input prices lead to a reduction in output? Does this result suggest why economists are not overly concerned about whether the profit-maximizing assumption is exactly correct? Explain.

9.9. Suppose that Keystone is a firm in the perfectly competitive ski resort business. If all of Keystone's input prices unexpectedly double, and at the same time the product price doubles, what will happen to Keystone's profit-maximizing level of output and its profit in the short run? In the long run? (Assume that Keystone begins from a position of long-run equilibrium.)

9.10. Starting from a long-run equilibrium, trace the effects of an unanticipated reduction in demand for (a) a constant-cost industry and (b) an increasing-cost industry. *Note:* This process is just the reverse of our derivation of the supply curves in Section 9.8, but it is very good practice to think through the process.

*9.11. In a constant-cost industry each firm's MC curve is upward-sloping, yet all the firms together—the industry—have a horizontal supply curve. Explain why there is no contradiction.

9.12. If each business school in the MBA education industry is operating where $LMC = P$, does it follow that the industry is in long-run equilibrium? Explain.

*9.13. "Suppose that the defense contracting business is perfectly competitive. In long-run equilibrium the price just covers average production cost, and every contractor makes zero profit. Thus, if the price goes down, even a little bit, due to a decrease in government defense spending, all contractors will go out of business." Discuss this statement.

9.14. Assume that the MBA education industry is constant-cost and is in long-run equilibrium. Demand increases, but due to strict accreditation standards, new firms are not permitted to enter the market. Analyze the determination of a new long-run equilibrium, showing the effects for a representative school as well as for the market as a whole.

9.15. For a given increase in demand, will output increase by more if the MBA education industry is constant-cost or increasing-cost? For a given decrease in demand, will output fall by more if the industry is constant-cost or increasing-cost?

9.16. How would each of the following phenomena affect the long-run supply curve of apples?
a. Workers in the apple industry form a union.
b. Consumers find out that apples cause cancer.

c. Hard-to-control bugs that eat apples invade from Mexico.
d. The government passes a law requiring apple trees to be planted at least 60 feet apart.
e. The government sets a maximum legal price (price ceiling) at which apples can be sold.
f. Immigration laws change to permit more itinerant apple pickers to enter the country.
g. The government passes a minimum wage law for apple pickers.

9.17. "Because agricultural demand is inelastic, a technological advance that lowers production costs will reduce total revenue. Thus, farmers have no incentive to introduce such a technique." True, false, or uncertain? Explain.

9.18. Can all schools in the MBA education market face constant returns to firm scale and yet the industry have an upward-sloping long-run supply curve? If the MBA education industry is constant-cost, what, if anything, does this imply about the returns to scale faced by the industry's individual schools?

9.19. As the industry moves from point B to C in Figure 9.11b, how can the industry's output increase yet NYU's output fall?

9.20. The American Red Cross is a supplier to the perfectly competitive domestic blood market. Unlike the other suppliers, however, the Red Cross is strictly nonprofit—its goal is to sell as much blood as possible without making a profit. Given this goal, is the Red Cross supply curve equal to its average variable cost curve? Explain why or why not.

9.21. Suppose that the gasoline retailing industry is perfectly competitive, constant-cost, and in long-run equilibrium. If the government unexpectedly levies a five-cent tax on every gallon sold by gasoline retailers, depict what will happen to the representative firm's cost curves. What will the effects of the tax be in the short run on industry output and price? Will the price rise by the full five cents in the short run? In the long run? How would your answers change if the industry was increasing-cost?

9.22. Suppose that Mensa Inc. is a representative firm operating in a perfectly competitive industry. Mensa's total cost of production, TC, is given by the equation $TC = 5,000 + 5q^2$, where q is Mensa's output. Based on this equation, Mensa's marginal cost is $10q$. If the output price is $100, what is Mensa's short-run profit-maximizing output? How much profit does Mensa make at that output?

9.23. Suppose that oil tankers fall into three classes: medium (tankers capable of carrying between 10,000 and 70,000 deadweight tons (DWT) of crude oil (approximately 170 million gallons)); large (tonnages between 70,000 and 175,000 DWT); and super (tonnages over 175,000 DWT). The total tonnage in each of the three classes is 53,000,000 in medium; 76,000,000 DWT in large; and 171,000,000 in super. Finally, suppose that the constant per unit annual operating cost per deadweight ton is $149 for medium; $107 for large; and $84 for super. Based on the preceding information, graph the short-run supply curves for each of the three tanker classes as well as for the overall oil shipping industry.

9.24. On October 13, 1993, as news of the potential merger between Bell Atlantic and Tele-Communications Inc. splashed across the front pages of newspapers, hordes of investors beseiged brokers with "buy" orders for TCI. The trouble was, TCI is the stock symbol for Transcontinental Realty Investors. TCI shares soared nearly 30 percent before the New York Stock Exchange caught on. It halted trading in the stock and sent out an advisory warning to members of the Exchange. Which assumption of perfect competition was violated by this episode?

9.25. Over the last two decades, the price of personal computers in real as well as nominal terms has declined markedly. Does this mean that the personal computer industry is decreasing-cost and that the long-run supply curve for personal computers is downward-sloping? Explain why or why not.

CHAPTER 10

Using the Competitive Model

The competitive model can be used to analyze a wide range of industries and the effects on them of government intervention. One example involves the manner in which taxicabs are licensed in many major city governments.

Chapter Outline

10.1 The Evaluation of Gains and Losses
Producer Surplus
Application 10.1 *The Allocation of Producer Surplus in Trucking*
Consumer Surplus, Producer Surplus, and Efficient Output *The Deadweight Loss of a Price Ceiling*

10.2 Excise Taxation
Who Bears the Burden of the Tax?
Application 10.2 *Why Cigarette Company Profits Did Not Get Smoked by a Recent Punitive-Damages Award*
The Deadweight Loss of Excise Taxation
Application 10.3 *The Long and the Short (Run) of the Deadweight Loss of Rent Control*

10.3 Airline Regulation and Deregulation
What Happened to the Profits? *After Deregulation*
Application 10.4 *The Contestability of Airline Markets*
The Push for Reregulation

10.4 City Taxicab Markets
The Illegal Market
Application 10.5 *Gypsy Vans and Super Shuttles*

10.5 Consumer and Producer Surplus, and the Net Gains from Trade
The Gains from International Trade
Application 10.6 *Should Imports of Sunlight Be Banned?*
The Link Between Imports and Exports

10.6 Government Intervention in Markets: Quantity Controls
Sugar Policy: A Sweet Deal
Application 10.7 *Evading Quantity Restrictions: Virgin Atlantic's Interest in the Airbus A380*
Summary

Learning Objectives

- Show how changes in market conditions or government policies affect the welfare of consumers, producers, and market participants as a whole.
- Analyze the effects of an excise tax on a specific good on the welfare of consumers, producers, and market participants as a whole.
- Detail how regulation of the U.S. airline industry affected fares, airline company profits, and service quality.
- Explain how the entry restrictions imposed by most major U.S. cities on taxis affects fares and the profits earned by licensed taxi owners.
- Understand the effects of international trade on consumer and producer surplus and why a net gain results to a country from either imports or exports.
- Explore how government-specified maximum quantities, or quotas, on sugar imports affect consumers, domestic producers, and the net welfare of the United States as well as other countries that produce sugar.

This chapter builds on the theory established in the previous chapter to show how the competitive model can be used to analyze particular industries and the effects on them of government intervention. The examples we will explore include gasoline taxes, airline regulation, taxicab licensing, and import quotas. The broad range of applications should illustrate the usefulness of the perfectly competitive model. The applications themselves will also indicate that while government intervention may be justified on the grounds of helping people, the effects of such intervention may end up being precisely counter to the objectives of the proponents of the intervention.

10.1   THE EVALUATION OF GAINS AND LOSSES

CONSUMER SURPLUS
a measure of the net gain to a consumer or group of consumers from purchasing a good arising from cost being below the maximum that consumers are willing to pay

PRODUCER SURPLUS
gains to producers from the sale of output to consumers, arising from price exceeding the minimum necessary to compensate the seller

Changes in market conditions or government policies always result in either gains or losses for participants in the market. For example, rent controls (that have been used in many cities) often benefit at least some tenants at the expense of landlords. But how large is the benefit to tenants and how large is the cost to landlords? In total, do the benefits outweigh the losses, or is the reverse true? To answer questions like these, we need a way to measure the gains and losses felt by market participants. In this section we will explain how we can use the concepts of consumer surplus and producer surplus to measure such gains and losses.

We have already explained the concept of consumer surplus. Recall that **consumer surplus** is a measure of the net gain to a consumer (or group of consumers) from purchasing a good. (You may wish to review how it is shown by areas under the demand curve; see Section 4.5.) The concept of producer surplus is an analogous measure of the net gain to those involved in producing and selling a good. Because this is a new concept, we will begin by explaining how it is related to the competitive supply curve.

Producer Surplus

Producers of goods often secure gains, called **producer surplus**, from the sale of output to consumers. The gain results because the price often exceeds the minimum amount that would be necessary to compensate the seller. To see how we can show the producer surplus in a competitive market, consider the long-run supply of sugar curve S in Figure 10.1. Assume that the sugar industry is at point E on the supply curve, output is Q, and sugar is being

FIGURE 10.1

Producer Surplus
Producer surplus is a measure of the net gain to producers from operating in a given market, and is shown as the area between the price line and the supply curve. It can be thought of as the sum of rectangles like A_2, B_2, and C_2, each of which is the net gain associated with the sale of a particular unit.

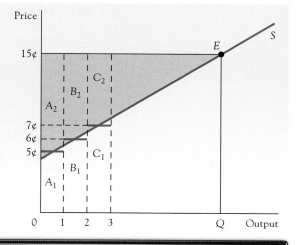

sold at a price of 15 cents per pound. What we will show is that the shaded triangular area is a measure of the net gain to sugar suppliers.

To explain this point, we begin by assuming that the industry takes a very simple form. Assume that each firm consists of only one person (the owner-manager-worker) who can produce only one unit of output. (We will drop this assumption later.) Now, consider the derivation of the supply curve, starting with an output of zero. At a price lower than 5 cents, no firm produces sugar—all potential firms can do better employing their resources elsewhere. At a price of 5 cents, firm A enters the market and produces one unit. At that price, firm A is just barely induced into this market, and so it makes no net gain from operating in this industry. If the price is 6 cents, however, firm B enters the market and produces one unit (so total output is two units). Firm B could have earned 6 cents elsewhere and so secures no net gain if the market price remains at 6 cents. Other firms enter the market at higher prices; in this way we trace out the industry supply curve as a steplike relationship.

Now consider the situation when the market price is 15 cents. At that price, firms A, B, C, and several more are selling one unit each at a price of 15 cents. How much does each firm benefit from selling in this market? Firm A would have been willing to sell one unit for a minimum of 5 cents; this is shown as rectangular area A_1. However, firm A sells the unit for 15 cents, shown as the rectangular area A_1 plus A_2, so it receives a net benefit of 10 cents—shown as area A_2. Area A_2 is the producer surplus realized by firm A. By similar reasoning, firm B receives a net benefit, or producer surplus, of area B_2 (9 cents) because its revenues are 15 cents and it would have been willing to sell for 6 cents. The net gain for each firm is therefore shown as a rectangular area like A_2, B_2, C_2, and so on. The sum of all these areas for the firms operating in the market is the total producer surplus realized by all the firms. Of course, if we assume more realistically that one unit of output is small relative to total output Q, so the rectangles become much narrower, then the supply curve approaches the smooth curve S. In that case, the total producer surplus is shown as the shaded area between the supply curve and the price line.

When we drop the assumption of one-person firms and consider the general case of a competitive industry, the triangular area shown continues to represent the total producer surplus. Now, however, we have to reconsider exactly who gets this surplus. Recall that economic profits are zero at every point on a long-run supply curve; producer surplus is not the same as economic profit. Indeed, owners of the firms may not receive any producer surplus at all. Producer surplus is the total net gain that goes to *anyone* involved in producing the good, and that includes the suppliers of inputs to the industry. To see what this implies, suppose that the sugar industry has an upward-sloping supply curve of labor, but a horizontal supply curve of every other input used to produce sugar. In this case, the sugar industry supply curve will be upward-sloping, as in Figure 10.1, because the wage rate will rise as the industry expands and employs more workers. What is producer surplus here? It is the net gain to the workers who would have been willing to work at the lower wage rates (when the industry output was smaller), but who are now receiving wage rates higher than the minimum necessary to induce them to work in the sugar industry. This total net gain will be shown by the shaded triangular area above the product supply curve for this market. No other input owners receive any producer surplus in this situation; only the workers.

Thus, the area between the product supply curve and the price line identifies the total producer surplus that accrues to *someone* engaged in the production of the good. Even though this area identifies the total net gain to "producers," we cannot tell from the supply curve alone exactly who receives this benefit. In general, producer surplus will accrue to some of the owners of inputs that have upward-sloping supply curves to the industry. Owners of inputs with horizontal supply curves to the industry receive no producer surplus. (Note that this conclusion implies there is no aggregate producer surplus for a constant-cost competitive industry when it is in long-run equilibrium.)

APPLICATION 10.1   THE ALLOCATION OF PRODUCER SURPLUS IN TRUCKING

From 1935 to 1975, federal regulation of interstate trucking included rate setting and strict controls on new entry into the industry. The regulation raised rates above competitive levels and generated producer surplus for regulated firms.

Based on an examination of workers' wages following the deregulation of interstate trucking in the late 1970s, it appears that unionized workers, represented by the powerful Teamsters Union, had been capturing at least two-thirds of the producer surplus created by the regula-tion.[1] According to the examination, deregulation re-sulted in annual losses of around $1.7 billion for the Teamsters ($6,400 in 2000 dollars per Teamsters driver). The remaining one-third of the producer surplus gener-ated by federal regulation of interstate trucking appears to have accrued to the owners of interstate trucking firms.

[1]Nancy L. Rose, "Labor Rent Sharing and Regulation: Evidence from the Trucking Industry," *Journal of Political Economy*, 95 No. 6 (Decem-ber 1987), pp. 1146–1178.

Consumer Surplus, Producer Surplus, and Efficient Output

In general, consumers and producers benefit from participation in a competitive market, and the size of that benefit is measured by their consumer surplus and producer surplus as seen in Figure 10.2a. The competitive equilibrium is at an output of Q and a price of $5. The net gain to consumers is shown as the shaded triangular area A between their demand curve and the price line. Similarly, the net gain to producers is shown as the shaded triangular area B above the supply curve up to the price line. The total net gain to those who participate in this market is therefore the sum of consumer surplus and producer surplus—area A plus area B. The sum of producer and consumer surplus is called the **total surplus**.

TOTAL SURPLUS
the sum of producer and consumer surplus

The total surplus, area A plus B in Figure 10.2a, is a measure of the aggregate net gain that is realized by participants in this market. Because it is the sum of the way the market af-fects the well-being of everyone participating in it, total surplus is often used as a measure of how well the market functions relative to its potential. The amount of total surplus will often be changed by government policies or by changes in market structure (e.g., if the mar-ket becomes monopolized). The change in total surplus in such cases is often taken as a measure of the gain or loss in well-being to market participants.

There is an alternative way to see that the sum of areas A and B in Figure 10.2a is equal to total surplus. This is illustrated in Figure 10.2b. The equilibrium quantity is once again Q. To identify the total surplus, we consider the net gain associated with each unit of output from zero to Q. It is important to recall that the height of the demand curve can be inter-preted as showing the marginal benefit of the good and the height of the supply curve can be interpreted as showing the marginal cost. Now consider the production of one unit. For the moment, we will think of the demand and supply curves as discrete, steplike relationships. The first unit received by consumers has a marginal benefit of $13, the sum of rectangular areas A_1 and A_2. Producers must be compensated by a minimum of $2; the marginal cost of the first unit is $2, shown as area A_1. The marginal benefit of the first unit is $11 greater than its marginal cost; there is a net gain associated with the first unit of $11, shown as area A_2, the difference between the marginal benefit of that unit and its marginal cost. The net gain is, of course, the total surplus associated with the first unit of output. Note, however, that this procedure does not identify who receives this surplus—producers or consumers.

Similarly, we see that there is a net gain from the second unit of output of area B_2, equal to the excess of marginal benefit over marginal cost for that unit. The sum of areas A_2 and

FIGURE 10.2

Competition Maximizes Total Surplus

(a) Consumer surplus equals area *A* and producer surplus equals area *B*; total surplus is the sum of consumer and producer surplus. (b) Total surplus can be thought of as the sum of the net gains (excess of marginal benefit over marginal cost) associated with the production of each unit of output from zero to *Q*.

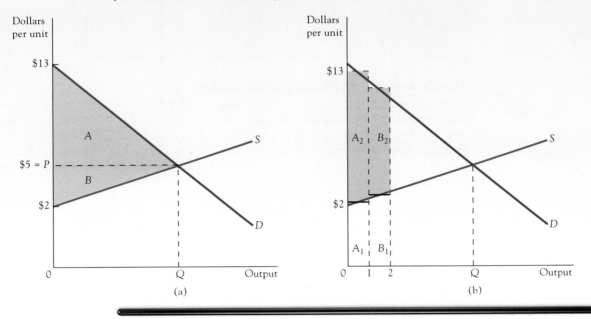

(a)   (b)

B_2 is the total surplus when two units are produced. By identifying the rectangular areas of net gain of each unit from zero to the quantity actually produced and summing the net gains over all units, we can determine the total surplus for quantity *Q*. When we let units of output become small relative to total output, the rectangles become narrower, and the demand and supply curves become the smooth curves shown as *S* and *D*. Then the sum of the net gains, the total surplus, will be shown as the shaded area in Figure 10.2b. Note that the total surplus arrived at by this reasoning is the same as that shown as the sum of consumer and producer surplus in Figure 10.2a.

We have explained two different ways of identifying the total surplus associated with the functioning of a market. The first way, illustrated in Figure 10.2a, involves determining the surpluses realized by producers and consumers separately and then adding them together. This approach has the advantage of showing how the overall net gain is distributed between consumers and producers (but recall it doesn't identify which producers benefit). The second way, illustrated in Figure 10.2b, involves determining the total surplus associated with each unit of output and summing over all units of output. It has the advantage of often being an easier procedure to use (as we will see later), but the disadvantage of not identifying the distribution of the net gain between producers and consumers.

Figure 10.2b shows why the equilibrium output of a competitive industry is also the efficient level of output. **Efficiency in output** requires that output be expanded to the point where the marginal benefit equals marginal cost. To say that the output level is efficient, moreover, is the same thing as saying that the net gain, or total surplus, from producing the good is as large as possible. Let's check to see if that is the case when output is *Q* in Figure

EFFICIENCY IN OUTPUT
the condition in which output is expanded to the point where marginal benefit equals marginal cost

10.2b. If output is expanded beyond Q, then the marginal benefit of additional units will be less than their marginal cost, so the net gain of these units is negative—that is, there is a net loss in total surplus associated with production beyond Q. Thus, the total surplus will be smaller than at output Q; it will be the shaded area minus the net loss on units in excess of Q. Any expansion of output beyond Q will therefore reduce the total surplus. Similarly, if output is less than Q, the total surplus will also be smaller than the shaded area. For example, if output is 2, the total surplus is the area between the demand and supply curves up to an output of 2 (roughly, the sum of rectangular areas A_2 and B_2), which is clearly smaller than the shaded area. Thus, an output of Q will maximize the total surplus, or net gain, of participants in the market. A competitive market achieves this result.

The Deadweight Loss of a Price Ceiling

To illustrate the use of these measures of surplus, we will consider again a price ceiling applied to rental housing, a policy we first examined in Section 2.4. In Figure 10.3a, the initial equilibrium involves a monthly price of $800 and a quantity of Q. The government then mandates a maximum price of $600. At that price, suppliers reduce output to Q_1, but consumers would like to purchase an amount of Q_2; the difference is the excess demand, or shortage, caused by the price ceiling.

How does the price ceiling affect the total surplus realized in this market? As we explained, there are different ways of evaluating total surplus and changes in it. The easiest

FIGURE 10.3

A Price Ceiling Reduces Total Surplus

(a) The price ceiling of P_C results in output of Q_1; there is a deadweight loss associated with producing less than the competitive output that is shown as area *BEC*. (b) The price ceiling results in a gain in consumer surplus shown by area *X* minus area *Y*, and a loss in producer surplus shown by area *X* plus area *Z*. Total surplus falls by the sum of the changes in consumer and producer surplus, area *Y* plus area *Z*.

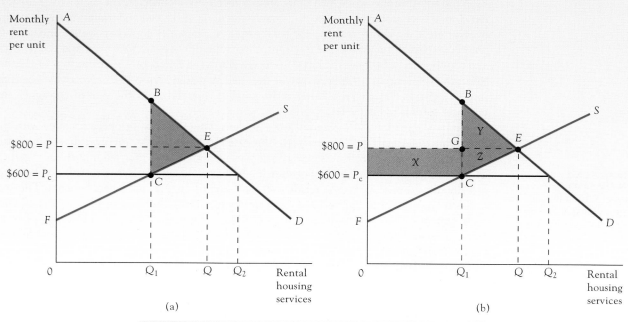

(a)

(b)

way, based on the approach of Figure 10.2b, is to evaluate total surplus without regard to its distribution between producers and consumers. Thus, in Figure 10.3a, total surplus before the price ceiling was area AEF, but after the price ceiling, when only Q_1 units are actually produced, total surplus is shown as area $ABCF$, the sum of the net gains on each unit from zero to Q_1.[2] Total surplus is therefore smaller under the price ceiling; the decrease in the size of total surplus is the area BEC. The loss in total surplus, area BEC, is the **deadweight loss** (also know as the welfare cost) of the price ceiling. As mentioned in Chapter 5, the deadweight loss is a measure of the aggregate loss in well-being of participants in the market. In this case, it is a measure of the loss due to production of an inefficient quantity of rental housing services.

Instead of comparing the total surplus with and without the price ceiling (for outputs Q and Q_1), we can arrive at the same conclusion by considering the change in total surplus caused by the reduction in output from Q to Q_1. Consider the units not produced (because of the price ceiling) between Q and Q_1. The marginal benefit of each of these units is shown by the height of the demand curve between Q and Q_1; similarly, the marginal cost is shown by the height of the supply curve. As you can see, each unit not produced has a marginal benefit greater than its marginal cost, so there is a net loss from not producing these units. The net loss is the difference between marginal benefit and marginal cost, and if these net losses are summed we arrive at area BEC as the aggregate net loss, or deadweight loss, of the price ceiling. (It may help if you think of the narrow rectangles, like area B_2 in Figure 10.2b, that make up the area BEC in Figure 10.3a.)

An alternative way to proceed, based on the approach used in Figure 10.2a, considers the effect on consumers and producers separately. This is illustrated in Figure 10.3b. Before the price ceiling, total consumer surplus was area AEP. After the price ceiling, when consumers are purchasing Q_1 units at a price of P_C, total consumer surplus is area $ABCP_C$, which is the sum of the net gain (marginal benefit less price) on each of the Q_1 units. Compared with the situation without the price ceiling, consumers have gained area X (rectangular area $PGCP_C$) and lost area Y (triangular area BEG). As drawn, area X is larger than area Y, so total consumer surplus has increased (by $X - Y$). Note that area X is the gain that consumers obtain from being able to purchase the Q_1 units at a lower price; the height of the rectangle is the reduction in price. But that is not the only way consumers are affected; they also end up consuming a lower quantity than before the price ceiling. Area Y is the consumer surplus they previously received on consumption from Q_1 to Q; they lose this net gain due to reduced production under the price ceiling. The net impact on consumer welfare depends on the size of these two separate effects.[3]

The effect on producers is easier to understand. Producer surplus before the price ceiling was area PEF. After the price ceiling, producer surplus is P_CCF. Thus, producer surplus falls by the sum of areas X and Z (the area of $PECP_C$). Producer surplus is unequivocally reduced by the price ceiling.

Because total surplus is the sum of consumer and producer surplus, we can determine the change in total surplus by summing the changes in consumer and producer surplus. In this case, the change in consumer surplus is $X - Y$, and the change in producer surplus is $-X - Z$ (where a minus sign indicates a loss in surplus). Thus, the sum of the changes in consumer

DEADWEIGHT LOSS
also called welfare cost, a measure of the aggregate loss in well-being of participants in a market resulting from an inefficient output level

---

[2]This does assume that the smaller quantity is rationed among consumers in such a way that the consumers who place the highest value on the rental housing actually get it. This may not be the case in the absence of a higher (i.e., black market) price to ration the rental housing among consumers. Then the total surplus under the price ceiling will be smaller than area $ABCF$.

[3]Whether area X is larger than area Y depends on the height of the price ceiling and the elasticities of the demand and supply curves. As these curves are drawn in Figure 10.3b, area X is larger, but it is possible for area Y to be larger (for example, imagine a price ceiling set below the level $F0$).

and producer surplus is $-Y - Z$. Total surplus falls by the sum of areas Y and Z, so that triangular area BEC identifies the loss in total surplus, or the deadweight loss, due to the price ceiling. Note that this is the same area identified in Figure 10.3a; these strategies are just different approaches to measuring the same thing.

One advantage to evaluating consumer and producer surplus changes separately is that it makes clear who gains and who loses. In this case, consumers gain area $X - Y$ and producers lose area $X + Z$; the gain to consumers is less than the loss to producers by area $Y + Z$—that is, the aggregate loss in total surplus. From this we see that finding a deadweight loss is not the same as saying that everyone is worse off. A deadweight loss measures the overall efficiency loss when the effects on everyone are summed, but the distribution of gains and losses may also be important to consider. If you view the well-being of consumers as sufficiently more important than the well-being of producers, you might favor the price ceiling in this case despite the fact that it produces a deadweight loss. (On the other hand, it is unlikely that all consumers benefit even here; the gain in consumer surplus is an aggregation over all consumers, some of whom may be made worse off by the rent control because they cannot find housing at the legal price.)

10.2   EXCISE TAXATION

The competitive model and the concept of efficiency introduced in the preceding section can be employed to analyze the effects of government policies on a wide variety of industries. Among the policies are the excise taxes levied on specific goods such as gasoline, cigarettes, and alcohol. For example, the 1993 Budget Reconciliation Bill increased the federal excise tax on gasoline by 4.3 cents per gallon. The increase raised $23 billion in government revenue from 1993 to 1998. State and local governments also use excise taxes. Such excise taxes applied to competitively produced products are easily analyzed using the industry supply and demand curves. It is instructive, however, to develop the analysis step by step, showing how the tax affects individual firms as well as the market, and examining how the short-run effects differ from those of the long run.

Let us analyze the federal government's excise tax on gasoline. In Figure 10.4, we assume that the industry is initially in long-run competitive equilibrium. Most government studies in fact indicate that the industry is close to perfectly competitive. Figure 10.4a shows a typical firm, Mobil, making zero economic profit at the market-determined price of $1.25 per gallon of gasoline. Price equals short-run and long-run marginal cost at Mobil's initial output of q_1. (We have not drawn in the long-run marginal cost curve or the short-run average cost curve. Throughout the analysis, we use only the relationships essential to the important points to avoid cluttering the diagrams.) Figure 10.4b identifies the original equilibrium price and output for the industry at $1.25 and Q_1, which is determined by the intersection of the long-run supply curve LS and the demand curve D at point A. The short-run supply curve SS passes through point A because it is the sum of the firms' SMC curves. Recall that SS is more inelastic than the long-run supply curve because expanding (or reducing) output is more costly in the short run (when some inputs are fixed) than in the long run (when all inputs are variable).

Now suppose that the government unexpectedly taxes each firm in the industry 20 cents per gallon of gasoline sold. Such a tax is a per-unit excise tax.[4] Let us first consider the immediate impact of the tax on the individual firm, Mobil. Before the tax, long-run average

---

[4]Another common form of excise tax is an *ad valorem* excise tax. An ad valorem tax is levied as a certain percentage of the market price. In contrast, a per-unit tax does not depend on the market price. The important economic effects of the two types of excise taxes are the same, however, and the per-unit tax is slightly easier to analyze.

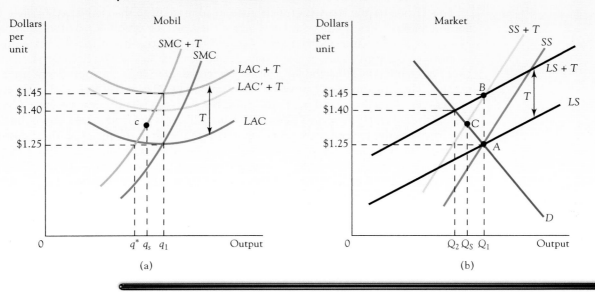

FIGURE 10.4

Effects of a Per-Unit Excise Tax
(a) The firm's cost curves shift upward by the amount of the tax, and, in the short run, the firm reduces output. (b) The industry supply curves also shift upward by the amount of the tax, and industry output declines. Output decreases by more in the long run so the price rises above its short-run level.

cost at output q_1 is \$1.25, but the tax increases Mobil's average cost of providing that output to \$1.45 per gallon. In fact, at every possible output, average cost is 20 cents higher than before. Note that the tax does not affect the cost of the resources required to produce the product but simply adds 20 cents per gallon to their cost. In Figure 10.4a, the 20 cent tax is shown as a parallel upward shift in the LAC curve to $LAC + T$, where T equals the 20 cent per-unit tax. All other per-unit cost curves, including the marginal cost curve, shift vertically upward also, because all per-unit production costs are increased by the amount of the tax.

If we temporarily assume that the gasoline price is unaffected, two important effects of the tax on the individual firm can be identified. First, Mobil will operate at an economic loss at q_1 because average cost (\$1.45) exceeds price (\$1.25). Second, at q_1, marginal cost, which has increased to \$1.45 at that output, exceeds the price. Mobil's immediate response will be to cut its loss by reducing output along its new short-run marginal cost curve $SMC + T$ to q^*, where marginal cost equals (the assumed unchanged) price. Mobil still incurs a loss at q^*, but the loss is smaller than if it keeps output at q_1.

Because the tax applies to all firms in the industry, they all incur a loss and have an incentive to cut output; this will affect the market price. Earlier, we assumed for the moment that the price was unchanged to trace out the individual firm's immediate response to the tax. Now let's see what happens to price when all firms in an industry reduce output. In Figure 10.4b, the initial short-run industry supply curve SS is the sum of the individual firms' SMC curves. Because the tax shifts the firms' marginal cost curves vertically upward by 20 cents, the SS curve also shifts vertically upward by 20 cents to $SS + T$ (distance BA equals 20 cents); $SS + T$ is the sum of the firms' $SMC + T$ curves. In other words, for the industry to supply any given rate of output, the price must be 20 cents higher than before because the tax has added 20 cents to unit costs. Of course, the industry will not continue to supply Q_1 gallons. In the short run, as firms cut output along their $SMC + T$ curves, industry output falls along the $SS + T$ curve. The short-run equilibrium occurs at point C, where $SS + T$ intersects D. Industry output is lower than the pre-tax equilibrium (Q_S versus Q_1) and price is higher (CQ_S versus AQ_1). In Figure 10.4a, Mobil is at point c on its $SMC + T$ curve and is still incurring a short-run loss.

This completes the analysis of the short-run adjustment to the excise tax. Because firms are still taking losses, however, we have not yet reached a position of long-run equilibrium. The losses provide an incentive for firms to exit the industry altogether, allowing resources to move to other industries where normal profits can be made. We can identify the new long-run equilibrium from the long-run supply curve. Like the short-run supply curve, the tax shifts the long-run supply curve vertically upward by 20 cents because it adds 20 cents to all per-unit costs, short- and long-run. Thus, the long-run supply curve becomes $LS + T$, passing through point B where distance BA equals 20 cents in Figure 10.4b. In the short run, the tax causes the industry to restrict output along $SS + T$; in the long run, the industry restricts production along $LS + T$. The final long-run equilibrium occurs at a price of $1.40 and an output of Q_2, where $LS + T$ intersects the unchanged demand curve. In the long run, the decrease in industry output is greater than in the short run (because firms have time to exit the industry and/or adjust their scales of plant), and consequently the price to consumers is higher.

As drawn in Figure 10.4b, the price to consumers has risen by only 15 cents (from $1.25 to $1.40) even though the per-unit tax is 20 cents. Thus, firms receive only $1.20 per unit ($1.40 minus 20 cents per unit) after paying the tax, less than they received before the tax was levied. Does this mean that firms are operating at a loss so that Q_2 is not really a long-run zero-profit equilibrium? No. We have assumed that the industry is an increasing-cost industry (with an upward-sloping long-run supply curve), which implies that some input prices fall as fewer of these resources are used. As a result, firms' cost curves shift downward as the industry contracts along its long-run supply curve. Figure 10.4a shows the situation from Mobil's viewpoint. As input prices fall, the $LAC + T$ curve shifts downward to $LAC' + T$, so Mobil makes zero economic profit at the $1.40 price.[5]

This step-by-step analysis shows how we can start with a firm's cost curves and determine the effects of a tax on an industry's supply and demand curves. It is possible, however, to analyze the effects by using just the demand and supply curves at the industry level. For example, if we are interested in only the industry-level effects in the long run, all we need to do is examine the consequences of the shift in the long-run supply curve from LS to $LS + T$ in Figure 10.4b. This immediately identifies the outcome: a lower output and higher price to consumers. However, the more systematic approach we have used helps reinforce the nature of the long-run adjustment process and emphasizes how the process affects individual firms. This is useful since it is not always obvious how an industry's supply curves will be affected; in many cases, it is important to develop the analysis by first examining how individual firms are affected.

Let's return to the economic effects of an excise tax and review two implications of the analysis. First, even though the tax is levied on and collected from firms, consumers bear a cost as a result of the higher price they pay for gasoline at the pump. In our specific example, the price to consumers rises by 15 cents in response to the 20-cent tax. As we will explain in

---

[5]Whether firms produce more or less than before the tax depends on how their LAC curves shift downward. If with lower input prices the minimum point on $LAC' + T$ occurs at the same output as before the tax (q_1), as drawn in the graph, firm output is the same as before the tax. The reduction in industry output then results from some firms exiting the industry. The minimum point on $LAC' + T$, however, can occur at a higher or lower output, depending on which input prices fall and the nature of a firm's production function.

the following subsection, the exact amount by which the price to consumers rises depends on the relative elasticities of the demand and (long-run) supply curves.

Second, after the long-run adjustment to the tax, firms once again make zero economic profits and do not suffer continuing losses. (In the short run they do lose money, but the losses are temporary.) After paying the tax, however, the firms net only $1.20 per gallon, less than they received before the tax was levied, so someone must suffer a continuing loss on the supply side of the market. But who? We can't say specifically, but we know that it will be the owners of inputs that are in less than perfectly elastic supply to the industry, because the owners of these inputs will receive lower prices for the services they provide. That is, as firms cut production and demand fewer inputs in response to the tax, prices for inputs with upward-sloping supply curves will fall. Consequently, in the increasing-cost case, the long-run burden of the tax is borne by consumers and certain input owners.

Who Bears the Burden of the Tax?

Our analysis shows that excise taxes reduce the output of the taxed good and increase its cost to consumers, but what determines *how much* output falls and *how much* the price to consumers rises? Asking how much the price to consumers rises is, of course, equivalent to asking how much of the tax burden is borne by consumers and how much by input owners. In our example we found that, in the long run, the price to consumers rose by 15 cents and the price to producers fell by 5 cents (to $1.20). In such a case economists would say that consumers bear 75 percent of the tax burden ($0.15 out of each $0.20 collected) and producers (more precisely, owners of inputs that are in less than perfectly elastic supply) bear the other 25 percent.

As we will see next, the quantitative effects on price and output depend on the elasticities of demand and supply, which we can show by using the industry demand and supply curves. Let's concentrate on the long-run effects. In Figure 10.5a, we examine how the *elas-*

FIGURE 10.5

How Elasticities Affect the Tax Burden
(a) With the more elastic supply curve, *LS*, the price increase to consumers is greater. With a perfectly elastic supply curve, such as *LS*, the price rises by the amount of the tax.
(b) With the more elastic demand curve, *D*, the price increase to consumers is smaller.

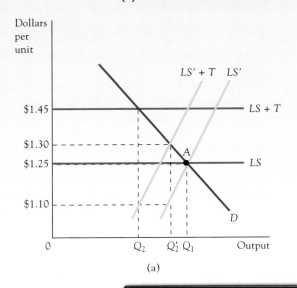

(a)

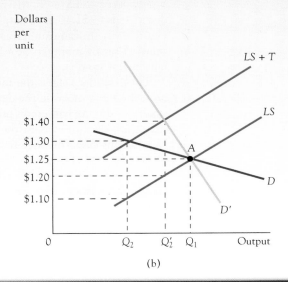

(b)

ticity of supply affects the outcome. Suppose that the industry is a constant-cost industry and has the horizontal long-run supply curve shown as *LS*. An excise tax shifts the supply curve vertically upward to *LS* + *T*. With the demand curve *D*, the tax reduces output to Q_2 and increases price to $1.45. In contrast to our earlier example, the price rises by the full amount of the per-unit tax, and firms continue to net $1.25 after remitting the tax to the government. Why are the effects of the tax different for a constant-cost industry? Recall that in the constant-cost case, when output is reduced, per-unit production costs do not decline, so output will continue to fall until the price has risen by the amount of the tax; only after this adjustment takes place will a new zero-profit equilibrium be achieved.

To illustrate the influence that different supply elasticities have on the distribution of the burden of the tax between buyers and sellers, consider Figure 10.5a once again and suppose that at the initial equilibrium point A the supply curve is less elastic, like supply curve *LS*′.[6] A tax of 20 cents per unit shifts *LS*′ vertically upward to *LS*′ + *T*. (Note that the vertical difference between each set of supply curves is the same; we are using the same tax per unit but varying the supply elasticity to isolate the effect of different supply elasticities on price.) In this case, equilibrium output declines to Q_2', the price to consumers rises to $1.30, and the net-of-tax price received by firms falls to $1.10. The consumer price does not rise by the full amount of the tax because as output falls, per-unit production costs decline and firms can make zero economic profits at a net-of-tax price lower than the initial $1.25 price. This also means that output does not have to fall as much to restore long-run equilibrium as in the constant-cost case.

These results suggest the following generalization: For a given demand curve and tax per unit, the more inelastic the supply curve, the smaller is the tax burden on consumers (price rises by less), the larger is the tax burden on producers (meaning the relevant input suppliers), and the smaller is the reduction in output. The only significant exception is in the unlikely case of a vertical demand curve. If the demand curve is vertical, the price to consumers would rise by the amount of the tax, regardless of the elasticity of the supply curve.

Now let's see how the *elasticity of demand* affects the outcome. In this case, we work with a given supply curve and tax per unit and then vary the demand elasticity. Figure 10.5b illustrates this analysis. Initially, we have the supply curve *LS* and demand curve *D*, so the before-tax equilibrium price and quantity are $1.25 and Q_1, respectively. The tax shifts the supply curve to *LS* + *T*, the price to consumers rises to $1.30, the net-of-tax price to producers falls to $1.10, and output declines to Q_2. Alternatively, suppose that demand is less elastic at the initial equilibrium point A, as shown by the *D*′ curve. Then the price to consumers rises by more (to $1.40), the price to producers falls by less (to $1.20), and output falls by less (to Q_2').

These results suggest the following generalization: For a given supply curve and tax per unit, the more inelastic the demand curve, the greater is the tax burden on consumers, the smaller is the tax burden on producers, and the smaller is the reduction in output. The only significant exception is in the case of a perfectly elastic supply curve—the constant-cost case. In this case, the price to consumers rises by the amount of the tax per unit, regardless of the elasticity of the demand curve.

In summary, the proportion of any excise tax borne by consumers depends on the relative sizes of the elasticities of demand and supply. These elasticities indicate how well consumers and producers can "substitute away" from a tax. The higher the elasticity, the greater the availability of substitutes in consumption or production, and the greater the ability to substitute away from the tax and impose the burden of the tax on the other party.

[6]It is important not to confuse slope and elasticity, but when we compare the elasticities of two curves at the same price-quantity combination, as we are doing here at point A, the steeper curve is the less elastic curve.

APPLICATION 10.2 WHY CIGARETTE COMPANY PROFITS DID NOT GET SMOKED BY A RECENT PUNITIVE-DAMAGES AWARD

In July 2000, a Florida jury levied a $145 billion punitive-damages award against tobacco manufacturers—the largest damage award in U.S. history—in a national class-action lawsuit brought on behalf of all addicted smokers injured by cigarettes.[7] Tobacco company stocks, however, hardly budged after news of the damage award broke.

Some analysts think that tobacco company shares did not fall in the wake of the bad news because investors had already anticipated the blockbuster award and believed that it would eventually be overturned on appeal. Other analysts attribute the absence of a negative stock effect to the fact that tobacco companies will not be the ones bearing the cost of the jury's punitive-damages award. Since the demand for cigarettes is much less elastic than the supply, cigarette manufacturers can more easily substitute away from the burden imposed by the jury's award than can consumers (the elasticity of demand for cigarettes is estimated to be roughly 0.3 while supply is close to perfectly elastic). Because smokers are so much less able than tobacco manufacturers to run away from the punitive-damages "tax" levied by the Florida jury, it is they, and not the tobacco companies, who will end up bearing the burden of the tax.

[7]This application is based on "Tobacco Companies Rail Against Verdict, Plan to Appeal $144.87 Billion Award," *Wall Street Journal* (July 17, 2000), pp. A3 and A6; "Yes, $145 Billion Deals Tobacco a High Blow, But Not a Killing One," *Wall Street Journal* (July 17, 2000), pp. A1 and A8; and Daniel A. Sumner and Michael K. Wohlgeront, "Effects of an Increase in the Federal Excise Tax on Cigarettes," *American Journal of Agricultural Economics*, Vol. 67 (May 1985), pp. 235–242.

The Deadweight Loss of Excise Taxation

As explained in Section 10.1, any deviation in output from the competitive level is inefficient and results in a deadweight loss. Because an excise tax results in an output that is lower than in the unfettered competitive market, it produces a deadweight loss. Let's consider why in more detail. Originally, price is P and output is Q_1 in Figure 10.6. An excise tax of T per unit causes the long-run supply curve to shift to $LS + T$, and the result is a reduction in quantity to Q_2 and an increase in price to P_1.

The easiest way to see that there is a deadweight loss is to consider the marginal benefit and cost associated with the change in output from Q_1 to Q_2. When output declines, each unit no longer produced has a marginal benefit that varies from P to P_1 to consumers. However, the cost saving associated with not producing each of these units is lower, ranging from P to P_2. Thus, there is a net loss associated with each of the units that is not produced (the marginal benefit sacrificed is greater than the marginal cost saved), and the sum of these net losses is shown as the triangular area BEC. Area BEC is the deadweight loss, and results from the excise tax because output is restricted to a level where the product's marginal benefit (P_1) exceeds the marginal cost of production (P_2); consumers would benefit from a higher output but the tax inhibits production of additional units beyond Q_2.

In explaining the deadweight loss, note that we continue to interpret the original supply curve as showing the marginal cost of production. From the firms' point of view, marginal cost is given by $LS + T$, but the tax is not a real cost to society. The tax simply transfers funds from market participants to the government; it does not reflect a use of scarce resources in production. Consider that if output was reduced from Q_1 to Q_2 before the tax, there would have been a cost saving (shown by the LS curve) in the form of less labor, capital, raw materials, and so on. When a tax leads to the same output reduction, the cost saving in terms of the value of resources no longer employed in the market is identical. The tax is

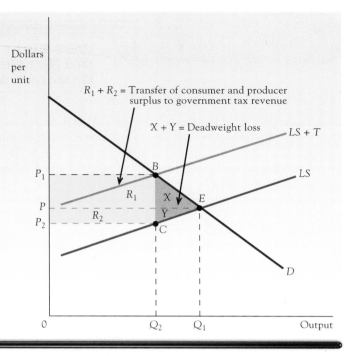

FIGURE 10.6

The Deadweight Loss of an Excise Tax
The excise tax reduces consumer surplus by area R_1 plus area X and producer surplus by area R_2 plus area Y. Part of the loss is transferred to the government as tax revenue, shown as R_1 plus R_2. The excess of the loss over the gain to the government is the decrease in total surplus or the deadweight loss, the triangular area X plus Y.

not a real cost to society, but it does influence firms' and consumers' decisions and that is why it produces a deadweight loss.

The deadweight loss of the tax can also be derived by relying on the concepts of consumer and producer surplus. The tax increases the price to consumers from P to P_1, thus decreasing consumer surplus by area P_1BEP. In addition, the tax reduces the net price received by producers from P to P_2, decreasing producer surplus by area $PECP_2$. Combining these two, we see that the reduction in consumer plus producer surplus equals area P_1BECP_2. However, of this loss, area P_1BCP_2 is received as tax revenue by the government. The tax revenue is also shown as the sum of rectangular areas R_1 and R_2, where R_1 is the direct burden of the tax on consumers and R_2 is the direct burden on producers.

Part of the loss in consumer plus producer surplus is a gain to the government in the form of tax revenue. However, the tax revenue is smaller than the loss in consumer plus producer surplus by the area BEC. Area BEC is the decrease in the total surplus (in this case, consumer plus producer plus government surplus) or the deadweight loss of the excise tax. Consumers and producers bear a burden (the loss in consumer plus producer surplus) that is greater than the revenue collected by the tax. That is why the deadweight loss is sometimes referred to as an **excess burden** when it is produced by a tax.

The excise tax produces a direct burden in the form of tax revenue collected, and also an additional, less obvious burden in the form of the deadweight loss (or excess burden). To get an intuitive understanding of the deadweight loss as something different from the burden of paying taxes, consider an excise tax that is so large that output falls to zero. In that case, there is no tax revenue collected. Nonetheless, there is a deadweight loss from the excise tax. What is the deadweight loss in this case? It is the total surplus that would have been generated by the market absent the tax.

Our analysis should not be taken to imply that excise taxes should be avoided. All taxes produce deadweight losses; they can't feasibly be avoided. However, the deadweight loss is still important because it tells us that if the public is to benefit from government expendi-

EXCESS BURDEN
another name for the deadweight loss produced by a tax

tures, more than a dollar in benefit has to be produced per dollar of government expenditure. For example, suppose that the gasoline excise tax revenue is $100 billion and the deadweight loss of the tax is $40 billion. Only if the spending of the $100 billion in tax revenue produces a benefit valued by the public at more than $140 billion does the spending compensate the public for all the costs of the excise tax.

APPLICATION 10.3

THE LONG AND THE SHORT (RUN) OF THE DEADWEIGHT LOSS OF RENT CONTROL

By reducing output below the competitive equilibrium, rent control results in a deadweight loss. Employing the competitive model to compare the short- and long-run effects of rent control allows us to see how the deadweight loss associated with a government-imposed price ceiling depends on the supply elasticity.

Figure 10.7 contrasts the short- and long-run effects of rent control. In the absence of a rent ceiling, the competitive (short- and long-run) equilibrium is a rent of P and quantity of Q. The short-run supply curve, SS, is drawn as being relatively price inelastic. This is so because if a city unexpectedly imposes rent control today, the quantity of rental units tomorrow will be virtually unaffected by the price change. It takes time for reduced construction and maintenance to have their full effects on durable goods like dwelling units. The adverse effects on the supply side thus are relatively small in the short

run. In response to a rent ceiling of P_c, for example, output decreases only a little bit in the short run to Q_1 and the resulting deadweight loss is given by triangular area BEC. Area BEC is the difference between the marginal benefit (the height of the demand curve) and marginal cost (the height of the short-run supply curve) summed over each unit of output between Q_1 and the competitive equilibrium of Q.

The long-run output adjustment to the rent ceiling is more substantial and begins as new construction falls and existing units are allowed to deteriorate. In the graph this is depicted by the long-run supply curve, LS, being more price elastic than the short-run supply curve, SS. In response to the rent ceiling, P_c, there is a long-run output reduction to Q_2 and a deadweight loss equal to triangular area FEG. Area FEG is the difference between the marginal benefit (the height of the demand

---

FIGURE 10.7

Supply Elasticity and the Deadweight Loss of Rent Control
With the rent ceiling P_c, the reduction in output in the short run is small, from Q to Q_1, along the short-run supply curve SS. The associated deadweight loss, triangular area BEC, is also small. The long-run effects of the rent ceiling are more significant. Output declines to Q_2 along the more elastic long-run supply curve LS. The associated deadweight loss is depicted by triangular area FEG.

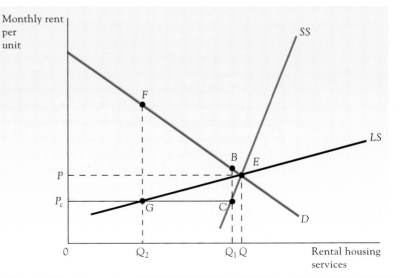

curve) and marginal cost (the height of the long-run supply curve) summed over each unit of output between Q_2 and the initial competitive equilibrium of Q.

As a result, rent control's deadweight loss is greater in the long run as suppliers have more time to reduce output in response to the price ceiling. All other things being equal, the greater the elasticity of supply and the larger the decline in output from the competitive equilibrium due to a price ceiling, the larger the deadweight loss. This suggests why elected local leaders may be less concerned than economists about rent control's adverse effects. Since city government officials typically hold office for only a few years, they are not around long enough to experience the long-run output adjustment to a rent ceiling. The relevant perspective on rent control to many elected officials may be closer to the one represented by the short-run supply curve in which the resulting deadweight loss is fairly small and the primary effect is a transfer of income from landlords to tenants. If tenants have more political clout than landlords, local policymakers may find the income transfer well worth the (small) short-run deadweight loss.

 ## 10.3   AIRLINE REGULATION AND DEREGULATION

Previously we mentioned that the perfectly competitive model remains extremely useful even if one or more of the conditions defining the model do not hold. In this section we show how this is the case in the U.S. experience with airline regulation and deregulation. During the period in which the domestic airline industry was regulated, entry into any given city-pair market in the industry was restricted. Carriers operating in a particular market were required to have an operating license from the Civil Aeronautics Board (CAB), and the CAB issued no new licenses to airlines requesting to enter an already served market. Even though the condition of free entry and exit was thus violated, the perfectly competitive model still can be employed to analyze the effects of regulation, as well as deregulation, on the airline industry.

From its formation in 1938 to the Congressional deregulation of the domestic airline industry in 1978, the CAB controlled, among other things, fares, routes that commercial airlines could serve, and entry of new firms into the industry. Analyzing the consequences of the regulations imposed by the CAB makes clear why there was widespread support for deregulation.

Our analysis will focus on the pricing policy followed by the CAB. The CAB closely regulated the fares airlines charged, and, it turns out, kept those fares well above the level that would have prevailed in an open market. Even when some airlines requested fare reductions, they were regularly denied. In effect, the CAB imposed a *price floor*, keeping the price above the competitive level.

Throughout the regulation era, persuasive evidence existed that regulated airline fares were artificially high. The CAB regulated only airlines engaged in interstate transportation; intrastate airlines were beyond its reach. The existence of unregulated airlines made possible some illuminating comparisons. For instance, intrastate airlines operating in California flew the Los Angeles–San Francisco route, a distance approximately the same as the interstate route between Washington, D.C., and Boston. The CAB-controlled fares on the Washington–Boston route, though, were twice as high as the uncontrolled fares from Los Angeles to San Francisco. In addition to actual price comparisons, the federal government's General Accounting Office estimated that, on average, fares were 22 to 52 percent higher due to the CAB's actions.

From this we might conclude that the CAB designed the regulations to help the airlines at the expense of passengers. Airlines, after all, were receiving much higher fares as a result of the CAB's price-setting policy. Now, however, we encounter a startling fact: Airlines were not particularly profitable during the period of regulation. In fact, over the 20 years prior to deregulation in 1978, the airline industry's accounting profits were slightly below the national average for all industries.

What Happened to the Profits?

The apparent profits to airlines were dissipated in three ways. First, the CAB required airlines to operate some unprofitable routes. These routes generally provided service between sparsely populated areas where demand was insufficient for the airline to make a profit. The airlines had to balance the losses on these runs against the profits on other routes. Second, airline worker unions were in a position to demand and get higher wages when the CAB kept fares above competitive levels, and so some of the potential profits went to employees.

The third reason is perhaps the most interesting because it would, in theory, eliminate profits even in the absence of the other two. It is nonprice competition. In any market where prices are set and suppliers cannot compete on the basis of price, another form of competition will emerge, as we saw with rent control in Chapter 2. What happened in the airline industry?

Airlines can make large profits at high prices only if they attract passengers. Under regulation, however, they could not cut prices to attract passengers away from their competitors. Each airline faced the problem of making itself more attractive than its competitors by some other means than lowering its fares. The solution was obvious: change the nature of the product to make it more appealing. So, airlines began to schedule more frequent flights so passengers could fly at times convenient to them. In addition, competition evolved among airlines to provide "frills": gourmet meals, movies, more and better attendants, complimentary Mickey Mouse ears for passengers en route to Disney World, and sometimes live entertainment. But all these things increased the airlines' cost of providing transportation. Costs rose, prices were fixed, and profits diminished. Indeed, economic theory would predict that in a competitive market the process would continue until airlines no longer made a profit at all. And so we see why the airline industry was not especially profitable despite artificially high prices.

Let's examine the process using graphs. Figure 10.8b shows the supply and demand curves for airline services. For simplicity, we assume the industry is constant-cost. (Economists call this a simplifying assumption: the results are not significantly different from the case of an increasing-cost industry, but the analysis is simpler.) In the absence of any regulation, price and quantity are P and Q, respectively. Then, the CAB sets the price P_{CAB}. Note that if the industry operated at point A on its supply curve, it would make a profit shown by the shaded area. Although this point is not the final outcome, it provides a convenient place to begin our analysis to understand why further adjustments must take place. Corresponding to point A in Figure 10.8b, a representative firm is at point a in Figure 10.8a, operating at the minimum point on its LAC and making a profit equal to the shaded area.

With all firms making a comfortable profit, why can't this point be an equilibrium? The answer is that each airline can make still more money if it expands output by drawing passengers away from other airlines. This is because an individual airline's profit-maximizing output is where LMC equals P_{CAB}. Because total quantity demanded is Q_1 and price cannot be lowered, an airline can gain passengers only by attracting them away from other airlines in some other way.

Suppose that the airline attempts to attract passengers by scheduling more frequent flights. Note that every airline has an incentive to initiate this practice, but more flights in total, with an unchanged total quantity demanded, means fewer passengers on each flight. Airlines will operate flights with empty seats, and to do so is in the interest of each airline. Why? At a price per passenger twice as high (P_{CAB}), it is profitable to schedule a flight even

FIGURE 10.8

Airline Regulation by the CAB

A price floor of P_{CAB} implies that a representative firm (a) and the industry (b) can earn profits shown by the shaded areas. However, the profits are dissipated through nonprice competition, which leads to cost curves shifting upward (*LAC* to *LAC'*).

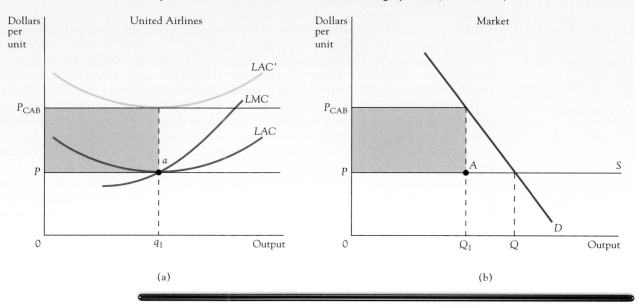

(a)   (b)

if only half the seats are filled. Flying half-filled planes, however, means a higher average cost per passenger. Thus, in Figure 10.8a the representative airline's *LAC* curve, showing the cost per unit of output, shifts upward as the number of passengers per flight declines. This shift continues until economic profit is eliminated. The final result is an average cost curve like *LAC'*, with the typical airline just covering its cost at the higher CAB price and with total output unchanged.[8]

After Deregulation

Since the domestic airline industry was deregulated, several significant changes have taken place. First, as our analysis would suggest, the cost of air travel to consumers has fallen. In real terms, airline ticket prices are almost 40 percent lower today than they were at the time of deregulation. In part because of the fare reductions, the number of passengers flown has risen by 250 percent since 1977. And the annual value of consumer surplus generated by deregulation is estimated to be $23 billion (2000 dollars).[9]

Second, a major restructuring of the industry has taken place since deregulation. For 40 years the CAB denied access to would-be entrants. Within a year of deregulation the number of airlines in interstate service rose from 36 to 98. The rapid expansion was a mixed

[8]This analysis neglects the way the quality change affects the demand curve. Presumably, more convenient flights with "frills" are worth more to consumers, so this practice shifts the demand curve rightward to some degree. Total industry output is then somewhat greater, but airlines still end up making zero economic profit.

[9]For a discussion of this and other consequences of airline deregulation, see Clifford Winston and Steven Morrison, *The Economic Effects of Airline Deregulation* (Washington, D.C.: Brookings Institution, 1997); and Adam D. Thierer, "20th Anniversary of Airline Deregulation: Cause for Celebration not Re-Regulation," Heritage Foundation Backgrounder, April 22, 1998.

blessing, however. From 1980 to 1982, the industry lost $1.4 billion—more than in any other prior year. Several established carriers, including Braniff, Pan Am, and Eastern, declared bankruptcy. A few other financially troubled airlines have been absorbed by stronger competitors.

Third, after deregulation many of the industry's new entrants operated at significantly lower costs than the established carriers. One reason for the cost differential was the union pay scales negotiated during regulation. As we mentioned earlier, potential profits from higher-than-competitive fares can be dissipated by paying above-market wages to union members. Between 1970 and 1978, for example, the Consumer Price Index increased by 68 percent, yet airline workers' wages rose by over 100 percent and fringe benefits increased by 300 percent. After deregulation the contrast in salaries paid by established airlines and newcomers was striking. In 1983, the average worker (typically union) at the established airlines made $39,000 a year, whereas workers (typically nonunion) at new airlines made an average of $22,000. Top (union) pilots received $150,000 per year from the established airlines, whereas the new entrants to the market paid their pilots only $45,000.

In an attempt to reduce labor costs in the deregulated environment, the established carriers have cut their workforces by the thousands and implemented a two-tier wage scale that pays new employees 30 to 50 percent less than current ones. Already, labor costs as a share of all expenses have fallen from 39 percent in 1979 to roughly 33 percent today. What this and other evidence makes clear is that unions were major beneficiaries of the CAB regulations and major losers from deregulation.

Fourth, service to small communities has, on average, increased with deregulation, but fares have gone up. Prior to deregulation, the CAB required airlines to provide service to small cities, but because the carriers used the same jets to serve small cities, they lost money on the small-city routes. After deregulation, the large carriers abandoned these unprofitable routes, but new commuter airlines using smaller, more fuel-efficient planes (e.g., turbo props and regional jets) have taken their place. In effect, the CAB regulations required airlines to use some of their potential profits to subsidize service to smaller communities, and deregulation ended the implicit subsidy.

APPLICATION 10.4 **THE CONTESTABILITY OF AIRLINE MARKETS**

Although deregulation has lowered fares, a question that has emerged—particularly in the wake of several recent mergers and bankruptcies—is, how many airlines are necessary in any city-pair market to ensure the competitive outcome? The number of existing suppliers may be irrelevant if airline markets are what economists term *contestable*. **Contestable markets** are those in which competition is so perfect that the market price is independent of the number of firms currently serving a market,

CONTESTABLE MARKETS
markets in which competition is so perfect that the market price is independent of the number of firms currently serving a market, because the mere possibility of entry suffices to discipline the actions of incumbent suppliers

because the mere possibility of entry suffices to discipline the actions of incumbent suppliers. (Remember that in perfect competition entry and exit are assumed to be frictionless so that incumbent suppliers must be wary of potential entry if they charge a price in excess of marginal cost.) For example, even though Delta Airlines may be the sole provider on the Atlanta–Birmingham (Alabama) air route, it will charge fares equal to marginal cost if the route is contestable. If Delta charged fares above marginal cost, other airlines could costlessly (that is, without friction) move into the market and take away Delta's passengers.

Although competition may be vigorous under deregulation, the available evidence suggests that it is not perfect and that airline markets are not contestable in the strict sense of the term. For example, holding other factors constant, average fares on routes with two competitors were about 8 percent lower in 1990 than the fares on routes served by a single airline.[10] A third competitor was associated with an additional decline in fares of 8 percent.

In a more specific illustration, researchers have examined the stock market effects of a series of announcements by People Express during 1984 to 1985 regarding particular routes the then-new airline was about to enter.[11] The researchers found that incumbent airlines operating in those markets suffered significant financial losses in the wake of the news. Since the pending People Express entry presumably lowered the prices charged and profits earned by incumbent airlines, the markets could not have been contestable as defined, with incumbents' pricing strategies already shaped by the mere possibility of entry by other firms. Given the definition of perfect competition, the People Express illustration also suggests the existence of some frictions to entry and exit—some costs that impeded the ability of potential competitors to constrain the pricing and profits of incumbent firms. These costs may consist of the advertising that must be done to announce one's arrival in a market, gate space that must be acquired and modified to an entering air-

line's specifications, and local staff that must be hired and trained with regard to company procedures.

Finally, the evidence suggests that there is an incentive in deregulated markets for additional entry—entry that will benefit consumers through lower prices. Recently, companies such as Southwest Airlines have made substantial inroads against more established firms because of their lower costs. For example, Southwest has achieved significantly lower operating costs than more established competitors by focusing on short-haul markets where the same type of fuel-efficient plane, a Boeing 737, can be used (thus lowering fuel, maintenance, and training costs); meals don't have to be served; expensive hubs and computerized reservations systems are unnecessary; and planes can be turned around quickly (in 20 minutes versus an hour or more for carriers such as United, American, and Delta, whose planes must sit on the ground at their hubs to await connecting passengers).

Lower costs have allowed Southwest to target underserved city pairs and offer frequent, low-fare service, often chasing out incumbents along the way. Until 1991, for example, TWA's one-way fare on the 255-mile St. Louis–Kansas City route was $295. Southwest jumped in with a fare of $59. Another example: in contrast to the existing one-way coach fare of $303 in the Los Angeles–San Francisco market, Southwest introduced a $20 fare between Oakland and Burbank in December 1990, virtually guaranteeing American Airlines' departure from the market. Southwest's success even prompted United Airlines to consider spinning itself off into one long-haul carrier plus four low-cost regional carriers modeled after the upstart airline.

[10]Severin Borenstein, "The Evolution of U.S. Airline Competition," *Journal of Economic Perspectives,* 6 No. 2 (Spring 1992), pp. 45–73.

[11]Michael D. Whinston and Scott C. Collins, "Entry and Competitive Structure in Deregulated Airline Markets: An Event Study Analysis of People Express," *Rand Journal of Economics,* 23 No. 4 (Winter 1992), pp. 445–462.

The Push for Reregulation

Not everyone is happy with the results of airline deregulation, and in recent years proposals to reinstitute regulation have surfaced. Some of the support for reregulation is understandable since it comes from groups that have suffered financially, such as the established airlines and their employees. Some, however, comes from groups concerned with other questions they believe to be associated with deregulation—namely, greater congestion at airports and issues of airline safety.

Not surprisingly, airports have been more congested following the surge in passenger traffic after deregulation, and with the congestion have come more delayed flights, lost luggage, and service complaints. Because deregulation has increased the number of passengers, it has contributed to these problems. But is reregulation the best way to deal with them? Let's consider some alternatives. Airport capacity, for example, could be expanded to handle the increased traffic. Indeed, in a fully competitive market, this would occur automatically, but it hasn't because airlines don't control airports. Airports are owned and operated primarily by local governments, and since deregulation there has been no significant expansion in airport capacity despite the fact that nearly twice as many passengers are using them. Prior to the completion of the Denver airport in 1995, the last new big-city airport, at Dallas–Fort Worth, was built in 1974. Part of the problem with expanding capacity is that the expansion often generates political opposition from zoning authorities, environmental groups, nearby residents, and perhaps the dominant airlines at the existing airport (which fear an increase in competition if capacity is expanded).

But even if local governments are unable or unwilling to expand airport capacity, there are other ways to deal with congestion problems. For instance, flight delays are as much a consequence of how airports manage landings and departures as they are a result of increased passenger service. Airlines schedule flights when consumers want them most (early morning, midday, and late afternoon), and these are the times when congestion is the worst. The amount of air traffic during peak hours can differ from the nonpeak hours by a factor of 10. Currently, the landing and takeoff fees charged to airlines by airports are usually the same regardless of whether they occur during peak or nonpeak hours. Economists would suggest increasing the peak-hour fees. Such a price differential would induce airlines and passengers to rearrange their schedules and reduce congestion during peak travel hours. (This technique is called *peak-load pricing* and is discussed more fully in Chapter 12.)

Congestion is also related to airline safety, because the probability of accidents increases with the number of airplanes in the sky at a given time. As we have seen, however, congestion is not entirely the result of deregulation, but results in part from the way airports are managed and priced by local governments. Nonetheless, the news media often suggest a possible connection between safety and deregulation whenever reporting an accident or near-miss. Actually, airline safety procedures are still regulated by the Federal Aviation Administration (FAA), just as they were before deregulation. If safety problems exist, it is not necessary to control air fares and routes to deal with them—the FAA could simply raise safety standards. In fact, some economists argue that the FAA isn't needed at all because airlines have an incentive to take safety into account due to the enormous costs they bear in the event of an accident.

The heightened concern over safety in recent years is somewhat puzzling because the data show clearly that safety has improved in the years following deregulation. According to the Department of Transportation, both fatality and accident rates were lower in the years after deregulation than in the years before. Another indication that air travel is at least as safe after deregulation is that the companies that stand to lose the most financially from crashes—insurance companies that insure airline carriers—have lowered the rates they charge the major carriers.

10.4 CITY TAXICAB MARKETS

Most major U.S. cities regulate taxis in some way. Usually, the regulations require taxis to have city-issued licenses. The licenses look like and are often called *medallions*. Typically, cities issue a fixed number of medallions and new entrants must purchase one from a current driver or cab company. The supply of cabs thus is limited by the number of issued medallions. The effects of such an entry restriction can be analyzed through the perfectly competitive model—much as the model allowed us to analyze the impact of domestic airline regulations limiting entry into individual city-pair markets.

To examine the operation of a taxicab market with a restricted number of licenses, consider Figure 10.9, which shows the supply and demand curves—S and D, respectively—for taxi service absent any regulation. The supply curve is drawn as a horizontal line—a constant-cost industry. Although we make this assumption partly to simplify the analysis, it is reasonable to assume that the supply of taxi services within a city is highly, if not perfectly, elastic. With the market conditions as illustrated, competition results in a per-mile fare (price) of

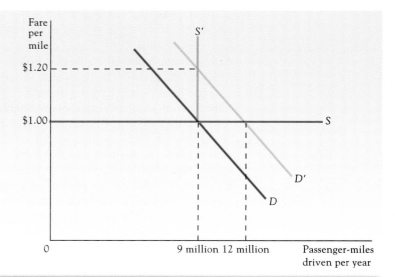

FIGURE 10.9

Licensing Taxicabs
Taxicab licensing makes the supply curve vertical (under our assumptions) at an output of 9 million passenger-miles. The result is higher fares and lower output than under unregulated conditions.

$1.00 and an annual output of 9 million passenger-miles. Suppose that this output is produced by 600 cabs, each of which transports passengers for 15,000 miles per year.

Next, suppose that the city requires taxis to have a medallion to operate, and it issues 600 medallions, giving one to each taxi. The medallions change nothing and have no effect on the market as long as supply and demand conditions remain the same. Now suppose that over a period of time the city's population grows and incomes rise, so demand shifts to D'. (The supply curve may also shift over time, but for simplicity we will assume that it does not.) Because the number of taxis is limited by the number of medallions, the supply curve is vertical at 9 million passenger-miles, as shown by S'. (We are assuming that each taxi continues to operate for the same number of passenger-miles as before.) Fares rise to $1.20 per mile while output remains unchanged. In contrast, if the market had not been regulated, output would expand along S to 12 million passenger-miles and the per-mile price would remain at $1.00.

The practice of licensing taxicabs restricts entry to the market and leads to higher consumer prices. Persons on the supply side of the market tend to benefit, but exactly who they are and how they benefit deserves some further discussion. Note that in the situation just described, operating a taxi for a year (15,000 miles) generates a profit of $0.20 per mile, or an annual profit of $3,000. To realize that profit, however, a person must own a medallion, so it is the owners of medallions who tend to benefit from licensing. More precisely, those who were originally given the medallions receive most, if not all, of the benefit. Current owners of medallions may not receive anything but competitive returns.

To see why, let's consider the factors determining a medallion's price. Suppose that a driver from another city wishes to purchase a medallion from a driver who owns one. (If you owned a medallion, what would you sell it for?) Because ownership of the medallion brings with it an annual gain of $3,000 (assuming market conditions remain unchanged), its value is the same as an asset yielding $3,000 per year. If the prevailing interest rate is 10 percent, a person needs a $30,000 investment to generate an income of $3,000 per year. Thus, the value of the medallion itself is $30,000. Buyers are willing to pay this amount because they could get as good a return by investing $30,000 in a medallion as by investing it where it yields an interest income of $3,000 per year.

The transferability of medallions at prices determined by the expected profitability of operating a taxi means that those who received the medallions free when they were first issued may get all the benefit from the licensing policy. To take an extreme example, suppose that all the original cab operators sell their medallions to others. If this occurs, those who benefited from the licensing policy are no longer in the market, and those who now operate taxis will receive only a normal return on their investment. Nonetheless, the fare is still above the real cost of producing taxi services; if the city allowed free entry into the market, cab fares would fall to $1.00, as indicated by the intersection of S and D', and the value of the medallions would fall to zero. Such a deregulation of cab markets would impose a large loss on the current owners of medallions—a loss valued at $30,000 each in our example—yet these cabdrivers may never have received any benefit from the restrictive policy.

A difficult ethical dilemma is implicit in this analysis: Is it fair to drivers to deregulate the market—that is, to allow unrestricted entry, lower prices, and higher output? Deregulation would impose a large loss on medallion owners, some of whom may never have shared in the economic profits created by the licensing policy. For example, in 2000 the price of a medallion in New York City was $250,000, so people who had invested their life savings or borrowed money to purchase a medallion would be devastated by a return to unrestricted entry, because that would leave them with no opportunity to earn the higher income that made the medallion worth the $250,000 they paid for it. If entry remains restricted, however, consumers continue to pay fares that are higher than necessary. As a further complication, the poor tend to be heavy users of taxis; they spend a larger portion of their incomes on taxi services than do higher-income groups, so they are especially burdened by higher fares.

We have emphasized the effects of the entry restriction created by taxicab licensing, but cities often regulate this market in other ways besides licensing. For instance, sometimes maximum fares are specified. This price ceiling creates shortages in certain parts of the city and at certain times of the day. For example, suppose that the maximum fare is $1.20 in Figure 10.9. Although that price might have no effect in the middle of the day, it can create a shortage during rush hour. At rush hour, congestion is greater and costs of operation are higher (traffic moves slower and it takes longer for a cab to travel a mile). Demand is also likely to be higher. If the quantity supplied is lower and the quantity demanded higher, and if a higher price is not permitted, a shortage results. Anyone who has tried to find a cab in New York City during rush hour knows what this means. Similarly, fare regulations can discourage cabs from operating in more remote or dangerous areas of a city. Because the regulated fares are not sufficiently high to cover the risk, drivers practice a form of nonprice rationing by avoiding passengers traveling to high-risk neighborhoods.

The Illegal Market

In many cities, licensing and fare regulations give rise to a thriving market in illegal transportation services. Illegal markets arise because of the mutual gains possible for their participants. As seen in Figure 10.9, taxi services can be profitably supplied at prices below $1.20 per mile (as shown by the horizontal supply curve S, which continues to show the cost of provision exclusive of the artificial medallion cost), and consumers also gain from a lower price.

By its very nature, an illegal market poses problems for investigators. This particular illegal market, however, is not as covert as some others are; the authorities tend to "look the other way," perhaps because transporting people without a taxi license is viewed as a crime without a victim. A Carnegie-Mellon study looked at the unlicensed (illegal) taxi market in Pittsburgh.[12] Two student "plants" got summer jobs driving illegal cabs—sometimes called

---

[12]Otto A. Davis and Norman J. Johnson, "The Jitneys: A Study of Grassroots Capitalism," *Journal of Contemporary Studies*, 7 (Winter 1984), pp. 81–102.

jitneys or *gypsies*—and they kept records about fares, areas serviced, drivers, and customers. In addition, the researchers also conducted field research by acting as customers and collecting information in that way.

Among the study's findings is that the size of the illegal market is larger than imagined. There are more than twice as many illegal cabs operating in Pittsburgh as there are licensed cabs. (In New York City, estimates indicate 25,000 gypsies compared with 12,000 licensed cabs.) The unlicensed cabs tend to provide service in areas, such as low-income neighborhoods, where the licensed cabs often do not operate. In addition, fares are lower for the unlicensed cabs. For instance, licensed cabs charged $2.52 (in 1980) for an average two-mile trip, while the same trip cost $2.00 in the unlicensed cabs. Tips are uncommon in the illegal market, which make the effective price spread greater. Moreover, the service quality provided by the unlicensed cabs tends to be better.

One concern about the illegal market has always been that it might be unsafe. For example, a paid advertisement in the *New York Times* warned riders: "Ignore unlicensed cabs. You may be putting yourself in the care of a murderer, a thief, or even a rapist."[13] The Pittsburgh study, however, finds the warning unwarranted. Much of the illegal market is organized around station houses, which act as central clearinghouses in the neighborhoods. The study notes, "It is apparent that station managers work hard to please customers by having courteous, safe, and reliable drivers who will not cheat on fares." In addition, there was no difference in traffic accidents between the licensed and the unlicensed drivers.

APPLICATION 10.5 GYPSY VANS AND SUPER SHUTTLES

Anyone who has recently landed at one of New York City's airports knows about the prevalence of gypsy cabs. Just outside the baggage claim area, between the terminal doors and the lines of licensed cabs, anxious-looking individuals query passenger after passenger: "Need a cab?"

Less commonly known around the "Big Apple" is the widespread presence of gypsy vans.[14] The privately operated vans race to scoop up passengers ahead of the city buses that are the only vehicles officially licensed to provide mass transit. Public officials estimate that over 2,500 private vans now operate in New York City. They charge passengers 15 cents less than the city bus fare (as of 1991), and deliver the passengers to their destinations ahead of scheduled city bus times. The phenomenon is spreading to other cities. In Miami, some of the 300 vans in operation even offer in-transit entertainment to their passengers consisting of soap opera videos.

A senior New York City Transit Authority official estimates that gypsy vans divert $30 million in annual revenue from public transportation. In 1991, van drivers were assessed fines of over $4 million for providing illegal mass transit services, although only $150,000 was collected on the assessed fines by city officials due to the failure of van drivers to appear at their court hearings.

Were it not for official sanctions, private vans would be more common providers of mass transit. This is evidenced by the spectacular growth of "Super Shuttles" when they have been allowed to ferry groups of different passengers to and from airports in certain major cities in the United States, such as Los Angeles and San Francisco. The Super Shuttles would provide even more wide-ranging mass transit services were they not restricted to routes where one of the endpoints of the route must be the city's airport.

[14]"Opportunistic Vans Are Running Circles Around City Buses," *Wall Street Journal* (July 24, 1991), pp. A1 and A17.

[13]Ibid., p. 97.

10.5 CONSUMER AND PRODUCER SURPLUS, AND THE NET GAINS FROM TRADE

So far, our look at the way markets work has not included international trade. However, it is a simple matter to incorporate such trade into the analysis. There are two important reasons to examine international trade. First, the economies of nations are becoming more interdependent. In 1960, for example, foreign trade accounted for less than 5 percent of U.S. gross national product; today the proportion exceeds 12 percent. Second, there are constant claims made in the political arena and the media that free trade is harmful to a nation's welfare. Microeconomic analysis can help us analyze the validity of these claims.

International trade arises because sellers and buyers located in different countries find it in their interests to deal with one another. To see what effects this has, consider Figure 10.10. In the left-hand panel we show the U.S. demand and supply curves for sugar as D_{US} and S_{US}, respectively. We assume that there is only one other country in the world, called Rest of the World (or RoW; this can be an aggregation of a number of other countries, of course). The right-hand panel shows the demand and supply curves for sugar in RoW as D_R and S_R, respectively. Without trade, each national market would attain equilibrium where its own demand and supply curves intersect. The result would be a price of P_3 in the United States and P_1 in RoW.

Now think about the incentives of buyers and sellers if trade becomes possible. Consumers in the United States have an incentive to buy sugar from RoW sellers, who are sell-

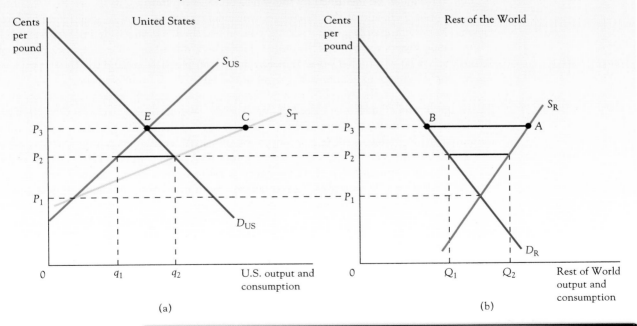

FIGURE 10.10

International Trade
The total supply curve of output available for sale in the United States is derived by adding to S_{US} an amount equal to the difference between quantity demanded and supplied in the RoW at each possible price; the result is S_T. The intersection of D_{US} and S_T determines price and total consumption in the United States; U.S. production is less than consumption by the amount of imports (q_2 minus q_1).

ing it at a lower price than U.S. sellers. Similarly, RoW sellers have an incentive to sell sugar in the United States, where the price is higher than they are getting in their domestic market. Therefore, we expect RoW producers to export sugar to the United States, and our task is to determine how much trade occurs and how it affects both markets. (Note that if the cost of transporting sugar is higher than P_3 minus P_1 per unit, there would be no trade. We will assume transportation costs are negligible.)

We will proceed by deriving the total supply curve, S_T, confronting U.S. consumers; this curve will show the total amount of sugar (from both U.S. and RoW producers together) that will be available in the United States at each possible price. Suppose that the price is P_3; how much will RoW producers offer to sell in the United States at that price? Figure 10.10b gives us the answer. At a price of P_3, RoW producers will produce at point A on their supply curve, a total amount of P_3A. Of this total, they will sell P_3B to consumers in RoW; the remainder, BA, is the amount they will export to the United States. The reason they sell P_3B to RoW consumers is that if they sold less, the price in RoW would be higher than P_3 and they would have an incentive to shift sales from the export market to their domestic market. Similarly, if they were selling more than P_3B to RoW consumers, the domestic price would be lower and they would have an incentive to shift sales to the export market. Thus, when the price is P_3, RoW producers will add BA to the output U.S. producers place on the market. Distance EC in Figure 10.10a is drawn equal to BA, so total output in the U.S. market is shown by the sum of domestic output, P_3E, and imports, EC, or P_3C. Point C is one point on the total supply curve, S_T, confronting U.S. consumers.

The remainder of S_T is derived in a similar fashion. At each possible price, we add to U.S. output (shown by S_{US}) the difference between the quantity that RoW producers would choose to sell at that price and the amount RoW buyers would purchase. The resulting curve S_T shows the total quantity available on the U.S. market at alternative prices. Note that this curve intersects the U.S. supply curve at P_1, the price that would prevail in the RoW in the absence of trade. This shows that if the U.S. price was the same as the RoW price in the absence of trade, there would be no exports from RoW to the United States. At a price lower than P_1, U.S. producers would become exporters of sugar.

Equilibrium can be identified by the intersection of S_T and D_{US} in Figure 10.10a. Thus, the U.S. price is P_2, and at that price U.S. consumers purchase q_2 units. However, U.S. producers are providing only q_1 units to U.S. consumers; the remaining q_1q_2 units represent imports. Trade lowers the price of all units sold in the United States because U.S. producers cannot sell sugar at a higher price than consumers can purchase it from the RoW, provided there is no difference in quality in the sugar produced by RoW and U.S. firms.

An important implication of this analysis is that both the U.S. and RoW markets must be in equilibrium. This is guaranteed by the way we constructed the S_T curve. Observe what has happened in RoW in Figure 10.10b. The price is P_2 in the RoW also. At that price, total output of RoW producers is Q_2, but consumption by RoW consumers is only Q_1. The difference, Q_1Q_2, is the amount exported to the United States. Q_1Q_2 in panel (b) is equal to q_1q_2 in panel (a); the amount that RoW producers want to export at P_2 is equal to the amount that U.S. consumers want to purchase as imports. Both markets are in equilibrium at a price of P_2, with production, consumption, and trade as indicated in the graphs. Note also that both markets can be in equilibrium only when the price is the same in both markets, because otherwise sellers in the lower-priced market would have an incentive to export to the higher-priced market.

This is a versatile model, but it must be handled carefully. For example, any change in demand or supply conditions in the RoW will cause the S_T curve to shift. If demand increases in the RoW, for instance, S_T will shift to the left and the price of sugar in the United States will increase. Similarly, changes in U.S. supply or demand conditions will result in changes in the uniform world price, and that will cause changes in RoW output, consumption, and consumption, and exports. When nations are linked by international trade, their markets are affected by one another in this way.

The Gains from International Trade

In the political arena and the media we frequently hear assertions that trade is harmful to national welfare. We can use our supply-demand model to show that these assertions are not well founded. Figure 10.11, based on the same supply and demand curves as Figure 10.10, illustrates the argument. The United States would be at point E in Figure 10.11a in the absence of trade. With trade, the price is reduced to P_2 and consumption increases, but domestic production falls. From the graph we see that consumer surplus increases by area P_3EKP_2—a trapezoid defined by the difference between the no-trade and with-trade price of sugar, P_3 minus P_2, from the vertical axis out to the domestic demand curve, D_{US}. Producer surplus falls by area P_3ELP_2—the difference between the no-trade and the with-trade price from the vertical axis out to the domestic supply curve, S_{US}. The gain in consumer surplus from the lower price exceeds the loss in producer surplus by area EKL. This area measures the net gain to the United States as a whole.

To say that there is a "net gain to the United States as a whole" does not mean, of course, that every U.S. citizen gains. Citizens involved in sugar production lose. That is why producer groups are among the most prominent supporters of trade restrictions. The gain to consumers is, however, larger than the loss to producers in the sense that consumers could fully compensate all those who lose on the supply side and still come out ahead (by area

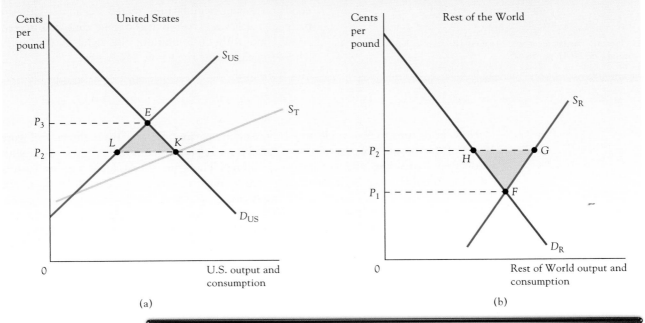

FIGURE 10.11

The Gains from Free Trade

(a) Trade increases consumer surplus in the United States by area P_3EKP_2 and decreases producer surplus by area P_3ELP_2. The difference, area EKL, is the net gain to the United States from trade. (b) For the RoW, the net gain from trade is shown by area HGF.

(a)

(b)

EKL). The fact that consumers could in principle pay compensation and still benefit is what the net gain from trade (in the case of an imported good) is all about. A fitting analogy involves any case of technological progress. For example, would an innovation such as the discovery of a low-cost cure for the common cold be a net gain for our country? The answer is yes in the same sense that free trade is a net gain for the United States: the cold cure would not benefit everyone (producers of aspirin and cold "remedies" would lose), but the gain in consumer surplus would exceed those losses.

APPLICATION 10.6   SHOULD IMPORTS OF SUNLIGHT BE BANNED?

To drive home the point that imports provide a net gain to a country as well as to satirize the frequent resistance by domestic producers to "unfair competition" from foreign suppliers, nineteenth-century French economist Frederic Bastiat penned the following hypothetical appeal from French candlemakers to the government.[15] The appeal asked for restrictions to be placed on the free sunlight driving French candlemakers out of business:

We are subjected to the intolerable competition of a foreign rival, who enjoys, it would seem, such superior facilities for the production of light that he can inundate our national market at so exceedingly reduced a price, that, the moment he makes his appearance, he draws off all custom from us; and thus an important branch of

French industry, with all its innumerable ramifications, is suddenly reduced to a state of complete stagnation. This rival is no other than the sun.

Our petition is, that it would please your honorable body to pass a law whereby shall be directed the shutting up of all windows, dormers, skylights, shutters, curtains, in a word, all openings, holes, chinks, and fissures through which the light of the sun is used to penetrate into our dwellings, to the prejudice of profitable manufactures which we flatter ourselves we have been enabled to bestow in gratitude upon the country; which country cannot, therefore, without ingratitude, leave us now to struggle unprotected through so unequal a contest. . . .

Does it not argue the greatest inconsistency to check as you do the importation of coal, iron, cheese, and goods of foreign manufacture, merely because . . . their price *approaches zero*, while at the same time you freely admit, and without limitation, the light of the sun, whose price is during the whole day *at zero*?

[15]Frederic Bastiat, *Economic Sophisms* (Princeton, N.J.: D. Van Nostrand Co., 1964), pp. 56–60.

Now let us turn to how trade affects our trading partner, RoW. This is shown in Figure 10.11b. RoW moves from its no-trade equilibrium at point F to a higher price of P_2, with production expanding and consumption falling. The gain in producer surplus is area P_2GFP_1—the difference between the with-trade and the no-trade price in RoW, P_2 minus P_1, from the vertical axis out to RoW's supply curve, S_R. The loss in consumer surplus is area P_2HFP_1—the difference between the with-trade and the no-trade price in RoW from the vertical axis out to RoW's demand curve, D_R. The gain in producer surplus exceeds the loss in consumer surplus by area HGF. This area measures the net gain to the RoW as a whole from trade in the same way that area EKL in Figure 10.11a measures the net gain for the United States. For the RoW, however, producers gain from trade, while in the United States consumers gain because in this case, RoW exports to the United States. In other industries, market conditions will result in the United States being an exporter. In that case, the effect on the U.S. market will be just like the effect on RoW in Figure 10.11b: trade will result in a gain in producer surplus that is larger than the loss in consumer surplus.

The Link Between Imports and Exports

Our analysis so far shows why both imports and exports make nations better off, on net, if supply and demand curves determine equilibrium prices and quantities. If the rest of the world is willing to supply a good at a lower price than would prevail without trade in the United States, our country as a whole is better off. And, if the rest of the world is willing to pay a higher price than would prevail in our domestic market without trade, our net national well-being is also enhanced.

Imports and exports, of course, are not independent of one another: Any time we import the rest of the world's goods, the dollars used to pay international suppliers for those goods must come back, by necessity, to our economy in the form of international demand for U.S. exports. To see why, suppose that the opposite was true—namely, that the dollars used to pay for U.S. imports never came back. Suppose, for example, that foreigners either stuffed the U.S. import dollars under their mattresses or, worse yet, burned them. If this was the case, we could run a tremendous scam on the rest of the world by simply printing up more pieces of paper, calling them dollars, and using them to import valuable goods such as Japanese cars and oil from Saudi Arabia, for free.

The only reason the rest of the world is willing to accept our dollars as payment for the goods we import from them is that those pieces of paper are worth something in return. Specifically, the dollars foreigners earn on U.S. imports can be employed to purchase U.S. goods.

Contrary to statements made in the political arena about how dollars spent on foreign products are "lost" to the U.S., free trade causes no such dissipation of currency. Currency is neither created nor destroyed in the process. The only thing that is created when other countries' products are purchased is a net gain to the United States as a whole—a net gain not only from the imports themselves but also from the exports that those imports serve to promote.

The difference between the political and economic views of trade is aptly summarized by Milton Friedman:[16]

> . . . *public opinion [on foreign trade overemphasizes] the visible [versus the] . . . invisible effects of government policy . . . steelworkers whose jobs are threatened by imports from Japan are highly visible. They . . . can see clearly the benefit to them from restricting [steel] imports. . . . The cost is large but spread thinly. Tens of thousands of buyers of objects made with steel would pay a bit more because of the restriction. The Japanese would earn fewer dollars here and, as a result, purchase fewer U.S. goods. But that cost too is invisible. The man who might have had a job producing a product the Japanese would have purchased if they had been permitted to sell more steel here will have no way of knowing that he has been hurt.*
>
> *Workers . . . [producing] products . . . sold to Japan to earn the yen used to buy Japanese steel are producing steel for the U.S. just as much as the men who tend the open-hearth furnaces in Gary [Indiana]. . . . We could produce bananas in hothouses, and no doubt would if the tariff on bananas was high enough. Would that make sense? Obviously not—we can produce them more efficiently indirectly by trading export goods for bananas from Central America. . . .*
>
> *As Adam Smith [noted in] The Wealth of Nations: "What is prudence in the conduct of every private family, can scarce be folly in that of a great Kingdom. If a foreign country can supply us with a commodity cheaper than we ourselves can make it, better buy it of them with some part of the produce of our own industry, employed in a way in which we have some advantage. The general industry of the country . . . will not thereby be diminished . . . but only left to find out the way in which it can be employed to the greatest advantage.*

[16]Milton Friedman, "In Defense of Dumping," *Newsweek* (February 20, 1978).

10.6 GOVERNMENT INTERVENTION IN MARKETS: QUANTITY CONTROLS

QUOTAS
government-imposed
maximum quantities
of goods

Price is not the only feature of markets that policy makers may wish to control. Quantity can also be the subject of government attention. For example, in Canada and much of Western Europe, there are government-specified maximum quantities, or **quotas**, on the amount of American-produced television that can be broadcast by local stations. In Singapore annual new car purchases are limited to 50,000 in an attempt to relieve congestion and improve air quality. In the United States, there are either voluntary or mandatory quotas on imports of such goods as steel, sugar, cars, computer chips, dairy products, and textiles. There are also legal limits on the number of people who can immigrate to the United States from any other country in the world in a given year.

To illustrate how the competitive model can be employed to analyze quantity controls, we focus on government-imposed maximum quantities—more specifically, the quota placed on sugar imports to the United States. The effects observed in the case of the sugar import quota can be generalized to other cases of government-legislated quotas. Moreover, the competitive model allows us to see why some of the economic effects of the quota may be contrary to the intentions of the policymakers implementing the quota.

Sugar Policy: A Sweet Deal

The U.S. climate is not well suited to the production of sugar, just as it is unsuited to the production of coffee and bananas. In the case of sugar, however, there is a thriving domestic industry; in most years we import less than 20 percent of the sugar we use. Why don't we import all the sugar we use, as we do with bananas and coffee? The answer is to be found in the policies adopted by our government toward the sugar industry—policies that include restrictions on imports from other countries.

Let's see how the sugar market would operate in the absence of government policy. In Figure 10.12a we show the U.S. demand and domestic supply curves for sugar as D_{US} and S_{US}. Figure 10.12b gives the supply and demand curves for the Rest of the World (RoW) as S_R and D_R, respectively; these are aggregated across many producing and consuming countries. From these relationships we can derive the total supply curve confronting U.S. consumers when there is free trade. The total supply curve is shown as S_T in Figure 10.12a. It is derived as the horizontal gap between D_R and S_R in Figure 10.12b, above P_1. It consists entirely of imports over the relevant range, because sugar can be produced at lower cost overseas than in the United States. With free trade, equilibrium is established at the intersection of S_T and D_{US}. The resulting uniform world price is P_2, with the United States importing all its sugar, an amount equal to Q_1Q_2 per year as shown in Figure 10.12b. There is no U.S. production; P_2 is not high enough to cover the cost of domestic production.

Suppose that to help domestic sugar producers the government places a quota of q_q pounds per year on imports. Then the total supply curve becomes the kinked line S'_T. The new total supply curve is the same as the previous total supply curve without the quota, S_T, out to the quota amount of q_q. At q_q, the new total supply curve becomes vertical until a sufficiently high price is reached, P_3, to encourage domestic production. Above P_3, the new total supply curve parallels the domestic supply curve, S_{US}, and has a magnitude that exceeds S_{US} by the amount of the quota, q_q.

The new total supply curve indicates that RoW suppliers will add an amount equal to q_q to domestic production at each possible price above P_1. Although RoW suppliers would like to sell more than this in the United States, they are not permitted to do so. The result of the import quota is a price for sugar of P_4 in the United States. This price is determined by the intersection of the U.S. demand curve, D_{US}, and the total supply curve, S'_T. At the price of

FIGURE 10.12

The Sugar Import Quota

With free trade, the uniform world price of sugar is P_2, with the United States importing Q_1Q_2 units of sugar and producing none. With an import quota of q_q, the price in the United States is P_4, production is q_1, consumption is q_2, and imports are q_1q_2. The price on world markets falls to P_5.

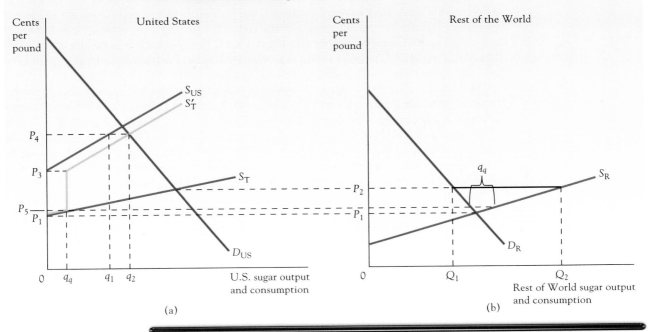

(a)

(b)

P_4, U.S. sugar output is q_1, domestic consumption is q_2, and imports equal q_1q_2, or the quota amount of q_q.

Domestic consumers, of course, bear the burden of the quota in the form of a higher price (P_4 versus P_2 in Figure 10.12a) for sugar. The estimated annual loss in domestic consumer surplus from the quota is $4 billion as of 2000, about $50 per family. Domestic sugar producers benefit from the quota. The estimated annual increase in producer surplus is $400 million as of 2000. Thus, the cost to consumers due to the quota is about $10 for each $1 of producer surplus gained by suppliers. The reason that the benefit to producers is so much less than the cost to consumers is that much of the consumer cost simply covers the significantly higher production cost of sugar in this country. In sum, contrary to the statements made by many political advocates of the quota, the United States is worse off on net because of the quota: domestic consumers are harmed more than domestic producers are helped.

Given that the sugar import quota imposes a deadweight loss on the United States, why does this policy remain in effect? The likely answer relates to the extent to which the benefits and costs of the sugar import quota are distributed. Although U.S. sugar producers may gain far less surplus than U.S. consumers lose, there are relatively few sugar producers and many sugar consumers. The gains from the sugar quota are thus much more concentrated, and each of the relatively small number of sugar producers has a strong incentive to lobby policymakers to retain the quota. In contrast, practically every family in the United States consumes sugar. The estimated annual loss per family is only $50—not much of an incentive for the typical family to lobby policymakers to repeal the quota.

Because their export markets are limited, producers in other countries are also harmed by the U.S. sugar policy. In Figure 10.12b, we see that when the United States adopts the import quota, the price on the world market falls from P_2 to P_5 (P_5 is the price at which the gap between the RoW supply and demand curves for sugar is exactly equal to the quota, q_q). This benefits consumers in other countries, but harms producers, and, in particular, sugar-producing countries. Ironically, many of the countries that produce sugar are less-developed countries, such as the Philippines and Haiti, that U.S. policymakers generally try to help. Moreover, the effects are substantial, as is suggested by the fact that in some years, the U.S. price has been more than five times the world market price!

The effects of the import quota do not stop with the sugar market. For example, with the domestic price of sugar so far above world levels, importing food products with high sugar content has become profitable because these foods can be produced more cheaply abroad using sugar purchased on the world market. Because this reduces domestic sugar purchases and puts downward pressure on the price of sugar in the United States, political pressure to apply import restrictions on imported goods that contain sugar has arisen. In 1985, import quotas were placed on a number of these goods, such as cake and pancake mixes.

Beyond imports, other market forces in the form of substitutes are at work, making maintenance of the price so far above competitive levels increasingly difficult. For example, production of a major substitute for sugar called high-fructose corn syrup (HFCS) has increased enormously, and this product has replaced sugar in many uses. (Today, HFCS is the major sweetening ingredient in soft drinks; 15 years ago sugar played this role.) Because HFCS is made from corn, corn producers have benefited from the import quota. As a consequence, we now see grain growers from the cornbelt lobbying alongside sugar growers from the South for preserving the quota.

The tremendous disparity between sugar prices in the United States and the rest of the world also creates some unusual attempts to evade the import quotas. According to the Department of Agriculture, some companies make money by importing products such as iced tea mix, separating out the sugar once the mix has safely crossed the U.S. border, and throwing away the remainder of the product. The sugar can then be sold at a cost to buyers still lower than if it had been purchased directly from a domestic producer.

The varied methods foreign producers employ in attempting to nullify the effects of U.S. import quotas are not peculiar to the case of sugar. For example, confronting limits on the number of computer chips they can sell in the U.S. market, foreign manufacturers get their chips into the United States in an indirect fashion. They install them onto personal computers and then export the personal computers to the United States. In response to limits on U.S. textile imports from Hong Kong, manufacturers there may move their production facilities to Indonesia. Faced with constraints on the number of immigrants that the United States will accept from Poland in any year, prospective Polish immigrants to the United States may first move to Canada or Italy, countries upon which the United States places less restrictive immigration quotas. And, under the "voluntary export restraints" on automobiles negotiated by the U.S. and Japanese governments, Japanese car producers have responded to the limit of 1.85 million cars that can be shipped to the U.S. market per year in a number of creative ways, including moving some of their production to the United States; tilting their product mix toward more luxurious car models such as Lexus and Acura that have higher per-unit profit margins; making standard previously optional features such as air conditioning, and adding the fee for the features into the base sticker price; and calling certain sport-utility vehicles such as the Suzuki Samurai and Isuzu Trooper "trucks," thereby avoiding the export restraint on "cars."

APPLICATION 10.7 — EVADING QUANTITY RESTRICTIONS: VIRGIN ATLANTIC'S INTEREST IN THE AIRBUS A380

Airbus Industries has been exploring the possibility of building a record-size passenger plane. Airbus calls the proposed plane A380. The behemoth jetliner would be a four-engine, double-deck jumbo seating up to 656 passengers—a capacity nearly 60 percent greater than rival manufacturer Boeing's most popular 747 model. Among the airlines expressing some interest in placing an order for the A380 is Virgin Atlantic. Virgin faces limits on the number of flights it can operate out of London's Heathrow and Gatwick airports to the United States. Although the quantity controls focus on the number of flights that Virgin can schedule on these lucrative routes, there is no limit on the number of seats per flight. The A380 thus could give Virgin an important means of evading the quantity restrictions it currently faces and fly more passengers on the popular transAtlantic routes.

SUMMARY

- A broad range of applications shows that while government intervention may be justified on the grounds of helping people, its effects may be precisely counter to the objectives of those favoring the intervention.
- Producer surplus, analogous to consumer surplus, is a gain that producers can realize from the sale of output to consumers when the price exceeds the minimum amount necessary to compensate the seller. In general, producer surplus will accrue to some of the owners of inputs that have upward-sloping supply curves to the industry.
- Total surplus is the total net gain to those who participate in a market—that is, the sum of consumer surplus and producer surplus.
- Price ceilings result in a deadweight loss, or welfare cost, which is the aggregate loss in well-being of all participants in a market.
- Excise taxes produce different effects in the short run and in the long run. In the short run, all firms incur a loss and have an incentive to cut output, increasing price. In the long run, some firms will exit the industry, output will drop further, and the final price to consumers will be higher than in the short run. In an increasing-cost industry, consumers and certain input owners will bear the burden of the tax.
- For a given supply curve and per-unit excise tax, the more inelastic the demand curve, the greater the tax burden on consumers, the smaller the tax burden on producers, and the smaller the reduction in output.
- In the case of a perfectly elastic supply curve, the constant-cost case, the price to consumers rises by the amount of the tax per unit, regardless of the elasticity of the demand curve.
- Because an excise tax results in an output lower than in an unfettered competitive market, it produces a deadweight loss by restricting output to a level where the product's marginal benefit exceeds the marginal cost of production.
- During the period in which the U.S. airline industry was regulated, the Civil Aeronautics Board (CAB) imposed, in effect, a price floor that kept price above the competitive level. Since suppliers could not compete on the basis of price, nonprice competition was waged, increasing costs and reducing profit despite high prices.
- Airline deregulation has resulted in lower ticket prices, a major restructuring of the airline industry, and lower costs for the firms that remain.
- In most major U.S. cities the supply of cabs is limited by an entry restriction in the form of a fixed number of city-issued licenses, or medallions, making the supply curve of passenger-miles fixed and vertical. As demand increases, prices rise. In many cities licensing and other forms of entry restriction such as maximum fares (a form of price ceiling) give rise to illegal markets in transportation services.
- The supply–demand model shows that international trade is beneficial to the United States as a whole, although in some situations individual producers or consumers may lose.
- Imports and exports are fundamentally linked in that the dollars that foreigners earn on U.S. imports must ultimately be employed to purchase U.S. goods.

• Governments may control quantity as well as price. Quantity is controlled by quotas and other legislation, whose economic effects are sometimes contrary to the intentions of policymakers. Restrictions on sugar imports, for instance, impose a deadweight loss in that the gains to domestic sugar producers are outweighed by the cost to consumers caused by the significantly higher cost of domestic sugar.

 ## REVIEW QUESTIONS AND PROBLEMS

Questions and problems marked with an asterisk have solutions given in Answers to Selected Problems at the back of the book (page 575).

10.1. What is producer surplus? What is consumer surplus? What is total surplus? Explain how each is shown in a supply and demand graph.

10.2. What is the relationship between the efficient level of output of a good and the size of total surplus achieved? Is total surplus greater if the output of the good is greater than the competitive output?

10.3. Define deadweight loss. How is it related to the concept of total surplus?

10.4. Using long-run supply and demand curves, analyze the effects of an ad valorem excise tax equal to 20 percent of the market (selling) price of gasoline. How do the effects differ from those of the per-unit excise tax discussed in the text?

*10.5. Suppose that the gasoline market is competitive and that the government grants a subsidy to the industry's firms of 20 cents per gallon. How will the subsidy affect price; output; and consumer, producer, government, and total surplus? Is there a deadweight loss associated with the subsidy? Does the price to consumers fall by more if the industry is increasing-cost or constant-cost? (*Hint:* This situation is the reverse of the excise tax analysis—the supply curve shifts down in height by 20 cents per gallon.)

10.6. Why is it not inconsistent to say that airline fares, as regulated by the CAB, were above the competitive level, and yet airlines did not realize economic profits?

10.7. The airlines generally favored CAB regulation and were opposed to fares being determined in open markets. Since airline profits apparently were not unusually high when the CAB regulated the industry, what reasons could account for this support?

*10.8. Suppose that New York City policymakers deregulate the taxicab market and, to avoid great harm to medallion owners, buy up outstanding medallions at the prevailing market price. Is this policy preferable to simply deregulating the market without buying up the medallions? In your answer, identify who would be harmed by the two alternative methods of deregulation.

10.9. How would each of the following affect the operation of a regulated taxi market and the price of a medallion?

a. A reduction in the maximum fare cabs can charge
b. An increase in the fares on subways and buses
c. An increase in parking fees in the downtown area
d. A police crackdown on the operation of illegal taxis
e. Announcement that the market will be deregulated in five years

10.10. Suppose that the gasoline industry is competitive and constant-cost. Suppose also that, due to an unexpected increase in demand, the industry's firms are making short-run economic profits. Using graphs, depict what would happen in the short and the long run if the government imposed a 50 percent "windfall profits tax" on the economic profits being earned by the industry's firms.

10.11. In the market for organs for transplant, such as kidneys and hearts, the price is constrained to equal zero. Opposition to any type of remuneration for donating organs has been all but absolute from physicians and legislators. Reliance on altruism, however, does not appear to be working. The number of people waiting for organ transplants (and dying if they do not receive them) is double the number of willing donors. Relying on graphs, explain the effect of the proscription of financial incentives for organ donations on the producer surplus and consumer surplus in this market.

10.12. Suppose that the low-skill job market is perfectly competitive and that the equilibrium wage and monthly output prevailing in the market absent government interference are $4.50 per hour and 1,000,000 hours, respectively. Assume that the demand and supply elasticity equal two and one, respectively. If the federal government mandates a minimum wage of $5.25 per hour, explain what happens to producer, consumer, and total surplus. Is there a deadweight loss associated with the minimum wage?

10.13. If all else is the same as in problem 10.12 but the demand elasticity equals zero, what is the effect of the minimum wage on producer, consumer, and total surplus? Is there a deadweight loss?

10.14. "Consumers understandably like lower prices, but they should understand there is a great difference between a lower price produced by a government price ceiling and a lower price that comes about through normal market channels; one benefits the consumer, the other may not." How does our analysis of rent control relate to this pronouncement?

10.15. Using a pair of graphs like Figure 10.10, illustrate a situation in which the United States would be an exporter of the good in question, and identify the equilibrium.

10.16. In the situation shown in Figure 10.10, assume that $P_3 - P_1$ equals 10 cents per pound, and that the cost of transporting sugar from the RoW to the United States is equal to 1 cent per pound. Explain the determination of equilibrium in this case.

10.17. If bad weather causes the supply of sugar in the RoW to fall, how will this affect the U.S. market if the import quota described by Figure 10.12 is in place? Does this explain why the U.S. and world prices can differ greatly from year to year?

10.18. Using Figure 10.12, show the effect on consumer and producer surplus of the sugar import quota (relative to free trade). Also show the changes in consumer and producer surplus in the RoW.

10.19. Suppose that sugar imports are completely prohibited by the U.S. government in Figure 10.12. What will be the new equilibrium in the United States and the RoW? Show the effect on consumer and producer surplus of the prohibition on imports (relative to free trade). Also show the changes in consumer and producer surplus in the RoW.

10.20. Mexico is a producer and exporter of crude oil. Since Mexico is a relatively small crude-oil-producing country, its actions do not affect world prices; as an exporter, Mexico faces a foreign demand curve that is perfectly elastic at a price of $15 per barrel. The equation for the domestic demand curve is $Q_d = 26 - P$ where price (P) is measured in dollars per barrel and quantity demanded (Q_d) is measured in billions of barrels per year. The equation for the domestic supply curve is $Q_s = 10 + P$ where quantity supplied (Q_s) is measured in billions of barrels per year.

a. Assuming free trade, show graphically how much crude oil will be produced, consumed, and exported by Mexico.
b. Graphically, show the gains from trade. Explain who wins and who loses, and show by how much in terms of producer and consumer surplus. Does everyone in Mexico benefit from free trade? Explain why or why not. Is Mexico as a whole better off? Explain.
c. Suppose that the Mexican government provides a $2 per-barrel subsidy for every barrel of Mexican crude oil bought by foreigners. Graphically, show the effects of the subsidy on domestic production; domestic consumption; exports; and the welfare of producers, consumers, the government, and Mexico as a whole.

10.21. If output is at an inefficient level, does it imply that consumer surplus is smaller than at the competitive output? Does it imply that producer surplus is smaller than at the competitive output?

10.22. Explain how an excise tax levied on a constant-cost industry produces a deadweight loss. Use a graph to show the loss in consumer and producer surplus from the excise tax. Is the loss in total surplus the same as the deadweight loss? If not, show the deadweight loss in the graph and explain the meaning of the remainder of the loss in total surplus.

10.23. States do not currently collect sales taxes on consumer purchases on the Internet. Who, consumers or suppliers, benefits from the absence of such taxes? Explain.

10.24. Most experts believe that electronic commerce cannot explain the low rate of price inflation in the United States. These experts point to the fact that online retail sales account for less than 1 percent of total retail sales as of 2000. Using the trade model we developed in this chapter, explain the basis for the experts' conclusion that electronic commerce cannot be exercising a significant amount of downward pressure on the prices of most goods.

CHAPTER 11

Monopoly

What price and output should a firm with some monopoly power select?

Chapter Outline

11.1 The Monopolist's Demand and Marginal Revenue Curves

11.2 Profit-Maximizing Output of a Monopoly

Graphical Analysis   *The Monopoly Price and Its Relationship to Elasticity of Demand*

Application 11.1 Demand Elasticity and Home Video Prices

11.3 Further Implications of Monopoly Analysis

Application 11.2 Life Is Not Always a Box of Chocolates

11.4 The Measurement and Sources of Monopoly Power

Measuring Monopoly Power   *The Sources of Monopoly Power*   *Barriers to Entry*

Application 11.3 Regulatory Barriers in the Philippines

Strategic Behavior by Firms: Incumbents and Potential Entrants

11.5 The Efficiency Effects of Monopoly

A Dynamic View of Monopoly and Its Efficiency Implications

Application 11.4 The Dynamics of Developing an AIDS Vaccine

11.6 Public Policy Toward Monopoly

Application 11.5 What Not to Say to a Rival on the Telephone

Application 11.6 Static versus Dynamic View of Monopoly and the Microsoft Antitrust Case

Regulation of Price

Learning Objectives

- Define monopoly and show what a monopolist's demand and marginal revenue curves look like.
- Explain why a monopolist's profit-maximizing output is where marginal revenue equals marginal cost.
- Describe why the extent to which a monopolist's price exceeds marginal cost is larger the more inelastic the demand faced by the monopolist.
- Understand why the shutdown condition applies to monopolies as well as to firms operating in a perfectly competitive market.
- Outline the potential sources of monopoly power: absolute cost advantages; economies of scale; product differentiation; and regulatory barriers.
- Explore the efficiency effects of monopoly from a static as well as a dynamic perspective.
- Overview public policy toward monopoly.

MONOPOLY
a market with a single seller

In perfect competition, firms are price takers. In other words, firms are numerous enough to ensure that no single seller affects the market price.

Monopoly is the polar opposite of perfect competition in that it describes a market with a single seller. A monopoly firm faces the market demand curve for its product because it is the sole seller of the product. Since it faces the market demand curve, the monopoly firm has control over the market price: It can choose any price–quantity combination on the market demand curve.

What price and output level should a profit-maximizing monopoly firm select? We will see that, relative to perfect competition, monopoly results in a higher price and a lower quantity. This has efficiency implications, and we discuss why it is illegal in the United States to monopolize a market.

Although pure monopoly is rare, markets where a small number of firms compete with one another are common. Chapters 13 and 14 more fully explore the strategic interactions between firms in such markets. In general, however, the firms may have some **monopoly power**: some control over price, some ability to set price above marginal cost. This chapter discusses the determinants of monopoly power, how to measure it, and its implications for product pricing.

MONOPOLY POWER
some ability to set price above marginal cost

11.1 THE MONOPOLIST'S DEMAND AND MARGINAL REVENUE CURVES[1]

A monopoly faces the market demand curve for its product because it is, by definition, the only seller of the product. Thus, a monopoly's demand curve slopes downward. This contrasts sharply with the horizontal demand curve faced by a competitive firm. While a competitive firm is a price taker, a monopoly is a **price maker**. A monopoly supplies the total market and can choose any price along the market demand curve it wants. Since the monopoly faces a downward-sloping demand curve, if it raises price, the amount it sells will fall. Much of the analysis of monopoly and the difference in output and price between a monopoly and a competitive industry stems from this difference in the demand curves.

Let's consider the co-stars of *Friends*, the most popular sitcom on television in recent years. Let's assume that the *Friends* co-stars face the demand curve depicted in Figure 11.1, are interested in maximizing profit, and must charge the same price for each new show produced per month. According to the last assumption, while the *Friends* co-stars can operate on any price-quantity point along the demand curve they face, once they select a price they must charge that same price for all shows sold.[2]

Under these assumptions, what price should the *Friends* co-stars choose? Is it better to select a very high price, produce little, but make a killing from each unit sold? For instance, if only one show is produced the *Friends* co-stars make $1 million per show. Or is it advisable to select a lower price and sell more shows, even though the price one can charge declines with output? The price the *Friends* co-stars obtain is only $400,000 if they supply seven shows.

In making its price and output decision, any profit-oriented firm will be concerned with the relationship between output and total revenue. Will more output increase total revenue and, if so, by how much? Recall that marginal revenue equals the change in total revenue associated with a one-unit change in output. Marginal revenue thus indicates how an output change affects total revenue. Understanding the significance of marginal revenue for a firm's output decision and the way marginal revenue is related to the firm's demand curve is central to analyzing monopoly and other noncompetitive market structures.

PRICE MAKER
a monopoly that supplies the total market and can choose any price along the market demand curve that it wants

---

[1]A mathematical treatment of some of the material in this section is given in the appendix at the back of the book (page 568).

[2]We leave to Chapter 12 the topic of price discrimination and what happens when a monopoly firm can charge different prices for the various units of output that it sells.

For a competitive firm facing a horizontal demand curve, marginal revenue is equal to the product's price (average revenue). With a downward-sloping demand curve, the situation is different: marginal revenue is always less than price. Figure 11.1 shows why. When price is $800,000, the *Friends* co-stars can sell three shows, and total revenue equals rectangle *PEQ0*, or $2,400,000. To sell four shows, the *Friends* co-stars must reduce their price to $700,000 since the demand curve slopes downward. Total revenue for 4 units sold is *P'E'Q'0*, or $2,800,000. Note how total revenue changes when output increases from three to four shows. The rectangular measure of total revenue decreases by area *A*: This area indicates how much revenue is lost on the first three shows when they are sold for $700,000 instead of $800,000 (area *A* equals $300,000). The rectangular measure of total revenue, however, also increases by area *B*—the amount added to total revenue from selling the fourth show for $700,000. Area *B* is equal to the new price the *Friends* co-stars have chosen, $700,000. When four shows are sold instead of three, total revenue rises by area *B* (the price received for the fourth show) minus area *A* (the reduced revenue from selling the first three shows at a lower price), or by $700,000 minus $300,000, or $400,000. The increase in total revenue is marginal revenue, and it is less than the price (area *B*) because the price of the first three shows must be reduced to sell four shows. This reasoning applies to any downward-sloping demand curve and shows why *marginal revenue is always less than price when the demand curve slopes downward*, except for the first unit sold.[3]

FIGURE 11.1

The Monopolist's (*Friends* co-stars) Demand Curve

The *Friends* co-stars confront a downward-sloping demand curve. Price exceeds marginal revenue with a downward-sloping demand curve. If price falls from $800,000 to $700,000, total revenue changes by area *B* (the price at which the fourth unit is sold) minus area *A*.

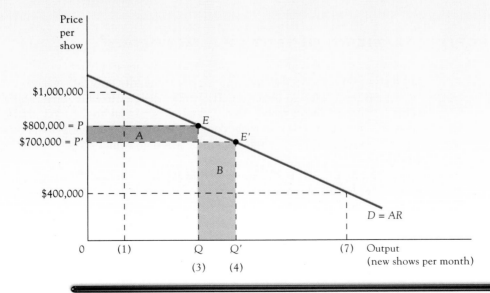

---

[3]In Table 11.1, where we assume that output can be produced only in whole units, marginal revenue equals price at an output of one. If we allow for output to be produced in ever-smaller and less than whole units, the marginal revenue and demand curves have the same height only at their intercepts on the vertical axis.

TABLE 11.1	DEMAND AND TOTAL, MARGINAL, AND AVERAGE REVENUES				
P	**Q**	**TR**	**MR**	**AR**
$1,100,000	0	$0	—	—
1,000,000	1	1,000,000	$1,000,000	$1,000,000
900,000	2	1,800,000	800,000	900,000
800,000	3	2,400,000	600,000	800,000
700,000	4	2,800,000	400,000	700,000
600,000	5	3,000,000	200,000	600,000
500,000	6	3,000,000	0	500,000
400,000	7	2,800,000	−200,000	400,000

Another way to see the relationship between price and marginal revenue is to recall that the demand curve is the same as the average revenue curve. If four shows are sold for $700,000 each, the average revenue per show is the same as the price. Viewed this way, the demand curve is a declining average revenue curve, and whenever the average is falling, the marginal curve associated with it must lie below the average.

Marginal revenue is not a fixed amount but varies with the quantity sold. Table 11.1 illustrates a hypothetical relationship between the *Friends* co-stars' demand schedule and total revenue (TR), marginal revenue (MR), and average revenue (AR). The first two columns reflect the assumption of a downward-sloping demand curve, with quantity sold (Q) rising as price (P) declines. $MR = P = AR$ for the first show sold, but for all other outputs price exceeds marginal revenue. When output rises from 1 to 2, for example, total revenue rises from $1,000,000 to $1,800,000. So MR for the second show is $800,000, but P is $900,000, according to the demand curve.

11.2 PROFIT-MAXIMIZING OUTPUT OF A MONOPOLY[4]

Demand and cost conditions jointly determine the most profitable output for a monopoly, just as they do for a competitive firm. Analytically, the only difference is that a monopoly faces a downward-sloping demand curve while a competitive firm faces a horizontal demand curve. Although the demand curve's slope depends on the market setting, the output-decision rule maximizing firm profit does not. In other words, both competitive and monopoly firms maximize profit by setting output where marginal revenue (MR) equals marginal cost (MC).

To see why the $MR = MC$ decision rule applies to monopolies as well as to competitive firms, consider the demand and cost data for a monopoly firm shown in Table 11.2. We know the firm is a monopoly from the demand data in the first two columns. These columns show that price must be lowered to sell more output, indicating that the firm's demand curve slopes downward. Multiplying price times quantity for each output yields total revenue, as shown in column (3). Column (4) identifies the long-run total cost (TC) of producing each output. Since profit (π) is the difference between total revenue and total cost, the firm selects the output where total revenue exceeds total cost by the largest possi-

---

[4]A mathematical treatment of some of the material in this section is given in the appendix at the back of the book (page 569).

TABLE 11.2

PROFIT MAXIMIZATION BY A MONOPOLIST (IN DOLLARS)

P	Q	TR	TC	π	AR	AC	MR	MC	
(1)	(2)	(3)	(4)	(5)	(6)	(7)	(8)	(9)	
10.20	0	0	0	0	—	—	—	—	
10.00	1	10.00	8.00	2.00	10.00	8.00	10.00	8.00 ⎫	
9.80	2	19.60	15.00	4.60	9.80	7.50	9.60	7.00	
9.60	3	28.80	21.00	7.80	9.60	7.00	9.20	6.00 ⎬ MR > MC	
9.40	4	37.60	27.50	10.10	9.40	6.88	8.80	6.50	
9.20	5	46.00	34.50	11.50	9.20	6.90	8.40	7.00	
9.00	6	54.00	41.80	12.20	9.00	6.97	8.00	7.30 ⎭	
8.80	7	61.60	49.39	12.21	8.80	7.056	7.60	7.59	MR ≈ MC
8.60	8	68.80	57.00	11.80	8.60	7.13	7.20	7.61 ⎫	
8.40	9	75.60	65.00	10.60	8.40	7.22	6.80	8.00 ⎬ MR < MC	
8.20	10	82.00	74.00	8.00	8.20	7.40	6.40	9.00 ⎭	

ble amount. This occurs at an output of 7 and a price of $8.80. At that output, profit is $12.21 and $MR \approx MC$.

To see that profit is maximized where $MR = MC$, note that marginal revenue exceeds marginal cost at output levels less than 7 units, indicating that the firm can increase profit by expanding output, but to do so, it must lower price. For example, the marginal revenue from selling the fourth unit ($8.80) exceeds the marginal cost ($6.50). Thus, profit will be $2.30 higher if the firm expands output from 3 to 4 units, as shown in the fifth column. At output levels greater than 7 units, marginal cost exceeds marginal revenue, and the firm can increase profit by reducing output and raising its price. For example, the marginal revenue from selling the tenth unit is $6.40, but the marginal cost of producing it is $9.00. Profit will be $2.60 higher if the firm reduces output from 10 to 9 units; that is, cost will fall by $2.60 more than revenue.

Graphical Analysis

Figure 11.2 depicts the profit-maximizing output for a monopoly. Panel (a) shows the monopoly's total revenue and total cost curves. Profit is maximized at the output where TR exceeds TC by the largest possible amount. In the figure, the profit-maximizing output is Q_1 (7 units in Table 11.2), where total revenue is AQ_1 ($61.60) and total cost is BQ_1 ($49.39). Total profit is shown by the distance AB ($12.21). Profit is smaller at every other output. Marginal cost and marginal revenue at output Q_1 are shown by the slopes of the TC and TR curves. Marginal cost is the slope of TC at point B (the slope of the line bb), and marginal revenue is the slope of TR at point A (the slope of the line aa). The slopes of the curves at these points are equal to one another since the most profitable output occurs where $MR = MC$.

Figure 11.2b depicts the most profitable output by using the per-unit cost and revenue curves. Because this approach is the more useful one—and the one we will use from now on in the text—we devote more attention to it. It is important to recognize, however, that the total and per-unit curve approaches are equivalent ways of looking at the same problem.

Figure 11.2b shows the monopolist's demand (average revenue) curve and the associated marginal revenue curve. As discussed in the previous section, for a negatively-sloped demand curve, marginal revenue is less than price at all output levels.

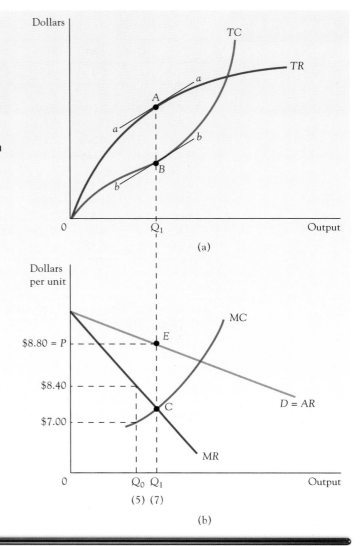

FIGURE 11.2

Profit Maximization: Total and Per-Unit Curves
(a) Profit is maximized when total revenue exceeds total cost by the largest amount possible. Maximum profit occurs at output Q_1, where the slopes of *TR* and *TC* (*MR* and *MC*) are equal. (b) The per-unit revenue and cost curves illustrate the same situation shown in part (a).

The monopolist's profit-maximizing output, Q_1 (7 units) in Figure 11.2b, is identified by the intersection of the *MR* and *MC* curves, at point C. The price charged by the monopolist ($8.80 based on the Table 11.2 data) is shown by point *E* on the demand curve. At any other output marginal revenue is not equal to marginal cost, and profit is lower. For example, at output Q_0 (5 units) marginal revenue is $8.40 and marginal cost is $7.00. Selling an additional unit of output thus adds more to revenue ($8.40) than to cost ($7.00), and profit will increase. At any output where marginal revenue exceeds marginal cost, the firm can increase profit by expanding output. So, in Figure 11.2b, output should be increased up to the point where the falling *MR* curve meets the rising *MC* curve, at point C.

Figure 11.2b identifies the most profitable output, but it does not show exactly how much profit is realized. To show the amount of profit explicitly, we must draw in the average cost

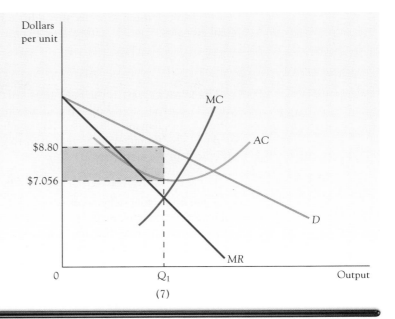

FIGURE 11.3

Profit Maximization
Total profit, the shaded area, is maximized at Q_1 where $MC = MR$.

(AC) curve. We do so in Figure 11.3. The most profitable output is, once more, Q_1, with a price of $8.80 charged. The difference between average revenue ($8.80) and average cost ($7.056) at Q_1 is the average profit per unit—in this case $1.744. Multiplying the average profit by the output, Q_1 (7 units), gives total profit ($12.21), shown in the diagram by the shaded area.

We have been implicitly using long-run cost curves, as shown by the fact that there are no fixed costs. But the same graphical analysis applies when we use short-run cost curves. As in the competitive case, a short-run analysis is appropriate when an unexpected or temporary change occurs in market conditions.

The Monopoly Price and Its Relationship to Elasticity of Demand

Our analysis of monopoly has shown that to maximize profit, output should be at the level where marginal revenue equals marginal cost, with price set above marginal cost as indicated by the demand curve. Suppose that you are a monopolist. How would you put this analysis to use in identifying the profit-maximizing price and output? It is plausible that you would know your marginal cost of production, but how do you find out what the demand curve for your product (and, hence, the marginal revenue curve) looks like? If you were operating in a competitive market, you would have no problem—you could simply observe the price charged by your competitors and recognize that you could sell all you want at that price. As a monopoly, however, you have no competitors and lack this source of information.

One way to proceed is to use your judgment and set a price, then observe the results. You could then experiment with raising and lowering the price, and through trial and error zero in on the profit-maximizing price. Obviously, you would make mistakes, and the mistakes could cost you a lot of money (in the form of sacrificed profit). Thus, you would like to find a way to more quickly arrive at the profit-maximizing price, and economic analysis suggests one such mechanism. Specifically, a little bit of algebra shows that if you know your marginal cost (MC) and demand elasticity (η), you should set price (P) such that:[5]

$$\frac{(P - MC)}{P} = \frac{1}{\eta}.$$

The left-hand side is the markup of price over marginal cost expressed as a percentage of price. This expression shows that to maximize profit, the price markup should equal the inverse of the demand elasticity. The smaller the demand elasticity, the greater the price markup. The formula can be rewritten to give price directly as a function of marginal cost and the demand elasticity:

$$P = MC/[1 - (1/\eta)].$$

If you know your demand elasticity and marginal cost, this expression can be used to calculate the profit-maximizing price.[6] For example, take the case of the only seller of gasoline on a particular corner of a major intersection; the seller is a monopolist due to the station's location. Suppose also that the station is located far from the airport (the importance of this assumption will be apparent shortly), marginal cost is \$1 per gallon, and the station's demand elasticity is 20 (a fairly high number due to the nearby presence of other stations) and is constant over all ranges of the demand curve.[7] Based on the inverse elasticity pricing formula, the station should charge a price equal to \$1/[1 − (1/20)] = \$1/(19/20) = \$(20/19) ≈ \$1.05. With a demand elasticity of 20, in other words, the profit-maximizing price-marginal cost markup is 5 percent.

Why do gas stations located near airports often charge more for gasoline than others who are not? Our inverse elasticity pricing rule suggests an answer. To avoid the hefty refueling charges levied by rental car companies on vehicles returned with a near-empty gas tank (almost double the going price) and because they may have little time to shop around before catching their flight, renters are willing to pay more per gallon if they haven't filled up prior to reaching the airport. These stations thus hold more monopoly power than do non-airport

---

[5]Refer to Figure 11.1 and note that the change in total revenue (ΔTR) associated with a change in quantity sold (ΔQ) is equal to area B minus area A. Area B equals $P (\Delta Q)$ and area A equals $Q(\Delta P)$. Thus:

$$\Delta TR = P(\Delta Q) - Q(\Delta P). \tag{1}$$

Since $\Delta TR/\Delta Q$ is marginal revenue, dividing (1) by ΔQ yields:

$$MR = P - (\Delta P/\Delta Q)Q. \tag{2}$$

Since the elasticity of demand η equals (when it is expressed as a positive number) $-(\Delta Q/Q)/(\Delta P/P)$, $\Delta P/\Delta Q$ equals $(-1/\eta)(P/Q)$. Substituting $(-1/\eta)(P/Q)$ for $\Delta P/\Delta Q$ in equation (2) produces:

$$MR = P + Q[(-1/\eta)(P/Q)] = P - (P/\eta) = P[1 - (1/\eta)]. \tag{3}$$

At the profit-maximizing output, MC = MR, so:

$$MC = P[1 - (1/\eta)]. \tag{4}$$

Subtracting P from both sides of equation (4) and then multiplying through by $-(1/P)$ yields:

$$(P - MC)/P = 1/\eta. \tag{5}$$

[6]The formula has one difficulty: it holds exactly only at the point of profit maximization, and because marginal cost and elasticity may vary with output, you may need to use this expression repeatedly to locate the profit-maximizing price. However, if marginal cost and elasticity vary only a little over the range of output you are considering, this formula can approximate the profit-maximizing price quite closely.

[7]Demand curves with a constant elasticity have the nonlinear, convex shape depicted in Figure 11.4. As explained in Section 11.3, the elasticity varies along a linear demand curve.

stations. The average consumer at an airport gas station is less price sensitive and the demand elasticity facing the typical airport gas station is smaller.

Say that because car renters are less price sensitive and account for a significant portion of airport gas station business, the typical airport gas station has a demand elasticity of 3. According to our inverse elasticity pricing rule, and with a marginal cost of $1 per gallon, the airport station's profit-maximizing price is $1/[1 − (1/3)] = $1/(2/3) = $(3/2) = $1.50. The airport station's price-marginal cost markup is thus 50 percent, 10 times greater than for the non-airport gas station examined earlier facing the same marginal cost but having a higher demand elasticity of 20.

Figure 11.4 illustrates MC, D, and MR curves for the airport and non-airport gas stations that we have just described. Since the non-airport station faces a more elastic demand, its price-marginal cost markup is lower than that of the airport station. In the limiting case, if the demand for non-airport stations was infinitely elastic (instead of equal to 20, as we have assumed), the inverse elasticity pricing formula shows that price equals marginal cost, a conclusion familiar from our analysis of perfectly competitive markets. This is shown in Figure 11.4 through the $D_{pc} = MR_{pc}$ curves. If the elasticity of a firm's demand curve is infinity, the price–marginal cost markup equals zero.

In sum, if you know your marginal cost, the only other thing you need to know is the demand elasticity to determine what price to charge. How can you determine the demand elasticity? One way is to estimate it statistically, as outlined in Chapter 4. Data from surveys or market experiments offer alternative methods. The important point is that you don't need to know the entire demand curve for your product; you need to know just how quantity demanded varies relative to price as summarized by the demand elasticity.

FIGURE 11.4

The Inverse Elasticity Pricing Rule
The more elastic demand is at the profit-maximizing output, the smaller the markup of price over marginal cost.

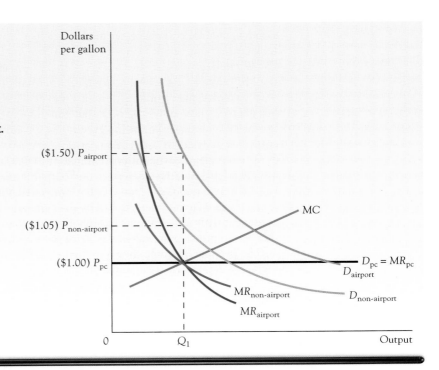

The price at which home videos are sold has been declining steadily over time but still varies across titles and studios. For example, Disney has maintained among the highest prices in the industry and has been reluctant to reduce the price of its home videos much below $19.[8] The thinking behind Disney's strategy appears to be the inverse elasticity pricing rule that we

have just outlined. The internal studies conducted by Disney indicate that consumer demand for its videos is more inelastic than the demand for other studios' films. Disney is the only brand in home videos that customers ask for by name. The Disney reputation for high-quality family entertainment has made its videos the top-selling products in the industry. As of 1993, the average U.S. household owned 29 videos, 14 of them Disney products. Because the demand for Disney videos is less elastic than for the videos produced by other studios, profit maximization dictates a higher price–marginal cost markup.

[8]This application draws on Louis Ashmallah, Sachiko Nagashima, Christopher Pating, Jose Sousa, Liz Steblay, and Michael Zabel, "Buena Vista Home Video," Integrative Competitive Strategy Project, USC MBA Program, November 15, 1993.

11.3 FURTHER IMPLICATIONS OF MONOPOLY ANALYSIS[9]

In this section we extend our discussion of monopoly to clarify several less obvious points:

1. We are so accustomed to analyzing markets in supply and demand terms that it is tempting to apply the same reasoning to a monopoly, but doing so can lead to mistakes. For example, if demand for a monopolist's product rises and the monopolist has an upward-sloping marginal cost curve, we might anticipate that both output and price will rise. Take a look again, however, at Figure 11.4. With demand $D_{\text{non-airport}}$, price is $P_{\text{non-airport}}$, and output is Q_1. When demand increases to D_{airport}, the new marginal revenue curve MR_{airport} intersects the MC curve at the original output. Output remains at Q_1, but price rises to P_{airport}.

To guard against thinking of supply and demand (appropriate for a competitive model but not for a monopoly), we note that a monopoly has no supply curve. A supply curve delineates the unique relationship between price and quantity supplied when firms have no control over price. In perfect competition, where firms are price takers, demand shifts trace out the unique price–quantity combinations (that is, the supply curve). There is no such unique relationship between price and output in monopoly because the output and price selected by a monopolist depend on both marginal cost and demand (the monopolist's marginal revenue curve is determined by the demand curve). A rise in demand can consequently lead to an increase in both price and quantity, an increase in quantity but no increase in price, or an increase in price but no increase in quantity (as in Figure 11.4).

The peculiar outcome shown in Figure 11.4 is not the typical response of a monopoly to increased demand. Instead, it occurs because the higher demand curve is much less elastic at the initial quantity. As a general proposition, we suspect that monopolies find it profitable to expand output when demand increases. For example, if the demand curve shifts outward parallel to the original curve, or if it rotates about the price axis, output will rise, as will price, so long as the marginal cost curve slopes upward.

[9]A mathematical treatment of some of the material in this section is given in the appendix at the back of the book (page 568).

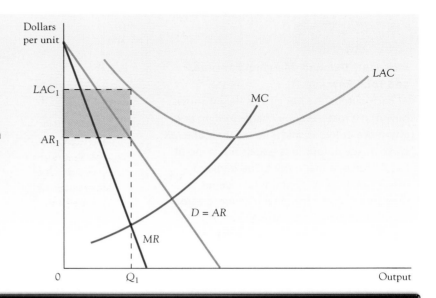

FIGURE 11.5

Monopoly and the Shutdown Condition

The shutdown condition applies to monopolies, just as it does to competitive firms. If *LAC* is greater than *AR* at the output, Q_1, where *MR* equals *MC*, zero is the most profitable output.

2. Monopolies are usually thought of as making huge profits, but in fact, they may not make a profit at all. A monopoly can always charge a price above cost, but it cannot force consumers to purchase at that price. The position of the demand curve ultimately limits its money-making ability. If the long-run average cost curve lies entirely above the demand curve, as depicted in Figure 11.5, any output the firm produces will have to be sold at a loss. Since average total cost lies above average revenue (that is, $LAC_1 > AR_1$) at the output (Q_1) where MR equals MC, the monopoly depicted in Figure 11.5 will do better to produce nothing in the long run. Just as in perfect competition, shutting down may be the best option.

Each year thousands of monopolists find out that monopoly power does not guarantee profits. This group includes those who receive patents on their inventions. Many items granted patents—which give the inventor the exclusive right to sell the product—are never marketed at all because businesses believe that potential customers will not pay enough to cover the production cost. For example, the following items have been given patents and not proven marketable: a chewing gum preserver, a safety coffin (with an escape tunnel and alarm so that people mistakenly buried alive can "on recovery of consciousness, ascend . . . or ring the bell [thus averting] premature death"), and goggles for chickens (to keep them from pecking one another in order to establish flock hierarchy, a pecking order).[10]

3. A monopoly's demand curve is elastic where marginal revenue is positive. An elastic demand curve means that a decrease in price and the associated increase in output will increase total revenue (total revenue moves in the same direction as output and in the opposite direction as price when demand is elastic) and when marginal revenue is greater than zero, total revenue, by definition increases as output rises. In Figure 11.6, the demand elasticity (η) exceeds unity along the upper portion of the straight-line demand curve (between the outputs of zero and Q_{trmax}) because marginal revenue is positive over this range. When marginal revenue is zero (at Q_{trmax}), total revenue remains constant when an additional unit is sold so demand is unit elastic (the effects of the decrease in price and the associated increase in output on total revenue exactly offset one another in the case where demand is unit elastic and total revenue thus remains unchanged as output increases).

[10]A. E. Brown and H. A. Jeffcott, Jr., *Absolutely Mad Inventions* (New York: Dover, 1960).

FIGURE 11.6

Monopoly Demand, Marginal Revenue, and Total Revenue

At each output, the *MR* curve's height shows how much total revenue changes when one unit more or less is sold. The height of the *MR* curve at any output thus equals the slope of the *TR* curve at that output. The demand elasticity equals unity and total revenue is maximized where marginal revenue is zero. The total-revenue maximizing price, P_{trmax}, is less than the profit-maximizing price, P_π.

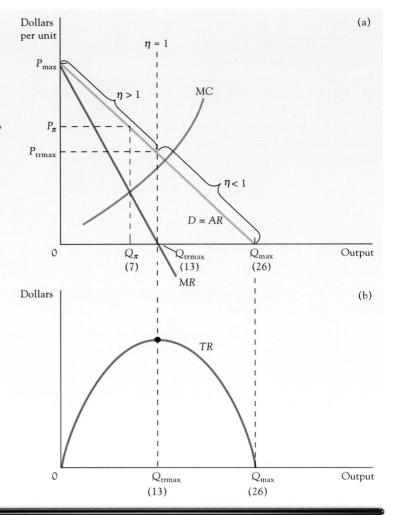

When marginal revenue is negative (at quantities beyond an output of Q_{trmax} in the graph), a decrease in price and the associated increase in output reduce total revenue so the demand curve is inelastic (the effect of the output increase on total revenue is less than the effect of the price decrease).

As shown in Figure 11.6b, in the case of a straight-line demand curve, a monopolist's total revenue curve has the shape of an upside-down bowl. Total revenue peaks at the output, Q_{trmax}, where marginal revenue is zero and demand is unit elastic. Total revenue equals zero in two cases: where at least P_{max} is charged and zero units are sold, or when a price of zero is charged and Q_{max} units are sold.

One bit of geometry may be useful to keep in mind when drawing marginal revenue curves for straight-line demand curves: the slope of the MR curve is, in absolute value, exactly twice the slope of the demand curve. The MR curve falls twice as fast and becomes zero at an output exactly halfway between the origin and the level of output where the demand curve intersects the quantity axis. In Figure 11.6a, marginal revenue becomes zero at Q_{trmax} (13 units) while the demand curve reaches zero at Q_{max} (26 units).

4. Monopolists are frequently thought to make more money if demand for their products is inelastic. Yet we can easily see that a profit-maximizing monopolist will always be selling at a price where demand is elastic. If, for some reason, a monopoly is producing an output where demand is inelastic, it can increase its profit by cutting back output and raising price. Lower output means higher total revenue (when demand is inelastic) and lower total cost, so profit will necessarily increase. The monopoly should reduce output until it is operating somewhere along the elastic portion of its demand curve. Another way to see this is by recalling that profit is maximized when marginal revenue equals marginal cost. Since marginal cost is always greater than zero, marginal revenue must be positive when profit is maximized. But a positive marginal revenue implies an elastic demand curve since it means that greater output (lower price) will increase total revenue.

Simple as this point is, notice how it allows us to see the inconsistency in the following statements: (a) "the oil companies collude with one another, charging a monopoly price for gasoline"; and (b) "gasoline is a virtual necessity that is in highly inelastic demand." These statements cannot both be correct. If gasoline is in inelastic demand at the current price, that price is not a monopoly price. If the price is a monopoly price, the demand must be elastic. Yet many people believe that both statements are correct.

APPLICATION 11.2 — LIFE IS NOT ALWAYS A BOX OF CHOCOLATES

Winston Groom, the author whose novel was the basis for the Academy Award-winning film, *Forrest Gump*, sold the rights to his novel to Paramount Pictures in return for 3 percent of the profit generated by the film.[11] Even though the film has generated more than $840 million in total revenue (making it one of the highest-grossing movies of all time), Groom has yet to realize much of a financial return from his literary efforts. According to Paramount's accounting statements, the film actually showed a loss of $62 million as of the end of 1994 (the year in which an overwhelming share of the total revenues were realized).

In 1995, Groom hired an attorney to investigate the legitimacy of Paramount's accounting standards. Because total profit is more easily misrepresented by a studio (by inflating costs), leading actors and directors prefer their contractual payments to be based on the total revenue associated with a movie (total revenue is easier for independent auditors to monitor). Indeed, in the case of *Forrest Gump*, lead actor Tom Hanks negotiated for a percentage of the film's total revenue and earned nearly $40 million from the arrangement.

While actors or directors may prefer to receive a percentage of a film's total revenue, such contractual arrangements create an inherent conflict in determining what price should be charged for a movie ticket. To see why, reconsider Figure 11.6, and think about the price of admission that should be set for a movie such as *Forrest Gump*. The movie studio will, of course, want to select the profit-maximizing price, P_π—the height of the demand curve at the quantity, Q_π, where MR equals MC. An actor such as Tom Hanks, who has negotiated for a percentage of the film's total revenue, however, will be best served by a lower price, P_{trmax}—the height of the demand curve at the quantity, Q_{trmax}, where total revenue is maximized. Because Tom Hanks' payment is based on total revenue, production cost does not matter to Hanks and he has an incentive to push for a lower-price/higher-output combination than the one preferred by the studio, which is interested in maximizing total profit.

[11]This application is based on: " 'Gump' a Smash, But Still in the Red, Paramount Says," *Los Angeles Times*, May 24, 1995, pp. A1 and A16; and **Internet Movie Database Limited**, 2000.

11.4 THE MEASUREMENT AND SOURCES OF MONOPOLY POWER[12]

As you might suspect, pure monopoly, in which there is only one supplier, is rare. More common are markets populated by at least several firms selling products that are reasonably close substitutes for one another. Even when there are several firms operating in the same market, however, each firm is likely to face a downward-sloping demand curve and thus have some *monopoly power*: some control over price, some ability to charge a price above marginal cost. In this section we explain why this is the case, as well as how the extent of any individual firm's monopoly power may be measured and the general sources of monopoly power.

Consider the aspirin market and suppose that Bayer is one of five (equal-sized) sellers in it. Suppose also that Bayer assumes that rival suppliers behave as competitive firms in determining their output. The latter assumption is a simplifying one, not meant to downplay other types of strategic behavior in which suppliers may engage when making price and output decisions. Chapters 13 and 14 more fully explore the strategic interactions between firms when the number of firms operating in a market is small. For now, however, we ignore alternative forms of strategic behavior to show that even when rival suppliers behave as competitive firms, an individual firm may have some monopoly power if the number of rivals is not too great.

Under these assumptions, Figure 11.7 shows how Bayer's demand curve, d, can be derived from the market demand curve, D, and the supply curve, S_O, of all *other* firms in the market. In Figure 11.7a, if Bayer produces nothing, the market price will be $10 per bottle, and Bayer's demand curve will begin at $10 on the vertical axis. How many bottles can Bayer

FIGURE 11.7

Monopoly Power When There Are Several Suppliers
Under the assumptions made in the text, Bayer's demand curve is *d*. It is derived by subtracting the quantity supplied by other firms (indicated by S_O) from the total amount consumers wish to purchase (shown by *D*) at each price.

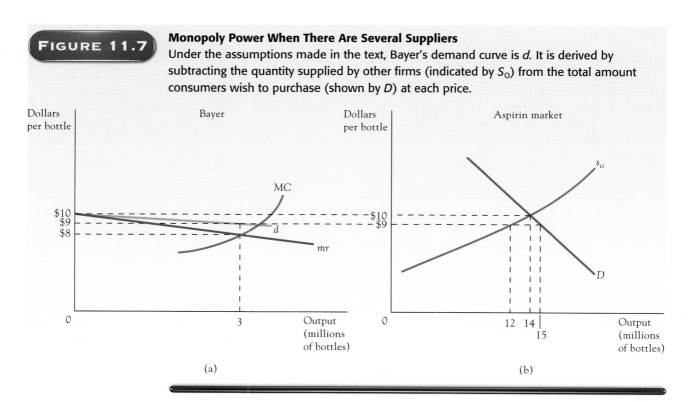

(a)   (b)

[12]A mathematical treatment of some of the material in this section is given in the appendix at the back of the book (page 568).

sell at a price of $9? At $9, other firms will supply 12 million bottles along their supply curve, but consumers are willing to purchase 15 million bottles, so Bayer can sell the difference, 3 million bottles. Now we have a second point on Bayer's demand curve, *d*. It is obviously highly elastic, with a point elasticity of $9 at an output of 3 million bottles. Although Bayer's demand curve is much more elastic than the market demand curve (the latter has a point elasticity of 0.6 at an output of 15 million bottles), the important point is that it is not perfectly elastic. And because its demand elasticity is less than infinity, Bayer has some monopoly power, some ability to set price above its marginal cost.

Given its demand curve, how much should Bayer produce to maximize profit? Once again, output should be set where *mr* = MC (3 million in Figure 11.7a). Bayer's profit-maximizing price is the height of its demand curve ($9) at the output where *mr* = MC. Note that the price exceeds Bayer's marginal cost ($8) and that Bayer thus has some monopoly power even though it is not a pure monopoly. The presence of four other suppliers limits Bayer's monopoly power but does not eliminate it.

Measuring Monopoly Power

LERNER INDEX
a means of measuring a firm's monopoly power that takes the markup of price over marginal cost expressed as a percentage of a producer's price

To measure a firm's monopoly power, economists often rely on the **Lerner index** (named after economist Abba Lerner). The Lerner index is nothing more than the markup of price over marginal cost, expressed as a percentage of a product's price:

$$\text{Lerner index of monopoly power} = (P - MC)/P.$$

We noted before that, at the profit-maximizing output, the price-marginal cost markup equals the inverse of the firm's demand elasticity, $(P - MC)/P = 1/\eta$. Thus, the smaller the firm's demand elasticity at the profit-maximizing output, the greater the price-marginal cost markup, and the larger the firm's degree of monopoly power as measured by the Lerner index.

The Lerner index varies between zero and one. In perfect competition, the elasticity of the firm's demand curve is infinite, and price equals marginal cost, so the Lerner index equals zero. The larger the Lerner index value, the greater a firm's monopoly power. In the aspirin example just discussed, Bayer's demand curve has an elasticity of 9 at the profit-maximizing output. The degree of Bayer's monopoly power, as measured by the Lerner index, thus equals the inverse of the elasticity or 1/9 (roughly 0.11).

The Sources of Monopoly Power

What factors determine the extent to which a firm has monopoly power? Our Bayer example suggests two: the elasticity of the market demand curve and the elasticity of supply by other firms. Note how, in Figure 11.7, as the price is dropped from $10 to $9 per bottle, the expansion of total purchases by consumers (by 1 million bottles) and the reduction in output by other firms (2 million bottles) determine how much Bayer can sell at the lower price. The size of the expansion in total purchases is determined by the elasticity of the market demand curve; the size of the reduction in output by other firms is determined by the elasticity of the other firms' supply curve. Thus, the more elastic *D* and S_O are, the greater the elasticity of Bayer's demand curve.

If the market demand curve is perfectly elastic, any individual supplier such as Bayer has no monopoly power. This would be the case even if Bayer were the only aspirin supplier and thus a pure monopolist. Even a pure monopolist, that is, would be unable to set price above marginal cost. Any attempt to do so would lead to total purchases equaling zero since consumers are hypersensitive to the price charged by the (albeit pure) monopolist if the market demand curve is perfectly elastic.

The monopoly power possessed by any one firm is also more limited the greater the number of rival firms. This is because as rivals become more numerous, the elasticity of supply by rival firms, as a group, tends to increase and the ability of any one firm to set price above marginal cost is impeded.[13] In Figure 11.7, for example, if S_O were more elastic such that production by other firms, as a group, falls to 1 million bottles as the price declines from $10 to $9, Bayer's demand curve would be much more price sensitive: the price decline would result in Bayer's sales rising from zero (at $10) to 14 million bottles (at $9).

Barriers to Entry

BARRIER TO ENTRY
any factor that limits the number of firms operating in a market and thereby serves to promote monopoly power

ABSOLUTE COST ADVANTAGE
a situation in which an incumbent firm's production cost (its long-run average total cost) is lower than potential rivals' production costs at all relevant output levels

ECONOMIES OF SCALE
a situation in which the long-run average total cost curve for all firms slopes downward over the entire range of market output

NATURAL MONOPOLY
an industry in which production cost is minimized if one firm supplies the entire output

PRODUCT DIFFERENTIATION
a means by which consumers may perceive the product sold by an incumbent firm to be superior to that offered by prospective rivals

REGULATORY BARRIERS
barriers to entry created by the government through vehicles such as patents, copyrights, franchises, and licenses

A **barrier to entry** is any factor that limits the number of firms operating in a market and thereby serves to promote monopoly power on the part of incumbent suppliers. Such factors fall into four general categories: absolute cost advantages, economies of scale, product differentiation, and regulatory barriers.

An **absolute cost advantage** occurs where an incumbent firm's production cost (its long-run average total cost) is lower than potential rivals' production costs at all relevant output levels. This cost disparity may be due to unique access to a production technique or an essential input. For example, Kentucky Fried Chicken has a proprietary recipe for "finger-lickin' good" chicken.[14] The Aluminum Company of America (Alcoa) was the sole producer of aluminum in the United States from the late nineteenth century until the 1940s, because it controlled all domestic sources of bauxite—the ore from which aluminum is made. In the field of music, Garth Brooks and Britney Spears have unique access to their personal singing abilities. Cisco is the leading maker of networks that use the Internet on account of the superior design technology for routers and servers that the company has proprietary access to.

All firms (incumbents as well as potential entrants) may have the same cost curves but the production technology may be such that one large firm can supply an entire market at a lower per-unit cost than several smaller firms that share the market. In other words, the long-run average total cost curve for all firms may slope downward over the entire range of market output. Consequently, to have more than one firm operating is wasteful since production cost is minimized if one firm supplies the entire output. The industry is thus characterized by **economies of scale** and is termed a **natural monopoly**.

Natural monopoly is common in the local distribution of power, water, and telephone services. It is cheaper, that is, to have one electric company serve an entire neighborhood than to have each home in the neighborhood rely on a separate company with its own distinct transmission lines. The single electric company dictated by economies of scale, however, has the potential to exercise monopoly pricing power.

Product differentiation is a third type of barrier to entry. Consumers may perceive the product sold by an incumbent firm to be superior to that offered by prospective rivals. Based on this perception, consumers are willing to pay more for the incumbent firm's product. For example, Ray-Ban sunglasses may be sufficiently differentiated in consumers' eyes to give the company some pricing latitude over potential competitors—even though the competitors have access to the same production technology.

Finally, a firm may have a limited number of rivals due to **regulatory barriers** such as government-granted patents, copyrights, franchises, and licenses. A patent, for example, grants the exclusive right to use some productive technique or to produce a certain product for a period of 17 years. Patents thus amount to the legal right to a temporary monopoly. Although patents are an instance of government-created monopoly power, there is an economic rationale for their use—namely, that firms and individuals will be less inclined to invest in the research and development of new products if others can immediately copy the results. As we will see in Chapter 19, this rationale is generally regarded as a valid argument

---

[13]We continue to ignore, for now, the strategic behavior in which firms may engage when selecting their price and output. As we will see in Chapters 13 and 14, it is possible for a large number of firms to collude in setting a monopoly price and a small number of firms to interact in such a manner as to ensure the competitive outcome. We will also see, however, why collusion tends to be less likely as the number of firms in a market grows.

[14]Reportedly, only two company officials know the recipe.

for granting some protection to inventors. But some economists believe that 17 years is too long; others believe that given the length of time needed to develop and market a product, 17 years is not long enough.

Governments also occasionally block entry by requiring firms to have a public operating license or franchise. Licensing is sometimes defended as a method of ensuring minimum standards of competency, but it can be (and many feel has been) used as a barrier to entry that insulates existing holders of licenses from new competition. For example, one cannot enter the mail delivery, broadcasting, public utility, or trucking markets without a public license. Similarly, hundreds of occupations require licenses, among them hair stylists, funeral directors, taxi drivers, contractors, bartenders, and tailors. Often these licenses are granted by state government boards composed largely of existing license holders.

In the case of cable television, the ability to provide service to any given community requires a franchise from the local city government. Until recently, these franchises were typically exclusive. Under exclusive franchising, no more than one operator is allowed to serve a community. Exclusive franchising is often predicated on the belief that economies of scale exist in local cable television distribution. However, studies have found that any such economies of scale are relatively minor, while the pricing power conferred by exclusive franchises appears to be substantial.[15] The average monthly basic service rate charged in "overbuild" communities (communities served by more than one operator) is 20 to 35 percent lower than in comparable communities served by only one cable operator.

Regulatory barriers can also take the form of the government making its purchases from particular firms or limiting nonprice forms of competition such as advertising. Restrictions on advertising exist in many states for products such as legal services, prescription drugs, health care, and eyeglasses. In general, prices are higher where there are limits on advertising. For example, researchers find that eyeglass prices are 25 to 30 percent higher in states with total advertising bans than in states with weak or no restrictions on advertising.[16]

APPLICATION 11.3   REGULATORY BARRIERS IN THE PHILIPPINES

During the time that the late Ferdinand Marcos was president of the Philippines, being his friend or relative tended to confer significant business advantages.[17] President Marcos used his power to benefit certain businesses over others, often to the detriment of foreign investors and most Filipinos. A golfing buddy's firm was awarded nearly every major government construction project. A domestic firm supplying cigarette filters won 90 percent of the local market when Marcos issued a decree slapping a 100 percent tax on a raw material used in filters by the company's domestic and international rivals. The company was owned by a relative of President Marcos. The domestic conglomerate buying 70 percent of the Philippine coconut crop was able, through government sanction, to effect a reduction of roughly 25 percent in its payments to the millions of coconut farmers in the country—farmers who are among the poorest of Filipinos. The president of the conglomerate was godfather to Marcos' son and grandsons. The flagrant favoritism displayed by the Marcos government in construction, cigarette filter, and coconut markets, among many others, helped lead to the president's downfall.

[17]"In Philippines, to Be President's Pal Can Be Boon for a Businessman," *Wall Street Journal* (November 4, 1983), pp. 1, 12.

[15]Thomas Hazlett, "Duopolistic Competition in Cable Television: Implications for Public Policy," *Yale Journal on Regulation*, 7 No. 1 (Winter 1990), pp. 65–119.

[16]Lee Benham, "The Effect of Advertising on the Price of Eyeglasses," *Journal of Law and Economics*, 15 No. 2 (October 1972), pp. 337–352.

Strategic Behavior by Firms: Incumbents and Potential Entrants

A common belief is that the degree of monopoly power exercised by firms in any market is related to the number of firms: the more firms there are, the less monopoly power each has. From our earlier discussion of the determination of Bayer's demand curve, it is easy to see why some such relationship might be expected. For instance, if there were four (equal-sized) firms instead of five in our example, then each firm would have a less elastic demand curve, and therefore more monopoly power. However, the relationship is not exact, and sometimes focusing on the number of firms can be misleading. The elasticity of each firm's demand curve depends not only on the number of competing firms, but also on the elasticity of the market demand, the elasticity of the supply curve for other firms, the extent to which the products produced by the various firms in the industry are homogeneous, and the nature of the competition among the firms. As we will see in Chapter 13, firms might choose not to compete perfectly in terms of the prices they charge. At the extreme, an industry's firms might even opt to form a cartel and behave in a collusive manner.

Another factor is likely to be of even greater importance: the possibility of entry by new firms into the market. After all, it is not only the number of firms already operating in a market that matters. The potential for entry and the elasticity of supply of such potential entrants can also play an influential role.

The possibility of entry by new firms can greatly constrain the exercise of monopoly power. To see how, suppose that you possess some monopoly power by virtue of ownership of a patent that enables you to produce CD-ROMs at a lower cost than other firms. Your marginal cost curve is shown as MC in Figure 11.8, and the market demand curve is shown as *TD*. If no other firms could sell CD-ROMs, you would maximize your profit by charging $20 per CD-ROM, and producing Q_M. However, suppose that other firms could sell them at a price of $16. At that price, they will sell whatever quantity consumers wish to purchase. How will this affect your price and output?

Obviously, if you try to charge a price higher than $16, other firms will enter the market and you will be undercut; you would not be able to sell any at a price above $16. The de-

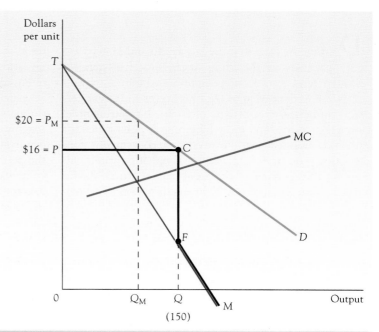

FIGURE 11.8

Potential Entry and Monopoly
The possibility of entry can affect a monopoly's price and output. If other firms are willing to sell the product at a price of *P*, then the monopoly's demand curve is *PCD*, and the monopoly will sell *Q* units at a price of *P* rather than Q_M units at a price of P_M.

mand curve you confront in this situation is basically horizontal at $16 out to the market demand curve. Any output between zero and Q units can be sold for a price of $16, but no higher, so the relevant demand curve is the horizontal line PC over that range of output. Higher levels of output beyond Q can still be sold for prices lower than $16, so the CD segment of the market demand curve is still relevant. As a result, your monopoly demand curve effectively becomes PCD on account of the threat of entry.[18]

When the demand curve changes, so does your marginal revenue curve. Over the range where the demand curve is horizontal, $P = MR$ since you can sell additional CD-ROMs without lowering price. Thus, PC is also your marginal revenue curve up to an output of Q. At greater output levels the original demand curve is unchanged, so the FM segment of the original marginal revenue curve associated with the CD portion of the demand curve is still relevant. The entire marginal revenue curve is therefore $PCFM$. The curve is discontinuous at an output of Q. Think about what the discontinuous (CF) segment of the new marginal revenue curve means. Suppose that Q is 150 units. If output increases one unit from 149 to 150, then the marginal revenue of the 150th unit is $16 (equal to CQ) since both the 149th and 150th units can be sold for $16. To sell 151 units, however, your firm must reduce price, say to $15.90. Thus, the marginal revenue of the 151st unit is only about $1 (equal to FQ).[19] Marginal revenue drops abruptly from $16 to $1 at an output of Q.

Once we recognize how the threat of entry affects the demand and marginal revenue curves, the rest of the analysis is straightforward. (However, note that we have not drawn in the average cost curve. For the analysis to be correct, we must assume that average cost is low enough for it to be profitable for the monopolist to continue to operate.) With the threat of entry, Q_M is no longer the profit-maximizing output; at this output marginal revenue (now $16) exceeds the unchanged marginal cost. This means that profit can be increased by expanding production. Note that marginal revenue exceeds marginal cost until output has increased to 150 units, implying that profit rises as output is expanded up to Q. But the marginal revenue associated with the sale of the 151st unit, FQ, is less than the marginal cost, so it does not pay to produce that unit. The new profit-maximizing output is Q.

Reflect carefully on the implications of the foregoing analysis. You are the only seller in this market, but your pricing power is rather limited. The threat of entry leads you to charge a lower price than you would if you could be assured entry would not occur. In general, depending on the conditions that would attract entry, you may have very little monopoly power—as suggested in the graph where your price is only slightly above marginal cost.

The example illustrates the important point that the threat of entry, as well as actual entry, can have a significant impact on the pricing behavior of firms. In addition, it shows why the number of firms operating in a market does not always have a direct relationship with the amount of monopoly power exercised.

11.5 THE EFFICIENCY EFFECTS OF MONOPOLY

The way a market structure affects the functioning of a market has always been a major concern in economics. Having examined competitive and monopoly markets separately, we should now turn to a careful comparison of the two market forms. To do so, we need to determine how a change in market structure—from competition, for example, to pure monopoly—will affect price and industry output.

---

[18]We are assuming that other firms effectively have a supply curve that is horizontal at $16. If their supply curve is upward-sloping, the PC portion of your demand curve will be negatively sloped but more elastic than the market demand curve.

[19]Total revenue from selling 150 units at $16 each is $2,400. Total revenue from selling 151 units at $15.90 each is $2,400.90. Thus, marginal revenue from selling the 151st unit is $0.90.

To make the comparison, let's reexamine the aspirin industry and assume that it is initially perfectly competitive and constant-cost. The constant-cost assumption means that input prices are the same under competition and monopoly and allows us to isolate more easily the impact of monopoly in the output market. In Figure 11.9, the market demand and supply curves are D and LS, so the competitive outcome is a price of P ($11) and output of Q (10 million bottles). The marginal revenue curve associated with the market demand curve is MR, but it plays no role in determining the competitive output since each firm adjusts to its own marginal revenue curve. With perfect competition, each of the numerous firms faces a horizontal marginal revenue curve at the market-determined price.

Now suppose that the aspirin industry becomes a pure monopoly. The monopoly faces the *industry's* demand and marginal revenue curves, but what about the monopoly's cost curves? If we assume that the monopoly can operate the separate plants at the same costs as those of the individual competitive firms, the competitive supply curve is the monopoly's average cost curve. Because this curve is horizontal, implying constant average cost regardless of output, marginal cost equals average cost. Thus, the horizontal competitive supply curve is the same as the monopoly's average and marginal cost curves.

At the initial competitive output Q, the monopoly's marginal cost (CQ) is greater than marginal revenue (EQ), so the monopolist is in a position to increase profit (from the zero-profit level of the competitive equilibrium) by reducing output. By restricting output, the monopolist is able to charge a higher price. The profit-maximizing output occurs where MR = MC at an output Q_M (5 million bottles). The monopoly will produce Q_M, charge a price of P_M ($15), and realize an economic profit of $P_M BAP$. For the same demand and cost conditions, price will be higher and output lower under monopoly than under competition. This is one of the most important and best-known conclusions of microeconomic theory.

Because a monopoly reduces the output of aspirin, from Q to Q_M in Figure 11.9, a net loss in total surplus results. The net loss is, of course, the *deadweight loss* of monopoly. To see why there is a net loss, note that at the monopoly output of Q_M, price ($15 per bottle) is above marginal cost ($11). Thus, consumers value additional aspirin bottles more than it costs the monopolist to produce. (Remember that the height of the demand curve at any quantity reflects the marginal value of a good.) If output is 5 million bottles, the incremental bottle is

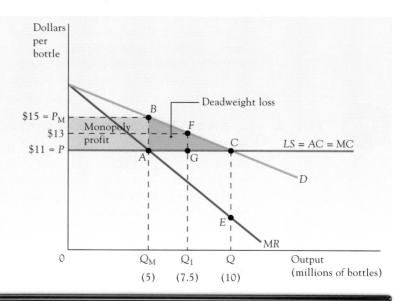

FIGURE 11.9

The Deadweight Loss of Monopoly
The competitive long-run supply curve is *LS*; if the industry is competitively organized, output is *Q* and price is *P*. With monopoly, *LS* is assumed to be the same as the monopolist's long-run *AC* and *MC* curves, and the profit-maximizing output is *Q*_M at a price of *P*_M. Price is higher and output lower under monopoly. The shaded rectangular area shows monopoly profit. Triangular area *BCA* is the deadweight loss associated with the reduced output under monopoly.

worth $15 to consumers, but it uses resources that can produce other goods worth only $11 (marginal cost). Consequently, a gain of $4, or BA, results if an additional bottle is produced. Each successive unit of output yields a smaller net benefit than the previous one until output reaches 10 million, where price equals marginal cost. For example, when the monopoly chooses not to produce the 7.5 millionth bottle, consumers lose a product worth FQ_1 ($13) to them; not producing that bottle permits the production of other goods to increase, but these goods are worth only GQ_1 to consumers ($11, equal to marginal cost), so a net loss of FG, or $2, on that bottle results.

The excess of value over cost associated with increasing output from 5 to 10 million is triangular area BCA. Area BCA is the sum of the loss in net benefits for all the aspirin bottles from 5 to 10 million. *This area is a measure of the deadweight loss due to the monopoly restriction of output.* The aspirin monopoly chooses not to produce these bottles, so consumers are unable to realize the potential net gain. Under competition, output expands to 10 million, where price is equal to marginal cost.

Another way to see that area BCA is a net loss is through the use of consumer and producer surplus. When the price rises from $11 to $15, consumer surplus falls by area P_MBCP. This area measures the loss to consumers from the monopoly price; it is *not* the deadweight loss because there is a corresponding gain in producer surplus accruing to the monopoly firm. The gain in producer surplus equals area P_MBAP, the difference between the monopoly price and marginal cost over the range of output (5 million) produced by the monopoly. However, the loss to consumers from the monopoly price, P_MBCP, is larger than the producer surplus gain to the monopoly, P_MBAP, by the area BCA. Consumers lose more than the monopoly gains, and the difference—area BCA—is the deadweight loss of monopoly.

The deadweight loss of monopoly, then, is due to an inappropriate level of production. Monopolies produce an inefficient (too low) level of output, and the triangular area BCA is a dollar measure of the net loss involved. Consumers bear this cost in addition to the cost they bear from paying the higher monopoly price for the product.

A Dynamic View of Monopoly and Its Efficiency Implications

STATIC ANALYSIS
a form of economic analysis that looks at the efficiency of a market at any one point in time

The preceding comparison of monopoly and perfect competition employs what economists term a **static analysis**. Basically we took a snapshot at one point in time. We started from a perfectly competitive outcome and assumed no changes in market demand and production cost. We then investigated what would happen if the industry moved from being perfectly competitive to monopolized. As we saw, price ended up being higher, output fell, and a deadweight loss was generated in the process.

DYNAMIC ANALYSIS
a form of economic analysis that looks, over time, at the efficiency of a market

While our static analysis indicates that, relative to perfect competition, monopoly imposes a deadweight loss on society, there is another important way of evaluating the efficiency effects of monopoly. This other way relies on **dynamic analysis**: looking over time at why monopolies are created in the first place. In contrast to the static analysis, dynamic analysis suggests an important reason why the existence of certain monopolies should be viewed more favorably from a social welfare perspective. Specifically, monopoly power may stem from firms generating better products through either devising ways to lower production cost (creating absolute cost advantages) or differentiating the product in consumers' eyes (product differentiation). If this is in fact the case, monopoly serves to enhance social welfare from a dynamic perspective since it reflects the creation of better products.

Figure 11.10 shows the market for personal computers and contrasts the dynamic view with the static perspective on monopolies that we have previously outlined. In the early 1970s, the market for personal computers was virtually nonexistent. The absence of a market at that time reflected the cost of producing such a good ($AC_{before} = MC_{before}$) being greater than the amount consumers were willing to pay for it. In other words, even though it was technologically possible to manufacture computers for personal use in the early 1970s,

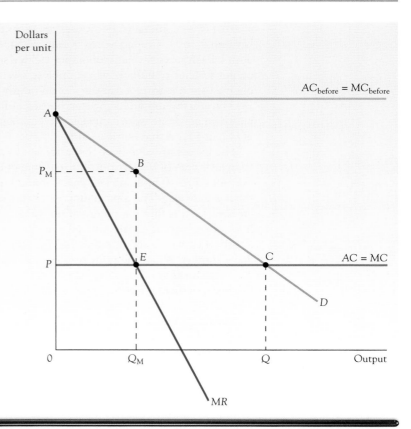

FIGURE 11.10

A Dynamic View of Monopoly
Relative to a world where production cost
($AC_{before} = MC_{before}$) exceeds the value
consumers place on a good (the height of
the D curve) and output is zero, a firm
possessing monopoly pricing power
because it has figured out a way to lower
production cost to $AC = MC$ serves to
increase total surplus by its actions. The
cost-reducing innovation increases
consumer surplus by ABP_M and producer
surplus by P_MBEP.

the minimum cost producers would have had to be paid to produce computers (as measured by the height of the $AC_{before} = MC_{before}$ curve) exceeded the maximum price consumers were willing to pay (as measured by the height of the demand curve) for them.

According to the dynamic perspective, a monopoly is created in this market when a company figures out a way to lower the production cost of personal computers—say, to a level of $AC = MC$. With this innovation, total surplus increases relative to the early 1970s outcome of no personal computers being marketed. There are two reasons for this. First, the company developing the lower-cost production method will be rewarded for its innovation by being able to exercise monopoly pricing power, charging a price of P_M and earning producer surplus equal to area P_MBEP. Second, consumers also benefit from the innovation. Relative to a world without personal computers, the monopoly outcome of Q_M increases consumer surplus from zero to an area equal to ABP_M. The increase in total surplus (producer plus consumer surplus) is $ABEP$.

Of course, once the lower-cost production technique is developed, the static perspective on monopolies still applies since competition would serve to further increase total surplus. That is, suppose that there are 20 firms with access to the same cost-reducing technology ($AC = MC$) as the innovating company, and 20 firms is sufficient to ensure the perfectly competitive price of P and output of Q. In this situation, relative to the monopoly price of P_M and output of Q_M, consumer surplus increases by P_MBCP, producer surplus decreases by P_MBEP, and total surplus increases by triangular area BCE. Just as from a dynamic perspective, innovation and pure monopoly are better than no firms possessing the lower-cost production technology, 20 firms and a perfectly competitive outcome are preferable, from the static perspective, to pure monopoly, once the lower-cost production method exists.

Which approach, the static or the dynamic, is the most appropriate to employ in analyzing monopoly? It turns out that both approaches have merit. As we will see in Chapter 20 regarding the debate on patents and the length of time for which they should be granted, monopolies should be encouraged to the extent that they result from the development of innovative products. *Ex post* monopoly pricing power provides an *ex ante* incentive to innovate. Exactly how much incentive should be provided to induce innovation, however, is an open question. The static perspective informs us that, relative to monopoly, competition increases total surplus once an innovation has been made. And the longer monopolies retain their pricing power, the more the total-surplus-enhancing benefits of competition are forestalled—even though such delays serve to induce innovation from a dynamic perspective.

The decision about which approach to employ in analyzing monopoly not only is of academic interest, but also has considerable policy relevance. The next section offers a brief overview of the role public policy has taken toward monopoly in the United States.

APPLICATION 11.4   THE DYNAMICS OF DEVELOPING AN AIDS VACCINE

The dynamic perspective on monopolies suggests that government policymakers walk a fine line if they attempt to spur competition in markets where firms either already have or will have monopoly pricing power. The pursuit of an AIDS vaccine provides a telling case in point.[20] Since U.S. policymakers have proposed reviewing the prices of "breakthrough drugs" and stimulating competition by ensuring that any know-how acquired by an innovating pharmaceutical company is shared quickly with competitors, some firms have either dropped out of or chosen not to enter the race to develop an AIDS vaccine.

[20]This application is based on: "Nog," *Wall Street Journal*, April 21 (1987), p. 38; and Robert J. Barro, "Attention Consumers: Creativity Never Comes Cheap," *Business Week*, October 2 (2000), p. 36.

11.6   PUBLIC POLICY TOWARD MONOPOLY

U.S. policy toward monopoly has been largely guided by the static view of monopoly. According to the static view, a monopoly results in an inefficient allocation of resources by producing too low a level of output. In comparison with a competitive market structure, it also transfers income from consumers to the monopoly owners. For both these reasons, it has been deemed desirable to use public policy to limit the acquisition and exercise of monopoly power. In the United States, the primary means to achieving these goals have been **antitrust laws**, a series of codes and amendments intended to promote a competitive market environment.

ANTITRUST LAWS
a series of codes and amendments intended to promote a competitive market environment

There are three major statutes governing antitrust policy. The first is the Sherman Act, passed in 1890. The Sherman Act makes illegal any activities "in restraint of trade or commerce among the several States." An example of forbidden activities is price fixing, whereby firms attempt to secure prices above the competitive level. The Sherman Act also states that "every person who shall monopolize, or attempt to monopolize . . . shall be deemed guilty of a felony." Although this appears to make being a monopolist illegal, this is not how the courts have actually interpreted the provision. Instead, being a monopolist is a crime only when certain practices are employed.

Partly because of vagueness in the Sherman Act's wording, Congress passed two more important pieces of antitrust legislation in 1914. The *Clayton Act* explicitly outlaws specific business practices believed to be monopolistic, such as price discrimination (examined in Chapter 12) and *predatory pricing* (pricing designed to drive competing firms out of business and/or deter prospective entrants so that the incumbent firm engaging in such behavior can eventually charge higher prices). However, these actions are illegal only if they "substantially lessen competition, or tend to create a monopoly." The *Federal Trade Commission Act* was also passed in 1914, creating a new federal agency charged with enforcing the antitrust laws (a duty it shares with the Justice Department) and having the authority to prohibit "unfair" methods of competition, such as deceptive advertising.

These laws form the cornerstone of antitrust policy. How well they have worked is a matter of some dispute, and assessing the evidence is beyond the scope of this book. Moreover, over the past two decades, the extent to which the antitrust laws have been applied to deter monopolies has diminished with the notable exception of some recent cases against Microsoft and Intel.

Part of the decline in the use of antitrust statutes is accounted for by the growing influence of the dynamic view of monopoly in the policymaking area. With international competition growing and the pace of technological change accelerating, any control by a supplier of a market at a given point in time is rendered more vulnerable, from a dynamic perspective, with the passing of time. For example, it is much harder for policymakers to attempt to prosecute General Motors or Ford today for having too large a share of domestic output given the stiff competition these companies now face from international rivals. An antitrust case against semiconductor chip manufacturer Intel is nowadays all the more difficult to prosecute given both the vigorousness of the competition Intel faces from overseas firms and the rapidity of technological innovation in the market for semiconductor chips (see Application 11.6).

Of course, the election and tenure of some conservative presidents over the 1980 to 1992 time period and more middle-of-the-road presidents since 1992 also partially explain the decline in the use of antitrust statutes. Well-publicized cases against companies such as IBM, AT&T, and top four ready-to-eat cereal manufactures were dropped during the 1980s following the election of Republican Ronald Reagan in 1980.

APPLICATION 11.5 WHAT NOT TO SAY TO A RIVAL ON THE TELEPHONE

One of the practices explicitly forbidden by the antitrust statutes is talking with one's rivals in a market about fixing prices. The following conversation between the CEOs of American (Robert Crandall) and Braniff (Howard Putnam) Airlines, who were engaged at the time in a fierce competition for passengers into and out of Dallas, provides an example of what one should *not* say to one's rival about prices:[21]

Crandall: I think it's dumb as hell . . . to sit here and pound the (deleted) out of each other and neither one

of us making a (deleted) dime. . . . We can both live here and there ain't no room for Delta. But there's, ah, no reason to put both companies out of business.
Putnam: Do you have a suggestion for me?
Crandall: Yes, I have a suggestion for you. Raise your (deleted) fares 20 percent. I'll raise mine the next morning. . . . You'll make more money and I will, too.
Putnam: We can't talk about pricing!
Crandall: Oh (deleted), Howard. We can talk about any (deleted) thing we want to talk about.

This conversation, secretly taped and turned over to the Justice Department by Putnam, led to price-fixing charges against Crandall and American Airlines,

[21]"American Air Accused of Bid to Fix Prices," *Wall Street Journal* (February 24, 1983), pp. 3 and 22.

charges Crandall vigorously and successfully fought (on the basis of no price having actually been agreed to) in federal court.

Whereas talking directly to one's rivals about fixing prices is explicitly forbidden by the Sherman Act, an airline industry tradition whose competitive implications are more difficult for antitrust authorities to assess is the practice of publishing fares with the Airline Tariff Publishing Company, a collectively owned computer network.[22] Centralizing the price data made it easier for airlines to convey information to travel agents about the over 100,000 domestic fare changes occurring daily in the industry. Critics of the system contended, however, that it enabled airlines to communicate pricing inten-

tions to one another. According to these critics, the most questionable practice involved one airline that was typically not the dominant provider of service in a particular city trying to increase its passenger traffic by lowering its fares. The lower fares were entered in the computer system. The dominant carrier at the affected airport not only matched the new fares but also lowered its fares in other markets served by the carrier initiating the fare decrease. The dominant carrier sometimes even attached special codes to the new fares to emphasize its message. For example, certain carriers prefixed their new fares with the impolite code letters "FU" to convey their displeasure. In the end, the carrier initiating the fare reduction often canceled the change and consumers ended up the losers. While airline officials denied any wrongdoing, the Justice Department scrutinized such fare games for their anticompetitive consequences and eventually found them to be in violation of antitrust statutes.

[22]"Airlines May be Using a Price-Data Network to Lessen Competition," *Wall Street Journal* (June 28, 1990), pp. A1 and A6.

APPLICATION 11.6 — STATIC VERSUS DYNAMIC VIEWS OF MONOPOLY AND THE MICROSOFT ANTITRUST CASE

The static versus dynamic views of monopoly were at the heart of the recent Microsoft antitrust case.[23] The Justice Department, which brought the antitrust case on behalf of the U.S. government, alleged that Microsoft monopolized the market for personal computer (PC) operating systems. As of the late 1990s, Microsoft accounted for more than 90 percent of the U.S. market for PC operating systems through the dominance of its Windows product. The Justice Department further alleged that Microsoft had attempted to extend its monopoly power from the PC operating system market to the market for Internet browsers by tying its Internet Explorer to Windows, at the expense of the rival Navigator product produced by Netscape.

In its defense, Microsoft pointed to the dynamic nature of competition in the market for computer hardware and software products. For example, manufacturers boast that they will have newer, faster models of their computers out every five months, and none nowadays would dare think of guaranteeing, as IBM did with its AT (Advanced Technology) desktop model in 1985, that a product will remain state-of-the-art for five years. Craig Barrett, CEO of leading chip manufacturer Intel, acknowledges that more than 90 percent of his company's multibillion-dollar annual product line becomes obsolete in less than a year. And software that may dominate a market at any given moment is constantly vulnerable to being overthrown by superior versions produced by rival suppliers. Take the case of WordStar, the leading word-processing software program in the early 1980s. WordStar lost its position of preeminence to WordPerfect in the late 1980s. WordPerfect, in turn, lost its market-leading position to Word by the mid-1990s. Likewise, Lotus 1-2-3, the leading electronic spreadsheet software program throughout most of the 1980s, lost its position to Excel in the 1990s.

[23]This application is based on David S. Evans, Franklin M. Fisher, Daniel L. Rubinfeld, and Richard L. Schmalensee, *Did Microsoft Harm Consumers? Two Opposing Views* (Washington, D.C.: AEI Press, 2000); Thomas L. Friedman, *The Lexus and the Olive Tree* (New York: Farrar, Straus, Giroux, 1999); Bill Gates; "We're Defending Our Right to Innovate," *Wall Street Journal* (May 20, 1998), p. A14; and Thomas W. Hazlett and George Bittlingmayer, "As Goes Microsoft, So Goes the Computer Industry," *Wall Street Journal* (May 26, 1998), p. A18.

On account of the dynamic nature of competition in PC hardware and software markets, Microsoft argued that, over time, consumers stand to gain a great deal (in terms of consumer surplus) from the innovations that result from intense competition between rival suppliers. Tying Internet Explorer to Windows, according to Microsoft, is but one example of such innovation that makes consumers better off. For example, numerous reviews from the trade press (*PC Magazine*, *PC Computing*, *Business Week*, and so on) praised Microsoft when it integrated Internet Explorer into Windows because of the benefits that were likely to accrue to consumers.

Moreover, Microsoft argued that government intervention against the exercise of monopoly power at any given point in time by a supplier who has brought a superior product to market hurts the producer of the product, as well as discouraging other firms from innovation,

and thereby harms consumers. Indeed, in a study by George Bittlingmayer and Tom Hazlett, the stock market valuation of a broad portfolio of computer companies is, in general, adversely affected by judicial and regulatory decisions against Microsoft.

The Justice Department's reasoning in the recent Microsoft antitrust case would predict the opposite effect. Microsoft's actions, according to the Justice Department, diminished competition in the software market and thereby harmed consumers. The stock prices of computer companies thus should *rise* when Microsoft is restrained by government intervention. The Bittlingmayer and Hazlett results, however, suggest that antitrust restraints against Microsoft may end up deterring competition and innovation in computer software markets and thereby diminishing consumer welfare.

Regulation of Price

Besides antitrust statutes, policymakers also rely on price regulation to deal with monopoly. In the case of local cable television distribution, for example, policymakers have relied on rate controls to limit the prices that can be charged by firms, of which there is typically only one per community. For example, whereas the profit-maximizing price might be \$20, policymakers can impose a ceiling, say \$16, on the rate a local cable monopoly charges its customers for monthly basic service.

We have already analyzed the effects of a price ceiling in a competitive market and have seen that the results include reduced output, a shortage at the controlled price, and nonprice rationing. A monopoly, however, may not respond to a price ceiling in the same way. Indeed, under certain conditions a mandatory price reduction for a monopoly may lead to increased output.

How can a lower price lead to greater output? Recall that a monopoly restricts output in order to charge a higher price. A price ceiling means that a restriction in output cannot result in a higher price, so the price ceiling eliminates the monopolist's reason for restraining output.

We can better understand the problem by focusing on how a price ceiling affects the profit-maximizing output of a local cable monopoly. In Figure 11.11, the demand curve is *TD* and the marginal revenue curve is *TM*. In the absence of any regulation, the most profitable output is Q_M, since marginal revenue and marginal cost are equal at that output, and the firm charges a \$20 price. Now the government imposes a maximum price of \$16. As a result, *the monopoly demand and marginal revenue curves effectively become* PCD *and* PCFM—as in the case of a monopoly confronting a threat of entry that we examined in Section 11.4. Once we recognize the way price regulation affects the demand and marginal revenue curves, the remainder of the analysis is straightforward.[24] With the price regulation, Q_M is no longer the profit-maximizing output; at this output, marginal revenue (now \$16) is greater than the unchanged marginal cost. What this means is that the monopoly can recoup some of the lost profit by expanding production. Note that marginal revenue exceeds marginal cost until output has been increased from Q_M to Q, implying that profit rises as output expands over that range. The new profit-maximizing output is Q.

---

[24]We again assume that average cost is low enough for it to be profitable for the monopolist to continue to operate.

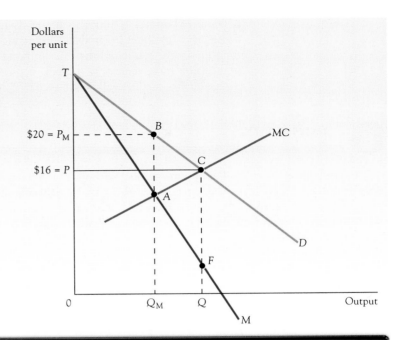

FIGURE 11.11

Price Ceiling Applied to Monopoly
When a price ceiling of *P* is applied to the monopoly, the demand curve becomes *PCD*, and the marginal revenue curve becomes *PCFM*. The most profitable output is *Q*, the efficient level of output.

In this case, the mandatory lower price leads to greater output and reduced profit for the monopoly. Although the firm recoups some of the initial loss in profit by expanding output from Q_M to Q, the net result is still a loss in profit. We can see this even without using the average cost curve, by noting that the monopoly could have chosen to produce Q at a price of $16 before the price control, but did not because profit was higher at Q_M and a price of $20. (In fact, profit is higher by the area *ACF*. Can you see why?) The regulation essentially confronts the monopoly with a horizontal demand curve over the zero-to-Q range of output, just like the demand curve facing a competitive firm, and therefore eliminates the reason for restricting output.

Thus, this price regulation reduces monopoly profit and benefits consumers by lowering price. But in this case it also does more: it increases output to the efficient level, eliminating the deadweight loss (from a static perspective) of monopoly! At the initial monopoly output, the deadweight loss is area *BCA*, the sum of the excess of the marginal value of units from Q_M to Q over their marginal cost. (This assumes that the monopoly marginal cost curve shows the relevant opportunity cost of the resources, which may not always be the case—but we will assume to be true here.[25]) By inducing an expansion in output to Q, the price regulation results in the monopoly reaching a level of production where the marginal value of the good is equal to marginal cost, as required for efficiency.

Of course, this beneficial outcome is not as easy to achieve as our analysis suggests. First, the outcome depends on where the price ceiling is set. In the diagram, if the price is set at either a higher or lower level than $16, the monopolist will choose to produce less. (You may want to confirm this.) From the point of view of promoting efficiency, the price should be set where the marginal cost curve intersects the demand curve, but because the government doesn't know the monopolist's marginal cost curve that outcome may not be achieved. Second, the price must not be lowered to the point where the monopolist suffers losses and

[25]For a discussion of the case when the monopoly's marginal cost curve is upward-sloping, see Edgar K. Browning, "Comparing Monopoly and Competition: The Increasing-Cost Case," *Economic Inquiry*, 25 No. 3 (July 1987), pp. 535–542.

goes out of business. Third, the monopoly has an incentive to skirt the price ceiling by reducing the quality of its product. Producing a lower-quality, lower-cost product is one way the monopolist can avoid the drop in profit that the price control otherwise causes. If the monopolist can pursue this strategy, a price ceiling will not achieve efficiency since the wrong-quality product will be produced.

SUMMARY

- A monopoly is the sole seller of some product without close substitutes.
- A monopoly confronts the market demand curve for the product it sells, and the demand curve will generally be downward-sloping.
- With a downward-sloping demand curve the monopoly's marginal revenue is less than price, because price must be reduced to sell a larger output.
- If a monopoly can select any price–quantity combination on its downward-sloping demand curve but must charge the same price to all customers, profit is maximized by producing the output for which marginal cost equals marginal revenue. The price of the product will be higher

and its output lower under monopoly than under competitive conditions.
- From a static perspective, the output restriction characteristic of monopoly represents a misallocation of resources and involves a deadweight loss. Because price is above marginal cost, greater output would be worth more to consumers than it would cost to produce.
- The size of the deadweight loss due to restricted output is shown by the triangular area between the demand and marginal cost curves from the monopoly output to the competitive output (where price equals marginal cost).
- Antitrust laws and price regulation are two policies that can, in principle, reduce monopoly's static deadweight loss.

REVIEW QUESTIONS AND PROBLEMS

Questions and problems marked with an asterisk have solutions given in Answers to Selected Problems at the back of the book (page 576).

11.1. Because they result in higher prices than perfect competition, monopolies are often blamed by policymakers for causing inflation, where inflation is a persistent increase in the general price level. Is it appropriate to assign such blame to monopolies? Explain.

11.2. Suppose that we, as consumers, have the option of having an AIDS vaccine produced by a monopoly or of not having the vaccine produced at all. Under which option would we be better off? Why?

11.3. "Because a monopoly is the only source of supply, consumers are entirely at its mercy. There is no limit to the price the monopoly can charge." Evaluate this statement.

11.4. Why will Disneyland never set its admission price at a level where its demand curve is inelastic? Use the total revenue and total cost curves to illustrate your answer.

11.5. At the profit-maximizing output the price of Tommy jeans is twice as high as marginal cost. What is the elasticity of demand? (*Hint:* Solve $MR = P[1-(1/\eta)]$ for η, and remember $MC = MR$.)

11.6. When a ski resort with some monopoly power is maximizing profit, price is greater than marginal cost. Thus, consumers are willing to pay more for additional lift tickets than the tickets

cost to produce. So why does the ski resort not charge a lower price per lift ticket and increase output?

11.7. "A competitive firm will never operate where marginal cost is declining, but a monopoly may." True or false? Explain.

*11.8. Show how the most profitable output and price are determined for a monopoly that can produce its product at zero cost ($MC = AC = 0$). Explain the deadweight loss that exists in this case.

11.9. Draw a diagram to show the deadweight loss of a monopoly with a marginal cost curve that is vertical at the profit-maximizing output level.

*11.10. "The concept of opportunity cost teaches us that producing more of any good, including a good produced by a monopoly, means that we must produce less of other goods. Thus, there is no objective basis for saying that an increase in a monopolist's output is worthwhile." Evaluate this statement.

11.11. Suppose that there is a single seller of gasoline in a particular town. Suppose that policymakers, outraged by the prices charged by this monopoly seller, impose a price ceiling. Will the seller's output increase? Explain your answer.

11.12. "Since the shutdown condition applies only to competitive firms, it is not a relevant factor when considering what profit-maximizing output level a monopolist such as Amazon.com should produce." Explain why you agree or disagree with this statement.

11.13. Suppose that the MC faced by Skechers is a constant $10 per shoe. If the demand elasticity for Skechers shoes is also constant and is equal to 5, what price should Skechers charge for its shoes?

11.14. Suppose that the (inverse) market demand curve for a new drug, Adipose-Off, designed to painlessly reduce body fat, is represented by the equation $P = 100 - 2Q$, where P is the price in dollars per dose and Q is the annual output. (The marginal revenue curve is thus given by the equation $MR = 100 - 4Q$.) Suppose also that there is a single supplier of the drug who faces a marginal cost, as well as average cost, of producing the drug, equal to a constant $20 per dose. What are the monopolist's profit-maximizing output and price? What is the resulting deadweight loss relative to the competitive outcome?

11.15. Suppose that in the preceding problem, the government levies an excise tax of $5 per dose on the monopolist. What would happen to the monopolist's profit-maximizing output and price? What would happen to consumer and producer surplus? How much money would the government collect due to the tax? What would be the size of the resulting deadweight loss relative to the competitive outcome?

11.16. Address all the questions in the preceding problem but assume that instead of a tax of $5 per dose the government offers a subsidy of $5 per unit.

11.17. "A monopolist like Spagos (a famous Hollywood restaurant frequented by movie stars) can fully pass on all marginal cost increases to its diners through higher prices since it is a price maker and can charge any price it wishes." Do you agree or disagree with this statement? Explain your answer.

11.18. Calculate the Lerner index for the monopoly described in question 11.14 above. How would the value of this index change when the tax described in question 11.15 is imposed on the monopolist? If the subsidy in question 11.16 is imposed instead?

11.19. "A monopoly's marginal cost curve is the monopoly's supply curve." True or false? Explain your answer.

11.20. Explain the determinants of a firm's monopoly power. How can a firm have monopoly power if it is not the sole supplier of a product?

11.21. Suppose that a monopoly is producing at an output where its average total cost of production is minimized and equals $50 per unit. If marginal revenue equals $60, is the monopoly producing at the profit-maximizing output level? Explain why or why not.

11.22. Provide an example of a firm with a Lerner index value of (a) zero and (b) unity. Why does the Lerner index take on a value between these two extremes? Explain why the Lerner index measures a firm's monopoly power.

11.23. Marin County Enterprises has a monopoly on the production of lunar-powered homes and has the normal U-shaped average cost curve. At its present profit-maximizing output and price, it is able to earn a positive economic profit. Show graphi-

cally the effects in the product market (output, price, profit, and so on) of each of the following changes:
a. Lunar-powered homes become a nationwide fad.
b. The cost of labor (a variable factor of production) rises.
c. The rent for the firm's office space (a fixed factor of production) rises.

If the Federal Alternative Power Commission can regulate the prices of lunar-powered homes and the promotion of efficiency is the commission's goal, what price should it set? What will happen to the output and profit of Marin County Enterprises as a result?

11.24. The City of Berkeley is currently considering alternative ways of providing cable service to its citizens. Based on an econometric analysis of several recently awarded cable franchises in other cities, economists have determined that the total cost, TC, and inverse demand, curves for a cable company in Berkeley would be:

$$TC = 2Q - 0.1Q^2 + 0.005Q^3 \text{ and}$$
$$P = 20 - 0.5Q;$$

where output, Q, is measured in thousands and P is the monthly basic tier price.
a. Given this information, what are the equations for the total and marginal revenue curves and what do these curves look like on a graph?
b. City Councilor A believes the city should own and operate a cable system for the purpose of making as much profit as possible. The profit would be used to lower the city government's deficit. If Councilor A gets her way, what will be the price and output of cable and by how much will the city-owned system be able to reduce the city's deficit?
c. Councilor B believes the city should produce as much cable service as possible without losing money (that is, the city should provide cable to its citizens on a nonprofit basis). If Councilor B gets his way, what output and price will result?
d. Councilor C believes that the private sector should provide cable to the city but that the single, private firm that gets the city's franchise should pay 10 percent of its total revenue back to the city in the form of an annual franchise fee. If Councilor C gets her way and the franchise is awarded to the firm promising to pay the largest franchise fee, what price and output will result? What will be the size of the annual franchise fee?

11.25. Suppose that the Berkeley City Council takes 10 years to award its first cable television franchise for the sake of ensuring that the price the franchised operator charges is as close to average cost as possible. Explain why such a strategy may do less to promote consumer surplus than the alternative strategy of awarding the franchise right away to an operator who will charge a monopoly price.

11.26. The prices of seats on major financial exchanges have plummeted dramatically in recent years. For example, at the Chicago Board of Trade, the world's biggest futures exchange, a membership seat sold for $495,000 in 1998, down 42 percent from a record of $858,000 not quite a year earlier. Explain, using a graph, why the decline in the value of such seats may be related to the growth of electronic trading.

CHAPTER 12

Product Pricing with Monopoly Power

Price discrimination, such as is practiced by airlines, can increase the profit of a firm with some monopoly power.

Chapter Outline

12.1 Price Discrimination

Other Degrees of Price Discrimination

Application 12.1 *Giving Frequent Shoppers the Second Degree*

Application 12.2 *The Third Degree by Car Dealers*

12.2 Three Necessary Conditions for Price Discrimination

Application 12.3 *Arbitrage in the International Phone Calling Market*

12.3 Price and Output Determination with Price Discrimination

Application 12.4 *Why Hotel and Apartment Building Owners Get Cable Television Service for a Lower Price*

Application 12.5 *The Cost of Being Earnest When It Comes to Applying to Colleges*

12.4 Two-Part Tariffs

Many Consumers, Different Demands

Application 12.6 *The Costs of Engaging in Price Discrimination*

12.5 Intertemporal Price Discrimination and Peak-Load Pricing

Application 12.7 *Yield Management by Airlines*

Application 12.8 *Priceline.com, Project Purple Demon, and Online Intertemporal Price Discrimination*

Peak-Load Pricing

Application 12.9 *Peak-Load Pricing Goes to College*

Learning Objectives

- Explain price discrimination, the various degrees of price discrimination, and how price discrimination can increase a firm's profit.
- Spell out the three necessary conditions for a firm to be able to engage in price discrimination.
- Demonstrate how, under third-degree price discrimination, market segments that have less elastic demand end up being charged a higher price all else being equal.
- Explore how two-part tariffs, a form of second-degree price discrimination, can increase a firm's profit.
- Show how intertemporal price discrimination, a type of third-degree price discrimination, can increase a firm's profit.

PRICE DISCRIMINATION the practice of charging different prices for the same product when there is no cost difference to the producer in supplying the product

O ur analysis of monopoly has thus far been based on the assumption that the monopolist charges a single price to all customers, and we have identified the profit-maximizing price and output based on this assumption. In many cases, however, firms with monopoly power charge different prices to different customers or even to the same customers depending on the quantity purchased. The practice of charging different prices for the same product when there is no cost difference to the producer in supplying the product is called **price discrimination**.

Examples of price discrimination include amusement parks, such as Disneyland, that use season passes to offer the first day of admission at a relatively high price and any additional day of admission for the rest of the year at a price of zero; the sale of discounted airline seats, hotel rooms, and rental cars through online merchants such as Travelocity; hotel chains and metropolitan bus services that feature discount rates for senior citizens; laundry services that charge more to dry clean women's blouses than men's shirts; book publishers that charge more for the early printings of a title (the hardback edition) than later printings (the paper-back edition); the frequent-flyer programs offered by airlines; and restaurants in Paris that list a higher price for a dish on the English version of their menu than they list for the same dish on the French version.

Why these more complicated pricing practices arise and what consequences they have are the subjects of this chapter. As we will see, price discrimination can increase a firm's profit as well as the total surplus (consumer surplus plus producer surplus) generated by a market.

12.1 PRICE DISCRIMINATION

Let's begin our discussion of price discrimination with a simple example. Consider a monop-oly that produces a product of which each consumer will purchase no more than one unit. An example might be a monthly fee to Internet access—few people would purchase two subscriptions to the same Internet access, even at a very low price. The demand curve con-fronting the monopoly, shown as D in Figure 12.1, slopes downward because consumers are willing to pay different prices for Internet access. At a lower price, a larger quantity of sub-scriptions can be sold as more consumers sign up for Internet access, but each consumer pur-chases only one subscription. Marginal cost is constant at $10 per subscription. If the monopoly must set one price for all consumers—the assumption we made in the previous chapter—price is $15, output is 100 units, and profit is given by the rectangular area A. (We have not drawn in the marginal revenue curve to keep the diagram simple.)

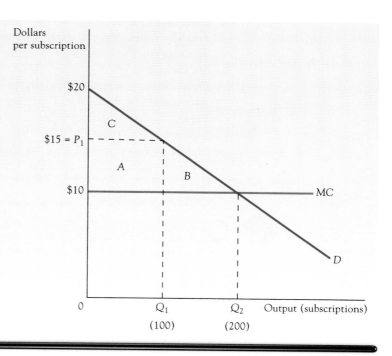

FIGURE 12.1

Price Discrimination Can Increase Profit
When a uniform price is charged, the maximum profit is shown by area *A*, assuming *MR* = *MC* at Q_1. However, if a different price can be charged for each unit sold, it may be possible to realize areas *A* plus *B* plus *C* as monopoly profit.

Now let's see how the monopolist might be able to increase its profit by charging nonuniform prices. Note that there is a person willing to pay just below the $15 price, say $14.95, for Internet access. If the monopoly could charge her $14.95 she would purchase the product. Moreover, the monopoly's profit would rise by $4.95 from the transaction ($14.95 minus the $10 marginal cost of the 101st unit) as long as the monopoly does not have to reduce the $15 price to the first 100 customers. (Recall that it is the lost revenue from lowering the price on initial sales that makes marginal revenue lower than price. If you don't have to lower the price on the first 100 units, the price received for the 101st unit is its marginal revenue.) But the monopolist doesn't have to stop there. If the 102nd unit can be sold for $14.90, then profit will rise by another $4.90 as long as the prices charged for the first 101 units are not lowered. Indeed, additional profit can be realized in this way all the way out to an output of 200: each unit can be sold for more than it costs to produce. In this way, the monopolist can increase profit by area B (which is the sum of the excess of price paid over marginal cost of each unit beyond 100).

Note that this pricing procedure doesn't have to be restricted to units from 101 to 200; all units can be priced at the maximum price each consumer will pay. The very first unit can be sold for, say, $20, the second for $19.95, and so on. Under these conditions, the marginal revenue curve relevant for the monopoly's output decision coincides with the demand curve, so the $MR = MC$ rule for profit maximization leads to an output of Q_2, as already explained. Then the monopoly's profit is given by the sum of areas A, B, and C, substantially higher than when the single price of $15 is charged for all units.

This pricing policy, in which each unit of output is sold for the maximum price a consumer will pay, is called **first-degree** or **perfect price discrimination**. It is perfect from the monopolist's point of view because the monopolist makes the maximum profit given the demand curve. If any higher price is charged on any unit, then that unit would not be sold and profit would be smaller. In effect, the monopoly has been able to appropriate all of the consumer surplus (which equals areas $A + B + C$) as its profit. A monopolist can do no better than that.

Perfect price discrimination, if a monopoly can practice it, has some notable consequences. In addition to increasing the monopolist's profit, the resulting output is efficient. This is in sharp contrast to the market outcome when a monopolist can charge only a single price and (at least from a static perspective) the monopoly output ends up being less than the efficient output. With perfect price discrimination, even though consumers receive no net benefit (or just the tiniest amount necessary to induce them to buy), every unit that has a marginal value to consumers greater than the marginal cost of producing it is, in fact, produced. All the potential net benefit from producing this good goes to the monopolist as profit, but it is just a transfer of income from consumers to the monopolist and not a net loss to society. All the potential benefit is realized by some member of society, which is what efficiency entails.

Implementing first-degree price discrimination is, as you might expect, not an easy task. It requires some mechanism by which a monopolist can determine the maximum amount each potential customer is willing to pay for the monopolist's product. Asking potential customers is no good because customers have an incentive to understate what they are willing to pay if they will be charged accordingly. Furthermore, there tends to be no indirect means of securing such information from potential customers. For example, car dealers do not (yet!) have a device that automatically registers the maximum amount a prospective customer is willing to pay for a car when the customer walks into the showroom.

Although perfect price discrimination may be rare (if not nonexistent), there are cases in which different consumers are charged different prices, and the preceding analysis ex-

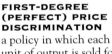

FIRST-DEGREE (PERFECT) PRICE DISCRIMINATION
a policy in which each unit of output is sold for the maximum price a consumer will pay

plains why they arise: Producers are trying to increase their profits by approximating this type of pricing. For example, lawyers and doctors often charge wealthy customers more than poor customers. Many car dealers also strive to approximate first-degree price discrimination. Although they are unable to perfectly estimate what each potential customer is willing to pay for a car, most dealers employ certain tactics to elicit at least a rough guess. For instance, the salesperson may claim to share the customer's goal of getting the best possible deal and promise to bargain very hard with the dealership owner on the customer's behalf. However, the sales representative will first attempt to get the customer to make an initial bid without committing the dealership to any selling price—all the while sizing up how badly the customer would like to buy a new car, how stuck the customer is on a particular model and color, the customer's financial resources, and so on. Once the customer is committed to a bid, the representative disappears (supposedly to meet with the owner of the dealership on the customer's behalf) and then reappears, typically to report that the customer's bid isn't quite good enough. The owner wants at least X dollars more, at a bare minimum. Another round of negotiation is initiated through which the salesperson attempts to get a higher bid from the customer. Because of this tactic, various buyers may pay a wide variety of prices for the same make and model of car, and dealers' profits are higher than they otherwise would be.

Other Degrees of Price Discrimination

Price discrimination occurs when different prices are charged for the same good, with the per-unit price varying either across consumers or across separate units purchased by the same consumer, or both. In the case of first-degree price discrimination, each consumer is charged a different price equal to the maximum amount he or she is willing to pay. In the case where consumers are willing to buy more than one unit, they are charged a different price for each successive unit, with the schedule of prices set to extract their entire consumer surplus.

As discussed in the preceding section, first-degree price discrimination is rare to nonexistent, if for no other reason than the difficulty of knowing each consumer's demand curve. Some pricing practices, however, represent rough attempts to approximate perfect price discrimination.

Second-degree price discrimination or **block pricing** is the name given to a schedule of prices such that the price per unit declines with the quantity purchased by a particular customer. It is distinguished from first-degree price discrimination in that the same price schedule confronts all consumers; the price schedule is not perfectly individually tailored as in the first-degree case.

An example of second-degree price discrimination is depicted in Figure 12.2. Suppose that an electric utility prices its product such that the first 100 kilowatt hours per month sell for $0.12 per kilowatt hour, the second 100 for $0.10, the third for $0.08, and so on. Just as in the first-degree case, block pricing can increase a firm's profit by extracting additional consumer surplus on initial units consumed. It also tends to result in greater (more efficient) output because heavy users pay prices closer or equal to marginal cost. It does not, however, convert all potential consumer surplus into monopoly profit—as perfect price discrimination does. To see this, note that based on the electricity consumer's demand curve depicted in Figure 12.2, the consumer is willing to pay more than $0.12 per unit for each kilowatt hour less than 100 and thus realizes some surplus when the utility charges only $0.12 per output unit. Likewise, the consumer is willing to pay more than $0.10 per hour for each kilowatt hour in excess of 100 but less than 200 and so realizes some added consumer surplus when the utility charges $0.10 per unit over this output range.

SECOND-DEGREE PRICE DISCRIMINATION (BLOCK PRICING)
the use of a schedule of prices such that the price per unit declines with the quantity purchased by a particular consumer

FIGURE 12.2

Second-Degree Price Discrimination: Block Pricing

An electric utility charges $0.12 per kilowatt hour per month for the first 100 units, $0.10 for the second 100 units, $0.08 for the third 100 units, and so on. The unit price (depicted by the step-like red curve) thus depends on the output quantity purchased by a consumer. This is an example of block pricing in second-degree price discrimination.

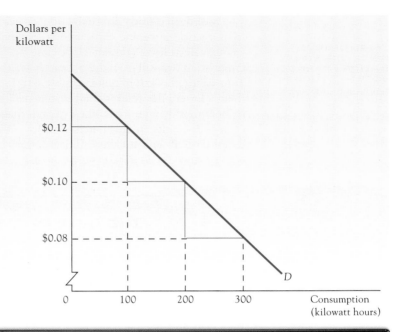

APPLICATION 12.1

GIVING FREQUENT SHOPPERS THE SECOND DEGREE

Second-degree price discrimination is actively practiced by most major airlines. Frequent flyers pay less as they fly more. Frequent-buyer programs are also employed by hotels, fast-food chains, airport parking lots, supermarkets, and financial services firms. For example, Marriott's Honored Guest program gives participating consumers a free weekend night at any domestic Marriott hotel after they have accumulated a certain number of points in the program (each dollar the customer spends on a Marriott guest room earns 10 points). Park and Fly, a chain that operates off-terminal parking lots near major airports in several major U.S. cities, has a "frequent-parker" program that offers customers a week's free parking after they have paid for 35 days.

Most major fast-food chains offer value packages whereby consumers are offered a discount the more food they order at any one point in time. McDonald's, for example, offers a "Value Meal" whereby the price of a Big Mac, french fries, and soft drink is lower if the items are purchased as a package than if each item is purchased separately.

Supermarkets also are moving toward a tiered-pricing system by offering lower prices to shoppers with greater loyalty. As of 2000, more than 70 percent of U.S. households belong to at least one supermarket frequent shopper club. Supermarkets relying on such programs employ computerized scanning systems that sort customers based on the volume of their purchases and dispense coupons at the checkout line accordingly.

In the financial services area, Merrill Lynch initiated a client-reward program in 1997 that bases the annual fee on the amount of money that investors maintain in Merrill accounts. "Bronze" investors who maintain at least $100,000 in accounts are charged an annual fee of 1.5 percent and are given 12 commission-free stock or bond trades per year. "Platinum" investors who maintain at least $5 million in Merrill accounts are charged an annual fee of 0.84 percent and receive 75 commission-free stock or bond trades per year.

THIRD-DEGREE PRICE DISCRIMI-NATION (MARKET SEGMENTATION) a situation in which each consumer faces a single price and can purchase as much as desired at that price, but the price differs among categories of consumers

Third-degree price discrimination or **market segmentation** occurs when each consumer faces a single price and can purchase as much as desired at that price, but the price differs among categories of consumers. Because this is probably the most common type of price discrimination, we will examine it more fully. There are many examples of this pricing practice. Your college bookstore quite possibly sells books to faculty members at a discount, charging them a lower price than it charges students for the same books. Telephone companies charge higher monthly rates for business phones than for home phones. Many drugstores offer senior citizens discounts on drug purchases. Movie theaters typically charge lower prices to children, senior citizens, and students. Grocery stores offer certain items at lower prices to customers with coupons. In all these cases the same product is sold to different groups for different prices.

APPLICATION 12.2   THE THIRD DEGREE BY CAR DEALERS

Professor Ian Ayres of Yale University employed a team of research assistants to explore whether car retailers priced their products differently on the basis of race or gender.[1] Apart from race and gender, the research assistants were selected for uniformity of age, education, economic class, occupation, address, and attractiveness. The research assistants were also all trained to use the same bargaining tactics.

Based on the study, Professor Ayres found that after multiple bargaining rounds, the lowest price offered by a dealer for a new car results in an average profit to the dealer of $362 per white male customer, $504 per white female customer, $783 per black male customer, and $1,237 per black female customer. The most likely explanation for this pattern is third-degree price discrimination, according to Ayres. To the extent that white men, on average, are believed by car dealers to have superior access to information about the car market and less aversion to bargaining, profit-maximizing behavior by car dealers would encourage precisely such a pricing pattern. Naturally, Ayres's conclusion presumes that information and competition in the market for new cars are sufficiently imperfect to allow an individual dealership some pricing power over individual customers.

[1]Ian Ayres, "Fair Driving: Gender and Race Discrimination in Retail Car Negotiations," *Harvard Law Review*, 104 No. 4 (February 1991), pp. 817–872.

12.2 THREE NECESSARY CONDITIONS FOR PRICE DISCRIMINATION

Although there are many examples of price discrimination, especially third-degree price discrimination, all of them are predicated on the satisfaction of certain conditions. First, the product seller must possess some degree of monopoly power, in the sense of confronting a downward-sloping demand curve. (It isn't necessary that the firm be a pure monopoly—that is, the only seller—just that the firm have some monopoly power.) In the absence of monopoly power a seller is not able to charge some customers higher prices than others.

Second, the seller must have some means of at least roughly approximating the maximum amount buyers are willing to pay for each unit of output. To practice third-degree price discrimination, for example, the seller must be able to separate customers into two or more identifiable market segments and the price elasticity of demand must differ among the segments. As we explain next in more detail, this condition makes it profitable for the seller to charge a higher price to the market segment with the more inelastic demand.

RESALE arbitrage of the product among market segments

Third, the seller must be able to prevent **resale** or arbitrage of the product among the market segments. If this condition is violated, the likelihood that a seller will be able to engage in price discrimination is significantly undermined. Suppose, for example, that General

Motors tries to price discriminate by selling automobiles to senior citizens at a 20 percent discount. How many automobiles would it sell at the higher, normal price? Very few, we would predict. Senior citizens would simply buy cars at a discount and then resell them at a higher price (still below GM's normal price). A similar result would occur if people got their parents or grandparents to purchase cars for them. Resale of the product undermines the seller's ability to sell at the higher price.

If resale of the product is relatively easy, price discrimination can't be very effective. How, then, can resale be prevented? Sometimes, the nature of the product itself prevents resale. Electricity provided to a local business can't be resold to a nearby homeowner. If you receive a medical checkup, there is no way you can transfer it to a friend. Children who attend movies cannot reproduce the entertainment for their parents. In general, goods that are immediately consumed—a common characteristic of services—are not as susceptible to resale. In contrast, manufactured items, like automobiles, appliances, and clothes, can be purchased by one person and later turned over to someone else. As a result, price discrimination is less common in the sale of manufactured goods.

APPLICATION 12.3   ARBITRAGE IN THE INTERNATIONAL PHONE CALLING MARKET

The price for an international call to the United States is 30 to 150 percent higher than the cost of making a comparable outbound call.[2] For example, it costs up to twice as much to call from Tokyo to Los Angeles as it does to call from Los Angeles to Tokyo. The differential pricing imposes roughly a $5 billion annual deficit on the U.S. balance of trade and results from the fact that most overseas phone companies are state-owned and face less competitive pressure because they are both the regulator and the provider of phone service.

The relatively high international rates provide an incentive for firms to resell calls at the U.S. rate to customers wishing to make calls from another country. That is, firms such as New York-based International Discount Telecommunications (IDT) allow callers to place calls from Malaysia at the same rates as if the calls originated in the United States.

Reselling works as follows: Suppose that a caller from Malaysia wishes to dial a number in San Francisco. The caller dials an IDT machine located in the United States, hangs up, and waits for the machine to call back. Using a telephone key pad, the caller then instructs the IDT machine to place a call to San Francisco. In this way, the caller is linked up with the intended contact at a cost savings of up to 50 percent.

[2]This application is based on "Foreign Calls Add $4 Billion to Trade Gap," *Los Angeles Times* (December 31, 1992), pp. D1 and D3.

12.3   PRICE AND OUTPUT DETERMINATION WITH PRICE DISCRIMINATION[3]

Imagine a monopoly that is initially selling 1,500 units of output at the uniform price of $10. Suppose that it can separate the customers into two identifiable market segments, segment A and segment B, and that resale of the product between the segments is not possible. Therefore, the monopolist may charge a different price to each segment. However, for price

[3]A mathematical treatment of some of the material in this section is given in the appendix at the back of the book (page 569).

discrimination to be worthwhile, the monopolist must be able to sell the 1,500 units for a higher total revenue by charging each segment a different price.

When the demand elasticities differ for the two market segments, the monopolist can increase total revenue from selling a given quantity by charging different prices. Suppose that when both segments are charged the $10 price, the elasticity of demand for segment A is 1.25 and for segment B it is 5.0. Recall from Chapter 11 that the formula for marginal revenue is $MR = P[1 - (1/\eta)]$.[4] A difference in elasticities means that the marginal revenue from selling in the two market segments differs. For segment A:

$$MR_A = \$10[1 - (1/1.25)] = \$2.$$

For segment B:

$$MR_B = \$10[1 - (1/5)] = \$8.$$

Thus, if one unit less is sold to segment A, the monopolist loses $2 in total revenue, but if that unit is sold to segment B, revenue from that segment will rise by $8. Consequently, transferring a unit of output from segment A to segment B increases total revenue by $6. Reducing sales to segment A raises the price to segment A, while segment B's price falls as sales increase there. This policy means that the segment with the more inelastic demand, segment A, pays a higher price.

Figure 12.3 illustrates the way to divide 1,500 units of output between the two segments to maximize total revenue. Segment A's demand curve is to the left of the origin, and segment B's is to the right. Initially, the monopolist charges a flat $10 price. At that price segment A purchases 500 units and segment B, 1,000 units. Total revenue is $15,000. Because segment A's demand curve is less elastic than segment B's, however, marginal revenue is lower for segment A ($2) than for segment B ($8). Shifting sales from the market segment where the marginal revenue is low to where it is high increases total revenue. As long as marginal revenue is higher for segment B, such reallocation will increase total revenue, so it should continue until the marginal revenues in the two market segments are equal.

When the monopolist transfers 200 units from segment A to segment B, marginal revenue in both market segments is equal at $7.50. The restriction of sales in segment A, where demand is less elastic, raises price sharply for this segment, to $12.75. But the increase in sales in market segment B, where demand is highly elastic, reduces price only slightly, to $9.75. The relative differences in the price changes explain why total revenue increases. Price rises sharply for the less elastic demand segment but falls only slightly for the highly elastic demand segment. With sales allocated so that the marginal revenues are equal, total revenue is now $15,525 [(300 × $12.75) + (1,200 × $9.75)], higher than the $15,000 in total revenue the monopolist earns when both market segments are charged the same price.

When the monopoly can charge different prices to the two segments, total revenue from the sale of any given output is highest when the marginal revenues are equal. This result always means a higher price for the segment with the less elastic demand. Note, however, that the rule of equating marginal revenues holds for any output, but it does not tell us what level of output is most profitable. Should the monopolist produce more than 1,500 units? The marginal revenue from an additional unit of output is now $7.50 in whichever market seg-

---

[4]See footnote 5 in Chapter 11. The formula implies that the more elastic the demand, the closer marginal revenue is to the price of the product. At the extreme, when the elasticity of demand is infinity (a horizontal demand curve), marginal revenue equals price: $MR = P[1 - (1/\infty)] = P(1 - 0) = P$. When demand is elastic ($\eta > 1$), marginal revenue is less than price but greater than zero. For example, when $\eta = 3$, marginal revenue is two-thirds the price: $MR = P[1 - (1/3)] = P(2/3) = (2/3)P$. When demand is unit-elastic, marginal revenue equals zero: $MR = P[1 - (1/1)] = P(0) = 0$. And when demand is inelastic ($\eta < 1$), marginal revenue is negative. For example, when $\eta = 1/2$, marginal revenue is equal to the negative of the price: $MR = P[1 - (1/0.5)] = P(1 - 2) = -P$.

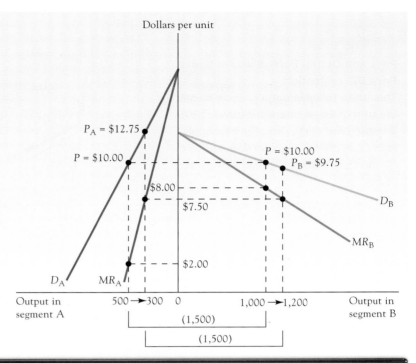

FIGURE 12.3

Gains from Price Discrimination
If demand elasticities differ and if the seller can segment a market, then it pays the seller to charge a higher price in the market segment with the less elastic demand. To maximize total revenue from the sale of 1,500 units, the seller divides output between the market segments so that the marginal revenues are equal: 1,200 units in segment B and 300 units in segment A. The seller charges a higher price in segment A ($12.75) than in segment B ($9.75).

ment it is sold, so if marginal cost is less than $7.50, profit will be higher if output increases. When sales are divided between market segments in this way, the decision of how much output to produce is made by comparing the common value of marginal revenue (because it is equal in both market segments) with marginal cost.

Figure 12.4 shows how the monopolist determines the most profitable level of total output. As we just explained, the monopolist should compare the marginal cost with the common value of marginal revenue for the two separate market segments. The common value of marginal revenue is derived by horizontally summing the separate marginal revenue curves, and the result is the darker curve ΣMR. This curve shows one value of marginal revenue (since it is the same in both separate segments) for each level of total output. The output level where MC equals ΣMR is consequently the most profitable output.

In the diagram the most profitable output is 1,500 units where marginal cost is $7.50 and equals the marginal revenue in both market segments. To determine how this total output is divided between segments A and B, we identify the output at which marginal revenue is equal to $7.50 in each segment. To do so, we move horizontally to the left from the intersection of MC and ΣMR until we reach each segment's separate marginal revenue curve. This occurs at points F and G, so sales to segment A are 300 units and sales to segment B are 1,200 units. Price is higher for A than for B.

Whether a monopolist who price discriminates is in any sense worse than one who charges a uniform price is not clear. Compared with a single-price monopoly, price discrimination benefits one group of consumers, those with the more elastic demand who are charged a lower price, and harms the other group of consumers. Frequently, those who benefit have lower incomes than those harmed because in some markets low-income persons are more sensitive to price (have higher demand elasticities), so perhaps this outcome is favorable. The monopoly also benefits from price discrimination by obtaining a higher profit (or else it wouldn't price discriminate), and that outcome is often regarded as undesirable in the

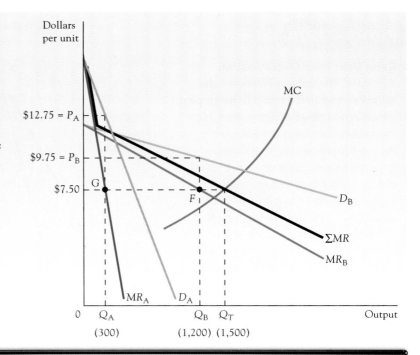

FIGURE 12.4

Price and Output Determination Under Price Discrimination
The most profitable output occurs where the sum of the separate *MR* curves, Σ*MR*, intersects *MC* at Q_T. Thus, the monopoly sells Q_B in market segment B at a price of P_B and Q_A in market segment A at a price of P_A.

public policy arena. Matters become more complicated when we recognize that total output may be greater (that is, more efficient) under price discrimination than under single-price monopoly. For these reasons no blanket condemnation of price discrimination seems appropriate, and each case should be separately judged.

The identities of the monopoly and its customers may also play a role in evaluating price discrimination, as a further example will suggest. Price discrimination is sometimes found in international markets when a firm charges a higher price in its domestic market than it charges abroad. This procedure is sometimes called *dumping*, and it occurs when the international demand for a product is more elastic than the demand in the domestic market. The difference in elasticities occurs because there is more competition in world markets. For instance, Japanese firms have been alleged to dump products in the United States by selling them at lower prices here than in Japan. In this case of price discrimination, U.S. consumers might applaud the practice because they are the ones who benefit. If we can get TVs, stereos, radios, steel, and cars from Japan more cheaply than we can produce them here, the average real income of U.S. consumers rises.

APPLICATION 12.4

WHY HOTEL AND APARTMENT BUILDING OWNERS GET CABLE TELEVISION SERVICE FOR A LOWER PRICE

L ocal cable television distributors often charge a lower price for basic service to owners of hotels and multiple-dwelling-unit apartment buildings than

they do to single-family residences. This situation occurs because, relative to single-family residences, hotel and apartment building owners find it more attractive to install satellite dishes to receive TV channels. That is, the per-residential-unit cost of a satellite dish is lower when the dish is employed to serve 50 apartment units versus just one home. Since hotel and apartment building owners' demand for cable service is more elastic, profit maximization by the franchised cable operator dictates a lower price for these more price-sensitive customers.

APPLICATION 12.5 — THE COST OF BEING EARNEST WHEN IT COMES TO APPLYING TO COLLEGES

Approximately 60 percent of the United States' 1,500 private four-year colleges use statistical analysis to determine how much financial aid to offer prospective students and thereby increase the schools' tuition revenue.[5] By offering less financial aid, a college in effect charges a higher tuition price to a prospective student. If the prospective student opts to attend, the college earns more revenue than it would have made by offering the student a more generous financial aid package.

Statistical models attempt to take into account the price sensitivity of various applicant groups. For example, eager applicants who apply for early admission tend to be less price sensitive and thus constitute a market segment that can be offered less financial aid (that is, charged a higher tuition price). Students who come for on-campus interviews are statistically more likely to enroll and so need less aid to entice them. Expressed premed majors also tend to be less price sensitive and thus can be offered less financial aid as well.

In contrast to basing financial aid offers overwhelmingly on a student's demonstrated financial need (as was the case in college admissions only a decade ago), taking into account a student's price sensitivity to college costs pays off for the colleges that take this route. Thomas E. Williams, the president of the National Center for Enrollment Management, one of the consulting groups that has sprouted up to develop the "financial-aid-leveraging" statistical models, states that his average client college in 1995 increased its tuition revenue by nearly $500,000 by factoring in applicants' price sensitivity.

[5]This application is based on "Colleges Manipulate Financial-Aid Offers, Shortchanging Many," *Wall Street Journal* (April 1, 1996), pp. A1 and A4.

12.4 TWO-PART TARIFFS

TWO-PART TARIFF
a form of second-degree price discrimination in which a firm charges consumers a fixed fee per time period for the right to purchase the product at a uniform per-unit price

ENTRY FEE
the fixed fee charged per time period in the case of a two-part tariff

A **two-part tariff** is a form of second-degree price discrimination. Under a two-part tariff a firm charges consumers a fixed fee (per time period) for the right to purchase the product at a uniform per-unit price. For example, consumers might have to pay $50 per month (regardless of how much of the product they purchase); having paid this **entry fee**, they can then purchase the product at $10 per unit. In this manner, consumers pay a lower average price per unit with the more units they purchase.

An example of a two-part tariff is a tennis club, for which you must pay an annual membership fee plus a charge each time you use the tennis courts. Another example is telephone service, for which you pay a monthly fee plus a charge for calls placed. Mail-order book retailers and member-based discount warehouses employ two-part tariffs when they charge a customer a fee to join their shoppers' clubs and then offer discounts (20 to 50 percent off the list price) on any purchase made.

To employ two-part tariffs, a firm must have a degree of monopoly power and must be able to prevent resale of the product; in these respects the situation is analogous to price discrimination. Resale must be prevented because consumers have incentives to avoid the entry fee by having one consumer pay the entry fee and then resell the product to other consumers who have not.

How does a firm that uses a two-part tariff decide how to set the entry fee and the per-unit price? Of course, the firm is guided by a desire to maximize its profit, but determining what combination of price and entry fee will maximize profit is often not an easy matter. In one case, however, it is simple: when all consumers have the same demand curve for the product, and the firm knows this demand curve. Figure 12.5 illustrates this case. In Figure 12.5a, a single consumer's demand curve for minutes of local telephone service (per month) is shown as D, and the marginal and average total costs to the firm providing local telephone service are assumed to be constant at $MC = ATC$. For the purpose of illustration we assume that the provider of local telephone service is not subject to any price regulation (as Chapter 15 will explain, this assumption is not valid in reality; public utility commissions limit the rates that local telephone suppliers can charge). To maximize profit, the firm charges an entry fee shown by the triangular shaded area T and a per-unit price of P. The consumer pays the entry fee and consumes Q minutes of local telephone service. The firm makes a profit (from this consumer) equal to the shaded area (the entry fee) because the revenue from selling at price P just covers the production cost.

How do we know that this combination of entry fee and price will maximize profit? In general, a monopolist cannot make a profit greater than the maximum consumer surplus that a consumer would attain if the product is priced at marginal cost. The maximum con-

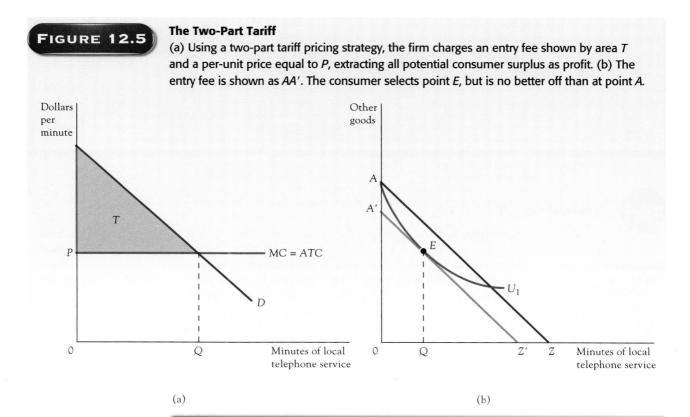

FIGURE 12.5

The Two-Part Tariff
(a) Using a two-part tariff pricing strategy, the firm charges an entry fee shown by area T and a per-unit price equal to P, extracting all potential consumer surplus as profit. (b) The entry fee is shown as AA'. The consumer selects point E, but is no better off than at point A.

sumer surplus is the shaded area, and in our example the firm realizes this amount as profit. In fact, the consumer receives no net gain at all from purchasing the product; all of the potential gain goes to the firm as profit. (Practically speaking, the firm might have to use a slightly lower entry fee to ensure that the consumer participates.) If the firm tried to raise the entry fee (with price fixed), the consumer would be better off not participating in this market at all. Similarly, if the firm tried to raise the price (with the entry fee fixed), the consumer would be better off exiting the market altogether.

The situation from the consumer's point of view can be clarified with the aid of Figure 12.5b. The consumer's income is given by A; line AZ has a slope equal to the price of the local telephone monopolist's product. AZ would be the consumer's budget line if the firm charged price P and no entry fee. Obviously, if the consumer could choose a point on AZ, he or she would be better off than if consuming none of the good at point A; there would be a net gain, or consumer surplus, in this case. The local telephone supplier, however, sets the entry fee to extract all this potential gain. In this case, the entry fee is given by AA'. After paying that entry fee the consumer can purchase the product along the $A'Z'$ budget line (which has a slope of P). Note that the entry fee is set so that the consumer's preferred point on $A'Z'$, point E, is on the same indifference curve the consumer realizes at point A: The consumer is indifferent between purchasing the product (and paying the entry fee) and not participating in this market at all (that is, staying at point A).

With many consumers who have identical demands, all would choose to participate and the local telephone provider would realize all the potential consumer surplus as its profit. In terms of the outcome, note that it is the same as when the firm can practice first-degree, or perfect, price discrimination. In both cases, the firm is able to capture all the consumer surplus as profit. In addition, the firm is producing the efficient rate of output, because it is producing where marginal cost equals the price (marginal benefit). All the potential gain from producing this product has been realized, but it has been realized by the firm as profit rather than by the consumers as consumer surplus.

Many Consumers, Different Demands

The firm would like to charge each consumer an entry fee that extracts the entire potential consumer surplus. When consumers have different demand curves, however, a different entry fee must be charged to each consumer. If that can be done, the outcome is the same as we have just explained. Typically, however, a firm may find that it must charge the same entry fee to all consumers, perhaps because it does not have enough knowledge of each consumer's demand curve, and acquiring such knowledge would be prohibitively expensive. In this case, the joint determination of the entry fee and a price that maximizes profit is more difficult. In fact, there is no general rule that determines the most profitable policy. Instead, firms have to proceed on the basis of trial and error, first setting an entry fee and then varying price, and vice versa, until they find the combination that maximizes profit. Let's consider what this combination is likely to look like.

Assume there are two consumers of local telephone service, Jennifer and Brad, with demand curves D_J and D_B, respectively, in Figure 12.6. (The analysis also applies, of course, if there are a large number of consumers, with equal numbers having each demand curve.) To simplify the analysis, we have drawn Brad's demand curve such that he would consume exactly twice as much as Jennifer at each possible price. The total demand curve facing the local telephone supplier is then D_T, and the supplier's marginal cost of production is assumed to be constant, as before. (The supplier is assumed to be free of any regulatory rate controls.) Now suppose that the local telephone supplier is initially charging a price equal to marginal cost and sets the entry fee equal to the shaded area (thereby extracting all of Jennifer's consumer surplus). Profit is equal to twice the shaded area because the entry fee is col-

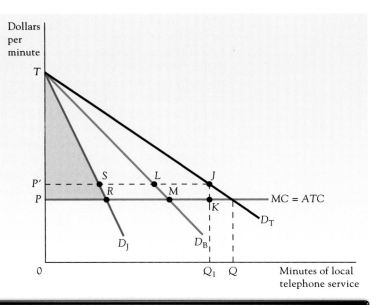

FIGURE 12.6

The Two-Part Tariff with Different Demands
When consumers have different demand curves, the entry fee is set lower and the price of the product is set above marginal cost. Here, we see that the firm will make a larger profit by charging price P' with entry fee TSP' instead of price P with entry fee TRP.

lected from both consumers. Note that if the entry fee is increased a small amount, Jennifer would drop out of the market and so profit would fall; only Brad would pay the entry fee.[6]

This combination of price and entry fee is not, however, the one that maximizes profit. To see why, suppose that the firm raises price to P' and simultaneously reduces the entry fee to ensure that both consumers remain in the market. (If the price is increased and the entry fee remains unchanged, Jennifer would exit the market. In Figure 12.5b, this would have the effect of making the budget line steeper at point A', and Jennifer would be better off at point A than at any point on the new budget line.) The maximum entry fee that can be charged and still keep Jennifer in the market is now the area TSP', so the entry fee has been reduced by area $P'SRP$. Our problem is to see whether this combination of a higher price and lower entry fee produces a larger profit for the firm. To see that it does, note that profit is now equal to area $P'JKP$ (from sales at a price above cost) plus twice the area TSP' (from the entry fee charged to each consumer). Compared with the initial situation, profit has increased by area $P'JKP$ minus twice the area $P'SRP$. Because area $P'JKP$ is larger than twice area $P'SRP$, profit has increased. (Because Brad's demand is exactly twice Jennifer's, twice the area $P'SRP$ exactly equals area $P'LMP$, so profit has increased by area $P'JKP$ minus $P'LMP$, or by area $LJKM$.)

Thus, the telephone supplier can increase its profit by reducing the entry fee and raising price above marginal cost. Note that this contrasts with our earlier analysis of the case where all consumers have the same demand curves. In that case, price was set equal to marginal cost. When demands differ, however, the firm has an incentive to alter both the entry fee and price. In Figure 12.6, for example, the firm has an incentive to continue reducing the entry fee and raising price as long as profit can be further increased. Where this process ends depends on the specific pattern of consumer demand curves confronting the firm, but we can show that the result will usually be a price lower than the simple monopoly price.

[6]If Brad's demand is more than twice as large as Jennifer's, it would pay the firm to raise the entry fee to extract all of Brad's consumer surplus and let Jennifer exit the market.

Consider Figure 12.7, in which the consumer demands and marginal cost are the same as in the previous graph. If the firm were a simple monopoly charging a uniform price and no entry fee, the price would be P and output, Q, would be half the competitive output (for linear demand curves and constant marginal cost). Profit would be shown by the rectangle $PJHN$. Now we can see that the firm can do better by using a two-part tariff, if that is feasible. If it charges an entry fee equal to the area TSP and continues to charge price P, profit will increase by twice the entry fee. Thus, a two-part tariff will result in larger profit than would a uniform price. However, it does not mean that this specific entry fee and price will maximize profit. In fact, we can show that an increase in the entry fee coupled with a price lower than P will increase profit.

Let us evaluate how an increase in the entry fee to TRP', coupled with a reduction in price to P', will affect the firm's profit. Ignoring the entry fee for the moment, we see that the price reduction will affect profit in two opposing ways. Profit will be increased by area $KFGH$ (additional output at a price above cost) and reduced by area $PJKP'$ (reduced profit on initial output). If the initial price P is the simple monopoly profit-maximizing price, these two areas will be approximately equal. (In other words, a small change in price in the neighborhood of the profit-maximizing price will have a negligible effect on total profit.) Thus, the profit from sales at a price above marginal cost is approximately unchanged by the price reduction. Recalling now that the firm also collects higher entry fees, equal to twice area $PSRP'$, we can see that the combination of a lower price and higher entry fee will increase total profit. (Proceeding more slowly, profit increases by area $KFGH$, minus area $PJKP'$, and plus twice area $PSRP'$ = area $PLMP'$. Thus, profit rises by area $KFGH$ minus area $LJKM$.)

This analysis is obviously somewhat complicated, and would be even more so if we considered a case with more than two consumers. Nevertheless, we have been able to reach some interesting conclusions about two-part tariffs. First, a firm can realize more profit by using this pricing strategy than by simply using a uniform price. Second, the price charged will be lower than the simple monopoly profit-maximizing price but higher than marginal cost. Third, and an implication of the second point, output will be higher than under simple monopoly and therefore the deadweight loss will be smaller.

FIGURE 12.7

Effect of Two-Part Tariff on Price
Profit can be increased by charging a price lower than the simple monopoly price when a two-part tariff is used. Here, we see that the firm will make a greater profit by charging price P' with entry fee TRP' rather than price P with entry fee TSP.

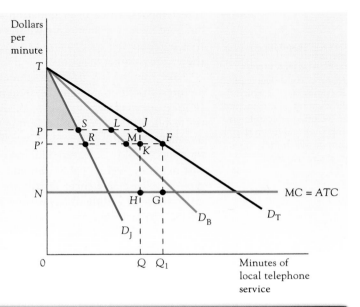

APPLICATION 12.6   THE COSTS OF ENGAGING IN PRICE DISCRIMINATION

Employing a pricing strategy such as a two-part tariff is not without its costs. The Disney theme parks provide a case in point.[7] Prior to 1980, Disney required customers to purchase a "passport" that granted admission to its theme parks, Disneyland and Disney World, and included a set number of tickets to each of the parks' various rides. Additional ride tickets could be purchased, with the price varying depending on the ride. Disney set the highest prices for "E" rides such as Space Mountain, since customers favoring such rides tended to be more fanatical (that is, less price sensitive) in their preferences. These fanatical riders could not be identified at the admission gate, but they could be sorted out through the two-part pricing scheme, and so Disney could extract more of their consumer surplus.

Despite the effectiveness of the two-part pricing scheme for extracting consumer surplus, Disney adopted a simpler, single-price admission policy in the early 1980s; the company began charging a higher entry fee but eliminated the additional ride charge. The reason was straightforward: Disney found that the cost of administering the more complicated two-part pricing scheme in terms of labor and paperwork (additional staff were needed to sell and collect tickets for the various rides) outweighed the benefit (the net revenue generated by the two-part pricing scheme). Although Disney's theme parks still employ other forms of price discrimination (multi-day and season passes, senior-citizen discounts, and so on), the two-part passport pricing strategy did not enhance company profit because of its administrative costs.

[7]This application draws on Walter Nicholson, *Intermediate Microeconomics*, 6th ed. (New York: Dryden Press, 1994).

12.5   INTERTEMPORAL PRICE DISCRIMINATION AND PEAK-LOAD PRICING

INTERTEMPORAL PRICE DISCRIMINATION

a form of third-degree price discrimination in which different market segments are willing to pay different prices depending on the time at which they purchase the good

Intertemporal price discrimination is a form of third-degree price discrimination. When different market segments are willing to pay different prices depending on the time at which they purchase the good, a firm can increase its profit by tailoring its prices to the demands of the various market segments.

Take the case of video programming. Distributors of television programs and motion pictures discriminate among audiences by releasing their products at different times (known as *windows*) and through different channels. Historically, movies were released through a series of "runs," beginning with first-run theaters in big cities and working down to small community theaters. Over the past decade, the typical domestic release sequence for a successful U.S. feature film has changed to cinema, home video, first cable run, broadcast network, second cable run, and syndication to local television stations. Through this type of release sequence, distributors allow buyers to sort themselves according to how much they are willing to pay to view the product at different points in time after the initial release of a program.

Figure 12.8 illustrates how a motion picture distributor can increase profit by engaging in intertemporal price discrimination versus charging the same markup of price over marginal cost irrespective of the viewing window. Suppose that consumers eager to view a new film as soon as it is released to theaters are represented by the demand and marginal revenue curves D_E and MR_E. In contrast, consumers willing to wait to view the film, on broad-

FIGURE 12.8

Intertemporal Price Discrimination
When two different market segments are willing to pay different prices based on the time that a good is purchased, a supplier can increase profit by employing a pricing strategy that takes this into account. Compared to charging a common price to the two segments, profit is increased by charging P_E to the market segment more eager to purchase the good and P_W to the segment willing to wait to make the purchase.

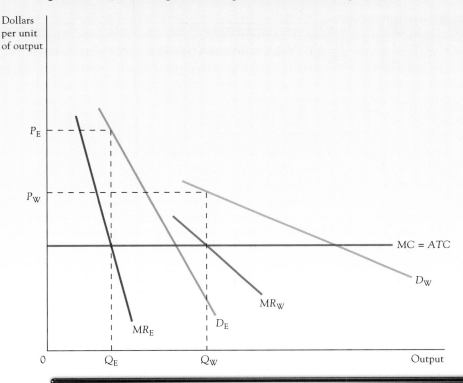

cast television perhaps, are represented by the demand and marginal revenue curves D_W and MR_W. Assume, for simplicity's sake, that the cost of serving all consumers is constant and equal to MC.

If resale can be prevented, the film distributor can increase profit by charging different prices to the two market segments: P_E to customers eager to see the film at a cinema as soon as it is released and P_W to customers opting to wait to view the film at home. Such third-degree price discrimination results in profit being greater than if a common price is charged to both market segments. As can be easily verified, charging a common price such as P_E or P_W, or a price in between P_E and P_W, yields lower total profit than if the two segments are charged different prices based on the outputs where their respective marginal revenue curves intersect the marginal cost curve.

Another example of intertemporal price discrimination involves different fares for seats on the same flight depending on how far in advance an airline ticket is purchased. Some economists believe that computer hardware manufacturers engage in intertemporal price discrimination when they introduce a new product. IBM, for instance, charged approximately $3,500 for a personal computer in the early 1980s when the product was first introduced. By the 1990s, however, the per-unit price had fallen below $2,000.[8] Book publishing provides another example. The paperback version of a book typically comes out six months to a year after the hardcover version and is priced much lower, not solely because of lower production cost but also in recognition of the fact that consumers willing to wait that long to read the book are more price sensitive than hardcover buyers.

APPLICATION 12.7   YIELD MANAGEMENT BY AIRLINES

To increase their profits, major airlines rely on "yield management:" sophisticated computer programs to determine how many seats on a given flight they should make available at a particular fare. Through a fare structure based on past demand for a flight (for example, 30 seats might be earmarked for sale at the lowest discount fare) and restrictions to prevent resale (advanced purchase requirements, Saturday-night stay conditions, cancellation penalties, and so on), airlines strive to take advantage of the fact that air travelers differ in their sensitivity to prices and restrictions. For example, the lowest-price fare typically requires an advance purchase of 21 days, necessitates a Saturday-night stay, and is nonrefundable. Such deep-discount fares generally are unattractive to business travelers, who are willing to pay more for a ticket (because the tickets are charged to an expense account) and cannot finalize their travel plans that far in advance or stay over a Saturday night. Prior to spinning it off as a separate unit in 1996, American Airlines estimated that SABRE, its computer-reservation system, accounted for 75 percent of the company's net worth thanks to its effectiveness at promoting price discrimination.

To exploit the fact that airlines release more lower-price fares whenever demand for seats on a flight is lower than expected, travel agents have begun relying on software programs that continuously scan a reservation system, snagging low fares as they become available. Airlines have retaliated by imposing hefty fees, based on the number of computer keystrokes made by the agencies, to discourage extensive fare searches.

Airlines' efforts to limit resale through their computer-reservation systems and travel restrictions have not proved entirely successful. For example, suppose that a business customer needs to travel twice from Atlanta to Chicago for meetings on two successive Wednesdays, on April 7 and 14. Rather than buying a ticket for each round-trip that originates in Atlanta on Tuesday afternoon and returns from Chicago on Wednesday night (fares that retail for $500 to $800), the travelers can buy two back-to-back Super-Saver tickets that require a Saturday night stay (each costing only $200 to $400): The first originates out of Atlanta on Tuesday, April 6, and returns from Chicago on Wednesday, April 14; and the second originates out of Chicago on Wednesday, April 7, and returns from Atlanta on Tuesday, April 13. In this manner, business travelers can circumvent the restrictions imposed by airlines while accessing the deepest-discount fares.

Individual airlines have recently begun cracking down on back-to-back ticketing ploys by refusing to let travelers board a flight if they do not plan to stay over on Saturday night at the destination city on a Super-Saver fare[9]—that is, when the carrier knows that the traveler has an overlapping ticket issued on the same airline. Whether the airlines ultimately will be able to prevent such arbitrage by business travelers is questionable, given that a business traveler can buy one back-to-back ticket from one airline and the other ticket from a competing airline.

[9]"Airlines Crack Down on Agents Over Fare Plays," *Wall Street Journal* (September 12, 1997), pp. B1 and B2.

---

[8]Increased competition in the personal computer market as well as falling production cost, however, might also explain the historical decline in prices.

APPLICATION 12.8   PRICELINE.COM, PROJECT PURPLE DEMON, AND ONLINE INTERTEMPORAL PRICE DISCRIMINATION

Notwithstanding the sophisticated yield management techniques practiced by airlines and detailed in the preceding application, about 30 percent of seats still go empty on any given day.[10] Rather than get nothing for them, airlines are increasingly turning to online distribution channels in an effort to entice bargain-minded travelers with special fares, referred to as *distressed inventory*, which aren't published in industrywide computer systems. For example, since the late 1990s, most major U.S. airlines have released, in the early hours of each Wednesday morning, e-mail or Web site lists of bargain fares on flights that remain largely unfilled. Passengers must leave on the coming Saturday and return on Monday or Tuesday. The savings can be substantial. For example, in 1998 American offered last-minute round-trip tickets from Chicago to Boston for $130 each online versus $1,000 for an unrestricted

coach ticket available through more traditional distribution channels.

Selling distressed inventory in the airline business, of course, is also the focus of *aggregator* companies such as Priceline.com, Travelocity.com, and Orbitz, which offer deeply discounted fares online for travel on a variety of different airlines. Priceline.com, the most successful of the aggregators as of the turn of the century, requires customers to name their price and masks the identity of the airline, the routing, and the precise time of day of the flights until the customers' offers are accepted. Priceline's annual revenue has grown from $35 million in 1998 to $1 billion by 2000.

Priceline's growth has, as one might expect, not gone unnoticed by the major carriers. In 1999, United, American, Northwest, Continental, US Airways, and America West, initiated a joint venture dubbed "Purple Demon" to compete with Priceline. Slated to launch in late 2000 as Hotwire.com, the joint venture intends to differ from Priceline in one key way: Consumers won't have to name their own price to get cheap tickets. Rather, Hotwire will allow consumers to select actual discount fares that will be posted online for various routes.

[10]This application is based on "Surf and Fly: Navigating Net Fares," *Business Week* (January 26, 1998), p. 102; and "Airlines to Offer Cheap Tickets on the Internet," *Wall Street Journal* (June 29, 2000), pp. B1 and B4.

Peak-Load Pricing

In Figure 12.8 we assumed that the marginal cost associated with selling output at various points in time is constant. Such an assumption is not always valid. Sometimes producers charge different prices at different points in time because, in addition to demand, the cost of producing the "same" product varies with the time it is produced. In such instances different prices reflect not only different demands (that is, price discrimination), but also different costs. An important case of this type involves the provision of telephone service.

Telephone usage varies greatly over a 24-hour period. Typically, total use is greatest in the daytime, during normal business hours. Residential use tends to be greater in the evening than during the day, but total use is lower in the evening than in the daytime. Late-evening use is lowest of all. (There are also often systematic variations in use over the year; telephone usage is lowest during vacation months such as August and skyrockets on specific dates such as Mother's Day.) Thus, a different demand curve exists for telephone service at different times of the day. Economists refer to the period when demand is highest as the "peak" period and when it is the lowest as the "off-peak" period.

Just as the demand for telephone service differs, so does the cost of producing it. If telephone switching capacity (the ability to connect one caller to another) could be stored at negligible cost, the marginal cost of providing telephone calls during peak and off-peak periods would not differ; that is, the telephone company could operate at a constant rate of production over the day, store the surplus switching capacity during the off-peak period, and sell it during the peak period. Unfortunately, however, switching capacity can't be stored; it has to be produced when it is used. Because production must be greater during the peak period than during the off-peak period, telephone companies must have the switching capacity to meet the peak demand. As a consequence, much of the switching capacity needed during periods of peak demand sits idle in off-peak periods. Moreover, the marginal cost of providing telephone service is higher during peak periods when capacity is strained and lower during off-peak periods when only the most efficient switching capacity is employed.

As we will see, charging a higher price for telephone service during the peak period than during the off-peak period serves to promote efficiency. We can compare the consequences of a uniform price for telephone service with prices set to reflect different demands and marginal costs of service over the day, with the aid of Figure 12.9. We assume a short-run setting in which the scale of operation has been selected; the switching capacity, buildings, and telephone lines are already built. The short-run marginal cost of telephone service is shown as SMC, and it slopes upward for reasons already explained in Chapter 8. We further assume that demand varies between two periods, with the demand curve for the peak period shown as D_1 and the demand curve for the off-peak period shown as D_2.

Now suppose that a public utility commission requires the provider of telephone service, a regulated monopoly, to sell output at the price P, which just covers the average cost of producing telephone service in peak and off-peak periods. At P, the monopoly will provide an output of Q_2 during the off-peak period, but what will be the most profitable output for the peak period? During the peak period the telephone company would like to produce an amount equal to PA, where $MC = MR (= P)$. Note, however, that if the telephone company produced PA, a shortage would result during the peak period. To avoid such a shortage, the public utility commission may require that the telephone company be able to meet the demand at the regulated rate. Thus, we assume that the monopoly will produce Q_1 during the peak period. However, because marginal revenue $(= P)$ is less than marginal cost at Q_1, the interests of the telephone company and the public utility commission, as well as the

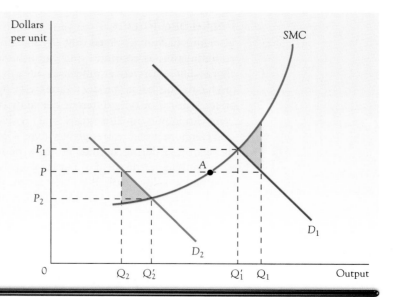

FIGURE 12.9

Peak-Load Pricing
With demand of D_1 in the peak period and D_2 in the off-peak period, peak-load pricing involves charging a price of P_1 in the peak period and P_2 in the off-peak period.

public, would be at odds. (In the case of electric utilities, where uniform pricing is much more common than for telephone service, some have argued that the occasional blackouts and brownouts during periods of heavy use are manifestations of suppliers' reluctance to provide adequate capacity to meet peak demand at regulated rates.)

In contrast to the uniform-price policy, **peak-load pricing** calls for a different price in peak and off-peak periods. If regulators wish to promote efficiency, the price in each period would be set where SMC intersects the relevant demand curve. Thus, price would be P_2 in the off-peak period and P_1 in the peak period. Faced with these prices, consumers would purchase Q_2' in the off-peak period and Q_1' in the peak period. With this price structure consumers have an incentive to be more economical in their use of telephone service at the time when the cost of providing it is highest. This situation may include shifting their telephone usage from the peak to the off-peak period.[11]

PEAK-LOAD PRICING
a pricing policy in which different prices are charged for peak and off-peak periods

Peak-load pricing has two advantages relative to uniform pricing. First, a more efficient distribution of telephone usage between the peak and off-peak periods results. Note that people curtail their telephone usage when it is more costly and increase their usage when it is less expensive, so the total cost of producing a given amount of telephone service is reduced. More formally, when use in the peak period falls from Q_1 to Q_1', total cost falls by the area under the SMC curve over this range, and total benefit falls by the area under the demand curve. Total cost falls by more than total benefit, however, so there is a net gain, as shown by the shaded area. Similarly, total benefit rises by more than total cost when consumption is increased in the off-peak period; the net gain is shown by the shaded area between D_2 and SMC. If the monopoly is regulated so that it makes zero economic profit, this efficiency gain will be realized by the consumers of telephone service. The gain to consumers is easiest to see if we assume that the total output of telephone service remains unchanged ($Q_2' - Q_2 = Q_1 - Q_1'$). Then, the total cost of producing this telephone service is reduced. If total revenue just covers total cost, total revenue from consumers also falls: The average price of telephone service is reduced by using peak-load pricing.

A second advantage of peak-load pricing becomes apparent when we turn from a short-run to a long-run setting. In choosing a scale of operation, the telephone company must have the capacity to meet the peak-period demand. Under uniform pricing, handling the peak demand means being able to produce Q_1. With peak-load pricing the quantity demanded in the peak period is less, so a smaller scale of operation is feasible. In terms of building adequate capacity, peak-load pricing means that the telephone company has to build and maintain less switching capacity. This cost saving also represents an efficiency gain from peak-load pricing.

To a significant extent, the efficiency gains from peak-load pricing depend on the ability of users to curtail their consumption when confronted with a higher price during the peak period. The options here are greater than might be imagined. Some adjustments are quite simple. In the case of electricity production in Vermont, for example, a system of peak-load pricing has been used since 1974. Vermont families commonly fill dishwashers after dinner but do not turn them on until late at night, when rates fall.

Businesses are also capable of adjusting their demand in response to a system of peak-load pricing. A case in point is provided by the Kohler Corporation, in Kohler, Wisconsin. When the daytime electricity price was raised to 2.03 cents per kilowatt hour and the night-

---

[11]The extent to which people shift telephone usage from the peak to the off-peak period will be greater than shown in the diagram because the demand curves themselves will shift. Demand curve D_1 is drawn for a given price of telephone service in the off-peak period—in this case, a price of P. When the price is P_2 in the off-peak period, the demand curve in the peak period will shift to the left since consumption in the two periods are substitutes. Similarly, demand in the off-peak period will rise. The interdependence between the demand curves is ignored in the text; taking it into account strengthens the case for peak-load pricing.

time price was lowered to 1.01 cents in 1977, Kohler responded by shifting 250 of its workers to the night-time shift. To compensate its workers for a less desirable work schedule, Kohler paid an extra $50,000 in wages, but cut its annual electric bill by about $464,000.

Although we have examined peak-load pricing in the context of regulated monopolies, it is also relevant for other forms of market organization. When the conditions are appropriate, it tends to arise naturally in unregulated markets. For example, hotels and motels in resort areas charge more during vacation periods when demand is high; restaurants charge more at dinner than at lunch; movie theaters charge more in the evening than in the afternoon; in many localities, public transportation costs less on weekends than during the week. In these and similar cases, the different prices charged result from the fact that demand and cost vary systematically over time and that cost varies over time because the product cannot be stored.

APPLICATION 12.9   PEAK-LOAD PRICING GOES TO COLLEGE

Faced with declining enrollment and pressures to become more self-sufficient, the State University of New York's trustees voted in 1996 to allow its 30 community colleges and 5 colleges of technology to set lower tuition rates for students taking courses at night, on weekends, during the summer, or at sites with vacant seats.[12] The technology-oriented colleges began offering a 23 percent reduction in tuition during the fall semester of 1996 to part-time students enrolled in classes at underutilized sites off campus. The off-peak pricing experiment "makes a lot of sense," according to Stanford economist William Massy: "When fixed-cost facilities are not being used heavily, why not charge a lower rate?" The State University of New York's facilities are used only 10 percent of the time on evenings and weekends.

[12]"Struggling Campuses Will Try Off-Peak Pricing Experiment," *New York Times* (September 28, 1996), pp. 1 and 20.

SUMMARY

• Monopolies can often engage in pricing tactics not available to competitive firms. One example is price discrimination, which is the charging of nonuniform prices.

• A firm with monopoly power has an incentive to engage in price discrimination because it can increase profit, provided it is not too costly to identify what different potential customers are willing to pay and that resale can be prevented.

• Perfect or first-degree price discrimination means selling each unit of output for the maximum price a consumer will pay. It is perfect from the monopolist's point of view because it produces the maximum amount of profit and reduces consumer surplus to zero.

• Second-degree price discrimination or block pricing occurs when the per-unit price declines as a function of the quantity purchased. Provided that such a declining per-unit pricing schedule does not reflect only cost considerations (for example, economies of scale), it can increase a monopoly's profit by allowing the firm to take advantage of the fact that it faces a downward-sloping demand curve.

• Third-degree pricing or market segmentation occurs when the price differs among categories of consumers. The same item may be sold to different market segments at different prices depending on such factors as a segment's demographic features and sensitivity to the time of purchase, as well as the extent to which the market segment is informed about the prices charged by competing firms.

REVIEW QUESTIONS AND PROBLEMS

Questions and problems marked with an asterisk have solutions given in Answers to Selected Problems at the back of the book (page 576).

*12.1. Apply the theory of price discrimination to a monopoly that faces a downward-sloping demand curve for its domestic sales but a horizontal demand curve for sales in international markets. (Do you see how tariffs and trade restrictions could produce this situation?)

12.2. Assume that all consumers have identical demand curves for local telephone service, and the producer of such service is a monopoly. Compare price, output, profit, and consumer surplus when (a) the monopoly sets a uniform price for the product; and (b) the monopoly uses a two-part tariff.

12.3. How can the supplier of local telephone service determine the optimal two-part tariff if its customers have different (but known to the supplier) demand curves?

12.4. In Figure 12.6, how will the profit realized by raising the price and reducing the entry fee be affected if Brad's demand curve is only slightly greater than Jennifer's (instead of twice as large, as shown in the graph)? In Figure 12.7, how will the profit realized by reducing the price and increasing the entry fee be affected if Brad's demand curve is only slightly greater than Jennifer's? What do these results suggest about how the profit-maximizing price and entry fee will vary in the two cases?

*12.5. Car rental firms often charge a daily rental fee for cars plus an additional cost per mile driven. Is this an example of a two-part tariff?

12.6. What is peak-load pricing? How is it similar to price discrimination? How is it distinguished from price discrimination?

*12.7. Food consumption peaks at dinnertime and is very small between midnight and 6:00 A.M. In view of this systematic variation in consumption over the day, why is peak-load pricing not used more extensively for food?

12.8. The text states that if conditions are appropriate, peak-load pricing arises naturally under competitive conditions. Explain why peak-load pricing will emerge, starting from a point where all firms are charging a uniform price.

12.9. "Suppose that Cornell University faces a downward-sloping, linear demand curve for the undergraduate education that it provides. If Cornell is able to engage in perfect, first-degree price discrimination (through obtaining detailed financial information from each prospective student and offering different levels of financial aid), then Cornell's marginal and average revenue curves will be identical." Explain why this statement is true, false, or uncertain.

12.10. The year is 2020 and the U.S. airline industry has been radically transformed through a recent wave of mergers. Only one company, MONO Airlines, has managed to survive the succession of price wars, labor–management disputes, and government policy reversal that plagued the industry in previous years. MONO now seeks to make the most of its exclusive hold on the market. To that end, it adopts a new slogan, "Fly MONO—or Walk," and then hires you as a consultant to offer advice on its pricing policy. Specifically, MONO asks you for advice on how much to charge for its one-way flight from Boston to New York City. You are informed that the one-way marginal cost for each passenger is $40. You are also told that there are two types of customers: well-paid business executives, and less-advantaged students and tourists. The demand by each of these types of customers is shown in the table.

Price of One-Way Ticket	One-Way Trips Demanded Per Year (in Thousands)	
	Executives	Students/Tourists
$140	0	0
$130	8	0
$120	9	1
$110	10	2
$100	11	3
$90	12	4
$80	13	5
$70	14	6

You recommend that MONO charge different prices to the two different customer groups. If MONO charges different fares, what fare would maximize the profit earned from each customer group?

12.11. Consider your answer to the preceding problem. Relative to the case where MONO charges a single price to all its passengers, would the price discrimination scheme you recommended raise or lower MONO's total profit? By how much?

12.12. Hard Bodies is a new entrant to the local health club scene. The owners of Hard Bodies realize that profit can be increased through price discrimination. Accordingly, the firm employs several different pricing schemes. For each of the following schemes explain whether it is price discrimination and, if so, what degree of price discrimination it is.

a. An annual membership to the club sells at a 50 percent discount of the total rate charged customers who choose to pay on a month-by-month basis (for example, the annual fee is $300 while the regular monthly rate is $50).

b. Obese customers weighing at least 300 pounds get a 20 percent discount on all regular rates.

c. Spouses of members belonging to the club qualify for a 30 percent discount on all regular rates.

d. Hard Bodies offers to beat (through a 20 percent discount) any rate that a customer is offered by a rival health club.

12.13. Besides price discrimination, can you think of any other reason to explain why dry cleaners typically charge more to dry clean a woman's blouse than a man's shirt?

12.14. Apart from shipping costs, would you expect the price of an item to be lower or higher if bought through a mail-order company versus through a store? Explain your answer.

12.15. A private golf club has two types of members. Serious golfers each have the demand curve $Q = 350 - 10P$, where Q represents the number of rounds played per year and P is the per-round price. Casual golfers have the demand curve $Q = 100 - 10P$. The club has 10 serious and 100 casual golfing members and faces a constant marginal cost of $5 per round played by either type of member. If the club can engage in third-degree price discrimination, what prices should it charge to the two types of members?

12.16. In the preceding problem, suppose that the club can employ a two-part pricing scheme but must charge all members the same annual membership (entry) fee. What entry fee and per-round price should the club charge?

12.17. Suppose that the golf club described in Problem 12.15 can employ a two-part pricing scheme and can charge different entry fees to different members. What entry fee and per-round price should the club charge to each member type?

12.18. Assume that the marginal cost to a grocery store of selling a particular bottle of salad dressing to customers who use coupons versus those who don't is identical and equal to $1.50. If the elasticity of demand of coupon users is 5 versus 1.25 for noncoupon users, how much of a per-unit discount should the store make available through coupons? What if coupon users have a demand elasticity equal to 2 versus 1.25 for noncoupon users?

12.19. A video game producer has costs of $25,000 per month that are fixed with regard to output. The firm's marginal cost is $5 per unit of output for output between 1 and 15,000 units.

Information available from the market research group indicates that 15,000 units could be sold each month in the firm's primary market if the price was set at $6.80 per unit and that 14,000 units could be sold at $7 per unit. The market research group also suggests that it is reasonable to assume that price and quantity demanded have a linear relationship in this market not only between those two points, but also well beyond them.

a. One officer of the firm feels that price should be set at the level that would maximize revenue. At what price would this objective be accomplished? What would price elasticity and marginal revenue be at this price? Is this the price the firm should establish? Why or why not?

b. Other officers are concerned with profit. What price should be set to maximize profit? What output will be taken from the market at this price? What would price elasticity and marginal revenue be at this price? What is the profit?

The firm has the opportunity to sell in a second market that is separated from the first in such a way that buyers in one market cannot resell to buyers in the other market. For the second market, the market research group has estimated the demand relationship to be:

$$P_2 = 7 - 0.00001Q_2;$$

where P_2 is the price in the second market and Q_2 is the quantity of the firm's product sold in that market each month.

c. Some officers of the firm believe this second market offers an opportunity for additional profit. They argue that if production is constrained to 15,000 units, the limit within which marginal cost is $5, it is worthwhile to sell some of these units in the second market. Should the firm sell any units in this market? Should it sell only units that would not be absorbed in the primary market at the profit-maximizing price? Should it divert some units from the primary to the secondary market? What price would you set in each market? What are the elasticity and marginal revenue in each market? What is the profit if your policy suggestion is followed? How much profit do you attribute to each market? Explain why your suggestion is the best policy.

d. One of the firm's production managers has pointed out that 15,000 units of output per month is not the absolute limit on production. The physical limit, he points out, may be closer to 30,000 units. The problem is that for each unit of output above the 15,000-unit level, marginal cost will rise by $0.001, so that unit 15,001 will increase total cost by $5.001, unit 15,002 will increase it by $5.002, and so on. He wonders if the two markets together could not advantageously absorb more than 15,000 units considering this production situation. What total output do you recommend? How much should go into each market? Is it worthwhile to push beyond 15,000 units of output per month? Why or why not?

12.20. You run a rather plush ride concession at an amusement park. It costs you $500 per day to have the ride available to patrons of the park. For each rider you have, the incremental cost is $1.

The patrons of the park appear to fall into one of two groups. Members of the first group are not concerned with taking a variety of rides but are quite responsive to ride price and will take the same ride many times. Members of the second group like variety in their rides and will pay a good deal to have at least one turn on a particular ride.

The daily demand for rides on your concession by a patron of the park in each of the two groups is shown in the table:

Price	Patron in Group 1	Patron in Group 2
$5.00	0	1
4.00	0	1
3.00	0	1
2.75	1	1
2.50	2	1
2.25	3	1
2.00	4	2
1.75	5	2
1.50	6	2
1.25	7	2
1.00	8	2
0.75	9	2
0.50	10	2

Each day each group includes about 100 patrons.

a. If the amusement park limited you to a one-part pricing structure that consisted only of a price per ride that was the same for every ride taken, then what price would you charge?

b. If you could charge a two-part tariff consisting of a fee for access to your concession plus a charge for each ride taken, then what access fee and ride charge would you set? How much would you be willing to pay to the amusement park to convince its owners to permit you to use this pricing structure?

c. If you could charge each patron a declining amount for each ride the patron took—that is, $3 for the first ride, $2.50 for the second, and so on—could you do better for yourself and for the amusement park than you could with either a single price or a two-part tariff? Explain why or why not.

12.21. Explain why magazine publishers sometimes offer a lower per-unit price to consumers who take a longer time to renew their subscription. Also explain why this is a profit-enhancing strategy as long as not too many customers realize that they can get a better deal by holding out.

12.22. Most cellular phone service providers offer prospective consumers several different plans from which to choose. For example, AT&T's Digital One Rate recently offered plans consisting of: an access charge of $59.99 for 450 minutes per month plus 35 cents for each additional minute beyond 450; $119.99 for 1,100 minutes plus 30 cents per each additional minute; and $199.99 for 2,000 minutes plus 25 cents for each additional minute. What degrees of price discrimination are being practiced by AT&T through such a menu of plans? Intuitively explain why AT&T finds it profitable to offer such a variety of plans.

CHAPTER 13

Monopolistic Competition and Oligopoly

What are the characteristics of monopolistic competition and oligopoly market structure models?

Chapter Outline

13.1 Price and Output Under Monopolistic Competition
Determination of Market Equilibrium   Monopolistic Competition and Efficiency
Application 13.1 *Ready-to-Regulate Ready-to-Eat*
Application 13.2 *Monopolistic Competition Is in the Eye of the Beholder*

13.2 Oligopoly and the Cournot Model
The Cournot Model   Evaluation of the Cournot Model
Application 13.3 *Strategic Interaction on Duopoly Air Routes*

13.3 Other Oligopoly Models
The Stackelberg Model   The Dominant Firm Model   The Elasticity of the Dominant Firm's Demand Curve
Application 13.4 *The Dynamics of the Dominant Firm Model in Pharmaceutical Markets*

13.4 Cartels and Collusion
Cartelization of a Competitive Industry
Application 13.5 *Will the Internet Promote Competition or Cartelization?*
Why Cartels Fail
Application 13.6 *The Difficulty of Controlling Cheating*
Application 13.7 *The Rolex "Cartel"*
Oligopolies and Collusion
Application 13.8 *Firm Count, Market Concentration, and Successful Collusion*
The Case of OPEC

Learning Objectives

- Explain how price and output are determined under monopolistic competition.
- Understand the characteristics of oligopoly.
- Explore several key non-cooperative oligopoly models: Cournot; Stackelberg; and dominant firm.
- Show how price and output are determined under the cooperative oligopoly model of cartels.

ompetition and pure monopoly lie at opposite ends of the market spectrum. Competition is characterized by many firms, unrestricted entry, and a homogeneous product, while a pure monopoly is the sole producer of a product. Yet many real-world market structures seem to be incompatible with either the competitive or the pure monopoly model. How do we analyze a situation, for example, if a dozen similar but slightly different brands of aspirin are on the market, or if only three companies supply breakfast cereals?

Falling between competition and pure monopoly are two other types of market structure: monopolistic competition and oligopoly. Monopolistic competition is closer to competition; it has many firms and unrestricted entry, like the competitive model, but the firms' products are differentiated. Fast-food chains, for example, may be viewed as monopolistic competitors. They supply the same general product, fast food, but one chain's specialty burger, say the Big Mac, is "different" from another's, such as the Whopper. Oligopoly is more like pure monopoly; it is characterized by a small number of large firms producing either a homogeneous product like steel or a differentiated product like automobiles.

This chapter examines monopolistic competition and oligopoly market structure models, noting the similarities with as well as the differences from perfect competition and pure monopoly. We also explore the case of cartels, whereby firms in an industry attempt to coordinate price and output decisions so as to act, in concert, as a pure monopoly and maximize their joint profit.

13.1 PRICE AND OUTPUT UNDER MONOPOLISTIC COMPETITION

MONOPOLISTIC COMPETITION
a market characterized by unrestricted entry and exit and a large number of independent sellers producing differentiated products

DIFFERENTIATED PRODUCT
a product that consumers view as different from other similar products

Monopolistic competition resembles both competition and monopoly. As with competition, entry into and exit from the industry are unrestricted, often resulting in a large number of independent sellers. However, in contrast to competition, the firms do not produce a homogeneous product. Instead, their products are heterogeneous, or differentiated. A **differentiated product** is one that consumers view as different from other similar products. For example, Wheaties and Cheerios are differentiated products in the general category of breakfast cereals. Consumers are not indifferent among brands of cereals; they perceive differences in taste, crunchiness, caloric content, and nutritional value. In a competitive market, by contrast, consumers view the product of one firm as identical to (a perfect substitute for) any rival firm's product.

Product differentiation may reflect *real* differences among products (Special K cereal is lower in fiber but higher in protein than Post Raisin Bran), or it may be based only on the *belief* that there are differences (a three-year-old may perceive Fruit Loops to be sweeter than Frosted Flakes but their sugar content is the same). The content of most aspirins is virtually identical, but many consumers believe that Bayer is superior to other brands. In blind taste tests, many consumers who claim to have strong preferences for Coca-Cola over Pepsi are unable to select their preferred brand. This outcome doesn't affect the theory, however; the important point is that consumers, or at least a substantial number of them, *believe* the products to be different.

There are many aspects to product differentiation. For example, products may be differentiated by physical features such as function, design, or quality, or by advertising, brand names, logos (such as a Macintosh apple), or packaging (such as Oscar Mayer Lunchables). They may also be differentiated by conditions related to the sale, such as credit terms, availability, or congeniality of sales help, location (have you ever shopped at a nearby 7-Eleven because of its convenience?), or service. As this list suggests, many of the goods you purchase are differentiated products. Clothing, drugs, cosmetics, restaurant meals, and many types of food products are prominent examples.

Determination of Market Equilibrium

The first step in analyzing monopolistic competition is understanding the demand curve that confronts a single firm. When a firm sells a differentiated product with close substitutes, it has some degree of monopoly power—hence, the "monopolistic" in monopolistic competition. In other words, the demand curve confronting the firm is downward-sloping. However, the degree of monopoly power will typically be slight because of the availability of close substitutes.

For instance, because McDonald's is the only firm selling Big Macs, the quantity of Big Macs sold is unlikely to fall to zero if McDonald's charges a *slightly* higher price than its competitors. But at a higher price for Big Macs, many consumers might switch to a Burger King Whopper or a Wendy's Double Bacon Cheeseburger. Thus, *the demand curve facing each firm in a monopolistically competitive market is downward-sloping but fairly elastic.*

Assume that the market for jeans is monopolistically competitive. In Figure 13.1a, we show the demand curve, D, for one firm in this market, Tight Jeans. The position of the demand curve depends strongly on the prices of other jeans, as well as the variety available. Thus, in drawing the demand curve for Tight Jeans, we assume that the number of other firms in this industry is fixed. Furthermore, we assume that the prices charged by other firms do not change when Tight Jeans varies its price. (Changes in the prices charged by other firms would cause Tight Jeans' demand curve to shift.) The basis for assuming other firms' prices as given is that Tight Jeans represents only a small part of the total jeans market. While a lower price for its jeans will cause some customers to shift from other brands, the loss for each brand will be small enough to be unnoticeable, or at least not to provoke a reaction.

Given the behavior of other firms in the market, let's consider how Tight Jeans determines price and output. Because its demand curve is downward-sloping, marginal revenue is less than price, and profit maximization calls for operating where marginal revenue equals marginal cost. If the firm has the cost curves shown in Figure 13.1a, it produces an output of Q_1 and charges a price of P_1. The resulting economic profit equals the shaded area.

In terms of the diagram, the position of the monopolistically competitive firm resembles that of a monopoly. However, there are two important differences. First, Tight Jeans is only one among a number of firms producing a similar product, and so the demand curve is not

FIGURE 13.1

Monopolistic Competition
(a) In the short run, a firm in a monopolistically competitive market may make a profit.
(b) Attracted by the prospect of profits, new firms enter the market. As entry continues, the demand curve for existing firms shifts downward until a zero-profit, long-run equilibrium is attained.

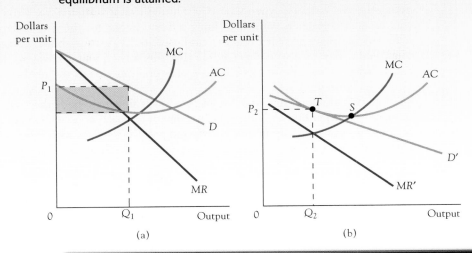

the market demand curve for jeans; it is only the demand curve for jeans produced by one firm. Second, under monopolistic competition, as distinct from pure monopoly, entry into the market is unrestricted. When existing firms are making profits, other firms are attracted to the market. Thus, the equilibrium in Figure 13.1a cannot be a long-run equilibrium because profits are being realized. It could represent a short-run equilibrium, but with the entry of other firms, the demand curves facing each existing firm will shift.

Under monopolistic competition, long-run equilibrium is attained as a result of firms entering (or leaving) the industry in response to profit incentives. In the present example, entry continues to occur until firms in the market are no longer making economic profits. How will the entry of other firms affect existing firms like Tight Jeans in Figure 13.1a? New firms will increase the total output of the industry, as well as provide for a wider variety of differentiated products. Both of these effects act to shift the demand curves of existing firms downward, leading to a general reduction in the level of prices in the industry and, from that, lower profits. (It is also possible that entry will lead to higher prices for some inputs, causing cost curves to shift upward as in an increasing-cost competitive industry, but we will ignore this possibility.) Entry and output adjustments by existing firms will continue until economic profits are zero; only then will there be no further incentive for other firms to enter the market.

Figure 13.1b shows a position of long-run equilibrium for Tight Jeans. The firm's demand curve has shifted down to D', a position where it is just tangent to the average cost curve at point T. (If the demand curve intersected the average cost curve, then there would be a range of output over which profit would be positive; the final equilibrium must be a tangency.) The profit-maximizing output is now Q_2 with a price of P_2; at this price and output Tight Jeans makes zero economic profit.[1] All rival firms will be in a similar situation, making zero economic profit in long-run equilibrium. Their cost and demand curves, however, need not be identical because they are not producing exactly the same products. For this reason, there may be a range of prices prevailing in equilibrium. Given the similarity among the differentiated products within a monopolistically competitive market, prices are likely to vary over a small range. A Big Mac and a Whopper need not be the exact same price, for example, but it would be surprising if the prices differed substantially.

Firms in a monopolistically competitive industry compete not only on price, but also by variations in their products intended to attract customers. The range of differentiated products in a market is not fixed, and firms often introduce new variations they believe will be profitable. For instance, when Coca-Cola introduced its caffeine-free Coke, it was betting that enough consumers wanted to limit caffeine intake for the line to be profitable. The company was right, and for a time it found itself in the position shown in Figure 13.1a, making a profit. But once it was recognized that this was a profitable way to differentiate cola drinks, other firms followed suit. Coca-Cola's profit eroded as the market moved toward a long-run equilibrium.[2]

Note that the long-run equilibrium position is similar to both the competitive and the monopolistic equilibria. As with perfect competition, each firm's demand curve is tangent to its long-run average cost curve, so economic profit is zero. As with monopoly, the demand curve is downward-sloping, so price exceeds marginal cost at the equilibrium. However, be-

[1] It is not a coincidence that marginal revenue and marginal cost are equal at the output where the demand curve is tangent to the average cost curve; it is a geometric necessity. Try depicting the equilibrium with total revenue and total cost curves to see why.

[2] Not all new product variations, of course, are successful. For example, McDonald's introduced the McLean burger during the 1980s, hoping that it would satisfy the tastes of health-conscious fast-food consumers. The McLean burger never proved profitable and came to be known as the "McFlopper" by industry analysts.

cause the firm's demand curve is relatively elastic, price will normally not exceed marginal cost by very much. For instance, demand elasticities for monopolistically competitive firms can easily exceed 10. If the firm's demand elasticity is 15, we can use the markup formula explained in Chapter 11 $[(P - MC)/P = 1/\eta]$ to see that when profit is being maximized, the markup would be only about 7 percent of price.

Monopolistic Competition and Efficiency

In Chapter 10, we saw that a competitive industry tends to be efficient, while in Chapter 11 we saw that a monopoly is inefficient (produces a deadweight loss). Because monopolistic competition combines elements of both monopoly and competition, it is natural to consider whether it is an efficient market structure, like competition, or inefficient, like monopoly.

Monopolistic competition has been charged with inefficiency in two respects. We can examine both with the aid of Figure 13.2, which shows a monopolistically competitive firm in long-run equilibrium (ignore the D^* demand curve for now). The first aspect of the alleged inefficiency involves the fact that the firm does not operate at the minimum point on its long-run average cost curve. In the diagram, the firm operates at point A, where average cost per unit is greater than at point S. Every firm in the monopolistically competitive industry is in a similar position. By contrast, firms in a competitive industry operate at the minimum points on their long-run AC curves. When firms fail to produce at lowest possible average cost, they are sometimes said to have **excess capacity**.

A failure to operate at minimum average cost is potentially inefficient because it is possible to produce the same *industry* output at a lower cost. To verify this notion, suppose that there are currently 10 firms like the one in Figure 13.2, each producing 100 units of output at an average cost of $15. The total cost of producing the 1,000 units would therefore be $15,000 (10 × 100 × $15). If the average total cost is at a minimum of, say, $11 per unit at an output of 125 units per firm, then 8 firms could produce the *same* 1,000 total output for less total cost. The total cost would now be $11,000 (8 × 125 × $11).

A monopolistically competitive market has also been alleged to be inefficient because it produces the wrong total output from a social perspective. (Note that in discussing excess capacity we were concerned with an unchanged total output.) Each firm is producing an output where price is greater than marginal cost. This condition suggests, by analogy to the

EXCESS CAPACITY
the result of firms failing to produce at lowest possible average cost

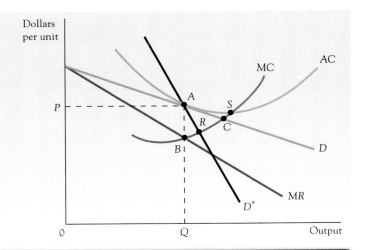

FIGURE 13.2

**Alleged Deadweight Loss
of Monopolistic Competition**
The monopolistic competitor's demand curve is *D* when it alone varies price; the demand curve *D** is relevant when all firms simultaneously change output. The deadweight loss is shown by area *ARB*; similar areas for the other monopolistically competitive firms can be added to this area to obtain the total deadweight loss due to restricted output in this market.

case of pure monopoly, that additional output is worth more to consumers than the cost of producing it. There is a deadweight loss from producing too little.

Figure 13.2 shows a monopolistically competitive firm producing an output of Q where price, AQ, is greater than marginal cost, BQ. It is tempting to apply the same reasoning we did in the case of pure monopoly and argue that the magnitude of the deadweight loss equals triangular area ACB. By performing the same calculation for each firm in the industry and adding up the results, we could arrive at the deadweight loss for the entire monopolistically competitive industry. Tempting as it is, this procedure is incorrect and overstates the industry's total potential deadweight loss.

To understand this, consider the firm in Figure 13.2 expanding output to the apparently efficient point C on its demand curve. Recall that the firm's demand curve is drawn on the assumption that rival firms keep their prices unchanged. This is the appropriate assumption if we are examining a price change by one firm alone. However, the prospective inefficiency here is that *all* firms in this industry are producing too little. If all expand their output, the demand curve confronting each firm must shift downward. Consequently, it is not desirable for every firm to expand output to the point where marginal cost intersects its *initial* demand curve, since that curve shifts in reaction to output and price changes by the other firms.

There is a complicated interdependence between individual firms' demand curves in an industry composed of several firms, and that interdependence must be accounted for in evaluating efficiency. (Note that this problem did not arise with pure monopoly because there was only one firm in the industry, or with a competitive market where we worked with industry, and not firm, demand curves.) One way to account for the interdependence is to draw the demand curve confronting the firm when it and all other firms in the industry simultaneously expand output. This demand curve, shown as D^* in Figure 13.2, captures the interdependence among the firms and shows that the marginal value, or price, of the firm's product falls more rapidly when rival firms are also producing more units. Point R now represents the efficient output of this firm, and this is consistent with every other firm also having expanded output to the point where their price is equal to marginal cost. We can thus sum the areas like ARB to arrive at the total deadweight loss resulting from each firm producing at a point where price exceeds marginal cost. Of course, the important point is that the industry's total deadweight loss is smaller than if we erroneously sum up the areas like ACB.

While monopolistic competition has been charged with being inefficient, there are three reasons why government intervention probably is not warranted. First, any deadweight loss associated with monopolistic competition is likely to be small, due to the presence of competing firms and free entry. Put differently, each firm's demand curve is relatively elastic, and so the excess of price over marginal cost is typically small. In the case of pure monopoly, this is not necessarily true. (Note that this excess, $P - MC$, is the height of the deadweight loss triangle, AB, in Figure 13.2.) For the same reason, the cost associated with excess capacity will also tend to be small.

Second, and, perhaps, most important, any possible inefficiency cost must be weighed against the product variety produced by monopolistic competition and the benefits of such variety to consumers. Similarly, it is probably desirable for firms to continue to have a dynamic incentive to introduce new differentiated products that better satisfy consumer tastes, and that incentive could be undermined by regulation.

Third, any sort of intervention has its own costs, which must also be balanced against the potential gain from expanding output. The costs of operating a regulatory agency may exceed the noted deadweight loss associated with monopolistic competition. Moreover, regulators can find it difficult to obtain the information necessary to achieve a more efficient output and mistakes may be made.

APPLICATION 13.1   READY-TO-REGULATE READY-TO-EAT

In the early 1970s, the Federal Trade Commission (FTC) initiated antitrust proceedings against the three leading ready-to-eat (RTE) cereal manufacturers. The three manufacturers accounted for more than 80 percent of RTE cereal sales and had been instrumental in increasing the number of nationally marketed brands from 27 in 1950 to 74 in 1971. The FTC argued that the product proliferation effectively precluded new entry and relied upon extensive advertising aimed at overly impressionable customers (kids) to differentiate cereals. While the typical industry devoted less than 1 percent of its sales revenue to advertising, the RTE cereal industry allocated more than 11 percent and ranked among the top five industries in terms of advertising intensiveness as of 1977. This is what one would expect from a monopolistically competitive market in which firms compete by varying (and advertising) the nature of their products in an effort to attract customers. The FTC proposed breaking up the three top RTE manufacturers into eight more evenly matched firms, regulating industry expenditures on advertising, and requiring licensing of significant cereal formulas and trademarks.

Although the FTC alleged that there was little fundamental difference between RTE cereal brands, manufacturers argued that the grain bases, shapes, flavors, nutritional values, and so on of the various brands ultimately reflected vigorous competition and the desire to better satisfy consumers' preferences for diversified breakfast fare. Furthermore, RTE manufacturers argued that the pricing discretion afforded to any individual brand by product proliferation was relatively minor— that is, the elasticity of demand for any particular brand was fairly high.

After spending several million dollars to prosecute the case, the FTC dropped its proceedings in 1982. The reversal partly resulted from the election of Ronald Reagan as president in 1980 and the appointment of more pro-business commissioners to the FTC. Moreover, the rapid growth in the late 1970s of health-oriented cereals that featured ingredients such as oat bran and were marketed by smaller firms, as well as growth in the number of house brand cereals sold by supermarkets, openly contradicted the FTC claims that product proliferation by the major cereal makers deterred new entrants to the industry.

APPLICATION 13.2   MONOPOLISTIC COMPETITION IS IN THE EYE OF THE BEHOLDER

Refractive eye surgery has become very popular in recent years.[3] In 2000 alone, more than 1 million people worldwide had the procedure in order to correct their vision. As the refractive eye surgery industry has grown, it has evidenced all the characteristics of monopolistic competition. Entry and exit into the industry is relatively unrestricted. There are a large number of independent sellers who do not produce a homogeneous product. For example, under the Lasik procedure, a surgeon creates a flap in the eye, then uses a laser on the area underneath to correct the vision. PRK, another form of laser eye surgery, consists of a surgeon using a laser on the eye's surface to correct vision. Some patients opt for corneal rings, prescription inserts that are intended to correct mild nearsightedness.

The various sellers of refractive eye surgery services tout the advantages of their differentiated product over what rivals are offering. As of 2000, it has been estimated that surgery centers are spending $200 per each eye corrected on advertising. For example, TLC Laser Eye Centers rely on Tiger Woods to advertise their ser-

[3]This application is based on: Randy Tucker, "Cost Cuts Debated by Doctors: Surgery Often 'On Sale'," *Cincinnati Enquirer*, November 15, 2000, p. B10; "Chat About the Risks of Laser Eye Surgery," *ABC-NEWS.com*, November 1, 2000; and "Turning Surgery Into a Commodity," *New York Times*, December 9, 2000, pp. B1 and B4.

vice. However, Dr. Penny Asbell, Director of the Cornea Service and Refractive Surgery Center in New York, urges prospective customers to be cautious when evaluating such promotions. Asbell notes that: "Just because someone is advertising doesn't necessarily mean that they're more qualified." She recommends relying on a surgeon who is associated with an academic medical center, such as a teaching hospital or one that is well known for advanced technology.

Dr. Steve Updegraff, medical director of Updegraff Lasik Vision in Tampa Bay, Florida, recommends choosing a doctor who is a Fellow of the American College of Surgeons. "The credentialling process there is pretty steep; also that group is diligent about advancing the field of surgery." Dr. Updegraff says that when something goes wrong during the flap cutting stage of Lasik, some less experienced surgeons may go ahead and perform the tissue removal anyway, instead of stopping surgery and trying again at a later date. He says that this is one reason for poor results.

Finally, sellers of refractive eye surgery services appear to also compete on price and respond to profit-based incentives for entry and exit. Whereas, the cost of laser eye surgery was as high as $6,000 in the late 1990s, it had fallen to less than $1,000 for surgery on both eyes as of 2000. Lasik Vision, a Canada-based corporation, has opened centers across the United States in recent years. When Lasik Vision entered the market in Cincinnati, Ohio, with an introductory offer of $1,000 for both eyes, its chief rival in town, a local firm, LCA-Vision, Inc., immediately matched its price.

13.2   OLIGOPOLY AND THE COURNOT MODEL

OLIGOPOLY
an industry structure characterized by a few firms producing all or most of the output of some good that may or may not be differentiated

Oligopoly is an industry structure characterized by a few firms producing all, or most, of the output of some good that may or may not be differentiated. The number of competitors is the distinguishing feature of this market structure. With competition (and monopolistic competition), there are "many" sellers, whereas with pure monopoly there is only one seller. Oligopoly falls between these extremes. In the United States, there are a number of examples of oligopolistic industries, including aluminum, cellular phone service, network television, and military aircraft.

When there are a small number of competitors, their marketing decisions will exhibit *strong mutual interdependence*, and this characteristic of oligopoly is what makes analysis of it difficult. By mutual interdependence, we mean that a firm's actions (setting price, for example) have a noticeable effect on its rivals, and so they are likely to react in some way. In this way, the firms are interdependent. As an example, suppose that General Motors (GM) is considering a 10 percent cut in the price of its Buick line. This action will have a significant effect on Ford and DaimlerChrysler. If they maintain their prices, they will lose sales to GM. If they cut prices, they can avoid losing sales, but they will make a smaller profit per car. To complicate matters further, Ford and DaimlerChrysler have the options of cutting prices by more or less than the 10 percent cut by GM.

Now consider what this situation means for GM: It cannot predict the results of its own 10 percent price cut without knowing how its rivals will respond. For instance, GM's sales will rise more if Ford and DaimlerChrysler maintain their prices than they would if those companies also reduce the prices of their cars. GM must base its decisions on some guess, or conjecture, about the responses of its competitors. What guess should it make? The problem for GM, and also for us as we try to understand the market, is that it is far from clear which prediction is appropriate. The market will function differently depending on which predictions about responses each firm makes and acts on. Furthermore, over time the firm may learn that some of its predictions were wrong and alter its behavior accordingly. But its competitors will also be learning and trying to outguess it. Complex questions of strategy arise in this setting.

In view of this complicated interdependence, it is perhaps not surprising that we do not have one agreed-upon theory of oligopoly. In fact, dozens of models have been suggested. Some of them appear to successfully explain the behavior in *some* industries over *some* periods of time, but none appears to explain all oligopolistic behavior. We will discuss a few of the more important models that have been developed, but be forewarned that determining when each model applies (if at all) is often difficult.

In addition to smallness in the numbers of competitors, there are two other features of oligopoly that are likely to have a bearing on how the market performs. First is whether the product is homogeneous or differentiated. Some oligopolies produce a homogeneous product, like aluminum or steel, while others produce differentiated products, like diapers or airline service in smaller city-pair markets. When the product is differentiated, advertising (which we will discuss in more detail in the following chapter) is likely to become a more important influence in the market.

A second important oligopoly feature is the nature of barriers to entry, if any. Oligopolistic firms are often thought to realize economic profits, and whenever there are profits there is incentive for entry. Something must impede entry for profits to persist. Moreover, just as in the case of monopoly (see Chapter 11), potential entry can influence oligopolists' pricing behavior.

The Cournot Model

We begin our discussion of oligopoly by considering one of the earliest models, introduced by French economist Augustin Cournot in 1838.[4] Cournot considered a **duopoly**, an industry with just two firms. To illustrate his analysis, Cournot assumed that the two firms sold water from the only two mineral springs in the area. To follow tradition, we will consider two firms that sell bottled water, Artesia and Utopia. No entry of new firms is possible. The bottled water is a homogeneous product, so that only one price can prevail in the market; that price is determined by the *combined* output of the two firms in conjunction with the market (industry) demand curve for bottled water. To further simplify the analysis, we assume that both firms have constant and equal long-run marginal cost curves, and that the market demand curve is linear.

The key element in the **Cournot model** is that *each firm determines its output based on the assumption that the other firm will not change its output.* This assumption (and it may be an unreasonable one, as we will see) allows us to determine the market price and output. To see how we can do this, consider Figure 13.3, where the *market* demand and marginal revenue curves are shown as D and MR, and each firm's marginal cost (MC) and average total cost (ATC) curves are assumed to be constant. Now let's examine Artesia's output decision. Artesia's most profitable output will depend on how much Utopia is producing, so first we consider how much Artesia will produce for each possible output of Utopia.

Suppose that Utopia produces nothing. In the Cournot model, Artesia assumes Utopia will continue to produce nothing whatever output Artesia chooses. In this situation, Artesia confronts the entire market demand curve and behaves as a monopolist, producing Q_M (48), where Artesia's marginal revenue curve (which coincides with the market marginal revenue curve in this case) intersects marginal cost. In the analysis that follows, it will be helpful to remember that with linear demand and constant marginal cost, the marginal revenue curve intersects marginal cost at an output half as large as that at which marginal cost intersects the demand curve. In this case, Artesia's output of 48 is half as large as the output that

DUOPOLY
an industry with just two firms

COURNOT MODEL
a model of oligopoly that assumes each firm in a duopoly determines its output based on the assumption that the other firm will not change its output

---

[4]Augustin Cournot, *Recherches sur les Principes Mathématiques de la Théorie des Richesses* (Paris, 1838), trans. Nathaniel Bacon (New York: Macmillan, 1897).

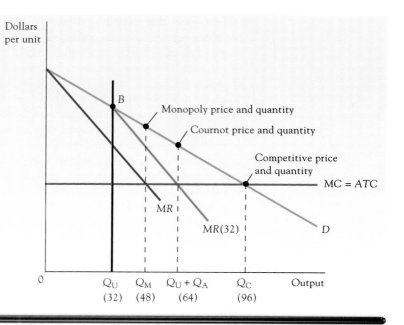

FIGURE 13.3

The Cournot Model
When Utopia's output is 32, the vertical axis relevant for Artesia's output decision is BQ_U, and Artesia's demand curve is the BD portion of the market demand curve. Artesia's marginal revenue curve is then $MR(32)$, and its most profitable output is 32, so combined output is 64.

would be produced under competition, 96, as shown by the intersection of demand and marginal cost.

Artesia's output depends on how much Utopia produces. We have just seen that Artesia will produce 48 units when Utopia produces nothing. Alternatively, suppose that Utopia produces 32 units. Then how much will Artesia produce? Artesia believes Utopia will continue to produce 32 units regardless of how much Artesia produces (and thus regardless of what happens to the market price, which will be determined by the two firms' combined output). At each price, Artesia can sell 32 fewer units than total quantity demanded as shown by the market demand curve. So Artesia's demand curve is the market demand curve shifted leftward by 32 units. This idea can be shown in a simpler, yet equivalent fashion by moving Artesia's vertical axis rightward by 32 units without repositioning the demand curve. Taking the origin for Artesia now to be Q_U, the demand curve confronting Artesia is the BD portion of the original demand curve. This makes sense. If Artesia produces nothing, total output will be 32 (Utopia's output), price will be BQ_U, and as Artesia produces and adds to Utopia's output, price will fall along the BD portion of the demand curve.

Confronted with the demand curve BD, Artesia's marginal revenue curve is $MR(32)$, the marginal revenue curve when Utopia's output is fixed at 32. In this situation, Artesia produces where its marginal revenue curve, $MR(32)$, intersects marginal cost; thus Artesia's output is 32 units, while the total output of the two firms is 64 units. Note that Artesia's output is half the difference between the competitive output (96) and Utopia's output (32); this is because $MR(32)$ intersects MC halfway between the new vertical axis for Artesia and the output at which MC intersects the demand curve.

We can now see how Artesia's output depends on how much Utopia produces. For each possible output by Utopia, Artesia will produce half the difference between Utopia's output and the output at which MC intersects D (96 units). If Utopia produces nothing, Artesia will produce 48; if Utopia produces 10, Artesia will produce 43; if Utopia produces 20, Artesia will produce 38; and so on. Now that we know what Artesia will do, what about Utopia? Because the firms have the same costs and because we also make the Cournot assumption for Utopia (that is, it will take Artesia's output as a given in determining its output), the same relationship holds for Utopia. In other words, Utopia will produce 48 units if Artesia produces nothing, 43 if Artesia produces 10, and so on.

So where will the market equilibrium be? Equilibrium is reached when neither firm has any incentive to change its output. This occurs when each firm is producing the output it prefers given the other firm's output. In this example, that occurs only when both firms produce 32 units. To check this, we note in Figure 13.3 that Artesia's most profitable output when Utopia produces 32 units is also 32 units. Because Utopia has the same marginal cost curve, it will also maximize profit by producing 32 units when Artesia produces 32. Neither firm has any incentive to change its output of 32 when the other firm is producing 32. (The implication of equal output here arises because the firms have the same costs; if costs differ, outputs will differ, but the reasoning remains the same.)

There is another way to arrive at this conclusion—by using reaction curves. Each firm's **reaction curve** shows its profit-maximizing output for each possible output by the other firm. In fact, we have already explained the relationships above. In Figure 13.4, R_A is Artesia's reaction curve. It shows that Artesia will produce 48 units when Utopia's output (measured on the vertical axis) is zero, will produce 36 when Utopia's output is 24, and so on. Utopia's reaction curve is R_U; it is the same relationship as for Artesia but looks different in the graph because the firms' outputs are on different axes. We can see how equilibrium can be attained in a step-by-step process, although this should not be thought of as the actual adjustment process, because if both firms started producing 32, there would be no reason for either to change. To begin, if Utopia produces nothing, then Artesia produces 48. When Artesia produces 48, however, we can see by looking directly above 48 to Utopia's reaction curve that it will produce 24. With Utopia producing 24, Artesia would prefer to change its output to 36. And with Artesia producing 36, Utopia will produce 30. The adjustments follow the arrows, and the firms are not *both* satisfied with their outputs until they reach the point where each is producing 32 units. Put differently, the Cournot equilibrium occurs at the *intersection* of the two reaction curves.

REACTION CURVE
a relationship showing one firm's most profitable output as a function of the output chosen by other firms

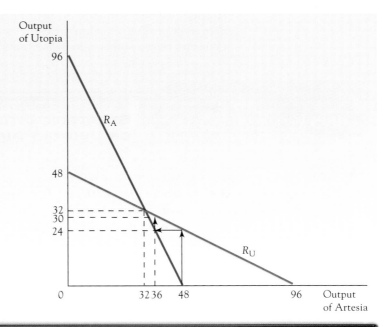

FIGURE 13.4

The Cournot Model with Reaction Curves
Each reaction curve shows one firm's most profitable output as a function of the other firm's output. For example, when Artesia's output is 48, R_U shows 24 to be Utopia's most profitable output. The Cournot equilibrium is shown by the intersection of the reaction curves, with each firm producing its most profitable output given the output of the other firm.

As depicted in Figure 13.3, the Cournot equilibrium involves a combined output of 64 units by the two firms in the industry. It is important to note that this amount is greater than the pure monopoly output (48 units) and less than the competitive output (96 units). A total output lying between that of pure monopoly and competition is characteristic of most oligopoly models. Some other things are clear from inspection of Figure 13.3. Price exceeds marginal cost, and because average cost equals marginal cost, price is above average cost and both firms realize economic profit. However, their combined profit is less than the maximum combined profit possible if the firms together produce the monopoly output. This fact is significant—it means that if the firms colluded instead of behaving independently as Cournot duopolists, they could increase their combined profit.

Evaluation of the Cournot Model

Is it reasonable for a firm to assume, in choosing its output, that the output of a rival remains constant? Not in the duopoly setting we have just studied, if the market is still adjusting toward the Cournot equilibrium. Away from the Cournot equilibrium—that is, when Artesia changes its output on the assumption that Utopia will keep its output fixed—it will observe that the assumption is wrong: Utopia does change its output in response to Artesia's actions. Yet at each step in the adjustment process, the firms continue to behave based on an assumption they can see is wrong. Thus, the key assumption of the Cournot model, that each firm takes the other firms' outputs as given, appears to be suspect if the market is still adjusting toward equilibrium.

While this criticism is significant, there are some things that can be said in defense of the Cournot model. First, note that if the equilibrium is somehow established, firms will not see the assumption invalidated. When Artesia sees Utopia producing 32 units, and decides on 32 for itself, based on the assumption that Utopia will not change its output, it will be right. The assumption becomes implausible only for adjustments to the equilibrium.

Second, the assumption is more plausible the larger the number of firms in the market. (The Cournot model can readily accommodate any number of firms greater than two and, in general, the greater the number of firms, the larger the total industry output as a percentage of the competitive output.) With 10 equal-sized firms, if one changes its output by, say, 10 percent, it will represent only a 1 percent change in industry output, which will have a small effect on price. The other firms may not associate such a small price change with the actions of one firm because other things, like shifting market demand, can also affect price.

APPLICATION 13.3   STRATEGIC INTERACTION ON DUOPOLY AIR ROUTES

A 1993 study examined the interaction between American and United Airlines over 1984–1988 on 16 Chicago-based air routes on which the two carriers could reasonably be characterized as a symmetric duopoly.[5] On these routes, the two carriers held a combined market share of over 90 percent, accounted for more

than one-third of the total passenger traffic each, and had very similar costs.

The study found that Cournot behavior most frequently characterized the interaction between the two air carriers on the selected duopoly routes. The Cournot outcome, however, did not always prevail. Changes in underlying costs and market demand influenced the strategic interaction between the two carriers. For example, a strike in 1985 by the pilots of United Airlines triggered an apparent price war and an outcome more

[5]James A. Brander and Anming Zhang, "Dynamic Oligopoly Behavior in the Airline Industry," *International Journal of Industrial Organization*, 11 (1993), pp. 407–435.

consistent with competition than with the Cournot model. The strike appeared to have increased the uncertainty each firm had (and thereby assumptions it made) about its rival's costs and strategic intentions.

The study acknowledged that some other factors may explain why, in terms of total output, the most frequently observed market outcome (consistent with Cournot behavior) lies between the pure monopoly and the perfectly competitive outcome. For example, because American and United Airlines interact in more than one market (that is, on different routes), such multiple points of contact may serve to restrain competition between the two firms on any given route. In other words, American may be wary of aggressively expanding output and lowering price on the Chicago–Des Moines (Iowa) route for fear that United may retaliate in kind across all the routes on which the two airlines compete.

On the other hand, while only two carriers may operate on any particular route, there is always the possibility of new entry. Just as we saw with monopoly in Chapter 11, the possibility of entry can strongly affect the operation of a market, and the same is certainly true in oligopoly markets. If American and United recognize that entry will occur if the price rises too much above cost, it may influence their output decisions. The threat of entry thus serves to push the observed market output away from the pure monopoly outcome and closer to the competitive outcome.

13.3 OTHER OLIGOPOLY MODELS

The Cournot model serves as a good introduction to oligopoly models by highlighting the importance of how firms handle the mutual interdependence in such markets. In this section we explore two other models of oligopoly. Although they by no means represent all the models that have been suggested, they do indicate some different assumptions a firm in an oligopoly market might make about rival firms' actions.

The Stackelberg Model

Recall that in the Cournot model each firm takes the other firm's output as constant in determining its own output. We saw, however, that this assumption may not be valid. So now suppose that in the same two-firm example, we have one firm that continues to behave in the naive Cournot fashion, while the other firm wises up and realizes that it should not assume its rival's output doesn't change. In fact, let's assume that Artesia realizes how Utopia chooses its output (from its reaction curve) and see whether Artesia can use that information to realize greater profit. Artesia is the "leader" firm in this case; it chooses its best output taking Utopia's reaction into account. Utopia is the "follower" firm; it selects output in exactly the same way as in the Cournot model, by taking the output of the other firm as given. This is the essence of the **Stackelberg model**: a leader firm selects its output first, taking the reactions of naive Cournot follower firms into account.[6]

Figure 13.5 illustrates the Stackelberg model as it operates for Artesia and Utopia. The marginal cost, average total cost, and market demand curves are shown in Figure 13.5a; they are the same as in Figure 13.3. Figure 13.5a shows how Artesia selects its output. Given Artesia's output, Utopia's output can be read off its reaction curve, R_U, reproduced directly below in Figure 13.5b. Remember that we are assuming that Artesia knows Utopia's reaction curve, so that it knows how much output Utopia will produce for each output Artesia may choose.

Our first task is to determine Artesia's demand curve under these conditions. This will not be the market demand curve, but what is referred to as a **residual demand curve**, which shows how much Artesia can sell at each price. The amount that Artesia can sell at each

STACKELBERG MODEL
a model of oligopoly in which a leader firm selects its output first, taking the reactions of follower firms into account

RESIDUAL DEMAND CURVE
a firm's demand curve based on the assumption that the firm knows how much output rivals will produce for each output the firm may choose

[6]Heinrich von Stackelberg, *Marktform und Gleichewicht* (Vienna: Julius Springer, 1934). As with the Cournot model, the Stackelberg model can readily be adapted to account for a larger number of firms.

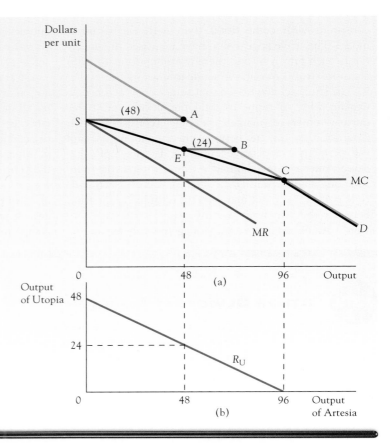

FIGURE 13.5

The Stackelberg Model
When Artesia knows that Utopia will choose output as in the Cournot model, Artesia confronts the demand curve *SCD*, and its most profitable output is 48. Utopia will produce 24, so total output is 72, higher than when both firms behave as Cournot duopolists.

price is less than total quantity demanded (as shown by the market demand curve) by the amount that Utopia produces. For example, suppose that Artesia produces zero. From Utopia's reaction curve, Artesia knows that Utopia will then produce 48 units. Thus, total (combined) output is 48 units when Artesia produces nothing, and the market price in Figure 13.5a will be S. At the other extreme, if Artesia produces 96 units, Utopia will produce nothing, and Artesia will be at point C in Figure 13.5a. That gives two points on Artesia's residual demand curve, S and C. Artesia's residual demand curve (with the assumed linear demand and cost conditions) is just the straight line connecting these points between outputs of zero and 96 units. Beyond 96 units of output, Artesia's residual demand curve coincides with the market demand curve (along *CD*), since Utopia will produce zero if Artesia produces in excess of 96 units.

To see that straight-line segment *SC* represents Artesia's residual demand curve for outputs between zero and 96 units, suppose that Artesia produces 48 units. From Utopia's reaction curve, Artesia knows that Utopia will produce 24, so total output will be 72. When total output is 72, the price will be given by point B on the market demand curve. Thus, Artesia can sell 48 units when price is at the height of point E (the same height as point B), which gives us a third point on Artesia's demand curve. Note that the horizontal distance between Artesia's demand curve and the market demand curve is the output of Utopia. As you can see, Utopia's output becomes smaller as Artesia increases output along its demand curve. In fact, for each one-unit increase in output by Artesia, Utopia reduces output by one-half unit (as can be seen from Utopia's reaction curve), so the two firms' total output increases by only half as much as the increase by Artesia. That is why price declines less rapidly along Artesia's residual demand curve than along the market demand curve (Artesia's demand curve is flatter; in fact, the slope is exactly half the slope of the market demand curve).

With knowledge of its demand curve, profit maximization by Artesia is straightforward. With demand curve SCD, the marginal revenue curve is MR, intersecting the marginal cost curve halfway between zero output and the output where marginal cost intersects demand. Therefore, Artesia's profit-maximizing output is 48 units, with price shown by the height of point E. Utopia is producing 24 units, so total industry output is 72 units.

Because we are using the same demand and cost conditions as we did with the Cournot model, it is instructive to compare the outcomes. Note that total output is higher with the Stackelberg model (72 versus 64), so price to consumers is lower. Output is closer to the competitive result than in the Cournot model, but still lies between the competitive and monopoly outputs. In addition, Artesia is making a larger profit and Utopia a smaller profit than in the case of a Cournot equilibrium. (This is not shown in the graphs but is easily verified.) This outcome is to be expected: Artesia is exploiting its superior knowledge of how Utopia will respond to make a larger profit at Utopia's expense.

Our discussion highlights a key point: namely, that the conjectures a firm makes in an oligopoly market about how its rivals will respond can affect firms' outputs and profits as well as total industry output. For example, total industry output is higher in a Stackelberg model than in a Cournot model. And the firm that is a Stackelberg leader can take advantage of its leadership position to set a larger (firm) output, thereby enhancing its profit at the expense of firms that follow its lead in naive Cournot fashion.

Whether the Stackelberg or Cournot model better describes an oligopoly depends on the particular market being examined. Where an oligopoly is composed of roughly equal-sized firms, none of which has superior knowledge or exercises a leadership position, the Cournot model is likely to be more apt. However, when one firm is more sophisticated about how rival firms will react and uses this information to operate as a leader in terms of output, pricing, and/or the introduction of new products, the Stackelberg model is more appropriate. The leadership role played by Intel in terms of setting price and introducing new products in the computer chip market during the 1990s provides a possible example of the latter case.

The Dominant Firm Model

In the Stackelberg model, the leader firm assumes that rivals display Cournot behavior and plans its output and price accordingly. We now will examine an alternative model in which the leader firm makes a different conjecture about the behavior of rival follower firms. In this model, known as the **dominant firm model**, the leader or dominant firm assumes that its rivals behave as competitive firms in determining their output. (Sometimes this model is referred to as the *dominant firm with a competitive fringe* model because the competitive firms are on the fringe.) The dominant firm model has been used by economists to analyze the performance of many industries.

Figure 13.6 shows how this market structure operates. To determine what price will maximize its profit, the dominant firm must know its demand curve. As with the Stackelberg model, the dominant firm's demand curve is a residual demand curve that shows what it can sell after accounting for other firms' output. In this case, the other firms in the market are assumed to behave as competitive firms: They will accept whatever price is set by the dominant firm and produce an output where their marginal cost equals that price. The output of the competitive fringe firms can therefore be determined from their supply curve because they collectively behave as a competitive industry. This supply curve is shown as S_F in the diagram. The market demand curve is DD'.

DOMINANT FIRM MODEL
a model of oligopoly in which the leader or dominant firm assumes its rivals behave like competitive firms in determining their output

FIGURE 13.6

The Dominant Firm Model

With the supply curve of fringe firms shown as S_F, the residual demand curve of the dominant firm is derived by subtracting the quantity supplied by fringe firms at each price from total quantity demanded at that price; the result is curve P_1AD'. The dominant firm maximizes profit by producing Q_D and charging price P; fringe firms produce Q_F at that price, so total output is Q_T.

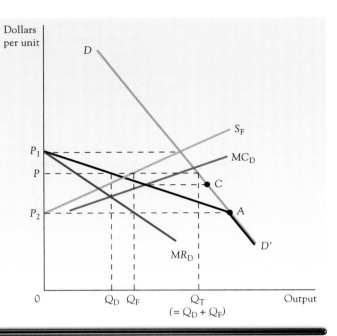

At any price, the dominant firm can sell an amount equal to the total quantity demanded at that price (as shown by DD') minus the quantity the fringe firms produce (as shown by S_F). For example, the dominant firm's demand curve begins at P_1 because at that price the fringe firms will supply as much as consumers wish to purchase, and the dominant firm could sell nothing. At the other extreme, if the dominant firm charges a price less than P_2, it faces the entire market demand curve because the fringe firms will produce nothing at such a low price. Between P_1 and P_2, the dominant firm's residual demand curve is P_1A, where the horizontal distance between this demand curve and the market demand curve at each possible price shows the output of the fringe firms.

Armed with a knowledge of its demand curve, P_1AD', the dominant firm also knows its marginal revenue curve, MR_D, and maximizes profit by producing where marginal revenue equals marginal cost. With a marginal cost curve shown as MC_D, the dominant firm's profit-maximizing output equals Q_D. The price is P, the height of the dominant firm's residual demand curve (not the market demand curve) at output Q_D. At price P, other firms produce Q_F as shown by their supply curve, and total output, Q_T, is the sum of their output and the dominant firm's output. At price P, consumers wish to purchase an output of Q_T, and so the market is in equilibrium. At the equilibrium, note that price is above marginal cost for the dominant firm, but it is equal to marginal cost for the fringe firms, S_F. This implies that total output is less than if the industry were competitive. The competitive output for the dominant firm is where MC_D intersects the residual demand curve; at that point both it and the other firms are producing where marginal cost equals price. Total output and price under competitive conditions are indicated by point C on the market demand curve.

One interesting implication of this model is that the share of total industry output produced by the dominant firm may not indicate how close output comes to the competitive result. For example, suppose that the supply curve of the fringe firms is perfectly elastic (as with a constant-cost competitive industry) at price P: The supply curve coincides with the horizontal dotted line in the graph. Then the dominant firm's residual demand curve is also given by this horizontal dotted line, and marginal revenue will equal P out to output Q_T.

The dominant firm will produce where its marginal cost curve intersects this horizontal line. Industry output will be the same, Q_T, but now the dominant firm is producing about 90 percent of it. Furthermore, price is equal to marginal cost, as under competition, even though one firm is contributing 90 percent of total output. This example illustrates the critical importance of the elasticity of the competitive firms' supply curve for the functioning of this sort of market structure.

Recall that this model differs from the Stackelberg model only in what the leader, or dominant, firm assumes about rival firms' output. In the Stackelberg model, the leader firm assumes Cournot behavior on the part of rivals; in this model, it assumes competitive behavior. The dominant firm model is more appropriate when there are a sufficiently large number of fringe firms for the assumption of competitive behavior to be plausible.

The Elasticity of the Dominant Firm's Demand Curve

Based on the fact that the dominant firm's output is equal to the total market output minus the quantity the fringe firms supply, we can derive the dominant firm's elasticity of demand as follows:

$$\eta_D = \eta_M\left(\frac{1}{MS}\right) + \varepsilon_{SF}\left(\frac{1}{MS} - 1\right); \tag{1}$$

where η_D is the elasticity of the dominant firm's demand, η_M is the elasticity of the market demand; MS is the dominant firm's market share; and ε_{SF} is the elasticity of supply of the fringe firms.[7] To see how to apply the formula, consider the case of the pharmaceutical firm Hoffman-La Roche (Roche for short), whose brand-name product Valium is the market-leading anti-anxiety drug. Suppose that Roche can be taken to be the dominant firm in the anti-anxiety market, that it has a 25 percent market share, that it faces a competitive fringe of firms that produce the generic equivalent of Valium, that the elasticity of supply by the competitive fringe is equal to 2, and that the elasticity of market demand for anti-anxiety drugs is equal to 1. Using these assumptions, we can calculate the elasticity of demand for the dominant firm's product, Valium, as follows:

$$\eta_D = 1\left(\frac{1}{0.25}\right) + 2\left(\frac{1}{0.25} - 1\right) = 10.$$

Even though its output is equal to one-fourth the entire market output, Roche faces a residual demand with an elasticity of 10. Thus, if the company raises Valium's price by just 5 percent, it will lose half its sales.

The formula for the elasticity of the dominant firm's demand shows that the elasticity of demand for this firm becomes larger when (1) the dominant firm's market share becomes

---

[7]To derive this formula, we start with the fact that the dominant firm's output (Q_D) equals the market output (Q_M) minus the output of the competitive fringe (Q_{SF}):

$$Q_D = Q_M - Q_{SF}.$$

This relationship also holds for a given change in output that results from a price change:

$$\Delta Q_D = \Delta Q_M - \Delta Q_{SF}.$$

Now divide by Q_D and multiply the two terms on the right by Q_M/Q_M and Q_{SF}/Q_{SF}, respectively:

$$\frac{\Delta Q_D}{Q_D} = \left(\frac{\Delta Q_M}{Q_M}\right)\left(\frac{Q_M}{Q_D}\right) - \left(\frac{\Delta Q_{SF}}{Q_{SF}}\right)\left(\frac{Q_{SF}}{Q_D}\right).$$

Dividing this expression by $\Delta P/P$ yields the formula in the text. Note that the minus sign on the right-hand side became a plus sign because we are treating the elasticity of demand as a positive number; Q_M/Q_D equals $1/MS$; and Q_{SF}/Q_D equals $(Q_M - Q_D)/Q_D$ or $(1/MS) - 1$.

smaller; (2) the elasticity of the market demand becomes greater; and (3) the elasticity of supply by the competitive fringe becomes greater. For example, if Roche's market share was 10 percent instead of 25 percent, the elasticity of demand for Valium would be greater: 28 [1(1/0.1) + 2((1/0.1) − 1)] versus the 10 already calculated. If the elasticity of the demand for anti-anxiety drugs was 5 instead of 1, the elasticity of demand for Valium would be 26 [5(1/0.25) + 2((1/0.25) − 1)] instead of 10. And if the elasticity of the fringe supply was 5 instead of 2, the elasticity of demand for Valium would be 19 [1(1/0.25) + 5((1/0.25) − 1)] instead of 10.

APPLICATION 13.4   THE DYNAMICS OF THE DOMINANT FIRM MODEL IN PHARMACEUTICAL MARKETS

As the patent on a brand-name pharmaceutical expires, the producer of the drug typically confronts competition from generic manufacturers. Generic manufacturers do little research of their own; rather, they specialize in copying brand-name products after their patents expire. Generic manufacturers tend to become both more numerous and more capable of expanding their output capacity the longer that a brand-name drug is "off-patent." In such a setting, therefore, the brand-name drug producer can be taken to be the dominant firm, with its market share decreasing and the competitive fringe's elasticity increasing the more years the brand-name drug is off-patent.

What does the dominant firm model predict about the price charged by a brand-name drug manufacturer and the sensitivity of consumers to the brand-name drug's price as the number of years that the drug has been off-patent increases? As the fringe supply curve tends to shift rightward (see Figure 13.6) as the time since the brand-name drug manufacturer's patent expired increases, it works to shift the dominant firm's residual demand curve leftward and put downward pressure on the price charged by the brand-name drug manufacturer. Moreover, as both the brand-name manufacturer's market share decreases and the elasticity of the fringe supply increases, equation (1) indicates that the

elasticity of demand facing the brand-name manufacturer tends to increase with the time since patent expiration. The available empirical evidence bears out these theoretical predictions generated by the dominant firm model.[8]

The empirical evidence also suggests that after patent expiration, brand-name manufacturers have pursued a market segmentation strategy—charging a lower price to hospitals and health maintenance organizations than to retail pharmacies. Hospitals and health maintenance organizations are more sensitive to price owing to their large volume of purchases and their greater knowledge about the (characteristically small) risks of substituting a generic drug for a brand-name product. Market segmentation, however, has not been without its costs. Retail pharmacists have sued pharmaceutical companies for conspiring to deny them the same price discounts offered to hospitals and health maintenance organizations. Brand-name drug manufacturers opted to settle one such suit in 1996 for $551 million.[9]

[8]Richard Caves, Michael Whinston, and Mark Horwitz, "Patent Expiration, Entry, and Competition in the U.S. Pharmaceutical Industry," *Brookings Papers on Economic Activity: Microeconomics 1991*, pp. 1–48.

[9]"Judge Agrees to Settlement in Drug Case," *New York Times*, June 22, 1996, p. 17.

13.4   CARTELS AND COLLUSION

In the oligopoly models we have examined so far, the individual firms were assumed to behave independently. Each firm makes a specific conjecture regarding how other firms will respond to its actions and then maximizes its own profit accordingly, without any concern for how it affects other firms' profits. An alternative class of oligopoly models is based on various types of cooperation among the firms. The firms coordinate their pricing and output decisions in an attempt to increase their combined profit, thereby increasing their individual profits as well.

The most important cooperative model of oligopoly is the cartel model. A **cartel** is an agreement among independent producers to coordinate their decisions so each of them will earn monopoly profit. Because cartels are illegal under the antitrust laws in the United States (though, surprisingly, not in many other countries), they are not common here. There have been a number of international cartels, however, and we examine one of the most famous, OPEC, later in this section. Familiarity with the cartel model is useful, because collusive practices that fall short of outright cartel agreements can be investigated with it. We begin by considering what happens if firms in a competitive industry form a cartel, and then extend the results to oligopolistic markets.

CARTEL

an agreement among independent producers to coordinate their decisions so each of them will earn monopoly profit

Cartelization of a Competitive Industry

Let's see how a group of firms in a competitive market can earn monopoly profits by coordinating their activities. We assume that the industry is initially in long-run equilibrium, and then we identify the short-run adjustments (with existing plants) that the industry's firms can make to reap monopoly profits for themselves. Figure 13.7b shows the industry equilibrium with a price of P and an output of 1,000 units. Figure 13.7a shows the competitive equilibrium for one of the firms in the industry. Note that initially, the firm faces the horizontal demand curve d at the market-determined price and produces an output of 50 units. To simplify matters, suppose that there are 20 identical firms in the industry, each producing 50 units of output.

FIGURE 13.7

A Cartel

Under competitive conditions industry output is Q and price is P. If the firms in the industry form a cartel, output is restricted to Q_1 in order to charge price P_1, the monopoly outcome. Each firm produces q_1 and makes a profit at price P_1.

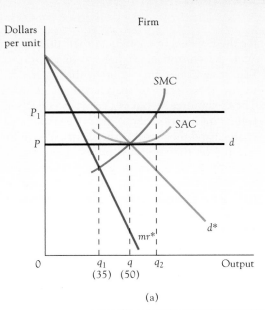

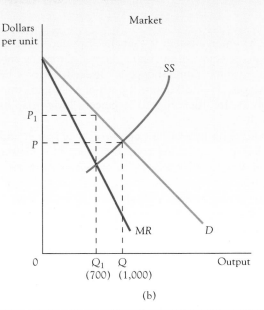

Next, the firms form a cartel and agree to restrict output to attain a higher price. Each firm agrees to produce an identical level of output, equal to one-twentieth of total industry output because there are 20 firms. The cartel agreement has the effect of changing the demand curve facing each firm. Before the agreement, if one firm alone reduced output, its action would not appreciably affect price, as shown by the firm's horizontal demand curve d. Now, however, other firms match a restriction in output by one firm, so when one firm cuts output by 15 units, all firms match the reduction, industry output falls by 300 units, and price rises significantly. The demand curve showing how price varies with output when firms' output decisions are coordinated in this way is the downward-sloping curve $d*$ in Figure 13.7a. At any price, the quantity on the $d*$ curve is 1/20 that on the industry demand curve.

Faced with this downward-sloping demand curve, the firm's profit-maximizing output occurs where its short-run marginal cost curve SMC intersects the new marginal revenue curve $mr*$. Output is 35 units, and because all 20 firms reduce production to the same output level, total output falls to 700 units and the price rises to P_1. Each firm is now making an economic profit. Indeed, *the idealized cartel result is just the same as if the industry were supplied by a monopoly that controlled the 20 firms*. Figure 13.7b illustrates the result, with the short-run supply curve SS (the sum of the SMC curves of the firms) intersecting the industry marginal revenue curve MR at an output of 700 units and a monopoly price of P_1. By forming a cartel and restricting output to achieve the monopoly equilibrium, the firms maximize their combined profit. Figure 13.7b shows the total market effect of the coordinated output reduction by the 20 firms; Figure 13.7a shows the effects on each firm individually.

Firms can always make a larger profit by colluding rather than by competing. Acting alone, competitive firms are unable to raise price by restricting output, but when they act jointly to limit the amount supplied, price will increase. As we will see in the next subsection, however, achieving a successful cartel in practice is not as simple as it may seem.

APPLICATION 13.5   WILL THE INTERNET PROMOTE COMPETITION OR CARTELIZATION?

The common wisdom is that the Internet serves to promote competition among suppliers, thereby creating bargains for surfing shoppers.[10] Indeed, a survey by Erik Brynjolfsson and Michael Smith of MIT finds that prices on the Internet are 9 to 16 percent lower than in retail outlets.

Although the Internet lowers the cost of search and thus makes it easier for buyers to shop around for a lower price, Hal Varian of U.C. Berkeley cautions that there is a good reason why the Web might actually result in *higher* prices for consumers. Namely, if there are only a few sellers, the availability of low-cost information about the prices they are charging could make it easier

for these sellers to coordinate their pricing through the Web. As a historical example, Varian points to the Joint Executive Committee set up by the major U.S. railroads in the 1880s prior to the enactment of antitrust laws. The Committee served as a cartel by collecting and publishing information about the prices individual railroads charged and their weekly shipments. The railroads often cheated on the published prices by offering lower rates to shippers in secret in exchange for more business. Such cheating would have been mitigated by a public Internet exchange, according to Varian, since each railroad could readily monitor the prices charged by others. Any attempt to offer a lower price could quickly be countered, thereby making the cartel less vulnerable to cheating.

A modern parallel to the activities of the Joint Executive Committee is the manner in which airlines post fares

[10]This application is based on Hal R. Varian, "Online Commerce Creates Strange Competition," *New York Times* (August 24, 2000), p. C2.

online: An airline will announce its rates and associated terms and then watch to see how competitors respond. In the late 1980s airlines began to use online reservation systems to signal their pricing intentions to each other. For example, United would post its intended fare changes at 2 A.M. on Thursday. If rival airlines followed suit by 6 A.M., United's price remained in effect. If not, United would return its price back to the pre-2A.M. level. In 1992, the Department of Justice brought an antitrust suit against several large airlines in an effort to limit the extent to which online reservations systems serve as a signaling device and thereby promote cartelization.

In the long run, the key will be the number of sellers in any online category of goods or services. If there are many sellers, the extra flow of information through the Internet is likely to work to the benefit of buyers, pushing prices down. But in Web-based exchanges where there are only a few sellers and many buyers, the availability of more timely price information may serve to promote cartelization, thereby increasing prices to consumers. The Federal Trade Commission is attempting to set some standards of behavior for online exchange to ensure that they promote competition rather than cartelization.

Why Cartels Fail

If cartels are profitable for the members, why aren't there many more? One reason is that in the United States they are illegal. But even before there were laws against collusive agreements, cartels were rare except when actually supported by government; when they did exist, they were short-lived. Three important factors appear to contribute to cartel instability.

1. *Each firm has a strong incentive to cheat on the cartel agreement.* A cartel achieves monopoly profit by having its members restrict output below the levels that each would individually choose, and this reduction results in a higher price. Once a higher price is achieved, individual cartel members could earn even more profit by expanding output. Each firm would like to enjoy the benefit of the cartel—a higher price—without incurring the cost—lower output. If only one firm expands output, price will not fall appreciably, but the additional sales at the monopoly price will add significantly to that firm's profit. It is thus in each firm's self-interest to violate the cartel agreement to restrict output.

Figure 13.7 illustrates the incentive to cheat on the cartel agreement. If the firm in Figure 13.7a adheres to the cartel agreement, it will produce q_1 and sell at price P_1. However, note what happens if the firm expands output beyond q_1 while the other firms continue to abide by the cartel agreement's restrictions. In this event the firm faces a horizontal demand curve at price P_1; that is, one firm expanding output alone will not affect price. Remember that the downward-sloping demand curve d^* is relevant only for simultaneous expansion and contraction of output by all firms. The firm acting alone can increase its profit significantly by expanding output, since marginal revenue (equal to price with the horizontal demand curve) is above marginal cost at q_1. Profit will be maximized if the firm increases sales to q_2 at the price of P_1.

Every firm has the same incentive to expand output and cheat on the cartel agreement. Yet if many firms do so, industry output will increase significantly, and price will fall below the monopoly level. It is in each firm's interest to have other firms restrict their output while it increases its own. Every firm's self-interest is therefore a threat to the survival of the cartel. To be successful, the cartel must have some means of enforcing and monitoring its agreement.

The foregoing suggests why government backing generally is so essential to ensuring a cartel's stability. Government provides the means of enforcing and monitoring a cartel agreement. A good example of this is provided by the caviar cartel.[11] Prior to the collapse of the Soviet Union, the Ministry of Fisheries in Moscow set stringent quotas for the annual sturgeon catch, the source of caviar, one of the world's most expensive delicacies. Close government monitoring limited poaching and illegal dealing in caviar. However, as the Soviet Union disintegrated, four new independent states and two autonomous regions appeared around the Caspian Sea—the location of over 90 percent of the world's sturgeon stocks. Central authority evaporated, and the independent actions of numerous poachers and illegal caviar traders began to rip the formerly tightly regulated cartel wide open. Caviar prices plummeted.

2. *Members of the cartel will disagree over appropriate cartel policy* regarding pricing, output, allowable market shares, and profit sharing. In Figure 13.7, we assumed that the firms have identical cost curves, making agreement on the profit-maximizing cartel output and price relatively easy. But when firms differ in size, cost conditions, and other respects, agreement will not come as easily since the firms will have different goals. If, for example, the cartel members' costs differ, they will disagree on what price the cartel should set. The problems become even more acute when the firms must make long-run investment decisions. Every cartel member will want to expand its capacity and share of total output and profit, but not all can be allowed to do so.

These problems are basically political, and no matter what policy the cartel follows, it will reflect some sort of compromise among divergent views. As happens with any compromise, some firms will be unhappy with the outcome, and those firms are all the more likely to refuse to join the cartel or join but violate the cartel policy and expand output.

Agreement will also be more difficult the less homogeneous the product. For example, in the United States there are two primary areas in which oranges are grown: Florida and California–Arizona. Through regulations instituted in 1937, the U.S. government (as an exception to antitrust laws) has allowed growers' cartels to control prices and supplies in the two areas. The organization of a growers' cartel has been much more problematic in Florida than in California–Arizona.[12] This reflects the longer growing season and greater varieties of oranges that can be produced in the climate and soil conditions there. Because there are more product dimensions that must be taken into account, Florida orange growers have been less successful at reaching an effective cartel agreement—despite the United States government's official approval of such an agreement.

3. *Profits of the cartel members will encourage entry into the industry.* If the cartel achieves economic profits by raising the price, new firms have an incentive to enter the market. If the cartel cannot block entry of new firms, price will be driven back down to the competitive level as production from the "outsiders" reaches the market. Indeed, if an increase in the number of firms in the market causes the cartel to break down, then price will temporarily fall below the cost of production, forcing losses on the cartel members. The prospect of entry by new competitors eager to share in the profits is probably the most serious threat to cartel stability.

To be successful, therefore, a cartel must be able to induce its members to comply with cartel policy (holding down output) and to restrict entry into the market. These tasks are not easily accomplished, and history is strewn with examples of cartels that flourished for a short time only to disintegrate because of internal and external pressures.

[11]"Bootleggers Thrive, Sturgeons Flounder, as Caviar Cartel Splits," *Washington Post* (June 1, 1992), pp. 1 and 8.

[12]Gary D. Libecap and Elizabeth Hoffman, "The Failure of Government-Sponsored Cartelization and the Development of Federal Farm Policy," *Economic Inquiry*, 33 No. 3 (July 1995), pp. 365–382.

APPLICATION 13.6 — THE DIFFICULTY OF CONTROLLING CHEATING

The Organization of Petroleum Exporting Countries (OPEC) has relied on such measures as accounting firms to monitor member nations' outputs to eliminate cheating on production quotas.[13] These measures, however, have not been entirely successful. This is perhaps not surprising, given that member states possess differing production costs, petroleum reserves, time horizons, and goals. Enforcing agreements is also difficult when member states are at war with one another, as in the case of Iran and Iraq in the 1980s.

To demonstrate the difficulties facing OPEC—or any other cartel—in fixing prices, Raymond Battalio, a Texas A&M professor, conducted an experiment with a class of 27 introductory economics students. In the experiment, each student was asked to write either a *0* or a *1* on a slip of paper. A *1* indicated a willingness to adhere to a collusive agreement, whereas a *0* signified a desire to cheat. There were real money payoffs associated with the game and they were structured so that if every-

one chose *1*, the total payoff to all the students would be maximized. The payoff to any individual student, however, was maximized if all other students opted for *1* and the individual cheated and selected *0*. If more than one student cheated, the payoff for cheating decreased as the number of cheaters increased, but was still greater than the payoff to noncheaters. Significantly, the payoffs associated with all possible outcomes were disseminated to students at the start of the experiment.

On the first round of the experiment, there were 6 noncheaters and 21 cheaters. Allowed to discuss the outcome, the students quickly realized that they could all be better off if they all voted to honor the agreement and place a *1* on their ballots. A student "leader" proposed, "Let's all put down *1*, and nobody cheat." After the students reached an explicit oral agreement to all vote *1* another vote was taken. There were 4 *1* votes and 23 *0* votes. The ringleader muttered: "I'll never trust anyone again as long as I live." Asked how he voted, the ringleader replied: "Oh, I voted *0*." The results suggest that in a cartel setting, self-interest leads to efforts to maximize returns individually even when the risk is great of lowering overall returns both to oneself and to one's "partners."

[13]This application is based on "OPEC May Monitor Members' Output On Site to Reduce Cheating on Quotas," *Wall Street Journal*, November 13, 1987, p. 44; and "All for One . . . One for All? Don't Bet on It," *Wall Street Journal* (December 4, 1986), p. 1.

APPLICATION 13.7 — THE ROLEX "CARTEL"

Although collusive agreements between different firms typically come to mind when cartels are mentioned, the model has wider applicability. Essentially, any firm with multiple production facilities or distribution channels and some market power faces a cartel management problem. The firm must coordinate the output and pricing decisions of its various plants and distribution channels to ensure that its total economic profit is maximized. To the extent, for example, that Rolex has some market power, it needs to ensure that one of its licensed dealers does not attempt to cheat on the Rolex "cartel" by selling more than a certain number of watches

at the agreed-upon price. Although such cheating may benefit the individual dealer, it undermines the overall profitability of the cartel. To limit the undermining, Rolex may set up exclusive territories for its various dealers, allot a set number of watches to each dealer, and specify a manufacturer's suggested retail price.

In the mid-1980s, Rolex became disgruntled with Carl Marcus, a Beverly Hills retailer of its watches.[14]

[14]"The Rolex War Rages on for Beverly Hills Jeweler," *Los Angeles Times* (November 13, 1987), pp. 1 and 17.

Marcus had been buying Rolex watches from other dealers around the country who were unable to sell their allocated number. He then sold these watches in the Beverly Hills area at a discount of 5 to 25 percent below the price most jewelers were charging for the same items.

Rolex launched an advertising campaign against Marcus alleging that he had sold a used watch to a customer while claiming it was new. The advertisements asked Marcus' former customers to have their watches inspected by Rolex to verify that they had not been similarly duped. The underlying motive of the advertising campaign was not so much to protect unsuspecting customers as it was to preserve Rolex's market power and profit. By offering to inspect the watches Marcus sold, Rolex could obtain the registration numbers and identify the dealers who had undermined the cartel by selling some of their allotments to Marcus.

Oligopolies and Collusion

Much of what has been said about the consequences of cartel formation in a competitive industry also applies when the industry is oligopolistic. Firms in an oligopolistic industry can increase their profits (they may already be making some pure economic profits to begin with) if they collude. The key to understanding this is our earlier finding that oligopoly output is usually greater than that of pure monopoly. This means that the combined profit of the oligopolistic firms can be increased if total output is restricted to the monopoly level, and with an appropriate sharing arrangement, each firm can realize greater profit. The incentive to collude—the prospect of higher profit—also exists in an oligopoly.

We generally expect collusion to be more common in oligopolies than in competitive markets because there are only a few firms in an oligopolistic industry. The limited number of firms means that fewer parties must participate in the collusive agreement, making reaching agreement easier. Additionally, monitoring is simpler when few firms are involved; it is easier to detect cheaters.

Nonetheless, factors that inhibit the formation and undermine the operation of cartels in competitive markets are also present when oligopolistic firms collude. Each party to the cartel agreement still stands to make more profit by cheating than by abiding by the cartel agreement. Even though one firm does not face a horizontal demand curve if it cheats—as does the competitive firm in Figure 13.7a—it will face a more elastic demand curve when cheating than when complying, so its profit will be greater if it cheats and the other firms abide by the agreement. Furthermore, the higher price achieved by collusion can still prompt entry by new firms, and that also undermines the success of the cartel.

A final point is important. It is not necessary for all the firms in a market to participate in the cartel for it to be worthwhile. Several firms that produce most of the output in an industry can increase their profit by colluding, although not by as much as when the entire industry is cartelized. In this case, the colluding firms will behave as if they were one giant firm and collectively exploit whatever monopoly power they have. The remaining firms then benefit from the higher price set by the colluding firms. In this case of partial cartelization of a market, the results can be analyzed using the dominant firm model illustrated earlier in Figure 13.6. In that graph, the marginal cost curve of the dominant firm is interpreted now as the summed marginal costs of the colluding firms, and they collectively maximize profit subject to the residual demand curve. Therefore, partial cartelization of an industry produces price and output that lie between those found with pure monopoly and competition. We will see an example of this application of the model in the next subsection.

APPLICATION 13.8

FIRM COUNT, MARKET CONCENTRATION, AND SUCCESSFUL COLLUSION

Despite the fact that fixing prices is forbidden by the Sherman Act, numerous price-fixing agreements have been documented in the United States. The striking of such agreements provides support for Adam Smith's well-known observation: "People of the same trade seldom meet together, even for merriment or diversion, but the conversation ends in a conspiracy against the public, or in some contrivance to raise prices."[15]

The ability to make a collusive arrangement stick appears to depend on the number of sellers and the degree of seller concentration in the relevant product or geographic market. Specifically, of the price-fixing conspiracies that were successfully prosecuted by the U.S.

Department of Justice between 1963 and 1972, 10 or fewer firms were involved in 79 percent of the cases.[16] In 78 percent of the documented cases, the top 4 firms involved in the conspiracy accounted for more than 50 percent of the total output in the relevant market. Thus, the combination of a small number of firms and a high degree of seller concentration appears to be more conducive to successful price collusion. In the relatively few cases in which a large number of firms have been involved, the conspiracies have been uncovered very rapidly. Indeed, details of some of the large-group organizational meetings have even been printed in local newspapers.

[15]Adam Smith, *The Wealth of Nations* (New York: The Modern Library), p. 128.

[16]George A. Hay and Daniel Kelly, "An Empirical Survey of Price-Fixing Conspiracies," *Journal of Law and Economics*, 17 No. 1 (April 1974), pp. 13–38.

The Case of OPEC

Few Americans took notice when OPEC was formed in 1960. Originally containing just 5 member nations, the cartel grew to an ominous 13 countries by 1973. During these years, however, OPEC could not be judged successful. World oil prices actually declined slightly in the 1960s. OPEC had not yet learned to use its potential market power.

All that changed in 1973 with the Arab–Israeli War. During the war the Arab members of OPEC temporarily cut off oil exports. The result was dramatic: oil prices nearly quadrupled in a matter of months. The estimated price of a barrel of oil on the world market was $2.91 in 1973 but jumped to $10.77 in 1974, providing a graphic demonstration of what an output restriction could accomplish. OPEC continued to hold down output after resuming exports; by accident, OPEC had learned how to run a cartel! After the war's end, oil prices remained relatively stable (in real terms) until they received another jolt in 1978, when revolution swept Iran. Iranian exports, which accounted for 20 percent of all OPEC exports, fell to almost zero. The world oil price rose to an average of $20.19 in 1979. Soon, thereafter, the Iran–Iraq War, which began in 1980, resulted in the widespread destruction of oil-producing facilities in both countries and reduced oil exports further. The world oil price jumped again to more than $30 per barrel in 1980 and averaged $35.10 in 1981.

Before continuing the historical saga of developments in the world oil market, let's examine the market as an example of a cartel. Specifically, because OPEC does not control all supply sources (in 1972, OPEC production was 64 percent of noncommunist world output), we will use the dominant firm model. In view of the history of OPEC, this is a bit of an oversimplification—OPEC has not always been monolithic enough to act as a single profit-maximizing firm. Nonetheless, we can gain insight into the way this market has functioned by treating OPEC as a dominant firm.

In Figure 13.8 we show world demand for oil as DD' and non-OPEC supply as S_F. These relationships should be interpreted as short-run, where the elasticities are relatively low. As we will see, low elasticities of demand and supply from fringe firms have a significant effect on the outcome. The marginal cost curve for OPEC is shown as MC_O, exhibiting substantially lower costs than other sources of supply, another characteristic of this market. OPEC's residual demand and marginal revenue curves are derived as before. Under competitive conditions (which prevailed before 1973), when OPEC and non-OPEC producers are producing where marginal cost equals price, price is P_C and total output is shown at point C on the demand curve. When OPEC behaves as a dominant firm, however, it produces where marginal cost equals its residual marginal revenue, an output of Q_O with a price of P. Note that price has risen sharply compared with the competitive price. This result should be contrasted with that shown earlier in Figure 13.6. In that representation of the dominant firm model, we assumed that demand and fringe supply were more elastic. A comparison of these graphs indicates why low elasticities of demand and fringe supply imply a higher cartel price. Equation (1) on page 367 also suggests this: decreases in the elasticity of the market demand and the fringe supply both work to lower the elasticity of demand faced by the dominant firm.

Because much of OPEC's early success was dependent on low elasticities, we need to be sure we understand why this was a characteristic of the world oil market.

The price elasticity of demand for oil is quite low in the short run. When oil prices rose, consumers were caught with a stock of energy-consuming capital designed for cheap oil. Houses, office buildings, and gas-guzzling automobiles could not be replaced overnight; it took time

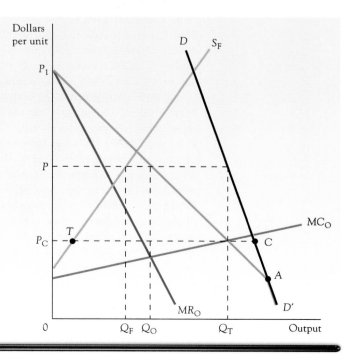

FIGURE 13.8

OPEC Cartel as a Dominant Firm
World oil demand is shown by DD' and non-OPEC supply as S_F. The residual demand curve confronting OPEC is then P_1AD'. With its marginal cost curve MC_O, OPEC produces Q_O at price P. Non-OPEC output at that price is Q_F, so total output is Q_T.

for higher energy prices to have a substantial effect on energy consumption. A low price elasticity means, of course, that moderate output restrictions will produce a large price increase, just what we see in Figure 13.8.

The price elasticity of supply of oil from non-OPEC suppliers is also quite low in the short run. The biggest threat to a cartel is increased production by noncartel members from either existing producers or entry of new firms. The ability of OPEC to raise oil prices successfully depended on total (OPEC and non-OPEC) output; if OPEC output restrictions were matched by substantial increases by others (as would happen with highly elastic non-OPEC supply), price would be largely unaffected. How much non-OPEC suppliers could increase output depended on their price elasticity of supply. Because non-OPEC producers were already producing at near-capacity levels, their immediate ability to increase output was limited. Furthermore, new oil fields could be brought into production only after a lengthy process of seismic exploration, drilling, and installation of pipelines requiring several years. Thus, non-OPEC producers were unable to respond quickly to the higher prices produced by the cartel.

These characteristics of the world oil market help explain OPEC's early success. In addition, OPEC also enjoyed another advantage: oil-importing nations frequently adopted policies that strengthened OPEC's position. In the United States, for example, price controls on oil kept the price received by domestic oil producers artificially low and discouraged production and exploration. Price controls on natural gas discouraged production of this alternative energy source. Similarly, tough environmental restrictions on the mining and use of coal slowed the transition to coal as another energy alternative. Finally, price controls on oil products such as gasoline and heating oil kept the prices of such products below world market levels and encouraged consumption. Encouraging domestic consumption and discouraging domestic production implies an increase in demand for oil from OPEC, and the United States inevitably became more dependent on imported oil during the 1970s.

Our story, however, does not end with the $35-per-barrel price of 1981. As economic theory tells us, long-run elasticities are greater than short-run elasticities. As time passed consumers responded to higher energy prices by switching to more energy-efficient homes, appliances, and cars, while non-OPEC suppliers increased output. Both responses put increased pressure on OPEC in the early 1980s. More specifically, world oil consumption fell from a 1979 high of 51 million barrels per day to less than 45 million in 1985 (particularly impressive since the prior long-run trend had been a 3 percent annual rate of increase in consumption). At the same time, non-OPEC production increased sharply, from 15 million barrels per day in 1977 to 24 million barrels in 1985. With total consumption down and non-OPEC production up, OPEC had to restrict its output sharply to try to hold the price up. Even though OPEC cut production from 31 million barrels per day in 1979 to barely 16 million barrels in 1985, the price of oil still fell below its previous level. The per-barrel price dropped to $32 in 1982 and to $27 in 1984, and it continued falling gradually until it stabilized at around $18 in 1987.

The experience of OPEC after 1981 was almost a textbook case of the operation of economic forces that undermine cartels. According to *Business Week*:[17] "The OPEC cartel is facing strains that it has never experienced before. . . . OPEC is so divided by cutthroat competition and internal political bickering that the organization is unlikely to find a way to agree anytime soon . . . Under-the-table discounts . . . are common."

---

[17]"The Leverage of Lower Oil Prices: On World Economies, on OPEC Countries, on the Oil Industry," *Business Week*, March 22, 1982, p. 69.

External pressures that diminished OPEC's power were also at work:[18] "Demand for OPEC oil . . . collapsed under the combined impact of . . . surprisingly high conservation, expanded use of alternative energy sources such as coal and gas, and rising non-OPEC production of oil from Mexico, the North Sea, and the North Slope of Alaska." (Long-run price elasticities of demand are higher than short-run price elasticities and were being felt as consumers switched to substitutes. Entry at the high cartel price was taking place.)

To illustrate in analytic terms how the passage of time affected the market, long-run demand and non-OPEC supply responses can be incorporated into Figure 13.8. To avoid cluttering the diagram, we have not done so, but we recommend that you work this out. Specifically, assume that the original competitive equilibrium was a long-run equilibrium. Then a more elastic long-run demand curve will pass through point C on the short-run demand curve, and a more elastic supply curve will pass through point T on the non-OPEC supply curve. With these curves, where will the long-run cartel equilibrium lie? You will find that in the long run, price will be lower, non-OPEC output will be greater, and OPEC output will be smaller (all compared to the short-run cartel equilibrium shown in our graph)—just the events we saw emerge in the 1980s.

Most observers concluded that OPEC's power had largely eroded by the late 1980s. In August 1990, however, Iraq invaded Kuwait and supply was disrupted again. The price of oil quickly rose to $40 per barrel, before falling back to about $20 per barrel after the United States defeated Iraq in the Gulf War in early 1991. These events do not mean that OPEC was exercising control, of course. Small changes in supply can have pronounced effects on price in a competitive market in the short run when short-run demand is very inelastic. As long as political turmoil pervades the Mideast, a major source of world oil, volatility is likely to characterize this market.

By 1998, the price of oil had fallen below $12 a barrel, the lowest level in a decade, because of increased global production and a decrease in OPEC's share of total output to 40 percent (from more than 50 percent in the early 1970s). The decline in the price of oil was arrested in 1999, due to a pact negotiated between the three largest exporters of oil to the United States: Saudi Arabia, Venezuela, and Mexico. The first two countries belong to OPEC, while Mexico does not. The three countries respectively account for 15, 18, and 14 percent of U.S. imports. The agreement, known as the *Riyadh Pact*, consisted of pledges to reduce output by 1.5 to 2.0 million barrels a day, about 2 to 3 percent of world production of 73 million barrels a day. The price of crude oil rose above $30 in the wake of the pact.

Mexican officials who were key to brokering the agreement, however, didn't hold any illusions about its long-run prospects. Then-president of Mexico, Ernesto Zedillo, recalled that when he was a graduate economics student at Yale University, one of his professors engaged his class in a game to test the limits of oligopolistic behavior (see Application 13.4).[19] "Within a few minutes, somebody would start cheating; it never failed," Zedillo observed. "No market with more than two participants can sustain a cartel."

[18]Ibid., p. 69.

[19]"'Big 3' Exporters' Pact to Cut Oil Output Signals Seismic Shifts," *Wall Street Journal* (June 23, 1998), pp. A1 and A10.

SUMMARY

• A monopolistically competitive market is one in which there are a large number of competing firms, but each firm produces a differentiated product.

• Each firm in a monopolistically competitive market confronts a demand curve that is fairly, but not perfectly, elastic.

• In long-run equilibrium, firms in a monopolistically competitive market make zero economic profits. They are not, however, producing at the minimum point on their long-run average cost curves since the LAC curve is tangent to a downward-sloping demand curve.

• Oligopoly is characterized by a few firms that together produce all or most of the total output of some product. A pronounced mutual interdependence among the decisions of firms in the industry results.

• What one firm does has a decided impact on other firms in an oligopoly, but the way that other firms will react is uncertain.

• There are three common oligopoly models: Cournot, Stackelberg, and dominant firm.

• Oligopoly firms can collude and operate as a cartel.

• The variety of models for studying oligopoly and the differences in their implications make generalizing about the effects of oligopoly difficult. In some cases, prices are predicted to be near the monopoly level. In other cases, they hover near the competitive level.

• Oligopolistic outcomes are likely to lie somewhere between the monopoly and competitive results, and the outcomes are likely to differ from one industry to another.

REVIEW QUESTIONS AND PROBLEMS

Questions and problems marked with an asterisk have solutions given in Answers to Selected Problems at the back of the book (page 576).

13.1. What are the assumptions of the theory of monopolistic competition? In what way do these assumptions differ from those of the perfectly competitive model?

13.2. Explain the relationship between the demand elasticity and the excess capacity that occurs for a monopolistic competitor.

13.3. Explain how, in the Cournot model, the output of one firm depends on the output of the other firm. Specifically, in Figure 13.3, what will be the output of Artesia if Utopia produces 32 units? If Utopia produces 48? If Utopia produces 64?

13.4. Starting from the Figure 13.3 Cournot equilibrium, suppose that the marginal and average total cost curves (which are the same for both firms) shift downward. Explain how the firms adjust to a new Cournot equilibrium.

13.5. How does the Stackelberg model differ from the Cournot model? Which model predicts that output will be higher?

13.6. Explain how the residual demand curve confronting the dominant firm in the dominant firm model is derived. In this derivation, what is assumed regarding how the output of other firms is determined? How does it differ from the Cournot assumption?

13.7. Explain how equilibrium is determined in the dominant firm model. If market demand increases, how will a new equilibrium be determined?

*13.8. Suppose that the supply curve of the "follower" firms in the dominant firm model is perfectly horizontal. Does the dominant firm still have the power to set the industry price?

13.9. "Because firms in any industry can always make greater profits by colluding there is an inevitable tendency for competitive industries to become cartels over time." Is the first part of this statement correct? Is the second part? Explain.

13.10. What problems usually make cartels collapse? How was OPEC able to avoid this fate, at least through the mid-1980s?

13.11. Consider the dominant firm model and treat OPEC as the dominant firm. Explain how OPEC would determine the price of oil and the level of output produced by the cartel. How would OPEC's price and output be affected by new discoveries of oil that shift the supply curve of oil for non-OPEC members to the right?

13.12. "There is no general theory of oligopoly." Explain this statement.

13.13. Under which oligopoly model does the outcome most nearly resemble that obtained with pure monopoly? Under which oligopoly model does the outcome most nearly resemble that obtained with perfect competition?

13.14. In an analysis of the automobile industry, what factors would you consider in determining whether to use the competitive model, the monopoly model, or one of the oligopoly models?

13.15. Suppose that there were three identical firms instead of only two under the cost and market demand conditions outlined in Section 13.2. What would be the Cournot equilibrium in terms of each firm's output as well as the total market output? If there were four identical firms sharing the market?

13.16. In a two-firm Stackelberg model of oligopoly, can both firms be "leaders"? Explain why or why not.

13.17. Suppose that Iran and Iraq are Cournot duopolists in the crude oil market and face the following market demand function:

$$P = 100 - (q_1 + q_2);$$

where q_i represents the output levels of the two countries with Iran being "1" and Iraq being "2" and P is the per-barrel price. The marginal revenue schedules facing the two countries are:

$$MR_1 = 100 - 2q_1 - q_2$$

$$MR_2 = 100 - 2q_2 - q_1.$$

Each country has a marginal cost curve of the form

$$MC_i = q_i;$$

where $i = 1, 2$.

a. Determine each country's reaction function.

b. Does a Cournot equilibrium exist? If so, find the outputs and prices of crude oil in the two countries.

c. Suppose that the two countries collude and become a cartel. What will be the resulting price and outputs for crude oil for the two countries? [Note that the market marginal revenue is $100 - 2(q_1 + q_2)$.]

d. Can it be said that because collusive profits are strictly greater, it is true that these countries should necessarily collude? Are there any potential pitfalls in such a collusive arrangement?

13.18. Suppose that Iraq is the Stackelberg leader in the preceding problem. What will be each country's reaction function? How much will each country produce and what will its profits be?

13.19. Repeat the preceding problem but assume that Iran is the Stackelberg leader.

13.20. It is the not too distant future and all important human needs have been eliminated. Thanks to the firm Bioeconotek, a miracle drug, Needless, has been invented that genetically suppresses a patient's desire to think in terms of having needs. The drug stimulates the patient's cognitive ability to perceive substitute products as being ever more attractive the greater the price of any item.

Needless does not come cheap. Given its curative powers, Bioeconotek charges $1,633 per dose and sells 62,020,000 doses annually despite the presence of a competitive fringe of generic suppliers, which collectively sell 51,650,000 doses annually at the same $1,633 price.

Bioeconotek managers estimate that the fringe supply curve is described by the equation:

$$P = 600 + \frac{Q_{FS}}{50,000};$$

and that the market demand is given by:

$$P = 13,000 - \frac{Q_M}{10,000}.$$

In the preceding equations P is the price per dose, Q_{FS} is the quantity supplied by the competitive fringe, and Q_M is quantity consumed in the total market.

The marginal cost associated with producing and distributing Needless is a constant $600 per dose. Bioeconotek initially invested $400 million in developing the drug but has faced no additional fixed costs since the initial investment.

a. At the current price of $1,633, a Bioeconotek manager estimates the demand elasticity for Needless as:

$$\text{Elasticity} = \left| \frac{\Delta Q}{\Delta P} \frac{P}{Q} \right| = \left| (-10,000) \left(\frac{1,633}{113,670,000} \right) \right|$$
$$= 0.14.$$

Since this value represents an inelastic demand, he argues that Needless' price should be raised. Is there something wrong with this reasoning? Briefly explain.

b. Write an equation that gives the demand for Bioeconotek's own output—that is, demand as seen by Bioeconotek given market demand and the fringe supply.

c. What is the profit-maximizing price for Bioeconotek to charge, given the current market demand and the current fringe supply behavior? (Recall that if a demand curve can be written as $P = a - bQ$, then $MR = a - 2bQ$.)

d. If Bioeconotek wants to implement a "limit-pricing" strategy that successfully eliminates fringe suppliers from the market, what annual output level does it need to select for its own product, Needless?

e. Another Bioeconotek manager worries about future growth of the fringe supply and argues that the company should set the price determined in part d so as to drive the current fringe out of business and eliminate any incentives for further entry. As briefly as possible, explain why this strategy cannot be more profitable than the pricing strategy you gave in part c.

13.21. Suppose that the market for Web search engines can best be characterized as monopolistically competitive. If this is the case, should firms that operate in the market such as Yahoo!, Alta Vista, and Excite be prosecuted by antitrust authorities on account of the potential inefficiency of the market outcome? Explain why or why not.

13.22. College textbooks have been increasing in price at a rate greater than the general price level over the past several decades. The reason for this phenomenon appears to be that publishers have realized that by having authors revise their texts more frequently, competition from used texts is reduced. Using the dominant firm model, explain how such a more-frequent-revision strategy leads to a higher price for a given textbook.

CHAPTER 14

Game Theory and the Economics of Information

How can we model choice under conditions of strategic interaction and what happens when decisionmakers have less than perfect information?

Chapter Outline

14.1 Game Theory
Determination of Equilibrium
Application 14.1 Dominant Strategies in Baseball

14.2 The Prisoner's Dilemma Game
Application 14.2 The Congressional Prisoner's Dilemma
The Prisoner's Dilemma and Cheating by Cartel Members   A Prisoner's Dilemma Game You May Play

14.3 Repeated Games
Application 14.3 Cooperation in the Trenches of World War I
Do Oligopolistic Firms Always Collude?   Game Theory and Oligopoly: A Summary

14.4 Asymmetric Information
The "Lemons" Model   Market Responses to Asymmetric Information
Application 14.4 Is There a Lemons Problem in Used Car Markets?

14.5 Adverse Selection and Moral Hazard
Adverse Selection
Application 14.5 Adverse Selection and the American Red Cross
Moral Hazard
Application 14.6 Moral Hazard in the S&L Industry
Application 14.7 Moral Hazard on the Road and at the Plate

14.6 Limited Price Information

14.7 Advertising
Advertising as Information
Application 14.8 A Newspaper Strike's Effect on Food Prices

Learning Objectives

- Understand the basics of game theory: a mathematical technique to study choice under conditions of strategic interaction.
- Describe the prisoner's dilemma and its applicability to oligopoly theory as well as many other situations.
- Explore how the outcome in the case of a prisoner's dilemma differs in a repeated-game versus a single-period model.
- Analyze asymmetric information and market outcomes in the case where consumers have less information than sellers.
- Explain how insurance markets may function when information is imperfect and there is the possibility of either adverse selection or moral hazard.
- Show how limited price information affects price dispersion for a product.
- Investigate advertising and the extent to which it serves to artificially differentiate products versus provide information to consumers about the availability of products and their prices and qualities.

This chapter covers two topics that have been intensively studied by economists in recent years: game theory and the economics of information. Game theory is a mathematical technique developed to study choice under conditions of strategic interaction. It has become the major approach to the study of oligopoly, and our discussion looks at how it has been adapted to give insight into problems of oligopolistic interdependence. In particular, we will see that it helps us understand the difficulties firms face in colluding to raise prices.

In most economic analysis, whether of competition or oligopoly, it is assumed that consumers have complete knowledge of prices and product characteristics. It is clear that this assumption is often violated in the real world, and recent research has begun to analyze what effect this has on the way markets function. When information is costly, consumers are not fully informed and lack either knowledge of the prices different firms charge or knowledge of the qualities of the products they sell, or both. Under these circumstances, the prices, quantities, and qualities of goods traded can be quite different than when consumers have "perfect information." Two especially interesting applications of the effects of costly information involve insurance markets and advertising. We discuss them later in the chapter.

14.1 GAME THEORY

GAME THEORY
a method of analyzing situations in which the outcomes of your choices depend on others' choices, and vice versa

Game theory is a method of analyzing situations in which the outcomes of your choices depend on others' choices, and vice versa. In these strategic situations, there is mutual interdependence among the choices made by the decisionmakers: each decisionmaker needs to account for how the others are affected by the choices made and how the other decisionmakers are likely to respond since their responses may affect what is the best choice to make. Among market structures, oligopoly is the setting in which such interactions are likely to be most important, and game theory has become widely used to analyze oligopolies.

Game theory is a general approach to analyzing strategic interactions, however, and it can be applied to issues other than oligopoly. For example, in determining the defense budget, the U.S. government must not only consider the impact of its budgetary decisions on the military decisions of potential enemies, but also recognize that these potential enemies are trying to predict how the United States will respond to their budgetary decisions. Similarly, a politician thinking about conducting negative campaign tactics must recognize that his or her opponent might respond in a variety of possible ways. Whether it is wise to pursue a negative campaign strategy depends on how the opponent is likely to respond. Game theory can be applied to a wide range of phenomena like these, but our main concern is with how it helps us understand the functioning of oligopolistic markets.

All game theory models have at least three elements in common: players, strategies, and payoffs. The **players** are the decisionmakers whose behavior we are trying to predict. In the case of oligopoly, the players are the firms. The **strategies** are the possible choices of the players. Outputs produced and prices charged are strategies in this sense, but so too are advertising budgets, new product introductions, and product differentiation. For oligopolistic firms, all of these actions can affect rivals. The **payoffs** are the outcomes, or consequences, of the strategies chosen. For firms, it is natural to express the outcomes as the profits or losses realized. It is important to remember, however, that a specific strategy (say, producing 300,000 microwave ovens) does not uniquely determine the profit (payoff) because that will depend on the strategies followed by the other players.

PLAYERS
in game theory, decisionmakers whose behavior we are trying to predict and/or explain

STRATEGIES
in game theory, the possible choices of the players

PAYOFFS
in game theory, the outcomes or consequences of the strategies chosen

Determination of Equilibrium

In addition to the players, strategies, and payoffs, other elements may play a role in determining the outcome in a game theory model, but for the moment, we'll use some simple examples to illustrate how the model links the various elements. Consider a market with just two firms, A and B. Each firm must choose either a low or a high output; these are the only possible "strategies." However, each firm's profit depends not only on its own output, but also on the output of the other firm.

To go further, we have to be precise about exactly how profits are affected by both firms' choices. To show the possibilities with some illustrative numbers, we will use a payoff matrix. A **payoff matrix** is a simple way of representing how each combination of choices affects firms' profits. Table 14.1 is the payoff matrix for our example. There are four cells in this case. The upper-left cell shows that profit is 10 for firm A and 20 for firm B when both firms choose the low-output strategy. The upper-right cell shows that profit is 9 for firm A and 30 for firm B when A chooses a low output and B chooses a high output. (Thus, when B increases its output from low to high and A holds its output constant at low, B's profit increases from 20 to 30, but A's falls from 10 to 9—perhaps because B's higher output reduces the demand confronting firm A.) Similarly, the lower-left cell shows what happens to profits when A's output is high and B's output is low. Finally, the lower-right cell shows the outcome when both firms choose a high output.

In interpreting this payoff matrix, we assume that firms act independently. Note that this means that firm A has only two possible strategies: It can choose one of the two horizontal rows in the payoff matrix. If it chooses the top row (low output), its profit will be either 10 or 9, depending on what B chooses. Firm A cannot choose which cell it will end up in because it doesn't control B's choice. In the same way, firm B can choose only between the two vertical columns. If it chooses the right column, for example, its profit will be either 30 or 25, but it doesn't know which unless it can predict A's output choice. (We assume that the firms select their outputs simultaneously so neither knows with certainty what the other's choice will be.)

The purpose of this exercise is, of course, to predict what the market equilibrium will be. So let's see if we can figure out what each firm will do. Consider firm A. If firm B chooses a low output, firm A is better off selecting a high output because its profit would then be 20 rather than 10. On the other hand, if B chooses a high output, A is also better off selecting a high output because its profit would then be 18 rather than 9. Consider carefully what this means: A is better off with a high output *regardless of what B does*. In this case A has a *dominant strategy* because the high-output choice is best no matter what B does. In this situation it is easy to predict that firm A will produce a high output.

PAYOFF MATRIX
a simple way of representing how each combination of choices affects players' payoffs in a game theory setting

TABLE 14.1

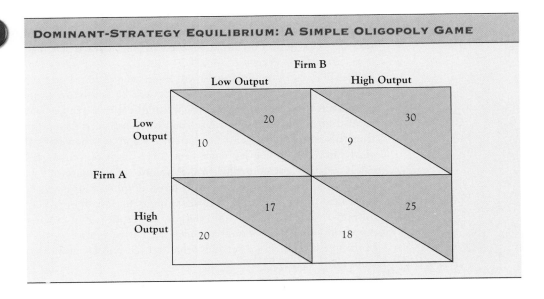

DOMINANT-STRATEGY EQUILIBRIUM: A SIMPLE OLIGOPOLY GAME

DOMINANT-STRATEGY EQUILIBRIUM

the simplest game theory outcome, resulting from both players having dominant strategies

Now apply the same reasoning to firm B. If firm A chooses a low output, B is better off selecting a high output because its profit would then be 30 instead of 20. Alternatively, if A chooses a high output, B is still better off selecting a high output because its profit would then be 25 rather than 17. Thus, B also has a dominant strategy: its high-output strategy is best regardless of what A does. We would predict that firm B will produce a high output.

In this example both firms have dominant strategies, and so we expect the equilibrium outcome to include high output from both firms. This is called a **dominant-strategy equilibrium** and is perhaps the simplest game that can be imagined. As you might expect, however, not all situations are so easily analyzed.

APPLICATION 14.1   DOMINANT STRATEGIES IN BASEBALL

In baseball, it is advantageous for any forced base runner (a runner who will be forced to advance to the next base if the batter gets on base) to run on the pitch when there are two outs and the count on the batter stands at three balls and two strikes.[1]

[1]This application is based on Avinash K. Dixit and Barry J. Nalebuff, *Thinking Strategically* (New York: W. W. Norton, 1991).

This is so because, if the batter does not hit the pitch, either the pitch is a third strike and the inning ends or it is a fourth ball and the runner and batter advance. If the batter fouls off the pitch, the runner simply returns to the initial base (if the foul isn't caught) or the inning ends (if the foul is caught). But if the batter hits a fair ball, a runner who left base on the pitch has a better chance of advancing or scoring. Thus, running on the pitch is a dominant strategy for a forced runner when there are two outs and the count is three balls and two strikes on the batter.

A slightly more involved situation is shown in Table 14.2. Here, we have changed only one number from the previous table. When both firms choose a low output (upper-left cell), A's profit is now 22 (rather than 10 as before). Now reconsider A's output choice. If B chooses a low output, A's best choice is a low output (profit of 22 rather than 20), but if B chooses a high output, A's best choice is a high output (profit of 18 rather than 9). Firm A now does not have a dominant strategy: its best choice depends on what firm B does. *What output should firm A choose?*

If firm A can predict what B will do, it would then know which choice was best. So A has to try to figure out what B's choice will be before it can make its own decision. This is characteristic of most game-theory applications: players have to evaluate and predict what their rivals will do because their own decisions depend on the rivals' choices. Note that this was not necessary in our first example, when both firms had dominant strategies. The best choice for each firm was a high output regardless of the actions of the other. So let's consider how firm A might try to figure out what firm B will do. In this case it is fairly simple. Firm B still has a dominant strategy. For B, a high output is best regardless of what A does. Thus, A might reasonably predict that B will choose a high output. And if B selects a high output, A's profit is higher when it also selects a high output. Consequently, our analysis suggests that two rational, profit-maximizing firms would both, in the Table 14.2 setting, select a high output, and that that would be the equilibrium in this game.

TABLE 14.2 · ANOTHER OLIGOPOLY GAME

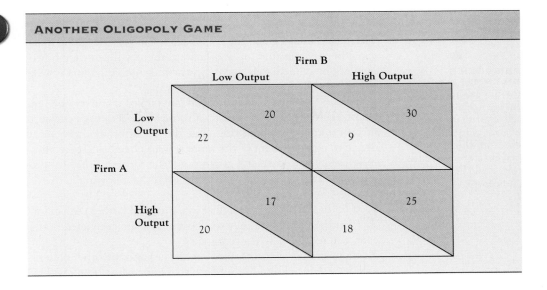

NASH EQUILIBRIUM
a set of strategies such that each player's choice is the best one possible given the strategy chosen by the other player(s)

The equilibrium we have identified in Table 14.2 is not a dominant-strategy equilibrium, however, because that term refers to a case where both firms have dominant strategies, and here only one does. To analyze the outcomes in many games, we need a more general concept of equilibrium than a dominant-strategy equilibrium. The concept most widely used is called a **Nash equilibrium**, after mathematician John Nash, who formalized the notion in 1951 and subsequently won the 1994 Nobel Prize in economics for his contribution.

A Nash equilibrium is a set of strategies such that each player's choice is the best one possible *given the strategy chosen by the other player(s)*. To see that the high output–high output set of strategies in Table 14.2 is a Nash equilibrium, we evaluate it as follows. What we want to see is whether firm A's best choice is high output *when firm B chooses high output*, and simultaneously whether firm B's best choice is high output *when firm A chooses high output*. If firm B chooses high output, then firm A is best off by choosing high output (profit of 18 rather than 9), so the lower-right cell passes the first part of the test. If A chooses high output, B is best off by choosing high output (profit of 25 rather than 17), so the lower-right cell passes the second part of the test also. The two strategies shown in the lower-right cell then, represent a Nash equilibrium.

If you apply this same reasoning to the equilibrium we identified in Table 14.1, you will see that the high output combination of strategies there is also a Nash equilibrium. A dominant-strategy equilibrium (as in Table 14.1) is a special case of a Nash equilibrium. That is, all dominant-strategy equilibria are also Nash equilibria, though not all Nash equilibria are dominant-strategy equilibria (as the example in Table 14.2 illustrates). Unfortunately, not all games have a Nash equilibrium. Thus, while the concept works in many cases, it does not let us determine the outcome in all strategic situations.

The Nash equilibrium is closely related to the analysis of the Cournot oligopoly model discussed in Chapter 13. Recall that the Cournot equilibrium is one in which each firm is producing its best output *given the outputs of other firms*. This is exactly the description of a Nash equilibrium, and sometimes the equilibrium in such a market situation is described as a Cournot–Nash equilibrium. More importantly, the application of game theory to the strategic interaction in that sort of model has provided a reason why firms might rationally choose to behave in the way Cournot described.

14.2 THE PRISONER'S DILEMMA GAME

PRISONER'S DILEMMA

the most famous game theory model in which self-interest on the part of each player leads to a result in which all players are worse off than they could be if different choices were made

The most famous game theory model is the **prisoner's dilemma**. We will first describe the game in the form that made it famous, thereby illustrating how it got its name. Although it may not be immediately apparent, the prisoner's dilemma is widely applicable—to oligopoly theory as well as many other situations.

Two individuals, Nancy and Sid, are picked up on a public nuisance charge. While questioning the suspects, the district attorney begins to suspect that they may be two key players in an international drug ring. The district attorney, however, does not have enough evidence to convict them of the more serious charge, so she comes up with the following ploy in an attempt to extract a confession. She separates the two prisoners so they cannot communicate with one another and tells each the following:

1. If both confess to drug trafficking, they will both go to jail for 10 years.
2. If neither confesses, they will be charged and convicted of the nuisance offense, and each will receive a 2-year sentence.
3. If one confesses (turns state's evidence) and the other does not, the one who confesses will get a reduced sentence of 1 year; the one who doesn't will be convicted and go to jail for 15 years.

Table 14.3 shows the relevant payoff matrix for this game. Now we can apply our knowledge of game theory to determine what each suspect will do. Let's look at the situation confronting Sid first. If Nancy confesses, Sid's best strategy is to confess also because he then gets 10 instead of 15 years. If Nancy doesn't confess, Sid's best strategy is still to confess because he then gets only 1 year instead of the 2 years he gets if he doesn't confess. *To confess is a dominant strategy for Sid:* Regardless of what Nancy does, Sid does better by confessing.

The situation is exactly symmetrical for Nancy. If Sid confesses, Nancy's best strategy is to confess (10 versus 15 years), and if Sid doesn't confess, Nancy still does better to confess (1 versus 2 years). Confession is a dominant strategy for Nancy also.

Thus, the dominant-strategy equilibrium (and a Nash equilibrium) is for both parties to confess, and that is the expected outcome. This may not seem surprising until you realize fully what it means. The predicted outcome is one where *both* suspects are worse off than

TABLE 14.3

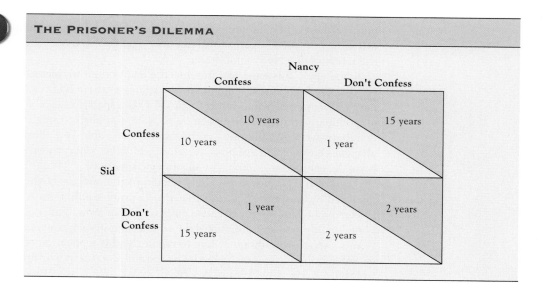

THE PRISONER'S DILEMMA

they would be if neither confessed (in which case they would get only 2 years each, the lower-right cell). Since they both know this, why do they confess? Because it is in each one's self-interest to confess, even though the *collective* outcome of each pursuing their self-interest is inferior for both. By the way, do not make the mistake of thinking that the reason each confesses is that they believe the other will also. The reason for the predicted outcome is stronger than that: it is in each suspect's interest to confess, regardless of the actions of the other.

When they first encounter the prisoner's dilemma, many people try to figure out some way in which the prisoners could realize the best all-around outcome, the 2-year sentence drawn if neither one confesses. By adding some additional elements to the scenario, it is indeed possible to spin a game-theoretic tale where both refuse to confess. For example, if Nancy and Sid are lovers, such that each feels as much pain if the other goes to jail as if they go to jail themselves, they would not confess. Another possibility might be that each suspect believes that if he or she is the only one to confess, the suspect who subsequently does 15 years would be willing to commit murder on release in revenge. In that case, there would probably be no confessions. (Note that the payoffs would be different than just the jail sentences shown in the table.) Taken on its own terms, however, the prisoner's dilemma does show how the individual pursuit of self-interest can, in certain situations, produce results that are inferior for all players.

The prisoner's dilemma has wide-ranging applicability. It has been used to model the interactions between the United States and the Soviet Union in the days of the Cold War. It has also been employed to explain political ticket-splitting (when voters cast ballots for candidates from different parties in various races in the same election) and why the U.S. health care system is so often characterized as being both overly expensive and bureaucratic. In this chapter we explore how the prisoner's dilemma can be applied to explain cheating by members of a cartel, the effects of a "curve"-based grading system on student study effort, and certain aspects of World War I trench warfare.

APPLICATION 14.2   THE CONGRESSIONAL PRISONER'S DILEMMA

Economist Russell Roberts of Washington University in St. Louis likens the difficulty the federal government has encountered in restraining spending over the last three decades to the case in which one's bill at a restaurant is spread evenly across the other 100 diners in the restaurant. If you were responsible for your entire bill, you would usually spend only $6 on a meal and wouldn't splurge on a second drink and dessert that would add $4 to the tab. On the other hand, adding the $4 drink and dessert costs only 4 cents when the bill is spread out evenly over all 100 patrons of the restaurant:

Splurging is easy to justify now. In fact, you won't just add a drink and dessert, you'll upgrade to the steak and add a bottle of wine. Suppose you and everybody else orders $40 worth of food. The tab

for the entire restaurant will be $4,000. Divided by the 100 diners, your bill will be $40. [While you'll get your "fair share"] this outcome is a disaster. When you dined alone, you spent $6. The extra $34 of steak and other treats were not worth it. But in competition with the others, you chose a meal far out of your price range whose enjoyment fell far short of its cost—self-restraint goes unrewarded. If you go back to ordering your $6 meal in hopes of saving money, your tab will be close to $40 anyway, unless the other 99 diners cut back also. The good citizen starts to feel like a chump. And so we read of the freshman Congressman eager to cut pork out of the budget but in trouble back home because local projects will also come under the knife. Instead of being proud to lead the way, he is forced to fight for the projects, to make sure his district gets its "fair share."[2]

In Roberts' judgment, therefore, the average representative confronts a prisoner's dilemma wherein pro-

moting spending on projects in one's district is a dominant strategy. The resulting equilibrium—an overall high level of government spending (and the taxes that must support such spending) across districts—is inferior to the outcome that would emerge if districts' representatives exercised more restraint in their pursuit of spending on government projects in their individual districts.

[2]Russell Roberts, "If You're Paying, I'll Have Top Sirloin," *Wall Street Journal* (May 18, 1995), p. A18.

The Prisoner's Dilemma and Cheating by Cartel Members

Firms in oligopolistic industries often find themselves in a prisoner's dilemma where each firm acting in its self-interest produces an outcome in which all firms are worse off. Consider a very simple setting, with just two firms in an industry. We will use the example developed in Chapter 13 to illustrate the Cournot model. Utopia and Artesia are the firms, and they sell a homogeneous product. We will consider the possibility that the two firms will coordinate their activities to increase their profits. In other words, the firms try to form a cartel. The cartel agreement would have each firm restrict its output so that the market price will be high. However, each firm might consider raising its output beyond the cartel quota (cheating on the agreement). Thus, for each firm the two possible strategies are to comply and to cheat. How will the firms decide which strategy to choose?

The firms' various alternatives are shown in Table 14.4. The numbers in the cells of the payoff matrix represent the firms' profits in each of the possible outcomes. Importantly, the numbers are not just arbitrarily chosen, but reflect the actual economic environment being investigated. (Or at least the relationship between the numbers, their rank ordering, reflects the problem being studied.) Let's see how we can apply economics to explain each firm's profit for each outcome.

Let's assume that Artesia and Utopia have the same cost curves so when they collude, they agree to produce the same output. Together they will produce the monopoly output for the industry because that maximizes their combined profit. With both producing the same

TABLE 14.4 **CHEATING IN A CARTEL**

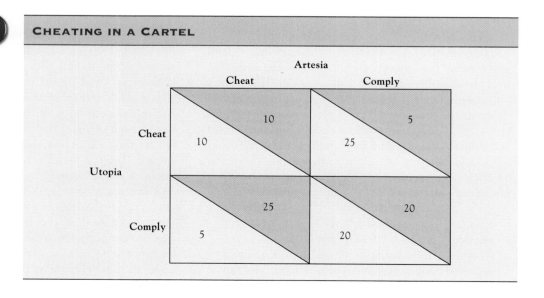

amount, each receives half the monopoly profit. This situation is shown in the lower-right cell where both firms restrict their output, thereby complying with the cartel agreement, and each realizes a profit of 20. Now consider the upper-left cell, where both firms cheat. Because cheating means producing a higher output, price will be lower and, more significantly, profits will be lower. Because the firms are identical, let's suppose that both firms have the same "cheating output" (which we might assume to be the Cournot output), and so will realize the same profit, which we take to be 10.

Now consider the lower-left cell, where Artesia cheats and Utopia complies. The easiest way to see how this affects the profit of each is to imagine starting with the perfect cartel outcome at the lower right. Then Artesia cheats. This increases Artesia's profit from 20 to 25 for the reason we discussed in Chapter 13 (the demand curve confronting a firm is more elastic when it changes output than when all cartel members simultaneously change output). This action, however, reduces Utopia's profit because its output is unchanged but the price of the product is reduced by Artesia's output expansion. Moreover, the reduction in profit for Utopia is greater than the increase for Artesia because we know their combined profit has to be less than 40, the maximum (monopoly) profit shown in the lower-right cell. Here, we assume profit is 5 for Utopia when it complies and Artesia cheats, although the important point is that Utopia's profit falls by more than Artesia's profit increases. Finally, by analogous reasoning, we obtain the figures in the upper-right cell, which is the mirror image of the lower-left cell.

Understanding why the payoffs are as shown, we can analyze the behavior of the two firms. For Artesia, cheating is better if Utopia either complies (profit of 25 versus 20) or cheats (profit of 10 versus 5). Thus, cheating is a dominant strategy for Artesia. For Utopia, cheating is better if Artesia either complies (profit of 25 versus 20) or cheats (profit of 10 versus 5), so cheating is a dominant strategy for Utopia also. Thus, we expect both firms to cheat, and they end up with a profit of 10 each, even though if they both complied they would realize a profit of 20 each. As you might suspect from the outcome, this situation is a version of the prisoner's dilemma game, so the outcome is not surprising. The model shows, in very clear fashion, why firms have an incentive to cheat on a cartel agreement.[3]

It would be a mistake, however, to conclude from this analysis that firms will never successfully form a cartel. Other factors not incorporated here can increase the likelihood of collusion. For example, suppose that cartel agreements are legal and will be enforced. If Artesia and Utopia enter into a contract stipulating that both will comply, each firm will have an incentive to sign since the cartel outcome is better than the outcome realized when both cheat. What this model makes clear, however, is that the agreement must be enforceable because each firm individually still has an incentive to cheat on the agreement. Of course, in the United States cartels are illegal, so if firms illegally enter into a collusive agreement they must have some way of enforcing the agreement on their own to prevent cheating. In other words, for a cartel to be stable, there must be some way to punish firms that cheat. We will consider how this goal might be accomplished in the next section.

This game theory model of cartel behavior can be extended to explain why cheating is more likely the higher the number of firms in the cartel. Suppose there are ten firms initially complying, with each firm making a profit of 20. Then one firm cheats. In our two-firm model, this action increases the cheater's profit from 20 to 25, but with ten firms involved

---

[3]Note that this example appears very similar to Table 14.1: in both cases there are two firms, each choosing between a "low" and a "high" output. Table 14.1 is not, however, a prisoner's dilemma, while Table 14.4 is. What accounts for the difference is that the interdependence is not as pronounced between the firms in Table 14.1. For example, it may be that they are producing goods that are not very good substitutes for one another, while in Table 14.4 the goods are perfect substitutes. Can you see why that would account for the difference in the payoffs shown in the two tables?

the increase in profit will be greater. This is simply because the cheater will confront a more elastic demand curve when it is one among ten firms than when it is one of two firms. (If one firm among ten increases its output by, say, 20 percent, price will fall by less than after an increase of 20 percent by one of two firms.) In addition, the damage the cheater does to the complying firms will be shared among the remaining nine, and so less noticeable for each individual, noncheating firm. For this reason, the more firms in the cartel, the more common we expect cheating to be. With more firms, cheating produces a greater increase in profit for the cheater while the loss for each complying firm is smaller and harder to detect. This game theory illustration supports our earlier explanation as to why collusion is likely to be less common among a larger number of competitors. Each member has a greater incentive to cheat and so undermine the cartel the greater the number of firms involved.

A Prisoner's Dilemma Game You May Play

To see an application of the prisoner's dilemma that may be relevant in your academic life, consider students competing for grades in a class. The professor grades "on the curve" and assigns a certain distribution of grades in the class regardless of what the absolute grades are. For example, the professor may assign 20 percent of the class a grade of "A" regardless of whether 20 percent or only 5 percent score above 90. The professor may have found that in the past about 20 percent of her students do "A" quality work. If on a particular test only 5 percent get grades above 90, she may reason that the test was unfairly difficult, or that she graded more harshly than usual. Thus, she sets the "A" range to include the top 20 percent even though that means giving an "A" to students with absolute scores below 90. If students' motivation for studying is to get a good grade, they will find themselves in a prisoner's dilemma in this class.

Consider two students, Kaitlyn and Scott—taken as representative of the entire class. In this class, grades are curved so that the average is a "B." If they each study four hours per week, they will both get an absolute score of 85 and a grade of "B," as shown in the lower-right cell of the Table 14.5 payoff matrix. However, if they each study only one hour per week, they both get an absolute score of 60, but still receive a grade of "B" because 60 is now the average score for the class and the average receives a "B." This outcome is shown in the upper-left cell. Although their letter grades are the same in both these cells, the students are better off in the upper-left cell: they have the same grades at a lower cost in study time.

TABLE 14.5

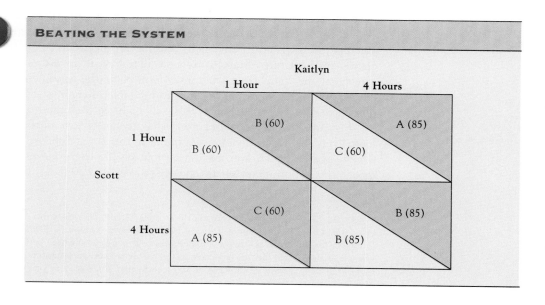

BEATING THE SYSTEM

However, if Kaitlyn studies one hour and Scott studies four hours, he will receive an "A" and she will receive a "C"—the lower-left cell. (Kaitlyn gets the same absolute score for the course, but ranks lower in the class now.) We will assume that a student prefers to earn an "A" with four hours of studying over a "B" with one hour. The same reasoning establishes the grades in the upper-right cell.

The way the students rank the Table 14.5 payoffs gives rise to the prisoner's dilemma. Each student acting independently has a dominant strategy: studying four hours per week. Thus, the outcome is the lower-right cell, a dominant-strategy equilibrium. However, the two students would be better off if they both studied one hour per week and attained the same "B" at a lower cost in time. Students might try to collude and attain the lower-right cell, but they would find enforcing the collusive agreement difficult because each student has an incentive to cheat (that is, studying four hours and "spoiling the curve"), and it is difficult to detect cheating and enforce sanctions. As a result, the students are caught in a prisoner's dilemma.

Does this model explain why students study as much as they do? Actually, it is clear that other factors play a role in studying decisions. For example, if a professor has strict absolute standards (even if you have the highest score in the class, you don't get an "A" unless it is above 90), there will be no prisoner's dilemma. A more serious objection to the analysis would be to question the assumption that students care only about the grades they receive. If they care more about learning than about the grades, there is no prisoner's dilemma. Because this is undoubtedly true in your economics classes, the model may not be applicable there. However, it may give you some insight into the behavior of students in some of your other classes.

14.3 REPEATED GAMES

Oligopolists often find themselves in a prisoner's dilemma if they attempt to collude so as to increase their profits. Because the prisoner's dilemma game has a dominant-strategy equilibrium where all firms cheat (that is, don't collude), it appears that successful collusion never occurs unless binding contracts are permitted and enforced by an external authority. To make this conclusion, however, is overreaching. As explained so far, the implicit assumption is that the prisoner's dilemma game is played only once: the decision to cheat or comply is made just once. This is an appropriate assumption in some settings (such as the situation in which Sid and Nancy found themselves), but it is often not appropriate when applied to firms' pricing and output decisions. Firms in an oligopoly play against one another repeatedly as they make decisions week after week. In the jargon of game theorists, the appropriate model for these market conditions is a **repeated-game model** rather than a single-period model.

REPEATED-GAME MODEL

a game theory model in which the "game" is played more than once

Let us now reconsider the prospects for effective collusion in a duopoly. We will use the data in Table 14.4 explained in the last section. Now, however, we want to imagine that the payoffs refer to the profits for Artesia and Utopia each week, and that each week the firms make a choice of either complying (low output) or cheating (high output). In the repeated-game setting, the range of strategies available to the firm increases enormously. It would be impossible to consider all the permutations, but one point should be clear: each firm now has a way to punish its rival for any past transgressions. Because the game is repeated, if Artesia cheats in the fourth week, then it is possible for Utopia to cheat in the fifth week, a tactic that imposes a cost on Artesia. In other words, the firms have a way of enforcing the cartel agreement by punishing one another for cheating.

What strategy will firms adopt in this setting, and what is the equilibrium likely to be? These are difficult questions without definitive answers, but we can easily see that collusion

TIT-FOR-TAT
a strategy in which each player mimics the action (e.g., cheat, comply) taken by the other player in the preceding period

is more likely in the repeated-game setting. Suppose that Utopia adopts a tit-for-tat strategy. Under a **tit-for-tat** strategy, Utopia will comply in a given week as long as Artesia complied in the previous week. However, if Artesia cheats in one week, the following week Utopia will cheat (tit-for-tat), and will continue cheating in each successive week until Artesia complies, after which Utopia will revert to complying. There is nothing sacrosanct about the tit-for-tat strategy, but it is simple and in a computer simulation turns out to be quite effective.[4] We can see why by considering the consequences of adopting this strategy.

Let's examine some of the options open to Artesia when Utopia plays the tit-for-tat strategy and Artesia is aware of it. Table 14.6 shows two possible scenarios that might unfold over a succession of weeks. In the first scenario, both firms comply in the first week and realize a profit of 20 (see Table 14.4 and the discussion there for the source of the profit numbers). In the second week, Utopia complies but Artesia cheats and obtains a higher profit of 25. In this scenario, we investigate the effects if Artesia continues cheating in the following weeks. In the third week, Utopia plays tit-for-tat and cheats. Artesia continues to cheat so both firms realize a profit of 10. As long as Artesia continues to cheat, so will Utopia, and they will continue to obtain a profit of 10 each.

Now imagine you are Artesia, and consider whether you would be better off following the strategy of Scenario 1 (comply in the first week and cheat thereafter) or complying every week. In Scenario 1, you get profits of 20, 25, 10, 10, and so on. If you comply, however, you get profits of 20, 20, 20, 20, and so on, because Utopia will continue to comply as long as you do. Clearly, you are better off by complying because the short-term gain you get by cheating in the second week is more than offset by the lower profits you suffer every week thereafter.

As an alternative, however, you might consider cheating one week and then complying in the next. Scenario 2 shows the evolution of the game when Artesia cheats in the second week and then complies in the third week, inducing Utopia to revert to complying in the fourth week. Once again, the sum of profits over time is higher for Artesia if it complies in every period than if it follows this strategy.[5]

This example illustrates why it is rational for Artesia to comply in every period when it knows that Utopia is playing a tit-for-tat strategy. This does not prove that the collusive

TABLE 14.6

CHEATING IN A REPEATED CARTEL GAME

Period	Scenario 1				Scenario 2			
	Artesia		Utopia		Artesia		Utopia	
Week 1	Comply	(20)	Comply	(20)	Comply	(20)	Comply	(20)
Week 2	Cheat	(25)	Comply	(5)	Cheat	(25)	Comply	(5)
Week 3	Cheat	(10)	Cheat	(10)	Comply	(5)	Cheat	(25)
Week 4	Cheat	(10)	Cheat	(10)	Comply	(20)	Comply	(20)
.	.	.	.		.	.	.	
.	.	.	.		.	.	.	
.	.	.	.		.	.	.	

[4]Of course, the effectiveness of any strategy depends on what strategy opposing players are using. Robert Axelrod, in *The Evolution of Cooperation* (New York: Basic Books, 1984), finds that, on average, tit-for-tat works better than any of the other strategies investigated.

[5]This conclusion depends on the sum of the profits in weeks 2 and 3 (cheat-comply and comply-cheat), here 30, being less than the sum of the profits when Artesia complies in both periods, here 40. Refer back to the discussion of the payoffs in Table 14.4 to see why the relationship between the payoffs must be this way.

outcome will result because we have just assumed that Utopia adopted this particular strategy and that Artesia is aware of it. It does, however, suggest why in a repeated-game setting the collusive outcome is more likely: firms will realize that if they cheat in the current period they are likely to suffer losses in subsequent periods, and that realization diminishes the incentive to cheat.

APPLICATION 14.3 — COOPERATION IN THE TRENCHES OF WORLD WAR I

Cooperation between rivals can emerge in some unlikely places. A poignant example involves the "live-and-let-live" system that surfaced in World War I trench warfare.[6] The system emerged despite the passions of battle and the military logic of "kill or be killed."

The situation along the Western Front of World War I can be represented as a repeated-game prisoner's dilemma. In any given locality, opposing units could either "cheat" (shoot to kill) or "cooperate" (withhold fire or shoot in such a way as to miss). Cheating was the dominant one-period-game strategy for both sides. This is so because weakening the enemy through cheating increased the cheating side's chances of survival. Cheating by both sides, however, resulted in an outcome—heavy losses inflicted on both sides for little or no gain—that was inferior to the one produced by cooperation. And opposing units interacted with each other for what appeared, at least to them, indefinite periods of time.

The diaries, letters, and reminiscences of the trench fighters testify to the "live-and-let-live" (that is, cooperative) equilibrium that eventually emerged. One British staff officer touring the trenches was "astonished to observe German soldiers walking about within rifle range behind their own lines. Our men appear to take no notice." A soldier commented: "It would be child's play to shell the road behind the enemy's trenches, crowded as it must be with ration wagons and water carts, into a bloodstained wilderness . . . but on the whole there is silence. After all, if you prevent your enemy from drawing his rations, his remedy is simple: he will prevent you from drawing yours." Another British officer recounted: "I was having tea with A Company when . . . suddenly a [German] salvo arrived but did no damage. Naturally, both sides got down and our men started swearing at the Germans, when all at once a brave German got on to his parapet and shouted out 'We are very sorry about that; we hope no one was hurt. It is not our fault, it is that damned Prussian artillery [behind the front lines].'"

Believing that tacit truces would undermine troop morale, the high commands of both sides began rotating troops and ordering raids (whose success or failure could be monitored by headquarters staff) in an effort to destroy the "live-and-let-live" system.

[6]Robert Axelrod, *The Evolution of Cooperation* (New York: Basic Books, 1984). The quotes that follow come from Chapter 4.

Do Oligopolistic Firms Always Collude?

Our analysis of the repeated prisoner's dilemma game seems to turn our earlier conclusions on their heads. The initial analysis suggested that firms would inevitably cheat, and now we have an analysis suggesting that over time collusion is likely. But the real world is, alas, even more complicated than the repeated-game model may suggest. It is well to consider the restrictive assumptions (not all explicit) underlying our repeated prisoner's dilemma game: there are only two firms, no entry into the market occurs, the firms have identical costs and produce a homogeneous product, each firm has complete knowledge of the payoffs for both firms for all strategy combinations, demand and cost conditions do not vary over time, and the game is repeated indefinitely. Relaxing almost any of these assumptions makes it less likely that collusion will be a stable outcome in an oligopolistic industry.

To see how changing one assumption can affect the outcome, consider the number of time periods the game is played. Our previous analysis implicitly assumed that the game was repeated forever. To contrast that, suppose that the two firms know that if they collude for ten weeks, new firms will have time to enter the market, and with new entry in the eleventh week, collusion will become ineffective. Artesia and Utopia then know that the game will last for ten weeks; there are ten time periods in which the data in Table 14.4 are relevant. The easiest way to see how this affects the analysis is to work backward by considering first the decisions of the firms in the last (tenth) week. In that week, it is rational for both firms to cheat because neither can be punished by the other after that, when the market will effectively be competitive. In the last period, the one-period prisoner's dilemma model that we initially discussed is relevant.

Both firms realize that it is in the other's interest to cheat in week 10. Now consider the choice in the ninth week. Because Artesia knows that Utopia will cheat in the tenth week, Artesia has no reason to comply in the ninth week. (The only reason for complying is to avoid its rival cheating in the next period, and it is going to do that anyway.) The same holds true for Utopia. Both firms will cheat in the ninth week, and both know this. Working backward in this way, we find that the firms' incentive is now to cheat in every period! This outcome occurs because of the common knowledge that the repeated game comes to an end at some point in the future.

Modifying the other assumptions in the repeated-game analysis also makes the collusive outcome more difficult to achieve. When demand conditions are variable, for example, the price each firm receives can change either because of cheating by its rival or because of falling market demand. How can the firm pinpoint the cause? If it assumes cheating whenever the price falls, the collusive arrangement can fall apart as the firms retaliate even though cheating may not have occurred.

Reaching a general conclusion about the repeated-game model of cartels is difficult because many factors can clearly influence the outcome. The analysis does, however, suggest how collusion might emerge and be enforced for at least some period of time. Still, the factors we emphasized in our discussion of cartels in Chapter 13—the possibility of entry, cheating, and the difficulty of reaching agreement, especially with heterogeneous firms and products—are forces that tend to undermine collusive arrangements.

Game Theory and Oligopoly: A Summary

We have given only a brief introduction to game theory as it relates to the study of oligopoly. Our purpose has been to convey the nature of this approach to studying markets in which strategic interactions are important. As is apparent from our discussion of collusion as a possible outcome in a repeated game, the strategic interactions become very complicated. Game theory provides a technique that is suited to investigate such interactions, but as applied in the research literature it is a far more mathematical treatment than might be suggested by our attempt to explain its nature in a simple way.

Because the game-theoretic approach has become the dominant approach to the analysis of oligopoly over the last few decades, let's examine its lessons. Unfortunately, the use of game theory has not produced a general theory of oligopoly—a theory that would tell us, for example, that a market characterized by factors A and B will operate as in the Cournot model, while a market characterized by factors C and D will operate as a dominant firm model. A large number of possible outcomes have been enumerated in game theory models, but we do not know when or whether these outcomes will occur in real-world markets. In this sense, the state of oligopoly theory is much as it was before the application of game-theoretic techniques.

Progress has been made, however, in illuminating more clearly the complexity of the whole topic of oligopoly analysis, and many theorists expect further research to provide the basis for a better understanding of the way oligopolistic markets function. For now, we have to be content with the recognition that the outcome in such a market may fall anywhere between the monopoly (the perfect cartel case) and the competitive outcome. And whether the outcome is closer to monopoly or to competition depends on the interplay of a wide variety of factors in ways that are not yet fully understood.

14.4 ASYMMETRIC INFORMATION

All of the models presented so far—the competitive model as well as the imperfectly competitive models—have been based on the assumption that market participants have all the information needed to make informed choices. For firms, this means knowing technology, input costs, and the prices consumers will pay for different products. For consumers, this means knowing product characteristics and prices. Although this assumption regarding knowledge is sometimes referred to as the *perfect information* assumption, the term is an exaggeration. Consumers and firms do not have to know everything for the analyses to be valid. Nonetheless, the assumption places meaningful restrictions on the models, and it is important to consider how markets function when market participants lack some information relevant to their decisions. We will begin by considering a common feature in many markets: when consumers have difficulty determining the quality of products prior to purchase.

The "Lemons" Model[7]

We are all familiar with "lemons": products that repeatedly break down or perform unsatisfactorily relative to what we expected. The model we will examine suggests that a high proportion of goods may be lemons in a market where buyers are less well informed about product quality than sellers. The basic assumption is one of **asymmetric information**: participants on one side of the market (in our case, sellers) know more about a good's quality than do participants on the other side (buyers). One market where this characteristic seems prevalent is the one for used cars. A seller of a used car normally has extensive experience using the car and can be expected to know its defects. It is often difficult for a prospective buyer to determine how good the car is until after having purchased and driven it for a while. At the time of the transaction, buyers are likely to have less information than sellers about product quality.

Before examining how asymmetric information affects the functioning of used car markets, let's first consider, for purposes of contrast, a market where all parties are fully informed. Suppose that there are only two types of used cars, "good" (high-quality) cars and "bad" (low-quality) cars. Consumers are willing to pay $12,000 for a good car and $6,000 for a bad car. To simplify, assume that the market demand curves are perfectly elastic at these prices. In this situation, there will be two markets, one for good cars and one for bad cars, and the prices will be $12,000 and $6,000, respectively. Assume also that sales of each type of car are 50,000. These markets will function as the competitive model predicts.

Now assume that buyers cannot distinguish between good and bad cars, but the sellers know the difference. How will this affect the market for used cars? Consider the buyers. Only one price will now prevail in the used car market because buyers cannot distinguish between good and bad cars at the time of purchase. Buyers do know, however, that the car may turn out to be either good or bad. How much the buyer is willing to pay for a used car will then depend on how likely it is that the car will be good or bad. To contrast this market with the full-information outcome given previously, let's initially suppose that consumers believe there is a 50 percent chance that the car they purchase will be a good one and a 50 percent chance it will be a bad one (because 50 percent of the cars sold in the full-information model were of each type). Then we expect the typical buyer to be willing to pay about $9,000 for a used car—because this is the average value of a used car when half turn out to be good (worth $12,000) and half turn out to be bad (worth $6,000).

ASYMMETRIC INFORMATION

a case in which participants on one side of the market know more about a good's quality than do participants on the other side

[7]The model explained in this section is based on George A. Akerlof, "The Market for 'Lemons': Quality Uncertainty and the Market Mechanism," *Quarterly Journal of Economics*, 84 No. 3 (August 1970), pp. 488–500.

From this discussion, we might expect that the used car market would now be in equilibrium at a single price of $9,000. But that is premature. We have not considered the response of the used car sellers. The sellers know the qualities of their cars. When sellers of high-quality used cars confronted a price of $12,000 (in the full-information model), we assumed they would choose to sell 50,000 units. Now these sellers will get only $9,000, and so we expect them to offer fewer units for sale. With an upward-sloping supply curve, fewer good cars will be sold when the price is lower. Similarly, if 50,000 bad cars would be sold at a price of $6,000, when the price is $9,000 we expect more owners of lemons to unload their cars. Suppose that at a price of $9,000, sales of good cars would be 25,000 and sales of bad cars would be 75,000.

If the price were $9,000, we would expect consumers to become aware that it is more likely they will get a low-quality car than a high-quality car in this market. That will affect their willingness to pay. If consumers perceive correctly that three-fourths of the time they get a bad car, they would be willing to pay only $7,500 for a used car (a weighted average of the $12,000 and $6,000 values of good and bad cars, with a weight of three-fourths on the $6,000 figure). But if the price is $7,500, this will decrease the quantities of both types of used cars. However, it is likely to increase the *proportion* of bad used cars in the market, leading to a further revaluation downward in the price consumers will pay.

Exactly where this process ends—where equilibrium will be reached—depends on the supply elasticities of good and bad used cars. It is possible that the process continues until only low-quality used cars are sold at a price of $6,000. It is also possible that there will be an equilibrium in which both good and bad cars are sold. Which outcome results is not as important as recognizing that *the proportion of used cars sold that are high quality will be lower than when consumers know the qualities before making the purchases*. Low-quality products tend to drive out high-quality products when there is asymmetric information.

Our use of used cars as an example should not be interpreted to mean that the analysis applies only to used products or that it applies to all used products. This analysis may apply in any market in which consumers have difficulty determining product quality. This is often true of the markets for technologically sophisticated products like personal computers, cellular phones, or VCRs. It is also true of some services: Did you know the quality of instruction at your college when you enrolled? The problem also often arises in purchasing the services of plumbers, carpenters, doctors, and dentists, to give only a few examples.

Market Responses to Asymmetric Information

Do low-quality products really drive out high-quality products? Certainly this is not always the case and may never be the case. The preceding analysis is intended to draw out the implications of the assumption that consumers have no way of judging quality. Consumers often do have ways of distinguishing low- from high-quality products. Before discussing a few of them, let's consider *why* the preceding analysis is incomplete. It is incomplete because it suggests there are substantial mutual gains to be realized if consumers seeking high-quality products can be paired with sellers of high-quality products. (In our example, sellers of good used cars would be better off selling them at, say, $10,000 than not selling any, and buyers would also be better off.) This means that people have the incentive to acquire (or disseminate) information that allows consumers to know when they are getting a high-quality product. Of course, information itself is a scarce good, and there are costs to acquiring and disseminating information. That is one reason why people are not fully informed: The benefits from acquiring information about product quality will not always be worth its costs.

The way in which information is acquired and used by consumers depends on many factors, including the nature of the product and its price, and therefore will differ from market to market. For low-priced products that are frequently purchased (for example, ball-point pens), personal experience may be the most economical source of information. When goods are higher priced and are purchased infrequently (automobiles, stereos, and so on), it becomes more important to not be stuck with a lemon, and consumers take some care before making a purchase. In the case of a used car, for example, they are likely to want a test drive and may take it to a mechanic whose quality they already know. For many products, consumers can consult publications like *Consumer Reports* for disinterested evaluations of product quality. Similarly, prospective college students may consult several of the available college guides before choosing a college. The opinions of people you know and trust can also provide useful information.

In many cases, it is more efficient for sellers to take the initiative in providing information about product quality. There are several ways to accomplish this goal. For example, sellers of high-quality products may offer guarantees or warranties. This step communicates to consumers that the products are high quality, and firms are willing to incur the costs of the guarantees because they can charge more when consumers believe they are getting a high-quality product. A key issue here is whether the information provided by the seller is believable. A guarantee is more believable if offered by an established firm than if offered by a stranger peddling "gold" watches on a street corner. In a similar fashion, many firms take actions to develop a reputation, or a brand name, for selling high-quality products. The brand name can provide reliable information about the quality of a firm's products. Finally, liability laws give firms an incentive to avoid at least the most serious quality defects because firms can be bankrupted by suits from consumers.

Do these various ways of acquiring and disseminating information imply that the lemons model tells us nothing about real-world markets? It would be a mistake, we think, to reach that conclusion. The provision and acquisition of information has its costs, and for products where these costs are high we would expect the lemons model to provide some insight. There are, for example, still many purveyors of "effortless weight loss" programs and wrinkle-removal creams, even though their "products" have been discredited (to the satisfaction of most people who have investigated them—but investigation has costs). Even where the cost of product quality information is relatively low and markets function well, it is worthwhile to understand that the markets do function differently than they would if consumers were fully informed without cost.

A final point is important. When a real-world market functions differently than it would if consumers were fully informed, it does not mean that the market is necessarily inefficient. Informing consumers is costly, and that usually means that it is efficient for consumers to be something less than fully informed. That is, the costs of informing consumers may be greater than the benefits produced.

APPLICATION 14.4   IS THERE A LEMONS PROBLEM IN USED CAR MARKETS?

For reasons we have explained, it is doubtful that bad cars will totally drive out good cars in used car markets. However, it is possible that asymmetric information has an effect on the way markets for used cars operate. One study examined this issue through the use of survey data.[8] The author reasoned that to the extent

the lemons problem was relevant, the quality of used cars should vary by type of seller. Cars purchased from used car dealers (who may provide warranties and have reputations at stake) and from friends or relatives should be of higher quality than those purchased from unknown individuals through a newspaper ad.

Quality is difficult to measure, of course; three different measures were designed for this study. One was based simply on a buyer's own evaluations of a car's mechanical condition using a 10-point scale, with 1 being a

[8]James M. Lacko, *Product Quality and Information in the Used Car Market*, Bureau of Economics Staff Report, Federal Trade Commission (Washington, D.C.: U.S. Government Printing Office, 1986).

lemon and 10 being a "gem." On this scale, the average used car's condition was rated at 6.65. After controlling for various factors (such as age and mileage), the researcher found that for cars between 1 and 7 years old there were few differences among the various types of sellers. This runs contrary to the lemons model. On the other hand, for older cars (8 to 15 years), cars purchased from dealers and friends were rated higher than those purchased through a newspaper ad from a stranger. Cars purchased from a used car dealer, for example, were rated 0.91 points higher than those purchased through an ad.

This study suggests that asymmetric information about the quality of used cars has no effect for cars less than 8 years old, and a limited effect for older cars. Apparently, consumers do obtain enough information through the sorts of channels we discussed to avoid the extreme outcome predicted by the lemons model.

14.5 ADVERSE SELECTION AND MORAL HAZARD

Our analysis of asymmetric information has emphasized markets in which consumers have less information than sellers. In some important instances, for example, insurance markets, it is the firms that are less well informed.[9] Our discussion in Chapter 5 of insurance markets was based on the assumption of full information (that is, both firms and consumers know the risks). Now let's see how insurance markets may function when this assumption is modified.

Adverse Selection

The most important information affecting the operation of insurance markets is the probability that the insured-against event will occur. Insurance companies have amassed statistical data that enable them to estimate these probabilities. They may find, for example, that one out of a thousand houses they insure burns down each year. What they often don't know is how the probability varies from one homeowner to another. Thus, it is quite possible that some homeowners have better information than the insurance companies. In the case of a potential arsonist, this is certain to be the case, but even in less extreme circumstances (people who store flammables alongside electrical wiring in their attics) consumers may know whether their risks are much higher than average. Thus, it is quite possible that at least some consumers have better information than the firms do. This asymmetric information can have profound effects on the operation of the market.

ADVERSE SELECTION

a situation in which asymmetric information causes higher-risk customers to be more likely to purchase or sellers to be more likely to supply low-quality goods

Assume that some homeowners are much more at risk of suffering fire damage to their homes, and that these homeowners know it. The insurance companies know the average risks based on their experience, and they have to charge premiums based on that. What consumers will find this an attractive deal? Clearly, the high-risk homeowners will find the price attractive; think of how much insurance an arsonist would buy when $100 in coverage can be purchased for $1, where this fee reflects the average risk. On the other hand, the insurance is much less attractive to low-risk homeowners. So the insurance companies will find most of their customers coming from the high-risk group; they get an **adverse selection** from the pool of potential customers. The "undesirable" customers, the high-risk homeowners, are more likely to want to deal in the market (this is the adverse selection), and the insurance companies cannot distinguish high-risk from low-risk homeowners when they sell policies.

[9]Another example is labor markets: when a firm hires workers it is less well informed about the quality of the workers' labor services than the workers.

Imagine where this process can lead. As mostly high-risk persons purchase insurance, the insurance company finds that it has to pay off on a larger share of policies than initially predicted. The average riskiness of its customers is thus higher than for the population as a whole, and this causes the price of insurance to rise. The higher cost of insurance drives away more low-risk customers and further raises the cost of providing the insurance. In the end, it is possible that only high-risk customers are served, and low-risk customers must go without insurance that could potentially benefit them if it reflected their true risk status. (In a full-information world, high- and low-risk customers would simply be charged different prices, reflecting the difference in risk.) This analysis should sound familiar, for it is essentially the lemons problem in a new setting. Adverse selection was the driving force in our used car example, also. There, sellers of low-quality used cars were adversely selected because buyers could not distinguish between good and bad cars. Here, high-risk customers are adversely selected because firms cannot distinguish between high- and low-risk customers.

The adverse selection problem may be important in many insurance markets. In life and medical insurance markets, customers often have a better idea of their risk status (from their own medical or family history) than do insurance companies. Similarly, automobile drivers who speed or drink and drive are more likely to have accidents, and they know more about their driving behavior than an insurance company does when providing them coverage. Doctors who purchase medical malpractice insurance may also be better informed of their risk of lawsuit than their insurance companies. In all these markets, it is possible that the adverse selection problem leads to a situation where mostly high-risk customers are insured and many low-risk customers choose to remain uninsured.

Of course, the outcome is not likely to be as dire as the analysis so far suggests, and the reason is the same as in the lemons model: there are potential gains to market participants from adjusting their behavior to take account of the adverse selection problem. For example, homeowners' insurance policies cover only the market value of structure and contents. By placing an upper limit on the potential losses, insurance companies reduce the costs imposed by high-risk customers, and this lowers the cost of insurance. (Imagine if potential arsonists could insure the family photo album for its "sentimental value" of $100,000.)

Other insurance company practices also make more sense when the adverse selection problem is understood. For health and life insurance policies, companies often require physical exams (to help distinguish high- from low-risk people) and a waiting period before a policy is in force (some maladies may not be apparent in a physical, even though the consumer is aware of them). In some cases, insurance companies use indirect measures to help identify the riskiness of customers. For instance, men aged 15 to 24 have car accidents with about twice the frequency of women the same age, so gender can be used as an indicator of riskiness. Similarly, women live longer than men and so are at lower risk of dying at any age; hence, life insurance is less costly for them.

Finally, group health plans have been developed partly in response to the adverse selection problem. These plans offer policies covering all the employees at a firm. Because all employees must be enrolled, there is a smaller likelihood that high-risk people will be overrepresented; the insured workers are more likely to be representative of the average population. Adverse selection can still occur (high-risk workers choose to work for firms with extensive coverage), but that is less likely to be a problem than in the sale of individual policies, so group plans can provide insurance coverage at lower costs. (There are also some other reasons for the lower cost of group plans, such as lower administrative costs.)

APPLICATION **14.5**   **ADVERSE SELECTION AND THE AMERICAN RED CROSS**

Fewer than 4 percent of all blood donors are paid for their donation. A key reason why so-called *commercial blood* is not more common is adverse selection.[10] Critics of for-profit giving argue that when people are

[10]This application is based on: Michael L. Katz and Harvey S. Rosen, *Microeconomics* (Boston: Irwin/McGraw Hill, 1998); and Alvin W. Drake, Stan N. Finkelstein, and Harvey M. Sapolsky, *The American Blood Supply* (Cambridge, MA: MIT Press, 1982).

motivated to donate blood for the sake of a financial reward, blood banks are more likely to attract donors who are desperate for the money because they are addicted to drugs or alcohol or have a serious infectious disease. Indeed, numerous studies have found that hepatitis, a disease that can be transmitted through blood transfusion and that inflames the liver and can occasionally be fatal, is much more likely to be present in commercially collected blood than in blood that is donated on a nonprofit basis.

Moral Hazard

MORAL HAZARD
a situation that occurs when, as a result of having insurance, an individual becomes more likely to engage in risky behavior

Moral hazard is another problem endemic to insurance markets. It occurs when, as a result of having insurance, an individual's behavior changes in such a way that the probability of the unfavorable outcome increases or its cost is greater when it does occur. An uninsured homeowner, for example, would take great precautions against fire. The homeowner might, for example, avoid the use of kerosene heaters, install smoke detectors, prohibit smoking, and have an electrician inspect the wiring frequently. The incentives become quite different if the costs of replacing the house are covered by an insurance policy. The benefits from avoiding a fire are now smaller, and so the homeowner is likely to devote fewer resources to that use. What this behavior means is that fires become more likely when the parties are insured, and this leads to higher prices of insurance coverage.

The extent of the moral hazard problem is likely to vary across individuals and types of insurable events. People with car insurance may be more careless about locking their cars or may park them in riskier neighborhoods. But does health insurance coverage lead people to exercise less, eat poorly, and smoke more? One reason the problem may be less severe in this instance is that health insurance does not cover all the costs of illness. Although it may cover all the medical costs, for many illnesses the costs to the patient of the pain, suffering, and disfigurement can be as much or greater. This gives people an incentive to take actions to avoid the illness even when the medical costs are covered. But the moral hazard problem is an important reason why you can't get insurance to compensate you fully for *all* (medical and other) costs you bear from illness: that sort of insurance would give you no reason for taking care of yourself.

The moral hazard problem arises when insurance companies lack knowledge of the actions people take that may affect the occurrence of the unfavorable events. If the actions are observable or verifiable, the policies can be made contingent on performance of those actions. This can work to the advantage of insurance companies as well as insured parties who receive more favorable rates. For instance, homes with security systems and smoke detectors may receive coverage at lower rates, giving homeowners incentives to take actions that lower the probability of theft and fire. Similarly, smokers are generally charged higher health insurance premiums than nonsmokers, making smokers bear the higher cost of medical care that results from their behavior, and at the same time giving them an incentive to quit smoking. "Good driver" policies reward automobile owners with unblemished records through lower rates.

Another type of moral hazard problem is particularly significant to health insurance. Consider a policy that covers all hospital costs. When a person is hospitalized, he or she will, in effect, face a zero price for treatment. This is likely to lead the patient to consume hospital services beyond the point where they are worth what they cost. Any form of medical care that has any benefit, no matter how small, will seem worthwhile if the insurance company is absorbing the expense. In this setting, doctors are likely to prescribe expensive tests and sophisticated treatments, knowing that financial responsibility falls to a faceless third party. But when patients and doctors behave this way, the cost of hospitalization goes up and insurance premiums rise to cover the cost.

A number of practices have evolved in the medical insurance market to deal with moral hazard. One is limitations on the services that insurance will cover (no more than three days in the hospital for an appendectomy, for example). Although patients may believe this reflects stinginess on the part of the insurer, it actually leads to lower insurance premiums and can be in the long-run interest of the insured. A second approach is to require the insured person to pay part of the costs. Patients might be required to pay 20 percent of the hospital bill; the share of the cost borne by the patient is called the *coinsurance rate*. Use of coinsurance reduces the cost of insurance directly, but also indirectly lowers it by giving patients incentive to be more economical in their use of hospital services. A third approach is the use of *deductibles*. Using a deductible means that a patient must pay, for example, the first $500 of hospital costs before insurance coverage is effective. This gives patients incentive to take account of all costs in the case of minor medical treatments, and also leads to lower insurance premiums.

Insurance markets are profoundly affected by asymmetric information, as this discussion indicates. There is no doubt that these markets function very differently from the way they would if all parties had perfect information. Understanding the problems that asymmetric information creates helps us see why certain practices aimed at mitigating them have emerged.

APPLICATION 14.6   MORAL HAZARD IN THE S&L INDUSTRY

The federal government's bailout of savings and loan institutions (S&Ls) ended up costing taxpayers over $150 billion.[11] While the monetary consequences of the bailout are sizable, the cause of the widespread bankruptcy in the S&L industry since the late 1980s is straightforward: moral hazard. During the late 1970s and early 1980s the availability of insurance for deposits at S&Ls was expanded by the government through institutions such as the Federal Deposit Insurance Corporation and the Federal Savings and Loan Insurance Corporation. The expanded availability of insurance, coupled with relaxations in other government regulations concerning S&Ls, implied that the government would insure virtually all accounts regardless of their size and no matter how risky the loans made. Predictably enough, S&Ls increased the riskiness of their loan portfolios during the early 1980s. The increased riskiness of the loan portfolios came back to haunt the S&Ls and ultimately the federal government, especially when the economy slid into recession during the late 1980s.

[11]Edward J. Kane, *The S&L Insurance Mess* (Washington, D.C.: The Urban Institute Press, 1989).

APPLICATION 14.7   MORAL HAZARD ON THE ROAD AND AT THE PLATE

Moral hazard is not limited to insurance markets. Consider the case of four-wheel-drive motor vehicles. Contrary to the claims of car makers and dealers about the safety of four-wheel drive vehicles, the drivers of such vehicles appear to be more likely to have an accident (holding other factors constant including the recent well-publicized failures of Bridgestone/Firestone tires on Ford sport utility vehicles).[12] The problem appears to be the behavior of drivers once they are behind the wheel of a four-wheel drive automobile. According to one Denver-based traffic investigator: "These people have it in their heads that they're driving Sherman tanks. As soon as snow hits the ground, they go speeding up the highway, and then two minutes later they're rolled over or skidding like crazy." A computer technician from Boston who recently wrecked his four-wheel-drive car notes, "When you're in a four-wheel drive, there is this sense of power and overconfidence that makes you forget everything else. You really don't realize your limitations until you hit something."

Another non-insurance-market example of moral hazard is the 1973 introduction of the Designated Hitter (DH) rule in the American League but not the National League of Major League Baseball. The DH rule relieved American League pitchers of their responsibility to appear at the plate as a hitter (another player could be designated to hit in place of the pitcher). Consequently, American League pitchers can throw at opposing hitters with greater impunity (lower cost) than National League pitchers, who must still take their turn at bat. American League pitchers are less likely to face direct retaliation (since they do not have to appear at the plate themselves) if they hit or come close to hitting an opposing batsman with a pitch. The result is as one would predict. Since the introduction of the DH rule, American League pitchers have been hitting 10 to 15 percent more batters with their pitches than National League pitchers (holding all other factors constant).

[12]This application is based on "Why Four-Wheel Drive Isn't Always Safer in Snow," *Wall Street Journal*, February 22, 1995, pp. B1 and B6; "Backlash on Insurance," *New York Times*, March 15, 1998, p. 10; Brian L. Goff, William F. Shughart II, and Robert D. Tollison, "Batter Up: Moral Hazard and the Effects of the DH Rule on Hit Batsmen," *Economic Inquiry*, 35 No. 3 (July 1997), pp. 555–561; and Brian L. Goff, William F. Shughart II, and Robert D. Tollison, "Moral Hazard and the Effects of the Designated Hitter Rule Revisited," *Economic Inquiry*, 36 No. 4 (October 1998), pp. 688–692.

14.6   LIMITED PRICE INFORMATION

Consumers may lack information about product prices as well as product qualities. In the competitive model, where consumers are fully informed, if one firm raises its price above the competitive level (the price charged by the other firms) it will lose all its sales because its customers know that the other firms charge a lower price and so will purchase from them. When consumers have perfect information about prices, all firms have to charge the same price and thus each firm faces a horizontal demand curve.

By contrast, if consumers do not know the prices at stores other than the one where they are currently shopping, retailers can raise prices without losing all customers. Consumers' lack of information about competitors' prices means that each store confronts a downward-sloping demand curve, which, in turn, gives it some market power. Exactly how such a market functions depends on a number of factors, including the extent of consumer ignorance and the cost of acquiring price information. In general, however, we expect that the firms in markets where many or all consumers are uninformed will be charging different prices. There is likely to be a range of prices or **price dispersion** for the same product.

Now consider consumer behavior in a market where there is price dispersion. Consumers wish to purchase from the firm offering the product for the lowest price, but they don't know which firm it is. They can find out, but there is a cost of acquiring the information. **Search costs** are the costs that consumers incur in acquiring information; they include such things as

PRICE DISPERSION
a range of prices for the same product, usually as a result of customers' lacking price information

SEARCH COSTS
the costs that customers incur in acquiring information

time (making telephone calls, buying newspapers, reading the ads) and transportation between stores. There is also a benefit from acquiring price information, of course, because consumers can buy the product for a lower price. However, consumers are unlikely to search until they are fully informed about all the prices being charged by various stores. The reason for this is that the expected marginal benefit from additional search declines the longer the search goes on.

A simple example illustrates this point. Suppose 20 stores sell a compact disc you want to purchase. You call one store and find its price is $12. Should you call a second store? If all stores charge different prices, the probability that the second store will charge a lower price is about one-half. So you call a second store and find its price is $13; you lost the coin flip. Now the probability that a third telephone call will generate a price lower than either of these is only about one-third. Even after calling 19 stores, there is a slight probability that the lowest-price store is the one you haven't called, but you would be unlikely to take the time to call all 20 stores just to guarantee you find the lowest price. In general, because the expected marginal benefit of additional search declines with the amount of search, you will not keep placing calls until you become fully informed. You may stop after three or four telephone calls and purchase from the lowest-priced source you have located, although that will often not be the lowest price available in the market.

For a given consumer, the amount of search undertaken will have no effect on the actual price dispersion in the market. But if many or all consumers increase search intensity, becoming better informed about price, the price dispersion will be reduced. As consumers become better informed, high-priced firms lose business relative to low-priced firms, and high-priced firms are forced to reduce their prices. Taken to the limit, if consumers become fully informed, only one price can prevail.

How does this help us understand the amount of price dispersion for a given product? The theory predicts that the dispersion falls when consumers search more (that is, become better informed). They will search more when the benefit from search is higher than the cost. A little thought will convince you that the benefit will be higher the greater the product's price. Finding a store that sells a compact disc for 1 percent less than another may not be worth an extra phone call, but saving 1 percent on the price of a car is likely to be worth it. Thus, it is not surprising that empirical studies have found less relative price dispersion (price variation compared with the average price) for higher-priced products. Prices are less widely dispersed for cars of the same make and model, for example, than for washing machines.[13]

Finally, we should not ignore the possibility that when consumers are not fully informed and there is price dispersion in a market, it may be in the interest of the low-price firms to inform consumers about price. This is one reason why firms advertise, which leads us to the next section.

14.7   ADVERTISING

Firms advertise in an attempt to increase the demand for their products. On that point economists agree. But there is some disagreement over whether advertising expenditures serve the useful function of providing information to consumers or the baleful function of wasting resources and distorting consumption choices.

Economists have a long tradition of skepticism regarding the benefits of advertising. In this view, competitive firms have no need to advertise because they can sell as much as they want at the market price (although this point is disputed), so the very existence of advertising implies that firms have some monopoly power. But advertising itself may not only be a symptom of market power—it can also help firms achieve and maintain market power. Firms may use Madison Avenue's tools of persuasion to convince consumers that their products are different from and better than those of competitors. This is sometimes referred to as **artificial product**

ARTIFICIAL PRODUCT DIFFERENTIATION
the use of advertising to differentiate products that are essentially the same

[13]George J. Stigler, "The Economics of Information," *Journal of Political Economy*, 69 No. 2 (June 1961), pp. 213–225.

differentiation and, if successful, increases the demand for the product and also makes demand more inelastic, conferring additional market power on the firm. For example, the chemical composition of Bayer aspirin is nearly indistinguishable from that of generic aspirin, but many consumers think Bayer is better and pay a substantially higher price for that brand.

It is also charged that advertising can operate as a barrier to entry. If a new firm attempts to enter a profitable industry, it may find that advertising by the established firms has created a captive audience of consumers who are reluctant to try a new brand. It may be necessary for an entrant to wage a massive advertising campaign to get consumers to give its product a try, and the prospect of that cost could be an effective deterrent. On the other hand, advertising can also be a means of breaking into an entrenched market, giving an entrant a way to increase sales quickly so that economies of scale can be realized.

In its most extreme form, criticism of advertising holds that it manipulates consumers and leads them to choose products they don't want or need. In this view, consumers' tastes are not formed independently, but are actually created by advertisers. Thus, instead of consumers' underlying wants being the factor behind the position of demand curves (and thereby the pattern of production), producers are held to play the central role of determining consumers' wants through their promotional activities.

Although few economists hold this extreme view on advertising today, there continues to be a belief that advertising may enhance market power, deter entry, and lead to more concentrated industries. Numerous studies have tried to find a connection between advertising and industrial concentration or profitability. By and large, their results have been inconclusive: about as many find advertising to be unassociated with industrial concentration or profitability as the reverse. This evidence has dispelled the worst fears of the critics of advertising, but there remains the possibility that advertising has harmful effects that are simply not large enough to be empirically identified.

Advertising as Information

A view that advertising is benign in its effects has more recently emerged as an outgrowth of research on the economics of information. Advertising is held to be a low-cost way of providing information to consumers about the availability of products and their prices and qualities. It may make markets more competitive and even lead to lower prices for consumers.

To see why, imagine an industry where there is no advertising. As we explained in the previous section, firms will then face downward-sloping demand curves because it is costly for consumers to find out about alternatives. In Figure 14.1, D_1 is a typical firm's demand curve when no firm in the industry advertises. Now if this firm *alone* advertises, its demand curve shifts outward to D_2 and may become more inelastic, as drawn. This appears to support the negative view of advertising—that market power is enhanced as demands become more inelastic. However, we must recognize that other firms are also free to advertise, and the effects of all firms advertising may be quite different from the effects when only one does. So, suppose that our typical firm continues to advertise, but now its competitors also try to persuade consumers of the virtues of their products. This will cause this firm's demand curve to shift leftward from D_2 and become more elastic, as shown by D_3, the demand curve when all firms are advertising. It is more elastic than demand when no firms advertise (D_1) because consumers will be more aware of the alternatives available on the market, and an increase in this firm's price will cause more consumers to shift to other products than when the consumers are not aware of the alternatives. Thus, it is possible that advertising, when undertaken by many or all competing firms, actually confronts firms with more elastic demand curves and reduces their market power.

In the previous section, we explained how price dispersion arises in a market when consumers are uninformed. The existence of price dispersion gives consumers an incentive to incur search costs to obtain information. It also, however, gives firms an incentive to advertise. For example, if some firms charge a higher price to uninformed consumers and if firms charging lower prices could inform consumers of this fact, the low-price firms can enhance

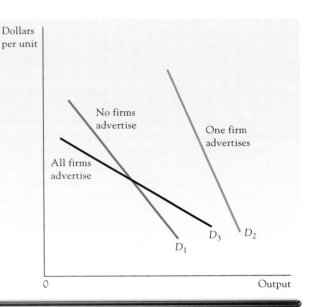

FIGURE 14.1

Advertising and the Firm's Demand Curve
When there is no advertising in an oligopoly, a firm's demand curve is D_1. If only this firm advertises, its demand curve shifts out to D_2. If all firms advertise, the firm's demand curve becomes D_3.

the demand for their products and potentially their profits. Moreover, if consumers switch from high-price to low-price firms, it will reduce the average price in the market. It could also lead the high-price firms to reduce their prices, which reduces the price dispersion and further lowers the average price. In this way, advertising can lead to lower prices.

It is also possible for advertising to solve the lemons problem discussed in Section 14.4. Recall that in this model, consumers cannot determine the quality of the product before purchase, and as a result low-quality products drive out high-quality ones. Through advertising, high-quality sellers can inform consumers that their products are of high quality. The problem arises in deciding whether such claims are true. Won't the low-quality sellers make the same claims? Possibly so, but surprisingly, high-quality sellers will normally have a greater incentive to advertise. Such is the importance of repeat purchases and word-of-mouth endorsements to a firm's future sales. A firm selling a lemon can at best convince a consumer to purchase one time, but it can be sure there will be no future sales to that customer, and it may lose future sales from other consumers that hear of this buyer's bad experience. By contrast, a firm selling a high-quality product can gain future sales in addition to the current sale, so it has a greater incentive to promote its product.

One interesting aspect of this analysis is that it suggests consumers may gain useful information from advertising even when that advertising does nothing more than assert a product is "great tasting" (that is, of high quality). Higher-quality (or higher-value) products will tend to be more heavily advertised, and if consumers are influenced by the amount of advertising they may be led to try the better products.

There is some evidence that advertising does work to the benefit of consumers, as this analysis suggests. For example, according to one study, the average price of eyeglasses in states permitting advertising is about 25 percent lower than the prices in states where such advertising is prohibited.[14] Eyeglass prices are also lower in states prohibiting advertisers from mentioning price, but permitting claims of high quality (prices are lowest in states where prices can be advertised). Thus, even when advertising does not mention prices, it can apparently contribute to lower prices for consumers. Other studies have also produced

[14]Lee Benham, "The Effect of Advertising on the Price of Eyeglasses," *Journal of Law and Economics*, 15 No. 2 (October 1972), pp. 45–74.

evidence that advertising about price lowers the average price consumers pay for products such as liquor, drugs, contact lenses, toys, and gasoline.

Even when advertising does not lead to lower prices, it may be advantageous for consumers. In the absence of advertising, consumers have to incur search costs to find out about products. The true prices they pay are then the sum of the money price and the search costs they bear; this is sometimes referred to as the **full price** of the product. One effect of advertising is that it is a substitute for the consumer's own search efforts. Thus, advertising can reduce consumers' search costs. Even if the money price is unchanged or rises somewhat, the full price consumers pay may fall as a result of advertising. For example, even if they do not lead to a decrease in the money price of products, advertisements on the Internet promise to significantly decrease the full price consumers pay for products by lowering consumers' search costs.

The advertising-as-information view suggests that advertising is a low-cost way of conveying useful information to consumers about alternative products and their prices, and thus makes markets work more efficiently. Not all economists accept this positive view, and television advertising has been singled out for special criticism. (Significantly, however, only 22 percent of all advertising expenditures are devoted to television; newspapers account for a larger share.) This is not surprising, because television advertising is more intrusive than most other forms and is more difficult to target to interested consumers than, say, advertising in specialized magazines. Moreover, there is the lingering suspicion that some consumers (of course, not us) may be swayed by the emphasis on visual images and emotional appeals.

In sum, probably each view of advertising contains an element of truth. It may be that advertising works well in certain types of markets and for certain types of products, but has more deleterious effects in other cases.

FULL PRICE
the sum of the money price and the search costs that consumers incur

APPLICATION 14.8   A NEWSPAPER STRIKE'S EFFECT ON FOOD PRICES

In the fall of 1979, a press operators' strike temporarily halted publication of New York City's three major dailies, the *Times, Post,* and *Daily News. Newsday,* in neighboring Long Island, continued publishing—and thus carrying local supermarkets' food advertisements. A study examining the prices of various food items in the New York City area during the first week of the strike found that prices increased by 3.4 percent less in supermarkets on Long Island than in other New York City boroughs ex-periencing reduced access to food advertisements.[15] Significantly, the difference in price changes was observed for supermarkets, which advertise in newspapers, but not for small fruit and vegetable stores, which do not. Thus, for supermarket food items in New York City, newspaper advertising appears to promote lower prices.

[15]Amihai Glazer, "Advertising, Information, and Prices—A Case Study," *Economic Inquiry,* 19 No. 3 (October 1981), pp. 661–671.

SUMMARY

• Game theory is a method of analyzing situations involving strategic interactions among decisionmakers, a setting characteristic of oligopolistic markets.

• A payoff matrix clarifies the nature of the problem confronting decisionmakers and helps us identify the equilibrium.

• Two types of equilibrium are dominant strategy and Nash.

• A particularly important type of game is the prisoner's dilemma, in which self-interest on the part of each player can lead to a result in which all players are worse off then they could be if different choices were made.

• The prisoner's dilemma game helps us see why firms have an incentive to cheat on a cartel agreement. When the game is repeated, however, the analysis becomes more complicated, and there is a greater possibility of collusion.

• Markets can work very differently when consumers or firms are not fully informed about prices and/or product characteristics. When consumers cannot determine the quality of a product before purchase, the lemons model suggests that low-quality products will predominate.

• Market forces limit the extent of the lemons problem. In the important case of the insurance industry, firms may have less information than do consumers. Adverse selection can then lead to only high-risk customers being insured.

• When consumers are not informed about the prices charged by all firms, it is possible for more than one price to prevail in the market. It is not necessary, however, for all customers to be fully informed for a single price to emerge. In general, the larger the proportion of informed consumers, the less the price dispersion in the market.

• Advertising is a particularly important way in which information is provided to consumers by firms. It can lead markets to operate more efficiently, but there is also the possibility that it can distort consumer choices and make it difficult for new firms to enter profitable industries.

REVIEW QUESTIONS AND PROBLEMS

Questions and problems marked with an asterisk have solutions given in Answers to Selected Problems at the back of the book (pages 576–577).

14.1. What is a dominant-strategy equilibrium? What is a Nash equilibrium? Is it possible for a Nash equilibrium to exist where neither player has a dominant strategy?

*14.2. Construct and explain the payoff matrix for two firms that operate in a competitive market. How does it differ from the situation illustrated in Table 14.1?

14.3. What is a prisoner's dilemma game? Why is it relevant in evaluating the likelihood of cheating in a cartel?

14.4. Tables 14.1 and 14.4 both involve two firms each choosing between low and high outputs, but only one of the tables illustrates the prisoner's dilemma. Explain why the nature of the market in which firms interact may sometimes produce a prisoner's dilemma and sometimes not.

14.5. Is a repeated- or single-period game more appropriate for the study of oligopolies? In which setting is collusion more likely to be a stable outcome? Explain your answer.

14.6. Construct a payoff matrix to examine the determination of outputs in the Cournot duopoly model. What type of equilibrium exists for this model? Does the game-theoretic approach make this model any more plausible?

14.7. Why do you think that game theory has become the preferred method of analyzing oligopolistic markets? What advantages does it have over simply assuming, say, Cournot behavior?

14.8. What is the basic assumption about information in the lemons model?

14.9. In the lemons model, there is only one price even though the products differ in quality. Why is that? What factors determine that price? How does the price affect the quantities traded of the different quality goods?

14.10. College instructors know more about the quality of their courses than prospective students. Does this mean that the lemons model is appropriate? How does this market differ from the one assumed in the pure lemons model?

14.11. What is adverse selection in insurance markets and how does it relate to the lemons model?

*14.12. Consider insurance covering the costs of cancer when there is no way to determine how likely it is that any given individual will contract the disease. How will the price of the policy be determined? Now suppose that it is determined that smokers have 10 times the risk of nonsmokers. How will the price be affected if insurance companies cannot determine who smokes and who doesn't?

14.13. How does the moral hazard problem differ from the adverse selection problem in markets for medical insurance?

14.14. Why don't consumers become fully informed about the prices different firms charge? If consumers are not fully informed, why is a firm likely to possess some degree of market power?

14.15. Suppose that a college town has a large number of firms selling a homogeneous product—pizza—and that there are two types of consumers in the town. The town's permanent residents are fully informed about the prices charged by all firms and always shop at the firm or firms with the lowest price. On the other hand, the students attending college in the town (temporary residents) are completely uninformed; they do not know anything about prices and simply choose among firms on a random basis. Explain why, in such a setting, a single price may prevail in the market for pizza.

14.16. How does advertising affect the demand curve confronting a single firm? How does the outcome depend on whether other firms also advertise? If all firms in an industry advertise, how will this shift the industry demand curve for the product?

*14.17. "Because advertising adds to firms' costs of production, it cannot lead to lower product prices." True or false? Explain.

14.18. According to the English poet Alfred Lord Tennyson, "Tis better to have loved and lost than never to have loved at all." Does Tennyson's observation imply that love is a dominant strategy? Explain why or why not.

14.19. In multidivision corporations where division heads are allocated an annual budget, explain why the "use-it-or-lose-it" phenomenon occurs and is a reflection of a prisoner's dilemma.

14.20. If there is asymmetric information between the owners of a baseball team for which a given player plays and other teams' owners, would you predict that players who opt to become free agents and end up getting traded to another team will spend more days on the disabled list, after being traded, than players who remain with their existing team? Explain why or why not.

CHAPTER 15

Using Noncompetitive Market Models

Noncompetitive models provide analytical frameworks for understanding the functioning of a variety of markets and certain pressing social problems.

Chapter Outline

15.1 The Size of the Deadweight Loss of Monopoly
  Other Possible Deadweight Losses of Monopoly
  Application 15.1 *Software and Soft-Money Political Contributions*
15.2 Do Monopolies Suppress Inventions?
  Application 15.2 *Hollywood and Home Videos*
15.3 Natural Monopoly
  Regulation of Natural Monopoly   Regulation of Natural Monopoly in Practice
  Application 15.3 *Regulating Natural Monopoly Through Public Ownership:
  The Case of USPS*
15.4 Government-Established Cartels: The Case of the British Columbia
  Egg Marketing Board
  *Estimating the Deadweight Loss: The First Round   Estimating the Deadweight Loss:
  The Second Round*
  Application 15.4 *The International Air Cartel*
15.5 More on Game Theory: Iterated Dominance and Commitment
  Iterated Dominance   Commitment
  Application 15.5 *Why It May Be Wise to Burn the Bridges Behind You*

Learning Objectives

- Determine the relative magnitude of the deadweight loss of monopoly.
- Ascertain the extent to which, if any, monopolies suppress innovations.
- Overview the extent to which government intervention can serve to promote efficiency in the case of natural monopoly.
- Analyze the deadweight loss associated with a government-established cartel such as the British Columbia Egg Marketing Board.
- Explore the concepts of iterated dominance and commitment in the context of game theory models.

In Chapters 11 through 14, we examined a number of models in which firms have varying degrees of market power. We found that prices tend to be higher and output lower than under competitive conditions. These models also provide analytical frameworks that can be used to examine other issues relevant to the functioning of noncompetitive markets and to understand certain pressing social problems. In this chapter we look at several examples, including the magnitude of the deadweight loss associated with monopoly and the effect of monopoly on innovation. We also examine how best to regulate monopolies that arise because economies of scale characterize the production of a good over the relevant range of market output. In such *natural monopoly* cases, average production cost is minimized if a single firm supplies the entire market.

15.1   THE SIZE OF THE DEADWEIGHT LOSS OF MONOPOLY

In Chapter 11, we explained how monopoly, at least from a static perspective, results in a deadweight loss. Figure 15.1 illustrates this analysis for a market that would be a constant-cost industry under competitive conditions. The competitive outcome is an output of Q (1,000) and a price of P ($1.00). If the industry becomes a pure monopoly and the monopoly can produce under the same cost conditions (so the competitive supply curve becomes the monopolist's marginal cost and average cost curves), the monopoly outcome is an output of Q_M (500) and a price of P_M ($2.00). The deadweight loss of monopoly is shown as the triangular area BCA.

Determining the magnitude of this deadweight loss is important for public policy reasons. This is so because, as we saw in Chapter 11, the deadweight loss indicates how much lower total (consumer plus producer) surplus is in a market on account of monopoly. Public policies promoting greater competition in such a market hence offer the potential for increasing total surplus and attaining efficiency in output.

Note that the deadweight loss is given by the area of the triangle BCA (at least when we assume linear demand and supply curves), and the area of a triangle equals one-half its base times its height. Thus, if we can determine the base and the height of the deadweight loss triangle, we can calculate the magnitude. The height of the triangle, distance BA in Figure 15.1, is the excess of the monopoly price over marginal cost of production ($P_M - MC$). The base of the triangle, distance AC, is the restriction in output due to the monopoly ($Q - Q_M$). This restriction in output can be calculated if we know price and marginal cost at the monopoly outcome and the price elasticity of demand (assuming marginal cost is constant). For example, the demand curve in Figure 15.1 has an arc elasticity of one between Q_M and Q, and because the monopoly price is 100 percent above the competitive price, we know the competitive output is 100 percent above the monopoly output (the ratio of the percentage change in output and percentage change in price equals the elasticity). Therefore, for the figures given in the graph, we can calculate the deadweight loss as ($\frac{1}{2}$)

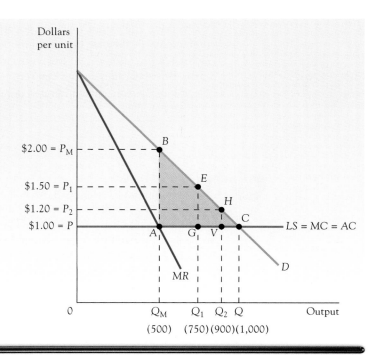

FIGURE 15.1

The Deadweight Loss of Noncompetitive Output
When price is P_M and output Q_M, the deadweight loss due to the monopolistic restriction of output is triangular area *BCA*. If the product is produced by an oligopoly, output is likely to be higher (say, Q_2) and the deadweight loss smaller (area *HCV*).

$(BA)(AC)$, or $(\frac{1}{2})(\$1)(500)$, or \$250. This is equal to one-fourth of the total consumer outlay on the product in our example.

Several economists have estimated the magnitude of the deadweight loss due to monopolistic restrictions in output in the real world. The first was Arnold Harberger, whose 1954 study concluded that the deadweight loss of monopoly in U.S. manufacturing corporations equaled a scant 0.1 percent (or one-thousandth) of gross national product (GNP).[1] (Manufacturing, however, accounted for only about one-fourth of GNP, so if monopoly is as important in other sectors as in manufacturing, the economy-wide deadweight loss would have been 0.4 percent.) A number of more recent studies, using different data and methodologies, have tended to support Harberger's conclusion that the deadweight loss is not large relative to GNP. A comprehensive survey of the research concludes that the deadweight loss of monopoly in the United States lies somewhere between 0.5 and 2 percent of GNP.[2]

There are several reasons why estimates of the deadweight loss of monopoly in relation to GNP are not large. One is that we are comparing the deadweight loss not to the size of the monopolized sector, but to the size of the whole economy (GNP). In our example in Figure 15.1, the deadweight loss is 25 percent of the total outlay in this market, but if only 20 percent of the economy is monopolized (to this degree), then the total deadweight loss relative to GNP would be one-fifth of 25 percent, or 5 percent.

An even more important factor is that there are few, if any, instances of pure monopoly in the United States. Most examples of noncompetitive markets involve markets dominated by several large firms (that is, oligopolies) rather than pure monopolies. Studies of the deadweight loss of monopoly are really examining monopoly power in industries such as soft drink manufacturing, as opposed to sole-producer industries.

Although we do not have a single satisfactory theory of oligopoly, recall that in most oligopoly models, the output is greater than the pure monopoly output. To see the importance of this point, suppose that output is actually three-fourths the competitive output in Figure 15.1—because the industry is an oligopoly. Then output is Q_1 (750) and the price is P_1, or \$1.50, because the demand curve is linear. The deadweight loss is then equal to area ECG, or $(\frac{1}{2})(\$0.50)(250)$, which equals \$62.50. Note that although the output restriction in this case (250) is half as large as the output restriction under pure monopoly (500), the deadweight loss is only one-fourth as large.

Of course, we cannot directly measure the restriction in output in any industry; we can observe only actual output. What we can try to measure directly is the excess of price over marginal cost—that is, the height of the deadweight loss triangle. This is what is done in practice, and the $P - MC$ estimates, along with estimated or assumed demand elasticities, allow us to infer the restriction in output. Unfortunately, it is far from straightforward to estimate how much the actual price exceeds marginal cost. If we assume that average cost and marginal cost are equal, as in our diagram, then the excess of price over marginal cost is also the economic profit per unit of output. Thus, data on profits may tell us how much higher than cost price is. But profit data always report accounting profits, and these typically exceed the pure economic profits we wish to measure. Nonetheless, looking at accounting profits data and making adjustments to try to estimate economic profits provide interesting clues to the excess of price over marginal cost in different industries.

Considering all U.S. corporations, how much accounting profit do you think businesses on average make per dollar of sales? The typical response from college students in a Gallup

---

[1]Arnold Harberger, "Monopoly and Resource Allocation," *American Economic Review*, 44 No. 2 (May 1954), pp. 77–87.

[2]Frederic M. Scherer and David Ross, *Industrial Market Structure and Economic Performance*, 3rd ed. (Boston, Mass.: Houghton Mifflin, 1990), p. 667.

opinion survey was 45 cents.[3] The correct answer is actually 5 cents of after-tax profit per dollar of sales. (In the same survey students also indicated that they thought a "fair" profit for corporations would be 25 cents per dollar of sales.) The 5 percent profit margin is based on the accounting definition of profit; the economic profit margin tends to be smaller. Of course, we are considering the average for all corporations, and for those with market power the profit margin can be much greater. But it turns out to be very rare for any industry to have a profit margin, even based on accounting data, as large as 20 percent. That is not really so surprising given that a 20 percent profit margin would be four times the average, and would constitute a powerful incentive for entry to occur in the market.

So, instead of basing our deadweight loss estimate on the output restriction, as we did in assuming output was three-fourths the competitive level, let's assume that in the industries with market power, price is 20 percent above marginal cost. This situation is shown in Figure 15.1 by an output of Q_2 and a price of P_2, or an output of 900 and price of $1.20. The deadweight loss is area HCV, which in this case is equal to $(\frac{1}{2})(\$0.20)(100)$, or $10. This is equal to about 1 percent of the industry's total revenue. However, the arc elasticity of demand between points H and C on the demand curve is only 0.58, and if we used the more commonly assumed value of 1 for our exercise, the deadweight loss would be nearly $20, or about 2 percent of the industry's total revenue. If one in five industries exercise this degree of monopoly power, the economy-wide deadweight loss from monopoly would be 0.4 percent of GNP.

These considerations have convinced many economists that the deadweight loss of monopolistic restrictions in output in the United States economy is almost certain to be less than 1 percent of GNP. Presumably, this is because most of the economy is reasonably competitive, with a relatively small number of exceptions. But there may be other types of deadweight loss associated with noncompetitive markets, as we will see next.

Other Possible Deadweight Losses of Monopoly

We have emphasized two consequences of monopoly widely viewed as undesirable: the restriction of output and the redistribution of income in favor of the owners of the monopoly. Only the restriction of output involves a net loss in total surplus, and both theory and the available evidence suggest it is not very large compared with GNP. Other potential effects of monopoly, however, should also be mentioned.

When comparing monopoly and competition, we assumed that the costs of production under monopoly would be the same as under competition. If the monopoly maximizes profit, this assumption is correct. For example, the monopoly would produce the 500 units of output in Figure 15.1 at a cost of $500. If profit is to be maximized, whatever output the firm produces must be produced at the lowest possible cost. The pressure on a monopoly to minimize production cost, however, is not as strong as the pressure on a competitive firm. If cost should increase because of slack cost controls in a competitive firm, the firm will start losing money and eventually close operations. For the monopolist, though, higher-than-necessary cost may just mean a smaller profit, not a loss. In the absence of competition with other firms, the monopolist is under less pressure to minimize cost. As Adam Smith observed, "monopoly . . . is a great enemy to good management."[4]

If production cost is unnecessarily high under monopoly, this is another deadweight loss. For instance, if in Figure 15.1 the monopoly produces 500 units at a cost of $1.50 per unit, the total cost of producing 500 units is therefore $250 higher under monopoly than it would be under competition. Part of the potential monopoly profit of $500 would be dissipated

---

[3]*Gallup Opinion Index*, Report No. 123 (Princeton, N.J., September 1975).

[4]Adam Smith, *The Wealth of Nations* (New York: Modern Library, 1937), p. 147.

through the cost increase. Some of the $500 profit rectangle, $P_M BAP$, no longer would be a transfer of income from consumers to the monopolist; instead, the money is absorbed by higher-than-necessary cost and is a net loss.

A similar outcome results if the monopoly incurs costs in acquiring or maintaining its market position. Our analysis implicitly assumed that production cost is the only cost of the monopoly. But a monopoly may have to expend resources to ensure continuation of its monopoly power. A lobbying effort may be necessary to secure favorable government policies to block competition by other firms. Management may spend more time worrying about protecting its market from encroachers than making business decisions regarding output and cost. Legal and accounting staffs may be required to fend off antitrust suits by the Justice Department. Because an average of seven years is needed to see an antitrust suit through to conclusion, litigation can be quite costly for both the government and the firm. For instance, in 1974 the Justice Department brought an antitrust suit against American Telephone and Telegraph (AT&T). By 1981, AT&T estimated that it had spent $250 million on the case—$25 million in direct legal costs, such as lawyers' fees and briefs, and another $225 million on supporting paperwork—and that pretrial proceedings had involved more than 40 million pages.[5] In January 1982, as the trial was nearing its conclusion, AT&T and the Justice Department settled the case out of court.

Due either to the absence of competitive pressures or to the expenses associated with securing monopoly power, cost may be higher than necessary under monopoly. Consequently, measures of the deadweight loss of monopoly based on the welfare triangle, which considers only the output restriction, may underestimate monopoly's true deadweight loss. We must emphasize that the analysis does not imply that cost *will* be higher under monopoly, only that it *may* be. There is little current evidence to suggest how quantitatively important this other deadweight loss really is. Moreover, as discussed in Chapter 11, it is important not to overlook the dynamic perspective on monopoly. While a monopolist may face less pressure to minimize cost than a competitive firm, monopoly power may have been acquired in the first place through discovering a way to build a better mousetrap or an existing mousetrap at lower cost. From a dynamic perspective, therefore, monopolies may be associated with a lower, rather than higher, production cost.

APPLICATION 15.1 SOFTWARE AND SOFT-MONEY POLITICAL CONTRIBUTIONS

Since being sued by the Department of Justice for antitrust violations in 1997, software giant Microsoft has ascended into the top tier of so-called soft-money contributors.[6] Whereas direct contributions to individual federal candidates are regulated, indirect contributions to such candidates through organizations such as national conventions and parties are unregulated and have been termed *soft money*. Between 1997 and 2000, for example,

Microsoft spent more than $14 million on a variety of Republican and Democratic political organizations, including federal candidates, national conventions, and the national parties. According to Microsoft President and CEO Steve Ballmer, the federal antitrust case has altered the way his company approaches politics: "We were caught unaware of the fact that our company doesn't function solely based on the technology we make. We're wide awake now, though. We've had a cold shower on the topic."

In donating to political parties, Microsoft has leaned Republican since 1997. This bias is based on the expec-

[6]This application is based on "Suit Has Affected Microsoft Contributions," *USA Today.com* (September 13, 2000).

[5]"Out of the Quagmire," *Wall Street Journal* (January 30, 1981), p. 1.

tation that a Republican presidential administration and Congress would be more sympathetic to Microsoft with regard to the antitrust proceedings.

Microsoft, of course, is not alone among computer-industry political contributors. Close behind in terms of giving has been rival Oracle, who with Sun Microsystems and Netscape sought in the late 1990s to build an indus-try alliance around a different set of software standards from the ones advocated by Microsoft. One of Oracle CEO Larry Ellison's stated objectives is being richer than Microsoft co-founder Bill Gates. Ellison has been a proponent of the federal antitrust case against Microsoft, and as you might expect, Oracle's soft money giving has leaned Democratic.

15.2   DO MONOPOLIES SUPPRESS INVENTIONS?

A common bit of folklore has it that firms sometimes suppress inventions that would benefit consumers. One version of this idea is the belief that manufacturers design products to wear out quickly (planned obsolescence) so that consumers will periodically have to replace them.

An economist would assess these beliefs by looking first at the internal consistency of the argument. The basic premise of this belief is that a business will make a larger profit by sup-pressing a worthwhile invention than by marketing it. Under what conditions will this premise be true?

To avoid ambiguity, we'll define a "worthwhile" invention as one that allows a firm to produce a higher-quality product at an unchanged cost or to produce the same-quality product at a lower cost. Suppression of invention in these cases would be unambiguously harmful.

Under competitive conditions a firm would never suppress a worthwhile invention. Sup-pose that the invention permits the production of the same-quality product at a lower cost. The first firm to introduce the process will have a lower production cost than its rivals, and this guarantees a profit. Even if the invention cannot be patented, the firm can earn a profit until other firms have had time to copy it.

What about the monopoly case? Let's look at an example and see whether it's likely a monopoly will suppress a worthwhile invention. Suppose that the market for light bulbs is monopolized and that the monopoly sells light bulbs that last for 1,000 hours. Then the mo-nopolist acquires an invention that permits production of bulbs that last for 10,000 hours at the same unit cost as the 1,000-hour bulbs. Obviously, consumers would purchase many fewer light bulbs per year if each one lasted 10 times as long. Does this mean that the mo-nopoly will make more money if it continues to sell the 1,000-hour light bulb and withholds the superior product?

The answer is no. To see why, suppose that consumers want 10,000 hours of light per year. Initially, they purchase 10 1,000-hour bulbs at $1.00 each, involving a total outlay of $10.00. If it costs the monopolist $0.50 to make each bulb, the firm makes a profit of $5.00 per consumer. Each consumer will be willing to pay at least $10.00 (more if convenience counts) for one 10,000-hour bulb, because a 10,000-hour bulb yields the same light as 10 1,000-hour bulbs that together cost $10.00. The monopolist, however, can produce each 10,000-hour bulb for $0.50, so profit is $9.50 on the sale of one 10,000-hour bulb but only $5.00 on the sale of 10 1,000-hour bulbs.

The foregoing example assumes that customers continue to purchase just enough light bulbs for 10,000 hours of light in both cases. While such an assumption may not be valid, the result that the monopolist will make more money by selling the superior light bulb continues to hold even when the assumption does not.[7] A graphical analysis shows why. There are two ways to proceed. One is to consider the demand curve for light bulbs but to recognize that the demand curve for 10,000-hour light bulbs differs from the curve for 1,000-hour bulbs. A simpler approach is to recognize that what consumers are really purchasing is the services of light bulbs—that is, hours of lighting—and the demand curve defined in this way does not shift. What changes when we switch from 1,000- to 10,000-hour bulbs is the cost and price per hour of lighting, not the demand curve itself.

Figure 15.2 illustrates this latter approach. On the horizontal axis we measure kilohours of lighting; each kilohour equals 1,000 hours, the service provided by each of the first type of bulbs. For simplicity, average and marginal cost are assumed to be constant at $0.50 per 1,000-hour bulb (per kilohour).

The initial pre-invention equilibrium at Q_1 involves 100 kilohours (100 1,000-hour bulbs) sold for $1.00 each. Each 1,000-hour bulb costs $0.50 to produce, so total profit is $50. The invention of the 10,000-hour bulb, which the firm can produce at the same unit cost ($0.50), means that the cost per kilohour falls to $0.05. Thus, the average cost curve if the new light bulb is produced is AC'. Operating with this lower-cost curve, the monopolist can make more profit, and the new profit-maximizing output of kilohours (not bulbs) is Q_2. Price falls to $0.75 per kilohour. Profit rises from $50 to $105: the cost per kilohour is $0.05, and the price is $0.75, so the profit per kilohour is $0.70; $0.70 times 150 kilohours yields a total profit of $105. Note that the new equilibrium corresponds to the sale of 15 10,000-hour bulbs at $7.50 each; fewer bulbs are sold.

FIGURE 15.2

Monopoly and Inventions
If a monopoly can produce a 10,000-hour light bulb at the same cost as a 1,000-hour bulb, the invention effectively reduces the cost per kilohour of light from $0.50 to $0.05. The monopoly will make a larger profit by producing and selling the superior bulb.

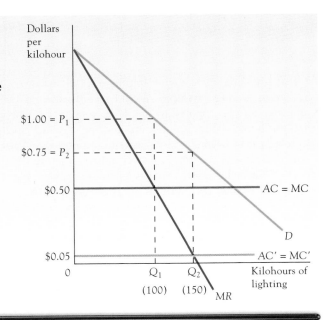

[7]Our analysis, of course, ignores the subtle complication that a consumer may want some amount of hours of light per year (such as 15,000) that is not a whole-number multiple of 10,000, while light from the superior bulbs must be purchased in 10,000-hour increments. Such a complication can still be addressed, however, to the extent that a consumer wants light in more than one year. That is, any excess light from a superior bulb not used in one year can be employed in the next year. A consumer who wants 5,000 hours of light in each of two years thus could use one of the 10,000-hour bulbs over the course of those two years rather than five of the 1,000-hour bulbs in each of the two years.

This analysis suggests that a monopolist has no reason to suppress a worthwhile invention—the reverse, in fact, is true. We have examined the more difficult case of a higher-quality product to show how we can analyze quality changes by focusing on product services (hours of lighting) rather than the product itself. We reach the same conclusion for an invention that lowers the cost of producing a product of unchanged quality. In that case the cost curves for an unchanged-quality product shift downward due to the invention, implying more profit for a monopolist.

Because a monopolist can increase profit by marketing a worthwhile invention, economists tend to be skeptical of allegations that businesses suppress them. As with many generalizations in economics, though, we can conceive of an exception, a case where a monopoly would find it profitable to suppress an invention. For instance, suppose the firm would lose its monopoly position by introducing the invention. Once the invention of the 10,000-hour light bulb becomes public knowledge, other firms could produce and sell it for $0.50. The monopoly would then find itself in a competitive market. If the firm can patent the invention, however, the monopoly may be able to retain its monopoly position and market the invention.[8]

There are many instances of worthwhile inventions being marketed, both by competitive firms and by firms with various degrees of monopoly power. Thus, the generalization that profit incentives will lead to the introduction of worthwhile inventions seems reliable. While there may be other deadweight losses associated with monopoly, widespread suppression of inventions does not appear to be one of them.

APPLICATION 15.2   HOLLYWOOD AND HOME VIDEOS

It is commonly assumed that major Hollywood motion picture producers should feel threatened by and therefore be opposed to the development of a market for home videos.[9] After all, renting a video and watching it at home is a substitute for going to see the same movie at a theater. However, motion picture producers now make nearly twice as much from home video sales and rentals ($20 billion in 2000) as from traditional theatrical exhibitions. And the explosive growth in ancillary markets such as home video, cable, and foreign television markets hasn't diminished overall theater revenues. Indeed, annual revenues from theatrical exhibitions grew from $2.8 billion in 1980 to $10 billion in 2000.

In much the same way that the advent of rental libraries in eighteenth century England spurred the demand for books, so has the development of the home video market helped increase demand for motion pictures. Although Hollywood was initially petrified by the invention of videotape recorders, and the television industry filed lawsuits to prevent home copying of broadcast programs, prerecorded videotapes have proven to be Hollywood's boon rather than the source of its demise. Most movie producers eventually realized that videotapes lowered distribution costs (as depicted in Figure 15.2) and thereby represented an opportunity to dramatically expand the markets for their products. According to economists Carl Shapiro and Hal Varian of the University of California, Berkeley, these prescient producers "succeeded beyond their wildest dreams, while those which stuck with the old model were consigned to the dustbins of history."[10]

[9]This application is based on: Carl Shapiro and Hal R. Varian, *Information Rules* (Boston: Harvard Business School Press, 1999); and James R. Jaeger II, "The Movie Industry," *www.mec.films.com/moviein.html.*

[10]Ibid., pp. 96–97.

---

[8]This is a long-run analysis. In the short run, firms, whether they are monopolistic or competitive, may not introduce an invention immediately. When the time comes to replace worn-out equipment, however (and that time will come more quickly when a lower-cost process is available), the firm will introduce the invention.

15.3   NATURAL MONOPOLY

In some cases monopoly results because one large firm can produce at a lower per-unit cost than several smaller firms together accounting for the same total output. If the production technology is such that economies of scale (declining average cost per unit of output) extend to very high output levels, a large firm can undersell small firms, and one or a few large firms will eventually dominate the industry. The extreme case is one in which the average cost of a single enterprise declines over the entire range of market demand. As mentioned earlier, this is called a **natural monopoly**.

Natural monopoly presents a challenging public policy dilemma. On the one hand, it implies that efficiency in production will be better served if a single firm supplies the entire market. On the other hand, natural monopoly results in the absence of any firms that actively compete with the monopolist. The monopolist thus will be tempted to exploit its natural monopoly power and to restrict output and raise price. And inefficiency in output (a deadweight loss) will occur if the monopolist takes these actions to increase its profit.

Figure 15.3 illustrates the natural monopoly case. Graphically, a natural monopoly exists when the long-run average cost curve of a single firm is still declining at the point where it intersects the total market demand curve for the product—at point A in the diagram. One firm can produce an output of Q_2 at an average cost of AQ_2. In this situation, the market, if unregulated, will be dominated by a single firm. If, instead, there are several small firms, each producing Q_1, for example, price will have to be at least P_1. Yet any one firm could expand output, sell at a lower price, and ultimately drive the smaller firms out. Monopoly is the "natural" result. Moreover, forcing a competitive structure on this market is undesirable in terms of attaining efficiency in production. The real cost of serving the market will be higher than necessary if there are several, small, high-cost firms.

Drawing cost curves that imply a natural monopoly is easy, but the important question is whether there are many cases of natural monopoly in the real world. In fact, natural monopoly conditions are not common, but they do exist for several products. Economists believe, for example, that natural monopoly conditions exist in the provision of electricity, water, natural gas, telephone services, and possibly cable television to specific geographic localities.

NATURAL MONOPOLY
the case in which the average cost of a single enterprise declines over the entire range of market demand

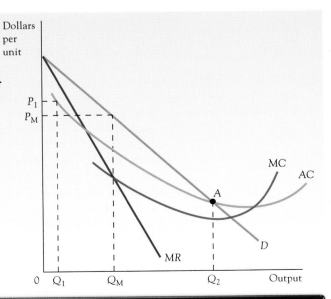

FIGURE 15.3

Natural Monopoly
When the average cost of producing a good declines over the entire range of market demand, a natural monopoly exists. It is less expensive for one firm to produce the entire market output than for several small firms to share the market. One firm can produce Q_2 at a unit cost of AQ_2, which is less than the cost when several firms each produce Q_1 at a unit cost of P_1. However, if the firm is allowed to produce monopolistically, output will be Q_M and price P_M.

Consider electricity. Providing it requires that homes be physically connected to the generating facility through underground or overhead lines. If several separate firms served homes in a given community, each firm would have to run its own connecting power lines. The cost of duplicating connecting lines (implying higher average costs) could be avoided by using just one set of lines. This situation is depicted in Figure 15.3. Unit costs are higher when several firms supply a few homes (Q_1) than when one operation provides electricity to all homes (Q_2).

When natural monopoly conditions exist, there are four ways public policymakers can deal with the situation. One is to leave the market alone. In this case a monopoly will result, and the monopoly will not choose to supply Q_2 at a cost of AQ_2 per unit (in Figure 15.3). Instead, it will choose the profit-maximizing output of Q_M with a price of P_M. The second option is to permit a monopoly to operate but to regulate its activities. The third option is to have government ownership and operation of the facility (the U.S. Postal Service, for example). A fourth option involves a government-sponsored competition for the right to operate a natural monopoly. Ideally, the operating right is awarded to the bidder promising to charge the lowest price. Competition for the right to be the sole supplier can serve to promote efficiency in output even though once the award is made, there is only one supplier.

In the United States the regulatory option has generally been pursued. A privately owned firm is given the legal right to a monopoly in the provision of the service, but a public agency is created to regulate the firm's behavior. How can such a natural monopoly be regulated?

Regulation of Natural Monopoly

The public agencies charged with regulating the behavior of natural monopolies, usually called public utilities, generally set the prices that may be charged. Before investigating how this is accomplished, let's examine the economic principles behind the price-setting approach.

In Figure 15.4, the natural monopoly's average and marginal cost curves are AC and MC (ignore AC′ for the moment). If we have complete knowledge of cost and demand conditions, two logical prices can be set. One is the price at the level where the average cost curve intersects the demand curve, a price of P_1. This solution is called *average-cost pricing*. If the monopoly produces Q_1, the price of P_1 just covers its average cost, implying zero economic profit. Moreover, the monopoly has an incentive to produce Q_1 if a maximum price of P_1 can be charged. As explained in Chapter 11, in the case of a price ceiling the demand curve facing the monopoly becomes P_1AD, so marginal revenue (equal to P_1 up to an output of Q_1) exceeds marginal cost as output expands to Q_1, but MR drops below MC at higher output levels. Indeed, when a price of P_1 is set, any output other than Q_1 yields a loss, because average cost is above P_1 at lower rates of output.

At an output of Q_1, price exceeds marginal cost (because average cost is falling at point A, marginal cost must be below it). Thus, consumers value additional units of output at more than they cost to produce, which suggests a second option—to set price at the level where the marginal cost curve intersects the demand curve (point B). This option is called *marginal-cost pricing*. There is, however, a major obstacle to marginal-cost pricing: if we set price at P_2, the monopoly incurs a loss. Because marginal cost is below average cost at Q_2, setting price equal to marginal cost will put the firm out of business. A subsidy can be used to enable the firm to produce Q_2 at a price of P_2, but the cost of implementing and financing the subsidy generally makes this solution impractical.

Consequently, the most practical alternative seems to be average-cost pricing. Output is greater than the unregulated monopoly output of Q_M, and because expansion of output from Q_M to Q_1 provides benefits to consumers that are greater than the additional production costs, there is an efficiency gain. (Said another way, part of the deadweight loss arising from

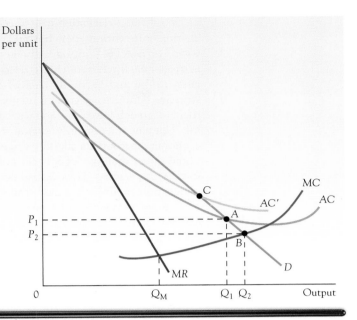

FIGURE 15.4

Regulation of Natural Monopoly
If price is set equal to *MC* at P_2, the monopoly cannot cover its production cost. If price is set equal to *AC* at P_1, output will be inefficient, the monopoly may have little incentive to minimize cost, and the average cost curve could rise to *AC'*.

restricted output by an unregulated monopoly is eliminated.) Price to consumers is lower than it is under unregulated monopoly, and the owners of the monopoly receive no monopoly profit.

Regulation of Natural Monopoly in Practice

In practice, regulators do not have complete knowledge of cost and demand conditions. They generally attempt to attain the average-cost-pricing outcome by focusing on the rate of return on invested capital (accounting profit) earned by a monopoly. It works this way: If the realized rate of return is higher than what is thought to be a normal return (suggesting economic profit), then the current price must be above average cost, and the result signals regulators to reduce the price. Conversely, if the realized rate of return is lower than normal (suggesting economic losses), regulators raise the allowed price. Proceeding in this trial-and-error fashion, regulators locate the price at which profit is normal—that is, where price equals average cost.

There are several problems with this approach, but perhaps the most serious is that it diminishes the monopolist's incentive to minimize cost. If cost rises, regulators permit a higher price so that the monopoly still earns a normal rate of return. Thus, managers have an incentive to pad expense accounts, pay themselves and their colleagues higher-than-necessary wages, and incur numerous other costs that would normally be avoided because they cut into profit. Unnecessary costs will not reduce profit if the regulatory agency permits a price increase to cover the costs.

Figure 15.4 also illustrates the consequences of this behavior. The AC curve continues to show minimum unit production cost, but cost padding shifts the actual cost curve to AC'. Because losses would occur at a price of P_1, regulators grant a price increase to cover the higher costs (point C). Most regulatory agencies recognize the perverse incentive of the regulation, and to overcome it, they frequently become involved in monitoring the costs of the monopoly. However, to determine the need for a particular cost is not easy, so average cost probably drifts upward to some degree.

This form of regulation may also lead the monopoly to suppress or slow down the introduction of inventions, which would not occur in an unregulated environment. The slowness with which AT&T introduced automated switching equipment is a good example. Automatic panel switches to replace operators were invented in the 1920s, but not until 50 years later, in the mid-1970s, did AT&T replace the old switches—even though the automatic switches permitted a greater number of connections and more rapid switching between them at a much lower cost and with much simpler maintenance. Recent advances in switching equipment, primarily digital technology, have produced further speed and cost economies, permitting additional services such as call waiting, call forwarding, and international direct dialing. AT&T did not convert all exchanges to digital switching until the turn of the century, however, so even though the relevant technology existed, some customers were unable to purchase these services for many years.

The slowness with which regulated monopolies introduce new products and technology may be a natural response to a price ceiling. If a monopoly discovers a cost-saving technology, it is unable to keep the increased profit because the regulatory agency will in turn reduce its rates. Similarly, the monopoly has reduced incentive to engage in research and development activities designed to decrease costs. Further, it is under no competitive pressure to offer new services to consumers quickly because its customers are unlikely to have a better alternative.

For these reasons, economists have become increasingly critical of the regulation of natural monopolies. One famous study compared electric rates in regulated and unregulated states between 1912 and 1937—before all states regulated rates—and found no difference in the rates charged.[11] However, the alternatives to regulation when natural monopoly conditions prevail—alternatives such as unregulated monopoly and government ownership—may not be particularly attractive either. Thus, there may be no completely satisfactory solution to the natural monopoly problem.

APPLICATION 15.3   REGULATING NATURAL MONOPOLY THROUGH PUBLIC OWNERSHIP: THE CASE OF USPS

An alternative to rate regulation in the case of natural monopoly is public ownership. This is the approach adopted in the case of mail collection and delivery in the United States. Namely, it is assumed that the average cost of service will be lower if there is a single designated producer—the United States Postal Service (USPS)—and that public ownership of production can be relied upon to ensure that price equals average cost.[12]

Public ownership, however, is associated with some notable drawbacks. For example, because one of the objectives of a public enterprise typically is to ensure that price equals average cost, the incentive to innovate and/or to encourage cost-minimization is attenuated. The managers of a public enterprise generally cannot benefit from the introduction of an innovative product and/or cost-saving technology since the profit of the enterprise is constrained to equal zero. This is in marked contrast to an unregulated, for-profit setting, where such improvements can translate into a healthier bottom line.

The absence of a profit motive likely explains why the USPS has been slow to allow for credit card payments, increase its hours of operation, and offer ancillary products (e.g., the packaging services supplied by for-

---

[12]This application is based on Mark A. Zupan, "Let the Market Deliver the Mail," *New York Times* (August 7, 1993), p. 11.

[11]George J. Stigler and Claire Friedland, "What Can Regulators Regulate?: The Case of Electricity," *Journal of Law and Economics*, 5 No. 2 (October 1962), pp. 1–16.

profit competitors such as Mail Boxes Etc.). The non-profit constraint also suggests why USPS was not the originator of overnight package delivery service (an innovation introduced by for-profit Federal Express). Finally, while economies of scale may be present in the collection and delivery of mail service, enshrining one publicly owned firm to provide the service at cost may result in costs not being minimized. Indeed, the USPS's own internal Postal Inspection Service indicates that on the 10 percent of all rural routes that are contracted out to private companies, the quality of service is greater and the cost is significantly lower (by over 50 percent) than it would be if the USPS provided the service. The difference in the cost of service between contracted-out and non-contracted-out routes is by and large due to wages and fringe benefits.

15.4 GOVERNMENT-ESTABLISHED CARTELS: THE CASE OF THE BRITISH COLUMBIA EGG MARKETING BOARD

As we saw in Chapter 13, a cartel has difficulty trying to maintain profits for its members, mostly due to the threat of entry and the incentive for cartel members to cheat. To be effective, a cartel must find some way to overcome these problems. One approach is to enlist the aid of government. That is, if government will help to organize the cartel and agree to punish cheaters, then cartel policy can be effectively enforced.

There are many instances in which generally competitive industries have been transformed into cartels with the aid of government. In Chapter 10, for example, we examined the effects of government regulation on the airline industry and taxicab markets. Although we treated both as competitive industries, we should recognize that government regulations produced higher prices and restricted output, just as a cartel would. Why, then, would government sanction a cartel? Usually, the reasons are well intentioned: to protect an industry from "ruinous competition," to guarantee consumer safety, to ensure product quality, and so on. The results, however, are often undesirable, as we saw in Chapter 10.

The Civil Aeronautics Board (CAB), for example, was created to protect the airline industry from "cutthroat competition," to guarantee passenger safety, and to develop standards for quality and service. To achieve these goals, the CAB was empowered to set air fares and to allocate routes among carriers. These regulations enabled the CAB to maintain identical air fares on the same routes and to deny entry to new carriers; in other words, the CAB effectively (and legally) set prices for the airline industry, established market-sharing route structures, and kept competitors from entering the industry, just as an effective cartel might do. Issuing medallions for taxicabs and regulating cab fares have similar effects and result in higher fares and restricted output.

Generally, government-established cartels have fewer problems than other cartels because they function within the law. Prices are set without fear of antitrust prosecution. Cheating is not as great a concern because cartel violations can be declared illegal and violators punished. Finally, entry can be limited by requiring licenses (taxis) or making entry conditional on government approval (airlines).

From this perspective, let's examine the operation of one such government-established cartel in Canada, the Egg Marketing Board of British Columbia. In Chapter 10, we examined the structural impact of regulation on the airline and cab markets; in this example, we want to focus on efficiency questions. The egg-marketing cartel is particularly well suited to this analysis because of the findings of a study by Thomas Borcherding, which estimates the deadweight loss of the egg-marketing policy.[13]

---

[13]Thomas Borcherding (with Gary W. Dorosh), *The Egg Marketing Board* (Vancouver, B.C.: The Fraser Institute, 1981).

British Columbia's Egg Marketing Board (BCEMB) was established in 1967 and consists of four members elected from the egg producers in British Columbia. In coordination with the federal Canadian Egg Marketing Agency, the BCEMB establishes a quota for the province as a whole as well as for individual producers. The quotas are expressed in units of 30 dozen eggs per week; the total number of quotas is fixed, and so is the maximum number of quotas possessed by an individual producer. It is illegal for egg producers to produce and sell eggs in excess of their individual quotas, and the BCEMB assesses heavy penalties for violations. In addition, egg prices are established by a complicated formula.

Clearly, the BCEMB has the power to act as a cartel because it can legally control the quantity of eggs supplied to the market. The stated intent of the Board is, however, not to raise prices, but to stabilize them, so as to avoid the uncertainties created by price fluctuations. How can we determine what effect the BCEMB has on the price of eggs? Borcherding provides several pieces of evidence that suggest BCEMB quotas have caused egg prices to rise above competitive levels. First, between 1965 (pre-BCEMB) and 1973, per capita egg consumption in Canada fell relative to the consumption in the United States, which indirectly suggests a jump in the relative price of eggs in Canada. Second, between 1961 and 1967, the average difference in egg prices between British Columbia and the adjacent state of Washington was only 1.4 cents per dozen, but over the 1973 to 1979 period the average price in British Columbia exceeded the price in Washington by 12.4 cents per dozen, a 20 percent differential.

A third piece of evidence is perhaps the most convincing. The quotas represent the legal right to produce eggs, and they have been transferable since 1976; that is, they can be bought and sold. If the operations of the BCEMB had led to a competitive environment for egg production, the market value of a quota would be zero. No one would actually pay for the right to earn a competitive return since that return could be realized in other industries without having to purchase quotas. In 1976, however, a unit of quota sold for $550; by 2000 the average price for a quota was $6,600. (Prices are in Canadian dollars throughout this section.) Explaining a positive market price for quotas is difficult except on the premise that a quota entitles a producer to sell eggs at a price above the cost of production. Therefore, the evidence suggests that the BCEMB policy has led to higher egg prices in British Columbia by restricting output through quotas.

Estimating the Deadweight Loss: The First Round

Figure 15.5 illustrates the consequences of the BCEMB policy on the (not unreasonable) assumption that the egg industry would be constant-cost under competitive conditions. In 1975, total egg output was 48.4 million dozen and output could not exceed that level because of the quotas, so the supply curve effectively becomes vertical at 48.4 million dozen, as shown by S'. The price of eggs, P_M, was $0.62. Because that price is above the cost of production, P, producers realized a profit of $P_M BAP$.

As we saw in Chapter 10, the profit is not a net loss to society but is, instead, an income transfer from consumers to producers. Area BCA is, however, a net loss, or deadweight loss. To estimate the size of this deadweight loss, we require two pieces of information: the height (BA) of the triangular area and the width of the base (AC). The height BA represents the excess of market price over production cost, and the distance AC represents how much greater egg purchases would have been if eggs were sold at a price equal to production cost.

Borcherding infers the price differential, $P_M - P$, from the market value of a quota. Knowing the value of a quota makes it simple to calculate this price differential since the weekly value tends to equal the excess profit attained on the sale of 30 dozen eggs per week. Quotas, however, are not sold on a weekly basis; a quota gives a producer the right to produce eggs indefinitely. Therefore, the market value of a quota is the present value of all fu-

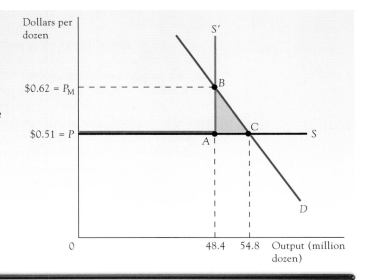

FIGURE 15.5

Deadweight Loss of BCEMB Quota Restrictions
Quotas restrict output to 48.4 million dozen, so price rises to $0.62. The deadweight loss triangle, *BCA*, can be estimated from knowledge of the price increment and the demand elasticity for eggs at point *B*.

ture profits. Calculating the price differential from this figure is still possible, however, by making appropriate assumptions about the interest rate used to discount future profits. Proceeding in this way, Borcherding estimates that P_M was 11 cents above the cost of production. Because the figure is similar to the difference in egg prices between British Columbia and the state of Washington, he has further support that the estimate falls in the correct range. An 11-cent price differential implies that the total annual producer profit is $5.3 million (48.4 million × $0.11).

The distance *AC* can be estimated if we know the elasticity of demand at point *B* and assume the demand curve is linear over the *BC* range. Based on several statistical studies, Borcherding assumes the elasticity of demand to be 0.75. To estimate *AC*, recall that the elasticity of demand equals $(\Delta Q/Q)/(\Delta P/P)$, so multiplying the percentage change in price ($\Delta P/P$, or 0.11/0.62) times elasticity yields the percentage change in quantity. Thus, we find that output would be 13.3 percent higher if price were 17.7 percent (0.11/0.62) lower, so the distance *AC* equals 6.4 million dozen per year.

With these two estimates for *AB* and *AC*, the deadweight loss triangle can be directly calculated as $\frac{1}{2}(AB \times AC)$, or $\frac{1}{2}($0.11 \times 6.4$ million), about $350,000. This sum is about 1 percent as large as the total consumer outlay on eggs ($30 million), and about 6 percent as large as the total profit realized by egg producers, as a group.

Estimating the Deadweight Loss: The Second Round

As we emphasized in Section 15.1, the exercise of monopoly power may produce some other type of deadweight loss in addition to the output restriction we have just examined. What is notable about the Borcherding study is that it investigates this other type of deadweight loss and, in fact, is able to estimate its approximate magnitude. Moreover, it tends to be substantially larger than the deadweight loss due to reduced output.

First, let's consider in theory how the operation of the BCEMB could produce a deadweight loss by inducing a higher-than-necessary cost of production. Not only does the BCEMB limit the total number of units of quota, but it also limits the number of quotas that can be held by a single producer. Specifically, a farm generally is not permitted to use more than 280 units of quota, so this restriction directly limits the scale of operation. If the size of operation is below the most efficient scale, the result is a higher-than-necessary production cost.

Figure 15.6 shows the results of such a restriction on individual farm size. In Figure 15.6a, the long-run average cost curve for a typical farm is shown as LAC. Without restrictions, the farm would produce an output of q_2 at the lowest point on LAC. The industry supply curve would be S_C in Figure 15.6b (recall that this is a constant-cost industry), and price would be P_C under competitive conditions. Now suppose that a maximum quota of q_1 per farm is established. The farm is constrained to operate at point G on LAC, and the unit cost of production is $P - P_C$ higher than necessary. If all farms have the same cost curves, the supply curve with this quota in place would be shown as S in Figure 15.6b, and horizontal at a price of P. Whatever output is supplied will now be produced at a higher cost than is necessary. More farms will operate, each at an inefficient scale of operation. In effect, the quotas make it impossible for the individual farm to take full advantage of economies of scale. If the total number of quotas is limited so that aggregate production can't exceed 48.4 million, the supply curve becomes vertical at that level of output. Price will then be P_M, and the individual farm makes a profit shown by area $P_M HGP$ in Figure 15.6a.

Previously, we estimated the deadweight loss as area BCA in Figure 15.6b. Now we see that this area underestimates the total deadweight loss. For the 48.4 million dozen eggs that are produced, the production cost is higher than necessary by an amount equal to $PAEP_C$. In addition, output is EF less than under competitive conditions, so there is a deadweight loss equal to BFE due to the output restriction. The total deadweight loss is $PAEP_C$ plus BFE.

Does the BCEMB limit quotas for individual farms at a level that entails higher unit costs, as in Figure 15.6? Some evidence suggesting it does comes from comparing individual farm sizes in British Columbia and the state of Washington. Washington has no restrictions on farm size, and about two-thirds of egg output is produced by farms with more than 50,000

FIGURE 15.6

Effects of the BCEMB on Production Cost and Welfare
With firms restricted to a maximum output of q_1 by the BCEMB quotas, a firm is forced to operate at point G on its LAC curve, involving a higher-than-necessary unit cost. The result is an additional deadweight loss, shown as the red-shaded area in part (b).

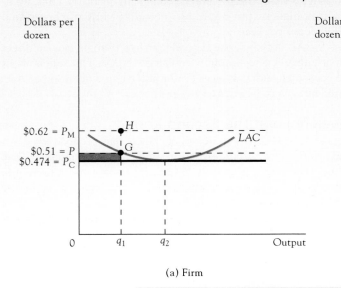

(a) Firm

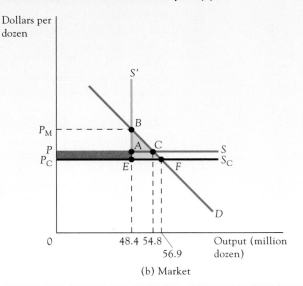

(b) Market

birds; in British Columbia less than 5 percent of output is produced by farms of this size.[14] The average flock size is also much smaller in British Columbia than in Washington. If farm size in Washington is any indication of the efficient scale of operation for producing eggs, then British Columbian farms are typically too small.

Using the results of a statistical study showing how production cost varies with the size of farms, together with the different distributions of farm size in Washington and British Columbia, Borcherding estimates that average production cost is 3.6 cents per dozen higher in British Columbia than it would be under competitive conditions. From this estimate we can infer that area $PAEP_C$ equals $1.7 million. This amount is nearly five times as large as the deadweight loss we estimated in the previous subsection. In addition, using the same elasticity assumption as earlier, we can estimate the deadweight loss due to restricted output (the area BFE) to be $620,000. The total deadweight loss arising from egg-marketing quotas is therefore on the order of $2.3 million.

Does such a large deadweight loss estimate mean that the BCEMB should be abolished? Not necessarily—the deadweight loss indicates only the magnitude of inefficiency that is involved. Don't forget that egg producers gain about $5.3 million in annual combined profit, and some have argued that preservation of the small family farm is a desirable goal in itself. What Borcherding shows is that consumers pay a high cost for this result. To transfer $5.3 million in income to egg producers, the BCEMB imposes a cost of $5.3 million plus the deadweight loss of $2.3 million, or $7.6 million, on consumers. Moreover, since egg consumption does not vary much by income, low-income consumers bear a large part of this cost. Significantly, this cost to low-income consumers and the deadweight loss imposed by the BCEMB have grown since the time of Borcherding's analysis (this can be inferred from the price of a quota being $6,600 in 2000 versus only $550 in 1976—the year in which Borcherding examined the BCEMB).

APPLICATION 15.4   THE INTERNATIONAL AIR CARTEL

The International Air Transport Association (IATA) is another example of a government-sponsored cartel. The IATA comprises more than 135 international airlines, controls 73 percent of all international air traffic, and is adept at fixing prices and limiting capacity.[15] On international routes covered by IATA agreements, such as between European countries, air fares are double those in the more competitive U.S. market for routes of similar length. Governments support IATA by awarding landing rights in accordance with IATA agreements, typically only to the national flag carriers of the two countries involved on any given international route (Alitalia and Air France on the Paris–Rome route, for example).

Although IATA has all the makings of a cartel, its members have consistently earned meager profits. Where are the receipts from exorbitant fares going? For one thing, price chiseling occurs. Some IATA members sell discount tickets, particularly for such heavily traveled routes as New York–London, through travel agencies known as "bucket shops." These bucket shops are often shut down in response to IATA member protests, only to reappear soon after. Estimates of consumer savings from the discounts at the expense of the cartel

[15]This application is based on Elden T. Chang and Mark A. Zupan, "International Fliers Could Use Takeoff on U.S. Deregulation," *Wall Street Journal* (October 8, 1985), p. 13; "French Delays 'Jeopardise Concorde'," *The Times* (October 12, 2000); and "Grounding the Highfliers," *Milwaukee Journal Sentinel* (August 17, 2000).

[14]A few farms are permitted to have outputs greater than the normal quota limit in British Columbia—namely, farms with over 50,000 birds, because 50,000 corresponds to about 700 units of quota. Only those farms that were already operating at that scale in 1967 are permitted these unusually large quotas.

range from $200 million to $1.5 billion annually. (Even with these discounts, however, fares per mile exceed those on domestic routes in the United States.)

Besides price cheating, IATA members compete on nonprice services. Although attempts have been made to standardize passenger service levels, international airlines continue to lure passengers with attractive and solicitous flight attendants, fine food and drink, extra-wide seats, and on-ground hotels and saunas between connecting flights. Nonprice competition has a singular effect on airline costs: it makes them higher than necessary.

The IATA profits are also low because most international airlines are government-owned and/or subsidized. So there is little incentive to minimize cost—which results in a deadweight loss of the type discussed earlier in this chapter. Some cartel profits are dissipated through excessive spending on advertising, costly ticket offices like those on Fifth Avenue in New York and the Champs Elysées in Paris, overstaffing, and high employee salaries and fringe benefits.

Revenues from international passengers are used to cross-subsidize intranational passengers. Passengers flying between European cities in the same country pay half the price of flights in the U.S. market on similar-length routes. This makes international airlines look good to those citizens who travel only within their na-

tion's borders. It also closely resembles a feature of the U.S. airline industry before it was deregulated: certain airlines were granted rights to operate profitable long-haul markets only if they provided service on certain unprofitable short-haul routes.

Because they tend to be publicly owned and/or subsidized, international airlines purchase aircraft for reasons other than rational economics. Political pressure to "buy local" sometimes persuades airlines to purchase domestically manufactured aircraft even if another aircraft better suits their needs. Due to pressures from their respective governments, for example, Air France and British Airways flew the Concorde extensively in the last quarter of the 20th century, despite annual operating losses of up to $10 million and $300 per passenger.

The Concorde has always held "prestige" value, however, and the airlines recognize its importance. On July 25, 2000, an Air France Concorde crashed just outside Charles De Gaulle airport, killing 113 people. British Airways promptly grounded its seven Concordes, but soon began complaining that French officials were slow to clear the jet's reputation, after it became known that debris from another airplane had caused the accident.

Both airlines had to weigh whether the costs of improving the safety of the quarter-century-old jet would be offset by its chief virtue—prestige.

15.5 MORE ON GAME THEORY: ITERATED DOMINANCE AND COMMITMENT

In the previous chapter, we introduced the basics of game theory and showed how it related to the study of noncompetitive markets. In all of the applications we covered in Chapter 14, at least one of the two players had a dominant strategy. We were therefore able to easily determine the equilibrium—either a dominant-strategy equilibrium (as in the case of the prisoner's dilemma game where both players had a dominant strategy of cheating/confessing) or the Nash equilibrium of Table 14.2 where only one of the two players had a dominant strategy.

What if neither player has a dominant strategy? Can a Nash equilibrium still emerge? The answer is "yes." In this section, we will show one way in which this can happen through the concept of *iterated dominance*. We will also examine the possibility that a player can make a *commitment* that alters the relevant payoff matrix in such a manner that a different equilibrium will emerge—an equilibrium that is more favorable to the player making the commitment. We thus can see that the usefulness of game theory is not limited to situations where at least one of the two players has a dominant strategy and that a player may have the ability to take an action that affects the strategies selected by other players.

Iterated Dominance

Suppose that only two companies, Circuit City and Best Buy, compete in the home entertainment market. The two firms each need to select one of three strategies regarding the price they charge for their products: high, medium, or low. The relevant payoff matrix, representing the profit of each firm based on the strategies selected by the two firms, is depicted in Table 15.1.

What equilibrium will emerge given the Table 15.1 payoff matrix? Clearly, neither company has a dominant strategy. If Circuit City chooses a high price, Best Buy's best strategy is a medium price (with a profit of 105). If Circuit City chooses a low price, Best Buy's best strategy is a high price (a profit of 11 versus a profit of 7 associated with choosing a medium price). Thus, Best Buy does not have a best strategy irrespective of Circuit City's strategy.

Likewise, Circuit City does not have a best strategy irrespective of Best Buy's strategy. For example, if Best Buy chooses a high price, Circuit City's best strategy is a medium price (with a profit of 105). If Best Buy chooses a low price, Circuit City's best strategy is a high price (a profit of 11 versus a profit of 7 associated with choosing a medium price).

With neither player having a dominant strategy in Table 15.1, we cannot as readily derive the equilibrium as we did in the games examined in Chapter 14 It turns out, however, that there is a Nash equilibrium associated with the Table 15.1 payoff matrix. To determine this equilibrium we need to rely on the concept of **iterated dominance**: *ruling out any strategy that is inferior to, or dominated by, another strategy.* That is, if a certain strategy yields lower payoffs for Circuit City than another strategy irrespective of the strategy selected by Best Buy, Circuit City would never select such a strategy. The strategy that is dominated by another strategy thus can be effectively eliminated from Circuit City's menu of strategic possibilities and the dimensions of the relevant payoff matrix thereby reduced. Whenever Circuit City has a strategy that is dominated by another strategy, eliminating the dominated strategy effectively reduces the number of rows in the Table 15.1 payoff matrix. Analogously, when Best Buy faces a strategy that is dominated by another strategy, eliminating Best Buy's dominated strategy effectively reduces the number of columns in the Table 15.1 payoff matrix.

Consider the low-price strategy for Circuit City. Irrespective of Best Buy's pricing strategy, a medium price consistently yields a higher payoff for Circuit City than does the low-price strategy. If Best Buy selects the high column, a medium price for Circuit City yields a payoff of 105 versus a payoff of 97 associated with a low price. If Best Buy opts for the medium column, a medium price for Circuit City yields a payoff of 50 versus a payoff of 40 associated with a low price. And, if Best Buy chooses the low price, a medium price remains a better choice for Circuit City than a low price (a payoff of 7 versus −10). Since Circuit City is never better off choosing the low price, the low row can effectively be eliminated from the Table 15.1 payoff matrix: It would never be selected by Circuit City in favor of the medium strategy.

Reasoning in a similar manner allows us to eliminate the low column for Best Buy. This strategy yields consistently lower payoffs than the medium option for Best Buy, regardless of

ITERATED DOMINANCE
the concept of eliminating any strategy that is inferior to or dominated by another strategy

TABLE 15.1 — A MORE COMPLEX GAME

		Best Buy		
		High Price	Medium Price	Low Price
Circuit City	High Price	90 / 90	105 / 44	97 / 11
	Medium Price	44 / 105	50 / 50	40 / 7
	Low Price	11 / 97	7 / 40	−10 / −10

Circuit City's pricing strategy. If Circuit City selects the high row, a medium price for Best Buy yields a payoff of 105 versus a payoff of 97 associated with a low price. If Circuit City opts for the medium row, the medium option for Best Buy yields a payoff of 50 versus a payoff of 40 associated with a low price. And, if Circuit City chooses a low price, the medium option remains a better choice for Best Buy than the low price (a payoff of 7 versus −10).

Once both the low row for Circuit City and the low column for Best Buy are eliminated from consideration, the three-by-three dimensional payoff matrix of Table 15.1 is reduced to the two-by-two matrix depicted in Table 15.2: both players have only two strategies from which to choose.

In the two-by-two payoff matrix of Table 15.2, both players have a dominant strategy. Circuit City's payoffs associated with the medium price are always greater than those associated with the high price (105 versus 90 if Best Buy opts for the high-price strategy, 50 versus 44 if Best Buy selects the medium price). Best Buy's payoffs associated with a medium price are also always greater than those associated with a high price (105 versus 90 if Circuit City opts for the high row, 50 versus 44 if Circuit City selects the medium row). Consequently, once we take the steps—or iterations—of eliminating players' dominated strategies, we end up with the prediction that the equilibrium associated with the Table 15.1 game will be both players selecting the medium-price strategy and, as a result, receiving a payoff of 50.

The predicted equilibrium for the Table 15.1 game is a Nash equilibrium. That is, each player's choice is the best one given the strategy chosen by the other player. Specifically, if, through the concept of iterated dominance, Best Buy finds that a medium price is the best strategy, Circuit City's best choice is the medium option (it generates the highest payoff for Circuit City when Best Buy chooses the medium column). Likewise, if Circuit City opts for a medium price, the medium option is Best Buy's best choice (it generates the highest payoff for Best Buy when Circuit City chooses the medium row).

By eliminating dominated strategies, therefore, the concept of iterated dominance allows us to predict what equilibrium will emerge in more complex games, such as the one depicted in Table 15.1. Even though neither of the players in Table 15.1 has a dominant strategy, a Nash equilibrium still exists once clearly inferior strategies are eliminated from consideration.

Commitment

The payoff matrix in Table 15.2 is another example of a prisoner's dilemma. Once the dominated low-price strategy of Table 15.1 is eliminated for both players, each player's dominant strategy is a medium price and results in a payoff of 50. The predicted outcome is one where both players are worse off than they would be if they both chose a high price and earned a payoff of 90. While choosing the medium option is in the self-interest of both players, the collective outcome of each player pursuing its self-interest is inferior for both.

TABLE 15.2

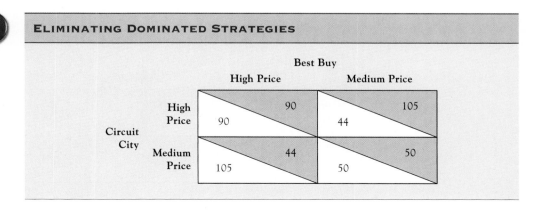

ELIMINATING DOMINATED STRATEGIES

COMMITMENT
the strategy of adopting a
particular course of
action, constraining one's
choice of other strategies,
in order to increase your
equilibrium payoff

Apart from the ways discussed in Chapter 14 by which players confronting a prisoner's dilemma game might overcome the problem and realize the best all-around outcome (through repeated games, altruism, and so on), there is another possible mechanism through which a player can ensure that acting on the basis of self-interest results in the maximum feasible payoff. Specifically, a player might find it desirable to make a **commitment** to a particular course of action and, by constraining one's choice of strategies, increase the player's equilibrium payoff.

It may seem paradoxical that constraining the set of strategic choices can generate a higher payoff. To see why this may be so, consider the case where both Circuit City and Best Buy vow that "they will not be undersold" in the context of Table 15.2. That is, if Circuit City chooses its medium row, Best Buy will not opt for a high-price strategy. Likewise if Best Buy chooses a medium price, Circuit City will not select a high-price strategy. The commitment to not be underpriced on the part of both players reduces the number of possible outcomes in this game from four to two: It effectively eliminates the northeast cell where Circuit City is underpriced by Best Buy and the southwest cell where Best Buy is underpriced by Circuit City. As depicted in Table 15.3, the only two possible outcomes that remain are if both players simultaneously opt for a high or low price. Thus, we can predict that both players will choose the high-price strategy and earn a profit of 90.

Note what the commitment to "not be undersold" on the part of Circuit City and Best Buy has accomplished. While appearing to promote competition in pricing, it allows the two players to overcome the prisoner's dilemma they previously confronted and results in consumers being charged the highest possible price to the benefit of the two sellers.

Of course, to be effective, a commitment must be credible. For example, Best Buy's vow not to be undersold implies that if Circuit City chooses a medium price in Table 15.3, Best Buy will not choose a high price, and vice versa for Circuit City if Best Buy chooses the medium option. To make their commitments credible, each player may promise to match or even beat (by, say, $25) the best price a customer is able to obtain for an appliance from the rival seller. In this manner, Best Buy and Circuit City effectively employ customers to bind them to their individual commitments to not be undersold—customers who, in the course of enforcing Best Buy's or Circuit City's commitments, end up promoting a high-price equilibrium.

Commitments need not be limited to vows to not be undersold. In many game-theoretic situations, a player can take other actions to alter the relevant payoff matrix so that it will be in the player's interest to follow through on a particular strategy. For example, to deter a political rival from entering a race, a politician may build up a substantial war chest—a money reserve that effectively binds the politician to competing vigorously to retain his or her elected post. On overnight, cross-country flights that are half-empty, after the airplane

---

TABLE 15.3

THE ROLE OF COMMITMENT

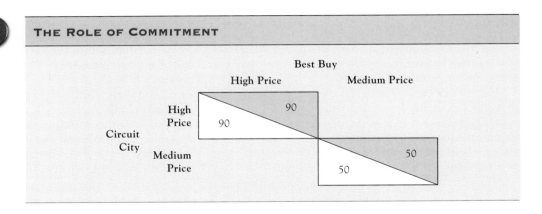

door is closed passengers usually scramble to sit in the middle seat of any empty row of three seats. Committing oneself to the middle seat diminishes the chances that a fellow passenger will choose either of the two empty seats next to you and increases the likelihood that you will have an empty row of seats in which to stretch out and sleep once the plane reaches a comfortable cruising altitude. As another example, Delco's shutting down of a production line that produces spark plugs specifically tailored for the Ford Motor Company may convince General Motors to divert more of its spark plug purchases to Delco because Delco can devote its attention to better satisfying General Motors' needs.

APPLICATION 15.5 WHY IT MAY BE WISE TO BURN THE BRIDGES BEHIND YOU

In invading Mexico in the sixteenth century, Spanish explorer Cortés ordered the fleet of ships that had carried his army to the New World burned. At first blush, his order may appear to be an act of madness, given that the Spanish army was vastly outnumbered. However, restricting the menu of strategic choices available to them committed Cortés' men to fighting. Not fighting and returning to Spain was no longer an option once the ships were burned. Upon being committed to fighting, Cortés' army successfully accomplished its objective of conquest.

SUMMARY

• Several examples illustrate the functioning of noncompetitive markets, the deadweight loss associated with monopoly, and the effect of monopoly on innovation.

• Public policies promoting greater competition in a monopoly market offer the potential for increasing total surplus and attaining efficiency in output. Thus, it is important to determine the relative magnitude of the deadweight loss of monopoly.

• If the product is produced by an oligopoly, output is likely to be higher and the deadweight loss smaller than in the case of monopoly.

• In addition to restriction of output, other deadweight losses may occur in cases of monopoly. For instance, with the absence of competition with other firms, the monopolist may be under less pressure to minimize costs of production or may incur costs in acquiring or maintaining its market position.

• Suppression of inventions does not appear to be a result of monopoly because a monopolist can increase profit by marketing a worthwhile invention.

• Natural monopoly exists when the average cost of a single enterprise declines over the entire range of market demand. This situation implies that the monopolist can serve the entire market more efficiently than many small firms but leads to the possibility that the firm will be tempted to exploit its power and restrict output and raise price.

• There are four policy options in dealing with natural monopolies: Leave the market alone; regulate the monopoly's activities; allow the government to own and operate the facility; or allow the government to sponsor a competition for the right to operate a natural monopoly, which goes to the bidder promising to charge the lowest price. In the United States, the second option has generally been chosen.

• In principle, average-cost pricing offers the most practical alternative for public agencies that regulate the behavior of natural monopolies.

• In practice, regulators lack complete knowledge of cost and demand conditions and seek to promote average-cost pricing by focusing on the rate of return on invested capital. The problem with this approach is that it diminishes the firm's incentive to minimize cost and to innovate.

• Some cartels operate with the help of the government. These function within the law, and prices are set without fear of antitrust prosecution. Deadweight losses typically result both from the restriction in output promoted by the cartel and diminished incentives to minimize production cost and to innovate.

• In a game-theory setting, iterated dominance allows us to assume that a firm will rule out any strategy that is inferior to, or dominated by, another strategy.

• Commitment to a particular course of action is another strategy that can increase one's equilibrium payoff in a prisoner's dilemma situation.

REVIEW QUESTIONS AND PROBLEMS

Questions and problems marked with an asterisk have solutions given in Answers to Selected Problems at the back of the book (page 577).

15.1. Explain why a certain triangular area is a measure of the deadweight loss of monopoly. What information do you require in order to calculate the size of this triangle?

*15.2. In an oligopolistic industry with constant marginal cost, output is 20 percent lower and price is 20 percent higher than competitive levels. How large is the deadweight loss as a percentage of the total consumer outlay on the product?

15.3. Studies have concluded that the deadweight loss of monopoly power in the United States is less than 0.5 percent of GNP. From your knowledge of the determinants of the deadweight loss, explain why such a small figure is plausible.

15.4. Suppose that the government levied a lump-sum tax on a monopolist. How would such a tax affect the monopolist's pricing and output decisions and profit?

15.5. Compare the effects of a $1-per-unit excise subsidy when applied to a monopoly and to a competitive industry with the same cost and demand conditions. In which case will price fall more? In which case will output increase more?

15.6. "If a business sells a product that wears out in a month, you will have to buy 12 a year, and the business will make 12 times as much money as it would selling a product that lasts a year." Evaluate this statement. Why don't businesses sell products that wear out in a day? In an hour?

15.7. Businesses frequently own patents on a number of products they do not produce and sell. This is sometimes cited as evidence that businesses suppress inventions. Is it?

15.8. Explain what natural monopoly is in terms of the relationship between cost curves and the demand curve. If the market is left to itself, what price and output will result?

15.9. Use a diagram to illustrate the "hoped for" result of natural monopoly regulation that attempts to set a price equal to average cost. What are the difficulties in achieving this outcome? Would an unregulated natural monopoly be preferable to a regulated natural monopoly?

*15.10. From the data given, can we determine whether the BCEMB has set its quotas at a level that will maximize the combined profit of producers? Can you think of reasons why the BCEMB would not try to maximize aggregate producer profit?

15.11. Suppose that the 3.6-cent cost differential shown in Figure 15.6 is due not to operation at the wrong place on the *LAC* curves but rather payment of higher-than-competitive wages to farm workers (perhaps because they are unionized). How large will the deadweight loss be in Figure 15.6 in this case?

15.12. In Table 15.2, if only Best Buy commits to not being undersold, what will be the outcome?

15.13. The manufacturer of a drug that has had a monopoly, due to patent protection, commits to pricing at cost and ensuring that no firm in the market will make a profit should a rival manufacturer enter the market once the drug's patent wears off. Is such a commitment credible? Explain.

15.14. Two companies each own property (and mineral rights) in an oil field. Each firm therefore has the legal right to drill for oil on its land and take out as much oil as it can. The problem, of course, is that one company's actions affect how much oil the other can produce.

The following matrix represents how each of these companies views the situation. The terms outside the matrix represent oil output by each firm (either low, medium, or high) while the numbers in each cell show the present value of all oil to be extracted by each company, given the two extraction policies. The first number represents the value to Company A and the second number represents the value to Company B.

As an example, if Company A pumps at a "low" rate and Company B pumps at a "low" rate, then the value to Company A of all the oil it expects to take over the life of the field is $100 while the value to Company B of its oil is $8.

		Company B's Extraction Rate		
		Low	Medium	High
Company A's Extraction Rate	Low	8 / 100	15 / 80	30 / 50
	Medium	5 / 125	10 / 110	22 / 55
	High	3 / 120	8 / 115	20 / 60

a. What extraction rates maximize the total value of the oil field?

b. Does the set of extraction rates of part a represent a stable situation? Explain.

c. Is there a dominant strategy (extraction rate) for either or both players? Explain.

d. Is there a Nash equilibrium set of extraction rates? If so, does it maximize the total value of the oil field?

e. Is there a mutually beneficial exchange inherent in this matrix—one that could solve the problem these two companies face? If Company A were to purchase Company B's oil rights, how much would it have to pay? Is this a feasible transaction?

15.15. If the latest computer chip produced by Intel has twice the storage capacity as the previous-generation chip, Intel would find it advantageous to market the new chip even though its sales of the old chip would plummet. True or false? Explain why. Would your answer change if Intel operated in a fully competitive market versus having monopoly power in the supply of computer chips?

15.16. Some have argued that the distribution of cable television service in a community is subject to economies of scale. Namely, it is cheaper to have just one company supply every household in the community with the service than to have several providers, each having to string separate cables throughout the community and each having to have their own satellite download facilities. On account of this apparent natural monopoly, communities employ franchise bidding to regulate local cable companies. Companies interested in supplying service to a community are required to bid ex ante for the right to be the sole supplier ex post. Explain why such franchise bidding competitions can serve to promote efficiency in markets characterized by natural monopoly.

CHAPTER 16

Employment and Pricing of Inputs

What determines the employment level and prices of inputs used to produce final products?

Chapter Outline

16.1 The Input Demand Curve of a Competitive Firm
The Firm's Demand Curve: One Variable Input   The Firm's Demand Curve: All Inputs Variable   The Firm's Demand Curve: An Alternative Approach

16.2 Industry and Market Demand Curves for an Input
A Competitive Industry's Demand Curve for an Input   The Elasticity of an Industry's Demand Curve for an Input
Application 16.1 *Explaining Sky-High Pilot Salaries under Airline Regulation*
The Market Demand Curve for an Input

16.3 The Supply of Inputs

16.4 Industry Determination of Price and Employment of Inputs
Process of Input Price Equalization Across Industries
Application 16.2 *The Net Benefits of High-Tech Immigrants*

16.5 Input Price Determination in a Multi-Industry Market

16.6 Input Demand and Employment by an Output Market Monopoly

16.7 Monopsony in Input Markets
Application 16.3 *Major League Monopsony*

Learning Objectives

- Explore the factors influencing the demand for an input by an individual competitive firm.
- Derive the market demand curve for an input by aggregating the demand curves of the various firms interested in hiring the input.
- Investigate the general shape of an input supply curve.
- Show how an input's price and employment level is determined in a multi-industry market.
- Examine input demand and employment by an output market monopoly.
- Define what is meant by monopsony in input markets.

In previous chapters we emphasized factors determining the output and price of final products. In this and the next two chapters we turn our attention to factors determining the employment level and prices of inputs used to produce final products. There are many similarities in the process of analyzing product markets and the process of analyzing input markets, since both involve the interaction of buyers and sellers. The leading actors' roles, however, are reversed. Firms are suppliers in product markets but demanders in input markets. Households and individuals are demanders in product markets and suppliers in input markets.

An examination of input markets helps us answer many interesting and important questions, such as "What determines a country's income level and distribution?", "Why do women earn less than men and African Americans less than whites?", "Why have the salaries of professional baseball players risen so rapidly during the past three decades?", "Why do entrepreneurs earn more than their non-entrepreneurial counterparts?", "Does immigration make the United States better off?", and "What are the effects of unions, and why have unions in the United States been declining in the private sector but growing in the public sector?"

This chapter discusses the basic principles common to all input market analysis, whether the input is labor, capital, land, or raw materials. We first examine the demand for inputs by competitive firms, then turn to the supply of inputs, and finally bring the two together to complete the general model. The chapter's final two sections analyze input markets under noncompetitive conditions.

16.1 THE INPUT DEMAND CURVE OF A COMPETITIVE FIRM[1]

The market demand curve for an input shows the total quantity of the input that will be purchased at various prices by all demanders as a group. To determine the market demand, we begin with the factors influencing the employment decision of the individual demander, usually a business firm. Then, we aggregate the demands of individual firms to obtain the total or market demand for the input. This treatment is similar to the derivation of the market demand curve for a consumer good. In that case, we first derived the individual consumer's demand curve; then, we combined those curves to obtain the market demand curve.

In this section we learn how a change in the price of some input will affect its use by a competitive firm. At the outset, note that there are no new assumptions in the analysis. We use the same competitive model developed in Chapters 8 and 9, but now our focus is on input rather than output markets. For example, we still assume the firm's goal is profit maximization, but now we want to see why profit maximization, along with the other assumptions of the competitive model, implies that a firm will employ more of an input when its price is lower.

How does a firm determine how many workers to hire when its goal is to maximize profit? For the moment we assume workers are homogeneous—that is, interchangeable as far as the firm is concerned—so the only question is how many the firm should employ. Each additional worker hired adds to the firm's cost, since the firm must pay the going wage rate. At the same time, each additional worker also adds to the firm's revenue, since a larger work force produces more output. Thus, benefits (greater revenue) and costs (wages) are associated with the firm's employment decision. The firm will increase profit by hiring additional workers as long as the additional revenue generated by the output expansion exceeds the wages paid. A comparison of the marginal benefit of hiring workers, in the form of added revenue, to the marginal cost of hiring workers, in the form of added wage costs, guides the firm's decision of how many workers to employ.

The Firm's Demand Curve: One Variable Input

Imagine a short-run setting where the quantities of nonlabor inputs (such as raw materials and machines) are fixed and only the number of workers can be varied. In this setting the law of diminishing marginal returns applies to labor: beyond some point, each additional worker results in a smaller addition to output. The contribution to output made by increasing the number of workers is an important determinant of the firm's demand for labor, and the marginal product curve (as described in Chapter 7) contains the relevant information.

---

[1]A mathematical treatment of some of the material in this section is given in the appendix at the back of the book (pages 569–570).

In Figure 16.1, the downward-sloping portion of the marginal product curve for labor is MP_L. The marginal product curve indicates that if the firm employs 20 workers per day, the output produced by an additional worker (MP_L) is three units; if employment increases to 25 workers, the marginal product of labor is lower (in this case two units) due to the law of diminishing marginal returns.

Starting from any given employment level, let's consider how hiring an additional worker affects the firm's total revenue. If 20 workers are employed, one more worker increases final output by 3 units. If the final output sells for a price, P, of $100 per unit, the additional 3 units of output generated by hiring another worker add $300 to revenue. Multiplying the marginal product by the price per unit of output ($MP_L \times P$) gives the marginal value product of labor (MVP_L). In general, the **marginal value product** measures *the extra revenue a competitive firm receives by selling the additional output generated when employment of an input is increased by one unit.*

A downward-sloping marginal value product curve is derived by multiplying the constant price of output (recall that we are dealing with a competitive firm; the price is unchanged when more output is sold) by the declining marginal product of labor. The marginal value product curve coincides with the marginal product curve. The only difference is that now we are measuring the marginal product of labor in terms of what it sells for on the vertical axis. For example, when 20 workers are employed and the price of output is $100, MP_L is 3 units and MVP_L is $300; when 25 workers are employed, MP_L falls to 2 units and MVP_L to $200.

The marginal value product curve is the firm's demand curve for a given input when all other inputs are fixed. To see this relationship, suppose that the daily wage rate is $300 per worker. The firm can hire as many workers as it wants at this wage rate, so each additional employee adds $300 to the firm's total cost. Every extra worker, however, also adds an amount equal to the marginal value product to the firm's total revenue. Comparing the cost and revenue effects tells the firm how many workers to hire. For instance, if the firm is currently employing 15 workers, the marginal value product of an additional worker is $400. Hiring another worker thus adds more to revenue ($400) than to cost ($300), so profit increases by employing more workers. The firm should expand employment up to the point where the marginal value product has fallen to $300, the wage rate. In Figure 16.1, the most profitable employment level is 20 workers when the wage rate is $300. If the firm hires more than 20 workers, total cost goes up by more than total revenue (the wage rate, $300, is greater than MVP_L beyond 20 workers), so profit declines.

MARGINAL VALUE PRODUCT (MVP)

the extra revenue a competitive firm receives by selling the additional output generated when employment of an input is increased by one unit

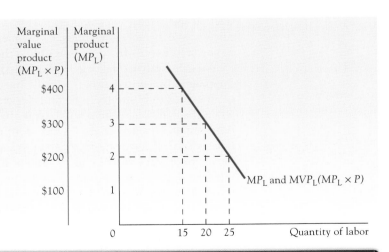

FIGURE 16.1

A Competitive Firm's Demand for Labor: One Variable Input

With labor as the only variable input, we can convert labor's marginal product curve, *MP*_L, into the marginal value product curve, *MVP*_L, by multiplying the marginal product of labor by the price of the commodity produced. The *MVP*_L curve is the competitive firm's demand curve for labor if other inputs cannot be varied.

Note that at a lower wage rate, hiring more workers is profitable. For instance, if the wage rate drops to $200 per day, the firm maximizes profit by expanding employment to 25 workers. At the initial employment level of 20 workers and the lower wage rate, the marginal value product of hiring another worker ($300) is now greater than the wage cost ($200), so the firm adds more to revenue than to cost by employing 5 more workers.

Two important conclusions emerge from this analysis. First, the marginal value product curve identifies the most profitable employment level for the input at each alternative cost. The firm will hire up to the point where the input's marginal value product equals its cost. Second, the marginal value product curve—the firm's demand curve when other inputs are not varied—slopes downward. This follows directly from the law of diminishing marginal returns: If an input's marginal product declines as more is employed, so must the marginal value product.

The preceding analysis assumes that the firm is a profit maximizer in a competitive market. It may be helpful to relate this analysis to the discussion in Chapter 9 that emphasized the most profitable output for the competitive firm. We have just seen that the firm maximizes profit by employing an input—in this case, labor—up to the point where its MVP equals the cost of the input—in this case, the wage rate w. When profit is at a maximum, therefore, the following condition holds:

$$w = MVP_L. \tag{1}$$

Because MVP_L equals $MP_L \times P$, if we divide both sides of equation (1) by MP_L we obtain:

$$w/MP_L = P. \tag{2}$$

Recall from Chapter 8 that the ratio w/MP_L is equal to the marginal cost (MC) of producing one more unit of output by using additional amounts of labor. Therefore, equation (2) is equivalent to the price-equals-marginal-cost condition for profit maximization in a competitive output market. *When the competitive firm is hiring workers so that $w = MVP_L$, then $MC = P$, and vice versa.* We have been looking at the same process of profit maximization that we examined in earlier chapters, but now from the perspective of its implications for the employment decisions of the firm.

The Firm's Demand Curve: All Inputs Variable

In identifying a firm's MVP curve as its demand curve for an input, we assumed that the quantities of other inputs are fixed. In general, however, a change in an input's price leads a firm to alter its employment of not only that input but also other inputs. For example, a reduction in the cost of computers may lead to the employment of more computer programmers as well as more computers. Consequently, an input demand curve should allow a firm to adjust its use of other inputs as well as the one whose price has changed.

We can easily extend the analysis to allow for variation in the quantities of all inputs. Suppose a competitive firm is initially in equilibrium, employing the appropriate quantities of all inputs. In Figure 16.2, the firm is operating at point A on MVP_L, employing 20 workers when the daily wage rate is $300. Note that the quantity of capital, assumed to be the only other input, is constant at 10 units at all points along MVP_L. Now suppose the wage rate falls to $200. If the quantity of capital is kept constant at 10 units, the firm increases its employment of workers to 25 units, at point B on MVP_L. This increased employment does not represent a complete adjustment to the lower wage rate, since it will normally be in the interest of the firm to expand its employment of capital, too.

An increase in the quantity of capital, though, shifts the MVP_L curve upward. If the quantity of capital increases to 12 units, the MVP_L curve shifts to MVP_L'. With 12 units of capital, each worker has more "tools" to work with than before, so the marginal productivity of workers is greater. The greater marginal productivity, coupled with an unchanged product

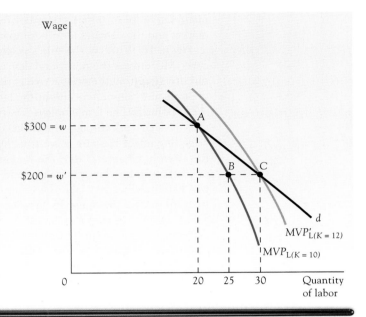

FIGURE 16.2

A Competitive Firm's Demand for Labor:
All Inputs Variable
When all inputs are variable, an input's *MVP* curve shifts with changes in the employment of other inputs. The firm's labor demand curve is then the *d* curve, which takes into account the way changes in the amount of capital employed affect the *MVP* of labor.

price, implies that the new marginal value product curve has a greater height at each possible employment level than before. The adjustment leads to a further increase in the employment of workers, to point C on the marginal value product curve for a constant 12 units of capital. Thus, the firm's full response to the lower wage rate is an employment increase from 20 to 30 workers.[2]

A and C are two points on the firm's labor demand curve, *d*, when the employment of all inputs can be varied in response to a change in the wage rate. The firm still employs workers up to the point where their marginal value product equals the wage rate, but we have now allowed for the effect of variations in the employment of other inputs on the marginal productivity of labor. We can think of the demand curve, *d*, therefore, as a generalized marginal value product curve. Since this curve allows the firm to vary all inputs, it is the competitive firm's long-run demand curve for an input. Note that in deriving this long-run demand curve, we assume that other inputs' prices are unchanged (only the quantities employed are variable) and that the final product's price is also constant.

The Firm's Demand Curve: An Alternative Approach

We can gain further insight into a firm's adjustment to an input price change with an alternative approach. Our first method has the advantage of linking the demand for an input to its marginal productivity but the disadvantage of obscuring what happens in the output market and the market for other inputs. The approach we develop next also shows that the de-

---

[2]Our analysis deals with the situation, thought to be typical, where labor and capital are complements. (Two inputs are complements if an increase in the quantity of one leads to an increase in the marginal product of the other.) When the firm uses more labor and the same amount of capital at point B, the marginal product curve of capital increases so the firm also expands its use of capital. The demand curve for labor, however, still slopes downward if the two inputs are substitutes. (They are substitutes if an increase in the quantity of one decreases the marginal product of the other.) In that case, when the firm increases labor (from point A to point B), the marginal product of capital declines and the firm employs less capital. A reduction in capital increases the marginal product of labor when the inputs are substitutes, so the MVP_L curve shifts upward in this case as well, just as it does in Figure 16.2.

mand curve for an input slopes downward, but pays more explicit attention to the output market and the demand for other inputs.

Figure 16.3b shows the firm's position, q_1, in its output market where its marginal cost curve MC crosses the horizontal demand curve at point E. Figure 16.3a shows the same initial situation from the perspective of the firm's employment of inputs. The least-cost method of producing output q_1 occurs at the tangency between the IQ_1 isoquant and the isocost line AZ at point E. The firm employs 20 workers and 10 units of capital at point E.

Now let's work through the effects of a reduction in the wage rate. First, how will a lower wage rate affect the firm if we *tentatively* assume it continues to produce the same output? Recall from Chapter 8 that the isocost line's slope equals the ratio of the wage rate to the price of capital. A lower wage rate and an unchanged price of capital imply that isocost lines will be flatter because labor becomes cheaper relative to capital when the wage rate falls. Isocost line A′Z′ in Figure 16.3a reflects the lower wage rate, and the least costly way of producing q_1 units of output occurs at E_1, where A′Z′ is tangent to isoquant IQ_1. *To produce an unchanged output, the firm uses more labor and less capital when the relative cost of labor falls; that is, the firm substitutes labor for capital.*

In Figure 16.3b, point E_1 on MC′ shows the same adjustment. A wage rate reduction lowers the entire marginal cost curve to MC′ (see Chapter 8 for a more detailed discussion), so when q_1 units are produced, the price of the product is greater than the marginal cost. The firm, therefore, has an incentive to expand output as a result of the lower wage rate. Now consider the subsequent effects as the firm expands output from q_1 to the new profit-

FIGURE 16.3

A Competitive Firm's Demand for Labor: All Inputs Variable
(a) A lower wage rate causes the firm to substitute toward labor and away from capital—the move from E to E_1. (b) At a lower wage rate, output expands from q_1 to q_2, as the lower wage rate shifts the marginal cost curve downward. This output effect further increases labor employment—the move from E_1 to E_2 in part (a).

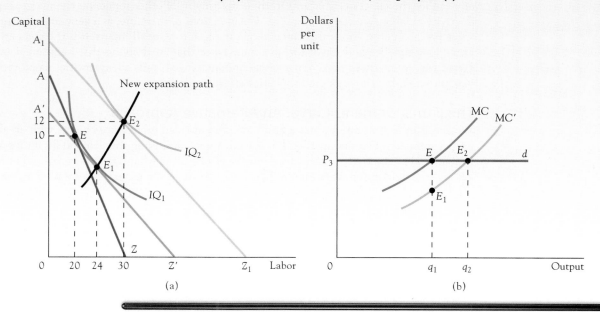

SUBSTITUTION EFFECT OF AN INPUT PRICE CHANGE
the change in input employment when output is held constant and one input is substituted for another in response to an input price change

OUTPUT EFFECT OF AN INPUT PRICE CHANGE
the change in input employment when output is altered in response to a change in the price of an input

maximizing level q_2. Figure 16.3a shows this effect as the movement along the new expansion path (based on the lower wage rate and unchanged price of capital) from point E_1 to point E_2. As the firm produces more output, it moves to a higher isocost line, A_1Z_1, and it employs more of both inputs than it did at point E_1. At E_2 the firm employs 30 workers and 12 units of capital. The wage rate reduction thus increases labor employment from 20 to 30 workers.

This approach to the demand curve for an input involves separating the total effect of an input price change into two components, similar to what we did with a consumer's demand curve. The change in input employment when output is held constant and one input is substituted for another is called the **substitution effect of an input price change**. The movement along the IQ_1 isoquant from point E to point E_1 (from 20 to 24 workers) shows the substitution effect in our case when the wage rate falls. The change in input employment when output is altered is called the **output effect of an input price change** and is shown by the movement along the new expansion path from point E_1 to point E_2 (from 24 to 30 workers).[3] When summed, these two effects identify a firm's full input employment response to an input price change.

Since the substitution and output effects both imply greater employment at a lower input price, the firm's input demand curve slopes downward. The firm employs more workers at a lower wage rate because it uses more labor per unit of output (the substitution effect) and because it is profitable to increase output when production cost falls (the output effect).

16.2 INDUSTRY AND MARKET DEMAND CURVES FOR AN INPUT

To derive the market demand curve for an input, we aggregate the demand curves of the various firms interested in hiring the input. Since an input such as labor is likely to be demanded by firms in many different industries, we proceed in two steps. First, we need to determine each industry's demand curve for labor. Second, we (horizontally) aggregate each industry's demand curve for labor to obtain the total or market demand curve for it.

A Competitive Industry's Demand Curve for an Input
In determining a particular industry's demand curve for an input such as labor, we must recognize one problem. When deriving the competitive firm's input demand curve, we assumed that the price of the product remained unchanged. Recall, though, that when the wage rate fell, the firm expanded output and sold the larger output at an unchanged price. The assumption of a given product price is appropriate when we are dealing with just one firm. But now we are interested in the response of all firms in an industry to a lower wage rate. *When all firms simultaneously increase output, they can sell more total industry output only at a lower price.*

Figure 16.4 illustrates how this factor affects the derivation of an industry's demand curve for an input. In Figure 16.4a, d is the labor demand curve for a single firm, assuming that the price, P, of the final product is $100 at all points along d. If the initial wage rate is $300, the firm in Figure 16.4a hires out to point A on its demand curve d and employs 20 workers. With 100 identical firms in the industry interested in hiring labor, total employment is

[3]In contrast to a consumer's demand curve, the firm's labor demand curve is not derived by pivoting the isocost line at point A in Figure 16.3a. That approach would be valid only if the firm continues operating at the same total cost, which is generally untrue. The most profitable total cost for the firm to incur depends on the demand and cost conditions shown in Figure 16.3b.

FIGURE 16.4

The Competitive Industry's Demand for Labor

(a) The competitive firm's demand curve for labor, *d*, assumes a given product price.
(b) In deriving the industry demand curve for labor, we must take into account that as industry output changes, so will the product price. The industry demand curve for labor is *D*.

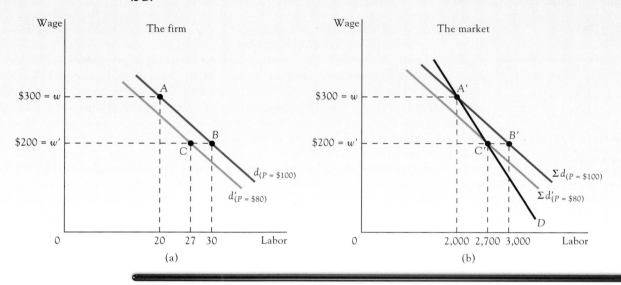

(a)

(b)

2,000 workers at the $300 wage rate, or point A′ in Figure 16.4b. Point A′ lies on the Σ*d* curve, which is the horizontal summation of the *d* curves of the firms in the industry.

By assumption, A′ in Figure 16.4b is a point on the industry demand curve for labor. The simple summation of the firms' demand curves, Σ*d*, does not, however, show the amount of labor demanded by the industry at other wage rates. To see this, suppose that the wage rate falls to $200. In Figure 16.4a, individual firms begin expanding employment from point A to point B, and in the process output rises. As industry output rises, the product price falls since consumers will buy the larger output only at a lower price. But a lower product price shifts each firm's labor demand curve downward, since labor's marginal value product curve is lower when the value (price) of the product is reduced. (Recall that the marginal value product of labor is equal to the marginal product of labor multiplied by the price of the output. Since the output price has fallen, the marginal value product of labor is lower for each level of input use.) If the product price falls to $80 per unit, for example, the firm's demand curve becomes *d*′ in Figure 16.4a, and the firm employs 27 workers. In Figure 16.4b, all the firms together begin by increasing employment from point A′ to point B′, but the increase is cut short by the falling product price, and they end up at point C′. Point C′ is a second point on the industry demand curve for labor, *D*.

This derivation of an industry's labor demand curve accounts for the effect of increased employment, and hence output, on the product price. The industry demand curve is less elastic than the Σ*d* curve, which is based on an unchanged product price, but it still slopes downward. This relationship becomes easier to see when we recognize that there are still substitution and output effects, implying greater employment at the lower wage rate even when the declining product price is taken into account. The product price falls only because more output is produced, and greater production involves the use of more labor (the output effect). In addition, firms use more labor per unit of output when the wage rate is lower because they substitute labor for other inputs (the substitution effect) at each given output level.

Note that we assume the demand curve for the final product is fixed when deriving an industry's demand curve for an input. In fact, economists often refer to an industry's input demand curve as a **derived demand**: the textile industry's demand for workers, for example, is derived from the demand of consumers for textiles. Firms will pay workers to produce textiles only because consumers are willing to pay for textiles. If the demand curve for textiles shifts, the textile industry's demand curve for workers also shifts. The consumer demand curve for a product is thus an important determinant of the industry demand curve for an input used in the production of the product.

The Elasticity of an Industry's Demand Curve for an Input

The price elasticity of an industry's demand for an input is defined and measured in the same way as a consumer demand curve. The magnitude of the price elasticity of demand for an input can be critical. For example, in evaluating the minimum wage law, whether a 10 percent increase in the legal minimum wage reduces employment of low-wage workers in the fast-food industry by 20 percent (an elasticity of 2.0) or 5 percent (an elasticity of 0.5) makes a big difference.

There are four major determinants of the elasticity of an industry's demand for an input. First, the greater the elasticity of demand for the product produced by the industry, the more elastic the input demand. Recall that an industry's input demand curve is a derived demand curve. If consumers will purchase a great deal more of the good at a slightly lower price (highly elastic product demand), firms in the industry will produce much more when an input price falls, and employment will increase sharply. An elastic product demand gives rise to a large output effect, which, in turn, contributes to the elasticity of the industry's demand for inputs. For instance, consider Figure 16.4b, and suppose the wage rate falls from $300 to $200. If the consumers' demand curve were perfectly elastic, the greater industry output could be sold at an unchanged $100 price. The firms would expand employment to point B', and, in fact, Σd would be the industry's demand curve for labor in this case.

Second, an industry's input demand is more elastic when it is easier to substitute one input for another in production. This condition refers to the technology of production reflected in the curvature of the production isoquants. When it is technically easy to substitute among inputs, the substitution effect of an input price change is large, implying a large (elastic) employment change. For example, if machines can adequately do the work performed by workers and at only a slightly higher cost, a wage increase can lead firms in an industry to switch entirely to machines and reduce employment of workers to zero—implying a highly elastic industry demand for workers.

Third, an industry's demand for a particular input is more elastic when the supply of other inputs to the industry is more elastic. If machine prices rise sharply when firms switch from workers to machines (implying an inelastic supply), only a limited amount of profitable switching can occur, giving rise to a small substitution effect and a low elasticity of demand for workers. The output effect reinforces this impact. If machines rise in price as more are used when output increases, the additional output firms can profitably produce as wage rates fall is limited.

Fourth, the longer the time allowed for adjustment, the more elastic an industry's demand for an input becomes. This is true because substitution possibilities among inputs become greater as firms in an industry have more time to alter their usage of various inputs. For example, a rise in the wage rate may mean that replacing workers with machines is profitable. It takes time, however, for machines to be built and installed, so in the short run few workers will be discharged.

DERIVED DEMAND
another name for an industry's input demand curve that reflects the fact that the industry's demand for an input ultimately derives from consumers' demand for the final product produced by that input

APPLICATION 16.1   **EXPLAINING SKY-HIGH PILOT SALARIES UNDER AIRLINE REGULATION**

As mentioned in Chapter 10, employee wages in the domestic airline industry were significantly higher when the industry was subject to regulation. For example, veteran union pilots at the major carriers made $150,000 per year in 1978, just prior to airline deregulation. By contrast, firms entering the industry following deregulation paid their top pilots only $45,000 per year.

The higher employee wages during regulation stemmed from the actions of the Civil Aeronautics Board (CAB). Specifically, the CAB limited competition between airlines on any given route during regulation. Only a few carriers were initially issued licenses to operate on each route and the CAB refused to grant additional licenses to other firms wanting to enter a market.

With limited competition, airlines with operating licenses for particular routes faced more inelastic demand curves for their output. More inelastic demands for final output implied that the derived demands for inputs, such as pilots, also were less price sensitive. In other words, because the cost of pilot salaries could more easily be passed on to an airline's customers in the form of higher air fares, domestic airlines were less price sensitive in their demand for pilots during regulation. Consequently, employee wages in the domestic airline industry were higher under regulation than after deregulation.

The Market Demand Curve for an Input

Once we have derived an industry's demand curve for an input, determining the market demand curve for the input is straightforward. What we need to do is recognize that firms in more than one industry may be vying for the services of a particular input. For example, the automobile industry is not the only buyer of steel or the only employer of engineers. The aerospace and construction industries also may compete for the services of the same inputs.

The market demand curve for an input is determined by (horizontally) aggregating the various industry demand curves for the input. The aggregation is analogous to the manner in which the demand curves of individual consumers are aggregated to obtain the market demand curve for a product. As we will see in a later section, it is the market demand for an input (the total demand of all industries using the input) that interacts with the total supply to all industries to determine input prices.

16.3   THE SUPPLY OF INPUTS

The supply side of input markets deals with the quantities of inputs available at alternative prices. This subject is somewhat complicated because the shape of the supply curve is likely to differ according to the type of input. In this section we make some general observations that are applicable to all inputs; we defer a discussion of specific inputs until the next chapter.

A broad definition of inputs might classify them as either labor, land, or capital. A narrow definition might distinguish between skilled and unskilled workers, land in New York City and Iowa, and buildings and trucks. The appropriate definition depends on the problem. The broad classification serves to make the general points here, but in the next two chapters we will see examples of cases for which it is fruitful to be more specific.

People own the inputs used by firms to produce goods. Our problem is to understand the conditions under which the owners of inputs will offer them for sale or rent. At the outset we should distinguish between the amount of inputs in existence at any given time—the stock of resources—and the amount offered for sale or rent. At any time, a fixed number of people are capable of working. There is a fixed area of land, and a fixed number of buildings, machinery, and other capital equipment. The amount in existence can differ significantly from the amount owners offer for use. Since the amount that owners offer depends on the price they are paid, we must be concerned with the supply curves of inputs, not just the stock of inputs in existence.

The general shape of an input supply curve depends critically on the market for which the supply curve is drawn. Consider the supply curve of labor to all industries in the economy. To simplify, suppose that all workers are identical, so there is only one wage rate. If the wage rate goes up, will the total amount of labor offered increase? We will give a fuller analysis in the next chapter, but here we simply note that the total amount of labor can increase only if workers decide to work longer hours or if more people enter the labor force. Such responses to a higher wage rate may be so small, though, that the supply curve of labor to all industries together will be approximately vertical, as in Figure 16.5a. A vertical supply curve indicates that an increase in the wage rate from w_1 to w_2 leaves the number of workers unchanged at 100 million. We are not asserting that the supply curve will necessarily be vertical, but it could be; so for the moment let's suppose it is.

Although the supply of labor to all industries taken together may be vertical, this does not imply that the supply curve of labor confronting *any particular industry* is vertical. While the total number of workers employed in the economy may not change, the number employed by a particular industry is subject to great variation. If the wage rate paid to software programmers increases, workers in other industries will leave their jobs to go to work as software programmers. This adjustment doesn't change the total number of workers employed, but it does change employment in the software programming industry. The supply curve of workers to the software programming industry thus slopes upward, as illustrated in Figure 16.5b. An increase in the software programming industry wage rate from w_1 to w_2 induces 10,000 workers to move from other jobs into the software programming industry.

Both labor supply curves in Figure 16.5 are correct in the sense that they can both exist simultaneously. Figure 16.5a shows the supply curve of labor *to the entire economy*; Figure

FIGURE 16.5

The Supply Curve of Labor to the Economy and to a Particular Industry
Distinguishing (a) the supply curve of an input to all industries together from (b) the supply curve of the input to one industry is important. The supply curve to one industry will always be more elastic than the supply curve to the economy as a whole.

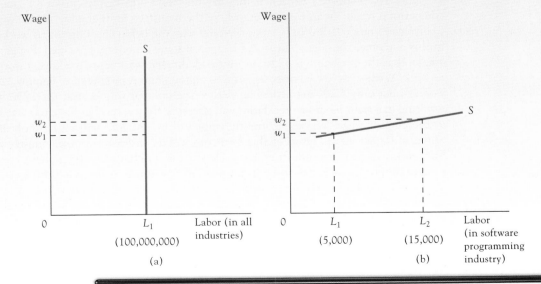

16.5b shows the supply curve of labor *to the software programming industry*. Because the software programming industry is only a small part of the entire (economy-wide) labor market, its labor supply curve is more price sensitive than the supply curve of labor for the economy. Indeed, if its share were as small as the numbers used in Figure 16.5, the software programming industry would likely face a virtually horizontal labor supply curve.

This discussion explains why referring to *the* supply curve of an input is ambiguous. We must always specify that it is the input supply curve to a particular set of demanders. Otherwise, we can fall into the trap of thinking that the supply curve of engineers to the defense contracting industry, for example, is vertical, because in the short run there are only a limited number of trained engineers. In fact, the supply curves of *most* inputs to *most* industries are likely to be upward-sloping, as in Figure 16.5b, regardless of the shape of the supply curve of the input to the economy as a whole, because most industries employ only a small portion of the total amount of any input.

This concept applies to other inputs besides labor. Although the total supply of land to the economy may plausibly be fixed (a vertical supply curve, as in Figure 16.5a), the supply available to any given industry is not. The corn industry can bid land away from other uses if it expands, just as homeowners can bid land away from farmers to build homes on.

Consequently, for individual industries, input supply curves will generally be quite elastic. However, supply curves of inputs to more broadly defined markets will be less elastic, and there are some types of situations where we should use this kind of supply curve. The proper pairing of supply and demand concepts is important to the analysis of input markets, as we will show in detailed examples ahead.

16.4 INDUSTRY DETERMINATION OF PRICE AND EMPLOYMENT OF INPUTS

Firms in an industry compete with one another to acquire inputs, and the industry demand curve for an input summarizes the way an input's price influences the firms' hiring decisions. Input owners provide resources to firms in the industry, and the supply curve of an input to the industry reflects the way the input owners' decisions depend on the price they receive. As with other competitive markets, the interaction of supply and demand determines the equilibrium price and quantity. Figure 16.6 illustrates this process, once again using labor as an example. As before, we assume that all workers are identical.

Figure 16.6b shows a particular industry's demand and supply curves for labor. Perfect competition results in an equilibrium where the industry's firms employ 10,000 workers at a (daily) wage rate of $300 ($w$). To understand why the behavior of firms and workers results in this outcome, consider what would happen if some other rate prevailed. Suppose, for example, that the wage rate is $250 ($w_1$) instead. At that wage, only 6,000 (L_0) workers agree to work. With such low labor costs, firms as a group find it profitable to employ 12,000 (L_1) workers, but only 6,000 are available. A shortage of labor will exist at the $250 wage rate, resulting in a tight labor market. Firms will advertise for workers but have too few applicants at the current wage. Workers currently employed by one firm will receive job offers from others at higher wages. Firms unable to recruit workers from within the industry will try to hire workers from other industries, but to do so, they will have to offer higher wages.

As a result, the wage rate will not stay at $250; it will rise. As firms bid the wage up, workers will quit their jobs in other industries to seize the better opportunity in this market, resulting in an increase in the quantity supplied—a movement up the supply curve. As the wage increases, firms will find that it is no longer profitable to try to fill 12,000 jobs, and the quantity demanded will decrease—a movement up the demand curve. The process will continue until the wage rate reaches the point where the number of workers willing and able to work for firms in the industry equals the number of workers firms are willing to employ. Graphically, the equilibrium is shown by the intersection of the industry demand and supply curves.

FIGURE 16.6

The Equilibrium Wage and Employment Level for a Competitive Industry
(a) The position of the firm in equilibrium is shown. Each firm faces a horizontal supply curve at the industry-determined wage rate of $300. (b) Supply and demand in an industry determine the equilibrium employment level and wage rate: 10,000 workers at $300 per day.

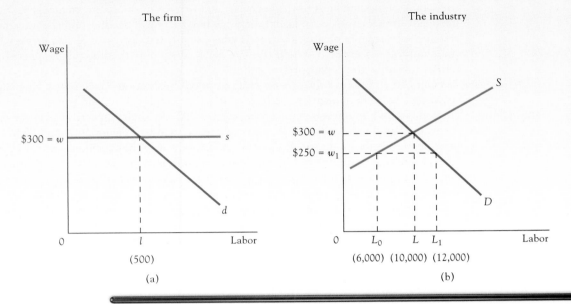

When the labor market for a particular industry is in competitive equilibrium, the situation from the perspective of an individual firm is that depicted in Figure 16.6a. The equilibrium wage rate is $300, and each firm faces a horizontal supply curve at that wage. The individual firm is a small part of the total market, so it has no option but to pay the going wage rate determined in the broader market (illustrated in Figure 16.6b). And at the equilibrium wage it can hire more or fewer workers without appreciably affecting the wage rate. Faced with the $300 wage, the firm in Figure 16.6a maximizes its profit by hiring 500 workers.

One implication of this analysis is that the market-determined input price equals the marginal value product of the input. Each firm is in the position shown in Figure 16.6a, employing an input quantity for which the marginal value product equals the input price. Recall that an input's marginal value product is the value consumers place on the addition to output made by the input. Thus, in a competitive market, input owners are compensated according to how much value the inputs they supply add to output. This happens because input demands are derived demands. Consumers, in their product purchases, are indirectly expressing how valuable the services of the inputs are to them.

Process of Input Price Equalization Across Industries

Several different industries often employ the same inputs. Most industries, for example, use land, electricity, unskilled labor, and buildings. To understand how the prices of these widely used inputs are determined, we must look beyond the boundaries of a single industry and recognize that there is competition among many industries for these inputs. We emphasize one characteristic of this situation here: the tendency for identical inputs to receive the same price, regardless of the industry employing them.

Suppose that the aerospace and telecommunications industries both employ computer programmers. Suppose also that for some reason wages are higher in the aerospace industry. The wage difference won't persist for long because programmers can move from one industry to another. Programmers in the low-paid telecommunications industry will leave their jobs and seek work in the aerospace industry, where pay is higher. This movement will simultaneously reduce the supply of programmers to the telecommunications industry and increase the supply of programmers to the aerospace industry. With more programmers seeking employment in the aerospace industry, the wage rate there will decline, and the wage rate will rise in the telecommunications industry, where supply has decreased. This process will continue until wages in the two industries are equal, since only then do programmers have no further incentive to change jobs.

Figure 16.7 illustrates the process of input price equalization. Let's assume that the aerospace and telecommunications industries together employ 1,500 programmers: aerospace employs 500 while telecommunications hires 1,000. At their respective levels of employment, the daily wage rate is $400 in the aerospace industry (Figure 16.7a) and $300 in the telecommunications industry (Figure 16.7b). To show why these markets are not in equilibrium and how they will ultimately adjust to an equilibrium, we use a specially defined supply curve. Consider the momentary, or very-short-run, supply curve of programmers that identifies the number of programmers in each industry at a specific time. These supply curves will be vertical; that is, at any given time each industry employs a certain number of programmers. These curves are not the supply curves we use in most applications. We use them here for the specific purpose of illustrating explicitly how the movement of programmers from one industry to another affects both markets.

FIGURE 16.7

Input Price Equalization Across Industries
When several industries employ the same input, the input tends to be allocated so that its price is equalized across industries. If this were not true—if, say, programmers were receiving $400 ($w_A$) in the aerospace industry and $300 ($w_T$) in the telecommunications industry—input owners would have an incentive to shift inputs to industries where pay is higher. This process tends to equalize input prices.

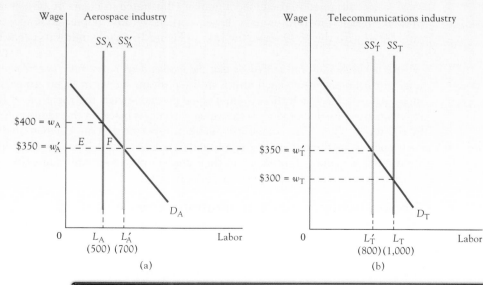

(a)

(b)

Initially, the momentary supply curve of programmers in the aerospace industry is SS_A, and in the telecommunications industry it is SS_T. Given the initial allocation of programmers between the industries, the wage rate of the 500 aerospace programmers is $400, and the wage rate of the 1,000 telecommunications workers is $300. Clearly, this result is not an equilibrium since telecommunications programmers have an incentive to quit their jobs and seek employment in the aerospace industry. Shifts in the SS curves show the movement of programmers between industries. The momentary supply curve in the telecommunications industry shifts to the left as programmers leave, and when these programmers seek jobs in the aerospace industry, the momentary supply curve there shifts to the right. The movement of workers decreases the difference in wages between the two industries: wages fall in aerospace and rise in telecommunications. Moreover, the movement of programmers will persist as long as the wage rate is higher in the aerospace industry, meaning it will continue until wages in the two industries are equal. In the diagram, equilibrium occurs when 200 programmers have moved from telecommunications to aerospace, and the common wage rate of $350 is established.

Note that this process works without requiring all programmers to change jobs in search of higher salaries. Relatively few programmers need to relocate to bring wages in the two industries into equilibrium. In our example, only 200 of the 1,500 programmers have to change jobs to produce a uniform wage rate. In fact, in some cases it is unnecessary for the workers to move, geographically speaking, at all. Suppose that the aerospace industry is in California and the telecommunications industry is in Colorado. Suppose also that programmers in Colorado are paid less but are unwilling to relocate to California. Labor immobility of this sort does not forestall the adjustment process. The wage differential creates an incentive for aerospace firms to relocate in Colorado and take advantage of the lower wage rate there, so the impact on wages will be the same as if workers had moved from Colorado to California—a uniform wage will be established.[4]

As this discussion suggests, competitive markets establish uniform input prices across firms, industries, and regions when identically productive inputs are compared. Competitive markets thus promote "equal pay for equal work." This conclusion is true if *equal work* is interpreted to mean equally productive work from the viewpoint of consumers—that is, equal in terms of marginal productivity. The possibility that discrimination by employers leads to differences in wage rates among equally productive workers, an exception to this conclusion, is discussed in Chapter 18.

APPLICATION 16.2   THE NET BENEFITS OF HIGH-TECH IMMIGRANTS

Since 1993, the information-technology sector has added more than 1 million net new jobs to the U.S. economy, at wages that average 75 percent more than in the rest of the economy.[5] The unemployment rate for information-technology workers is below 2 percent, and the Commerce Department estimates the nation will require at least 1.3 million new information-technology workers over the coming decade.

To fill the need for workers, high-tech companies have been lobbying for lifting the government restrictions on the number of skilled workers who can obtain H-1B visas in the United States. In 1999, the number of such visas was nearly doubled to 115,000 per year. In

[5]This application is based on Laura D'Andrea Tyson, "Open the Gates Wide to High-Skill Immigrants," *Business Week* (July 5, 1999), and "Bill on High-Tech Visa Advances," *Arizona Daily Star* (October 4, 2000), pp. D1 and D6.

[4]In some cases, wages can differ between locations because of workers' geographic preferences, but we defer that topic to the next chapter.

2000, Congress again raised the immigration limit—this time to 200,000 skilled foreign workers per year.

The net benefit associated with less-restricted immigration of high-tech workers to the United States is illustrated by Figure 16.7a. "Consumers" of labor in the United States are better off by the sum of areas E and F—the difference between the old and the new wage rate (w_A versus w'_A) out to the labor demand curve in the United States.[6] Recall that the height of the demand curve for any product—in this case, labor—reflects the maximum consumers are willing to pay for that product. Due to immigration and the fall in the wage rate, or price of labor, the L_A workers hired in the United States prior to immigration are now cheaper to employ by the amount of the wage rate decline. Consumers of labor in the United States thus benefit from the lower wage rate by rectangular area E on the first L_A workers hired. Moreover, U.S. labor employment rises from L_A to L'_A. On

these newly employed workers, consumers of labor realize a net benefit equal to the difference between the height of the demand curve (the marginal value product of the workers) and the cost of hiring the new employees (the wage rate of w'_A). Consequently, a net benefit equal to triangular area F accrues to consumers of U.S. labor on the additional workers hired from L_A to L'_A.

What about the native suppliers of labor represented by the pre-immigration labor supply curve SS_A? They are harmed by immigration since it leads to a decline in the going wage rate and thereby reduces their earnings. The decline in the total earnings accruing to native laborers is represented by rectangular area E—the difference between the old and new wage rate out to the initial labor supply curve SS_A. As might be expected, union organizations representing domestic high-skill workers have been vehemently opposed to any loosening of immigration restrictions by Congress.

On net, however, immigration makes initial U.S. residents better off by triangular area F if Figure 16.7a appropriately reflects the U.S. labor market. The gain to labor consumers from immigration (area E plus area F) outweighs the loss imposed by immigration on native laborers (area E).

---

[6]The *consumers* of labor who benefit from the lower wage rate need not be the firms hiring the labor. For example, to the extent that product markets are perfectly competitive, the gains from the lower wage rate will be passed on to consumers of the final products produced by the firms hiring the labor.

16.5 INPUT PRICE DETERMINATION IN A MULTI-INDUSTRY MARKET

When several industries compete for the available supply of a particular input, the impact of any one industry on the input's price is likely to be slight, since it usually composes only a small part of the total demand for the input. The broader multi-industry conditions of demand and supply determine the input's price. Now we wish to see how a single industry fits into this broader input market and, in particular, to identify the factors that determine the shape and position of the input supply curve confronting each industry.

Let's consider the hypothetical market for engineers, workers we assume to be identical. Several industries employ engineers. Industry B's demand curve for engineers is D_B in Figure 16.8b, and D_A in Figure 16.8a reflects the demand for engineers by all other industries, *excluding* industry B. Think of industry A as a *group* of industries; each has a demand curve for engineers, and their demands are aggregated as D_A. Therefore, A and B together constitute the total market demand for engineers. The total market demand curve for engineers, the sum of D_A and D_B, is D_T in Figure 16.8c. The market supply curve of engineers to all industries together is S_T, and we have drawn it as upward sloping on the assumption that higher wage rates will be needed to encourage more people to enter the engineering profession. (Note that we are looking at a time period long enough for people to complete their training. In the short run the market supply curve for engineers will be more inelastic.) *The interaction between the number of people willing and able to work as engineers and the total demand for engineers by all firms and industries determines the wage rate for engineers.* This interaction is shown in Figure 16.8c, with an equilibrium involving employment of 6,000 engineers at a daily wage rate of w, or $350. Each individual industry will then employ the number of engineers it wants at that wage. Industry B will hire 1,000 engineers and industry A will hire 5,000, for a total of 6,000.

FIGURE 16.8

Input Price Determination in a Multi-Industry Setting
Total labor demand D_T is the sum of the demands of industries A and B, and it intersects with total supply S_T in part (c) to determine the uniform wage rate. In part (b) the supply curve confronting industry B alone is derived by assuming that D_B increases. Supply curve S_B is highly elastic because industry B is a small part of the total labor market.

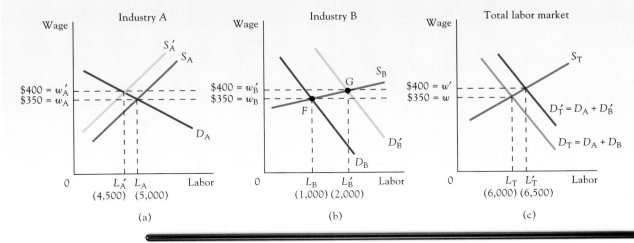

Our primary purpose in this section is to explain what determines the shape of the supply curve of engineers to a particular industry—in this example, industry B. We have already identified one point on this supply curve, point F in Figure 16.8b. At F, 1,000 engineers are willing to work in industry B at a wage of $350. Recall that we derive the supply curve of *output* for an industry by assuming a shift in the demand curve and tracing the consequences. We can use the same approach to derive the supply curve of an *input* to an industry—that is, the supply curve of engineers to industry B.

Let's assume that the demand for engineers in industry B increases to D_B', perhaps because of an increase in consumer demand for the output in industry B. As a result, the total market demand for engineers increases, but the effect on the market demand is proportionately less because demand has increased in only one segment of the market. With the market demand rising to D_T' (equal to D_A plus the new demand by B, D_B'), the wage rate of engineers is bid up to w', and total employment increases to 6,500. At the new wage of $400, industry B will hire 2,000 engineers, at point G. Point G is a second point on the supply curve of engineers to industry B; that is, at a wage of $400, 2,000 engineers are willing to work in industry B. In industry A, where the demand curve has not shifted, employment falls to 4,500 when the wage rate rises to $400.

Note that the additional 1,000 engineers employed in industry B come partly from industry A, where 500 fewer are employed, and partly from an expansion in the total number of engineers from 6,000 to 6,500. In effect, as industry B bids for more engineers by offering higher wages, it attracts some from industry A and also induces some new entrants into the engineering profession. Having derived the supply curve of engineers to industry B, we can understand more easily why the supply curve of an input to a particular industry will normally be highly elastic. In the example given here, when the wage rate in industry B rose from $350 to $400, the number of engineers willing to work there increased from 1,000 to 2,000, implying an elasticity of supply of about 5 (using the formula for arc elasticity). The elasticity of the supply curve of engineers to the total market, however, is only about 0.6. The reason for this difference is straightforward: industry B is only a part of the market for engineers, and it can bid some away from other industries—perhaps only a few from each of dozens of industries—without greatly affecting the general wage level for them all. *The smaller the share of the total market accounted for by an industry, the more elastic its input supply curve.* In our example, industry B initially employed one-sixth of the total number of engineers, but this proportion rose to nearly one-third after the demand increase. In many real-world cases, a single industry will compose a much smaller part of the total market, so its input supply curve can easily be perfectly elastic (horizontal). Recall the significance of high input supply elasticities for the elasticity of the output supply curve, discussed in Chapter 9.

We should also note that the increase in demand by industry B causes the supply curve of engineers to industry A to shift. An input supply curve to a given industry is based on given demand conditions in other industries (in drawing S_B, we assumed D_A was fixed). When other industries compete more aggressively for inputs, industry A will find its workers being bid away, causing a reduction in input supply to industry A. The result is a higher wage in industry A as well. Remember that input prices will be equalized across industries, so industry A will be unable to retain engineers if it pays less than industry B.

If we were concerned solely with industry B, we would simply need to consider Figure 16.8b. We should, however, integrate the supply of an input to a particular industry into the broader market for the input, a market that usually contains several industries. Indeed, the concept of an industry—a group of firms producing the same product—was designed primarily to study how output markets work. For that purpose, grouping the firms producing the same product makes sense. Relying on the same classification scheme when analyzing input markets is much less helpful since many different industries compete for the same supply of inputs. The notion of a multi-industry input market (Figure 16.8c) is more appropriate.

16.6 INPUT DEMAND AND EMPLOYMENT BY AN OUTPUT MARKET MONOPOLY[7]

A monopoly is defined as a firm that is the sole seller of some product, but a firm that has monopoly power in its output market does not necessarily have market power in its input markets. A firm can be the sole seller of a product and still compete with a large number of firms in hiring inputs. In that case, the firm is a monopoly in its output market and a competitor in its input markets; this situation is the subject of this section's discussion.

Like a competitive firm, a monopoly bases its decisions about input use on the way profit is affected. It expands input employment as long as hiring one more unit adds more to revenue than to cost. The price that must be paid for an input measures the added cost of employing it—just as it did for a competitive firm. The difference in the two market settings rests on the way hiring one more input unit affects the firm's revenue.

For a competitive firm, employing one more input unit adds to revenue an amount equal to the marginal value product. The marginal value product is the additional output produced multiplied by the price at which it can be sold. For a monopoly, one more input unit also adds to revenue by expanding output, but revenue does not increase by the price at which the additional output is sold. Recall that to sell more, a monopoly must reduce the price for all its output; that is, the price received for the hundredth unit of output, for example, is greater than its contribution to revenue. Marginal revenue, which is always lower than price, measures the effect on revenue of selling one more unit of output. Consequently, for a monopoly, the contribution to revenue from employing one more input unit is the additional output (the input's marginal product) multiplied by the marginal revenue associated with the additional output. The product of marginal product and marginal revenue is called the input's **marginal revenue product**.

MARGINAL REVENUE PRODUCT

the product of an input's marginal product and the marginal revenue that can be derived from selling that marginal product

[7]A mathematical treatment of some of the material in this section is given in the appendix at the back of the book (page 570).

Consider a situation in which all inputs but labor are fixed in quantity for the firm. In Figure 16.9, the marginal value product curve, MVP_L, would be the demand curve for the input under competitive conditions, as we explained in Section 16.1. If the firm is a monopoly, the marginal revenue product curve, MRP_L, is the demand curve for the input. For a monopoly, marginal revenue is below price at each level of output and at each level of labor employment, so the MRP_L curve lies below the MVP_L curve. The monopoly's demand curve for labor, the MRP_L curve, slopes downward for two reasons. First, the marginal product of labor declines as more labor is employed (this relationship also holds true in the competitive case). Second, the marginal revenue associated with selling more output also declines as more labor is employed, since the additional output can be sold only at a lower price.

In Figure 16.9, at a wage rate of $400, the monopoly employs L_1 workers. This amount is the profit-maximizing level of employment. At any lower level of employment the revenue generated by hiring another worker exceeds the cost ($MRP_L > w$), so profit increases if employment increases to L_1, where $MRP_L = w$. If the monopoly employed more workers, they would add more to cost (w) than to revenue (MRP_L), and profit would be lower.

Employment of labor, or any other input, is lower under monopoly than competition. Under competition, L_2 workers are employed at the point where $w = MVP_L$; only L_1 workers are employed under monopoly. This result should come as no surprise, since it was already implicit in our conclusion in Chapter 11 that a monopoly produces less output than a competitive industry. To produce less, it uses fewer inputs. Figure 16.9 therefore depicts the monopolistic reduction in output from the perspective of the input market.

Figure 16.9 also shows an output market monopoly's deadweight loss. The marginal value product of labor measures how much one more worker's output is worth to consumers. At the monopoly outcome, L_1, MVP_L equals $700, indicating that consumers are willing to pay more for another worker than it costs the monopolist to hire the worker (a wage of $400). The benefit to consumers of more output is greater than the cost of producing the output, but the monopoly does not hire more workers to expand output. This discussion describes the same deadweight loss due to monopoly explained in Chapter 11, but focuses on the input side of the picture.

We can extend the analysis of the monopoly demand for an input to a case where all inputs are variable in the same manner as we did for the competitive firm. No significant new conclusions emerge, and two important points remain. First, the input demand curves of an output monopoly slope downward, both because the input's marginal productivity declines

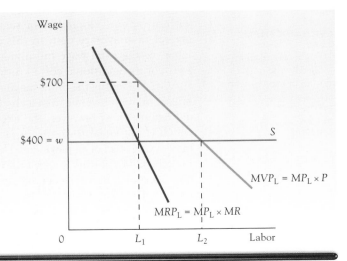

FIGURE 16.9

An Output Monopolist's Demand for an Input
When only one input is variable, we derive a monopoly's input demand curve by multiplying the input's marginal product by the marginal revenue, *MR*, from selling the commodity produced: $MRP_L = MP_L \times MR$. The marginal revenue product curve MRP_L is the monopoly's demand curve, and it lies below the competitive demand curve, MVP_L.

and because marginal revenue from selling output declines as more of any input is consumed. Second, the input demand curves of a monopoly are lower than they would be if the output market were competitive.

Finally, it is important to note that our focus in this section has been on the input demand curve of a firm that is a monopoly in its output market. *An output market monopoly is not the same as an input market monopoly.* The latter involves a single seller of an input confronting the entire market demand curve for the input (where the market demand curve for an input is derived by aggregating the demands for the input across various firms operating in either competitive or monopoly output markets). We address the topic of input market monopoly in the next chapter in the context of labor unions.

16.7   MONOPSONY IN INPUT MARKETS

MONOPSONY
an input market in which a firm is the sole purchaser of an input

Monopsony means "single buyer." Pure monopsony in input markets occurs when a firm is the sole purchaser of an input. An example of pure monopsony is purchases by General Motors of an automobile part that has been uniquely tailored by suppliers for GM cars. As a sole buyer, a monopsony faces the market supply curve of the input, a curve that is often upward-sloping. An upward-sloping supply curve means that the monopsonist has market power in the input market and can reduce the price paid without losing all the input.

An input market monopsony is analogous to an output market monopoly. An output market monopoly has some discretion over the price charged for its product (as determined by the downward-sloping demand curve), while an input market monopsony has some discretion over the price paid for an input (as determined by the upward-sloping supply curve of the input).

Graphically, an upward-sloping supply curve for an input confronting the firm indicates the presence of monopsony. We'll use labor once more as an example. An upward-sloping supply curve means that the firm must pay a higher wage rate to increase the number of workers it employs. (Up until now, we have assumed that every firm faces a horizontal supply curve for each input.) When the firm faces an upward-sloping input supply curve, **marginal input cost** is not the same as **average input cost**. For example, suppose that a firm employs 10 workers at a wage of $300, but to employ 11 workers, the firm must pay a wage rate of $310 to them all. The marginal cost of hiring the eleventh worker is therefore $410, because total labor cost rises from $3,000 to $3,410 when employment increases by one worker. Put differently, we can think of the wage rate as the average cost of labor (AC_L). When the average cost rises as more workers are employed (as is the case with an upward-sloping labor supply curve), the marginal cost of labor (MC_L) must be greater than average cost. In this case the $310 wage rate is equal to the average cost of labor, or the total wage bill divided by the number of workers, and the marginal cost is $410, or the additional cost of hiring an extra worker.

MARGINAL INPUT COST
the cost of using an additional unit of an input

AVERAGE INPUT COST
the total cost of an input divided by the units of that input used by a firm

We can identify the profit-maximizing employment level of a monopsony by comparing the impact on total revenue from a change in employment with the effect on total cost, just as we did before. Now, however, the effect on cost is determined by the marginal cost of labor, which is not equal to the wage rate. Figure 16.10 illustrates how we determine the profit-maximizing level of employment. The demand curve of the firm indicates the amount that hiring an additional worker adds to revenue. (The demand curve will be the MVP_L curve if the firm is a competitor in its output market; it will be the MRP_L curve if the firm is a monopoly in its output market. Conceivably, a firm could be competitive in its output market and be a monopsony in its labor market, although this situation is unlikely.) The supply curve to the firm slopes upward—the graphical characteristic of monopsony—so the marginal cost of labor curve, MC_L, lies above the supply curve. Note that the average cost of labor curve, AC_L, is identical to the supply curve if the firm can select any employment level along the labor supply

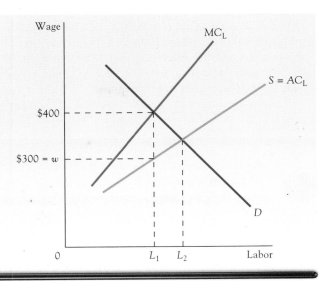

FIGURE 16.10

An Input Market Monopsony
An input market monopsony faces an upward-sloping input supply curve, so the marginal cost of employing the input is greater than the input price (the average cost of the input): MC_L lies above $S = AC_L$. The intersection of MC_L and D determines employment, but the wage rate is determined by the height of the supply curve.

curve. But once the level is selected, each worker hired is paid the same wage. For example, if each worker is paid $300 per day, the average daily wage per worker is also $300.

The firm maximizes profit by employing L_1 workers. At that point the marginal cost of labor equals the addition to total revenue from hiring one more worker. The firm, however, does not pay an amount equal to the worker's marginal contribution to revenue ($400). Instead, the firm pays a wage of $300. The intersection of MC_L and the demand curve determines the most profitable employment level, while the wage rate is determined by the height of the supply curve at the corresponding level of employment.

In comparison with competitive input market conditions, employment is lower under monopsony and so is the wage rate. If there were competition in the input market in Figure 16.10, employment would be L_2, and the wage would be higher, since the supply curve slopes upward. A similarity between monopsony and monopoly becomes apparent. An output market monopoly restricts output to obtain a higher price; an input market monopsony restricts employment to pay a lower wage. An output market monopoly is able to charge a higher price because it faces a downward-sloping demand curve for its product; an input market monopsony is able to pay a lower wage because it faces an upward-sloping input supply curve.

APPLICATION 16.3   MAJOR LEAGUE MONOPSONY

U ntil arbitration led to its dismantling in 1975, a provision in major league baseball known as the *reserve clause* limited players to negotiating salary with the first team to sign them.[8] That is, unless the first team to offer a player a contract terminated or traded him, he was at the mercy of the team's owners. The reserve clause thus effectively tied each player to one team and eliminated competition between teams for individual players.

As the monopsony model predicts, when the reserve clause was in effect, players' salaries were lower than their contributions to total revenues (as measured by gate receipts, broadcast fees, concession sales, and so on). In the late 1960s, for example, superstar hitters re-

[8]This application draws on: Susan Lee, "The Baseball Strike Is a Monopolists' Slugfest," *Wall Street Journal* (June 30, 1981), p. 15; and Gerald W. Scully, "Pay and Performance in Major League Baseball," *American Economic Review*, 64 No. 6 (December 1974), pp. 915–930.

ceived an average salary of $68,000 per season but contributed $384,000 to their teams' total revenues (net of any training and transportation costs). Superstar pitchers averaged annual salaries of $86,000, but added $480,000 to their teams' total revenues.

The dismantling of the reserve clause in 1975 and resulting competition between teams over individual play-ers has caused a fly-up in players' salaries. As of 1976, players who have served a team for five years are eligible to become free agents and sell their skills to the highest bidder. Average annual salaries shot up by 175 percent between 1975 and 1980, from $53,000 to $146,000. By 1999, the average salary of a Major League baseball player had risen to $1,572,000.

SUMMARY

• A competitive firm's demand for any input slopes downward. This can be shown either by focusing on the marginal value product curve or by considering the substitution and output effects of a change in the input's price.
• A competitive industry's demand curve for an input is derived by aggregating firms' demand curves for the input, but this summation is not a simple one, since a product's price changes as total industry employment and thus output vary.
• In terms of input supply, the demander or set of demanders needs to be specified. Firms that are perfect competitors in input markets face horizontal input supply curves.
• The supply curve to an industry may be either horizontal or upward-sloping.
• The supply curve to the economy as a whole may be very inelastic.
• In competitive markets the interaction of supply and demand determines input prices and employment, although the relevant market is frequently broader than a single industry.

• When many industries employ the same input, the input price tends to be equalized across them, and the supply curve of the input to any single industry will be very elastic; no single industry will have much effect on the input price.
• Firms that are monopolies in output markets also have downward-sloping demand curves, termed marginal revenue product curves.
• Compared with competitive firms, output market monopolies have lower input demand curves. This outcome does not necessarily imply, however, that an output market monopoly will pay lower prices for inputs, since it may face a horizontal input supply curve and thus have to pay the market price for an input.
• An input market monopsony is the sole employer of the input, and so it faces the market supply curve. If that supply curve slopes upward, the monopsony's employment decision affects the price of the input: The monopsonist has market power in the input market.
• Compared to the competitive outcome, the price and employment of an input will be lower with input market monopsony.

REVIEW QUESTIONS AND PROBLEMS

Questions and problems marked with an asterisk have solutions given in Answers to Selected Problems at the back of the book (page 577).

16.1. The data in Table 7.1 relate total output to the amount of labor employed when the amounts of other inputs such as capital are held constant. Use it to answer the following: If the price of final output is $10 and the wage rate is $120, how many workers will be hired? (Assume that the output market is competitive.) Illustrate your answer with a graph similar to Figure 16.1.

16.2. What factors (other than the wage rate) affect the amount of labor a firm that operates in perfectly competitive

output markets will hire? How will a change in each of these factors affect the firm's demand curve for labor?

16.3. "The law of demand does not apply to professional baseball players. Since each team already has the maximum number of players allowed on its squad, a reduction in the wage rate that must be paid for baseball players would not lead to any more being hired." Evaluate this statement.

*16.4. If the demand for personal computers rises, the productivity of workers engaged in making personal computers does not necessarily increase. Why, then, does the demand for such workers increase?

16.5. Distinguish between the short-run and the long-run supply curves of geologists to the domestic economy. Which curve will be more inelastic? Why?

16.6. Rank the following labor supply curves in terms of their elasticities. How does your answer depend on whether you consider short-run or long-run supply curves? Explain your answer.
a. The supply of economists to the federal government.
b. The supply of taxi drivers to Chicago.
c. The supply of college professors to Ohio State University.

16.7. Discuss the determination of equilibrium input price and employment by a competitive industry. Concerning the equilibrium, firms would prefer to pay a lower price for the input; why don't they? Owners of inputs would prefer to receive a higher price; why don't they refuse to supply the input unless the price is higher?

*16.8. "Employers set wage rates equal to marginal value products." True or false? Explain.

*16.9. "If the supply of labor increases and depresses wages in a competitive industry, this outcome will benefit firms at the expense of workers." True or false? Explain.

*16.10. Writing about the late nineteenth century, C. Vann Woodward observes: "There was nothing but the urging of conscience and the weak protest of labor to keep employers from cutting costs at the expense of their workers." Analyze this statement. Was it conscience that kept wage rates from being zero?

16.11. "College teachers are no more productive today than they were 50 years ago, yet they are paid three times as much today. They are obviously not being paid according to their marginal productivity." Discuss.

*16.12. If the demand for automobiles rises sharply, how will the price of refrigerators be affected? (Steel is an important input in the production of both products.)

16.13. "The demand for videocassette recorders has increased rapidly in recent years, while the demand for radios has scarcely increased at all. Therefore, the fact that workers are better paid in the VCR industry is not surprising." Would you be surprised if the assertion about wage rates turned out to be correct? Support your position with a graphical analysis.

16.14. "If among many good-hearted employers there is one that is determined to exploit workers, the actions of the single employer may suffice to neutralize the good-heartedness of the rest. This is because if a single employer succeeds in screwing down wages below the rate previously current, his fellow-employers may have no alternative but to follow suit, or to see themselves undersold in the product market." Why is this statement wrong?

16.15. "If Mexicans are allowed to immigrate to the United States, they will take jobs away from U.S. citizens." Evaluate this statement.

16.16. Explain why an output market monopoly will employ more of an input when its price is lower in terms of the substitution and output effects of the lower input price. (*Hint:* How would Figures 16.3a and 16.3b be different for a monopoly?)

16.17. Do output market monopolies cause unemployment?

16.18. What is a monopsony? Graphically, what distinguishes a monopsony from a competitive employer of inputs? What does this difference imply for the relative levels of employment and input prices under monopsony versus competition?

16.19. "Along a downward-sloping competitive industry's demand curve for labor, such as the one depicted in Figure 16.4, firm profits will be greater the lower the wage rate is." Explain why this statement is true, false, or uncertain.

16.20. Workers belonging to the Malevolent Association of Microeconomics Teaching Assistants Union at your school are disgruntled over their salaries and would like to request a $100 increase in their weekly wage. Is their request more or less likely to be honored if alternative means of assisting faculty in the instruction of economics become more plentiful, such as study guides, videotapes, and robots? If the demand for the undergraduate education provided by your school becomes more price elastic due to greater competition from other schools?

16.21. Bad Breath, Inc., sells its output at $1 per unit into competitive markets. Bad Breath's factory is the only employer of labor in Gilroy, California (garlic capital of the world). It faces a supply from competitive workers of $Q_L = w$ where Q_L is the number of workers hired per year and w is the annual wage. Each additional worker hired adds one less unit of output than was added by the previous worker. The 30,000th worker adds nothing to total output. Bad Breath must pay all workers the same wage and, because it has to raise wages to get more labor, each additional worker costs the company $2Q_L$ dollars per year. To maximize profit, how much labor should Bad Breath hire and what wage should it pay? Does efficiency prevail in the Gilroy labor market? If not, what is the size of the deadweight loss?

16.22. If nominal wages in the South are less than in the North, does this imply that the economic theory of labor mobility is invalid? Explain why or why not.

16.23. Per capita income is 600 percent higher in the United States than in Mexico. No other two countries sharing a border have a wider disparity in income levels. Explain why this leads to immigration of workers from Mexico to the United States. Is such immigration beneficial, on net, to the United States?

16.24. Due to OPEC, the price of jet fuel increased by over 700 percent between 1970 and 1980. Explain why airlines responded hardly at all to the increase in the price of jet fuel in the short run (an estimated demand elasticity of between 0 and 0.15). Also explain why the long run response was more substantial and involved substituting Boeing 737s and 767s for 727s and 747s and investing in superior tracking systems whereby a take-off can be delayed until a landing slot is assured at the destination city.

CHAPTER 17

Wages, Rent, Interest, and Profit

How are wages, rent, interest, and profit determined?

Chapter Outline

17.1 The Income-Leisure Choice of the Worker
Is This Model Plausible?

17.2 The Supply of Hours of Work
Is a Backward-Bending Labor Supply Curve Possible?   *The Market Supply Curve*

17.3 The General Level of Wage Rates
Application 17.1 The Malaise of the 1970s

17.4 Why Wages Differ
Compensating Wage Differentials
Application 17.2 Twelve Hours' Pay for Ten Minutes' Work
Differences in Human Capital Investment
Application 17.3 The Returns to Investing in a BA and an MBA
Differences in Ability
Application 17.4 What's on the Outside Also Counts

17.5 Economic Rent
Application 17.5 The Bay Area Real Estate Frenzy: Economic Rents at Ground Zero

17.6 Monopoly Power in Input Markets: The Case of Unions
Application 17.6   The Decline and Rise of Unions

17.7 Borrowing, Lending, and the Interest Rate

17.8 Investment and the Marginal Productivity of Capital
The Investment Demand Curve

17.9 Saving, Investment, and the Interest Rate
Equalization of Rates of Return

17.10 Why Interest Rates Differ

17.11 Valuing Investment Projects
Application 17.7   Why Lottery Winners May Not Be "Millionaires"

Learning Objectives

- Investigate a worker's decision concerning how many work hours to supply.
- Examine the income and substitution effects of a higher wage rate and whether the net result of a wage increase involves a worker supplying more work hours.
- Analyze the general level of wage rates and why wages differ among jobs.
- Define what economists mean by the term "rent."
- Explore selling or monopoly power in input markets and show how unions attempt to exercise such power in labor markets.
- Explain how the interest rate is determined through the interplay of the supply of and demand for capital.
- Overview why interest rates differ across specific credit markets.
- Describe the net present value method for analyzing the desirability of undertaking investment projects.

The general principles discussed in Chapter 16 apply to the analysis of the market for any type of input. However, some special issues arise in conjunction with particular input markets, and these deserve further attention. In this chapter, we extend the general analysis to specific input markets to see how wages, rent, interest, and profit are determined. Because labor earnings account for about 75 percent of total U.S. national income, we continue to emphasize labor markets.

17.1 THE INCOME-LEISURE CHOICE OF THE WORKER

In our discussion of consumer demand in Chapters 3 and 4, we assumed the consumer's income to be fixed. For most people, however, income is not fixed; among other things, it depends on the decision about how much time to spend working. To investigate the worker's decision concerning how many work hours to supply, we will assume that the individual worker is paid a fixed hourly wage and can work any number of hours desired at that wage.

LEISURE
the portion of a worker's
time when he or she is not
receiving compensation
from an employer

This analysis utilizes the indifference curve–budget line technique developed in Chapters 3 and 4 for the analysis of consumer choice. In Figure 17.1, the vertical axis measures the individual worker's total weekly income, and the horizontal axis, from left to right, measures the worker's leisure time. The term **leisure** refers to the portion of the worker's time when he or she is not receiving compensation by an employer. Any worker has 168 hours a week available, 24 hours a day, 7 days a week. We divide this time into two mutually exclusive categories, work and leisure. Working time plus leisure time per week must equal 168 hours. In Figure 17.1, Z is the total time available, and the point L_1 indicates that the individual

---

FIGURE 17.1

Income-Leisure Choice of the Worker
Measuring leisure from left to right is the
same as measuring hours worked from
right to left from point Z. The budget line
AZ has a slope equal to the hourly wage
rate. The optimal point is E, with the
individual working ZL_1 hours and earning
$800 per week.

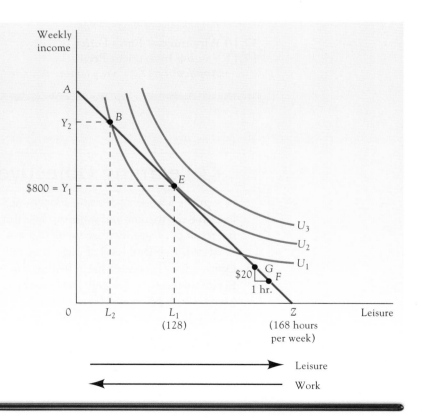

consumes L_1 hours of leisure and supplies the remaining time, ZL_1 hours, to an employer as work effort. Measuring leisure in this way, from left to right, is therefore equivalent to measuring work effort (hours of labor supplied) to the left from point Z.

With income and leisure measured on the axes, a worker's budget line reflects the wage rate received per hour of work provided. In the diagram, the budget line is AZ, and it shows the combinations of income and leisure available to the worker. Note that the more hours the individual works (that is, the less leisure time consumed), the higher the worker's income. For example, if ZL_1 hours are worked (leisure of L_1), income is Y_1, but if work effort increases to ZL_2 hours (leisure decreases to L_2), income rises to Y_2. If no work is done (point Z), income is zero since we assume that the worker has no nonlabor sources of income. Also observe that *the slope of this budget line equals the worker's wage rate*. For example, a movement from point F to point G indicates that the worker is providing one more hour of labor (giving up one more hour of leisure) and in return receives an additional \$20 in wage income. Thus, the hourly wage rate is \$20.

To the worker, both income and leisure are desirable economic goods. For a given amount of leisure, more income is preferred to less, and for a given amount of income, more leisure is preferred to less. As we pointed out in Chapter 3, whenever economic goods are measured on the axes, indifference curves have their normal shapes (downward-sloping, convex, and nonintersecting). The slope of an indifference curve relating income and leisure measures the willingness of the worker to give up leisure for more money income and therefore indicates the relative importance of these two goods to the individual. Figure 17.1 shows three of the worker's income-leisure indifference curves.

The optimal point for the worker is E since this point represents the most preferred combination of income and leisure from among those on the budget line. Work effort is ZL_1 (40 hours per week) and weekly income is Y_1 (\$800). As usual, the optimal point involves a tangency between the budget line and an indifference curve. In this case the tangency indicates that the subjective marginal valuation of the worker's own leisure time is equal to the market valuation of the individual's work time, the wage rate. At point E the worker must be paid at least \$20 to give up one more hour of leisure, since the marginal rate of substitution (MRS) between income and leisure is \$20 per hour at that point.

Note that the optimal point in Figure 17.1 does not result in the worker's income being maximized. For example, the worker could earn a higher income by working longer hours, such as at point B. But the extra Y_1Y_2 income is worth less than the L_1L_2 hours of leisure time that must be sacrificed to earn the additional income, as shown by the fact that point B is on a lower indifference curve than point E. The worker thus is better off by forgoing the higher income (point B) for the sake of more leisure (point E). At point B, the marginal value of leisure exceeds the opportunity cost of leisure (forgone income); thus the worker will increase his or her utility by pursuing additional leisure until the MRS between income and leisure just equals the wage rate.

Is This Model Plausible?

This analysis rests on the assumption that the worker is able to choose how many hours to work. A common objection to the model is that workers don't really have the ability to vary their work hours. Most employment contracts specify that employees will work a certain length of time—perhaps 35 hours per week, for example. Even if an individual employee prefers a 30-hour week combined with a one-seventh reduction in pay, the employer may not provide that option. In short, the argument holds that the workweek is fixed by the employer and beyond the control of the individual worker. There is an element of truth to this point, but it is a less serious criticism than it might appear on first glance.

One way to justify the assumption of variable work effort is to recognize that most workers can, in fact, exercise some degree of control over how much they work, although perhaps not on a daily or weekly basis. Overtime, vacation leave, leaves without pay, moonlighting, sick leave, and early retirement are options available to many workers. At a more basic level, each person has a wide range of options in selecting a job in the first place. Some jobs entail long hours, some short, and some permit considerable variation in work effort. For example, it is not unusual for software programmers to average 80-plus hours of work per week in today's high-tech startups striving to bring new products to market. Many of the same programmers could opt for less demanding information-technology-related jobs in the nonprofit or public sectors that, while requiring fewer hours of work per week, are associated with less promising financial rewards.

Another justification for the variable work effort assumption is that at a more fundamental level the analysis may still be valid for many purposes, even if it is impossible for a worker to vary his or her workweek even slightly. Although the employer fixes the workweek, consider the economic factors that determine the level at which it is set. Employers are profit maximizers, and it is therefore in their interest to cater to the preferences of workers, just as they are led by profit motives to cater to the preferences of consumers. If a firm's employees prefer a 30-hour workweek, but the firm requires them to work 35 hours, it will lose workers to other firms that do a better job of satisfying the employees' preferences. Competition for workers thus leads firms to set workweeks that correspond to worker preferences. So, the assumption that workers can choose how much they will work should yield a reasonably correct analysis, although it does not precisely describe reality.

One qualification should be mentioned. Employers have an incentive to cater to workers' preferences on average, but not necessarily to each employee's preferences. The technology of production requires most firms to have a common workweek for all employees (though it can, and does, differ among firms). A fixed workweek means that workers with preferences different from the group average will not like the workweek schedule. Thus, our model may not be strictly accurate for any specific worker, but it does provide a basis for analyzing work effort decisions involving groups of workers.

17.2　THE SUPPLY OF HOURS OF WORK

Will workers work longer hours at a higher wage rate? The work-leisure choice model can help answer this question. Figure 17.2 examines the effect of a higher wage rate for a particular worker. When the hourly wage rate is $20, the budget line is AZ, and the worker's preferred point is E with ZL_1 work hours supplied. Remember that we measure work effort from right to left in the diagram. If the hourly wage rate rises to $25, the budget line rotates about point Z and becomes steeper. The new budget line is $A'Z$ with a slope of $25 per hour. Note that at the higher wage rate income is greater for any level of work effort. Given the specific preferences of this worker, when confronted with the higher wage rate, the new optimal point E' involves an increase in hours of work, from ZL_1 to ZL_2.

Does a higher wage rate always lead a worker to work more? The answer is no, and we can see why by considering the income and substitution effects associated with a change in the wage rate.

The *substitution effect* of a higher wage rate encourages a worker to supply more hours of labor. When the hourly wage rate rises from $20 to $25, the sacrifice for leisure consumption is greater, since each hour of leisure now means giving up $25 in income instead of $20. Since leisure has become more costly in terms of income lost, the worker is encouraged to substitute away from leisure toward income—that is, to work more.

An *income effect* is also associated with a higher wage rate but has an opposite result on work effort from the substitution effect. A wage increase makes the individual better off, permitting the worker to reach a higher indifference curve. A higher real income tends to

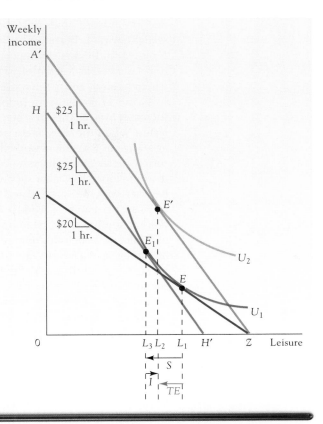

FIGURE 17.2

Worker's Response to a Change in the Wage Rate
A higher wage rate pivots the budget line from AZ to $A'Z$ and work effort increases from ZL_1 to ZL_2. We show the income and substitution effects of the change in the wage rate by using the hypothetical budget line HH' that is parallel to the $A'Z$ budget line but just tangent to the initial indifference curve U_1. The substitution effect, L_1L_3, involves more work, but the income effect, L_3L_2, involves less. In this case the combined effect implies greater work effort at the higher wage rate.

increase the consumption of all normal goods, and leisure for most people is a normal good. The income effect of a wage rate increase thus encourages the consumption of leisure and leads the worker to work less. Because of the higher wage, the worker can afford to work less; it is possible to work fewer hours and still achieve a higher money income than before the wage increase.

Figure 17.2 shows that *the substitution effect of a higher wage rate encourages more work, and the income effect encourages less work.* The hypothetical budget line HH' is drawn tangent to the worker's original indifference curve U_1. Its slope reflects the higher wage rate of $25. The substitution effect is shown as the movement along U_1 from E to E_1. Because leisure has become more costly, the worker consumes less, and work effort increases from ZL_1 to ZL_3. The income effect is shown as the movement from E_1 to E' when we allow the individual to move from the HH' budget line to the parallel $A'Z$ budget line, reflecting the increase in real income associated with the rise in the wage rate. Since leisure is a normal good, the income effect involves more leisure, from L_3 to L_2, which is the same as saying it encourages less work—that is, ZL_2 instead of ZL_3. The total effect of the higher wage rate is the sum of the income and substitution effects. Although these effects operate in opposite directions, in this case the substitution effect is larger, so the total effect is an increase in work hours from ZL_1 to ZL_2.

Is a Backward-Bending Labor Supply Curve Possible?

For the worker whose preferences are depicted in Figure 17.2, the supply curve of work hours slopes upward, at least between wage rates of $20 and $25, since a higher wage leads to a greater quantity of labor supplied. This outcome need not always be the case, however. The income effect of a higher wage may be larger than the substitution effect, resulting in a reduction in work hours at higher pay. The intuition behind such an alternative outcome is straightforward. Beyond some point individuals may prefer to work a little less, take some time off, and enjoy the higher income made possible by a higher salary. For example, 30 hours a week at a wage of $25 per hour means more income and more leisure time with which to enjoy the income when compared to 40 hours at a wage of $5 per hour.

Figure 17.3a shows an individual who will choose to work longer hours when the wage increases from $20 to $25 but will then decide to work somewhat less when the wage rises again. When the wage increases from $20 to $25, work hours increase from ZL_1 to ZL_2, but at a wage of $30, hours worked falls to ZL_3. (We have not separated the income and substitution effects in the diagram, but you may wish to do so.) Figure 17.3b shows the same information plotted as a labor supply curve of weekly work hours. The supply curve slopes upward between wage rates of $20 and $25 but bends backward as the wage rate rises further.

A supply curve of work hours can thus be backward-bending beyond some wage rate. Note that a backward-bending labor supply curve does not depend on an unusual set of circumstances, as does an upward-sloping demand curve; rather, *it just requires that the normal income effect of a higher wage rate exceed the substitution effect.* Leisure is a normal good, so the income and substitution effects always work in opposing directions in the case of a labor supply curve because the worker is a *seller* of labor services. A rise in the price of something an individual sells (such as labor services) has a positive effect on the individual's income and thus leads to greater consumption of all normal goods, including leisure. (In contrast, when the price of something you purchase as a *buyer* increases, the effect on your income is negative. The negative income effect reinforces, rather than counteracts, the substitution

FIGURE 17.3

An Individual Worker's Weekly Supply of Work
(a) An individual's choices of how much to work at three different wage rates are represented by *E*, *E′*, and *E″*. (b) These labor supply choices are plotted as the supply curve of weekly work hours. When the income effect exceeds the substitution effect, the supply curve becomes backward-bending.

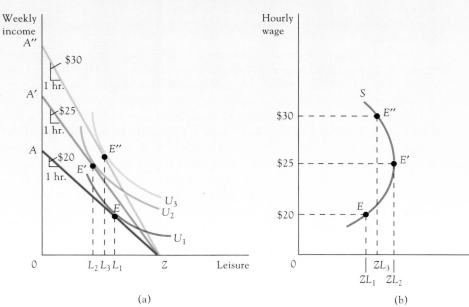

(a)   (b)

effect for a normal good.) Moreover, the income effect of a change in pay is likely to be large relative to the substitution effect since most income derives from providing labor.

The Market Supply Curve

To go from an individual's supply curve of work hours to the market supply curve, we need only horizontally sum the responses of all workers competing in a given labor market. Thus, the market supply curve can also slope upward, bend backward, or show a combination of the two, as shown in Figure 17.3b. Theoretical considerations alone do not permit us to predict the exact shape of the market supply curve. Empirical evidence, however, suggests that it slopes upward (at least for wage rates near present levels), with an elasticity somewhere between 0.1 and 0.3.[1] An elasticity of 0.1 means that a 10 percent increase in the wage rate increases the quantity of labor supplied by 1 percent. Such an inelastic supply curve slopes upward and is almost vertical.

A highly inelastic aggregate supply curve, as suggested by the empirical evidence, appears plausible. Casual observation suggests that the amount of time most people work stays the same over moderate periods of time despite changes in wage rates. If individual supply curves were sharply upward sloping or backward bending, we would see substantial changes in individuals' work hours in jobs where market forces have produced large wage rate changes. Work hours per worker in most jobs seem to be quite stable over time, suggesting that the effect of wage rate changes on work hours is not pronounced. This result does not mean that people are completely unresponsive to wage rate changes, only that the responses that occur are modest.

When should we use the aggregate labor supply curve? In the preceding chapter we emphasized that the labor supply curve *to a particular industry or occupation* is likely to slope upward and be quite elastic. We must distinguish that type of labor supply curve, however, from the one discussed here. In looking at the supply to an industry or occupation, we see that the quantity of labor services *can* increase sharply with a rise in the wage rate in that job, but the increase results mainly from an influx of workers from other jobs or industries and not from a change in work hours of current workers. The supply curve of labor to a specific job or industry therefore depends mainly on how the number of workers varies with wage rates in those specific occupations.

The aggregate labor supply curve is used in cases when the movement of workers between jobs is likely to be significant but the possible change in the hours supplied by workers in their current jobs is. For example, how would a 10 percent increase in all wage rates affect the total quantity of labor supplied? Since all jobs will pay proportionately more, people will have little incentive to change jobs. The only way the total labor supply will increase, therefore, is if people work longer hours (which includes the possibility that some people will enter the labor force for the first time at the higher wage rate). For this type of aggregate analysis, which involves the total quantity of labor supplied across all industries, the market supply curve of work hours is appropriate. We discuss an example using this supply curve in the next section and offer more examples in Chapter 18.

17.3 **THE GENERAL LEVEL OF WAGE RATES**

In analyzing the determination of wage rates, it is convenient to divide the subject into two parts: determination of the general level of wage rates and consideration of why they differ among jobs. In this section we focus on the factors that influence the level of real wages, or

---

[1] For a representative survey of the empirical evidence see U.S. Congressional Budget Office, *An Analysis of the Roth-Kemp Tax Cut Proposal* (Washington, D.C.: U.S. Government Printing Office, 1978).

the average wage rate; we defer until the next section a discussion of the factors that cause a variation in wage rates around the average.

Supply and demand are still the applicable concepts for investigating the level of wage rates. The supply curve of labor indicates the total quantity of labor supplied by all persons at various wage levels. The appropriate supply concept is therefore the aggregate supply curve of work hours discussed in the previous section. This supply curve is probably quite inelastic, like curve S_1 in Figure 17.4.

The aggregate demand curve for labor reflects the marginal productivity of labor to the economy as a whole. Indeed, it is convenient to think of the wage rate as being paid in units of national output (each unit composed of the combination of goods consumed by the average person) to emphasize that we are dealing with the level of *real* wage rates. In constructing the demand curve relevant for a particular time period, the following factors are held constant: capital (including land, buildings, and equipment), technology, and the skills, knowledge, and health of the labor force. If these factors are fixed, an increase in the total quantity of labor is subject to the law of diminishing marginal returns. Consequently, the aggregate marginal product curve slopes downward and is the aggregate demand curve for labor.

At any particular time, if the supply curve is S_1 and the demand curve is D_1 as in Figure 17.4, then the (average) real wage rate is w_1 and employment is L_1. At the high degree of aggregation used in this analysis, the model is necessarily abstract and ignores a multitude of factors that could influence the positions of the demand or supply curves. Yet it highlights the importance of the productivity of labor in determining the level of wages. National output and national income are two sides of the same coin, and with labor receiving about 75 percent of national income (output), it is clear that the factors that determine the output level produced from a given quantity of labor play a central role in the analysis. These factors are primarily (but not exclusively) technology, the skill level of the labor force, and the amounts of other inputs, which in this example we refer to as *capital*.

This concept explains why real wages are so much higher in the United States than in less developed countries: the (marginal) productivity of labor is greater. Marginal productivity is higher because of the factors determining the position of the demand curve: capital, technology, and skills. In U.S. manufacturing industries the amount of capital per worker is about $125,000, contributing to high average and marginal productivity of labor. Technological knowledge is superior in this country, and the U.S. labor force is well educated and

---

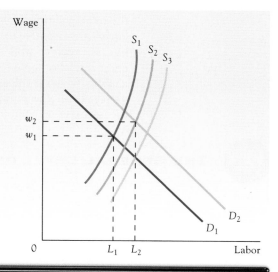

FIGURE 17.4

Determination of the General Wage Level
The aggregate demand curve for labor interacts with the aggregate supply curve to determine the general wage level. Over time, normally both supply and demand increase. If demand increases faster than supply, wage rates tend to rise over time.

highly skilled by international standards. Consequently, output per worker in the United States is much higher. Other factors, such as climate, efficiency of the economic system in allocating the available resources, the degree of political stability, and attitudes toward work, play a role in determining national real wage levels. We can analyze their influence on the productivity of the labor force by examining the way they affect the positions of the demand or supply curves.

Over time, both the demand and supply curves generally shift. Because of saving and investment, the amount of capital tends to grow over time, and this growth shifts the demand curve outward: more capital per worker at each employment level increases marginal productivity. Similarly, technological progress and improvements in the labor force's skill level also increase marginal productivity. On the supply side, the supply curve shifts to the right as the population grows over time. Whether these changes lead to rising or falling real wage rates depends on how much demand shifts relative to supply. In Figure 17.4, if demand increases relatively more, to D_2, while supply increases to S_2, the real wage goes up to w_2. Such an outcome has been the experience in most industrial countries over the past two centuries. Because of capital accumulation, technological progress, and the availability of workers with greater skills, the demand for labor has increased faster than the supply, pulling real wages and living standards up in the process. Unfortunately, this happy outcome is not inevitable.

APPLICATION 17.1 THE MALAISE OF THE 1970s

To most U.S. consumers, who had become accustomed to uninterrupted economic progress since the 1930s, the decade of the 1970s was a shock. Foremost among the decade's economic woes was a failure of many families' incomes to keep pace with inflation. Median family income in constant dollars increased by 33 percent in the 1950s and again in the 1960s. In the 1970s, however, real median family income increased less than 1 percent before taxes. After taxes were paid, many families lost ground.

What went wrong with the U.S. economy in the 1970s? Observers point to a variety of possible culprits: inflation, higher energy prices, reduced national saving and investment, Japanese imports, increased government taxes and regulation, and others. The basic problem was a failure of real wage rates to rise as much as they had in previous decades. Thus, an explanation of the situation should focus on what happened to the supply of and demand for labor. Focusing on supply and demand conditions doesn't rule out the possibility that some of the factors mentioned above could have caused wages to grow less rapidly, but it suggests that a major role may have been played by a factor that most commentators fail to recognize.

During the 1970s the labor force in the United States grew dramatically. Following increases of 12 percent in the 1950s and 19 percent in the 1960s, the labor force grew by 29 percent in the 1970s—the largest increase on record in a single decade. Referring to Figure 17.4, we can see the consequences of such a large increase in the labor force. If the normal increase in supply due to labor force growth over a decade is from S_1 to S_2 (by about 15 percent, for example), then the increase during the 1970s would be shown as the much greater shift in labor supply from S_1 to S_3. With the same increase in demand from D_1 to D_2, the abnormally large increase in labor supply means that over that period wage rates will not rise as much as usual, or might not rise at all.

Table 17.1 provides data on the growth in the labor force and real hourly earnings for the 1950 to 1980 period. A large increase in the labor force in the 1970s was associated with a 2.3 percent decline in real wages over the entire decade. Simple supply and demand forces appear to have been at work.

The increase in the labor force in the 1970s was primarily the result of two factors. First, the number of young persons reaching working age during the decade was unusually large. The "baby boom" generation of the

TABLE 17.1 | **SIZE OF LABOR FORCE AND WAGE RATES, 1950–1980**

	Labor Force (Millions)	Increase over Previous Period (Percentage)	Index of Real Hourly Earnings (1971 = 100)	Increase over Previous Period (Percentage)
1950	62.2	–	64.0	–
1960	69.6	11.9	81.4	27.2
1970	82.8	19.0	95.7	17.6
1980	106.9	29.1	93.5	−2.3

Source: *Economic Report of the President*, 1982.

1950s had grown up. Second, the share of females in the labor force increased from 43 percent in 1970 to 52 percent in 1980. (The labor force participation rate of females had never exceeded 40 percent before 1966.) Each of these factors was significant in itself, but together they spelled an unusually large increase in labor supply. Labor markets, however, adjusted to accommodate this influx of workers, and employment increased by millions more than it had in any previous decade. The relatively large shift in supply meant that wage rates rose less than in previous decades.

What roles did inflation, energy prices, decreased saving, and the other factors so frequently mentioned play in affecting real wage rates? Several caused the demand for labor to grow less rapidly than it had in previous decades and thus reinforced the tendency for wage rates to rise more slowly. For example, a reduced rate of investment and a higher price of oil—an input purchased in large quantities from other countries—both depressed the rate of increase in labor demand. Theory suggests, however, that some of the other factors frequently mentioned, like inflation and higher imports of consumer goods from Japan, would have little effect, since they do not significantly affect productivity. The exact quantitative contribution of each of these factors to the slowdown in the growth of real wages is an unresolved issue and has been the subject of some debate among economists.

The role of other factors notwithstanding, the massive increase in the number of workers in the labor force appears to have had a significant impact on real wages during the 1970s in the United States. Moreover, the supply–demand model appears to offer the correct approach to the question of what caused the decline in real wages during this period.

17.4   WHY WAGES DIFFER

From the market forces that determine the general level of wage rates, we turn now to the question of why there is such wide variation in the wages received by different individuals. In Chapter 16, we explained why wage rates across firms or industries tend to equalize. That analysis depended on the assumptions that workers were identical and that they evaluated the desirability of the jobs only in terms of the money wage rates. Dropping these assumptions, as we must for a fuller understanding of labor markets, suggests that wage rates can differ among jobs and among people employed in the same line of work. People are different in the type of work they are both able and willing to perform, and these differences on the supply side of labor markets produce differences in wage rates.

Perhaps the best way to see what is involved is to take a hypothetical, but plausible, example. Figure 17.5a shows the labor market for clerks, and Figure 17.5b shows the labor market for engineers. Under competitive conditions, the intersection of supply and demand curves in each market yields a wage rate for engineers that is twice that for clerks. We suggest that these markets are in full equilibrium with no tendency for the wage rates to equal-

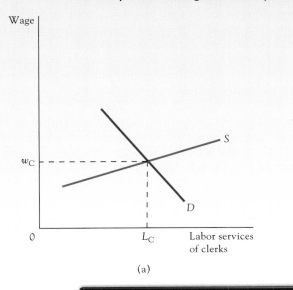
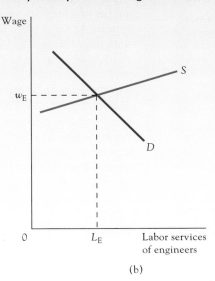

FIGURE 17.5

Equilibrium Wage Differences

(a) The labor market for clerks results in wage rate w_C. (b) The labor market for engineers results in wage rate w_E. Although the wage rate for engineers is higher, there is no tendency for these wage rates to equalize: they are equilibrium wage differences.

(a)

(b)

ize. Is this result possible, and if so, why? Why don't some clerks leave their low-paying jobs and become engineers, a movement that would tend to equalize wage rates in the two occupations? Why don't employers of engineers seek out workers presently employed as clerks and offer them engineering jobs at better pay (but at wage rates slightly below w_E) since their demand curve indicates they would be willing to hire more engineers at a lower wage?

Thinking about these questions suggests several possible answers. First, workers currently employed as clerks may prefer their jobs despite the financial difference; that is, they don't want to work as engineers. Second, acquiring the skills to become an engineer may have a significant cost. The wage for engineers may not be sufficiently high to compensate clerks for the training costs they would have to bear to become engineers. Third, even if there were no training costs, clerks may not have the aptitude for science and mathematics necessary to work as engineers.

Training costs as well as differences in workers' abilities and/or preferences for particular jobs can lead to *equilibrium differences in wage rates* among persons and jobs; there is no tendency toward adjustments that would wipe out wage differentials due to such factors. Now let's take a somewhat more detailed look at these factors.

Compensating Wage Differentials

Monetary compensation is not the only factor, and sometimes not even the most important factor, influencing individuals' job choices. People routinely make decisions to take jobs paying less in monetary terms than they might earn elsewhere. Many academic economists, for example, could earn 50 percent more working for government or industry but choose to remain in a scholarly environment. Similarly, some people might agree to work at the same job for less money if they could live in the Sun Belt instead of the Northeast.

When workers view some jobs as intrinsically more attractive than others, the forces of supply and demand produce differences in the wages paid. These differences are called **compensating wage differentials** because the less attractive jobs must pay more to equalize the real (monetary and nonmonetary) advantages of employment across jobs.

COMPENSATING WAGE DIFFERENTIALS
differences in wages paid that are created by the forces of supply and demand when workers view some jobs as intrinsically more attractive than others

We can illustrate the implications of differences in job attractiveness. Suppose a certain number of potential workers are identical in their abilities to work as police officers or fire fighters. At equal wage rates, they would all prefer to be fire fighters, perhaps because they think police work is a thankless task. Only if the wage rate for police work is at least 25 percent higher than that of fire fighting will they choose to enter the police force. If market conditions determine wage rates, then wage rates for police officers will be 25 percent higher than those for fire fighters. Only then would the *real* wage, in the eyes of the workers, be the same for the two jobs.

Differences in money wage rates are necessary to equate the quantity of labor supplied and demanded in different occupations when the nonmonetary attractiveness of jobs differs. Some cities have ignored this fact and set the same wage rates for police officers and fire fighters. The outcome? A surplus of recruits for fire fighters' positions and a shortage of applicants for the police force.

APPLICATION 17.2   **TWELVE HOURS' PAY FOR TEN MINUTES' WORK**

Each year hundreds of "jumpers" or "glow boys" are hired by public utilities to fix steel pipes in aging power plants.[2] The jumpers work for only 10 minutes at a time and are paid the equivalent of 12 hours of average maintenance wages in addition to free travel and per diems. The only catch is the job site: the pipes are located inside nuclear power plants where radiation is so intense that a jumper can stay for only a limited period of time before, in industry parlance, "burning out." The maximum amount of radioactivity to which a jumper may be exposed is 5,000 millirems per year (the equivalent of 250 chest X-rays). The Nuclear Regulatory Commission, which sets the limit, estimates that if workers are exposed to even that level for 30 years, 5 percent will die of cancer as a result. The high pay earned by jumpers thus illustrates a compensating wage differential: riskier jobs pay more.

[2]"Ten Minutes' Work for 12 Hours' Pay? What's the Catch?," *Wall Street Journal* (October 12, 1983), pp. 1 and 21.

Differences in Human Capital Investment

Our ability to perform useful services can be augmented by training, education, and experience. People can become more productive workers, and more productive workers receive higher wage rates. The process by which people augment their earning capacity is sometimes called **human capital investment.** In these terms, human beings are viewed as capable of generating a flow of productive services over time, much as capital assets can. When they bear the costs of training or education themselves, they are investing in their own earning capacity by attempting to increase the productive services they can provide as workers.

HUMAN CAPITAL INVESTMENT
the process by which people augment their earning capacity

Education and training are much like other investments. Initially, people incur costs. For college students, for example, the explicit and implicit costs include tuition, fees, and forgone income. The payoff to the investment comes several years later; then, you find out how profitable the investment was. If earning capacity has increased sufficiently, the higher earnings in later years cover the initial investment cost. No student needs to be told that this form of investment, like many others, is risky.

Jobs requiring large human capital investments tend to pay higher wages. The reason is simple: if the wages weren't higher, few people would be willing to incur the training costs. The higher wages associated with highly skilled work are, in part, the returns on past investments in human capital. According to this view, it is no accident that college graduates on average earn more than high school graduates or that neurosurgeons earn more than typists.

In terms of our labor supply–demand model, the supply curve tells us that the amount of labor supplied to jobs requiring large investments in human capital will be forthcoming only at higher wage rates. Thus, in Figure 17.5, the supply curve of engineers is positioned higher (vertically) than the supply curve for clerks.

APPLICATION 17.3   THE RETURNS TO INVESTING IN A BA AND AN MBA

A lthough investing in a college education involves some risk, the average return, net of any costs, appears to be greater than ever.[3] As of 1998, according to the U.S. Census Bureau, workers with a college degree made 71 percent more than workers with only a high school diploma. As recently as 1988, college degree holders made just 48 percent more than workers with only a high school diploma. Researchers estimate that as much as 30 to 50 percent of the relative wage gains made by college graduates over the past decade reflect the spread of computer technology and the fact that college-educated workers tend to be more proficient at using computers than their non-college-educated counterparts.

The Census Bureau does not track the median annual income for holders of an MBA degree. According to *Business Week*, however, pursuing an MBA at one of the top 30 schools appears to be a profitable investment. Graduates of these schools landed jobs with median starting salaries of $126,900 in 2000. Prior to enrolling in an MBA program, the same graduates had median earnings of $47,350 per year.

[3]This application is based on: U.S. Department of Commerce, *Money Income in the United States: 1998* (Washington, D.C.: U.S. Government Printing Office, 1999); "The Payoff from Computer Skills," *Business Week* (November 3, 1997), p. 30; and "The Best Business Schools," *Business Week* (October 2, 2000).

Differences in Ability

Workers' productive capacities depend not only on their training and experience (human capital investment) but also on certain inherited traits. The relative importance of these two factors is greatly disputed. For years people have debated whether genetic or environmental factors are more important in explaining IQs. There is no doubt, however, that inherited traits play a significant role in determining what we are capable of doing. No amount of training could turn all of us into nuclear physicists, basketball stars, entertainers, models, politicians, or business executives. People differ in strength, stamina, height, mental ability, physical attractiveness, motivation, creativity, and numerous other traits. These traits, or the lack of them, influence the work we are capable of accomplishing.

Similarly, possessing abilities that are scarce is no guarantee of a high wage. For example, the ability to wiggle your ears may be uncommon but is unlikely to generate a high income. What matters is the supply of persons with abilities required to perform certain jobs relative to the demand for their services. If consumers were unwilling to pay to watch athletes throw balls through a hoop, being able to slam-dunk in 12 different ways would not command a million-dollar salary. Obviously, then, some human abilities are in limited supply relative to demand, and, as a result, those endowed with such abilities can command higher wages.

APPLICATION 17.4   **WHAT'S ON THE OUTSIDE ALSO COUNTS**

A recent study indicates that beauty tends to be rewarded by the labor market.[4] Using interviewers' ratings of respondents' physical appearance, the study found that good-looking people earn higher wages than average-looking people, who in turn earn higher wages

[4]Daniel S. Hamermesh and Jeff E. Biddle, "Beauty and the Labor Market," *American Economic Review*, 84 No. 5 (December 1994), pp. 1174–1194.

than plain-looking people. The wage premium paid by the labor market for good looks is roughly 5 to 10 percent relative to average looks and 10 to 20 percent relative to plain (below average) looks. The wage premium for beauty holds across occupations and for both women and men (if anything, the premium is larger for men than for women). Thus, contrary to the well-known saying, it's not just what's on the inside that counts when determining the wages earned by different workers.

17.5 ECONOMIC RENT

ECONOMIC RENT
that portion of the payment to an input supplier in excess of the minimum amount necessary to retain the input in its present use

In ordinary usage, *rent* refers to payments made to lease the services of land, apartments, equipment, or other durable assets. Economists use the term differently. **Economic rent** is defined as that portion of the payment to an input supplier in excess of the minimum amount necessary to retain the input in its present use. The economic rent accruing to suppliers in input markets is thus analogous to the concept of producer surplus in output markets.

In the history of economics, the term *rent* was originally associated with the payments to landowners for the services of their land. To see why, let's suppose that the supply of land is fixed, so its supply curve is vertical. (This assumption is a slight exaggeration since the supply of usable land is not absolutely fixed; without care land can erode, become overgrown, or lose its fertility.) A vertical supply curve means that landowners will place the same quantity on the market regardless of its price. Even at a zero price the same amount of land would be available. Thus, the minimum payment necessary to retain land in use is zero, and any actual payment above zero exceeds the minimum amount necessary to call forth the supply. *All the payments to landowners therefore satisfy the definition of economic rent.*

Figure 17.6 illustrates this point. The vertical supply curve of land interacts with the demand curve to determine the equilibrium price. The price and quantity are specified per month to indicate that we are concerned not with the sale price of the land but rather with the price for the services yielded by the use of land. The shaded area indicates the monthly income received by land suppliers.[5] The shaded area also equals the economic rent received by landowners, because all payments for the services of land exceed the (zero) amount necessary to have a supply of Q. The position of the demand curve determines the amount of economic rent. If demand increases, the price of land services goes up and the shaded area becomes larger, but the larger shaded area would still be all rent.

Because nineteenth-century economists regarded the supply of land as fixed, they viewed payments to landowners as economic rent. Today economists recognize that suppliers of other inputs may receive economic rent as well. The prices received by the owners of any

[5]In practice, owners often do not receive the income from the use of their land in monetary form. Homeowners, for example, secure the services of the land on which their houses rest. Since they own the land, the income from its use is in the form of these services directly received, but these services have a monetary value determined by supply and demand.

FIGURE 17.6

FIGURE 17.6

Economic Rent with a Vertical Supply Curve
When the input supply curve is vertical, the entire remuneration of
the input (the shaded area) represents economic rent, since the
same quantity would be available even at a zero price.

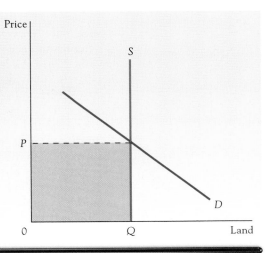

input in fixed supply are entirely rent, and part of the prices received by inputs with upward-sloping supply curves are also rent. Consider the supply of university professors. For clarity, let's examine the discrete case involving a small number of persons. The supply curve is then the step-like relationship in Figure 17.7. In equilibrium, five professors are working: individuals A, B, C, D, and E. We assume that they are identically productive as professors but not identical in their abilities to perform other jobs.

Individual A will be *willing* to work as a professor if paid area A_1. Even at a very low wage he will opt for the academic life because his next best employment opportunity is as a dishwasher, where he would earn very little. Individual B has a better alternative; she could sell used cars. She will work in academe if she receives at least area B_1. And so we progress up the supply curve. The supply curve slopes upward because to attract more people, colleges must bid them away from increasingly more attractive alternative employments.

FIGURE 17.7

Economic Rent with an Upward-Sloping Supply Curve
With an upward-sloping input supply curve, part of the
payment to input owners represents rent. In this case
individuals A, B, C, and D receive rent equal to areas
A_2, B_2, C_2, and D_2, respectively.

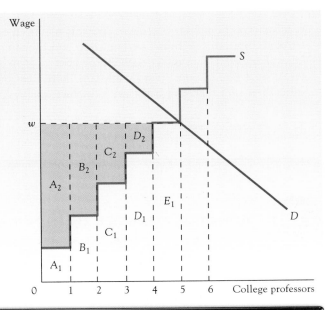

When this labor market is in competitive equilibrium, individuals A to E will all be paid a wage of w. A wage equal to w means that individual A receives an amount greater than the minimum necessary to induce him to work as a professor. Recall that the minimum amount is area A_1, but he is being paid area A_1 plus area A_2, so area A_2 represents an economic rent. Individuals B, C, D, and E receive rents equal to areas B_2, C_2, D_2, and zero, respectively. Individual E receives just enough pay to induce him to supply his services as a professor. If the wage were any lower, he would work elsewhere, so none of his earnings represents rent.

In this example, part of the earnings of professors (except for E) are economic rent, and the remainder is the payment required to keep the individuals from leaving their academic jobs and working elsewhere. The total rent received is the sum of the colored areas. Whenever the supply curve of any input slopes upward, part of the payment to inputs will be rent, as in this example. The more inelastic the supply curve, the larger the rent as a fraction of the total payment to an input. In the extreme case of perfectly inelastic supply (Figure 17.6), all the payment represents rent.

APPLICATION 17.5   **THE BAY AREA REAL ESTATE FRENZY: ECONOMIC RENTS AT GROUND ZERO**

Although labor—*human capital*—has been the primary input in the ongoing development of the high technology industry, land still plays a role in the production process. After all, it takes office space to bring together the engineers, software programmers, and entrepreneurs who have been the wellspring of success for firms such as Oracle, Cisco, Hewlett-Packard, Intel, Yahoo!, Netscape, Apple, and Silicon Graphics.

As an input in the high technology production process, land has garnered heightened economic rents on account of the industry's growth—notably in epicenters of the industry such as San Francisco and Silicon Valley. For example, in the late 1990s, the price of commercial real estate more than doubled in both areas.[6] Annual rents for high-end San Francisco office space—

bayfront properties that overlook the bridges and offer dazzling views—were nearing $100 per square foot in 2000, while the vacancy rate for such space was a tiny 0.78 percent. Rents in Palo Alto, in the heart of Silicon Valley, were running as high as $120 per square foot annually, while the vacancy rate was at 0.19 percent. At $120 per square foot, a 50-by-100-foot space costs $600,000 per year in office rental costs.

With the dramatic rise in commercial real estate rates, even office space in San Francisco's neighborhoods known for drug trafficking and homeless problems were being renovated and leased. Some entrepreneurs interested in a San Francisco location opted to launch venture operations in garages of family members or friends, or in rented two-room apartments, with one room being reserved for sleeping quarters and the other serving as the basis of operations for the new venture.

[6]"S.F. Space Race: Commercial Real Estate Scarce," *SJMercury.com* (July 30, 2000).

17.6   MONOPOLY POWER IN INPUT MARKETS: THE CASE OF UNIONS

In Chapter 16 we examined the hiring of inputs by firms operating in either perfectly competitive or monopoly output markets. We also explored the effects of buying or monopsony power in input markets. We did not, however, address selling or monopoly power in input markets. We do so here by focusing on labor unions. If effectively organized, labor unions are the sole supplier of an input—namely, the labor services of the union's members—and thus have some influence over the wages union members are paid. Much as a monopolist in a product market seeks a price and an output level so as to maximize profit, a labor union may seek a wage and employment level so as to maximize the economic rent accruing to its members.

Consider Figure 17.8, where the demand and supply of labor to a market are given by the curves D and S. These curves depict the quantity of labor services demanded and supplied, respectively, at various possible wage rates absent any monopsony or monopoly power. Under competitive conditions, L_C workers are hired at a wage rate of w_C.

Now suppose that workers unionize and effectively cartelize the supply side of the market depicted in Figure 17.8. By organizing, the union's members acquire monopoly power and

FIGURE 17.8

The Effect of an Input Market Monopoly
An effectively organized union represents a monopoly in the market for labor services. To maximize economic rent, the union selects the employment level where the marginal revenue, in terms of additions to the union's wage bill, from having an additional worker hired (the height of the *MR* curve) equals the opportunity cost needed to induce the worker to work (the height of the *S* curve). The union employment level is L_U at a wage rate of w_U. The economic rent accruing to the union equals area $w_U ABF$.

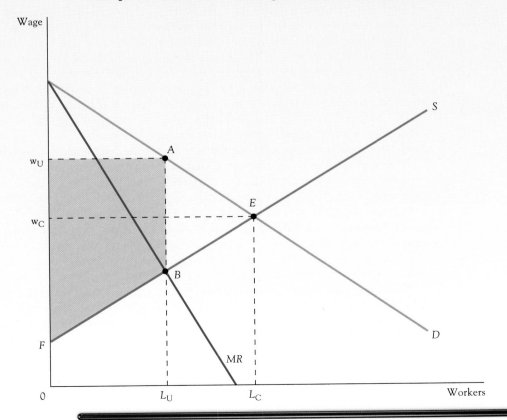

can exercise that power by selecting any wage–employment level combination on the demand curve for labor services confronting the union.[7]

What point on the demand curve for their services should a union's members select if they are interested in maximizing their economic rent? Analogous to the case of monopoly power in output markets, the union needs to take into account the marginal revenue curve, MR, associated with the demand curve for its services. The marginal revenue curve represents the additional wages earned by the union membership as a whole when an incremental worker is hired. The marginal revenue curve lies below the demand curve at all employment levels since the hiring of an additional worker requires the union to lower the wage level paid to all previously employed workers. The reduced payments to previously employed workers must be subtracted from the wage earned by the incremental worker (the height of the demand curve) to derive the additional wages earned by the union as a whole (the height of the marginal revenue curve) when the incremental worker is hired.

To maximize economic rent, the union compares the additional wages resulting from the hiring of another worker (MR) with the bare minimum the worker needs to be paid to work in this market—the worker's opportunity cost. The height of the supply curve represents the bare minimum that needs to be paid to induce an incremental worker to work at various possible total employment levels and thus is effectively the union's marginal cost curve. Much as profit in an output market is maximized by setting marginal revenue equal to marginal cost, the economic rent earned by a labor union's members is maximized by selecting an employment level, L_U, where MR intersects S in Figure 17.8. Up to L_U, every worker contributes more to the union's total wage payments than it costs to induce him or her to work. The wage rate set by the union-monopoly is w_U and the economic rent accruing to the union membership as a whole is depicted by area $w_U ABF$—the excess of the wage rate over workers' opportunity costs from zero to the quantity of labor services sold, L_U, by the union-monopoly.

Note that in Figure 17.8 fewer workers end up being employed as a result of the union than under competitive conditions. This is because the union is presumed to be interested in maximizing the economic rent accruing to its membership rather than the number of workers having jobs. The economic rent from the monopoly outcome of L_U and w_U (area $w_U ABF$) exceeds the economic rent associated with the competitive outcome of L_C and w_C (area $w_C EF$).

By restricting output in the market for labor and raising the prevailing wage rate, the union illustrated in Figure 17.8 produces a deadweight loss similar to the one resulting from monopoly in output markets. Triangular area AEB is the deadweight loss associated with the labor union. This can be seen by noting that in order to maximize economic rent, the union restricts labor employment to L_U from L_C. Each worker between L_U and L_C can generate more in terms of the value of output produced (the height of the D curve) than it costs to induce the worker to work (the height of the S curve). These potential net gains are not realized, however, because a labor union interested in maximizing economic rent does not care about the total value of the output produced by an incremental worker (the height of the demand curve). Rather, such a union cares about the incremental worker's contribution to the union's total wage bill (the height of the MR curve).

While acknowledging the potential deadweight loss associated with unions, some economists have argued for a more benign evaluation of their role since they may be organized to counteract monopsony power possessed by input-buying firms.[8] For example, in this view, the United Auto Workers union arose out of the need to protect workers' rights and wages

---

[7]For ease of discussion we assume that the union cannot engage in price discrimination, securing different wages for its various members. When an input supplier can price discriminate, an analysis analogous to the one presented in Chapter 12 on price discrimination in output markets is applicable.

[8]See, for example: "Unions Need Not Apply," *New York Times* (July 26, 1999), pp. C1 and C14; and Richard B. Freeman and James L. Medoff, *What Do Unions Do?* (New York: Basic Books, 1984).

from the actions of the "Big Three" automobile companies. Furthermore, to the extent that unions set up effective grievance procedures and give workers a "voice" with their employers, they may actually make workers more satisfied and productive on the job (the height of the labor demand curve shifts upward if workers become more productive, all else equal).

There is some empirical evidence that, controlling for other factors, union workers not only receive higher wages but also are more productive than nonunion workers. Most economists, however, are skeptical that unions actually improve workers' productivity. One would expect the value of the final output produced by an additional worker to increase the fewer the number of workers hired. Fewer workers have more of the other, nonlabor inputs to share between themselves and thus, if the law of diminishing returns holds, have higher marginal products.

In Figure 17.8, for example, the height of the labor demand curve reflects the value of the final output produced by an incremental worker and could be used as a measure of worker productivity. According to such a measure, workers are more productive at the union employment level of L_U than at the competitive level of L_C. This does not imply, however, that the union has made each worker more productive. The height of the demand curve at an employment level L_U is just as high under a union-monopoly as it is with perfect competition. Once again it is important to distinguish between a movement along a given demand curve (in this case a labor demand curve) and a potential shift of the entire demand curve.

APPLICATION 17.6   THE DECLINE AND RISE OF UNIONS

Labor unions in the United States have undergone dramatic membership changes over the past few decades.[9] In the private sector, the percentage of nonagricultural wage and salary workers who are union members has plummeted from 38 percent in the early 1950s to 9 percent in the late 1990s. By contrast, over the same time period, public sector union membership has skyrocketed from 10 to 37 percent.

What accounts for the different fortunes of private and public sector unions in the United States over the past few decades? Public sector unions have grown in relative importance due to changes in labor laws favorable to the unionization of government workers at all levels of government throughout the 1960s and 1970s. Prior to the 1960s, collective bargaining by most government workers was illegal.

In the private sector, the rapid growth of the high technology sector explains some of the overall decline in union membership in the United States. Only a small fraction of the 5 million employees who work for computer semiconductor and software companies are

unionized. This is due to demand for such workers growing much more quickly than the supply and companies promising generous salaries and stock options to recruit and retain workers—rewards that diminish the relative benefits workers could obtain through unionization.

Furthermore, growing international competition in certain industries, such as automobile production, and the enhanced competitiveness of other deregulated industries, such as trucking and airlines, have made the output demand curves for firms operating in these industries more price elastic. As we saw in the previous chapter, one of the factors that determines the elasticity of demand for an input (and hence the monopoly power of sellers of that input) is the elasticity of the demand for the final product produced by the input. For example, the monopoly power possessed by the United Auto Workers has been lessened as American car manufacturers have faced growing foreign competition. In the 1950s, when foreign competition was more limited, the demand for General Motors (GM) cars was more price inelastic and any wage increase demanded by the United Auto Workers from GM could more readily be passed on to final consumers and so agreed to by GM.

[9]"Public and Private Unionization," *Journal of Economic Perspectives*, 2 No. 2 (Spring 1988), pp. 59–110.

17.7   BORROWING, LENDING, AND THE INTEREST RATE

INTEREST RATE
(1) the price paid by
borrowers for the use of
funds, and (2) the rate of
return earned by capital
as an input in the
production process

This chapter has so far focused on labor markets. We now turn to the market for another critical input, capital. We begin our discussion with a term, **interest rate**, that has two apparently different meanings in economics. *Interest rate* sometimes refers to the price paid by borrowers for the use of funds. When a person borrows $100 this year and must return $110 to the lender a year later, the additional $10 is interest, and the ratio of the interest to the principal amount, 10 percent, is the annual interest rate. *Interest rate* can also refer to the rate of return earned by capital as an input in the production process. When a person purchases a machine for $5,000, and the use of that machine generates $500 in income each year thereafter, the rate of return is 10 percent. Economists designate both the return on loaned funds and the return on invested capital as *interest rates* because there is a tendency for these returns to become equal.

To explore the determinants of the interest rate, let's start with a simple example. Suppose that no capital investment is taking place; that is, no investors are using borrowed funds to finance building construction or equipment purchases. Although there is no borrowing for investment purposes, there will still be people who wish to lend money and others who wish to borrow. Households whose current incomes are high in comparison with their expected future incomes may be willing to lend to others and use the repayment of the loan to augment their otherwise lower ability to consume in the future. Other households may wish to borrow in order to consume more than their current income in the present, repaying the loan in the future. These households are the potential suppliers and demanders of consumption loans, and their interaction determines a price, or interest rate, for borrowed funds.

The level of the interest rate affects both the quantity supplied and quantity demanded of loanable funds. The suppliers of funds are saving—that is, consuming less than their current income allows. As noted in Chapter 5, a higher interest rate has opposing income and substitution effects on the amount saved. The substitution effect encourages less present consumption (more saving) because each dollar saved returns more in the future. The income effect, however, increases the real incomes of savers, encouraging more present consumption and less saving. On balance, a higher interest rate may lead to more or less saving. The supply of loanable funds from savers is likely to slope upward at low interest rates but can become backward bending at sufficiently high interest rates. This curve is analogous to the supply curve of hours of work.

On the other side of the market, the demand curve for funds from borrowers must slope downward. To a borrower, a higher interest rate has income and substitution effects, both of which reduce the level of desired borrowing. The substitution effect reflects the fact that a higher interest rate makes it more expensive to finance increased consumption from borrowed funds, inhibiting borrowing. The income effect reflects the fact that a higher interest rate reduces the real income of borrowers, so they cannot afford to borrow as much.

Figure 17.9 illustrates the interaction of borrowers and lenders in the market for consumption loans. The supply of saving (funds to lend) is S_S, and the demand for these funds by borrowers for consumption purposes is D_C. Equilibrium occurs when lenders provide $10 million to borrowers in the present time period, with borrowers agreeing to repay the loans at an interest rate of 5 percent.

In this simple example the funds saved are not used in a way that increases the output of goods through capital accumulation. Yet saving is productive. It provides the means for borrowers to have a consumption pattern over time that is more to their liking than having to live within their incomes each year, and these preferences explain why borrowers are willing to pay for the use of borrowed funds. A positive interest rate emerges because lenders must receive compensation for sacrificing their use of the funds for present consumption.

FIGURE 17.9

A Borrowing-Lending Equilibrium
If there is no investment demand for funds, the demand for consumption loans and the supply of saving determine the interest rate. Here people borrow $10 million to finance present consumption with the commitment to repay it plus 5 percent interest.

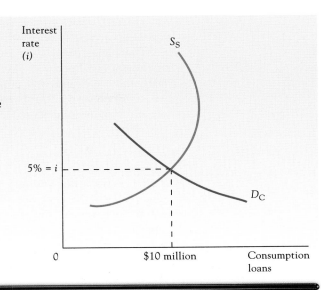

17.8 INVESTMENT AND THE MARGINAL PRODUCTIVITY OF CAPITAL

In the consumption loan example, the only outlet for the funds supplied by savers is the borrowing by other households to finance consumption. Now let's expand the analysis to account for the fact that saving also provides funds used to finance investments. Firms may borrow money for the purpose of enlarging their stock of capital equipment, and they must compete for the limited supply of saving with households that are borrowing to finance consumption.

Why are firms willing to incur interest costs to finance investments in capital? Basically, the reason is that capital contributes sufficiently to production to repay the interest costs. For example, if Robinson Crusoe fishes by hand, he may be able to catch 20 fish per week. If he takes one week off to weave a net, he can then catch 25 fish a week with the net until it wears out in 10 weeks. Unfortunately, Crusoe is going to get very hungry if he doesn't eat for a week. However, if he borrows 10 fish from his Man Friday, on the condition that he pays back the 10 fish plus an extra 5 fish, he can catch an additional 5 fish a week.

The 5 additional fish caught per week for 10 weeks (50 fish) are a measure of the **gross marginal productivity** of the net. Whether the net (the capital) is productive depends on whether the gain in output outweighs the cost of not fishing for a week so he could weave a net. Since Crusoe could have caught 20 fish that week, the cost of the net is a sacrifice of 20 fish plus the 5 fish paid as interest on the 10 borrowed fish. (The 10 borrowed fish are not a cost; he borrowed 10 and returned 10, so the cost is zero.)

By sacrificing 25 fish, Crusoe gains 50 fish over the life of the net, representing a gain of 25 fish. In this example, capital—the net—is productive in the sense that its **net** (no pun intended) **marginal productivity** is 25 fish. When the capital's net marginal productivity is positive, investment—the act of adding to the amount of capital—allows Crusoe to produce a larger output even after "netting" out the cost of the capital. (Note as a brief aside that Man Friday also benefits, as he picks up an extra 5 fish for his trouble.)

Next, we need a measure for the net productivity of investment in capital that allows us to compare the productivities of various projects. The annual percentage rate of return is

GROSS MARGINAL PRODUCTIVITY
the total addition to productivity that capital investment contributes

NET MARGINAL PRODUCTIVITY
the total addition to productivity that capital investment contributes, less the cost of capital

convenient for this purpose. Suppose a machine costs $100 to construct this year and its use next year will add $120 to output. For simplicity we will let the machine wear out after one year's use. Then the net gain is $20 in one year, an annual rate of return on the initial $100 investment of 20 percent. The 20 percent figure is the net marginal productivity of investment, and it measures how much the capital investment will add to output one year hence per unit of present cost. It is essentially the rate of return on the investment. Denoting this rate of return measure of productivity by g, we can calculate it from the formula:

$$C = R/(1 + g) \qquad or$$

$$\$100 = \$120/(1 + g); \tag{1}$$

where C is the initial cost and R is the resulting addition to output (capital's gross marginal value product) the next year. When capital equipment yields services over more than one year, the normal case, the principle is the same but the formula is slightly more complicated. Suppose the equipment lasts for 2 years before wearing out and adds $60 to output after one year (R_1) and $81 in the second year ($R_2$). Then, we calculate the rate of return from:

$$C = [R_1/(1 + g)] + [R_2/(1 + g)^2] \qquad or$$

$$100 = [\$60/(1 + g)] + [\$81/(1 + g)^2]. \tag{2}$$

Given the initial cost of the equipment and the contribution to output in each year, we can solve this expression for g. In this example the rate of return is 0.25, or 25 percent per year.[10]

The Investment Demand Curve

The net productivity of a capital investment, g, depends on the value of additional output generated (the R terms) and on the initial cost (the C term). In turn, the C and R terms depend on many factors, among them the size and skills of the labor force, the amount and costs of other inputs such as natural resources, technology, and the degree of political stability. When we hold these other factors constant, the net productivity of investment also depends on the rate of investment undertaken per time period. The greater the rate of investment, the lower the net *marginal* productivity of still more investment.

Consider the rate of investment for the economy as a whole. As investment increases, each additional dollar's worth of capital adds less to output than the previous dollar's worth because of the law of diminishing marginal returns; more capital applied to a given labor force and quantity of land causes its marginal product to decline. This factor reduces the R terms in the formula and contributes to a lower rate of return. In addition, an increase in investment also means more demand for machinery, vehicles, buildings, and other types of capital, which tends to raise their prices. This factor increases the initial cost of investment, the C term, and also contributes to a lower rate of return.

Taken together, these factors imply that a lower rate of return will be associated with a greater amount of investment, other things being equal. The downward-sloping D_1 curve in Figure 17.10 illustrates this point. When investment is at a level of I_0, g is equal to 15 percent. If investment increases to I_1, the rate of return on invested capital falls to 10 percent.

The D_1 curve, indicating the rate of return generated by different investment levels, is the **investment demand curve.** This idea is easiest to understand if we suppose that firms and individuals finance their investments by borrowing. If the interest rate is 10 percent, investment expands to I_1, where the return on the investment just covers the cost of the borrowed funds. At any lower investment level, the rate of return on investment will be higher

INVESTMENT DEMAND CURVE
the relationship between the rate of return generated and various levels of investment

---

[10]In the general case where equipment lasts n years, the formula is: $C = [R_1/(1 + g)] + [R_2/(1 + g)^2] + [R_3/(1 + g)^3] + \ldots + [R_n/(1 + g)^n]$.

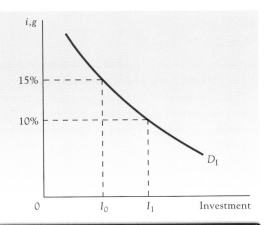

FIGURE 17.10

Investment Demand Curve
The D_I curve shows the rate of return generated by alternative investment levels. It is the investment demand curve, and it shows the amount invested at various interest rates.

(15 percent at I_0, for example), yielding a pure economic profit to firms and individuals who are only paying 10 percent for the funds they are investing. An expansion in investment will occur as long as the rate of return is greater than the cost of borrowed funds, and such an expansion causes the rate of return to fall. Equilibrium results when investments yield a return just sufficient to cover the interest rate on borrowed funds, at I_1 when the interest rate is 10 percent. *Thus, the rate of return on capital investment* (g) *tends to equal the interest rate for borrowed funds* (i).

Even if investment is not financed by borrowing, I_1 still is the equilibrium investment level if the interest rate is 10 percent. For example, a firm with $1 million in retained earnings can use this sum to finance an equipment acquisition, but it will not do so unless the investment yields at least 10 percent. Why? Because the firm can lend the $1 million at the 10 percent interest rate; if the investment project yields less than 10 percent, the firm can do better by lending funds rather than investing them. The opportunity cost of investing is the same whether the funds are borrowed or acquired in any other way, so the 10 percent interest rate guides investment decisions in either case.

Our discussion of investment decisions assumes that firms and individuals know the rate of return generated by investments. In most cases, however, investors do not know, since rates of return depend on what happens in the future. The investment demand curve reflects what investors *expect* the outcome of investment projects to be. After the fact, some investments expected to yield 10 percent fail to do so, and others do better. For given expectations on the part of actual and potential investors, the demand curve still slopes downward. A change in expectations causes the entire curve to shift. If investors expect nationalization of industry or violent revolution to occur in a country, the demand shifts far to the left, one reason firms are reluctant to invest in countries with unstable political regimes.

17.9 SAVING, INVESTMENT, AND THE INTEREST RATE

Households with a demand for consumer loans, and firms and persons with investment projects, compete for funds supplied by savers. So far we have discussed these elements separately; Figure 17.11 brings them together. The demand curve for consumer loans is D_C, and D_I is the investment demand curve. The horizontal summation of these curves yields D_T, the total demand for funds supplied by savers. The total demand in conjunction with the supply of savings determines the interest rate. At the market-determined interest rate of 10 percent,

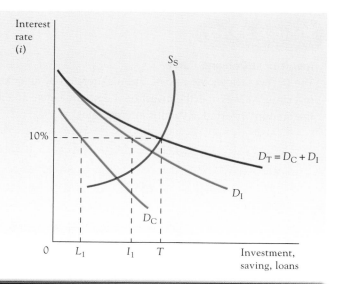

FIGURE 17.11

The Equilibrium Levels of Saving, Investment, Consumer Loans, and the Interest Rate

The total demand for funds supplied by savers, D_T, is the sum of the investment demand curve, D_I, and the demand for consumer loans, D_C. The intersection of D_T and S_S determines the interest rate. Investment is I_1, saving is T, and consumer loans are L_1.

consumer loans are L_1 and investment is I_1, with the sum equal to T. As drawn, the investment demand is much greater than consumer loan demand. This tends to be the real-world case.

In this model, the gross saving of households and firms, T, is not equal to investment, I_1; consumer loans account for the difference. Economists sometimes define saving as net of consumer loans ($T - L_1$), and in that definition net saving equals investment. (We have also ignored the government's demand for funds to help finance budget deficits. Including that factor would create another demand for funds supplied by savers.)

The Figure 17.11 analysis corresponds to the aggregate labor demand and supply model since we are talking about the supply and demand for funds aggregated across all saving-lending and borrowing-investment markets. It is important to recognize that there is not just one big special market that determines the interest rate but many closely interrelated markets that we are summarizing. Bond markets, stock markets, mortgage borrowing, credit card loans, bank deposits and loans, investment of retained earnings by firms, and other markets are all involved in this process of allocating funds, provided by a multitude of sources, among different competing uses. We lose some detail by using an aggregated model (as we did in the labor market model), but we gain the important advantage of emphasizing the common underlying factors affecting all the interrelated markets: namely, the willingness to consume less than current income and the existence of profitable investment opportunities.

Investment in excess of the amount required to replace worn-out capital adds to the stock of productive capital, which, in turn, increases the productive capacity of the economy in subsequent periods. Figure 17.12 illustrates this effect. In the present year, a society's production possibility frontier (PPF) relating the attainable output of consumer goods and capital goods is FF'. The production of capital goods requires the use of resources (inputs) that can otherwise be used to produce consumer goods, so if more capital goods are produced, fewer consumer goods are available, and vice versa. The market forces summarized in Figure 17.11 determine where we are located on this frontier. Investment of I_1 in Figure 17.11 means an addition to the stock of capital of that amount and corresponds to a point

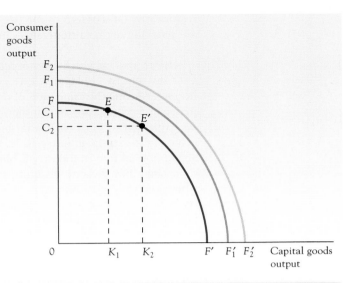

FIGURE 17.12

The Level of Investment and Productive Capacity
Greater investment in the present—E' rather than
E—means less current consumption—C_2 versus
C_1—but greater capacity to produce goods in the
future. When K_1 is invested in year 1, the
production frontier in year 2 is F_1F_1'; if K_2 is
invested, it is F_2F_2'.

such as K_1 in Figure 17.12. With more capital available the following year, the productive
capacity of the economy increases. When K_1 is invested in year 1, the *PPF* becomes F_1F_1' in
year 2. If investment were greater in year 1—for instance, at K_2 (point E')—then the *PPF*
would move out even farther, to F_2F_2'. The effect of capital investment on the position of
the *PPF* in subsequent periods is due to the productivity of capital discussed in Section 17.8.
(There are also other reasons why the *PPF* shifts over time—most importantly, growth in
the labor force, investment in human capital, and technological progress.)

Investing more in the present time period thus means that incomes and consumption are
greater in the future. Still, we should avoid drawing the conclusion that an ever-increasing
expansion in investment is desirable. To invest more, less must be consumed; that is, for an
increase in investment from K_1 to K_2, consumption must fall from C_1 to C_2. Thus, the cost
of greater investment (yielding higher future income) is increased saving (reduced consumption) in the present. The saving supply curve shows how much households must be paid in
return for providing funds for investment purposes. At the Figure 17.11 optimal point,
households will supply more saving than T only if they receive an interest rate higher than
10 percent. Investors, however, will be unwilling to pay savers more than 10 percent for additional funds since the increased investment yields less than a 10 percent return. As a result, the market is in equilibrium with investment of I_1.

Equalization of Rates of Return
There is a tendency for capital to be allocated among firms and across industries so that the
rate of return is equal everywhere. This tendency parallels the tendency of labor to be allocated so that wage rates are equal. In the case of labor, however, we pointed out a number of
reasons why wages differ because of differences in the productivities and preferences of people. With capital, fewer qualifications are necessary. A firm purchasing a machine is indifferent to the source of funds for financing; one person's money can purchase as much capital as
another's. Moreover, a person supplying funds usually doesn't care whether the funds are
used to finance a computer in the aerospace industry or a truck in the construction industry;
lenders care only about the rate of return earned on the saving. There are, of course, some

reasons why rates of return won't be exactly equal, such as differing degrees of risk, but they are generally not quantitatively as important as the factors that produce differences in wage rates.

The process by which rates of return tend to equalize is much like the process for labor. Let's say that two industries, *E* (for entertainment) and *S* (for steel), are initially in equilibrium, earning the same rates of return on invested capital. Next, let an unexpected shift in demand occur. Suppose consumers' demand for *E* increases and their demand for *S* falls. As explained in Chapter 9, the short-run effects are economic profits in industry *E* and economic losses in industry *S*. In terms of the return to capital, capital now earns an above-normal rate in industry *E* but a below-normal rate in industry *S*. (A normal rate of return signifies the rate of return investors can expect to earn on capital invested elsewhere and thus represents the opportunity cost of capital.) The owners of capital in industry *S* have an incentive to shift their investments to industry *E*, where the return is higher. As capital (and other resources, too) moves from *S* to *E*, the output of industry *E* expands, and price falls until the industry earns a normal return (zero profit). The opposite happens in industry *S*: the industry contracts, investors withdraw capital, price rises, and once again the industry earns a normal return. This process describes how industries adjust in response to a change in consumer demand from the perspective of the market for the input, capital.

17.10   WHY INTEREST RATES DIFFER

Although we have been discussing *the* rate of interest and its relationship to *the* rate of return on capital, you should realize that this description is a simplification, just as it was when we discussed *the* wage rate in the aggregate labor supply–demand model. There is, in fact, a range of interest rates, and *the* interest rate in an aggregate model is best thought of as shorthand for "the general level of interest rates." In that sense the model developed in the preceding sections is extremely helpful in pinpointing important determinants of the level of interest rates.

Differences can exist in specific interest rates in equilibrium, although the differences are less pronounced than differences in wage rates. The four most important reasons for differences in interest rates are as follows:

1. *Differences in risk.* There is always the possibility that a loan will not be repaid. The greater the risk that a borrower will default, the higher the interest rate that a lender will charge. If there is a one-in-five chance of a default, for example, the lender will have to charge an interest rate about 25 percent higher than for no-risk loans to receive the same expected return. For this reason corporate bonds pay higher interest rates than do government bonds, and loans secured by collateral (like home mortgages) involve lower interest rates than installment credit.
2. *Differences in the duration of the loan.* Borrowers will generally pay more for a loan that does not have to be repaid for a long time since it gives them greater flexibility. Usually, lenders must also receive a higher interest rate to part with funds for extended periods. This is one reason why savings accounts, where the funds can be withdrawn on short notice, pay lower interest rates than six-month certificates of deposit.
3. *Cost of administering loans.* A small loan usually involves greater bookkeeping and servicing costs per dollar of the loan than a large loan. Loans repaid in frequent installments, such as automobile loans, also involve higher administrative costs. When greater costs are associated with administering loans, the borrower must cover these costs and thus pay a higher interest rate.

4. *Differences in tax treatment.* The way the tax system treats interest income and investment income is very complex, and it sometimes leads to divergences in interest rates that would otherwise be more nearly equal. For example, the interest paid by state and local governments on municipal bonds is not taxable under the federal income tax, but the interest on otherwise comparable corporate bonds is. The after-tax returns are what guide lenders' decisions, and they will tend to be brought into equality, implying a difference in the before-tax (market) rates of interest. The result is that state and local governments can borrow at lower rates of interest than corporations.

Although these factors lead to divergences in interest rates in specific credit markets, they should not obscure the common factors that affect all interest rates. For example, if the public decides to save less (a leftward shift in the S_S curve), all these rates would go up, as would the rate of return on invested capital.

17.11 VALUING INVESTMENT PROJECTS

Our discussion of interest rates suggests a means by which profit-maximizing firms or individuals can determine if undertaking a particular investment is worthwhile. To see how investment projects may be valued, let's use an extremely simple example: namely, let's discard any differences between specific interest rates due to risk, tax considerations, and the like. There is only one interest rate, i, that reflects the annual rate at which one can borrow or lend money. Furthermore, let's assume that there is no change in the price level over time, so that i reflects both the nominal and the real rate of interest. In such a setting, consider the case of a hospital administrator contemplating a $1.4 million investment in a CAT (computerized axial tomography)-scanning machine. The machine will generate $500,000 in annual net revenue in each of the first three years before wearing out. Should the administrator make the investment?

As with most other questions in economics, the correct answer is, "It depends." In our specific example, the answer depends on the level of the interest rate, i—the opportunity cost of using money over time. If i equals zero and there is no opportunity cost to using money over time, then the investment in the CAT-scanning machine is clearly worthwhile. In such a case, a payoff of $1 a year from now is worth the same as a dollar in the bank today; $1 saved in the bank (or invested in capital, for that matter) generates zero interest and consequently still equals $1 at the end of the year. The $500,000 payoff generated by the CAT-scanning machine a year into the investment thus is equivalent to $500,000 in the bank at the present time. The additional $500,000 generated 2 years into the investment is also equivalent to $500,000 in the bank at the present time (since the interest rate or opportunity cost of using money for each of the first 2 years is zero percent). The same logic applies to the third-year payoff. In total, if the interest rate is zero, the machine provides a payoff equivalent to $1.5 million in terms of present dollars ($500,000 in each of the first 3 years) and therefore generates more in net revenue than the $1.4 million investment cost confronting the administrator.

If the interest rate is greater than zero, the answer is less clear-cut. Suppose, for example, that the annual interest rate, i, is 10 percent. One dollar invested in the bank today generates $1(1 + i) = \$1(1 + 0.1) = \$1.10$ a year from now. Moreover, the **present discounted value** (*PDV*) of $1 paid a year from now is the amount of money, X_1, placed in the bank today that will yield $1 a year from now at the interest rate, i. Since we are looking for the sum X_1 that when multiplied by $(1 + i)$ will yield $1 a year from now, we can solve for X_1 as follows:

$$X_1 = PDV \text{ of } \$1 \text{ paid a year from now} = \$1/(1 + i).$$

PRESENT DISCOUNTED VALUE OF $1
the amount of money, X_t, placed in the bank today that will yield $1 t years from now at interest rate i

At an interest rate of 10 percent, the present discounted value of $1 paid a year from now thus equals $1/1.1 \approx $0.91 paid today; $1 paid a year from now is worth only $0.91 today when the opportunity cost of using money over time is 10 percent. This relationship makes intuitive sense. When money can be put to productive use over time (when the interest rate is positive), then $1 a year from now is worth less than $1 in hand today. The dollar in hand today can be invested and will yield more than $1 a year from now.

The foregoing formula can readily be employed to determine the present discounted value of $500,000 paid a year from now. The *PDV* is simply $500,000 discounted by the factor $1/(1 + i)$ or $500,000/(1 + i)$. If the interest rate is 10 percent, the *PDV* of $500,000 paid a year from now is thus $500,000/1.1 \approx $454,545.45.

The logic we have just employed can also be used to determine the *PDV* of $1 paid two years from now, X_2. Since the dollar amount that needs to be placed in the bank today, X_2, to equal $1 two years from now will yield $X_2(1 + i)$ a year from now and $X_2(1 + i)(1 + i)$ two years from now, we know that $X_2(1 + i)^2 = $1 paid two years from now. Consequently:

$$X_2 = PDV \text{ of } \$1 \text{ paid two years from now} = \$1/(1 + i)^2.$$

At an interest rate of 10 percent, the *PDV* of $1 paid 2 years from now is $1/(1.1)^2 \approx $0.83; $1 paid two years from now is worth only $0.83 in the bank today. Note that with a payment of $1 that is two years versus one year away, we need less money in the bank today ($0.83 versus $0.91) to be able to equal the payment. Furthermore, the *PDV* of $500,000 paid two years from now can be derived by simply multiplying $500,000 by the discount factor of $1/(1.1)^2$. With a 10 percent interest rate, $500,000 paid two years from now equals $500,000/(1.1)^2 \approx $413,223.14.

The *PDV* of $1 paid three years from now, X_3, can be derived in an analogous fashion, as can the *PDV* of $1 paid n years from now, X_n. The correct formulas are as follows:

$$X_3 = PDV \text{ of } \$1 \text{ paid three years from now} = \$1/(1 + i)^3, \text{ and}$$

$$X_n = PDV \text{ of } \$1 \text{ paid } n \text{ years from now} = \$1/(1 + i)^n.$$

Based on the formula for X_3, the $500,000 payoff three years into the CAT-scanner investment with an interest rate of 10 percent has a present discounted value of $500,000/(1.1)^3 \approx $375,657.40.

We can now put all the foregoing pieces together to determine a general rule for whether the stream of payments associated with an investment project such as the CAT scanner is worth the investment cost. Specifically, the **net present value** (*NPV*) of a project takes into account the initial investment cost (a negative present value) and the *PDV* of any future payoffs. The *NPV* of the CAT scanner is thus:

NET PRESENT VALUE (NPV)
the present discounted value of any future payoffs from an investment minus the initial investment cost of a project

$$NPV = -\$1,400,000 + \$500,000/(1 + i) + \$500,000/(1 + i)^2 + \$500,000/(1 + i)^3.$$

With an interest rate of 10 percent, the *NPV* of the CAT scanner turns out to be:

$$NPV = -\$1,400,000 + \$454,545.45 + \$413,223.14 + \$375,657.40$$

$$= -\$156,574.01.$$

This implies that, based on the opportunity cost of capital over time, investing in the CAT scanner is not profitable when the interest rate is 10 percent. The same $1.4 million that it would take to purchase the CAT scanner yields a higher return if invested in the bank than if invested in the CAT scanner when the interest rate is 10 percent. *As a general rule, if the net present value of an investment project is negative, then the funds required by the project could be better employed elsewhere. When the NPV of a project is positive, then the project represents a profitable employment of capital at capital's prevailing opportunity cost.*

While extremely straightforward, the mechanism just outlined for valuing investment projects has wide-ranging applicability. Among other things, it can be employed to price stocks and bonds that entail an up-front purchase price but promise future returns such as a stream of dividends and coupon payments, determine the value of lost earnings when an individual is involved in an accident, and evaluate the cost of a home mortgage or car loan.

APPLICATION 17.7   WHY LOTTERY WINNERS MAY NOT BE "MILLIONAIRES"

Most state lotteries offer jackpots of $1 million or more. Thus, the lucky winners are often called "millionaires."[11] Because of the manner in which winnings are paid out by state lottery commissions, however, winning $1 million does not make you a millionaire in present discounted value terms. The California State Lottery Commission, for example, awards all million-dollar prizes over a 20-year period: the winner is paid $50,000 immediately and $50,000 in each succeeding year for the next 19 years. By paying off on the installment plan, the Commission pays a $1-million-winner much less than $1 million in present discounted value terms. If the prevailing interest rate is 10 percent, for instance, the present discounted value of $1 million paid out in equal installments of $50,000 each over 20 years is slightly less than $426,000.

[11]This application is based on *www.calottery.com/winnersgallery/stories.html*.

SUMMARY

• The aggregate labor supply curve identifies the total number of hours of work that will be supplied to the economy as a whole at different wage rate levels. It is derived from the income-leisure choices of individual workers.

• Since the income and substitution effects operate in opposite directions, the aggregate labor supply curve is likely to be quite inelastic and probably bends backward above some wage rate.

• A major application of the aggregate labor supply curve, in connection with the aggregate labor demand curve, is in analyzing the determination of the general level of real wages. The aggregate demand curve is essentially the marginal product of labor curve. Its position depends on the amount of other inputs available (such as capital), the level of technology, and the productive characteristics of the labor force.

• Wage rates can differ among jobs and workers for several reasons, with no tendency for the rates to become equal. Equilibrium wage differences can be due to compensating wage differentials, differences in human capital investments, and/or differences in ability.

• Economic rent arises whenever the supplier of an input is paid more than the minimum amount necessary to retain the input in its present use. Supply and demand analysis shows that part of an input's price will represent rent whenever the input is in less than perfectly elastic supply.

• Borrowing-lending and saving-investment markets interact to determine both the interest rate on loaned funds and the rate of return on invested capital. In equilibrium, the interest rate on loaned funds and the rate of return on invested capital tend to be equal, ignoring any differences in risk, tax treatment, and the like. The interest rate thus acts to equalize the willingness of people to give up present consumption for future consumption (marginal rates of substitution) and the real net marginal productivity of investment.

• The equilibrium interest rate may be used to determine the net present value associated with various types of investment projects. Profit maximization dictates that projects with a positive net present value should be undertaken.

REVIEW QUESTIONS AND PROBLEMS

Questions and problems marked with an asterisk have solutions given in Answers to Selected Problems at the back of the book (pages 577–578).

17.1. Edie chooses to work 90 hours per week when the wage rate is $16 per hour. If she is offered time-and-a-half ($24 per hour) for "overtime work" (that is, hours in excess of 90 per week), will she choose to work longer hours? Support your results with a diagram.

17.2. If workers differ widely in their preferred hours of work at a given wage rate, would you expect to see all firms set the work-week at the average preferred level? Why or why not?

*17.3. Jeeves works 40 hours a week at a $7.50 wage rate. He unexpectedly inherits a trust fund that pays him $200 per week. How does inheritance of the trust fund affect his budget line? Will he continue to work 40 hours a week? Will his total income rise by $200 a week?

*17.4. Can a person choose to work so much less at higher wage rates that his or her total earnings decline? To answer, show the income and substitution effects that are implied by that outcome.

17.5. "Kevin (a highly skilled business manager) earns $150,000 a year. If he were to return to his home country of New Guinea (where there are more limited business opportunities), Kevin would be able to earn only $5,000 a year. This proves both that Kevin doesn't deserve his high salary and that wages are arbitrarily set in the United States." Evaluate this statement.

17.6. In general, the aggregate demand for and the supply of labor increases over time. Can we predict what will happen to real wage rates and employment over time? What factors are responsible for the shift in the demand curve? In the supply curve?

*17.7. "Since only a few people have the ability to become nuclear physicists, the long-run supply curve of nuclear physicists is vertical." True or false? Explain.

17.8. Discuss the three reasons for equilibrium wage rate differences given in the text. Which one, or more, accounts for differences in wage rates between engineers and elementary school teachers? College professors and high school teachers? Basketball superstars and basketball coaches? Doctors and lawyers?

17.9. If workers had identical preferences and were equally able to perform any job, would all wage rates be equal?

17.10. If Wayne Gretzky's supply curve of hours of work to professional hockey is vertical, does this imply that all of his labor earnings represent economic rent?

17.11. What do we mean when we say that capital is productive? How do we measure this productivity? What does productivity have to do with the investment demand curve?

17.12. "In equilibrium, the interest rate equates the willingness of people to give up present goods in return for future goods and the ability of the economy to transform present goods into future goods." Explain.

17.13. How does the interest rate serve to bring into equality the desired rate of saving and the desired rate of investment? Would the interest rate serve this function if the government placed an upper limit on the interest rate lenders could charge? How would such a law affect the amount of investment undertaken?

*17.14. In Figure 17.12, will the aggregate demand for labor in year 2 be higher if investment is K_1 or K_2 in year 1? Why?

17.15. If the union depicted in Figure 17.8 wishes to maximize the total wage payments made to its members, what wage and employment levels should the union select? Explain your answer.

17.16. In the example of the hospital administrator and the CAT scanner discussed in Section 17.11, is the net present value of the investment project positive if the interest rate is 5 percent?

17.17. Suppose that you are considering purchasing a corporate bond promising to pay a $1,000 "coupon" in each of the next five years. If the relevant interest rate is 10 percent, what will be the price for such a bond if the bond market is competitive? Will the bond's price rise or fall if the interest rate rises to 20 percent? What do your answers imply about the nature of the relationship (inverse or direct) between bond prices and the interest rate?

17.18. A speeding car swerves to avoid a rattlesnake slithering across a road but accidentally runs over and kills a lawyer walking along the side of the road. The lawyer was expected to make $90,000 per year over the next and final 10 working years of her life before her untimely demise. If the relevant interest rate is 10 percent and the lawyer's family sues the driver, for how much can the family sue for in terms of lost earnings due to the accident?

17.19. A Fijian island resort offers customers the opportunity to buy 30 vacation days at current prices with the opportunity to spend the purchased days on the island anytime over the next 5 years. The money on any days not spent on the island, plus 10 percent annual interest, is refundable at the end of the 5 years. If the interest rate over the same period on a typical money market fund is expected to be only 5 percent, is investing in the vacation days a good idea? Explain your answer.

17.20. Why might a medical doctor who has established a lucrative practice reduce her patient load and spend more time on the golf course or tennis court? Explain using a graph of a labor supply curve.

17.21. In 1999, tobacco companies agreed to settle a lawsuit brought by attorneys general from 46 states. According to the terms of the settlement, the companies are required to pay $206 billion to the states over 25 years in equal annual installments. Explain why the net present value of the settlement to the states is likely to be far less than $206 billion.

17.22. At any one point in time the supply of lawyers in the United States is relatively fixed. Since lawyers are an input to structuring new companies and business transactions, explain why the growth of the Internet economy has generated some economic rents for lawyers. (*Note*: Whereas law firms historically had taken their cues regarding salaries from established New York partnerships, by the late 1990s Silicon Valley firms had become the trend-setters. In 1999, for example, several Silicon Valley law firms began offering starting salaries of $125,000 to first-year attorneys in contrast to the $91,000 offered by established New York partnerships. The New York partnerships had to play catch-up with their Silicon Valley counterparts.)

CHAPTER 18

Using Input Market Analysis

Input market analysis can help us examine a variety of institutions and policies affecting the incomes of workers.

Chapter Outline

18.1 The Minimum Wage Law

Further Considerations   *How Large Are the Effects of the Minimum Wage?*

Application 18.1 *The Disemployment Effect of the 1990–1991 Minimum Wage Hike*

The Minimum Wage: An Example of an Efficiency Wage?

18.2 Who Really Pays for Social Security?

But Do Workers Bear All the Burden?

Application 18.2 *Mandated Retirement Benefits and Corporate America's Increasing Reliance on "Permatemps"*

18.3 The NCAA Cartel

An Input Buyers' Cartel   *The NCAA as a Cartel of Buyers*   *Eliminate the Cartel Restrictions on Pay?*

Application 18.3 *The "Collusion Era" in Major League Baseball*

18.4 Discrimination in Employment

What Causes Average Wage Rates to Differ?

Application 18.4 *Male Versus Female Earnings Among Self-Employed Workers*

Learning Objectives

- Analyze the effects of the minimum wage on the employment of unskilled workers.
- Determine the extent to which employers versus employees bear the burden of the Social Security program.
- Explain the benefits to firms from colluding in hiring some input through examining the NCAA cartel.
- Show how employment discrimination can affect usage rates and employment.

S ome of the most interesting and important issues in economics center on the way input markets function. This is not surprising. People understandably have great interest in the market (or markets) to which they supply inputs, since the functioning of that market largely determines their standard of living. As consumers, we have only a small stake in each of many product markets, but as producers, we have a great interest in one or a few. For example, few consumers are sufficiently motivated to stage demonstrations over milk price supports raising the price of milk by 20 percent, but the prospect of a 20 percent gain or loss in your salary will not leave you so unmoved.

In addition to our interest in matters affecting our personal incomes, we are affected by the operation of input markets generally. The way input markets work strongly influences an economy's income distribution. Some people are poor because the wage rates they receive are low; others are wealthy because their wage rates are high. Many public policies have been designed to redistribute income toward low-income households, and input market analysis is vital to understand the consequences of such policies. This chapter uses input market analysis to examine institutions and policies affecting the incomes of workers. These include the minimum wage, Social Security, discrimination, and the NCAA cartel.

18.1   THE MINIMUM WAGE LAW

In 1938, Congress passed the Fair Labor Standards Act, which established a nationwide minimum wage of $0.25 per hour. The federal minimum wage has been raised periodically since its establishment: from $3.35 to $4.25 an hour in 1990, to $4.70 in 1996, and to $5.15 in 1997. As of 2000, a further increase was being contemplated by Congress. Although the recent increases in the minimum wage may seem large, we should view them relative to the increase in average wage rates since 1938, which have risen greatly as a result of both inflation and real productivity gains. In 1938 the minimum wage of $0.25 represented 40 percent of the average manufacturing wage, while in 2000 the minimum wage of $5.15 represented about 37 percent of the average manufacturing wage.

Most people think of the minimum wage as a policy designed to help low-wage workers. If some people are poor because of low wage rates, requiring employers to pay a "living wage" seems a straightforward remedy. Some simple economic analysis (together with extensive empirical evidence), however, suggests that a minimum wage may not be the best way to help the poor.

Just 15 percent of all workers have wage rates low enough to be directly affected by the current minimum wage. For convenience we refer to this group as *unskilled workers*. The remaining 85 percent of workers, the *skilled workers*, would have wages in excess of the minimum even without the law. Therefore, our analysis of the minimum wage law focuses on the unskilled labor markets where wages normally would be below the legally specified level.

For simplicity, let's assume that unskilled workers are identical in all relevant respects so that a single wage rate prevails; we will relax this assumption later. Figure 18.1 depicts the labor market for unskilled workers. Almost all jobs and industries are covered by the minimum wage law; that is, by law they must pay the minimum wage. A few industries and jobs are exempt, such as domestic workers, babysitters, hospital and nursing home employees, and workers in seasonal amusement parks. Because of the law's broad coverage, an aggregate analysis is appropriate. As a result, the supply curve of unskilled labor to all jobs is fairly inelastic. In the absence of the minimum wage, let's assume that the wage rate is $4.00 per

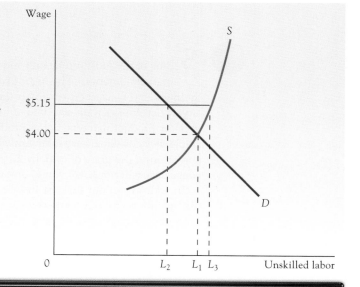

FIGURE 18.1

The Minimum Wage
A minimum wage of $5.15 per hour reduces employment of unskilled workers from L_1 to L_2 and increases the quantity of labor supplied from L_1 to L_3. The difference between quantity demanded and quantity supplied, L_2L_3, is the unemployment created by the minimum wage.

hour and total employment is L_1. Next, let the government impose a minimum wage of $5.15. In accordance with the law of demand, employers hire fewer workers at a higher wage rate. Employment falls from L_1 to L_2. This predictable response of employers to a higher wage rate is frequently overlooked in discussions of the minimum wage. Economists refer to the reduction in employment of L_1L_2 as the **disemployment effect** of the minimum wage. Note also that at the $5.15 wage, the number of workers looking for work has increased to L_3, which exceeds the number employed, L_2, by L_2L_3. This is the unemployment created by the minimum wage.[1] The higher wage rate has induced more people to enter the job market, but because of the increase in the wage rate, employers will hire fewer people.

DISEMPLOYMENT EFFECT
the tendency of employers to respond to a higher wage rate by hiring fewer workers

Do unskilled workers benefit from the minimum wage? On the basis of this analysis, an unqualified answer is not possible. Workers able to secure employment at the $5.15 wage do indeed benefit, but another group of workers—those who lose their jobs or are unable to find jobs—are left worse off. Some people argue that if the total earnings of unskilled workers as a group rise, we should say that they gain as a group. (Note that this outcome depends on the elasticity of demand for unskilled workers. If demand is inelastic, total earnings rise after a wage rate increase.) Whether or not the total earnings of unskilled workers as a group rise, however, you should recognize that certain unskilled workers are made worse off, and, individually, suffer a major loss.

We gain more insight into who is likely to lose jobs when we drop the assumption that all unskilled workers are identical. For example, suppose that in the absence of the minimum wage, some unskilled workers earn slightly below the minimum, $5.00 per hour, while others earn much less, $2.00 per hour. With a minimum wage of $5.15 per hour the wage rate for employees formerly earning $5.00 per hour rises by 3 percent, but for workers earning $2.00 per hour the wage rate employers must pay more than doubles. Employment therefore will decline much more for workers whose wages are initially the lowest because the minimum wage increases most sharply the cost of hiring these workers. In other words, the most disadvantaged, unproductive workers are the ones most likely to lose their jobs and be priced entirely out of the market by the minimum wage. The especially harmful effects on this group of unskilled workers presumably most in need of assistance need to be taken into account by any overall evaluation of the minimum wage.

Apart from those who lose their jobs, who else bears a cost from the minimum wage? Most people assume that employers bear the cost of paying the higher wage. This conclusion is unlikely to be true. The costs of the minimum wage are certain to be spread more widely through society in the form of higher prices for products produced by unskilled workers and lower input prices for complementary factors of production. No one knows exactly who ultimately bears these costs. Perhaps the most accurate statement is that the rest of society (other than the unskilled workers) is the ultimate employer of unskilled workers, so it must bear the cost of a higher wage rate in some form.

Further Considerations

We ignored several complications in the preceding analysis. Among them are the following:

1. The reduction in employment can take the form of a reduction in hours each worker is employed rather than a reduction in the number of workers employed. In other words, instead of one out of ten workers losing a job, each worker might be able to work only 90 percent as many hours as desired. Whatever is more profitable to employers determines the

[1]Official statistics may not measure this unemployment accurately. Some workers unable to find jobs at the $5.15 wage may stop looking for work. Since the government records as unemployed only workers who are actively seeking but unable to find work, those who have dropped out of the labor force are not counted.

outcome. Since overhead costs are associated with each worker hired, independent of hours worked, employers will probably cut back on workers rather than on work hours. Nonetheless, there is some evidence of reductions in hours per worker. For example, about half of all low-wage workers work only part-time—although this practice is surely, at least in part, a matter of choice.

2. When the government requires firms to pay a higher money wage, employers will respond, if possible, by reducing fringe benefits of employment. The fringe benefits that may be reduced include pensions, health insurance, and on-the-job training. Reducing fringe benefits means that the real wage employers pay rises by less than the money wage. Although employment will not fall as much, the intended impact of the minimum wage is mitigated: If employers reduce fringe benefits, the real wage (minimum wage plus fringe benefits) may not change at all. The importance of this reaction is unclear, but it could partly explain why low-wage workers tend to have such poor private pension and health insurance coverage and the on-the-job training provided by employers to their workers has fallen over the past several decades.

3. Our analysis assumed that the minimum wage law covers all unskilled jobs. Actually, not all employers must pay the minimum wage; 15 percent of all unskilled workers have uncovered jobs. For the 85 percent of unskilled workers in covered jobs, the analysis of Figure 18.1 holds: employment falls. With an uncovered sector, workers who are unable to find jobs at the minimum wage in the covered sector may seek employment in uncovered jobs. As the supply of workers to the uncovered sector increases, the wages prevailing in that sector go down, thereby harming workers already employed in the uncovered sector. However, the uncovered sector is now so small that we cannot say how important it is in absorbing workers who can't find jobs in the covered sector at the minimum wage. In the past the uncovered sector was much larger: nearly 50 percent of jobs were uncovered in the 1950s.

4. With a surplus of workers created by the minimum wage (L_2L_3 in Figure 18.1), employers can be more selective about whom they hire. If employers have prejudices relating to the gender, race, age, weight, or religion of their workers, they are in a better position to indulge their "tastes." When there is a glut of workers from which to choose, employers can more easily hire someone with characteristics they prefer. That is, if there are more applicants than jobs, the cost of discriminating falls. Insofar as employers have prejudices, the harmful effects of the minimum wage are more likely to be borne by workers with characteristics considered undesirable in the eyes of employers.

How Large Are the Effects of the Minimum Wage?

Most of the economic research on the minimum wage has concentrated on its effect on employment. Does the minimum wage reduce employment and, if so, by how much? Researchers have conducted numerous studies, and the evidence generally supports the proposition that the minimum wage reduces employment, especially among the least skilled workers. But no consensus has been reached concerning the size of the disemployment effect.

Most studies have attempted to identify groups of workers who are, on average, less skilled and who should be most affected by the law. For example, Yale Brozen of the University of Chicago concentrated on teenage employment, since teenagers frequently lack the skills, experience, and long-term job attachment necessary to earn high wages. Brozen found that teenage unemployment rates typically rose following each increase in the legal minimum. Other more sophisticated econometric studies have supported Brozen's results.[2]

Particularly striking has been the trend in teenage unemployment rates among African Americans relative to whites. In 1948, when the minimum wage was about 40 percent of

[2]Yale Brozen, "The Effects of Statutory Minimum Wage Increases on Teen-Age Unemployment," *Journal of Law and Economics*, 12 No. 1 (April 1969), pp. 109–122; also see Finis Welch, *Minimum Wages* (Washington, D.C.: American Enterprise Institute, 1978).

the average manufacturing wage and 50 percent of jobs were covered, African American and white teenage unemployment rates were nearly the same: 9.4 percent for African Americans and 10.2 percent for whites. By the late 1970s, when the minimum wage was 50 percent of the average manufacturing wage and 85 percent of jobs were covered, white teenage unemployment stood at 15 percent, but African American teenage unemployment was 35 percent. Whether unemployment among African American teens rose more sharply because as a group they are relatively less skilled (possibly because of poor schooling) or because of the way the minimum wage lessens the cost of discrimination is not clear. Other factors, such as changing attitudes about what jobs are acceptable, may also be involved, but most economists believe the minimum wage played at least a partial role in increasing African American teenage unemployment rates.

More recently, several studies have examined wage rate and income data to obtain a clearer picture of just who is likely to benefit from minimum wages.[3] The results were surprising. The studies found that low wage rates and low family incomes are not closely correlated. Among workers with wage rates low enough to be affected by the minimum wage, 50 percent were members of families in the wealthier half of the income distribution. This result occurs because some high-income families have individual members who work at low wages, such as teenage children. Moreover, many poor families have low incomes not because of low wage rates but because they are unemployed or work only part-time. (A third of low-income households, for example, are elderly and retired.) Furthermore, less than 20 percent of families in the bottom fifth of the income distribution have members who work at a wage rate as low as the minimum wage, so only a minority of low-income families stand to benefit from the minimum wage.

Most economists believe that the minimum wage is an unwise policy, not because they oppose helping the poor but because the minimum wage is such a blunt policy instrument when it comes to targeting assistance to low-income families (many middle-class teenagers benefit in the process). Most low-income families are not poor because of low wage rates, and some of those who are may well end up with a zero wage rate (unemployed) as a result of the policy.

APPLICATION 18.1 — THE DISEMPLOYMENT EFFECT OF THE 1990–1991 MINIMUM WAGE HIKE

The debate over certain recent studies of the effects of an hourly minimum wage increase from $3.35 to $4.25 between 1990 and 1991 suggests why there is no general consensus on the extent of the disemployment effect of the minimum wage.[4] The studies are controversial because of both their unorthodox approach and their findings. For example, economists Lawrence Katz of Harvard and Alan Kreuger of Princeton conducted a telephone survey of fast-food chain managers in Texas and found that only 11 percent of the surveyed chains reduced their employment of nonmanagement workers following the minimum wage hike in the spring of 1991. The authors argue that the results indicate a fairly minor disemployment effect associated with the minimum wage hike.

Critics of the Katz-Kreuger study contend that it underestimates the disemployment effect because not

[4]This application is based on: "Forging New Insight on Minimum Wages and Jobs," *New York Times*, June 29, 1992, pp. C1 and C7; Alan Reynolds, "Cruel Costs of the 1991 Minimum Wage," *Wall Street Journal*, July 7, 1992, p. A14; and Gary S. Becker, "It's Simple: Hike the Minimum Wage and You Put People Out of Work," *Business Week*, March 6, 1995, p. 22.

[3]See William R. Johnson and Edgar K. Browning, "The Distributional and Efficiency Effects of Increasing the Minimum Wage: A Simulation," *American Economic Review*, 73 No. 1 (March 1983), pp. 204–211; and Edward M. Gramlich, "Impact of Minimum Wages on Other Wages, Employment and Family Income," *Brookings Papers on Economic Activity*, 2 (1976), pp. 409–451.

all other factors have been held constant. Namely, the demand for labor appears to have been unusually strong in the period examined; as a result of rising exports to Mexico, the overall unemployment level in Texas declined from 6.9 to 5.8 percent. Moreover, three to four months may not be sufficient time to gauge the full effects of the minimum wage hike. While they may not fire existing workers, employers may reduce new hiring. Furthermore, the study does not account for the fact that the reduction in employment may occur in the form of fewer hours per worker, reduced fringe benefits, or an increase in employee productivity per hour worked. As one manager of several fast-food restaurants put it: "Our head count didn't increase or decrease. . . . [We're] just going to manage a lot more tightly to get more out of the people we've got."

In contrast to the Katz-Kreuger results, a statistical study by Donald Deere and Finis Welch of Texas A&M and Kevin Murphy of the University of Chicago finds a much more sizable disemployment effect associated with the hike in the minimum wage from 1990 to 1991. The Deere, Murphy, and Welch study finds that, holding constant other factors, the 27 percent increase in the minimum wage (from $3.35 to $4.25) appears to have decreased the employment of male and female teenagers by 12 and 18 percent, respectively.

The Minimum Wage: An Example of an Efficiency Wage?

EFFICIENCY WAGE
a wage higher than the prevailing market-determined level that serves to increase firms' profits by lowering the costs of searching for, selecting, and training new workers

Some analysts have argued that the minimum wage represents an **efficiency wage:** a wage higher than the prevailing market-determined level that serves to increase firms' profits.[5] According to this theory, paying an above-market wage may be profitable to a firm if there are costs associated with searching for, selecting, and training new workers. Facing these types of costs, a firm may want to pay higher wages to reduce labor force turnover and the costs associated with it. Additionally, if there is imperfect information in labor markets and if a higher wage is likely to attract a larger pool of more-qualified job applicants, a firm may find it profitable to raise wages above the level needed to attract qualified applicants. The increased quality in job applicants may more than offset the costs. Moreover, if hired workers are prone to moral hazard (see Chapter 14) and working below their fullest capacity upon being given an employment contract, a wage exceeding the prevailing market level may induce a greater increase in productive effort than the wage premium—provided that workers are motivated by the higher pay to put forth the additional effort.

Henry Ford's 1914 decision to institute a $5-per-day wage for workers in his automobile factory, twice the prevailing market rate, is often cited as an example of an efficiency wage. The benefits of the higher wage included 75 percent declines in worker turnover and absenteeism, a dramatic increase in the number and quality of applicants for positions in the factory, and a productivity improvement of roughly 50 percent in the year following the wage increase. The annual profitability of Ford's company doubled in the wake of the wage hike.

Although Ford's $5-per-day pay contract may be a striking example, the evidence that a government-legislated minimum wage represents a similar efficiency wage is more tenuous. Moreover, if the minimum wage is indeed an example of an efficiency wage, the question arises of why the government has to legislate a minimum wage for unskilled workers in the first place. An efficiency wage implies that firms will have an incentive to pay an above-market wage without any government intervention; an above-market wage will increase profits.

[5]George Akerlof and Janet Yellen, eds., *Efficiency Wage Models of the Labor Market* (Cambridge, England: Cambridge University Press, 1986).

18.2 WHO REALLY PAYS FOR SOCIAL SECURITY?

The U.S. Social Security system was begun during the Great Depression and is intended to provide older citizens with a secure source of income after retirement. The payments made to retired workers under the system are financed by a payroll tax composed of two equal-rate levies, one collected from current employers and the other from employees. In 2000, each rate was 7.65 percent. Workers earning $20,000 per year, then, have $1,530 deducted from their paychecks to cover the employee portion of the tax, and this amount is matched by a $1,530 payment collected from their employers. The total tax is thus $3,060.

By splitting the tax between current employers and employees, Congress apparently intended to divide the burden of the Social Security program between them. Whether this has actually been accomplished is far from clear. Economists believe that the way the tax is divided into employer and employee portions has no effect on who actually bears its cost.

Before discussing who actually pays the Social Security tax, we need to see whether the division of the tax into employer and employee portions makes a difference to wage rates and employment levels. We will compare the two extreme cases: one where employees pay the entire tax and the second where employers pay it. In Figure 18.2, before any tax is levied, the supply and demand curves for labor are S and D, the wage rate is $10 per hour, and employment is L_1. Now suppose the government levies a payroll tax on *employers*, which requires them to pay $2.00 to the government for each hour of labor they employ.

To understand how we incorporate the tax into the analysis, recall that the demand curve for labor shows the maximum amount per hour that employers will pay for each alternative quantity of labor. For example, the demand curve in Figure 18.2 means that employers will pay a maximum of $10.00 per hour to hire L_1 units of labor. With the tax in place, employers will still pay no more than $10.00 per hour for the quantity L_1, but since they must pay $2.00 to the government, the amount that employers will be willing to pay for L_1 units of labor falls to $8.00 per hour. In the diagram the effect of the tax is thus shown as a vertical shift downward by $2.00 in the demand curve to D'. The downward shift in the demand curve means that with a $2.00-per-hour tax, employers pay $2.00 less to workers at each level of employment. With the supply curve S, the tax reduces employment to L_2, and the wage rate paid to workers falls to w_A, or $8.50. To employers, the cost of labor *including* the tax is now $10.50 per hour.

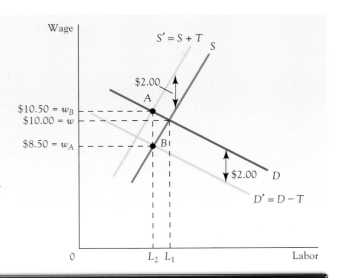

FIGURE 18.2

Tax on Employers Versus Tax on Employees
A tax of $2.00 per hour of employment has the same effect regardless of whether it is collected from employees or employers. When collected from employers, it is analyzed with a $2.00 downward shift in demand to D'; when collected from employees, it is analyzed with a $2.00 upward shift in supply to S'. In both cases workers receive $8.50 per hour and firms pay $10.50 per hour.

Alternatively, if employees pay the $2.00-per-hour tax entirely, the supply curve shifts vertically upward by $2.00, or to S', without affecting the demand curve. The shift in supply reflects the fact that workers must receive $2.00 more per hour to yield the necessary after-tax wage to compensate them for supplying each alternative quantity of labor. For example, if workers must pay the $2.00-per-hour tax, they will continue to supply L_1 hours of labor only if they receive a net (after-tax) payment of $10.00 per hour. When the workers pay the tax, the intersection of S' and D determines the new equilibrium, involving employment of L_2 and a wage rate of $10.50. Since workers must remit $2.00 to the government, their take-home pay is $8.50.

Note that the real effects of the tax are exactly the same whether the tax is collected from employers or employees. When collected from employers, employment is L_2, and firms incur a labor cost of $10.50 per hour, with $2.00 going to the government and the remaining $8.50 to workers. When employees pay the tax, employment is again L_2, and firms pay $10.50 as before; although the workers receive $10.50, they keep only $8.50 and must remit $2.00 to the government. In both cases the $2.00-per-hour tax, distance AB, reflects the difference between the gross-of-tax cost of labor to employers and the net-of-tax payment to workers.

The way the tax is collected gives the government no control over who ultimately bears its cost. The results are the same whether employers or employees pay the tax. Although we have shown that the effects are identical for the extreme cases (when the employer or the employee pays the entire tax), this conclusion holds for the intermediate cases, too. For instance, if $1.00 of the tax is collected from employers and $1.00 from employees, firms would pay $9.50 to workers (plus $1.00 to the government for a total unit cost of labor of $10.50, as before), and workers would receive a gross wage of $9.50 and get to keep $8.50, since they would turn over $1.00 to the government.

But Do Workers Bear All the Burden?

We have just shown that the real effects of the payroll tax are the same regardless of its division, for collection purposes, between employers and employees. This is not the same as saying that workers bear all the burden of the tax. Note that in our example the $2.00-per-hour tax led to a $1.50 reduction in the net wage rate ($10.00 to $8.50), so in that case workers did not bear the full burden of the tax in the form of a lower wage rate. Most economists specializing in tax analysis, however, believe that workers bear most, if not all, of the cost of the tax in the form of reduced wages.

Exactly how far (net-of-tax) wages fall when a payroll tax is collected depends on the elasticities of supply and demand. Of particular importance in the case of the payroll tax is the elasticity of supply. In Figure 18.2, the labor supply curve is drawn as moderately elastic, with lower wage rates leading to significant reductions in the quantity of labor supplied. This is done to simplify the graph for the point being made. Now let's look more closely at the labor supply curve relevant for analyzing the payroll tax.

The payroll tax applies to virtually all jobs, industries, and occupations. Since it applies across the economy, the relevant supply curve for use in analyzing the payroll tax is the aggregate supply curve of hours of work. As explained in Chapter 17, the aggregate labor supply curve is likely to be quite inelastic and, in fact, is vertical if income and substitution effects exactly offset one another. Consequently, let's examine the impact of the payroll tax when the supply curve is vertical.

Figure 18.3 illustrates this case. In the absence of the tax, employment is L_1 and the wage rate is $10. Next, the government levies a tax of $2 per hour. Since it makes no difference if it is collected from employers or workers, let's assume employers pay the entire tax. As a result, the demand curve shifts vertically downward by $2 to D'. With a vertical supply curve

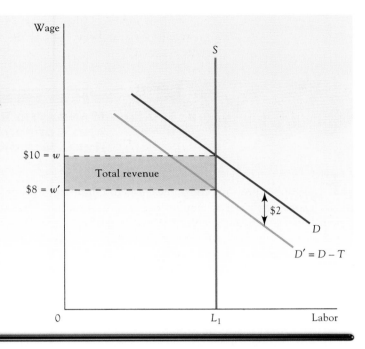

FIGURE 18.3

The Burden of the Social Security Tax
When the supply curve of labor is vertical, a tax on wage income reduces the hourly wage rate workers receive by the amount of the tax, from $10 to $8.

the wage rate received by workers falls by $2—the amount of the tax—to $8. Employment, however, does not fall, because workers choose to supply the same number of hours at the lower wage rate. *When the supply curve is vertical, the net wage rate received by workers falls by the full amount of the tax, so workers bear the entire burden of the tax.*[6]

Note that the cost of labor, including the tax to employers, has not risen; it is still $10. Now, however, $2 goes to the government and $8 to workers, rather than $10 to workers. Since labor costs have not risen, there is no effect on product prices. Much popular discussion in the media of payroll taxes, especially the employer portion, holds that higher employer payroll taxes add to labor costs and thus contribute to higher prices. The analysis here indicates that total labor costs do not rise: when taxes go up, wage rates go down.

This analysis suggests two conclusions, both important and both routinely misunderstood in most discussions of the Social Security payroll tax. First, whether the tax is collected from employers or employees makes no difference. The employer portion is no more borne by business than is the employee portion. Second, if the aggregate supply of labor is highly inelastic, workers bear all, or virtually all, of the burden of the tax in the form of lower after-tax wage rates. In particular, workers bear the cost of the employer portion to the same degree that they bear the cost of the employee portion. Many people are unaware of the existence of the employer portion of the tax, but it depresses their take-home pay just as much as the employee portion of the tax. These points are important to keep in mind. Recent advocates of national health insurance, for example, have proposed financing the program through increased payroll taxes, with employers paying a disproportionately larger share. As

[6]If the tax is collected from the workers, the supply curve shifts vertically upward by $2, which means that it does not visibly shift at all. Workers still continue supplying L_1, and employers still pay $10 per hour. But after sending $2 per hour to the government, workers keep $8 per hour, just as when the tax is collected from employers.

our analysis indicates, the cost of any health insurance scheme financed through payroll taxes will be borne by workers in the form of lower wages, regardless of how the tax is initially assigned.

APPLICATION 18.2   **MANDATED RETIREMENT BENEFITS AND CORPORATE AMERICA'S INCREASING RELIANCE ON "PERMATEMPS"**

Federal law prevents companies from discriminating against any group of employees in giving out retirement benefits.[7] As our analysis of the payroll tax associated with Social Security suggests, however, one effect of government-mandated benefits is to lower the after-tax wage rates received by workers. Another effect is to encourage firms to outsource their work to temporary workers ("temps") to the extent that government-mandated benefits do not have to be provided to temps. Corporate America's reliance on temporary workers who work full-time but do not receive benefits has grown

substantially over the past decade. A 1997 study by the Conference Board, a business research group, estimates that as many as 20 percent of U.S. firms use temps for more than 10 percent of their work force. As many as 40 percent of all workers in Silicon Valley are temps, according to an AFL-CIO Labor Council study.

Relying on temps, however, is not without its problems. Microsoft, which relies on temps for 27 percent of its workforce in the Seattle area, has recently been sued by some former employees whom the firm first fired and then offered to rehire only if they signed up through a third-party staffing agency. The protracted 1997 strike at United Parcel Service (UPS) stemmed primarily from UPS's reliance on "permatemps"—full-time, temporary employees.

[7]This application is based on "Microsoft Testing Limits on Temp Worker Use," *Los Angeles Times*, December 7, 1997, pp. D1, D14.

18.3 THE NCAA CARTEL

In Chapter 13, we explained why a group of firms had an incentive to reach a collusive agreement, or a cartel, to limit production and raise the price of their product. In that chapter, we examined a cartel in the output market; it is also possible to have a cartel among buyers in input markets. The motivation is the same: By colluding, firms can make higher profits. When firms collude in hiring some input, the goal is to reduce the price paid for the input, which in turn lowers production costs. In effect, firms that collude are attempting to exercise their collective monopsony power in input markets. If effective, it has a detrimental effect on the price and economic rent received by suppliers of the input facing the buyers' cartel.

This section examines an effective input buyers' cartel: the National Collegiate Athletic Association (NCAA) regulation of student-athlete compensation. To fully understand the effects of this regulation, we need to first discuss the theory relating to the exercise of monopsony power in input markets by cartels.

An Input Buyers' Cartel

We'll begin with a competitive equilibrium in an input market and then explain how collusion among the firms would increase their profits. Figure 18.4b shows the market demand and supply curves for a certain type of labor, with an equilibrium wage rate of w and employment level of L_1. Figure 18.4a shows the equilibrium from the viewpoint of one of the com-

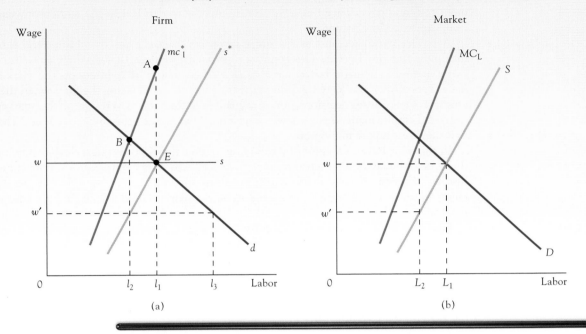

FIGURE 18.4

An Input Buyers' Cartel

Under competitive labor market conditions, the wage rate is *w*, with each firm facing a horizontal supply curve at that wage rate and employing l_1 workers. If the firms form a cartel, total employment is restricted to L_2, permitting firms to pay a lower wage, *w'*.

petitive firms in the market. As noted in Chapter 16, in a competitive environment the firm faces a horizontal supply curve, *s*, for the input at the market wage rate *w*, so with a demand curve of *d*, the firm employs l_1 workers.

Each firm acting alone has no incentive to reduce the number of workers it employs, since a single firm's decision to hire fewer workers will not affect the wage rate—all that will happen is that the firm produces less output and sees its profits fall. If all firms simultaneously reduce employment, however, the combined effect of their actions reduces the wage rate if the market supply curve is upward–sloping, as it is in this example. Lower wages (that is, lower production costs) are what an input buyers' cartel tries to achieve. To show the consequences somewhat more formally, assume for simplicity that the firms are identical and that they agree to coordinate employment decisions so they simultaneously increase or reduce employment. The cartel agreement has the effect of changing the labor supply curve facing each firm.

If one firm reduces employment, all other firms will as well, and the combined effect depresses the wage rate. With coordinated hiring decisions, the individual firm faces the upward-sloping supply curve *s** in Figure 18.4a. This curve is each firm's *pro rata* share of the total labor market supply curve *S* in Figure 18.4b. It reflects the firm's average cost of labor at alternative employment levels, provided that all firms coordinate their hiring decisions.

Because each firm's labor supply curve is upward-sloping with collusion, the marginal cost of employing labor is greater than the average cost, or wage rate, as shown by mc_L^* in Figure

18.4a. Firms find that at their initial level of employment, the marginal cost of hiring labor, Al_1, is greater than the marginal value product of labor, El_1. Thus, profits can be increased by reducing employment, since labor cost will fall by more than revenue. The profit-maximizing employment level is where the marginal cost of labor equals the marginal value product—that is, where mc_L^* intersects the demand curve d. Firms therefore reduce employment to l_2 and pay a wage rate of w'. This outcome is identical to the monopsony equilibrium explained in Chapter 16.

A buyers' cartel acts just as if a single buyer controlled hiring by all firms and acted to maximize combined profit. This result is illustrated in Figure 18.4b, which shows how the cartel, acting as a single buyer, employs L_2 workers where MC_L intersects the market demand curve. MC_L and S are the sum of the mc_L^* and s^* curves facing the firms when they coordinate their hiring decisions, reflecting the fact that the buyer side of the market has restricted employment to pay a lower wage rate. That is, the firms are collectively behaving as if they were a pure monopsony.

In this way, buyers can profit by colluding to force down prices of goods they purchase. If this type of behavior is so advantageous to buyers, why aren't buyer cartels more common? Just like seller cartels, buyer cartels are difficult to organize and maintain. In Chapter 13, we identified three reasons why seller cartels in output markets tend to fail; they are relevant in this case as well.

First, firms have an incentive to cheat on the cartel agreement. Each firm, acting individually, can raise its profit still further by increasing employment to l_3 at wage rate w' in Figure 18.4a. If many firms cheat, the cartel will fail. Second, participating firms will find it difficult to reach agreement on the levels of permitted employment (l_2) and the wage rate, w'. This is especially true when firms differ in size, structure, and aspiration. Third, the lower wage rate invites entry into the market by other firms that are not parties to the cartel, making it more difficult for the cartel to restrict competition for labor and hold the wage rate down.

Two additional factors, unique to input markets, hinder input buyers' cartels. First, an input market is often composed of many firms in several different industries. Coordinating hiring decisions among a large number of firms within and across industries is difficult. Second, every firm usually hires many different inputs, and the potential profit from reducing the price of only one input may not be significant. Typically, a firm stands to gain more by increasing the price of what it sells (usually one or a few items) than by reducing the price of one input.

For these reasons the effective exercise of monopsony power by an input buyers' cartel is uncommon. There are, however, a few interesting examples, and we discuss one of these next.

The NCAA as a Cartel of Buyers

The NCAA is a private organization empowered to regulate various aspects of college athletics. Currently, nearly 800 colleges and universities belong to the NCAA. When founded in 1906, the NCAA's goal was to control violence in college football, but its powers gradually expanded over time. As athletics became a major source of revenue for many colleges, the NCAA began to promulgate first voluntary guidelines and later rules governing recruitment and financial aid. Today the NCAA limits the number of athletic scholarships schools may award as well as the amount of financial assistance they may give. Basically, student-athletes can receive assistance only for room, board, and tuition (although this oversimplifies the NCAA's 411-page rulebook).

In essence, the NCAA determines the maximum financial reward a student-athlete can receive and the number of student-athletes who may be recruited with scholarships at each school. If the rules are effectively enforced, the NCAA thus has the power to operate a buyers' cartel on behalf of member schools. We can see this by reinterpreting Figure 18.4 as it applies to the NCAA. The NCAA sets total "employment" by restricting the number of student-athletes receiving scholarships, and it controls the maximum "wage" by limiting assistance to room, board, and tuition. Each school is given a quota (l_2) smaller than the number of student-athletes it would like to hire (l_3) at the lower wage.

Applying a model developed for profit-maximizing firms to the nonprofit world of higher education may seem strange, but there is no doubt that some colleges and universities try to maximize the "profit" from their athletic programs. College athletic programs generate annual revenues equaling roughly $2 billion in ticket sales and television rights. A winning basketball or football team (the only true money-making sports) can provide enough revenue to finance the entire athletic program, so it is not surprising that some schools treat athletics as a business.

The NCAA rules clearly have the potential to be used to establish a monopsony-like result for college athletics, but are the rules really applied strictly enough to produce this outcome? We have several pieces of evidence that they are. First, let's consider the marginal value products (or marginal revenue products) of college athletes. As shown in Figure 18.4a, the wage paid to an athlete is below the athlete's marginal value product (the height to the demand curve, or Bl_2) in a monopsony equilibrium. A number of estimates for selected college athletes have shown how much revenue they personally generated for their colleges. Doug Flutie, for example, is credited with bringing in $3 million in television revenue during his last two years on the football team at Boston College, and there are many other cases of college "superstars" generating revenues in excess of $1 million a year for their schools. Clearly, these athletes are paid far less than they are worth to their colleges.

A second piece of evidence is the significant number of NCAA rules violations by colleges and universities. Recall that any individual school has an incentive to cheat on the cartel agreement, since superior athletes are worth more to the school than the NCAA permits them to be paid. If the sports press can be believed, rules violations are common. Reports of athletes receiving cash payments, cars, apartments, free tickets, jobs without work requirements, and so on are widespread. Between 1977 and 1985 for instance, seven football players at Texas Christian University were paid between $35,000 and $45,000 apiece to attend the school. Such instances of cheating all indicate that the official wage permitted by the NCAA is below the market-clearing level.

Why doesn't cheating cause the demise of the NCAA cartel? If cheating could not be controlled, disintegration would be the likely result, but the NCAA can apply sanctions to punish cheaters who are caught, and these sanctions have become increasingly severe. For instance, the NCAA can reduce the number of athletic scholarships a school can grant. The NCAA can also limit television appearances and prohibit a school from appearing in lucrative post-season tournaments. An appearance in the national championship football bowl game can be worth more than $15 million (as of 2000) to a school. In an extreme example of the penalty the NCAA can impose on a school, Southern Methodist University's entire 1987 football schedule was canceled. The NCAA clearly has powers enabling it to enforce, at least partially, the employment restrictions necessary to achieve the monopsony outcome.

Eliminate the Cartel Restrictions on Pay?

Should colleges be permitted to pay student-athletes? That question cannot be answered by economics alone since, as the "should" in the question indicates, value judgments as well as positive analysis are involved. The topic is too provocative and interesting to ignore, however, so let's consider some of the relevant issues. Positive economic analysis indicates that NCAA policies result in a monopsony-like market for student-athletes. Thus, we know that student-athletes are paid less than they are worth as revenue generators. So if student-athletes are harmed by the NCAA restrictions on pay, who benefits? At a general level, colleges and universities with big-time athletic programs gain: they receive sizable revenues without having to pay the people largely responsible for generating them. But since colleges are nonprofit institutions, tracking down the ultimate beneficiaries is difficult. Perhaps non-revenue-generating sports are subsidized from the profits, perhaps tuition is a bit lower, or perhaps the salaries of coaches and economics professors are higher.

What is clear, however, is that those who benefit from the low pay of college athletes are wealthier than those who are harmed by it. Student-athletes typically come from poorer households than the average college student; often they come from quite disadvantaged backgrounds. One justification for the imbalance between revenue generators and revenue receivers is that student-athletes will soon be making megabucks as professional athletes. This is incorrect; fewer than 1 percent of college athletes make it to the pros. Thus, not only does the NCAA impede the smooth functioning of this labor market, but those who are most obviously harmed are also often relatively poor. These income distribution implications are the reason why certain analysts support breaking up the NCAA cartel. Others remain unconvinced, so let's briefly examine three of the most commonly heard arguments in favor of the current system.

1. *Some schools would have to drop their athletic programs if they had to pay their athletes a competitive "wage".* Although this might be true for some schools, since more student-athletes would participate in college sports at a higher wage, many schools could operate the same size or expanded athletic programs. Nonetheless, someone must bear the cost when schools lose "profits" made as a result of not paying their student-athletes what they are worth. If a school currently uses its basketball and football programs' profit to subsidize other sports, for example, these programs will suffer. The basic issue is whether the student-athletes in profitable sports should bear the cost of supporting other, less profitable, programs.

2. *Paying college athletes would destroy their amateur status and turn college athletics into a business.* Giving schools the option of paying student-athletes does not imply that every institution would have to participate in this market. If a school wanted to maintain an amateur athletic program, it could, and probably many would choose this option. Some student-athletes might actually prefer this alternative, although schools choosing not to pay athletes a competitive wage would have difficulty attracting the very best athletes. Under the current system, however, student-athletes are forced to be amateurs rather than having a choice.

3. *Paying athletes might adversely affect the education they receive.* Currently, less than one-third of athletes in the revenue-producing sports graduate from college, and of those that do, many take unchallenging courses, so the situation is already cause for concern. The joke about the university basketball coach telling a player who received four Fs and a D, "Looks like you're spending too much time on one subject," may be a more accurate reflection of the priorities of some college athletic departments than they care to admit. Perhaps the goals of having exciting sports programs with superb athletes and providing a quality college education to those athletes are incompatible. Whether or not this is true, it is not clear that permitting colleges to pay athletes makes it harder for them to require athletes to perform well academically and complete their education.

Although these remarks do not dispose of all the objections to permitting the wage rate of college athletes to be determined in an open market, they suggest how an economic approach to the question might help in understanding some of the issues.

APPLICATION 18.3 — THE "COLLUSION ERA" IN MAJOR LEAGUE BASEBALL

The end of the reserve clause and the onset of free agency in major league baseball (see Chapter 16 for more details) substantially increased the salaries and economic rents earned by players. Between 1976 and 1985, for example, the average player's salary rose 700 percent to $369,000. This upward spiral was temporarily arrested from 1985 to 1988 in what has come to be known as the *collusion era*.[8] During the collusion era, the free agency market dried up as far as players' prospects were concerned, while team profits soared. Baseball teams, as a group, earned their first pretax operating profit in eight years in 1986, the first of the collusion years. Over the next year, average players' salaries declined 2 percent while overall operating profit increased tenfold, to $103 million.

The ability of major league baseball teams to effectively organize during the collusion era reflected the leadership of Peter Ueberroth, elected league commissioner in 1984. Upon assuming office, Ueberroth doubled the number of meetings between team owners and the commissioner (to four per year) and used them to openly berate owners for their lack of business sense in going after free agents while ignoring their own bottom lines. Ueberroth also got the owners to open up their books to one another for the first time ever at a meeting in 1985

[8]This application is based on "How Peter Ueberroth Led the Major Leagues in the 'Collusion Era'," *Wall Street Journal* (May 20, 1991), pp. A1 and A6.

and made them financially justify each of their hiring decisions. The exercise allowed owners to tacitly signal their intentions for any player up for free agency and forged a group dynamic among the owners whereby bidding competitions over players were shunned. Ueberroth also raised the maximum fine that could be levied by the league against a team violating the commissioner's rulings from $5,000 to $250,000. Finally, Ueberroth began using a central fund, based on licensing and merchandising fees, to award up to $500,000 per year to teams acting in consonance with the commissioner's wishes.

The consensus established through Ueberroth's tactics was amazingly strong. For example, of the eight free agents who refused to re-sign with their initial teams by a league-set deadline of January 1987, choosing instead to seek outside offers, most found the market barren and ended up returning to their old teams with pay docked for refusing to re-sign on time. The average free agent's salary that year declined 16 percent.

In the end, however, the implicit consensus proved to be too successful for its own good. The owners lost several grievance procedures filed by the players' union and had to pay $280 million in damages for acting too closely in concert with one another. Peter Ueberroth lost interest in seeking reelection for a second five-year term as commissioner. And the owners reverted to their usual ways of competing aggressively over players. Average player pay rose again, by 50 percent between 1990 and 1991.

18.4 DISCRIMINATION IN EMPLOYMENT

Discrimination can take many forms, but in this section we are concerned with only one aspect of this complex issue: how employment discrimination can affect wage rates and employment. Our main concern is whether, and under what circumstances, wage rates of equally productive workers will differ because of discriminatory hiring practices on grounds unrelated to a person's productivity, such as race, religion, or gender. If wage differentials unrelated to productivity can result from discrimination, we need to qualify the analysis in Chapter 16, where we concluded that wages have a tendency to equalize.

We will examine this issue by considering a labor market in which some employers discriminate and others do not. To be specific, we will assume that a fixed total of 2,000 equally productive workers wish to work in this market. Of these workers, 1,200 are men and 800 are women. Half of the employers (group A) are prejudiced against women workers and will not hire them under any circumstances; the other employers (group B) don't care whether their workers are male or female. What will be the wage rates paid to men and women in this market, and how many will be employed by group A and group B employers, respectively?

To answer this question, it will simplify matters to assume that no employers discriminate, identify a nondiscriminatory labor market equilibrium, and then work out the consequences when group A employers begin to discriminate against women. In Figure 18.5, the demands for labor by groups A and B are shown in separate graphs as D_A and D_B, respectively. In the initial nondiscriminating equilibrium, workers will be divided between the two markets so that the wage rates are equal, as shown by the supply curves S_A and S_B. The wage rate is w, or $10, in both markets, and 1,000 workers are employed by each group. Since this market does not include any discrimination yet, we assume that men and women are employed by groups A and B in proportion to their total labor market representation—that is, each group of employers hires 600 males and 400 females (600M + 400F).

When employers do not discriminate, equally productive men and women receive the same wage rates. Now let us suppose that group A employers begin to discriminate against

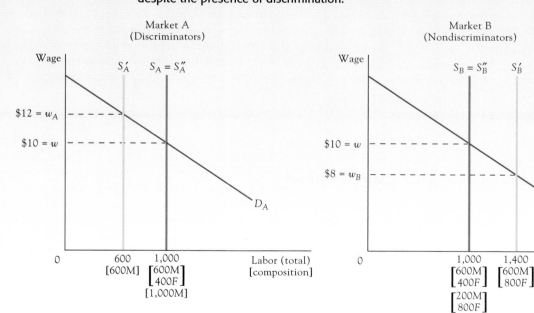

FIGURE 18.5

Discrimination in Labor Markets

When employers in market A begin to discriminate against women, the initial effect is a leftward shift in the total labor supply curve in market A, S_A, and a simultaneous rightward shift in S_B, as the discharged women move to the nondiscriminating market. This trend creates incentives for men in market B to move to market A, reversing the initial supply curve shifts. The final result is that wage rates of men and women are equal despite the presence of discrimination.

women. They fire their 400 female employees. In the graph, the immediate, or very short-run, effect of this action would be shown as a shift in the supply curve of labor to the A market from S_A to S_A': the total supply is now 600 men. The wage rate in the A market paid to men will be bid up to w_A, or $12. What happens to the 400 discharged women employees? Of course, they will look for work elsewhere—in this case, in the B market. Their availability increases the total supply of labor to the B market, shown as a shift in supply from S_B to S_B'. The result is a lower wage rate of w_B, or $8, and an increase in total employment in market B to 1,400. All of the women are now employed by nondiscriminating employers and none by discriminating employers.

This position is not, however, the final labor market equilibrium. Indeed, it may not materialize at all, as incentives for other changes simultaneously affect the behavior of market participants. To see that the position described is not an equilibrium, consider the 600 *men* still employed in market B. They are now receiving an $8 wage rate—while the wage rate in market A is $12 *and market A is not discriminating against men.* Thus, men in market B would look for jobs in market A. (Alternatively, employers in market A would try to lure male employees away from market B because they wouldn't have to pay the men as much as their current $12 wage.) The shift of male workers from B to A is shown as a rightward shift in S_A' and a simultaneous leftward shift in S_B'. This trend will tend to reduce the wage rate in A and increase it in B. How far will this process continue? As long as the wage rate remains higher in market A and any men continue to work in market B, male workers in market B have incentive to move to market A. The process continues until the wage rates are the same in the two markets.

The final discriminating equilibrium occurs when S_A' has shifted to S_A'' (coinciding with S_A) and S_B' has shifted to S_B'' (coinciding with S_B). Wage rates are the same in both markets, and each market employs 1,000 workers—just as in the case when no employers discriminate. The difference appears in the composition of employment in the two markets. The discriminating employers now employ 1,000 workers—all men; the nondiscriminating employers now employ 1,000 workers—200 men and 800 women.

This effect is a remarkable, and little understood, implication of basic economic analysis. It demonstrates that widespread discrimination can exist, and yet have no effect on the wage rates of the discriminated-against group. Discrimination will tend to produce segregated employment patterns, but not wage differentials.

Can discrimination by employers ever lead to lower wage rates for discriminated-against groups? In our model, this result is possible if the proportion of employers who discriminate is sufficiently large relative to the size of the discriminated-against group. Specifically, if women represent 40 percent of the relevant labor force and discriminating employers account for more than 60 percent of total employment, then discrimination could reduce the wage rates of women (and raise those of men). But as this analysis makes clear, discrimination must be very widespread to affect wage rates. In the case of a small minority like African Americans, who account for about 12 percent of the total labor force, discriminating employers would have to control an even larger portion of total employment (more than 88 percent in that case) for discrimination to produce lower wage rates. The key issue is whether enough nondiscriminating employers exist to absorb the discriminated-against group.

Even if discrimination is prevalent enough to produce lower wage rates for the discriminated-against group, a second market force tends to limit its consequences—the profit motive. Firms that engage in discrimination bear a cost in the form of sacrificed profits. Suppose, for example, that widespread discrimination against women produces lower wage rates for female workers. To be specific, assume that firms can hire male workers for $35,000 per year and can hire equally productive female workers for $25,000 per year. For every male worker hired in this situation, a firm loses $10,000 in profit because it incurs a higher cost than necessary. If the firm is a profit maximizer, it would hire only female workers, which would give it a cost advantage over (discriminating) firms that hire only males. This incentive for firms—to employ the lowest-cost available inputs (of comparable productivity)—works to promote equality in input prices.

The stronger the profit motive, the less likely that discrimination will exist or influence wage rates. Even a moderate difference in wage rates creates the opportunity for a firm to greatly increase its profit by not discriminating. On average, labor costs account for approximately 70 percent of all production costs, while before-tax profits average about 9 percent. If the average firm could reduce its labor cost by just 15 percent, it could nearly double its profit. How many businesses would be willing to forgo doubling their profits just to discriminate against certain groups of workers?

These arguments do not mean that discrimination in employment is nonexistent or that it cannot affect wage rates, particularly when we recognize that discrimination in employment can reflect preferences of consumers or co-workers rather than employers' prejudices. (Employers may discriminate against certain groups of workers if customers are likely to refuse to purchase goods or services provided by that group of workers or if other workers are unwilling to work with them.) The analysis does suggest, however, that discriminatory attitudes must be widespread and that discriminators must be willing to bear nontrivial reductions in profit to indulge their prejudices, if significant wage rate differentials are to be maintained.

What Causes Average Wage Rates to Differ?

It is well known that average incomes and earnings differ among groups. In recent years, for example, the average earnings of African American males have been about 70 percent as much as those of white males. Among full-time workers, women also earn about 70 percent as much as men. To many people, these and similar numbers provide evidence of discrimination and its consequences. Our theoretical analysis does not prove this view to be wrong, but it does suggest that we should consider other possible explanations for these differences. Average wage rates of groups can differ for reasons other than discrimination. Differences may exist in the average current labor market productivity among groups, for example. Although productivity is notoriously difficult to measure directly, we can measure a number of characteristics thought to be related to productivity.

The median age of African Americans, for example, is 22; for whites, the median age is 30. Productivity and earnings tend to rise with age and experience, so whites would be expected to have higher average earnings when the entire groups are compared. Half of all African Americans, but a much lower percentage of white Americans, live in the South, where wage rates (and living costs) are lower. The careers of African Americans, especially if they are older, may also bear the lingering effects of past discrimination by schools and labor unions. On average, whites have slightly more schooling than African Americans (though the difference has been narrowing in recent decades); since education is related to earnings, this discrepancy produces a difference in group average earnings (22 percent of whites over the age of 25 have four or more years of college compared with 12 percent of African Americans). African Americans also score lower on standardized tests on average than whites, and some believe that these test scores reflect productive potential. Even marriage patterns can play a role in determining earnings. The percentage of African American men who are single is double the percentage for white men, and single men in general work 20 percent fewer hours per week than married men. These differences between the two groups would produce differences in average wage rates even if there was no discrimination.

What about women? Perhaps the most important factor here is the different ways that marriage and child-rearing affect men and women. Statistically, married men make more money than single men, but married women make less than single women. Perhaps this result occurs because, historically, marriage has freed men of household duties and permitted them to give more single-minded attention to their jobs, whereas it has had the opposite effect for women. For whatever reason, men work 10 to 20 percent longer hours than women, even when only full-time workers are taken into account. To test whether marriage and choices made within marriages may be responsible for much of the difference in average wages, we may consider only men and women young enough that marriage and procreation are not so widespread. It turns out that young women earn substantially more relative to young men than older women do relative to older men. If we compare single women and single men, single women earn 91 percent as much as single men. To highlight another factor, a recent study compared the starting salaries of male and female college graduates. On average, women received 83 percent as much as men. When women were compared with men who had the same major subject in college, however, the female workers were found to receive 97 percent as much as their male counterparts. Women tended to choose lower-paying majors, which accounted for almost all of the difference in average starting salaries.

In trying to determine whether wage differences are due to discrimination, we should compare groups of workers who are equally capable, motivated, and experienced. Such a comparison is not easy, given the numerous factors that affect the current earnings of any worker. Using statistical techniques, economists and other social scientists have tried to take into account easily measured factors like age, years of education, region, and hours of work. They have generally found that from one-half to three-fourths of the overall differences in earnings between African Americans and whites, and between men and women, can be explained by these factors.[9] Whether the remaining differences reflect discrimination or something else remains a controversial issue.

APPLICATION 18.4   MALE VERSUS FEMALE EARNINGS AMONG SELF-EMPLOYED WORKERS

Since no self-employed person discriminates against himself or herself, economists have argued that if employer discrimination were the main reason for the earnings gap between men and women, self-employed women should find their earnings to be much closer to those of similarly productive self-employed men than do women who work for employers other than themselves. The data actually indicate that the gender earnings gap among the self-employed is, if anything, slightly larger than it is among regular-wage and salaried employees.[10] This finding suggests that reasons other than employer discrimination may explain the gender earnings gap.

[10]Victor Fuchs, "Women's Quest for Economic Equality," *Journal of Economic Perspectives*, 3 No. 1 (Winter 1989), pp. 25–41; and Robert L. Moore, "Employer Discrimination: Evidence from Self-Employed Workers," *Review of Economics and Statistics*, 85 No. 3 (August 1983), pp. 496–501.

[9]Ronald Ehrenberg and Robert Smith, *Modern Labor Economics*, 3rd ed. (Glenview, Ill.: Scott, Foresman, 1988). All of the difference in gross earnings between young African American and white males has been explained in a study that takes account of the results of achievement tests administered by the military since World War I—achievement tests used by the armed services to test individuals for fitness for military service. The tests measure verbal and mathematical skills and reflect the quality of schooling received as well as the effects of parental background. See June O'Neill, "The Role of Human Capital in Earnings Differences Between Black and White Men," *Journal of Economic Perspectives*, 4 No. 4 (Fall 1990), pp. 25–45.

SUMMARY

- The way input markets work strongly influences an economy's income distribution.
- The 1938 Fair Labor Standards Act established a nationwide minimum wage, which, by 2000, had been increased to $5.15 per hour. Although the minimum wage policy was designed to help low-wage workers, economic analysis suggests that it may not be the best way to do so. Employers' response to the minimum wage is often to hire fewer workers, according to the law of demand. The resulting disemployment effect of the minimum wage, and the fact that the cost of paying the higher wage is spread widely through society in the form of higher goods prices, makes it difficult to assess the minimum wage as an unqualified success in assisting unskilled workers in the labor market.
- Social Security is intended to provide older citizens with a secure source of income after retirement by taxing both those currently employed and their employers. Economists believe that the way the tax is divided has no effect on who actually bears the cost of Social Security and that employees in fact bear most (but not all) of the burden in the form of lower after-tax wage rates, particularly if the aggregate supply of labor is highly inelastic.
- The National Collegiate Athletic Association is an input buyers' cartel that, in essence, determines the maximum financial reward a student-athlete can receive and the number of student-athletes who can be recruited with scholarships at each school. At the same time, its policies result in a monopsony-like market for student-athletes, who are paid less than they are worth as revenue generators for their schools.
- Economic analysis shows that widespread employment discrimination can exist yet have no effect on the wage rates of the group that is discriminated against. Even if discrimination is prevalent enough to produce lower wage rates for a particular group, firms that fail to hire workers in that group pay higher labor costs than necessary and realize correspondingly lower profits.

REVIEW QUESTIONS AND PROBLEMS

Questions and problems marked with an asterisk have solutions given in Answers to Selected Problems at the back of the book (page 578).

18.1. "Proponents of minimum wage laws stress society's obligation to act through its elected representatives to ensure an adequate standard of living for all working citizens." Evaluate the extent to which minimum wages achieve this goal.

18.2. Why does economic theory imply that the most harmful effects of the minimum wage law will fall on the most disadvantaged and least productive workers?

*18.3. "The employer Social Security tax is just like any other labor cost to firms. A higher employer tax will thus increase labor costs, reduce employment, and increase prices." Explain why this reasoning is incorrect.

18.4. When the Social Security Administration attempts to compare the retirement benefits a worker receives with the taxes paid, it usually bases the comparison on only the employee portion of the tax. Do you think this comparison is appropriate?

18.5. As the owner of a retail store, you would like to be able to pay your salespeople lower wages. What problems would you confront if you attempt to establish a cartel among employers to force down wage rates?

18.6. Articulate and defend your position regarding paying college athletes. What is the role played by positive analysis versus value judgments in your argument?

18.7. You are a business manager, and you believe that the differences in wages between men and women and between African Americans and whites reflect discrimination and not productivity differences. What type of employment policy should you adopt?

*18.8. Suppose that some consumers of personal training services refuse to purchase such services from health clubs that employ any members of a minority group, the Amazons. How will this refusal affect the employment and wage rates of Amazons and other (assumed equally productive) workers?

18.9. Suppose that all employers in a perfectly competitive industry do not have a preference for discriminating against African Americans but that all the employees at one firm do. Describe what will happen to the profit-maximizing output level of this firm in the long run if the employees' racial preferences influence the firm's hiring decisions.

18.10. If the prevailing market wage for low-skilled workers is $7.00 per hour and a minimum wage law is passed dictating $6.00 per hour, what will be the effect of the law on employment and the prevailing wage rate?

18.11. One of the authors of this book typically pays twice the prevailing market wage for research assistants. Why might such a policy be rational?

18.12. Suppose that Korean Americans on average earn more than Polish Americans. Does this imply that Polish Americans are discriminated against by employers relative to Korean Americans?

CHAPTER 19

General Equilibrium Analysis and Economic Efficiency

How is equilibrium determined in all markets simultaneously and to what extent do markets promote the well-being of the members of a society as a whole?

Chapter Outline

19.1 Partial and General Equilibrium Analysis Compared

The Mutual Interdependence of Markets Illustrated   When Should General Equilibrium Analysis Be Used?

19.2 Economic Efficiency

Efficiency as a Goal for Economic Performance

19.3 Conditions for Economic Efficiency

19.4 Efficiency in Production

The Edgeworth Production Box   The Production Contract Curve and Efficiency in Production   General Equilibrium in Competitive Input Markets

19.5 The Production Possibility Frontier and Efficiency in Output

Efficiency in Output   An Economy's PPF and the Gains from International Trade

***Application 19.1** The Effects of Trade Restrictions on an Economy's Consumption and Production Possibilities*

19.6 Competitive Markets and Economic Efficiency

The Role of Information

***Application 19.2** Can Centralized Planning Promote Efficiency?*

19.7 The Causes of Economic Inefficiency

Market Power   Imperfect Information

***Application 19.3** Deterring Cigarette Smoking*

Externalities/Public Goods

Learning Objectives

- Delineate the difference between partial and general equilibrium analysis.
- Explain the concept of economic efficiency.
- Outline the three conditions necessary for the attainment of economic efficiency.
- Examine efficiency in production and what this implies about input usage across different industries.
- Show how efficiency in output is related to the production possibility frontier.
- Demonstrate how perfect competition satisfies all three conditions for economic efficiency.
- Spell out the reasons why economic efficiency may not be achieved.

The analysis developed in previous chapters focused on individual markets in isolation. Price and quantity in each market, whether it was a product or an input market, were determined by supply and demand conditions in that specific market. The analysis largely ignored events in other markets.

We know, of course, that markets are interrelated. Changes in the market for gasoline, for example, affect the automobile market, and changes in the automobile market in turn affect the gasoline market. Consequently, an analysis that focuses on one market in isolation is incomplete. To see how the interdependence of individual markets can be taken into account, this chapter provides a brief introduction to **general equilibrium analysis**, the study of how equilibrium is determined in all markets simultaneously.

GENERAL EQUILIBRIUM ANALYSIS
the study of how equilibrium is determined in all markets simultaneously

In addition to exploring their interdependence, this chapter also evaluates the extent to which markets promote the well-being of the members of a society as a whole. We revisit the concept of economic efficiency first introduced in Chapter 6, and discuss the conditions that must be met for an economy to ensure efficiency in allocation of inputs across firms, distribution of products among consumers, and output mix. We show how perfect competition satisfies these conditions as well as consider the reasons why markets may fail to promote efficiency.

19.1   PARTIAL AND GENERAL EQUILIBRIUM ANALYSIS COMPARED

PARTIAL EQUILIBRIUM ANALYSIS
the study of the determination of an equilibrium price and quantity in a given product or input market viewed as self-contained and independent of other markets

In previous chapters we have employed partial equilibrium analysis almost exclusively. **Partial equilibrium analysis** focuses on the determination of an equilibrium price and quantity in a given product or input market, where the market is viewed as largely self-contained and independent of other markets. An analysis of the gasoline market using supply and demand curves, for instance, is a partial equilibrium analysis. The supply and demand curves for gasoline are drawn on the assumption of given and unchanging prices in other product and input markets. In effect, these assumptions allow us to focus on the gasoline market and ignore others.

Characteristic of a partial equilibrium approach is the assumption that *some things—like other prices—that conceivably could change do not*. In many situations this assumption may be reasonable. For example, a tax on gasoline that raises its price is unlikely to have a measurable effect on the price of wristwatches. A change in the price of gasoline could conceivably cause a change in the price of wristwatches by raising or lowering their demand, but in a partial equilibrium analysis of the gasoline market, we assume it does not. In contrast, a higher gasoline price would probably have a significant effect on the market for automobiles. In that case the partial equilibrium assumption that the price of automobiles does not change could be seriously flawed.

Partial equilibrium analysis therefore tends to ignore some of the interrelationships among prices and markets. Formally, this is accomplished through the "other things equal" assumption. By contrast, in a general equilibrium analysis all prices are considered variable, and the analysis focuses on the simultaneous determination of equilibrium in all markets.

The Mutual Interdependence of Markets Illustrated

Before turning to the discussion of a model of general equilibrium, let's examine what is meant by the interrelationships, or *mutual interdependence*, among markets. Consider two markets where the interdependence on the demand side is likely to be fairly pronounced— the markets for margarine and butter. Margarine and butter are close substitutes, so a higher price for margarine shifts the demand curve for butter upward; similarly, a higher price for butter causes the demand for margarine to increase.

Figure 19.1a shows the margarine market, and Figure 19.1b shows the butter market. Initially, assume both markets are in equilibrium, with the price of margarine at $2.00 per pound and the price of butter at $3.00 per pound. From our earlier analysis of demand curve relationships, recall that the prices of other goods are assumed to be fixed at all points along a given demand curve, as are consumers' incomes and tastes. Our emphasis here will be on prices in other markets. Thus, at all points along D_M the price of butter is $3.00 per pound, and at all points along D_B the price of margarine is $2.00 per pound.

To illustrate the significance of mutual interdependence, let's examine the effects of an excise tax of $0.75 per pound on margarine. Using the familiar partial equilibrium approach,

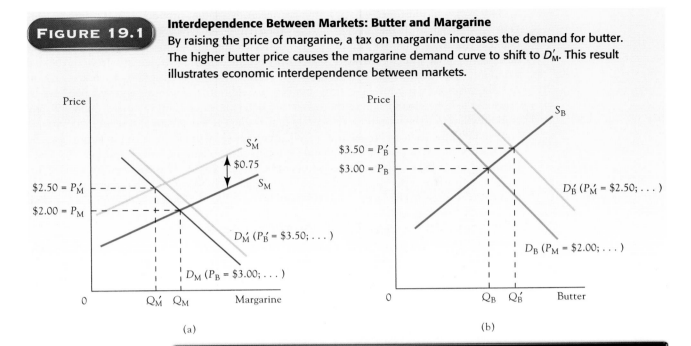

FIGURE 19.1

Interdependence Between Markets: Butter and Margarine
By raising the price of margarine, a tax on margarine increases the demand for butter. The higher butter price causes the margarine demand curve to shift to D'_M. This result illustrates economic interdependence between markets.

(a)

(b)

we could analyze an excise tax by shifting the supply curve in Figure 19.1a upward to S'_M, which causes the price to rise to $2.50 and the quantity to fall to Q'_M. Now, however, let's see how the partial equilibrium approach ignores the mutual interdependence between the margarine and butter markets and what implications this procedure has for the analysis.

The foregoing partial equilibrium analysis neglects two types of consequences. *First, the change in the margarine market has a* **spillover effect** *on other markets, which disrupts the equilibria there.* In our example, the higher margarine price causes the demand for butter to rise because butter and margarine are substitutes. Don't forget that in drawing D_B we held the price of margarine fixed at $2.00 per pound; when the tax raises the price of margarine to $2.50 per pound, we must redraw the demand curve for butter on the basis of the higher margarine price. Thus, D'_B is the demand for butter when the margarine price is $2.50. In short, the tax on margarine leads to an increase in the demand for butter, which in turn increases the price of butter to $3.50 per pound.

If this type of spillover effect from the margarine market to the butter market were the only effect neglected by partial equilibrium analysis, there would be little cause for concern. The analysis of the margarine market would remain exactly correct. But there is a *second ef*-*fect neglected: The induced change in the butter market has a* **feedback effect** *on the margarine market.* So far, the tax on margarine has led to a higher price for butter. Now consider the demand curve for margarine once again. We constructed the original demand curve, D_M, on the assumption that the price of butter was $3.00. Since the price of butter has risen, the demand curve for margarine will shift upward. When the price of butter is $3.50, for example, the demand curve for margarine is D'_M. So the partial equilibrium analysis of the margarine market, which identified P'_M and Q'_M as the equilibrium price and quantity, does not correctly identify the final result. Partial equilibrium analysis, by assuming that prices in other markets remain unchanged, rules out the possibility of such a feedback effect.

SPILLOVER EFFECT
a change in equilibrium in one market that affects other markets

FEEDBACK EFFECT
a change in equilibrium in a market that is caused by events in other markets that, in turn, are the result of an initial change in equilibrium in the market under consideration

This example illustrates what economists mean by mutual interdependence among markets: what happens in one market affects others (spillover effects) and is affected by other markets (feedback effects). The margarine–butter example is a simple case of mutual interdependence since just two markets, related only on the demand side, are involved. In the real world a change in one market may affect the operation of hundreds of other markets and, in turn, be affected by conditions in those markets. In addition, the interdependence need not be restricted to the demand side of the markets. The employment and pricing of inputs in one market will affect the supply curves in others that employ the same or closely related inputs. For example, the increase in defense spending promoted by the Reagan administration in the 1980s led to an expansion in the demand for inputs such as land in Boston and southern California, where a large number of defense contractors are based. This increase in demand for land made it more expensive for other industries such as banking, entertainment, and education to do business in the same cities and shifted their respective output supply curves leftward.

When Should General Equilibrium Analysis Be Used?

The first 18 chapters of this book concentrated on partial equilibrium analysis, and it would not have received such emphasis if economists believed that it was an unreliable framework for analysis. Yet we have seen that partial equilibrium analysis neglects some market interdependencies that can affect the way a given market functions. General equilibrium analysis, in contrast, accounts for the interrelationships among markets. On these grounds, the general equilibrium approach would appear superior, so it is worthwhile to explain why economists continue to rely on partial equilibrium analysis to study many issues.

Partial equilibrium analysis explicitly ignores some factors that could have a bearing on the analysis, but in many cases these neglected factors may be *quantitatively* unimportant in the sense that if they were taken into account, the conclusions would be affected only to a trivial degree. For instance, in our butter–margarine example, the excise tax on margarine may affect the price of butter only slightly, and this in turn will have an even smaller effect on the demand curve for margarine. In that case, ignoring the market interdependencies and assuming that the margarine demand curve "stays put" yields a result that is a sufficiently close approximation to the true outcome.

This does not imply that partial equilibrium analysis can always be used. There are cases where the implications of a partial and general equilibrium analysis differ significantly. A reasonable guideline is that partial analysis is usually accurate in cases involving a change in conditions primarily affecting one market among many, with repercussions on other markets dissipated throughout the economy. When a change in conditions affects many, or all, markets at the same time and to the same degree, however, general equilibrium analysis tends to be more appropriate.

An example will clarify this distinction. Suppose that a price control is applied to one product—say, rental housing. Rent control is sure to have a major impact on the rental housing market, but the impact on other markets is likely to be slight and uncertain. Most economists would agree that a partial equilibrium analysis focusing on the rental housing market is adequate to investigate this issue.

By contrast, imagine that the government applies price controls to all goods simultaneously. With all markets affected at the same time, and to a large degree, a general equilibrium analysis is required. In fact, a partial equilibrium analysis may give misleading results. Suppose, for example, that the government mandates a 50 percent reduction in the prices of all goods except rental housing and a 5 percent reduction for that. If we looked at the rental housing market using partial equilibrium analysis, we would be tempted to say the output of rental housing would fall and a shortage would result. The opposite is more likely to be the case because this set of price controls *increases the relative price* of rental housing compared with all other goods. Resources would shift from industries where prices are most depressed to those where they are least depressed, increasing output in the latter. Only a general equilibrium analysis is capable of accurately evaluating this situation.

Thus, both general and partial equilibrium approaches are quite valuable, with their relative usefulness depending on the issue under investigation. Earlier chapters give numerous examples of topics that can be fruitfully studied by using the partial equilibrium approach. This section has shown how the separate markets form an interconnected system and attain a general equilibrium. In the remainder of this chapter we will see how we can use the general equilibrium model to evaluate the efficiency with which an economy allocates resources. Chapter 6 first introduced the concept of economic efficiency in the context of the distribution of fixed quantities of goods among consumers. Now we are concerned with *efficiency* in a more general sense. In our discussion the terms *efficient* and **Pareto optimal** are used interchangeably; the latter term is named after the Italian economist Vilfredo Pareto, who first gave careful attention to the concept.[1]

PARETO OPTIMAL
the condition in which it is not possible, through any feasible change in resource allocation, to benefit one person without making some other person or persons worse off

19.2 ECONOMIC EFFICIENCY

Let's begin with a formal definition of economic efficiency and its corollary, economic inefficiency. *An allocation of resources is* **efficient** *when it is not possible, through any feasible change in resource allocation, to benefit one person without making some other person, or persons, worse off.* In other words, when the economy is operating efficiently, there is no scope for further improvements in anyone's welfare or well-being unless they are benefited at the expense of other people.

An allocation of resources is **inefficient** *when it is possible, through some feasible change in the allocation of resources, to benefit at least one person without making any other person worse off.* Inefficiency implies waste, in the sense that the economy is not satisfying the wants of people as well as it could.

These abstract definitions become clearer when we employ a diagram. To simplify matters, let's assume that society consists of only two people, Scrooge and Tiny Tim, although we can easily extend the analysis to larger numbers. In Figure 19.2, Scrooge's welfare is measured horizontally and Tiny Tim's welfare vertically. Since no objective way exists to attach units of measurement to a person's utility or welfare, the welfare measure is entirely ordinal. In other words, a rightward movement in the diagram implies that the resource allocation has changed in a way beneficial to Scrooge, but it does not tell us how much better off Scrooge is. All we know from the diagram is that the farther to the right we are, the higher is the indifference curve Scrooge attains. Upward movements similarly imply a change beneficial to Tiny Tim.

The levels of well-being attained by Scrooge and Tiny Tim depend on their consumption of goods. There are limits, though, to how much they can consume, because limited quantities of resources are available to produce those goods. Scarcity places upper limits on the well-being of Scrooge and Tiny Tim, and these limits are shown in Figure 19.2 by the welfare frontier WW'. The **welfare frontier** separates welfare levels that are attainable from those that cannot be reached, given the available resources. Any point on or inside the frontier is attainable. For example, different allocations of resources would place Scrooge and Tiny Tim at points A, B, C, D, E, or F. Any point beyond the frontier, like L, is unattainable. The economy cannot produce enough goods and services to make Scrooge and Tiny Tim as well off as the point indicated by L.

A welfare frontier illustrates how the allocation of resources affects the well-being of members of society. To use it correctly, we must understand how it is derived from the un-

EFFICIENT
carries the same meaning as Pareto optimal

INEFFICIENT
the condition in which it is possible, through some feasible change in the allocation of resources, to benefit at least one person without making any other person worse off

WELFARE FRONTIER
a curve that separates welfare levels that are attainable from those that cannot be reached given the available resources

---

[1]Vilfredo Pareto, *Manuel d'Economie* (Paris: V. Giard and E. Briere, 1903).

FIGURE 19.2

The Welfare Frontier
The welfare frontier shows how any resource allocation affects the well-being of both consumers. Any point on the frontier is an efficient point. Points inside the frontier, like point D, are inefficient since both parties can be made better off.

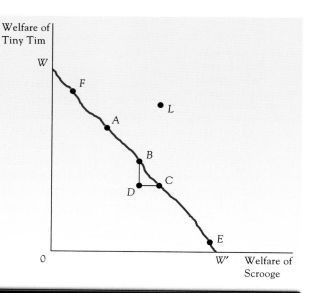

derlying characteristics of an allocation of resources, and we will do this in the remainder of the chapter. For now, let's take the existence of the frontier for granted and use it to illustrate several points about the nature of economic efficiency.

Any resource allocation resulting in a point on the WW′ frontier is efficient, or optimal; that is, it satisfies the definition of efficiency given earlier. Consider point A, for example. Since it is impossible to move beyond the frontier, there is no move from point A that can benefit one person without making the other worse off. The same is also true of point B; any move from point B harms at least one of the two persons. Thus, point B also represents an efficient allocation of resources. Indeed, *every point lying on the welfare frontier satisfies the definition of economic efficiency.* In fact, all points on the frontier are equally efficient, and no point on the frontier is more efficient than any other.

Any point inside the welfare frontier represents an inefficient resource allocation. Point D, for instance, is inefficient because resources can be reallocated so as to benefit one person without harming the other. A vertical move from D to B makes Tiny Tim better off and leaves Scrooge's welfare unchanged. Alternatively, a horizontal move from D to C benefits Scrooge without harming Tiny Tim. *Every point lying inside the welfare frontier represents an inefficient allocation of resources.* Note, also, that an inefficient point means it is possible to reallocate resources in a way that makes *all* parties better off, such as a move from point D to a point between B and C on the welfare frontier.

Efficiency as a Goal for Economic Performance

The notions of efficient and inefficient resource allocations, as summarized by the points on and inside the welfare frontier, naturally lead to an emphasis on the factors that affect the level and distribution of well-being. But this focus does not allow us to identify one resource allocation as being better than any other. To see why, consider a choice among the points on the welfare frontier, all of which are efficient. Is one better than another? Note that the points differ in terms of the distribution of well-being; a movement from one point to another—for example, from E to B—benefits one person and harms another. Since there is no objective way to compare one person's gain with another person's loss—interpersonal utility comparisons cannot be made objectively—economics must remain silent on this issue. As individuals we might believe for normative reasons that B is superior to E, but we can't rest our judgment on positive, efficiency-based considerations.

To see that economic efficiency is a reasonable goal, notice what an inefficient allocation of resources, like point D, implies. Inefficiency indicates that it is possible to change the allocation of resources in a way that benefits some, perhaps all, people without harming anyone, a noble goal. Since a move from inside the frontier at D to a point on the frontier between B and C benefits both parties, would anyone oppose such a change? In this context we must realize that when we talk about people being better off, we mean better off according to their own preferences: Tiny Tim views himself as better off at B than at D. Accepting efficiency as a goal means accepting the premise that each person is the best judge of his or her own welfare. One could quarrel with this view, but it appears a reasonable assumption in most situations. If granted, we could conclude that changes benefiting some and harming no one—that is, movements from inefficient to efficient points—are desirable, which is why we use efficiency as a goal.

We cannot conclude, however, that *any* efficient position is better than *any* inefficient position. For example, although a move between points D and E is a change from an inefficient to an efficient allocation, the change in this case greatly benefits Scrooge while impoverishing Tiny Tim. In comparing these points, we cannot simply note that one is efficient and the other inefficient; we must also take into account the change in the distribution of well-being. Taking equity considerations into account, we might judge point D to be superior to point E. By making such a judgment, however, we recognize that efficiency is not the only goal: the distribution of well-being counts, too. Even so, efficiency goals are not irrelevant since there are still efficient points between B and C making both Scrooge and Tiny Tim better off than point D.

Almost all real-world resource allocation changes involve both a move to a more (or less) efficient position and a change in the distribution of well-being, like the move from D to E in the diagram. In these cases, demonstrating that there is a gain in efficiency does not prove that the change is desirable, since distributional effects are important as well. Consequently, economists are generally reluctant to claim that one resource allocation is superior to any other. Economics can sometimes prove that one situation is more efficient than another, but there are other goals besides efficiency.

19.3 CONDITIONS FOR ECONOMIC EFFICIENCY

Notwithstanding the importance of other goals, such as distributional equity, let us turn now to deriving the conditions necessary for achieving economic efficiency. In general, any economy must solve three fundamental economic problems:

1. How much of each good to produce.
2. How much of each input to use in the production of each good.
3. How to distribute goods among consumers.

Each of these problems can be solved in different ways, but not all solutions are equally efficient. For example, consider the distribution of goods among consumers, an issue we discussed in Chapter 6. Recall that in a simple two-person, two-good setting, an Edgeworth exchange box shows all possible distributions of goods between consumers. Only some of these distributions, however, are efficient. The contract curve identifies which distributions of goods across consumers are efficient; distributions located off the contract curve are inefficient. At all points along the contract curve, the marginal rate of substitution (MRS) between any two goods is the same across consumers. Thus, we can concisely express the condition for efficiency in the distribution of goods as:

$$MRS^1 = MRS^2 = \ldots = MRS^i; \tag{1}$$

where the superscripts 1, 2, . . . i represent the i consumers in an economy. If this condition does not hold, at least some consumers can be made better of without harming other consumers by a change in the distribution of goods.

We now turn to developing similar conditions for efficiency in both production and output. We do so by employing the now-familiar constructs of an Edgeworth box and a production possibility frontier (*PPF*).

19.4 EFFICIENCY IN PRODUCTION

To address the issue of efficiency in production, think about a simplified world in which there are only two inputs (labor and land) and two possible consumer goods produced with the inputs (food and clothing). Assume that consumers' incomes are earned through the sale of the services of their labor and land and are spent on food and clothing. All inputs are homogeneous; each worker, for instance, is interchangeable with any other. Most importantly, the overall quantities of land and labor are taken to be in fixed supply. In other words, the aggregate labor and land supply curves are vertical. Finally, although the total supply of each input is fixed, the amount employed in each industry is not. The food industry can employ more labor, for instance, but only by bidding workers away from the clothing industry, since the total employment by the two industries together is fixed.

Although these assumptions describe about the simplest economy imaginable, understanding how the pieces fit together is still complex. Note that there are six identifiable markets: labor employed in producing food, labor employed in producing clothing, land employed in producing food, land employed in producing clothing, and the two product markets for food and clothing. Moreover, these markets are interrelated for the food industry to expand, for example, it will have to bid away inputs from the clothing industry. Consequently, we must determine a pattern of prices and quantities in which the quantities demanded and supplied in each of the six markets are brought into equality simultaneously—that is, a general equilibrium.

The Edgeworth Production Box

An **Edgeworth production box** (analogous to the Edgeworth exchange box introduced in Chapter 6) identifies all the ways labor and land can be allocated between the food and clothing industries in our simplified economy. As shown in Figure 19.3, the length of the box indicates the amount of labor employed by the two industries, in this case 80 units; the height of the box shows the amount of land employed by the two industries, 50 units.

Through the Edgeworth production box we can determine the quantities of labor and land employed by both industries. Let's measure the employment of labor in clothing production horizontally from the southwest corner, point 0_C, and the employment of land in clothing production vertically from the same point. Point B, for example, indicates that 40 units of labor (*L*) and 10 units of land (*A*) are used in clothing production; point C implies 60 units of labor and 20 units of land. Because the total available input quantities are shown by the dimensions of the box, a given point also identifies employment levels in the food industry. Since total employment of labor in both industries together is 80 units, if the clothing industry employs 40 units, the food industry must be employing the remaining 40 units. In the diagram we measure the employment of labor and land in the food industry to the left and down, respectively, from the northeast corner, point 0_F. Thus, at point B the clothing industry employs 10*A* and 40*L*, and the food industry employs the remaining 40*A* and 40*L*. A move from B to C would indicate an expansion in employment of both inputs in clothing production to 20*A* and 60*L*, coupled with a decline in employment of both inputs in food production to 30*A* and 20*L*. Put differently, a move from B to C shows that the clothing industry has bid 20 labor units and 10 land units away from the food industry, although the total employment in both industries together remains unchanged.

EDGEWORTH PRODUCTION BOX
a diagram that identifies all the ways two inputs such as labor and land can be allocated between industries in a simplified economy

FIGURE 19.3

Edgeworth Production Box

With fixed total input supplies, we can show all the possible ways of allocating inputs between food and clothing production with an Edgeworth production box. Point B, for example, indicates employment of 10 units of land (A) and 40 units of labor (L) in clothing production; the remaining inputs, 40 units of land and 40 units of labor, are employed in food production.

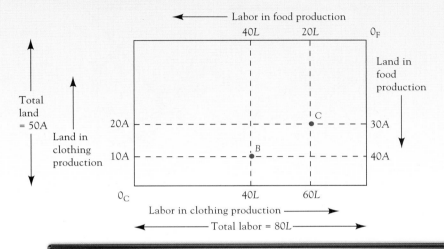

Having shown how the allocation of inputs is indicated by a point in the Edgeworth production box, we next want to identify the levels of food and clothing output corresponding to each possible input allocation. This is accomplished by incorporating clothing and food isoquants into the diagram, since these curves identify the output level associated with each combination of inputs. In Chapter 7 we explained how a *firm's* production function could be graphed as a set of isoquants. Here, though, isoquants are used to represent the production function of an entire *industry* composed of all the separate firms producing each good. The industry isoquants have the same characteristics as those of individual firms.

Figure 19.4 incorporates the clothing and food isoquants into the Edgeworth production box. For clothing, several isoquants are drawn with their origin at point 0_C—100C, 150C, 160C, and so on—each labeled to indicate the amount of clothing produced with each combination of land and labor. Note that the isoquants have the familiar shapes discussed in Chapter 7. The food isoquants—100F, 220F, 260F, and so on—are drawn relative to the origin at point 0_F, with the employment of labor measured to the left and the employment of land measured down from 0_F. In effect, the food isoquants are turned upside down, which accounts for their unconventional appearance. Nonetheless, the food isoquants embody the familiar properties, with isoquants lying closer to the origin at point 0_F representing lower food output.

With the isoquants drawn in, each point in the Edgeworth production box indicates the employment of labor and land in both industries as well as the output of food and clothing. For example, point B implies employment of 40L and 10A by the clothing industry, with an output of 100 clothing units; point B also indicates employment of 40A and 40L by the food industry (see point B in Figure 19.3 to understand this explicitly; to avoid cluttering the diagram, we have not shown these input employment levels on the Figure 19.4 axes), with an output of 300 food units. In the same way, point D shows employment of 20A and 10L producing 100 units of food, with the remaining 30A and 70L used to produce 200 units of clothing.

FIGURE 19.4

General Equilibrium in Input Markets
A competitive equilibrium involves an input allocation lying somewhere on the contract curve connecting points of tangency between food and clothing isoquants. Input prices depend on exactly where on the contract curve the equilibrium lies.

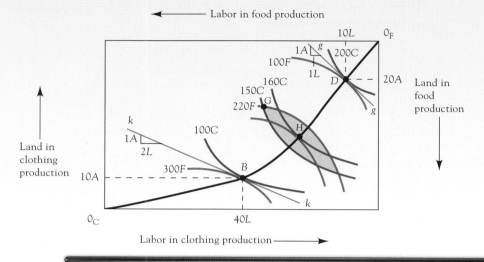

The Production Contract Curve and Efficiency in Production

The Figure 19.4 box diagram shows every conceivable way of allocating labor and land between the two industries. Still, only some of these resource allocations are *efficient* in the sense that the output of one good cannot be increased without decreasing the output of the other. Indeed, *only input allocations where the isoquants are tangent to one another represent efficient resource allocations.* The *production contract curve* running from one origin to the other and passing through points B, H, and D connects all the points where food and clothing isoquants are tangent.

To see why only points on the production contract curve represent efficient input allocations, consider point G, where a food (220F) and a clothing (150C) isoquant intersect. At point G, a lens-shaped area lies between the intersecting food and clothing isoquants. The significance of the lens-shaped area is that every allocation of inputs identified by a point inside the area involves larger outputs of both goods than at point G. For instance, point H implies greater production of both clothing (160) and food (260) than point G (150 clothing units and 220 food units). Thus, a move from point G to H, which involves shifting some labor from the food to the clothing industry and some land from the clothing to the food industry, will increase the output of both goods at no additional cost. This result is true at every point in the box diagram where isoquants intersect. Thus, any point where food and clothing isoquants intersect, which includes all points not on the production contract curve, cannot represent efficiency in production.

General Equilibrium in Competitive Input Markets

If perfect competition prevails in input markets, a point on the production contract curve (that is, efficiency in production) will be attained. To see why, recall from Chapter 16 that in competitive markets, the price of an input tends to be equalized across firms and industries. Here, this tendency means that the wage rate earned by laborers will be the same in the clothing and food industries, and similarly for the rental price of land. Furthermore, every firm will minimize cost by employing inputs in quantities so that the ratio of marginal products (MP) equals the ratio of input prices (Chapter 6). For a wage rate of w and a rental price of land of v, the condition for cost minimization is:

$$w/v = MP_L/MP_A = MRTS_{LA}. \tag{2}$$

Geometrically, this equality is shown by the tangency between an isocost line, with a slope of w/v, and an isoquant where the isoquant's slope, the marginal rate of technical substitution ($MRTS_{LA}$), is equal to the ratio of marginal products (MP_L/MP_A).

In a competitive equilibrium, each food producer operates at a point where the slope of its food isoquant equals the ratio of input prices, w/v. In addition, each clothing producer operates at a point where the slope of its clothing isoquant also equals the *same* input price ratio. *Therefore, the slopes of the clothing and food isoquants must equal one another since both are equal to the same input price ratio.* Consequently, the equilibrium must lie on the contract curve, which identifies resource allocations where the slopes of clothing and food isoquants are equal. For example, if the wage rate is half the rental price of land, isocost lines have a slope of $1/2$, as illustrated by line *kk* in Figure 19.4. To minimize the cost of producing 100 clothing units, clothing producers would operate at point *B* where the 100C isoquant is tangent to *kk*. Similarly, food producers also minimize the cost of producing 300 food units when they use the remaining inputs, since the 300F isoquant is also tangent to *kk* at point *B*. Only when the isoquants are tangent can both industries be minimizing cost when confronted with the same input prices.

For these reasons the competitive equilibrium can exist only at a point on the production contract curve in Figure 19.4. Exactly where on the contract curve the equilibrium will lie depends on the consumers' demands for clothing and food. If the demand for clothing is relatively high, for example, equilibrium will occur at a point like *D*, where a large quantity of clothing and very little food is produced. On the other hand, if the demand for clothing is relatively small (which is equivalent to saying that the demand for food is relatively great), not much clothing and a large quantity of food will be produced, as at point *B*.

19.5 THE PRODUCTION POSSIBILITY FRONTIER AND EFFICIENCY IN OUTPUT

To bring the output markets for food and clothing clearly into focus, we use a concept introduced in Chapter 1, the *production possibility frontier* (PPF). The PPF shows the alternative combinations of food and clothing that can be produced with fixed supplies of labor and land. The same information is already contained in the Edgeworth production box, but the PPF presents it more clearly. Glance once again at the contract curve in Figure 19.4. Each point identifies a certain combination of food and clothing output that can be produced with available inputs. A movement between points on the contract curve, as from *B* to *H*, shows that as more clothing is produced, food output must fall.

The PPF is derived from the contract curve in Figure 19.4 by plotting the various possible output combinations directly. In Figure 19.5, the frontier is the bowed-out curve ZZ'. Points *B*, *H*, *D*, and *G* in Figure 19.5 correspond to these same points in Figure 19.4. For example, point *B* indicates an output combination of 100C and 300F in both diagrams. The frontier slopes downward, indicating that more clothing can be produced only by giving up food output, since land and labor must be transferred from the food to the clothing industry to produce more clothing.

With the available quantities of labor and land, firms can produce any combination of output lying on or inside the PPF. Points lying inside the frontier represent allocations that are production inefficient. That is, in Figure 19.5 a point like *G* inside the frontier corre-

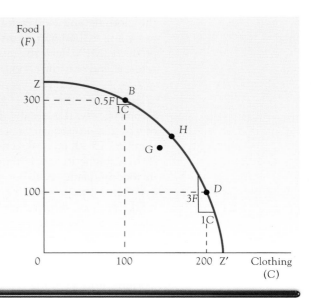

FIGURE 19.5

The Production Possibility Frontier Revisited
The *PPF* plots the output combinations from the contract curve in Figure 19.5. It is normally bowed out from the origin. The slope of the frontier, called the *marginal rate of transformation*, shows how much of one good must be given up to produce more of the other.

MARGINAL RATE OF TRANSFORMATION
the rate at which one product can be "transformed" into another

sponds to a point where isoquants intersect in the box diagram of Figure 19.4; more of both goods can be obtained from the available resources, such as at point *H*.

As discussed in Chapter 1, the *PPF* is typically bowed out, or concave to the origin. The *PPF* slope thus becomes more steep in absolute value as we move down the curve from point *Z* to point *Z'*. Like many slopes in economics, the *PPF* slope has a special name, the **marginal rate of transformation**, or *MRT*. At any point on the frontier, the *MRT* indicates the rate at which one product can be "transformed" into the other. Of course, once food is produced, it cannot usually be changed into clothing, but clothing output can be increased by transferring land and labor from food to clothing production, thereby gaining more clothing at a cost of reduced food output. At point *B* the marginal rate of transformation is 0.5F/1.0C, indicating that production of one more clothing unit requires removing resources from food production by an amount that will reduce food output by 1/2 unit. Further down the frontier, at point *D*, the *MRT* is 3F/1C, implying that increasing clothing output by one unit necessitates a sacrifice of three food units.

As Chapter 1 shows, the marginal rate of transformation, or the *PPF* slope, reflects the opportunity cost of one good in terms of the other. The marginal rate of transformation also equals the ratio of the monetary marginal cost (MC) of clothing production to the monetary marginal cost of food production. *At any point on the frontier, the slope, or* MRT, *equals* MC_C/MC_F. To see why, suppose that at current output levels the marginal costs of clothing and food are \$100 and \$200, respectively. How much food would we have to give up to produce one more clothing unit? (That is, what is the *MRT* between clothing and food?) Producing one more clothing unit utilizes \$100 worth of resources (labor and land), so MC_C = \$100. If we remove \$100 worth of resources from food production, food output falls by half a unit since the marginal cost of a food unit is \$200. Thus, we must give up half a food unit to produce one more clothing unit—that is, *MRT* = 0.5F/1.0C = 1F/2C. This ratio is also equal to the marginal cost ratio: MC_C/MC_F = \$100/\$200 = 1F/2C.

When the marginal cost of food is twice that of clothing, we know that one more clothing unit requires a sacrifice of half a unit of food. Point *B* illustrates this situation. As we move down the frontier, the marginal cost of clothing increases as more is produced, and the marginal cost of food declines as less is produced. (This means that the ratio MC_C/MC_F rises since the numerator increases and the denominator decreases.) At point *D*, for example,

$MC_C/MC_F = 3F/1C$, showing that the marginal cost of clothing is three times the marginal cost of food, so three food units must be given up to produce one more clothing unit.[2]

Efficiency in Output

Now we come to the question of where on the *PPF* we should operate—that is, what combination of food and clothing should be produced? Producing an efficient output mix requires balancing the subjective wants, or preferences, of consumers with the objective conditions of production. More specifically, efficiency in output is attained when the rate at which consumers are willing to exchange one good for another (the marginal rate of substitution, or *MRS*, of those consumers) equals the rate at which, on the production side, one good can be transformed into another (the marginal rate of transformation, or *MRT*):

$$MRS^1 = MRS^2 = \ldots = MRS^i = MRT; \tag{3}$$

where the superscripts refer to an economy's *i* consumers.

To see why the foregoing equality needs to be satisfied to ensure efficiency in output, recall from Chapter 4 that, in the context of our example, MRS_{CF} reflects a consumer's willingness to pay for an additional unit of clothing by consuming less food. As we saw in the preceding section, MRT_{CF} represents the ratio of the marginal cost of clothing relative to the marginal cost of food.

Now, suppose that the MRS_{CF} is identical across all consumers (that is, we have achieved efficiency in distribution) and equal to three units of food per clothing unit, while the MRT_{CF} equals one unit of food per clothing unit. Such an outcome would not represent an efficient output mix. When consumers' MRS_{CF} is $3F/1C$, then the marginal benefit to a consumer of one more clothing unit is equal to three units of food—this is the maximum amount of food that a consumer is willing to give up for one more clothing unit. In contrast, when MRT_{CF} is $1F/1C$, the marginal cost of one more clothing unit is only one food unit. Thus, when MRS_{CF} is greater than MRT_{CF}, the marginal benefit to consumers of more clothing output exceeds the marginal cost of producing it—both expressed in units of food. Additional clothing is worth more to consumers than it costs to produce, and consumers can be made better off by moving along the *PPF* to a point where more clothing and less food is produced.

As more clothing and less food is produced, MRT_{CF} rises, and as consumers consume more clothing and less food, their marginal rates of substitution tend to decline. The process of producing more clothing and less food tends to bring MRT_{CF} and MRS_{CF} closer together. This movement along the production frontier can continue to benefit consumers until the two terms are exactly equal. In sum, *it is always possible to change the output mix and leave consumers better off whenever their common marginal rates of substitution are not equal to the marginal rate of transformation.*

We can illustrate the preceding analysis with a diagram. In Figure 19.6, the points on the production possibility frontier *ZZ'* all represent efficient input allocations in our two-good economy. Of these points, an efficient output mix is represented by a point such as *P* on the frontier. At point *P*, the marginal rate of transformation between food and clothing (MRT_{CF}) equals the slope of a representative consumer's indifference curve, the marginal rate of substitution between food and clothing (MRS_{CF}), at the optimal consumption point, *E*, chosen by the consumer. The slope of the production frontier at *P* is reflected by the slope of line *gg* and is equal to two units of food per one clothing unit. The slope of the representa-

---

[2]As mentioned in Chapter 1, it is possible for the *PPF* to be a straight line with a constant slope. This situation occurs when both industries are constant-cost so that each good's marginal cost is constant over all output levels. The ratio MC_C/MC_F is constant at all output combinations, implying a linear production frontier.

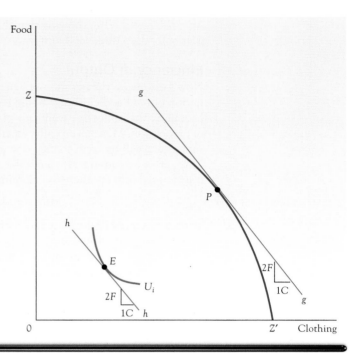

FIGURE 19.6

Efficiency in Output
The output mix at point *P*, together with the consumption point *E* selected by a representative consumer, satisfy the condition for efficiency in output. For efficiency in output to be realized, the slope of the *PPF* (the marginal rate of transformation) must equal the slope of all consumers' indifference curves (the marginal rates of substitution) at their selected consumption points.

tive consumer's indifference curve U_i at consumption point E is represented by the slope of the line *hh* and also equals two units of food per clothing unit.[3]

By calling for the marginal rates of substitution and transformation to be equal, the condition for efficiency in output is simply restating what we discussed earlier in Chapter 10: namely, efficiency in output requires the output of any good to be expanded to the point where marginal benefit (*MRS*) equals marginal cost (*MRT*). The only difference of note is that in Chapter 10 we employed a partial equilibrium perspective and showed how, at any given output level, the marginal benefit to consumers from a good is represented by the height of the demand curve, while the height of the supply curve represents the marginal cost. Relying on a partial equilibrium approach, we saw how efficiency in output thus is realized where the demand and supply curves intersect.

In this chapter we have adopted a general equilibrium approach and avoided the assumption that we can treat the market for any good in isolation. The heights of demand and supply curves for a good at any given output level can be influenced by the operation of markets for other goods.

An Economy's *PPF* and the Gains from International Trade
Our general equilibrium analysis has been developed for a society that does not trade with other countries. It can, however, be easily extended to show the consequences of international trade. In fact, a general equilibrium approach provides a particularly vivid demonstration of the sense in which a country can be said to gain from participation in international trade.

In Figure 19.7, suppose that we are a nation initially isolated from world trade and in equilibrium at point *B* on our production possibility frontier, *ZZ′*. The assumed pre-trade price ratio between the two goods is shown by the slope of *gg*, or 2F/1C. Now assume that

---

[3]Figure 19.6 does not rule out the possibility that consumers differ in their incomes and, from that, in how far removed their budget lines may be from the origin. For efficiency in output mix to result, all that is necessary is that, at the consumption points selected by individual consumers, the slopes of various consumers' indifference curves be identical and equal to the slope of the *PPF*.

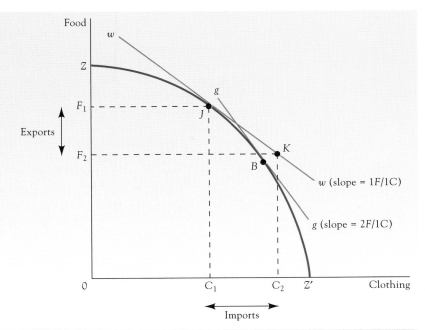

FIGURE 19.7

The *PPF* and the Gains from International Trade

Without trade, equilibrium is at point *B*. When trade becomes possible at terms of $1F/1C$, production takes place at point *J*, and exports of F_1 minus F_2 food units are exchanged for imports of C_2 minus C_1 clothing units. The country can attain more of both goods through trade (at point *K*) than it did without trade (at point *B*).

we begin engaging in international trade. The terms on which other countries are willing to trade are measured by the world price ratio. If that ratio is, for instance, $1F/1C$, then other countries are willing to supply us with one food unit for each clothing unit we supply to them, or to sell us one clothing unit for one food unit. In this model we view our exports of one product as paying for our imports, with the world price ratio indicating how much of one product can be exchanged for the other. (In reality, money is used to pay for imports, but since the money received by international sellers is used to purchase our exports, exports are really being exchanged for imports.)

If the opportunity for international trade at a price ratio of $1F/1C$ exists and the domestic price ratio is initially $2F/1C$, then the domestic economy will undergo a number of changes to adjust to a new equilibrium position. With the world price of clothing lower than the domestic price, clothing consumers will switch from domestic to imported apparel and expand total clothing purchases. As a consequence, the domestic clothing industry will lose customers and have to contract its output. (In partial equilibrium terms, the domestic industry moves down its supply curve until it operates where the domestic price equals the world price.)

At the same time that the clothing industry contracts in the face of foreign competition, the food industry expands. Since the world price of food (one C for one F) is higher than the initial domestic price (one-half C for one F), food producers can make higher profits by exporting food. Food production will expand until the domestic food price rises to equal the world price of food.

So, domestic clothing production falls and domestic food production rises until the domestic price ratio equals the world price ratio. These adjustments are illustrated in Figure 19.7. The world price ratio is equal to the slope of line *ww*. Since domestic production adjusts until the domestic price ratio equals the world price ratio, the output mix produced by the economy shifts to point *J* on the production frontier; at point *J*, the slope of ZZ' equals the slope of *ww*, the world price ratio. Point *J* thus identifies the output mix produced by the economy. It does not, however, identify the domestic consumption of food and clothing since the country can, by engaging in trade, consume a different bundle of products than it produces. In fact, through trade the country may consume any output combination along line *ww*.

Exactly where on ww consumption will take place depends on domestic demands for the two products, which are not shown in the diagram. Suppose, however, that consumers choose to consume at point K. To arrive at K, an amount of food equal to F_1 minus F_2 is exported and used to pay for clothing imports of C_2 minus C_1. *Note that consumption of both products is greater at point K than at the no-trade equilibrium of point B.* This difference shows clearly the nature of the gain made possible when a nation engages in international trade: it is possible to consume more of all goods. In effect, trade makes possible the consumption of goods beyond the domestic production possibility frontier.

Does this analysis demonstrate that trade is beneficial for the country as a whole? As discussed in Chapter 10, the answer to this question depends on what is meant by "country as a whole." Not everyone is likely to benefit. Since the adjustment to trade implies that the domestic clothing industry will contract, the owners of resources specialized in clothing production are likely to find their real incomes reduced. Alternatively, in our general equilibrium model, as the output of food expands at the expense of clothing (see Figure 19.4), the wage rate falls relative to the rental price of land, so workers may lose. Our analysis shows that trade makes it possible for everyone to consume more of all goods, not that everyone actually will. This idea has significant policy implications. The analysis indicates, for example, that the trade liberalization brought about by the North American Free Trade Agreement (NAFTA) and the General Agreement on Tariffs and Trade (GATT) may not result in all Americans consuming more of all goods, though it does make it possible for them to do so. Trade liberalization raises the average standard of living, but not everyone is average.

APPLICATION 19.1 THE EFFECTS OF TRADE RESTRICTIONS ON AN ECONOMY'S CONSUMPTION AND PRODUCTION POSSIBILITIES

In terms of Figure 19.7, trade restrictions prevent a country from moving between points B and J on the production side—a movement that permits access to greater consumption possibilities such as at point K along the free-trade price-ratio line of ww. The effects on a country's consumption possibilities and welfare from such trade restrictions can be substantial. For example, the Smoot-Hawley Tariff Act enacted by the United States in 1930, and similar "beggar-thy-neighbor" protectionist policies adopted at the same time by other countries, arguably exacerbated the severity and length of the worldwide Great Depression.[4]

In addition to the effect of protectionism on a country's overall consumption possibilities, the tradeoffs implied on the production side can be quite sizable.[5] For

example, consider the case of voluntary export restraints (VERs) on sales of Japanese cars in the United States. Since 1981, Japanese car manufacturers have "voluntarily" restricted their exports of cars to the United States to 1.7 million cars per year. Robert W. Crandall of the Brookings Institution estimates that under this program 26,000 automotive manufacturing jobs have been saved in the United States at an annual cost of $4.3 billion in diminished U.S. car consumer surplus. The annual cost per domestic auto job preserved by VERs is thus $160,000 ($4.3 billion/26,000) in terms of reduced consumer spending on other, non-automotive goods.

The same type of calculations reveal similarly substantial production-side tradeoffs in the case of other domestic industries protected from international competition. For example, tariffs on imports have been estimated to save 116,000 jobs in the domestic clothing industry at an annual consumer surplus cost of $45,000 per job saved. The cost of preserving a job in the domestic steel industry through government protection from international competition has been estimated at $750,000 per year.

[4]Jagdish Bhagwati, *Protectionism* (Cambridge, Mass.: The MIT Press, 1988).

[5]"The $750,000 Job," in *The Economics of Public Issues,* 9th ed., by Roger L. Miller, Daniel K. Benjamin, and Douglass C. North (New York: HarperCollins Publishers, 1993), pp. 228–233.

19.6   COMPETITIVE MARKETS AND ECONOMIC EFFICIENCY

Economists tend to be advocates of perfect competition because it satisfies all three conditions for economic efficiency. Let's consider each of the three conditions in turn and show why this is the case.

1. As shown in Chapter 6, a perfectly competitive economy results in an efficient distribution of products among consumers. To see why this is the case, recall that, in maximizing utility, each consumer will select a basket of goods where the consumer's *MRS* between any two goods (say, food and clothing) equals the ratio of the prices of the two goods, or:

$$P_C/P_F = MRS_{CF}. \tag{4}$$

Since competitive markets establish a uniform price for each good, the ratio P_C/P_F confronting all consumers is the same. Because all consumers equate their individual marginal rates of substitution to the same price ratio, the marginal rates of substitution between goods will end up being the same across consumers:

$$MRS^1_{CF} = MRS^2_{CF} = \ldots = MRS^i_{CF}; \tag{5}$$

where the superscripts signify the *i* consumers in an economy. This is the condition for an efficient distribution of goods across consumers. A competitive equilibrium therefore implies an efficient distribution of goods.

2. A perfectly competitive economy results in efficiency in production. This point was covered in Section 19.4. Recall that each firm producing a good minimizes cost by employing inputs in quantities such that the marginal rate of technical substitution between the inputs equals the input price ratio. In the context of a two-input economy (labor and land), each firm thus equates:

$$w/v = MRTS_{LA}. \tag{6}$$

Since competitive markets equalize input prices across firms and industries, the ratio w/v is the same for all firms. Therefore, the marginal rates of technical substitution end up being the same across all firms and industries:

$$MRTS^1_{LA} = MRTS^2_{LA} = \ldots = MRTS^j_{LA}; \tag{7}$$

where the superscripts indicate the *j* producers in an economy. This is the condition for efficiency in production. The condition requires that we end up on the contract curve of the economy's Edgeworth production box and that the slopes of all producers' isoquants are identical.

3. A perfectly competitive economy results in efficiency in output. This can be shown by considering the equilibrium conditions of firms in output markets and the equilibrium conditions of consumers. When clothing producers produce the profit-maximizing outputs, they operate where marginal cost equals price, or:

$$P_C = MC_C. \tag{8}$$

For food producers, the profit-maximizing condition is:

$$P_F = MC_F. \tag{9}$$

Dividing equation (8) by (9) yields:

$$P_C/P_F = MC_C/MC_F. \tag{10}$$

We know that MC_C/MC_F equals the marginal rate of transformation between food and clothing (MRT_{CF}) and that utility-maximizing consumers will equate their marginal rates of substitution between food and clothing to the ratio of prices of these two goods (that is, $MRS_{CF} = P_C/P_F$). By substitution, therefore, we obtain:

$$MRS_{CF}^1 = MRS_{CF}^2 = \ldots = MRS_{CF}^i = MRT_{CF}; \tag{11}$$

where the superscripts refer to an economy's i consumers. This is the condition for efficiency in output.

The preceding formal manipulations show that *if perfect competition prevails, then all three conditions for economic efficiency are satisfied.* Perhaps the most intuitive way of understanding why perfect competition efficiently solves the three basic economic problems of distribution, production, and output is to note that a competitive economy relies on voluntary exchanges. Whenever any possible change in the allocation of either inputs or goods promises mutual benefits to market participants, people have an incentive to work out exchanges to realize these gains. If all mutually beneficial exchanges are consummated, as they are in competitive markets, then no further change will benefit some without harming others. The outcome is efficient.

This discussion is proof, at an abstract level, of Adam Smith's famous "invisible hand" theorem: namely, that people pursuing their own ends in competitive markets promote an important social goal—economic efficiency—that is not actually their intention and that they may not even understand. In terms of our welfare frontier construct, it means that competitive markets attain a point on the frontier. Although the one point on the welfare frontier that represents a competitive equilibrium is not the only efficient resource allocation, we should recognize that competitive markets get us to a point on the welfare frontier, no easy task.

The Role of Information

Before closing our discussion of economic efficiency and why perfect competition attains it, we should emphasize the important role of information in the process. When showing what an efficient resource allocation looks like, we assumed that all the relevant information was known: consumer preferences, production functions, and the quantities and productive capabilities of inputs. Clearly, in the real world, with millions of consumers, firms, and products, no one person knows or could possibly ever know all the relevant information needed to attain economic efficiency. Take the case of even a simple lead pencil. Producers of pencils purchase wood, graphite, steel, paint, and rubber from other people. Pencil producers cannot produce these inputs themselves. Despite the fact that no one individual knows how to make a pencil, much less an automobile or a personal computer, these items are produced. How?

The answer lies in the nature of a market system: partial bits of information possessed by many different people are coordinated to produce a result that no one fully comprehends. The only information individual consumers or producers need to know about the rest of the economy to adjust their behavior accordingly is conveyed through prices. For example, if the supply of cotton expands while the supply of wool declines, the price of cotton clothing will fall relative to the price of wool clothing. Buyers will substitute cotton for wool in their apparel, using more of the plentiful fabric and economizing on the scarce. This efficient response can, and probably will, occur without anyone knowing why prices changed the way they did.

A market system can function efficiently without any single individual understanding how. In this sense markets economize on the information that people individually require to coordinate their economic activities. An immense amount of information must be utilized to achieve an efficient allocation of resources. Perhaps the most significant implication of our analysis is that, in principle, an efficient outcome can be accomplished by decentralized, voluntary transactions among people, each of whom has only a tiny portion of the requisite information.

APPLICATION 19.2   CAN CENTRALIZED PLANNING PROMOTE EFFICIENCY?

During the early part of this century, economists Oscar Lange and Abba Lerner argued that it would be possible to attain Pareto optimality through central planning. All that was necessary to attain such an outcome, according to them, was individual consumers and producers reporting to a central planning board information about underlying consumer preferences, production technology, input availability, and so on. The central planning board could then specify the amount of each commodity to be produced, the input usage levels to be used in production, and the distribution of goods among consumers. The scheme proposed by Lange and Lerner gave credence to the fascist and communist governments coming into power at that time and raised the possibility that such forms of government might be more effective in promoting efficiency than governments relying on decentralized, market-based economies.

Among the earliest critics of the hypothesis advanced by Lange and Lerner was Austrian economist Friedrich Hayek.[6] Hayek argued that central planning inevitably must fail because it can never fully accommodate the particular and changing information about costs and/or demand possessed by individual consumers and producers. Moreover, central planning also undermines the incentive consumers and producers have to acquire information and to act on the information they have acquired. As Hayek stated:

[Knowledge of this kind] cannot be conveyed to any central authority in statistical form. The statistics which such a central authority would have to use would have to be arrived at precisely by abstracting from minor differences between the things, by lumping together, as resources of one kind, items which differ as regards location, quality, and other particulars, in a way which may be very significant for the specific decision. It follows from this that central planning based on statistical information by its nature cannot take direct account of these circumstances of time and place and that the central planner will have to find some

way or other in which the decisions depending on them can be left to the "man on the spot." . . . [T]he ultimate decisions must be left to the people who are familiar with these circumstances, who know directly of the relevant changes and of the resources immediately available to meet them. We cannot expect that this problem will be solved by first communicating all this knowledge to a central board which, after integrating all knowledge, issues its orders. We must solve it by some form of decentralization.

[Where] knowledge of the relevant facts is dispersed among many people, prices can act to coordinate the actions of separate people. . . . The marvel is that in a case like the scarcity of one raw material, without an order being issued, without more than perhaps a handful of people knowing the cause, tens of thousands of people whose identity could not be ascertained by months of investigation, are made to use the material or its products more sparingly. . . . I have deliberately used the word "marvel" to shock the reader out of the complacency with which we often take the working of this [price] mechanism for granted. I am convinced that if it were the result of deliberate human design, and if the people guided by the price changes understood that their decisions have significance far beyond their immediate aim, this mechanism would have been acclaimed as one of the greatest triumphs of the human mind. Its misfortune is the double one that it is not the product of human design and that the people guided by it usually do not know why they are made to do what they do. But those who clamor for "conscious direction" [i.e., central planning]—and who cannot believe that anything which has evolved without design (and even without our understanding it) should solve problems which we should not be able to solve consciously—should remember this: The problem is precisely how to expand the span of our utilization of resources beyond the span of control of any one mind; and, therefore, how to dispense with the needs of conscious control and how to provide inducements which will make the individuals do the desirable things without having to tell them what to do.

[6]Friedrich A. Hayek, "The Use of Knowledge in Society," *American Economic Review*, 35 No. 4 (September 1945), pp. 519–530.

19.7   THE CAUSES OF ECONOMIC INEFFICIENCY

A market may fail to satisfy the conditions for Pareto optimality for several reasons, including market power, imperfect information, and externalities/public goods. We briefly discuss each of these reasons in sequence.

Market Power

The preceding section showed that competitive markets, without government intervention, will result in the attainment of Pareto optimality. This will not be the outcome, however, if producers or consumers have some market power and perfect competition does not prevail. To see why monopoly or monopsony power results in economic inefficiency, consider the case of a monopoly in an output market. Suppose, for example, that in our simplified two-good economy, the food industry is competitive while the clothing industry is controlled by a monopoly seller.

The clothing monopoly maximizes its profit by reducing output below the competitive level and setting the per-unit clothing price above the marginal cost. Since the price of food equals its marginal cost (we assumed that the food market is competitive), the relative price of clothing exceeds its relative marginal cost:

$$P_C/P_F > MC_C/MC_F. \tag{12}$$

The preceding inequality indicates that an output market monopoly violates the output efficiency condition. With a monopoly seller in the clothing market, the rate at which consumers are willing to trade food for clothing (MRS_{CF}, which equals P_C/P_F provided consumers are utility maximizers) exceeds the marginal rate of transformation between food and clothing on the production side (MRT_{CF}, or MC_C/MC_F).[7]

More clothing and less food should be produced since the marginal benefit of more clothing, in terms of food, exceeds its marginal cost at the monopoly equilibrium. Such a change in output mix, however, will not occur, because it would be contrary to the profit-maximizing interest of the monopoly clothing supplier.

A similar inefficiency results in the case of monopoly in input markets. For example, suppose that the market for labor in the clothing industry is monopolized by a union. This implies that in our simple, two-good economy, the ratio of the labor wage rate (w) to the rental price of land (v) will be higher in the clothing industry than in the food industry (provided that competition characterizes all other input markets):

$$w_C/v > w_F/v. \tag{13}$$

Since profit-maximizing firms equate their $MRTS$ between labor and land to the relative input costs (that is, $MRTS_{LA} = w/v$), the rate at which producers are willing to exchange land for labor units ($MRTS_{LA}$) will be greater in the clothing than in the food industry. In equilibrium, that is, labor is relatively more productive if employed in clothing manufacturing than in food production. The input-pricing actions of the union, however, prevent the movement of labor from the food to the clothing industry.

In the context of a *PPF* such as that in Figure 19.5, the union's action results in an outcome such as point G inside the frontier. Note that this outcome occurs not because resources are unemployed (since we assume that all inputs are employed), but because of an inefficient allocation of inputs between the food and the clothing industries—inefficiency in

---

[7]In the context of Figure 19.6, the clothing monopoly results in a point on the *PPF* being realized somewhere between Z and P (less than the optimal amount of clothing is produced). The slope at the *PPF* at the realized point is less than the slope of all consumers' indifference curves (as indicated by line *hh* in Figure 19.6). That is, the rate at which consumers are willing to trade food for clothing (given by the slope at line *hh*) is greater than the marginal rate of transformation between food and clothing (as indicated by the slope of the *PPF* at the realized point between Z and P with a clothing monopoly).

production. Total output is lower than it could be, as is total consumption. At least in terms of total economic surplus, society is not as well off at point G as it could be if it were operating on the production frontier.

Imperfect Information

If consumers or producers are not accurately informed, they may take actions that run counter to the dictates of Pareto optimality. For example, consumers may mistakenly think that a certain "miracle" gel can help reverse hair loss. Upon applying the gel to their scalps, the consumers may be disappointed to find that their hair continues to thin. Worse yet, some consumers may end up bald. Likewise, if a computer manufacturer is unaware that a particular chip has a computational glitch, it may use the chip extensively in the production of computers.

Of course, the existence of imperfect information does not in and of itself imply that government intervention can best remedy the problem. After all, information may be considered to be just another good for which private markets provide better production and consumption incentives than do government edicts.

APPLICATION 19.3   DETERRING CIGARETTE SMOKING

Since the early part of this century, increasingly strong scientific evidence has shown that smoking cigarettes is harmful to one's health. As the evidence has mounted, the presumption that government is best able to inform consumers about these effects has prevailed. Since 1965, for example, all cigarette packages have been required by the Federal Trade Commission to carry a warning from the Surgeon General. Carriage of the same warnings on all cigarette advertisements has been mandated since 1972.

Economist John Calfee, formerly of the Federal Trade Commission, has examined the historical role played by the government in improving information about the health risks associated with cigarettes.[8] Calfee's examination suggests that, at least in this case, the presumption that government is best able to diminish informational imperfections may not be warranted. For example, from the 1920s through the 1950s, while smoking was considered glamorous by many, it was also widely described in such unglamorous terms as "coffin nails," "smoker's cough," "gasper," and "lung duster"— despite a lack of scientific evidence about smoking's mortal long-term effects.

Rather than suppressing smokers' fears or arguing that they were unfounded, cigarette manufacturers re-

lied on these fears as an advertising tool. Among the slogans employed by particular brands were "Not a cough in a carload" (Chesterfield), "Not a single case of throat irritation due to smoking Camels," and "Why risk sore throats?" (Old Gold).

In the early 1950s, two well-designed scientific studies sponsored by the American Cancer Society linked smoking with lung cancer. Newspapers and magazines such as *Reader's Digest* provided extensive coverage of the academic studies and *Consumer Reports* began publishing tar and nicotine ratings for all cigarette brands. Cigarette producers, notably the smaller firms, began introducing brands with filters that greatly reduced tar and nicotine. Filtered brands grew from 1 to 10 percent of the total cigarette market between 1950 and 1954. The companies selling them sought to spur their sales by scaring smokers about rival brands: "Filtered smoke is better for your health" (Viceroy), "just what the doctor ordered" (L&M), and "[Kent] takes out more nicotine and tars than any other leading cigarette—*the difference in protection is priceless.*" Television advertisements showed the dark smoke left by competing unfiltered brands on Kent's filter.

Producers' actions thus had the unintended consequence of better informing smokers about the health risks associated with cigarettes in general. According to Calfee, these actions, coupled with the reports in the popular press, did more to deter smoking through the

---

[8]John E. Calfee, "The Ghost of Cigarette Advertising Past," *Regulation*, 10 No. 2 (November/December 1986), pp. 35–45.

early 1960s than the actions of the government. If anything, Calfee argues, government actions actually hindered the dissemination of information about smoking's risks after a 1955 Federal Trade Commission regulation forbidding producers from making any tar and nicotine claims until "it has been established by competent scientific proof that the claim is true, and if true, that such difference or differences are significant." Although the guidelines explicitly permitted the advertising of taste and pleasure, any references to the presence or absence of physical effects of smoking were banned.

Predictably, cigarette advertisements changed to stressing taste and pleasure rather than the fear associated with smoking. Kent advertisements changed from "significantly less tars and nicotine" to "satisfies your appetite for a real good smoke." Duke, one of the new low-tar brands, switched from "lowest in tars" to "designed with your taste in mind." Cigarette sales ended their several-year decline in 1955 and rose significantly in the ensuing decade. In 1966, acceding to appeals from the American Cancer Society, the Federal Trade Commission reversed its policy and authorized tar and nicotine advertising.

Externalities/Public Goods

Sometimes, in the process of producing or consuming certain goods, harmful or beneficial side effects called *externalities* are borne by people not directly involved in the market activities. Take the case of a motorist choosing to travel an urban freeway during rush hour. The motorist may impose congestion costs on other drivers, costs for which the motorist is not directly accountable. Other goods, known as *public goods*, simultaneously provide benefits to multiple consumers. For example, the same parade, park, or B-1 bomber may enhance the well-being of more than one consumer.

Because the benefits or costs of a good may not be fully accounted for by market actors, externalities and public goods can result in inefficiency—even if competitive markets prevail. In the following chapter, we extensively discuss the reasons why as well as the best mechanisms for promoting efficiency in the case of externalities and public goods.

 SUMMARY

• Partial equilibrium analysis concentrates on one market at a time, viewing that market as independent from other markets.

• In contrast, general equilibrium analysis views the economy as a network of interconnected markets, with events in one market affecting others and, in turn, being affected by others. Mutual interdependence among markets is emphasized.

• The concept of economic efficiency, or Pareto optimality, plays a central role in the analysis because it defines a situation in which no person's well-being can be further improved unless someone else is harmed.

• Three conditions determine whether an economy is operating efficiently. First, the goods produced must be efficiently distributed among consumers. Efficient distributions occur at points on the contract curve in an Edgeworth exchange box.

• Second, inputs must be allocated efficiently in the production of goods. Efficiency in production is shown by points on the contract curve in an Edgeworth production box or, equivalently, by the economy's operation on, rather than inside, its production possibility frontier.

• Third, the output mix produced must be efficient. Efficiency in output is identified by a point on the production frontier where, when the outputs are distributed among consumers, each consumer's marginal rate of substitution between any two goods equals the marginal rate of transformation between those two goods.

• If perfect competition prevails, all three efficiency conditions are satisfied and an economy will end up at a point on its welfare frontier. The reasons why economic efficiency may not be realized include market power, imperfect information, externalities, and public goods.

REVIEW QUESTIONS AND PROBLEMS

Questions and problems marked with an asterisk have solutions given in Answers to Selected Problems at the back of the book (page 578).

19.1. What do economists mean when they say markets are *mutually interdependent*? Give an example to support your explanation.

*19.2. In the butter–margarine example of Figure 19.1, would there be any spillover effect on the butter market from the margarine market if the supply curve of margarine were horizontal?

19.3. What does the contract curve in an Edgeworth production box signify? Why do competitive markets generate equilibriums that lie on the contract curve?

19.4. What is the relationship between the *PPF* and the contract curve in an Edgeworth production box?

*19.5. If all industries are in competitive equilibrium, and the price of personal computers is 10 times the price of cellular telephones, what is the *MRT* between the two goods?

19.6. The domestic computer chip manufacturing industry argues that permitting free trade will cost the jobs of thousands of computer chip workers. How does general equilibrium analysis help in responding to this argument?

19.7. What factors are important in deciding whether a particular economic issue can be adequately analyzed by using a partial equilibrium approach rather than a general equilibrium approach?

19.8. Is every efficient allocation of resources preferred to every inefficient allocation of resources?

19.9. Explain why, when all markets are competitive and in equilibrium, all three conditions for efficiency are satisfied. Does this result indicate that society's welfare is maximized?

*19.10. According to Albert Einstein, "The economic anarchy of capitalist society as it exists today is, in my view, the main cause of our evils. Production is carried on for profit, not for use." Is there a conflict between "production for profit" and "production for use"?

19.11. If Cisco has a monopoly in the server market, what efficiency condition is violated? Would the regulation of Cisco and the elimination of Cisco's profit lead to a more efficient allocation of resources? Will all members of society benefit?

*19.12. Ignoring rationing problems and black markets, under rent control (or any price ceiling that produces a shortage) the price paid by consumers equals the marginal cost of producing the good. Does this mean the output level is efficient? Explain.

19.13. "Using efficiency as a criterion biases the analysis in favor of the status quo, since any change is certain to harm someone." Discuss.

19.14. In each of the cases below, state whether one of the conditions for economic efficiency is violated. "Uncertain" is an acceptable response. If one of the efficiency conditions is violated, indicate which one and whether the resources in question are overused or underused.
a. The Rapid Transit District charges reduced bus fares to its senior citizens.
b. There is a limit to the number of people who can legally immigrate to the United States from India per year.
c. Some neighborhood families do not regularly mow their lawns.
d. The market for hot dogs is perfectly competitive. Michael Jordan's consumption of a hot dog leaves fewer hot dogs available for the rest of the world.
e. The Federal Trade Commission provides free pamphlets helping potential used car buyers identify whether a car's odometer has been rolled back.
f. A per-unit tax is applied to clothing in the context of a two-good (food-and-clothing), two-input (labor-and-capital) economy.
g. A selective minimum wage is imposed by the government on labor employed in clothing production in the context of a two-good (food-and-clothing), two-input (labor-and-capital) economy.

19.15. Why might a resource allocation that achieves efficiency in production not satisfy the condition for efficiency in output? Provide a real-world example.

19.16. Suppose that in the production of computer software, the marginal rate of technical substitution between engineers and marketers is 5 for IBM and 3 for Microsoft. Explain why this outcome violates the condition for efficiency in production and how a voluntary exchange could make both companies better off.

19.17. Most former communist governments of Eastern Europe subsidized food production (both in absolute terms and relative to any subsidies provided other goods). Explain the effect of this policy on the relationship between the typical Eastern European consumer's marginal rate of substitution between food and all other goods (treated as a composite good) and the marginal rate of transformation between food and all other goods.

*19.18. In the international trade example, we implicitly assumed that the world price ratio was unaffected when the domestic country engaged in trade. Under what conditions is this assumption reasonable? If the world price ratio is affected, how will it change? How will this change affect the analysis?

CHAPTER 20

Public Goods and Externalities

How may public goods and externalities adversely affect the way resources are allocated by markets and what are the possible remedies, government regulation among others, to such impediments to economic efficiency?

Chapter Outline

20.1 What Are Public Goods?

The Free-Rider Problem

***Application 20.1** Paying for NATO*

***Application 20.2** An Online Horror Tale*

20.2 Efficiency in the Provision of a Public Good

***Application 20.3** Promoting Truthful Revelation in China*

Efficiency in Production and Distribution Patents

***Application 20.4** Napster: Nipping or Nudging Economic Efficiency?*

20.3 Externalities

External Costs

***Application 20.5** Cures for Traffic Externalities*

External Benefits

20.4 Externalities and Property Rights

***Application 20.6** Radio Waves and Property Rights*

The Coase Theorem

***Application 20.7** Coasean Bargaining in Movie Making*

20.5 Controlling Pollution, Revisited

The Market for Los Angeles Smog

Learning Objectives

- Explain what economists mean by the term "public goods" and how the free-rider problem inhibits the provision of the efficient output level of such goods.
- Define external benefits and external costs and show how their presence results in nonoptimal output levels for goods characterized by such aspects.
- Show how clearly defined and enforced property rights can resolve externality problems and thereby ensure an efficient outcome.
- Demonstrate how air pollution can more efficiently be controlled through the establishment of an overall industry pollution target and the assignment of tradeable emissions permits to the industry's firms.

PUBLIC GOODS
those goods that benefit all consumers, such as national defense

EXTERNALITIES
the harmful or beneficial side effects of market activities that are borne or realized by participants in the market

As we have seen in several of this book's preceding chapters, government intervention in markets may fail to promote economic efficiency. For example, Chapter 10 showed how rent control and a quota on sugar imports can diminish the total surplus realized by market participants as a group. Without discounting the impediments to efficiency that may be associated with government intervention, this chapter looks at two important reasons why markets left to themselves may also not function efficiently: public goods and externalities. **Public goods** are those that benefit all consumers, such as national defense. A public good will be undersupplied by a market when consumers cannot be excluded from sharing in its benefits and thus have no incentive to pay for its production.

Externalities are present when all of the costs or benefits of a good are not fully borne by the participants in the market for it. For example, an oil refinery may not have to pay for some of the air pollution generated by its production process and may consequently produce more oil than is economically efficient. Individuals may not obtain a flu shot if some of the benefits of the vaccination against such a communicable disease accrue to society at large rather than fully to them.

When public goods or externalities lead markets to generate an inefficient allocation of resources, government can intervene, at least in theory, with an appropriate policy that will improve things. This chapter analyzes how public goods and externalities may adversely affect the way resources are allocated by markets as well as the remedies, government regulation among others, to such impediments to economic efficiency.

20.1 WHAT ARE PUBLIC GOODS?

The term *public good*, as used by economists, does not necessarily refer to a good provided by the government. Instead, economists define a public good by the characteristics of the good itself. Two are important: nonrival consumption and nonexclusion.

A good is **nonrival in consumption** if, with a given level of production, consumption by one person need not diminish the quantity consumed by others. Although this definition may sound peculiar, such goods do exist. Consider a nuclear submarine that reduces the likelihood of enemy attack. Your property and person are protected, and so are others'. The protection you receive in no way diminishes the extent to which others are protected. Another example is a flood control project that reduces the probability of flood damage. Less flood damage to one home does not mean more flood damage to another; all persons in a given area simultaneously benefit in the form of a reduced likelihood of flooding.

NONRIVAL IN CONSUMPTION
a condition in which a good with a given level of production, if consumed by one person, can also be consumed by others

In effect, nonrival consumption means potential simultaneous consumption of a good by many persons. By contrast, most goods are rival in consumption. For a given level of production of shoes (or soft drinks, T-shirts, cars, or hamburgers), the more you consume, the less is available for others. In these cases consumption is rival because the economic system must ration output among competing (rival) consumers. When a good is nonrival in consumption, the good need not be rationed. Once it is produced, the good can be made available to all consumers without affecting any individual's consumption level.

The second characteristic of a public good is nonexclusion. **Nonexclusion** means that confining a good's benefits (once produced) to selected persons is impossible, or prohibitively costly. Thus, a person can benefit from a good's production regardless of whether he or she pays for it. Although the concepts of nonrivalry and nonexclusion often go together, they are distinct. Nonrivalry means that consumption by one person *need not* interfere with consumption of others; although a good may be nonrival in consumption, restricting consumption to selected persons may still be possible.

NONEXCLUSION
a condition in which confining a good's benefits, once produced, to selected persons is impossible or prohibitively costly

For example, when a Web site is posted, anyone with Internet access can go to the Web site and view its contents without interfering with another person's ability to view the same site. (An exception would be if the site suddenly got a huge number of hits, overloading the server.) It is possible to deliberately exclude access to a Web site, however, and in fact, it is often done. The Web site for the *Wall Street Journal*, for instance, *www.wsj.com*, includes "Free Content" that may be accessed by anyone. However, only subscribers can access more detailed information, such as front-page stories from the *Journal*. Clicking on those areas brings up the message, "The page you requested is available only to subscribers." Subscribers must supply a user number and a password, and nonsubscribers are denied access. The Web illustrates how some things can be nonrival and yet have the possibility of exclusion. Thus, it does not meet the criteria to be a public good.

In contrast, national defense is an example of a good with both characteristics. A given defense effort protects (or endangers) everyone simultaneously, and to limit the protection to certain people is impossible. The benefits of defense are thus nonrival to the population, and exclusion of selected persons is infeasible.

A good that is nonrival in consumption and has high exclusion costs creates problems for a market system. Once such a good is produced, many people will automatically benefit regardless of whether they pay for it, because they cannot be excluded. As we will see, this feature makes it unlikely that private producers will provide the good efficiently.

The Free-Rider Problem

Even when a public good is worth more to people than it costs to produce, private markets may fail to provide it. To see why, consider the construction of a dam that will lessen the probability of flooding for a community's residents; the dam is a public good for the residents. It may have a total cost of $1,000,000, and business firms will be willing to build it if someone will provide the funds. If 10 persons live in the community and the benefit of the dam to each person is $200,000, then the total benefit of the dam to all 10 residents is $2,000,000—twice as much as it costs. All 10 people would be better off if each contributed $100,000 to finance construction costs, since each would then receive a benefit valued at $200,000 from the dam.

Even though it is in each resident's interest to have the dam constructed, there is a good chance that it won't be built if private markets are relied upon to organize the construction. To finance the dam, residents must jointly agree to contribute, but many will realize that they get the benefit of the dam once built, regardless of whether they make a contribution toward its construction. *Each resident, therefore, has an incentive to understate what the dam is worth in an effort to secure the benefit at a lower, or zero, cost.* If enough people behave in this way—as a **free rider**—voluntary contributions will be insufficient to finance the dam and it won't be built. Viewing the provision of public goods as a prisoner's dilemma, free riding is the equivalent of "cheating" in the prisoner's dilemma game discussed in Chapter 14.

When public goods are involved, free riding is rational, but it hinders the ability of private markets to cater efficiently to the demand for a public good. In the example just discussed, enough people could conceivably contribute so that the dam would be financed by voluntary agreements. With just 10 people involved, only a small number need to agree to contribute. The severity of the free-rider problem, however, varies with the number of people involved. The larger the number of people receiving benefits from a public good, the less likely that voluntary cooperation will ensure its provision.

As the group size increases, it is more likely that everyone will behave like a free rider, and the public good will not be provided. To illustrate, let's change our example slightly and assume that a dam now benefits 1,000 people, each by $2,000. (Note that the total benefit is still $2,000,000, just as before.) In this case, faced with deciding whether or how much to contribute voluntarily, each person will realize that one single contribution has virtually no effect on whether the dam is built. Put differently, the outcome depends mainly on what the other 999 people do, and whether any one person contributes will not affect the others' decisions. In this case each person gets the same benefit whether or not any contribution is made, and choosing not to contribute is the most rational behavior. Because this is true for everyone, few people will contribute, and the good likely will not be provided.

Many real-world examples provide evidence of free-rider behavior with public goods. A particularly clear-cut example occurred in 1970 (before mandatory pollution controls) when General Motors tried to market pollution control devices for automobiles at a price of $20. The emission controls would have reduced the pollution emitted by 30 to 50 percent. Pollution abatement is, of course, a public good, at least over a certain geographic area. It is reasonable to suppose that the benefits of a 30 to 50 percent reduction in automobile pollution far outweighed the cost of $20 per car. Yet GM withdrew the device from the market because of poor sales. This example illustrates the large-group free-rider problem at work. Everyone might have been better off if all drivers used the device, but it was not in the in-

FREE RIDER
a consumer who has an incentive to underestimate the value of a good in order to secure its benefits at a lower, or zero, cost

terest of any single person to purchase it because the overall level of air quality would not be noticeably improved as a result of any one individual's action.

When the benefits of a public good are nonrival over a large group, private markets probably will not provide it. Even if some amount of the public good is provided through the contributions of a few people, it will be at a suboptimal quantity. This result is true even when it is in the interest of people to have the good provided—that is, even when the benefits exceed the costs. Competitive markets cannot in general supply public goods efficiently. This fact provides a major justification for considering governmental alternatives. In the dam example of 1,000 persons, for instance, the government could levy a tax of $1,000 on each person and use the $1,000,000 in tax revenue to finance the dam. Each person would be made better off by this policy, receiving $2,000 of benefit from the dam at a cost of $1,000 in taxes. The government expenditure of $1,000,000 on the dam would lead to a more efficient allocation of resources than reliance on private markets.

APPLICATION 20.1 PAYING FOR NATO

A military alliance such as the North Atlantic Treaty Organization (NATO) is a public good for the countries belonging to the alliance.[1] NATO's ability to prevent aggressive military actions against its member states by the former Soviet Union served to benefit all the countries belonging to NATO. That is, protecting West Germany from invasion also forestalled the Soviet military threat to Belgium, the United States, France, and so on.

We would expect free riding to be less likely by NATO nations that have more to gain from successful provision of the public good that is the goal of the alliance—an effective defense. This is indeed what a study by the RAND Corporation finds. Of the 14 NATO members as of 1964, the 7 with the greatest economic stake, in terms of total GNP, in deterring the Soviet Union, spent 7.8 percent of their combined GNP on defense. The 7 nations with the smallest GNPs spent only 4.3 percent. The United States, by far the largest economic member of NATO at the time (accounting for 60 percent of the total GNP across the 14 nations), devoted 9 percent of its GNP to defense. In contrast, Luxembourg, the nation with the smallest GNP (0.4 percent of the total) devoted only 1.7 percent to defense.

[1]This application draws on Jack Hirshleifer and Amihai Glazer, *Price Theory and Applications*, 5th ed. (Englewood Cliffs, N.J.: Prentice Hall, 1992), p. 467.

APPLICATION 20.2 AN ONLINE HORROR TALE

In 2000, horror writer Stephen King became the first major author to self-publish online.[2] King asked readers to pay him a dollar for each chapter of a serial e-novel titled "The Plant," they downloaded and warned that he would not post new installments unless he received payments for at least 75 percent of the downloads. Voluntary contributions for King's e-novel appeared to be plagued by the free-rider problem as only 46 percent of the downloads were paid for. King promptly called it quits on publishing "The Plant" online in order to work on other, more conventional books from which it is easier to exclude non-payers.

[2]"A Stephen King Online Horror Tale Turns Into a Mini-Disaster," *New York Times on the Web*, November 29, 2000.

20.2 EFFICIENCY IN THE PROVISION OF A PUBLIC GOOD

What is the efficient output of a public good? As usual, we must compare the marginal benefit and marginal cost associated with different levels of output. The marginal cost of a public good is the opportunity cost of using resources to produce that good rather than others, just as it is in the case of the nonpublic, or private, goods discussed in previous chapters. Because of the nonrival nature of the benefits of a public good, though, its marginal benefit differs from that of a private good. With a good like a cheeseburger, the marginal benefit of producing an additional unit is the value of the cheeseburger to the single person who consumes it. With a public good like defense, the marginal benefit is not the marginal value to any one person alone because many people benefit simultaneously from the same unit. Instead, we must add the marginal benefits of every person who values the additional unit of defense, and the resulting sum indicates the combined willingness of the public to pay for more defense—that is, its marginal benefit.

SOCIAL MARGINAL BENEFIT CURVE
the demand curve for a public good

Figure 20.1 shows how we derive the demand, or **social marginal benefit curve** for a public good like submarines. For simplicity, assume that only two people, Ted and Jane, benefit from the defense services of submarines. Each person has a demand curve for submarines, shown as d_T and d_J. These demand curves are derived from each person's indifference curves, just as would their demand curves for a private good. Recall that the height of a consumer's demand curve indicates the marginal benefit of another unit of the good. *To derive the social, or combined, demand curve, we must add the marginal benefits of the two consumers.* Geometrically, the combined demand curve involves a **vertical summation** of the consumers' demand curves. For example, the marginal benefit to Ted of the first submarine ($400) is added to the marginal benefit Jane receives from the first submarine ($250) to determine the social marginal benefit ($650) for the first unit. This vertical addition of marginal benefits identifies one point on the social marginal benefit curve, indicating that the combined marginal benefit of Ted and Jane for the first submarine is $650. At alternative quantities of submarines, we continue to add the heights of each consumer's demand curve to trace out the entire social marginal benefit curve, MB_S.

VERTICAL SUMMATION (OF DEMAND CURVES)
the derivation of a social marginal benefit curve through the summing of consumers' marginal benefit curves

We can now determine the efficient output of submarines. At any output level where MB_S lies above the marginal cost curve MC—drawn here for simplicity as horizontal at

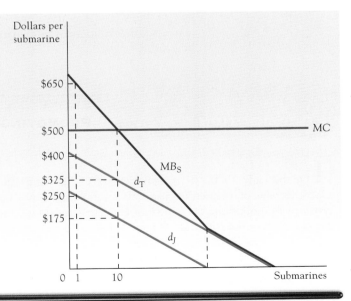

FIGURE 20.1

The Efficient Output of a Public Good
Because the benefits of a public good are nonrival, the social marginal benefit is the sum of the marginal benefits of the separate consumers. Graphically, the social marginal benefit curve is constructed by vertically summing the consumers' demand curves. The efficient output is identified by the intersection of MB_S and MC.

$500—Ted and Jane are willing to pay more for an additional unit than its marginal cost, so efficiency requires a higher output. Thus, an additional unit could be financed in a way that makes both of them better off—with each contributing somewhat less than the maximum amount he or she is willing to pay. When MC lies above MB_S, however, too much of the public good is being produced—the combined marginal benefit as shown by MB_S is less than marginal cost over this output range. Thus, the efficient output is 10 submarines, where Ted's marginal benefit of $325 plus Jane's marginal benefit of $175 just equals the marginal cost of $500.

In general, the efficient output of a public good occurs where MB_S, *obtained by vertically summing the demand curves of all consumers, intersects the marginal cost curve.* There is no presumption, however, that this output will be the actual, or equilibrium, output. In fact, we have already seen that the free-rider problem will generally mean that private markets will not produce the efficient output. The government has the power to finance the efficient output from tax revenues, but whether it actually does so depends on how political forces determine public policy.

Government financing of a public good overcomes one aspect of the free-rider problem—the tendency of people to withhold payment. There is another aspect of free riding that government financing does not overcome: people have no incentive to accurately reveal their demands for the public good—especially if they will be taxed commensurate to the benefits they report receiving. To determine the efficient output, we must know every person's demand curve so that we can vertically add them to obtain MB_S. How can we determine the true worth of a public good like defense to millions of people? Needless to say, obtaining this information is problematic.

For example, to obtain the efficient level of output of a public good such as the one depicted in Figure 20.1, the government can tax people according to the heights of their reported marginal benefit curves. Thus, for 10 submarines, Ted is taxed $325 per unit while Jane must remit $175 per unit. The total amount paid in taxes ($500 per submarine) is just sufficient to cover the marginal cost of producing an additional submarine at the efficient output of 10.

Where citizens are taxed according to their reported marginal benefit curves, however, they have an incentive to understate their benefits. For example, Jane may be tempted to say that she gets no benefit from submarines (and thus pays no taxes) and free ride on any payments made by Ted—since any submarines paid for by Ted through taxes also will benefit Jane. Ted has the same incentive to understate the benefit he gets from submarines. Understatement of demand would imply less than optimal provision of the public good.

APPLICATION 20.3   PROMOTING TRUTHFUL REVELATION IN CHINA

In the early 1900s, the government of China used the value of a citizen's house and land-holdings as a proxy to determine the tax levied for benefits derived by the citizen from the public goods provided by the government. To promote truthful reporting by citizens of the value of their property, the Chinese government employed a creative enforcement mechanism. It reserved the right to purchase a citizen's property at the value of the property reported by the citizen for tax reasons. Any incentive to understate property values for tax reasons thus was counteracted by the potential that one's property could be confiscated at a loss by government authorities.

Efficiency in Production and Distribution

In Chapter 19, we pointed out that there are three conditions for efficiency. These conditions also apply to public goods. So far, we have emphasized only the condition for an efficient level of output. A second condition is that the output be produced by using the least costly combination of inputs. In Figure 20.1, that condition is implicit in the assumption that a marginal cost of $500 is the minimum cost necessary to produce a submarine. The third condition relates to the efficient distribution of the good among consumers. For a private good this condition requires an equality of marginal rates of substitution. But how is a public good rationed efficiently?

With a public good there is no rationing problem. If 10 submarines are produced, both Ted and Jane simultaneously benefit, and the benefit to one in no way diminishes the benefit to the other. For example, suppose it were possible in some hard-to-imagine way to have Ted protected by 10 submarines but Jane protected by only 5. In other words, if exclusion were possible, would there be any advantage in excluding Jane from the services of all 10 submarines? The answer is no, because when 10 submarines are available, Jane's receiving the services of only 5 does not make any more submarines available for Ted. Consequently, Jane is harmed, and no one benefits. By definition, this outcome is clearly inefficient.

Recall our definition of a public good as one characterized by nonrival consumption and nonexclusion. When a good has both characteristics, it would be impossible to exclude anyone from its benefits, even if we wanted to. What about a good with nonrival benefits where exclusion is possible? The analysis above suggests that *it is inefficient to exclude anyone even if we could.* Before accepting that as a general rule, let's examine an important public policy issue dealing with a good where benefits are nonrival but exclusion is possible.

Patents

As explained in Chapter 11, a patent grants temporary legal monopoly power to an inventor. A patent gives the inventor the right to make and sell some new product or to use some new production process for a period of 17 years. But what do patents have to do with the exotic world of nonrival benefits and nonexclusion? Surely, you say, a vibrating toilet seat (patent number 3,244,168, granted in 1966) is not a public good.

Admittedly, most of the products granted patents are not themselves public goods. But what about the knowledge required to make, for example, a vaccine to prevent AIDS? This knowledge of "how to do it" has nonrival benefits. Once the knowledge exists, any number of people can use it without interfering with each other's use. One person's use of this special knowledge does not leave less for someone else. Simultaneous consumption of knowledge is therefore possible, but could people be excluded from its use? Whether exclusion is possible depends on the type of knowledge involved, but in some cases the use of knowledge can be prohibited if producing or selling its tangible embodiment is made illegal. For example, if it is illegal for you to manufacture and sell the AIDS vaccine, you would be effectively excluded from using the knowledge of how to make it. This is exactly what patents do. They exclude all but the inventor from making use of the knowledge he or she produced.

Thus, at least some types of knowledge have nonrival benefits, but exclusion is possible. Now let's consider efficiency in resource allocation in connection with knowledge. Although new knowledge is sometimes produced accidentally, much of it results from the use of resources devoted to research and development. The efficient output of new knowledge requires that resources be devoted to producing it and is accomplished by equating the vertically summed marginal benefits with marginal cost, just as in Figure 20.1. Yet once the knowledge exists, using it efficiently requires that no one be excluded. Both aspects of efficiency are important.

To see how this discussion relates to patents, suppose that the inventor of an AIDS vaccine could not exclude others from copying and selling the product. Would the inventor devote a million dollars to develop such a vaccine? If this investment were successful, others would immediately copy and sell it, driving the price down to a level that just covered production cost and leaving no way for the inventor to recoup research costs. For this reason inventors would have little financial incentive to produce the knowledge in the first place, even though that knowledge might be highly beneficial. Too few resources would be devoted to research and development, because those who bear the costs could not charge others who use the knowledge for the benefit they receive. In other words, private markets would not produce the efficient quantity of the public good, new knowledge.

Patents can encourage a greater, more efficient output of new knowledge. Because inventors receive a temporary monopoly right, they get a return above the cost of producing new products to compensate for the research costs. The prospect of this gain stimulates inventors to devote resources to the production of new knowledge. This example illustrates how private markets can produce a good with nonrival benefits when exclusion is possible.

Encouraging a greater, more efficient output is the beneficial result of using patents, but there is a cost. Once the new knowledge is produced, it is inefficiently employed, since some people are legally excluded from using it. That is, the AIDS-preventing vaccine will be monopolistically produced for 17 years, which inefficiently restricts the use, or consumption, of the vaccine. This cost must be weighed against the gain—namely, that the vaccine might never have been developed without the incentive created by patent protection.

Private markets can produce goods with nonrival benefits when exclusion is possible, as the patent example shows. Private markets, however, would probably not function with perfect efficiency because of the exclusion of some people who could potentially benefit. Whether it is possible to devise some arrangement that works better is uncertain and requires a more detailed case-by-case evaluation. In any event, the degree of inefficiency in market provision for a nonrival good will be far less when exclusion is possible than when it is not. The combination of the nonrival and nonexclusion characteristics creates more severe problems for market provision, and in this case a more active role for government may be required. No one has determined, for example, how national defense could be provided by private markets.

APPLICATION 20.4   NAPSTER: NIPPING OR NUDGING ECONOMIC EFFICIENCY?

Copyrights are intended to encourage the production of music, literature, and art by granting creators an exclusive right to publish, sell, and reproduce their works for a set period of time. Like patents, copyrights require a dynamic versus static efficiency trade-off. This is the case because while copyrights promote the production of music, literature, and art from a dynamic perspective, once a work has been produced, copyrights also exclude some people who might benefit from hearing a particular song or reading a given novel.

Napster provides a recent example of the (sometimes subtle) efficiency considerations associated with copyrights.[3] The brainchild of 18-year-old college drop-out Shawn Fanning, Napster was launched in 1999 as an Internet service letting users download songs at no charge from other users' hard drives. The first example of a peer-to-peer (P2P) Internet service, Napster acquired 25 million users within a year of its inception and quickly drew the attention of the $40-billion-in-annual-revenues music industry.

[3]This application is based on *Time.com* (October 2, 2000); "Napster Should be Playing Jailhouse Rock," *Wall Street Journal* (July 31, 2000), p. A2; and Carl Shapiro and Hal R. Varian, *Information Rules* (Boston: Harvard Business School Press, 1999).

Represented by the Recording Industry Association of America (RIAA), the music industry argued that Napster facilitated the theft of musical property, had cost the industry more than $300 million in lost sales as of the year 2000, and should be shut down. The band Metallica and rapper Dr. Dre brought lawsuits against Napster for copyright infringement. In support of the argument that Napster would diminish the incentive to produce music, the RIAA presented evidence from retail-store tracker SoundScan. The evidence showed that compact disc sales fell in the year 2000 by 13 percent at stores within one mile of *Wired* magazine's Top-40 "wired" colleges and those near colleges with Napster-induced network overloading problems.

Not all artists, however, opposed the continued growth of Napster. In fact, the band Limp Bizkit and rapper Chuck D. argued that Napster would spur sales revenue by providing a try-before-you-buy service to individuals who might not otherwise become exposed to a particular artist's work. Chuck D. pointed to overall compact disc sales growing by $500 million in 2000, the same year that witnessed the dramatic increase in users of Napster and rival P2P service providers such as Gnutella and Aimster.

Indeed, it could be argued that the lower reproduction and distribution costs brought about by the Internet and technological innovations such as Napster may, over the long run, represent more of an opportunity than a threat to the music industry. By analogy, economists Hal Varian and Carl Shapiro of the University of California at Berkeley point out that, contrary to leading to the demise of the movie industry as initially predicted, video cassette recorders have proven to be a boon to it. Similarly, the Internet and technological innovations such as Napster promise to broaden the market for music. Industry sales and profits thus may increase as long as producers are adept at setting the terms and conditions that maximize the value of their intellectual property—that is, as long as exclusion remains possible.

20.3 EXTERNALITIES

Sometimes, in the process of producing or consuming certain goods, harmful or beneficial side effects called externalities are borne by people not directly involved in the market exchanges. These side effects of ordinary economic activities are called **external benefits** when the effects are positive and **external costs** when they are negative. The term *externality* is used because these effects are felt beyond, or are external to, the parties directly involved in generating the effects.

Immunization against a contagious disease is a good example of a consumption activity that involves external benefits. For instance, if Barney decides to get an inoculation, he benefits directly because his chance of contracting the disease is reduced. This benefit is not the external benefit, since Barney himself receives it. The external benefit is the one other people receive in the form of a reduced likelihood they will catch the disease because an inoculated Barney is less likely to transmit it. The central point is that Barney's decision about whether to be inoculated is unlikely to be swayed by how his inoculation affects other people: he is concerned mainly with the effect on his own health. Thus, the benefit his inoculation creates for others is external to, and doesn't influence, his decision.

Pollution provides a classic example of an external cost. Driving a car or operating a factory with a smoking chimney pollutes the atmosphere that others breathe; thus, the operation of a car or factory imposes costs on people not directly involved in the activity. Similarly, operating a boom box or motorcycle produces a level of noise that is often irritating to those nearby, just as the noise level of an airplane may be annoying to people living near airports. Congestion is also an external cost: when a person drives during rush hour, the road becomes more congested, not only for this person but for other drivers as well.

At a formal level, externalities and public goods are very similar, and recognizing the similarity makes understanding externalities easier. If Barney is inoculated against a conta-

EXTERNAL BENEFITS
positive side effects of ordinary economic activities

EXTERNAL COSTS
negative side effects of ordinary economic activities

gious disease, there are nonrival benefits: both he and others simultaneously benefit from his inoculation. In addition, to exclude other people from the benefits would be very difficult. When a person produces new knowledge, this action confers an external benefit on others who can use the knowledge profitably. Pollution is also like a public good (except here it should perhaps be called a public bad) since there are nonrival costs. A large number of people are simultaneously harmed if the atmosphere is polluted, and, obviously, to have the atmosphere in a particular area polluted for some and not for others would be difficult. The sole distinction between externalities and public goods is that external effects are *unintended* side effects of activities undertaken for other purposes. People don't pollute because they enjoy breathing polluted air; they simply want to transport themselves conveniently in a car from one place to another.

Externalities are likely to lead to an inefficient allocation of resources, just as public goods do. Market demands and supplies will reflect the benefits and costs of market participants only; the benefits and costs that fall on others will not be taken into account in determining resource allocation. For example, Barney may decide against being inoculated because the improvement in his health is not worth the extra cost. If the benefits of improved health for others are added to his benefit, the combined benefit might exceed the cost. In this case Barney's decision to not be inoculated would represent an inefficient use of resources.

External Costs

A closer look at a case involving external costs will help clarify the issues involved. Suppose that firms in a constant-cost competitive industry produce some type of waste materials as a byproduct of their activities. They dispose of these wastes by dumping them in a nearby river. From the firms' point of view, this method of disposal is the least costly. People living downstream, however, suffer, because the river no longer serves recreational purposes. The firms impose external costs on those living downstream. Because these external costs are not taken into account by the firms, the allocation of resources is inefficient.

Let's see how this situation appears diagrammatically. In Figure 20.2, the competitive demand and supply curves, where of course the supply curve is the private marginal cost curve, are D and MC_P. The equilibrium output is Q_1 with a price of $20 per unit. Each unit of output generates a specific quantity of wastes, so the greater the industry output, the greater the amount of water pollution. The harm done by the pollution is shown by the marginal exter-

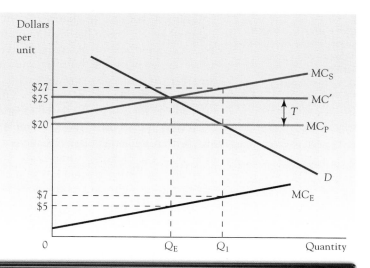

FIGURE 20.2

External Costs and Taxes
The marginal external cost curve, MC_E, shows the external cost associated with production of the good. Vertically adding this curve to the private marginal cost curve, MC_P, yields the social marginal cost curve, MC_S. Its intersection with the demand curve identifies the efficient output, Q_E, which is less than the market equilibrium output, Q_1.

nal cost, or MC_E, curve. It slopes upward, reflecting the assumption that additional amounts of pollution inflict increasing costs on people living downstream. (The marginal external cost curve results from vertically summing the marginal cost of each person harmed, since the harmful effects are nonrival over many persons.) At the market output of Q_1, the marginal external cost is $7, implying that people downstream would be $7 better off with one unit less of the product and the waste associated with it.

With external costs, the competitive output is too large from a social perspective. Firms expand output to where the price consumers pay just covers *their* private production costs (as reflected by the private marginal cost curve, MC_P), but the resulting price does not cover *all* production costs, since pollution is also a cost of producing the product. At Q_1, firms incur a cost of $20 per unit, which is just covered by the price paid by consumers, but there is also a $7 per-unit pollution cost borne by people downstream. At the competitive output, Q_1, the product is not worth what it costs to produce. The social, or combined, marginal cost of production is $27, whereas the marginal benefit to consumers is only $20. The social marginal cost of production is shown by the curve MC_S, obtained by vertically summing the MC_E curve and the private marginal cost curve, MC_P. It identifies all the costs associated with producing the product, not just the costs borne by producers. Efficiency requires that output be expanded to the point where the marginal benefit to consumers equals the social marginal cost of production. This point is shown by the intersection of D and MC_S at an output of Q_E.

Competitive market pressures, however, lead to an output of Q_1, larger than the efficient output. The government can do several things to improve the situation. One approach would be to levy a tax on the product to induce firms to produce at the efficient level. A tax of $5 per unit would shift the private marginal cost curve up by $5 to MC_P', and firms would curtail production to Q_E, with consumers paying a price of $25. The result is the efficient output level, where the marginal benefit to consumers equals the social marginal cost of production. Note that pollution is not completely eliminated; it is simply reduced to the point where a further reduction in production and pollution would cost more than it is worth. In general, external costs should not be totally eliminated even though those who are harmed might like to see them reduced to zero. Instead, the gain from reduced pollution to people downstream must be weighed against the cost to consumers of reduced output.

In this example we assumed that each unit of output is invariably associated with a certain amount of pollution. In the more general case the amount of pollution per unit of output is variable. Automobiles, for example, can produce various amounts of emissions. When this situation is the relevant case, as it usually is, the tax should be levied on pollution itself, not on the product. Then, as discussed in Chapter 8, firms have an incentive to curtail pollution—the external cost—in the least costly manner.

APPLICATION 20.5   CURES FOR TRAFFIC EXTERNALITIES

While an individual motorist's decision to drive at rush hour may cost only a few extra minutes of commuting time, the external congestion costs imposed by such motorists as a group can add up to millions of dollars per year in a major urban area. A recent study, for example, estimated that congestion in the Los Ange-les area costs local motorists a total of $7.7 billion annually in terms of the opportunity cost of their time spent delayed by traffic.[4]

[4]Michael W. Cameron, "Efficiency and Fairness on the Road," unpublished study (Washington, D.C.: Environmental Defense Fund, 1993).

In addition to congestion costs, rush-hour commuters pay for only a fraction of what they impose on the community at large in terms of road construction and pollution costs.[5] For example, significant road construction subsidies exist to better accommodate the needs of rush-hour drivers. According to one study, this subsidy totals over $500 per year for every rush-hour commuter in the Los Angeles area. Overall, California state gasoline taxes amount to only one-sixtieth of the estimated cost that rush-hour drivers impose on the community at large in terms of congestion, road construction, and pollution costs.

Some examples from overseas suggest mechanisms by which motorists could be held more fully accountable for the burden they impose on a community. Hong Kong, for example, undertook an Electronic Road Pricing experiment in the mid-1980s. Cars were equipped with an electronic license plate (at a cost of $20 each) making them automatically detectable to computerized sensors located throughout the city's streets. A computer recorded their movements and tallied the tolls exacted on different city streets, billing car owners monthly based on streets traveled, days of the week, and times of day.

Singapore's efforts to control traffic are legendary for promoting free-flowing roads and cleaner air and also for their draconian methods of enforcement.[6] Whereas the neighboring capitals of Southeast Asia such as Bangkok,

Thailand, and Jakarta, Indonesia, are notorious for their smog and day-long gridlock, Singapore's policies keep the skies clean and even rush-hour traffic delays to a minimum. Among the policies employed to achieve these objectives is a requirement that cars entering the city center pay an Electronic Road Price (ERP) that varies in amount depending on the time of day. For example, the ERP is: $2.50 from 8–9 AM; $2 for 9–9:30 AM and 6–6:30 PM; $1.50 from 5:30–6 PM; $1 from 9:30–10 AM, 12:30–5:30 PM, and 6:30–7 PM; $0.50 from 7:30–8 AM; and free at all other times.

The government of Singapore also adds on more than 200 percent in duties to every auto's purchase price. Moreover, every car owner must pay a sizable annual road use tax (analogous to a registration fee in the United States) to operate a vehicle. The road tax on a small Toyota is $800. When even the sizable costs of purchasing an automobile failed to curb the growth in car ownership, Singapore began limiting the absolute number of cars that can be sold in any year to 50,000. The quota is designed to keep new purchases to 4 percent of the total cars on the road.

The top speed limit on the island of Singapore is set at 45 miles per hour, to promote safe driving and thereby minimize the chance of accident-related traffic jams. Taxis are required to have a chime built into their dashboards that sounds continuously and annoyingly when the speed limit is violated. Trucks are mandated to have a yellow light on their roofs that is activated when the speed limit is exceeded. Police, as well as hidden cameras hooked up to remotely operated radars, are employed to catch traffic violators. If speeding is caught on camera, a ticket is sent to the violator by mail within days of the infraction.

[5]Jonathan Marshall, "How to Break Up Traffic Jams," *Wall Street Journal*, September 15, 1986, p. 32.

[6]"In Singapore, Driving Is Easy But Owning a Car Isn't," *Los Angeles Times* (August 17, 1991), pp. A1 and A14; and *www.gov.gg/lta/2_ERP/Main.html*.

External Benefits

External benefits can be analyzed in a similar fashion. Let's suppose that the consumption of some product generates external benefits—that is, people other than the direct consumers of the product benefit from its consumption. Some economists have argued that education may be such a product if a better-educated citizen not only makes himself or herself better off in the process but also the society of which he or she is a part. In Figure 20.3, the competitive supply and demand curves where demand identifies the private marginal benefit, are S and MB_P. The private marginal benefit curve, MB_P, reflects the marginal benefits of the good only to the consumers of the product, and its intersection with the supply curve determines the market equilibrium with an output of Q_1 and a price of $10. The marginal external benefit curve, MB_E, shows the external benefits per unit of consumption. This curve is derived by vertically summing the demands of people other than the immediate consumers of the product. Vertical summation is used because people other than direct consumers simultaneously receive benefits—that is, the benefits are nonrival.

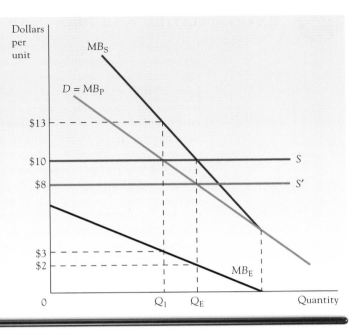

FIGURE 20.3

External Benefits and Subsidies
The marginal external benefit curve, MB_E, shows the external benefits generated by consumption of the good. Vertically adding this curve to the private marginal benefit curve, MB_P, yields the social marginal benefit curve, MB_S. Its intersection with the supply curve identifies the efficient output, Q_E, which is greater than the market equilibrium output, Q_1.

When external benefits exist, the competitive output is inefficient. At Q_1, the marginal benefit to consumers of another unit of the product is $10, as given by the height of the MB_P curve. If another unit is consumed, people other than the direct consumers also receive a marginal benefit valued at $3, as shown by the height of MB_E at Q_1. Thus, the combined marginal benefit for all those affected by consumption of another unit is $13, and this amount exceeds the $10 marginal cost of producing an additional unit. The combined, or social, marginal benefit is shown by MB_S, which is derived by vertically adding MB_P and MB_E (again because the benefits are nonrival).[7] The competitive output is too small because the marginal benefit of additional units of output exceeds the marginal cost of producing them. Yet there is no tendency for competitive pressures to produce a larger output, because the additional benefit to the direct consumers is less than the $10 price they must pay per unit. Thus, it is not in the consumers' interest to purchase more than Q_1 units; only when the *combined* benefits to consumers and other people are considered is it apparent why greater production is worthwhile.

Figure 20.3 illustrates the general tendency of an activity to be underproduced when external benefits are involved and when production is determined in competitive markets. The competitive output is Q_1, whereas the efficient output is Q_E, where MB_S intersects S. To achieve the efficient output, the government could step in with a policy designed to increase output beyond the market-determined level. In this case, a subsidy would be appropriate. If the government pays firms $2 for every unit of output sold, the supply curve confronting consumers would shift to S'. Although the marginal cost of production is still $10, the government in effect bears $2 of the cost through the subsidy, so consumers pay only $8. At the lower price, consumers purchase Q_E units, the efficient output.

---

[7]At an output in excess of the level at which the marginal external benefit becomes zero, the MB_S and MB_P curves coincide. When consumption is so great that additional consumption yields zero marginal benefits to other people, the only ones who receive any benefits from further increasing consumption are the direct consumers themselves, and their marginal benefits are shown by the MB_P curve.

20.4   EXTERNALITIES AND PROPERTY RIGHTS

External effects may appear intrinsically different from normal costs and benefits, but that appearance is partly misleading. When a firm uses your labor services, it imposes a cost on you, since you sacrifice the option to use your time in other ways. When a firm pollutes the river passing by your home, it imposes a cost on you, since you sacrifice the option to use the river for recreation. These costs are not fundamentally different: they both imply that you are unable to use economic resources in other, valuable, ways. Why, then, do we call pollution, but not the firm's employment of your labor services, an external cost?

One glaring difference in these two cases is that the firm must pay you for your labor services, but you are not compensated when the river is polluted. Since the firm must pay you at least enough to persuade you to give up alternative uses of your time, it will have an incentive to take this cost into account in deciding whether to employ you; that is, when the firm bears a direct cost associated with the use of a resource, that cost enters into its production decision. But if the firm can use the river in a way that harms you without compensating you for the damage, it has no reason to consider this cost in making its output decision—the firm treats the river as a zero-priced input.

Why must the firm pay to use your labor services but not to use the river? Fundamentally, the answer to this question involves property rights to the use of economic resources. You have well-defined and legally enforceable rights to your own labor services, meaning that no one can use them without securing your permission, which is normally acquired by paying you. There are, however, no such clearly defined property rights to the water that flows past your home. In fact, ownership of the river and who has the right to decide how it will be used are uncertain. Consequently, the firm can use it as a convenient garbage dump. If you had property rights to pure water flowing past your home, the firm would have to buy your permission to dump waste in the river. The firm might still pollute, but would do so only if the gain from polluting was greater than the compensation required to be paid. The situation would then be just analogous to the case of labor services. Pollution would no longer be a cost external to the firm's calculations; the cost would be taken into account, and the allocation of resources would be efficient.

Reasoning along these lines suggests that externalities are intimately connected with the way property rights are defined. Indeed, in most cases dealing with externalities, we can usually trace the source of the problem to an absence or inappropriate assignment of property rights. Accordingly, the government may not need to use taxes, subsidies, or regulation at all; it may only have to define and enforce property rights, and the resulting market exchanges will produce an efficient resource allocation.

As an example, imagine a beautiful beach on the California coast and suppose that no one owns it, just as no one owns the river. How will this scarce economic resource be used? It is not beyond fancy to conceive of masses of people crowding the beach trying to enjoy the sand, sun, and surf. Radios could blare, dune buggies roar up and down the beach, dirt bikes spray sand, litter lie strewn across the beach, and surfboards crash into swimmers. Externalities would be rampant.

Most would agree that this is not an efficient use of scarce oceanfront property, but because no one owns it, no one has an incentive to see the beach used in the most valuable way. The situation is far different when someone has property rights to the beach. In that case, use of the property will be guided by whoever pays the most for its use—that is, by who benefits most. The owner may still use the property as a beach, but now it will be operated differently. Admission might be charged, which will diminish the overcrowding that reduces the attractiveness of the nonowned beach. The owner might enforce rules regarding radios, litter, surfboards, and so on, further enhancing the benefits to consumers. In short, the external cost is no longer external when someone owns the beach. The owner has an incentive to see that the beach yields as much benefit to consumers as possible, since they will then pay more for its use.

The beach example is hypothetical, but it helps explain why some highways, parks, and beaches are overcrowded and inefficiently utilized. "Publicly owned" property is, in effect, sometimes owned by no one, in the sense that no one has the incentive and the right to see that it is used in the most valuable way.

APPLICATION 20.6 RADIO WAVES AND PROPERTY RIGHTS

R adio began to be used commercially near the beginning of the twentieth century. In the early years there was no government involvement at all. Anyone who wanted to broadcast a message could build or buy a transmitter and broadcast on any frequency. The result was described by one observer as follows:

> The chaos . . . as more and more enthusiastic pioneers entered the field of radio was indescribable. Amateurs crossed signals with professional broadcasters. Many of the professionals broadcast on the same wavelength and either came to a gentlemen's agreement to divide the hours of broadcasting or blithely set about cutting one another's throats by broadcasting simultaneously. Listeners thus experienced the annoyance of trying to hear one program against the raucous background of another.[8]

The market could not function properly because no one owned the resources involved—the individual wave-

lengths. The "chaos" could have been avoided by creating legally enforceable property rights in wavelengths and letting the market determine who would use the various frequencies.

The Federal Radio Commission (FRC) was established in 1927 to assign and enforce property rights in frequencies. It was succeeded by the Federal Communications Commission (FCC) in 1934. Eventually, the two agencies ended up taking a more active role in regulating the broadcast spectrum than advocated by most economists. For example, instead of assigning and enforcing property rights to the spectrum based on the willingness of various broadcasters to pay for it, the regulatory agencies set aside specified amounts of bandwidth for various types of uses (that is, a certain amount of bandwidth for radio broadcasting, VHF television broadcasting, UHF television broadcasting, and eventually services such as cellular telephones). Moreover, license awards and the approval of license sales came to be based on the extent to which broadcasters were deemed by the government regulatory agencies to serve the "public interest" rather than just economic efficiency.

[8]Ronald H. Coase, "The Federal Communications Commission," *Journal of Law and Economics*, 2 No. 2 (October 1959), pp. 1–40.

The Coase Theorem

These examples suggest that the assignment of property rights can make an important contribution to resolving issues involving externalities—but who is to have exactly what right to use the resource in question? Should a factory have the right to discharge smoke into the atmosphere, or should a nearby resident have the right to pure air? A case can certainly be made that both of these parties have a reasonable claim to use the atmosphere for their own purposes, yet giving the resident the right to clean air denies the factory the right to use a smokestack, and vice versa.

Ronald Coase addressed this issue in one of the most widely read papers in the history of economics.[9] Coase developed his analysis by considering a rancher and a farmer with adjoining properties. The rancher's cattle occasionally stray onto the farmer's property and destroy some of the crops—an external cost associated with cattle raising if this cost is not properly taken into account. Now suppose the farmer has the right to grow crops in a trample-free

[9]Ronald H. Coase, "The Problem of Social Cost," *Journal of Law and Economics*, 3 No. 2 (October 1960), pp. 1–45.

environment. The rancher would then be legally liable for the damage caused by the straying cattle. Since the rancher will have to compensate the farmer for the crop damage, the cost of straying cattle will become a direct cost to the rancher and will be taken into account in the rancher's production decision. An efficient outcome will result, probably one involving fewer straying cattle.

This conclusion is familiar, but Coase went further and argued that even if the rancher were not liable for damages, an efficient outcome would still result! This situation corresponds to giving the rancher the right to allow his or her cattle to stray. Coase explained that the farmer then has an incentive to offer to pay the rancher to reduce the number of straying cattle because a reduction in crop damage increases the farmer's profit. The harm done by straying cattle necessarily implies that the farmer will be willing to pay something to avoid that harm. An agreement would therefore be struck that would reduce cattle straying to the efficient level.

COASE THEOREM
the idea that as long as property rights are clearly defined and enforced, bargaining between two parties can ensure an efficient outcome

As far as efficiency is concerned, the **Coase theorem** states that whether the farmer or the rancher is initially assigned the property rights doesn't matter. *As long as the rights are clearly defined and enforced, bargaining between the parties can ensure an efficient outcome*. The *distributional* effects, though, depend on the exact definition of property rights. If the rancher is liable, the rancher will compensate the farmer; alternatively, if the rancher is not liable, the farmer will pay the rancher to reduce the cattle straying. In both cases cattle straying and crop damage are reduced to the efficient level, but different people bear the cost and secure the benefit.

Simply assigning property rights, however, will not resolve all externality problems. In the case discussed earlier, a firm pollutes a river and *many* people living downstream are harmed. If downstream residents are given the right to have clean river water, would bargaining between parties lead to an efficient level of water pollution? Most likely not. This is because thousands of people are affected by the pollution, and a firm would have to negotiate an agreement with all of them simultaneously to be allowed to pollute. *Whenever the effects are nonrival over a large group and exclusion is not feasible, the free-rider problem hinders the process of achieving agreement among all concerned*. The negotiation process likely would be so costly and time consuming as to become a practical impossibility. Consequently, with such an assignment of property rights, there would be no pollution in the river—but that may be as inefficient as (or perhaps even more inefficient than) allowing the firm to pollute freely.

Our earlier conclusion that markets would be inefficient is correct, therefore, in the case where the external effects simultaneously fall on many people. Assigning property rights can solve externality problems when there are small numbers of parties involved but not as readily when there are large numbers, because of the free-rider problem. Many issues of great importance, such as defense, pollution, and police protection, are large-group externalities or public goods, and private markets are thus unlikely to function effectively in these areas without some form of government intervention.

APPLICATION 20.7   COASEAN BARGAINING IN MOVIE MAKING

When film crews rent a house to shoot a scene for a movie, an external cost is imposed on neighboring households.[10] The neighbors' parking spaces may be

[10]This application is based on "LA Residents Grow Even More Negative Toward Film Crews," *Wall Street Journal*, March 30, 1990, pp. A1 and A11.

occupied or driveways blocked by film trucks. Neighbors' cars may be towed if a film crew obtains a permit to clear the street. As one neighbor of a house used during the filming of *Robocop 2* complained, "It's like Beirut here. There are bright lights and explosions at night. We can't sleep. It's total harassment."

To get film crews to pay for some of the costs that they impose on others, neighbors have been known to go to unusual lengths. Since film crews desperately need quiet at the moment they are shooting a scene, leaf blowers may be turned on, lawn mowers revved up, foghorns blown, and metal garbage-pail lids banged against iron gates, all to pressure filmmakers into making cash payments. One film crew in Pasadena paid a neighboring home owner $1,000 per day not to use her vacuum cleaner. The owner of a saloon adjacent to a film site in Santa Monica received $400 per hour not to have rock music blaring from his stereo prior to the bar's opening hours. And the owner of a nearby weightlifting shop in Los Angeles turned up on location with a loud buzzing chainsaw, threatening to interfere with the film unless paid $50 per hour to turn it off. So widespread are the harass-for-cash extortion schemes that legislation has been introduced in the California State Assembly to allow off-duty police officers to ticket nuisance-mongers and take them to court.

20.5 CONTROLLING POLLUTION, REVISITED

Perfect competition ensures efficiency in industry output if demand and supply curve heights reflect the full marginal benefits and costs associated with a particular product. There are cases, however, where assuming that demand and supply curve heights reflect a product's full marginal benefits and costs is not valid. Oil refineries, for example, may not be fully accountable for the costs associated with their productive activities. The refineries, that is, may not have to pay for the air pollution caused by their operations and imposed on surrounding communities.

As we saw earlier in this chapter, when demand and supply curve heights do not reflect a product's full marginal benefits and costs, the industry output attained by perfect competition is generally not efficient. Still, even if an industry does not attain efficiency in output because certain benefits and costs are external to the decisionmaking of consumers and firms, perfect competition results in efficiency in production. The industry output that is produced, in other words, is produced at lowest possible cost even though it may not be the efficient output.

To see how competition ensures production efficiency even if output efficiency is not attained, reconsider the case of two oil refineries first introduced in Chapter 8. Refineries A and B are located in the Los Angeles basin. Suppose they impose air pollution costs that they do not have to pay for on their surrounding communities. As a result, the firms' individual output decisions are based on only part of the costs associated with their productive activities and (as we saw in Section 20.3) the realized industry output is not efficient.

Policymakers may seek to ensure that the refineries account for the costs of their air pollution by levying a tax per unit of air pollution emitted. The tax creates an incentive for each refinery to curtail pollution, because the refinery saves the amount of the tax per unit of pollution not emitted. If reducing pollution by one unit costs the refinery less than the tax, the refinery has an incentive to engage in pollution abatement.

The appropriate tax that policymakers should levy per unit of pollution to ensure efficiency in output may, of course, be difficult to determine. Regardless of the amount of the tax, however, the total amount of pollution abatement across all refineries in response to the tax will be produced at lowest possible cost (will achieve efficiency in production) if perfect competition prevails.

Say that a tax of $3,000 per unit of air pollution emitted is imposed on refinery A. Figure 20.4 shows how such a tax would affect the level of air pollution. As in Chapter 8, pollution is measured from right to left, and the refineries' marginal cost curves for pollution abatement are shown as MC_A and MC_B. (Ignore refinery B for the moment.) A tax of $3,000 per unit of pollution can be shown as a horizontal line at $3,000. A refinery's total tax liability is

FIGURE 20.4

A Tax on Pollution

A per-unit tax on pollution makes refineries competitive producers of pollution abatement. With a tax of $3,000 per unit of pollution, refinery A produces P_1X_1 abatement units ($0X_1$ pollution units), and refinery B produces P_2X_2 abatement units ($0X_2$ pollution units).

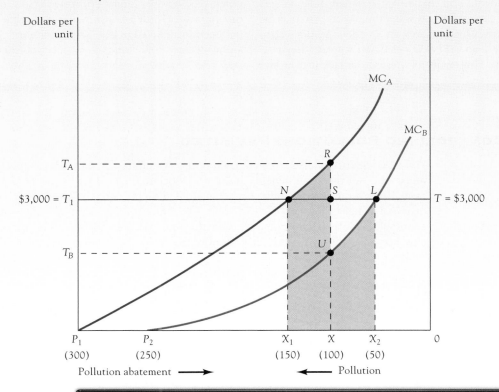

$3,000 times the number of units of air pollution. If refinery A continues to pollute at its initial level, $0P_1$ (when there was no pollution tax), it will have to pay a tax equal to $0T$ ($3,000) times $0P_1$, which is the area $0TT_1P_1$.

The tax gives refinery A an incentive to curtail pollution, because each abatement unit saves $3,000 in taxes. Looked at from left to right, the horizontal line T_1T is like a demand curve for pollution abatement: It shows a gain in net revenue of $3,000 per unit of abatement produced. Thus, refinery A faces a horizontal demand curve for abatement, and its marginal cost curve indicates the cost of abatement. To maximize profit, the refinery has a strong incentive to curtail pollution. Specifically, if the refinery can eliminate a unit of pollution for less than $3,000, doing so adds more to net revenue (reducing taxes by $3,000) than it adds to cost. In the interest of profit, refinery A will curtail pollution to $0X_1$ (producing P_1X_1 in abatement), where the marginal cost of abatement exactly equals the $3,000 per-unit tax. Cutting back further is not worthwhile because the cost of more abatement exceeds the tax saving. With pollution of $0X_1$ refinery A still pays total taxes of $0TNX_1$, but this sum is significantly less than the tax cost associated with the initial pollution level $0P_1$.[11]

---

[11]This analysis does not show how the pollution tax affects the refinery in its product market. Of course, the tax increases production cost and shifts the cost curves upward. To be accurate here, we should explicitly assume that the tax is not so large that it becomes unprofitable for the refinery to stay in business.

Now let's turn to refinery B. The same analysis is relevant for refinery B, which has an incentive to cut back pollution to $0X_2$, where its marginal cost of abatement equals the $3,000 per-unit tax. Note what this means: refinery A and refinery B are both operating at an abatement level where marginal cost equals $3,000. Their marginal costs are the same, which implies that the total amount of abatement of 350 units ($P_1X_1 = 300 - 150 = 150$ units by refinery A plus $P_2X_2 = 250 - 50 = 200$ units by refinery B) is achieved in the least costly way. And this outcome happens without the government's knowing either refinery's marginal cost curve. By applying the same tax to both refineries, the government gives each refinery the same incentive to curtail pollution. The result is efficient coordination of their independent production decisions.

To better understand why the total cost of achieving 350 abatement units is minimized by relying on incentives and competitive market forces, consider a reallocation of abatement units among the two refineries. For example, consider what happens if refinery A produces 50 additional units and refinery B produces 50 fewer units (so combined output remains unchanged). Refinery A's production cost goes up by the sum of the marginal cost of each unit from 151 to 200, shown by area X_1NRX. Refinery B's production cost falls by the sum of the marginal cost of each unit it ceases to produce, shown by area $XULX_2$. Because refinery A's cost increase exceeds refinery B's cost saving (as can be seen in Figure 20.4 by recalling that the widths of the shaded areas are equal), the total cost of producing 350 abatement units is higher under such a reallocation. Similar reasoning shows that any other way of having the refineries produce a total of 350 abatement units results in a higher total production cost than that achieved by the competitive refineries individually choosing their profit-maximizing outputs.

The foregoing discussion indicates why many economists favor taxation as a pollution control strategy. Notwithstanding the difficulty of determining the "appropriate" level of the tax that will result in efficiency in output (a tax that equals the marginal external costs associated with pollution), a pollution tax effectively creates market incentives for firms to reduce pollution in the least costly manner and thereby ensures efficiency in production. Moreover, the size of the tax can be changed to regulate the amount of pollution: a larger tax per unit will reduce pollution further.

In the United States, most environmental policies rely on a command-and-control approach: regulations and quantity limitations rather than taxes. Many economists have been critical of these non-market-oriented policies, in part because they believe the taxation approach can achieve the same results at lower cost. And the taxation approach is more than a theorist's pipe dream. Germany, for example, has successfully used pollution taxes to regulate waste discharge into the Ruhr River for more than 50 years.

The Market for Los Angeles Smog

An alternative market-oriented approach to controlling pollution involves the setting of an overall industry pollution level, with each firm receiving permits to emit a certain amount of pollution units and allowing firms to exchange their permits. This Coasean approach has recently been adopted by policymakers in an attempt to control smog in the Los Angeles basin. Tradable permits to pollute have been issued to each of the 390 companies producing four or more tons of emissions annually. The overall emission level allowed through the permits is set below the existing level and will be further reduced each year so that by the year 2003, nitrogen oxides are cut by 75 percent and sulfur oxides by 60 percent. Pollution permits are allocated across firms more or less according to their existing emissions.

The recently established L.A. smog market allows an overall emission target to be achieved in the least costly manner. To see why, suppose that in our simple example the goal is to reduce air pollution by 350 units (the same reduction achieved by a tax of $3,000 per emission unit) and that the two refineries are issued tradable permits to emit 100 pollution units each (200 total units across the two refineries). As shown in Figure 20.4, with no pollution control whatsoever, 550 pollution units would be produced—300 by refinery A ($0P_1$) and 250 by refinery B ($0P_2$).

Under the tradable-permit scheme, the potential exists for mutual gains from trade between the two refineries. This is because at its allotted 100 emission units, refinery A's marginal abatement cost (T_A) exceeds refinery B's abatement cost (T_B). Since, at the margin, refinery A is willing to pay more to increase its emission (cutting its abatement cost T_A) than refinery B needs to be paid to decrease its emission (incurring abatement cost T_B), there is room for the two refineries to exchange pollution permits for a price somewhere between T_A and T_B, making both sides better off.

Of course, the exact price at which the permits will be exchanged will depend on, among other things, the bargaining abilities of the two refineries. Moreover, the bounds around the exchange price will narrow as more permits are sold by refinery B to refinery A. The bounds around the exchange price will narrow because as refinery A buys more permits, the maximum amount it is willing to pay per permit declines from T_A; the cost of abatement to refinery A decreases as it pollutes more and moves to the left along its marginal cost of abatement curve. In addition, as refinery B sells additional permits, the minimum amount it needs to be paid for each rises from T_B; the cost of abatement to refinery B rises as it pollutes less and moves right along its marginal cost curve.

How many permits will be exchanged? The total will be 50 in the case depicted in Figure 20.4. When refinery B sells this many permits to refinery A, their marginal costs of abatement are identical. Refinery B, because it has the lower marginal cost of abatement curve, ends up emitting $0X_2$ (50) pollution units, abating P_2X_2 (250 − 50 = 200) units, and having a marginal cost of abatement of T_1. Refinery A ends up emitting $0X_1$ (150) pollution units, abating P_1X_1 (300 − 150 = 150) units, and having a marginal cost of abatement of T_1. The price for the fiftieth exchanged pollution permit equals $3,000 since it is perfectly constricted by the two refineries' marginal costs of abatement (that is, T_1).

By generating the "proper" marginal permit price ("proper" in terms of achieving an overall level of 200 pollution units and 350 units of pollution abatement) and confronting both refineries with that price, the L.A. smog market ensures attainment of the overall emission target in the least costly way. If, instead of allowing permit trading, regulators limited each refinery to 100 pollution units, the total abatement cost would be higher. That efficiency in production would not be served through such a command-and-control device is evidenced by the fact that in Figure 20.4 the cost to refinery A of reducing its pollution from 150 to 100 units (area X_1NRX) exceeds the cost to refinery B of reducing its pollution from 100 to 50 units (area $XULX_2$). The same overall emission target of 200 units can thus be achieved at lower total cost if refinery A is allowed to emit 150 units and refinery B is permitted 50 units.

In summary, market-based pollution control mechanisms such as tradable emission permits or per-emission-unit taxes promote efficiency in production. Although such mechanisms do not necessarily guarantee the attainment of efficiency in output, they do ensure that whatever amount of abatement is produced by an industry is produced at lowest possible cost.

The cost savings associated with market-based pollution control mechanisms can be substantial in the real world. For example, economists have estimated that the L.A. smog market saves $1,000 per year in abatement costs per resident household relative to a policy of mandating proportional, across-the-board reductions in emissions and not allowing pollution permit trading.[12] Significant abatement cost savings could also be realized if emission

---

[12]David Harrison, Jr. and Albert L. Nichols, *Market-Based Approaches to Reduce the Cost of Clean Air in California's South Coast Basin* (Cambridge, Mass.: National Economic Research Associates, November 1990).

trading programs were more broadly implemented on a national as well as international basis. For example, according to the consulting firm Charles River Associates, the cost for reducing greenhouse-gas emissions according to the Kyoto Protocol (a greenhouse-gas reduction treaty signed in 1997 as part of the United Nations Framework Convention on Climate Change) is estimated to be $280 per ton if no trading in emissions permits is allowed. By contrast, the estimated cost drops to $60 per ton if a completely open market in emissions permits is authorized.[13]

Among some of the other market-oriented pollution control mechanisms with which policymakers have experimented over the past three decades are "bubbles," through which a firm can treat an existing plant with multiple emission sources as if it were a single source—a bubble allows a firm to adjust its various emission sources to meet an overall emission target for the plant in the least costly manner; banking of pollution abatement credits, whereby a firm can hold onto emission reduction credits for future use or sale; and offsetting—a major new emission source in regions failing to meet national air quality standards can compensate for its added pollution with emission reductions of an equal or greater amount achieved through internal or external trades. All of these market-based approaches promise significant efficiencies in production over the more commonly employed command-and-control mechanisms for dealing with pollution.

SUMMARY

• Public goods are characterized by nonrival consumption and nonexclusion. When a good has these two characteristics, the free-rider problem arises and makes it difficult to ensure that the efficient quantity will be produced through voluntary arrangements.

• An efficient output of a public good is that at which the vertically summed demand curves of individuals intersect the marginal cost, or supply, curve.

• Externalities are the harmful or beneficial side effects of market activities that are borne or realized by people not directly involved in the market exchanges. They represent costs or benefits that are not incorporated in the private supply and demand curves that guide economic activity. Once again, the result is an inefficient resource allocation.

• In some cases it is only necessary to define property rights appropriately for externalities to be taken into account. In other cases, principally those involving large numbers of people, this solution will likely not work and other types of government policies should be considered.

• With regard to accounting for the externalities associated with air pollution, there are two types of government policies: taxes and tradable permits to emit a certain amount of pollution.

REVIEW QUESTIONS AND PROBLEMS

Questions and problems marked with an asterisk have solutions given in Answers to Selected Problems at the back of the book (pages 578–579).

20.1. What two characteristics define a public good? Which of the following are public goods: parks, police services, welfare payments to the poor, production of energy, space exploration?

20.2. Why will private markets produce an inefficient output of a public good? Explain how the efficient level of a public good is determined.

20.3. What is meant by the "free-rider" problem? How does it relate to the provision of public goods? How can it be overcome?

***20.4.** Suppose there are three consumers—two "hawks" and one "dove." The dove receives negative benefits from (is harmed by) national defense, but the hawks value defense. Show graphically how an efficient output of defense is determined in this case.

20.5. From a public good perspective, critique the use of patents.

---

[13]"Letting the Free Market Clear the Air," *Business Week*, November 6, 2000, pp. 200–204.

20.6. "External costs are bad, and government intervention to reduce them is justified. External benefits, however, are good, and there is no reason for government intervention in this case." Evaluate these statements.

20.7. Education is sometimes cited as a source of external benefits. In what way, if at all, does your receiving a college education benefit other people?

*20.8. Suppose that property rights change so that students no longer have exclusive rights to the use of lecture notes they take in classes. (All notes are collected after class, and anyone can borrow notes for 24 hours on a first-come, first-served basis.) How would this policy affect note taking, class attendance, and studying? Would students learn more or less? What does this example illustrate about the relationship between externalities and property rights?

20.9. A piece of state legislation proposes banning smoking in nearly all public facilities and private businesses. The major argument for the bill is that it "is needed to protect nonsmokers from the health hazards of cigarettes." Prepare an evaluation of the economic case for this legislation. (Assume that smoking adversely affects the health of nearby nonsmokers.)

*20.10. "When public goods or externalities lead to inefficient resource allocation, government intervention is justified." Is it? Why?

20.11. In an otherwise competitive economy there is an externality in the form of pollution. Show what the private market equilibrium implies in terms of where we are on (or inside of) the welfare frontier.

20.12. In Figure 20.2, suppose the government placed a quota instead of a tax on the output of the product that limited output to a maximum of Q_E. Would this policy achieve an efficient allocation of resources?

20.13. In discussing Figure 20.3, the text states that the private equilibrium output, Q_1, is inefficient. By definition, inefficiency is supposed to mean that everyone could be better off with a different allocation of resources. Does the subsidy shown in the diagram benefit everyone, including the taxpayer who pays to finance it? If not, what type of policy could be used that would benefit everyone?

20.14. A miracle drug that cures obesity is developed and produced competitively at a constant cost to producers of 10 cents per dose. The companies that produce the drug, however, discharge chemical wastes resulting from the production process into the nation's rivers. The damage to the economy in terms of reduced commercial and recreational use of the waterways is estimated to be 1 cent per dose. The social demand for the drug is $Q = 1,000,000 - 10,000P$, where Q indicates the number of doses produced and P is the price per dose measured in cents.
a. How much of the miracle drug is produced? At what price? Give both numerical and graphical answers.
b. An economist testifies before Congress that obesity cures are being overproduced and sold too cheaply. What price and

quantity do you think the economist would advocate? What is she likely to estimate as the cost to the economy of the supposed overproduction? Give numerical and graphical answers.
c. The economist argues that a tax should be placed on every unit of output that is accompanied by a waste discharge. What size tax per unit of output would an efficiency-seeking economist advocate? With this tax, what would the price and output be for the miracle drug? Give both numerical and graphical answers.

20.15. Suppose that in the preceding problem drug producers invent another production process that discharges no waste and can be used at a constant cost of 10.6 cents per dose.
a. What will the price and output of the miracle drug be if the tax advocated in part c of the preceding problem is imposed?
b. What will the price and output be if the no-discharge process had a cost of 11.4 cents per dose?
c. Suppose that the producer's cost under the new process rises to 13 cents per unit and producers are forbidden to use the original waste-discharging process. What price and output will result? By the economist's criteria, are there appropriate amounts of obesity cures and pollution? What is the deadweight loss, if any, that results? Give both numerical and graphical answers.

20.16. Comment on the following hypothetical remarks by the Congressional representatives who questioned the economist in Problem 20.14. Do you agree or disagree? (You don't have to play the role of an economist in your answer.)

Senator Anthony: "No value can be placed on the benefit this drug brings to humanity."
Senator Loeb: "The cure for obesity should be provided freely to all who need it."

20.17. Distinguish between efficiency in production and efficiency in output. Can an industry achieve efficiency in production and still produce at an inefficient output level? Explain.

20.18. Explain why efficiency in production is not realized if both refineries in Figure 20.4 are limited to emitting 100 pollution units each.

20.19. A clothing factory is located downwind from a copper smelting plant. The copper smelting plant emits particulates into the air that cause $100,000 in damage per year to the clothing factory in terms of fabric discoloration. The plant could eliminate its emissions of particulates by installing a superior scrubbing technology at a cost of $50,000 per year. Existing regulations do not prohibit the emission of these particulates. The only way to remedy the inefficiency associated with the emissions is through government intervention. True or false? Explain your answer.

20.20. The defense services provided by submarines are a public good. Suppose that the equation relating the marginal benefit Ted derives from the quantity of submarines produced (Q) is $MB = 600 - 10Q$. The equation relating the marginal benefit

Jane derives from submarines is $MB = 400 - 10Q$. The marginal cost of producing each submarine is a constant \$400.

a. If Ted and Jane are the only two individuals who benefit from the defense services provided by submarines, what is the efficient output of submarines?

b. Without any coordination between Ted and Jane and/or government intervention, what will be the output of submarines? Explain your answer. What will be the size of any resulting inefficiency?

c. Suggest a taxing scheme to ensure the attainment of efficiency in the provision of submarines.

d. Suppose that the defense services afforded by submarines are still nonrival in consumption but that the cost of excluding a demander is zero. If submarines are produced by a monopolist practicing third-degree price discrimination (that is, a producer that charges different prices to different demanders), what will be the profit-maximizing output and price that the monopolist will charge Ted and Jane? How does your answer compare to that in part a?

20.21. Much public debate has focused on the external costs associated with smoking. Explain why there may also be an external benefit from smoking in that smokers die at an earlier age than nonsmokers.

20.22. The United Nations Kyoto Protocol of 1997 requires most industrial nations to reduce their carbon dioxide and other greenhouse-gas emissions during the ensuing decade to about 5 percent of 1990 levels. Explain why such a policy is inefficient.

20.23. As cellular or mobile phones proliferate rapidly, with more than 100 million U.S. users, so do complaints about cell phone rudeness. "No Cell Phones" signs are popping up all over. Restaurants, theaters, libraries, museums, and doctors' offices have banned the devices. Explain why, using the concept of externalities.

20.24. As of the late 1990s, there had been instances of Russians shooting at Japanese, Tunisians shooting at Italians, and Portuguese shooting at Spaniards. This is just a partial list of the heated conflicts occurring on the high seas between aggressive fishing fleets and well-armed navy and coast guard vessels jealously protecting a lucrative and declining resource. At the source of the conflict appears to be the inability to define property rights to fish. Explain why.

20.25. Using the concept of property rights, explain why the buffalo nearly became extinct in the late 1800s while cow herds proliferated.

A. Mathematical Appendix

The Mathematical Appendix is designed to show how some of the more important conclusions of microeconomic theory can be developed mathematically with the aid of calculus. The material included here is organized according to the relevant sections in the text.

Chapter 2

SECTION 2.5 • ELASTICITIES (PP. 32–40)

In the text we defined the *price elasticity of demand* as the percentage change in quantity demanded divided by the percentage change in price for a movement along a demand curve. As the price change approaches zero in the limit, the calculus counterpart to this definition is:

$$\eta = \frac{dQ/Q}{dP/P} = \frac{dQ}{dP}\frac{P}{Q}; \tag{1}$$

where the demand curve is expressed as $Q = f(P)$.

Two points should be noted about this definition. First, expressing Q as a function of P is the reverse of the usual procedure, and graphically would be equivalent to putting Q on the vertical axis. Thus, dQ/dP is the slope of the demand curve as thus positioned. If P is expressed as a function of Q (the normal procedure), dQ/dP is the reciprocal of the slope of the demand curve. Second, dQ/dP will always be negative for a downward-sloping demand curve, and since P/Q will always be positive, the elasticity as defined by equation (1) will be negative. As noted in the text, economists often take the absolute value of price elasticity, and so define elasticity as $(-)dQ/dP \times P/Q$. In mathematical manipulations it is often important to be careful of the sign convention that is being used.

Now let's apply this definition to determine the price elasticity for two commonly used types of demand curves. If the demand curve is *linear*, it can be expressed as:

$$Q = a - bP; \tag{2}$$

where a and b are positive constants. (Alternatively, if P is taken as the dependent variable, the demand curve would be $P = a/b - Q/b$.) Note that the derivative of equation (2), dQ/dP, is $-b$; this is the reciprocal of the slope of the linear demand curve (a demand "line"?). From equation (1), we see that the price elasticity of demand at any point is given by

$$\eta = -b\frac{P}{Q}. \tag{3}$$

(Since b, P, and Q are positive, elasticity will always be negative; if we use the convention of taking the absolute value, the elasticity is bP/Q.) Since P/Q is different at every point on a downward-sloping demand curve, equation (3) thus indicates that the price elasticity varies along a linear demand curve. Moreover, P/Q becomes larger as we move up a demand curve, so elasticity will be greater (in absolute value) as we move up the demand curve.

The price elasticity differs at every point on a linear demand curve. Sometimes it is convenient to approximate the demand curve with a relationship where the price elasticity is the same at all points along the demand curve. Such a demand curve is given by the curvilinear relationship:

$$Q = kP^{-\alpha}; \tag{4}$$

where k and α are positive constants. With this type of demand curve, the price elasticity will be the same at all points on the curve and will equal $-\alpha$ (or just α if treated as a positive number). To verify this, we take the derivative:

$$\frac{dQ}{dP} = -\alpha kP^{-\alpha-1} \tag{5}$$

Then price elasticity equals this term multiplied by P/Q, or:

$$\eta = -\alpha kP^{-\alpha-1}\frac{P}{Q} = -\frac{\alpha kP^{-a}}{Q} = -\alpha; \tag{6}$$

where the last step follows since $kP^{-\alpha}$ in the numerator equals Q from equation (4). Thus, the demand curve given by equation (4) has a price elasticity equal to α at every point on the demand curve. This is easy to see if we let α equal 1, since then equation (4) is the equation for a rectangular hyperbola with $PQ = k$, so total expenditure equals k regardless of the price (a characteristic of unitary price elasticity).

Finally, we can easily verify the relationship between price elasticity of demand and how total expenditure varies with the price of the product. Total expenditure, E, is given by:

$$E = PQ. \tag{7}$$

To determine how E varies with P, let's take the derivative dE/dP using the product rule and remembering that Q is a function of P:

$$\frac{dE}{dP} = Q + P\frac{dQ}{dP}$$
$$= Q\left(1 + \frac{P}{Q}\frac{dQ}{dP}\right)$$
$$= Q(1 - \eta). \tag{8}$$

In equation (8), we treat price elasticity as positive. Note that if price elasticity is unity, then dE/dP equals 0, which shows that a change in price has no effect on total expenditure; total expenditure is unchanged. When price elasticity is greater than 1, dE/dP is negative, which shows that an increase in price with elastic demand causes total expenditure to fall. When price elasticity is less than 1, dE/dP is positive, which shows that an increase in price with inelastic demand causes total expenditure to rise.

Chapter 3

SECTION 3.1 • PREFERENCES OF THE CONSUMER (PP. 46–55)

We assume that a consumer's well-being depends on the quantities of compact discs and movies consumed. The preferences of the consumer can then be represented by a utility function, which gives utility (well-being) as a function of the quantities of the goods consumed:

$$U = U(C, M). \tag{9}$$

In the text, preferences are represented by a set of indifference curves. Along an indifference curve, total utility (U) is a constant, so specifying some fixed level for U would transform equation (9) from a general function into the equation for an indifference curve. To consider the relationship to indifference curves in more detail, take the total differential of equation (9):

$$dU = \frac{\partial U}{\partial C} dC + \frac{\partial U}{\partial M} dM. \tag{10}$$

[Note that the partial derivatives in equation (10), $\partial U/\partial C$ and $\partial U/\partial M$, are the marginal utilities of the two goods.] For a movement along a given indifference curve, total utility is unchanged, so we may set $dU = 0$ and obtain:

$$\frac{\partial U}{\partial M} dM = -\frac{\partial U}{\partial C} dC. \tag{11}$$

Thus:

$$\frac{dM}{dC} = -\frac{\partial U/\partial C}{\partial U/\partial M}. \tag{12}$$

Equation (12) shows that the slope of an indifference curve, dM/dC, equals (minus) the ratio of the marginal utilities. Of course, this is the same as saying that the marginal rate of substitution equals the ratio of the two marginal utilities (as explained in Section 3.6) since $-dM/dC$ equals the MRS.

SECTION 3.2 • THE BUDGET LINE (PP. 55–59)

A consumer spends his or her entire income, I, on C units of compact discs and M units of movie passes at prices of P_C and P_M. Consumer purchases must satisfy the budget constraint (the algebraic representation of the budget line), which is given by:

$$I = P_C C + P_M M. \tag{13}$$

This relationship indicates that expenditures on compact discs ($P_C C$) and movies ($P_M M$) sum to total income. With income

and prices fixed, the quantity of movies purchased can be expressed as a function of the quantity of compact discs purchased:

$$M = \frac{I}{P_M} - \frac{P_C}{P_M} C. \tag{14}$$

Taking the derivative of M with respect to C then yields:

$$\frac{dM}{dC} = -\frac{P_C}{P_M}. \tag{15}$$

This shows the slope of the budget line (dM/dC) to be equal to the negative of the price ratio, as explained in Section 3.2.

SECTION 3.3 • THE CONSUMER'S CHOICE (PP. 59–64)

The condition for the consumer's optimal choice can be derived as follows. The consumer's problem is to select the quantities of the two goods that yield him or her the greatest utility possible given the limitation posed by a fixed income. Mathematically, this can be expressed as a problem of constrained maximization: maximize utility subject to the budget constraint. The Lagrangian multiplier technique is the most straightforward way to solve the problem.

We begin by forming the Lagrangian expression (Z):

$$Z = U(C, M) + \lambda(I - P_C C - P_M M). \tag{16}$$

In equation (16), λ is known as the Lagrangian multiplier since it is multiplied by the equation for the budget constraint (in the form $I - P_C C - P_M M = 0$). With the constraint incorporated in this way, maximizing Z will also maximize U when the constraint is satisfied since the parenthetical expression will equal zero. The first-order conditions for a maximum are that the partial derivatives with respect to the three variables, C, M, and λ, must be equal to zero:

$$\frac{\partial Z}{\partial C} = \frac{\partial U}{\partial C} - \lambda P_C = 0; \tag{17}$$

$$\frac{\partial Z}{\partial M} = \frac{\partial U}{\partial M} - \lambda P_M = 0; \tag{18}$$

and

$$\frac{\partial Z}{\partial \lambda} = I - P_C C - P_M M = 0. \tag{19}$$

These conditions provide more instructive insights after some slight manipulation. Dividing equation (17) by equation (18) yields:

$$\frac{\partial U/\partial C}{\partial U/\partial M} = \frac{P_C}{P_M}. \tag{20}$$

Equation (20) shows that the ratio of marginal utilities must equal the ratio of prices if the consumer is to be maximizing utility. In other words, the MRS (ratio of marginal utilities) must equal the slope of the budget line (ratio of prices). In addition, the consumer's choice must lie on the budget line since equation (19) must also be satisfied. Thus, these conditions are the counterpart to the graphical treatment with the consumer's choice shown as a tangency between an indifference curve and the budget line.

Chapter 4

SECTION 4.1 • PRICE CHANGES AND CONSUMPTION CHOICES (PP. 82–86)

The demand curve of a consumer for some product can be derived from the first-order conditions determining the consumer's optimal choice, as given by equations (17) through (19) since these conditions must hold whatever the prices of the products or income of the consumer. Note that these expressions represent three equations in three unknowns (C, M, and λ); normally, with the number of equations and unknowns equal, it is possible in principle to solve for the unknowns. In general, when we solve for the quantity of some product demanded, we find that the quantity is a function of the price of the product, and this relationship gives the consumer's demand curve for the product.

Obviously, a consumer's demand curve depends on the exact nature of his or her preferences, that is, on the specific utility function that represents those preferences. Thus, the best we can do is illustrate how demand curves can be derived from a specific utility function. For this purpose, suppose a consumer's utility function is given by:

$$U = C^\alpha M^{1-\alpha}; \qquad (21)$$

where α is a constant with a value between 0 and 1. This functional form, called a *Cobb-Douglas function,* has played a large role in empirical economic analysis since it is both simple and is thought to approximate some actual economic relationships. You may wish to verify that the indifference curves derived from this utility function are, as we argue in the text, downward-sloping and convex toward the origin.

To derive the consumer's demand curves for compact discs and movies, we begin by forming the Lagrangian expression:

$$Z = C^\alpha M^{1-\alpha} + \lambda(I - P_C C - P_M M). \qquad (22)$$

Taking the partial derivatives and setting them equal to zero yields:

$$\frac{\partial Z}{\partial C} = \alpha C^{\sigma-1} M^{1-\alpha} - \lambda P_C = 0; \qquad (23)$$

$$\frac{\partial Z}{\partial M} = (1 - \alpha)C^\alpha M^{-\alpha} - \lambda P_M = 0; \qquad (24)$$

and

$$\frac{\partial Z}{\partial \lambda} = I - P_C C - P_M M = 0. \qquad (25)$$

Now we can solve these equations for C and M. One way to proceed is by multiplying both sides of equation (23) by C and then solving for C:

$$C = \frac{\alpha C^\alpha M^{1-\alpha}}{\lambda P_C}. \qquad (26)$$

Similarly, by multiplying both sides of equation (24) by M and then solving for M we obtain:

$$M = \frac{(1 - \alpha)C^\alpha M^{1-\alpha}}{\lambda P_M}. \qquad (27)$$

Since these expressions contain the unknown, λ, we must go further. We need to substitute equations (26) and (27) into equation (25) and solve for λ:

$$\lambda = \frac{C^\alpha M^{1-\alpha}}{I}. \qquad (28)$$

And, finally, we substitute equation (28) back into equations (26) and (27):

$$C = \frac{\alpha I}{P_C}; \qquad (29)$$

and

$$M = \frac{(1 - \alpha)I}{P_M}. \qquad (30)$$

Equations (29) and (30) are the demand *functions* that give the quantity demanded for any α, income, and price. The demand *curves* are determined by specifying particular values for α and I; then the quantity demanded varies with price when these other factors are held constant. Note that, with the numerators thus held constant, the quantity demanded of each good is an inverse function of its price: the higher the price, the lower is quantity demanded. Thus, the utility function we use here implies downward-sloping demand curves for both products. In fact, the demand curves are rectangular hyperbolas, implying that the price elasticity of demand for each product is unity, regardless of the price. (For compact discs, this can be seen by multiplying both sides of equation (29) by the price of compact discs. This shows that $P_C C$, the consumer's total expenditure on compact discs, is equal to αI regardless of the price of compact discs.)

Chapter 6

SECTION 6.2 • EFFICIENCY IN THE DISTRIBUTION OF GOODS (PP. 151–154)

In Section 6.2 of the text we explained that an efficient distribution of goods among consumers requires that the marginal rates of substitution of the consumers be equal. We can use the Lagrangian technique to demonstrate this conclusion formally.

We investigate the issue here in the same setting used in Section 6.3. There are two consumers, Edge and Worth, and two goods, football tickets and ballet passes. The utility function of the consumers are $U^E(F_E, B_E)$ and $U^W(F_W, B_W)$, indicating that the well-being of each consumer depends on his or her consumption of the two goods. Our problem is to determine the condition for an efficient distribution of fixed quantities of football tickets and ballet passes between the two consumers. Recall that an *efficient distribution* can be described as one that makes one consumer as well off as possible for a given level of well-being for the other consumer. Stated another way, an efficient distribution is one that maximizes the utility of one consumer subject to the constraint that the utility of the other is held fixed at some level. We set up the problem as the maximization of Edge's utility subject to the constraint that Worth attain a specified level of utility. This constraint can be expressed as:

$$U^W(F_W, B_W) = k. \tag{31}$$

In equation (31), the constant k is any arbitrary level of utility. For example, it could be U_3^W, as we assumed in discussing Figure 6.2a.

In addition to this constraint, we must recognize that the total quantities of the two goods are fixed. Thus, there are two more constraints, which are given by:

$$F_E + F_W = F^*; \tag{32}$$

and

$$B_E + B_W = B^*; \tag{33}$$

where F^* and B^* are the fixed quantities of the goods.

Thus, we wish to maximize Edge's utility subject to these three constraints. The relevant Lagrangian expression to be maximized is:

$$Z = U^E(F_E, B_E) + \lambda_1[k - U^W(F_W, B_W)]$$
$$+ \lambda_2(F^* - F_E - F_W)$$
$$+ \lambda_3(B^* - B_E - B_W). \tag{34}$$

The first-order conditions for a maximum involve setting the seven partial derivatives of equation (34) (with respect to F_E, B_E, F_W, B_W, λ_1, λ_2, and λ_3) equal to zero. We only need to use the first four of these partial derivatives:

$$\frac{\partial Z}{\partial F_E} = \frac{\partial U^E}{\partial F_E} - \lambda_2 = 0; \tag{35}$$

$$\frac{\partial Z}{\partial B_E} = \frac{\partial U^E}{\partial B_E} - \lambda_3 = 0; \tag{36}$$

$$\frac{\partial Z}{\partial F_W} = -\lambda_1 \frac{\partial U^W}{\partial F_W} - \lambda_2 = 0; \tag{37}$$

and

$$\frac{\partial Z}{\partial B_W} = -\lambda_1 \frac{\partial U^W}{\partial B_W} - \lambda_3 = 0. \tag{38}$$

Next, we divide equation (35) by (36) and equation (37) by (38) to obtain:

$$\frac{\dfrac{\partial U^E}{\partial F_E}}{\dfrac{\partial U^E}{\partial B_E}} = \frac{\lambda_2}{\lambda_3}; \tag{39}$$

and

$$\frac{\dfrac{\partial U^W}{\partial F_W}}{\dfrac{\partial U^W}{\partial B_W}} = \frac{\lambda_2}{\lambda_3}. \tag{40}$$

Note that the terms on the left-hand sides of equations (39) and (40) are the ratios of marginal utilities, which, as we have seen, are simply MRS_{FB}^E and MRS_{FB}^W, respectively. Since both MRSs are equal to λ_2/λ_3, they must be equal to each other. Thus, we have shown that the consumers' MRSs must be equal for the distribution of products to be efficient. This is the same conclusion we reach in the text, where the efficient distributions are shown as positions of tangency between the consumers' indifference curves in the Edgeworth box diagram; that is, positions where the MRSs are equal.

Chapter 7

SECTION 7.2 • PRODUCTION WHEN ONLY ONE INPUT IS VARIABLE (PP. 167–173)

When all inputs except for one are held constant, output can be expressed as a function of that one input alone, as in:

$$Q = Q(L); \tag{41}$$

where output is shown to depend on the quantity of labor, with it understood that the quantities of other inputs (such as capital and land) are held constant, as is technology. In this case the marginal and average products of the variable input, labor, are given by:

$$MP_L = \frac{dQ}{dL}; \tag{42}$$

and

$$AP_L = \frac{Q}{L} = \frac{Q(L)}{L}. \tag{43}$$

The relationship between marginal and average product can now be derived easily. Consider how the average product varies with the quantity of labor by differentiating AP_L with respect to L using the quotient rule, since both the numerator and denominator of equation (43) are functions of L:

$$\frac{dAP_L}{dL} = \frac{d(Q/L)}{dL} = \frac{\left(L\dfrac{dQ}{dL} - Q\right)}{L^2}. \tag{44}$$

Now we factor out $(1/L)$ to obtain:

$$\frac{dAP_L}{dL} = \frac{1}{L}\left(\frac{dQ}{dL} - \frac{Q}{L}\right)$$

$$= \frac{1}{L}(MP_L - AP_L). \tag{45}$$

Equation (45) conveniently summarizes the relationship between marginal and average product. Note that whenever MP_L is greater than AP_L, the right-hand side is positive, implying that average product increases with the use of additional units of labor (below 4 units of labor in Figure 7.1). Whenever MP_L is less than AP_L, the right-hand side is negative, implying that average product decreases with increased use of labor (above 4 units of labor in Figure 7.1). Finally, for AP_L to be at a maximum, the derivative must equal zero, so equating the right-hand side of equation (45) to zero we find this happens when MP_L equals AP_L.

SECTION 7.3 • PRODUCTION WHEN ALL INPUTS ARE VARIABLE (PP. 173–177)

Assume that two inputs are used in production and consider a time period in which both are variable. In this case output can be expressed as a function of both inputs with the production function:

$$Q = Q(L, K); \tag{46}$$

where L and K are the quantities of the two inputs, labor and capital, with technology assumed fixed. In this situation, note that the marginal products are now given by partial derivatives, $\partial Q/\partial L$ and $\partial Q/\partial K$, since marginal product measures the additional output produced when only one input is varied and other inputs are held constant.

To see the relationship between the production function and the isoquants used to represent it graphically in the text, take the total differential of equation (46):

$$dQ = \frac{\partial Q}{\partial L}\,dL + \frac{\partial Q}{\partial K}\,dK. \tag{47}$$

Along an isoquant there is no change in total output, so $dQ = 0$; thus, the right-hand side of equation (47) equals zero along an isoquant, and this implies:

$$\frac{\partial Q}{\partial K}\,dK = -\frac{\partial Q}{\partial L}\,dL; \tag{48}$$

or:

$$\frac{dK}{dL} = -\frac{\partial Q/\partial L}{\partial Q/\partial K}. \tag{49}$$

Equation (49) shows that the slope of an isoquant, dK/dL, equals (minus) the ratio of the marginal products of the inputs. Of course, this is the same as saying that the marginal rate of technical substitution equals the ratio of marginal products since $-dK/dL$ equals the MRTS.

SECTION 7.4 • RETURNS TO SCALE (PP. 178–182), AND SECTION 7.5 • EMPIRICAL ESTIMATION OF PRODUCTION FUNCTIONS (PP. 182–185)

A production function that exhibits constant returns to scale is called a *linear homogeneous function* (also the mathematical term for what economists refer to as a *constant returns to scale function*). For a production function given by $Q = Q(L, K)$ to be a linear homogeneous production function, it must satisfy the following condition:

$$sQ = Q(sL, sK); \tag{50}$$

for s equal to any positive constant. In other words, equation (50) just says that a proportionate increase in both inputs must increase output in the same proportion. For instance, if $s = 2$, then equation (50) indicates that a doubling of both inputs exactly doubles output.

Linear homogeneous production functions have played a large role in economic analysis, both because there is a certain intuitive plausibility about the relationship and because empirical evidence suggests that many production relationships are close to being constant returns to scale.

A commonly used production function is the Cobb–Douglas production function:

$$Q = L^\alpha K^{1-\alpha}; \tag{51}$$

where α is a positive constant with a value between 0 and 1. Such a Cobb–Douglas production function is a linear homogeneous function. To show this, consider how increasing both inputs by the factor s affects output:

$$Q(sL, sK) = (sL)^\alpha (sK)^{1-\alpha}$$

$$= s^{\alpha+1-\alpha} L^\alpha K^{1-\alpha} = sQ. \tag{52}$$

Thus, increasing both inputs by the factor s increases output by the same factor, implying that the Cobb–Douglas function is a linear homogeneous function.

Linear homogeneous production functions have several properties that are useful to keep in mind. One of these is that the marginal product of each input depends only on the proportion in which inputs are used (K/L). Although we do not show here that this relationship holds for all linear homogeneous functions, we can easily demonstrate that it is true for the foregoing Cobb–Douglas function.

The marginal product of labor is given by

$$MP_L = \frac{\partial Q}{\partial L} = \alpha L^{\alpha-1} K^{1-\alpha}$$

$$= \alpha(K/L)^{1-\alpha}. \tag{53}$$

Equation (53) shows the marginal product to depend only on the ratio K/L and not on the absolute amount of labor; that is, doubling both K and L will leave the marginal product unaffected. (The same can be shown for the marginal product of capital.) This makes good sense since it means the marginal product depends on how scarce the input is relative to the other input. Graphically, in an isoquant diagram, this implies that the marginal products of both inputs are unchanged as we move outward along any ray through the origin (thus keeping K/L unchanged).

A second important property of linear homogeneous production functions is that the $MRTS$ depends only on the proportion in which inputs are used. This is already clear from equation (53) since the $MRTS$ is the ratio of the marginal products, and with each marginal product depending on only the ratio K/L, the $MRTS$ also depends on only the same ratio. Graphically, this relationship means that the slopes of isoquants are equal along a ray through the origin.

Chapter 8

SECTION 8.3 • SHORT-RUN COST CURVES (PP. 194–197)

The geometrical relationship between average and marginal cost curves is easily derived mathematically. Formally, the analysis is analogous to the way we derived the relationship between marginal and average product curves.

Average cost is simply total cost (C) divided by total output (Q):

$$AC = \frac{C}{Q}. \tag{54}$$

Now let's take the derivative of average cost with respect to output, recalling that both the numerator and denominator of equation (54) are functions of output:

$$\frac{dAC}{dQ} = \frac{d(C/Q)}{dQ} = \frac{(Q \, dC/dQ - C)}{Q^2}.$$

Factoring out $1/Q$ gives us:

$$\frac{1}{Q}\left(\frac{dC}{dQ} - \frac{C}{Q}\right) = \frac{1}{Q}(MC - AC). \tag{55}$$

Equation (55) conveniently summarizes the relationship between the AC and MC curves. It shows that the slope of the AC curve (dAC/dQ) is negative when marginal cost is less than average cost [since this makes the right-hand side of equation (55) negative]. Equation (55) also shows that the slope of the average cost curve is positive when MC is greater than AC [making the right-hand side of equation (55) positive], and that the slope is zero when MC equals AC.

Note that the relationship derived here holds regardless of whether we are dealing with long-run or short-run cost curves; the geometrical relationship is the same in either case.

SECTION 8.4 • LONG-RUN COST OF PRODUCTION (PP. 197–203)

As explained in the text, the firm's input choices can be viewed as either maximizing output for a given level of total cost or equivalently minimizing the cost necessary to produce a given output. Let's consider both ways of approaching the problem, starting with output maximization subject to a cost constraint.

Suppose that the firm has a fixed sum, C^0, to spend on labor and capital, which are available at per-unit costs of w and r. Then the firm is restricted to purchasing combinations of labor and capital that satisfy:

$$C^0 = wL + rK. \tag{56}$$

In other words, equation (56) is the cost constraint, and the firm wants to produce as much output as possible while satisfying this constraint. Thus, the firm wants to maximize output, as given by $Q(L, K)$, subject to the cost constraint.

As before, we begin by forming the Lagrangian expression:

$$Z = Q(L, K) + \lambda(C^0 - wL - rK). \tag{57}$$

The first-order conditions for a maximum involve setting the three partial derivatives (with respect to the variables, L, K, and λ) equal to zero:

$$\frac{\partial Z}{\partial L} = \frac{\partial Q}{\partial L} - \lambda w = 0; \tag{58}$$

$$\frac{\partial Z}{\partial K} = \frac{\partial Q}{\partial K} - \lambda r = 0; \tag{59}$$

and

$$\frac{\partial Z}{\partial \lambda} = C^0 - wL - rK = 0. \tag{60}$$

To see that these conditions describe the same solution explained in geometrical terms in the text, let's divide equation (58) by equation (59) to obtain

$$\frac{\partial Q/\partial L}{\partial Q/\partial K} = \frac{w}{r}. \tag{61}$$

The left-hand side of equation (61) is the ratio of the marginal products of the inputs, or the $MRTS$; the right-hand side is the ratio of the input prices. Since these ratios are, respectively, the slope of an isoquant and an isocost line, equation (61) just formalizes the result in the text that a firm will choose a combination of inputs such that there is a tangency between an isoquant and isocost line.

Equations (58) and (59) can also be rearranged as follows:

$$\frac{\partial Q/\partial L}{w} = \frac{\partial Q/\partial K}{r} = \lambda. \tag{62}$$

Expressed in this form, equation (62) shows that the firm should be allocating its funds so that the marginal products per dollar's worth of all inputs are equal. Note, too, that the Lagrangian multiplier for this problem is equal to this common value of the additional output per dollar's worth of all inputs.

Now let's show how the problem can be formulated as a constrained minimization problem. Suppose the firm wants to produce a given output at the lowest possible cost. In other words, the firm wants to minimize total cost, $wL + rK$, subject to the constraint that output be some fixed level, or:

$$Q^0 = Q(L, K). \tag{63}$$

The Lagrangian for this problem is:

$$Z = wL + rK + \lambda[Q^0 - Q(L, K)]. \quad (64)$$

The first-order conditions for a constrained minimum are, of course, the same as for a maximum, and involve setting the three partial derivatives equal to zero:

$$\frac{\partial Z}{\partial L} = w - \lambda \frac{\partial Q}{\partial L} = 0; \quad (65)$$

$$\frac{\partial Z}{\partial K} = r - \lambda \frac{\partial Q}{\partial K} = 0; \quad (66)$$

and

$$\frac{\partial Z}{\partial \lambda} = Q^0 - Q(L, K) = 0. \quad (67)$$

Note what we get when we divide equation (65) by equation (66):

$$\frac{w}{r} = \frac{\partial Q/\partial L}{\partial Q/\partial K}. \quad (68)$$

Equation (68) is the same as equation (61), which we derived using the output maximization approach; both approaches tell us that the firm should select a point of tangency between an isoquant and an isocost line. Or, as noted in the text, points of tangency show the maximum output attainable at a given cost as well as the minimum cost necessary to produce that output.

SECTION 8.8 • USING COST CURVES: CONTROLLING POLLUTION (PP. 213–216)

In the text we explained that for pollution to be reduced at the lowest possible cost, each firm must be operating where the marginal cost of pollution abatement is the same. This conclusion can also be derived using the Lagrangian technique since the problem is really one of constrained minimization.

Each of two firms, A and B, have cost functions for providing pollution abatement, which we indicate as $C_A(PA_A)$ and $C_B(PA_B)$. Our problem is to minimize the sum of the costs of the two firms:

$$C = C_A(PA_A) + C_B(PA_B). \quad (69)$$

However, cost is to be minimized subject to the constraint that only a certain quantity of pollution be permitted, that is, that pollution abatement equal a specified level:

$$PA_A + PA_B = PA*. \quad (70)$$

Thus, we want to minimize equation (69) subject to the constraint specified by equation (70), so the relevant Lagrangian expression is:

$$Z = C_A(PA_A) + C_B(PA_B)$$
$$+ \lambda(PA* - PA_A - PA_B). \quad (71)$$

The first-order conditions are:

$$\frac{\partial Z}{\partial PA_A} = \frac{\partial C_A}{\partial PA_A} - \lambda = 0; \quad (72)$$

$$\frac{\partial Z}{\partial PA_B} = \frac{\partial C_B}{\partial PA_B} - \lambda = 0; \quad (73)$$

and

$$\frac{\partial Z}{\partial \lambda} = PA* - PA_A - PA_B = 0. \quad (74)$$

In equations (72) and (73), note that $\partial C_A/\partial PA_A$ and $\partial C_B/\partial PA_B$ are the marginal costs of pollution abatement of firms A and B, respectively. Moreover, since equations (72) and (73) show that both marginal costs must equal the same Lagrangian multiplier, they must also be equal to one another, which is precisely the condition for producing pollution abatement efficiently explained in the text.

Chapter 9

SECTION 9.4 • SHORT-RUN PROFIT MAXIMIZATION (PP. 229–234), AND SECTION 9.7 • LONG-RUN COMPETITIVE EQUILIBRIUM (PP. 241–245)

Using calculus we can easily show that a competitive firm must produce where price equals marginal cost to maximize profit. The total profit (π) of a firm is equal to the difference between total revenue (R) and total cost (C):

$$\pi = R - C. \quad (75)$$

Both R and C are functions of output. Total revenue equals price times output, or PQ. For a *competitive* firm, price is a constant, which we indicate as P_0. Thus, the total profit of a competitive firm is given by:

$$\pi = P_0Q - C. \quad (76)$$

The first-order condition for finding the profit-maximizing output requires that the first derivative of the total profit function be equal to zero:

$$\frac{d\pi}{dQ} = P_0 \frac{dQ}{dQ} - \frac{dC}{dQ} = 0$$
$$= P_0 - MC = 0. \quad (77)$$

[In equation (77), note that dC/dQ equals marginal cost.] Thus, the competitive firm should produce an output where $MC = P_0$.

In deriving equation (77), we make no distinction between long-run and short-run profit maximization. Both require production where price equals the relevant marginal cost, either short-run or long-run marginal cost. To formulate the problem so that it applies explicitly to a short-run setting, we would let the firm's total cost equal the sum of total variable cost (VC) and fixed cost (F). Then profit equals $P_0Q - VC - F$ and the first derivative equals $P_0 - dVC/dQ - dF/dQ$. In this case, dVC/dQ is short-run marginal cost and dF/dQ equals zero since F is a constant. Thus, we obtain the same condition for profit maximization.

The condition that the firm produce a level of output where marginal cost and price are equal is only the first-order condition for a maximum; there is also a second-order condition. Although we have previously ignored second-order conditions, we can easily derive and interpret it in this case. The second-order condition for profit maximization requires that the second derivative of the total profit function be negative:

$$\frac{d^2\pi}{dQ^2} = 0 - \frac{d^2C}{dQ^2} < 0. \tag{78}$$

[In equation (78), the second derivative of revenue with respect to output is zero since price is constant.] From equation (78), we see that d^2C/dQ^2 must be positive for profit to be at a maximum. This relationship means that at the point where price equals marginal cost, the marginal cost curve must have a positive slope since d^2C/dQ^2 is the slope of the marginal cost curve. This condition arises because it is possible for the marginal cost curve to intersect the price line at more than one point. For example, with a U-shaped marginal cost curve, there may be two intersections. The first, where marginal cost is declining, is not a position of maximum profit (it is a position of minimum profit), and the second-order condition tells us to ignore that intersection in seeking the profit-maximizing output.

SECTION 9.9 • WHEN DOES THE COMPETITIVE MODEL APPLY? (PP. 253–254), AND SECTION 11.4 • THE MEASUREMENT AND SOURCES OF MONOPOLY POWER (PP. 308–313)

We can use calculus to derive a formula relating the price elasticity of demand confronting one firm to the market price elasticity of demand, the firm's market share, and the price elasticity of supply of other firms. We begin with the fact that the output of one firm, q_i, equals total industry output, Q_T, minus the output of other firms, Q_0:

$$q_i = Q_T - Q_0. \tag{79}$$

Now we can take the derivative with respect to the (common) market price:

$$\frac{dq_i}{dP} = \frac{dQ_T}{dP} - \frac{dQ_0}{dP}. \tag{80}$$

By manipulating equation (80), we can express the relationship in terms of the three relevant elasticities. Let's start by multiplying both sides by P/q_i since this converts the left-hand side of the equation to η_i:

$$\eta_i = \frac{dQ_T}{dP}\frac{P}{q_i} - \frac{dQ_0}{dP}\frac{P}{q_i}. \tag{81}$$

If we examine the two terms on the right in view of the formulas for the market price elasticity of demand and the price

elasticity of supply of other firms, we see that multiplying the first term by Q_T/Q_T and the second term by Q_0/Q_0 results in the required elasticities:

$$\eta_i = \frac{Q_T}{q_i}\left(\frac{dQ_T}{dP}\frac{P}{Q_T}\right) - \frac{Q_0}{q_i}\left(\frac{dQ_0}{dP}\frac{P}{Q_0}\right). \tag{82}$$

The terms in the parentheses on the right are now the price elasticity of the market demand (η) and the price elasticity of supply of other firms (ε_0), respectively, and Q_T/q_i is the reciprocal of firm i's market share (S_i). Thus, with due respect to our convention of taking the absolute value of elasticity of demand, equation (82) is the formula behind some of the intuition given in the text.

Chapter 11

SECTION 11.1 • THE MONOPOLIST'S DEMAND AND MARGINAL REVENUE CURVES (PP. 296–298), AND SECTION 11.3 • FURTHER IMPLICATIONS OF MONOPOLY ANALYSIS (PP. 304–307)

Now let's consider some relationships between marginal revenue and demand. Total revenue is equal to price times quantity:

$$R = PQ. \tag{83}$$

Since we are dealing with the market demand curve, price is not taken as a constant but as an inverse function of output (that is, $P = f(Q)$ and $dP/dQ < 0$). Marginal revenue is simply the derivative of total revenue with respect to Q, which we find by using the product rule:

$$\frac{dR}{dQ} = MR = P + Q\frac{dP}{dQ}. \tag{84}$$

Equation (84) shows that marginal revenue is always less than price for a downward-sloping demand curve since P is positive and dP/dQ is negative. (When the demand curve is horizontal, as it is for a competitive firm, dP/dQ equals zero, and marginal revenue equals price.) Moreover, marginal revenue is less than price by an amount equal to $Q(dP/dQ)$. This corroborates our discussion of Figure 11.1 in the text where marginal revenue is shown to equal area B minus area A. Area B corresponds to P in equation (84) and area A—the reduction in revenue on the original units from an increase in output—corresponds to $Q(dP/dQ)$.

By factoring out P, we can rearrange equation (84) to give the relationship between price, marginal revenue, and price elasticity of demand:

$$MR = P\left(1 + \frac{Q}{P}\frac{dP}{dQ}\right)$$
$$= P(1 - 1/\eta). \tag{85}$$

Equation (85) is the formula given in the text. Once again, recall that we are treating price elasticity as a positive number.

SECTION 11.2 • PROFIT-MAXIMIZING OUTPUT OF A MONOPOLY (PP. 298–304)

Profit maximization by a monopolist is handled in the same way as the competitive case considered earlier, except that price is no longer considered a constant but instead an inverse function of output. Profit is given by:

$$\pi = R - C; \tag{86}$$

where π, R, and C are profit, total revenue, and total cost, respectively, as before. All three variables are functions of the quantity of output. The first-order condition for maximum profit involves setting the first derivative with respect to output (Q) equal to zero:

$$\frac{d\pi}{dQ} = \frac{dR}{dQ} - \frac{dC}{dQ} = 0. \tag{87}$$

Equation (87) shows that marginal revenue (dR/dQ) must equal marginal cost (dC/dQ) for output to be at the profit-maximizing level.

An alternative derivation is helpful in relating this to the competitive case. We change equation (86) to express revenue as price times quantity:

$$\pi = PQ - C. \tag{88}$$

Now we take the first derivative, recalling that P is a function of Q:

$$\frac{d\pi}{dQ} = P + Q\frac{dP}{dQ} - \frac{dC}{dQ} = 0. \tag{89}$$

Equation (89) is general and applies whether the firm is a competitive firm or a monopoly. If the firm is competitive, dP/dQ equals zero (horizontal demand curve), and equation (89) reduces to the price-equals-marginal-cost rule. If the firm is a monopoly, equation (89) indicates that marginal revenue (which will be less than price) must equal marginal cost since $P + Q(dP/dQ)$ is equal to marginal revenue, as we saw above. Finally, note that price will be above marginal cost at the monopoly profit-maximizing equilibrium. Can you see why from equation (89)?

Chapter 12

SECTION 12.3 • PRICE AND OUTPUT DETERMINATION WITH PRICE DISCRIMINATION (PP. 331–335)

A monopolist practicing price discrimination is assumed to have the same goal as any other firm: to maximize profit. The profit-maximizing conditions are easily derived. Assume the monopoly sells in two markets, A and B, as in the text. The profit of the monopolist is the sum of revenues from sales in the two markets less total cost of production, or:

$$\pi = R_A + R_B - C$$
$$= P_A Q_A + P_B Q_B - C. \tag{90}$$

In equation (90), total cost is understood to be a function of total output, $Q_A + Q_B$.

The first-order conditions for profit maximization involve setting the two partial derivatives of the profit function with respect to Q_A and Q_B equal to zero; the marginal profit from output in each market must be zero:

$$\frac{\partial \pi}{\partial Q_A} = \frac{\partial R_A}{\partial Q_A} - \frac{\partial C}{\partial Q_A} = 0; \tag{91}$$

and

$$\frac{\partial \pi}{\partial Q_B} = \frac{\partial R_B}{\partial Q_B} - \frac{\partial C}{\partial Q_B} = 0. \tag{92}$$

Equation (91) simply indicates that the monopolist should operate where the marginal revenue from selling in market A ($\partial R_A/\partial Q_A$) equals the marginal cost of producing for that market ($\partial C/\partial Q_A$). An equivalent condition holds for market B. But recall that the marginal cost terms will be equal since marginal cost depends on total output; given any total output, the marginal cost of selling to either market is the same and is equal to the marginal cost of producing another unit. Thus, both marginal revenues must equal the same marginal cost, so the profit-maximizing condition can be written concisely as:

$$MR_A = MR_B = MC. \tag{93}$$

Note that this condition is satisfied at the equilibrium identified in Figure 12.4 in the text.

We can go somewhat further by recalling that marginal revenue equals $P(1 - 1/\eta)$. Thus, equation (93) implies:

$$P_A\left(1 - \frac{1}{\eta_A}\right) = P_B\left(1 - \frac{1}{\eta_B}\right). \tag{94}$$

Equation (94) shows that price will be lower in the market with the more elastic demand curve. In addition, note that if the elasticities are the same, then the prices charged will be the same; in this case, there is no gain from being able to charge different prices.

Chapter 16

SECTION 16.1 • THE INPUT DEMAND CURVE OF A COMPETITIVE FIRM (PP. 436–441)

A simple variation on our earlier discussion of the determination of the profit-maximizing output of a competitive firm allows us to determine the profit-maximizing employment of inputs. Once again, the objective of the firm is to maximize profit, or the difference between revenue and cost. Total cost is equal to total payments to input owners, so if labor and capital are the only two inputs, total cost is $wL + rK$. Profit is then given by:

$$\pi = PQ - (wL + rK). \tag{95}$$

Note that both total revenue and total cost are functions of the quantities of inputs used, so profit is a function of the quantities of inputs used. [Total revenue is a function of input employment because output is a function of input employment: $Q = Q(L, K)$.] To maximize profit, the partial derivatives of the profit function with respect to both inputs must be equal to zero:

$$\frac{\partial \pi}{\partial L} = P \frac{\partial Q}{\partial L} - w = 0; \qquad (96)$$

and

$$\frac{\partial \pi}{\partial K} = P \frac{\partial Q}{\partial K} - r = 0. \qquad (97)$$

(In taking the partial derivatives, P, r, and w are treated as constants since we are dealing with a competitive firm.) Equations (96) and (97) can be rewritten as:

$$P \frac{\partial Q}{\partial L} = w, \textit{ or } MVP_L = w; \qquad (98)$$

and

$$P \frac{\partial Q}{\partial K} = r, \textit{ or } MVP_K = r. \qquad (99)$$

Equations (98) and (99) indicate that a competitive firm maximizes profit by hiring each input up to the point where the input's marginal value product equals its price, a conclusion explained in the text. The second-order condition here, which is easily verified, is that the MVP curve be negatively sloped.

SECTION 16.6 • INPUT DEMAND AND EMPLOYMENT BY AN OUTPUT MARKET MONOPOLY (PP. 452–454)

Determination of the profit-maximizing levels of employment of inputs for a monopoly differs only slightly from that for a com-

petitive firm. Consider equation (95), which gives the total profit of a firm as the difference between total revenue and total cost. This relationship remains true when the firm is a monopoly. However, what differs from the competitive case is that price is not treated as a constant. When the firm is a monopoly, price is a function of output, and output is a function of the quantities of inputs employed. (Input prices are still treated as constants.) When this difference is taken into account, the relevant partial derivatives (to be set equal to zero for a maximum) become:

$$\frac{\partial \pi}{\partial L} = P \frac{\partial Q}{\partial L} + Q \frac{\partial P}{\partial Q} \frac{\partial Q}{\partial L} - w = 0; \qquad (100)$$

and

$$\frac{\partial \pi}{\partial K} = P \frac{\partial Q}{\partial K} + Q \frac{\partial P}{\partial Q} \frac{\partial Q}{\partial K} - r = 0. \qquad (101)$$

These equations can be rewritten as:

$$\frac{\partial Q}{\partial L} \left(P + Q \frac{\partial P}{\partial Q} \right) = w; \qquad (102)$$

and

$$\frac{\partial Q}{\partial K} \left(P + Q \frac{\partial P}{\partial Q} \right) = r. \qquad (103)$$

Examining these equations reveals that they represent equalities between marginal revenue product and input price. Recall that the parenthetical terms equal marginal revenue; see equation (84).

Answers to Selected Problems

Chapter 1

1.5. False. The opportunity cost of the land to RAND equals the amount RAND could sell the land for. This amount is likely to be substantial, given the prime location of the land.

Chapter 2

2.1. First, because the increase in the overall price level over the year is not given, it is not clear how the relative price of textbooks has changed. Second, it is possible that the demand curve has shifted over the year, perhaps due to such things as changes in college enrollments or greater interest in economics and business courses.

2.5. (a) $0.70 and 120,000. (b) The demand curve confronting producers becomes DAD_1. Output will be 140,000 with consumers purchasing 110,000 and the government 30,000 (equal to the output consumers do not purchase—140,000 less 110,000). (c) Consumer demand becomes $D''D'''$, and the demand curve confronting producers becomes $D''A'D_1$. Total output and price do not change, but consumer purchases rise to 121,000 and government purchases fall to 19,000 (140,000 less 121,000).

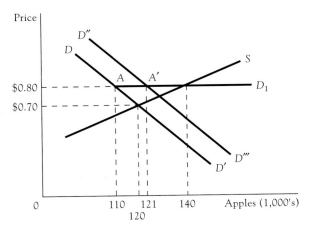

2.8. (a) Will increase demand. (b) Will increase demand. (c) Will reduce supply. (d) Will increase demand and reduce supply. (e) Will increase demand. (f) Will increase demand.

2.10. False. The demand elasticity for a more narrowly defined good (such as a particular cigarette brand) is always greater than for a less narrowly defined good (cigarettes in general).

2.14. The price of crack cocaine would rise and so would the total consumer outlay on crack cocaine since its demand is inelastic. Since the funds to purchase crack cocaine are obtained by stealing, the amount of crime would rise.

Chapter 3

3.2. The budget constraint is AMZ, kinked at point M. Along the AM portion the slope is $10/1V while the slope is $5/1V along the MZ portion.

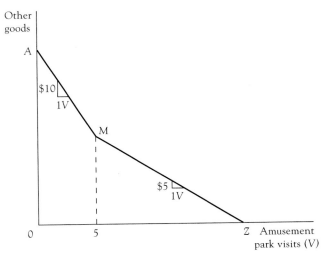

3.3. Income is $60, the price of hamburgers times the hamburger intercept. The price of french fries is $2, income of $60 divided by the french fries intercept, 30. The slope is 20H/30F $= P_F/P_H = $2/$3$.

3.9. Marilyn would be at point N on the budget line (see next page for a graph). At this point, her MRS $< P_C/P_F$: the slope of the indifference curve at N is 1F/1C while the budget line's slope is 3F/1C. Thus, N is not an optimal consumption point for Marilyn. The optimal point is M.

3.10. Not necessarily. Seat belts have costs as well as the benefit of reduced risk of injuries, and if motorists considered the marginal cost of purchasing and using seat belts greater than the marginal benefit, they would be rational not to purchase them. This would be shown as a corner equilibrium, as in Figure 3.12.

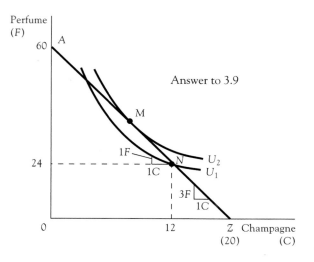

Answer to 3.9

3.13. Yes; at a higher income it is possible for a consumer to purchase more of all goods. No; since all income is spent on something (remember, saving is considered one of the goods), at a higher income more of at least one good must be purchased.

3.14. Market baskets are shown as points A and B. If good V is a normal good, MRS_{VO}—the slope of the indifference curve—must be greater at B, as shown in the diagram. Otherwise the consumer would not purchase more V at a higher income. If V is an inferior good, MRS_{VO} at point B would be less than at point A.

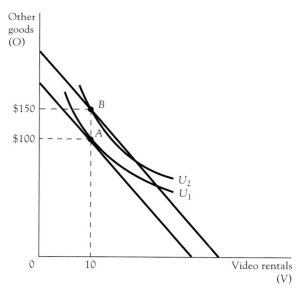

Chapter 4

4.4. If Joe could purchase as much gas as desired at a price of $1.50, the budget line would be AZ. However, since only 25 gal-

lons can be acquired at that price, the budget line is AMG', and Joe's optimal consumption point is M. Since the MRS at M is greater than $1.50 per gallon, Joe will pay more than $1.50 to get additional gasoline beyond 25 gallons.

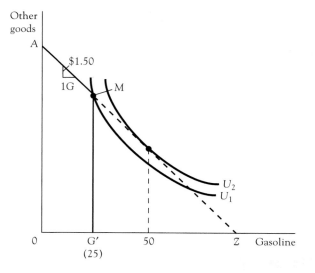

4.6. The budget line pivots from AZ to A'Z. The income effect implies greater car maintenance consumption (with maintenance a normal good), while the substitution effect implies less consumption of car maintenance, so we cannot predict the overall effect. (That illustrates why income must be held constant in drawing a demand curve; in the present case, the demand curve has shifted outward.) However, both the income and substitution effects imply greater consumption of other goods.

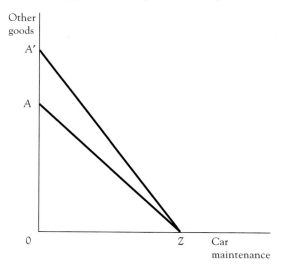

4.16. Fabio will be better off and consume less gasoline. The price increase changes the budget line from AZ to AZ' and distance ET = $500 (= 1,000 gallons times $0.50). Thus, a cash transfer of $500 shifts the budget line to A_1Z_1, which passes through point E since $A_1A = ET = \$500$.

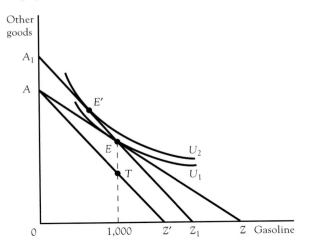

Chapter 5

5.2. Kate will be better off with food stamps but will consume more food with the excise subsidy. Her optimal point with the food stamps is E on budget line $AA'Z'$, with the $100 cost shown by the distance ET. Her optimal point with the excise subsidy is E' on budget line AZ_1 with the $100 cost equal to $E'T'$. The trick is to locate the size of the excise subsidy per unit that costs exactly $100, and this implies that the optimal point with the excise subsidy is where Kate's price-consumption curve intersects $A'Z'$. Note that with a larger excise subsidy per unit (lower price), total cost would exceed $100, and vice versa.

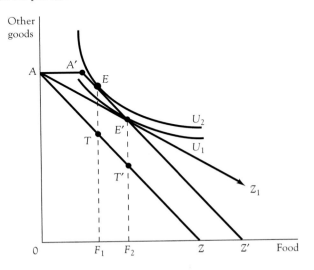

5.11. The initial endowment point is N, AZ is the budget line, and Leona's optimal point is E. When year one earnings fall to $4,000,000$, the endowment point shifts to N' and the budget

line becomes $A'Z'$. With consumption in both years normal goods, consumption in both years will fall due to the income effect (there is no substitution effect), as shown by the new optimal point E'. Borrowing has increased, so year 1 consumption has fallen by less than the reduction in earnings.

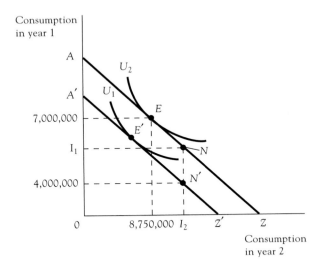

Chapter 6

6.3. At point A, John would be willing to give up three gallons of gasoline for one bag of sugar and remain equally well off. Thus giving up two gallons of gasoline for one bag of sugar as in a move from point A to point B would make John better off (John would end up on a higher indifference curve, U_2^J versus U_1^J). Maria would be willing to participate in the trade represented by the move from point A to point B since she is willing at point A to give up one gallon of gasoline in exchange for one bag of sugar. A move from point A to point B results in Maria getting two gallons of gasoline for one bag of sugar and makes Maria better off (she ends up on indifference curve U_2^M versus U_1^M at point A).

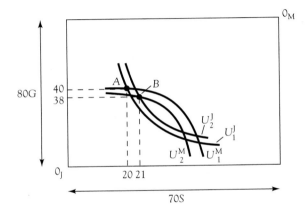

6.5. The question describes the situation shown at point A on one of the sides of the box diagram.

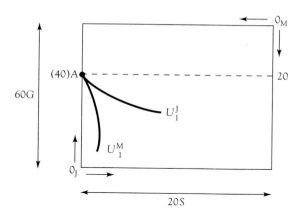

Although the MRSs differ, the distribution is efficient since there is no way to move without harming one of the two persons. The equality-of-MRSs' condition is necessary for efficiency only when both parties consume some positive amount of both commodities.

6.7. No. John will pay a maximum of 4G for one S, so after the tax is collected, that leaves only one G for one S, which is less than Maria requires to part with one S. Both John and Maria are harmed by the tax since they don't get the potential gain from exchange; no one is benefited since the government collects no tax revenue.

6.9. An equal distribution is shown at the midpoint of the diagonal line connecting the origins. This distribution would be efficient only if the consumers' MRSs happen to be equal at that point. If the consumers have different preferences, this will not be so.

6.11. Voluntarism in trade includes the right to stop trading with someone if you can do better disposing of the good in another way. Presumably, the apartment owner and the future purchasers of condominiums will both benefit from the conversion if the owner's judgment is correct. Note that this situation is no different in principle from the situation when you stop eating at McDonald's and patronize Burger King instead.

6.15. No. It only implies that both children would consider themselves better off after the trade. The parent may wish to override their wishes on the ground that the children don't appreciate the benefits of a more balanced diet.

Chapter 7

7.3. The average and marginal product curves would co-incide and be a horizontal line: AP and MP are constant regardless of the amount of input used. If the law of diminishing marginal returns holds, the total product curve would not have this shape.

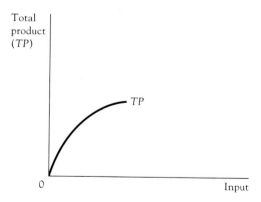

7.4. The total product curve has a slope that becomes flatter right from the start, as shown in the above diagram. The marginal and average product curves are depicted below. Note that AP = MP for the first unit.

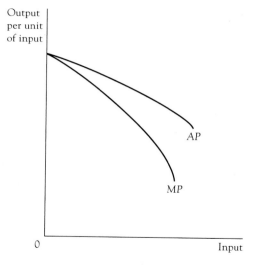

7.5. Since the marginal product indicates how much output will rise if the worker is hired, the firm should be concerned with the marginal product.

7.9. The isoquant might have a slope of (minus) one at this point, but it does not have to. If it does, this implies that the marginal products of both inputs are equal when equal quantities are employed. Remember that the slope of the isoquant equals the ratio of the marginal products.

7.11. Eighteen units of output.

Chapter 8

8.2. With MP falling from the start, MC and AC are rising from the start (as shown on the next page). If MP first rises and then falls, the cost curves have their conventional U shapes.

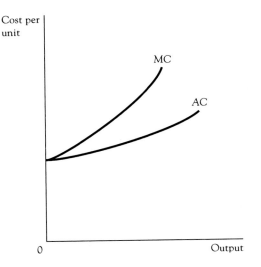

8.4. Basically, the reason is that we assume firms attempt to maximize profit. If the same output can be produced at a lower total cost, a firm would make a larger profit by doing so. This reasoning does not provide a basis for assuming that the Postal Service and the American Red Cross minimize cost since they are not profit-making operations.

8.9. Coldwell Banker is at point N on isocost line AZ. At point N, the isoquant has a slope of $50C/4L = 12.5$, which is flatter than the isocost line with a slope of $4,000C/12L = 333.33$. By operating at point M on the lower isocost line $A'Z'$, Coldwell Banker can produce the same output at a lower cost.

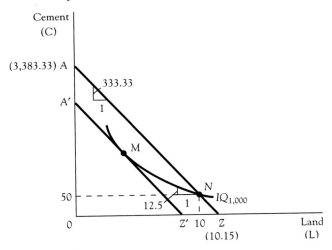

Chapter 9

9.3. (a) Output is zero and losses equal the fixed cost of $60,000 (profit equals minus $60,000) since the firm cannot cover AVC. (b) Output is seven units and the firm loses $28,000 (profit

equals minus $28,000), but this is less than it would lose if it shut down.

9.7. False. The difference between price and marginal cost is the change in profit (positive or negative) that would be realized by a unit change in output. The firm wishes to maximize total profit, which implies that price minus marginal cost equals zero.

9.11. The industry long-run supply curve is not the sum of the firms' marginal cost curves. The industry has a horizontal supply curve in the constant-cost case because new firms can enter the market and produce at the same average cost as existing firms, and entry does not increase input prices.

9.13. False. Enough defense contractors need to exit such that the short-run industry supply curve shifts sufficiently to the left to ensure that the price can once again cover average cost for the contractors remaining in the industry.

Chapter 10

10.5. With a constant-cost industry, with LS_1 and D, P and Q are the equilibrium price and quantity. The subsidy shifts LS_1 to $LS_1 - S$ and price falls to P_1, or by the amount of the subsidy per unit S (20 cents). The deadweight loss is equal to triangular area ABC. With an increasing-cost industry, the supply curve is LS_2 and shifts to $LS_2 - S$ when the subsidy is applied. Price falls by less in this case (to P_2).

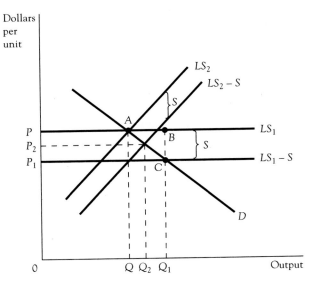

10.8. Either method of deregulation would lead to a competitive market in taxi services, but the cost would be imposed on different people. With the government purchasing the medallions, the cost is borne by taxpayers; without purchases, the cost would be borne by the current owners of the medallions. To decide which is better, a value judgment must be made concerning who should bear the cost.

Chapter 11

11.8. In this case, total revenue is equal to profit, so the monopolist produces where total revenue is at a maximum, or where marginal revenue equals zero. Thus, output is Q and price is P in the diagram. The deadweight loss is shown by the area ADQ.

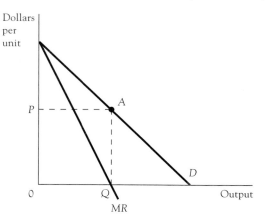

11.10. The deadweight loss due to monopoly means that consumers would be willing to give up the necessary quantities of other goods to have more of the monopolized product. This is shown by the fact that at the monopolist's output, price (the marginal value to consumers) is greater than marginal cost (the value of other goods produced by the resources required to produce another unit of the monopolist's product).

Chapter 12

12.1. The ΣMR curve is ABD_2. Total output is Q_2. Q_1 is sold in the home market at P_2, while $Q_2 - Q_1$, or Q_1Q_2, is sold in the international market at the lower price, P_1.

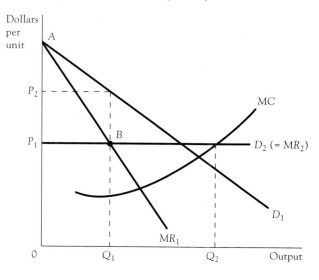

12.5. Probably not. There are a large number of car rental firms, and the presumption is that the market is competitive; competitive firms cannot use monopolistic pricing tactics. Note that there are costs to the firms from renting cars independent of how much they are driven (depreciation, some maintenance, insurance, administrative overhead, and so on), and the daily fee may simply cover these costs while the mileage fee covers the additional costs associated with driving the automobiles.

12.7. Food need not be consumed at the same time it is purchased; it can be stored. The peak-load phenomenon occurs only when production and consumption must occur simultaneously, and there is a systematic variation in demand over time.

Chapter 13

13.8. With the supply curve of the follower firms shown as S_0, the dominant firm faces a demand curve PAD and marginal revenue curve $PALM$. The dominant firm can only affect the price if it sets a price below P. If the dominant firm's marginal cost curve is MC_1, price will be P with both the dominant firm and other firms supplying a total output of Q. If MC_2 is the cost curve, the dominant firm supplies the entire market at P and produces Q. Only if the MC curve is lower than MC_3 will price and total output differ from P and Q. In most cases, a horizontal supply curve of other firms means the dominant firm will have no effect on price and output.

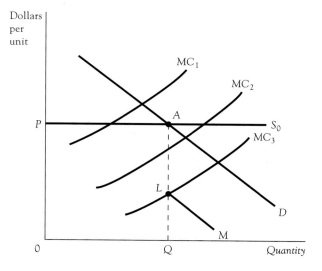

Chapter 14

14.2. Assuming "high output" is the long-run competitive equilibrium output for each firm, the matrix would look something like the one depicted below.

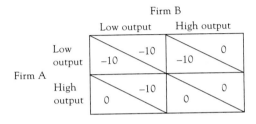

Each firm's profit depends only on its own output; changes in one firm's output have no effect on the other firm's profit. There is no interdependence between the firms to take account of, so game theory is not necessary or useful.

14.12. If one in fifty people gets cancer, the cost of a policy would be about one-fiftieth of the cost of medical care in a competitive market. If the probability is one in a hundred for non-smokers and one in ten for smokers, and smokers know this, then insurance would become much more attractive for smokers; there would be an adverse selection of smokers. Firms would find that they have to pay out on more than one in fifty policies, and the price would rise. In the limit, the price would rise to one-tenth the cost of medical care and only smokers would purchase insurance.

14.17. There are at least three reasons why the statement is false. First, price may be above average cost in the absence of advertising, and equal to average cost when advertising increases competition. Second, the firm may operate at a lower point on the higher average cost curve as a result of advertising. Even though advertising results in the firm operating on AC' rather than AC, the firm may be at point B with advertising and point A without advertising (because advertising leads to more elastic demand curves). Third, even if the money price of the product does rise as a result of advertising, the full price may still be lower.

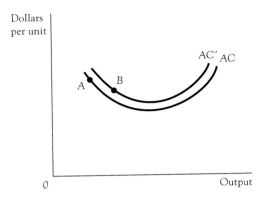

Chapter 15

15.2. Let P and Q be the competitive price and quantity, respectively. The oligopoly price and output are therefore $1.20P$ and

$0.8Q$, respectively. Thus, the deadweight loss is $0.5(0.2P)(0.2Q)$, or $0.02PQ$. Because the total outlay on the product equals $(1.2P)(0.8Q)$, or $0.96PQ$, the deadweight loss is 2.1 percent as large as the total consumer outlay.

15.10. The demand elasticity estimate was 0.75. A monopolist, or cartel, that maximizes the combined profit of its members will never operate in the inelastic region of the demand curve. Thus, if the elasticity estimate is correct, combined profit is not being maximized.

Chapter 16

16.4. The marginal value product of any given number of workers will be higher when product demand increases since consumers pay a higher price for the product.

16.8. False. Each employer must take the market wage rate as given. Employers expand employment at the market-determined wage rate up to the point where MVP equals that wage rate.

16.9. In the short run, an unanticipated increase in labor supply will lead to economic profits for firms and somewhat lower prices for consumers. In the long run, economic profits of the firms will be zero. Consumers, who can get the product at a lower price, are the primary beneficiaries of an increase in labor supply in the long run.

16.10. No single firm except a monopsony has the ability to cut wage rates without losing employees. This quotation illustrates the common error of treating thousands of separate firms as if they could collude to form one gigantic monopsony. One could just as well argue that consumers force down the prices of products they buy at the expense of enormous losses to firms.

16.12. If the supply curve of steel confronting the combined automobile and refrigerator industries is upward-sloping, the price of refrigerators will rise. The analysis would be the same as in Figure 16.8. However, steel is used by a number of other industries, so the share of total steel output used by these two may be fairly small, in which case the steel supply curve will be horizontal and the price of refrigerators would not be affected.

Chapter 17

17.3. Initially, Jeeves is at point E on AZ (below). The inheritance produces a parallel shift in the budget line to $A'Z'Z$, where $Z'Z = \$200$. There is only an income effect here since the wage rate has not changed. If leisure is a normal good, Jeeves will consume more of it—that is, work less. For example, the new optimal point might be at E', and his total weekly income would be $400, up only $100 because he is earning $100 less than before.

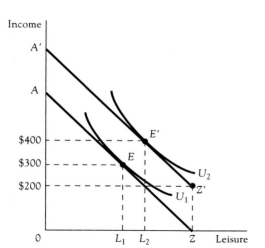

17.4. If money income is a normal good, a worker will always choose to earn more of it when the wage rate rises, so there is a limit on how backward-bending a labor supply curve can be. A higher wage rate has an income effect implying greater consumption of money income (if it is a normal good) and a substitution effect in favor of money income also, so the net effect is unambiguous.

17.7. False. Not everyone who has the ability to be a nuclear physicist is one. At a higher wage for physicists, others with the requisite ability would be attracted to the profession. At a lower wage rate, fewer would.

17.14. Aggregate labor demand will be higher if investment is K_2 in year 1. The more investment today, the greater the amount of capital per worker in the future. More capital per worker means the marginal productivity of workers will be greater, and hence demand for workers will be greater too.

Chapter 18

18.3. Labor costs will not increase if the money wages that must be paid go down by the amount of the increase in employer tax. As explained in the text, if the supply curve of labor is perfectly vertical, this will happen.

18.8. No Amazons would be employed by health clubs catering to discriminating customers (Type A clubs); all the Amazons would be employed by Type B clubs serving nondiscriminating customers. Wage rates for non-Amazons and Amazons will remain equal, however, unless there are fewer non-Amazons initially employed by Type B clubs than there are Amazons employed by Type A clubs. To see this, imagine that wage rates did go down in Type B clubs and up in Type A clubs. Then the non-Amazons initially in Type B clubs have an incentive to shift to Type A clubs, and this process would continue until the wage rates at the two types of clubs were again equal.

Chapter 19

19.2. No, at least not from the demand side of the market since the price of margarine would not change in this case, and thus the demand curve for butter would not shift.

19.5. Ten cellular telephones per personal computer. The MRT is equal to the ratio of marginal costs, and since marginal cost equals price in equilibrium, the MRT equals the ratio of the price of personal computers to the price of cellular telephones.

19.10. No, if markets are competitive.

19.12. No. Consumers cannot purchase as much as they want at the controlled rent, and so the controlled rent does not measure the marginal value (or MRS) of rental housing to consumers. The marginal value of rental housing would be greater than marginal cost, so output is too low.

19.18. If the domestic country's exports and imports are a small part of total world trade in these products, then the participation of the domestic country in world trade would have a negligible effect on world prices. If the world price ratio is affected, the relative price of the good imported by the domestic country will rise. In Figure 19.12, for example, if the world price prior to trade is 1F/1C, the final price might be 1F/1.5C after the domestic country begins to trade. The gain to the domestic country from trade is less in this case.

Chapter 20

20.4. The dove, individual C, has a negative demand for defense. This must be added vertically to the demands of the hawks A and B. The result, Σd, is lower than it would be if we summed the demands of A and B only. The intersection of Σd and MC identifies the efficient output. (See graph.)

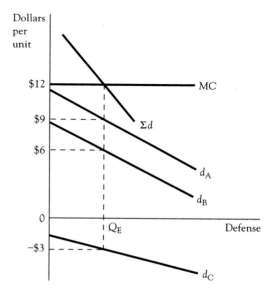

20.8. We would predict that class attendance would rise, poorer notes would be taken (but maybe carbon paper would be used?), and students would study the text more. Students would probably learn less.

20.10. No. Government intervention could make a bad situation worse. Only an explicit analysis of the effects of government intervention could show whether it would improve matters, in the sense of leading to a more efficient resource allocation.

Index

A380, 291
Abowd, John, 227
Absolute cost advantage, 310
Absolute price, 4
Accounting costs, 8
Acre-foot, 158
Ad valorem tax, 266n
Adverse selection, 400–402
Advertising, 405–409
Advertising-as-information view, 406–408
AFC, 192
AFC curve, 194, 196
African American workers, 508
Aggregate demand curve, 95–97
Aggregator companies, 343
AIDS vaccine, 317
Air bags, 63
Air France, 428
Air pollution. *See* Pollution control
Airbus Industries, 291
Airline industry, 274–279
    cartelization, 370–371
    congestion, 278–279
    contestability of markets, 277–278
    deregulation, 276–277
    distressed inventory, 343
    duopoly air routes, 362–363
    frequent-buyer programs, 329
    international air cartel, 427–428
    price fixing, 318–319
    profits, 275–276
    regulation, 274–276, 444
    safety, 279
    yield management, 342
Airline Tariff Publishing Company, 319
Airport gas station, 302–303
Akerlof, George A., 397n
Alcohol abuse, 84–85
Alfred, Lord Tennyson, 409
Allen, Paul, 5
Aluminum Company of America (Alcoa), 310
America Online (AOL), 105
American Airlines, 201–202, 318, 342, 362–363
Anheuser-Busch, 212
Annual rates of return, 134
Answers to selected problems, 571–579
Antitrust laws, 317–320

AOL, 105
AOL-Time Warner merger, 217
AR, 229
Arc elasticity formula, 35
Arithmetical relationships, 179
Artificial product differentiation, 405
Asbell, Penny, 358
Aspirin market, 308–309
Assumptions
    composite-good convention, 62
    consumer preferences, 46–47
    demand curve, 19
    market participants, 5–6
    perfect competition, 224–225
    production, 173
    use of, 2
Astaire, Fred, 143
Asymmetric information, 397–399, 533
AT&T, 415, 422
AT&T Digital One Rate, 349
ATC, 192
ATC curve, 194, 196
Automated teller machines (ATMs), 108
Automobile industry
    emission standards, 215
    first-degree price discrimination, 328
    import quotas, 290
    third-degree price discrimination, 330
    tradable emission permits, 555–557
    used car market, 397–400
    VERs on sale of Japanese cars, 528
AVC, 192
AVC curve, 194, 196
Average cost, 566
Average-cost pricing, 420–421
Average fixed cost (AFC), 192
Average fixed cost (AFC) curve, 194, 196
Average input cost, 454
Average-marginal cost curve relationships, 196–197
Average product, 168
Average product curve, 168–170
Average product of labor, 170
Average profit per unit (π/q), 230
Average revenue (AR), 229

Average total cost (ATC), 192
Average total cost (ATC) curve, 194, 196
Average variable cost (AVC), 192
Average variable cost (AVC) curve, 194, 196
Axelrod, Robert, 394n, 395
Ayres, Ian, 330

B2B e-commerce, 147–148
Babysitters, 25
Ballmer, Steve, 415
Bandwagon effect, 105–106, 209
Barrett, Craig, 319
Barriers to entry, 310–311
Baseball
    collusion era, 505
    DH rule, 404
    dominant strategies, 386
    field size, 206
    home run hitters, 170
    player salaries, 455–456, 505
    reserve clause, 455
Bastiat, Frederic, 286
Battalio, Raymond, 373
Bayer, 308–309, 406
Beer industry, 212
Best fitting, 111
Bittlingmayer, George, 320
Black market, 30
Bliss, Michael, 32
Block pricing, 328–329
Blood donors, 402
Boeing, 142
Book publishing, 342
Borcherding, Thomas, 423–425
Borrowing, 128–134
Borrowing–lending equilibrium, 478–479
Brand-name drug manufacturers, 368
British Airways, 428
British Columbia Egg Marketing Board, 423–427
Broadly defined goods, 68
Brooks, Garth, 310
Brozen, Yale, 494
Bryant, Kobe, 187
Brynjolfsson, Erik, 370
Bubbles, 557
Bucket shops, 427
Budget constraint, 55

Budget line
  defined, 55
  geometry of, 56–57
  income changes, and, 57–58
  income-leisure choice, 460–461
  incomplete analysis, 125
  intertemporal, 121, 123
  mathematical appendix, 562
  price changes, and, 58–59
  shifts in, 57–59
Buffett, Warren, 5
Building demolition, 206
Burger King, 68, 113
Business schools, 251
Business-to-business (B2B) e-commerce, 147–148
Buyers' cartel, 500–502

C2C e-commerce, 147
CAB, 274–277, 423, 444
Cable TV
  demand elasticity, 36
  growth, 101
  price discrimination, 334–335
  public operating license, 311
Calfee, John, 533–534
California
  electrical bills, 239–241
  state lottery, 487
  water allocation, 158
California gold rush, 136, 236
Calorie theory, 2–3
Canada
  British Columbia Egg Marketing Board, 423–427
  health care, 32
  tax-plus-rebate program, 89–92
  television quantity controls, 70–71
Carnegie, Andrew, 74
Cartels, 368–378
  cheating, 373, 390–392
  defined, 369
  egg-marketing, 423–427
  failure of, 371–372
  government-established, 423–427
  input buyers, 500–502
  international air travel, 427–428
  NCAA, 502–503
  OPEC, 375–378
  prisoner's dilemma, 390–392
  Rolex, 373–374
Case, Steve, 217
Cash grant, 119–120
Caviar cartel, 372
Cellular phone service, 64

Central heating, Moscow, 122
Central planning, 531
CEO compensation, 227
Charitable giving, 74
Child care expenses, 118
China, property valuation, 542
Chuck D., 545
Cigarettes
  demand elasticity, 38
  deterring smoking, 533–534
  P-C curve, 104–105
  punitive damages award, 271
Cisco Systems, 310
Civil Aeronautics Board (CAB), 274–277, 423, 444
Clayton Act, 317
Close substitutes, 37
Coase, Ronald, 551–552
Coase theorem, 552
Cobb, Charles W., 183n
Cobb-Douglas production function, 183, 563
Coca-Cola, 212, 354
Coin flipping, 141
Coldwell Banker, 204–205
Colleges
  athletics, 502–504
  commencement tickets, 71–72
  consumer's demand curve, 83
  financial aid, 335
  hockey teams, 206
  peak-load pricing, 346
  young techies say no, 85–86
Commencement tickets (college), 71–72
CommerceOne, 148
Commercial blood, 402
Commitment, 430–432
Commuting to work, 176–177
Compact discs, 65
Company health benefits, 120
Compartmentalization, 181
Compensating wage differentials, 470
Competition, 224
Competitive equilibrium, 155–158, 523
Competitive model, 222–293
  airline regulation/deregulation, 274–279
  applicability of, 253–254, 568
  constant-cost industry, 245–247
  decreasing-cost industry, 249–251
  demand curves, 227–229
  economic efficiency, 529–530
  excise taxation, 266–274
  increasing-cost industry, 247–249

input market analysis, 436–449.
  See also Input market analysis
international trade, 283–287
long-run competitive equilibrium, 241–245, 567–568
long-run industry supply curve, 245–253
operating at loss in short run, 232–234
profit maximization, 225–226
quantity controls, 288–291
short-run firm supply curve, 234–237
short-run industry supply curve, 237–239
short-run profit maximization, 229–234, 567–568
shutdown point, 235
taxicab licensing, 279–282
very-short-run firm supply curve, 236
Complements, 18
Composite good, 62
Composite-good convention, 61–63
Concave-shaped PPF, 11
Concorde, 428
Congressional prisoner's dilemma, 389–390
Constant-cost industry, 245–247
Constant returns to scale, 178, 181
Constrained minimization problem, 566–567
Consumer choice theory, 44–79, 116–143
  budget constraint, 55–59. See also Budget line
  changes in income/consumption choices, 64–71
  composite-good convention, 61–63
  consumer preferences, 46–55, 562
  consumer's choice, 59–63, 562
  corner solution, 61
  excise subsidies, 118–122
  garbage collection, 125–128
  indifference curves, 47–49. See also Indifference curves
  investor choice, 134–142
  perfect substitutes/complements, 54
  public schools, 122–125
  saving/borrowing, 128–134
  selfishness, 72–74
  utility approach, 74–77
Consumer preferences, 46–55, 562
Consumer price index (CPI), 4

Consumer Reports, 399
Consumer surplus
    defined, 98, 260
    efficient output, 262–264
    excise subsidy, 121–122
    free TV, 101
    indifference curves, 102
    international trade, 285
    overview, 98–101
    price ceiling, 265–266
    rationing by waiting, 161
Consumer-to-consumer (C2C)
    e-commerce, 147
Consumer's choice, 59–63, 562
Consumption choices
    income changes, 64–71
    price changes, 82–86, 563
Contestable markets, 277
Continental Airlines, 232, 234
Contract curve, 152–153
Copyrights, 544
Corner solution, 61
Cortés' invasion of Mexico, 432
Cost curves
    geometry of, 197
    input price changes, 204–205
    long-run, 207–210
    market structure, and, 210–212
    short-run, 194–197, 566
Cost estimation, 217–218
Cost minimization, 200–202
Cost of production, 188–221
    economies of scope, 216
    estimating cost, 217–218
    expansion path, 199, 202
    golden rule of cost minimization,
      200
    input price changes/cost curves,
      204–205
    isocost lines, 197–199
    long-run, 197–203, 566
    long-run cost curves, 207–210
    market structure/cost curves,
      210–212
    minimum efficient scale, 210–213
    nature of cost, 190–191
    pollution control, 213–215, 567
    short-run, 191–193
    short-run cost curves, 194–197,
      566
Cournot, Augustin, 359
Cournot firm model, 359–362
Cournot-Nash equilibrium, 387
CPI, 4
Crandall, Robert W., 201–202,
    318–319, 528

Cross-price elasticity of demand, 39
Cubic total cost function, 217–218
Customer surveys, 109–110

DaimlerChrysler, 167, 173
Deadweight loss, 121
    defined, 265
    egg-marketing cartel, 424–427
    excise taxation, 271–273
    monopolistic competition,
      355–356, 412
    monopoly, 314–315, 412–415
    noncompetitive output, 412
    oligopoly, 412
    price ceiling, 264–266
    rent control, 273–274
    unions, 476
Decreases in demand, 19
Decreasing-cost industry, 245, 249–251
Decreasing returns to scale, 178–181
Deere, Donald, 496
Demand curve
    advertising, 406–407
    competitive firm, 227–229
    dominant firm, 367–368
    downward slope, 16–17, 86
    general remarks, 84
    input (competitive firm),
      436–441, 569–570
    input (competitive industry),
      441–443
    investment, 480–481
    market, 95–97
    monopoly, 296–297
    shifts in, 17–19
Demand elasticity. *See* Price elasticity
    of demand
Demand estimation, 109–113
    experimentation, 109
    McDonald's vs. Burger King, 113
    regression analysis, 110–113
    surveys, 109–110
Democracy in America (Tocqueville), 74
Demolishing a building, 206
Deregulation
    airline, 276–278
    electricity, 239–241
Derived demand, 443
Desirability, 4
DH rule, 404
Differentiated product, 352
Diminishing marginal returns, 172
Diminishing marginal utility, 75
Diminishing MRS, 50–51
Discrimination in employment, 505–509
Diseconomies of scale, 208

Diseconomies of scope, 216
Disemployment effect, 493, 495–496
Disequilibrium, 22
Dismal science, 187
Disney, 304
Disney theme parks, 340
Diversification, 141–142
Division of labor, 178
Dominant firm model, 365–368
Dominant-strategy equilibrium,
    385–386
Douglas, Paul H., 183n
Dr. Dre, 545
Driving speed, 176–177
Duopoly, 359
Dynamic analysis, 315

e-49ers, 137
eBay, 147
Econometric estimation, 217
Econometrics, 110
Economic "bads," 47, 53
Economic cost, 6, 8
Economic efficiency, 144–163, 517–533
    competitive equilibrium/efficient
      distribution, 155–158
    competitive markets, 529–530
    conditions for, 519–520
    contract curve, 152–153
    defined, 146, 517
    Edgeworth exchange box,
      148–151
    Edgeworth production box,
      520–521
    efficiency as goal for economic
      performance, 518–519
    efficiency in distribution of goods,
      151–154, 563–564
    efficiency in output, 523–528
    efficiency in production, 520–523
    equity, 154
    information, 530–531
    rationing, 159–161
    two-person exchange, 146–151
Economic "good," 47
Economic inefficiency, 517, 532–534
Economic "neuter," 53
Economic rent, 472–474
Economic theory, 2–3
Economics of information, 397–408
    adverse selection, 400–401
    advertising, 405–409
    asymmetric information, 397–399,
      533
    limited price information, 404–405
    moral hazard, 402–403

Economies of scale, 208–209, 310
Economies of scope, 216
Edgeworth exchange box, 148–151
Edgeworth production box, 520–521
Education
        colleges. *See* Colleges
        private vs. public schools, 203
        public schools, 122–125
Efficiency, 152, 517. *See also* Economic
        efficiency
Efficiency in output, 263
Efficiency wage, 496
Efficient distribution, 151–158,
        563–564
Efficient rationing, 160
Egg-marketing cartel, 423–427
Einstein, Albert, 535
Elastic, 33, 40
Elasticities, 32–40
        cross-price elasticity, 39
        defined, 32
        excise taxation, and, 269–270
        income elasticity, 39
        mathematical appendix, 561
        price elasticity. *See* Price elasticity
                of demand
        supply elasticity, 39–40
Elasticity of supply, 39–40
Electricity, 37
Electricity deregulation (California),
        239–241
Ellison, Larry, 5, 74, 227, 416
Employment discrimination, 505–509
Endowment point, 129
Entrepreneurship, 136
Entry fee, 335
Equilibrium
        borrowing–lending, 479–480
        competitive input markets,
                522–523
        defined, 22
        efficient distribution, 155–158
        employment level/wage rate, 447
        game theory, 384–387
        general equilibrium analysis,
                514–517
        long-run (competitive model),
                241–245, 567–568
        monopolistic competition,
                352–355
        partial equilibrium analysis, 514
        supply-demand model, 22–23
Equity, 154
Estimating cost, 217–218
Estimating demand. *See* Demand
        estimation

Estimating production functions,
        182–185, 565
Excess burden, 272
Excess capacity, 355
Exchange. *See* Economic efficiency
Excise subsidies, 118–122
Excise tax, 89
Excise taxation, 266–274
Exclusive franchising, 311
Expansion path, 199, 202
Expected return, 137
Expected utility, 137
Experimentation, 109
Explicit costs, 6, 190
Exports, 287
External benefits, 545, 548–549
External costs, 545–547
Externalities, 545–552. *See also*
        Pollution control
        defined, 537
        external benefits, 548–549
        external costs, 546–547
        property rights, 550–552

FAA, 279
Factors of production, 166
Facts, 2
Fair Labor Standards Act, 492
Fairness, 154
Fanning, Shawn, 544
Fast-food industry
        monopolistic competition,
                353–354
        recession, 68
        value packages, 329
Federal Aviation Administration
        (FAA), 279
Federal Communications Commission
        (FCC), 551
Federal Trade Commission Act, 318
Feedback effect, 515
Finance professors, 251
Fire insurance, 139–141
First-degree price discrimination,
        327–328
Fixed inputs, 167
Flipping coins, 141
Flow variable, 55n
Food, 68
Food stamp program, 68–70
Ford, Henry, 496
Forrest Gump, 307
Four-wheel drive vehicles, 404
49ers, 136
Free entry and exit, 224
Free rider, 539

Free-rider problem, 539–540
Free television, 101
Frequent-buyer programs, 329
Friedman, Milton, 287
Full price, 408

Gambling (Las Vegas), 139n, 140
Game theory, 384–395
        commitment, 430–432
        defined, 384
        dominant-strategy equilibrium,
                385–386
        equilibrium, 384–387
        iterated dominance, 428–430
        Nash equilibrium, 387
        prisoner's dilemma, 388–393
        repeated games, 393–395
Ganett, Corey, 86
Garbage collection, 125–128
Garbage in, garbage out, 113
Gasoline
        consumption of, and driving
                speed, 176–177
        demand elasticity, 38
        excise tax, 266–269
        rationing, 159–161
        Washington, D.C., gas tax, 38
        Western Europe, 26–27
Gates, Bill, 5, 74, 227
Gates, Melinda, 74
GATT, 528
Gender earnings gap, 508–509
General Agreement on Tariffs and
        Trade (GATT), 528
General equilibrium analysis, 514–517
General Motors, 539
Generalizability, 109
Giffen, Robert, 92
Giffen good, 92, 94, 95
Global warming, 215–216
Glow boys, 470
Goal-oriented behavior, 5
Gold rush, 136, 236
Golden rule of cost minimization, 200,
        205
Government-established cartels,
        423–427
Government intervention
        effects, 260
        gasoline coupon rationing, 160
        price controls, 27–32
        quantity controls, 288–291
        regulatory barriers, 310–311
Greenhouse gas emission, 215–216
Groom, Winston, 307
Gross marginal productivity, 479

Group health plans, 401
Gypsy vans, 282

Haggling, 155
Hallway medicine, 32
Hamburger, 67, 93
Hanks, Tom, 307
Hayek, Friedrich, 531
Hazardous industries, 181–182
Hazlett, Tom, 320
Health care
    Canadian system, 32
    company health benefits, 120
    demand elasticity, 38
    financing of, through payroll
        taxes, 499–500
    group health plans, 401
    moral hazard, 403
    physician reimbursement, 31–32
    subsidies, 118–119
    supply–demand model, 27
Herring, Eli, 7
HFCS, 290
High-fructose corn syrup (HFCS), 290
High-tech immigrants, 449–450
Hockey rinks, 206
Home delivery portals, 7
Home run hitters, 170
Home videos, 304, 418
Homeowner's insurance, 139–141
Homogeneous product, 224, 254
Hong Kong, traffic control, 548
Hong Kong Hilton, 8
Horizontal summation, 96
Hotwire.com, 343
Houseplants, 172–173
Housing prices, 9
Human capital investment, 470
Hurricane Andrew, lumber prices, 40

IATA, 427–428
IBM, 341
Immigration (high-tech workers),
    449–450
Immigration quotas, 290
Immunization, 545
Implicit costs, 6, 190
Import quotas, 288–290
Imports, 287
Income changes
    budget line, 57–58
    consumption choices, 64–71
    optimal consumption choice, 65
    rising stock market, 132
    saving/borrowing, 130–131
Income–consumption curve, 64

Income effect
    defined, 87
    gasoline-tax-plus-rebate program,
        89–92
    higher wage rate, 462–463
    inferior goods, 92–94
    interest rate charges, 133–134
    normal good, 88–89
Income elasticity of demand, 39
Income–leisure choice, 460–461
Income tax code, 118
Increase in demand, 19
Increase in supply, 22
Increasing-cost industry, 245, 247–249
Increasing returns to scale, 178–181
Indifference curves
    cellular phone services, 64
    characteristics, 47–49
    composite-good convention, 62–63
    consumer surplus, 102
    curvature, 49–51
    defined, 47
    economic "bad," 53
    economic "neuter," 53
    Edgeworth exchange box, 149–151
    entrepreneurship, 136
    income–leisure choice, 460–461
    incomplete analysis, 125
    isoquants, and, 174
    perfect complements, 54
    perfect substitutes, 54
    preferences, and, 52
    return–risk tradeoff, 135
    saving/borrowing, 129
    utility approach, and, 76–77
Indifference map, 48–49
Inefficient/inefficiency, 153, 517. See
    also Economic inefficiency
Inelastic, 33, 40
Inferior goods
    characteristics, 66–67
    defined, 18
    economic "bad," contrasted, 66
    Giffen goods, 92
    income changes/consumption
        choices, 66–68
    income/substitution effects, 92–94
Information. See Economics of
    information
Information technology industry, 249
Input buyers' cartel, 500–502
Input demand curve
    competitive firm, 436–441,
        569–570
    competitive industry, 441–443
    market demand curve, 444

Input market analysis, 434–457. See
    also Labor market
    equilibrium in competitive input
        markets, 522–523
    input demand (output market
        monopoly), 452–454, 570
    input demand curve (competitive
        firm), 436–441, 569–570
    input demand curve (competitive
        industry), 441–443
    input market monopoly (unions),
        475–477
    input price determination (multi-
        industry market), 450–452
    input price equalization, 447–449
    market demand curve for input,
        444
    monopsony in input markets,
        454–455
    supply of inputs, 444–446
Input market monopoly, 475–477
Input market monopsony, 454–455
Input markets, 435
Input price equalization, 447–449
Input substitution effect, 205
Input supply curve, 444–446
Inputs, 166, 444
Insurance, 140–141
Insurance markets
    adverse selection, 400–401
    moral hazard, 402–403
Intertemporal price discrimination,
    340–343
Interdependence between markets,
    514–516
Interest rates
    borrowing/lending, 478–479
    defined, 478
    difference in, 484–485
    saving/borrowing, 132–134
    saving/investment, 481–484
International Air Transport
    Association (IATA), 427–428
International Discount
    Telecommunications (IDT), 331
International phone, 331
International trade, 283–287,
    526–528
Internet
    B2B e-commerce, 147
    C2C e-commerce, 147–148
    cartelization, 370–371
    e-49ers, 137
    Napster, 544–545
    online intertemporal price
        discrimination, 343

Internet (*Continued*)
   online shopping, 7
   surfing (delays), 31
   World Wide Web, 209
Interpersonal comparisons of utility, 154
Intertemporal budget line, 121, 123
Inventions, 416–418
Inverse elasticity pricing rule, 303–304
Investment
   marginal productivity of capital, 478–481
   saving/interest rate, 481–484
   valuation of projects, 485–487
Investment demand curve, 480–481
Investor choice. *See* Stock market investments
Invisible hand, 155, 530
Isocost line, 197–199
Isoquants
   characteristics, 175
   convexity, 175
   defined, 173
   gasoline/commuting time, 177
   graphical representation of production function, 173–174
   indifference curves, and, 174
   returns to scale, 181
   slope, 175
Iterated dominance, 428–430

Jackson, Henry "Scoop," 142
Jefferson, Thomas, 220
Jensen, Michael, 227
Job attractiveness, 469–470
Joint Executive Committee, 370
Jumpers, 470

Katz, Lawrence, 495
Kentucky Fried Chicken, 310
King, Stephen, 540
Koch, Ed, 29
Kohler Corporation, 345–346
Kreuger, Alan, 495
Kyoto Protocol, 557, 559

Labor market. *See also* Input market analysis
   African American workers, 508
   employment discrimination, 505–509
   gender earnings gap, 508–509
   general level of wage rates, 465–466
   income–leisure choice, 460–462
   market supply curve, 465

   minimum wage, 492–496
   payroll tax, 497–499
   supply of hours of work, 462–465
   why wages differ, 468–472, 508–509
Labor unions, 475–477
LAC curve, 207, 209–210
Lagrangian expression
   consumer's choice, 562
   efficiency in distribution of good, 564
   long-run cost of production, 566, 567
   pollution control, 567
   price changes/consumer choices, 563
Lagrangian multiplier, 562, 566
Landing fees (airports), 163
Landon, Alf, 109
Lange, Oscar, 531
Large-scale technologies, 179
Las Vegas casino, 139n, 140
Lasik Vision, 358
Law of demand, 16
Law of diminishing marginal returns, 172
Law of diminishing returns, 184
Law of supply, 20
LCA-Vision, Inc., 358
Legal services industry, 212
Leisure, 460
Lemons model, 397–400
Lerner, Abba, 309, 531
Lerner index, 309
Levin, Gerald, 217
Li Ka-Shing, 8
Licensing, 311
Limited price information, 404–405
Limp Bizkit, 545
Linear homogeneous function, 565–566
Live and let live (WWI), 395
LMC curve, 207
Lockheed Corporation, 142
Long run, 173, 209
Long-run average cost (LAC) curve, 207, 209–210
Long-run competitive equilibrium, 241–245, 567–568
Long-run cost curves, 207–210
Long-run cost of production, 197–203, 566
Long-run industry supply curve, 245–253
Long-run marginal cost (LMC) curve, 207

Long-run profit maximization, 242
Long-run total cost (LTC) curve, 207
Lopez, Jennifer, 143
Los Angeles
   smog, 555–556
   traffic congestion, 547–548
Los Angeles Lakers, 187
Lotteries, 139, 487
Lottery tickets, 139
Lotus 1-2-3, 319
Low-income families, 120
LTC curve, 207
Lumber prices (Hurricane Andrew), 40
Lump-sum medisave accounts, 120
Lump-sum transfer, 118–120

Macroeconomics, 2
Mail-order shopping, 7
Major league baseball. *See* Baseball
Malthus, Thomas, 187
Managerial compensation, 227
Marcos, Ferdinand, 311
Marcus, Carl, 373–374
Marginal-average cost curve relationships, 196–197
Marginal benefit, 60, 98
Marginal cost (MC), 60, 192
Marginal cost (MC) curve, 194–195
Marginal-cost pricing, 420
Marginal input cost, 454
Marginal product, 168, 171
Marginal product curve, 168–170
Marginal rate of substitution (MRS), 50
Marginal rate of technical substitution (MRTS), 175
Marginal rate of transformation (MRT), 524
Marginal revenue (MR), 229
Marginal revenue product, 452
Marginal utility, 75
Marginal value product (MVP), 437
Marginal value product curve, 437–438
Maris, Roger, 170
Market baskets, 47
Market demand curve, 95–97
Market power, 532
Market segmentation, 330
Markets, 4
Marriott's Honored Guest program, 329
Massy, William, 346
Mathematical appendix, 561–570
   applicability of competitive model, 568
   budget line, 562
   consumer preferences, 562

consumer's choice, 562
efficient distribution, 563–564
elasticities, 561
empirical estimation of
    production functions, 565
input demand curve (competitive
    firm), 569–570
input demand/employment
    (output market monopoly), 570
long-run competitive equilibrium,
    567–568
long-run cost of production,
    566–567
monopolist's demand/marginal
    revenue curves, 568
monopoly (profit-maximizing
    output), 569
monopoly analysis, 568
monopoly power, 568
pollution control/cost curves, 567
price changes/consumption
    choices, 563
price discrimination (price/output
    determination), 569
production when all inputs
    variable, 565
production when one input
    variable, 564–565
returns to scale, 565
short-run cost curves, 566
short-term profit maximization,
    567–568
Maximizing profit. *See* Profit
    maximization
MBA program, 6–7, 97, 251, 471
MC, 192
MC curve, 194–195
McDonald's, 68, 115, 329, 353
McGwire, Mark, 170
McKinsey Company, 182
Measuring economic costs/benefits, 9
Measuring intangibles, 9
Meat, 67–68
Medallions, 279
Medical care. *See* Health care
Medisave accounts, 120
Merrill Lynch, 329
Metallica, 545
Microeconomic theory, 3
Microeconomics, 2
Microsoft
    antitrust case, 108, 319–320
    market dominance, 209
    soft-money contributor, as,
        415–416
    Windows operating system, 108

Minimum efficient scale, 210–213
Minimum wage, 3, 492–496
Misreporting, 110
Monopolistic competition, 352–356
    deadweight loss, 355–356, 412
    defined, 352
    efficiency, 355–356
    equilibrium, 352–355
Monopoly, 294–349
    antitrust laws, 317–320
    barriers to entry, 310–311
    clarification of less obvious points,
        304–307, 568
    deadweight loss, 314–315,
        412–415
    defined, 295
    demand curve, 296–297, 568
    dynamic vs. static analysis,
        315–317
    efficiency effects, 313–317
    elasticity of demand, 301–303
    input demand (output market
        monopoly), 452–454
    intertemporal price
        discrimination, 340–343
    inventions, 416–418
    marginal revenue, 296–298, 568
    monopoly power, 308–313, 568
    natural, 419–423
    peak-load pricing, 343–346
    price discrimination, 326–334. *See
        also* Price discrimination
    price regulation, 320–322
    profit-maximizing output,
        298–303, 569
    shutdown condition, 305
    threat of entry, 312–313
    two-part tariff, 335–340
    unions (input market monopoly),
        475–477
Monopoly power, 296, 308–313, 568
Monopsony, 454
Moore, Gordon, 187
Moore's law, 187
Moral hazard, 402–404
Moscow, central heating, 122
Mother Teresa, 5–6
Motion picture distribution,
    340–341
Movement along a given demand
    curve, 19
Movement along a given supply curve,
    22
Movie production, 552–553
MR, 229
MRS, 50

MRT, 524
MRTS, 175
Murphy, Kevin, 227, 496
Mutual interdependence of markets,
    514–516
MVP, 437

NAFTA, 528
Napster, 544–545
Narrowly defined good, 37
Nash, John, 387
Nash equilibrium, 387
National Center for Enrollment
    Management, 335
National defense, 538
NATO, 540
Natural monopoly, 310, 419–423
NCAA, 502
NCAA cartel, 502–503
Negative U.S. savings rate, 132
Net marginal productivity, 479
Net present value (NPV), 486
Network effects
    bandwagon effect, 105–106
    defined, 105
    snob effect, 106–107
    Windows operating system, 108
Network society, 208–209
New entrant technique, 217
New York City
    gypsy vans, 282
    newspaper advertising/supermarket
        food prices, 408
    rent control, 27–32
Nominal price, 4
Nonexclusion, 538
Nonprice rationing
    gasoline coupon rationing,
        160–161
    rationing by waiting, 161
    rent control, 30
Nonrival in consumption, 538
Nonsatiation, 47
Normal goods
    defined, 18
    income changes/consumption
        choices, 64–66
    income effect, 88–89
    substitution effect, 88–89
Normative analysis, 4
North American Free Trade
    Agreement (NAFTA), 528
North Atlantic Treaty Organization
    (NATO), 540
NPV, 486
Nunn, Sam, 142

O'Neal, Shaquille, 8
Oil shipping, 181
Oligopoly, 358–378
  cartels, 368–378. *See also* Cartels
  collusion, 374, 395–396
  Cournot model, 359–362
  deadweight loss, 412
  defined, 358
  dominant firm model, 365–368
  game theory, 396–397
  Stackelberg model, 363–365
OLS, 111–112
Omidyar, Pierre, 147
O'Neal, Shaquille, 187
Online intertemporal price
  discrimination, 343
Online shopping, 7, 25
OPEC, 373, 375–378
Opportunity cost, 6–8
Optimal consumption choice
  consumer's choice, 60
  corner solution, 61
  income changes, 65
  saving/borrowing, 130
  utility approach, 75–76
Oracle, 416
Orange growers, 372
Ordinal ranking, 48
Ordinary least-squares (OLS), 111–112
Organization of Petroleum Exporting
  Countries (OPEC), 373, 375–378
Output effect of an input price change,
  441
Output market monopoly, 452–454

P-C curve, 82–83, 104
Pareto, Vilfredo, 151n, 517
Pareto optimality, 151–154, 517. *See
  also* Economic efficiency
Park and Fly, 329
Parking meters, 25
Parking spaces, 23–24
Parking structures, 205
Partial equilibrium analysis, 514
Partnerships, 141
Patents, 310, 543–544
Payoff matrix, 385
Payoffs, 384
Payroll tax, 497–499
Peak-load pricing, 343–346
People Express, 180, 278
Pepsi, 212
Per-unit curves, 231
Perfect competition, 224–225. *See also*
  Competitive model
Perfect complements, 54

Perfect price discrimination, 327–328
Perfect substitutes, 54
Perkasie, Pennsylvania (garbage
  collection), 125–127
Permatemps, 500
Pharmaceutical industry, 368
Philanthropy, 74
Picasso paintings, 40
"Plant, The" (King), 540
Players, 384
Point elasticity formula, 34–35
Pollution, 545–546
Pollution control, 553–557
  bubbles, 557
  cost analysis, 213–215, 567
  greenhouse gases, 215–216
  taxes, 546–547, 553–555
  tradable emission permits,
    555–557
Positive analysis, 3
Positive economic profit, 243
PPF, 9–11, 523–524
Preferences, 18. *See also* Consumer
  preferences
Present discounted value of $1, 485
Price, 4
Price ceiling, 27, 161, 264–266,
  320–322
Price changes
  budget line, 58–59
  consumption choices, 82–86, 563
  input price changes/cost curves,
    204–205
  rationing function, 159
  short-term firm supply curve,
    236–237
  youth alcohol abuse, 84–85
Price-consumption curve, 82–83, 104
Price controls, 27–32
Price discrimination, 326–334
  defined, 325
  first-degree, 327–328
  intertemporal, 340–343
  price/output determination,
    331–334, 569
  required conditions, 330–331
  second-degree, 328–329
  third-degree, 330
Price dispersion, 404–408
Price elasticity of demand, 32–38
  cable TV, and, 36
  calculating, 34–35
  close substitutes, 37
  defined, 32
  estimating, 37–38
  excise taxation, and, 270

home videos, 304
industry input demand curve, 443
monopoly price, and, 301–303
price-consumption curves, 104
time period for adjustment, 37
Washington, D.C., gas tax, and,
  38
Price elasticity of supply, 39–40
Price floor, 27
Price gouging, 40
Price maker, 296
Price taker, 155, 228
Price theory, 2
Priceline.com, 343
Principal-agent problem, 227
Prisoner's dilemma, 388–393
Private schools, 203
Private vs. public provision, 203
Problems, answers to, 571–579
Producer surplus, 260–261
  defined, 260
  efficient output, 262–264
  international trade, 285
  price ceiling, 265–266
  trucking industry, 262
Product curves, 168–171
Product differentiation, 310, 352
Product homogeneity, 224–225, 254
Production, 164–187
  cost. *See* Cost of production
  efficiency in, 520–523
  estimating production functions,
    182–185, 565
  isoquants, 173–175
  law of diminishing marginal
    returns, 172
  product curves, 168–171
  production function, 166
  relating output to inputs, 166
  returns to scale, 178–181, 565
  with all inputs variable, 172–177,
    565
  with one input variable, 167–173,
    564–565
Production contract curve, 522
Production function, 166
Production function estimation,
  182–185, 565
Production isoquants. *See* Isoquants
Production possibility frontier (PPF),
  9–11, 523–524
Profit maximization, 165
  competitive model, 225–226,
    229–234, 567–568
  defined, 225
  long-run, 242

monopoly, 298–303, 569
short-run, 229–234, 567–568
Property rights, 550–552
Protectionism, 528
Public goods
    characteristics, 538
    defined, 537
    efficient output, 541–542
    efficient production/distribution, 543
    free-rider problem, 539–540
Public operating license, 311
Public ownership of natural monopolies, 422–423
Public schools, 122–125, 203
Public sector unions, 477
Public vs. private provision, 203
Purple Demon, 343
Putnam, Howard, 318

Quadratic total cost function, 218
Quantity controls, 70, 288–291
Quantity demanded, 16
Quantity supplied, 21
Queues, 140
Quotas, 288

Radio, 551
Rates of return of financial assets, 134
Rational behavior, 6
Rationing. *See* Nonprice rationing
Rationing by waiting, 161
Rats, 95
Razing a building, 206
Reaction curve, 361
Ready-to-eat (RTE) cereal manufacturing, 357
Reagan, Ronald, 357
Real price, 4
Real rate of return, 134
Recording Industry Association of America (RIAA), 545
Rectangular hyperbola, 33n
Recycling, 128
Refractive eye surgery, 357–358
Regression analysis, 110–113, 182, 183
Regulatory barriers, 310–311
Rent control, 27–32, 273–274
Repeated-game model, 393
Repeated games, 393–395
Resale, 330
Reselling of international phone calls, 331
Residual demand curve, 363
Return–risk tradeoff, 135
Returns to scale, 178–181, 565

Risk aversion
    defined, 138
    entrepreneurs, 136
    insurance, 140
    nature of, 137–139
    standing in line, 140
    total utility curve, 138
Risk loving, 138–140
Risk neutral, 138, 139
Risk reduction techniques, 140–142
Risk–return tradeoff, 135
Riyadh Pact, 378
Roberts, Russell, 389–390
Rockefeller, John D., 5, 74
Rolex cartel, 373–374
Roosevelt, Franklin Delano, 109
RTE cereal manufacturing, 357
Ruth, Babe, 170

S&L industry, 403
SABRE, 342
Saloner, Garth, 108
San Francisco Bay Area housing market, 25
San Francisco office space, 474
Saving, 128–134, 482
Savings and loan institutions (S&Ls), 403
Savings rate (U.S.), 132
Scale economies, 208–209
Scarce resources, 6
Scope diseconomies, 216
Scope economies, 216
Scully, Gerald, 13
Search costs, 404
Seattle, garbage collection, 128
Second-degree price discrimination, 328–329
Selfishness, 72–74
Senior executive compensation, 227
Sexual activity, 110
Shapiro, Carl, 209, 418, 545
Shepard, Andrea, 108
Sherman Act, 317
Shift in demand, 19
Shift in supply, 22
Short run, 173, 209
Short-run cost curves, 194–197, 566
Short-run cost of production, 191–193
Short-run firm supply curve, 234–237
Short-run industry supply curve, 237–239
Short-run profit maximization, 229–234, 567–568
Short-run total cost curve, 194
Shortage, 22

Shovels (California gold rush), 236
Shutdown point, 235
Silicon Valley, 249, 474
Simplexis.com, 137
Singapore, traffic control, 548
Single-line system (queuing), 140
Small plane business, 182
Smith, Adam
    division of labor, 178–179
    invisible hand, 155, 530
    monopoly, 414
    philanthropy, 74
    pin production, 178–179
    price collusion, 375
Smith, Michael, 370
Smoot-Hawley Tariff Act, 528
Snob effect, 106–107
Social marginal benefit curve, 541
Social Security, 497–499
Soft drink industry, 212
Soft-money political contributions, 415–416
Southwest Airlines, 278
Spears, Britney, 310
Specialization and division of labor, 178
Speed limit, 177
Speeding, 20
Spillover effect, 515
Springsteen, Bruce, 143
Stackelberg, Heinrich von, 363n
Stackelberg model, 363–365
Standing in line, 140
Start-up company, 142
State lotteries, 139, 487
State University of New York, 346
Static analysis, 315
Steel, 209
Stigler, George, 217n
Stock market investments, 134–142
    diversification, 141–142
    historical rates of return, 134
    return–risk tradeoff, 135
    rising stock prices, 132
    risk tolerance, 137–140
Stock variable, 55n
Strategies, 384
Student-athletes, 502–504
Subletting, 30
Subsidies
    company health benefits, 120
    excise, 118–122
    external benefits, 124–125
    food stamp program, 68–70
    health care, 118–119
    income tax code, 118

Subsidies (*Continued*)
　　lump-sum transfer, 118–120
　　public schools, 122–125
　　voucher program, 124–125
Substitutes, 18, 37
Substitution effect
　　defined, 87
　　excise subsidy, 120
　　gasoline-tax-plus-rebate program, 89–92
　　higher wage rate, 462–463
　　inferior goods, 92–94
　　interest rate changes, 133–134
　　normal good, 88–89
Substitution effect of an input price change, 441
Sugar, 100
Sugar import quota, 288–290
Sunk costs, 8
Sunlight, 286
Super Bowl tickets, 163
Super shuttles, 282
Supermarkets, 329
Supply curve
　　labor, 462–465
　　long-run industry, 245–253
　　shifts in, 21–22
　　short-run firm, 234–237
　　short-run industry, 237–239
　　upward slope, 20–21
Supply–demand model, 14–43
　　adjustment to changes, 24–25
　　demand curve, 16–17
　　demand estimation, 109–113
　　elasticities, 32–40. *See also* Elasticities
　　equilibrium, 22–23
　　explaining market outcomes, 26–27
　　market demand curve, 95–97
　　price controls, 27–32
　　shifts in demand curve, 17–19
　　shifts in supply curve, 21–22
　　supply curve, 20–21
Supply elasticity, 39–40
Supply of inputs, 444–446
Suppression of invention, 416–418
Surplus, 23
Surveys, 109–110
Survivor principle, 226
Survivor technique, 217

T-bills, 134–135
Taco Bell, 68
Tangency points, 200
Tastes, 18

Tax-plus-rebate program, 89–92
Taxicab licensing, 279–282
TC, 192
Technological improvements, 250
Technologically efficient, 166
Teenage drinking, 85
Telephone service, 343–344
Television
　　cable. *See* Cable TV
　　Canadian content rules, 70–71
　　free TV, 101
Temporary workers, 500
TFC, 191
Theory, 2–3
Third-degree price discrimination, 330
Ticket scalping, 163
Time Warner, 6
Time Warner–AOL merger, 217
Tit-for-tat, 394
Titanic, 181, 182
TLC Laser Eye Centers, 357
Tobacco industry, 104. *See also* Cigarettes
Tocqueville, Alexis de, 74
Total benefit, 98
Total cost (TC), 192
Total fixed cost (TFC), 191
Total product, 167
Total product curve, 168–171, 193
Total profit, 230
Total revenue (TR), 229
Total surplus, 262–263
Total utility, 75
Total variable cost (TVC), 191
Total variable cost (TVC) curve, 193
Toyota, 6
TR, 229
Tradable emission permits, 555–557
Trade liberalization, 528
Trade restrictions, 528
Trade, international, 283–287, 526–528
Traffic externalities, 547–548
Traffic schools, 20
Transferring income to another person, 73
Transitivity, 47
Trash collection services, 125–128
Treasury bills, 134–135
Trucking industry, 262
TV. *See* Television
TVC, 191
TVC curve, 193
Two-part tariff, 335–340
Two-person exchange, 146–151

Ueberroth, Peter, 505
Unions, 475–477
Unit elastic, 33, 40
United Airlines, 278, 362–363, 371
United Auto Workers, 477
United Parcel Service (UPS), 500
United States Postal Service (USPS), 203, 422–423
U.S. saving rate, 132
Universities. *See* Colleges
Updegraff, Steve, 358
Used car market, 397–400
Utility approach to consumer choice, 74–77
Utility-maximizing market basket, 76

Value judgment, 4
Variable inputs, 173
Varian, Hal, 209, 370, 418, 545
Vending machines, 25
Vermont, peak-load pricing (electricity), 345
Vertical summation (of demand curves), 541
Very-short-run firm supply curve, 236
Video programming, 340
Vintage Jaguar cars, 107
Virgin Atlantic, 291
Voluntary exchange, 146. *See also* Economic efficiency
Voucher programs, 124–125

Wages. *See* Labor market
Waiting, 161
Water allocation (California), 158
Wealth of Nations (Smith), 74, 178
Welch, Finis, 496
Welfare cost, 265. *See also* Deadweight loss
Welfare frontier, 517–518
Welfare payments, 120
Williams, Thomas E., 335
Windows, 340
Windows operating system, 108
Woods, Tiger, 357
WordPerfect, 319
WordStar, 319
Work–leisure choice model, 460–464
World Wide Web, 209. *See also* Internet

Yield management, 342
Youth alcohol abuse, 84–85

Zedillo, Ernesto, 378
Zero economic profit, 242–243

APPLICATIONS

11.1 Demand Elasticity and Home Video Prices

11.2 Life is Not Always a Box of Chocolates

11.3 Regulatory Barriers in the Philippines

11.4 The Dynamics of Developing an AIDS Vaccine

11.5 What Not to Say to a Rival on the Telephone

11.6 Static Versus Dynamic View of Monopoly and the Microsoft Antitrust Case

12.1 Giving Frequent Shoppers the Second Degree

12.2 The Third Degree by Car Dealers

12.3 Arbitrage in the International Phone Calling Market

12.4 Why Hotel and Apartment Building Owners Get Cable Television Service for a Lower Price

12.5 The Cost of Being Ernest When It Comes to Applying to Colleges

12.6 The Cost of Engaging in Price Discrimination

12.7 Yield Management by Airlines

12.8 Priceline.com, Project Purple Demon, and Online Intertemporal Price Discrimination

12.9 Peak-Load Pricing Goes To College

13.1 Ready-to-Regulate Ready-to-Eat

13.2 Monopolistic Competition is in the Eye of the Beholder

13.3 Strategic Interaction on Duopoly Air Routes

13.4 The Dynamics of the Dominant Firm Model in Pharmaceutical Markets

13.5 Will the Internet Promote Competition of Cartelization?

13.6 The Difficulty of Controlling Cheating

13.7 The Rolex "Cartel"

13.8 Firm Count, Market Concentration, and Successful Collusion

14.1 Dominant Strategies in Baseball

14.2 The Congressional Prisoner's Dilemma

14.3 Cooperation in the Trenches of World War I

14.4 Is There a Lemons Problem in Used Car Markets?

14.5 Adverse Selection and the American Red Cross

14.6 Moral Hazard in the S&L Industry

14.7 Moral Hazard on the Road and at the Plate

14.8 A Newspaper Strike's Effect on Food Prices